ONBAKING

COMPREHENSIVE TEACHING

▶ FOR THE INSTRUCTOR

POWERPOINT PRESENTATIONS AND INSTRUCTOR'S MANUAL

Available on Prentice Hall's online catalog and at www.prenhall.com/pineapple, adopters may access, free of charge, PowerPoint presentations featuring lecture outlines for the entire textbook and an Instructor's Manual with answers to each chapter's Questions for Discussion, problem-based learning exercises and examination questions. The Instructor's Manual is also available in print.

TESTGEN (COMPUTERIZED TEST BANK)

The TestGen contains text-based questions in a format that enables instructors to select questions and create their own examinations.

BAKING YIELDS, MEASUREMENTS AND PERCENTAGES VIDEO

An all-new video simplifies and presents in a visual format the basics of yields, scaling and baker's percentages and is available for purchase.

▶ FOR THE STUDENT

CD-ROM

The **ValuSoft MasterCook CD-ROM** contains all recipes from *On Baking* and is packaged with each copy of the textbook. This software allows users to modify recipes, convert recipe quantities and search for recipes using various data fields. Short video clips illustrating basic techniques and nutritional analysis of the recipes are included.

STUDENT STUDY GUIDE

A paperback Student Study Guide is available for purchase. The Study Guide assists students in learning terminology and theory. It includes review questions with answers to help the student comprehend the techniques and processes illustrated within the textbook.

AND LEARNING PACKAGE

▶ ONLINE RESOURCES

Today's learning environment requires materials that incorporate technology into the classroom. With this new edition, we are seeking to meet the needs of all instructors and students with flexible, easy-to-use online offerings filled with rich content resources.

COMPANION WEBSITE

Prentice Hall's **Companion Website** provides an interactive learning environment for students and supplies support resources for instructors. The **Companion Website** is an invaluable technological offering for this textbook. This website (www.prenhall.com/labensky) is a free site that will enable students to take practice exams, link up to other culinary websites, and allow the instructor to post an online syllabus.

For additional information on media resources
or instructor materials, please contact
Prentice Hall faculty services at 1-800-526-0485

▶ ADDITIONAL KEY FEATURES

LEARNING OBJECTIVES

Each chapter begins with clearly stated objectives. Students can refer to these objectives while reading to make sure they understand the material.

CHAPTER INTRODUCTION

Each chapter begins with a brief overview of the topics to be covered. Students can use this introduction to improve their understanding of the concepts.

AFTER STUDYING THIS CHAPTER, YOU WILL BE ABLE TO:

▶ prepare a variety of cakes and tortes

▶ prepare a variety of frostings

▶ assemble cakes using basic finishing and decorating techniques

Cakes and tortes are popular in most bakeshops because a wide variety of finished products can be created from only a few basic cake, filling and frosting formulas. Many of these components can even be made in advance and assembled into finished desserts as needed. Cakes are also popular because of their versatility: They can be served as unadorned sheets in a high-volume cafeteria or as the elaborate centerpiece of a wedding buffet.

Cake making need not be difficult or intimidating, but it does require an understanding of ingredients and mixing methods. This chapter begins by explaining how typical cake ingredients interact. Each of the traditional mixing methods is then explained and illustrated with a recipe. Information on panning batters, baking temperatures, determining doneness and cooling methods follows. The second portion of this chapter presents methods for assembling and decorating a variety of cakes and tortes using many of the icing formulas discussed in the previous chapter. An array of creams and mousses suitable for filling certain cakes and tortes are discussed in Chapter 15, Custards and Creams. A selection of cake and torte formulas, which can be used throughout this book, concludes the chapter.

MARGIN DEFINITIONS

Important terms are defined in the margins to help students master new terminology. A phonetic pronunciation guide is also provided for non-English terms.

SAFETY ALERTS

Brief notes remind students of safety concerns and encourage them to incorporate food safety and sanitation into their regular kitchen activities.

SAFETY ALERT

EGG PRODUCTS IN UNCOOKED MOUSSES

Pasteurized egg products are recommended for most mousse formulas since mousses require no further cooking. One exception is Italian meringue. The hot sugar syrup cooks the egg whites to a temperature that makes them safe for consumption.

TABLES

Tables and charts offer visual support and organization of material to enhance students' understanding of the material.

Table 14.3 CAKE PAN SIZES

PAN SHAPE AND SIZE	QUANTITY OF BATTER	BUTTER/HIGH-FAT	EGG FOAM	NO. OF SERVINGS FOR 2-LAYER CAKE
Round, 2 in. deep				
6 in.	1 pt.	8–10 oz.	5–6 oz.	6
8 in.	3 c.	12–16 oz.	8–10 oz.	12
10 in.	1½ qt.	24–32 oz.	16–18 oz.	20
12 in.	1 qt. + 3½ c.	32–36 oz.	18–22 oz.	30
14 in.	2½ qt.	40–48 oz.	24–30 oz.	40
Square, 2 in. deep				
8 in.	1 qt.	16–18 oz.	10–12 oz.	16
10 in.	1½ qt.	24–30 oz.	16–18 oz.	20
12 in.	2½ qt.	40–48 oz.	26–30 oz.	36
14 in.	3 qt. + 1½ c.	48–52 oz.	32–40 oz.	48
Rectangular, 2 in. deep				
6 in. × 8 in.	2½ c.	10–12 oz.	6–8 oz.	12
9 in. × 13 in.	2 qt.	32–36 oz.	20–24 oz.	24
18 in. × 13 in.	2 qt. + 3 c.	3.5–4 lb.	28–32 oz.	48
18 in. × 26 in.	5 qt.	6–8 lb.	2.5–3 lb.	96

*Quantities given are approximate and are based on filling the pans two-thirds full of batter. The weight of cake batter needed to properly fill a pan will vary depending on the type of batter, additional flavor ingredients and the amount of air incorporated during mixing.

SIDEBARS

Sidebars present additional information on food history, food in culture and the background of professional foodservice. These sidebars help students to understand the culinary arts in a wider social context.

CONVENIENCE PRODUCTS

A wide selection of prepared icings, glazes and toppings are available. Often, chocolate and vanilla fudge-based icings are purchased and then flavored or colored as needed. Foam icings can be purchased in powder form, to which you simply add water and whip. Ready-to-use glazes and flat icings are formulated for many types of applications—brushing over cakes, sweet dough pastries or doughnuts in particular. Even prepared "buttercreams" are available in shelf-stable or frozen forms, although they contain little or no real butter.

Prepared icings are often exceedingly sweet and overpowered by artificial flavors and chemical preservatives. These products save time and offer consistent results but often cost more than their counterparts made from scratch. They should be used only after balancing the disadvantages against the benefits for your particular operation.

Prepared syrups used to flavor coffee drinks may be used in place of simple syrup in a pinch when the syrup is used to moisten a spongecake or torte. The variety of flavors is limitless and exotic; espresso, hazelnut, kiwi or anise, for example. But making sugar syrup from scratch is preferred when making caramel or buttercream. Popular sauces such as caramel, butterscotch, hot fudge and strawberry have been available for many years, usually sold for use at ice cream stands. With the broad appeal of plated desserts, more varieties of sauces and products containing less sugar and more natural ingredients are now available. Convenience reached a new level when fruit sauces for plated desserts became available in ready-to-pour plastic applicator bottles.

CHAPTER SUMMARY

Each end-of-chapter Conclusion reviews the main topics covered.

CONCLUSION	Few techniques in the bakeshop produce the visible and flavorful results that lamination does. Puff pastry demonstrates the wonders of science in the kitchen, that mere steam and fat can leaven dough. The ability to create quality croissants and Danish pastries depends on an understanding of ingredient functions as well as experience with lamination techniques. The information and techniques discussed in this chapter and in Chapter 7, Yeast Breads, will enable any baker to prepare a variety of dessert and breakfast pastry classics.

QUESTIONS FOR DISCUSSION

Questions for Discussion appear at the end of each chapter in order to encourage students to integrate theory and technique into a broader understanding of the material. Web-based activities, as indicated by the WWW icon, encourage them to do original research and seek answers from outside their primary classroom material.

QUESTIONS FOR DISCUSSION	1 Briefly describe the procedure for making a rolled-in dough, and give two examples of products made from rolled-in doughs. 2 Name the leaveners used in laminated dough. 3 Describe the effect that docking has on puff pastry and why this technique would be used. 4 What can happen if croissants and Danish pastries are proofed at high temperatures? 5 Describe one roll-in method for making croissant or Danish dough.

HALLMARK FEATURES

► KEY FEATURES

- over 615 recipes
- inclusion of convenience items where appropriate
- recipe variations
- over 700 photographs and line drawings

- chapter on Healthful and Special-Needs Baking (18)
- chapter on Mise en Place (5)

PROCEDURES

Step-by-step color photographs of various stages in the preparation of dishes and ingredients help students visualize unfamiliar techniques and encourage them to review classroom or kitchen activities whenever necessary.

4 Rolling out the dough.

5 Folding the dough in thirds to complete a turn.

6 Cutting rectangles of Danish dough.

PRODUCT IDENTIFICATION

Hundreds of original color photographs help students recognize and identify ingredients. Students can explore a huge variety of items such as fruits, berries, chocolates, and fresh herbs.

Calimyrna Figs

FIGS

Figs (Fr. *figues*) are the fruit of ficus trees. They are small, soft, pear-shaped fruits with an intensely sweet flavor and rich, moist texture made crunchy by a multitude of tiny seeds. Fresh figs can be served on tarts or baked, poached and simmered to make jams, preserves or compotes.

Dark-skinned figs, known as Mission figs, are a variety planted at Pacific Coast missions during the 18th century. They have a thin skin and small seeds and are available fresh, canned or dried. The white-skinned figs grown commercially include the White Adriatic, used principally for drying and baking, and the all-purpose Kadota. The most important domestic variety, however, is the Calimyrna. These large figs have a rich yellow color and large nutty seeds. Fresh Calimyrna figs are the finest for eating out of hand; they are also available dried.

For the best flavor, figs should be fully ripened on the tree. Unfortunately, fully ripened figs are very delicate and difficult to transport. Most figs are in season from June through October; fresh Calimyrna figs are available only during June.

LINE DRAWINGS

Detailed line drawings illustrate tools and equipment without brand identification.

Balance or Baker's Scale

This feature makes measuring accurately more convenient. Electronic scales are considered more accurate than mechanical ones and are often required where foods are priced for sale by weight, as in a retail bakery.

Any scale must be properly used and maintained to provide an accurate reading. Never pick up a scale by its platform, as this can damage the balancing mechanism.

VOLUME MEASURES

Ingredients may be measured by volume using measuring spoons and measuring cups, though most professional bakeshops use scales to measure all but the smallest quantities. Measuring spoons sold as a set usually include ¼-teaspoon, ½-teaspoon, 1-teaspoon and 1-tablespoon units (1.25-, 2.5-, 5- and 15-milliliter units). Liquid measuring cups are available in capacities from 1 cup to 1 gallon (or the metric equivalent). They have a lip or pour spout above the top line of measurement to prevent spills. Though more commonly used in the home kitchen, measuring cups for dry ingredients are sometimes used in the professional kitchen, especially for converting home recipes or measuring small amounts of items such as chopped nuts and spices. They are usually sold in sets of ¼-, ⅓-, ½-, and 1-cup units. They do not have pour spouts, so the top of the cup is level with the top measurement specified. To ensure an accurate measurement of dry ingredients, fill the cup and then level off the top with a knife or flat spatula. Glass measuring cups are not recommended because they can break. Avoid using bent or dented measuring cups as the damage may distort the measurement capacity.

Measuring Spoons

Liquid Measuring Cup

Dry Measuring Cups

LADLES

Long-handled ladles are useful for portioning liquids such as sauces, custards and syrups. The capacity, in ounces or milliliters, is stamped on the handle.

PORTION SCOOPS

Portion scoops (also known as dishers) resemble ice cream scoops. They come in a range of standardized sizes and have a lever-operated blade for releasing their contents. Scoops are useful for portioning muffin batters and cookie dough or other soft foods. A number, stamped on either the handle or the release mechanism, indicates the number of level scoopfuls per quart. The higher the scoop number, the smaller the scoop's capacity. See Table 2.1.

Portion Scoop

Ladles

Dough Hook

Whip

Flat Paddle

20-Quart Mixer and Attachments

► RECIPE

MEASUREMENTS

All recipes are written in both U.S. and metric measurements. Metric equivalents are also provided for all temperatures, pan sizes and length measurements throughout the text. Includes baker's percentages as appropriate.

ILLUSTRATIONS

Recipes are illustrated frequently with both sequential pictures showing fabrication and assembly of dishes to enhance instruction, as well as many finished plated photos that show students the authors' finished work created while testing the recipes.

VARIATIONS

Recipe variations show students how to modify recipes to create new flavor profiles and new dishes.

CHOCOLATE ANGEL FOOD CAKE

Yield: 1 Tube Cake, 10 in. (25 cm)   **Method:** Egg foam   Sugar at 100%

Ingredient	U.S.	Metric	%
Cocoa powder, alkalized	1 oz.	30 g	8%
Water, warm	2 fl. oz.	60 ml	16%
Vanilla extract	0.3 fl. oz. (2 tsp.)	9 ml	2.5%
Granulated sugar	12 oz.	360 g	100%
Cake flour, sifted	3.5 oz.	105 g	29%
Salt	0.05 oz. (¼ tsp.)	1.5 g	0.4%
Egg whites	1 lb. (16 whites)	480 g	133%
Cream of tartar	0.3 oz. (2 tsp.)	9 g	2.5%
Total batter weight:	2 lb. 3 oz.	1055 g	291%

1 Combine the cocoa powder and water in a bowl. Add the vanilla and set aside.
2 In another bowl, combine 5 ounces (150 grams) of the sugar with the flour and salt.

1 Folding the egg-white-and-cocoa mixture into the whipped egg whites.

2 Folding in the flour.

...ing the cake upside down in ...an.

4 Removing the cake from the pan.

VARIATIONS:

Vanilla Angel Food Cake—Omit the cocoa powder and warm water from the formula. Increase the amount of vanilla extract to 0.5 fluid ounce (15 milliliters/4%) and fold it in at the end of Step 5.

Lemon Angel Food Cake—Omit the cocoa powder and warm water from the formula. Add 0.14 ounces (2 teaspoons/4 grams/1%) fresh lemon zest to the sugar-and-flour mixture. Add 0.15 fluid ounces (1 teaspoon/5 milliliters/1%) lemon extract, folding it and the vanilla extract in at the end of Step 5.

Approximate values per ¹/₁₀-cake serving: **Calories** 210, **Total fat** 0.5 g, **Saturated fat** 0 g, **Cholesterol** 0 mg, **Sodium** 150 mg, **Total carbohydrates** 44 g, **Protein** 7 g, **Claims**—low fat; no saturated fat; no cholesterol

NUTRITIONAL ANALYSIS

All recipes include a nutritional analysis prepared by a registered dietician.

ON BAKING

ON BAKING

► A TEXTBOOK OF BAKING AND PASTRY FUNDAMENTALS

SARAH R. LABENSKY, CCP
Mississippi University for Women Culinary Arts Institute

with

EDDY VAN DAMME
Houston Community College

PRISCILLA MARTEL

KLAUS TENBERGEN, CMB, CEPC, ASBPB
The School of Culinary Arts at Kendall College

Photographs by Richard Embery
Drawings by Stacey Winters Quattrone and William E. Ingram

PEARSON

Prentice
Hall

Upper Saddle River, New Jersey 07458

Library of Congress Cataloging-in-Publication Data

On baking : a textbook of baking and pastry fundamentals / Sarah R. Labensky … [et al.];
photographs by Richard Embery ; drawings by Stacey Winters Quattrone and William E. Ingram.
    p. cm.
Includes bibliographical references and index.
ISBN 0-13-533647-3
1. Baking. I. Labensky, Sarah R.

TX763.B3233 2005
641.8'15-dc22   2003070744

Editor in Chief: Stephen Helba
Executive Editor: Vernon R. Anthony
Executive Assistant: Nancy Kesterson
Editorial Assistant: Beth Dyke
Director of Manufacturing and Production: Bruce Johnson
Managing Editor: Mary Carnis
Creative Director: Cheryl Asherman
Interior Design: Cheryl Asherman
Manufacturing Buyer: Ilene Sanford
Senior Production Editor: Adele Kupchik
Full-Service Project Management: Linda Zuk, WordCrafters Editorial Services, Inc.

Developmental Editor: Mark Huth and Triple SSS Press
Senior Marketing Manager: Ryan DeGrote
Marketing Assistant: Elizabeth Farrell
Marketing Coordinator: Adam Kloza
Composition: Carlisle Communications, Inc.
Printer/Binder: R. R. Donnelley & Sons Co.
Cover Design: Cheryl Asherman
Cover Photos: Richard Embery: chef coat by Marjory Dressler
Cover Printer: Lehigh Press

Photo Credits:

Ancient Egyptian sculpture (p. 4): National Geographic; 19th-century bakery in France (p. 5): Corbis/Bettmann; portrait of Antonin Carême (p. 7): courtesy of Barbara Wheaton; portrait of Auguste Escoffier (p. 8): courtesy of Musée de l'Art Culinaire, Villeneuve-Loubet (Village), France; photo of Gaston Lenôtre (p. 9): Corbis/Sygma, © Sophie Bassouls; photo of Lionel Poilâne Bakery (p. 10): AP/Wide World Photos; rolling pin (p. 24), baking sheet (p. 31), and baker's peel (p. 39): courtesy of TriMark United East, South Attleboro, MA; spiral mixer (p. 37), dough sheeter (p. 41), and deck oven (p. 38): courtesy FBM Baking Machines, Inc., Cranbury, NJ; photos pages 567 and 571: from *Fancy Cake Baking* by Henry Heide, © 1926, Henry Heide Incorporated.

Photos from Ambria Restaurant in Chicago (pages 468-69, 591 [top], 594 [top left], and 598) are not subject to reuse by any other parties without express written consent of the copyright holder.

Pearson Education LTD.
Pearson Education Singapore, Pte. Ltd
Pearson Education, Canada, Ltd
Pearson Education-Japan

Pearson Education Australia PTY, Limited
Pearson Education North Asia Ltd
Pearson Educación de Mexico, S.A. de C.V.
Pearson Education Malaysia, Pte. Ltd

10 9 8 7 6 5 4 3 2 1
ISBN 0-13-533647-3

CONTENTS

CHAPTER 20

RESTAURANT DESSERTS   585

CHAPTER 21

CHOCOLATE AND DECORATIVE WORK   605

APPENDIX I

MEASUREMENT AND CONVERSION CHARTS   645

APPENDIX II

HIGH-ALTITUDE BAKING   648

APPENDIX III

FRESH FRUIT AVAILABILITY CHART   649

APPENDIX IV

PROFESSIONAL ORGANIZATIONS   650

PREFACE

Building on the successful approach developed in *On Cooking: A Textbook of Culinary Fundamentals, On Baking* is a carefully designed text intended to teach both the principles and practices of baking and the pastry arts. Although it contains more than 600 recipes for a wide range of traditional and contemporary bakeshop items, the focus of this book is on the underlying baking principles and skills necessary to produce a wide array of baked goods and confections. Throughout the text, we discuss both the how and why of baking. Extensive step-by-step photographs help you visualize the techniques used to form bread dough or shape cookies or temper chocolate, for example, while recipes illustrate the baking principle and procedures. Throughout the book, we also provide extensive illustrated sections identifying bakeshop ingredients and equipment. We believe that a thorough understanding of the function of ingredients will serve you well throughout your baking career.

Numerous professional bakers, pastry chefs and educators throughout the country contributed recipes to this book, usually illustrated with a photograph of the item as it was actually prepared in their kitchens. These recipes and illustrations allow you to explore different techniques and presentation styles. As in *On Cooking,* informative sidebars provide background on the rich historical and cultural traditions of the bakeshop. And professionals share their insights and technical knowledge in brief comments scattered throughout the book.

Chapter 18 is devoted to alternative baking for consumers with special dietary needs in the hope that today's well-trained baker will understand how and why to adapt formulas to this clientele. As a working professional, you may encounter convenience products in use in many restaurants, hotels or institutions. Therefore, each chapter of *On Baking* includes practical information on convenience products, providing information on the selection, storage, handling and use of these items.

We wish you much success throughout your professional career and hope that this book serves to inspire and inform you for many years to come.

► A NOTE ON RECIPES AND FORMULAS

Recipes throughout this text are designed to reinforce and explain techniques and procedures presented in the text. Recipes intentionally produce lower yields used typically in small schools and teaching kitchens. Volume measurements are provided only when the quantity of an ingredient would be difficult to weigh without specialized equipment—less than ½ ounce of salt, leavening or spices, for example. All ingredients are listed in both U.S. and metric measurements. In most instances the metric equivalents are rounded off to even, easily measured amounts. You should consider these ingredient lists as separate recipes or formulas; do not measure some ingredients according to the metric amounts and other ingredients according to the U.S. amounts or the proportions will not be accurate and the intended result will not be achieved.

Baker's percentages are also included for many of the recipes in this text. Widely used in the professional bakeshop, baker's percentages are very useful for increasing or decreasing yields as needed. Yields are provided in either total batch weight or total yield, offering suggested portion sizes where appropriate.

Detailed procedures for standard techniques are presented in the text and are generally not repeated in each recipe (for example, "apply egg wash" or "divide the dough"). No matter how detailed the written recipe, however, we must assume that you possess certain knowledge, skills and judgment.

Variations appear at the end of selected recipes. These variations enable you to see how one set of techniques or procedures can be used to prepare different dishes with only minor modifications. Variations also provide the advanced baker or pastry chef the opportunity to customize recipes for different applications.

A registered dietician analyzed all of the recipes in this book using nutritional analysis software that incorporates data from the U.S. Department of Agriculture, research laboratories and food manufacturers. The nutrient information provided here should be used only as a reference, however. A margin of error of approximately 20 percent can be expected because of natural variations in ingredients. Preparation techniques and serving sizes may also significantly alter the values of many nutrients. In the nutritional analysis for a recipe that offers a choice of ingredients, the first-mentioned ingredient is the one used unless stated otherwise. Ingredients listed "as needed" are omitted from the analysis. Corn oil and whole milk are used throughout for "vegetable oil" and "milk," respectively. In cases of a range of ingredient quantities or numbers of servings, the average is used.

Throughout this book various recipes are marked with a pyramid symbol. This symbol identifies dishes that are particularly low in calories, fat, saturated fat or sodium; if appropriate, they may also be a good source of vitamins, protein, fiber or calcium.

The World Wide Web icon appears next to end-of-chapter Questions for Discussion whose answers may be researched on the web.

It is most important to remember that baking is both an art and a science. It is best learned through hands-on experience combined with study of the principles that underlie each technique. You should rely on the knowledge and skills of your instructor for guidance. Although some skills and an understanding of theory can be acquired through reading and study, no book can substitute for repeated, hands-on preparation and observations.

▶ ACKNOWLEDGMENTS

This book would not have been possible without the assistance and support of many people. Special thanks go to photographer Richard Embery for his talent, professionalism and commitment to quality; and to Sharon Salomon, MS, RD, for preparation of Chapter 18, "Healthful and Special-Needs Baking." The nutritional analysis was prepared by Mindy Herman, MS, RD, whose thoroughness and prompt replies were greatly appreciated. Thanks also go to Stacey Winters Quattrone and Bill Ingram for their artistry. We are also grateful to the many chefs, restaurateurs, writers and culinary professionals who provided recipes and essays for this book.

Sarah offers her sincere thanks and appreciation to her co-authors for adding their expertise, insight and artistry to this text. She would also like to recognize Mississippi University for Women, especially the faculty, staff and students of the

Culinary Arts Institute, for supporting and encouraging this project. She dedicates this book to her late husband David Moline.

Eddy would like to thank his parents and sister for recognizing his passion and "gently" guiding him into the pastry field. He would like to recognize his colleagues Joris Bundervoet and Roland De Mits for strengthening his enthusiasm for finer and better pastry work. Eddy would also like to recognize Houston Community College, for supporting his work, Dr. Morandi for his encouragement and support of this book and President Patricia Williamson for her dedication and vision of excellence for the program.

Priscilla would like to recognize the personal and professional support of Victor Frumolt, Jacques Pépin, Carole Pierce, Alain Sailhac and Lee White with this project. She would also like to thank Chef Daniel Chong-Jiménez, The Spa at Norwich Inn; Mary Beth Cothern and Tad Graham-Handley, Connecticut Culinary Institute; Dennis Hibdon, Technical Service, Bunge Corporation; Warren Patterson, General Mills; and Bill Weekley, Lesaffre Yeast Corporation, for their professional help with this project. And special thanks to Charles van Over for always keeping the wood oven stoked.

Klaus would like to thank his wife Bea and his children Kimberly and Sebastian for their continued support. He would like to express his appreciation to Kendall College for allowing the use of its facilities for shooting photographs for this book, and to the faculty and students for their support during the project. He dedicates his work to the memory of his late son Benjamin and to his late father and his mother in Germany. Finally, he wishes to thank all the friends that he has made in the United States and South Africa for their support as he worked on this book.

The authors wish to thank the following companies for their generous contributions to the production of this book: Terry Noyes, Executive Chef, SYSCO Hartford, Connecticut; Houston Community College, Houston, Texas; Kendall College, Evanston, Illinois; and Alan Hause and Fabulous Food Catering, Phoenix, Arizona.

Finally we wish to thank everyone involved in this project at Prentice Hall, including Vernon Anthony, Executive Editor; Mark Huth and Triple SSS Press, Developmental Editor; Linda Zuk, Production Editor; Cheryl Asherman, Creative Director; Mary Carnis, Managing Editor; Adele Kupchik, Senior Production Editor; and Ryan DeGrote, Senior Marketing Manager. We also remain indebted to Robin Baliszewski, Acquisitions Editor of the first edition of *On Cooking* and current President of the Career, Health, Education & Technology Division, for her support and friendship.

The authors would like to acknowledge the following reviewers for their comments and assistance with this book: Robert Axel, The Art Institute of Philadelphia; Robert Beighey, Sullivan University; Robert Brown, Paul Smith's College; Vince Donatelli, Ashville-Buncombe Technical College; Amy Felder, Johnson & Wales University; Peter Fendt, Quality Pastry Shop, Inc.; Carol Gunter, Purdue University; Catherine Hallman, CEPC, Walters State Community College; Audrey Langenhop, York Technical College; and Marilyn Mook, Michigan State University. These reviewers provided many excellent suggestions and ideas for improving the text.

RECIPES

CHAPTER 15   CUSTARDS AND CREAMS

CHAPTER 16   ICE CREAM AND FROZEN DESSERTS

CHAPTER 17   FRUITS

CHAPTER 21   CHOCOLATE AND DECORATIVE WORK

ONBAKING

THE RANKS OF EVERY PROFESSION CONCERNED WITH THE SALE OR PREPARATION OF FOOD, INCLUDING COOKS, CATERERS, CONFECTIONERS, PASTRY COOKS, PROVISION MERCHANTS AND THE LIKE, HAVE MULTIPLIED IN EVER-INCREASING PROPORTIONS. . . . NEW PROFESSIONS HAVE ARISEN; THAT, FOR EXAMPLE, OF THE PASTRY COOK—IN HIS DOMAIN ARE BISCUITS, MACAROONS, FANCY CAKES, MERINGUES. . . . THE ART OF PRESERVING HAS ALSO BECOME A PROFESSION IN ITSELF, WHEREBY WE ARE ENABLED TO ENJOY, AT ALL TIMES OF THE YEAR, THINGS NATURALLY PECULIAR TO ONE OR OTHER SEASON.

—Jean-Anthelme Brillat-Savarin, French writer, politician and philosopher (1755–1826)

PROFESSIONALISM

AFTER STUDYING THIS CHAPTER, YOU WILL BE ABLE TO:

▶ discuss the development of the baker and pastry chef professions

▶ explain the organization of the professional kitchen brigade

▶ appreciate the role of the professional pastry chef and baker in modern food service operations

▶ understand the attributes a student chef needs to become a professional

▶ recognize how to maintain a safe and sanitary work environment

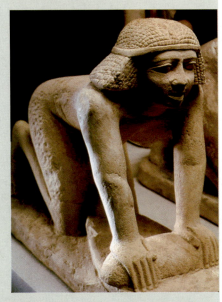

Ancient Egyptian sculpture depicting kneading bread dough

▶ **confectionery**—transforming sugar into sweets; it also refers to the trade of candy making

Like any fine art, great cookery requires taste and creativity, an appreciation of beauty and a mastery of technique. Like the sciences, successful cookery demands knowledge and an understanding of basic principles. And like any successful leader, today's food service professionals must exercise sound judgment and be committed to achieving excellence in their endeavors.

This book describes foods and cooking equipment, explains baking and culinary principles and cooking techniques and provides recipes using these principles and techniques. No book, however, can provide taste, creativity, commitment and judgment. For these, you must rely upon yourself.

▶ BAKERS, CHEFS AND RESTAURANTS

The culinary student studying the baking arts is entering a world rich in cultural heritage. Knowledge of this heritage is an important part of a culinary education, one that serves as a source of inspiration and professional pride.

BREAD MAKING SINCE ANCIENT TIMES

The first bread products were firm porridges made from grasses and grains cooked on flat stones heated by an open fire. The earliest form of wheat used for bread making, *Triticum dioccum,* thrived in the fertile basin of the Nile River valley. The use of a stone oven for bread making dates to the Neolithic period (4000 B.C.E.). Remarkably, the ovens discovered in archaeological ruins from that time closely resemble the domed beehive-shaped ovens still used today. It is believed that the Egyptians discovered the effect of yeast in leavening bread and perfected bread making to achieve consistent results. What historians interpret as organized bakeries are depicted in hieroglyphics, sculptures and tomb paintings discovered throughout Egypt, where as many as 70 kinds of bread were consumed in the first millennia B.C.E.

Bread making and **confectionery** were the first labor activities organized into specialized trades. Pharaohs employed skilled bakers to provide bread for their private consumption. Among the trades recognized by the highly organized Greek society of the fourth and third centuries B.C.E. were the wafer makers *(oblaten)* and the pastry cooks. The religion of ancient Greece focused on the worship of multiple deities and included the offering of gifts to these gods, especially around critical times, to ensure plentiful harvests, adequate rain and prosperity. As is customary today, certain breads and sweets were eaten to commemorate special occasions. Historians credit the ancient Greeks with spreading the profession of the skilled baker throughout the Mediterranean basin. According to the Greek historian Herodotus, writing in the fourth century B.C.E., bakers accompanied roving Greek armies on their raids. When Roman armies conquered them, Greek soldiers and bakers remained in what is now Italy. Roman occupation then helped to spread the techniques for cultivating grains, milling and baking bread products throughout the western world.

Bread and pastry making found a fertile home on the European continent. In the northern regions including Austria, Germany, the Netherlands, Scandinavia

19th-century bakery in France

and Great Britain, where a cool, damp climate was inhospitable to wheat grow-ing, rye grain products took hold. In the 17th century, the Dutch and British debuted the use of pans in which to bake bread, paving the way for the devel-opment of the sandwich.

Until the process for milling flour was perfected in the 1830s, white flour was expensive and most bread was made from relatively coarse ground grains. These grains baked into rough-textured solid loaves quite unlike their light and crusty descendants eaten today. The milling process was labor intensive, involving grinding the grain between heavy millstones then sifting the flour manually through cloth to remove the coarse bran. The finest and whitest flour, the small-est quantity produced after many stages of sifting, made the softest products and was available only to the wealthy.

In the mid-19th century, advances were made in the production of a stable form of yeast to leaven bread. Once perfected by a Viennese distiller, this yeast paste popularized the production of a wider variety of breads. Simultaneously, improved mechanical kneading machinery appeared, making the task of large-scale bread mixing possible.

REFINED SUGAR AND THE ART OF CONFECTIONERY

Humans share a strong appetite for sweet foods; it is the only universally innate taste preference. For much of prehistory, historians assume that fruits were hu-mans' primary source of sweet foods. Honey was the first concentrated sweet-ener to be widely used, a position it held on the European continent and Great Britain until well into the middle ages. Egyptian hieroglyphs from the 15th cen-tury B.C.E. depicting clay beehives document the cultivation of bees for their honey. In ancient Egypt, Greece and Rome, honey was used to season both sa-vory and sweet dishes and as a preservative.

While many candies and sweet confections can be made from honey, it was not until refined sugar became readily available that the pastry and confectionery trades evolved. Without refined sugar, many of the candies and sweets widely consumed today would not be possible. Sugar cane produces a liquid syrup that when boiled down hardens and crystallizes. Sugar's ability to be both a liquid and solid makes it indispensable for candy and pastry making.

The process of extracting sugar from a large tropical grass now known as sugar cane began in India around 500 B.C.E. Arabs perfected the cultivation and refining of sugar around 600 C.E. Arab conquests of the Mediterranean region, international trade and the travels of the crusaders spread the use of refined sugar throughout

Europe during the 13th through 15th centuries. It remained an expensive luxury until the ability to extract and refine sugar cane became more common. (See Chapter 4, Bakeshop Ingredients). Venice was one of the first European cities to set up its own sugar refineries in the 15th century, making refined cane sugar available throughout the region. Many confections from that time, such as sugared fruits, sugared almonds and marzipan, are still prepared in the same manner today.

During his travels to the New World, Columbus carried sugar cane from the Canary Islands to Santo Domingo, where it flourished. As sugar cane became more dispersed geographically, the cost of production dropped, causing sugar to lose status as a luxury item while increasing its importance as a basic nutrient. During the 16th through 19th centuries sugar confectionery began to take hold in Europe.

THE BIRTH OF THE RESTAURANT

The culinary crafts of the baker, butcher, distiller and pastry cook evolved during the Middle Ages under the European guild system. The guild system was a method of organizing the production and sale of goods produced outside the home. Guilds ensured quality manufacturing methods and consistent pricing. Each guild had a monopoly on preparing certain items. For example, during the reign of Henri IV of France (1553–1610), there were separate culinary guilds for *rôtisseurs* (who cooked *la grosse viande*, the main cuts of meat), *pâtissiers* (who cooked poultry, pies and tarts), *tamisiers* (who baked breads), *vinaigriers* (who made sauces and some stews, including some restoratives), *traiteurs* (who made ragouts) and *porte-chapes* (caterers who organized feasts and celebrations).

The French claim that the first modern restaurant opened one day in 1765 when a Parisian tavern keeper, a Monsieur Boulanger, hung a sign advertising the sale of his special restorative, a dish of sheep feet in white sauce. His establishment closed shortly thereafter as the result of a lawsuit brought by a guild whose members claimed that Boulanger was infringing on their exclusive right to sell prepared dishes. Boulanger triumphed in court and later reopened.

Boulanger's establishment differed from the inns and taverns that had existed throughout Europe for centuries. These inns and taverns served foods prepared (usually off premises) by the appropriate guild. The food—of which there was little choice—was offered by the innkeeper as incidental to the establishment's primary function: providing sleeping accommodations or drink. Customers were served family style and ate at communal tables. Boulanger's contribution to the food service industry was to serve a variety of foods prepared on premises to customers whose primary interest was dining.

Several other restaurants opened in Paris during the succeeding decades, including the Grande Taverne de Londres in 1782. Its owner, Antoine Beauvilliers (1754–1817), was the former steward to the Comte de Provence, later King Louis XVIII of France. He advanced the development of the modern restaurant by offering his wealthy patrons a menu listing available dishes during fixed hours. Beauvilliers's impeccably trained wait staff served patrons at small, individual tables in an elegant setting.

The French Revolution (1789–1799) had a significant effect on the budding restaurant industry. Along with the aristocracy, guilds and their monopolies were generally abolished. The revolution also allowed the public access to the skills and creativity of the well-trained, sophisticated chefs who had worked in the aristocracy's private kitchens. Although many of the aristocracy's chefs either left the country or lost their jobs (and some their heads), a few opened restaurants catering to the growing urbanized middle class.

As the 19th century progressed, more restaurants opened, serving a greater selection of items and catering to a wider clientele. By midcentury, several large, grand restaurants in Paris were serving elaborate meals, decidedly reminiscent of the **grande cuisine** (also known as *haute cuisine*) of the aristocracy. *Grande*

RESTORATIVES

The word *restaurant* is derived from the French word *restaurer* ("to restore"). Since the 16th century, the word *restorative* had been used to describe rich and highly flavored soups or stews capable of restoring lost strength. Restoratives, like all other cooked foods offered and purchased outside the home, were made by authorized guild members.

▶ **grande cuisine**—the rich, intricate and elaborate cuisine of the 18th- and 19th-century French aristocracy and upper classes. It is based on the rational identification, development and adoption of strict culinary principles. By emphasizing the how and why of cooking, *grande cuisine* was the first to distinguish itself from regional cuisines, which tend to emphasize the tradition of cooking

MARIE-ANTOINE (ANTONIN) CARÊME (1783–1833)

Carême, known as the "cook of kings and the king of cooks," was an acknowledged master of French *grande cuisine*. Abandoned on the streets of Paris as a child, he worked his way from cook's helper in a working-class restaurant to become one of the most prestigious chefs of his (or, arguably, any other) time. During his career, he was chef to the famous French diplomat and gourmand Prince de Talleyrand, the Prince Regent of England (who became King George IV), Tsar Alexander I of Russia and Baron de Rothschild, among others.

His stated goal was to achieve "lightness," "grace," "order" and "perspicuity" in the preparation and presentation of food. As a pâtissier, he designed and prepared elaborate and elegant pastry and confectionery creations, many of which were based on architectural designs. He is credited with the invention of croquembouche, millefeuile and pulled sugar work. As a showman, he garnished his dishes with ornamental *hâtelets* (skewers) threaded with colorful ingredients such as crayfish and intricately carved vegetables, and presented his creations on elaborate *socles* (bases). As a saucier, he standardized the use of roux as a thickening agent, perfected

Courtesy of Barbara Wheaton

recipes and devised a system for classifying sauces. As a *garde-manger*, Carême popularized cold cuisine, emphasizing molds and aspic dishes. As a culinary professional, he designed kitchen tools, equipment and uniforms.

As an author, he wrote and illustrated important texts on the culinary arts, including *Le Maître d'hotel français* (1822), describing the hundreds of dishes he personally created and cooked in the capitals of Europe; *Le Pâtissier royal Parisian* (1825), containing fanciful designs for *les pieces montées*, the great decorative centerpieces that were the crowning glory of grand dinners; and his five-volume masterpiece on the state of his profession, *L'Art de la cuisine au XIXe siècle* (1833), the last two volumes of which were completed after his death by his associate Plumerey. Carême's writings almost single-handedly refined and summarized 500 years of culinary evolution. But his treatises were not mere cookbooks. Rather, he analyzed cooking, old and new, emphasizing procedure and order and covering every aspect of the art known as grande cuisine.

Carême died before age 50, burnt out, according to Laurent Tailhade, "by the flame of his genius and the coal of the spits."

cuisine, which arguably reached its peak of perfection in the hands of Antonin Carême, was characterized by meals consisting of dozens of courses of elaborately and intricately prepared, presented, garnished and sauced foods. Carême was known for advancing the art of the **pâtissier** by creating elaborate showpieces made with pastillage and pulled sugar. A great innovator, he is credited with perfecting nougat, meringue, croquembouche and millefeuille.

▶ **pâtissier**—French for pastry chef; the person responsible for all baked items, including breads, pastries and desserts

THE LATE 19TH CENTURY—ESCOFFIER AND CUISINE CLASSIQUE

Following the lead set by the French in both culinary style and the restaurant business, restaurants opened in the United States and throughout Europe during the 19th century. Charles Ranhofer (1836–1899) was the first internationally renowned chef of an American restaurant, Delmonico's in New York City. In 1893, Ranhofer published his "franco-american" encyclopedia of cooking, *The Epicurean*, containing more than 3500 recipes.

One of the finest restaurants outside France was the dining room at London's Savoy Hotel, opened in 1898 under the direction of Cesar Ritz (1850–1918) and Auguste Escoffier. Escoffier is generally credited with refining the *grande cuisine* of Carême to create *cuisine classique* or **classic cuisine.** By doing so, he brought French cuisine into the 20th century.

▶ **classic cuisine**—a late 19th- and early 20th-century refinement and simplification of French *grande cuisine*. Classic (or classical) cuisine relies on the thorough exploration of culinary principles and techniques, and emphasizes the refined preparation and presentation of superb ingredients

AUGUSTE ESCOFFIER (1846–1935)

Escoffier's brilliant culinary career began at age 13 in his uncle's restaurant and continued until his death at age 89. Called the "emperor of the world's kitchens," he is perhaps best known for defining French cuisine and dining during La Belle Époque (the "Gay Nineties").

Unlike Carême, Escoffier never worked in an aristocratic household. Rather, he exhibited his culinary skills in the dining rooms of the finest hotels in Europe, including the Place Vendôme in Paris and the Savoy and Carlton Hotels in London.

Escoffier did much to enhance the *grande cuisine* that arguably reached its perfection under Carême. Crediting Carême with providing the foundation for great—that is, French—cooking, Escoffier simplified the profusion of flavors, dishes and garnishes typifying Carême's work. He also streamlined some of Carême's overly elaborate and fussy procedures and classifications. For example, he reduced Carême's elaborate system of classifying sauces into the five families of sauces still recognized today. Escoffier sought simplicity and aimed for the perfect balance of a few superb ingredients. Some

consider his refinement of *grande cuisine* to have been so radical as to credit him with the development of a new cuisine referred to as *cuisine classique* (classic or classical cuisine).

His many writings include *Le Livre des menus* (1912), in which, discussing the principles

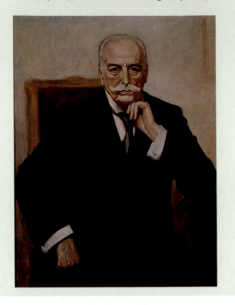

of a well-planned meal, he analogizes a great dinner to a symphony with contrasting movements that should be appropriate to the occasion, the guests and the season, and *Ma cuisine* (1934), surveying *cuisine bourgeoisie*. But his most important contribution is a culinary treatise intended for the professional chef entitled *Le Guide culinaire* (1903). Still in use today, it is an astounding collection of more than 5000 classic cuisine recipes and garnishes. In it, Escoffier emphasizes the mastery of techniques, the thorough understanding of cooking, principles and the appreciation of ingredients—attributes he considered to be the building blocks professional chefs should use to create great dishes.

Escoffier was honored as a Chevalier of the French Legion of Honour in 1920 for his work in enhancing the reputation of French cuisine. Escoffier's most famous recipe was Peach Melba, created for Australian opera star Nellie Melba (1861–1931) when she was staying at the Savoy in 1893. Dame Melba also liked her toast made in the way that today bears her name: Melba toast.

THE MID-20TH CENTURY—POINT AND NOUVELLE CUISINE

The mid-20th century witnessed a trend toward lighter, more naturally flavored and more simply prepared foods. Fernand Point was a master practitioner of this movement. But this master's goal of simplicity and refinement was carried to even greater heights by a generation of chefs Point trained: principally, Paul Bocuse, Jean and Pierre Troisgros, Alain Chapel, Francois Bise and Louis Outhier. They, along with Michel Guérard and Roger Vergé, were the pioneers of **nouvelle cuisine** in the early 1970s. In the world of the pâtissier, Gaston Lenôtre made inroads by taking the classic pastries of *grande cuisine* and adapting them to a brighter, fresher style of pastry making.

▶ **nouvelle cuisine**—French for "new cooking"; a mid-20th-century movement away from many classic cuisine principles and toward a lighter cuisine based on natural flavors, shortened cooking times and innovative combinations

Their culinary philosophy was principled on the rejection of overly rich, needlessly complicated dishes. These chefs emphasized healthful eating. The ingredients must be absolutely fresh and of the highest possible quality; the cooking methods should be simple and direct whenever possible. The accompaniments and garnishes must be light and contribute to an overall harmony; the completed plates must be elegantly designed and decorated. Following these guidelines, some traditional cooking methods have been applied to untraditional ingredients, and ingredients have been combined in new and previously unorthodox fashions.

RETURN TO CRAFTSMANSHIP AND THE ARTISAN BREAD MOVEMENT

During this period, a number of Parisian bread bakers, notably Lionel Poilâne, sought to return simplicity to quality bread making. The bread most often associated with France—the long, golden brown baguette with the white fluffy interior—

GASTON LENÔTRE (1920–   )

Gaston Lenôtre started in the baking trade in the heart of Normandy in the 1930s. By age 15, he had passed his professional exams and set off to work in his hometown. In 1947, he bought the boulangerie/pâtisserie of his boss in Pont Audemer. His bakery became a destination for sophisticated Parisians on their way to their country estates. In 1957 he was enticed to open a shop in Paris at 44, rue d'Auteuil in the 16th *arrondissement*, one of the city's most stylish sections. It was the first of more than a baker's dozen of locations, plus a vast catering business, which literally catered to "le tout Paris."

Lenôtre chose the village of Plaisir outside Paris for his third location—a vast production kitchen that became the heart of his expanding empire. He saw that to realize his expansion plans, he needed to train workers in his methods. In 1971, he began an in-house school, L'École Lenôtre. But here is where Gaston Lenôtre has shown himself to be much more than a talented baker and inspired businessman: There was a crisis in the trade at the time due to a lack of qualified bakers so Lenôtre opened the school, a few years later, to the entire professional community. For a fee, even his competi-

tors could come learn from his *Meilleurs Ouvriers de France*—chefs recognized by the French government as the best artisans in the trade.

As befitting a native of Normandy, the heart of France's dairy industry, Lenôtre's innovations came in the area of Bavarians, Charlottes and fruit mousses. Many of his cakes and tortes became modern classics, copied by pastry chefs worldwide. La Feuille d'Automne, Le Concorde,

L'Opéra and the Charlotte Cécile seemed to be in all the Parisian bakeries in the early 1980s. Lenôtre mastered the technique of freezing, using it with respect to protect the quality of his products without adulterating them. He used the latest technology and had a staff of laboratory experts working full-time to maintain the integrity of his products. Proper freezing preserves the product, extending its shelf life without having to use chemicals and preservatives common in industrial food production. Many professionals believe that Lenôtre single-handedly saved the pastry profession when it was threatened by mass production.

Lenôtre is considered by many as the father of modern French pastry, and his impact is worldwide. By the early 1980s he had 18 stores in Japan as well as outposts in Germany, Switzerland and England. Today, whether you go to Rio de Janeiro, Disney World in Florida, Lebanon or Las Vegas, you will find Lenôtre's name on the marquee.

—Alex Miles, pastry chef and culinary educator, Dijon, France

---

is a 20th-century invention. In the 1920s a new mixing technique was introduced, which produced lighter, softer bread than what had been available previously. During World War II, severe shortages forced bread rationing in France. The scarce bread that was available during the war was made from whole grains extended with inferior ingredients such as ground beans. According to French historian Jérôme Assire, this bread's offensive taste made the longing for pure white bread even more intense. Following the war, the demand for the fluffy white bread was greater than ever. New dough mixing methods and rack ovens capable of handling large numbers of loaves produced plenty of bread to meet this demand.

In the 1960s Lionel Poilâne began working at his father's bakery where he learned to make an old-style loaf of bread like that sold by bakers in 18th-century Paris. Using a blend of whole-meal flours and long fermentation (rising) times, he learned to bake breads on the stone floor of a wood-fired oven. Following his lead, other bakers in Paris were similarly inspired to rediscover traditional ways of making flavorful bread. These bakers inspired an international interest in producing what is called **artisan** bread, bread made in traditional ways with the purest of ingredients.

THE LATE 20TH CENTURY—AN AMERICAN CULINARY REVOLUTION

During the last 30 years, broad changes have affected the culinary landscape in the United States. During this period, restaurateurs and chefs began Americanizing the principles of French *nouvelle cuisine*. When Alice Waters opened Chez Panisse in Berkeley, California, in 1971, her goal was to serve fresh food, simply prepared. Rejecting the growing popularity of processed and packaged foods,

▶ **artisan**—a person who works in a skilled craft or trade; one who works with his or her hands. Applied to bread bakers and confectioners who prepare foods using traditional methods

LIONEL POILÂNE (1945–2002)

"What many bakers don't realize is that good wheat can make bad bread. The magic of bread baking is in the manipulation and the fermentation. What has been lost . . . is this method."
Lionel Poilâne

Called a true visionary and an ambassador of bread, Lionel Poilâne is credited with elevating the craft of bread baking and the appreciation of traditional artisan ways of making bread in our time. At age 14, he began working in his father's small bakery on a project that would become his life's passion. His father had started making a large dark rustic loaf, like that which was common in Paris before the light baguette style bread captivated the city in the 1920s. Enchanted by this old-style bread, Poilâne dedicated himself to reviving traditional regional breads. Renowned for his attention to detail and appreciation of the craft of the baker, in the early 1980s he set out to document regional

bread recipes. Captured in his book, *Guide de l'Amateur de Pain*, these breads were fading memories before he rediscovered them. His

book is used as a reference text in schools throughout France to this day.

Thousands of loaves of *pain Poilâne*, the name for his singular crusty round loaf, are made each day in a production bakery outside of Paris. This bread is sold in restaurants and shops throughout Paris and flown to the United States and more than a dozen other countries daily. While the production is large, it is not industrialized. He believed in what he called "retro-innovation," combining the best of the old techniques with modern advances. Two bakers work at each of 24 wood-fired stone ovens, forming the loaves by hand. The original shop at 8 rue du Cherche-Midi is situated on the site of an 18th-century monastery and houses ovens dating from that time. The shop, which still sells fresh pain Poilâne and a limited selection of other baked goods, is a Mecca for serious bread lovers from around the world.

▶ **New American cuisine**—a late-20th-century movement that began in California but has spread across the United States; it stresses the use of fresh, locally grown, seasonal produce and high-quality ingredients simply prepared in a fashion that preserves and emphasizes natural flavors

▶ **fusion cuisine**—the blending or use of ingredients and/or preparation methods from various ethnic, regional or national cuisines in the same dish; also known as transnational cuisine

▶ **national cuisine**—the characteristic cuisine of a nation

Waters wanted to use fresh, seasonal and locally grown produce in simple preparations that preserved and emphasized the foods' natural flavors. Chez Panisse and the many chefs who passed through its kitchen launched a new style of cuisine that became known as **New American cuisine.**

As Waters's culinary philosophy spread across the United States, farmers and chefs began working together to make fresh, locally grown foods available, and producers and suppliers began developing domestic sources for some of the high-quality ingredients that were once available only from overseas. European-style cultured butter from Vermont and goat cheese from Sonoma, California, are just two examples.

Pastry chefs and bakers followed Waters's lead. Those who fell under her direct influence, including Lindsey Shire and Steve Sullivan, and others such as Nancy Silverton, traveled to France to study as Waters had done. They returned with European skills and a desire to serve desserts with freshness and simplicity. Pastry chefs and bakers, exposed to the work of Lenôtre and Poilâne on their travels, brought these influences into kitchens throughout this country.

By the mid-1980s, American chefs began a period of bold experimentation. They began to combine ingredients or preparation methods of a variety of cuisines. Their work resulted in **fusion cuisine.** With fusion cuisine, ingredients or preparation methods associated with one ethnic or regional cuisine are combined with those of another. French pastry cream flavored with star anise served with a banana spring roll and kiwi Napoleon are examples of fusion style preparations.

Others worked to rediscover American cooking and baking traditions. Lacking professional reference texts on the subject, professionals turned to cookbooks written for home consumers for inspiration. Talented pastry chefs such as Maida Heatter, whose 1974 book *Maida Heatter's Book of Great Desserts* became a well-thumbed reference in professional kitchens in the 1970s and 1980s, introduced the restaurant public to homey desserts including Palm Beach Brownies and Sweet Potato Pecan Pie.

Along with this new interest in and appreciation for American ingredients and American tastes has come a new respect for American chefs. Many European and

American food writers and pundits now consider American chefs among the best in the world, a fact they often triumph at the same time they express their concern about the general decline of French cuisine and the exodus of European chefs to America. In addition, the American public has taken food to heart.

Many chefs have been elevated to celebrity status; an entire cable television network is devoted to cooking. Bookstore and library shelves are jammed with cookbooks, and newspapers and magazines regularly review restaurants or report on culinary trends. With gourmet shops and cookware stores in most malls, cooking has become both a hobby and a spectator sport. All this has helped to inspire a generation of American teenagers to pursue careers behind the stove—and in front of the camera.

▶ THE BAKESHOP AND FOOD SERVICE OPERATION

Professional bakeshops may be small sections within a restaurant kitchen or a separate kitchen composed of many departments with its own staff and operating budget. No matter the size, the organizational concepts are the same. To function efficiently, a food service operation must be well organized and staffed with appropriate personnel. This staff is sometimes called a **brigade.** Escoffier is credited with developing the kitchen brigade system used in large restaurant kitchens. From the chaos and redundancy found in the private kitchens of the aristocracy, he created a distinct hierarchy of responsibilities and functions for commercial food service operations.

▶ **brigade**—a system of staffing a kitchen so that each worker is assigned a set of specific tasks; these tasks are often related by cooking method, equipment or the types of foods being produced

Today most food service operations use a simplified version of Escoffier's kitchen brigade. The **executive chef** coordinates kitchen activities and directs the kitchen staff's training and work efforts. The executive chef plans menus and creates recipes. He or she sets and enforces nutrition, safety and sanitation standards and participates in (or at least observes) the preparation and presentation of menu items to ensure that quality standards are rigorously and consistently maintained. He or she is also responsible for purchasing food items and, often, equipment. In some food service operations, the executive chef may assist in designing the menu, dining room and kitchen. He or she trains the dining room staff so that they can correctly answer questions about the menu. He or she may also work with food purveyors to learn about new food items and products, as well as with catering directors, equipment vendors, food stylists, restaurant consultants, public relations specialists, sanitation engineers, nutritionists and dietitians.

The executive chef is assisted by a **sous-chef** or executive sous-chef, who participates in, supervises and coordinates the preparation of menu items. His or her primary responsibility is to make sure that the food is prepared, portioned, garnished and presented according to the executive chef's standards. The sous-chef may be the cook principally responsible for producing menu items and supervising the kitchen.

Large hotels and conference centers with multiple dining facilities may have one or more **area chefs,** each responsible for a specific facility or function. There could be, for instance, a restaurant chef and a banquet chef. Area chefs usually report to the executive chef. Each area chef, in turn, has a brigade working under him or her. **Assistants** and **apprentices** are assigned where needed to assist and learn the area.

The **pastry chef** (Fr. *pâtissier*) is responsible for developing recipes for and preparing desserts, pastries, frozen desserts and breads. He or she reports directly to the executive chef and is usually responsible for purchasing the food items used in the bakeshop. In a large operation, there may be an **executive pastry chef** overseeing a staff of pastry specialists. A classic kitchen brigade would include a pastry chef, who supervises the **bread baker** (Fr. *boulanger*) who makes the breads, rolls and baked dough containers used for other menu items (for example, bouchées and feuilletés); the **confectioner** (Fr. *confiseur*), who makes candies and petits fours; the **ice cream maker** (Fr. *glacier*), who makes all chilled and frozen desserts; and the **decorator** (Fr. *décorateur*), who makes showpieces and special cakes. An executive pastry chef possesses the same authority and responsibility within his or her area of expertise as would an executive chef.

The independent retail pastry shop or bakeshop is organized into departments according to the tasks required. A **head baker** directs the mixing and baking of all baked goods. He or she may purchase all ingredients and train the staff on preparation. One group of bakers may be responsible for baking the bread while another group mixes all the yeast dough and laminated dough to make breads and pastries. A cake decorator fills and ices cakes according to the style of the operation.

A bakeshop may employ a **master baker** (Fr. *maître boulanger*, Gr. *Bäckermeister*). This title recognizes the highest level of achievement; only highly skilled and experienced bakers who have demonstrated their professional knowledge in written and practical exams are entitled to use it. This title recalls the European guild tradition still alive in many countries today. In France and Germany, for example, a baker must pursue many years of classroom and job training, work as an apprentice and pass numerous examinations before acquiring the right to call himself or herself a "master baker." In the United States, several professional organizations administer programs leading to certification as a master baker. (See Appendix IV.)

THE PROFESSIONAL PASTRY CHEF AND BAKER

Although there is no one recipe for producing a good professional chef, with knowledge, skill, taste, judgment, dedication and pride a student chef will mature into a professional chef.

KNOWLEDGE

Pastry chefs and bakers must be able to identify, purchase, utilize and prepare a wide variety of foods. They should be able to train and supervise a safe, skilled and efficient staff. To do all this successfully, professional pastry chefs and bakers must possess a body of knowledge and understand and apply certain scientific and business principles. Schooling helps. A professional culinary program should, at a minimum, provide the student chef with a basic knowledge of foods, food styles and the methods used to prepare foods. Student chefs should also have an understanding of sanitation, nutrition and business procedures such as food costing.

This book is designed to help teach these basics as applied to the pastry and baking profession. The study begins with extensive sections identifying equipment, tools and ingredients. Throughout this book, basic baking principles are discussed while formulas illustrate these principles in action. Whenever possible, whether it be preparing puff pastry or ice cream, the focus of the material is on the general procedure, highlighting fundamental principles and skills, both the how and why of baking. Only then are specific applications and sample formulas given. In order for the student to gain a sense of the rich tradition of food and the baking and pastry arts, informative sidebars on food history, chef biographies and other topics are scattered throughout the book.

In this way, the materials in this book follow the trail blazed by Escoffier, who wrote in the introduction to *Le Guide culinaire* that his book is not intended to be a compendium of recipes slavishly followed, but rather his treatise should be a tool that leaves his colleagues "free to develop their own methods and follow their own inspiration; . . . the art of cooking . . . will evolve as a society evolves, . . . only basic rules remain unalterable."

AN HONEST LOAF

It is astonishing that the word *artisan* as it applies to bread baking remains so challenging to define. "I know it when I see it," "Bread made all by hand," "Bread made by hand except for mechanical mixing and an oven," and "Bread made from the soul of the baker" all have been presented by various spokespeople. I once heard someone call artisan bread "an honest loaf" and it made me think of all the implications of our craft—not the inference of the word but the impact of a lifelong quest for the bread they call "honest."

To today's artisanal baker, the creation of an honest loaf goes beyond man versus machine. It's about respect. Respect for everything that occurs before the baker creates the loaf and respect for everything that the loaf means after it leaves the bakery. Today's baker knows the source of the wheat, sometimes the name of the farmer who planted it and has respect for the methodology used to sustain the wheat field. Today's artisanal baker knows where the wheat was milled and has a good understanding of complicated scientific tests that predict the quality of the grain. To bake an honest loaf the baker maintains the integrity of the bread-baking process, facing day-to-day challenges without taking shortcuts. The baker realizes that his or her art is on display not in a museum but in a home, around the family dinner table sharing all the joy and pain of reality. Finally being a prideful sort, today's artisanal baker realizes that unselfishly teaching others, sharing information, and setting an example of professional discipline are the cornerstones of sustaining the honest loaf.

A famous singer once compared herself to Rembrandt. "It's not easy to be a performing artist. Rembrandt only had to paint *Return of the Prodigal Son* once. I have to paint it every time I perform." The same could be said about the artisanal baker. The quest for the honest loaf is eternal.

—Greg Mistell, owner, Delphina's Bakery and Pearl Bakery, Portland, Oregon; past chairman, Bread Bakers Guild of America

As with any profession, an education does not stop at graduation. The acquisition of knowledge continues after the student joins the ranks of the employed. He or she should take additional classes on pastry traditions and techniques, nutrition, business management or specialized skills. He or she should regularly review some of the many periodicals and books devoted to baking and the pastry arts. Well-rounded food professionals should travel and should try new dishes to broaden their culinary horizons. The professional pastry chef and baker should also become involved in professional organizations (see Appendix IV) in order to meet his or her peers and exchange ideas.

SKILL

Culinary schooling alone does not make a student a pastry chef or baker. Nothing but practical, hands-on experience will provide even the most academically gifted student with the skills needed to produce, consistently and efficiently, quality foods or to organize, train, motivate and supervise a staff.

Many food service operations recognize that new workers, even those who have graduated from culinary programs, need time and experience to develop and hone their skills. Therefore, many graduates start in entry-level positions. Do not be discouraged; advancement will come, and the training pays off in the long run. Today, culinary styles and fashions change frequently. What does not go out of fashion are well-trained, skilled and knowledgeable chefs. They can adapt.

TASTE

No matter how knowledgeable or skilled the chef, he or she must be able to produce foods that taste great, or the consumer will not return. A chef can do so only if he or she is confident about his or her own sense of taste.

Our total perception of taste is a complex combination of smell, taste, sight, sound and texture. All senses are involved in the enjoyment of eating; all must be considered in creating or preparing a dish. The chef should develop a taste memory by sampling foods, both familiar and unfamiliar. The chef should also think about what he or she tastes, making notes and experimenting with flavor combinations and cooking methods. But a chef should not be inventive simply for the sake of invention. Rather, he or she must consider how the flavors, appearances, textures and aromas of various foods will interact to create a total taste experience.

WORDS TO SURVIVE IN A PROFESSIONAL KITCHEN

So you want to be a pastry chef and spend your life trying to satisfy the nation's insatiable sweet tooth? No one has more friends than a pastry chef, but getting there is hard work and only for the very dedicated. However, if you are the kind of person who can't fall asleep at night because you're distracted by a new dessert you thought up using figs, crème brûlée base, cheddar cheese ice cream and a port reduction, then this may be the art form for you.

You may have discovered your love for baking at your mom's knee, but she's not coming into the pro kitchen with you. So make sure you chose it for the right reason—because you can't imagine doing anything else. Keep in mind that everyone has something to teach you, even your chef. As you truss yourself into your apron, feel confident, feel strong, play well with others in the sandbox and teach your hands to work like a surgeon's, in consort with your mind. Constantly try new recipes and solve problems, not make them. Scrape your mixing bowl often, more often than you really want to and check your math twice when scaling up a recipe.

The main thing is to always, always, always wear comfortable shoes. If your feet are happy you'll be happy and you'll be successful at this glorious form of expression called Pastry.

—Gale Gand, pastry chef and co-owner, Tru, Chicago, IL

JUDGMENT

Creating a pastry menu, determining how much of what item to order, deciding whether and how to combine ingredients and approving finished items for service are all matters of judgment. Although knowledge and skill play a role in developing judgment, sound judgment comes only with experience. And real experience is often accompanied by failure. Do not be upset or surprised when a dish does not turn out as expected. One can learn from mistakes as well as from successes; these experiences help develop sound judgment.

DEDICATION

Becoming a pastry chef and baker is hard work; so is being one. The work is often physically taxing; the hours, often in the early morning, are usually long and the pace is frequently hectic. Despite these pressures, the professional is expected to efficiently produce consistently fine products that are properly prepared and presented. To do so requires pastry chefs and bakers who are dedicated to the job.

Dedication means never faltering. The bakery and food service industry is competitive and depends on the continuing goodwill of an often fickle public. One bad dish, one pale loaf or one off night can result in a disgruntled customer and lost business. The pastry chef and baker should always be mindful of the food prepared and the customer served.

The true professional is dedicated to his or her staff. Virtually all bakeries and food service operations rely on teamwork to get the job done well. Good teamwork requires a positive attitude and dedication to a shared goal.

PRIDE

Professional bakers and pastry chefs share a sense of pride in doing their jobs well. Pride should also extend to personal appearance and behavior in and around the kitchen. The professional should be well groomed and in uniform when working.

The pastry chef wears the same uniform as that worn by a professional chef: comfortable shoes, trousers (either solid white, solid black, black-and-white checked or black-and-white striped), a white double-breasted jacket, an apron and a neckerchief usually knotted or tied cravat style. The uniform has certain utilitarian aspects: Checked trousers disguise stains; the double-breasted white jacket can be rebuttoned to hide dirt, and the double layer of fabric protects from scalds and burns; the neckerchief absorbs facial perspiration and the apron protects the uniform and insulates the body.

The professional baker's uniform varies from that of the professional chef. While comfortable shoes are the foundation of any food professional's uniform, the baker may wear white trousers and a short-sleeved white shirt. The choice of white is utilitarian; it does not show the presence of flour as would a dark-colored uniform. The uniform should be worn with pride. Shoes should be polished; trousers and jacket should be pressed.

The crowning element of the uniform is the **toque.** A toque is the tall white hat worn by chefs almost everywhere. Although the toque traces its origin to the monasteries of the 6th century, the style worn today was introduced at the end of the 19th century. Most chefs now wear a standard 6- or 9-inch-high toque, but historically, a cook's rank in the kitchen dictated the type of hat worn. Beginners wore flat-topped calottes; cooks with more advanced skills wore low toques and the master chefs wore high toques called *dodin-bouffants*. Culinary lore holds that the toque's pleats—101 in all—represent the 101 ways its wearer can successfully prepare eggs. Traditionally, the baker wears a flat-topped baker's cap. Its derivation is quite simple; bending and working close to the bread oven would prevent a tall cap from staying in place.

▶ SAFETY AND SANITATION

Like all food service professionals, pastry chefs and bakeshop workers must have a thorough understanding of sanitation principles and practices. The threat of transmitting food-borne illnesses is of serious concern to all food professionals. Providing consumers with well-prepared and safe food is the primary responsibility of all cooking professionals.

Microorganisms that cause food-borne illnesses can be destroyed or their growth severely limited by proper food-handling procedures. Bacteria, molds, yeasts, viruses and fungi are **microorganisms** that thrive on certain foods. These foods are referred to as potentially hazardous foods (PHF). By observing proper handling and sanitation procedures, kitchen workers can stop the spread or growth of these microorganisms.

SAFE FOOD-HANDLING PRACTICES

Learning about food contaminants, how they are spread and how they can be prevented or controlled can help ensure customer safety. **Temperature** is the most important factor in the **pathogenic** bacteria's environment because it is the factor most easily controlled by food service workers. Most microorganisms are destroyed at high temperatures. Freezing slows but does not stop growth, nor does it destroy bacteria.

Most bacteria that cause food-borne illnesses multiply rapidly at temperatures between 60°F and 120°F (16°C and 49°C). Therefore, the broad range of temperatures between 40°F and 140°F (4°C and 60°C) is referred to as the **temperature danger zone.** See Figure 1.1. Keeping foods out of the temperature danger zone decreases the bacteria's ability to thrive and reproduce.

To control the growth of any bacteria that may be present, it is important to maintain the internal temperature of food at 140°F (60°C) or above, or 40°F (4°C) or below. Simply stated: Keep hot foods hot and cold foods cold. Potentially hazardous foods should be heated or cooled quickly so that they are within the temperature danger zone as briefly as possible. This is known as the time-and-temperature principle.

Keep hot foods hot. The high internal temperatures reached during proper cooking kill most of the bacteria that can cause food-borne illnesses. Once properly heated, hot foods must be held at temperatures of 140°F (60°C) or above. Foods that are to be displayed or served hot must be heated rapidly to reduce the time within the temperature danger zone. When heating or reheating foods:

- ▶ Heat small quantities at a time.
- ▶ Stir frequently.
- ▶ Heat foods as close to service time as possible.
- ▶ Use preheated ingredients whenever possible to prepare hot foods.
- ▶ Never use a steam table for heating or reheating foods. Bring reheated food to an appropriate internal temperature (at least 165°F/74°C) before placing it in the steam table for holding.

Keep cold foods cold. Foods that are to be displayed, stored or served cold must be cooled rapidly. When cooling foods:

- ▶ Refrigerate semisolid foods at 40°F (4°C) or below in containers that are less than 2 inches deep. (Increased surface area decreases cooling time.)
- ▶ Avoid crowding the refrigerator; allow air to circulate around foods.
- ▶ Vent hot foods in an ice-water bath, as illustrated in Chapter 5, Mise en Place.
- ▶ Prechill ingredients such as pastry cream before preparing cold foods.
- ▶ Store cooked foods above raw foods to prevent cross-contamination.

POTENTIALLY HAZARDOUS FOODS

A potentially hazardous food (PHF) is any food or food ingredient that will support the rapid growth of infectious or toxigenic microorganisms, or the slower growth of *Clostridium botulinum*. Potentially hazardous foods include the following:

- Food from an animal source (for example, meat, fish, shellfish, poultry, milk and eggs)
- Food from a plant that has been heat-treated (for example, cooked rice, beans, potatoes, soy products and pasta)
- Raw seed sprouts
- Cut melons
- Garlic in oil mixtures that are not acidified or otherwise appropriately modified at a processing plant
- Foods containing any of the preceding items (for example, custards, sauces and casseroles)

▶ **microorganisms**—single-celled organisms as well as tiny plants and animals that can be seen only through a microscope

▶ **pathogen**—any organism that causes disease; usually refers to bacteria

THE TEMPERATURE DANGER ZONE

The temperature danger zone is a broad range of temperatures in which most of the bacteria that cause food-borne illnesses multiply rapidly. The 2000 Model Food Code of the Food and Drug Administration (FDA) indicates that the temperature danger zone begins at 41°F (5°C) and ends at 140°F (60°C). Regulations in some localities state that the danger zone begins at 45°F (7°C) or ends at 130°F (54°C), however. Here we use the broader range recommended by the U.S. Department of Agriculture (USDA)—40°F to 140°F (4°C to 60°C)—since this provides a slightly greater margin of safety.

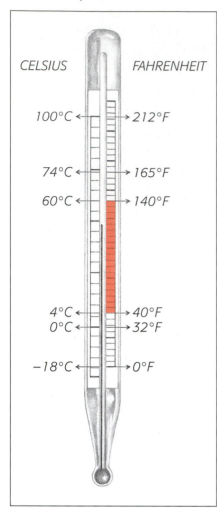

CELSIUS   FAHRENHEIT

100°C ←   → 212°F

74°C ←   → 165°F
60°C ←   → 140°F

4°C ←   → 40°F
0°C ←   → 32°F

−18°C ←   → 0°F

FIGURE 1.1 ▶ The temperature danger zone

Keep frozen foods frozen. Freezing at 0°F (−18°C) or below essentially stops bacterial growth but will not kill the bacteria. Do not place hot foods in a standard freezer. This will not cool the food any faster, and the release of heat can raise the temperature of other foods in the freezer. Only a special blast freezer can be used for chilling hot items. If one is not available, cool hot foods as mentioned earlier before freezing them. When frozen foods are thawed, bacteria that are present will begin to grow. Therefore:

▶ Never thaw foods at room temperature.
▶ Thaw foods gradually under refrigeration to maintain the food's temperature at 40°F (4°C) or less. Place thawing foods in a container to prevent cross-contamination from dripping or leaking liquids.
▶ Thaw foods under running water at a temperature of 70°F (21°C) or cooler.
▶ Thaw foods in a microwave only if the food will be prepared and served immediately.

Bacteria need moisture to thrive. Dry foods such as flour, sugar and crackers are rarely subject to bacterial infestations. However, when a dry food such as beans is cooked and moistened it becomes a breeding ground for the growth of any bacteria that may be present. Bacteria do not thrive in foods that are high in acid such as lemon juice or vinegar. Simply adding acid, however, should not be relied on to destroy bacteria or to preserve foods.

CROSS-CONTAMINATION

Generally, microorganisms and other contaminants cannot move by themselves. Rather, they are carried to foods and food contact surfaces by humans, rodents or insects. This transfer is referred to as **cross-contamination.** Humans provide the ideal environment for the growth of microorganisms. Everyone harbors bacteria in the nose and mouth. These bacteria spread easily by sneezing or coughing or not washing hands frequently and properly.

Observing proper cleaning procedures prevents cross-contamination. You can do several things to decrease the risk of an illness being spread by poor personal hygiene:

▶ Wash your hands frequently and thoroughly. Gloves are not a substitute for proper hand washing.
▶ Keep your fingernails short, clean and neat. Do not bite your nails or wear nail polish.
▶ Keep any cut or wound antiseptically bandaged. An injured hand should also be covered with a disposable glove.
▶ Bathe daily, or more often if required.
▶ Keep your hair clean and restrained.
▶ Wear work clothes that are clean and neat. Avoid wearing jewelry or watches.
▶ Do not eat, drink, smoke or chew gum in food preparation areas.

Cross-contamination is preventable by observing proper cleaning and sanitizing procedures. Soiled cutting boards, knives and side towels are major sources of cross-contamination. For example, when a cutting board that has been used to cut raw poultry is used to slice fruit for a salad, the fruit can become exposed to microorganisms present in the poultry.

Cleanliness refers to removing visible soil and food residue. Sanitizing refers to removing harmful substances to safe levels. Something that may be clean may not always be sanitary; the visible dirt can be removed but the disease-causing microorganism may remain. The cleaning of dishes, pots, pans and utensils in a food service operation involves both removing soil and sanitizing. Soil can be

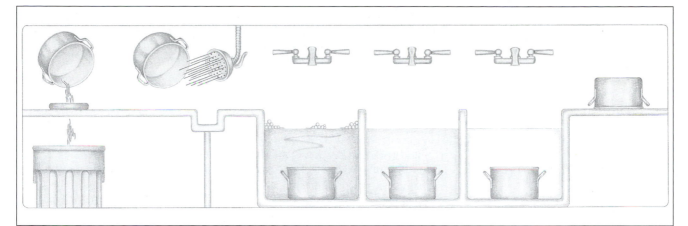

FIGURE 1.2 ▶ The three-compartment sink procedure—scrape, spray, wash, rinse, sanitize and air-dry each item.

removed manually or by machine. Sanitizing can be accomplished with heat or chemical disinfectants.

Procedures for manually washing, rinsing and sanitizing dishes and equipment generally follow the three-compartment sink setup shown in Figure 1.2. The dish washer must do the following:

1 Scrape and spray the item to remove soil.

2 Wash the item in the first sink compartment using an approved detergent. A brush or cloth may be used to remove any remaining soil.

3 Rinse the item in the second sink compartment using clear, hot water.

4 Sanitize the item in the third sink compartment by either:

    a. immersing it in 171°F (77°C) water for at least 30 seconds, or

    b. immersing it in an approved chemical sanitizing solution used according to the manufacturer's directions.

5 Empty, clean and refill each sink compartment as necessary, and check the water temperature regularly.

Food service items, dishes, silverware and utensils should always be allowed to air-dry, as towel drying might recontaminate them.

Chemical products used to clean and sanitize equipment should be stored well away from clean equipment and foodstuffs to avoid contaminating foodstuffs with these chemicals.

Pest control is of special concern in the bakeshop as insect and rodent infestation of bulk ingredients such as flour and grains can introduce harmful contaminants to otherwise safe ingredients. An insect or rodent infestation is usually considered a serious health risk and should be dealt with immediately and thoroughly. Pests must be controlled by (1) building them out of the facility, (2) creating an environment in which they cannot find food, water or shelter and (3) relying on professional extermination.

The best defense against pests is to prevent infestations in the first place by building them out. Any crack—no matter how small—in door frames, walls or windowsills should be repaired immediately, and all drains, pipes and vents should be well sealed. Inspect all deliveries thoroughly, and reject any packages or containers that contain evidence of pests.

Flies are a perfect method of transportation for bacteria because they feed and breed on human waste and garbage. Use screens or "fly fans" (also known as air curtains) to keep them out in the first place. Controlling garbage is also essential because moist, warm, decaying organic material attracts flies and provides favorable conditions for eggs to hatch and larvae to grow.

PROPER HAND-WASHING PROCEDURE

- Use hot running water.
- Wet hands and forearms.
- Apply an antibacterial soap.
- Rub hands and arms briskly with soapy lather for at least 20 seconds.
- Scrub between fingers and clean nails with a clean nail brush.
- Rinse thoroughly under hot running water.
- Reapply soap and scrub hands and forearms for another 5–10 seconds.
- Rinse again.
- Dry hands and arms using a single-use towel.
- Use the towel to turn off the water.
- Discard the towel in a trash receptacle.

Pest management also requires creating an inhospitable environment for pests. Store all food and supplies at least 6 inches off the floor and 6 inches away from walls. Rotate stock often to disrupt nesting places and breeding habits. Provide good ventilation in storerooms to remove humidity, airborne contaminants, grease and fumes. Do not allow water to stand in drains, sinks or buckets, as cockroaches are attracted to moisture. Clean up spills and crumbs immediately and completely to reduce their food supply.

Despite your best efforts to build pests out and maintain proper housekeeping standards, it is still important to watch for the presence of pests. For example, cockroaches leave a strong, oily odor and feces that look like large grains of pepper. Cockroaches prefer to search for food and water in the dark, so seeing any cockroach on the move in the daylight is an indication of a large infestation.

Rodents (mice and rats) tend to hide during the day, so an infestation may be rather serious before any creature is actually seen. Rodent droppings, which are shiny black to brownish gray, may be evident, however. Rodent nests made from scraps of paper, hair or other soft materials may be spotted.

Should an infestation occur, consult a licensed pest control operator immediately. With early detection and proper treatment, infestations can be eliminated. Be very careful in attempting to use pesticides or insecticides yourself. These chemicals are toxic to humans as well as to pests. Great care must be used to prevent contaminating food or exposing workers or customers to the chemicals.

THE SAFE WORKER

Food service professionals are also responsible for their own personal safety as well as that of their customers and fellow workers. Kitchens are filled with objects that can cut, burn, break, crush or sprain the human body. The best ways to prevent work-related injuries are proper training, good work habits and careful supervision.

The federal government enacted legislation designed to reduce hazards in the work area, thereby reducing accidents. The Occupational Safety and Health Act (OSHA) covers a broad range of safety matters. Employers who fail to follow its rules can be severely fined. Unfortunately, human error is the leading cause of accidents, and no amount of legislation can protect someone who doesn't work in a safe manner.

Safe behavior on the job reflects pride, professionalism and consideration for fellow workers. The following list should alert you to conditions and activities aimed at preventing accidents and injuries:

▶ Clean up spills as soon as they occur.
▶ Learn to operate equipment properly; always use guards and safety devices.
▶ Wear clothing that fits properly; avoid wearing jewelry, which may get caught in equipment.
▶ Use knives and other equipment for their intended purposes only.
▶ Walk, do not run.
▶ Keep exits, aisles and stairs clear and unobstructed.
▶ Always assume pots and pans are hot; handle them with dry towels.
▶ Position pot and pan handles out of the aisles so that they do not get bumped.
▶ Get help or use a cart when lifting or moving heavy objects.
▶ Avoid back injury by lifting with your leg muscles; stoop, don't bend, when lifting.
▶ Use an appropriately placed ladder or stool for climbing; do not use a chair, box, drawer or shelf.

- Keep breakable items away from food storage or production areas.
- Warn people when you must walk behind them, especially when carrying a hot pan.

Some accidents will inevitably occur, and it is important to act appropriately in the event of an injury or emergency. This may mean calling for help or providing first aid. Every food service operation should be equipped with a complete first-aid kit. Municipal regulations may specify the exact contents of the kit. Be sure that the kit is conveniently located and well stocked at all times.

The American Red Cross and local public health departments offer training in first aid, cardiopulmonary resuscitation (CPR) and the Heimlich maneuver used for choking victims. All employees should be trained in basic emergency procedures. A list of emergency telephone numbers should be posted by each telephone.

CONCLUSION

The art and science of baking and cookery form a noble profession with a rich history and long traditions. With knowledge, skill, taste, judgment, dedication and pride, the student chef can become part of this profession. This book provides the basic knowledge and describes the techniques in which a pastry chef or baker must become skilled. Dedicate yourself to learning this information and mastering your skills. Once you have done so, take pride in your accomplishments. Good luck.

QUESTIONS FOR DISCUSSION

1 Describe the influences on the baker and pastry chef in the 20th century.
2 What are the roles of the executive chef and the pastry chef in the modern kitchen brigade?
3 Discuss the importance of proper sanitary practices in the professional bakery and kitchen.
4 Numerous professional organizations hold competitions for pastry chefs and bread makers each year. Use the Internet to research recent bread-making and pastry competitions. Discuss the winning entries and the people who succeeded in these competitions.

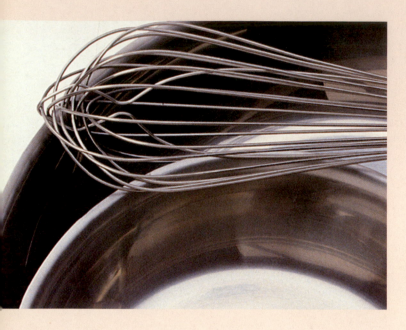

COOKING IS AT ONCE CHILD'S PLAY AND ADULT JOY.
AND, COOKING DONE WITH CARE IS AN ACT OF LOVE.
—*Craig Claiborne, American restaurant critic and
cookbook author (1920–2000)*

TOOLS AND EQUIPMENT FOR THE BAKESHOP

AFTER STUDYING THIS CHAPTER, YOU WILL BE ABLE TO:

▶ recognize a variety of professional bakeshop tools

▶ recognize major equipment used in the bakeshop

▶ understand how a professional bakeshop is organized

Having the proper tools and equipment for a particular task may mean the difference between a job well done and one done carelessly, incorrectly or even dangerously. This chapter introduces most of the tools and equipment typically used in a professional bakeshop. Items are divided into categories according to their function: hand tools, knives, measuring and portioning devices, cookware and bakeware, strainers and sieves, processing equipment, storage containers, heavy equipment and safety equipment.

A wide variety of specialized tools and equipment is available to today's baker and pastry chef. Breading machines, dough dividers and doughnut glazers are designed to speed production by reducing handwork. Much of this specialized equipment is quite expensive and found only in specialized kitchens or food manufacturing operations; a discussion of it is beyond the scope of this chapter. Other devices—a chocolate tempering machine or madeleine pan, for example—are used only for unique tasks. Brief descriptions of some of these specialized devices are, however, found in the Glossary and in the chapters on yeast breads, chocolate and decorative work.

Before using any equipment, study the operator's manual or have someone experienced with the particular item instruct you on proper procedures for its use and cleaning. And remember to always think safety first.

▶ STANDARDS FOR TOOLS AND EQUIPMENT

NSF International (NSF), previously known as the National Sanitation Foundation, promulgates consensus standards for the design, construction and installation of kitchen tools, cookware and equipment. Many states and municipalities require that food service operations use only NSF-certified equipment. Although NSF certification is voluntary, most manufacturers submit their designs to NSF to show that they are suitable for use in professional food service operations. Certified equipment bears the NSF mark shown in Figure 2.1.

NSF standards reflect the following requirements:

1 Equipment must be easily cleaned.

2 All food contact surfaces must be nontoxic (under intended end-use conditions), nonabsorbent, corrosion resistant and nonreactive.

3 All food contact surfaces must be smooth, that is, free of pits, cracks, crevices, ledges, rivet heads and bolts.

4 Internal corners and edges must be rounded and smooth; external corners and angles must be smooth and sealed.

5 Coating materials must be nontoxic and easily cleaned; coatings must resist chipping and cracking.

6 Waste and waste liquids must be easily removed.

FIGURE 2.1 ▶ The NSF mark

► SELECTING TOOLS AND EQUIPMENT

In general, only commercial food service tools and equipment should be used in a professional kitchen and bakeshop. Household tools and appliances not NSF-certified may not withstand use in a professional kitchen. Look for tools that are well constructed and up to the rigors of repeated use. For example, joints should be welded, not bonded with solder; handles should be comfortable, with rounded borders; plastic and rubber parts should be seamless.

► HAND TOOLS

Hand tools are designed to aid in cutting, shaping, moving or combining foods. They have few, if any, moving parts. The essential hand tools in the bakeshop are the spatulas, dough scrapers, whisks, tongs and specialized cutters used every day for routine preparations. Sturdiness, durability and safety are the watchwords when selecting hand tools. Choose tools that can withstand the heavy use of a professional kitchen and those that are easily cleaned.

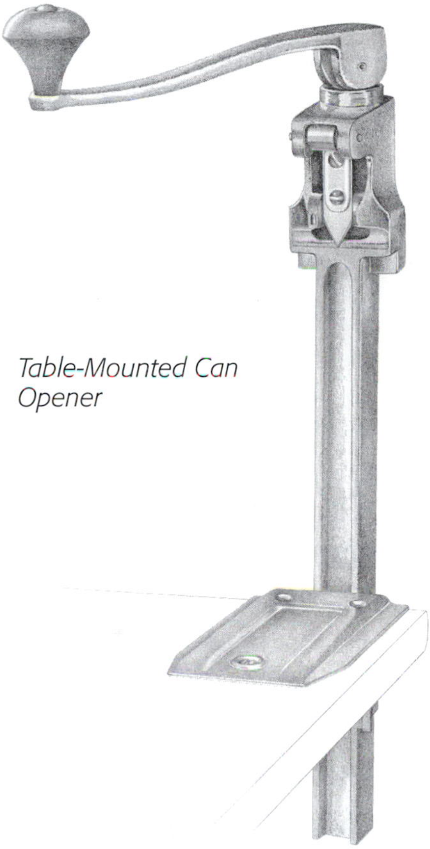

Table-Mounted Can Opener

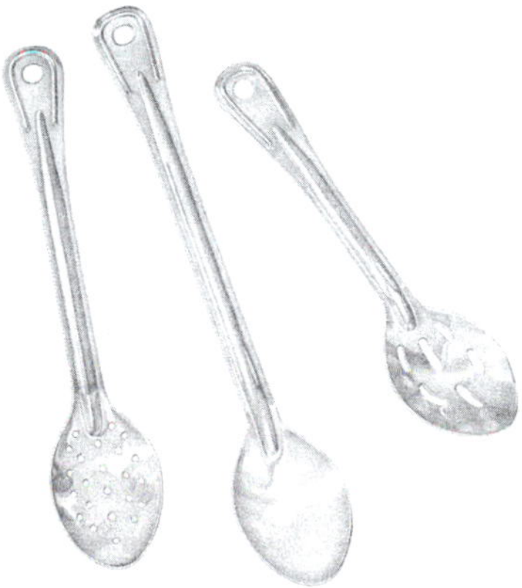

Vegetable Peeler

Perforated, Plain and Slotted Spoons

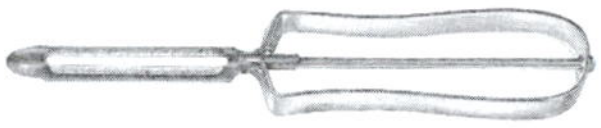

Zester

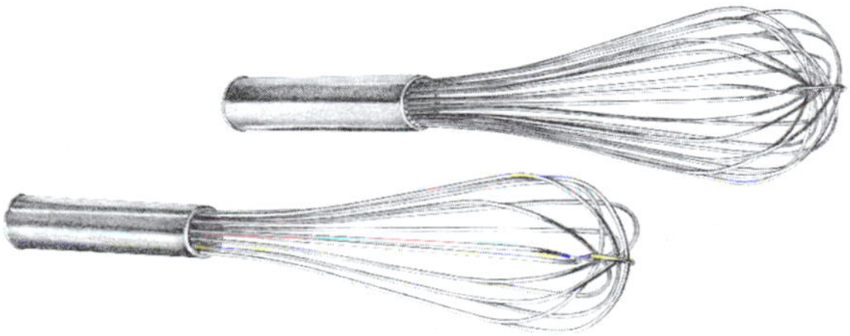

Balloon and Rigid Whisks

Melon Ball Cutter

Straight Spatula (Cake Spatula)

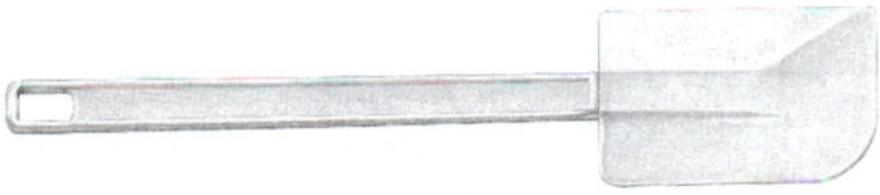

Rubber Spatula

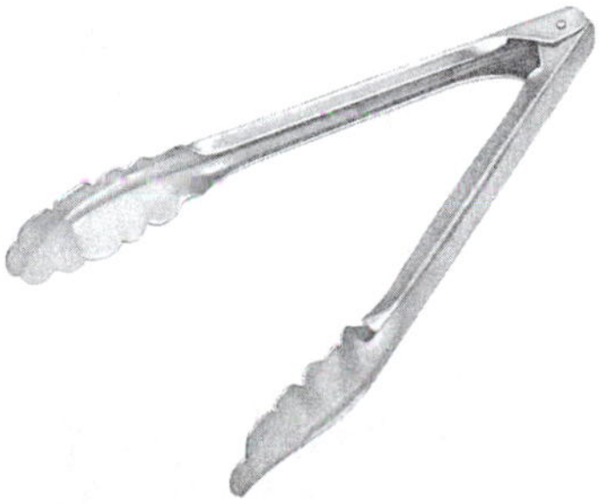

Straight Tongs

GRATERS

A variety of graters are used to shred ingredients into small uniform pieces so that they will blend or melt easily when cooked. The most common grater is the four-sided box grater. Made from tin or stainless steel, each side is punched with small holes of varying sizes. A handle on top secures the grater while the open bottom permits foods to be released. A flat metal grater with tiny, razor-sharp holes resembling a woodworker's rasp is now available for the bakeshop. These graters are especially useful for removing the zest from citrus fruits without any of the bitter pith. Handheld or table-mounted rotary graters are used for grating chocolate and nuts into a fine powder. Graters designed specifically for nutmeg and ginger are widely used.

PASTRY BRUSHES

Brushes are used in the bakeshop to apply coatings onto bakeware or to glaze foods before or after cooking. A **bench brush** helps remove flour from the bakeshop worktable. With a long-handled **oven brush,** the baker can safely sweep the floor of a pizza or deck oven to prevent bits of flour or cornmeal from burning. Oven brushes must be made from special materials so they don't burn. Natural bristles do not burn as easily as nylon ones but brushes with synthetic bristles are easier to keep clean and sanitize.

ROLLING PINS

Rolling pins help flatten or spread dough to a uniform thickness before cutting and baking. They also assist kneading and flattening lumps of dough. Common rolling pins are made from hardwoods that resist splitting, such as maple or beechwood, and are mounted on ball bearings with handles at either end. The dowel or French rolling pin is a solid piece of wood, straight or slightly tapered at each end. While durable, wooden rolling pins should never be soaked in water. Teflon-coated rolling pins are handy for rolling marzipan and pastillage for decorative work. Marble rolling pins are useful when working with buttery dough because they may be chilled before using.

Rolling Pin

CUTTERS

Cutting tools help the pastry chef and baker save time and produce uniform products. Most kitchens have a set of round biscuit cutters and a rolling cutter. Made from stainless steel, chrome plated metal, tin or plastic, pastry cutters come in sets of graduated sizes, with either fluted or smooth edges. A wide variety of shapes are also sold individually. The bottom edge is sharp for cutting and the top edge is reinforced to take pressure. Miniature aspic cutters are made to cut decorative pieces of garnish to be placed on small cakes and petits fours. A doughnut cutter is a 4-inch round cutter with a smaller circular cutter mounted in the center. A lever on the cutter releases a small piece of dough, which becomes the doughnut hole once fried.

Rolling cutters consist of one or more round blades mounted in a handle. They are used to portion pizzas, trim edges on pastry before baking or leave a decorative impression on dough. Also known as a pastry wheel, those with multiple blades cut several strips of dough at one time. Other common cutters in this category include the croissant cutter and the bear claw cutter.

Rolling Cutter (in foreground), Croissant Cutter (to the right)

▶ KNIVES

Good quality knives are expensive but will last for many years with proper care. Select easily sharpened, well-constructed knives that are comfortable and balanced in your hand. Knife construction and commonly used knives are discussed here.

KNIFE CONSTRUCTION

A good knife begins with a single piece of metal, stamped, cut or—best of all—forged and tempered into a blade of the desired shape. The following substances are generally used for knife blades:

1 **Carbon steel**—An alloy of carbon and iron, it is traditionally used for blades because it is soft enough to be sharpened easily. It corrodes and discolors easily, however, especially when used with acidic foods.

2 **Stainless steel**—It will not rust, corrode or discolor and is extremely durable. A stainless steel blade is much more difficult to sharpen than a carbon steel one, although once an edge is established, it lasts longer than the edge on a carbon steel blade.

3 **High-carbon stainless steel**—An alloy combining the best features of carbon steel and stainless steel, it neither corrodes nor discolors and can be sharpened almost as easily as carbon steel. It is now the most frequently used metal for blades.

4 **Ceramic**—A ceramic called zirconium oxide is now used to make knife blades that are extremely sharp, very easy to clean, rustproof and nonreactive. With proper care, ceramic blades will remain sharp for years, but when sharpening is needed, it must be done professionally on special diamond wheels. Material costs and tariffs make ceramic-bladed knives very expensive. Although this ceramic is highly durable, it does not have the flexibility of metal, so never use a ceramic knife to pry anything, to strike a hard surface or to cut against a china or ceramic surface.

A portion of the blade, known as the tang, fits inside the handle. The best knives are constructed with a full tang running the length of the handle; they also have a bolster where the blade meets the handle (the bolster is part of the blade, not a separate collar). Less expensive knives may have a ¾-length tang or a thin "rattail" tang. Neither provides as much support, durability or balance as a full tang.

Knife handles are often made of hard woods infused with plastic and riveted to the tang. Molded polypropylene handles are permanently bonded to a tang without seams or rivets. Stainless steel handles welded directly to the blade are durable but very lightweight. Any handle should be shaped for comfort and ground smooth to eliminate crevices where bacteria can grow.

KNIFE SHAPES

You will collect many knives during your career, some with specialized functions not described here. This list includes only the most basic knives and sharpening equipment used in the bakeshop.

FRENCH OR CHEF'S KNIFE

An all-purpose knife used for chopping and slicing. Its rigid 8- to 14-inch long blade is wide at the heel and tapers to a point at the tip.

French or Chef's Knife

UTILITY KNIFE

An all-purpose knife used for cutting and carving. Its rigid 6- to 8-inch-long blade is shaped like a chef's knife but narrower.

Utility Knife

Paring Knife

PARING KNIFE

A short knife used for detail work or cutting fruits; the most common knife used in the bakeshop. The rigid blade is from 2 to 4 inches long. A tournée or **bird's-beak knife** is similar to a paring knife but with a curved blade; it is used to cut curved surfaces.

Bread Knife

BREAD KNIFE OR CAKE KNIFE

A knife with a long, serrated blade that cuts easily through bread crust or pastry items. The tip may be round or pointed, and the blade may be flexible or rigid. (A similar knife with a smooth edge is used for slicing cooked meat.)

Lame for Scoring Bread

LAME OR BREAD SLASHER

The bread baker uses a lame or bread slasher to score the surface of bread dough before baking. This knife may have a fixed blade or a holder for a replaceable razor blade.

▶ MEASURING AND PORTIONING DEVICES

Recipe ingredients must be measured precisely, especially in the bakeshop. Batters and doughs should be measured before baking to provide uniform baking times and to control portion size and cost. Accuracy in measurement is key to producing quality and consistent results. Scales, temperature gauges and measuring devices make up a well-equipped kitchen. The devices used to measure and portion foods are, for the most part, hand tools designed to make food preparation and service easier and more precise. The accuracy they afford prevents the cost of mistakes made when accurate measurements are ignored.

Measurements may be based on weight (for example, grams, ounces, pounds) or volume (for example, teaspoons, cups, gallons) as discussed in Chapter 5, Mise en Place. Therefore, it is necessary to have available several measuring devices, including a variety of scales and liquid and dry measuring cups. Thermometers and timers are also measuring devices discussed here. When purchasing any measuring device, look for quality construction and accurate markings.

SCALES

Scales are necessary to determine the weight of an ingredient or a portion of food (for example, individual pieces of dough for dinner rolls). Weighing ingredients in the bakeshop ensures the most accurate results. Balance scales (also known as baker's scales) use a two-tray and free-weights counterbalance system. A curved hopper holds dry ingredients on one side of the scale. Counterweights graduated in ¼-ounce increments balance the weight on the other side. When both trays are level, the desired quantity has been measured.

Portion scales use a spring mechanism, round dial and single flat tray. They are available calibrated in grams, ounces or pounds. Capacity varies; portion models accommodate up to 2 pounds in ¼-ounce increments, while larger-capacity scales measure in ½-pound increments up to 25 pounds or their metric equivalents. Electronic scales also use a spring mechanism but provide digital readouts in ¹⁄₁₀- or ¼-ounce increments. An automatic tare feature allows the user to ignore the weight of any container used to hold loose ingredients on the scale.

Portion Scale

Balance or Baker's Scale

This feature makes measuring accurately more convenient. Electronic scales are considered more accurate than mechanical ones and are often required where foods are priced for sale by weight, as in a retail bakery.

Any scale must be properly used and maintained to provide an accurate reading. Never pick up a scale by its platform, as this can damage the balancing mechanism.

VOLUME MEASURES

Ingredients may be measured by volume using measuring spoons and measuring cups, though most professional bakeshops use scales to measure all but the smallest quantities. Measuring spoons sold as a set usually include ¼-teaspoon, ½-teaspoon, 1-teaspoon and 1-tablespoon units (1.25-, 2.5-, 5- and 15-milliliter units). Liquid measuring cups are available in capacities from 1 cup to 1 gallon (or the metric equivalent). They have a lip or pour spout above the top line of measurement to prevent spills. Though more commonly used in the home kitchen, measuring cups for dry ingredients are sometimes used in the professional kitchen, especially for converting home recipes or measuring small amounts of items such as chopped nuts and spices. They are usually sold in sets of ¼-, ⅓-, ½-, and 1-cup units. They do not have pour spouts, so the top of the cup is level with the top measurement specified. To ensure an accurate measurement of dry ingredients, fill the cup and then level off the top with a knife or flat spatula. Glass measuring cups are not recommended because they can break. Avoid using bent or dented measuring cups as the damage may distort the measurement capacity.

Measuring Spoons

Liquid Measuring Cup

Dry Measuring Cups

LADLES

Long-handled ladles are useful for portioning liquids such as sauces, custards and syrups. The capacity, in ounces or milliliters, is stamped on the handle.

PORTION SCOOPS

Portion scoops (also known as dishers) resemble ice cream scoops. They come in a range of standardized sizes and have a lever-operated blade for releasing their contents. Scoops are useful for portioning muffin batters and cookie dough or other soft foods. A number, stamped on either the handle or the release mechanism, indicates the number of level scoopfuls per quart. The higher the scoop number, the smaller the scoop's capacity. See Table 2.1.

Portion Scoop

Ladles

Table 2.1	**PORTION SCOOP CAPACITIES**			
SCOOP NUMBER	**VOLUME**		**APPROXIMATE WEIGHT***	
	U.S.	**METRIC**	**U.S.**	**METRIC**
6	⅔ c.	160 ml	5 oz.	160 g
8	½ c.	120 ml	4 oz.	120 g
10	3 fl. oz.	90 ml	3–3½ oz.	85–100 g
12	⅓ c.	80 ml	2½–3 oz.	75–85 g
16	¼ c.	60 ml	2 oz.	60 g
20	1½ fl. oz.	45 ml	1¾ oz.	50 g
24	1⅓ fl. oz.	40 ml	1⅓ oz.	40 g
30	1 fl. oz.	30 ml	1 oz.	30 g
40	0.8 fl. oz.	24 ml	0.8 oz.	23 g
60	½ fl. oz.	15 ml	½ oz.	15 g

*Weights are approximate because they vary by food.

Instand-Read Thermometer

Candy Thermometer

HOW TO CALIBRATE A STEM-TYPE THERMOMETER

All stem-type thermometers should be calibrated at least weekly as well as whenever they are dropped. To calibrate a stem-type thermometer, fill a glass with shaved ice, then add water. Place the thermometer in the ice slush and wait until the temperature reading stabilizes. Following the manufacturer's directions, adjust the thermometer's calibration nut until the temperature reads 32°F (0°C). Check the calibration by returning the thermometer to the slush. Then repeat the procedure, substituting boiling water for the ice slush, and calibrate the thermometer at 212°F (100°C).

THERMOMETERS AND GAUGES

Various types of thermometers and gauges are used in the bakeshop to determine when foods are fully cooked and when working with yeast dough, chocolate, sugar and other ingredients.

Stem-type or probe thermometers, including instant-read models, are inserted into foods to obtain temperature readings. Temperatures are shown on either a dial noted by an arrow or a digital readout. An instant-read thermometer is a small stem-type model, designed to be carried in a pocket and used to provide quick temperature readings. An instant-read thermometer should not be left in foods that are cooking because doing so damages the thermometer. Sanitize the stem of any thermometer before use in order to avoid cross-contamination.

Candy and fat thermometers measure temperatures up to 400°F (204°C) using mercury in a column of glass. A back clip attaches the thermometer to the pan, keeping the chef's hands free. Many models include helpful notations on their casing to indicate critical stages for cooking candy or fat. Be careful not to subject glass thermometers or gauges to quick temperature changes as the glass may shatter.

Specialty gauges that look like thermometers are used when making sugar mixtures for candies, syrups and creams. Known as a syrup-density meter or Baumé hydrometer, this tool measures the amount of sugar dissolved in a solution (see page 348).

Electronic probe thermometers are now reasonably priced and commonly used in food service facilities. These thermometers provide immediate, clear, digital readouts from a handheld unit attached to a metal probe. Other models can be programmed to beep when a set temperature is reached, which is useful for chocolate and sugar work. A chocolate thermometer is highly calibrated and designed to use while stirring and tempering chocolate. It measures up to 130°F (54°C) in 1-degree gradations.

The latest advancement in thermometers relies on infrared sensors with laser sightings. Infrared thermometers can instantly monitor the surface temperature of foods during cooking or holding, and the temperature of goods at receiving and in storage. Units can respond to a wide range of temperatures in less than a second without actually touching the food, thus avoiding any risk of cross-contamination. These thermometers are especially useful as maintenance tools to monitor the efficiency of refrigeration equipment.

Because proper temperatures must be maintained for holding and storing foods, many health departments require the use of oven and refrigerator thermometers. Select thermometers with easy-to-read dials or column divisions.

TIMERS

Portable kitchen timers are useful for any busy chef. Small digital timers can be carried in a pocket; some even time three functions at once. Select a timer with a loud alarm signal and long timing capability.

▶ COOKWARE AND BAKEWARE

Cookware for the bakeshop includes the saucepans used on the stove top as well as the baking sheets, cake pans and specialty molds used inside the oven. The term *bakeware* is also used to refer to items used inside the oven. Cookware and bakeware should be selected for its size, shape, ability to conduct heat evenly and overall quality of construction.

MATERIALS AND HEAT CONDUCTION

Cookware and bakeware that fails to distribute heat evenly may cause hot spots that burn foods. Because different metals conduct heat at different rates, and thicker layers of metal conduct heat more evenly than thinner ones, the most important considerations when choosing cookware are the type and thickness (known as the *gauge*) of the material used. Copper, aluminum and stainless steel are the most versatile and useful materials for cookware and bakeware in the bakeshop. No one cookware or material suits every process or need, however; always select the most appropriate material for the task at hand.

COPPER

Copper is an excellent conductor: It heats rapidly and evenly and cools quickly. Indeed, unlined copper pots are unsurpassed for cooking sugar and fruit mixtures. But copper cookware is extremely expensive. It also requires a great deal of care and is often quite heavy. Moreover, because copper may react with some foods, copper cookware usually has a tin lining, which is soft and easily scratched. Because of these problems, copper is now often sandwiched between layers of stainless steel or aluminum in the bottom of pots and pans. (One exception is the unlined copper mixing bowl designed for beating eggs; it is believed that egg white foam is more stable when beaten in contact with copper.)

ALUMINUM

Aluminum is the metal used most commonly in commercial utensils. It is lightweight and, after copper, conducts heat best. Aluminum is a soft metal, though, so it should be treated with care to avoid dents. Do not use aluminum containers for storage or for cooking acidic foods because the metal reacts chemically with many foods. Light-colored foods, such as custard sauce, may be discolored when cooked in aluminum, especially if stirred with a metal whisk or spoon.

Anodized aluminum has a hard, dark, corrosion-resistant surface that helps prevent sticking and discoloration.

STAINLESS STEEL

Although stainless steel conducts and retains heat poorly, it is a hard, durable metal particularly useful for holding foods and for low-temperature cooking where hot spots and scorching are not problems. Stainless steel pots and pans are available with aluminum or copper bonded to the bottom or with an aluminum-layered core. While expensive, such cookware combines the rapid, uniform heat conductivity of copper and aluminum with the strength, durability and nonreactivity of stainless steel. Stainless steel is also an ideal material for storage containers because it does not react with foods.

CERAMICS

Ceramics, including earthenware, porcelain and stoneware, are used primarily for baking dishes, soufflé cups, casseroles and baking stones because they conduct heat uniformly and retain temperatures well. Ceramics are nonreactive, inexpensive and generally suitable for use in a microwave oven (provided there is no metal in the glaze). Ceramics are easily chipped or cracked, however, and should not be used over a direct flame. Also, quick temperature changes may cause the cookware to crack or shatter.

PLASTIC

Plastic containers are frequently used in commercial kitchens for food storage or service, but they cannot be used for heating or cooking except in a microwave oven. Plastic microwave cookware is made of phenolic resin. It is easy to clean, relatively inexpensive and rigidly shaped, but its glasslike structure is brittle, and it can crack or shatter.

OTHER MATERIALS

Cast-iron, glass and enamel cookware are popular for home cooking but have few applications in the professional kitchen. Cast-iron cookware distributes heat evenly and holds high temperatures well. It is often used in griddles and large skillets but it must be seasoned properly and maintained carefully to prevent rust. Glass retains heat well but conducts it poorly. It does not react with foods. Tempered glass is suitable for microwave cooking provided it does not have any metal band or decoration. But commercial operations rarely use glass cookware because of the danger of breakage. Pans lined with enamel should not be used for cooking; in many areas, law prohibits their use in commercial kitchens. The enamel can chip or crack easily, providing good places for bacteria to grow.

NONSTICK COATINGS

Without affecting a metal's ability to conduct heat, a polymer (plastic) known as polytetrafluoroethylene (PTFE) and marketed under the trade names Teflon and Silverstone may be applied to many types of cookware and bakeware. It provides a slippery, nonreactive finish that prevents food from sticking and allows the use of less fat in cooking. Cookware with nonstick coatings requires a great deal of care, however, since the coatings can scratch, chip and blister. Do not use metal spoons or spatulas in cookware with nonstick coatings. Some nonstick coatings give pans a charcoal-colored finish. This dark color may affect the browning of cookies or cakes baked on such pans, giving delicate baked goods an unpleasantly dark crust.

COMMON COOKWARE

POTS

Pots are large round vessels with straight sides and two loop handles. Available in a range of sizes based on volume, they are used on the stove top for making custards and cooked fillings, or for boiling or simmering foods, particularly where rapid evaporation is not desired. Flat or fitted lids are available. The double boiler, a small pan that sits snugly on top of a pot filled with simmering water, is useful when melting chocolate or cooking delicate creams.

Rondeau/Brazier

Saucepot

PANS

Pans are round vessels with one long handle and straight or sloped sides. They are usually smaller and shallower than pots. Pans are available in a range of diameters and are used for general stove top cooking, especially sautéing, frying or reducing liquids rapidly. Common pans in the bakeshop include pans for making pancakes and crepes.

Sautoir (Straight Sides)

Saucepan

Sauteuse (Sloped Sides)

COMMON BAKEWARE

Baking pans and molds are used for shaping or holding various batters and dough. Some pans such as baking sheets and hotel pans are standard items in the professional kitchen. Others, such as brioche or savarin molds, are specialty bakeshop items named for the cake or pastry baked in them.

SHEET PANS, SHEET TRAYS OR BAKING SHEETS

Sheet pans are shallow rectangular trays with a 1-inch lip on all four sides. The most common are made from aluminum, and come in two standard sizes: 18 inches × 26 inches (45 cm × 65 cm) (full size) and 13 inches × 18 inches (32.5 cm × 45 cm) (half size). Some baking sheets may be rimless or have a rim on one side; this makes it easy to slide items off the sheet after baking. For making cookies, bright shiny baking sheets promote even browning. Perforated sheet pans may be used when baking bread and pastries in a convection oven; the holes allow more air to come in direct contact with the dough, resulting in a crisp crust. Adjustable metal frames, the same dimension as sheet pans, are available to increase the height of the pan so they may be used for baking large sheet cakes.

Full-Size Sheet Pan

Hotel Pans

HOTEL PANS

Hotel pans (also known as steam table pans) are rectangular stainless steel pans designed to hold food for service in steam tables. Hotel pans are also used for baking, roasting or poaching inside an oven. Perforated pans useful for draining, steaming or icing down foods are also available. The standard full-size pan is 12 inches × 20 inches (30 centimeters × 50 centimeters) with pans one-half, one-third, one-sixth and other fractions of this size available. Hotel pan depth is standardized at 2 inches (referred to as a "200 pan"), 4 inches, 6 inches and 8 inches (4, 10, 15, and 20 centimeters).

TART PANS

Tart pans come in individual or large sizes and in round, rectangular or square shapes. Some have fluted edges and removable bottoms, making removing the baked pastry from the pan easier. (See Chapter 10, Pies and Tarts.)

CAKE PANS

Properly designed cake pans heat evenly to allow delicate batters to rise properly. Most cake pans are made from a heavy-gauge aluminum in a variety of round sizes. Angel food, Bundt and kugelhopf pans are known as tube pans. They are round pans with a hollow cone in the middle. This design brings heat to the center of the batter and is beneficial when baking heavy batters as well as delicate egg foam cakes.

Springform pans have a removable bottom and sides that release with the flip of a spring mechanism. Cheesecakes and fragile desserts that would be difficult to unmold are often best baked in springform pans.

Flan rings or ring molds are strips of coated steel curved and formed into rings. They look like bottomless cake pans. When placed on a baking sheet, these rings are used to mold or to contain mousses and ice creams before chilling. Layers of baked cake and filling may be placed in a ring mold to make a European-style torte. Once the ring is removed the mousse or cake maintains its perfect shape.

Muffin pans make it possible to bake a number of individual pastries at one time. Large sheets or plaques of smaller molds, such as those used to make popovers, tartlets or madeleine cookies, speed the production of pastries.

MOLDS

Unique shapes give bakeshop products enhanced eye appeal. Buttery yeast dough can take on a totally different appearance and taste when baked in different-shaped molds. Molds are made from a variety of materials including tinned steel, stainless steel, silicone and aluminum. The assortment of molds available to the pastry chef is limitless, from individual baba molds to drum-shaped molds for panettone or charlottes. A creative chef can improvise many molds from products found at any local hardware store.

Timbale molds are small (about 4 ounces/120 milliliters) metal or ceramic containers used for molding or baking individual portions of mousse or custard. Their slightly flared sides allow the contents to release cleanly when inverted. Oven-baked custards and puddings are usually made in ceramic molds called ramekins, custard cups or soufflé cups.

Timbales

SILICONE BAKEWARE

In the 1980s, flexible silicone baking materials became available to the pastry chef. Made from pure silicone or fiberglass impregnated with food-grade silicone, this light material resists sticking and can withstand temperatures from freezing to 485°F (251°C). Baking pan liners made from silicone materials rarely require greasing and are useful for baking as well as candy and chocolate work. Sheets of baking molds made from these materials are used to form individual cakes, petits fours and desserts as well as ice cream and frozen desserts. Many of the tortes in Chapter 14, Cakes and Tortes, are produced using silicone molds. Often these pans are called by the brand names used by their manufacturers, among them Silpats, Flexipan, Gastroflex, Silform and Elastomold. In this book, silicone baking products are referred to as silicone mats, silicone molds or silicone pans.

▶ STRAINERS AND SIEVES

Strainers and sieves are used primarily to aerate and remove impurities from dry ingredients and drain or purée cooked foods. Strainers, colanders, drum sieves and china caps (chinois) are nonmechanical devices with a stainless steel mesh or screen through which food passes. The size of the mesh or screen varies from extremely fine to several millimeters wide; select the fineness best suited for the task at hand.

CHINA CAP/CHINOIS

The china cap and the chinois are cone-shaped metal strainers. Their conical shape allows liquids to filter through small openings. The body of a china cap is perforated metal; a chinois is made of very fine mesh. Either style is used for straining liquids and sauces, with the fine-screened chinois being particularly useful for removing seeds from fruit purées. A china cap can also be used with a pestle to purée soft foods.

Round Mesh Strainer

China Cap

Chinois

SKIMMER AND SPIDER

Both the skimmer and spider are long-handled tools used to remove foods or impurities from liquids. The flat, perforated disk of a skimmer is used for removing whole foods from poaching liquids. The spider has a finer mesh disk, which makes it better for retrieving items from hot fat.

CHEESECLOTH

Cheesecloth is a loosely woven cotton gauze used for straining liquids and sauces and for draining cream and cheese products. Cheesecloth is also indispensable for making sachets to hold spices used to flavor syrups, creams and poaching liquids. Always rinse cheesecloth thoroughly before use; this removes lint and prevents the cheesecloth from absorbing other liquids.

Skimmer

Spider

FOOD MILL

A food mill purées and strains food at the same time. Food is placed in the hopper and a hand-crank mechanism turns a blade in the hopper against a perforated disk, forcing the food through the disk. Most models have interchangeable disks with various-sized holes. Choose a mill that can be taken apart easily for cleaning.

Food Mill

Drum Sieve (Tamis)

Flour Sifter

FLOUR SIFTER

A sifter is used for aerating, blending and removing impurities from dry ingredients such as flour, cocoa and leavening agents. The 8-cup hand-crank sifter shown here uses four curved rods to brush the contents through a curved mesh screen. The sifter should have a medium-fine screen and a comfortable handle. The French tamis is a drum-shaped sieve useful for sifting ingredients as well as for straining thick purées to remove lumps and seeds.

▶ DECORATING AND FINISHING TOOLS

Like the sculptor, painter or fine woodworker, the pastry and bakeshop artist uses a wide variety of tools to help decorate cakes and pastries. (Many of these tools appear in photographs throughout this book and in Figure 2.2.) **Pastry bags** help the chef dispense fillings, frosting and batters into uniform and decorative patterns. They may be made from plastic-coated cotton, nylon, or disposable heavy-gauge plastic. The **dispensing tips** are stainless steel, plastic or

FIGURE 2.2 ▶ Clockwise from center back: cake turntable, cake pans, flan ring, tartlet pans, cannoli forms, offset spatulas, flat cake spatula, blade for scoring breads, flower nail, rectangular tartlet pans, piping bag and tips, metal spatula, dough cutter, rolling pin, springform pan, copper sugar pot (on cooling rack), nest of round cutters

chrome-plated metal cones. Once slipped inside the pastry bag, the tips produce unique shapes when paste or icing is squeezed through them. Pastry tips come in a wide variety of sizes and are numbered according to the size and shape of the piping produced. The most common pastry tips are the plain tip, used to pipe batters for baking or frying, and the open or closed star tip. A pastry chef can pipe icing onto a decorator's nail when making roses or flowers for cake garnishes.

Cake combs are flat metal or stiff plastic tools with teeth cut along each edge. When dragged across the surface of a frosted cake, they leave parallel lines in the icing. The **cake-decorating turntable** is a round metal or plastic platform seated on a heavy stand. It makes applying an even layer of icing or decorative piping on a layer cake fast and easy.

An assortment of disposable paper and other products help put the finishing touches on pastries. Silicone-coated greaseproof paper called parchment paper is used to line baking sheets. Its nonstick surface makes removing baked goods easier. This paper is formed into liners for muffin pans and chocolate work. Special disposable paperboard containers are available for baking in the oven, making the purchase of costly specialized pans unnecessary. Light corrugated cardboard cake rounds and sheets in a wide variety of sizes are used under cakes to make them easy to frost and transport. Clear strips of plastic acetate can line ring molds to protect the edges of layered tortes and pastries and can be used to create chocolate decorations.

▶ PROCESSING EQUIPMENT

Processing equipment includes both electrical and nonelectrical mechanical devices used to chop, purée, slice, grind or mix foods. Before using any such equipment, be sure to review its operating procedures and ask for assistance if necessary. Always turn the equipment off and disconnect the power before disassembling, cleaning or moving the appliance. Any problems or malfunctions should be reported immediately. *Never place your hand into any machinery when the power is on. Processing equipment is powerful and can cause serious injury.*

SLICER

An electric slicer is used to cut bread, cheese or raw fruits, not to mention meat and vegetables, into uniform slices. It has a circular blade that rotates at high speed. Food is placed in a carrier and then passed (manually or by an electric motor) against the blade. The distance between the blade and the carrier determines slice thickness. Because of the speed with which the blade rotates, foods can be cut into extremely thin slices very quickly. An electric slicer is convenient for preparing moderate to large quantities of food, but the time required to disassemble and clean the equipment makes it impractical when slicing only a few items.

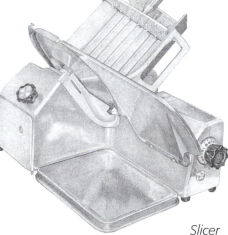

Slicer

MANDOLINE

A mandoline is a manually operated slicer made of stainless steel with adjustable slicing blades. It is also used to make julienne and waffle-cut slices. Its narrow, rectangular

Mandoline

body sits on the work counter at a 45-degree angle. Foods are passed against a blade to obtain uniform slices. It is useful for slicing small quantities of fruits or vegetables when using a large electric slicer would be unwarranted. To avoid injury, always use a hand guard or steel glove when using a mandoline.

FOOD PROCESSOR

A food processor has a motor housing with a removable bowl and S-shaped blade. It is used, for example, to purée cooked foods, chop nuts, and emulsify sauces. Special disks can be added that slice, shred or julienne foods. Bowl capacity and motor power vary; select a model large enough for your most common tasks.

Food Processor

BLENDER

Though similar in principle to a food processor, a blender has a tall, narrow food container and a four-pronged blade. Its design and whirlpool action is better for processing liquids or liquefying foods quickly. A blender is used to prepare smooth drinks, purée sauces, blend batters and chop ice. A **vertical cutter/ mixer** (VCM) operates like a very large, powerful blender. A VCM is usually floor-mounted and has a capacity of 15 to 80 quarts.

Heavy-Duty Blender

IMMERSION BLENDER

An immersion blender—as well as its household counterpart called a hand blender or wand—is a long shaft fitted with a rotating four-pronged blade at the bottom. Operated by pressing a button in the handle, an immersion blender is used to purée a soft food or sauce or blend directly in the container in which it was prepared, eliminating the need to transfer the food from one container to another. This is especially useful when working with hot foods. Small cordless, rechargeable models are convenient for puréeing or mixing small quantities or beverages, but larger heavy-duty electric models are more practical in commercial kitchens.

Immersion Blender

MIXER

A vertical mixer is indispensable in the bakeshop and most kitchens. The U-shaped arms hold a metal mixing bowl in place; the selected mixing attachment fits onto the rotating head. The three

20-Quart Mixer and Attachments

Flat Paddle

Whip

Dough Hook

common mixing attachments are the whip (used for whipping eggs or cream), the paddle (used for general mixing) and the dough hook (used for kneading bread). Most mixers have several operating speeds; depending on the manufacturer, table or bench models may have three to six speeds. Bench models range in capacity from 4.5 to 20 quarts, while floor mixers can hold as much as 140 quarts. Some mixers can be fitted with shredder/slicers, meat grinders, juicers or power strainers, making the equipment more versatile. In larger bakeshops, a spiral mixer or **orbital mixer** may be used for bread dough. Mounted on casters on the floor, the mixing bowl rotates along with the dough attachment when the machine is in operation.

Spiral Mixer

JUICER

Two types of juicers are available: reamers and extractors. Reamers, also known as citrus juicers, remove juice from citrus fruits. They can be manual or electric. Manual models use a lever arm to squeeze the fruit with increased pressure. They are most often used to prepare small to moderate amounts of juice for cooking. Juice extractors are electrical devices that create juice by liquefying raw fruits, vegetables and herbs. They use centrifugal force to filter out fiber and pulp.

Citrus Juicer

▶ HEAVY EQUIPMENT

COOKING AND BAKING

The professional kitchen is designed to accomplish the rapid cooking and service of hot meals. The cooking requirements of the bakeshop are somewhat different. More often than not, pastries, breads, desserts, and common bakeshop items will be prepared in a separate area and at a different time from meals designed for immediate service. While the cook stove is the centerpiece of the professional kitchen, the oven is one of the more significant pieces of cooking equipment in the bakeshop. Most pastries, breads and bakeshop foods, even custards, are baked in some type of oven. The type of products made in the bakeshop determine what types of ovens may be used.

OVENS

An oven is an enclosed space where food is cooked by being surrounded by hot air. Convection ovens use internal fans to circulate hot air over and around foods placed on adjustable wire racks inside the oven's cavity. This tends to cook foods more quickly and evenly. Convection ovens are almost always freestanding units, powered either by gas or electricity. Because convection ovens cook foods more quickly, temperatures may need to be reduced by 25°F to 50°F (10°C to 20°C) from those recommended for conventional ovens. Convection ovens can reduce cooking time, but the air currents may damage delicate products such as spongecake or puff pastry.

Conventional ovens are often located beneath a stove top. They have a heating element located at the unit's bottom or floor. Conventional ovens may also be

Gas Burner and Flat-Top Range with Dual Ovens and an Overhead Broiler (Salamander)

separate, freestanding units or decks stacked one on top of the other. In stack or deck ovens, pans are placed directly on the deck or floor and not on wire racks. Breads and pizzas may be placed directly on the heated surface of the deck oven.

Stack Oven

Specialty deck ovens designed for artisan bread bakeries have steam-injecting devices installed. Steam injection ovens use conventional heat flow but allow the baker to automatically add steam to the cooking chamber as needed to produce crisp-crusted breads. Although expensive, steam injection ovens are a necessity for commercial bakeries and most larger restaurant and hotel bakeshops. Commercial bakeries may use more specialized ovens including revolving ovens, rotating rack ovens and tunnel conveyor ovens.

Baking instructions in the following chapters are based on the use of a conventional oven. If a convection oven is used instead, remember that the temperature and baking time may need to be reduced.

Commercial Deck Oven

BAKER'S PEEL OR TRANSFER PEEL

A baker's peel is a wooden or metal shovel used to slide breads and pizza onto the floor of the deck oven. It is a necessity when baking breads or pizza on the floor of a hearth oven.

WOOD-BURNING OVENS

The ancient practice of baking in a retained-heat masonry oven has been revived in recent years, with many upscale restaurants and artisan bakeries installing brick or adobe ovens for baking pizzas and breads as well as roasting fish, poultry and vegetables. These ovens have a curved interior chamber that is usually recessed into a wall. Although gas-fired models are available, wood firing is more traditional and provides the aromas and flavors associated with brick ovens. A wood fire is built inside the oven to heat the brick chamber. The ashes are then swept out and the food is placed on the flat oven floor. Breads and pizzas baked in direct contact with the hot masonry rise better than in a conventional oven and develop a unique crisp crust. The combination of high heat and wood smoke adds distinctive flavors to foods.

MICROWAVE OVENS

Microwave ovens are electrically powered ovens used to cook or reheat foods. They are available in a range of sizes and power settings. Microwave ovens will not brown foods unless fitted with special browning elements, however. In the bakeshop, microwave ovens are useful as a convenience device for melting chocolate or butter.

COOK STOVES

Stove tops or ranges have one or more burners powered by gas or electricity. The burners may be open or covered with a cast-iron or steel plate. Open burners supply quick, direct heat that is easy to regulate. A steel plate, known as a **flat top,** supplies even but less intense heat. Although it takes longer to heat than a burner, the flat top supports heavier weights and makes a larger area available for cooking. Many stoves include both flat tops and open burner arrangements.

BROILER, SALAMANDER AND BLOWTORCH

A top browning is given to sugar-coated custards and some baked goods before serving. A broiler, salamander or blowtorch is used for this purpose. For a broiler, the heat source is above the food. Most broilers are gas powered. A **salamander** is a small overhead broiler primarily used to finish or top-brown

Baker's Peel

Wood-Burning Oven

▶ **hearth oven**—an oven whose floor is made from stone or masonry; bread, pizzas or other items are baked directly on its heated stone surface; also known as a deck oven

INDUCTION—A NEW HEAT WAVE

Induction cooking uses special conductive coils called inductors placed below the stove top's surface in combination with flat-bottomed cookware made of cast iron or magnetic stainless steel. The coil generates a magnetic current so that the cookware is heated rapidly with magnetic friction. Heat energy is then transferred from the cookware to the food by conduction. The cooking surface, which is made of a solid ceramic material, remains cool. Only the cookware and its contents get hot. This means that induction systems are extremely efficient with instant response time because power is directed into the cooking utensil, not the surrounding air.

Induction cooking is gaining acceptance in professional kitchens because of the speed with which foods can be heated and the ease of cleanup. Induction burners are useful in the bakeshop where there may be only a limited need for direct-heat cooking; they are portable and maintain a safer, cooler cooking environment.

Induction Cooktop

foods. A handheld **blowtorch** such as that used in the plumbing trade may be used for this purpose. Be sure to select a blowtorch with a simple ignition and an easily changed fuel cartridge.

DEEP-FAT FRYERS

Deep-fat fryers are used to cook foods in a large amount of hot fat. Doughnuts are the most common bakeshop items cooked in a deep-fat fryer. Fryers are sized by the amount of fat they hold. Most commercial fryers hold between 15 and 82 pounds. Fryers can be either gas or electric and are thermostatically controlled for temperatures between 200°F and 400°F (90°C and 204°C).

When choosing a fryer, look for a fry tank with curved, easy-to-clean sloping sides. Some fryers have a cold zone (an area of reduced temperature) at the bottom of the fry tank to trap particles. This prevents them from burning, creating off-flavors and shortening the life of the fryer fat.

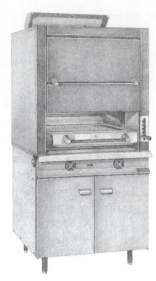

Overhead Broiler

Deep fryers usually come with steel wire baskets to hold the food during cooking. Fryer baskets are usually lowered into the fat and raised manually, although some models have automatic basket mechanisms. A doughnut fryer is wide but shallow and it includes a submerging screen to hold the doughnuts below the fat so that the batter cooks and browns evenly.

The most important factor when choosing a deep fryer is **recovery time.** Recovery time is the length of time it takes the fat to return to the desired cooking temperature after food is submerged in it. When food is submerged, heat is immediately transferred to the food from the fat. This heat transfer lowers the fat's temperature. The more food added at one time, the greater the drop in the fat's temperature. If the temperature drops too much or does not return quickly to the proper cooking temperature, the food may absorb excess fat and become greasy.

PROOF BOX

Bread dough and yeast-based pastries need a warm, moist environment in which to rest before baking. The proof box is used for this purpose. A simple proof box is a metal cabinet lined with shelves spaced to hold full-size and half-size sheet pans. Heat and humidity are generated from a small pan of water sitting on the bottom, heated by an electric coil. In a hotel bakeshop or small commercial bakery, the proof box may be large enough to accommodate one or more rolling racks, with temperature and humidity automatically controlled. Larger bakeries may invest in entire rooms specially steam-heated for fermenting yeast dough products.

REFRIGERATORS AND FREEZERS

Proper refrigeration space is an essential component of any kitchen. Many foods must be stored at low temperatures to maintain quality and safety. Most commercial refrigeration is of two types: walk-in units and reach-in or upright units.

A walk-in is a large, room-sized box capable of holding hundreds of pounds of food on adjustable shelves. A separate freezer walk-in may be positioned nearby or even inside a refrigerated walk-in.

Reach-ins may be individual units or parts of a bank of units, each with shelves approximately the size of a full sheet pan. Reach-in refrigerators and freezers are usually located throughout the kitchen to provide quick access to foods. Small units may also be placed beneath the work counters. Freezers and refrigerators are available in a wide range of sizes and door designs to suit any operation.

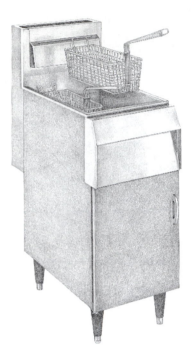

Deep-Fat Fryer

Other forms of commercial refrigeration include chilled drawers located beneath a work area that are just large enough to accommodate a hotel pan, and display cases used to show foods to the customer. Large bakeries may include blast freezers and special chill units. In open kitchens and retail bakeries, refrigerated display cases may be required for soft pies and filled pastries.

ICE CREAM FREEZER

Ice cream freezers or ice cream machines incorporate air while freezing a sweetened cream or fruit mixture. These machines come in two styles, manual and automatic, with a wide range of capacities. The simplest manual machine is the one our grandparents used, a table model with a metal canister for the cream mixture sitting inside a larger container for crushed ice and rock salt. A chilled mixture is poured into the metal container, then a flat blade called a dasher is inserted and a hand crank is attached. When the crank is turned, the mixture is stirred, adding air and minimizing the formation of ice crystals as the mixture freezes. In newer models, a coolant is sealed in the walls of the metal cylinder and frozen before using. This eliminates the need for crushed ice. Electrified table models are available. These small appliances make batches of ice cream or sherbet ranging in capacity from 1 quart to 1 gallon. Larger commercial ice cream machines may make batches of ice cream or may be fully automated machines. The soft-serve machine, for example, churns, aerates and dispenses the frozen dessert in one continuous process.

SHEETER

The sheeter is an electric appliance that mechanically rolls dough and pastry to a uniform thickness. The device consists of a cloth conveyor belt that moves beneath a stationary rolling pin. The height of the pin is adjusted to change the thickness of the product. Table and floor models are available, as are reversible models that automatically move the dough back and forth beneath the roller. Larger bakeshops and bakeries will have a sheeter for rolling out puff pastry and croissant dough.

Dough Sheeter

DISHWASHERS

Mechanical dishwashers are available to wash, rinse and sanitize dishware, glassware, cookware and utensils. Small models clean one rack of items at a time, while larger models can handle several racks simultaneously on a conveyor belt system. Commercial bakeshops may have a pan washer designed to accommodate full-size sheet trays. Sanitation is accomplished either with extremely hot water (180°F/82°C) or with chemicals automatically dispensed during the final rinse cycle. Any dishwashing area should be carefully organized for efficient use of equipment and employees, and to prevent recontamination of clean items.

WORK SURFACES, STORAGE AND ORGANIZATION

In the professional kitchen, stainless steel is the preferred material for all tables and work surfaces. It meets all sanitation standards as it is nontoxic (under intended end-use conditions), nonabsorbent, corrosion resistant, and nonreactive. Wooden-topped tables have a special place in the bakeshop, however. Because wood is a poor heat conductor, it is a great surface to maintain the optimal dough temperature when handling yeast dough. The somewhat soft surface of a wooden-topped table is preferred for rolling out pastry dough by hand. When kept clean, smooth and free from cracks and crevices, hardwood is a sanitary surface approved by the NSF for use in the bakeshop.

Marble or granite tabletops are also used in some pastry kitchens. They stay cool, a useful feature when working with candy and chocolate.

Storage Containers

STORAGE CONTAINERS

Proper storage containers are necessary for keeping leftovers and opened packages of food safe for consumption. Proper storage can also reduce the costs incurred by waste or spoilage.

Although stainless steel pans such as hotel pans are suitable and useful for some items, the expense of stainless steel and the lack of airtight lids makes these pans impractical for general storage purposes. Aluminum containers are not recommended because the metal can react with even mildly acidic items. Glass containers are generally not allowed in commercial kitchens because of the hazards of broken glass. The most useful storage containers are those made of high-density plastics such as polyethylene and polypropylene.

Storage containers must have well-fitting lids and should be available in a variety of sizes, including some that are small enough to hold even minimal quantities of food without allowing too much exposure to oxygen. Round and square plastic containers are widely available. Flat, snap-on lids allow containers to be stacked for more efficient storage. Containers may be clear or opaque white, which helps protect light-sensitive foods. Some storage containers are marked with graduated measurements so that content quantity can be determined at a glance.

Large quantities of dry ingredients, such as flour, sugar and rice, can be stored in rolling bins. The bins should be seamless with rounded corners for easy cleaning. They should have well-fitting but easy-to-open lids and should move easily on well-balanced casters.

RACKS

Rolling racks are metal frames designed to hold a number of sheet trays in a space-saving manner. They are useful for storing trays of items waiting to be placed in the oven or for receiving hot pans directly from an oven. To retain their distinctive textures, cakes, pastries and breads are often cooled on wire racks before using. A rolling shelf unit made from wire racks is used for cooling a large quantity of breads after baking.

SAFETY EQUIPMENT

Certain items are critical to the well-being of a food service operation although they are not used in food preparation. These are safety devices, many of which are required by federal, state or local law. Failing to include safety equipment in a kitchen or failing to maintain it properly endangers workers and customers.

FIRE EXTINGUISHERS

Fire extinguishers are canisters of foam, dry chemicals (such as sodium bicarbonate or potassium bicarbonate) or pressurized water used to extinguish small fires. They must be placed within sight of and easily reached from the work areas in which fires are likely to occur. Different classes of extinguishers use different chemicals to fight different types of fires. The appropriate class must be used for the specific fire; see Table 2.2. Fire extinguishers must be recharged and checked from time to time. Be sure they have not been discharged, tampered with or otherwise damaged.

VENTILATION SYSTEMS

Ventilation systems (also called ventilation hoods) are commonly installed over cooking equipment to remove vapors, heat and smoke. Some systems include fire extinguishing agents or sprinklers. A properly operating hood makes the kitchen more comfortable for the staff and reduces the danger of fire. The system should be designed, installed and inspected by professionals, then cleaned and maintained regularly.

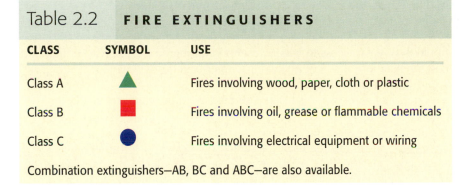

Table 2.2	**FIRE EXTINGUISHERS**	
CLASS	**SYMBOL**	**USE**
Class A	▲	Fires involving wood, paper, cloth or plastic
Class B	■	Fires involving oil, grease or flammable chemicals
Class C	●	Fires involving electrical equipment or wiring
Combination extinguishers—AB, BC and ABC—are also available.		

FIRST-AID KITS

First-aid supplies should be stored in a clearly marked box, conspicuously located near food preparation areas. State and local laws may specify the kit's exact contents. Generally, the kit should include a first-aid manual, bandages, gauze dressings, adhesive tape, antiseptics, scissors, cold packs and other supplies. The kit should be checked regularly and items replaced as needed. In addition, cards with emergency telephone numbers should be placed inside the first-aid kit and near a telephone.

▶ THE PROFESSIONAL BAKESHOP

Professional bakeshops may be small sections within a restaurant kitchen or a separate kitchen composed of many departments with its own staff and operating budget. No matter the size, the organizational concepts are the same. Creating an efficient operating space with proper workflow is the key to designing a successful kitchen and bakeshop environment.

In France, the pastry kitchen is called a *laboratoire* or laboratory. As its name suggests, the classic French bakeshop is a controlled environment where specialized operations take place under exacting conditions and to high standards. As discussed in Chapter 1, Professionalism, the classic pastry shop brigade consists of numerous cooks and chefs each skilled in different disciplines, from chocolate tempering and confectionery making to ice cream and bread making. The layout of such a structured pastry kitchen ideally includes separate kitchens for each department. The mixing of bread and pastry dough would be separate from the hot baking areas. Chocolate and ice cream making would take place in temperature-controlled spaces. In most small bakeshops or in those that form part of a restaurant, space may be scarce. The pastry department often consists of a small worktable, possibly shared during the hours when meals are served.

In order to properly plan the layout of a professional bakeshop, the tasks performed must be identified and the work assigned. The goal of designing a bakeshop is the efficient use of space so that each task has a designated area or **work station** where similar tasks are performed. The bakeshop should have an efficient flow from one section to the other. Ideally work stations should be designed to minimize the steps necessary to perform the task. The task of baking is divided into four stages: the measuring and mixing of ingredients, the makeup of the product before baking, the baking and the final assembly. Professional bakeshops are arranged to give enough space for each of these stages.

Measuring and mixing requires easy access to ingredients and ample room in which to maneuver large quantities of finished dough. Flour, sugar and other bulk items might be stored in covered rolling bins underneath a worktable. Large bags of unopened ingredients might be stored off the floor on pallets in a secure storeroom near the mixing area. Smaller quantities of items such as spices, flavorings and baking powder may be stored on shelving above a worktable. The scale and mixer should be placed near each other and the entire work station should have easy access to water, an important ingredient in bread dough and other preparations that require mixing. Larger bakeries will have a metering device to portion water adjacent to the mixer.

Dough make-up requires a large surface area on which to divide and roll dough. Operations where a large volume of Danish and croissant pastries are produced require wide open tables on which dough is rolled or portioned. These same tables may be used for cutting out doughnuts, forming bagels and assembling cakes as long as the work schedule prevents overlaps when the space is required for multiple tasks. In a small independent bakery, such a worktable or workbench may be positioned in a central location to be shared between different departments throughout the day. Bread dough might be divided into loaves then rolled and formed on the table early in the morning; then cakes might be filled and frosted in the same place in the afternoon.

The baking stage requires ample room for loading and unloading the oven. Because an oven generates intense heat, positioning it away from other bakery activities is desired. Where large quantities of bread, muffins and pastries are baked, the ovens might be in a separate room. Space is also allotted for large wire cooling racks on wheels, which are used to cool the breads before packaging or service.

The final assembly stage includes the filling and frosting of cookies, pastries and cakes. Because of the perishability of many of the creams, icings, custards and fruits used in the bakeshop, pastry assembly should take place in a cool, dry, dust-free environment far from the heat of the oven. Many specialized tools are needed to perform these tasks: piping bags, turntables, decorative stencils and color spray guns, to name a few. Accessible and safe storage for these items must be provided.

In addition to production areas, a typical bakeshop and professional kitchen includes areas dedicated to the following:

1 *Receiving and storing foods and other items.* Most kitchens will need freezer, refrigerator and dry-goods storage facilities. Each should have proper temperature, humidity and light controls in order to properly and safely maintain the stored items. Typically there is a combination of central and section storage, with smaller quantities stored at a work station and bulk storage separate. Additional storage space will be needed for cleaning and paper supplies, dishes and other service ware.

2 *Washing dishes and other equipment.* Dish-washing and equipment-washing facilities should have their own sinks. Food-preparation and hand-washing sinks must be separate.

3 *Employee use.* Restrooms, locker facilities and an office are also found in most food service facilities.

The guiding principle behind good kitchen design is to maximize the flow of goods and staff from one area to the next and within each area itself. Maximizing flow creates an efficient work environment and helps reduce preparation and service time.

Governmental building, health, fire and safety codes will dictate, to a degree, certain aspects of a professional kitchen's design. But to make the most of these spaces, the well-designed kitchen should reflect a sound understanding of the tasks to be performed and the equipment necessary to perform them efficiently.

CONCLUSION

Hundreds of tools and pieces of equipment can help you prepare, cook, store and present food. These tools make the efficient preparation of a variety of pastries possible. Some simplify complex processes, while other tools ensure that food is prepared and stored safely and under proper sanitary conditions. Every year, manufacturers offer new or improved items. Throughout your career, you will use many of them. Select those that are well constructed, durable and best suited for the task at hand. Then use them in a safe and efficient manner.

The way in which equipment is arranged and stored in a kitchen is also important. Good kitchen design emphasizes the efficient flow of goods and staff from one work section to another as well as within each work section or station.

QUESTIONS FOR DISCUSSION

1 What is NSF International? What is its significance with regard to commercial kitchen equipment?

2 List four materials used to make cookware and bakeware for the bakeshop and describe the advantages and disadvantages of each.

3 Describe the types of equipment used to mix ingredients in the bakeshop.

4 List three classes of fire extinguishers. For each one, describe its designating symbol, and identify the type or types of fire it should be used to extinguish.

5 Explain the relationship between work sections and work stations and the kitchen brigade system discussed in Chapter 1, Professionalism.

6 Assume that you have been asked to select a new oven for a small commercial bakery. You must research the industry and find a bakery oven supplier who can provide you with specialized equipment for your establishment. Find a few Internet sites of companies that can assist you with this research. List the questions you must be able to answer in order to purchase this equipment.

THE FINE ARTS ARE FIVE IN NUMBER, NAMELY:
PAINTING, SCULPTURE, POETRY, MUSIC AND
ARCHITECTURE, THE PRINCIPAL BRANCH OF THE
LATTER BEING PASTRY.

—Marie-Antoine (Antonin) Carême, French chef
(1783–1833)

PRINCIPLES
OF BAKING

AFTER STUDYING THIS CHAPTER, YOU WILL BE ABLE TO:

▶ understand the various mixing methods used in the bakeshop

▶ understand how heat affects batters and doughs, the basis of most bakeshop items

▶ identify and understand the basic cooking methods employed in the bakeshop

▶ **gluten**—an elastic network of proteins created when wheat flour is moistened and manipulated; it gives structure and strength to baked goods and is responsible for their volume, texture and appearance

▶ **aerate**—to incorporate air into a mixture through sifting and mixing; to whip air into a mixture to lighten such as beating egg whites to a foam

▶ **formula**—standard term used throughout the industry for a bakeshop recipe; formulas rely on weighing to ensure accurate measuring of ingredients

Baking is a science that relies on a good understanding of the basic principles of the baking and cooking process. Once a student understands that the actions that take place when a mixture of flour, fat and water becomes a finished product are a function of scientific principals, he or she will be able to select ingredients and work with formulas with greater ease. While a degree in chemistry or physics is not a prerequisite for working in the bakeshop, a good understanding of the everyday science of the kitchen makes for a well-rounded professional. Throughout this book different aspects of the principles discussed in this chapter are demonstrated and expanded upon.

▶ MIXING METHODS

The first step in the production of all baked goods is the measuring of ingredients; see Chapter 5, Mise en Place. Once the ingredients are measured, all baked goods must be mixed. The techniques used to mix or combine ingredients affect the baked good's final volume, appearance and texture. Mixing distributes ingredients evenly. Mixing activates the proteins in wheat flour causing the formation of the elastic structure called **gluten,** which is discussed more fully in Chapter 4, page 57. Mixing incorporates air into (**aerates**) a mixture to help it rise and develop a light texture when baked. Different mixing methods ensure that ingredients are combined in the proper order to achieve the desired results. Future chapters in this book explore how different mixing methods and different combinations of basic ingredients create a variety of distinct baked items.

Several mixing methods—**beating, blending, creaming, cutting, folding, kneading, sifting, stirring** and **whipping**—are used throughout this book, especially in procedure discussions and **formulas.** (See Table 3.1.) Learn the difference in these mixing methods, then use the designated method with the appropriate equipment or tool to ensure a good-quality finished product.

Baked goods are made from doughs and batters. A **dough** has a low water content. The water-protein complex known as gluten forms the continuous medium into which other ingredients are embedded. A dough is usually prepared by beating, blending, cutting or kneading and is often stiff enough to cut into various shapes.

A **batter** generally contains more liquids, fat, and sugar than a dough. Gluten development is minimized and liquid forms the continuous medium in which other ingredients are dispersed. A batter bakes into softer, moister products. A batter is usually prepared by blending, creaming, stirring or whipping and is generally thin enough to pour.

▶ COOKING METHODS

Foods can be cooked in air, fat, water or steam. These are collectively known as cooking media. There are two general types of cooking methods: dry heat and moist heat. See Table 3.2.

Dry-heat cooking methods use air or fat and are the principal methods employed to cook batter and dough. These methods are baking and frying, meth-

Table 3.1 MIXING METHODS

METHOD	PURPOSE	EQUIPMENT
Beating	Vigorously agitating foods to incorporate air or develop gluten	Spoon or electric mixer with paddle attachment
Blending	Mixing two or more ingredients until evenly distributed	Spoon, rubber spatula, whisk or electric mixer with paddle attachment
Creaming	Vigorously combining softened fat and sugar while incorporating air	Electric mixer with paddle attachment on medium speed
Cutting	Incorporating solid fat into dry ingredients only until lumps of the desired size remain	Pastry cutters, fingers or an electric mixer with paddle attachment
Folding	Very gently incorporating ingredients such as whipped cream or whipped eggs into dry ingredients, a batter or cream	Rubber spatula or balloon whisk
Kneading	Working a dough to develop gluten	Hands or electric mixer with dough hook. If done by hand, the dough must be vigorously and repeatedly folded and turned in a rhythmic pattern
Sifting	Passing one or more dry ingredients through a wire mesh to remove lumps, combine and aerate	Rotary or drum sifter or mesh strainer
Stirring	Gently mixing ingredients by hand until evenly blended	Spoon, whisk or rubber spatula
Whipping	Beating vigorously to incorporate air	Whisk or electric mixer with whip attachment

Table 3.2 COMMON BAKESHOP COOKING METHODS

METHOD	MEDIUM	BAKESHOP PRODUCTS	EQUIPMENT
Dry-Heat Cooking Methods			
Baking	Air	Doughs, batters for breads, cakes, cookies, pastries; fruits	Oven, convection oven
Broiling	Air	Fruits; glazed custards	Overhead broiler, salamander
Deep-frying	Fat	Doughnuts, fritters	Deep-fat fryer
Pan-frying	Fat	Batters for griddlecakes	Stove top
Sautéing	Fat	Fruit	Stove top
Moist-Heat Cooking Methods			
Boiling	Water or other liquids	Creams, sauces, fruits	Stove top
Poaching	Water or other liquids	Fruits, fresh and dried	Stove top, oven
Simmering	Water or other liquids	Creams, sauces, fruits	Stove top, oven

ods used to cook many foods including yeast bread, cakes and doughnuts. Dry-heat cooking methods also include those cooking methods associated with the savory kitchen—grilling, roasting, sautéing and pan-frying. These are, for the most part, of secondary importance in the bakeshop.

Moist-heat cooking methods are those using water or steam. They are poaching, simmering and boiling, techniques regularly used to cook fruits and other pastry components, as well as steaming. Moist-heat cooking methods are used to tenderize foods and enhance their natural flavor. They are also used to heat liquids to encourage evaporation, resulting in an intensified liquid or

▶ **reduction**—a liquid cooked until a portion of it evaporates, reducing the volume of the liquid; used to concentrate flavor and thicken liquids

reduction such as for a syrup or sauce. Moist-heat methods such as simmering are used to gently heat mixtures so that proteins set and the mixture thickens such as for custards and creams. Detailed procedures and formulas applying these methods to specific foods are found throughout this book.

▶ THE BAKING PROCESS

Many changes occur in a dough or batter as it bakes. A pourable liquid solidifies into a tender, light cake; a sticky mass becomes chewy cookies; a soft, elastic dough becomes firm, crusty French bread. These physical changes are the result of the ingredients used, the mixing methods employed and the effect of heat applied during the baking process. Namely, gases form and are trapped within the dough or batter; starches, proteins and sugars cook; fats melt; moisture evaporates and staling begins.

By learning to control these changes, the student baker also learns to control the final product. Control can be exerted in the selection of ingredients and the methods by which those ingredients are combined, as well as the baking temperature and duration.

STAGES OF BAKING

Batters and dough pass through nine stages during and after the baking process.

1 Gases form

2 Gases are trapped

3 Starches gelatinize

4 Proteins coagulate

5 Fats melt

6 Water evaporates

7 Sugars caramelize

8 Carryover baking

9 Staling

THE SCIENCE OF BAKING A CAKE, CIRCA 1806

"The heat of the oven is of great importance for cakes, especially those that are large. If not pretty quick, the batter will not rise. Should you fear its catching by being too quick, put some paper over the cake to prevent its being burnt. If not long enough lighted to have a body of heat, or it is become slack, the cake will be heavy. To know when it is soaked, take a broad bladed knife that is very bright, and plunge it into the very center, draw it instantly out, and if the least stickiness adheres, put the cake immediately in, and shut up the oven."

—Maria Eliza Ketelby Rundell, 1745–1828. From *A New System of Domestic Cookery: Formed upon Principles of Economy, and Adapted to the Use of Private Families* (Exeter, N.H.: Norris & Sawyer, 1808).

GASES FORM

A baked good's final texture is determined by the amount of leavening or rise that occurs both before and during baking. This rise is caused by the gases present in the dough or batter. These gases are carbon dioxide, air and steam. Air and carbon dioxide are present in doughs and batters before they are heated. (Air may be incorporated during the mixing process. Carbon dioxide is released as a by-product of leaveners used in the mixture.) Other gases are formed when heat is applied. For example, steam is created as the moisture in a dough is heated; yeast and baking powder rapidly release additional carbon dioxide when placed in a hot oven. These gases then expand and leaven the product. Additional information on the effects of baking powder and baking soda is found in Chapter 6, Quick Breads. Yeast is discussed in detail in Chapter 7, Yeast Breads.

GASES ARE TRAPPED

The stretchable network of proteins created in a batter or dough, either egg proteins or gluten, traps gases in the product. Without an appropriate network of proteins, the gases would just escape without causing the mixture to rise.

STARCHES GELATINIZE

Starches are complex carbohydrates present in plants and grains such as potatoes, wheat, rice and corn. Flour made from these and other grains is the primary ingredient in most baked goods. When starch granules in a batter or dough reach a temperature of approximately 140°F (60°C), they absorb additional moisture—up to 10 times their own weight—and expand. This contributes to the baked good's structure.

PROTEINS COAGULATE

Gluten and dairy and egg proteins begin to coagulate (solidify) when the dough or batter reaches a temperature of 160°F (71°C). This process provides most of the baked good's structure.

Proper baking temperatures are important for controlling the point at which proteins coagulate. If the temperature is too high, proteins will solidify before the gases in the product have expanded fully, resulting in a product with poor texture and volume. If the temperature is too low, gases will escape before the proteins coagulate, resulting in a product that may collapse.

FATS MELT

As fats melt, steam is released and fat droplets are dispersed throughout the product. These fat droplets coat the starch (flour) granules, thus moistening and tenderizing the product by keeping the gluten strands short. Fats melt at different temperatures. It is important to select a fat with the proper melting point for the product being prepared. See Chapter 4, Bakeshop Ingredients.

WATER EVAPORATES

Throughout the baking process, the water contained in the liquid ingredients will turn to steam and evaporate. This steam is a useful leavener; see Table 3.3. As steam is released the dough or batter dries out starting from the outside and the result is the formation of a crust.

SUGARS CARAMELIZE

The process of cooking sugar is known as **caramelization.** Sugars are simple carbohydrates used by all plants and animals to store energy. Sugars are found in eggs, dairy products and other ingredients in a formula, not just in refined sugar and liquid sweeteners. As sugars are heated above 320°F (160°C), they caramelize, adding flavor and causing the product to darken.

Table 3.3	LEAVENING AGENTS IN BAKED GOODS	
LEAVENING AGENT	**PRESENT IN**
Air	All products, especially those containing whipped eggs or creamed fat
Steam	All products when liquids evaporate or fats melt
Carbon dioxide	Products containing baking soda, baking powder, baking ammonia or yeast

Caramelization of sugars is responsible for most of the flavors associated with baked goods. Because high temperatures are required for caramelization, most foods will brown only on the outside and only through the application of dry heat.

CARRYOVER BAKING

The physical changes in a baked good do not stop when it is removed from the oven. The residual heat contained in the hot baking pan and within the product itself continues the baking process as the product cools. This is why a crisp-style cookie or biscuit may be soft and seem a bit underbaked when removed from the oven; it will finish baking as it cools.

STALING

Staling is a change in a baked good's texture and aroma caused by both moisture loss and changes in the structure of the starch granules. Stale products have lost their fresh aroma and are firmer, drier and more crumbly than fresh goods.

▶ **starch retrogradation**—the process whereby starch molecules in a batter or dough lose moisture after baking. The result is baked goods that are dry or stale

Staling is not just a general loss of moisture into the atmosphere; it is also a change in the location and distribution of water molecules within the product. This process, known as **starch retrogradation,** occurs as starch molecules cool, becoming more dense and expelling moisture.

In breads, this moisture migrates from the interior to the drier crust, causing the crust to become tough and leathery. If the product is not well wrapped, moisture will escape completely into the surrounding air. In humid conditions, unwrapped bread crusts absorb moisture from the atmosphere, resulting in the same loss of crispness. The flavor and texture of breads can be revived by reheating them to approximately 140°F (60°C), the temperature at which starch gelatinization occurs. Usually, products can be reheated only once without causing additional quality loss.

The retrogradation process is temperature-dependent. It occurs most rapidly at temperatures of approximately 40°F (4°C). Therefore, baked products should not be refrigerated unless they contain perishable components such as cream fillings. It is better to store products frozen or at room temperature, as long as food safety is not of concern.

Products containing fats and sugars, which retain moisture, tend to stay fresh longer. Commercial bakeries usually add chemical emulsifiers, modified shortening or special sweeteners to retard staling, but these additives are not as practical for small-scale production.

A solid understanding of the scientific principles that underlie cooking and baking serves the pastry chef and cook throughout his or her career. During preparation and baking, doughs and batters go through many physical changes. Knowing how and why these changes take place allows the baker to adjust formulas as needed to compensate for different work conditions and different ingredients. When the pastry chef and baker seeks to test new ideas, an understanding of the principles of baking will help avoid costly and frustrating mistakes. Learning to recognize the cause and effect of various mixing, baking and cooking methods makes the work in the bakeshop easier.

1 Discuss the various mixing methods and the tools used.
2 What are the various cooking methods employed in the bakeshop and for which products are they commonly used?
3 What elements in baked goods make them rise?
4 List and describe the nine steps in the baking process.
5 Explain what process causes staling. List the ways to minimize staling of breads and cakes.

No one who cooks, cooks alone. Even at her most solitary, a cook in the kitchen is surrounded by generations of cooks past, the advice and menus of cooks present, the wisdom of cookbook writers.

—Laurie Colwin, cookbook author and American writer (1944–1992)

BAKESHOP
INGREDIENTS

AFTER STUDYING THIS CHAPTER, YOU WILL BE ABLE TO:

▶ identify different types of flours, sweeteners and fats

▶ understand gluten and its importance in the bakeshop

▶ understand the function of many bakeshop ingredients

Flour, sugar, eggs, milk, butter, flavorings—with this simple list of ingredients a seemingly endless variety of delectable bakeshop sweets are made: breads to sauces to pastries to ice cream. But to produce consistently good brioche, Bavarians, biscuits or the like, the baker must pay careful attention to the character and quantity of each ingredient, the way the ingredients are combined and how heat is applied to them. Although substituting ingredients may have little or no effect on some dishes (carrots may replace turnips in a stew, for instance), this is not the case with baked goods. Different flours, fats, liquids and sweeteners function differently. Bread flour and cake flour are not the same, nor are shortening and butter. When substituting one ingredient for another, the results will be different.

Understanding ingredients, why they function the way they do and how to adjust for their differences will make the baking experience more successful and consistent. This chapter covers most of the ingredients used in the bakeshop, from the most common, flour, to more unusual specialty flavorings. Ingredients are grouped according to the function they perform. Fruits are discussed in detail in Chapter 17, Fruits. Chemical leavening agents, without which there would be neither biscuits nor muffins, are discussed in Chapter 6, Quick Breads. Yeast and natural leaveners are discussed in Chapter 7, Yeast Breads. Chocolate is discussed in detail in Chapter 21, Chocolate and Decorative Work.

▶ FLOURS

Flour provides bulk and structure to baked goods. Some flours are used to thicken liquids in items such as puddings and pie fillings, or to prevent foods from sticking during preparation and baking. Flour is produced when grain kernels are milled or ground into a powder. Grains are grasses that bear edible seeds. Corn, rice and wheat are the most significant grains for human consumption but the most frequently used—and therefore the most important ingredient in the bakeshop—is wheat flour.

WHEAT FLOUR

Wheat flour (Fr. *farine*) is produced by milling wheat kernels (berries). A wheat kernel has an outer covering called bran. It is composed of several layers that protect the endosperm, which contains starches and proteins. The innermost part is the germ, which contains fat and serves as the wheat seed (see Figure 4.1). During milling, the kernels first pass through metal rollers to crack them, then the bran and germ are removed through repeated stages of sifting and separation. The remaining endosperm is then ground into flour. Flour made from

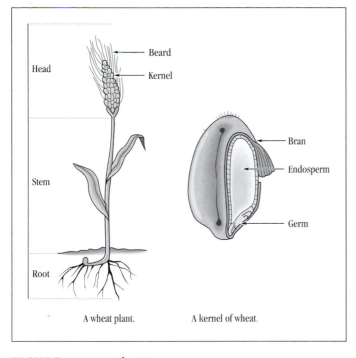

Head

Beard

Kernel

Stem

Bran

Endosperm

Germ

Root

A wheat plant.

A kernel of wheat.

FIGURE 4.1 ▶ Wheat

the portion of the endosperm closest to the germ (also known as patent flour) is finer; flour made from the portion of the endosperm nearer the bran (clear flour) is coarser and darker.

COMPOSITION OF FLOUR

Flour consists primarily of five nutrients: fat, minerals, moisture, starches and proteins. Fat and minerals each generally account for less than 1 percent of flour's content. The moisture content of flour is also relatively low—when packaged, it cannot exceed 15 percent under government standards. But its actual moisture content varies depending on climatic conditions and storage. In damp areas, flour absorbs moisture from the atmosphere.

Starches constitute 63 to 77 percent of flour, and are necessary for the absorption of moisture during baking. This process, known as gelatinization, occurs primarily at temperatures above 140°F (60°C). Starches also provide food for yeast during fermentation.

Flour proteins are of crucial importance because of their gluten-forming potential. Gluten is the tough, rubbery substance created when wheat flour is mixed with water. Gluten strands are both plastic (that is, they change shape under pressure) and elastic (they resume their original shape when that pressure is removed). Gluten is responsible for the volume, texture and appearance of baked goods. It provides structure and enables dough to retain the gases given off by leavening agents. Without gluten, there could be no raised breads. The gases created by yeast fermentation or chemical leaveners would simply escape if there were no network of gluten strands to trap them in the dough.

In general, the higher a flour's protein content, the greater that flour's gluten-forming potential. In some cases, however, flour with, for example, 13% protein may perform better than one with 14% protein because the proteins in the flour are of superior quality. The proteins responsible for gluten formation are glutenin and gliadin. Flour does not contain gluten; only a dough or batter can contain gluten. Gluten is produced when glutenin and gliadin are moistened and manipulated, as when they are stirred or kneaded. In order to make a chewy product such as a crusty French loaf, a flour with a high protein content must be used. Lower-protein flours are used for tender soft products such as cakes and

Table 4.1	**PROTEIN CONTENT OF FLOURS**	
TYPE OF FLOUR	**PERCENT PROTEIN**	**USES**
Cake	6–8	Tender cakes
Pastry	7.5–9.5	Biscuits, pie crusts
All-purpose	10–13	General baking
Bread	12–15	Yeast breads
Whole-wheat	13–14	Breads
High-gluten	14–15	Bagels, used to increase protein content of weaker flour such as rye, whole-grain or specialty flours
Vital wheat gluten (Gluten flour)	40–85	Added to flour to increase protein content of weaker flours such as rye, whole-grain or specialty flours

muffins. Table 4.1 lists the protein content and uses for several common flours. Substituting one type of flour for another may be acceptable in some formulas as long as the ratio of fats, moisteners and other ingredients is adjusted accordingly. In many cases, such as substituting cake flour for bread flour in a loaf of crusty bread, substituting one type of flour for another will result in a changed and probably less desirable product.

Gluten development is affected by a number of factors, including mixing time and the presence of fat. Generally, the longer a substance is mixed, the more gluten will develop. Extreme overmixing in industrial equipment can break down the gluten structure, however. The type and balance of ingredients in a formula will also affect gluten development. Fats coat the protein in the flour, inhibiting the formation of the gluten bond. A high-fat cookie dough that contains very little liquid will bake into a crumbly or **friable** product, not a light and chewy one. Flour needs to absorb liquid in order for the proteins to bond into gluten. Firm bread dough that can be kneaded and shaped before baking requires a high-protein flour. When this dough is made with water it will bake into a product with a solid structure. When whole milk is used in the same formula, the product will be more tender because the milkfat weakens the gluten bond. The factors that affect gluten development in the bakeshop will be studied throughout this book.

▶ **friable**—easily crumbled; said of a baked good with a low moisture and high fat content such as a butter cookie

The character of the wheat determines the character of the flour. Wheat is classified as soft or hard depending on the kernel's hardness. The harder the wheat kernel, the higher its protein content. Soft wheat yields a soft flour with a low protein content. **Soft flour,** also called **weak flour,** is best for tender products such as cakes. Hard wheat yields a **hard flour** with a high protein content. Hard flour, also known as **strong flour,** is used for yeast breads.

Various types of flour are created by mixing or blending flours from different varieties of wheat. All-purpose flour, a blend of hard and soft flours, is designed for use in a wide range of foods. It is also referred to throughout this book because it is readily available in quantities appropriate for small food service operations. Large bakeshops rarely use all-purpose flour; instead, they choose flours specifically milled and blended for specific characteristics.

AGING AND BLEACHING

Any flour develops better baking qualities if allowed to rest for several weeks after milling. Freshly milled flour produces sticky doughs and products with less volume than those made with aged flour. During aging, flour turns white through a natural oxidation process referred to as bleaching.

Natural aging and bleaching are somewhat unpredictable, time-consuming processes, however, so chemicals are often used to do both. Potassium bromate and chlorine dioxide gas rapidly age flour. Chlorine dioxide and other chemicals bleach flour by removing yellow pigments in order to obtain a uniform white color. Bleaching destroys small amounts of the flour's naturally occurring vitamin E. Many artisan bakers use unbleached and unbromated flours exclusively. (It should be noted, however that potassium bromate has been identified as a possible carcinogen and may not be added to flour milled and sold in Canada or Europe.)

SPECIALTY FLOURS

Whole-wheat flour is made by milling the entire wheat kernel, including the bran and nutritious germ. Whole-wheat flour has a nutty, sweet flavor and brown, flecked color. Products made with whole-wheat flour will be denser, with less volume than those made with white flour; bran particles cut through the gluten strands in the dough, resulting in a heavier crumb. A newer strain of white whole wheat produces a lighter-colored whole-wheat flour with the nutritional benefits of whole wheat. Whole-wheat flour has a reduced shelf life because fats in the germ can become rancid during storage. Whole-wheat pastry and high-gluten flours are available. Graham flour is a type of coarse whole-wheat flour used to add texture to crackers and baked goods.

Whole-Wheat Flour

Though not a flour, **wheat germ** is often used in place of some flour in recipes for flavor and fiber. Wheat germ, preferably toasted, can be used in place of up to one-third of the wheat flour in a dough formula. The finished product will have a denser texture, however.

Vital wheat gluten (gluten flour) is the pure protein extracted from wheat flour. With an average protein content of 75%, it is used to boost the protein content of weaker flours such as rye and whole-wheat flour. It must be blended with other ingredients to form a dough or batter.

Self-rising flour is an all-purpose flour to which salt and a chemical leavener, usually baking powder, have been added. It is not recommended for professional use. Chemicals lose their leavening ability over time and may cause inconsistent results. Furthermore, different formulas call for different ratios of salt and leaveners; no commercial blend is appropriate for all purposes.

Nonwheat flours, also referred to as **composite flours,** are made from grains, seeds or beans. Corn, soybeans, rice, oats, buckwheat, potatoes and other items provide flours, but none of them contain the gluten-forming proteins of wheat flour. Composite flours are generally blended with a high-protein wheat flour for baking. Substituting composite flour for wheat flour changes the flavor and texture of the product.

Rye flour is commonly used in bread baking. It is milled from the rye berry much as wheat flour is milled from the wheat berry. Rye flour comes in four grades or colors: white, medium, dark and rye meal. White rye flour is made from only the center of the rye berry. Medium and dark rye flours are made from the whole rye berry after the bran is removed and have the most intense rye flavor. Rye meal is the entire rye berry milled into a flour of different granulations, most often a coarse-textured flour. Some mills refer to their rye meal as pumpernickel flour. Others use pumpernickel to describe dark rye flour. All rye flours have a warm, pungent flavor similar to caraway and a gray-brown color. Although rye flour contains proteins, they will not form gluten, so bread made with 100% rye flour will be dense and flat. Therefore, rye flour is usually blended with a high-protein wheat flour to produce a more acceptable product. White rye flour can be substituted successfully for up to 40% of wheat flour in a recipe without significant loss of volume. Medium and dark rye flours should be limited to no more than 30% and 20% of the total amount of flour, respectively.

Rye Flour

Cornmeal

Blanced Almond Flour

Cornmeal is made by grinding a special type of corn known as dent, which may be yellow, white or blue. Cornmeal is often added to breads to lend a crunchy texture. It is also sprinkled on a baker's peel to help pizza and bread slide into a hearth oven.

Oats are one of the most common grains consumed in America, usually in the form of a hot breakfast cereal. Added to bread, oats lend texture, taste and nutrition to many products. An oat groat is the whole oat kernel with only the husk removed. It contains both the bran and germ. *Steel-cut oats* are groats that are toasted and then cut into small pieces with steel blades. *Rolled oats* are groats that have been steamed, then rolled into flat flakes. *Quick-cooking oats* are simply rolled oats that are cut into smaller pieces to reduce cooking time.

Oats

Finely ground almonds, hazelnuts, pistachios and other nuts are called **nut flours** and are used in the bakeshop. Containing no protein-forming gluten, these flours lend a delicate taste and texture to cakes and cookies in which they are added. See Chapter 5, Mise en Place, page 100. Because of their high fat content, nut flours are prone to rancidity. They should be stored under refrigeration.

PURCHASING AND STORING

Most flours are purchased in 50- and 100-pound bags. They should be stored in a lit, ventilated room at temperatures no higher than 80°F (27°C). Flour can be stored in a refrigerator or freezer if necessary to prevent the onset of rancidity. Refrigeration may cause the flour to absorb moisture, however, which will limit the flour's ability to absorb additional moisture during actual use. An open bag of flour should be transferred to a closed container to prevent contamination. Even unopened bags of flour should not be stored near items with strong odors, as flour readily absorbs odors. Whole grains should be stored in airtight containers in cool, dry, dark conditions. Coolness inhibits insect infestations; dryness prevents mold. Using airtight containers stored in darkness helps prevent nutrient loss.

▶ SUGAR AND SWEETENERS

Sugar (Fr. *sucre*) and other sweeteners serve several purposes in the bakeshop: They provide flavor and color, tenderize products by weakening gluten strands, provide food for yeasts, serve as a preservative and act as a creaming or foaming agent to assist with leavening. (Artificial sweeteners are discussed in Chapter 18, Healthful and Special Needs Baking.)

SUGAR

Sugars are carbohydrates. They are classified as either (1) single or simple sugars (monosaccharides), such as glucose and fructose, which occur naturally in honey and fruits, or (2) double or complex sugars (disaccharides), which may occur naturally, such as lactose in milk, or in refined sugars. See Table 4.2.

Table 4.2	**S U G A R S**
MONOSACCHARIDES	**DISACCHARIDES**
Glucose (blood sugar)	Lactose (milk sugar)
Fructose (fruit sugar)	Maltose (malt sugar)
Galactose (part of milk sugar)	Sucrose (table sugar)

The sugar most often used in the kitchen is **sucrose,** a refined sugar obtained from both the large tropical grass called sugar cane (*Saccharum officinarum*) and the root of the sugar beet (*Beta vulgaris*). Sucrose is a disaccharide, composed of one molecule each of glucose and fructose. The chemical composition of beet and cane sugars is identical. The two products taste, look, smell and react the same. Sucrose is available in many forms: white granulated, light or dark brown granulated, molasses and powdered.

SUGAR MANUFACTURING

Common refined or table sugar is produced from sugar cane or sugar beets. The first step in sugar production is to crush the cane or beet to extract the juice. This juice contains tannins, pigments, proteins and other undesirable components that must be removed through refinement. Refinement begins by dissolving the juice in water, then boiling it in large steam evaporators. The solution is then crystallized in heated vacuum pans. The uncrystallized liquid by-product, known as molasses, is separated out in a centrifuge. The remaining crystallized product, known as raw sugar, contains many impurities; the USDA considers it unfit for direct use in food.

Raw sugar is washed with steam to remove some of the impurities. This yields a product known as turbinado sugar. Refining continues as the turbinado is heated, liquefied, centrifuged and filtered. Chemicals may be used to bleach and purify the liquid sugar. Finally, the clear liquid sugar is recrystallized in vacuum pans as granulated white sugar.

Pure sucrose is sold in granulated and powdered forms and is available in several grades. Because there are no government standards regulating grade labels, various manufacturers' products may differ slightly.

TYPES OF SUGAR

Turbinado sugar, sometimes called Demerara sugar, is the closest consumable product to raw sugar. It is partially refined, light brown in color, with coarse crystals and a caramel flavor. It is sometimes used in beverages and certain baked goods. Because of its high and variable moisture content, turbinado sugar is not recommended as a substitute for granulated or brown sugar.

Sanding sugar has a large, coarse crystal structure that prevents it from dissolving easily. It is used almost exclusively for decorating cookies and pastries.

Granulated sugar is the all-purpose sugar used throughout the kitchen. The crystals are a fine, uniform size suitable for a variety of purposes. **Sugar cubes** are formed by pressing moistened granulated sugar into molds and allowing it to dry. Most cubes are used for beverage service.

Brown sugar is simply regular refined cane sugar with some of the molasses returned to it. Light brown sugar contains approximately 3.5 percent molasses; dark brown sugar contains about 6.5 percent. Molasses adds moisture and a distinctive flavor. Brown sugar can be substituted for refined sugar, measure for measure, in any formula where its flavor is desired. Because of the added moisture, brown sugar tends to lump, trapping air into pockets. Always store brown sugar in an airtight container to prevent it from drying and hardening.

Superfine or castor sugar is granulated sugar with a smaller-sized crystal. It can be produced by processing regular granulated sugar in a food processor for a few moments. Superfine sugar dissolves quickly in liquids and produces light and tender cakes.

Powdered sugar (Fr. *sucre en poudre*) or confectioner's sugar is made by grinding granulated sugar crystals through varying degrees of fine screens. Powdered sugar cannot be made in a food processor. It is widely available in various degrees of fineness: 10X is the finest and most common; 6X and 4X are progressively coarser. Because of powdered sugar's tendency to lump, 3 percent cornstarch is added to absorb moisture. Powdered sugar is most often used in icings and glazes and for decorating baked products.

▶ **sucrose**—the chemical name for common refined sugar; it is a disaccharide, composed of one molecule each of glucose and fructose

Clockwise from top left: Demerara sugar cubes, light brown sugar, powdered sugar, sugar cubes, brown sugar crystals, granulated sugar

Glucose

Honey

Fructose is a simple sugar (monosaccharide) that occurs naturally in honey, fruits and vegetables. Fructose is normally a liquid; however, a free-flowing crystalized fructose powder can be made from invert sugar or glucose syrup, discussed shortly. Fructose is nearly twice as sweet as sucrose. Fructose attracts more water than does sugar; therefore, fructose-sweetened products tend to be moist. Baked products made with fructose will be darker than those made with sucrose.

LIQUID SWEETENERS

Except for leavening, liquid sweeteners can be used to achieve the same benefits as sugar in baked goods. Most of these liquids have a distinctive flavor as well as sweetness. Some liquid sweeteners are made from sugar cane; others are derived from other plants, grains or the activities of bees.

Corn syrup is produced by extracting starch from corn kernels and treating it with acid or an enzyme to develop a sweet syrup. This syrup is extremely thick or viscous and less sweet-tasting than honey or refined sugar. Its viscosity gives foods a thick, chewy texture. It stabilizes products made with sugar, preventing them from recrystalization. Corn syrup is available in light and dark forms; the dark syrup has caramel color and flavor added. Corn syrup is a hygroscopic (water-attracting) sweetener, which means it will attract water from the air on humid days and lose water through evaporation more slowly than granulated sugar. Thus, it keeps products moister and fresher longer.

Glucose is a thick syrup extracted from the starch in corn, potatoes, rice or wheat in a process known as hydrolysis. Like corn syrup, glucose is less sweet-tasting than sugar and is hygroscopic. It is an invert sugar widely used in the confectionery industry for its ability to prevent sugar crystallization. Light corn syrup may be used interchangeably for glucose in recipes in this book.

Invert sugar is a dense sugar syrup produced by refining sucrose with an acid. When sucrose is heated and combined with an acid it "inverts" or partially breaks down into glucose and fructose. This inversion makes it more difficult for crystals to form. Invert sugar is about 20 to 30 percent sweeter than regular sucrose and it is extremely hygroscopic. Honey and corn syrup are naturally occurring invert sugars and invert sugar syrup, similar to corn syrup, is available commercially. Like glucose, invert sugar syrup is widely used in the confectionery industry and when making pulled sugar and other decorative sugar work.

Honey (Fr. *miel*) is a strong sweetener consisting of fructose and glucose. It is created by honeybees from nectar collected from flowers. Its flavor and color vary depending on the season, the type of flower the nectar came from and its age. Commercial honey is often a blend, prepared to be relatively neutral and consistent. Like corn syrup, honey is highly hygroscopic. Its distinctive flavor is found in several ethnic foods such as baklava and halvah, and beverages such as Drambuie and Benedictine.

Malt is a liquid sweetener produced from germinated barley or wheat grains. The enzymes (called alpha-amylase) in malts aid in the fermentation of many types of bread. Often European bread formulas, especially those with rye flour, include malt that acts as a quick yeast food. Malt also enhances the elasticity of bread dough and retains moisture in the crumb.

Maple syrup is made from the sap of sugar maple trees. Sap is collected during the spring, then boiled to evaporate its water content, yielding a sweet brown syrup. One sugar maple tree produces about 12 gallons of sap each season; 30–40 gallons of sap will produce 1 gallon of syrup. Pure maple syrup must weigh not less than 11 pounds per gallon; it is graded according to color, flavor and sugar content. The more desirable products, Grades AA and A, have a light amber color and delicate flavor. Pure maple syrup is expensive, but it does add a distinct flavor to baked goods, frostings and, of course, pancakes and waffles. Maple-flavored syrups, often served with pancakes, are usually corn syrups with artificial colorings and flavorings added.

As mentioned earlier, **molasses** (Fr. *mélasse*) is the liquid by-product of sugar refining. Edible molasses is derived only from cane sugar, as beet molasses has an unpleasant odor and bitter flavor. Unsulfured molasses is not a true by-product of sugar making. It is intentionally produced from pure cane syrup and is preferred because of its lighter color and milder flavor. Sulfured molasses is a by-product and contains some of the sulfur dioxide used in secondary sugar processing. It is darker and has a strong, bitter flavor.

The final stage of sucrose refinement yields blackstrap molasses, which is somewhat popular in the American South. Blackstrap molasses is very dark and thick, with a strong, unique flavor that is unsuitable for most purposes.

Sorghum molasses is produced by cooking down the sweet sap of a brown corn plant known as sorghum, which is grown for animal feed. The flavor and appearance of sorghum molasses are almost identical to unsulfured sugar cane molasses.

Molasses

COOKING SUGAR

Sugar can be incorporated into a prepared item in its dry form or first liquefied into a syrup. Sugar syrups (not to be confused with liquid sweeteners such as molasses) take two forms: simple syrups, which are mixtures of sugar and water, and cooked syrups, which are made of melted sugar cooked until it reaches a specific temperature. The making and handling of liquid sugar is discussed in Chapter 13, Syrups, Icings and Sauces.

▶ FATS

Fat is the general term for butter, lard, margarine, shortening and oil. Fats provide flavor and color, add moisture and richness, assist with leavening, help extend a product's shelf life and shorten gluten strands, producing tender baked goods.

The flavor and texture of a baked good depends on the type of fat used and the manner in which it is incorporated with other ingredients. In pastry doughs, solid fat shortens or tenderizes the gluten strands; in bread doughs, fat increases loaf volume and lightness; in cake batters, fat incorporates air bubbles and helps leaven the mixture. Fats should be selected based on their flavor, melting point and ability to form emulsions.

Most bakeshop ingredients combine completely with liquids; fats do not. Fats will not dissolve but will break down into smaller and smaller particles through mixing. With proper mixing, these fat particles are distributed, more or less evenly, throughout the other ingredients causing fat and liquid to blend or **emulsify.**

▶ **emulsify**—to combine a fat and a liquid into a homogeneous mixture by properly blending ingredients

BUTTER

Butter is a fatty substance produced by agitating or churning cream. Its flavor is unequaled in sauces, breads and pastries. Butter contains at least 80% milkfat, not more than 16% water and 2–4% milk solids. It may or may not contain added salt. Butter is firm when chilled and soft at room temperature. It melts into a liquid at approximately 93°F (33°C) and reaches the smoke point at 260°F (127°C). Butter is prized in the bakeshop for its flavor; however, its low melting point makes it difficult to handle in certain applications, and it burns easily. Unsalted butter is preferred for baking because it tends to be fresher, and additional salt might interfere with product formulas.

Salted butter is butter with up to 2.5% salt added. This not only changes the butter's flavor, it also extends its keeping qualities. When salted butter is used, the salt content must be considered in the total recipe.

▶ **whole butter**—butter that is not clarified, whipped or reduced-fat

European-style butter contains more milkfat than regular butter, usually from 82 to 86%, and very little or no added salt. It is often churned from cultured cream, giving it a more intense, buttery flavor.

Whipped butter is made by incorporating air into the butter. This increases its volume and spreadability, but also increases the speed with which the butter will become rancid. Because of the change in density, whipped butter should not be substituted in recipes calling for regular butter.

Clarified butter is butter that has had its water and milk solids removed by a process called clarification. Although **whole butter** can be used for cooking or sauce making, sometimes a more stable and consistent product will be achieved by using clarified butter. The clarification process is described in Chapter 5, Mise en Place.

STORAGE

Butter should be well wrapped and stored at temperatures between 32°F and 35°F (0°C and 2°C). Unsalted butter is best kept frozen until needed. If well wrapped, frozen butter will keep for up to nine months at a temperature of 0°F (18°C).

LARD

Lard (Fr. *saindoux*) is rendered pork fat. It is a solid white product of almost 100 percent pure fat; it contains only a small amount of water. Lard yields flaky, flavorful pastries, such as pie crusts, but is rarely used commercially because it turns rancid quickly.

MARGARINE

Margarine is manufactured from animal or vegetable fats or a combination of such fats. Flavorings, colorings, emulsifiers, preservatives and vitamins are added, and the mixture is firmed or solidified by exposure to hydrogen gas at very high temperatures, a process known as hydrogenation. Generally, the firmer the margarine, the greater the degree of hydrogenation and the longer its shelf life. Like butter, margarine is approximately 80% fat and 16% water. But even the finest margarine cannot match the flavor of butter. Margarine melts at a slightly higher temperature than butter, making it useful for some rolled-in doughs such as puff pastry or Danish. Because it requires higher temperatures to melt, margarine and other vegetable-based shortenings can leave a greasy taste on the tongue.

Lard

MARGARINE: FROM LABORATORY BENCH TO DINNER TABLE

A French chemist invented margarine in 1869 after Napoleon III offered a prize for the development of a synthetic edible fat. Originally produced from animal fat and milk, margarine is now made almost exclusively from vegetable fats.

In *On Food and Cooking: The Science and Lore of the Kitchen,* Harold McGee recounts the history of margarine. He explains that margarine caught on quickly in Europe and America, with large-scale production underway by 1880. But the American dairy industry and the U.S. government put up fierce resistance. First, margarine was defined as a harmful drug and its sale restricted. Then it was heavily taxed; stores had to be licensed to sell it and, like alcohol and tobacco, it was bootlegged. The U.S. government refused to purchase it for use by the armed forces. And, in an attempt to hold it to its true colors, some states did not allow margarine to be dyed yellow (animal fats and vegetable oils are much paler than butter); the dye was sold separately and mixed in by the consumer. World War II, which brought butter rationing, probably did the most to establish margarine's respectability. But it was not until 1967 that yellow margarine could be sold in Wisconsin.

Margarine packaged in tubs is softer and more spreadable than solid products and generally contains more water and air. Indeed, diet margarine is approximately 50% water. Because of their decreased density, these soft products should not be substituted for regular butter or margarine in baking.

Specially formulated and blended margarine is available for commercial use in making puff pastry, croissant doughs, frostings and the like.

SHORTENINGS

Any fat is a **shortening** in baking because it shortens gluten strands and tenderizes the product. What is generally referred to as shortening, however, is a type of solid, white, generally flavorless fat, specially formulated for baking. Shortenings are made from animal fats and/or vegetable oils that are solidified through hydrogenation. These products are 100 percent fat with a relatively high melting point (see Table 4.3). Solid shortenings are ideal for greasing baking pans because they are flavorless and odorless. When substituting shortening in a formula calling for butter, additional liquid must be added to compensate for the lack of moisture in the shortening.

Emulsifiers may be added to regular shortening to assist with moisture absorption and retention as well as leavening. **Emulsified shortenings,** also known as high-ratio shortenings, are used in the commercial production of cakes and frostings where the formula contains a large amount of sugar. If a formula calls for an emulsified shortening, use it. If you substitute any other fat, the product's texture suffers.

Oils may be extracted from a variety of plants including corn, cottonseed, peanuts, rapeseeds (canola), and soybeans by pressure or chemical solvents. Vegetable oils are virtually odorless and have a neutral flavor. Because they contain no animal products they are cholesterol-free. Oils extracted from a variety of nuts, including walnuts and hazelnuts, are prized for their distinctive flavors.

Unlike butter and other fats, oil blends thoroughly throughout a mixture. It therefore coats more of the proteins, and the gluten strands produced are much shorter, a desirable result in fine-textured products such as muffins or chiffon cakes. For baking, select a neutral-flavored oil unless the distinctive taste of olive oil is desired, as in some breads. Never substitute oil in a formula requiring a solid shortening.

Table 4.3	**MELTING POINT OF FATS***
Butter, whole	92°F–98°F (33°C–36°C)
Butter, clarified	92°F–98°F (33°C–36°C)
Cocoa butter	88°F–93°F (31°C–34°C)
Lard	89°F–98°F (32°C–36°C)
Margarine, solid	94°F–98°F (34°C–36°C)
Shortening, all-purpose vegetable	120°F (49°C)
Shortening, emulsified vegetable	115°F (46°C)
Shortening, heavy-duty fryer	97°F–107°F (36°C–42°C)

*The melting point of any fat depends on its specific ratio of fatty acids. Natural products such as butter and lard will vary more from one lot to the next than will manufactured products such as margarine.

This information was obtained from a variety of manufacturers and assumes that the fat is pure and previously unused.

▶ **lactose**—a disaccharide that occurs naturally in mammalian milk; milk sugar

▶ MILK AND DAIRY PRODUCTS

Milk provides texture, flavor, volume, color and nutritional value for cooked or baked items. Highly perishable, milk is an excellent bacterial breeding ground. Care must be exercised when handling and storing milk and other dairy products.

Whole milk—that is, milk as it comes from the cow—consists primarily of water (about 88%). It contains approximately 3.5% milkfat and 8.5% other milk solids (proteins, milk sugar **[lactose]** and minerals).

Whole milk is graded A, B or C according to standards recommended by the U.S. Public Health Service. Grades are assigned based on bacterial count, with Grade A products having the lowest count. Grades B and C, though still safe and wholesome, are rarely available for retail or commercial use. Fresh whole milk is not available raw, but must be processed as we describe shortly.

PROCESSING TECHNIQUES

PASTEURIZATION

By law, all Grade A milk must be pasteurized prior to retail sale. Pasteurization is the process of heating something to a sufficiently high temperature for a sufficient length of time to destroy pathogenic bacteria. This typically requires holding milk at a temperature of 161°F (72°C) for 15 seconds. Pasteurization also destroys enzymes that cause spoilage, thus increasing shelf life. Milk's nutritional value is not significantly affected by pasteurization.

ULTRA-PASTEURIZATION

Ultra-pasteurization is a process in which milk is heated to a very high temperature (275°F/135°C) for a very short time (2 to 4 seconds) in order to destroy virtually all bacteria. Ultra-pasteurization is most often used with whipping cream and individual creamers. Although the process may reduce cream's whipping properties, it extends its shelf life dramatically.

ULTRA-HIGH-TEMPERATURE PROCESSING

Ultra-high-temperature (UHT) processing is a form of ultra-pasteurization in which milk is held at a temperature of 280°F–300°F (138°C–150°C) for 2 to 6 seconds. It is then packed in sterile containers under sterile conditions and aseptically sealed to prevent bacteria from entering the container. Unopened UHT milk can be stored without refrigeration for at least three months. Although UHT milk can be stored unrefrigerated, it should be chilled before serving and stored like fresh milk once opened. UHT processing may give milk a slightly cooked taste, but it has no significant effect on milk's nutritional value. Long available in Europe, it is now gaining popularity in the United States.

HOMOGENIZATION

Homogenization is a process in which the fat globules in whole milk are reduced in size and permanently dispersed throughout the liquid. This prevents the fat from clumping together and rising to the surface as a layer of cream. Although homogenization is not required, milk sold commercially is generally homogenized to ensure a uniform consistency, a whiter color and a richer taste.

MILKFAT REMOVAL

Whole milk can also be processed in a centrifuge to remove all or a portion of the milkfat, resulting in reduced-fat, low-fat and nonfat milks. Reduced-fat or less-fat milk is whole milk from which sufficient milkfat has been removed to produce a liquid with 2% milkfat. Low-fat or little-fat milk contains 1% milkfat.

Nonfat milk, also referred to as fat-free, no-fat or skim milk, has had as much milkfat removed as possible. The fat content must be less than 0.5%. Nonfat milk should not be substituted for whole milk in most baked-good formulas without the addition of fat to compensate for that removed.

Pasteurized milk needs to be heated to 200°F (93°C) to destroy certain milk enzymes that are known to weaken gluten structure, resulting in sticky, difficult to handle dough. For convenience, dry milk powder is often used instead since it requires no heating and is easily stored. Yogurt, buttermilk and UHT milk require no preheating to destroy this enzyme.

STORAGE

Fluid milk is a potentially hazardous food and should be kept refrigerated at or below 40°F (4°C). Its shelf life is reduced by half for every five-degree rise in temperature above 40°F (4°C). Keep milk containers closed to prevent absorption of odors and flavors. Freezing is not recommended.

CONCENTRATED MILKS

Concentrated or condensed milk products are produced by using a vacuum to remove all or part of the water from whole milk. The resulting products have a high concentration of milkfat and milk solids and an extended shelf life.

Evaporated milk is produced by removing approximately 60 percent of the water from whole, homogenized milk. The concentrated liquid is canned and heat-sterilized. This results in a cooked flavor and darker color. Evaporated skim milk, with a milkfat content of 0.5%, is also available. A can of evaporated milk requires no refrigeration until opened, although the can should be stored in a cool place. Evaporated milk can be reconstituted with an equal amount of water and used like whole milk for cooking or drinking.

Sweetened condensed milk is similar to evaporated milk in that 60 percent of the water has been removed. But unlike evaporated milk, sweetened condensed milk contains large amounts of sugar (40 to 45 percent). Sweetened condensed milk is also canned; the canning process darkens the color and adds a caramel flavor. Sweetened condensed milk cannot be substituted for whole milk or evaporated milk because of its sugar content. Its distinctive flavor is most often found in puddings, fudge and other confections.

Dry milk powder is made by removing virtually all the moisture from pasteurized milk. Dry whole milk, nonfat milk and buttermilk are available. The lack of moisture prevents the growth of microorganisms and allows dry milk powders to be stored for extended periods without refrigeration. Powdered milks can be reconstituted with water and used like fresh milk. Milk powder may also be added to foods directly, with additional liquid included in the recipe. This procedure is typical in bread making and does not alter the function of the milk or its flavor in the finished product.

CREAM

Cream is a rich, liquid milk product containing at least 18% fat. It must be pasteurized or ultra-pasteurized and may be homogenized. Cream has a slight yellow or ivory color and is more viscous than milk. It is used throughout the kitchen to give flavor and body to sauces, soups and desserts. Cream is marketed in several forms with different fat contents, as described here.

Half-and-half is a mixture of whole milk and cream containing between 10% and 18% milkfat. It is often served with cereal or coffee, but does not contain enough fat to whip into a foam.

Light cream, coffee cream and **table cream** are all products with more than 18% but less than 30% milkfat. These products are often used in baked goods or soups as well as with coffee, fruit and cereal.

IMITATION AND ARTIFICIAL DAIRY PRODUCTS

Coffee whiteners, imitation sour cream, whipped topping mixes and some whipped toppings in pressurized cans are made from nondairy products. These products usually consist of corn syrup, emulsifiers, vegetable fats, coloring agents and artificial flavors. These products are generally less expensive and have a longer shelf life than the real dairy products they replace, but their flavors are no match. Imitation and artificial products may be useful, however, for people who have allergies or are on a restricted diet. If you choose to use these products, you cannot claim to be using real dairy products on menus or labels.

Light **whipping cream** or, simply, whipping cream, contains between 30% and 36% milkfat. It is generally used for thickening and enriching sauces and making ice cream. It can be whipped into a foam and used as a dessert topping or folded into custards or mousses to add flavor and lightness.

Heavy whipping cream or, simply, **heavy cream,** contains not less than 36% milkfat. It whips easily and holds its whipped texture longer than other creams. It must be pasteurized, but is rarely homogenized. Heavy cream is used throughout the kitchen in the same ways as light whipping cream.

Clotted cream is a thick spreadable cream with 55% milkfat made from unpasteurized whole milk. The milk is heated, then the thick cream clumps and floats to the top when the milk cools, and the dense clotted cream is removed. It is served as a spread or filling for scones, cakes and other pastries. Clotted cream is also referred to as Devon or Devonshire cream, named for two English counties where it is made.

STORAGE

Ultra-pasteurized cream will keep for six to eight weeks if refrigerated at or below 40°F (4°C). Unwhipped cream should not be frozen. Keep cream away from strong odors and bright lights, as they can adversely affect its flavor.

CULTURED DAIRY PRODUCTS

Cultured dairy products such as yogurt, buttermilk and sour cream are produced by adding specific bacterial cultures to fluid dairy products. The bacteria convert the milk sugar lactose into lactic acid, giving these products their body and tangy, unique flavors. The acid content also retards the growth of undesirable microorganisms; thus cultured products have been used for centuries to preserve milk. With their mild acidity, these products are most often used in baked goods for their distinctive taste.

Buttermilk originally referred to the liquid remaining after cream was churned into butter. Today, buttermilk is produced by adding a culture (*Streptococcus lactis*) to fresh, pasteurized skim or low-fat milk. This results in a tart milk with a thick texture.

Sour cream is produced by adding the same culture to pasteurized, homogenized light cream. The resulting product is a white, tangy gel used to give baked goods a distinctive flavor. Sour cream must have a milkfat content of not less than 18%.

Crème fraîche is a cultured cream popular in French cuisine. Although thinner and richer than sour cream, it has a similar tart, tangy flavor and adds depth of flavor when added to chilled custard sauces and for ice cream base. It is easily prepared from the recipe on page 69.

Yogurt is a thick, tart product made from milk (either whole, low-fat or nonfat) cultured with *Lactobacillus bulgaricus* and *Streptococcus thermophilus*. Though touted as a health or diet food, yogurt contains the same amount of milkfat as the milk from which it is made. Yogurt may also contain a variety of sweeteners, flavorings and fruits. Yogurt may be used in baked products and frozen desserts.

STORAGE

Cultured products are potentially hazardous foods and should be kept refrigerated at or below 40°F (4°C). Under proper conditions, sour cream will last up to four weeks, yogurt up to three weeks and buttermilk up to two weeks. Freezing is not recommended for these products, but dishes prepared with cultured products generally can be frozen.

CRÈME FRAÎCHE

Yield: 1 pint (500 ml)

Heavy cream	16 fl. oz.	500 ml
Buttermilk, with active cultures	1 fl. oz.	30 ml

1 Heat the cream (preferably not ultra-pasteurized) to approximately 100°F (38°C).

2 Remove the cream from the heat and stir in the buttermilk.

3 Allow the mixture to stand in a warm place, loosely covered, until it thickens, approximately 12 to 36 hours.

4 Chill thoroughly before using. Crème fraîche will keep for up to 10 days in the refrigerator.

Approximate values per 1-oz. (30-g) serving: **Calories** 90, **Total fat** 10 g, **Saturated fat** 6 g, **Cholesterol** 35 mg, **Sodium** 10 mg, **Total carbohydrates** 1 g, **Protein** 1 g, **Vitamin A** 10%, **Claims—** very low sodium

CHEESES

Cheese (Fr. *fromage;* It. *formaggio*) is one of the oldest and most widely used foods known to humans. It is ideal served alone with bread or in many bakeshop preparations including cakes, breads and other baked goods. Cheese starts with a mammal's milk; cows, goats and sheep are the most commonly used. The milk proteins (known as casein) are coagulated with the addition of an enzyme, usually rennet, which is found in calves' stomachs. As the milk coagulates, it separates into solid curds and liquid whey. After draining off the whey, either the curds are made into fresh cheese, such as ricotta or cottage cheese, or the curds are further processed by cutting, kneading and cooking. The resulting substance, known as "green cheese," is packed into molds to drain. Salt or special bacteria may be added to the molded cheeses, which are then allowed to age or ripen under controlled conditions to develop the desired texture, color and flavor.

Some cheeses, such as Brie or Camembert, develop a natural rind or surface because of the application of bacteria (bloomy rind) or by repeated washing with brine (washed rind). Most natural rinds may be eaten if desired. Other cheeses, such as Gouda and Cheddar, are coated with an inedible wax rind to prevent moisture loss. Fresh cheeses have no rind whatsoever.

Moisture and fat contents are good indicators of a cheese's texture and shelf life. The higher the moisture content, the softer the product and the more perishable it will be. Low-moisture cheeses such as Parmigiano-Reggiano and pecorino romano may be used for grating and will keep for several weeks if properly stored. (Reduced water activity levels prohibit bacterial growth.) Fat content ranges from low fat (less than 20% fat) to double cream (at least 60% fat) and triple cream (at least 72% fat). Cheeses with a high fat content will be creamier and have a richer flavor and texture than low-fat products.

FRESH OR UNRIPENED CHEESES

Fresh cheeses are uncooked and unripened with many uses in sweet and savory bakeshop preparations. Referred to as *fromage blanc* or *fromage frais* in French, they are generally mild and creamy with a tart tanginess. They should not taste acidic or bitter. Fresh cheeses have a moisture content of 40 to 80% and are highly perishable. A few of the more common fresh cheeses used in the bakeshop are featured here.

Mascarpone

Cream cheese is a soft cow's-milk cheese containing approximately 35% fat. It is available in various-sized solid white blocks or whipped and flavored. A popular spread for bagels and toast, cream cheese is used in cheesecakes, pastry fillings and icings.

Farmer's cheese, baker's cheese, and **quark** are traditional, fresh soft cheeses made from cow's milk with a light taste and a smooth texture. They may be used interchangeably. Quark, German for curd, is like a cross between mild cream and cream cheese. If quark is not available, substitute an equal amount of farmer's cheese, baker's cheese, or cream cheese. Add enough milk to soften the cheese to a yogurtlike consistency. Yogurt may also be used in place of quark.

Mascarpone (mas-cahr-POHN-ay) is a soft cow's-milk cheese originally from Italy's Lombard region. It contains 70 to 75% fat and is extremely smooth and creamy. Mascarpone is highly perishable and is available in bulk or in 8- or 16-ounce tubs. With its pale ivory color and rich, sweet flavor, it is useful in sweet sauces, ice creams and fillings.

Ricotta (rih-COH-tah) is a soft Italian cheese, similar to American cottage cheese, made from the whey left when other cow's-milk cheeses are produced. It contains only 4 to 10% fat. It is white or ivory in color and fluffy, with a small grain and sweet flavor. Ricotta is an important ingredient in Italian cheesecake and as a filling for cannoli pastries. It can be made easily with the following recipe.

RECIPE 4.2   **RICOTTA CHEESE**

THE ART INSTITUTE OF WASHINGTON, ARLINGTON, VA
Chef John Harrison

Yield: 8 oz. (240 g)

| Milk | 1 qt. | 960 ml |
| Fresh lime juice | 3 fl. oz. | 90 ml |

1 Allow the milk to reach room temperature in a covered container.

2 In a stainless steel saucepan slowly heat the milk to 180°F (82°C), stirring often. Hold the heated milk at 180°F (82°C) for 5 minutes.

3 Remove the milk from the heat and gently stir it while adding the lime juice. Continue to stir until curds form.

4 Gently pour the curds into a strainer or china cap lined with new, rinsed cheesecloth. Allow the whey (liquid) to separate and drain away from the curds (solids). Discard the whey.

5 Allow the cheese to rest undisturbed for 1 hour. For a firm, dry ricotta, lift the corners of the cheesecloth and tie them together with twine. Suspend the bag

1 Heat milk to 180°F (82°C).

2 Gently stir in the lime juice.

3 Strain the mixture through the cheesecloth.

4 The finished ricotta.

in a tall, covered container, place it in the refrigerator and allow the cheese to drain for 4 hours or overnight.

6 Unwrap the cheese. Season it with salt if desired. Use the cheese as you would use commercially produced ricotta.

Approximate values per 1-oz. (30-g) serving: **Calories** 80, **Total fat** 4 g, **Saturated fat** 2.5 g, **Cholesterol** 15 mg, **Sodium** 60 mg, **Total carbohydrates** 7 g, **Protein** 4 g, **Calcium** 15%

STORAGE

Most cheeses are best kept refrigerated, well wrapped to keep odors out and moisture in. Firm and hard cheeses can be kept for several weeks; fresh cheeses will spoil in 7 to 10 days because of their high moisture content. Some cheeses that have become hard or dry may still be grated for cooking or baking. Freezing is possible but not recommended because it changes the cheese's texture, making it mealy or tough.

▶ EGGS

Eggs flavor, leaven and thicken items in the bakeshop. They enrich and tenderize yeast breads and extend the shelf life of some baked goods.

FRESH EGGS

COMPOSITION

The primary parts of an egg are the shell, yolk and albumen. See Figure 4.2. The **shell,** composed of calcium carbonate, is the outermost covering of the egg. It prevents microbes from entering and moisture from escaping, and also protects the egg during handling and transport. The breed of the hen determines shell color; for chickens, it can range from bright white to brown. Shell color has no effect on quality, flavor or nutrition.

The **yolk** is the yellow portion of the egg. It constitutes just over one-third of the egg and contains three-fourths of the calories, most of the minerals and vitamins and all the fat. The yolk also contains lecithin, the compound responsible for emulsification in products such as sabayon sauce and French buttercream icing. Egg yolk solidifies (coagulates) at temperatures between 149°F and 158°F (65°C and 70°C). Although the color of a yolk may vary depending on the hen's feed, color does not affect quality or nutritional content.

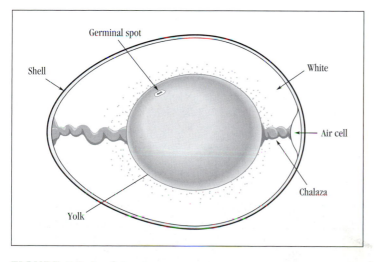

FIGURE 4.2 ▶ An egg

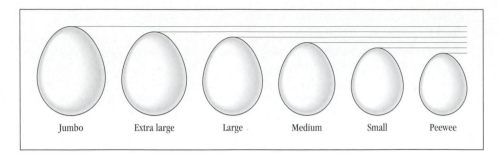

FIGURE 4.3 ▶ Egg sizes

The **albumen** is the clear portion of the egg and is often referred to as the egg white. It constitutes about two-thirds of the egg and contains more than half of the protein and riboflavin. Egg white coagulates, becoming firm and opaque, at temperatures between 144°F and 149°F (62°C and 65°C).

An often-misunderstood portion of the egg is the **chalazae cords.** These thick, twisted strands of egg white anchor the yolk in place. They are neither imperfections nor embryos. The more prominent the chalazae, the fresher the egg. Chalazae do not interfere with cooking or with whipping egg whites.

Eggs are sold in Jumbo, Extra Large, Large, Medium, Small and Peewee sizes, as determined by weight per dozen. (See Figure 4.3.) Food service operations generally use large eggs, which weigh 24 ounces per dozen including the shell. Other sizes are based on plus or minus 3 ounces per dozen; Medium eggs weigh 21 ounces per dozen while Extra Large eggs weigh 27 ounces per dozen. All recipes in this book call for large eggs. The average weight of a large egg once shelled is 1.6 ounces (50 grams). A large egg white weighs 1 ounce (30 grams) and a large egg yolk weighs 0.6 ounce (20 grams).

GRADING

Eggs are graded by the USDA or a state agency following USDA guidelines. The grade AA, A or B is given to an egg based upon interior and exterior quality, not size. The qualities for each grade are described in Table 4.4. Grade has no effect on nutritional values.

Table 4.4 EGG GRADES

	GRADE AA	GRADE A	GRADE B
Spread*	Remains compact	Spreads slightly	Spreads over wide area
Albumen	Clear, thick and firm; prominent chalazae	Clear and reasonably firm; prominent chalazae	Clear; weak or watery
Yolk	Firm; centered; stands round and high; free from defects	Firm; stands fairly high; practically free from defects	Enlarged and flattened; may show slight defects
Shell	Clean; of normal shape; unbroken		Slight stains permissible; abnormal shape; unbroken
Use	Any use, especially frying, poaching and cooking in shell		Baking; scrambling, used in bulk egg products

*Spread refers to the appearance of the egg when first broken onto a flat surface.

STORAGE

Improper handling quickly diminishes egg quality. Eggs should be stored at temperatures below 40°F (4°C) and at a relative humidity of 70 to 80 percent. Eggs will age more during one day at room temperature than they will during one week under proper refrigeration. As eggs age, the white becomes thinner and the yolk becomes flatter. Although this will change the appearance of poached or fried eggs, age has little effect on nutrition or behavior during cooking procedures.

Do not use dirty, cracked or broken eggs, as they may contain bacteria or other contaminants. Cartons of fresh, uncooked eggs will keep for at least four to five weeks beyond the pack date if properly refrigerated. Hard-cooked eggs left in their shells and refrigerated should be used within one week. Store eggs away from strongly flavored foods to reduce odor absorption. Rotate egg stock to maintain freshness. Frozen eggs should be thawed in the refrigerator and used only in dishes that will be thoroughly cooked, such as baked products.

SANITATION

Eggs are a potentially hazardous food. Rich in protein, they are an excellent breeding ground for bacteria. Salmonella is of particular concern with eggs and egg products because the bacteria are commonly found in a chicken's intestinal tract. Although shells are cleaned at packinghouses, some bacteria may remain. Therefore, to prevent contamination, it is best to avoid mixing a shell with the liquid egg.

Inadequately cooking or improperly storing eggs may lead to food-borne illnesses. USDA guidelines indicate that pasteurization is achieved when the whole egg stays at a temperature of 140°F (60°C) for 3½ minutes. Custards thickened with eggs and ice cream products are especially fertile breeding grounds for bacteria. Heat these products above 145°F (63°C). Chill these products over an ice bath as a soon as they are made and keep them refrigerated below 40°F (4°C). Never leave an egg dish at room temperature for more than one hour, including preparation and service time. Never reuse a container after it has held raw eggs without thoroughly cleaning and sanitizing it.

EGG PRODUCTS

Bakeries and large food service operations often want the convenience of buying eggs out of the shell in the exact form needed: whole eggs, yolks only or whites only. These processed items are called **egg products** and are subject to strict pasteurization standards and USDA inspections. **Pasteurized eggs** are recommended when the preparation requiring eggs will not be cooked, such as for an unbaked meringue pie topping (see page 268). Egg products can be frozen, refrigerated or dried. Frozen and refrigerated egg products may be used interchangeably with fresh eggs weight for weight. Plain dried egg products need to be reconstituted in water before use according to manufacturer's directions, although dried egg whites are often added to liquid egg whites to stabilize egg foams when making meringues. Some dried egg products contain additional ingredients to aid whipping and to compensate for changes to the product during drying. Follow manufacturer's directions when reconstituting these products.

Concerns about the cholesterol content of eggs have increased the popularity of **egg substitutes.** There are two general types of substitutes. The first is a complete substitute made from soy or milk proteins. It should not be used in recipes where eggs are required for thickening. The second substitute contains real albumen, but the egg yolk has been replaced with vegetable or milk products. Egg substitutes have a different flavor from real eggs, but may be useful for people on a restricted diet.

1 Egg whites whipped to soft peaks.

2 Egg whites whipped to stiff peaks.

3 Spongy, overwhipped egg whites.

WHIPPED EGG WHITES

Egg whites are often whipped into a foam that is then incorporated into cakes, custards, soufflés, pancakes and other products. The air beaten into the egg foam gives products lightness and assists with leavening.

▶ PROCEDURE FOR WHIPPING EGG WHITES

1 Use fresh egg whites that are completely free of egg yolk and other impurities. Warm the egg whites to room temperature before whipping; this helps a better foam to form.

2 Use a clean bowl and whisk. Even a tiny amount of fat can prevent the egg whites from foaming properly.

3 Whip the whites until very foamy, then add salt or cream of tartar as directed.

4 Continue whipping until soft peaks form, then gradually add granulated sugar as directed.

5 Whip until stiff peaks form. Properly whipped egg whites should be moist and shiny; overwhipping will make the egg whites appear dry and spongy or curdled.

6 Use the whipped egg whites immediately. If liquid begins to separate from the whipped egg whites, discard them; they cannot be rewhipped successfully.

▶ THICKENERS

STARCHES

Starches are often used as thickening agents in bakeshop products. Cornstarch, arrowroot and flour can be used as thickeners for pastry creams, sauces, custards and fruit fillings. **Cornstarch** is a grain-based starch. It must be dissolved in cold water, then added to a mixture to be thickened. Once it reaches just below boiling point it must be cooked for 3 minutes to thicken into an opaque gel. Products thickened with cornstarch should not be vigorously stirred once cooled or they can break down and soften. They also tend to separate when thawed after freezing.

Arrowroot is dissolved in cold water and added to a liquid to thicken it. Used primarily to thicken hot sauces, arrowroot can break down if overcooked, making it most appropriate for thickening sauces that will be served immediately.

Although less commonly encountered in professional bakeshops, tapioca can be used to thicken a variety of pastry products. **Tapioca** is a starch produced from the root of the tropical cassava (manioc) plant. It is available as a flour or as balls, referred to as pearls. Tapioca flour can be used in the same manner as cornstarch to thicken sauces and fruit mixtures. Pearl tapioca is used to thicken milk for tapioca pudding, or to thicken fruit pie fillings. Most pearl tapioca must be soaked in a cold liquid for several hours before cooking. Instant tapioca, which is smaller, needs to soak for only 20 to 30 minutes before cooking.

Pearl Tapioca

GELATIN

One of the most commonly used thickeners in the bakeshop is **gelatin,** a natural product derived from collagen, an animal protein. It is available in two forms: granulated gelatin and sheet (also called leaf) gelatin. A two-step process is necessary to use either form: The gelatin must first be softened in a cold liquid, **bloomed,** then dissolved in a hot liquid.

Granulated gelatin is available in bulk or in ¼-ounce (7-gram) envelopes (slightly less than 1 tablespoon). One envelope is enough to set 1 pint (500 milliliters) of liquid into a firm gel for aspic or decorating or 3 cups (720 milliliters) of liquid into a softer mousse consistency. Granulated gelatin should be softened in four times its weight of cold liquid for at least five minutes, then heated gently to dissolve. The initial softening in a cold liquid is necessary to separate the gelatin molecules so that they will not lump together when the hot liquid is added. Melting over a double boiler prevents scorching.

Sheet or **leaf gelatin** is available in 1-kilogram boxes, sometimes further packaged in envelopes containing five or six sheets. The sheets are produced in varying thicknesses and weights; the average weighs about ¹⁄₁₀ ounce (3 grams) per sheet. They must be separated and soaked in ice water until very soft, at least 15 minutes. They are then removed from the water, squeezed to remove excess moisture and stirred into a hot liquid until completely dissolved. When sheet gelatin is added to a hot liquid it is not necessary to melt it first.

Granulated and sheet gelatin can be substituted weight for weight in any formula. Sheet gelatin, though more expensive, is preferred for its lack of flavor and color. It also tends to dissolve more readily and evenly and has a longer shelf life than the granulated form. Once incorporated into a product such as a Bavarian, gelatin can be frozen, or melted and reset once or twice, without a loss of thickening ability. Because it scorches easily, gelatin and mixtures containing gelatin should not be allowed to boil. Products thickened with gelatin, such as mousse or custard, can become rubbery after a few days in the refrigerator.

▶ **bloom**—to soften granulated gelatin in a liquid before melting and using

Granulated Gelatin

▶ PROCEDURE FOR USING SHEET GELATIN

1 Gelatin sheets are submerged in ice water for several minutes to soften.

2 Softened gelatin sheets are then removed from the ice water and incorporated into a hot liquid.

SUBSTITUTING GRANULATED AND SHEET GELATIN

When a formula in this book is created using granulated gelatin, the ingredient list will specify "granulated gelatin" and the ingredient list will include the amount of water necessary to dissolve the gelatin. See the recipe for Lime

Chiffon, page 448. If substituting sheet gelatin in that formula, simply submerge the sheet gelatin in ice water until it is soft and pliable. Drain the sheets and add them to the warm liquid to melt. The additional water will not be required. Do not use it in the formula.

When a formula in this book is created using sheet gelatin, the ingredient list will specify "sheet gelatin, softened." See the recipe for Fresh Fruit Bavarian, page 446. To substitute granulated gelatin for sheet gelatin, additional water will be needed to dissolve the gelatin. To calculate how much water will be required to soften the granulated gelatin, multiply the weight of the gelatin called for in the formula by 4. First, let the granulated gelatin bloom (soften) in that amount of water. Then, melt the softened granulated gelatin over very low heat and add it to the recipe. For example, if the recipe calls for "½ ounce (15 grams) sheet gelatin, softened," bloom ½ ounce (15 grams) of granulated gelatin in 2 fluid ounces (60 milliliters) of water, then melt the gelatin over low heat and continue with the recipe.

▶ FLAVORINGS

Many flavoring ingredients are used in the bakeshop. Practically any herb, spice, beverage or extract can be used to give baked goods, creams and confections their characteristic flavors. As with all baking ingredients, select flavoring components for overall quality and freshness, and combine flavorings carefully to achieve a balanced, good-tasting finished product.

SALT

Salt (Fr. *sel*) is the most basic seasoning, used to enhance the flavor and sweetness of other ingredients in food. The presence of salt can be tasted easily but not smelled. Salt suppresses bitter flavors, making the sweet and sour ones more prominent. In yeast dough, salt slows yeast fermentation. Salt also strengthens the gluten structure in bread dough. Omitting or reducing the amount of salt can cause the dough to rise too quickly, adversely affecting the shape and flavor of bread.

Culinary or **table salt** is sodium chloride (NaCl), available from several sources, each with its own flavor and degree of saltiness. **Table salt** is produced by pumping water through underground salt deposits, then bringing the brine to the surface to evaporate, leaving behind crystals. Chemicals are usually added to prevent table salt from absorbing moisture and thus keep it free flowing. Iodized salt is commonly used in the United States. The iodine has no effect on the salt's flavor or use; it is added simply to provide an easily available source of iodine, an important nutrient, to a large number of people.

For baking, use finely ground salt from whichever source is preferred, as it will dissolve readily in all mixtures. Weighing is the only way to measure salt accurately, as different granulations of salt will have different volume measurements.

Rock salt, mined from underground deposits, is available in both edible and nonedible forms. It is used in ice cream churns, for thawing frozen sidewalks and, in edible form, in salt mills.

Sea salt is obtained, not surprisingly, by evaporating seawater. Unlike other table salts, sea salt contains additional mineral salts that give it a stronger, more complex flavor and a grayish-brown color. The region where it is produced can also affect its flavor. Sea salt is considerably more expensive than other table salts and is often reserved for finishing a dish or used as a condiment. Fleur de sel and sel gris are two distinctive types of unrefined sea salt.

Rock Salt

"Fleur de Sel" (Sea Salt)

Kosher salt has large, irregular crystals and is used in the "koshering," or curing, of meats. It is purified rock salt that contains no iodine or additives. It can be substituted for common kitchen salt.

Because it is nonorganic, salt keeps indefinitely. It will, however, absorb moisture from the atmosphere, which prevents it from flowing properly. Salt is a powerful preservative; its presence stops or greatly slows down the growth of many undesirable organisms.

Kosher Salt

EMULSIONS AND EXTRACTS

Emulsions and extracts are liquid flavoring agents derived from various flavoring oils **(essential oils)** taken from fruits, beans, spices or seeds.

Emulsions are flavoring oils mixed into water with the aid of emulsifiers. Lemon and orange are the most common emulsions. Emulsions are much stronger than extracts and should be used carefully and sparingly. **Extracts** are mixtures of flavoring oils or essential oils and ethyl alcohol. Vanilla, almond and lemon are frequently used extracts. An extract may be made with pure flavoring oils or with artificial flavors and colors. Contents are regulated by the FDA, and package labels must indicate any artificial ingredients. Emulsions and extracts are highly volatile. They should be stored in sealed containers in a cool area away from direct light.

▶ **essential oils**—pure oils extracted from the skins, peels and other parts of plants used to give their aroma and taste to flavoring agents in foods, cosmetics and other products

VANILLA

Vanilla (Fr. *vanille*) is the most frequently used flavoring in the bakeshop. It comes from the pod fruit, called a bean, of a vine in the orchid family. Vanilla beans are purchased whole, individually or by the pound. They should be soft and pliable, with a rich brown color and good aroma. The finest vanilla comes from Tahiti and Madagascar.

To use a vanilla bean, cut it open lengthwise with a paring knife. Scrape out the moist seeds with the knife's tip and stir them into the mixture being flavored. The seeds do not dissolve and will remain visible as small black or brown flecks. After all the seeds have been removed, the bean can be stored in a covered container with sugar to create vanilla sugar. Because the intensity of vanilla extract varies, it is difficult to recommend an equivalent in vanilla beans. Generally, ½ fluid ounce (15 milligrams) of vanilla extract can be substituted for 1 vanilla bean; however, taste should be the ultimate guide.

Vanilla beans should be stored in an airtight container in a cool, dark place. During storage, the beans may develop a white coating. This is not mold, but rather crystals of vanilla flavor known as vanillin. It should not be removed.

Pure vanilla extract is an easy and less expensive way to give bakeshop products a true vanilla flavor. It is dark brown and aromatic, and comes in several strengths referred to as folds. The higher the number of folds, the stronger the flavor of the extract. Any product labeled "vanilla extract" must not contain artificial flavorings and must be at least 35 percent alcohol by volume. Vanilla extract should be stored at room temperature in a closed, opaque container. It should not be frozen.

Artificial or imitation vanilla flavoring is made with synthetic vanillin. Artificial flavoring is available in a clear form, which is useful for white buttercreams where the dark brown color of pure vanilla extract would be undesirable. Although inexpensive, artificial vanilla is, at best, weaker and less aromatic than pure extract. It can also impart a chemical or bitter taste to foods.

Scraping seeds from the interior of a vanilla bean.

CHOCOLATE

Chocolate is one of the most popular flavorings—perhaps the most popular—for candies, cookies, cakes and pastries. Chocolate is also served as a beverage and is an ingredient in the traditional spicy Mexican molé sauce. Chocolate is available in a variety of forms and degrees of sweetness. Chocolate and cocoa are discussed in Chapter 21, Chocolate and Decorative Work.

COFFEE

Green Coffee Beans

Coffee (Fr. *café*) is equally important for flavoring pastries as it is for accompanying them. Its smoky richness marries well with chocolate, cinnamon, mint and nuts in mousses, candies and ice creams. Ground coffee may be steeped in milk or cream to be used in a formula, then strained. Brewed coffee may be reduced to a potent syrup for use as a flavoring. Commercially prepared coffee extract is also available.

Coffee begins as the fruit of a small tree grown in tropical and subtropical regions throughout the world. The fruit, referred to as a cherry, is bright red with translucent flesh surrounding two flat-sided seeds. These seeds are the coffee beans. When ripe, the cherries are harvested by hand, then cleaned, fermented and hulled, leaving the green coffee beans. The beans are then roasted, blended, and ground for brewing.

French-Roast Beans

TEA

Tea (Fr. *thé*) is used to flavor creams and custards. The leaves may be steeped in the milk used for ice cream, for example, then strained before chilling and freezing. Tea is the name given to the leaves of *Camellia sinensis,* a tree or shrub that grows at high altitudes in damp tropical regions. Although tea comes from only one species of plant, there are three general types of tea—black, green and oolong. **Black tea** is amber-brown and strongly flavored. Its color and flavor result from fermenting the leaves. Black tea leaves are named or graded by leaf size. Because larger leaves brew more slowly than smaller ones, teas are sorted by leaf size for efficient brewing. Souchong denotes large leaves, pekoe denotes medium-sized leaves and orange pekoe denotes the smallest whole leaves, not a citrus flavor. Broken tea is smaller, resulting in a darker, stronger brew, and is most often used in tea bags.

For **green tea** the leaves are not fermented, resulting in a yellowish-green colored beverage with a bitter flavor. **Oolong tea** is partially fermented to combine the characteristics of black and green teas.

HERBS AND SPICES

Herbs refer to the large group of aromatic plants whose leaves, stems or flowers are used to add flavors to other foods. Most herbs are available fresh or dried. Because drying alters their flavors and aromas, fresh herbs are generally preferred and should be used if possible. Spices are the bark, roots, seeds, buds or berries of plants, most of which grow naturally only in tropical climates. Spices are almost always used in their dried form, rarely fresh, and can usually be purchased whole or ground. Some plants—dill, for example—can be used as both an herb (its leaves) and a spice (its seeds).

Most herbs are associated with the savory kitchen. But many, including basil, parsley, chives, oregano and dill, do find a place in savory breads and pizza. When chopped finely, they may be added directly to dough or applied as a topping before baking. Spices are more commonly associated with baked goods. Creative pastry chefs are expanding the uses for many herbs and spices, incorporating them or infusing syrups, custards and chocolates with their distinctive aromas. A selection of herbs and spices that are used in sweet preparations are featured here. Recommendations for bakeshop uses for herbs and spices can be found in Table 4.5.

HERBS

Lavender (Fr. *lavande*) is an evergreen with thin leaves and tall stems bearing spikes of tiny purple flowers. Although lavender is known primarily for its aroma, which is widely used in perfumes, soaps and cosmetics, the flowers are also used as a flavoring, particularly in Middle Eastern and Provençal cuisines. These flowers have a sweet, lemony flavor and can be crystallized and used as a garnish. Lavender is also used in jams and preserves and to flavor teas and tisanes.

Lavender

Peppermint

Mint (Fr. *menthe*), a large family of herbs, includes many species and flavors (even chocolate). **Spearmint** is the most common garden and commercial variety. It has soft, bright green leaves and a tart aroma and flavor. Mint has an affinity for chocolate. It can also be brewed into a beverage or used as a garnish.

Peppermint has thin, stiff, pointed leaves and a sharper menthol flavor and aroma. Fresh peppermint is used less often in cooking or as a garnish than spearmint, but peppermint oil is a common flavoring in sweets and candies.

Spearmint

EDIBLE FLOWERS

Many specialty produce growers offer edible pesticide-free blossoms to be used as cake or pastry decorations. (Fresh violets coated in sugar and then dried are sold as candied violets.) Some flowers such as nasturtiums, calendulas and pansies are raised and picked specifically for eating. Others such as roses and violets may be grown for ornament only. Be certain to use only flowers raised for consumption.

Nasturtiums

Calendulas

Pansies

SPICES

Allspice (Fr. *toute-épice*), also known as Jamaican pepper, is the dried berry of a tree that flourishes in Jamaica, and one of the few spices still grown exclusively in the New World. Allspice is available whole; in berries that look like large, rough, brown peppercorns; or ground. Ground allspice is not a mixture of spices, although it does taste like a blend of cinnamon, cloves and nutmeg. Allspice gives a distinctive taste to spiced cookies and gingerbread.

Allspice

Anise (Fr. *anis*) is native to the eastern Mediterranean, where it was widely used by ancient civilizations. Today, it is grown commercially in warm climates throughout India, North Africa and southern Europe. The tiny, gray-green egg-shaped seeds have a distinctively strong, sweet flavor, similar to licorice and fennel. When anise seeds turn brown, they are stale and should be discarded.

Anise Seeds

Table 4.5   BAKESHOP USES FOR SOME COMMON HERBS AND SPICES

FLAVORING	FORM	SUGGESTED USES
Allspice	Dry ground	Fruits, quick breads and spice cookies
Anise	Dry, whole or ground	Pastries and breads
Basil	Fresh or dried	Savory bread, pizzas and bagels
Caraway	Whole or ground	Rye breads, bagel topping
Cardamom	Ground	Sweet dough, cookies and pastries
Cinnamon	Whole	Infused in syrups and poaching liquid
	Ground	Pies, pastries, breads and ice cream
Cloves	Whole or ground	Poaching liquids for fruit, spice breads and muffins
Dill	Whole seeds or fresh	Breads, bread toppings
Ginger	Fresh root	Infused in syrups, ice cream and custards
	Powder	Cakes, cookies, muffins and gingerbread
Mace	Ground	Spice breads and cookies
Mint	Fresh	Infused in sauces and syrups, garnish
Nutmeg	Ground	Custards, spice breads and cookies
Pepper	Whole	Infused in wine for poaching fruit
	Ground	Spice blends for cakes and gingerbread

Caraway Seeds

Cardamom Pods

*Ground Cinnamon
and Cinnamon Sticks*

Anise is used in pastries and in alcoholic beverages (for example, Pernod, Sambuca and ouzo).

Caraway (Fr. *carvi*) is perhaps the world's oldest spice. Its use has been traced to the Stone Age, and seeds have been found in ancient Egyptian tombs. The caraway plant grows wild in Europe and temperate regions of Asia. It produces a small, crescent-shaped brown seed with the peppery flavor of rye. Seeds may be purchased whole or ground. (The leaves have a mild, bland flavor and are rarely used in cooking.) Caraway is a very European flavor, used extensively in the rye breads of Germany and Austria. It is also used in alcoholic beverages and cheeses. It is said to have preservative qualities extending the shelf life of breads made with it.

Cardamom (Fr. *cardamome*) is one of the most expensive spices, second only to saffron in cost. Its seeds are encased in ¼-inch- (6-millimeter-) long light green or brown pods. Cardamom is highly aromatic. Its flavor, lemony with notes of camphor, is quite strong and is used in both sweet and savory dishes. Cardamom is widely used in India and the Middle East to flavor coffee. Scandinavians use cardamom to flavor breads and pastries. Ground cardamom loses its flavor rapidly, so it is best to purchase whole seeds and grind your own as needed.

Cinnamon (Fr. *cannelle*) and its cousin cassia are among the oldest known spices: Cinnamon's use is recorded in China as early as 2500 B.C.E. and the Far East still produces most of these products. Both cinnamon and cassia come from the bark of small evergreen trees, peeled from branches in thin layers and dried in the sun. High-quality cinnamon should be pale brown and thin, rolled up like paper into sticks known as quills. Cassia is coarser and has a stronger, less subtle flavor than cinnamon. Consequently, it is cheaper than true cinnamon. Cinnamon is usually purchased ground because it is difficult to grind. Cinnamon sticks are used when long cooking times allow for sufficient flavor to be extracted (for example, in poaching liquids). Cinnamon's flavor is most often associated with pastries and sweets. Labeling laws do not require that packages distinguish between cassia and cinnamon, so most of what is sold as cinnamon in the United States is actually cassia, blended for consistent flavor and aroma.

Cloves (Fr. *girofles*) are the unopened buds of evergreen trees that flourish in muggy tropical regions. When dried, whole cloves have hard, sharp prongs that can be used to push them into other foods, such as onions or fruit, in order to provide flavor. Cloves are extremely pungent, with a sweet, astringent aroma.

Cloves

A small amount provides a great deal of flavor. Cloves are usually blended with other spices for cakes and cookies. They may be purchased whole or ground.

Coriander Seeds

Coriander (Fr. *coriander*) seeds come from the cilantro plant. They are round and beige, with a distinctive sweet, spicy flavor and strong aroma. Unlike other plants in which the seeds and the leaves carry the same flavor and aroma, coriander and cilantro are very different. Coriander seeds are available whole or ground and are frequently used in sweet dough and cookie recipes.

Fresh Ginger Root

Ginger (Fr. *gingembre*) is a well-known spice obtained from the root of a tall, flowering tropical plant. Fresh ginger root is known as a "hand" because it looks vaguely like a group of knobby fingers. It has grayish-tan skin and a pale yellow, fibrous interior. Fresh ginger should be plump and firm with smooth skin. It should keep for about a month under refrigeration. Its flavor is fiery but sweet, with notes of lemon and rosemary. Ginger is also available peeled and pickled in vinegar, candied in sugar or preserved in alcohol or syrup. Dried, ground ginger is a fine yellow powder widely used in pastries. Its flavor is spicier and not as sweet as fresh ginger.

Nutmeg (Fr. *muscade*) and mace come from the yellow plumlike fruit of a large tropical evergreen. These fruits are dried and opened to reveal the seed known as nutmeg. A bright red lacy coating or aril surrounds the seed; the aril is the spice mace. Whole nutmegs are oval and look rather like a piece of smooth wood. The flavor and aroma of nutmeg are strong and sweet, and a small quantity provides a great deal of flavor. Nutmeg should be grated directly into a dish as needed; once grated, flavor loss is rapid. Nutmeg is used in pastries and sweets in many European cuisines.

*Whole Nutmegs with
Ground Mace (left)
and Ground Nutmeg (right)*

Mace

Mace (Fr. *macis*) is an expensive spice, with a flavor similar to nutmeg but more refined. It is almost always purchased ground and retains its flavor longer than other ground spices. Mace is used primarily in pastry items.

Peppercorns (Fr. *poivre*) are the berries of a vine plant (*Piper nigrum*) native to tropical Asia, not to be confused with the chile (capsicum) peppers. Black and white peppercorns are produced from the same plant, but are picked and processed differently. For black peppercorns, the berries are picked when green and simply dried whole in the sun. Black pepper has a warm, pungent flavor and aroma. For white peppercorns, the berries are allowed to ripen until they turn red. The ripened berries are allowed to ferment, then the outer layer of skin is washed off. White pepper has fewer aromas than black pepper but is useful where the appearance of black speckles is undesirable. Green peppercorns and pink peppercorns, actually the berries of a South American tree, are also available.

*Black Pepper (left)
and White Pepper (Right)*

Poppy seeds (Fr. *pavot*) are the ripened seeds of the opium poppy, which flourishes in the Middle East and India. (When ripe, the seeds do not contain any of the medicinal alkaloids found elsewhere in the plant.) The tiny blue-gray seeds are round and hard with a sweet, nutty flavor. Poppy seeds are used in pastries and breads, often combined with honey and citrus rind.

Poppy Seeds

Sesame seeds, also known as benne seeds, are native to India. They are small, flat ovals with a creamy white color. Their taste is nutty and earthy, with

Sesame Seeds

a pronounced aroma when roasted or ground into a paste (known as tahini). Sesame seeds are the source of sesame oil, which has a mild, nutty flavor and does not go rancid easily. Sesame seeds are often toasted and used in confections and cookies and as a garnish for breads.

NUTS

Nuts (Fr. *noix*) provide texture and flavor in baked goods and are often substituted for all or part of the wheat flour in a pastry such as linzer tart (page 281) or a dacquoise (page 299). A nut is the edible single-seed kernel of a fruit surrounded by a hard shell. A hazelnut is an example of a true nut. The term is used more generally, however, to refer to any seed or fruit with an edible kernel in a hard shell. Walnuts and peanuts are examples of non-nut "nuts" (peanuts are legumes that grow underground; walnuts have two kernels). Nuts are high in fat, making them especially susceptible to rancidity and odor absorption. Nuts should be stored in nonmetal, airtight containers in a cool, dark place. Most nuts may be kept frozen for up to one year.

Nuts are often roasted in a low (275°F/135°C) oven or in a sauté pan over low heat before being used in order to heighten their flavor. Allowing roasted nuts to cool to room temperature before grinding prevents them from releasing too much oil. Some nuts such as hazelnuts, pistachios, almonds, peanuts and cashews are ground into nut butters used to flavor pastries. When sweetened, nut butter is referred to as a paste and is used to flavor chocolates, ice creams and other baked items.

Almond Paste

Almonds (Fr. *almande*) are the seeds of a plumlike fruit, native to western India, that was first cultivated by the ancient Greeks. It is now a major commercial crop in California. Almonds are available whole, sliced, slivered or ground. Blanched almonds have had their brown, textured skins removed; natural almonds retain their skins. Unless the brown color of natural almond skin is undesirable, the two types can be used interchangeably in recipes. Almonds are frequently used in pastries and candies and are the main ingredient in almond paste and marzipan.

Brazil Nuts

Brazil nuts (Fr. *noix du Brésil*), sometimes referred to as cream nuts, are the large, oval-shaped seeds of huge trees that grow wild in the rain forests of Central and South America. Their high oil content gives them a rich, buttery flavor and a tender texture. Brazil nuts are available both in-shell and shelled, and are eaten raw, roasted, salted and in ice creams and bakery and confectionery products.

Cashews (Fr. *noix de caju*), native to the Amazon, are actually the seeds of a plant related to poison ivy. Because of toxins in the shell, cashews are always sold shelled. They are expensive and have a pronounced flavor. Cashews make a wonderful addition to cookies and candies.

Almonds

Cashews

Chestnuts (Fr. *marrons*) are true nuts that must be cooked before using. Available steamed, dried, boiled or roasted, they are often sold as a canned purée, with or without added sugar. Candied or glazed chestnuts

Chestnuts

are also available. Most chestnuts are grown in Europe, primarily Italy, but new varieties are beginning to flourish in North America. Their distinctive flavor is found in many sweet dishes and pastries.

Coconuts (Fr. *noix de coco*) are the seeds from one of the largest of all fruits. They grow on the tropical coconut palm tree. The nut is a dark brown oval, covered with coarse fibers. The shell is thick and hard; inside is a layer of white,

Coconuts

moist flesh. The interior also contains a clear liquid known as **coconut water.** (This is not the same as **coconut milk** or **coconut cream,** both of which are prepared from the flesh.) Coconut has a mild aroma, a sweet, nutty flavor and a crunchy, chewy texture. Fresh coconuts are readily available but require some effort to use. Coconut flesh is available shredded or flaked, with or without added sugar. Coconut purée is sold as a pastry ingredient and in ethnic markets. Coconut is most often used in pastries and candies and is also an important ingredient in Indian and Caribbean cuisines. A good fresh coconut should feel heavy; you should be able to hear the coconut water sloshing around inside. Avoid cracked, moist or moldy coconuts.

Hazelnuts (Fr. *noisette*) are true nuts that grow wild in the northwestern and upper midwestern states. The cultivated form, known as a filbert, is native to temperate regions throughout the Northern Hemisphere. A bit larger than the hazelnut, the filbert has a weaker flavor than its wild cousin. Both nuts look like smooth brown marbles. Filberts are more abundant, so are generally less expensive. Their distinctive flavor goes well with chocolate and coffee.

To remove the hazelnut's skin, roast whole nuts at 275°F (135°C) for 12 to 15 minutes. They should give off a good aroma and just begin to darken. While still hot, rub the nuts in a dry towel or against a mesh sifter to remove the skin.

Hazelnut paste (Fr. *praline*) is a smooth composition made from finely ground roasted hazelnuts and sugar. It is used to flavor creams, chocolates and icings. Gianduja [zhahn-DOO-yah] refers to chocolate blended with hazelnut paste. It is used as a filling or in candies.

Hazelnut Paste

Hazelnuts

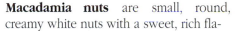

Macadamia nuts are small, round, creamy white nuts with a sweet, rich flavor and high fat content, native to Australia. The shell is extremely hard and must be removed by machine, so the macadamia is always sold out of the shell. Its flavor blends well with fruit, coconut and white and dark chocolate.

Peanuts (Fr. *arachide*), also known as groundnuts, are actually legumes that grow underground. The peanut is native to South America; it made its way into North America via Africa and the slave trade.

Macadamias

Peanuts

▶ **coconut water**—the thin, slightly opaque liquid contained within a fresh coconut

▶ **coconut milk**—a coconut-flavored liquid made by pouring boiling water over shredded coconut; may be sweetened or unsweetened. Do not substitute cream of coconut for coconut milk

▶ **coconut cream**—(1) a coconut-flavored liquid made like coconut milk but with less water; it is creamier and thicker than coconut milk; (2) the thick fatty portion that separates and rises to the top of canned or frozen coconut milk. Do not substitute cream of coconut for true coconut cream

▶ **cream of coconut**—a canned commercial product consisting of thick, sweetened coconut-flavored liquid; used for baking and in beverages

Pecans

They may be eaten raw or roasted and are available shelled or unshelled, with or without their thin red skins. Peanuts are ubiquitous ground with a bit of oil into peanut butter.

Pecans (Fr. *noix de pacane*), native to the Mississippi River valley, are perhaps the most popular nuts in America. Their flavor is rich and mapley and appears most often in breads, sweets and pastries. They are available whole in the shell or in various standard sizes and grades of pieces.

Pine nuts (Fr. *pignon*), also known as piñon nuts and pignole, are the seeds of several species of pine tree. The small, creamy white, teardrop-shaped nuts are commonly used in pastries from Spain, Italy and the American Southwest. They are rarely chopped or ground because of their small size, and will need roasting only if being used in a dish that will not receive further cooking.

Pine Nuts

Pistachios (Fr. *pistaches*) are native to central Asia, where they have been cultivated for more than 3000 years. California now produces most of the pistachios marketed in the United States. Pistachios are unique for the green color of their meat. When ripe, the shell opens naturally at one end, aptly referred to as "smiling," which makes shelling the nuts quite easy. Red pistachios are dyed, not natural. Pistachios are sold whole, shelled or unshelled and are used in pastries and confections.

Pistachios

Walnuts

Walnuts (Fr. *noix*), relatives of the pecan, are native to Asia, Europe and North America. The black walnut, native to Appalachia, has a dark brown meat and a strong flavor. The English walnut, now grown primarily in California, has a milder flavor, is easier to shell and is less expensive. Walnuts are more popular than pecans outside the United States. They are used in baked goods and are pressed for oil.

ALCOHOLIC BEVERAGES

Liquors, liqueurs, wines and brandies are used to either add or enhance flavors in products made in the bakeshop. When added to doughs and pastes that will be baked, most of the alcohol in these products evaporates during cooking. Liquors such as rum, bourbon or whiskey can be used for their own distinctive flavors or to blend with other flavors such as chocolate and coffee. Liqueurs are also selected for their specific flavors: for example, kirsch for cherry, amaretto for almond, Kahlúa for coffee, crème de cassis for black currant and crème de cacao for chocolate. Wine, both still and sparkling, is used as a flavoring (for example, in sabayon sauce) or as a cooking medium (for example, pears poached in red wine). Brandy, especially the classic orange-flavored Grand Marnier, is another common bakeshop flavoring. Brandy complements fruits and rounds off the flavor of custards and creams.

When selecting an alcoholic beverage for baking, make quality your first concern. Only high-quality products will enhance the flavor and aroma of your baked goods.

Ingredients play a major role in determining the appearance and taste of baked goods and pastries. Understanding the function of ingredients and their selection is of great importance to the pastry chef and baker. The proper type of flour must be chosen for a formula. Sweeteners may be crystalline like granulated sugar or fluid like corn syrup. Substituting one for the other in a formula will result in significantly different results. Fats require special handling and storage, as do highly perishable items such as eggs and dairy products. A myriad of herbs and flavorings are available to the baker and pastry chef. The baker and pastry chef must know how to use, select and store these ingredients properly.

1 What is the importance of protein in flour for bread making? Name the general types of flours available and their different uses in the bakeshop.
2 What is milkfat, and how is it used in classifying milk-based products?
3 Discuss the four functions of sugar and sweeteners in baked goods.
4 Why are eggs pasteurized? What precautions can the pastry cook and baker take to ensure food safety when handling raw egg products?
5 Many varieties of fat and shortening are available to today's baker and pastry chef. Discuss which fats are preferred for various bakeshop applications.
6 Use the Internet to locate a U.S. producer of European-style pastry ingredients. What type of flavorings and nut products do they produce and market?

THE KITCHEN IS A COUNTRY IN WHICH THERE ARE ALWAYS DISCOVERIES TO BE MADE.

—*Grimod de la Reynière, French writer and gastronome (1758–1837)*

MISE EN PLACE

AFTER STUDYING THIS CHAPTER, YOU WILL BE ABLE TO:

▶ understand measurement systems and how to measure ingredients

▶ organize and plan your work more efficiently

▶ understand basic flavoring techniques

▶ prepare items needed prior to actual cooking

The French term *mise en place* (meez ahn plahs) means "put in place." In the professional kitchen it means having everything in place necessary for the successful preparation of a meal. In the bakeshop, mise en place means accurate selection and measurement of ingredients, and preparation of all the components and equipment needed to prepare the final product. Mise en place is as much a mental exercise as it is the physical act of preparing to cook. Anticipating the steps required to prepare a formula, from identifying the tools and ingredients necessary, to setting the oven to the proper temperature, saves time and prevents mishaps.

In this chapter we discuss many of the basics that must be in place before baking begins: measuring ingredients, preparing pans for baking, clarifying butter, toasting nuts and flavoring ingredients. The proper handling and care of knives, often overlooked in the bakeshop, is also discussed.

▶ FORMULAS AND RECIPES

As in the scientific laboratory, many basic recipes in the bakeshop are referred to as formulas, perhaps in reference to the scientific nature of what seems like the magic of baking. Using the same preparation method, a product may bake into an entirely different one when the ratio of ingredients is altered. For example, if the amount of fat in a formula for pie dough is increased but the type and quantity of other ingredients are not adjusted, the result may be a product that bears no resemblance to what was intended.

The first step when making bakeshop items is to become familiar with the formula and the intended result. Careful reading of a formula alerts the baker or pastry chef to any special steps that might be required. Equipment must be identified and readied for use. Ingredients must be selected and prepared. Often these ingredients, such as butter for creaming into a butter cake, need to be brought to the proper temperature, which requires forethought and planning.

Many finished pastries consist of several components. For example, a lemon meringue pie requires three components—dough for the crust, lemon filling and an egg white meringue topping. The dough needs to be made and then chilled before rolling so that it will be easier to handle. Because it contains a precooked filling, the pie crust must then be baked before the lemon filling is added. And the meringue topping deflates easily, especially in humid conditions, so it should be prepared and applied close to serving time. A careful, thoughtful reading of the entire formula will alert the baker to the steps required and the best order for completing the work. Similarly, a formula for sourdough rye bread requires a sourdough starter, which can take as long as a week to develop. Sourdough bread formulas may deceive if the time to prepare this essential ingredient is overlooked.

It is equally important to follow bakeshop formulas carefully and completely. Unlike other types of cooking, baking mistakes often cannot be discovered until the product is finished, by which time it is too late to correct them. If the salt is omitted when preparing a stew, the mistake can be corrected by adding salt at service time. If the salt is omitted from a loaf of bread, however, the mistake cannot be corrected after the bread has baked, and its texture and flavor may be ruined. It is probably more important to follow a written formula, measure ingredients precisely and combine them accurately in the bakeshop than anywhere else in the kitchen.

▶ MEASURING INGREDIENTS

The precise, accurate measurement of ingredients is extremely important for bakeshop products. To reproduce products consistently and for the same cost day after day, it is important that the ingredients be measured accurately each time. In a kitchen, measurements may be made in three ways: weight, volume and count.

Weight refers to the mass or heaviness of a substance. It is expressed in terms such as grams, ounces, pounds, kilograms and tons. Weight may be used to measure liquid or dry ingredients (for example, 2 pounds of eggs for a bread recipe) and portions (for example, 3 ounces of hot fudge for a sundae). Weight is the most accurate form of measurement and the one most commonly used in the bakeshop.

Volume refers to the space occupied by a substance. This is mathematically expressed as height × width × length. It is expressed in terms such as cups, quarts, gallons, teaspoons, fluid ounces, bushels and liters. Volume is most commonly used to measure liquids. It may also be used for dry ingredients when the amount is too small to be weighed accurately without specialized equipment (for example, ¼ teaspoon of salt).

Cooks who assume that 8 ounces of flour is the same as 1 cup of flour commonly make errors in the bakeshop. In fact, 1 cup of flour may weigh from 3 to 5 ounces (90 to 150 grams) depending on the flour and how it was scooped into the measuring cup. Measuring ingredients by weight, commonly referred to as **scaling,** is more accurate; therefore, baking formulas often use weight, even for liquid ingredients.

It is not unusual to see both weight and volume measurements used in a single formula. When a formula ingredient is expressed in weight, weigh it. When it is expressed as a volume, measure it. Like most rules, however, this one has exceptions. The weight and volume of water, butter, shortening, eggs and milk are, in each case, the same. For these ingredients use whichever measurement is most convenient.

Because accurate weights are so important, balance scales are commonly employed in the bakeshop. Once the basic procedures are understood, it will be faster than measuring by volume.

Table 5.1 COMMON ABBREVIATIONS

teaspoon	=	tsp.
tablespoon	=	Tbsp.
cup	=	c.
pint	=	pt.
quart	=	qt.
gram	=	g
milliliter	=	ml
liter	=	lt
ounce	=	oz.
fluid ounce	=	fl. oz.
pound	=	lb.
kilogram	=	kg

▶ **scaling**—measuring ingredients on a scale before mixing a batter or dough

Liquids can be measured by volume in liquid measuring cups, which may be marked in U.S. and/or metric units.

Small amounts of dry ingredients are measured by overfilling the appropriate measuring spoon, then leveling the ingredient.

▶ PROCEDURE FOR USING A BALANCE SCALE

1 To use a balance scale to weigh an ingredient, place an empty container on the left, then set a counterbalance to that container on the right. Use weights and the sliding beam weight to add an amount equal to the amount of the ingredient needed.

2 Place the ingredient on the left side of the scale until the two platforms are balanced.

Count refers to the number of individual items. Count is used in formulas (for example, 4 grapefruits) and in portion control (for example, 1 poached pear). Count is also commonly used in purchasing to indicate the size of the individual items. For example, a "96 count" case of lemons means that a 40-pound case contains 96 individual lemons; a "115 count" case means that the same 40-pound case contains 115 individual lemons. So, each lemon in the 96-count case is larger than each lemon in the 115-count case. When placing an order, the chef must specify the desired count.

MEASUREMENT SYSTEMS

The measurement formats of weight, volume and count are used in both the U.S. and metric measurement systems. Both of these systems are used in modern bakeshops, so today's pastry chef and baker should be able to prepare formulas written in either one.

The **U.S. system** is actually the more difficult system to understand. It uses ounces and pounds for weight and cups for volume.

The **metric system** is the most commonly used system in the world. Developed in France during the late 18th century, it was intended to fill the need for a mathematically rational and uniform system of measurement. The metric system is a decimal system in which the gram, liter and meter are the basic units of weight, volume and length, respectively. Larger or smaller units of weight, volume and length are formed by adding a prefix to the words gram, liter or meter. Some of the more commonly used prefixes in food service operations are *deca-* (10), *kilo-* (1000), *deci-* ($\frac{1}{10}$) and *milli-* ($\frac{1}{1000}$). Thus, a kilogram is 1000 grams; a decameter is 10 meters; a milliliter is $\frac{1}{1000}$ of a liter. Because the metric system is based on multiples of 10, it is extremely easy to increase or decrease amounts.

Knowledge of the metric system is useful for bakers and pastry chefs interested in European formulas. Luckily, most modern measuring equipment is calibrated in both U.S. and metric increments and there is no need to convert amounts from metric to the U.S. measuring system. The need to convert amounts will arise only if the proper equipment is unavailable. What is most important is to prepare a formula using one set of measurements. If a formula is written in metric units, use metric measuring equipment; if it is written in U.S. units, use U.S. measuring equipment.

CONVERTING GRAMS AND OUNCES

Being familiar with metric conversions allows the baker in the United States to understand, at a glance, the yield and quantities in a metric formula. As you can see from Table 5.2, 1 ounce equals 28.35 grams. Likewise, 1 fluid ounce equals 28.35 milliliters. This number is often rounded to 30 for convenience, however. So, to convert ounces/fluid ounces to grams/milliliters, multiply the number of ounces by 30.

$$8 \text{ oz. } \times 30 = 240 \text{ g}$$
$$8 \text{ fl. oz. } \times 30 = 240 \text{ ml}$$

To convert grams/milliliters to ounces/fluid ounces, divide the number of grams/milliliters by 30.

$$240 \text{ g} \div 30 = 8 \text{ oz.}$$
$$240 \text{ ml} \div 30 = 8 \text{ fl. oz.}$$

To develop a framework for judging conversions, remember that:

▶ A kilogram is about 2.2 pounds
▶ A gram is about $\frac{1}{30}$ ounce
▶ A pound is about 480 grams
▶ A liter is slightly more than a quart
▶ A centimeter is slightly less than $\frac{1}{2}$ inch
▶ 0°C (32°F) is the freezing point of water
▶ 100°C (212°F) is the boiling point of water

Table 5.2	COMMON EQUIVALENTS
Dash	= $\frac{1}{8}$ teaspoon
3 teaspoons	= 1 tablespoon
2 tablespoons	= 1 fl. oz.
4 tablespoons	= $\frac{1}{4}$ cup (2 fl. oz.)
5$\frac{1}{3}$ tablespoons	= $\frac{1}{3}$ cup (2$\frac{2}{3}$ fl. oz.)
16 tablespoons	= 1 cup (8 fl. oz.)
2 cups	= 1 pint (16 fl. oz.)
2 pints	= 1 quart (32 fl. oz.)
4 quarts	= 1 gallon (128 fl. oz.)
2 gallons	= 1 peck
4 pecks	= 1 bushel
1 gram	= 0.035 ounces ($\frac{1}{30}$ oz.)
1 ounce	= 28.35 grams (often rounded to 30 for convenience)
454 grams	= 1 pound
2.2 pounds	= 1 kilogram (1000 grams)
1 teaspoon	= 5 milliliters
1 tablespoon	= 15 milliliters
1 fluid ounce	= 28.35 milliliters (often rounded to 30 for convenience)
1 cup	= 0.24 liters
1 gallon	= 3.80 liters

These approximations are not a substitute for accurate conversions, however. Appendix I contains additional information on equivalents and metric conversions. There is no substitute for knowing this information.

The formulas in this book were developed using the equivalent of 1 ounce equals 30 grams. While 28.35 is a more mathematically accurate representation of the number of grams in a U.S. ounce, rounding the numeral to 30 produces more usable formulas. If, for example, formulas are converted using 28.35 grams per ounce, then 4 ounces of butter would become 113.4 grams of butter. Likewise, 1000 grams of flour would be 35.27 ounces of flour. In each case, expensive, highly specialized scales would be necessary to measure ingredients. The U.S. and metric formulas in this book may not yield identical amounts. They should each be treated as separate formulas.

TEMPERATURE MEASUREMENTS

Temperature may be expressed in the Fahrenheit temperature scale, which is the standard system used in the United States, or in the Celsius temperature scale, which is used in most of the rest of the world and by the scientific community. In the Fahrenheit scale, the freezing point of pure water is indicated at 32°F and the boiling point is reached at 212°F. Named after the Swedish astronomer who invented it in the 18th century, the Celsius scale measures 100 degrees between the freezing (0°C) and boiling point (100°C) of pure water. The system is sometimes referred to as the centigrade system. To convert Fahrenheit to Celsius, subtract 32 from the Fahrenheit temperature, then multiply the resulting number by 5 and divide that result by 9.

$$140°F - 32 = 108 \times 5 = 540 \div 9 = 60°C$$

▶ FORMULA CONVERSIONS

Whether it produces 6 servings or 60 servings, 3 pounds or 30 pounds of dough, every formula is designed to produce or **yield** a specific amount of product. The yield may be expressed in volume, weight or servings (for example, 1 quart of sauce; 8 pounds of bread dough; 8 ½-cup servings). If the expected yield of a formula is not what is needed, the ingredient amounts must be converted (that is, increased or decreased) to produce the desired quantity. Increasing (decreasing) a formula yield is also referred to as **scaling up** (down).

It is just as easy to change yields by uneven amounts as it is to double or halve formulas. The mathematical principle is the same: Each ingredient is multiplied by a conversion factor. Do not take shortcuts by estimating formula amounts or conversion factors. Inaccurate conversions lead to inedible foods, embarrassing shortages or wasteful excesses. Take the time to learn and apply proper conversion techniques.

▶ **yield**—the total amount produced by a formula expressed in total weight, volume or number of units of the product

▶ **scale up (down)**—to increase (decrease) a recipe or formula mathematically

CONVERTING TOTAL YIELD

When portion size is unimportant or remains the same, formula yield is converted by a simple two-step process:

Step 1 Divide the desired (new) yield by the formula (old) yield to obtain the conversion factor (C.F.).

new yield ÷ old yield = conversion factor

Step 2 Multiply each ingredient quantity by the conversion factor to obtain the new quantity.

old quantity × conversion factor = new quantity

EXAMPLE 5.1

A formula for grapefruit sorbet must be scaled down. The present formula yields 1½ quarts but only ¾ quart is needed.

Step 1 Determine the conversion factor:

$$0.75 \text{ quart} \div 1.5 \text{ quarts} = 0.5$$

Note that any unit can be used, as long as the same unit is used with both the new and the old formula. For example, the same conversion factor would be obtained if the formula amounts were converted to fluid ounces:

$$24 \text{ fluid ounces} \div 48 \text{ fluid ounces} = 0.5$$

Step 2 Apply the conversion factor to each ingredient in the sorbet formula:

GRAPEFRUIT SORBET

	old quantity	×	C.F.	=	new quantity
Fresh grapefruit juice	1 qt.	×	0.5	=	½ qt.
Granulated sugar	8 oz.	×	0.5	=	4 oz.
Lemon juice	1 fl. oz.	×	0.5	=	½ fl. oz.
Corn syrup	1 Tbsp.	×	0.5	=	1½ tsp.

CONVERTING PORTION SIZE

Formula conversion is sometimes complicated by portion size conversion. For example, it may be necessary to convert a formula that initially produces 24 2-ounce servings of ice cream into a formula that produces 62 4-ounce servings.

Sometimes the amount of food served as a portion must be changed. For example, a new muffin pan holds less dough than one it is replacing, or a new plated dessert may require a smaller portion of ice cream than a single serving of ice cream by itself. A few additional steps are necessary to convert formulas when portion sizes must also be changed. This is easy to understand in terms of the total amount of a food item that is needed in relation to the total amount of that item (yield) produced by the current formula. The key is to find a common denominator for the new and old formula: ounces, grams, cups, servings and so on. Any unit can be used, as long as the same unit is used with both the new and the old formula.

Step 1 Determine the total yield of the existing formula by multiplying the number of portions by the portion size.

original portions × original portion size = total (old) yield

Step 2 Determine the total yield desired by multiplying the new number of portions by the new portion size.

desired portions × desired portion size = total (new) yield

Step 3 Obtain the conversion factor as described earlier.

total (new) yield ÷ total (old) yield = conversion factor

Step 4 Multiply each ingredient quantity by the conversion factor.

old quantity × conversion factor = new quantity

EXAMPLE 5.2

Returning to the grapefruit sorbet, the original formula produced 1½ quarts or 24 2-ounce servings. Now you need 36 3-ounce servings.

Step 1 Total original yield is 24 × 2 = 48 ounces.
Step 2 Total desired yield is 36 × 3 = 108 ounces.

Step 3 The conversion factor is calculated by dividing total new yield by total old yield:

$$108 \div 48 = 2.25$$

Step 4 Old ingredient quantities are multiplied by the conversion factor to determine the new quantities:

GRAPEFRUIT SORBET

	old quantity	×	C.F.	=	new quantity
Fresh grapefruit juice	1 qt.	×	2.25	=	2.25 qt.
Granulated sugar	8 oz.	×	2.25	=	18 oz.
Lemon juice	1 fl. oz.	×	2.25	=	2.25 fl. oz.
Corn syrup	1 Tbsp.	×	2.25	=	2.25 Tbsp.

BAKER'S PERCENTAGE

Many commercial formulas, especially those for cookies, cakes and breads, list ingredients as a percentage in addition to, or in place of, a specific weight or volume measurement. Percentages make accurate formula conversions possible, and percentages are also a convenient type of shorthand. At a glance, the baker who is familiar with the function of ingredients can tell how rich, moist or crisp a finished product will be. For example, a cookie dough with a high percentage of fat in relation to flour will bake into a more crumbly pastry than cookie dough containing a lower percentage of fat. The simplest bread dough made with flour, water, salt and yeast will bake into a crusty loaf with a crisp crust. When even a small percentage of fat is added, the loaf will become more tender and the crust will be less crisp. When formulas list ingredients in proportion to other ingredients, the experienced baker can select formulas with the proper ratios for the product desired.

The percentage may represent the true percentage or the baker's percentage. In the **true percentage** method, the percent of each ingredient is calculated based on the total weight of all ingredients in a formula, with the total being 100%.

The percentage formula most commonly used in the bakeshop is called the **baker's percentage.** When using baker's percentage, the quantity of each ingredient is expressed as a percentage of the total amount of flour used in the formula. The flour in the formula is always 100%. If a formula calls for two or three types of flour, the total of all the flours must equal 100%.

To calculate the baker's percentage in a formula:

▶ **baker's percentage**—a system for measuring ingredients in a formula by expressing them as a percentage of the total flour weight

Step 1 Identify the weight of the flour in the formula. This weight will be 100%.

Step 2 Divide the weight of each of the other ingredients in the formula by the weight of the flour.

weight of ingredient ÷ weight of flour

Step 3 Multiply the number obtained by 100% to calculate the baker's percentage for each ingredient.

weight of ingredient ÷ weight of flour × 100% = baker's percentage of ingredient

EXAMPLE 5.3
The formula for Sugar Cookie Dough shown in Figure 5.1 needs to be converted to baker's percentage so that it can be scaled up.

Step 1 Determine the weight of the flour, which is 100%.

1 pound (16 ounces) of flour = 100%

Here is an example of how a formula written in baker's percentage might look. The column to the right indicates the relationship of all ingredients in this formula to the quantity of total flour in the formula. The total batch weight and baker's percentage are used to scale a formula up or down.

Sugar Cookie Dough
Yield: 20 Cookies, 1½ oz. each

	Quantity	**Baker's Percentage**
Flour	1 lb.	100%
Granulated sugar	6 oz.	37.5%
Butter	7 oz.	43.7%
Vanilla extract	1 fl. oz.	6.2%
Total:	1 lb. 14 oz.	187.4%

FIGURE 5.1 ▶ Baker's percentage formula

Step 2   Divide the weight of the sugar by the weight of the flour.

$$6 \div 16 = 0.375$$

Step 3   Multiply the number obtained by 100 to obtain the baker's percentage for the sugar.

$$0.375 \times 100 = 37.5\%$$

Step 4   Calculate the baker's percentage for each of the remaining ingredients in the formula as outlined in Steps 1, 2 and 3.

$$\text{butter } 7 \div 16 = 0.437 \times 100 = 43.7\%$$
$$\text{vanilla extract } 1 \div 16 = 0.062 \times 100 = 6.2\%$$

An experienced baker will know at a glance that this sugar cookie with 44% butter will be more tender and crumbly than one made from a formula with just 20% butter. With 37.5% sugar, this cookie will be sweet and somewhat crisp but not as brittle as a similar cookie with 60% sugar. The baker can also easily customize this formula by using percentages. Seeing that the vanilla extract is 6.2%, the baker knows that adding 5 or 6% of another flavoring, ground nuts or chocolate chips will transform this cookie without significantly altering the texture of the finished product. Note that the total baker's percentage for a formula is always calculated. It is used to scale a formula up or down using the baker's percentages.

CONVERTING A FORMULA USING BAKER'S PERCENTAGE

With baker's percentage the relationship or ratio of ingredients remains unchanged, making it very easy to scale a formula up or down. To convert a formula using baker's percentage, first the new formula yield must be determined. Then the total baker's percentage for the original formula is divided by 100 to obtain a baker's percentage conversion factor. The new formula yield is multiplied by the conversion factor to obtain the quantity of flour needed for the new scaled formula. Once the total amount of flour has been determined, it is easy to calculate the quantities of other ingredients in the formula. The remaining ingredient quantities are determined by multiplying the new flour weight by the baker's percentage for each ingredient.

Step 1   Determine the new formula yield required. Converting the yield to ounces (grams) ensures accuracy.

Step 2   Divide the total baker's percentage for the original formula by 100 to obtain the baker's percentage (BP) conversion factor for the formula.

$$\text{total baker's percentage} \div 100 = \text{BP conversion factor}$$

Step 3 Divide the new formula yield by the BP conversion factor.

new formula yield ÷ BP conversion factor = quantity of flour for new formula

Step 4 Compute the quantity of other ingredients required by multiplying the baker's percentage for each ingredient by the new flour weight.

EXAMPLE 5.4

The formula for Sugar Cookie Dough yields 20 cookies at 1.5 ounces each (1 pound 14 ounces of dough). Four dozen cookies weighing 1.5 ounces each are needed (4.5 pounds of dough). See Figure 5.2.

Step 1 Calculate the new formula yield.

4.5 lb. × 16 oz. per lb. = 72 oz.

Step 2 Divide the total baker's percentage for the original formula by 100 to obtain the baker's percentage conversion factor for the formula.

187.4 ÷ 100 = 1.874

Step 3 Divide the new formula yield by the BP conversion factor.

72 ÷ 1.874 = 38.42 oz. flour

Step 4 Compute the quantity of other ingredients required by multiplying the new flour weight by the baker's percentage for each ingredient.

38.42 × 37.5% = 14.4 oz. sugar

38.42 × 43.7% = 16.7 oz. butter

38.42 × 6.2% = 2.3 fl. oz. vanilla extract

Note that the weight of ingredients may be rounded to make scaling more efficient.

Baker's percentage is included in formulas in this book when flour is a primary ingredient. In the few formulas for which baker's percentage is provided but flour is not the dominant ingredient, the formula will indicate this. In formulas where baker's percentage is used, the percentages are what dictate the quantity of ingredients in either the U.S. or metric column. The metric formulas are not always exact equivalents of the U.S. measurement using the conversion of 1 ounce to 30 grams as discussed on page 91. Quantities are rounded to the nearest whole number to make the formulas usable. An exception is made for significant ingredients when their weight is less than 5% of the weight of flour, however.

Sugar Cookie Dough **Yield:** 20 Cookies, 1½ oz. each			**New Yield:** 48 Cookies, 1½ oz. each	
	Old Quantity	**Baker's Percentage**	**New Quantity**	**Rounded**
Flour	1 lb.	100%	38.5 oz.	39 oz.
Granulated sugar	6 oz.	37.5%	14.4 oz.	14 oz.
Butter	7 oz.	43.7%	16.7 oz.	17 oz.
Vanilla extract	1 fl. oz.	6.2%	2.3 fl. oz.	2 fl. oz.
Total:	1 lb. 14 oz.	187.4%	71.9 oz. 4 lb. 7.9 oz.	72 oz. 4 lb. 8 oz.

FIGURE 5.2 ▶ Scaling up using baker's percentage

ADDITIONAL CONVERSION PROBLEMS

When making significant changes to a formula's yield—for example, from 5 to 25 portions or 600 to 300 portions—additional problems can arise. The mathematical conversions described here do not take into account changes in equipment, evaporation rates, unforeseen formula errors or cooking times. Pastry chefs and bakers learn to use their judgment, knowledge of cooking principles and skills to compensate for these factors.

EQUIPMENT

When the size of a formula changes, the equipment necessary to produce it must change as well. Problems arise, however, when the production techniques previously used no longer work with the new quantity of ingredients. For example, if a small muffin formula can be mixed by hand, an increased batch size might require the use of a mixer. But if mixing time remains the same, the batter may become overmixed, resulting in poor-quality muffins. Trying to prepare a small amount of product in equipment that is too large for the task can also affect its quality.

EVAPORATION

Equipment changes can also affect product quality because of changes in evaporation rates. Increasing a custard formula may require substituting a large, shallow pot for a deep, narrow saucepan. But because the shallow pot provides more surface area for evaporation than does a deep saucepan, reduction time must be decreased to prevent overthickening the cream. The increased evaporation caused by increased surface area may also alter the strength of the flavoring used.

FORMULA ERRORS

A formula may contain errors in ingredients or techniques that are not obvious when it is prepared in small quantities. When increased, however, small mistakes often become big (and obvious) ones, and the final product suffers. The only solution is to test formulas carefully and rely on your knowledge of cooking principles to compensate for unexpected problems.

TIME

Do not multiply time specifications given in a formula by the conversion factor used with the formula's ingredients. All things being equal, cooking time will not change when baking a larger batch. For example, if the pan and portion size remains the same, a muffin requires the same amount of baking time whether you prepare 1 dozen or 14 dozen. Of more significance is the effect that changing equipment has on cooking time. If the muffin pan size is increased, cooking time may increase. Conversely, a smaller pan may take noticeably less time to bake. And an oven filled to capacity may lose more heat, thus slowing the baking time. Cooking time will also be affected by changes in evaporation rate or heat conduction caused by equipment changes. A larger batch of milk for custard cooking in the same size pan will take longer to heat than the original formula. Mixing time may change when formula size is changed. Different equipment may perform mixing tasks more or less efficiently than previously used equipment.

► PREPARING EQUIPMENT

Pans, baking sheets and molds to be used in the bakeshop require preparation before using. In order to prevent baked goods from sticking, most baking pans are coated with fat, a nonstick baking parchment or both.

In kitchens where a great deal of baking is done, it may be more convenient to prepare quantities of pan coating to be kept available for use as needed. Pan coating is a mixture of equal parts oil, shortening and flour that can be applied to cake pans with a pastry brush. It is used whenever pans need to be greased and floured. Pan coating will not leave a white residue on a baked crust, as a dusting of flour often does. Apply sparingly as a thick coating may leave a discernible taste. Make small batches so the mixture does not turn rancid before it can be used.

RECIPE 5.1	**PAN COATING**

Yield: 3 lb. (1440 g)

Vegetable oil	1 lb.	480 g
All-purpose shortening	1 lb.	480 g
Bread flour	1 lb.	480 g

1 Place all the ingredients in a mixer fitted with the paddle attachment. Blend on low speed for 5 minutes or until smooth.
2 Store in an opaque airtight container at room temperature for up to 1 month.
3 Apply to baking pans in a thin, even layer using a pastry brush.

▶ KNIFE SKILLS

Basic knife skills are the backbone of the techniques used in a professional kitchen. In the pastry kitchen, dough must be cut, chocolate must be chopped and fruit must be sliced. Sharp knives in skilled hands are just as critical to work in the bakeshop as they are in the kitchen. Here we outline some of the basics of safe knife handling.

USING KNIVES SAFELY

The first rule of knife safety is to focus on the task at hand. Other basic rules of knife safety are as follows:

1 Use the correct knife for the task at hand.
2 Always cut away from yourself.
3 Always cut on a cutting board. Do not cut on glass, metal or marble. Secure the cutting board by placing a damp towel underneath it to prevent it from sliding.
4 Keep knives sharp; a dull knife is more dangerous than a sharp one.
5 When carrying a knife, hold it point down, parallel and close to your leg as you walk.
6 A falling knife has no handle. Do not attempt to catch a falling knife; step back and allow it to fall.
7 Never leave a knife in a sink of water; anyone reaching into the sink could be injured and other pots and utensils could dent the knife.

CARING FOR KNIVES

A sharpening stone called a **whetstone** is used to put an edge on a dull blade. To use a whetstone, place the heel of the blade against the whetstone at a 20-degree angle. Keeping that angle, press down on the blade while pushing it away from you in one long arch, as if to slice off a thin piece of the stone. The entire length of the blade should come in contact with the stone during each sweep. Repeat the procedure on both sides of the blade until sufficiently sharp.

When sharpening a knife against a three-sided whetstone, go from the coarsest to the finest surface.

Honing a knife against a steel straightens the blade between sharpenings.

With a triple-faced stone, such as that shown here, you progress from the coarsest to the finest surface. Any whetstone can be moistened with either water or mineral oil, but not both. Do not use vegetable oil on a whetstone since it will soon become rancid and gummy.

A **steel** does not sharpen a knife. Rather it is used to hone or straighten the blade immediately after and between sharpenings. To use a steel, place the blade against the steel at a 20-degree angle. Then draw the blade along the entire length of the steel. Repeat the technique several times on each side of the blade.

Do not wash knives in commercial dishwashers. The heat and harsh chemicals can damage the edge and the handle. The blade can also be damaged if it knocks against cookware or utensils. In addition, the knife could injure an unsuspecting worker. Always wash and dry your knives by hand immediately after each use.

▶ PREPARING INGREDIENTS

CLARIFYING BUTTER

Unsalted whole butter is approximately 80% fat, 16% water and 4% milk solids. When the water and milk solids are removed from butter through a process known as **clarification,** the butter does not burn as quickly and is more stable than whole melted butter. Unsalted or salted butter may be clarified. Clarified butter is often added to egg foam cakes such as genoise (Chapter 14, Cakes and Tortes) to add flavor without additional liquid. Clarified butter will keep for extended periods in either the freezer or refrigerator.

Skimming milk solids from the surface of the melted butter.

▶ PROCEDURE FOR CLARIFYING BUTTER

1 Slowly warm the butter in a saucepan over low heat without boiling or agitation. As the butter melts, the milk solids rise to the top as a foam and the water sinks to the bottom.

2 When the butter is completely melted, skim the milk solids from the top.

3 When all the milk solids have been removed, ladle the butterfat into a clean pan, being careful to leave the water in the bottom of the pan.

4 The clarified butter is now ready to use. One pound (480 grams) of whole butter will yield approximately 12 ounces (360 grams) of clarified butter—a yield of 75%.

Ladling the butterfat into a clean pan.

Toasting sesame seeds in a dry sauté pan on the stove top.

TOASTING NUTS AND SPICES

Nuts are often toasted lightly before being used in baked goods and confections. Whole spices are sometimes toasted before being ground for a sauce or custard. Toasting not only browns the food, it brings out its flavor and makes it crispier and crunchier. When toasting nuts or spices on the stove top or in the oven, they should be watched closely as they can develop scorched flavors and burn easily.

BLANCHING NUTS

The skin on many nuts, especially almonds or hazelnuts, can taste bitter and discolor baked goods such as butter cakes and cookies. Nuts with skins such as almonds and hazelnuts are blanched to remove the skins before using. (They may also be purchased blanched.) To blanch whole almonds, cover the nuts with boiling water and let them soak for 3 to 5 minutes. Drain the nuts then squeeze each one to remove its skin. Since the moistened skins may discolor the nuts, remove them promptly.

To blanch hazelnuts, place the nuts on a baking sheet. Heat them at 275°F (135°C) for 12 to 15 minutes, just until the nuts start to become fragrant. Remove the nuts from the oven and place them in a clean cloth towel. Briskly rub the nuts in the towel and most of the skin will come off.

PREPARING NUT FLOUR

Finely ground nuts, especially almonds and hazelnuts, are substituted for some or all of the wheat flour in a number of recipes, particularly torte and egg foam cakes such as dacquoise (page 299), joconde (page 418) and almond macaroons (page 572). While nut flour may be purchased as an ingredient from a bakery or pastry ingredient supplier, it may also be made in small quantities in most bakeshops. Using a handheld or table model rotary grater makes a finely ground nut flour. The raw nuts, with or without their skins, are placed in the grater and the crank is turned. A food processor may also be used to prepare nut flour, but care must be taken to keep the nuts from overheating and turning into nut butter. When grinding nuts in a food processor, the friction caused by the blade heats the nuts, extracting some of their oil. Adding some granulated sugar while grinding the nuts and pulsing the machine during processing helps minimize this.

▶ PROCEDURE FOR GRINDING NUTS INTO FLOUR USING A FOOD PROCESSOR

1 Place whole blanched (skins removed) almonds or hazelnuts in the bowl of a food processor fitted with a metal blade. Add ½ ounce (15 grams) of sugar or 10 percent of the sugar called for in the formula to the nuts.
2 Turn on the machine and grind the nuts for 10 seconds. Turn off the machine, then pulse it on and off at 15- to 20-second intervals during grinding to keep heat from building up.
3 Once the nuts are ground, to obtain finer flour, sift the nut flour through a medium-mesh strainer or tamis.

MAKING BREAD, CAKE OR COOKIE CRUMBS

Crumbs are used to make fillings for pastries and crusts for pies and cheesecake. Depending on the application, almost any bread or pastry, including leftover baked Danish and croissant pastries, may be ground and used as a crumb. (Often bakers will grind unsold Danish pastries and add them to fillings for the next day's batch.) **Fresh crumbs** are made from fresh bread, plain cookies or plain

1 Grind chunks of bread in a food processor.

2 Pass the crumbs, if desired, through a tamis or sieve so that they will be the same size.

cake trimmings that are slightly dried out, approximately two to four days old. If the products are too fresh the crumbs will be gummy and stick together. If the products are stale the crumbs will taste stale. **Dry crumbs** are made from bread, cake trimmings, broken plain cookies or baked pastries that have been dried out in the oven. Ground graham crackers, vanilla cookies, plain butter cookies and spice cookies make excellent crusts for cheesecake (see page 442).

To make crumbs, the product is cubed or torn into pieces and ground in a food processor. Dried crumbs can be processed to a finer consistency than can fresh crumbs. After processing, the crumbs should be passed through a tamis and stored in a tightly closed container in a cool, dry place.

▶ PREPARING TO BAKE

Ingredients are often flavored before being used in bakeshop formulas. Creams and syrups may be **infused** with the aroma of an herb or spice. Dried fruits and ingredients may be perfumed with an extract or liqueur.

Although most fruits are edible raw and typically served that way, many fruits are enhanced by soaking (**macerating**) them in a flavored syrup or liqueur with added spices and flavorings. When macerating fruits, be certain they are well washed and bruise-free. Drying the fruits after washing prevents diluting the macerating liquid with water.

▶ **infuse**—to flavor a liquid by steeping it with ingredients such as tea, coffee, herbs or spices

▶ **macerate**—to soak foods in a flavorful liquid, usually alcoholic, to soften them

STEEPING

Steeping is the process of soaking dry ingredients in a liquid (usually hot) in order to infuse their flavor into the liquid. Spices, vanilla and coffee beans and nuts are often steeped in hot milk to extract their flavors. The milk is then used to flavor other foods during cooking. For example, coffee beans can be steeped in hot milk and then strained out, with the coffee-flavored milk being used to make a custard sauce.

Note that the steeping mixture is generally covered and removed from the heat to avoid evaporation or reduction of the liquid.

CONDITIONING DRY FRUIT

Dry fruits such as raisins, currants, candied peel and other similar ingredients benefit from a short or overnight soaking in liquid before using in order for them to remain tender once baked in bread and muffin dough. Typically the softened

Steeping a vanilla bean and cinnamon sticks in warm milk to extract their flavors.

Conditioning raisins in hot water to rehydrate.

fruits will be used in a formula and the liquid discarded. This is called **conditioning.** To condition dry fruit with water, cover the dry fruit with 80°F (27°C) water and let it sit for 5 minutes. Drain the fruit in a strainer or colander, then let the fruit sit for four hours before using. The last step allows the fruit to plump and absorb any moisture remaining on the outer skin. To condition and flavor dried fruit for certain types of baked products, soak it overnight in sugar syrup, rum, lemon essence or other fruit juice. Drain the fruit before adding to the dough or batter. The soaking liquid may be used in place of up to 10% of the liquid in the formula.

BLANCHING AND PARBOILING

Some foods, especially fruit and herbs such as mint being used in a sauce, are **blanched** or **parboiled.** To do so, they are immersed in a large quantity of boiling unsalted water. This parcooking assists in their preparation (for example, it loosens skins from peaches and other fruit), removes some bitterness, preserves color, softens fruit and shortens final cooking time. The only difference between blanching and parboiling is total cooking time. Blanching is done quickly, usually only a few seconds. Parboiling lasts longer, usually several minutes. The water may be changed, as when parboiling citrus rind, to remove off-flavors from the cooking liquid. Foods that are blanched or parboiled in water are **shocked** or refreshed in ice water to halt the cooking process.

MAKING AN ICE BATH

Because of the risk of food-borne illness, it is important to cool food quickly to a temperature below 40°F (4°C) before storing it in the refrigerator. An ice bath is an easy, efficient way to do so. An ice bath is also necessary for stopping the cooking of delicate mixtures such as custards and for shocking or refreshing blanched or parcooked fruit or herbs. An ice bath is simply a container of ice cubes and cold water. The combination of ice and water will chill foods more rapidly than a container of ice alone. The food being chilled will also cool faster if it is in a metal container, rather than one made of plastic.

▶ **blanching**—very briefly and partially cooking a food in boiling water; used to assist preparation (for example, to loosen skin from fruit), as part of a combination cooking method or to remove undesirable flavors

▶ **parboiling**—partially cooking a food in boiling or simmering liquid; similar to blanching but the cooking time is longer

▶ **shocking**—also called refreshing; the technique of quickly chilling blanched or parcooked foods in ice water; prevents further cooking and sets colors

Chilling a cream sauce in an ice bath

What may seem like extra steps at the start of a day in the bakeshop pays off in mistakes avoided. Proper mise en place—setting up and preparing ingredients before starting to cook and bake—helps ease some of the work in the bakeshop. Ingredients must be measured for accuracy, with weighing the preferred method of measuring. When formulas need to be adjusted, increased or decreased, using a conversion formula is the most effective way of calculating the quantity of ingredients required. Use the tips and procedures in this chapter to make the most effective use of your time in the bakeshop.

1 Why is it so important to weigh ingredients used in the bakeshop? What types of ingredients may be accurately measured using volume?

2 Describe the proper procedures for sharpening a knife.

3 Explain the process used to scale up a formula. Why is it important to follow the procedures described in this chapter when scaling a bakeshop formula up or down?

4 Select a formula from Chapter 15, Custards and Creams, and describe the mise en place for that item.

WHEN I AM IN TROUBLE, EATING IS THE ONLY THING THAT CONSOLES ME . . . AT THE PRESENT I AM EATING MUFFINS BECAUSE I AM UNHAPPY. BESIDES, I AM PARTICULARLY FOND OF MUFFINS.

—Oscar Wilde, Irish dramatist and writer (1854–1900)

QUICK BREADS

MISSISSIPPI UNIVERSITY FOR WOMEN CULINARY ARTS INSTITUTE,
Columbus, MS
Chef Sarah R. Labensky, CCP

AFTER STUDYING THIS CHAPTER, YOU WILL BE ABLE TO:

▶ use chemical leavening agents properly

▶ prepare a variety of quick breads using the biscuit method, muffin method and creaming method

▶ prepare a variety of griddlecakes, pancakes and waffles

Buttermilk biscuits, blueberry muffins, banana nut bread and currant scones are all quick breads. Why they are called quick breads is obvious: They are quick to make and quick to bake. With only a few basic ingredients and no yeast, almost any food service operation can provide its customers with fresh muffins, biscuits, scones and loaf breads.

The variety of ingredients is virtually limitless: cornmeal, whole wheat, fruits, nuts, spices and vegetables all yield popular products. And the use of these products is not limited to breakfast service—they are equally appropriate for lunch, snacks and buffets. This chapter looks at these basic quick breads as well as formulas for griddlecakes such as pancakes and waffles.

▶ CHEMICAL LEAVENING AGENTS

Quick breads are made with chemical leavening agents, principally baking soda and baking powder. This sets them apart from breads that are made with yeast and require additional time for fermentation and proofing, as discussed in Chapter 7, Yeast Breads. Understanding how chemical leavening agents operate is essential to successfully producing quick breads.

Chemical leavening agents release gases (primarily carbon dioxide) through chemical reactions between acids and bases contained in the formula. These gases form bubbles or air pockets throughout the dough or batter. As the product bakes, these gases expand, causing the product to rise. The proteins in the dough or batter then set around these air pockets, giving the quick bread its rise and texture.

BAKING SODA

Sodium bicarbonate ($NaHCO_3$) is more commonly known as household baking soda. Baking soda is an alkaline compound (a base), which releases carbon dioxide gas (CO_2) if both an acid and moisture are present. Heat is not necessary for this reaction to occur. Therefore, products made with baking soda must be baked at once, before the carbon dioxide has a chance to escape from the batter or dough.

Acids commonly used with baking soda are buttermilk, sour cream, lemon juice, honey, molasses and fruits high in acid such as citrus. Generally, the amount of baking soda used in a formula is only the amount necessary to neutralize the acids present. If more leavening action is needed, baking powder, not more baking soda, should be used. Too much baking soda causes the product to taste soapy or bitter; it may also cause a yellow color and brown spots to develop.

BAKING POWDER

Baking powder is a mixture of sodium bicarbonate and one or more acids, generally cream of tartar ($KHC_4H_4O_6$) and/or sodium aluminum sulfate ($Na_2SO_4 \cdot Al_2[SO_4]_3$). Baking powder also contains a starch to prevent lumping and balance the chemical reactions. Because baking powder contains both the acid and the base necessary for the desired chemical reaction, the quick bread formula does not need to contain any acid. Only moisture is necessary to induce the release of gases.

There are two types of baking powder: single-acting and double-acting. An excess of either type produces undesirable flavors, textures and colors in baked products.

Single-acting baking powder requires only the presence of moisture to start releasing gas. The eggs, milk, water or other liquids in the formula supply this moisture. As with baking soda, products using single-acting baking powder must be baked immediately.

Double-acting baking powder is more popular. With double-acting baking powder, there is a small release of gas upon contact with moisture and a second, stronger release of gas when heat is applied. Products made with double-acting baking powder need not be baked immediately, but can sit for a short time without loss of leavening ability. All formulas in this book rely on double-acting baking powder.

Both baking soda and baking powder are sometimes used in one formula. This is because baking soda can release CO_2 only to the extent that there is also an acid present in the formula. If the soda/acid reaction alone is insufficient to leaven the product, baking powder is needed for additional leavening.

BAKING AMMONIA

Baking ammonia (ammonia bicarbonate or ammonia carbonate) is also used as a leavening agent and to add crispness in some baked goods, primarily cookies and crackers. Baking ammonia releases ammonia and carbon dioxide very rapidly when heated. The strong odor it releases as it bakes dissipates once the product is cooked above 140°F (60°C). It is suitable for low-moisture products with large surface areas that are baked at high temperatures, such as crackers and biscotti. Consequently, it is rarely used in quick breads.

PURCHASING AND STORING

Purchase chemical leaveners in the smallest unit appropriate for your operation. Although a large can of baking powder may cost less than several small ones, if not used promptly the contents of a larger container can deteriorate, causing waste or unusable baked goods.

Chemical leavening agents should always be kept tightly covered. Not only is there a risk of contamination if left open, but they can also absorb moisture from the air and lose their effectiveness. They should be stored in a cool place, as heat deteriorates them. A properly stored and unopened container of baking powder or baking soda has a shelf life of several years.

▶ MIXING METHODS

Quick breads are generally mixed by the **biscuit method,** the **muffin method** or the **creaming method.** The mixing method employed is directly related to the type and consistency of fat used in the formula. Cold solid fats, such as butter, lard or vegetable shortening, are used in the biscuit method to produce flaky products. Fats that are soft but not liquid are used in the high-fat creaming method. Liquid fats, such as oil or melted butter, are used in the muffin method to produce very moist, tender products. See Table 6.1.

Table 6.1 **QUICK BREAD MIXING TECHNIQUES**

MIXING TECHNIQUE	FAT	RESULT
Biscuit method	Solid (chilled)	Flaky dough
Muffin method	Liquid (oil or melted butter)	Soft, tender, cakelike texture
Creaming method	Softened (room temperature)	Rich, tender, cakelike texture

BISCUITS AND SCONES: A GENEALOGY

Biscuit is a French word used to describe any dry, flat cake, whether sweet or savory. It was, perhaps, originally coined to describe twice-baked cakes (*bis* = twice, *cuit* = cooked). Crusader chronicles, for example, mention soldiers eating a "bread called 'bequis' because it is cooked twice" and still, today, the Reims biscuit is returned to the oven for further baking after it is removed from its tin.

Over the centuries, the French began to use the term *biscuit* generically and appended modifiers to identify the particular type of dry, flat cake. For example, a *biscuit de guerre* was the very hard, barely risen product of flour and water used from the time of the Crusades to the era of Louis XIV as an army ration (*guerre* is French for "war"); *biscuit de Savoie* is a savory spongecake; *biscuit de pâtisserie* is a sweet biscuit.

To the British, a biscuit is what Americans call a cracker or cookie. Yet there appears to be no British quick bread quite comparable to the American biscuit—the closest relative would be the scone. But because a scone contains eggs and butter, it is much richer than a biscuit.

Elizabeth Alston, in *Biscuits and Scones,* proposes that the biscuit is an American variant of the scone. She theorizes that early British colonists in America brought with them traditional scone recipes. Unable to find or afford the necessary fresh butter and eggs, these practical bakers substituted lard and omitted the eggs. What they created, however, were not mock scones, but rather a new product, different from scones but still delicious. Alston further speculates that French cooks initially called the new American product "biscuit de something" and eventually dropped the "de something."

▶ **crumb**—the interior of bread or cake; may be elastic, aerated, fine or coarse grained

Quick breads are tender products with a soft **crumb.** To keep gluten development to a minimum, flour is mixed into quick breads swiftly and gently.

BISCUIT METHOD

The biscuit method is used for biscuits, shortcakes and scones and is very similar to the technique used to make flaky pie doughs. The goal is to create a baked good that is light, flaky and tender.

▶ PROCEDURE FOR PREPARING PRODUCTS WITH THE BISCUIT METHOD

1 Measure all ingredients.
2 Sift the dry ingredients together.
3 Cut in the fat, which should be in a solid form.
4 Combine the liquid ingredients, including any eggs.
5 Add the liquid ingredients to the dry ingredients. Mix just until the ingredients are combined. Do not overmix, as this causes toughness and inhibits the product's rise.
6 Place the dough on the bench and knead it lightly 10 or 15 times (approximately 20 to 30 seconds). The dough should be soft and slightly elastic, but not sticky. Too much kneading toughens the biscuits. Use a slow speed and a short mixing time when kneading biscuit dough in a mixer.
7 The dough is now ready for **make-up** and baking.

▶ **make-up**—the cutting, shaping and forming of dough products before baking

▶ MAKE-UP OF BISCUIT-METHOD PRODUCTS

1 Roll out the dough on a floured surface to a thickness of ½ to ¾ inch (1.2 to 1.8 centimeters). Be careful to roll it evenly. Biscuits should double in height during baking.
2 Cut into the desired shapes. Cut straight down; do not twist the cutters, as this inhibits rise. Space cuts as close together as possible to minimize scraps.
3 Position the biscuits on a lightly greased or paper-lined sheet pan. If placed with sides nearly touching, the biscuits will rise higher and have softer sides. Place farther apart for crusty sides.
4 Reworking and rerolling the dough may cause tough, misshapen biscuits. Nevertheless, it may be possible to reroll scraps once by pressing the dough together gently without kneading.

5 Tops may be brushed with egg wash before baking or with melted butter after baking. Bake immediately in a hot oven.

6 Cool the finished products on a wire rack.

COUNTRY BISCUITS   RECIPE 6.1

Yield: 36 Biscuits, 2¼ oz. (66 g) each   **Method:** Biscuit

All-purpose flour	2 lb. 8 oz.	1200 g	100%
Salt	0.75 oz.	24 g	2%
Granulated sugar	2 oz.	60 g	5%
Baking powder	2 oz.	60 g	5%
Unsalted butter, cold	14 oz.	420 g	35%
Milk	1½ pt.	720 ml	60%
Total weight:	5 lb. 2 oz.	2484 g	207%

1 Sift the dry ingredients together, making sure they are blended thoroughly.

2 Cut in the butter. The mixture should look mealy; do not overmix.

3 Add the milk and stir, combining only until the mixture holds together.

4 Transfer the dough to a lightly floured work surface; knead until it forms one mass, approximately five or six kneadings.

5 Roll out the dough to a thickness of ½ inch (1.2 centimeters). Cut with a floured cutter and place the biscuits on a paper-lined sheet pan.

6 Bake at 425°F (220°C) until the tops are light brown, the sides almost white and the interiors still moist, approximately 10 to 12 minutes. Internal heat will continue to cook the biscuits after they are removed from the oven.

7 Remove the biscuits to a wire rack to cool.

Approximate values per biscuit: **Calories** 210, **Total fat** 10 g, **Saturated fat** 6 g, **Cholesterol** 25mg, **Sodium** 240 mg, **Total carbohydrates** 27 g, **Protein** 4 g, **Vitamin A** 10%

1 Sifting the dry ingredients together.

2 Cutting in the fat.

3 Kneading the dough.

4 Cutting the biscuits.

MUFFIN METHOD

Muffins are any small, cakelike baked good made in a muffin tin (pan). Batters for muffins and loaf quick breads are generally interchangeable. For example, banana muffin batter may be baked in a loaf pan, provided the baking time is altered.

When preparing baked goods by the muffin method, the goal is to produce a tender product with an even shape and an even distribution of fruits, nuts or other ingredients. The most frequent problem encountered with muffin-method products is overmixing. This causes toughness and may cause holes to form inside the baked product, a condition known as **tunneling** (see Table 6.2).

▶ **tunneling**—large tubular holes in muffins and cakes, a defect caused by overmixing

Table 6.2	TROUBLESHOOTING CHART FOR MUFFINS AND QUICK BREADS	
PROBLEM	**CAUSE**	**SOLUTION**
Soapy or bitter flavor	Chemical leaveners not properly mixed into batter	Sift chemicals with dry ingredients
	Too much baking soda	Adjust formula
Elongated holes (tunneling)	Overmixing	Do not mix until smooth; mix only until moistened
Crust too thick	Too much sugar	Adjust formula
	Oven temperature too low	Adjust oven
Flat top with only a small peak in center	Oven temperature too low	Adjust oven
Cracked, uneven top	Oven temperature too high	Adjust oven
No rise; dense product	Old batter	Bake promptly
	Damaged leavening agents	Store new chemicals properly
	Overmixing	Do not overmix

▶ PROCEDURE FOR PREPARING PRODUCTS WITH THE MUFFIN METHOD

1 Measure all ingredients.

2 Sift the dry ingredients together.

3 Combine the liquid ingredients, including melted fat or oil. Melted butter or shortening may resolidify when combined with the other liquids; this is not a cause for concern.

4 Add the liquid ingredients to the dry ingredients and stir just until combined. Do not overmix. The batter will be lumpy.

5 The batter is now ready for make-up and baking.

▶ MAKE-UP OF MUFFIN-METHOD PRODUCTS

1 Muffin pans and loaf pans should be greased with butter, shortening or commercial pan grease. Paper liners may be used and will prevent sticking if the batter contains fruits or vegetables. Paper liners, however, inhibit rise.

2 A portion scoop is a useful tool for ensuring uniform-sized muffins. Be careful not to drip or spill batter onto the edge of the muffin cups; it will burn and cause sticking.

3 Allow muffins and loaf breads to cool for several minutes before attempting to remove them from the pan.

4 Cool the finished products on a wire rack.

RECIPE 6.2   **BLUEBERRY MUFFINS**

Yield: 12 Muffins, 2½ oz. (75 g) each   **Method:** Muffin

All-purpose flour	8 oz.	240 g	100%
Granulated sugar	5 oz.	150 g	62%
Baking powder	0.3 oz. (2 tsp.)	9 g	4%
Salt	0.05 oz. (¼ tsp.)	1.5 g	0.6%
Eggs	3.3 oz. (2 eggs)	100 g	41%
Milk	8 fl. oz.	240 ml	100%
Unsalted butter, melted	2 oz.	60 g	25%
Vanilla extract	0.15 fl. oz. (1 tsp.)	5 ml	2%
Blueberries	5 oz.	150 g	62%
Lemon zest	0.2 oz. (1 Tbsp.)	6 g	2.5%
Total weight:	2 lb.	961 g	399%

1 Combining the liquid ingredients.　　**2** Folding in the blueberries.　　**3** Portioning the batter.

1 Sift together the dry ingredients (flour, sugar, baking powder, salt).

2 Stir together the liquid ingredients (eggs, milk, melted butter, vanilla).

3 Stir the liquid mixture into the dry ingredients. Do not overmix. The batter should be lumpy.

4 Gently fold in the blueberries and lemon zest.

5 Portion into greased or paper-lined muffin cups and bake at 350°F (180°C) until light brown and set in the center, approximately 18 minutes.

6 Cool the muffins in the pan for several minutes before removing.

VARIATIONS:

Cranberry Orange Muffins—Substitute fresh orange zest for the lemon zest and 4 ounces (120 grams/50%) of dried cranberries for the blueberries.

Pecan Spice Muffins—Omit the blueberries and lemon zest. Add 4 ounces (120 grams/50%) of chopped pecans, 0.04 oz. (1/2 teaspoon/1 g/0.4%) of cinnamon and 0.02 oz. (1/4 teaspoon/0.5 gram/ 0.2%) each of nutmeg and ground ginger to the batter.

Approximate values per muffin: **Calories** 180, **Total fat** 6 g, **Saturated fat** 3 g, **Cholesterol** 50 mg, **Sodium** 150 mg, **Total carbohydrates** 29 g, **Protein** 4 g

CREAMING METHOD

The creaming method is comparable to the mixing method used for many butter cakes. In fact many butter cake formulas may be baked in muffin pans and served as muffins. The softened fat and granulated sugar should be properly creamed to incorporate air, which will help leaven the product as it bakes. The final product will be cakelike, with a fine texture. There is less danger of overmixing with this method because the higher fat content shortens gluten strands and tenderizes the batter.

▶ PROCEDURE FOR PREPARING PRODUCTS WITH THE CREAMING METHOD

1 Measure all ingredients.

2 Sift the dry ingredients together.

3 Combine the softened fat and sugar in a mixer bowl. Cream on low speed until the color lightens and the mixture fluffs.

4 Add eggs gradually, mixing well.

5 Add the dry and liquid ingredients to the creamed fat alternately. In other words, a portion of the flour is added to the fat and incorporated, then a portion of the liquid is added and incorporated. These steps are repeated until all the liquid and dry ingredients are incorporated. By adding the liquid and dry ingredients alternately, you avoid overmixing the batter and prevent the butter and sugar mixture from curdling.

6 The batter is now ready for make-up and baking.

▶ MAKE-UP OF CREAMING-METHOD PRODUCTS

Panning and baking procedures are the same as those for quick breads prepared with the muffin method.

RECIPE 6.3

SOUR CREAM MUFFINS

Yield: 12 Muffins, 3¼ oz. (100 g) each   **Method:** Creaming

Unsalted butter,			
room temperature	8 oz.	240 g	80%
Granulated sugar	8 oz.	240 g	80%
Eggs	3.3 oz. (2 eggs)	100 g	33%
All-purpose flour	10 oz.	300 g	100%
Baking powder	0.14 oz. (1 tsp.)	4 g	1.4%
Baking soda	0.14 oz. (1 tsp.)	4 g	1.4%
Salt	0.2 oz. (1 tsp.)	6 g	2%
Sour cream	10 oz.	300 g	100%
Vanilla extract	0.15 fl. oz. (1 tsp.)	5 ml	1.5%
Total weight:	2 lb. 7 oz.	1199 g	399%

1 Cream the butter and sugar until light and fluffy. Add the eggs.

2 Sift the dry ingredients together.

3 Stir the dry ingredients and sour cream, alternately, into the butter mixture in three additions. Stir in the vanilla.

4 Portion and bake at 350°F (180°C) until light brown and set, approximately 20 minutes.

5 Allow the muffins to cool briefly in the pan before removing.

VARIATIONS:

▶ **streusel**—a crumbly mixture of fat, flour, sugar and sometimes nuts and spices; used to top baked goods

Sour cream muffins can be topped with **streusel** or flavored with a wide variety of fruits or nuts by adding approximately 4–6 ounces (1 cup/120–180 grams/ 40–60%) fresh or frozen drained fruit to the batter. Blueberries, dried cherries, candied fruits, pecans and diced pears yield popular products. To make basic spice muffins, add 0.04 ounces. (½ teaspoon/1 gram/0.3%) each of cinnamon and nutmeg.

Approximate values per muffin: **Calories** 290, **Total fat** 17 g, **Saturated fat** 10 g, **Cholesterol** 70 mg, **Sodium** 260 mg, **Total carbohydrates** 31 g, **Protein** 4 g, **Vitamin A** 15%

1 Creaming the butter and sugar.

2 Adding the sour cream.

3 Topping the muffins with the streusel.

STREUSEL TOPPING

RECIPE 6.4

Yield: 5 lb. 4 oz. (2528 g)

All-purpose flour	2 lb.	960 g	100%
Cinnamon, ground	0.25 oz.	7 g	0.8%
Salt	0.2 oz. (1 tsp.)	6 g	0.6%
Brown sugar	8 oz.	240 g	25%
Granulated sugar	1 lb. 8 oz.	720 g	75%
Whole butter, cold	1 lb. 4 oz.	595 g	62%
Total weight:	5 lb. 4 oz.	2528 g	263%

1 Combine the dry ingredients. Cut in the butter until the mixture is coarse and crumbly.

2 Sprinkle on top of muffins or quick breads prior to baking. Streusel topping will keep for several weeks under refrigeration and may be frozen for longer storage. There is no need to thaw before use.

Approximate values per 1-oz. (30-g) serving: **Calories** 190, **Total fat** 8 g, **Saturated fat** 5 g, **Cholesterol** 20 mg, **Sodium** 45 mg, **Total carbohydrates** 29 g, **Protein** 2 g

CONVENIENCE PRODUCTS

Prepared quick bread and muffin mixes and batters are available in a number of formats. Dry powdered muffin mixes or muffin bases require the addition of liquid, some oil and sometimes eggs. Attention to mixing remains the same as for a muffin batter made from scratch. Select mixes with natural ingredients and flavorings and less sugar.

Ready-to-use quick bread batters are sold in 1- and 5-gallon containers, designed to be scooped out, panned then baked. These batters offer the bakeshop the flexibility of baking small batches of muffins on an as-needed basis. Additionally, the bakeshop can customize a basic batter by adding fruits, nuts and seasonings of their own choice. These batters also come in plastic tubes, designed to be piped directly from their packaging into prepared pans. Prepared batters must be refrigerated or frozen and thawed as directed and leftovers must be stored according to the manufacturer's directions. Improper storage, panning or baking will impact final product quality.

CONCLUSION

First you must master the three mixing methods used in producing quick breads (biscuit, muffin and creaming) and understand the interaction between chemical leaveners and other ingredients. Then, with an imaginative use of flavoring ingredients, you can successfully produce a wide array of fresh-baked breads for almost any food service operation.

QUESTIONS FOR DISCUSSION

1 Name two chemical leavening agents, and explain how they cause batters and doughs to rise. Describe the purpose of leavening agents in baked goods. Explain why baking soda is used with an acid in baked goods.

2 List three common methods used for mixing quick breads. What is the significance of the type of fat used for each of these mixing methods?

3 What is the most likely explanation for discolored and bitter-tasting biscuits? What is the solution?

4 What happens when muffin batter has been overmixed?

5 Visit the Web sites for King Arthur Flour and White Lily Foods to learn more about the varieties of flours and flavoring ingredients that are available for use in biscuits and muffins. What are each of these companies famous for? How do the products of these two regional flour manufacturers differ?

RECIPE 6.5

SARAH R. LABENSKY, CCP

Chef Sarah R. Labensky is founding director of the Culinary Arts Institute at Mississippi University for Women. She teaches cooking courses and administers MUW's four-year baccalaureate degree program in culinary arts. Before joining MUW, she was a professor of culinary arts at Scottsdale (Arizona) Community College and had worked as a chef and caterer.

Her career has not always been focused on the kitchen, however. Chef Sarah was once a practicing attorney with a J.D. degree from Vanderbilt University School of Law.

She is the co-author of this book and *On Cooking: A Textbook of Culinary Fundamentals,* now in its third edition, as well as a co-author of *Webster's New World Dictionary of Culinary Arts.*

CREAM SCONES

Note: This dish appears in the chapter opening photograph.

Yield: 24 Scones, 1½ oz. (45 g) each   **Method:** Biscuit

All-purpose flour	1 lb.	480 g	100%
Granulated sugar	1.5 oz.	45 g	9%
Baking powder	0.4 oz. (1 Tbsp.)	12 g	2.5%
Baking soda	0.14 oz. (1 tsp.)	4 g	0.9%
Salt	0.2 oz. (1 tsp.)	5 g	1%
Unsalted butter, cold	4 oz.	120 g	25%
Egg yolks	1.3 oz. (2 yolks)	40 g	8%
Half-and-half	11 fl. oz.	330 ml	69%
Total weight:	2 lb. 2 oz.	1036 g	214%

1 Combine ingredients using the biscuit method.
2 Roll out the dough to a thickness of approximately ½ inch (1.2 centimeters). Cut as desired.
3 Bake at 400°F (200°C) for approximately 10 minutes.
4 Brush the tops with butter while hot.

VARIATIONS:

Add 4 ounces (120 grams/25%) of raisins, sultanas or currants to the dry ingredients.

Approximate values per scone: **Calories** 130, **Total fat** 6 g, **Saturated fat** 3.5 g, **Cholesterol** 35 mg, **Sodium** 160 mg, **Total carbohydrates** 17 g, **Protein** 3 g

RECIPE 6.6

SHORTCAKES

Yield: Approximately 48 Pieces,   **Method:** Biscuit
2¾ oz. (83 g) each

All-purpose flour	4 lb.	1920 g	100%
Baking powder	3.75 oz.	115 g	6%
Salt	0.4 oz. (2 tsp.)	12 g	0.6%
Granulated sugar	13 oz.	385 g	20%
Unsalted butter, cold	1 lb. 12 oz.	845 g	44%
Eggs	11.5 oz. (7 eggs)	350 g	18%
Milk	18 fl. oz.	540 ml	28%
Whole butter, melted	as needed	as needed	
Granulated sugar	as needed	as needed	
Total dough weight:	8 lb. 10 oz.	4167 g	216%

1 Combine ingredients using the biscuit method.
2 Cut into 3-inch (7.5-centimeter) circles and space 2 inches (5 centimeters) apart on a paper-lined sheet pan.
3 Bake at 400°F (200°C) until lightly browned, approximately 15 to 18 minutes.
4 Remove from the oven and brush the tops with melted butter, then sprinkle with granulated sugar.

Approximate values per shortcake: **Calories** 310, **Total fat** 15 g, **Saturated fat** 9 g, **Cholesterol** 65 mg, **Sodium** 250 mg, **Total carbohydrates** 38 g, **Protein** 5 g, **Vitamin A** 15%

BASIC BERRY MUFFINS

STOUFFER STANFORD COURT HOTEL, San Francisco, CA

Former Executive Chef Ercolino Crugnale

Yield: 60 Muffins, 2½ oz. (75 g) each   **Method:** Muffin

Eggs	13.3 oz. (8 eggs)	400 g	28%
Heavy cream	1 qt.	925 ml	66%
Lemon zest, finely grated	0.2 oz. (1 Tbsp.)	6 g	0.4%
Nutmeg, ground	0.02 oz. (¼ tsp.)	0.5 g	0.04%
Granulated sugar	1 lb. 4 oz.	590 g	42%
Baking powder	2.5 oz. (6 Tbsp.)	70 g	5%
Cake flour	3 lb.	1400 g	100%
Kosher salt	0.5 oz. (1 Tbsp.)	14 g	1%
Fresh berries or nuts*	1–1½ lb.	460–700 g	33–50%
Unsalted butter, melted	1 lb.	460 g	33%
Total weight:	9 lb. 4 oz.	4325 g	308%

1 Whisk the eggs, cream and zest together by hand.

2 Sift the dry ingredients together. Add the berries or nuts, tossing to coat them evenly with the flour mixture.

3 Add the dry ingredients to the egg mixture and stir until about two-thirds mixed. Add the melted butter and finish mixing.

4 Portion into greased muffin tins and bake at 375°F (190°C) for approximately 15 to 18 minutes.

*Blueberries, blackberries, raspberries, chopped pecans or walnuts may be used, as desired.

Approximate values per muffin: **Calories** 260, **Total fat** 13 g, **Saturated fat** 8 g, **Cholesterol** 70 mg, **Sodium** 135 mg, **Total carbohydrates** 31 g, **Protein** 3 g, **Vitamin A** 15%, **Claims**—low sodium

MORNING GLORY MUFFINS

Yield: 18 Large Muffins, 5 oz. (150 g) each   **Method:** Muffin

All-purpose flour	1 lb.	480 g	100%
Granulated sugar	18 oz.	540 g	112%
Baking soda	0.6 oz. (4 tsp.)	20 g	4%
Cinnamon, ground	0.3 oz. (4 tsp.)	10 g	2%
Carrots, grated	14 oz.	420 g	88%
Raisins	6 oz.	180 g	38%
Pecan pieces	4 oz.	120 g	25%
Coconut, shredded	4 oz.	120 g	25%
Apple, unpeeled, grated	6 oz.	180 g	38%
Eggs	10 oz. (6 eggs)	300 g	62%
Corn oil	10.5 oz.	315 g	65%
Vanilla extract	0.6 fl. oz. (4 tsp.)	20 ml	4%
Total weight:	5 lb. 10 oz.	2705 g	563%

1 Sift the dry ingredients together and set aside.

2 Combine the carrots, raisins, pecans, coconut and apple.

3 Whisk together the eggs, oil and vanilla.

4 Toss the carrot mixture into the dry ingredients. Then add the liquid ingredients, stirring just until combined.

5 Bake in well-greased muffin tins at 350°F (180°C) until done, approximately 25 minutes.

Approximate values per muffin: **Calories** 520, **Total fat** 27 g, **Saturated fat** 5 g, **Cholesterol** 70 mg, **Sodium** 310 mg, **Total carbohydrates** 63 g, **Protein** 6 g, **Vitamin A** 45%, **Claims**—good source of fiber

RECIPE 6.9

BASIC BRAN MUFFINS

Yield: 24 Muffins, 2 oz. (60 g) each   **Method:** Muffin

Toasted wheat bran	6 oz.	180 g	50%
All-purpose flour	12 oz.	360 g	100%
Granulated sugar	4 oz.	120 g	33%
Baking powder	0.6 oz. (4 tsp)	18 g	5%
Salt	0.2 oz. (1 tsp.)	6 g	1.6%
Milk	12 fl. oz.	360 ml	100%
Honey	3 oz.	90 g	25%
Molasses	3 oz.	90 g	25%
Eggs	3.3 oz. (2 eggs)	100 g	27%
Vanilla extract	0.15 fl. oz. (1 tsp.)	5 ml	1.2%
Unsalted butter, melted	4 oz.	120 g	33%
Total weight:	4 lb.	1449 g	400%

1 Combine all ingredients using the muffin method.

2 Scoop into greased or paper-lined muffin tins. Bake at 350°F (180°C) until lightly brown and firm, approximately 20 minutes.

VARIATIONS:

Up to 6 ounces (180 grams/50%) of raisins or chopped nuts may be added to the batter if desired.

Approximate values per muffin: **Calories** 170, **Total fat** 5 g, **Saturated fat** 2.5 g, **Cholesterol** 30 mg, **Sodium** 110 mg, **Total carbohydrates** 26 g, **Protein** 4 g, **Claims**—low sodium; good source of fiber

RECIPE 6.10

PUMPKIN MUFFINS

Yield: Approximately 48 Muffins,   **Method:** Muffin
$2^3/_4$ oz. (83 g) each

All-purpose flour	1 lb. 4 oz.	600 g	100%
Baking soda	0.6 oz. (4 tsp.)	18 g	3%
Salt	0.4 oz. (2 tsp.)	12 g	2%
Baking powder	0.3 oz. (2 tsp.)	9 g	1.5%
Nutmeg	0.14 oz. (2 tsp.)	4 g	0.7%
Allspice	0.14 oz. (2 tsp.)	4 g	0.7%
Cinnamon	0.14 oz. (2 tsp.)	4 g	0.7%
Cloves, ground	0.07 oz. (1 tsp.)	2 g	0.3%
Granulated sugar	2 lb. 10 oz.	1260 g	210%
Vegetable oil	8 oz.	240 g	40%
Eggs, beaten	13.3 oz. (8 eggs)	400 g	66%
Pumpkin purée	2 lb.	960 g	160%
Orange juice	12 fl. oz.	360 ml	60%
Total weight:	8 lb. 1 oz.	3873 g	645%

1 Sift the flour, baking soda, salt, baking powder and spices together twice. Set aside.

2 Cream the sugar and oil together until fluffy. Add the eggs and pumpkin to the creamed mixture. Fold in the dry ingredients, being careful not to overmix. Stir in the orange juice.

3 Scoop into well-greased muffin pans.

4 Bake at 350°F (180°C) until brown and firm, approximately 20 to 25 minutes. Muffins should still be moist and steamy inside.

Approximate values per muffin: **Calories** 200, **Total fat** 6 g, **Saturated fat** 1 g, **Cholesterol** 35 mg, **Sodium** 230 mg, **Total carbohydrates** 36 g, **Protein** 3 g, **Vitamin A** 80%

LEMON POPPY SEED MUFFINS

Yield: 48 Muffins, 2¾ oz. (83 g) each   **Method:** Creaming

Pastry flour	2 lb.	960 g	80%
Bread flour	8 oz.	240 g	20%
Baking soda	0.14 oz. (1 tsp.)	4 g	0.3%
Baking powder	0.14 oz. (1 tsp.)	4 g	0.3%
Poppy seeds	3 oz.	90 g	7.5%
Unsalted butter, room temperature	1 lb.	480 g	40%
Granulated sugar	1 lb. 10 oz.	780 g	65%
Glucose or honey	4 oz.	120 g	10%
Olive oil	4 fl. oz.	120 ml	10%
Eggs	20 oz. (12 eggs)	600 g	50%
Salt	0.4 oz. (2 tsp.)	12 g	1%
Vanilla extract	1 fl. oz.	30 ml	2.5%
Lemon zest, grated	0.5 oz.	15 g	1.25%
Sour cream	1 lb.	480 g	40%
Total weight:	8 lb. 3 oz.	3935 g	328%

1 Sift together the flours, baking soda and baking powder. Stir in the poppy seeds and set aside.

2 Using a mixer fitted with the paddle attachment, cream the butter until lump-free and fluffy. Add the sugar, glucose or honey and olive oil and cream until light.

3 Gradually add the eggs followed by the salt, vanilla, lemon zest and sour cream. Then stir in the sifted dry ingredients.

4 Scale the muffins into 5-ounce (150-gram) portions using a scale or #6 scoop and place in greased or paper-lined muffin tins.

5 Bake at 425°F (220°C) until the centers of the muffins bounce back when lightly pressed, approximately 15 to 18 minutes.

Approximate values per muffin: **Calories** 580, **Total fat** 29 g, **Saturated fat** 14 g, **Cholesterol** 155 mg, **Sodium** 310 mg, **Total carbohydrates** 72 g, **Protein** 9 g, **Vitamin A** 15%, **Vitamin C** 15%

ZUCCHINI BREAD

Yield: 2 Loaves, 9 in. × 5 in. (24 cm × 12 cm)   **Method:** Muffin

Whole eggs	5 oz. (3 eggs)	150 g	36%
Corn oil	7 oz.	210 g	50%
Granulated sugar	1 lb. 2 oz.	540 g	128%
Vanilla extract	0.15 fl. oz. (1 tsp.)	5 ml	1.1%
Cinnamon, ground	0.14 oz. (2 tsp.)	4 g	1%
Salt	0.2 oz. (1 tsp.)	6 g	1.4%
Baking soda	0.14 oz. (1 tsp.)	4 g	1%
Baking powder	0.07 oz. (½ tsp.)	2 g	0.5%
All-purpose flour	14 oz.	420 g	100%
Zucchini, coarsely grated	11 oz.	330 g	78%
Pecans, chopped	4 oz.	120 g	28%
Total weight:	3 lb. 11 oz.	1791 g	425%

1 Combine all ingredients using the muffin method.

2 Bake in two greased loaf pans at 350°F (180°C), approximately 1 hour.

Approximate values per 2-oz. (60-g) serving: **Calories** 260, **Total fat** 16 g, **Saturated fat** 2 g, **Cholesterol** 30 mg, **Sodium** 190 mg, **Total carbohydrates** 27 g, **Protein** 2 g

RECIPE 6.13

IRISH SODA BREAD

Yield: 1 Round Loaf, 8 in. (20 cm) **Method:** Muffin

Currants	2 oz.	60 g	16%
Irish whiskey	1.5 fl. oz.	45 ml	12.5%
All-purpose flour, sifted	12 oz.	360 g	100%
Salt	0.2 oz. (1 tsp.)	6 g	1.6%
Baking powder	0.2 oz. (1 ½ tsp.)	6 g	1.6%
Baking soda	0.14 oz. (1 tsp.)	4 g	1%
Brown sugar	0.5 oz. (1 Tbsp.)	14 g	4%
Low-fat buttermilk	1 pt.	480 ml	133%
Total weight:	2 lb.	975 g	269%

1 Soak the currants in the whiskey until plump, at least 1 hour.
2 Sift the dry ingredients together. Stir in the currants and whiskey.
3 Stir in the buttermilk, making a stiff batter.
4 Spread the batter in a greased 8-inch (20-centimeter) round cake pan. Bake at 350°F (180°C) until well browned and firm, approximately 45 minutes.

Approximate values per 3-oz. (90-g) serving: **Calories** 150, **Total fat** 1 g, **Saturated fat** 0 g, **Cholesterol** 0 mg, **Sodium** 480 mg, **Total carbohydrates** 31 g, **Protein** 5 g, **Calcium** 10%, **Claims**—low fat; no cholesterol; no saturated fat

RECIPE 6.14

BASIC CORN MUFFINS

Yield: 30 Muffins, 2½ oz. (75 g) each **Method:** Muffin

Yellow cornmeal	12 oz.	360 g	50%
All-purpose flour	12 oz.	360 g	50%
Granulated sugar	10 oz.	300 g	42%
Baking powder	0.4 oz. (1 Tbsp.)	12 g	1.6%
Baking soda	0.14 oz. (1 tsp.)	4 g	0.6%
Salt	0.15 oz. (¾ tsp.)	4 g	0.6%
Buttermilk	24 fl. oz.	720 ml	100%
Eggs	10 oz. (6 eggs)	300 g	42%
Unsalted butter, melted	6 oz.	180 g	25%
Total weight:	4 lb. 10 oz.	2240 g	311%

1 Combine ingredients using the muffin method.
2 Portion into greased muffin tins, filling two-thirds full.
3 Bake at 375°F (190°C) until done, approximately 20 to 25 minutes.

VARIATION:
Southern-Style Cornbread—Omit the sugar. Pour the batter into cast-iron skillets or molds that are preheated and well greased with shortening or bacon fat. Bake at 425°F (220°C) until golden.

Approximate values per muffin: **Calories** 180, **Total fat** 6 g, **Saturated fat** 3.5 g, **Cholesterol** 55 mg, **Sodium** 140 mg, **Total carbohydrates** 28 g, **Protein** 4 g

BLUE CORN MUFFINS

Yield: Approximately 60 Muffins,
2½ oz. (75 g) each

Method: Creaming

All-purpose shortening	1 lb.	480 g	50%
Granulated sugar	1 lb. 8 oz.	720 g	75%
Blue cornmeal	1 lb.	480 g	50%
Whole eggs	1 lb. (10 eggs)	480 g	50%
All-purpose flour	2 lb.	960 g	100%
Baking powder	1.25 oz.	40 g	4%
Salt	1.5 oz.	45 g	5%
Vanilla extract	0.5 fl. oz.	15 ml	1.5%
Honey	1 lb. 2 oz.	540 g	56%
Buttermilk	1 qt.	960 ml	100%
Total weight:	9 lb. 13 oz.	4720 g	491%

1 Using a mixer fitted with the paddle attachment, cream the shortening, sugar and cornmeal until light and fluffy. Add the eggs. Mix on low speed for 1 minute.

2 Sift the remaining dry ingredients together.

3 Stir the vanilla and honey into the buttermilk.

4 Add the dry ingredients and buttermilk mixture, alternately, to the creamed mixture. Mix on low speed for 2 minutes, scraping down the bowl as necessary.

5 Portion into well-greased muffin pans. Bake at 325°F (160°C) until done, approximately 15 minutes.

Note: Blue cornmeal is derived from variegated Indian corn. Its natural blue-gray color is a result of a high lysine content. Blue corn has a stronger flavor than white or yellow corn and is popular in southwestern cuisine.

Approximate values per muffin: **Calories** 230, **Total fat** 9 g, **Saturated fat** 2.5 g, **Cholesterol** 25 mg, **Sodium** 310 mg, **Total carbohydrates** 35 g, **Protein** 4 g

RECIPE 6.16

HUSH PUPPIES (DEEP-FRIED CORNBREAD)

Yield: 60 Pieces, 2 in. (5 cm) each   **Method:** Muffin

Yellow cornmeal	1 lb.	480 g	66%
All-purpose flour	8 oz.	240 g	34%
Baking powder	0.4 oz. (1 Tbsp.)	12 g	1.6%
Salt	0.6 oz. (1 Tbsp.)	18 g	2.5%
Black pepper	0.2 oz. (1 Tbsp.)	6 g	0.8%
Granulated sugar	2 oz.	60 g	8%
Onions, minced	8 oz.	240 g	34%
Eggs	6.75 oz. (4 eggs)	200 g	28%
Milk	1 pt.	480 ml	66%
Total weight:	3 lb. 10 oz.	1736 g	241%

1 Combine all ingredients using the muffin method.

2 Drop small scoops (using a #60 or #70 portion scoop) into deep fat at 375°F (190°C), allowing the batter to swim freely in the fat. Deep-fry until golden brown.

3 Remove from the fat and drain. Serve immediately.

Approximate values per piece: **Calories** 70, **Total fat** 3 g, **Saturated fat** 1 g, **Cholesterol** 5 mg, **Sodium** 120 mg, **Total carbohydrates** 10 g, **Protein** 1 g

1 Scooping the hush puppy batter into the deep-fat fryer.

2 Draining the cooked hush puppies.

LEMON TEA BREAD

Yield: 12 Muffins, 2½ oz. (75 g) each, or 1 Loaf   **Method:** Creaming

Unsalted butter, softened	3 oz.	90 g	50%
Granulated sugar	10 oz.	300 g	166%
Eggs	3.3 oz. (2 eggs)	100 g	55%
Milk	4 fl. oz.	120 ml	66%
All-purpose flour	6 oz.	180 g	100%
Baking powder	0.14 oz. (1 tsp.)	4 g	2.3%
Salt	0.1 oz. (½ tsp.)	3 g	1.6%
Lemon zest, grated	0.2 oz. (1 Tbsp.)	6 g	3%
Lemon juice	4 fl. oz.	120 ml	66%
Total weight:	1 lb. 14 oz.	923 g	510%

1 Cream the butter with 7 ounces (210 grams) of the sugar. Add the eggs and milk. Mix well.

2 Sift the flour, baking powder and salt together and add to the butter mixture. Fold in the lemon zest. Portion into lightly greased pans.

3 Bake at 350° (180°C) until a tester comes out clean, approximately 35 to 40 minutes for a large loaf or 12 to 15 minutes for muffins. Remove the bread from the pan(s) and place on a cooling rack.

4 Combine the remaining 3 ounces (90 grams) of sugar with the lemon juice. Heat until the sugar dissolves and the mixture is hot. Slowly pour or brush the glaze over the hot bread.

Approximate values per serving: **Calories** 220, **Total fat** 7 g, **Saturated fat** 4 g, **Cholesterol** 50 mg, **Sodium** 115 mg, **Total carbohydrates** 36 g, **Protein** 3 g

RECIPE 6.18

GINGERBREAD

Yield: 3 Loaves, 4 in. × 11 in. (10 cm × 26 cm)   **Method:** Creaming

Unsalted butter	10 oz.	300 g	38%
Brown sugar	12 oz.	360 g	46%
Eggs	6.75 oz. (4 eggs)	195 g	25%
Salt	0.4 oz. (2 tsp.)	12 g	1.5%
Molasses	12 oz.	360 g	46%
Sour cream	1 lb. 4 oz.	600 g	77%
Bread flour	1 lb. 10 oz.	780 g	100%
Baking powder	0.3 oz. (2 tsp.)	8 g	1%
Baking soda	0.3 oz. (2 tsp.)	8 g	1%
Cinnamon	0.4 oz. (2 Tbsp.)	12 g	1.5%
Ginger	0.4 oz. (2 Tbsp.)	12 g	1.5%
Cloves	0.1 oz. (1½ tsp.)	3 g	0.4%
Total weight:	5 lb. 8 oz.	2650 g	339%

1 Cream the butter in a mixer fitted with the paddle attachment. Add the brown sugar and cream to blend. Add the eggs one at a time, then stir in the salt, molasses and sour cream.

2 Sift the remaining ingredients together and then add to the creamed mixture.

3 Bake in three buttered and floured loaf pans at 375°F (190°F) until the cake bounces back when lightly pressed, approximately 45 minutes.

Approximate values per ¹/₁₂-loaf serving: **Calories** 240, **Total fat** 11 g, **Saturated fat** 6 g, **Cholesterol** 50 mg, **Sodium** 250 mg, **Total carbohydrates** 32 g, **Protein** 4 g, **Iron** 10%

RECIPE 6.19

SOUR CREAM COFFEECAKE

Yield: 1 Tube Cake, 10 in. (25 cm)   **Method:** Creaming

Filling:			
All-purpose flour	0.4 oz. (1½ Tbsp.)	12 g	5.7%
Cinnamon, ground	0.2 oz. (1 Tbsp.)	6 g	2.8%
Brown sugar	6 oz.	180 g	86%
Pecans, chopped	4 oz.	120 g	57%
Unsalted butter, melted	1 oz.	30 g	14%
Cake:			
Unsalted butter	4 oz.	120 g	57%
Granulated sugar	8 oz.	240 g	114%
Eggs	3.3 oz. (2 eggs)	100 g	47%
Sour cream	8 oz.	240 g	114%
Cake flour, sifted	7 oz.	210 g	100%
Salt	0.05 oz. (¼ tsp.)	1 g	0.7%
Baking powder	0.14 oz. (1 tsp.)	4 g	2%
Baking soda	0.14 oz. (1 tsp.)	4 g	2%
Vanilla extract	0.15 fl. oz. (1 tsp.)	5 ml	2.1%
Total weight:	2 lb. 10 oz.	1272 g	604%

1 To make the filling, blend all the filling ingredients together in a small bowl. Set aside.

2 To make the cake batter, cream the butter and sugar. Add the eggs one at a time, beating well after each addition. Add the sour cream. Stir until smooth.

3 Sift the sifted flour, salt, baking powder and baking soda together twice. Stir into the batter. Stir in the vanilla.

4 Spoon half of the batter into a greased tube pan. Top with half of the filling. Cover the filling with the remaining batter and top with the remaining filling. Bake at 350°F (180°C) for approximately 35 minutes.

Approximate values per ¹/₁₆-cake serving: **Calories** 240, **Total fat** 13 g, **Saturated fat** 6 g, **Cholesterol** 40 mg, **Sodium** 130 mg, **Total carbohydrates** 29 g, **Protein** 2 g

JAMAICAN SPICED BANANA BREAD   RECIPE 6.20

Yield: 3 Loaves, 8½ oz. (255 g) each   **Method:** Creaming

Unsalted butter, room temperature	2 oz.	60 g	30%
Granulated sugar	2 oz.	60 g	30%
Brown sugar	2.5 oz.	70 g	36%
Eggs	1.6 oz. (1 egg)	45 g	23%
Ripe banana	6.5 oz.	180 g	89%
Cake flour	3.5 oz.	100 g	50%
Pastry flour	3.5 oz.	100 g	50%
Baking powder	0.07 oz. (½ tsp.)	2.5 g	1.2%
Baking soda	0.07 oz. (½ tsp.)	2.5 g	1.2%
Salt	0.05 oz. (¼ tsp.)	1 g	1%
Ground cinnamon	0.04 oz. (½ tsp.)	1 g	0.5%
Buttermilk	2 fl. oz.	55 ml	28%
Walnuts, chopped	1.75 oz.	50 g	24%
Total weight:	1 lb. 9 oz.	727 g	363%

1 Cream the butter and both sugars in a mixer fitted with the paddle attachment until light, pale and fluffy. Add the egg, then mash the banana and add to the mixture.

2 Sift the flours with the baking powder, baking soda, salt and cinnamon. Add to the banana mixture, alternating with the buttermilk. Stir in the walnuts.

3 Divide the batter between three prepared 5 × 4 × 1½-inch (12.5 × 10 × 3.7-centimeter) loaf pans and bake at 375°F (190°C) until light brown, approximately 25 to 30 minutes.

VARIATION:

Chocolate Chip Banana Cake—Add 4 ounces (115 grams/57%) chocolate chips to the batter along with the walnuts.

Approximate values per ¼-cake serving: **Calories** 180, **Total fat** 7 g, **Saturated fat** 3 g, **Cholesterol** 30 mg, **Sodium** 130 mg, **Total carbohydrates** 27 g, **Protein** 3 g

GRIDDLECAKES

Pancakes and waffles are types of griddlecakes or griddle breads. They are usually leavened with baking soda or baking powder and are quickly cooked on a very hot griddle or waffle iron using very little fat. Griddlecakes should be more than just an excuse for eating butter and maple syrup, however. They should have a rich flavor and a light, tender, moist interior.

Pancake and waffle batters may be flavored with tangy buckwheat flour, fruits, whole grains or nuts. Both pancakes and waffles are usually served with plain or flavored butter and fruit compote or syrup. Waffles must be cooked in a special waffle iron, which gives the cakes a distinctive gridlike pattern and a crisp texture. Electric waffle irons are available with square, round and even heart-shaped grids. The grids should be seasoned well, then never washed. (Follow the manufacturer's directions for seasoning.) Belgian waffles are especially light and crisp because of the incorporation of whipped egg whites and/or yeast. They are often made in a waffle iron with extra deep grids and are served for breakfast or as a dessert, topped with fresh fruit, whipped cream or ice cream.

▶ PROCEDURE FOR MAKING PANCAKES

1 Prepare the batter.

2 Heat a flat griddle or large sauté pan over moderately high heat. Add clarified butter.

3 Portion the pancake batter onto the hot griddle using a portion scoop, ladle or adjustable batter dispenser. Pour the portioned batter in one spot; it should spread into an even circle. Drop the batter so that no two pancakes will touch after the batter spreads.

4 Cook until bubbles appear on the surface and the bottom of the cake is set and golden brown. Flip the pancake using an offset spatula.

5 Cook the pancake until the second side is golden brown. Avoid flipping the pancake more than once as this causes it to deflate.

RECIPE 6.21

BUTTERMILK PANCAKES

Yield: 24 Pancakes, 2 oz. (60 g) each

Flour	1 lb.	480 g	100%
Granulated sugar	0.9 oz. (2 Tbsp.)	28 g	6%
Baking powder	0.4 oz. (1 Tbsp.)	12 g	2.5%
Salt	0.3 oz. (1 ½ tsp.)	9 g	2%
Buttermilk	1 ½ pt.	720 ml	150%
Unsalted butter, melted	2 oz.	60 g	12.5%
Eggs, beaten	5 oz. (3 eggs)	150 g	31%
Clarified butter	as needed	as needed	
Total batter weight:	3 lb.	1459 g	304%

1 Sift the flour, sugar, baking powder and salt together.

2 Combine the buttermilk, melted butter and eggs and add them to the dry ingredients. Mix just until the ingredients are combined.

3 If the griddle is not well seasoned, coat it lightly with clarified butter. Once its temperature reaches 375°F (190°C), drop the batter onto it in 2-fluid-ounce (60-milliliter) portions using a ladle, portion scoop or batter portioner.

4 When bubbles appear on the pancake's surface and the bottom is browned, flip the pancake to finish cooking.

VARIATIONS:

Blueberry Pancakes—Gently stir 1 pound (480 grams/100%) of fresh or frozen blueberries into the batter. If using frozen berries, drain them thoroughly, then pat dry with paper towels before adding them to the batter. Serve with blueberry syrup or compote.

Apple-Pecan Pancakes—Gently fold 4 ounces (120 grams/25%) of chopped cooked apples, 0.02 ounces (¼ teaspoon/0.5 gram/0.01%) of cinnamon and 1 ounce (30 grams/6.2%) of finely chopped pecans into the batter.

Approximate values per pancake: **Calories** 120, **Total fat** 4 g, **Saturated fat** 2.5 g, **Cholesterol** 35 mg, **Sodium** 250 mg, **Total carbohydrates** 17 g, **Protein** 4 g

RECIPE 6.22

DUTCH BABY PANCAKES

Dutch baby pancakes are a cross between a soufflé, a crêpe and a pancake. Because only the edges rise during baking, the center can be filled with sautéed apples, pears or peaches just before service. The plain pancake is also delicious sprinkled with powdered sugar and fresh lemon juice.

Yield: 1 Pancake, 10 in. (25 cm)

Flour	5 oz.	150 g	100%
Milk	8 fl. oz.	240 ml	160%
Eggs	5 oz. (3 eggs)	150 g	100%
Granulated sugar	1.5 oz.	45 g	30%
Salt	0.05 oz. (¼ tsp.)	1.5 g	1%
Vanilla extract	0.15 fl. oz. (1 tsp.)	5 ml	3%
Whole butter	0.5 oz.	15 g	10%
Powdered sugar	as needed	as needed	
Fresh lemon juice	0.5 fl. oz.	15 ml	10%
Total batter weight:	1 lb. 4 oz.	621 g	414%

1 Place the flour in a large mixing bowl. In a separate container blend the milk, eggs, granulated sugar, salt and vanilla. Whisk the egg mixture into the flour, beating until well blended and smooth.

2 Place the butter in a heavy 10-inch (25-centimeter) skillet and put the skillet into a hot oven. When the pan is hot and the butter melted but not burned, remove the pan from the oven and immediately pour in the batter. Return the pan to a 425°F (220°C) oven and bake until puffed, dry and lightly browned, approximately 25 minutes.

3 Dust with powdered sugar and sprinkle with lemon juice and serve immediately.

Approximate values per ¼-pancake serving: **Calories** 290, **Total fat** 9 g, **Saturated fat** 4.5 g, **Cholesterol** 175 mg, **Sodium** 220 mg, **Total carbohydrates** 40 g, **Protein** 10 g, **Calcium** 10%, **Iron** 10%

WAFFLES

RECIPE 6.23

Yield: 20 Waffles, 2¾ oz. (83 g) each

All-purpose flour	18 oz.	540 g	100%
Salt	0.4 oz. (2 tsp.)	12 g	2.2%
Baking powder	1.25 oz. (3 Tbsp.)	38 g	7%
Granulated sugar	2 oz.	60 g	11%
Eggs	6.75 oz. (4 eggs)	200 g	37%
Milk, warm	24 fl. oz.	720 ml	133%
Unsalted butter, melted	5 oz.	150 g	28%
Vanilla extract	0.3 fl. oz. (2 tsp.)	9 ml	1.6%
Total batter weight:	3 lb. 9 oz.	1729 g	319%

1 Mix the dry ingredients together in a large bowl.

2 Whisk the eggs together in a separate bowl; add the milk, butter and vanilla.

3 Pour the liquid mixture into the dry ingredients, stirring to blend. Keep refrigerated until ready to use. Batter may be made up to one day in advance.

4 Cook in a preheated waffle iron according to the manufacturer's directions. Serve waffles immediately with your choice of toppings.

VARIATION:

Pecan Waffles–Sprinkle 0.3 ounces (1 Tablespoon/9 grams/1.6%) of chopped pecans over the batter as soon as it is poured onto the waffle iron. Substitute 0.15 fluid ounces (1 teaspoon/5 millileters/0.8%) of pecan flavoring for the vanilla extract if desired.

Approximate values per waffle: **Calories** 190, **Total fat** 8 g, **Saturated fat** 4.5 g, **Cholesterol** 65 mg, **Sodium** 480 mg, **Total carbohydrates** 25 g, **Protein** 5 g, **Calcium** 20%

BREAD DEALS WITH LIVING THINGS, WITH GIVING LIFE, WITH GROWTH, WITH THE SEED, THE GRAIN THAT NURTURES. IT IS NOT COINCIDENCE THAT WE SAY BREAD IS THE STAFF OF LIFE.

—Lionel Poilâne, France's most celebrated baker (1946–2002)

7

YEAST BREADS

KENDALL COLLEGE SCHOOL OF CULINARY ARTS, Evanston, IL
Chef Klaus Tenbergen

AFTER STUDYING THIS CHAPTER, YOU WILL BE ABLE TO:

▶ select and use yeast properly

▶ perform the 10 steps involved in yeast bread production

▶ mix yeast doughs using the straight dough method and the sponge method

▶ mix yeast dough using preferments and sourdough techniques

▶ prepare bagels, flatbreads and other specialty breads

Bread making is an art that dates back to ancient times. Over the centuries, bakers have learned to manipulate the basic ingredients—flour, water, salt and leavening—to produce a vast variety of breads. Thin-crusted baguettes, tender Parker House rolls, crisp flatbreads and chewy bagels derive from careful selection and handling of the same key ingredients. A renewed interest in the traditional craft of baking has seen many new bread bakeries open in recent years. Customers are demanding and more restaurants are servings exciting bread assortments to their guest with each meal. Although few baked goods intimidate novice bakers as much as yeast breads, few baked goods are actually as forgiving to prepare. By mastering a few basic procedures and techniques, restaurants and bakeshops can offer their customers delicious, fresh yeast products.

Yeast breads can be divided into two major categories: lean doughs and rich doughs. Lean doughs, such as those used for crusty French and Italian breads, contain little or no sugar or fat. Traditional sourdough and rye breads are lean doughs that require special handling to bring out their unique flavor. Rich doughs, such as brioche and challah, contain significantly more sugar and fat than lean doughs. Rich dough bakes into softer products with a tender crust and interior crumb and are discussed in Chapter 8, Enriched Yeast Doughs. A specific type of rich, flaky dough is made by incorporating layers of fat and flour and is covered in Chapter 12, Laminated Doughs.

This chapter covers in detail the basic production techniques for making lean and sourdough bread products. The principles discussed in this chapter apply to working with all types of yeast-raised products, however. Rereading the discussion of the function of ingredients found in Chapter 4, Bakeshop Ingredients, is recommended before beginning this chapter.

▶ YEAST

Yeast is a living organism: a one-celled fungus. Various strains of yeast are present virtually everywhere. Yeast feeds on carbohydrates present in the starches and sugars in bread dough, converting them to carbon dioxide and ethanol, an alcohol, in an organic process known as **fermentation:**

Yeast + Carbohydrates = Alcohol + Carbon Dioxide

When yeast releases carbon dioxide gas during bread making, the gas becomes trapped in the dough's gluten network. (See Chapter 4, Bakeshop Ingre-

▶ **fermentation** the process by which yeast converts sugar into alcohol and carbon dioxide; it also refers to the time that yeast dough is left to rise—that is, the time it takes for carbon dioxide gas cells to form and become trapped in the gluten network

THE RISE OF YEAST BREADS

How and when the first yeast-leavened breads came into being, no one knows. Perhaps some wild yeasts—the world is full of them—drifted into a dough as it awaited baking. Perhaps some ancient baker substituted fermented ale or beer for water one day. In any case, the resulting bread was different, lighter and more appetizing.

Based on models, images and writings found in excavated tombs, historians are fairly certain that the ancient Egyptians saved a bit of fermented dough from one day's baking to add to the next day's. This use of sourdough starter continues today, enjoying widespread popularity.

Other cultures developed their own leavening methods. The Greeks and Romans prepared a wheat porridge with wine, which caused their doughs to ferment. The Gauls and Iberians added the foamy head from ale to their doughs. Both methods resulted in lighter breads that retained their fresh textures longer. Since ancient times, bread baking has been one of the first household tasks readily turned over to professionals. The first cooks to work outside homes during the Greek and Roman empires were bakers. The bakery trade flourished during the Middle Ages, with a wide variety of breads being produced. Yeast-leavened breads remained the exception, not the norm, until well into the

17th century, however. The first real collection of bread recipes is found in Nicolas Bonnefon's *Les Délices de la campagne,* published in 1654. Bonnefon's instructions, meant for those dissatisfied with commercial products of the time, included the use of beer yeast. By the end of the 17th century, published works included recipes for breads leavened with sourdough starter and the yeasts used in breweries.

Louis Pasteur finally identified yeast as a living organism in 1857. Soon after, a process for distilling or manufacturing baker's yeast was developed. By 1868, commercial baking yeast was available in stores.

Table 7.1	**TEMPERATURE FOR YEAST DEVELOPMENT**	
TEMPERATURE		**YEAST DEVELOPMENT**
34°F	(2°C)	Inactive
60°F–70°F	(16°C–21°C)	Slow action
75°F–95°F	(24°C–35°C)	Best temperature for yeast activity
85°F–100°F	(29°C–38°C)	Best water temperature for hydrating instant yeast
100°F–110°F	(38°C–43°C)	Best water temperature for hydrating active dry yeast
138°F	(59°C)	Yeast dies

dients, page 57.) The trapped gas leavens the bread, providing the desired rise and texture. The small amount of alcohol produced by fermentation evaporates during baking.

As with most living things, yeast is very sensitive to temperature and moisture. It prefers temperatures between 75°F and 95°F (24°C and 35°C). At temperatures below 34°F (2°C), it becomes dormant; above 138°F (59°C), it dies. See Table 7.1. Moisture activates the yeast cells, helping the yeast convert carbohydrates in the dough into food.

Salt is used in bread making because it conditions gluten, making it stronger and more elastic. Salt also affects yeast fermentation. Because salt inhibits the growth of yeast, it helps control the dough's rise. Too little salt and not only will the bread taste bland, it will rise too rapidly. Too much salt, however, and the yeast will be destroyed. By learning to control the amount of food for the yeast and the temperatures of fermentation, you can learn to control the texture and flavor of yeast-leavened products.

TYPES OF YEAST

Baker's yeast, *Saccharomyces cerevisiae,* is available in three forms: compressed, active dry and instant. (Do not be confused by a product called brewer's yeast; it is a nutritional supplement with no leavening ability.)

Compressed Yeast

Dry Yeast

COMPRESSED YEAST

Compressed yeast is a mixture of yeast and starch with a moisture content of approximately 70 percent. Also referred to as fresh yeast, compressed yeast must be kept refrigerated. It should be creamy white and crumbly with a fresh, yeasty smell. Do not use compressed yeast that has developed a sour odor, brown color or slimy film. Compressed yeast is softened in twice its weight in warm water at 100°F (38°C) before being added to bread dough. Some bakers even add compressed yeast directly to the dry mix.

Compressed yeast is available in 1-pound (450-gram) blocks. Under proper storage conditions, compressed yeast has a shelf life of 2 to 3 weeks. When fresh, it may be frozen and stored for one month. Frozen compressed yeast will lose about 5 percent of its activity when thawed.

ACTIVE DRY YEAST

Active dry yeast differs from compressed yeast in that virtually all the moisture has been removed by hot air. The absence of moisture renders the organism dormant and allows the yeast to be stored without refrigeration for several months. When used in preparing doughs, dry yeast is generally rehydrated in a lukewarm (approximately 110°F [43°C]) liquid before being added to the other ingredients.

Dry yeast is available in ¼-ounce (7-gram) packages and 1- or 2.2-pound (500-gram or 1-kilogram) vacuum-sealed bags. It should be stored in a cool, dry place and refrigerated after opening.

INSTANT DRY YEAST

Instant dry yeast has gained popularity because of its ease of use; it is added directly to the dry ingredients in a bread formula without rehydrating. The water in the formula activates it. Like all yeasts, instant dry yeast is a living organism and will be destroyed at temperatures above 138°F (59°C). (See Table 7.1.) While instant yeast can be added to flour without hydration, some bakers still prefer to hydrate instant yeast before using it in certain types of formulas. When doughs are mixed briefly or are very firm, such as bagel or croissant dough, instant dry yeast may not fully dissolve during mixing. In such cases the yeast is moistened in four to five times its weight of water. Deduct this amount of water from the total water called for in the formula.

SUBSTITUTING YEASTS

The flavors of dry and compressed yeasts are virtually indistinguishable, but dry yeasts are at least twice as strong. Because too much yeast can ruin bread, always remember to reduce the specified weight for compressed yeast when substituting dry yeast or active dry yeast in a formula. Likewise, if a formula specifies dry or active dry yeast, increase the quantity specified when substituting compressed yeast. Any type of yeast may be used in the formulas in this book. Use the formulas in Table 7.2 to convert one type of yeast to another.

NATURAL YEAST LEAVENERS—SOURDOUGH STARTER

Prior to commercial yeast production, bakers relied on natural yeast leaveners, also called starters, to make bread rise. Early starters were simple mixtures of

Table 7.2   YEAST SUBSTITUTIONS

Use these formulas to convert from one type of yeast to another	Compressed (fresh) yeast	×	0.5	=	Active dry yeast
	Compressed (fresh) yeast	×	0.33	=	Instant yeast
	Active dry yeast	×	2	=	Compressed (fresh) yeast
	Active dry yeast	×	0.75	=	Instant yeast
	Instant yeast	×	3	=	Compressed (fresh) yeast
	Instant yeast	×	1.33	=	Active dry yeast

flour and a liquid (water, potato broth, milk) left to capture wild yeasts and beneficial acid-producing bacteria from the environment. Once the mixture fermented, it was used to leaven bread and contribute a distinctive flavor, from mild and buttery to sharp and tangy, to the finished product. Only a portion of the starter was used at a time. The rest was kept for later use, replenished periodically with additional flour and liquid so that the yeast activity could continue. Over time and in different regions, bakers developed numerous strategies for using natural yeast starters to create different flavors and textures in bread.

The making of a natural starter begins by combining equal parts flour and water into a wet mixture. A small amount of grapes, apple peels or orange rinds may be added to seed the mixture with natural yeast spores. Or some prepared yeast may be used to get the mixture going. After several hours bubbles will appear on the surface, indicating that yeast activity has begun. Within 12 to 24 hours, yeast activity should be noticeable and the mixture will double or triple in volume. Over time, the starter will develop a mellow flavor with some noticeable acidity.

To maintain a natural starter, frequently replenish or feed it with more flour and water. When making bread in a production bakery, feed the starter as often as every eight hours to keep the yeast active. The amount of flour and water necessary to feed a starter varies, but never add more flour and water than would double the mixture at one time. Yeast is more active in a wet starter than a dry one; add more flour when the starter will not be used for an extended period of time. More water can be added to activate the starter on the day when it will be used.

Starter activity at three stages: just mixed (lower right), 3 hours after mixing (left) and 12 hours later (upper right).

SIMPLE SOURDOUGH STARTER
RECIPE 7.1

Yield: 3 lb. 12 oz. (1850 g)

Active dry yeast	0.15 oz. (1 tsp.)	5 g	0.5%
Water, warm	4 fl. oz.	120 ml	12%
Water, room temperature	24 fl. oz.	720 ml	75%
All-purpose flour	2 lb.	960 g	100%
Total weight:	3 lb. 12 oz.	1805 g	187%

1 Combine the yeast and warm water. Let stand until foamy, approximately 10 minutes.

2 Stir in the room-temperature water, then add the flour, 2 ounces (60 grams) at a time.

3 Blend by hand or with the paddle attachment of an electric mixer on low speed 2 minutes.

4 Place the starter in a warmed bowl and cover with plastic wrap. Let stand at room temperature 8 to 12 hours. The starter should triple in volume but still be wet and sticky. Refrigerate until ready to use.

5 Each time a portion of the starter is used, it must be replenished and activated. Remove the starter from the refrigerator several hours before using. Replenish the starter to activate the yeast cells, then use. To replenish the starter, stir in equal amounts by volume of flour and warm water. Then allow the mixture to ferment at room temperature for several hours or overnight before using again or refrigerating.

Approximate values per fluid ounce (30 ml): **Calories** 100, **Total fat** 0 g, **Saturated fat** 0 g, **Cholesterol** 0 mg, **Sodium** 0 mg, **Total carbohydrates** 22 g, **Protein** 3 g

Note: If liquid rises to the top of the starter, it can be drained off or stirred back into the mixture. If the starter develops a pink or yellow film, it has been contaminated and must be discarded.

▶ PRODUCTION STAGES FOR YEAST BREADS

The production of yeast breads can be divided into 10 stages:

1 Scaling the ingredients
2 Mixing and kneading the dough
3 Fermenting the dough
4 Punching down the dough
5 Portioning the dough
6 Rounding the portions
7 Make-up: Shaping the portions
8 Proofing the products
9 Baking the products
10 Cooling and storing the finished products

STAGE 1: SCALING THE INGREDIENTS

As with any other bakeshop product, it is important to scale or measure ingredients accurately and to have all ingredients at the proper temperature when making a yeast bread. Liquids such as water, milk and eggs may all be weighed to ensure accuracy in a formula. When a minute quantity of an ingredient is required, such as for salt and spices, a volume measurement may be preferred.

The amount of flour required in yeast bread may vary depending on the humidity level, storage conditions of the flour and the accuracy with which other ingredients are measured. Flour from different mills or from different batch lots may **absorb** more or less water depending on the type of wheat used. Flour with a higher protein content will absorb more liquid than one with a lower protein content. Even switching flour batches will affect the amount of water needed in a formula. The amount of flour stated in most formulas is to be used as a guide. Have additional flour available before mixing. Experience will teach when more or less flour is actually needed.

▶ **absorption** the ability of flour to absorb moisture when mixed into dough, which varies according to protein content, growing and storage conditions

OBTAINING THE PROPER DOUGH TEMPERATURE

Yeast activity is most beneficial when the finished bread dough reaches a temperature range of 75°F to 80°F (24°C to 27°C) after mixing. The temperature of the flour and water, the temperature in the bakeshop and the heat built up by friction during mixing all affect the final dough temperature. The ingredients in the formula must be adjusted to the proper temperature before mixing yeast dough.

Temperatures vary widely in most bakeshops depending on the time of the year, the local climate and the location of hot ovens inside the bakery. Some commercial bakeries are temperature controlled, but in most bakeries the temperature fluctuates frequently. The bakeshop and flour temperature are not easily changed but they can be gauged with a thermometer. The friction produced when the dough is kneaded by machine (**friction factor**) depends on the specific equipment used in the bakeshop. Most equipment user manuals indicate what the friction factor is for the specific equipment.

Of all the variables, the easiest to control is water temperature. Consequently, when scaling water the baker adjusts the water temperature according to a formula. The formula is to multiply by three the desired dough temperature after mixing. Then the temperature of the flour, the room temperature and the friction factor are subtracted from this number. The result is the temperature to which the water should be adjusted before mixing the dough. See the formula in Table 7.3. The desired dough temperature of 77°F (25°C) is used for most yeast dough although some enriched dough may be mixed to 80°F (27°C) as discussed in Chapter 8, Enriched Yeast Doughs. Often in hot weather, cold water will be required and ice cubes will be used to chill water to the desired temperature.

Table 7.3	**FORMULA FOR ADJUSTING WATER TEMPERATURE FOR YEAST BREAD DOUGH**

FORMULA	EXAMPLE	
Multiply the desired dough temperature times 3	77°F × 3 (25°C × 3) =	231°F (75°C)
Subtract the total of the room temperature, the flour temperature and the mixer friction factor	Room temperature Flour temperature Mixer friction factor Less subtotal	77°F (25°C) 68°F (20°C) 25 (14) 170°F (59°C)
Water temperature should be	Ideal water temperature	61°F (16°C)

In this example, for a yeast dough that is to be mixed immediately, the water temperature should be 61°F (16°C).

Note: The friction factor of 25 (14) is different when working in Fahrenheit or Celsius. The difference takes into account the variances between the two measuring systems.

The friction factor is a number that, when added to the formula for obtaining proper water temperature, adjusts for the temperature increase during machine mixing. A friction factor of 25 (14), which is used in Table 7.3, works for many machines. Consult the user guide or test the mixer. To determine the friction factor of a specific mixer, scale the ingredients for a batch of dough. Use a friction factor of 35 (2) to determine the temperature for the water. Mix the dough 7 to 8 minutes on medium speed. Take the temperature of the dough. If the dough is too cold (hot), reduce (increase) the temperature of the friction factor by 5°F (1°C) and test again on another batch of dough. Repeat testing as required to determine the friction factor for that equipment.

The formulas in this book requiring water that is adjusted by using this formula are indicated as "temperature controlled."

STAGE 2: MIXING AND KNEADING THE DOUGH

The way ingredients are combined affects the outcome of the bread. Yeast dough must be mixed and kneaded properly in order to combine the ingredients uniformly, distribute the yeast and develop the gluten. If the dough is not mixed properly, the bread's texture and shape suffer.

Yeast breads are usually mixed by either the **straight dough method** (direct method) or one of several **pre-fermentation methods** in which the dough is mixed in several stages: the **sponge method**, the **old dough method** and the **sourdough starter method**. (Another method used for rich, flaky doughs, the lamination or rolling-in method, is discussed later in Chapter 12, Laminated Doughs.)

Once the ingredients are combined, the dough must be kneaded to develop gluten, the network of proteins that gives bread its shape and texture. Kneading achieves certain key results. It helps the protein hydrate, ensuring development of the gluten web in the bread dough, and it warms the dough to a temperature conducive to keeping the yeast active. Kneading can be done by hand or by an electric mixer with its dough hook attachment. The goal is to create a dough that is smooth and moderately elastic.

▶ PROCEDURE FOR KNEADING DOUGH BY HAND

1 First, bring a portion of the dough toward you.

2 Then push the dough away with your fist.

3 Repeat until the dough is properly kneaded.

Having the dough at the proper temperature when mixing is complete is one key to controlling the bread-making process. The final dough temperature is important because a higher dough temperature will increase the rate of fermentation. Conversely, a lower temperature will slow yeast activity. The rate of fermentation affects the characteristics and flavor of the finished bread.

Mixing is done in two stages. In the first stage (pickup stage) the ingredients are combined on low speed until a rough dough is formed, approximately 2 to 3 minutes. At this point, the baker makes any required adjustments to the formula, adding more liquid or flour if necessary depending on the flour's absorption. When the dough appears too soft, additional flour may be added; when the mixture seems dry and will not form a dough, more water can be added. Be warned, however, that dough hydrates and softens during mixing. What appears to be a dry dough at the outset may be a perfect supple dough once kneaded. The baker uses his or her experience with mixing dough and with the particular formula to determine whether to add more flour or liquid.

Once the ingredients are combined, the dough is kneaded (mixing stage) on medium speed approximately 5 to 10 minutes. The goal is to properly develop the gluten structure in the dough and to warm the dough to the ideal temperature. The dough should look smooth. In many cases, the dough will clear away from the machine bowl toward the end of the kneading process.

Bakers check to see when bread dough is properly kneaded and its gluten structure is fully developed by performing the **windowpane test.** To do this, turn off the mixer and take a small piece of dough from the bowl. Using both hands, gently stretch the dough apart. If it stretches without tearing and becomes nearly translucent (like bubble gum or a latex glove), the dough has reached its optimum development. The windowpane test is used on dough made with wheat flours that contain enough protein to form gluten; bread dough with a high percentage of rye and other low-protein flours may not achieve this stage of elasticity.

▶ **windowpane test** a procedure to check that yeast dough has been properly kneaded; a piece of the kneaded dough is pulled to see if it stretches without breaking apart

MIXING METHODS

Straight Dough Method

The simplest and most common method for mixing yeast doughs is known as the straight dough method. With this method, all ingredients are simply combined and mixed. Once the ingredients are combined, the dough is kneaded until it is smooth and elastic. Kneading time varies according to the kneading method used and the type of dough being produced. The straight dough method is illustrated by Soft Yeast Dinner Rolls (page 146).

Pre-Fermentation Methods

A number of mixing methods—the sponge, old dough and sourdough starter methods—employ a two-step process often referred to as a pre-fermentation technique. First a batter, dough or starter is prepared to allow the yeast to begin fermentation. Then this mixture is turned into a finished dough. Pre-fermentation helps improve the flavor, texture, crust and color of the finished loaf and is discussed more fully in the section on fermentation (page 136).

Sponge Method   The sponge method of mixing yeast dough has two stages. During the first stage the yeast, liquid and approximately half the flour are combined to make a thick batter known as a **sponge** (Fr. *poolisch*, It. *biga*). The sponge is allowed to rise until bubbly and doubled in size. During the second stage, the remaining ingredients are added. The dough is kneaded and allowed to rise again. These two fermentations give sponge method breads a somewhat different flavor and a lighter texture than breads made with the straight dough method.

The sponge method is often used to improve the texture of heavy doughs such as rye and some enriched yeast doughs as discussed in Chapter 8, Enriched Yeast Doughs. The first-stage sponge is usually prepared only for the specific formula and is not reserved for later use. In a high-volume or commercial bakery, however, an all-purpose sponge may be made to streamline production, as long as it is used within a short time period as illustrated on page 155. The sponge method is illustrated by Light Rye Bread (page 148).

Old Dough Method   Old dough (Fr. *pâte fermentée*) is nothing more than a piece of dough saved from a previous batch of bread and added to a new batch to improve the aroma and flavor of the bread. Since the old dough has been fermented, to keep production flowing a bakery may use the old dough method to add flavor without compromising a production schedule. Up to an equal amount of old dough can be added to a new batch of dough. Since the old dough is fully developed, it is added near the end of the mixing period. An all-purpose bread dough formula is provided to use as old dough in the formulas calling for it. But any similar dough may be used for this purpose. Old dough may be omitted in any formulas that call for it. Yield on the finished dough will be that much less, however. Old dough keeps for at least three days under refrigeration. The old dough method is illustrated by Traditional French Baguettes (page 149).

Sourdough Starter Method   The true sourdough starter method of mixing bread has three stages. First a sourdough culture or mother (Fr. *chef*) is prepared. Because natural yeasts may be less concentrated in the starter, a second-stage mixture called a **levain** is prepared to add more yeast food and encourage yeast activity. In the third stage, the final dough is mixed. True sourdough bread contains no commercially prepared yeast. Today, however, many bread doughs made with starters are often fortified with yeast to provide consistency and reliability. The starter provides flavor and other qualities to the dough while the yeast ensures timely bread production. Bread dough with a high percentage of rye flour benefits from the inclusion of starters because rye ferments quickly. The three-stage sourdough mixing method is illustrated by Pain au Levain (Traditional French Sourdough Bread) (page 174).

▶ **levain** the French term for leavening; it is dough made from a sourdough culture that forms the basis for French-style sourdough bread

KNEADING

Mixing and kneading times given in formulas should be used only as a guide. Reaching the correct dough temperature and creating dough that passes the windowpane test are the goals of proper mixing. Care should be taken not to overknead the dough. Overkneading results in dough that is, at best, difficult to shape and, in extreme cases, sticky and inelastic.

When the desired dough temperature is not reached after mixing the dough, the baker has several options. If the temperature is too low by a few degrees, knead the dough another minute to increase the dough temperature. If the dough is still too cool after the additional mixing, flatten the dough and let it rise in a warm area. (Increased surface area makes dough warm or cool more quickly.) When the dough temperature is 2 or 3 degrees higher than desired after kneading, flatten the dough and place it in a cool area to rise. When the dough temperature is more than 5 degrees higher than required, it may have been overkneaded. Overkneaded dough will become wet and sticky because the gluten breaks down, causing water that was absorbed during mixing to be released. Discard overkneaded dough or use it for Old Dough (page 155).

Ingredients such as raisins, nuts and other add-ins should be incorporated after the dough has fully developed in order to maintain their integrity in the finished bread.

STAGE 3: FERMENTING THE DOUGH

As mentioned earlier, fermentation is the natural process by which yeast converts sugar into alcohol and carbon dioxide. Fermentation begins the moment the dough is finished mixing and continues until the dough is baked and reaches a temperature high enough to kill the yeast cells—138°F (59°C). Fermentation also refers to the period when yeast dough is left to rise—that is, the time it takes carbon dioxide gas to form and become trapped in the gluten network. Fermentation is divided into two stages. **Bulk fermentation** refers to the rise given to the entire mass of yeast dough before the dough is shaped and **proofing** refers to the rise given to shaped yeast products just prior to baking.

Dough develops characteristics during fermentation that will enhance the taste and texture of the finished bread. As it feeds on the sugars and starches in the dough, the yeast converts them to flavorful enzymes and bacteria. The gluten strengthens during fermentation, ensuring a bread that will hold its structure when baked. For fermentation, place the kneaded dough into a container large enough to allow the dough to expand, or scrape the dough onto a floured workbench. The surface of the dough may be oiled to prevent drying. Cover the dough and place it in a draft-free place at a temperature between 75°F and 85°F (24°C and 29°C).

Fermentation is complete when the dough has approximately doubled in size and no longer springs back when pressed gently with two fingers. The time necessary varies depending on the type of dough, the temperature of the room and the temperature of the dough. Generally lean dough will ferment 1 to 3 hours until it is roughly doubled in bulk. Longer fermentation times at cool temperatures are recommended for flavor development in lean bread doughs and certain enriched doughs. Bread doughs that rely on a starter for leavening may require even longer fermenting because natural yeast may be less concentrated than commercially prepared yeast.

CONTROLLING FERMENTATION

The ingredients in the formula, the dough temperature and the temperature of the environment in which the dough ferments will affect the total fermentation time. Bakers use different strategies to regulate fermentation time to achieve desired results.

Ingredients

▶ **no-time dough** dough formulated with more yeast to speed fermentation

▶ **dough conditioner** enzymes, emulsifiers and yeast foods added to bread dough to improve gluten development or to soften the dough for faster mixing and shorter fermentation times; available as a powdered blend

Dough with more yeast and more yeast food will ferment more quickly. Increasing the yeast in a formula will increase the rate of fermentation, thus speeding production time. Adding sugar, malt, honey or other yeast food will speed fermentation also, although too much sugar can actually slow yeast's activity; enriched dough formulas often include a higher percentage of yeast for this reason.

No-time dough refers to formulas in which the quantity of yeast is increased to such an extent that fermentation time is reduced significantly. **Dough conditioners** are added to these formulas to ensure that the dough ferments properly in the brief time allotted.

Dough Temperature

Using warmer water in the dough and fermenting it in a warm environment will speed up the fermentation process. Conversely, kneading the dough to the proper dough temperature and then letting it ferment in a cool environment will slow down this process. Wintertime baking in colder climates must take this into consideration.

Room Temperature

Bakeries often extend the fermentation time of certain doughs in a specially designed refrigerator called a retarder. **Retardation** describes the stage when dough is put in a cool place, usually between 38°F and 50°F (3°C and 10°C), for anywhere from 2 to 36 hours. The cool temperature slows down the yeast activity, giving the dough the maximum opportunity to develop its flavor. The cool temperature inhibits or retards the yeast activity, yet leaves it with enough strength for the final proofing stage after the loaves are formed. Formed bread dough may also be retarded before proofing, which can be extremely helpful in scheduling production and baking.

STAGE 4: PUNCHING DOWN THE DOUGH

After fermentation, the dough is gently folded down to expel and redistribute the gas pockets with a technique known as punching down. The procedure reactivates the yeast cells, encouraging more yeast activity. Punching down dough also helps even out the dough's temperature and relaxes the gluten.

STAGE 5: PORTIONING THE DOUGH

The dough is now ready to be divided into portions. For loaves, the dough is scaled to the desired weight. For individual rolls, the dough can be rolled into an even log from which portions are cut with a chef's knife or dough cutter. Weighing the cut dough pieces on a portion scale ensures even-sized portions. When portioning, work quickly and keep the dough covered to prevent it from drying out.

STAGE 6: ROUNDING THE PORTIONS

The portions of dough must be shaped into smooth, round balls in a technique known as rounding. Rounding stretches the outside layer of gluten into a smooth coating. This helps hold in gases and makes it easier to shape the dough. Unrounded rolls rise unevenly and have a rough, lumpy surface. At this stage some breads may be left on the worktable for a short period of **bench rest.** This relaxes the gluten, making the shaping process easier.

STAGE 7: MAKE-UP: SHAPING THE PORTIONS

Lean doughs and some rich doughs can be shaped into a variety of forms: large loaves, small loaves, free-form or country-style rounds or individual dinner rolls. Free-form loaves are often placed between the floured folds of heavy linen canvas (**couche**) to hold their shape while proofing. Or these loaves may be placed in linen-lined baskets (**bannetons**) or coiled willow or plastic baskets (**brotform**). These baskets hold the loaves' shape and leave a distinctive imprint on the loaves when they are removed from them before baking. Some shaping techniques are shown here. Other doughs, particularly brioche, croissant and Danish, are usually shaped in very specific ways. Those techniques are discussed and illustrated in Chapter 8, Enriched Yeast Doughs, and Chapter 12, Laminated Doughs.

▶ **retardation** chilling a yeasted dough product under refrigeration to slow yeast activity and to extend fermentation or proofing time

Rounding bread dough.

▶ **banneton** (BAN-tahn) a traditional willow basket, often lined with canvas, in which yeast bread is placed to rise before baking

Bread dough being placed in a canvas couche before being proofed.

▶ **brotform** (BROT-form) a traditional woven basket in which yeast bread is placed to rise before baking. The basket leaves marks in the dough. Heavy plastic versions are available for commercial food service use

Taking a rounded piece of dough, molding it and placing it in a brotform.

▶ PROCEDURE FOR FORMING AN OBLONG LOAF

1 Round a portion of dough into a ball by rolling it under cupped hands across the surface of the workbench.
2 Flatted the rounded dough into a disk.
3 Fold up the bottom edge of the dough ⅔ of the way, then fold the top edge down. Press to seal.
4 Rotate the dough 180° and fold again in the same manner as in Step 3.
5 Flatten the dough into a rectangle.
6 Fold the right and left edges over, then roll the dough into a tight cylinder.
7 Place the dough with the seam facing up into a flour-dusted brotform or banneton. Or, place the dough seam side down on a cornmeal-dusted sheet pan.

Forming, then rolling a long loaf or baguette.

▶ PROCEDURE FOR ROLLING A LONG LOAF OR BAGUETTE

1 Round a portion of dough into a ball by rolling it under cupped hands across the surface of the workbench.
2 Roll out the ball of dough into a short cylinder.
3 With both hands together, roll the dough until it gradually begins to lengthen.
4 Roll to the desired length.

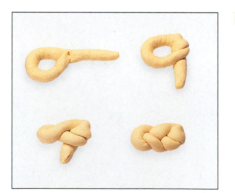

Forming a twisted knot loaf.

▶ PROCEDURE FOR FORMING A TWISTED KNOT ROLL OR LOAF

1 Roll a portion of dough into a long rope. Form a loop by attaching the left end to the middle of the rope. Pinch to seal the dough.
2 Pass the right end of the rope through the loop.
3 Fold down the top of the loop and twist slightly.
4 Thread the loose end of the loaf through the loop.

▶ PROCEDURE FOR FORMING A BOW KNOT ROLL

1 Roll a portion of dough into a short rope.
2 Pick up one end of the dough. Cross it over the other end of the dough.
3 Tie a simple knot in the dough.
4 Tuck the end of the dough underneath and pinch to seal it.

Forming a bow knot roll.

▶ PROCEDURE FOR FORMING A FOLDED LOAF

1 Round a portion of dough into a ball by rolling it under cupped hands across the surface of the workbench.
2 Flatten the portion of dough into a 10-inch (25-centimeter) oval approximately 1 inch (2.5 centimeters) thick.
3 Brush the top of the dough with water and fold in half.

Fully proofed folded loaf (top), daisy loaf (left) and star loaf (right) before baking.

Baked folded loaf (right), daisy loaf (top) and star loaf (left) after baking.

▶ PROCEDURE FOR FORMING A DAISY LOAF

1 Round a 16-ounce (480-gram) portion of dough into a ball by rolling it under cupped hands across the surface of the workbench. Round a 1½-ounce (45-gram) portion of dough.
2 Sprinkle the top of the larger portion of dough with flour. Using a thin rolling pin, press down on the dough to divide it into eight equal parts without separating the pieces. Release the rolling pin with a twisting motion.
3 Wet the bottom of the smaller portion of dough. Place it in the center of the larger portion, firmly pressing the ball into place.

Scoring a star loaf with scissors before proofing.

▶ PROCEDURE FOR FORMING A STAR LOAF

1 Divide the dough into one 5-ounce (150-gram) and nine 2½-ounce (76-gram) portions. Round the dough and bench rest, covered, for 5 minutes.

2 Place one of the smaller portions of dough in the center of a flour-dusted sheet pan. Moisten the surface of four more portions of dough, then dip them in grated cheese or sesame, caraway or other seeds. Place them evenly around the small portion of dough on the sheet pan without touching. Roll the four remaining smaller portions of dough into ovals. Moisten them with water, then dip them in poppy seeds, sea salt or other seeds of a contrasting color or texture. Position them evenly between the rounds.

3 Slightly flatten the remaining larger portion of dough with a rolling pin, then place it in the center of the star-shaped bread. Score the star loaf with scissors before proofing. The loaf may be left plain. The decorative scoring will create a pattern on the bread once the loaf bakes.

▶ PROCEDURE FOR MAKING A THREE-STRAND BRAIDED LOAF

1 Divide the dough into three equal pieces. Roll the pieces into three long ropes of equal length. Press the three strands together at one end.

2 Cross the left strand over the center strand. Then cross the right strand over the new center strand.

3 Repeat this pattern until the strands are all braided. Tuck the ends underneath and pinch to seal the braid.

1 Pressing the three strands together.

2 Crossing the strips one over the other to make the braid.

3 Rolling the ends together to seal the braid.

▶ PROCEDURE FOR MAKING A FOUR-STRAND BRAIDED LOAF

1 Divide the dough into two equal pieces. Roll each piece into a long strand.

2 Lay the two strands of dough out perpendicular to each other. Twist the two ends of the horizontal strand, bringing the right end up and the left end down.

3 Repeat this motion with the vertical strand. Continue crossing the strands until the dough forms a tight loaf. Tuck the ends underneath and pinch to seal the braid.

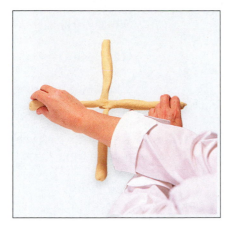

1 Forming a cross with two strands of dough.

2 Twisting the ends of the dough.

3 Tucking the ends of the dough underneath to form a tight loaf.

▶ PROCEDURE FOR MAKING A TURBAN BRAIDED LOAF

1 Divide the dough into six equal pieces. Roll the pieces into six narrow ropes. Make two thick ropes by laying three narrow ropes side by side and pinching the ends together to seal.

2 Place one thick dough rope perpendicular to the other. Fold one end of A down, crossing over the horizontal strip of dough. Bring D under B and over A.

3 Repeat the pattern, bringing C over D and under A.

4 Tuck the ends underneath and pinch to seal the braid.

1 Crossing the two ropes of dough and folding one end down.

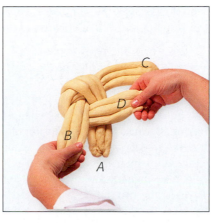

2 Bringing the left end D under B and over A.

3 The finished turban braided loaf.

Table 7.4	PAN SIZE	
PAN	**APPROXIMATE SIZE**	**WEIGHT OF DOUGH***
Sandwich loaf	16 in. × 4 in. × 4½ in. (40 cm × 10 cm × 11.2 cm)	4 lb. (1920 g)
Pullman	13 in. × 4 in. × 3 in. (32.5 cm × 10 cm × 7.5 cm)	3 lb. (1440 g)
Large	9 in. × 5 in. × 3 in. (22.5 cm × 12.5 cm × 7.5 cm)	2 lb. (960 g)
Medium	8 in. × 4 in. × 2 in. (20 cm × 10 cm × 5 cm)	1 lb. 8 oz. (720 g)
Small	7 in. × 3 in. × 2 in. (17.5 cm × 7.5 cm × 5 cm)	1 lb. (480 g)
Miniature	5 in. × 3 in. × 2 in. (12.5 cm × 7.5 cm × 5 cm)	8 oz. (240 g)

*Weights given are approximate; variations may occur based on the type of dough used as well as the temperature and length of proofing.

Underproofed bread dough (top), fully proofed bread dough (center) and overproofed bread dough (bottom).

▶ **oven spring** the rapid rise of yeast goods when first placed in a hot oven resulting from the temporary increase of yeast activity and the expansion of trapped gases

STAGE 8: PROOFING THE PRODUCTS

Proofing is the final rise of shaped or panned yeast products before baking. For most bread, the temperature should be between 80°F and 115°F (27°C and 46°C), slightly higher than the temperature for fermentation. Some humidity is also desirable to prevent the dough from drying or forming a crust. Temperature and humidity can be controlled with a special cabinet known as a **proof box.**

Most products are proofed until the dough doubles in size and springs back slowly when lightly touched. Underproofing results in poor volume and texture. Overproofing results in a sour flavor, poor volume and a paler color after baking. Some doughs made with low-protein flours such as rye or multigrains and some enriched yeast doughs may be proofed less, until expanded only 50 to 70 percent in volume. The weaker gluten structure and the heavy weight of the fats in such doughs makes them fragile. Proofing these doughs until doubled in volume can result in loaves that collapse in the oven.

STAGE 9: BAKING THE PRODUCTS

As yeast breads bake, a variety of chemical and physical changes turn the dough into an edible product. These changes are discussed in Chapter 3, Principles of Baking. Because of the expansion of gases, yeast products experience a sudden rise, referred to as **oven spring,** when first placed in a hot oven. As the dough's temperature increases, the yeast dies, the gluten fibers become firm, the starches gelatinize, the moisture evaporates and, finally, the crust forms and turns brown. To assist the rise during baking and to improve their appearance when baked, loaves may be brushed with a wash and/or scored before baking.

WASHES

The appearance of yeast breads can be altered by applying a glaze or wash to the dough before baking. The crust is made shiny or matte, hard or soft, darker or lighter by the proper use of washes. Washes are also used to attach seeds, wheat germ, oats or other toppings to the dough's surface.

The most commonly used wash is an egg wash, composed of whole egg and water, usually one part water to three parts egg. Yeast products can also be topped with plain water, a mixture of egg and milk, plain milk or richer glazes containing sugar and flavorings. Even a light dusting of white flour can be used to top dough. (This is commonly seen with potato rolls.) Rye breads are often coated with a starch wash (page 173), made from cornstarch cooked in water, which produces a dark shiny crust. (See Table 7.5.)

Washes may be applied before or after proofing. If applied after proofing, be extremely careful not to deflate the product. Avoid using too much wash, as it can burn or cause the product to stick to the pan. Puddles or streaks of egg wash on the dough will cause uneven browning.

Occasionally, a formula will specify that melted butter or oil be brushed on the product after baking. Do not, however, apply egg washes to already baked products, as the egg will remain raw and the desired effect will not be achieved.

Applying egg wash with a commercial sprayer.

Dipping bread in seeds and coatings before baking.

Rolls baked with various washes: egg yolk and water, egg yolk and cream, egg white, egg white and milk (top row from left to right); whole egg and salt, whole egg and milk, whole egg and water (bottom row from left to right).

Table 7.5	WASHES FOR YEAST PRODUCTS
WASH	**USE**
Whole egg and water	Shine and color
Whole egg and milk	Shine and color with soft crust
Egg white and water	Shine with firm crust
Egg yolk and cream or milk	Shine and color with soft crust
Milk or cream	Color with soft crust
Water	Crisp crust
Flour	Texture and contrast
Starch wash	Shine and color

Scoring a round loaf with a lame.

▶ **docker** a hand tool designed to pierce holes in the surface of bread, cracker, pastry and pizza dough before baking to release air bubbles so the product bakes evenly

SCORING AND DOCKING

The shape and appearance of some breads can be improved by cutting their tops with a sharp knife or razor (lame) just before baking. (A lame is pictured in the photograph on page 26 and at left.) This is referred to as scoring or slashing. Hard-crusted breads are usually scored to allow for continued rising and the escape of gases after the crust has formed. Breads that are not properly scored will burst or break along the sides. Scoring can also be used to make an attractive design on the product's surface. Some flatbreads such as pizza and crackers may be docked, or pricked with small holes to prevent the formation of irregular air bubbles in the finished product. A tool called a **docker** is used for this purpose. By contrast, pita bread is not docked so that its distinctive pocket will form. Even a hard-crusted loaf of bread can be gently docked after proofing to create an attractive design on the crust.

Docking a risen loaf of raisin bread with a docker before baking.

Unmolding a loaf from a brotform onto a sheet pan (in the foreground), the scored loaf (in the center) and an unscored loaf (at the top).

STEAM IN THE OVEN

The crisp crust desired for certain breads and rolls is achieved by introducing moisture into the oven during baking. Steam revitalizes the yeast in the dough and keeps the surface of the dough soft so that it can rise fully in the oven. The steam also contributes to the chemical changes of the starch and sugar on the surface of the dough, producing a thin crust and brown color. Steam is introduced into the oven in the early baking stages only. Excessive steam will produce a crust that is pale and thick. Professional bakers' ovens have built-in steam injection jets to provide moisture as needed. Steam must not be present during the final stages of baking so the bread can brown.

To create steam in any oven, spray or mist the bread with water several times during baking, or place a pan on the oven's lowest rack to receive hot water. Then pour ½ to ¾ cup (120 to 180 milliliters) of hot water into the pan just before placing the bread in the oven. This creates a burst of steam and a moist oven during the first few minutes of baking. (To remove any trace of steam in the oven, slightly open the oven door or the vent in a deck oven [the damper] during the last few minutes of baking to let any condensed steam escape.) Rich doughs, which do not form crisp crusts, are usually baked without steam.

Many bakeries bake their breads directly on the flat heated surface of a deck oven. Usually made from masonry material, the hearth or deck traps heat and releases it directly onto bread baked on it. Bakers slide the bread onto the hearth using a flat wooden or metal peel. These ovens usually include automated steam systems to provide the moisture necessary for making crisp-crusted breads.

DETERMINING DONENESS

Baking time is determined by a variety of factors: the product's size, the oven thermostat's accuracy and the desired crust color. Larger items require a longer baking time than smaller ones. Lean dough products bake faster and at higher temperatures than enriched dough products.

Fully baked lean bread dough should reach an internal temperature of 190°F to 210°F (88°C to 99 °C). Rich bread dough is fully baked when it reaches an internal temperature of 180°F to 190°F (82°C to 88°C). The internal temperature can be gauged with great accuracy using an instant-read thermometer. However, bread loaves are commonly tested for doneness by tapping them on the bottom and listening for a hollow sound. This indicates that air, not moisture, is present inside the loaf. If the bottom is damp or heavy, the loaf probably needs more baking time. The texture and color of the crust are also a good indication of doneness, particularly with individual rolls. Browning (caramelization) on the outside of bread flavors the entire loaf. A pale loaf will have less flavor than a well-browned one. The baking times indicated in these formulas are estimates only and may vary depending on the equipment used. Experience will teach how to determine doneness without strict adherence to elapsed time.

STAGE 10: COOLING AND STORING THE FINISHED PRODUCTS

The quality of even the finest yeast products suffers if they are cooled or stored improperly. Yeast products should be cooled on racks at room temperature and away from drafts. Yeast breads and rolls should be removed from their pans for cooling unless indicated otherwise. Allow loaves to cool completely before slicing. This allows the internal structure to settle and evaporates any excess moisture remaining after baking.

Once cool, yeast products should be stored at room temperature or frozen for longer storage. Do not refrigerate yeast breads, as refrigeration promotes staling. Do not wrap crisp-crusted breads such as Italian or French loaves, as this causes the crust to soften.

▶ PROCEDURE FOR PREPARING YEAST BREAD

Straight Dough Method

1 Scale ingredients. Adjust water temperature and rehydrate yeast if necessary.

2 Combine all ingredients in the bowl of a mixer fitted with a dough hook on low speed to moisten; this is the pickup stage.

3 Adjust the mixture with more water or flour if needed to correct dough consistency.

4 Knead the dough on medium speed to properly develop the dough, approximately 5 to 10 minutes.

5 Ferment the dough until double in bulk, then punch down to release gases.

6 Scrape the dough onto the workbench, then divide and scale into uniform pieces. Round each piece into a smooth ball, then rest before rolling into desired shapes. Pan the formed dough as desired.

7 Proof the dough. Brush with egg wash and score the dough, if necessary.

RECIPE 7.2   **SOFT YEAST DINNER ROLLS**

Yield: 64 Rolls, approximately 1¼ oz. (38 grams) each

Method: Straight dough

Fermentation: 1 hour.

Proofing: 30 to 45 minutes.

Water (temperature controlled)	1 lb. 4 oz.	595 ml	45%
Active dry yeast	2 oz.	60 g	4.5%
Bread flour	2 lb. 12 oz.	1320 g	100%
Salt	1 oz.	30 g	2.3%
Granulated sugar	4 oz.	120 g	9%
Nonfat dry milk powder	2 oz.	60 g	4.5%
Shortening	2 oz.	60 g	4.5%
Unsalted butter, softened	2 oz.	60 g	4.5%
Eggs	3.3 oz. (2 eggs)	100 g	7.5%
Egg wash	as needed	as needed	
Total dough weight:	5 lb.	2405 g	182%

1 Combine the water and yeast in a bowl. Combine the flour, salt, sugar, milk powder, shortening, butter and eggs in the bowl of a mixer fitted with a dough hook.

2 Add the water-and-yeast mixture to the mixer bowl; stir to combine.

3 Knead on medium speed 10 minutes or until the dough reaches 77°F (25°C).

4 Transfer the dough to a lightly greased bowl, cover and place in a warm spot. Ferment until doubled, approximately 1 hour.

5 Punch down the dough. Let it rest a few minutes to allow the gluten to relax.

6 Divide the dough into 1¼-ounce (38-gram) portions and round. Shape as desired and arrange on paper-lined sheet pans. Proof until doubled in size.

7 Carefully brush the proofed rolls with egg wash. Bake at 400°F (200°C) until medium brown, approximately 12 to 15 minutes.

Approximate values per roll: **Calories** 90, **Total fat** 1.5 g, **Saturated fat** 0.5 g, **Cholesterol** 10 mg, **Sodium** 160 mg, **Total carbohydrates** 15 g, **Protein** 3 g, **Claims**—low fat; low saturated fat; low cholesterol

▶ PROCEDURE FOR PREPARING YEAST BREAD

Sponge Method

1 Scale ingredients. Adjust water to proper temperature and rehydrate yeast if necessary.

2 Mix the sponge from a portion of the flour, the water and the yeast. Usually half the total flour weight is used.

3 Ferment the sponge until bubbly and approximately double in bulk, approximately 1 hour.

4 Add remaining ingredients, then knead the dough on medium speed until properly developed, approximately 5 to 10 minutes.

5 Ferment the dough until double in bulk, then punch down to release gases.

6 The dough is now ready for scaling, shaping, proofing and baking.

▶ **bagel** a dense, donut-shaped yeast roll; it is cooked in boiling water, then baked, which gives it a shiny glaze and chewy texture

▶ **bun** any of a variety of small, round yeast rolls; can be sweet or savory

▶ **club roll** a small oval-shaped roll made of crusty French bread

▶ **Kaiser roll** a large round yeast roll with a crisp crust and a curved pattern stamped on the top; used primarily for sandwiches

1 Mixing the soft yeast dough: (a) Combining the ingredients in a mixer bowl with the dough hook attached.

(b) Adding the yeast-and-water mixture.

2 Kneading the dough.

3 The dough before fermenting.

4 Punching down the risen dough: (a) Pressing down on the center of the dough with your fist.

(b) Folding the edges of the dough in toward the center.

5 Scaling the dough.

6 Rounding the rolls.

7 Brushing the rolls with egg wash.

RECIPE 7.3   **LIGHT RYE BREAD**

1 Rye bread sponge.

2 Mixing the rye dough.

3 Shaping the rye loaves.

Yield: 2 Large Loaves   **Method:** Sponge

Fermentation: Sponge, 1 hour. Dough, 45 minutes to 1 hour.

Proofing: 45 minutes.

Unbleached wheat flour	1 lb.	480 g	66%
Medium rye flour	8 oz.	240 g	34%
Dark molasses	3 oz.	90 g	12.5%
Water (temperature controlled)	20 fl. oz.	600 ml	83%
Active dry yeast	0.5 oz.	15 g	2%
Nonfat dry milk powder	1.5 oz.	45 g	6%
Caraway seeds, crushed	0.6 oz.	20 g	3%
Kosher salt	0.5 oz.	15 g	2%
Unsalted butter, melted	0.5 oz.	15 g	2%
Egg wash	as needed	as needed	
Total dough weight:	3 lb. 2 oz.	1520 g	210%

1 Stir the flours together and set aside.

2 To make the sponge, combine the molasses, water and yeast. Add 8 ounces (240 grams) of the flour mixture. Stir vigorously for 3 minutes. Cover the bowl and set aside to ferment until doubled and very bubbly, approximately 1 hour.

3 Stir the milk powder, caraway seeds, salt and butter into the sponge.

4 Transfer the dough to the bowl of a mixer fitted with a dough hook.

5 Gradually add the remaining flour to the sponge. Mix on low speed and continue adding flour until the dough is stiff but slightly tacky. Knead 5 minutes on low speed until the dough reaches 77°F (25°C).

6 Transfer the dough to a lightly greased bowl, cover and place in a warm place until doubled, approximately 45 to 60 minutes.

7 Punch down the dough and divide into two equal pieces. Shape each piece into a round loaf and place on a sheet pan that has been dusted with cornmeal or lightly oiled. Brush the loaves with egg wash and let rise until doubled, approximately 45 minutes.

8 Score the tops with a razor or knife. Bake at 375°F (190°C) until golden brown and crusty, approximately 25 minutes.

Approximate values per $^{1}/_{10}$-loaf serving: **Calories** 160, **Total fat** 1.5 g, **Saturated fat** 0 g, **Cholesterol** 15 mg, **Sodium** 370 mg, **Total carbohydrates** 31 g, **Protein** 6 g, **Claims**—low fat; no saturated fat; low cholesterol

▶ PROCEDURE FOR PREPARING YEAST BREAD

Old Dough Method

1 Prepare the old dough and ferment. (If using old dough that has been refrigerated, bring it to room temperature before using.)

2 Scale other ingredients. Adjust water to proper temperature and rehydrate yeast if necessary.

3 Combine the flour, yeast, salt and water and mix until moistened, then knead on medium speed until the dough is almost fully developed. Divide the old dough into small pieces and add to the new dough in the mixer. Knead another 1 or 2 minutes until the old dough is fully incorporated.

4 Ferment the dough until double in bulk, approximately 1 to 3 hours.

TRADITIONAL FRENCH BAGUETTES

RECIPE 7.4

Yield: 4 Loaves, approximately 12 oz. (360 g) each   **Method:** Old dough

Fermentation: Old dough, 4 to 6 hours. Final dough, 1 to 2 hours.

Proofing: 30 to 45 minutes.

Old Dough (page 155), room temperature	1 lb.	480 g	84%
Bread flour	1 lb. 3 oz.	570 g	100%
Instant yeast	0.15 oz. (1 tsp.)	4.5 g	0.8%
Water (temperature controlled)	12 fl. oz.	360 ml	63%
Salt	0.5 oz.	15 g	2.6%
Total weight:	3 lb.	1430 g	250%

1 The dough is portioned, then rolled into baguettes in two stages.

1 Prepare the old dough and allow it to ferment at least 4 hours. Or remove the old dough from the refrigerator and bring it to room temperature 2 to 4 hours before mixing.

2 Place the flour, yeast, water and salt in the bowl of a mixer fitted with a dough hook. Mix on low speed until blended. Then knead on medium speed until the dough is almost fully developed and reaches 75°F (24°C), approximately 7 to 10 minutes. Add the old dough in small pieces. Continue kneading until the dough is fully developed and reaches approximately 77°F (25°C).

3 Place the dough on a floured surface or in a large bowl. Cover the dough and ferment until doubled in size, approximately 1 to 2 hours.

4 Punch down the dough and divide into four equal pieces. Round the dough, cover and bench rest 10 minutes.

5 Shape each piece of dough into a 10-inch (25-centimeter) cylinder. Cover the dough and rest several minutes before rolling it into 24-inch- (60-centimeter-) long baguettes.

6 Place the rolled dough seam side down onto a canvas couche lightly dusted with rice or bread flour or in prepared baguette pans. Proof until the loaves increase 55 to 65 percent in volume, approximately 30 to 45 minutes.

7 Remove the proofed loaves from the proof box and let the bread's surface dry for 5 minutes. Use the canvas to roll the bread onto sheet pans or leave in the baguette pans. Score several diagonal cuts in each piece of dough.

8 Bake at 450°F (230°C), with steam injected into the oven during the first few minutes of baking, until golden brown, approximately 20 to 22 minutes.

2 The proofed loaves are scored to allow steam to escape.

Approximate values per ¹/₇-loaf serving: **Calories** 100, **Total fat** 0 g, **Saturated fat** 0 g, **Cholesterol** 0 mg, **Sodium** 280 mg, **Total carbohydrates** 20 g, **Protein** 3 g

VARIATION:

Olive Bread—Once the dough is mixed, knead in 0.25 ounce (8 grams/1.3%) finely chopped fresh oregano and 12 ounces (360 grams/63%) pitted and finely chopped Kalamata olives. Knead only to incorporate the ingredients. Ferment, then divide and shape the dough as desired.

3 The finished baguettes.

▶ QUALITIES OF BREAD

Bread is judged by its external and internal appearance, flavor, aroma and keeping properties. Well-crafted bread has a pleasing uniform brown surface color. The crust is neither too thick nor too thin, depending on the type of formula. The crust is crisp or tender without being leathery and excessively thick. With the exception of long-fermented sourdough, the crust should be uniform and free from surface blisters. The interior (crumb) of a tender-crusted bread or enriched-dough product should be even and moist without being sticky. A long-fermented country bread or sourdough may contain an irregular cell structure characteristic of this type of bread. Well-crafted bread has good keeping properties; improperly made bread will stale in a matter of hours. Use Table 7.6 to troubleshoot dough mixing and baking.

Table 7.6 TROUBLESHOOTING CHART

PROBLEM	CAUSE	SOLUTION
Dense, leaden dough	Too much flour forced into the dough	Gradually add water; adjust formula
Crust too pale	Oven temperature too low	Adjust oven
	Dough overproofed	Proof only until almost doubled, then bake immediately
	Too much steam	Adjust steam
Crust too dark	Oven too hot	Adjust oven
	Too much sugar in the dough	Adjust formula or measure sugar carefully
Top crust separates from loaf	Dough improperly shaped	Shape dough carefully
	Crust not scored properly	Score dough to a depth of ½ in. (1.2 cm)
	Dough dried out during proofing	Cover dough during proofing; increase humidity in proof box
Sides of loaf are cracked	Bread expanded after crust formed in oven	Score top of loaf before baking
	Bread underproofed	Proof until loaf almost doubled
Dense texture	Not enough yeast	Adjust formula or measure yeast carefully
	Not enough fermentation time	Let dough rise until doubled or as directed
	Improper molding technique	Handle dough gently
	Too much salt	Adjust formula or measure yeast carefully
Ropes of undercooked dough running through product	Insufficient kneading	Knead dough until smooth and elastic and passes windowpane test, or as directed
	Insufficient rising time	Allow adequate time for proofing
	Oven too hot	Adjust oven
Free-form loaf spreads and flattens	Dough too soft	Adjust formula or measure carefully
Large holes in bread	Too much yeast	Adjust formula or measure yeast carefully
	Overkneaded	Knead only as directed
	Inadequate punch-down	Punch down properly to knead out excess air before shaping
Blisters on crust	Too much liquid	Measure ingredients carefully
	Improper shaping	Knead out excess air before shaping
	Too much steam in oven	Reduce amount of steam or moisture in oven

CONVENIENCE PRODUCTS

The popularity of freshly baked bread has led to the introduction of many products designed to make fresh bread within the reach of all types of food service establishments. Bread mixes are dry blends of flours, salt and other ingredients. In the bakeshop, yeast and water are added, then the product is mixed and fermented as for scratch dough. Mixes allow the baker to prepare a variety of breads with few additional ingredients. Bread mixes may be made from all-natural ingredients or they can include dough conditioners and additives to speed mixing and fermentation times and ease shaping.

Bread bases are dry blends of specialty ingredients that must be added to a scratch bread formula or a mix. Bases are added to a formula in a ratio of from 25 to 50 pounds of base for each 50 pounds of flour. Bread bases come in varieties such as multigrain, cracked wheat, oatmeal, potato and herb among countless others. A small bakery that would otherwise offer a scratch product might use a base to expand the variety of breads offered. Waste is avoided since large bags of unusual flours, grains or nuts that might not be used quickly are replaced by smaller quantities of bases. Check the ingredient label to determine whether the mix or base meets the requirements of your bakeshop. With bread mixes and bases, careful measuring and temperature control of water is still a skill required to achieve the best results. Consult the manufacturer's recommendations because mixing and fermentation times may be different for breads prepared from these products. Forming, proofing and baking, however, are the same as for scratch products.

Powdered sourdough starters give breads the tangy flavor of sourdough without the effort of preparing and nurturing natural yeast. Made from a starter mixture that has been dried and pulverized, these prepared starters are simply added to the dry ingredients in a yeast dough formula. Commercial yeast leavens the dough while the starter lends its tangy flavor.

Frozen bread dough enables the restaurant operator or smaller bakeshop to offer freshly baked bread even when time, space or staff are limited. The dough comes already fermented. It needs only thawing, proofing and baking. Frozen bread dough may be purchased in bulk; 10- and 20-pound cases are common. Once thawed, the dough is portioned, shaped, proofed and baked. Nuts, seeds, herbs, spices, dried fruit or other flavoring ingredients can be kneaded into the dough to customize the product. From the same dough, a restaurant can offer dinner rolls, bread sticks, pizza and sandwich bread. Fresh refrigerated bread dough is also available. Frozen dough also comes portioned and formed into loaves and rolls. It requires panning and then careful thawing, usually under refrigeration.

Much of the guesswork in the proofing and baking process has been removed with parbaked bread. This is bread dough that has been formed and then baked only long enough to stop all yeast activity and solidify the starches without browning the crust. The parbaked bread is then flash-frozen. The restaurant operator simply pans and thaws the parbaked loaves or rolls, then finishes the baking. With parbaked bread it is essential to bake at the temperatures and for the time indicated by the manufacturer. Fully baked frozen breads, rolls, bread sticks and other products are the ultimate convenience, if not the ultimate in flavor. Inattentive reheating and cooling will destroy the flavor, texture and appearance of these yeast breads, however.

CONCLUSION

Fresh yeast breads are a popular and inexpensive addition to any menu and are surprisingly easy to prepare. A solid grasp of the 10 production stages described in this chapter enables the student baker to prepare many types of yeast breads. After mixing a few batches of dough, the student baker will quickly learn to recognize the ideal texture of properly kneaded bread dough. With practice, forming and shaping loaves will become routine.

QUESTIONS FOR DISCUSSION

1 Explain the differences between active dry yeast, instant dry yeast and compressed yeast. Describe the correct procedures for working with these yeasts.

2 Explain the differences between a sponge and a sourdough starter. How is each of these items used?

3 Describe the straight dough mixing method and give two examples of products made with this procedure.

4 List the 10 production stages for yeast breads. Which of these production stages would also apply to quick bread production? Explain your answer.

5 Locate a professional organization for bread bakers. What services are available to its members?

6 Locate two recipes each for typical French, German and Italian yeast breads and determine whether they are made with the straight dough, sponge or other pre-fermentation method.

The formulas provided here are grouped according to bread types: Tender-Crusted Bread; Hard-Crusted Breads; Multigrain, Rye and Sourdough Breads; and Specialty Breads. To help production planning, guidelines at the beginning of each formula indicate approximate times for fermentation, proofing and baking. Be aware that times may need to be adjusted according to the conditions in the bakeshop. Adjusting the quantity of yeast used, the temperature of the water and other ingredients in the formulas and changing the mixing time will all affect production. As discussed in this chapter, fermentation and proofing may be accelerated or slowed to accommodate a particular schedule. Using old dough gives many types of bread a full flavor, however it may be omitted when called for in formulas in this book. Following the chapter opening photo formula, the first formulas in this section are for a natural starter, basic sponge and old dough that may be required in some formulas.

RECIPE 7.5

TURKISH PIDE BREAD

CHEF KLAUS TENBERGEN, CMB, CEPC, ASBPB
KENDALL COLLEGE SCHOOL OF CULINARY ARTS, EVANSTON, IL

In Old World European fashion, Klaus Tenbergen started his baking career in 1977 as an apprentice baker in Germany. After working in Germany, Namibia, Bophuthatswana and South Africa, where he owned a bakery and confectionery shop for 9 years, he brought his skills as Bäckermeister to the United States in 1994. Klaus joined the Kendall College School of Culinary Arts in Evanston, Illinois, in 1998 as Chef Instructor in the Baking and Pastry Department, where he is responsible for developing the bread-baking curriculum. One of his main interests is building relationships with the baking industry to provide his students with internship opportunities. In 1998 he was a member of the Baking Team USA. He frequently publishes baking-related articles for national and international publications. He is a noted speaker on baking trends and an active member of the Retail Baker's Association and the Research Chef's Association, as well as the proud father of two children who he hopes someday will follow in his footsteps.

KENDALL COLLEGE SCHOOL OF CULINARY ARTS, EVANSTON, IL
Chef Klaus Tenbergen

Note: This bread is featured in the chapter opening photograph.

Yield: 3 Loaves   **Method:** Sponge

Fermentation: Sponge, 3 hours. Final dough, bench rest 50 minutes.

Proofing: 35 minutes.

Compressed yeast	0.75 oz.	20 g	2%
Water, cool	3.5 fl. oz.	100 ml	10%
Bread flour	2 lb.	900 g	90%
Light rye flour	3.5 oz.	100 g	10%
Dough conditioner (optional)	0.3 oz. (2 tsp.)	10 g	1%
Salt	0.6 oz.	20 g	2%
Water (temperature controlled)	20.5 fl. oz.	580 ml	58%
Egg wash	as needed	as needed	
Sesame seeds	as needed	as needed	
Total dough weight:	4 lb. 6 oz.	2000 g	200%

1 Pressing dowel into Turkish pide bread.

2 Spraying egg wash on Turkish pide bread.

3 The finished Turkish pide bread.

1 Make the sponge by dissolving the yeast in the cool water in the bowl of a mixer fitted with a dough hook. Add 7 ounces (210 grams) of the bread flour. Mix 5 minutes at medium speed. Cover the sponge and ferment at room temperature until active and bubbling, approximately 3 hours.

2 Add the remaining bread flour, light rye flour, dough conditioner, if using, salt and temperature-controlled water to the sponge. Mix on low speed to combine all the ingredients, approximately 3 to 4 minutes. Stop the machine and scrape down the bowl. Knead the dough on medium speed until fully developed, 7 to 10 minutes to make a soft, pliable dough.

3 Scrape the dough onto a lightly floured workbench. Cover the dough and ferment 30 minutes. Divide the dough into three equal pieces. Round the dough, cover and bench rest another 20 minutes.

4 Flatten the portioned dough on a cornmeal-dusted workbench into a 12-inch (30-centimeters) circle. Press a thin rolling pin or dowel, measuring approximately 1 inch (2.5 centimeters) in diameter, into the dough, making rows of parallel lines. Repeat in the opposite direction to create a diamond pattern on the surface of the bread.

5 Place the dough on paper-lined sheet pans. Brush or spray the bread with egg wash. Sprinkle the loaves with sesame seeds. Proof until doubled in bulk, approximately 30 to 40 minutes.

6 Bake at 450°F (230°C) until dark golden brown, 12 to 15 minutes. Cool on racks.

Approximate values per $^1/_{14}$-loaf serving: **Calories** 90, **Total fat** 0.5 g, **Saturated fat** 0 g, **Cholesterol** 5 mg, **Sodium** 180 mg, **Total carbohydrates** 18 g, **Protein** 3 g

NATURAL SOURDOUGH STARTER (CHEF)

Yield: 1 lb. 5 oz. (630 g)

Spring water, 70°F (21°C)	9 fl. oz.	270 ml	100%
Organic grapes	3 oz.	90 g	33%
Bread flour	9 oz.	270 g	100%
Total weight:	1 lb. 5 oz.	630 g	233%

1 Combine 3 fluid ounces (90 milliliters) of the water and the grapes. Add 3 ounces (90 grams) of the flour and mix together using a rubber spatula. The dough will be somewhat firm. Transfer the mixture to a container with a tight-fitting lid or cover tightly with plastic wrap.

2 Store at room temperature, 70°F to 75°F (21°C to 24°C), 24 hours.

3 Remove the grapes. Stir in 3 ounces (90 grams) of the flour and 3 fluid ounces (90 milliliters) of the water and mix energetically.

4 Cover tightly and store at room temperature until the starter is bubbling, 24 hours.

5 Add the remaining flour and water to the bubbly dough and mix energetically.

6 Cover well, and store at room temperature 24 hours.

7 By the third day, the starter is ready to use to make Pain au Levain (page 174). The chef may be refrigerated for 2 to 3 days, and then may be made into a levain or used in any recipe calling for a sourdough starter.

8 To keep the starter alive and fresh over a long period of time, every 2 to 4 days remove it from the refrigerator. Feed the starter with 3 fluid ounces (90 milliliters) water and 3 ounces (90 grams) flour. Mix, then let the starter sit at room temperature 6 to 8 hours. Use the starter at that time or refrigerate it.

Approximate values per 1-oz. (30 g) serving: **Calories** 50, **Total fat** 0 g, **Saturated fat** 0 g, **Cholesterol** 0 mg, **Sodium** 0 mg, **Total carbohydrates** 10 g, **Protein** 2 g

ALL-PURPOSE SPONGE (POOLISCH)

To streamline production, larger bakeries may use an all-purpose sponge for a variety of formulas. When this sponge is refrigerated after fermentation, it may be kept up to 24 hours before using.

Yield: 1 lb. 4 oz.

Fermentation: 4 to 6 hours

Bread flour, room temperature	10 oz.	300 g	100%
Water, 70°F (20°C)	10 fl. oz.	300 ml	100%
Instant yeast	0.07 oz. (½ tsp.)	2 g	0.7%
Total weight:	1 lb. 4 oz.	602 g	200%

1 Combine all ingredients. Mix until thoroughly blended, approximately 2 minutes. Lightly dust the surface of the dough with flour and then cover it with plastic film.

2 Ferment the dough at room temperature until doubled, approximately 4 to 6 hours. Use immediately or refrigerate the sponge overnight and use it within 24 hours.

3 To use the sponge, remove from the refrigerator 2 hours before needed, so that it reaches room temperature before use. Or cut the dough into small pieces and place on a well-floured sheet pan in a warm area or proof box to speed warming.

Approximate values per 1-oz. (30-g) serving: **Calories** 50, **Total fat** 0 g, **Saturated fat** 0 g, **Cholesterol** 0 mg, **Sodium** 0 mg, **Total carbohydrates** 10 g, **Protein** 2 g

OLD DOUGH (PÂTE FERMENTÉE)

Yield: 1 lb. 1 oz. (507 g)

Fermentation: 4 to 6 hours

Bread flour	10 oz.	300 g	100%
Instant yeast	0.15 oz. (1 tsp.)	4.5 g	1.5%
Water, 70°F (21°C)	6.5 fl. oz.	195 ml	65%
Salt	0.25 oz. (1¼ tsp.)	7.5 g	2.5%
Total weight:	1 lb. 1 oz.	507 g	169%

1 Combine the ingredients in the bowl of a mixer fitted with a dough hook. Knead on medium speed until a perfect windowpane has been reached, approximately 8 minutes. Lightly dust the dough with flour and cover it with plastic film.

2 Ferment the dough until fully doubled, approximately 4 to 6 hours.

3 Use the dough immediately or retard it in the refrigerator up to 4 days.

4 Remove the dough from the refrigerator 2 hours before needed so that the dough warms to room temperature, approximately 70°F (21°C), before use.

Approximate values per 1-oz. (30-g) serving: **Calories** 60, **Total fat** 0 g, **Saturated fat** 0 g, **Cholesterol** 0 mg, **Sodium** 170 mg, **Total carbohydrates** 13 g, **Protein** 2 g

TENDER-CRUSTED BREADS

RECIPE 7.9   **WHITE SANDWICH BREAD**

Yield: 2 Large Loaves   **Method:** Straight dough

Fermentation: 1 to 1½ hours.   **Proofing:** 30 minutes to 1 hour.

Water (temperature controlled)	12 fl. oz.	360 ml	50%
Nonfat dry milk powder	1.25 oz.	35 g	5%
Granulated sugar	1 oz.	30 g	4%
Salt	0.4 oz. (2 tsp.)	12 g	1.6%
Active dry yeast	0.5 oz.	15 g	2%
Bread flour	1 lb. 8 oz.	720 g	100%
Unsalted butter, softened	1 oz.	30 g	4%
Eggs	3.3 oz. (2 eggs)	100 g	14%
Total weight:	2 lb. 11 oz.	1302 g	180%

1 Combine the water, milk powder, sugar, salt, yeast and 12 ounces (360 grams) of the flour. Blend well. Add the butter and eggs and beat 2 minutes.

2 Stir in the remaining flour, 2 ounces (60 grams) at a time. Knead 8 minutes or until the dough reaches 77°F (25°C).

3 Place the dough in a lightly greased bowl, cover and ferment at room temperature until doubled, approximately 1 to 1½ hours.

4 Shape into loaves and proof until doubled.

5 Bake at 400°F (200°C) if free-form or small loaves; bake at 375°F (190°C) if larger loaves. Bake until brown and hollow-sounding, approximately 35 minutes for small loaves and 50 minutes for large loaves.

VARIATION:

Whole-Wheat Sandwich Bread—Substitute up to 12 ounces (360 grams/50%) whole-wheat flour for an equal amount of the bread flour.

Approximate values per 2-oz. (60-g) serving: **Calories** 150, **Total fat** 2 g, **Saturated fat** 1 g, **Cholesterol** 25 mg, **Sodium** 250 mg, **Total carbohydrates** 28 g, **Protein** 6 g, **Vitamin A** 4%, **Claims**—low fat

PULLMAN LOAVES

Yield: 2 Loaves, 1¾ lb. (840 g) each   **Method:** Straight dough

Fermentation: Bench rest, 25 minutes.

Proofing: 30 minutes to 1 hour.

Dry milk powder	0.75 oz.	20 g	2%
Bread flour	1 lb. 2 oz.	500 g	50%
High-gluten flour	1 lb. 2 oz.	500 g	50%
Water (temperature controlled)	19 fl. oz.	530 ml	53%
Compressed yeast	2.5 oz.	70 g	7%
Granulated sugar	0.3 oz. (2 tsp.)	10 g	1%
Salt	0.75 oz.	20 g	2%
Dough conditioner (optional)	0.75 oz.	20 g	2%
Unsalted butter, room temperature	1.75 oz.	50 g	5%
Total weight:	3 lb. 13 oz.	1720 g	172%

1 Stir the dry milk powder into the flours in the bowl of a mixer fitted with a dough hook. Add the remaining ingredients and mix on low speed to combine. Stop the machine and scrape down the bowl. The dough should be soft and smooth. Add more water if the dough appears to be dry. Increase speed to medium and knead the dough until it is fully developed and passes the windowpane test, approximately 7 minutes. The dough should reach 77°F (25°C).

2 Scrape the dough onto a lightly floured work bench and cover. Bench rest 10 minutes. Punch down the dough, then cover and bench rest another 5 minutes.

3 Divide the dough into two equal pieces, then round them, cover with plastic and bench rest 10 minutes. Shape the dough into long loaves and place the dough into greased Pullman or loaf pans. Or divide the dough into four equal pieces, shape into long loaves and twist two pieces together before placing them in greased pans.

4 Grease the interior of the Pullman pan lids or the bottoms of two half-sheet pans. Place the lids on the pans or the greased sheet pans on top of the loaves. Proof the dough until it is 1 inch away from the top of the pan.

5 Bake at 375°F (190°C) until well browned, approximately 60 to 65 minutes.

Approximate values per ¹/₁₇-loaf serving: **Calories** 120, **Total fat** 1.5 g, **Saturated fat** 1 g, **Cholesterol** 5 mg, **Sodium** 250 mg, **Total carbohydrates** 23 g, **Protein** 4 g

1 Twisting the Pullman dough before placing in the pan.

2 Pullman loaf after proofing.

3 Fully baked Pullman loaves.

RECIPE 7.11
WHOLE-WHEAT BREAD

Yield: 2 Large Loaves or 35 Dinner Rolls   **Method:** Straight dough

Fermentation: 1 to 2 hours.   **Proofing:** 30 minutes to 1 hour.

Salt	0.4 oz. (2 tsp.)	12 g	1.5%
Nonfat dry milk powder	1.25 oz.	40 g	5%
Whole-wheat flour	1 lb. 10 oz.	780 g	100%
Water (temperature controlled)	18 fl. oz.	540 ml	69%
Active dry yeast	0.5 oz.	15 g	2%
Honey	3 oz.	90 g	12%
Unsalted butter, softened	1 oz.	30 g	4%
Whole butter, melted (optional)	as needed	as needed	
Total dough weight:	3 lb. 2 oz.	1507 g	193%

1 Combine the salt and milk powder with 12 ounces (360 grams) of the flour in a large mixer bowl.
2 Stir in the water, yeast, honey and softened butter. Beat until combined into a thick batterlike dough.
3 Add the remaining flour, 2 ounces (60 grams) at a time. Knead on medium speed approximately 8 minutes until the dough reaches 77°F (25°C).
4 Place the dough in a lightly greased bowl and cover. Let the dough ferment in a warm place until doubled.
5 Punch down, portion and shape as desired.
6 Let the shaped dough proof until doubled. Bake at 375°F (190°C) until firm and dark brown, approximately 1 hour for loaves and 20 minutes for rolls. Brush the tops of the loaves or rolls with melted butter after baking, if desired.

Approximate values per 1½-oz. (45-g) serving: **Calories** 170, **Total fat** 2 g, **Saturated fat** 1 g, **Cholesterol** 5 mg, **Sodium** 250 mg, **Total carbohydrates** 32 g, **Protein** 6 g, **Claims**—low fat; low saturated fat; low cholesterol; good source of fiber

RECIPE 7.12
ENGLISH MUFFIN LOAVES

Yield: 2 Large Loaves   **Method:** Straight dough

Fermentation: 30 minutes to 1 hour.

Active dry yeast	0.5 oz.	15 g	2%
Granulated sugar	0.4 oz. (1 Tbsp.)	13 g	1.7%
Baking soda	0.03 oz. (¼ tsp.)	0.75 g	0.1%
Salt	0.4 oz. (2 tsp.)	13 g	1.7%
All-purpose flour	1 lb. 8 oz.	720 g	100%
Milk	1 pt.	480 ml	67%
Water	4 fl. oz.	120 ml	17%
Cornmeal	as needed	as needed	
Total batter weight:	2 lb. 13 oz.	1362 g	190%

1 Stir together the yeast, sugar, baking soda, salt and 12 ounces (360 grams) of the flour.
2 Combine the milk and water and heat to 120°F (49°C).
3 Stir the warm liquids into the dry ingredients, beating well. Add enough of the remaining flour to make a stiff batter.
4 Spoon the batter into loaf pans that have been greased and dusted with cornmeal. Proof until doubled.
5 Bake at 400°F (200°C) until golden brown and done, approximately 25 minutes.

Approximate values per 1/12-loaf serving: **Calories** 119, **Total fat** 1 g, **Saturated fat** 0.5 g, **Cholesterol** 3 mg, **Sodium** 202 mg, **Total carbohydrates** 23 g, **Protein** 4 g

AMERICAN HAMBURGER OR HOT DOG ROLLS

Yield: 32 Rolls, 2 oz. (60 g) each   **Method:** Straight dough

Fermentation: Bench rest, 25 minutes. **Proofing:** 20 to 30 minutes.

Compressed yeast	3.5 oz.	100 g	10%
Water (temperature controlled)	15.5 fl. oz.	440 ml	44%
Salt	0.5 oz.	16 g	1.6%
Bread flour	2 lb. 3 oz.	1000 g	100%
Dough conditioner (optional)	0.5 oz.	15 g	1.5%
Vegetable shortening or lard	3.5 oz.	100 g	10%
Granulated sugar	3.5 oz.	100 g	10%
Dry milk powder	1 oz.	25 g	2.5%
Vital wheat gluten	0.5 oz.	15 g	1.5%
Eggs	3.3 oz. (2 eggs)	100 g	10%
Egg wash	as needed	as needed	
Total dough weight:	4 lb. 2 oz.	1911 g	191%

1 Dissolve the yeast in half of the water and set aside.

2 Dissolve the salt in the remaining water in the bowl of a mixer fitted with a dough hook. Add flour, dough conditioner (if using), shortening, sugar, milk powder, gluten and eggs. Stir in the yeast mixture and mix to combine the ingredients 3 minutes at low speed. Stop the machine and scrape down the bowl. Add more flour or water to make a soft dough. Increase speed to medium and knead the dough until fully developed, approximately 7 to 9 minutes. The dough should reach 77°F (25°C).

3 Scrape the dough onto a lightly floured work bench and cover. Bench rest 10 minutes. Punch down the dough, cover and bench rest another 5 minutes.

4 Divide the dough into 2-ounce (60-gram) pieces. Bench rest another 10 minutes. Round the rolls, then bench rest another 10 minutes.

5 Make up the dough into rolls for hamburger buns, then flatten slightly and place them on paper-lined sheet pans. For hot dog rolls, roll the dough into oblongs 6 inches (15 centimeters) long.

6 Brush with egg wash, then proof the rolls until doubled, 20 to 30 minutes. Bake at 450°F (230°C), with steam injected into the oven during the first few seconds of baking, until golden brown, approximately 9 to 12 minutes.

Approximate values per roll: **Calories** 160, **Total fat** 4 g, **Saturated fat** 1 g, **Cholesterol** 15 mg, **Sodium** 180 mg, **Total carbohydrates** 27 g, **Protein** 5 g

RECIPE 7.14

TENDER POTATO HERB ROLLS

Yield: 35 Rolls, 2 oz. (60 g) each   **Method:** Straight dough

Fermentation: Approximately 1 hour.   **Proofing:** 30 minutes to 1 hour.

Bread flour	2 lb. 2 oz.	1020 g	92%
Potato flour	3 oz.	90 g	8%
Instant yeast	1 oz.	30 g	3%
Water (temperature controlled)	21 fl. oz.	630 ml	57%
Eggs	3.3 oz. (2 eggs)	100 g	9%
Dry milk powder	1.5 oz.	45 g	4%
Granulated sugar	2.5 oz.	75 g	7%
Salt	0.75 oz.	22 g	2%
Olive oil	3 fl. oz.	90 ml	8%
Fresh parsley, chopped fine	1 oz.	30 g	3%
Fresh chervil, chopped fine	0.5 oz.	15 g	1.5%
Fresh rosemary, chopped fine	0.14 oz. (2 tsp.)	4 g	0.4%
Black pepper	0.2 oz. (1 Tbsp.)	6 g	0.5%
Egg wash	as needed	as needed	
Onion slices, $\frac{1}{8}$ inch (3 millimeters) thick (optional)	35	35	
Kosher salt	as needed	as needed	
Total dough weight:	4 lb. 7 oz.	2157 g	195%

1 Place the flours, yeast, water, eggs, milk powder, sugar, salt and oil in the bowl of a mixer fitted with a dough hook. Mix on low speed to combine. Knead on medium speed until a perfect windowpane has been reached and the dough reaches 77°F (25°C), approximately 7 to 9 minutes. Mix in the herbs and pepper just until evenly distributed in the dough.

2 Cover the dough and ferment until doubled in bulk, approximately 1 hour.

3 Punch down the dough and divide into 2-ounce (60-gram) pieces. Round and place on paper-lined sheet pans.

4 Proof until the rolls increase 70 to 80 percent in volume.

5 Brush the proofed rolls carefully with egg wash and place a slice of onion on top of each roll (if using). Sprinkle with kosher salt.

6 Bake without steam at 375°F (190°C) until golden brown, approximately 16 to 18 minutes.

Approximate values per roll: **Calories** 150, **Total fat** 3.5 g, **Saturated fat** 0.5 g, **Cholesterol** 10 mg, **Sodium** 250 mg, **Total carbohydrates** 26 g, **Protein** 5 g

POTATO CHEDDAR CHEESE BREAD

STOUFFER STANFORD COURT HOTEL, SAN FRANCISCO, CA
Former Executive Chef Ercolino Crugnale

Yield: 7 Loaves, 1 lb. 4 oz. (600 g) each   **Method:** Straight dough

Fermentation: Approximately 2 hours.   **Proofing:** 45 minutes.

Active dry yeast	2 oz.	60 g	2.7%
Water, warm (100°F/38°C)	8 fl. oz.	240 ml	11%
Potatoes, boiled and peeled	2 lb.	950 g	44%
Bread flour	4 lb. 8 oz.	2160 g	100%
Kosher salt	1.5 oz.	45 g	2%
Cracked pepper	1 oz.	30 g	1.4%
Unsalted butter, melted	3 oz.	90 g	4%
Cheddar cheese, grated	1 lb.	475 g	22%
Water, room temperature	1 pt.	475 ml	22%
Total weight:	9 lb. 7 oz.	4525 g	209%

1 Dissolve the yeast in the warm water and set aside.

2 Pass the potatoes through a ricer. Combine the riced potatoes with the flour, salt, pepper, butter and cheese in a mixer bowl. Blend on low speed 2 to 3 minutes.

3 Slowly add the room-temperature water and the yeast mixture. Knead on medium speed 8 to 10 minutes.

4 Allow the dough to ferment in a warm spot until doubled, approximately 2 hours. Punch down the dough and divide into seven equal loaves.

5 Proof in a flour-dusted banneton until doubled in size, approximately 45 minutes. Remove the proofed dough from the banneton and bake at 350°F (180°C) until brown, approximately 20 to 30 minutes.

Approximate values per 1½-oz. (45-g) serving: **Calories** 150, **Total fat** 3.5 g, **Saturated fat** 2 g, **Cholesterol** 10 mg, **Sodium** 280 mg, **Total carbohydrates** 25 g, **Protein** 6 g, **Calcium** 10%, **Claims**—low cholesterol

RECIPE 7.16 **BLACK PEPPER CHEDDAR BREAD**

Yield: 4 Loaves, approximately 1 lb. 4 oz. (600 g) each

Method: Sponge and old dough

Fermentation: Sponge and old dough, 4 to 6 hours. Final dough, about 1 hour.

Proofing: 30 to 45 minutes.

Bread flour	1 lb. 12 oz.	840 g	100%
Instant yeast	0.75 oz.	25 g	3%
Water (temperature controlled)	13 fl. oz.	395 ml	47%
Salt	0.75 oz.	25 g	3%
All-Purpose Sponge (page 155), room temperature	1 lb. 4 oz.	600 g	71%
Old Dough (page 155), room temperature (optional)	1 lb.	480 g	57%
Black pepper	0.25 oz. (1 Tbsp.)	7.5 g	0.9%
Cheddar cheese, large dice	12 oz.	360 g	43%
Total weight:	5 lb. 10 oz.	2732 g	325%

1 Combine the flour, yeast, water and salt with the sponge in the bowl of a mixer fitted with a dough hook. Mix on low speed to blend the ingredients. Knead on medium speed until dough is almost fully developed. Add the old dough in small pieces (if using) and knead until proper dough temperature is reached. Add pepper and cheese and mix until well combined.

2 Cover the dough and ferment until doubled, approximately 1 hour.

3 Punch down the dough and divide into four equal loaves.

4 Proof the dough at 80°F (25°C) until the loaves increase 50 percent in volume, approximately 30 to 45 minutes.

5 Score the loaves. Bake at 400°F (200°C), with steam injected into the oven during the first few minutes of baking, until well browned, approximately 45 minutes.

VARIATION:

Blue Cheese–Red Onion Bread—Reduce the black pepper to 0.07 ounces (1 teaspoon/2 grams/0.2%). Omit the Cheddar cheese. Once the dough is well kneaded, add 0.75 ounces (25 grams/3%) chopped fresh parsley, 6 ounces (180 grams/21%) coarsely chopped red onion and 10 ounces (300 grams/35%) blue cheese. Mix only to evenly distribute the ingredients through the dough.

Approximate values per 2-oz. (60-g) serving: **Calories** 160, **Total fat** 3.5 g, **Saturated fat** 2 g, **Cholesterol** 10 mg, **Sodium** 330 mg, **Total carbohydrates** 25 g, **Protein** 6 g, **Iron** 10%

CARROT BREAD WITH HERBS

Yield: 3 Loaves, approximately 1 lb. 8 oz. (720 g) each

Method: Straight dough or old dough

Fermentation: Old dough, 4 to 6 hours. Final dough, 1 hour.

Proofing: 35 to 40 minutes.

Water (temperature controlled)	21 fl. oz.	625 ml	65%
Olive oil	1.5 fl. oz.	45 ml	5%
Salt	0.75 oz.	22 g	2.3%
Granulated sugar	0.75 oz.	22 g	2.3%
Bread flour	2 lb.	960 g	100%
Instant yeast	0.5 oz.	15 g	1.5%
Old Dough (page 155), room temperature (optional)	1 lb.	480 g	50%
Fresh parsley, chopped fine	2 oz.	60 g	6%
Fresh thyme, chopped fine	0.5 oz.	5 g	1.5%
Onion, chopped fine	5 oz.	150 g	16%
Carrots, grated coarse	8 oz.	240 g	25%
Total weight:	5 lb. 8 oz.	2624 g	274%

1 Place the water, oil, salt and sugar in the bowl of a mixer fitted with a dough hook. Add the flour and yeast. Blend on low speed to combine. Knead at medium speed until the dough is almost fully developed.

2 Add the old dough in small pieces (if using) and continue mixing until the dough is smooth and elastic. The dough should reach 77°F (25°C) and pass the windowpane test. Knead in the herbs and vegetables on low speed just to incorporate.

3 Cover the dough and ferment until doubled, approximately 1 hour.

4 Punch down the dough, divide into three equal pieces and shape as desired.

5 Proof at 80°F (25°C) until the loaves increase 50 percent in volume, approximately 30 to 45 minutes.

6 Score the loaves. Bake at 400°F (200°C), with steam injected into the oven during the first few minutes of baking, until well browned, approximately 40 to 45 minutes.

Approximate values per 2-oz. (60-g) serving: **Calories** 120, **Total fat** 1.5 g, **Saturated fat** 0 g, **Cholesterol** 0 mg, **Sodium** 250 mg, **Total carbohydrates** 22 g, **Protein** 4 g, **Vitamin A** 40%

RECIPE 7.18   **TIGER BREAD**

1 Spreading topping over proofed bread.

2 The finished tiger bread.

This light wheat bread takes its name from the distinctive crackled pattern its coating gives the finished loaf. The coating may be used on any tender-crust, mild wheat bread.

Yield: 4 Loaves, approximately 13 oz. (390 g) each

Method: Straight dough

Fermentation: Approximately 2 hours.

Proofing: Approximately 25 minutes.

Dough:

Bread flour	2 lb. 3 oz.	1000 g	100%
Dough conditioner (optional)	0.75 oz.	20 g	2%
Shortening	0.3 oz. (2 tsp.)	10 ml	1%
Salt	0.75 oz.	20 g	2%
Compressed yeast	0.75 oz.	20 g	2%
Granulated sugar	0.3 oz. (2 tsp.)	10 g	1%
Water (temperature controlled)	18 fl. oz.	520 ml	52%
Total dough weight:	3 lb. 7 oz.	1600 g	160%

Topping:

Rice flour	1.75 oz.	50 g
Bread crumbs, dry	1.75 oz.	50 g
Compressed yeast	0.2 oz. (1 tsp.)	5 g
Granulated sugar	0.25 oz. (2 tsp.)	7 g
Vegetable oil	0.25 fl. oz. (2 tsp.)	7 ml
Water (temperature controlled)	3.5 fl. oz.	100 ml
Total weight:	7 oz.	219 g

1 Prepare the dough by combining all the dough ingredients in the bowl of a mixer fitted with a dough hook. Mix on low approximately 3 minutes. Stop the machine and scrape down the bowl. Add additional flour to make a firm dough if needed. Increase speed to high and knead approximately 6 to 7 minutes. The dough will be smooth yet somewhat firm and should reach 77°F (25°C).

2 Cover the dough and ferment 1 hour.

3 Divide the dough into four equal pieces. Round the dough, cover and bench rest 45 minutes.

4 Form the dough into short baguettes 12 inches (30 centimeters) long. Proof on a parchment-lined sheet pan until loaves have increased 75 percent in volume.

5 While the dough is proofing, prepare the topping. Place all the topping ingredients in the bowl of a mixer fitted with a paddle. Mix until well blended, approximately 2 to 3 minutes. The mixture should be somewhat wet and sticky but not loose. Cover the topping and ferment in a warm place 30 minutes.

6 Place the topping in a piping bag fitted with a medium plain tip. Pipe the topping over the proofed loaves, then use an offset spatula to spread it smoothly over the bread, covering the entire surface of each loaf down to the parchment paper. Resume proofing the loaves until the topping begins to crack, approximately 10 to 15 minutes.

7 Bake at 450°F (230°C) with steam injected into the oven during the first few seconds of baking. Immediately reduce the oven temperature to 375°F (190°C) and bake until crisp and browned, approximately 30 to 35 minutes.

Approximate values per ⅑-loaf serving: **Calories** 110, **Total fat** 1 g, **Saturated fat** 0 g, **Cholesterol** 0 mg, **Sodium** 230 mg, **Total carbohydrates** 22 g, **Protein** 3 g

HARD-CRUSTED BREADS

KAISER OR VIENNA ROLLS

Yield: 28 Rolls, 2 oz. (60 g) each   **Method:** Straight dough

Fermentation: Bench rest, 30 minutes.   **Proofing:** 35 to 45 minutes.

Bread flour	2 lb. 3 oz.	1000 g	100%
Dough conditioner (optional)	0.75 oz.	25 g	2%
Vegetable shortening	1 oz.	30 g	3%
Salt	0.75 oz.	20 g	2%
Compressed yeast	1.75 oz.	50 g	5%
Water (temperature controlled)	19.5 fl. oz.	550 ml	55%
Vegetable oil	as needed	as needed	
Poppy seeds	as needed	as needed	
Sesame seeds	as needed	as needed	
Caraway seeds	as needed	as needed	
Coarse salt	as needed	as needed	
Total dough weight:	3 lb. 10 oz.	1670 g	167%

Stamping the Kaiser roll.

1 Combine the flour, dough conditioner (if using), shortening, salt, yeast and water in the bowl of a mixer fitted with a dough hook. Mix on low speed 3 to 4 minutes, until blended. Stop the machine and scrape down the bowl. The dough should be somewhat soft and smooth. Add more water if the dough appears dry. Increase the speed to medium and knead until the dough is fully developed and reaches 77°F (25°C), approximately 7 to 9 minutes.

2 Scrape the dough onto a lightly floured workbench and cover. Ferment 10 minutes. Punch down the dough and fold over to release gases. Cover and bench rest another 10 minutes.

3 Divide the dough into 2-ounce (30-gram) pieces. Round the dough, cover and bench rest another 10 minutes. Place the formed dough onto paper-lined sheet pans, spaced 2 inches (5 centimeters) apart. Brush the tops of the dough with oil and proof until doubled in size, approximately 20 to 30 minutes.

4 Dip a Kaiser roll stamp in flour and press into each proofed roll. Spray the rolls lightly with water and sprinkle them with poppy, sesame or caraway seeds combined with no more than 10 percent coarse salt. Proof another 15 minutes.

5 Bake at 450°F (230°C), with steam injected into the oven during the first few minutes of baking, until golden brown, approximately 12 to 14 minutes.

Approximate values per roll: **Calories** 130, **Total fat** 1.5 g, **Saturated fat** 0 g, **Cholesterol** 0 mg, **Sodium** 280 mg, **Total carbohydrates** 24 g, **Protein** 4 g

RECIPE 7.20

ONION RING LOAVES

1 Coating the onion ring in flour before proofing.

2 The finished onion ring loaves.

Yield: 6 Loaves, 10 oz. (300 g) each   **Method:** Straight dough

Fermentation: Bench rest, approximately 35 minutes.

Proofing: 20 to 30 minutes.

Bread flour	2 lb. 2 oz.	950 g	95%
Light rye flour	1.75 oz	50 g	5%
Water (temperature controlled)	19.5 fl. oz.	550 ml	55%
Compressed yeast	0.7 oz.	25 g	2%
Toasted onion flakes	3.5 oz.	100 g	10%
Salt	0.6 oz.	18 g	1.8%
Dough conditioner (optional)	0.3 oz. (2 tsp.)	10 g	1%
Vegetable shortening	0.5 oz.	15 g	1.5%
Rye flour	as needed	as needed	
Total dough weight:	3 lb. 12 oz.	1718 g	171%

1 Combine all the ingredients in the bowl of a mixer fitted with a dough hook. Mix on low speed to combine. Stop the machine and scrape down the bowl. Add more water if the dough appears dry. Increase speed to medium and knead until the dough is fully developed and reaches 77°C (25°C), approximately 7 to 8 minutes.

2 Scrape the dough onto a lightly floured workbench and cover. Rest 15 minutes. Punch down the dough and fold over to release gases. Cover and bench rest another 10 minutes.

3 Divide the dough into 10-ounce (300-gram) pieces. Round, cover and bench rest another 10 minutes.

4 Roll the dough pieces into 12-inch- (30-centimeter-) long ropes as for baguettes. Moisten each end of a piece of dough lightly with water. Press the ends together to form a ring.

5 Place the rings, top-side down, onto a sheet pan lined with a very wet, clean towel. Then dip each moistened ring in rye flour and place flour side up on paper-lined sheet pans. Cover and proof until doubled in size, approximately 20–30 minutes.

6 Score each ring four times in a crosshatch pattern.

7 Bake at 420°F (215°C), with steam injected into the oven during the first 2 minutes of baking, until well browned, approximately 15 to 20 minutes. Open the oven door slightly during the last 5 minutes of baking to remove any trace of steam.

Approximate values per ⅙-loaf serving: **Calories** 120, **Total fat** 1 g, **Saturated fat** 0 g, **Cholesterol** 0 mg, **Sodium** 260 mg, **Total carbohydrates** 23 g, **Protein** 4 g

ONION WALNUT BREAD

Yield: 4 Loaves, 1 lb. 6 oz. (660 g) each

Method: Sponge and old dough

Fermentation: Sponge and old dough, 4 to 6 hours. Final dough, about 1 hour.

Proofing: 45 minutes to 1 hour.

Topping:

Onions, peeled	12 oz.	360 g	
Powdered sugar	as needed	as needed	
Kosher salt	as needed	as needed	

Dough:

All-Purpose Sponge (page 155), room temperature	1 lb. 4 oz.	600 g	62%
Bread flour	1 lb. 8 oz.	720 g	75%
Dark rye flour	4 oz.	120 g	12.5%
Whole-wheat flour	4 oz.	120 g	12.5%
Instant yeast	0.75 oz.	22 g	2.3%
Water (temperature controlled)	16 fl. oz.	480 ml	50%
Salt	1 oz.	30 g	3%
Old Dough (page 155), room temperature (optional)	1 lb.	480 g	50%
Walnuts, chopped	6 oz.	175 g	19%
Total dough weight:	5 lb. 11 oz.	2747 g	286%

1 Cut the onions into ⅛-inch- (3-millimeter-) thick slices. Place them on paper-lined sheet pans. Lightly dust with powdered sugar and sprinkle with kosher salt. Bake the onions at 375°F (190°C) until lightly browned. Set aside.

2 Place the sponge, flours, yeast, water and salt in the bowl of a mixer fitted with a dough hook. Mix on low speed to combine the ingredients. Then knead on medium speed until the dough is smooth and elastic and reaches 77°F (25°C), approximately 7 to 10 minutes.

3 Add the old dough in small pieces (if using). Continue kneading until the dough is fully developed. Mix in 8 ounces (240 grams) of the cooked onions and the walnuts until combined.

4 Ferment the dough until doubled, approximately 1 hour.

5 Punch down the dough and divide into four equal pieces. Shape into loaves and place seam side down on a floured canvas, banneton or sheet pan. Proof in a warm area until the loaves increase 50 percent in volume, approximately 45 minutes to 1 hour.

6 Flip the loaves onto a baking sheet or peel, if necessary. Score the top and then garnish with the remaining onions. Bake at 425°F (220°C), with steam injected into the oven during the first few minutes of baking, until golden brown, 40 to 45 minutes.

Approximate values per 2-oz. (60-g) serving: **Calories** 140, **Total fat** 3.5 g, **Saturated fat** 0 g, **Cholesterol** 0 mg, **Sodium** 290 mg, **Total carbohydrates** 24 g, **Protein** 5 g, **Iron** 10%

RECIPE 7.22

FRENCH OR ITALIAN BREAD

Yield: 4 Loaves, 1 lb. 7 oz. (690 g) each   **Method:** Straight dough

Fermentation: 1 to 3 hours.   **Proofing:** 30 to 45 minutes.

Water, warm	1 qt.	955 ml	53%
Active dry yeast	1 oz.	28 g	1.6%
Bread flour	3 lb. 12 oz.	1.8 kg	100%
Salt	1 oz.	28 g	1.6%
Total weight:	5 lb. 14 oz.	2811 g	156%

1 Combine the water and yeast in the bowl of a mixer fitted with a dough hook. Add the remaining ingredients and mix on low speed until all the flour is incorporated.

2 Increase to medium speed and knead the dough until it is smooth and elastic.

3 Ferment the dough until doubled. Punch down, divide, shape and score as desired. Proof the loaves until doubled.

4 Bake at 400°F (200°C), with steam injected during the first few minutes of baking, until the crust is well developed and golden brown and the bread is baked through, approximately 12 minutes for rolls and 20 minutes for small loaves.

Approximate values per 1½-oz. (45-g) serving: **Calories** 80, **Total fat** 0 g, **Saturated fat** 0 g, **Cholesterol** 0 mg, **Sodium** 135 mg, **Total carbohydrates** 16 g, **Protein** 3 g, **Claims**—fat free; low sodium; no sugar

RECIPE 7.23

FRENCH COUNTRY LOAF (PAIN DE CAMPAGNE)

Yield: 3 Loaves, 1 lb. 6 oz. (660 g) each

Method: Old dough or straight dough

Fermentation: Old dough, 4 to 6 hours. Final dough, 1 to 2 hours.

Proofing: 35 to 40 minutes.

Bread flour	1 lb. 2 oz.	540 g	90%
Dark rye flour	2 oz.	60 g	10%
Instant yeast	0.5 oz.	15 g	2.5%
Water (temperature controlled)	13 fl. oz.	390 ml	65%
Salt	0.5 oz.	15 g	2.5%
Old Dough (page 155), room temperature (optional)	2 lb.	960 g	160%
Total weight:	4 lb. 2 oz.	1980 g	330%

1 Place the flours, yeast, water and salt in the bowl of a mixer fitted with a dough hook. Mix on low speed until blended. Increase the speed to medium and knead until the dough is smooth and elastic, approximately 7 to 10 minutes. Add the old dough in small pieces (if using). Continue kneading until the dough is fully developed and reaches 77°F (25°C).

2 Cover the dough and ferment until doubled in size, 1 to 2 hours.

3 Punch down the dough and divide into four equal pieces. Shape into round loaves, then place the dough seam side down on flour-dusted canvas or a sheet pan lightly dusted with rice flour, coarse cornmeal or bread flour. Proof until the loaves increase 55 to 65 percent in volume, approximately 30 to 45 minutes.

4 Remove the dough from the proof box and uncover the loaves to allow the surface of the bread to dry slightly. Use the canvas to roll the bread onto sheet pans. Score the loaves.

5 Bake at 450°F (230°C), with steam injected into the oven during the first few minutes of baking, until the crust is a deep dark brown, approximately 38 to 40 minutes.

VARIATION:

Walnut Bread—Once the dough is mixed, knead in 12 ounces (360 grams/60%) coarsely chopped walnuts. Knead just long enough to incorporate the walnuts without crushing them. Ferment, then divide the dough and shape into round loaves or rolls.

Approximate values per ¹/₇-loaf serving: **Calories** 90, **Total fat** 0 g, **Saturated fat** 0 g, **Cholesterol** 0 mg, **Sodium** 250 mg, **Total carbohydrates** 18 g, **Protein** 0 g

CUBAN-STYLE BREAD   RECIPE 7.24

This plump loaf is unique because a strip of wet palmetto leaf is applied to the top of the bread before baking. Scoring is not necessary as the leaf helps the loaf burst open during baking. When palm leaves are not available, the bread is scored down the middle. Popular with the Cuban community in Tampa, Florida, this bread is ideal eaten buttered or layered with ham, roast pork and cheese and then pressed for the classic Cubano sandwich.

Yield: 3 Loaves, approximately 1 lb. 4 oz. (600 g) each

Method: Straight dough

Fermentation: 2 hours 15 minutes. **Proofing:** Approximately 1 hour.

Compressed yeast	0.3 oz. (2 tsp.)	10 g	1%
Water (temperature controlled)	23 fl. oz.	650 ml	65%
Bread flour	1 lb.	500 g	50%
High-gluten flour	1 lb.	500 g	50%
Salt	0.75 oz.	20 g	2%
Dough conditioner (optional)	1 oz.	30 g	3%
Dry malt	0.3 oz. (2 tsp.)	10 g	1%
Shortening	0.14 oz. (1 tsp.)	4 g	0.4%
Palmetto leaves	3	3	
Total dough weight:	3 lb. 13 oz.	1724 g	172%

1 Dissolve the yeast in the water in the bowl of a mixer fitted with a dough hook. Add the flours, salt, dough conditioner (if using), malt and shortening and mix on low speed 2 minutes. Scrape down the bowl and knead another 5 minutes at high speed until dough is smooth and elastic and reaches 77°F (25°C).

2 Cover the dough and ferment 1 hour. Punch down the dough, then bench rest another 60 minutes.

3 Scrape the dough onto a lightly floured workbench. Divide the dough into three equal pieces. Round the dough, cover and bench rest 15 minutes.

4 Roll the dough into oblong loaves 10 inches (25 centimeters) long and place into bannetons lined with washed palmetto leaves. Or place the formed loaves onto cornmeal-dusted sheet pans. Brush the surface with water and place a palmetto leaf on top.

5 Proof the loaves at low humidity until doubled, approximately 1 hour. If palmetto leaves are not available, score the bread lengthwise after proofing. Bake at 450°F (230°C), with steam injected into the oven during the first few seconds of baking. Immediately reduce the temperature to 350°F (180°C) and bake until browned, approximately 35 to 40 minutes. Remove the palmetto leaf before serving.

Approximate values per ¹/₁₂-loaf serving: **Calories** 100, **Total fat** 0.5 g, **Saturated fat** 0 g, **Cholesterol** 0 mg, **Sodium** 230 mg, **Total carbohydrates** 21 g, **Protein** 4 g

MULTIGRAIN, RYE AND SOURDOUGH BREADS

This category of breads requires special handling. The low protein and coarse texture of whole grains cuts into the gluten strands that develop when kneading dough. Higher-protein flours such as high-gluten flour as well as vital wheat gluten (see Chapter 4, Bakeshop Ingredients) are added to strengthen multigrain and rye doughs.

Rye grows well in colder northern climates and was for centuries the primary grain available for bread making in Europe. German, Austrian and other central European bakers have mastered working with this challenging grain. The protein in rye flour is not usable to form the gluten structure necessary to make rye loaves rise; bread formulas with more than 40 percent rye flour will be dense, flat and uneven when baked. Combining rye with higher-protein flour compensates for this while preserving rye flavor. Sourdough starters add flavor to rye breads and their chemical properties help rye ferment, something rye flour does rapidly. Rye doughs are mixed and baked relatively quickly and can overproof easily.

RECIPE 7.25	NINE-GRAIN BREAD

Yield: 3 Loaves, 1 lb. 9 oz. (750 g) each

Method: Straight dough or old dough

Fermentation: Old dough, 4 to 6 hours. Final dough, 1 to 1½ hours.

Proofing: 30 to 45 minutes.

*Nine-grain mix	8 oz.	240 g	33%
Water, room temperature	10 oz.	300 g	42%
High-gluten flour	1 lb. 8 oz.	720 g	100%
Vital wheat gluten	1.25 oz.	36 g	5%
Instant yeast	0.75 oz.	22 g	3%
Salt	0.75 oz.	22 g	3%
Water (temperature controlled)	16 fl. oz.	485 ml	67%
Old Dough (page 155), room temperature (optional)	1 lb.	480 g	66%
Total weight:	4 lb. 12 oz.	2305 g	319%

1 Soak the nine-grain mix in the room-temperature water in a mixer bowl 1 hour.

2 Sift the flour and gluten into the soaked grains. Add the yeast, salt and temperature-controlled water to the flour mixture. Mix on low speed to combine, then knead at medium speed until the dough is smooth and pulls away from the sides of the bowl and reaches 77°F (25°C).

3 Add the old dough in small pieces (if using) and continue mixing until a perfect windowpane is reached.

4 Ferment the dough until doubled in bulk, 1 to 1½ hours.

5 Punch down the dough and divide into 26-ounce (780-gram) pieces. Mold the dough into plump oval loaves. Place them on paper-lined sheet pans or on floured canvas. Proof the dough in a warm area until the loaves increase 50 percent in volume, approximately 30 to 45 minutes.

6 Gently use the canvas to turn the loaves onto a floured peel or baking sheet. Score the loaves.

7 Bake at 400°F (200°C), with steam injected during the first few seconds of baking, until the crust is a deep dark brown, approximately 40 to 45 minutes.

*Nine-grain mix is a blend of various grains including cracked wheat, barley, cornmeal, millet, rolled oats, rye, triticale, brown rice, soy flour and flax seeds. Any combination of these grains will work in this recipe.

Approximate values per 2-oz. (60-g) serving: **Calories** 120, **Total fat** 1 g, **Saturated fat** 0 g, **Cholesterol** 0 mg, **Sodium** 290 mg, **Total carbohydrates** 24 g, **Protein** 5 g

MULTIGRAIN SOURDOUGH BREAD   RECIPE 7.26

Yield: 2 Loaves, 9 in. × 5 in. (22 cm × 13 cm)   **Method:** Straight dough

Fermentation: 2 to 3 hours.   **Proofing:** 30 to 45 minutes.

Cracked wheat	4.5 oz.	135 g	22%
Water, hot	8 fl. oz.	240 ml	40%
Whole butter, melted	2 oz.	60 g	10%
Molasses	1.5 oz.	45 g	7.5%
Honey	1.5 oz.	45 g	7.5%
Salt	0.2 oz. (1 tsp.)	6 g	1%
Nonfat dry milk powder	2 oz.	60 g	10%
Flax seeds	2 oz.	60 g	10%
Sunflower seeds, roasted	2 oz.	60 g	10%
Sourdough starter	1 lb. 6 oz.	660 g	110%
Active dry yeast	0.15 oz. (1 tsp.)	4.5 g	0.7%
Whole-wheat flour	10 oz.	300 g	50%
Bread flour	10 oz.	300 g	50%
Egg wash	as needed	as needed	
Total dough weight:	4 lb. 1 oz.	1975 g	328%

1 Combine the cracked wheat and water in the bowl of an electric mixer. Add the butter, molasses, honey, salt and milk powder. Set aside to cool.

2 When the mixture has cooled to lukewarm, stir in the flax seeds, sunflower seeds, starter and yeast. Stir in the whole-wheat flour, then gradually add the bread flour. When the dough begins to stiffen, attach the bowl to a mixer fitted with a dough hook and continue adding the bread flour. Knead until the dough is smooth and elastic, approximately 5 minutes.

3 Place the dough in a lightly oiled bowl, cover and ferment until doubled.

4 Punch down the risen dough, cover and ferment again.

5 After the second rise, punch down the dough and divide into two equal portions. Place the dough into two well-greased loaf pans, cover and proof the dough until doubled again.

6 Brush the surface of each loaf with egg wash and make two or three cuts across the top of each loaf. Bake at 375°F (190°C) until done, approximately 30 minutes.

Approximate values per 1/16-loaf serving: **Calories** 150, **Total fat** 3.5 g, **Saturated fat** 1 g, **Cholesterol** 5 mg, **Sodium** 90 mg, **Total carbohydrates** 26 g, **Protein** 5 g, **Iron** 10%, **Claims—** good source of fiber and iron

RECIPE 7.27   **GERMAN MASON'S BREAD**

This is a typical German sourdough with a mild sour flavor and rustic appearance. To develop its taste, the bread is baked until deeply browned; the caramelization of the crust intensifies the flavor of the crumb. Like many breads made with rye flour, this loaf is best eaten 24 hours after it is baked; the resting time allows the flavor to develop.

Yield: 4 Loaves, approximately 14 oz. (420 g) each

Method: Sourdough starter

Fermentation: Sourdough sponge, overnight, 15 to 20 hours. Final dough, 30 minutes.

Proofing: 1 hour.

Sourdough starter	0.7 oz.	20 g	2%
Water, cool	5.5 fl. oz.	160 ml	16%
Light rye flour	10.5 oz.	300 g	30%
Bread flour	1 lb. 8 oz.	700 g	70%
Dough conditioner (optional)	0.7 oz.	20 g	2%
Compressed yeast	1.5 oz.	40 g	4%
Salt	0.6 oz.	18 g	1.8%
Shortening	0.3 oz. (2 tsp.)	10 g	1%
Water (temperature controlled)	1 pt.	460 ml	46%
Clarified butter	as needed	as needed	
Starch Wash (recipe follows)	as needed	as needed	
Total dough weight:	3 lb. 11 oz.	1728 g	173%

1 The day before making the finished bread, make the sourdough sponge. Combine the starter, cool water and 7 ounces (210 grams) of the rye flour. Mix to combine ingredients, cover and ferment at room temperature approximately 15 to 20 hours.

2 Combine the sponge with the remaining rye flour, the bread flour, dough conditioner (if using), yeast, salt, shortening and temperature-controlled water in the bowl of a mixer fitted with a dough hook on low speed. Mix approximately 3 minutes to combine all ingredients. Stop the machine and scrape down the bowl. Knead the dough on medium speed until it is smooth and comes away from the sides of the bowl, 5 to 7 minutes. The dough will be elastic and somewhat sticky and should reach 77°F (25°C) after kneading.

3 Cover the dough and ferment 15 minutes.

4 Punch down the dough and divide into four equal pieces. Round the dough, cover and bench rest 15 minutes. Round the loaves and place them seam side down into rye-flour-dusted bannetons. Proof at room temperature until the loaves have increased 75 percent in volume, approximately 1 hour.

5 Flip the loaves onto a sheet pan or peel lightly dusted with cornmeal. Place into an oven preheated to 425°F (220°C), with steam injected into the oven during the first few minutes of baking. Immediately reduce temperature to 350°F (180°C) and bake to a deep, rich brown, approximately 30 to 35 minutes. (To avoid a soggy crust, slightly open the oven door or vent during the last few minutes of baking to let any condensed steam escape.)

6 Brush the baked loaves with clarified butter or starch wash as soon as they are removed from the oven.

Approximate values per ⅑-loaf serving: **Calories** 100, **Total fat** 0.5 g, **Saturated fat** 0 g, **Cholesterol** 0 mg, **Sodium** 210 mg, **Total carbohydrates** 21 g, **Protein** 3 g

STARCH WASH

Yield: 8 fl. oz. (240 ml)

Cornstarch	0.3 oz. (1 Tbsp)	9 g
Water, cold	8 fl. oz.	240 ml

1 Dissolve the cornstarch in 2 fluid ounces (60 milliliters) of the water. Set aside. Bring the remaining water to a boil in a small saucepan. Stir in the dissolved cornstarch, stirring constantly. Cook the starch mixture until it thickens and loses its opaqueness, approximately 3 minutes.

2 Remove the starch from the heat. Cool and use immediately to glaze breads after baking. Store the starch wash, covered, in the refrigerator up to 3 weeks.

PLIÉ BRETON (BRITTANY FRENCH RYE)

RECIPE 7.28

Brittany rye bread folded before proofing and baking.

Yield: 4 Loaves, approximately 1 lb. (480 g) each

Method: Sourdough starter

Fermentation: Sourdough sponge, overnight, 15 to 20 hours. Final dough, bench rest 30 minutes.

Proofing: 25 to 30 minutes.

Sourdough starter	1.75 oz.	50 g	5%
Water, cool	2.75 fl. oz.	80 ml	8%
Light rye flour	3 oz.	100 g	10%
Bread flour	2 lb.	900 g	90%
Dough conditioner (optional)	0.75 oz.	20 g	2%
Compressed yeast	0.75 oz.	20 g	2%
Salt	0.6 oz.	18 g	1.8%
Quark, farmer's cheese or			
baker's cheese	2.5 oz.	75 g	7.5%
Water (temperature controlled)	20.5 fl. oz.	580 ml	58%
Total weight:	4 lb.	1843 g	184%

1 The day before making the finished bread, make the sourdough sponge. Combine the starter, cool water and rye flour. Mix to combine the ingredients. Cover the sponge and ferment at room temperature approximately 15 to 20 hours.

2 Combine the sponge with the remaining ingredients in the bowl of a mixer fitted with a dough hook on low speed. Mix 3 minutes to combine the ingredients. Stop the machine and scrape down the bowl. Knead on medium speed until smooth and elastic, approximately 5 to 7 minutes. The dough should reach 77°F (25°C) after kneading.

3 Cover the dough and ferment 15 minutes.

4 Punch down the dough and divide into four equal pieces. Round the dough, cover and bench rest 15 minutes.

5 Flatten each piece of dough with a rolling pin into a 10-inch (25-centimeter) oval approximately 1 inch (2.5 centimeters) thick. Brush the tops of the ovals with water and fold them in half. Place each loaf on lightly floured sheet pans. Proof until doubled in size, approximately 25 to 35 minutes.

6 Dust the loaves lightly with rye flour. Bake at 450°F (230°C), with steam injected into the oven during the first few seconds of baking. Immediately reduce the temperature to 375°F (190°C) and bake until well browned and cooked through, approximately 30 to 35 minutes.

The finished plié Breton.

▶ **quark** —a fresh white curd cheese, with the texture and flavor of sour cream, commonly eaten in Germany

Approximate values per ⅑-loaf serving: **Calories** 100, **Total fat** 0.5 g, **Saturated fat** 0 g, **Cholesterol** 0 mg, **Sodium** 250 mg, **Total carbohydrates** 20 g, **Protein** 3 g

RECIPE 7.29

SAN FRANCISCO SOURDOUGH BREAD

STOUFFER STANFORD COURT HOTEL, SAN FRANCISCO, CA
Former Executive Chef Ercolino Crugnale

Yield: 1 Loaf

Method: Straight dough

Fermentation: 1 to 3 hours.

Proofing: 45 minutes to 1 hour.

Active dry yeast	0.5 oz.	15 g	3%
Water, warm (120°F/49°C)	8 fl. oz.	240 ml	50%
Sourdough starter	6 oz.	180 g	37%
Bread flour	1 lb.	480 g	100%
Kosher salt	0.5 oz.	15 g	3%
Cornmeal	as needed	as needed	
Egg white, beaten	1.6 oz. (1 white)	50 g	
Total dough weight:	2 lb.	930 g	193%

1 Sprinkle the yeast over 2 fluid ounces (60 milliliters) of the water and set aside until dissolved and foamy.

2 In the bowl of a mixer fitted with a dough hook, combine the starter and the remaining water. Add 6 ounces (180 grams) of the flour.

3 Stir until a dough forms, then add the yeast mixture. Knead 5 minutes on medium speed.

4 Add the remaining flour and the salt. Knead until the dough is smooth and elastic, approximately 10 minutes.

5 Place the dough in a lightly greased bowl and cover with a damp cloth. Ferment in a warm place, approximately 80°F to 90°F (27°C to 32°C), until doubled.

6 Punch down the dough and shape it into a round loaf. Place the loaf on a greased and cornmeal-dusted sheet pan.

7 Proof the dough in a warm place, covered with a damp cloth, until it has risen to 2½ times its original size.

8 Brush the risen loaf with the beaten egg white and score the top of the loaf with a sharp knife.

9 Bake at 450°F (230°C), with a pan of boiling water underneath the oven rack, for 10 minutes.

10 Reduce the oven temperature to 375°F (190°C), remove the water and continue baking until the loaf is well browned, approximately 35 to 45 minutes.

Approximate values per 2-oz. (60-g) serving: **Calories** 135, **Total fat** 0.5 g, **Saturated fat** 0 g, **Cholesterol** 0 mg, **Sodium** 355 mg, **Total carbohydrates** 27 g, **Protein** 4 g, **Claims**—low fat; no saturated fat; no cholesterol

RECIPE 7.30

PAIN AU LEVAIN (TRADITIONAL FRENCH SOURDOUGH BREAD)

Yield: 3 Loaves, approximately 1 lb. 6 oz. (660 g) each

Method: Sourdough starter

Fermentation: Levain, 8 to 12 hours. Final dough, approximately 2 hours.

Proofing: 45 minutes to 1 hour.

Levain:

Natural Sourdough Starter (page 154)	1 lb. 2 oz.	540 g	360%
Bread flour	5 oz.	150 g	100%
Total levain weight:	1 lb. 7 oz.	690 g	460%

Dough:

Dough:			
Levain	1 lb. 7 oz.	690 g	88%
Bread flour	1 lb. 10 oz.	780 g	100%
Water (temperature controlled)	18 fl. oz.	540 ml	69%
Salt	0.75 oz.	22 g	3%
Total weight:	4 lb. 3 oz.	2032 g	260%

1 To make the levain, combine the starter and flour in the bowl of a mixer fitted with a dough hook. Knead on medium speed until combined.

2 Scrape the mixture into a large bowl or plastic container and cover. Store at room temperature 8 to 12 hours.

3 To make the dough, place the levain mixture in the bowl of a mixer fitted with a dough hook. Add the flour, water and salt. Mix on low speed until well combined. Increase speed to medium and knead until the dough is smooth, elastic and fully developed, approximately 7 to 8 minutes.

4 Cover the dough and ferment 2 hours.

5 Punch down the dough and divide into three equal pieces. Round the dough, cover and bench rest 10 minutes.

6 Shape the dough into plump oval loaves slightly tapered at each end. Place the loaves seam side down on paper-lined sheet pans or in flour-dusted bannetons.

7 Proof until the loaves increase 70 percent in volume.

8 Unmold the loaves from the bannetons (if using) and then score them lengthwise with three slashes. Bake at 425°F (220°C), with steam injected into the oven during the first few minutes of baking, until the crust is a deep dark brown, approximately 40 to 45 minutes.

VARIATIONS:

Pain au Levain with Nuts—Add 3 ounces (90 grams/11%) walnuts, 3 ounces (90 grams/11%) whole toasted almonds and 3 ounces (90 grams/11%) whole toasted hazelnuts to the dough once it has been fully kneaded. Mix just to distribute the nuts throughout the dough.

Pain au Levain with Garlic and Herbs—Bake 3 whole heads of garlic, wrapped in aluminum foil, at 350°F (180°C), approximately 1 hour. Cool, then peel the baked garlic. Add the baked garlic cloves and 0.05 ounce (15 grams/2%) finely chopped fresh rosemary to the dough once it has been fully kneaded.

Pain au Levain with Three Cheeses—Dice 8 ounces (240 grams/30%) each of Parmesan, mozzarella and Gruyère cheese into $5/8$-inch (1.5-centimeter) cubes and add to the dough once it has been fully kneaded.

Pain au Levain with Walnuts and Cranberries—Add 10 ounces (300 grams/38%) walnuts and 10 ounces (300 grams/38%) dried cranberries to the dough once it has been fully kneaded.

Approximate values per $1/12$-loaf serving: **Calories** 100, **Total fat** 0 g, **Saturated fat** 0 g, **Cholesterol** 0 mg, **Sodium** 220 mg, **Total carbohydrates** 20 g, **Protein** 3 g

SPECIALTY BREADS

ENGLISH MUFFINS

KENDALL COLLEGE SCHOOL OF CULINARY ARTS, Evanston, IL

Chef Instructor Mike Artlip, CEC, CCE

Yield: 18 Muffins, approximately 3 oz. (90 g) each **Method:** Sponge

Fermentation: Sponge, 15 minutes. Dough, bench rest 30 minutes.

Proofing: 20 to 30 minutes.

Milk	9.25 fl. oz.	290 ml	29%
Compressed yeast	0.75 oz.	25 g	2.5%
Pastry flour	1 lb.	500 g	50%
Bread flour	1 lb.	500 g	50%
Baking powder	0.4 oz. (1 Tbsp.)	12 g	1.25%
Granulated sugar	1.25 oz.	35 g	3.5%
Salt	0.25 oz. (1¼ tsp.)	8 g	0.8%
Unsalted butter, room temperature	1.5 oz.	50 g	5%
Water (temperature controlled)	9.25 fl. oz.	290 ml	29%
Cornmeal	as needed	as needed	
Total dough weight:	3 lb. 6 oz.	1710 g	171%

1 Heat the milk to 75°F (24°C). Stir the yeast into the milk until it dissolves. Mix in 7 ounces (210 grams) of the pastry flour. Cover the sponge and ferment 15 minutes.

2 Sift the remaining pastry flour and the bread flour with the baking powder. Set aside.

3 Place the sponge, flour mixture, sugar, salt, butter and water in the bowl of a mixer fitted with a dough hook. Mix 3 minutes on low speed to moisten the ingredients, then beat on high speed another 7 minutes. The dough will be soft and somewhat sticky.

4 Cover the dough and rest 20 minutes. Punch down the dough and rest another 10 minutes.

5 Roll out the dough until it is 1 inch (2.5 centimeters) thick. Cut the dough into circles with a 3¼-inch (8.1-centimeter) cutter. Place the cut pieces on cornmeal-dusted sheet pans and proof 20 to 30 minutes.

6 Bake the muffins on a lightly greased griddle heated to 375°F (190°C) until golden brown, approximately 7 minutes per side.

Approximate values per muffin: **Calories** 220, **Total fat** 3.5 g, **Saturated fat** 1.5 g, **Cholesterol** 10 mg, **Sodium** 170 mg, **Total carbohydrates** 43 g, **Protein** 7 g, **Iron** 15%

BREAD STICKS

Yield: 24 Bread Sticks

Method: Straight dough

Fermentation: 20 to 30 minutes.

Active dry yeast	0.5 oz.	15 g	3%
Water, warm	10 fl. oz.	300 ml	55%
Granulated sugar	1 oz.	30 g	5%
Olive oil	4 fl. oz.	120 ml	22%
Salt	0.4 oz. (2 tsp.)	10 g	2%
Bread flour	1 lb. 2 oz.	540 g	100%
Egg wash	as needed	as needed	
Sesame seeds	1 oz. (3 Tbsp.)	30 g	
Total dough weight:	2 lb. 1 oz.	1015 g	187%

1 Rolling bread stick dough.

1. Stir the yeast, water and sugar together in a mixer bowl.
2. Blend in the oil, salt and 8 ounces (240 grams) of the flour.
3. Gradually add the remaining flour. Knead the dough until it is smooth and cleans the sides of the bowl, approximately 5 minutes.
4. Remove the dough from the bowl and rest a few minutes. Roll the dough into a rectangle about ¼ inch (6 millimeters) thick.
5. Cut the dough into 24 equal pieces. Roll each piece into a rope and twist; bring the ends together, allowing the sides to curl together. Place on a paper-lined sheet pan.
6. Brush with egg wash and top with sesame seeds. Let the bread sticks rise until doubled, approximately 20 minutes.
7. Bake at 375°F (190°C) until golden brown, approximately 12 to 15 minutes.

2 Twisting bread stick dough.

VARIATIONS:

Garlic Bread Sticks—Knead 1 ounce (30 grams/5%) grated Parmesan and 1 ounce (2 tablespoons/30 grams/5%) minced garlic into the dough.

Herbed Bread Sticks—Knead 0.3 ounce (3 tablespoons/9 grams/2%) chopped fresh herbs such as basil, parsley, dill and oregano into the dough.

Approximate values per bread stick: **Calories** 60, **Total fat** 5 g, **Saturated fat** 1 g, **Cholesterol** 10 mg, **Sodium** 190 mg, **Total carbohydrates** 2 g, **Protein** 1 g, **Claims**—low saturated fat; low cholesterol

RECIPE 7.33

PLAIN BAGELS

Assortment of plain and flavored bagels

Yield: 14 Bagels, approximately 2¾ oz. (80 g) each

Method: Straight dough

Fermentation: 30 minutes to 1 hour.

Proofing: Approximately 25 minutes.

Dough:

High-gluten flour	1 lb. 8 oz.	720 g	100%
Vital wheat gluten	1.25 oz.	36 g	5%
Water (temperature controlled)	1 pt.	475 ml	66%
Instant yeast	0.75 oz.	22 g	3%
Barley malt or honey	0.5 oz.	15 g	2%
Salt	0.5 oz.	15 g	2%
Total dough weight:	2 lb. 11 oz.	1283 g	178%

Poaching liquid:

Water	1 gal.	4 lt
Honey	3 oz.	90 g
Baking soda	1 oz.	30 g
Sesame, poppy or caraway seeds, chopped onions, kosher salt	as needed	as needed

1 Combine all dough ingredients in the bowl of a mixer fitted with a dough hook. Mix on low speed to blend the ingredients. Increase the speed to medium and knead the dough until it is smooth but firm and fully developed. The dough should reach 77°F (25°C).

2 Place the dough on an unfloured workbench. Cover and ferment until not quite doubled, approximately 30 minutes.

3 Flatten the dough into a large rectangle. Cut the dough into 5-inch- (12.5-centimeter-) wide strips the length of the rectangle. Divide each strip of dough into 3-ounce (90-gram) pieces.

4 Roll the portioned dough into 10-inch- (25-centimeter-) long ropes. Wrap one rope of dough around one hand, overlapping the ends 1 inch (2.5 centimeters) to form a ring. Pinch the ends to seal the dough. Roll the dough back and forth on the workbench to even the shape and thickness of the bagel.

5 Place the formed bagels on a lightly floured canvas or paper-lined sheet pans. Proof until the bagels have increased 20 percent in volume.

6 Combine the water, honey and baking soda in a wide shallow pot for the poaching liquid. Bring it to a full rolling boil. Just before adding the bagels to the liquid, reduce the heat so that the water simmers. Add as many bagels as the pot will comfortably hold.

7 Poach each batch of bagels 45 seconds to 1 minute. Flip the bagels with a skimmer and poach them another 45 seconds on the other side. Remove them from the liquid with the skimmer and drain them in a colander. Place the poached bagels on paper-lined sheet pans, leaving enough space between each bagel for further expansion. Sprinkle with toppings if desired.

8 Bake at 450°F (230°C) until amber-colored, approximately 18 to 20 minutes.

VARIATIONS:

Long-Fermented Bagels—Form the bagels, then place them on sheet pans generously sprinkled with flour or cornmeal. Retard the formed bagels overnight, then bring them to room temperature before proofing, boiling and baking. Or, retard the bagels after poaching, then let them sit 90 minutes at room temperature before baking.

Tomato Basil Bagels—Add 6 ounces (180 grams/25%) coarsely chopped sun-dried tomatoes and 0.75 ounce (22 grams/3%) finely chopped fresh basil to the dough toward the end of the kneading process. Garnish each poached bagel with a thin slice of fresh tomato. Brush with olive oil and sprinkle with salt before baking.

Onion Walnut Bagels—Cut 8 ounces (240 grams/33%) peeled onions into 1/8-inch- (3-millimeter-) thick slices. Place on a sheet pan. Dust lightly with powdered sugar and bake at 375°F (190°C) until lightly browned. Cool, then add to the dough near the end of the kneading process along with 8 ounces (240 grams/33%) chopped walnuts. Slice 2 more peeled onions thinly and place on top of the poached bagels. Sprinkle with kosher salt, black pepper and poppy seeds, then bake immediately.

Cinnamon Raisin Bagels—Increase the instant yeast to 1 ounce (30 grams/4%). Add 2 ounces (60 grams/8%) granulated sugar to the dough in the first step. Add 0.25 ounce (8 grams/1%) ground cinnamon and 8 ounces (240 grams/33%) raisins to the dough toward the end of the kneading process. Remove from the mixer when the dough is still streaked with cinnamon. When the bagels come out of the oven, bush them with melted butter and dip in cinnamon sugar.

Approximate values per bagel: **Calories** 190, **Total fat** 0.5 g, **Saturated fat** 0 g, **Cholesterol** 0 mg, **Sodium** 400 mg, **Total carbohydrates** 39 g, **Protein** 9 g, **Iron** 15%

FOCACCIA (ROMAN FLATBREAD)

RECIPE 7.34

Yield: 1 Half-Sheet Pan, 12 in. × 18 in. (30 cm × 45 cm)

Method: Straight dough

Fermentation: 1 to 2 hours.   **Proofing:** 15 minutes.

Granulated sugar	0.4 oz. (1 Tbsp.)	11 g	2%
Active dry yeast	0.4 oz. (1 Tbsp.)	11 g	2%
Water, lukewarm	12 fl. oz.	350 ml	66%
All-purpose flour	1 lb. 2 oz.	540 g	100%
Kosher salt	0.3 oz. (2 tsp.)	10 g	1.7%
Onion, chopped fine	3 oz.	90 g	17%
Olive oil	0.5 fl. oz.	15 ml	3%
Fresh rosemary, crushed	0.2 oz. (2 Tbsp.)	5 g	1%
Total weight:	2 lb. 2 oz.	1032 g	193%

Topping the flatbread dough with crushed rosemary.

1 Combine the sugar, yeast and water. Stir to dissolve the yeast. Stir in the flour, 4 ounces (120 grams) at a time.

2 Stir in 1½ teaspoons (7 milliliters) of the salt and the onion. Mix well, then knead on a lightly floured board or in the bowl of a mixer fitted with a dough hook until smooth.

3 Place the dough in an oiled bowl, cover and ferment until doubled.

4 Punch down the dough, then flatten it onto an oiled sheet pan. It should be no more than 1 inch (2.5 centimeters) thick. Brush the top of the dough with the olive oil. Let the dough proof until doubled, approximately 15 minutes.

5 Sprinkle the crushed rosemary and remaining ½ teaspoon (2 milliliters) of salt on top of the dough. Bake at 400°F (200°C) until lightly browned, approximately 20 minutes.

Approximate values per 1-oz. (30-g) serving: **Calories** 100, **Total fat** 0.5 g, **Saturated fat** 0 g, **Cholesterol** 0 mg, **Sodium** 230 mg, **Total carbohydrates** 21 g, **Protein** 3 g, **Claims**—low fat; no saturated fat; no cholesterol

RECIPE 7.35

PIZZA DOUGH

Yield: 1 Large Pizza or 8 Individual Pizzas   **Method:** Straight dough

Fermentation: 30 minutes.

Active dry yeast	0.4 oz. (1 Tbsp.)	12 g	3%
Water, warm	2 fl. oz.	60 ml	14%
Bread flour	14 oz.	420 g	100%
Water, cool	6 fl. oz.	180 ml	43%
Salt	0.2 oz. (1 tsp.)	6 g	1.4%
Olive oil	1 fl. oz.	30 ml	7%
Honey	0.75 oz.	20 g	5%
Total weight:	1 lb. 8 oz.	728 g	173%

1 Stir the yeast into the warm water to dissolve. Add the flour.

2 Stir the remaining ingredients into the flour mixture. Knead with a dough hook or by hand until smooth and elastic, approximately 5 minutes.

3 Place the dough in a lightly greased bowl and cover. Ferment the dough in a warm place 30 minutes. Punch down the dough and divide into portions. The dough may be wrapped and refrigerated up to 2 days.

4 On a lightly floured surface, roll the dough into very thin rounds and top as desired. Bake at 400°F (200°C) until crisp and golden brown, approximately 8 to 12 minutes.

Approximate values per 2-oz. (60-g) serving: **Calories** 220, **Total fat** 4 g, **Saturated fat** 0.5 g, **Cholesterol** 0 mg, **Sodium** 290 mg, **Total carbohydrates** 41 g, **Protein** 6 g, **Claims**—low saturated fat; no cholesterol

RECIPE 7.36

PITA BREAD

Yield: 18 Individual Loaves   **Method:** Straight dough

Fermentation: Bench rest, 45 minutes.   **Proofing:** 25 to 30 minutes.

Compressed yeast	2.75 oz.	80 g	8%
Water (temperature controlled)	19 fl. oz.	530 ml	53%
Bread flour	2 lb. 4 oz.	1000 g	100%
Salt	0.75 oz.	20 g	2%
Vegetable oil	3 fl. oz.	85 ml	8.5%
Total weight:	3 lb. 13 oz.	1715 g	171%

1 Dissolve the yeast in the water in the bowl of a mixer fitted with a dough hook. Add the remaining ingredients and mix on low speed 3 minutes. Scrape down the bowl. Add more flour, if necessary, to make a stiff dough. Knead the dough on high speed until it is smooth and comes away from the sides of the bowl, approximately 7 more minutes. The dough should reach 77°F (25°C).

2 Cover the dough and rest 15 minutes. Punch down the dough and rest another 10 minutes.

3 Divide the dough into 3-ounce (90-gram) pieces. Round and lightly oil each piece. Cover the oiled dough and bench rest 20 minutes. Flatten each dough ball into a 6-inch (15-centimeter) circle. Place the dough on paper-lined sheet pans. Proof the dough in a warm, dry place until doubled in size, approximately 25 to 30 minutes.

4 Bake at 475°F (250°C) until puffed and lightly browned, approximately 8 to 10 minutes. Cool on racks to preserve the pocket in the dough.

Approximate values per loaf: **Calories** 250, **Total fat** 6 g, **Saturated fat** 0.5 g, **Cholesterol** 0 mg, **Sodium** 410 mg, **Total carbohydrates** 42 g, **Protein** 1 g, **Iron** 15%

NAAN (INDIAN FLATBREAD)

Yield: 6 Loaves, approximately 10 oz. (300 g) each   **Method:** Sponge

Fermentation: Sponge, 3 hours. Final dough, 3½ hours.   **Proofing:** 1 hour.

Ingredient	US	Metric	%
Compressed yeast	0.18 oz. (1 tsp.)	5 g	0.5%
Water (temperature controlled)	17 fl. oz.	470 ml	47%
Bread flour	1 lb. 8 oz.	670 g	67%
Whole-wheat flour	12 oz.	330 g	33%
Yogurt	10.5 oz.	300 g	30%
Olive oil	1 fl. oz.	30 ml	3%
Baking powder	0.07 oz. (½ tsp.)	2 g	0.2%
Baking soda	0.07 oz. (½ tsp.)	2 g	0.2%
Salt	0.7 oz.	20 g	2%
Vegetable or olive oil	as needed	as needed	
Black sesame seeds	as needed	as needed	
Fresh parsley, chopped	as needed	as needed	
Total dough weight:	4 lb. 1 oz.	1829 g	182%

1 To prepare the sponge, dissolve 0.04 ounce (1 gram/0.1%) of the yeast in 6 fluid ounces (160 milliliters/16%) of the water in the bowl of a mixer fitted with a dough hook. Add 8 ounces (220 grams/22%) of the bread flour and mix until well incorporated. Cover and set aside. Ferment at room temperature until cracks appear on the surface of the starter, approximately 3 hours.

2 Place the sponge and the remaining bread flour, water, the whole-wheat flour, yogurt, olive oil, baking powder and baking soda in the bowl of a mixer fitted with a dough hook. Mix on low speed 3 minutes. Stop the mixer and scrape down the bowl. Add the remaining 0.14 ounce (4 grams/0.4%) of the yeast and mix on high speed another 3 minutes. Add the salt, then mix until the dough is fully developed and reaches 77°F (25°C), approximately 5 more minutes.

3 Cover the dough and ferment 3 hours.

4 Punch down the dough and divide into six equal pieces. Round the portioned dough. Cover and bench rest 30 minutes.

5 Stretch each piece of dough out until it measures 12 inches (30 centimeters) long. Place the dough on flour-dusted sheet pans and proof until doubled, approximately 50 minutes.

6 Dimple the surface of the dough with your fingertips. Brush the dough with oil and sprinkle it with black sesame seeds or chopped fresh parsley. Place the dough directly on the heated surface of a deck oven at 485°F (255°C) or place the sheet pan of dough on a rack in the oven. Bake until the bread is well browned and crisp, approximately 10 to 12 minutes. To prevent a soggy crust, open the oven door or vent during the last 2 minutes of baking to remove any excess steam that may build up in the oven.

Approximate values per 1½ oz. (45-g) serving: **Calories** 100, **Total fat** 1 g, **Saturated fat** 0 g, **Cholesterol** 0 mg, **Sodium** 230 mg, **Total carbohydrates** 19 g, **Protein** 4 g

BREAD, MILK AND BUTTER ARE OF VENERABLE
ANTIQUITY. THEY TASTE OF THE MORNING OF THE
WORLD.

—Leigh Hunt, British writer (1784–1859)

8

ENRICHED YEAST DOUGHS

AFTER STUDYING THIS
CHAPTER, YOU WILL BE
ABLE TO:

▶ understand the mixing and
handling requirements for
making enriched yeast breads

▶ prepare brioche, challah and
a variety of enriched yeast
dough products

▶ prepare a variety of specialty
breakfast pastries made from
sweet dough

Enriched yeast doughs, as the name indicates, have a higher percentage of fat, eggs, milk and/or sweeteners than traditional yeast bread doughs. Fats and sweeteners interfere with the development of gluten in these types of dough, resulting in breads, rolls and pastries with a soft crust and tender crumb. Because they are usually softer and stickier than lean yeast bread dough, enriched yeast doughs are handled somewhat differently from the lean doughs discussed in the preceding chapter. But a good understanding of the techniques and terms covered in Chapter 7, Yeast Breads, is necessary for successful preparation of these breads as well.

In many parts of the world, breakfast includes some version of the breads and pastries discussed in this chapter. Buns, babka and coffeecake, as well as croissants and Danish pastries, discussed in Chapter 12, Laminated Doughs, are all considered enriched yeast dough products. Popular breakfast items such as sticky buns and brioche rely on large quantities of butter to make these flavorful crusty yet tender pastries.

▶ ENRICHED YEAST DOUGH

Enriched yeast dough, also referred to as sweet dough, bakes into the most popular breakfast pastries such as sticky buns, coffeecake, sweet rolls and doughnuts. Among the breads featured in this chapter are stollen, panettone and challah, festive breads served around the world to mark holidays and celebratory occasions. Enriched yeast doughs are made with a good proportion of fat and sugar, though not all are sweet. Savory breads rich with cheese, such as Jalapeño Cheese Bread (page 197), are included in this category.

INGREDIENTS FOR ENRICHED YEAST DOUGH

The ingredients used to make enriched yeast doughs are the same as those used in any yeasted dough product. It is the quantity of the ingredients that differs. Enriched yeast doughs may be made with all-purpose, bread or high-gluten flour. As the amount of fat and sweeteners in the formula increases, a higher-protein flour may be needed. Fats added while the dough is mixing will coat the flour, inhibiting the development of gluten. A stronger flour compensates for this. In some enriched yeast dough products, such as brioche, the amount of eggs and fat makes the dough quite heavy. Higher-protein flour develops the gluten structure needed to support the weight of these ingredients.

Dairy products, butter, shortening, oil and eggs may be added in varying proportion according to the specific formula. Pasteurized milk contains enzymes that can weaken gluten, resulting in a sticky dough that is difficult to handle. For best results, heat milk to 200°F (93°C) to destroy these enzymes. Since dry milk powder requires no heating, it is frequently used in place of liquid milk in bread formulas for convenience. Yogurt, buttermilk and UHT milk require no preheating to destroy this enzyme. Butter is the preferred fat in these products because of its flavor and browning ability. To make up for the large amount of eggs in many enriched dough formulas, the quantity of liquid is reduced.

As discussed in Chapter 7, Yeast Breads, sugar is a yeast food that, when present in large quantities, can slow yeast activity and gluten formation. To compensate, enriched yeast dough formulas may contain slightly higher amounts of yeast than normally found in leaner bread doughs. Barley malt, honey or other sweeteners are often used in enriched yeast dough formulas along with or in place of sugar. Beneficial enzymes in these liquid sweeteners aid fermentation without overfeeding the yeast.

Some bakers prefer to hydrate instant dry yeast before it is used in an enriched yeast dough formula because dry yeast may not fully dissolve during mixing. Instant dry yeast may be dissolved in a portion of the water called for in the formula before adding it to the dry ingredients.

Dried fruit, especially raisins and currants, enhance many enriched yeast doughs. In order for dried fruit to remain tender after the dough is baked, the fruit should be softened or **conditioned** to increase its moisture content before being mixed into the dough. This technique is described in Chapter 5, Mise en Place.

MIXING ENRICHED YEAST DOUGHS

Enriched yeast doughs are mixed using either the straight dough method or the sponge method. (A third method for incorporating fat into enriched dough is discussed in Chapter 12, Laminated Doughs.) The straight dough method is used for enriched bread dough where the percentage of fat and sugar is not so great as to interfere with gluten development. See Challah (page 186), Jumbo Cinnamon Buns (page 200) or Hot Cross Buns (page 204). The sponge method works well in formulas with the highest percentage of fat and eggs, such as Stollen (page 206), Parisian Brioche (page 198) and Sweet Bun Dough (page 188). The sponge improves the texture of enriched doughs and enhances the flavor of bread made from these doughs. Fermentation begins in the sponge before the fat prevents access to the yeast food in the flour. Whether using the straight dough or sponge method, some enriched doughs such as Rum Babas (page 199) and brioche are kneaded until the gluten is developed before the fat is added.

When mixing the enriched doughs in this chapter, the temperature of the water is adjusted according to the formula discussed in Chapter 7, Yeast Breads. To accelerate yeast activity, enriched dough may be mixed to a slightly warmer dough temperature than lean bread dough, approximately 80°F (27°C). Any butter or fat should be at room temperature so that it blends easily into the dough during kneading. Because fat and sugar slow gluten development, enriched doughs often require longer kneading for the gluten to fully develop. Use the windowpane test to judge when these doughs have been kneaded sufficiently. Long cool fermentation, often in a refrigerator or retarder, brings out the flavor of these bread doughs. Chilling the dough before forming also makes these sticky doughs easier to handle.

FORMING ENRICHED YEAST DOUGHS

Most enriched dough products are divided and formed using the methods described in Chapter 7, Yeast Breads, page 145. See Milk Bread (page 194) and Sweet Bun Dough (page 188). Braiding is a commonly used technique because it helps these soft and rich doughs hold their shape during baking. Because they are tender and delicate, many types of sweet doughs are molded and baked in pans. Brioche, **babas, savarin, kugelhopf,** stollen, **panettone** and many breads in this chapter are associated with special shapes and molds. Pans should be well greased or lined with parchment paper before using. Cool these breads thoroughly before unmolding to help keep their soufflé-like texture intact.

▶ **baba** small, light yeast cake soaked in rum syrup; traditionally baked in individual cylindrical molds, giving the finished product a mushroom shape

▶ **savarin** rich, yeasted cake prepared from baba dough baked into a small round ring, the center of which may be filled with whipped cream and candied fruit

▶ **kugelhopf** (KOO-guhl-hopf) a light, buttery yeast cake studded with nuts and raisins and baked in a special fluted mold; a specialty of Germany, the Alsace region of France and other central European countries

▶ **panettone** (pan-eh-TONE-nay) sweet Italian yeast bread filled with raisins, candied fruits, anise seeds and nuts; traditionally baked in a rounded cylindrical mold and served as a breakfast bread or dessert during the Christmas holidays

PROOFING AND BAKING ENRICHED YEAST DOUGH

Care must be taken to properly proof enriched yeast doughs. These fragile doughs collapse easily if overproofed. In many cases—Jalapeño Cheese Bread (page 197) and Stollen (page 206), for example—a slight underproofing ensures that enough yeast energy remains to leaven these heavy doughs. Brushing with egg wash before proofing keeps the dough moist so that it expands fully during baking. Proofing in a hot environment, above 85°F (29°C), may melt the butter in sticky bun or brioche dough and is not recommended. As the sugar rapidly caramelizes during baking, enriched dough browns easily. Bake these doughs at moderate temperatures, 350°F to 375°F (180°C to 190°C), to ensure fully baked bread without burning.

The procedure for mixing an enriched yeast dough using the straight dough method is illustrated by Challah (below). The procedure for mixing an enriched yeast dough using the straight dough method with fat added later in the mixing is illustrated by Sweet Bun Dough (page 188).

▶ PROCEDURE FOR PREPARING ENRICHED YEAST DOUGH

STRAIGHT DOUGH METHOD

1 Scale ingredients. Adjust water to proper temperature and rehydrate yeast if necessary.

2 Combine all ingredients in the bowl of a mixer fitted with a dough hook on low speed to moisten. The flour may be added a small amount at a time in order to form a soft dough. Scrape down the bowl.

3 Knead dough on medium speed to properly develop dough, approximately 5 to 10 minutes.

4 Ferment the dough until double in bulk, then punch down to release gases.

5 Scrape dough onto workbench, then divide and scale into uniform pieces. Round each piece into a smooth ball, then rest before rolling into desired shapes. Pan the formed dough as desired.

6 Proof the dough. Brush with egg wash and score the dough, if necessary, then bake.

| RECIPE 8.1 | CHALLAH |

Challah (HAH-la) is the traditional bread for Jewish Sabbath and holiday celebrations, rich with eggs and flavored with honey. Time-honored tradition dictates that challah be braided or formed into a turban-shaped loaf as described in Chapter 7, Yeast Breads. Topped with poppy or sesame seeds, challah is excellent for toast or sandwiches.

Yield: 2 Large Loaves   **Method:** Straight dough

Fermentation: 1 to 1½ hours.   **Proofing:** 45 minutes.

Honey	6 fl. oz.	180 ml	21%
Salt	0.6 oz.	18 g	2%
Bread flour	1 lb. 12 oz.	840 g	100%
Active dry yeast	0.5 oz.	15 g	1.8%
Water, hot (90°F/32°C)	4 fl. oz.	120 ml	14%
Water (temperature controlled)	10 fl. oz.	300 ml	36%
Eggs	6.75 oz. (4 eggs)	200 g	24%
Unsalted butter, melted	4 oz.	120 g	14%
Egg wash	as needed	as needed	
Sesame or poppy seeds	as needed	as needed	
Total dough weight:	3 lb. 11 oz.	1793 g	213%

1 Stir together the honey, salt and 8 ounces (240 grams) of the flour in the bowl of a mixer fitted with a dough hook. Dissolve the yeast in the hot water. Add the yeast mixture, temperature-controlled water, eggs and butter to the mixer bowl. Stir until smooth.

2 Knead the dough on medium speed, adding the remaining flour 2 ounces (60 grams) at a time, until smooth and elastic, approximately 5 minutes.

3 Place the dough in a lightly greased bowl, cover and ferment until doubled, approximately 1 to 1½ hours.

4 Punch down the dough and divide into six equal portions. Form the dough into two three-strand braided loaves (page 140). Place the loaves on a paper-lined sheet pan.

5 Brush the loaves with egg wash and sprinkle with sesame or poppy seeds. Proof until doubled, approximately 45 minutes.

6 Bake at 350°F (180°C) until the loaves are golden brown and sound hollow when thumped, approximately 40 minutes.

Approximate values per 2-oz. (30-g) serving: **Calories** 156, **Total fat** 4 g, **Saturated fat** 2 g, **Cholesterol** 44 mg, **Sodium** 145 mg, **Total carbohydrates** 25 g, **Protein** 6 g

SWEET DOUGH OR BUN DOUGH

For many years in the United States and Great Britain, a small yeast roll or bun was a staple item in every bakeshop. The dough used to prepare this slightly sweet, deeply browned roll is referred to as "sweet dough" or "bun dough" by many bakers. While there is no single formula for sweet dough, all formulas are sweeter and richer than that used to make dinner rolls or Pullman loaves but with less fat than brioche. Most sweet dough has fewer eggs than challah but a higher percentage of fat. Sweet dough is more tender and less elastic than challah when baked. Sweet dough is often kneaded into a fully developed dough before the fat is added.

Sweet dough bakes into aromatic bread with a golden color and buttery taste. Raisins, candied fruit or chopped nuts can be kneaded into the dough before fermenting and baking. Sweet dough or bun dough works equally well when formed into plain rolls or decorative pastries. The dough can be rolled out flat with a rolling pin, then spread with streusel, fruit preserves, poppy seeds or other fruit and nut fillings. Once coated with filling, the dough can be rolled up and baked in a loaf or cake pan. See Sweet Dough Coffeecakes (page 195). The dough may also be made up as for the braided Danish coffee cake illustrated on page 330 in Chapter 12, Laminated Doughs. Because the dough holds its shape well, sweet dough or bun dough can be divided and shaped into braided loaves, its appearance and taste enhanced with sweet and decorative icings after the dough is baked.

▶ PROCEDURE FOR PREPARING ENRICHED YEAST DOUGH

STRAIGHT DOUGH METHOD WITH FAT ADDED AFTER GLUTEN IS DEVELOPED

1 Scale ingredients. Adjust water to proper temperature and rehydrate yeast if necessary.

2 Combine all ingredients except the fat in the bowl of a mixer fitted with a dough hook on low speed to moisten. The flour may be added a small amount at a time in order to form a soft dough. Scrape down the bowl.

3 Knead on medium speed to properly develop the dough, approximately 5 to 10 minutes.

4 Add the fat, a small amount at a time, and mix until it is fully incorporated into the dough.

5 Ferment the dough until double in bulk, then punch down to release gases.

6 Portion, shape and proof the dough.

7 Brush with egg wash and score the dough, if necessary, then bake.

RECIPE 8.2

SWEET BUN DOUGH

BENNISON BAKERY, EVANSTON, IL

Chef Jory Downer

Yield: 36 Buns, approximately 2 oz. (60 g) each   **Method:** Straight dough

Fermentation: 12 to 24 hours under refrigeration.

Proofing: 20 to 30 minutes.

Compressed yeast	2 oz.	50 g	5%
Water (temperature controlled)	15 fl. oz.	420 ml	42%
Dry milk powder	2 oz.	55 g	5.5%
Bread flour	1 lb. 11 oz.	750 g	75%
Pastry flour	9 oz.	250 g	25%
Granulated sugar	7.5 oz.	210 g	21%
Baking powder	0.5 oz.	14 g	1.4%
Salt	0.5 oz.	14 g	1.4%
Eggs	3.3 oz. (2 eggs)	100 g	10%
Unsalted butter, room temperature	3.6 oz.	100 g	10%
Vegetable shortening	3.6 oz.	100 g	10%
Egg wash	as needed	as needed	
Basic Sugar Glaze (page 360)	as needed	as needed	
Nuts, chopped	as needed	as needed	
Total dough weight:	4 lb. 10 oz.	2063 g	206%

1 Soften the yeast in the water in the bowl of a mixer fitted with a dough hook.

2 Stir the milk powder into the flours. Add the flour mixture to the bowl along with the sugar, baking powder, salt and eggs. Mix the dough 2 minutes at low speed until the ingredients are moistened. Stop the machine and scrape down the bowl. Add additional flour if needed to make a firm yet sticky dough. (The dough will soften as it kneads.) Increase the speed to medium and knead the dough 3 more minutes.

3 Add the butter and shortening and mix until the soft dough is smooth and fully developed, approximately 3 more minutes. The dough should reach 77°F (25°C) after kneading.

4 Cover the dough and bench rest 45 minutes.

5 Divide the dough into two equal pieces. Round them and place on a paper-lined sheet pan. Cover the rounded dough and refrigerate a minimum of 12 hours, but no longer than 24 hours.

6 Remove the dough from the refrigerator and rest at room temperature 20 minutes. Divide each piece of dough into 18 portions to make a total of 36 portions. Form into smooth rolls and place the rounded rolls onto paper-lined sheet pans.

7 Proof until doubled in size, approximately 20 to 30 minutes.

8 Brush the rolls with egg wash and bake at 350°F (180°C), with a short burst of steam at the beginning of baking, until golden brown and baked through, approximately 18 to 20 minutes.

9 Brush the hot rolls with glaze and sprinkle with chopped nuts. Cool on a cooling rack.

VARIATIONS:

Quick Fermented Sweet Bun Dough Rolls—For shorter fermentation times increase the amount of yeast to 3 ounces (75 grams/8%). Ferment the dough until doubled, approximately 45 minutes. Shape, proof and bake.

Cardamom Sweet Bun Dough—Add 0.07 ounces (1 teaspoon/2 grams/0.2%) ground cardamom to the flour before mixing. Mix, ferment, proof and bake.

Approximate values per 1½-oz. (45-g) serving: **Calories** 140, **Total fat** 4.5 g, **Saturated fat** 2 g, **Cholesterol** 15 mg, **Sodium** 150 mg, **Total carbohydrates** 21 g, **Protein** 3 g

BRIOCHE

Brioche (bree-OHSH) is a rich, tender bread made with a generous amount of eggs and butter. The high ratio of fat makes this dough difficult to work with, but the flavor is well worth the extra effort.

Brioche dough is mixed using a two-stage method. First, the flour, liquid, yeast and eggs are kneaded into a soft bread dough. Then the softened butter is added. This unique kneading process allows the protein structure to be developed in the dough before the fat can interfere. Once kneaded, the dough is fermented, then stored in the refrigerator overnight (retarded) before make-up, proofing and baking. Brioche may also be mixed using the sponge method. See Parisian Brioche (page 198).

Brioche is traditionally baked in fluted pans and has a cap or topknot of dough; this shape is known as brioche à tête. The molded dough is washed with beaten egg or egg yolks and milk or cream before and after proofing. It is important to keep the wash from touching the sides of the pan, where it could coagulate and prevent the dough from rising when baked. The dough may also be baked in a loaf pan, making it perfect for toast or canapés. Savory brioche dough is popular as a casing for pâté and **coulibiac,** the stuffed salmon dish of Russian origin.

▶ **coulibiac** a creamy mixture of salmon fillet, rice, hard-cooked eggs, mushrooms, shallots and dill enclosed in a pastry envelope usually made of brioche dough

▶ PROCEDURE FOR MIXING BRIOCHE DOUGH

1 Have all ingredients at room temperature.

2 Hydrate the yeast, then combine it with the flour, salt, sugar and eggs. Mix until a soft dough is formed.

3 Knead the dough on medium speed for 15 to 20 minutes until it is smooth and shiny.

4 Add the butter in small increments, kneading until the butter is incorporated before adding more. Continue this process until all of the butter has been absorbed into the dough, approximately 8 to 15 minutes.

5 Cover the dough and ferment at room temperature until doubled.

6 Punch down the dough, then cover and refrigerate overnight.

7 Divide and mold the chilled brioche dough into desired shapes. Brush with egg wash or cover lightly and proof until doubled in volume. Do not proof brioche in a very warm place; the butter may melt out of the dough before proofing is complete.

8 Bake in a moderate oven until the crust is deep golden brown. Cool in pans on racks for 10 minutes to prevent the loaves from collapsing, then remove bread from pans and finish cooling on racks.

RECIPE 8.3   BRIOCHE

1 Combining the ingredients for brioche.

2 Adding the yeast-and-water mixture to the dough.

3 Brioche dough after kneading for 20 minutes.

4 Adding the butter to the brioche dough.

Yield: 3 Large Loaves or 60 Rolls   **Method:** Straight dough

Fermentation: 1 to 2 hours at room temperature, then overnight under refrigeration.

Proofing: 30 minutes to 1½ hours.

All-purpose flour	4 lb. 7 oz.	2130 g	100%
Eggs	2 lb. 6 oz. (24 eggs)	1130 g	53%
Salt	1.75 oz.	50 g	2.5%
Granulated sugar	7 oz.	210 g	10%
Active dry yeast	1.75 oz.	50 g	2.5%
Water (temperature controlled)	7 fl. oz.	210 ml	10%
Unsalted butter, room temperature	3 lb.	1430 g	67%
Total weight:	10 lb. 14 oz.	5210 g	245%

1 Place the flour, eggs, salt and sugar into the bowl of a mixer fitted with a dough hook. Stir the ingredients together.

2 Combine the yeast and water and add to the dough.

3 Knead approximately 20 minutes on medium speed. The dough will be smooth, shiny and moist. It should not form a ball.

4 Slowly add the butter to the dough. Knead only until all the butter is incorporated. Remove the dough from the mixer and place it into a bowl dusted with flour. Cover the dough and ferment at room temperature until doubled.

5 Punch down the dough, cover tightly with plastic wrap and refrigerate overnight.

6 Portion and shape the chilled dough as desired. Place the shaped dough in well-greased pans and proof at room temperature until doubled.

7 Bake at 375°F (190°C) until the brioche is a dark golden brown and sounds hollow. Baking time will vary depending on the temperature of the dough and the size of the rolls or loaves being baked.

VARIATIONS:

Raisin Brioche—Gently warm 3 fluid ounces (90 milliliters/4%) rum with 6 ounces (180 grams/8%) raisins. Set aside until the raisins are plumped. Drain off the remaining rum and add the raisins to the dough after the butter is incorporated.

Brioche for Sandwiches or Coulibiac—Reduce the sugar to 3 ounces (90 grams/4%). Ferment the dough, then retard it overnight. Mold in a rectangular loaf pan for slicing, or use the dough to wrap salmon and fillings for coulibiac.

Savory Cheese and Herb Brioche—Reduce the sugar to 3 ounces (90 grams/4%). Add 4 ounces (120 grams/5%) grated Parmesan and 4 ounces (120 grams/5%) grated Gruyère cheese, 0.02 ounces (¼ teaspoon/0.5 grams) black pepper, and 0.02 ounces (¼ teaspoon/0.5 grams) dry thyme to the dough with the flour. Mold in rectangular or conical pans. Serve sliced thinly with smoked salmon, pâté or other savory spreads.

Approximate values per 4-oz. (120-g) serving: **Calories** 475, **Total fat** 30 g, **Saturated fat** 17 g, **Cholesterol** 192 mg, **Sodium** 138 mg, **Total carbohydrates** 43 g, **Protein** 9 g, **Vitamin A** 30%, **Iron** 16%

5 The finished brioche dough ready for fermentation.

6 Shaping brioche à tête.

7 Panning the rolls.

8 A finished loaf of brioche baked in a Pullman pan.

CONVENIENCE PRODUCTS

As with the yeast dough discussed in Chapter 7, many varieties of prepared mixes for enriched yeast dough are available. Most manufacturers sell mixes that are formulated for making sweet dough, which can be used to make everything from rolls to sticky buns to filled coffee cake. The baker adds yeast and water, then mixes, forms, proofs and bakes the products. Better flavors can be achieved from mixes that call for the addition of fresh eggs and butter according to the manufacturer's recommendation.

Mixes are formulated to perform well under specific mixing and baking conditions. The combination of ingredients in a doughnut mix, for example, is selected to withstand cooking in hot oil without burning. The amount and type of fat and sweeteners is adjusted to produce evenly browned products when fried. Do not be tempted to use a sweet dough mix to make doughnuts unless it is recommended by the manufacturer. Similarly, adding eggs to a sweet dough mix will not necessarily produce challah dough, a product recognized by the subtle sweetness of honey, eggs and fats.

Frozen brioche dough is sold in 2- to 10-pound blocks, rolled into sheets or portioned into individual pastries. Some manufacturers use pure butter, others vegetable shortening. As with other frozen doughs, care must be taken to thaw frozen brioche dough, usually under refrigeration overnight. If thawed at room temperature, the exterior of the dough will be warm while the center remains frozen. Yeast activity will be uneven, affecting the quality of the finished bread made from the dough.

Frozen sweet dough usually comes portioned and formed into filled or plain rolls, buns or pastries. The dough requires panning and then careful thawing, usually under refrigeration, before proofing and baking. The baker applies toppings and glazes after baking the dough. Frozen fully baked sweet dough products such as sticky buns, rum babas and doughnuts are also available. These products are simply defrosted and then glazed or iced as desired. As with similar products, the advantages of convenience and time savings must be weighed against the flavor and quality of freshly made products.

CONCLUSION

The enriched doughs in this chapter are those that bake into breads with a tender crust. These breads contain a higher percentage of fat, sugar and eggs than the lean bread doughs covered in Chapter 7, Yeast Breads. When baked, the enriched doughs in this chapter are light in texture with a tender crumb and distinct flavor of butter or fat and a rich golden color from eggs. Enriched yeast doughs bake into some of the most popular pastries in bakeshops. The popularity of the bakery café has increased consumer demand for pastries such as the brioche and sticky buns featured in this chapter. Basic sweet doughs are versatile and offer the operator many types of products from a limited number of formulas. Handling these rich, sticky doughs is an easily mastered skill well within the grasp of student bakers who first have a solid understanding of the principles of yeast bread baking discussed in Chapter 7, Yeast Breads.

QUESTIONS FOR DISCUSSION

1 Describe the kinds of flour used to make enriched and sweet yeast doughs such as brioche or challah. What characteristics of flour are important to consider when making these doughs?

2 Discuss the mixing methods used to make enriched and sweet doughs.

3 What effect will using firm butter have on the mixing of enriched yeast doughs such as brioche?

4 What issues does the baker face when making brioche or other enriched sweet yeast doughs in a hot and humid climate? Discuss techniques that the baker can employ under such working conditions.

PAIN DE MIE (SANDWICH BREAD)　　　　　RECIPE 8.4

More tender than a Pullman loaf, pain de mie is an even-crumb loaf baked in a rectangular pan with lid.

Yield: 2 Loaves, 1 lb. 14 oz. (900 g) each　　**Method:** Straight dough

Fermentation: 45 minutes.　　**Proofing:** Approximately 30 to 45 minutes.

Instant yeast	0.7 oz.	20 g	2%
Water (temperature controlled)	19 fl. oz.	570 ml	56%
Bread flour	2 lb. 2 oz.	1020 g	100%
Dry milk powder	1 oz.	30 g	3%
Granulated sugar	1.3 oz.	40 g	4%
Salt	0.7 oz.	20 g	2%
Unsalted butter, room temperature	4 oz.	120 g	12%
Egg wash	as needed	as needed	
Total dough weight:	3 lb. 12 oz.	1820 g	179%

1. Moisten the yeast in the water in the bowl of a mixer fitted with a dough hook. Mix in the flour, milk powder, sugar and salt on medium speed. Mix until a soft dough is formed, approximately 3 minutes. Cut the butter into eight pieces and add it to the dough. Mix until the dough is smooth and elastic and passes the windowpane test, approximately 5 minutes.

2. Place the dough on a lightly floured surface and ferment until doubled in size, approximately 45 minutes.

3. Punch down the dough and divide into 2 uniform pieces. Round the portions, cover and bench rest 5 minutes.

4. Shape the dough into cylinders and place the formed dough into buttered loaf pans with lids (Pullman pans). (When no lids are available, grease a half-sheet pan and place it over the loaves.)

5. Proof until the loaves have increased 70 to 80 percent in volume, approximately 30 to 45 minutes. Brush with egg wash. Close the lids or set the greased sheet pans on top of the loaves.

6. Bake at 375F (190°C) until golden brown, approximately 40 minutes. Remove the lids and cool the loaves in their pans for 10 minutes before unmolding.

Approximate values per 1½-oz. (45-g) serving: **Calories** 120, **Total fat** 2.5 g, **Saturated fat** 1.5 g, **Cholesterol** 5 mg, **Sodium** 190 mg, **Total carbohydrates** 19 g, **Protein** 3 g

RECIPE 8.5   **MILK BREAD**

Milk bread rolls

Milk bread baked into various loaf shapes

▶ **pearl sugar** large-grain sugar formed into opaque pellets for decorating cookies and breads

Milk bread dough may be baked in many forms, including loaves for slicing or individual rolls (see Chapter 7, Yeast Breads). The make-up method illustrated in this formula produces small loaves composed of several individual rolls that stick together during proofing and baking. After baking the loaves may be served intact or the segments pulled apart into individual rolls after cooling.

Yield: 7 Loaves, approximately 10 oz. (300 g) each

Method: Straight dough

Fermentation: Bench rest, 20 minutes.   **Proofing:** 30 minutes.

Milk	20 fl. oz.	550 ml	55%
Compressed yeast	2.25 oz.	60 g	6%
Bread flour	1 lb. 2 oz.	500 g	50%
Pastry flour	1 lb. 2 oz.	500 g	50%
Shortening	4.5 oz.	120 g	12%
Granulated sugar	3.6 oz.	100 g	10%
Dough conditioner (optional)	0.5 oz.	15 g	1.5%
Salt	0.5 oz.	15 g	1.5%
Eggs	3.3 oz. (2 eggs)	100 g	10%
Egg wash	as needed	as needed	
Sliced almonds	as needed	as needed	
Pearl sugar	as needed	as needed	
Total dough weight:	4 lb. 6 oz.	1960 g	196%

1 Warm the milk to 200°F (93°C), then cool it to room temperature.

2 Dissolve the yeast in the milk in the bowl of a mixer fitted with a dough hook. Mix in the flours, shortening, sugar, dough conditioner (if using), salt and eggs on low speed until combined, approximately 3 minutes.

3 Stop the mixer, scrape down the bowl and check the dough consistency. Add more flour if necessary to make a soft dough. Increase the speed to medium and knead until the dough is fully developed and reaches 80°F (27°C), approximately 7 minutes.

4 Scrape the dough onto a lightly floured workbench and cover. Bench rest 15 minutes. Punch down the dough, then cover and bench rest another 5 minutes.

5 Divide the dough into 2-ounce (60-gram) pieces. Round the rolls, cover and bench rest 5 minutes. Shape each piece of dough into a small oval. Place five pieces of the formed dough side by side on a paper-lined sheet pan with their long sides touching. Repeat until seven loaves have been formed. Brush the dough with egg wash.

6 Proof until doubled in size, approximately 30 minutes. Score the loaves and sprinkle them with sliced almonds or pearl sugar.

7 Bake at 375°F (190°C) until golden brown, approximately 8 to 10 minutes. The loaves can be served intact or pulled apart into individual rolls after cooling.

Approximate values per 1½-oz. (45-g) serving: **Calories** 130, **Total fat** 4 g, **Saturated fat** 1 g, **Cholesterol** 10 mg, **Sodium** 140 mg, **Total carbohydrates** 21 g, **Protein** 4 g

SWEET DOUGH COFFEECAKES   RECIPE 8.6

Yield: 2 Coffeecakes, approximately 2 lb. (960 g) each

Method: Straight dough   **Proofing:** Approximately 1 hour.

Cardamom Sweet Bun Dough (page 189)	3 lb.	1440 g
Unsalted butter, melted	4 oz.	120 g
Cocoa Streusel (page 279)	1 lb.	480 g
Fondant Glaze (page 370)	as needed	as needed
Basic Sugar Glaze (page 360)	as needed	as needed
Nuts, chopped	as needed	as needed

1 Grease two 8-inch (20-centimeter) cake pans and line with parchment paper. Set aside.

2 Divide the dough into two equal pieces. Roll out each piece of dough into a 10-inch (25-centimeter) rectangle. Brush the dough with the melted butter and sprinkle with 8 ounces (240 grams) of the Cocoa Streusel.

3 Roll up each piece of dough into a cylinder, then coil the cylinders and place in the prepared cake pans. Sprinkle the dough with the remaining Cocoa Streusel.

4 Proof the cakes until doubled in volume, approximately 1 hour. Bake at 350°F (180°C), with a short burst of steam at the beginning of baking, until golden brown and baked through, approximately 25 to 30 minutes.

5 Remove the coffeecakes from their pans. Brush the hot cakes with Fondant Glaze. Cool the cakes on a cooling rack. Decorate the cooled cakes with Basic Sugar Glaze and chopped nuts.

Approximate values per 2-oz. (60-g) serving: **Calories** 290, **Total fat** 18 g, **Saturated fat** 11 g, **Cholesterol** 50 mg, **Sodium** 160 mg, **Total carbohydrates** 29 g, **Protein** 4 g, **Vitamin A** 10 %

CHOCOLATE CHERRY BABKAS   RECIPE 8.7

Yield: 2 Loaves, approximately 2 lb. 4 oz. (1080 g) each

Method: Straight dough   **Proofing:** Approximately 1 hour.

Sweet Bun Dough (page 188)	3 lb.	1440 g
Unsalted butter, softened	4 oz.	120 g
Bittersweet chocolate, chopped	8 oz.	240 g
Cherries, dried	8 oz.	240 g
Walnuts, lightly toasted, chopped	8 oz.	240 g
Cinnamon, ground	0.2 oz. (1 Tbsp.)	6 g
Basic Sugar Glaze (page 360)	as needed	as needed
Crystal sugar	as needed	as needed

1 Grease two 10-inch (25-centimeter) loaf pans and line the bottom and sides with parchment paper. Set aside.

2 Divide the dough into four equal pieces. Roll out each piece of dough into a 10-inch (25-centimeter) log. Flatten each piece of dough slightly. Spread the butter over the dough. Press the chocolate, cherries and walnuts into the surface of the dough. Sprinkle with the cinnamon. For each loaf, twist two pieces of chocolate-coated dough together and place in the prepared pan.

3 Proof the dough until doubled in volume, approximately 1 hour. Bake at 350°F (180°C), with a short burst of steam at the beginning of baking, until golden brown and baked through, approximately 25 to 30 minutes.

4 Remove the babkas from their pans. Cool the babkas on a cooling rack. Decorate the cooled babkas with Basic Sugar Glaze and crystal sugar.

Approximate values per 2-oz. (60-g) serving: **Calories** 240, **Total fat** 17 g, **Saturated fat** 8 g, **Cholesterol** 35 mg, **Sodium** 115 mg, **Total carbohydrates** 19 g, **Protein** 4 g

CONCHAS

LA PETITE PASTRY SHOP, Chicago, IL
Chef Bill Goebel, Owner

These sweet rolls are a Mexican specialty, popular at breakfast. The plump rolls are usually topped with a brightly colored sugar paste that, when baked, cracks open to resemble a seashell.

Yield: 36 Rolls, 2 oz. (60 g) each   **Method:** Straight dough

Fermentation: Bench rest, 3 hours.   **Proofing:** 30 minutes to 1 hour.

Dough:

Compressed yeast	3.6 oz.	100 g	10%
Water (temperature controlled)	3 fl. oz.	80 ml	8%
Bread flour	2 lb. 4 oz.	1000 g	100%
Eggs	1 lb. (10 eggs)	450 g	45%
Granulated sugar	9.75 oz.	270 g	27%
Unsalted butter or lard, room temperature	6.5 oz.	180 g	18%
Vanilla extract	0.25 fl. oz. (1½ tsp.)	7.5 ml	0.7%
Salt	0.15 oz. (¾ tsp.)	5 g	0.5%
Total dough weight:	4 lb. 11 oz.	2092 g	209%

Topping:

Bread flour	16 oz.	450 g	100%
Powdered sugar	10 oz.	280 g	63%
Shortening or lard	10 oz.	280 g	63%
Water	1 fl. oz.	30 ml	7%
Cocoa powder or food coloring (optional)	as needed	as needed	
Total topping weight:	2 lb. 5 oz.	1040 g	233%
Melted shortening or lard	1.5 oz.	45 g	
Granulated Sugar	as needed	as needed	

1 To prepare the dough, soften the yeast in the water in the bowl of a mixer fitted with a dough hook. Add the remaining dough ingredients and mix 3 minutes on low speed. Scrape down the bowl. Restart the mixer on medium speed and knead until the dough is soft and smooth, approximately 7 more minutes. The dough should reach 80°F (27°C) after kneading.

2 Place the dough on a lightly floured workbench, cover and bench rest 30 minutes.

3 Punch down the dough. Bench rest another 30 minutes. Repeat this process two more times for a total of 3 hours bench rest.

4 While the dough is resting, prepare the topping. Combine the flour, sugar, shortening and water in the bowl of a mixer fitted with a paddle. Beat to combine the ingredients into a smooth paste. Add enough cocoa powder or food coloring (if using) to tint the topping to the desired shade. Set aside.

5 Scale the dough into 2-ounce (60-gram) pieces. Shape each piece into a round ball and place on a paper-lined sheet pan. Brush each piece with melted shortening or lard.

6 Divide the topping into ½-ounce (15-gram) pieces. Spread each ball of dough with a piece of the topping. Dip a concha cutter, pizza wheel or Kaiser roll stamp in flour. Use it to stamp a series of five lines into the dough in a pattern resembling a shell. Sprinkle the rolls with sugar.

7 Proof at 80°F (25°C) until the rolls triple in volume, approximately 1 hour.

8 Bake the rolls at 375°F (190°C), with steam injected into the oven during the first few minutes of baking, until golden brown, approximately 8 to 10 minutes.

Approximate values per roll: **Calories** 340, **Total fat** 15 g, **Saturated fat** 5 g, **Cholesterol** 60 mg, **Sodium** 60 mg, **Total carbohydrates** 45 g, **Protein** 6 g, **Iron** 10%

JALAPEÑO CHEESE BREAD   RECIPE 8.9

Yield: 4 Loaves, approximately 1 lb. 6 oz. (660 g) each

Method: Straight dough

Fermentation: 1 to 1½ hours.   **Proofing:** 30 to 45 minutes.

Bread flour	2 lb. 3 oz.	1050 g	100%
Water (temperature controlled)	1 pt.	480 ml	46%
Eggs	6.75 oz. (4 eggs)	200 g	19%
Instant yeast	1 oz.	30 g	3%
Dry milk powder	1 oz.	30 g	3%
Granulated sugar	3 oz.	90 g	9%
Salt	0.75 oz.	22 g	2%
Olive oil	3 fl. oz.	90 ml	9%
Jalapeño peppers, seeded and chopped	10 oz.	300 g	29%
Cilantro, chopped fine	1.5 oz.	45 g	4%
Onions, fine dice	2 oz.	60 g	6%
Cheddar cheese, large dice	10 oz.	300 g	29%
Total weight:	5 lb. 10 oz.	2697 g	259%

1 Place the flour, water, eggs, yeast, milk powder, sugar, salt and oil in the bowl of a mixer fitted with a dough hook. Mix on low speed until the ingredients are combined into a firm dough. Increase the speed to medium and knead until the dough is fully developed, approximately 7 to 9 minutes. Add the jalapeños, cilantro, onions and cheese and mix just until blended into the dough. The dough should reach 80°F (27°C) after kneading.

2 Cover the dough and ferment until doubled, approximately 1 to 1½ hours.

3 Punch down the dough and divide into four equal pieces. Round the dough, cover and bench rest 10 minutes.

4 Roll the dough into cylinders and place them seam side down into greased or paper-lined loaf pans.

5 Proof until the formed loaves increase 75 to 80 percent in volume, approximately 30 to 45 minutes.

6 Brush with egg wash and bake at 375°F (190°C) until golden brown, approximately 50 minutes. Cool the loaves in their pans for 30 minutes to prevent the loaves from collapsing.

Approximate values per 1½-oz. (45-g) serving: **Calories** 110, **Total fat** 3.5 g, **Saturated fat** 1.5 g, **Cholesterol** 15 mg, **Sodium** 170 mg, **Total carbohydrates** 14 g, **Protein** 4 g

RECIPE 8.10

PARISIAN BRIOCHE

Yield: 3 Loaves, approximately 1 lb. 9 oz. (750 g) each   **Method:** Sponge

Fermentation: Sponge, 2 hours. Final dough, 1 hour.   **Proofing:** 1 hour.

Sponge:

Instant yeast	0.5 oz.	15 g	6%
Water, warm	4 fl. oz.	120 ml	50%
Bread flour	8 oz.	240 g	100%
Eggs	8 oz. (5 eggs)	240 g	100%
Granulated sugar	1 oz.	30 g	12%
Total sponge weight:	1 lb. 5 oz.	645 g	268%

Dough:

Instant yeast	0.25 oz. (1 1/2 tsp.)	8 g	1%
Water, warm	1 fl. oz.	30 ml	4%
Sponge	1 lb. 5 oz.	645 g	80%
High-gluten flour	1 lb. 10 oz.	780 g	100%
Granulated sugar	4 oz.	120 g	15%
Eggs, lightly beaten	13 oz. (8 eggs)	390 g	50%
Salt	0.75 oz.	23 g	3%
Unsalted butter, room temperature	13 oz.	390 g	50%
Egg wash	as needed	as needed	
Total dough weight:	4 lb. 15 oz.	2386 g	303%

1 Prepare the sponge by combining the yeast, water, flour, eggs and sugar. Mix on low speed until well combined and very smooth. Cover with plastic and ferment 2 hours, or until doubled.

2 To prepare the dough, dissolve the yeast in the water. Add it to the sponge along with the flour, sugar, 6 ounces (180 grams) of the eggs and the salt. Mix on low speed until a soft dough forms, approximately 3 minutes.

3 Add the remaining eggs in six increments, waiting for the eggs to be fully incorporated before adding more to the dough.

4 Add the butter in six increments, waiting for the butter to be fully incorporated before adding more to the dough.

5 Cover the dough and ferment 45 minutes to 1 hour.

6 Punch down the dough, divide into 4 3/4-ounce (142-gram) pieces and round.

7 Generously butter three large brioche pans. Fill each brioche pan with five rounded pieces of dough. First position four rounded pieces of dough in the bottom of each pan and then taper one side of the fifth piece of dough and place it in the center on top of other four pieces, tapered end down.

8 Proof at 85°F (30°C), until the loaves have increased 70 percent in volume, approximately 1 hour.

9 Gently brush the loaves with egg wash. Bake at 375°F (190°C) until deeply browned, approximately 38 to 40 minutes.

Approximate values per 1 1/2-oz. (45-g) serving: **Calories** 130, **Total fat** 7 g, **Saturated fat** 4 g, **Cholesterol** 55 mg, **Sodium** 170 mg, **Total carbohydrates** 14 g, **Protein** 4 g

RUM BABAS WITH CRÈME CHANTILLY   RECIPE 8.11

Yield: 18 Babas, 2½ oz. (75 g) each   **Method:** Straight dough

Fermentation: 45 minutes to 1 hour   **Proofing:** Approximately 1 hour.

Instant yeast	0.5 oz.	15 g	3%
Water (temperature controlled)	12 fl. oz.	360 ml	75%
Eggs	8.3 oz. (5 eggs)	250 g	52%
Granulated sugar	1 oz.	30 g	6%
Salt	0.3 oz. (1½ tsp.)	10 g	2%
Vanilla extract	0.15 fl. oz. (1 tsp.)	5 ml	1%
Bread flour	1 lb.	480 g	100%
Unsalted butter, room temperature	6 oz.	180 g	37%
Total dough weight:	2 lb. 12 oz.	1330 g	276%
Simple Syrup (page 349)	3 qt.	3 lt	
Dark rum	2 fl. oz.	60 ml	
Crème Chantilly (page 445)	1 pt.	480 ml	
Fresh fruit, as desired	1 lb. 4 oz.	600 g	

1 Dissolve the yeast in the water in the bowl of a mixer fitted with a dough hook. Add the eggs, sugar, salt, vanilla and flour and mix on low speed until the dough is smooth and elastic, approximately 6 to 10 minutes. The dough should reach 80°F (27°C) after kneading.

2 Break the butter up into several pieces and place it on top of the dough. Mix the dough about 20 to 30 seconds on low speed, just enough to distribute the butter throughout the dough without completely incorporating it into the dough.

3 Ferment the dough in the bowl of the mixer, covered, until it doubles in size, approximately 45 minutes.

4 Restart the mixer on medium speed and knead the dough 2 to 3 minutes to completely mix the butter into the dough. The dough will be very soft, smooth and elastic when fully kneaded.

5 Place the dough in a pastry bag fitted with a large plain tip. Pipe buttered baba or savarin molds one-third to one-half full with the dough. Use scissors to cut the dough away from the pastry tip.

6 Proof until doubled in size. Bake at 375°F (190°C) until golden brown, approximately 15 minutes. Cool to room temperature.

7 Bring the Simple Syrup to a boil in a large saucepan. Reduce the heat to a low simmer. Place the babas in the simmering syrup, allowing ample room for them to expand. After 1 minute flip the pastries, then leave them to soak up the syrup for 1 minute on the other side. When fully soaked, the babas will expand by approximately 25 percent.

8 Remove the babas from the syrup using a slotted spoon and place them on a serving plate. (Strain and reserve any leftover syrup for another use.) Sprinkle or brush each baba with the dark rum. Decorate with Crème Chantilly and fresh fruit. Babas may be served warm or at room temperature.

VARIATION:

Babas in Exotic Syrup—Prepare babas. Make a simple syrup using 1 quart (1 liter) water, 10 fluid ounces (300 milliliters) orange juice, 4 fluid ounces (120 milliliters) passion fruit juice, 2 fluid ounces (60 milliliters) lime juice, 0.5 fluid ounce (15 milliliters) vanilla extract and 2 pounds (960 grams) sugar. Soak the babas in this syrup. Brush the babas with exotic fruit liqueur instead of rum.

Approximate values per baba: **Calories** 340, **Total fat** 20 g, **Saturated fat** 11 g, **Cholesterol** 105 mg, **Sodium** 230 mg, **Total carbohydrates** 34 g, **Protein** 5 g, **Vitamin C** 30%

RECIPE 8.12   **JUMBO CINNAMON BUNS**

Yield: 24 Large Rolls   **Method:** Straight dough

Fermentation: 1 to 2 hours. **Proofing:** Approximately 1 hour.

Dough:

Water, warm	1 qt.	960 ml	40%
All-purpose flour	5 lb.	2400 g	100%
Granulated sugar	12 oz.	360 g	15%
Active dry yeast	1 oz.	30 g	1.2%
Dry milk powder	1.25 oz.	40 g	1.6%
Salt	0.25 oz. (1¼ tsp.)	7 g	0.3%
Whole butter, softened	10 oz.	300 g	12%
Total dough weight:	8 lb. 8 oz.	4097 g	170%

Filling:

Whole butter, softened	6 oz.	180 g
Cinnamon, ground	0.25 oz. (4 tsp.)	7 g
Brown sugar	6 oz.	180 g
Raisins	4 oz.	120 g
Powdered Sugar Glaze (recipe follows)	11 fl. oz.	330 ml

1 Combine all the dough ingredients in the large bowl of a mixer fitted with a dough hook. Knead the dough until it is smooth, approximately 6 to 8 minutes.

2 Place the dough in a lightly oiled bowl, cover and ferment until doubled.

3 Punch down the dough and roll it out on a lightly floured surface. Shape into a rectangle, approximately 18 inches × 30 inches (45 centimeters × 75 centimeters).

4 To make the filling, spread the butter over the surface of the dough. Combine the cinnamon, sugar and raisins and sprinkle this mixture over the butter, covering the dough evenly.

5 Starting with the longer side, roll the dough into a spiral. Cut into 24 pieces, each approximately 1½ inches (3.7 centimeters) thick. Place the rolls close together, cut side up, on a paper-lined sheet pan and allow them to rise until doubled.

6 Bake at 300°F (150°C) until golden brown and done, approximately 30 minutes.

7 Cool slightly, then top with Powdered Sugar Glaze.

Approximate values per roll: **Calories** 656, **Total fat** 16 g, **Saturated fat** 10 g, **Cholesterol** 42 mg, **Sodium** 132 mg, **Total carbohydrates** 117 g, **Protein** 11 g, **Vitamin A** 11%, **Iron** 27%

POWDERED SUGAR GLAZE

Yield: 11 fl. oz. (330 ml)

Powdered sugar, sifted	1 lb.	450 g
Vanilla extract	0.3 fl. oz. (2 tsp.)	10 ml
Lemon juice	0.3 fl. oz. (2 tsp.)	10 ml
Water, warm	1 fl. oz.	30 ml

1 Combine all ingredients in a small bowl. Stir to blend thoroughly and dissolve any lumps. Cover and store at room temperature.

Approximate values per 1-fl.-oz. (30-ml) serving: **Calories** 160, **Total fat** 0 g, **Saturated fat** 0 g, **Cholesterol** 0 mg, **Sodium** 0 mg, **Total carbohydrates** 41 g, **Protein** 0 g

PECAN STICKY BUNS

Yield: 12 to 15 Buns   **Method:** Straight dough

Fermentation: 1 to 2 hours. Bench rest, 10 minutes.

Proofing: 20 minutes.

Dough:

Active dry yeast	1 oz.	30 g	7%
Granulated sugar	2 oz.	60 g	14%
Salt	0.1 oz. (½ tsp.)	3 g	0.7%
Milk	0.5 fl. oz.	15 ml	3.6%
Buttermilk	5.5 fl. oz.	165 ml	39%
Vanilla extract	0.15 fl. oz. (1 tsp.)	5 ml	1%
Lemon zest, grated	0.2 oz. (1 Tbsp.)	6 g	1.4%
Lemon juice	0.15 fl. oz. (1 tsp.)	5 ml	1%
Egg yolks	1.3 oz. (2 yolks)	40 g	9%
All-purpose flour	14 oz.	420 g	100%
Unsalted butter, very soft	8 oz.	240 g	57%
Total dough weight:	2 lb.	989 g	233%

Topping:

Honey	6 fl. oz.	180 ml	
Brown sugar	6 oz.	180 g	
Pecans, chopped	3 oz.	90 g	

Filling:

Cinnamon	0.07 oz. (1 tsp.)	2 g	
Pecans, chopped	3 oz.	90 g	
Brown sugar	4 oz.	120 g	
Unsalted butter, melted	3 oz.	90 g	

1 Brushing melted butter over the sticky bun dough.

2 Rolling up the filling in the sticky bun dough.

3 Cutting and panning the sticky buns.

1 To make the dough, stir the yeast, sugar, salt and milk together in a small bowl. Set aside.

2 Stir the buttermilk, vanilla, lemon zest and lemon juice together and add to the yeast mixture.

3 Add the egg yolks, flour and butter to the liquid mixture. Knead until the butter is evenly distributed and the dough is smooth and fully developed, approximately 6 minutes. Cover and ferment until doubled.

4 Prepare the topping and filling mixtures while the dough is fermenting. To make the topping, cream the honey and sugar together. Stir in the pecans. This mixture will be very stiff. To make the filling, stir the cinnamon, pecans and sugar together.

5 Lightly grease muffin cups, then distribute the topping mixture evenly, about 1 tablespoon (15 milliliters) per muffin cup. Set the pans aside at room temperature until the dough is ready.

6 Punch down the dough and rest 10 minutes. Roll out the dough into a rectangle about ½ inch (1.2 centimeters) thick. Brush with the melted butter and top evenly with the filling mixture.

7 Starting with either long edge, roll up the dough. Cut into slices about ¾ to 1 inch (1.8 to 2.5 centimeters) thick. Place a slice in each muffin cup over the topping.

8 Let the buns proof until doubled, approximately 20 minutes. Bake at 325°F (160°C) until very brown, approximately 25 minutes. Immediately invert the muffin pans onto paper-lined sheet pans to let the buns and their topping slide out.

Approximate values per bun: **Calories** 480, **Total fat** 26 g, **Saturated fat** 11 g, **Cholesterol** 75 mg, **Sodium** 100 mg, **Total carbohydrates** 55 g, **Protein** 5 g, **Vitamin A** 15%, **Iron** 15%

PECAN STICKY BUNS

Sweet dough filled with a cinnamon and nut filling and a sticky topping is one of the most popular forms of sweet dough preparations. Almost any sweet dough can be used to form the dough for this pastry, including Sweet Bun Dough (page 188) or Brioche (page 190). The dough in this formula is rich and buttery. Buttermilk, lemon zest and lemon juice give it a pleasant tang to contrast with the gooey filling.

RECIPE 8.14 **CINNAMON SWIRL RAISIN BREAD**

Yield: 3 Loaves, 1 lb. 10 oz. (780 g), each   **Method:** Sponge

Fermentation: Sponge, 2 hours. Final dough, about 1 hour.

Proofing: 1 hour.

Sponge:

Bread flour	8 oz.	240 g	100%
Water	4 fl. oz.	120 ml	50%
Instant yeast	0.15 oz. (1 tsp.)	5 g	2%
Total sponge weight:	12 oz.	365 g	152%

Dough:

Sponge	12 oz.	365 g	63%
Bread flour	1 lb. 3 oz.	570 g	100%
Potato flour or additional bread flour	3 oz.	90 g	16%
Dry milk powder	1.5 oz.	45 g	8%
Eggs	5 oz. (3 eggs)	150 g	26%
Granulated sugar	3 oz.	90 g	16%
Vanilla extract	0.15 fl. oz. (1 tsp.)	5 ml	0.8%
Salt	0.75 oz.	22 g	4%
Corn syrup or glucose	1.75 oz.	50 g	9%
Instant yeast	0.75 oz.	22 g	4%
Water (temperature controlled)	10 fl. oz.	300 ml	52%
Unsalted butter, room temperature	6 oz.	180 g	32%
Raisins	1 lb. 4 oz.	600 g	105%
Total dough weight:	5 lb. 2 oz.	2489 g	436%
Cinnamon, ground	0.07 oz. (1 tsp.)	2 g	
Granulated sugar	4 oz.	120 g	
Egg wash	as needed	as needed	

1 To make the sponge, combine the flour, water and yeast. Cover and ferment 2 hours.

2 Place the sponge in the bowl of a mixer fitted with a dough hook. Add the flours, milk powder, eggs, sugar, vanilla, salt, corn syrup, yeast and water to the sponge. Mix on medium speed until well blended, about 5 minutes. Once the dough has reached approximately 75°F (24°C), gradually add the butter. Knead until the dough is fully developed and passes the windowpane test. Add the raisins and gently mix into the dough.

3 Cover the dough and ferment until doubled, approximately 1 hour.

4 Punch down the dough and divide into three equal pieces. Round the dough, then bench rest 5 minutes.

5 Flatten each piece of dough into a rectangle measuring approximately 10 inches by 6 inches (25 centimeters by 15 centimeters). Combine the cinnamon and sugar, then sprinkle each piece with the mixture. Roll up tightly and place seam side down into buttered or paper-lined loaf pans.

6 Proof at 80°F (25°C) until the loaves have increased 75 to 80 percent in volume, approximately 1 hour. Brush with egg wash.

7 Bake at 375°F (190°C) until well browned, approximately 40 to 45 minutes. Cool the loaves in their pans for about 30 minutes to prevent them from collapsing.

Approximate values per $^1/_{17}$-loaf serving: **Calories** 150, **Total fat** 3.5 g, **Saturated fat** 2 g, **Cholesterol** 20 mg, **Sodium** 170 mg, **Total carbohydrates** 26 g, **Protein** 3 g

QUARK STUTEN
(GERMAN SWEET SPICE AND RAISIN BREAD)

RECIPE 8.15

Yield: 5 Loaves, 1 lb. (480 g) each   **Method:** Straight dough

Fermentation: Bench rest, 40 minutes.   **Proofing:** 30 to 45 minutes.

Compressed yeast	2 oz.	60 g	6%
Water (temperature controlled)	13.75 fl. oz.	390 ml	39%
Bread flour	2 lb. 3 oz.	1000 g	100%
Dough conditioner (optional)	0.3 oz. (2 tsp.)	10 g	1%
Granulated sugar	5.25 oz.	150 g	15%
Cardamom, ground	0.17 oz. (2½ tsp.)	5 g	0.5%
Salt	0.7 oz.	20 g	2%
Shortening or margarine	3.5 oz.	100 g	10%
Quark, farmer's cheese or baker's cheese	10.5 oz.	300 g	30%
Orange zest, grated fine	3.5 oz.	100 g	10%
Golden raisins	10.5 oz.	300 g	30%
Total weight:	5 lb. 5 oz.	2435 g	243%
Clarified unsalted butter	as needed	as needed	
Granulated sugar	as needed	as needed	

1 Dissolve the yeast in the water in the bowl of a mixer fitted with a dough hook. Mix in the flour, dough conditioner (if using), sugar, cardamom, salt, shortening, quark and orange zest. Mix at low speed until the ingredients are combined, approximately 3 minutes. Knead on medium speed until fully developed, approximately 7 minutes. Add the raisins and knead just until incorporated.

2 Scrape the dough onto a lightly floured workbench. Cover the dough and bench rest 20 minutes. Punch down the dough and bench rest another 10 minutes.

3 Divide the dough into five uniform pieces and round. Cover and bench rest another 10 minutes. Shape each piece of dough into an oval and place the loaves on paper-lined sheet pans.

4 Cover and proof until doubled, approximately 30 to 45 minutes. Dock the surface of the loaves. Bake at 400°F (200°C), with steam injected into the oven during the first few seconds of baking, until the loaves are golden brown and baked through, approximately 35 to 40 minutes.

5 Brush the baked loaves with clarified butter and roll in granulated sugar. Cool on racks.

Approximate values per 2-oz. (60-g) serving: **Calories** 160, **Total fat** 3.5 g, **Saturated fat** 1 g, **Cholesterol** 0 mg, **Sodium** 220 mg, **Total carbohydrates** 29 g, **Protein** 4 g

HOT CROSS BUNS

Bread often plays a major role in holiday and religious observances. The hot cross bun is traditional Lenten bread, its exact origins unknown. Some say that it has pagan origins, the cross representing the moon and its four quarters. Anglo-Saxons ate the sacramental buns in honor of their goddess Eastore. When the Romans arrived in Britain, the clergy tried to stop the use of the sacramental buns, but could not. So they blessed them and gave the cross on the buns a Christian meaning.

Traditionally these buns are decorated with dough piped across the top before baking, not a sweet icing as is commonly seen. A thin glaze brushed over the hot buns provides the added sweetness.

Yield: 30 Rolls, Approximately 3½ oz. (105 g) each

Method: Straight dough

Fermentation: 45 minutes. **Proofing:** 1 hour.

Dough:

Golden raisins	10 oz.	300 g	30%
Dark raisins	10 oz.	300 g	30%
Candied orange peel	3 oz.	80 g	8%
Bread flour	2 lb. 4 oz.	1000 g	100%
Shortening	4 oz.	120 g	12%
Granulated sugar	3.5 oz.	100 g	10%
Dough conditioner (optional)	0.3 oz. (2 tsp.)	10 g	1%
Dry milk powder	2 oz.	50 g	5%
Compressed yeast	2.75 oz.	80 g	8%
Salt	0.6 oz. (1 Tbsp.)	18 g	1.8%
Eggs	3.3 oz. (2 eggs)	100 g	10%
Vanilla extract	0.15 fl. oz. (1 tsp.)	5 ml	0.5%
Cardamom, ground	0.07 oz. (1 tsp.)	2 g	0.2%
Allspice, ground	0.07 oz. (1 tsp.)	2 g	0.2%
Ginger, ground	0.14 oz. (2 tsp.)	4 g	0.4%
Cinnamon, ground	0.2 oz. (1 Tbsp.)	6 g	0.6%
Water	19 fl. oz.	520 ml	52%

Cross dough:

Pastry flour	4 oz.	110 g	11%
Shortening	0.75 oz.	22 g	2.2%
Milk	3.5 fl. oz.	100 ml	10%
Bun Glaze (recipe follows)	5 fl. oz.	150 ml	
Total dough weight:	6 lb. 7 oz.	2929 g	293%

1 Place the raisins and orange peel in a small bowl and cover with hot water. Let soften in the water for 5 minutes. Drain the water and let the fruit condition 2 to 4 hours before using. Set aside.

2 Place the flour, shortening, sugar, dough conditioner (if using), milk powder, yeast, salt, eggs, vanilla and spices in the bowl of a mixer fitted with a dough

hook. Add the water and mix the dough on low speed 3 minutes until moistened. Stop the machine and scrape down the bowl. Add additional flour if necessary to create a soft dough. Mix the dough on medium speed 6 to 7 minutes until it is soft and pliable.

3 Add the conditioned fruit and mix the dough on low speed until the fruit is well distributed in the dough. If necessary, dust the dough lightly with more flour to help the fruit incorporate.

4 Scrape the dough onto a flour-dusted workbench. Cover and ferment 30 minutes. Deflate the dough and fold it into thirds, then rest another 15 minutes.

5 Divide the dough into 3½-ounce (105-gram) pieces. Round the dough into tight rolls with a smooth top surface. Place the formed rolls seam side down on a paper-lined half-sheet pan. Position them in rows on the tray, five rolls by six rolls, so that the rolls touch when fully proofed.

6 Proof the rolls with low humidity until doubled in size, approximately 50 minutes.

7 While the rolls proof, prepare the cross dough. Combine the pastry flour, shortening and milk in the bowl of a mixer fitted with a paddle. Mix on medium speed until the shortening is well blended and the dough is lump-free.

8 When the rolls have proofed, scoop the cross dough into a pastry bag fitted with a plain tip. Quickly pipe a cross over the surface of each roll.

9 Bake at 375°F (190°C) until the rolls are a rich brown color, approximately 15 minutes.

10 Brush the hot rolls generously with the chilled Bun Glaze, making certain they are well coated so that no dry spots appear when the glaze dries.

BUN GLAZE

Yield: 5 fl. oz. (150 ml)

Water	1.75 fl. oz.	50 ml
Granulated sugar	3.5 oz.	100 g
Ginger, ground	0.02 oz. (¼ tsp.)	0.5 g
Lemon juice	0.15 fl. oz. (1 tsp.)	5 ml
Lemon zest, finely grated	0.07 oz. (1 tsp).	2 g
Cream of tartar	pinch	pinch

1 Place all ingredients in a heavy saucepan. Bring the mixture to a boil, stirring until the sugar dissolves. Continue boiling 5 minutes until the mixture reduces into a light syrup.

2 Strain the glaze into a bowl and allow it to cool, then refrigerate the glaze until it is well chilled.

Approximate values per bun: **Calories** 280, **Total fat** 6 g, **Saturated fat** 1.5 g, **Cholesterol** 15 mg, **Sodium** 260 mg, **Total carbohydrates** 53 g, **Protein** 6 g, **Iron** 15%

RECIPE 8.17

1 Placing the log of marzipan on the flattened stollen dough.

2 Finished Stollen

STOLLEN

Yield: 4 Loaves, 1 lb. 4 oz (600 g) each   **Method:** Sponge

Fermentation: Sponge, 2 hours. Final dough, 1 hour.

Proofing: 45 minutes to 1 hour.

Sponge:

Bread flour	7 oz.	210 g	100%
Water	5 fl. oz.	150 ml	71%
Instant yeast	0.25 oz. (1½ tsp.)	7.5 g	3.5%
Total sponge weight:	12 oz.	367 g	174%

Dough:

Sponge	12 oz.	367 g	122%
Bread flour	10 oz.	300 g	100%
Water (temperature controlled)	3 fl. oz.	90 ml	30%
Instant yeast	0.5 oz.	15 g	5%
Granulated sugar	2 oz.	60 g	20%
Glucose or corn syrup	0.75 oz.	22 g	0.7%
Salt	0.5 oz.	15 g	5%
Egg	1.6 oz. (1 egg)	50 g	1.6%
Egg yolk	0.6 oz. (1 yolk)	20 g	6%
Dry milk powder	1 oz.	30 g	10%
Vanilla extract	0.15 fl. oz. (1 tsp.)	5 ml	0.2%
Unsalted butter, softened	6 oz.	180 g	60%
Hazelnuts, toasted and chopped	5 oz.	150 g	20%
Dried cherries	3 oz.	90 g	30%
Raisins, soaked in rum 12 hours	1 lb.	480 g	160%
Candied orange peel	2.5 oz.	75 g	25%
Pistachios, chopped	5.5 oz.	165 g	55%
Marzipan	6 oz.	180 g	60%
Egg wash	as needed	as needed	
Unsalted butter, melted	as needed	as needed	
Powdered sugar	as needed	as needed	
Total dough weight:	4 lb. 12 oz.	2294 g	710%

1 To make the sponge, combine the flour, water and yeast. Cover and ferment 2 hours.

2 Place the sponge in the bowl of a mixer fitted with a dough hook. Add the flour, water, yeast, sugar, glucose, salt, egg, egg yolk, milk powder and vanilla. Once incorporated, mix on medium speed until the dough is fully developed, approximately 7 to 8 minutes. The dough should reach 77°F (25°C).

3 Gradually knead in the butter on medium speed until the dough is completely smooth. Add the hazelnuts, cherries, raisins, orange peel and pistachios, kneading just until combined.

4 Cover the dough and ferment until doubled in bulk, approximately 1 hour.

5 Divide the dough into four equal pieces. Round the dough and place it seam side up on a lightly floured workbench. Cover and bench rest 15 minutes.

6 Scale the marzipan into 1½ ounce (45-gram) pieces. Roll each piece into an 8-inch (20-centimeter) cylinder. Set aside.

7 Flatten each piece of dough into an oval. Place a log of marzipan in the middle of each piece of flattened dough. Fold the dough lengthwise to cover the marzipan. Press the dough together with a dowel placed parallel to the marzipan. Transfer the formed loaves to paper-lined sheet pans and proof at 85°F (30°C) until the loaves have increased 60 to 70 percent in volume, 45 minutes to 1 hour.

8 Brush with egg wash and bake at 375°F (190°C) until well browned, approximately 40 minutes. While still warm, brush each loaf generously with melted butter. Dust the cooled loaves with powdered sugar.

Approximate values per 2-oz. (60-g) serving: **Calories** 190, **Total fat** 9 g, **Saturated fat** 2.5 g, **Cholesterol** 20 mg, **Sodium** 150 mg, **Total carbohydrates** 26 g, **Protein** 4 g

ITALIAN PANETTONE

RECIPE 8.18

Yield: 2 Loaves, approximately 1 lb. 12 oz. (840 g) each

Fermentation: 1½ to 2 hours.   **Proofing:** 35 minutes to 1 hour.

Unsalted butter	4 oz.	120 g	16%
Granulated sugar	4 oz.	120 g	16%
Active dry yeast	0.75 oz.	22 g	3%
Water (temperature controlled)	8 fl. oz.	240 ml	33%
Salt	0.2 oz. (1 tsp.)	6 g	0.8%
Eggs	3.3 oz. (2 eggs)	100 g	14%
Egg yolks	2 oz. (3 yolks)	60 g	8%
Cake flour	1 lb. 8 oz.	720 g	100%
Dried pineapple, diced	4 oz.	120 g	16%
Raisins	6 oz.	180 g	25%
Lemon zest	0.14 oz. (2 tsp.)	4 g	0.6%
Pine nuts, chopped	3 oz.	90 g	12%
Anise seeds (optional)	0.07 oz. (1 tsp.)	2 g	0.3%
Vegetable oil	as needed	as needed	
Total dough weight:	3 lb. 11 oz.	1784 g	244%

1 Melt the butter and sugar in a small saucepan. Set aside to cool.

2 Sprinkle the yeast over the water in a mixer bowl and stir to dissolve. Add the butter-and-sugar mixture, salt, eggs and egg yolks and 12 ounces (360 grams) of the flour. Mix well. Add the fruit, lemon zest, nuts and anise seeds (if using).

3 Add the remaining flour, a small amount at a time, until a soft dough forms. Knead the dough on medium speed until smooth and elastic, approximately 7 to 10 minutes. Add only enough flour to keep the dough from sticking. The dough should reach 77°F (25°C) after kneading.

4 Place the dough in a lightly oiled bowl, cover and ferment until doubled, about 1½ to 2 hours.

5 Punch down the dough and turn it out onto a floured work surface. Divide the dough into two equal portions. Cover and bench rest 5 minutes. Grease and paper the bottoms of two panettone molds or two clean 1-pound (480-gram) coffee cans. Form the dough into smooth balls and place one in each pan.

6 Brush the tops of the dough with vegetable oil and proof until doubled in bulk, approximately 35 to 50 minutes.

7 Bake at 350°F (180°C) until well browned and baked through, approximately 35 to 45 minutes. Cool for 5 minutes in the pans, then unmold and cool completely before slicing.

Approximate values per 2-oz. (60-g) serving: **Calories** 190, **Total fat** 6 g, **Saturated fat** 2.5 g, **Cholesterol** 45 mg, **Sodium** 90 mg, **Total carbohydrates** 31 g, **Protein** 4 g, **Iron** 15%

RECIPE 8.19

YEAST-RAISED DOUGHNUTS

1 Cutting the rolled dough into round doughnut shapes before frying.

2 Frying the doughnuts and doughnut holes.

Yield: 40 Doughnuts, 2½ oz. (75 g) each   **Method:** Straight dough

Fermentation: 1½ to 2 hours.   **Proofing:** 30 minutes to 1 hour.

Granulated sugar	8 oz.	240 g	14%
Salt	1 oz.	30 g	1.8%
Bread flour	3 lb. 8 oz.	1680 g	100%
Dry milk powder	3 oz.	90 g	5.5%
Cinnamon	0.04 oz. (½ tsp.)	1 g	0.07%
Mace	0.25 oz. (3½ tsp.)	7 g	0.4%
Shortening	6 oz.	180 g	11%
Eggs	10 oz. (6 eggs)	300 g	18%
Buttermilk	6 fl. oz.	180 ml	11%
Vanilla extract	1 fl. oz.	30 ml	1.8%
Instant yeast	1 oz.	30 g	1.8%
Water, warm (95F/35C)	1 pt.	470 ml	28%
Total dough weight:	6 lb. 12 oz.	3238 g	193%

Topping:

Granulated sugar	6 oz.	180 g	
Cinnamon	0.2 oz. (1 Tbsp.)	6 g	

1 Combine the sugar, salt, flour, milk powder, cinnamon, mace and shortening in the bowl of a mixer fitted with a dough hook. Mix briefly to blend the spices throughout the dry mixture. Beat the eggs lightly and then add them to the flour mixture along with the buttermilk and vanilla.

2 Dissolve the yeast in the water and add to the flour. Mix on low speed about 2 to 3 minutes, adding additional flour if needed to make a soft dough. Scrape down the bowl and increase speed to medium. Knead the dough 5 to 7 minutes until it is smooth, soft and elastic.

3 Ferment the dough until doubled, approximately 1½ to 2 hours.

4 Divide the dough into four equal pieces. Place three portions of the dough on a lightly floured sheet pan, cover and refrigerate while making up the first piece of dough. Roll the dough out into a rectangle ½ inch (1.2 centimeters) thick. Cut out individual pieces with a doughnut cutter and place them on lightly floured sheet pans.

5 Portion the remaining dough, then cover and proof until it has increased 75 percent in volume.

6 Fry the doughnuts in batches in deep fat heated to 385°F (196°C). Cook until puffed and browned, approximately 1 minute. Flip the doughnuts using a long wooden skewer and cook another minute until browned. Remove from the fat and drain on absorbent paper.

7 Combine the sugar and cinnamon in a flat pan. Toss the hot doughnuts in this mixture.

VARIATIONS:

Jelly-Filled Doughnuts—Divide the fermented dough into 2½-ounce (75-gram) pieces. Round, proof and fry. Cool the doughnuts before filling. Place jelly or doughnut filling in the bowl of a mixer fitted with a paddle and mix on medium speed to soften. Scrape jelly into a doughnut pump or pastry bag fitted with a small plain tip. Pierce a hole in one side of each doughnut with a metal skewer. Insert the tip into the doughnut and fill each with jelly. Dust with powdered sugar.

Bismarcks—Prepare the doughnuts as for jelly doughnuts. Cut the cooled doughnuts three-quarters of the way through horizontally. Fill with Crème Chantilly (page 445) or Pastry Cream (page 436). Dust with powdered sugar.

Approximate values per doughnut: **Calories** 320, **Total fat** 15 g, **Saturated fat** 3 g, **Cholesterol** 25 mg, **Sodium** 300 mg, **Total carbohydrates** 41 g, **Protein** 7 g, **Iron** 10%

CHOCOLATE BEIGNETS

HERBSAINT BAR AND RESTAURANT, New Orleans, LA
Chef Donald Link

Beignets (ben-YEA) are leavened, deep-fried doughnutlike pastries smothered in powdered sugar. They are served piping hot 24 hours a day in New Orleans' French Quarter. Chef Link has added chocolate to the traditional formula for this dessert presentation.

Yield: 60 Pieces   **Method:** Straight dough

Fermentation: 30 minutes.

Chocolate Ganache (page 362)	2 lb.	960 g	123%
Dried cherries	2 oz.	60 g	8%
All-purpose flour	1 lb. 10 oz.	780 g	100%
Cocoa powder	1.75 oz.	55 g	7%
Granulated sugar	4 oz.	120 g	15%
Salt	0.1 oz. (½ tsp.)	3 g	0.4%
Active dry yeast	0.9 oz. (2 Tbsp.)	27 g	3.5%
Milk, warm	6 fl. oz.	180 ml	23%
Eggs	11.5 oz. (7 eggs)	345 g	44%
Unsalted butter, room temperature	5 oz.	150 g	19%
Egg wash	as needed	as needed	
Powdered sugar	as needed	as needed	
Total dough weight:	5 lb. 9 oz.	2680 g	343%

1 Prepare the Chocolate Ganache and allow it to rest at room temperature until it begins to firm. Or if refrigerated, warm the ganache over a pot of warm water until it is soft enough to pipe. Place the ganache in a pastry bag fitted with a large plain tip, then pipe it into ½-ounce (15-gram) "kisses" on a paper-lined sheet pan. Refrigerate.

2 Steep the cherries in hot water for 5 minutes, then drain and chop.

3 Sift the flour with the cocoa powder, then stir in the sugar and salt.

4 Combine the yeast with the milk. Add the yeast and milk to the dry ingredients in the bowl of a mixer fitted with a dough hook. Mix the ingredients at low speed, adding the eggs a small amount at a time. Mix the dough until the gluten develops, approximately 7 to 10 minutes.

5 Rest the dough 5 minutes. Then mix the dough on medium speed, adding the butter a small piece at a time. Let the butter mix in after each addition. When all of the butter has been added and the dough is pulling away from the sides of the bowl, add the cherries and mix until incorporated. Rest the dough in the refrigerator 30 minutes before using.

6 Roll a portion of the dough into a long rectangle, approximately 2 inches (5 centimeters) wide and ⅛ inch (3 millimeters) thick. Mark a centerline down the length of the dough with the back of a chef's knife. Brush the dough with egg wash. Place a row of ganache kisses on the lower half of the dough, spaced approximately 2 inches (5 centimeters) apart. Fold the upper half of the dough over the ganache. Press the dough together around the ganache kisses, ravioli-style. Cut the dough between the ganache kisses to form individual pillows. Place the beignets on a paper-lined sheet pan and freeze.

7 Place several frozen beignets in a deep-fryer basket. Place another deep-fryer basket over the beignets to keep them submerged in the fat as they cook. Deep-fry the frozen beignets at 325°F (160°C) approximately 3 to 4 minutes. Drain, toss in powdered sugar and serve.

Approximate values per 3-piece serving: **Calories** 870, **Total fat** 54 g, **Saturated fat** 30 g, **Cholesterol** 225 mg, **Sodium** 170 mg, **Total carbohydrates** 93 g, **Protein** 17 g, **Vitamin A** 30%, **Calcium** 10%, **Iron** 35%

IF MORE OF US VALUED FOOD AND CHEER AND SONG ABOVE HOARDED GOLD, IT WOULD BE A MERRIER WORLD.
—*J. R. R. Tolkien, British author and scholar (1892–1973)*

COOKIES AND BROWNIES

FAIRYTALE BROWNIES, Phoenix, AZ
Eileen Spitalny and David Kravetz, Owners

AFTER STUDYING THIS
CHAPTER, YOU WILL BE
ABLE TO:

▶ prepare a variety of cookie
doughs and batters

▶ understand the various make-
up methods for cookies,
biscotti and brownies

▶ assemble a variety of
decorated cookies and
brownies

Assortment of Cookies

Cookies need no introduction. These portable sweets are an American favorite. Brought here by early Dutch settlers—*koekje* means "little cake" in Dutch—sweet, dry biscuits have been assimilated and adapted by generations of immigrants. Sugar cookies, Italian biscotti, gingersnaps and other varieties from around the world are common in bakeshops across the country. With a good profit margin and all-around customer appeal, these products are a bakeshop staple.

This chapter examines the fundamental techniques for making a wide variety of basic cookies and all-American brownies. More elaborate and specialty cookies are discussed in further detail in Chapter 19, Petits Fours.

▶ COOKIES

Cookies are small, flat pastries usually eaten alone (although not singularly) as a snack or with coffee at the end of a meal. The proliferation of cookie shops in malls and office buildings attests to the popularity of freshly baked cookies. They are indeed one of America's best-loved foods.

The pleasure of cookies comes from their versatility. They may be eaten as a midmorning snack or as the elegant end to a formal dinner. Inventive cookie plates, often baked to order, appear on contemporary dessert menus alongside more traditional desserts. Cookies also provide the finishing touch to a serving of ice cream, custard or fruit. Flavors are limited only by the baker's imagination: chocolate, oatmeal, cornmeal, fresh and dried fruit and nuts all find their way into several types of cookies.

MIXING METHODS

Most cookies are made from a rich dough that is mixed by the creaming method used for quick breads and cake batters. (See Chapter 6, Quick Breads, and Chapter 14, Cakes and Tortes.) However, because cookie dough contains less liquid than these batters, the liquid and flour need not be added alternately. Cookies can be leavened with baking soda, baking powder or just air and steam. Most cookies are high in fat, which contributes flavor and tenderness and extends shelf life. In cookie formulas with a high percentage of fat and low moisture content, overdevelopment of gluten is usually not a problem. However, careless mixing can produce tough and dense cookies. When there are eggs or liquid in the dough, the flour is blended in gently to minimize gluten development. Add-ins such as chopped nuts, chocolate and pieces of fruit are stirred into the dough for this same reason.

▶ PROCEDURE FOR MIXING COOKIE DOUGHS

1 Cream the fat and sugar together to make a lump-free mixture and to blend the ingredients completely.

2 Add the eggs gradually, scraping down the bowl as needed.

3 Stir in the liquid ingredients.

4 Stir in the flour, salt, spices and leaveners.

5 Fold in any nuts, chocolate chips or chunky ingredients by hand or in a mixer on slow speed, taking care not to overmix the dough.

CHOCOLATE CHIP COOKIES

RECIPE 9.1

Yield: 50 Cookies, approximately 2 oz. (60 g) each

Method: Drop cookies

Granulated sugar	8 oz.	240 g	40%
Brown sugar	12 oz.	360 g	60%
Vegetable shortening, softened	1 lb.	480 g	80%
Eggs	6.75 oz. (4 eggs)	200 g	34%
Vanilla extract	0.3 fl. oz. (2 tsp.)	10 ml	1.5%
All-purpose flour	20 oz.	600 g	100%
Baking soda	0.3 oz (2 tsp.)	10 g	1.5%
Salt	0.4 oz (2 tsp.)	12 g	2%
Pecans, chopped	8 oz.	240 g	40%
Chocolate chips	2 lb.	960 g	160%
Total weight:	6 lb. 7 oz.	3112 g	519%

1 Cream the sugars and shortening in the bowl of a mixer fitted with a paddle. Beat until light, approximately 5 minutes at medium speed.

2 Add the eggs to the creamed mixture one at a time. Add the vanilla.

3 Stir the flour, baking soda and salt together and add to the creamed mixture.

4 Stir in the pecans and chips.

5 Portion the dough using a #20 scoop onto a parchment-lined sheet pan and bake at 350°F (180°C) for 10 to 12 minutes.

Approximate values per 2-oz. (60-g) cookie: **Calories** 310, **Total fat** 20 g, **Saturated fat** 7 g, **Cholesterol** 20 mg, **Sodium** 160 mg, **Total carbohydrates** 35 g, **Protein** 3 g

MAKE-UP METHODS

Cookie varieties are usually classified by the way in which the individual cookies are prepared once the dough has been made. This section describes six preparations or make-up techniques: **drop, icebox, bar, cut-out** or **rolled, pressed** and **wafer.**

DROP COOKIES

Drop cookies are made from a soft dough that is spooned or scooped into mounds for baking. Chunky cookies such as Chocolate Chip Cookies (above), Spiced Oatmeal Cookies (page 221) and Chocolate Jumbles (page 221) are common examples. Although a uniform appearance is not as important for drop cookies as for other types, uniform size and placement results in uniform baking time. A portion scoop is recommended for portioning the dough. See page 646 for recommended scoops and sizes. Rolling the ball of dough between moistened palms will make a more uniform shape in the finished cookie. Often the surface of a drop cookie is flattened slightly with a fork before baking. Moistening the fork with water or dipping it in sugar before pressing is helpful. The tines of the fork give peanut butter cookies their distinctive surface pattern. Drop cookies tend to be thick with a soft or chewy texture.

ICEBOX COOKIES

Icebox cookies are made from dough that is shaped into logs or rectangles, chilled thoroughly, then sliced into individual pieces and baked as needed. Logs of icebox cookies are often rolled in sugar or nuts before slicing, giving a flavorful decorative edge to the cookie once it bakes. Icebox cookies can be as simple as a log of chocolate chip dough or as sophisticated as elegant pinwheel and checkerboard cookies assembled with two colors of short dough. This method

Drop Cookies

Icebox Cookies

usually produces uniform, waferlike cookies with a crisp texture. The formed dough freezes nicely and can be stored when well wrapped with plastic for up to 1 month before using. Thaw this type of dough in the refrigerator overnight before using as directed. Checkerboard Cookies (page 224) and Bergamot Shortbread (page 225) illustrate the procedures for making icebox cookies.

BAR COOKIES

Bar cookie dough is pressed or layered in shallow pans and cut into portions after baking, usually in squares or rectangles to avoid waste or scraps. This category, also known as sheet cookies, contains a wide variety of layered or fruit-filled products. Often a short dough such as that used for a fruit tart or shortbread cookie forms the base of the bar cookies, then a topping is layered on the cookie before or after baking. See Mirror Cookies (page 230) and Lemon or Lime Bars (page 228). Brownies, often considered a bar cookie, are discussed later in this chapter. Other bar cookies can be produced by baking a traditional pastry in a shallow sheet pan and then cutting it into bars. Graham-cracker-crust cheesecake, Linzer and ganache tarts are good examples of this technique.

CUT-OUT OR ROLLED COOKIES

Cut-out or rolled cookies are made from a firm dough that is rolled out into a sheet and then cut into various shapes before baking. Many of the rich tart doughs in Chapter 10, Pies and Tarts, can be used as a cut-out cookie dough. Dough for rolled or cut-out cookies freezes well and can be stored well wrapped in the freezer for up to 1 month. This dough should be thawed in the refrigerator overnight before using as directed in the formulas. See Sugar Cookies (page 231) and Crisp and Chewy Ginger Cookies (page 226).

A seemingly infinite selection of cookie cutters is available, or you can use a paring knife or pastry wheel to cut the dough into the desired shape. Always start cutting cookies from the edge of the dough, working inward. Cut the cookies as close to each other as possible to avoid scraps. While scraps of dough can sometimes be reworked and rerolled, often this results in a tougher dough and a tougher baked cookie.

Sliced nuts, coarse granulated sugar or other garnishes can be pressed into the cookie dough before baking. Doing this as soon as the cookies are rolled will help ensure that the ingredients adhere to the surface. Cut-out cookies are usually baked on an ungreased pan to keep the dough from spreading. After baking, cut-out cookies are sometimes decorated with sugar glaze or colored frostings, an especially popular bakery offering during holiday seasons. See Decorative Cookie Icing (page 371).

Another type of rolled cookie is made from a stiff dough that is hand-shaped into spheres, crescents or other traditional shapes. See Rugelach (page 234) and Swedish Yule Logs (page 235).

Bar Cookies

Cut-Out or Rolled Cookies

PRESSED COOKIES

Also referred to as bagged or **spritz** cookies, these products are made with a soft dough that is forced through a pastry tip or **cookie press.** Pressed cookies are usually small with a distinct, decorated shape. The task of piping out dozens of identical cookies may seem daunting but the skill can be mastered with practice and an understanding of doughs. Doughs for pressed cookies often use eggs as their only liquid. Eggs, which are a toughener, contribute body and help the cookies retain their shape. Using too much fat or too soft a flour (that is, one low in protein) can cause the cookies to spread and lose their shape. Overcreaming can also result in dough that will not retain distinctive piping marks in a pressed cookie. See Spritz Cookies (page 236).

WAFER COOKIES

Wafer cookies are extremely thin and delicate. They are made with a thin batter that is poured or spread onto a baking sheet and baked. Then while still hot, the wafer is molded into a variety of shapes. The most popular shapes are the tightly rolled cigarette; and the cup-shaped tulipe also known as the tuile. Wafer batter, also known as **stencil batter,** is sweet and buttery and is often flavored with citrus zest or ground nuts. See Russian Cigarettes (page 239) and Tulipe Cookies (page 238).

PANNING AND BAKING

Proper panning and baking ensures that cookies will bake to the proper texture and color. For consistent results, roll cookie dough to a uniform thickness. Use a tablespoon measure or small scoop to evenly portion drop cookie dough. With practice and a steady hand, pressed cookies will be easy to pipe uniformly. Leave the same amount of space between cookies on the baking sheet to allow heat and air to circulate so cookies will brown evenly. For some cookies such as Biscotti (page 240), doubling the sheet pans protects the cookies from burning on the bottom. A filled sheet pan is simply placed on top of a clean pan before baking. The extra pan and the air trapped between them insulates the bottom of the cookies. Depending on the equipment used, sheets of cookies may require rotation during baking to ensure even browning. Most cookies should be removed from their pans once baked and cooled on a rack. Carryover cooking may cause them to burn and they may stick once cooled. However, some fragile cookies may need to be briefly cooled on their pans so that they set up before moving to prevent breaking. Wafer cookies must be formed while still hot. Test baking times with a small batch of cookies in your equipment until you achieve the desired results.

TROUBLESHOOTING

A great deal of the pleasure and taste in a cookie comes from its distinctive texture. The textures associated with cookies—crispness, softness, chewiness and spread—are affected by various factors, including the ratio of ingredients in the formula, the oven's temperature during baking and the pan's coating. Understanding these factors allows you to adjust formulas or techniques to achieve the desired results. See Table 9.1.

CRISPNESS

Low oven temperatures will increase baking time, making cookies drier and crisper. An extreme example of this is baked meringue. Smaller and thinner cookies can usually be baked more crisp than thick cookies. If more or less crispness is desired, examine the options described in Table 9.1. A cookie that spreads more is usually crisper.

Pressed Cookies

▶ **cookie press** (also known as a **cookie gun**), a hollow tube fitted with a plunger and an interchangeable decorative tip or plate. Soft cookie dough is pressed through the tip to create shapes or patterns.

Wafer Cookies

Table 9.1   COOKIE TEXTURES

DESIRED TEXTURE	FAT	SUGAR	LIQUID	FLOUR	SIZE OR SHAPE	BAKING
Crispness	High	High; use granulated sugar	Low	Strong	Thin dough	Well done; cool on baking sheet
Softness	Low	Low; use hygroscopic sugars	High	Weak	Thick dough	Use parchment-lined pan; underbake
Chewiness	High	High; use hygroscopic sugars	High	Strong	Not relevant; chilled dough	Underbake; cool on rack
Spread	High	High; use coarse granulated sugar	High; especially from eggs	Weak	Not relevant; room-temperature dough	Use greased pan; low temperature

▶ **humectant** a substance such as corn syrup, glucose or honey that absorbs moisture, making baked goods soft and tender

SOFTNESS AND CHEWINESS

For softer, chewier cookies, replace 10 to 15 percent of the sugar with invert sugar, glucose, honey or corn syrup. These sugars act as **humectants,** absorbing moisture and resulting in a softer baked cookie. Bake at slightly higher temperatures and underbake the cookies slightly. Wrap cookies or the entire sheet pans while still warm with food film. This helps the cookies retain moisture and stay soft. Spreading has a large effect on tenderness or chewiness; cookies that have spread too much are usually not tender or chewy.

SPREAD

Ingredients play a major role in increasing or decreasing spread. If more spread is desired, add additional baking soda or baking powder. For less spread, reduce the leaveners. Choosing flour with a lower protein content will increase spread; flour with a higher protein content will have the opposite effect. Powdered sugar decreases spread; granulated sugar increases it. Mixing methods also affect spread. Insufficient creaming of the batter will reduce spread; overcreaming will increase it. Buttering the sheet pan or parchment paper will aid spreading.

Baking temperatures also affect spread. If the oven temperature is too low the cookies will spread more because gelatinization takes longer. If the temperature is too high the exterior crust will form before the dough can spread appropriately.

FINISHING

Once cookies are baked, the further possibilities for embellishing them are endless. Sandwich cookies are made with two identical cookies spread with a thin layer of filling or ice cream and pressed together. Icebox and cut-out cookies lend themselves to being sandwiched with fillings such as thick jam, melted chocolate, buttercream, ganache, nut butter or fruit curd. Some pressed cookies are indented before baking and filled with jam, chocolate or fruit purée.

Baked, cooled cookies may be garnished with a thin drizzle or a thick dipping of melted dark or white chocolate. Fondant, royal icing or glaze can be piped, poured or spread on, provided that the color and flavor selected offers an appropriate contrast to the cookie itself.

STORING

Most cookies can be stored up to 1 week in a cool dry place when packed in an airtight container. Do not store crisp cookies with soft cookies in the same container, however. The crisp cookies will absorb moisture from the soft cookies, ruining the texture of both. Do not store strongly flavored cookies, such as spice, with those that are milder, such as shortbread. Most baked cookies freeze well if wrapped airtight to prevent moisture loss or freezer burn. Raw dough can also be frozen, either in bulk or shaped into individual portions.

▶ BROWNIES

Where do you draw the line between cakes and brownies? The decision must be a matter of texture and personal preference, for the preparation methods are nearly identical. Brownies are generally chewy and fudgy, sweeter and denser than even the richest of butter cakes. Brownies are a relatively inexpensive and easy way for a food service operation to offer its customers a fresh-baked dessert. Although not as sophisticated as an elaborate gâteau, a well-made brownie can always be served with pride (and a scoop of ice cream).

MIXING METHODS

Brownies are prepared using the same procedures as those for high-fat cakes. Eggs and air incorporated during the mixing process are usually the only leaveners in a traditional brownie formula. Good brownies are achieved with a proper balance of ingredients: A high percentage of butter to flour and not too many eggs produces a dense, fudgy brownie. The fat coats the flour, preventing the protein from developing into gluten. Less butter produces a more cakelike brownie. Increasing the eggs produces a brownie with a crumb structure that more closely resembles a true cake.

Likewise, the higher the ratio of sugar, the gooier the finished brownie will be. In some formulas, the fat is creamed to incorporate air, as with butter cakes. In others, the fat is first melted and combined with other liquid ingredients. Brownies are rarely made with whipped egg whites, however, as this makes their texture too light and cakelike.

▶ PROCEDURE FOR PREPARING BROWNIES

1 Melt unsweetened or bittersweet chocolate and butter over a double boiler.
2 Whip eggs and sugar until light and aerated.
3 Stir in the melted chocolate mixture.
4 Stir in flour and nuts or other add-ins.
5 Bake until the batter is set but not dry. Cool the brownies completely in the pan before cutting.

RECIPE 9.2

CLASSIC BROWNIES

Yield: 8 Dozen 2-in. (5-cm) Squares, 1 Sheet Pan   **Method:** Bar cookies

Unsweetened chocolate	2 lb.	985 g	123%
Unsalted butter	2 lb.	985 g	123%
Eggs	2 lb. (20 eggs)	985 g	123%
Granulated sugar	5 lb. 12 oz.	2832 g	354%
Vanilla extract	2 fl. oz.	60 ml	8%
All-purpose flour	1 lb. 10 oz.	800 g	100%
Pecan pieces	1 lb.	490 g	61%
Powdered sugar	as needed	as needed	
Total batter weight:	14 lb. 8 oz.	7137 g	892%

1 Melt the chocolate with the butter over a double boiler.

2 While the chocolate is melting, whip the eggs and sugar in the large bowl of a mixer fitted with a paddle for 10 minutes.

3 Add the melted chocolate and vanilla to the eggs. Stir to blend completely. Stir in the flour and nuts.

4 Spread the batter evenly onto a parchment-lined and buttered sheet pan. The pan will be very full. Bake at 325°F (160°C) for 40 minutes, rotating the pan after the first 20 minutes.

5 Cool completely before cutting. Dust the brownies with powdered sugar, if desired.

Approximate values per 2-in. (5-cm) square: **Calories** 343, **Total fat** 18 g, **Saturated fat** 9 g, **Cholesterol** 70 mg, **Sodium** 16 mg, **Total carbohydrates** 41 g, **Protein** 4 g

FLAVORING BROWNIES

Each customer and cook has his or her own idea of the quintessential brownie. Some prefer a cloyingly sweet brownie, with a creamy texture and an abundance of chocolate; others prefer a bitter and crisp brownie. Whatever style, once the batter is made brownies may be flavored in a number of ways to please many palates. See German Chocolate Layered Brownies (page 241). The procedure for flavoring brownies illustrates the many ways in which a basic brownie can be customized. It is not necessary to use all these techniques for each brownie; sometimes a dusting of powdered sugar is all that's necessary to make a simple brownie sensational.

Techniques for Flavoring Brownies

▶ Prepare the brownie batter. Flavor brownie batter with an extract, liqueur or flavoring oil. Almond, anise, cherry, coffee, hazelnut, lemon and orange work especially well with chocolate.

▶ Fold nuts, chunks of white or dark chocolate, raisins, dried fruit, coconut or diced pieces of almond paste into the batter before panning. Diced pieces of toffee, broken candy bars or miniature marshmallows all make excellent additions to brownies.

▶ Once panned, place large spoonfulls of jam over the surface of the batter. Marbleize the batter with the jam. Raspberry or strawberry jam, orange marmalade, peanut or almond butter or softened cream cheese complement many chocolate brownie batters.

▶ Layer the panned brownie batter with a toffee or coconut filling, as for German Chocolate Layered Brownies (page 241).

▶ Once baked and cooled, ice the brownies with flavored cream cheese icing, buttercream or melted chocolate. Select a topping that contrasts with the sweetness and texture of the brownie. The slight sourness of a cream cheese icing balances what otherwise might be a cloying sweetness.

▶ Garnish iced brownies with nuts, streusel or toasted coconut.

▶ Cut the brownies into bars, squares or triangles.

STORING

Baked brownies can be frozen 2 to 3 months if well wrapped.

CONVENIENCE PRODUCTS

Prepared dry mixes and prepared dough are common convenience products to assist in making cookies or brownies. Dry mix, especially for brownies, requires the addition of water, and frequently oil and eggs.

Cookie dough comes packaged in bulk 2- and 5-gallon buckets, refrigerated or frozen. This offers the bakeshop the convenience of a premixed dough to which additional items may be added to customize the mix. Frozen dough is also sold in portioned units, in bulk or already positioned on parchment paper ready for placing on a baking sheet and baking.

Select products with quality ingredients. Pure butter, nuts, natural flavorings, a high percentage of fruit and chocolate and few preservatives are good indications of quality. Refrigerated and frozen products must be properly stored and thawed according to manufacturer's recommendations, usually under refrigeration. Once thawed, these dough products perform much like a scratch product. You must pan, bake and cool using the same care as you would a scratch product.

CONCLUSION

Cookies, bars and brownies are both homey and refined pastries, part of every bakeshop and restaurant repertoire. Cookie dough may be used for individual pastries or as components in more elaborate dessert presentations. The techniques used to assemble and garnish cookies presented in this chapter introduce the student to basic concepts for dessert presentation used throughout this book. Using cookie making as a guide, the aspiring baker and pastry chef can learn about the function of ingredients and basic baking principles while applying creativity to make unique products.

QUESTIONS FOR DISCUSSION

1 Discuss the effect that changing ingredients has on cookie products. What results can you expect when cake flour is used as opposed to all-purpose flour in an icebox cookie, for example?

2 Describe the different effect that creaming will have on cookie dough after it is baked.

3 Describe three garnishing techniques for icebox cookies, before and after baking.

4 What are the proper cooling methods for various types of cookies? How does proper cooling affect the qualities and characteristics of these different types of cookies?

5 Design a cookie plate to be included on a restaurant dessert menu. Include at least five different cookies and explain the reasoning behind your selection.

Note: Fairytale Brownies appear in the chapter opening photograph.

FAIRYTALE BROWNIES, PHOENIX, AZ
Eileen Spitalny and David Kravetz, Owners

Childhood friends Eileen Spitalny and David Kravetz started Fairytale Brownies in a borrowed kitchen with a secret 45-year-old heirloom recipe. Now just 10 years later, their small local startup ships brownies worldwide through Internet and catalog sales. Their commitment to quality ingredients, imported chocolate and pure butter, combined with their business savvy, helped Fairytale Brownies live up to its name as a dream come true for its two founders. While their recipe is a guarded secret, we hope that the story of these brownies will inspire you to invent your own fantasy brownies using the formulas we provide on pages 241 to 243.

RECIPE 9.3

CHOCOLATE JUMBLE COOKIES

Yield: 34 Cookies, 1 oz. (30 g) each   **Method:** Drop cookies

Coffee or espresso	2 fl. oz.	60 ml	45%
Unsweetened chocolate	2 oz.	60 g	45%
All-purpose flour, sifted	4.5 oz.	135 g	100%
Salt	0.05 oz. (¼ tsp.)	1 g	1%
Unsalted butter, softened	3 oz.	90 g	66%
Vanilla extract	0.08 fl. oz. (½ tsp.)	2.5 ml	1.8%
Granulated sugar	8 oz.	240 g	178%
Eggs	3.3 oz. (2 eggs)	100 g	73%
Walnuts, chopped	6 oz.	175 g	1.3%
Milk chocolate chips	6 oz.	175 g	1.3%
Total weight:	2 lb. 2 oz.	1038 g	512%

1 Combine the coffee and chocolate and melt over a bain marie.

2 Stir the flour and salt together and set aside.

3 Cream the butter, vanilla and sugar together until fluffy. Add the eggs one at a time. Add the chocolate mixture, stirring to blend well.

4 Stir the flour into the chocolate mixture, then fold in the nuts and chocolate chips.

5 Portion into 1-ounce (30-gram) mounds using a #20 portion scoop. Place on parchment-lined baking sheets and refrigerate at least 1 hour before baking. Bake at 375°F (190°C) until set, approximately 12 minutes.

Approximate values per cookie: **Calories** 130, **Total fat** 8 g, **Saturated fat** 3 g, **Cholesterol** 20 mg, **Sodium** 25 mg, **Total carbohydrates** 14 g, **Protein** 2 g

SPICED OATMEAL COOKIES

Yield: 3 Dozen Cookies, 1⅓ oz. (40 g) each   **Method:** Drop cookies

All-purpose shortening	6 oz.	180 g	86%
Brown sugar	6 oz.	180 g	86%
Granulated sugar	6 oz.	180 g	86%
Eggs	3.3 oz. (2 eggs)	100 g	47%
Orange juice concentrate	1 fl. oz.	30 ml	14%
All-purpose flour	7 oz.	210 g	100%
Baking soda	0.14 oz. (1 tsp.)	4 g	2%
Baking powder	0.14 oz. (1 tsp.)	4 g	2%
Salt	0.2 oz. (1 tsp.)	6 g	3%
Cinnamon, ground	0.07 oz. (1 tsp.)	2 g	1%
Allspice, ground	0.03 oz. (½ tsp.)	1 g	0.4%
Nutmeg, ground	0.03 oz. (½ tsp.)	1 g	0.4%
Regular oats	6 oz.	180 g	86%
Dark raisins	6 oz.	180 g	86%
Golden raisins	6 oz.	180 g	86%
Total weight:	3 lb.	1438 g	686%

1 Cream the shortening and sugars until light and fluffy. Add the eggs and orange juice concentrate.

2 Sift the flour, baking soda, baking powder, salt and spices together and add them to the creamed mixture.

3 Blend in the oats and raisins.

4 Portion the dough onto lightly greased sheet pans and bake at 325°F (160°C) until almost firm, approximately 12 minutes.

Approximate values per cookie: **Calories** 150, **Total fat** 5 g, **Saturated fat** 1.5 g, **Cholesterol** 10 mg, **Sodium** 105 mg, **Total carbohydrates** 24 g, **Protein** 2 g, **Claims**—low cholesterol; low sodium

FLOURLESS CHOCOLATE CHEWIES

Yield: 2 Dozen Cookies, approximately 3¾ oz. (112 g) each

Method: Drop cookies

Ingredient			Sugar at 100%
Powdered sugar	2 lb. 14 oz.	1300 g	100%
Cocoa powder	6 oz.	170 g	13%
Salt	0.5 oz.	15 g	1%
Vanilla extract	0.5 fl. oz.	15 ml	1%
Egg whites	12 oz. (12 whites)	340 g	26%
Walnuts or any other nut, chopped coarse	1 lb. 12 oz.	795 g	61%
Total weight:	5 lb. 13 oz.	2635 g	202%

1 In the bowl of a mixer fitted with a paddle, combine the powdered sugar, cocoa powder, salt, vanilla and egg whites. Mix 2 minutes on medium speed, then add the nuts.

2 Using a #8 portion scoop, portion the batter onto paper-lined sheet pans. Space 3 inches (7.5 centimeters) apart to allow room for the cookies to spread.

3 Bake at 400°F (200°C) until the centers of the cookies are just set, about 12 to 14 minutes. When perfectly baked, the cookies will be chewy yet crisp.

Approximate values per cookie: **Calories** 450, **Total fat** 23 g, **Saturated fat** 2.5 g, **Cholesterol** 0 mg, **Sodium** 250 mg, **Total carbohydrates** 63 g, **Protein** 8 g

RECIPE 9.6

CINNAMON BUTTER COOKIES

Yield: 40 Cookies, 1 oz. (30 g) each   **Method:** Drop cookies

Pastry flour	14 oz.	420 g	100%
Baking powder	0.14 oz. (1 tsp.)	4 g	1%
Cinnamon, ground	0.25 oz. (3½ tsp.)	8 g	2%
Unsalted butter, softened	8 oz.	240 g	57%
Granulated sugar	6 oz.	180 g	43%
Brown sugar	8 oz.	240 g	57%
Eggs	3.3 oz. (2 eggs)	100 g	23%
Vanilla extract	0.5 fl. oz.	15 ml	4%
Salt	0.4 oz. (2 tsp.)	12 g	3%
Total dough weight:	2 lb. 8 oz.	1219 g	290%

Topping:

Granulated sugar	2 oz.	60 g	
Cinnamon, ground	0.14 oz. (2 tsp.)	4 g	

1 To prepare the cookie dough, sift together the flour, baking powder and cinnamon. Set aside.

2 Cream the butter and sugars until light and fluffy. Beat in the eggs, one at a time, then add the vanilla and salt. Gradually add the flour mixture, beating just until well combined.

3 Drop the dough in 1-ounce (30-gram) mounds onto paper-lined sheet pans. Flatten the dough using the bottom of a cup to ½ inch (1 centimeter). Combine the sugar and cinnamon and sprinkle the cookies generously with the mixture.

4 Bake at 400°F (200°C) until golden brown but still moist, approximately 9 to 11 minutes.

Approximate values per cookie: **Calories** 90, **Total fat** 4 g, **Saturated fat** 2.5 g, **Cholesterol** 15 mg, **Sodium** 100 mg, **Total carbohydrates** 14 g, **Protein** 1 g

RECIPE 9.7

PEANUT BUTTER SANDIES

Yield: 4½ Dozen Cookies, 1⅓ oz. (40 g) each   **Method:** Drop cookies

Pastry flour	24 oz.	720 g	100%
Baking soda	0.14 oz. (1 tsp.)	4 g	0.6%
Baking powder	0.14 oz. (1 tsp.)	4 g	0.6%
Unsalted butter, softened	1 lb.	475 g	66%
Granulated sugar	1 lb.	475 g	66%
Eggs	3.3 oz. (2 eggs)	100 g	14%
Peanut butter	10 oz.	300 g	42%
Salt	0.4 oz. (2 tsp.)	12 g	1.7%
Granulated sugar	as needed	as needed	
Peanut halves	2 oz.	60 g	8%
Total dough weight:	4 lb. 8 oz.	2150 g	299%

1 Sift together the flour, baking soda and baking powder. Set aside. Cream the butter. Add the sugar and continue creaming. Gradually add the eggs, followed by the peanut butter and salt.

2 Add the dry ingredients to the butter mixture and mix to make a firm dough.

3 Scale the dough into 1-pound (480-gram) pieces. Roll the dough into 12-inch (36-centimeter) logs. Cut into 1-inch (3-centimeter) pieces.

4 Roll each cookie into a ball and place on a sheet pan. Press each ball down using the bottom of a measuring cup to slightly less than ½ inch (1 centimeter). The edges of the cookies will develop some cracks, which is a desired look.

5 Using a fork, press criss-cross markings on the surface of the cookie. Lightly brush the cookies with water. Sprinkle lightly with granulated sugar and press one peanut half into each cookie.

6 Bake at 400°F (200°F) until golden brown, approximately 12 minutes.

Approximate values per cookie: **Calories** 190, **Total fat** 12 g, **Saturated fat** 5 g, **Cholesterol** 20 mg, **Sodium** 160 mg, **Total carbohydrates** 22 g, **Protein** 3 g

TEA-SCENTED CHERRY COOKIES   RECIPE 9.8

Yield: 7 Dozen Cookies, approximately ⅔ oz. (20 g) each

Method: Icebox cookies

Unsalted butter, softened	1 lb. 2 oz.	540 g	95%
Powdered sugar	10 oz.	300 g	53%
Vanilla extract	0.5 fl. oz.	15 ml	2.7%
Salt	0.2 oz. (1 tsp.)	6 g	1%
Almond extract	0.3 fl. oz. (2 tsp.)	10 ml	1.6%
Earl Grey tea bags, single-serving size	3	3	
Dried cherries, chopped coarse	6 oz.	180 g	32%
Pastry flour	1 lb. 3 oz.	570 g	100%
Egg wash	as needed	as needed	
Almonds, chopped	as needed	as needed	
Three Red Fruit Jam (recipe follows)	as needed	as needed	
Total dough weight:	3 lb. 6 oz.	1621 g	285%

1 Blend the butter and sugar in the bowl of a mixer fitted with a paddle. Thoroughly mix in the vanilla, salt, almond extract and contents of the tea bags. Add the cherries and flour and mix until just combined.

2 Divide the dough into four equal portions, approximately 12½ ounces (375 grams) each. Roll each piece into a 10-inch- (25-centimeter-) long cylinder. Freeze until hard (approximately 30 minutes).

3 Remove from the freezer and lightly brush the dough with egg wash. Roll the dough in chopped almonds and cut into ⅜-inch- (1-centimeter-) thick slices.

4 Place the cookies on paper-lined sheet pans. Indent the center of each cookie with the back of a spoon and fill the indentation with Three Red Fruit Jam.

5 Bake at 375°F (190°C) until cookies are golden brown, approximately 18 minutes.

THREE RED FRUIT JAM

Yield: 2 lb. 6 oz. (1140 g)

Strawberries, fresh or IQF	8 oz.	240 g
Raspberries, fresh or IQF	8 oz.	240 g
Cherries, fresh or IQF	8 oz.	240 g
Granulated sugar	1 lb.	480 g
Pectin	0.3 oz. (2 tsp.)	10 g
Citric acid (optional)	as needed	as needed

1 Heat the fruits in a stainless steel pan to 120°F (49°C). Using an immersion blender, chop the softened fruit into small pieces.

2 Blend the sugar with the pectin and add to the fruit. Bring to a boil while stirring constantly. Boil about 10 minutes. Remove from the heat. Add a small amount of citric acid (if using). Store this jam in the refrigerator because of its reduced sugar content.

Approximate values per cookie: **Calories** 110, **Total fat** 5 g, **Saturated fat** 3 g, **Cholesterol** 15 mg, **Sodium** 30 mg, **Total carbohydrates** 16 g, **Protein** 1 g

RECIPE 9.9   **CHECKERBOARD COOKIES**

Yield: 160 Cookies, approximately ¾ oz. (25 g) each

Method: Icebox cookies

Vanilla dough:

Unsalted butter, softened	1 lb.	475 g	66%
Powdered sugar	13 oz.	390 g	54%
Eggs	6.75 oz. (4 eggs)	200 g	28%
Salt	0.4 oz. (2 tsp.)	12 g	1.6%
Vanilla extract	0.5 fl. oz.	15 ml	2%
Almond extract	0.15 fl. oz. (1 tsp.)	5 ml	0.6%
Almond flour	6 oz.	180 g	25%
Pastry flour	24 oz.	720 g	100%
Total weight:	4 lb. 2 oz.	1997 g	277%

Chocolate dough:

Unsalted butter, softened	1 lb.	480 g	70%
Powdered sugar	15 oz.	450 g	65%
Eggs	6.75 oz. (4 eggs)	200 g	29%
Salt	0.4 oz. (2 tsp.)	12 g	1.7%
Vanilla extract	0.5 fl. oz.	15 ml	2%
Almond extract	0.15 fl. oz. (1 tsp.)	5 ml	0.6%
Almond flour	3 oz.	90 g	13%
Cocoa powder	3 oz.	90 g	13%
Pastry flour	1 lb. 7 oz.	690 g	100%
Total weight:	4 lb. 3 oz.	2032 g	294%

1 For the vanilla dough, cream the butter and powdered sugar until light and fluffy. Add the eggs one at a time, scraping well between additions. Beat in the salt, vanilla, almond extract and almond flour. Add pastry flour and beat until just combined.

2 Wrap tightly and chill the dough until firm.

3 Prepare the chocolate dough following the same procedure used for the vanilla dough. Add the cocoa powder with the almond flour. Wrap tightly and chill the dough until firm.

4 On a well-floured surface roll the vanilla and chocolate doughs into rectangles ¼ inch (1.25 centimeters) thick. Cut the dough into 2-inch- (5-centimeter-) wide strips.

5 Brush a strip of chocolate dough lightly with water; place a vanilla strip on top. Repeat with a second chocolate strip and end with a strip of vanilla dough. Refrigerate until firm.

6 Using a long French knife, cut the block of dough lengthwise into four equal strips.

7 Place a cut strip flat side down on a paper-lined sheet pan. Lightly moisten with water. Place another cut strip onto the first, making certain that the chocolate and vanilla bands are touching. Repeat with two more strips for a total of four. This block of dough may be wrapped in a ⅛-inch- (3-centimeter-) thick sheet of dough if desired.

8 Freeze until hard. Cut crosswise in ¼-inch (6-millimeter) slices. Place on a paper-lined sheet pan. Bake at 375°F (190°C) until golden brown, about 14 to 16 minutes.

Approximate values per cookie: **Calories** 120, **Total fat** 7 g, **Saturated fat** 3.5 g, **Cholesterol** 25 mg, **Sodium** 70 mg, **Total carbohydrates** 14 g, **Protein** 2 g

1 Marking the layered block of chocolate and vanilla dough for slicing.

2 Cutting the dough into narrow strips to reveal alternating layers of dough.

3 Stacking the striped layers of dough to form a checkerboard pattern.

4 Wrapping a layer of chocolate dough around the log of checkerboard dough.

5 Slicing the block of checkerboard dough into cookies before baking.

BERGAMOT SHORTBREAD

RECIPE 9.10

Yield: 7 Dozen Cookies, approximately ½ oz. (15 g) each

Method: Icebox cookies

Unsalted butter, softened	1 lb.	480 g	84%
Powdered sugar	8 oz.	240 g	42%
Vanilla extract	0.5 fl. oz.	15 ml	3%
Salt	0.2 oz (1 tsp.)	5 g	1%
Essential oil of bergamot	12 drops	12 drops	
Pastry flour	1 lb. 3 oz.	570 g	100%
Egg wash	as needed	as needed	
Decorating sugar	as needed	as needed	
Total dough weight:	2 lb. 11 oz.	1310 g	230%

▶ **bergamot** a member of the citrus family resembling an orange with inedible flesh; edible oil extracted from its skin gives a mellow orange flavor to candies, chocolates and Earl Grey tea

1 Blend the butter and sugar in a mixing bowl without creaming. Stir in vanilla, salt and oil of bergamot, mixing thoroughly. Add the flour and mix until just combined.

2 Divide the dough into four equal portions. Roll each piece into a 10-inch- (25-centimeter-) long cylinder. Freeze until hard (approximately 30 minutes).

3 Remove from the freezer and unwrap, then lightly brush the cylinders with egg wash and roll them in the sugar. Cut the cylinders into ½-inch- (1.2-centimeter-) thick slices, then place the slices cut side down on paper-lined sheet pans. Dock the cookies with a fork.

4 Bake at 375°F (190°C) until pale golden brown, approximately 15 to 20 minutes.

VARIATIONS:

Traditional Shortbread—Omit the oil of bergamot. Divide the dough into four equal portions. Roll the dough into circles and cut each circle into eight wedges. Dock the cookies, then brush with egg wash and bake.

Approximate values per cookie: **Calories** 70, **Total fat** 4.5 g, **Saturated fat** 3 g, **Cholesterol** 10 mg, **Sodium** 30 mg, **Total carbohydrates** 8 g, **Protein** 1 g

RECIPE 9.11

CHOCOLATE HAZELNUT SHORTBREAD

Yield: 10 Dozen Cookies, approximately ½ oz. (15 g) each

Method: Icebox cookies

Hazelnuts, toasted	12 oz.	360 g	63%
Unsalted butter, softened	1 lb. 10 oz.	780 g	137%
Powdered sugar	11 oz.	330 g	58%
Vanilla extract	0.5 fl. oz.	15 ml	3%
Salt	0.2 oz. (1 tsp.)	6 g	1%
Eggs	5 oz. (3 eggs)	150 g	26%
Pastry flour	1 lb. 3 oz.	570 g	100%
Egg wash	as needed	as needed	
Coarse sugar crystals	as needed	as needed	
Milk or semisweet chocolate, melted and tempered	as needed	as needed	
Total dough weight:	4 lb. 9 oz.	2211 g	388%

1 Chop the toasted hazelnuts and set aside.

2 Blend the butter and sugar in a mixing bowl without creaming. Add the vanilla, salt and eggs and mix on low speed until well incorporated. Add the chopped hazelnuts and flour and mix until just combined.

3 Divide the dough into four equal portions. Roll each piece into a 10-inch- (25-centimeter-) long cylinder. Freeze until hard (approximately 30 minutes).

4 Remove from the freezer and unwrap, then lightly brush the cylinders with egg wash and roll them in the sugar crystals. Cut the cylinders into ⅛-inch- (3-millimeter-) thick slices, then place them cut side down on paper-lined sheet pans. Dock the cookies with a fork.

5 Bake at 350°F (180°C) until golden brown, approximately 17 to 20 minutes. Cool completely, then dip half of each cookie in tempered chocolate.

Approximate values per cookie: **Calories** 70, **Total fat** 4.5 g, **Saturated fat** 3 g, **Cholesterol** 10 mg, **Sodium** 30 mg, **Total carbohydrates** 8 g, **Protein** 1 g

▶ **tempering** a process of melting chocolate during which the temperature of the cocoa butter is carefully stabilized; this keeps the chocolate smooth and glossy

RECIPE 9.12

CRISP AND CHEWY GINGER COOKIES

Yield: 7 Dozen Cookies, approximately ½ oz. (15 g) each

Method: Icebox cookies

Bread flour	1 lb. 1 oz.	510 g	100%
Baking powder	0.2 oz. (1½ tsp.)	6 g	1.2%
Baking soda	0.07 oz. (½ tsp.)	2 g	0.4%
Unsalted butter, softened	8 oz.	240 g	47%
Granulated sugar	1 lb.	480 g	94%
Glucose or corn syrup	1 oz.	30 g	6%
Eggs	3.3 oz. (2 eggs)	100 g	19%
Vanilla extract	0.3 fl. oz. (2 tsp.)	10 ml	2%
Ginger, ground	0.3 oz. (1½ Tbsp.)	10 g	2%
Lemon oil	3 drops	3 drops	
Orange oil	3 drops	3 drops	
Total weight:	2 lb. 14 oz.	1388 g	271%
Egg wash	as needed	as needed	
Granulated sugar	as needed	as needed	

1 Sift together the flour, baking powder and baking soda. Set aside.

2 Cream the butter, sugar and glucose until light and fluffy. Gradually add eggs and all flavorings. Add the flour mixture, beating just until well combined.

3 Divide the dough into 11-ounce (330-gram) pieces. Roll each piece into a 10-inch- (25-centimeter-) long log. Freeze until hard, about 30 minutes.

4 Remove from the freezer and unwrap, then lightly brush the cylinders with egg wash and roll them in the sugar. Cut into ½-inch- (12-millimeter-) thick slices and place them cut side down on paper-lined sheet pans. Indent the center of each sliced cookie.

5 Bake at 400°F (200°C) about 15 minutes. Lightly baked, these cookies will be soft; medium baked they will still be chewy but will also be somewhat crisp. For completely crisp cookies, bake slightly longer.

Approximate values per cookie: **Calories** 90, **Total fat** 2.5 g, **Saturated fat** 1.5 g, **Cholesterol** 10 mg, **Sodium** 20 mg, **Total carbohydrates** 16 g, **Protein** 1 g

OATMEAL CHOCOLATE CHIP BAR COOKIES   RECIPE 9.13

Yield: 3 Dozen Bars, 1 Half-Sheet Pan   **Method:** Bar cookies

Pastry flour	1 lb.	480 g	100%
Baking soda	0.3 oz. (2 tsp.)	8 g	1.8%
Cinnamon, ground	0.14 oz. (2 tsp.)	4 g	0.8%
Unsalted butter, softened	1 lb.	480 g	100%
Brown sugar	1 lb.	480 g	100%
Granulated sugar	8 oz.	240 g	50%
Eggs	6.75 oz. (4 eggs)	200 g	42%
Buttermilk	3 fl. oz.	90 ml	19%
Salt	0.2 oz (1 tsp.)	6 g	1.2%
Vanilla extract	0.5 fl. oz.	15 ml	3%
Rolled oats	1 lb.	480 g	100%
Chocolate chunks	1 lb. 10 oz.	780 g	162%
Walnuts, chopped	10 oz.	300 g	62%
Total weight:	7 lb. 6 oz.	3563 g	742%

1 Sift together the pastry flour, baking soda and cinnamon. Set aside. Cream the butter and sugars. Gradually add the eggs, then mix in the buttermilk, salt, vanilla and oats. Add the flour mixture, beating just until well combined. Stir in the chocolate chunks and nuts.

2 Spread the batter on a greased and floured half-sheet pan and bake at 375°F (190°C) until golden, approximately 45 minutes.

3 After cooling, slide the sheet of cookies onto a workbench, then cut into 2-inch × 3-inch (5-centimeter × 7.5-centimeter) bars.

Approximate values per cookie: **Calories** 410, **Total fat** 23 g, **Saturated fat** 11 g, **Cholesterol** 50 mg, **Sodium** 150 mg, **Total carbohydrates** 51 g, **Protein** 6 g

RECIPE 9.14

LEMON OR LIME BARS

Yield: 80 Cookies, 1½ in. (4 cm) Square, 1 Half-Sheet Pan

Method: Bar cookies

Sweet Tart Dough (page 249), plain or coconut variation, chilled	2 lb. 8 oz.	1200 g
Egg wash	as needed	as needed
Filling:		
Granulated sugar	1 lb. 6 oz.	640 g
Eggs	13.3 oz. (8 eggs)	400 g
Pastry flour	2 oz.	60 g
Lemon or lime juice	11 fl. oz.	330 ml
Milk	5 fl. oz.	150 ml
Salt	0.1 oz. (½ tsp.)	3 g
Powdered sugar	4 oz.	120 g

1 Roll the chilled dough out on parchment paper to fit the sides and bottom of a half-sheet pan. Flip the parchment-covered dough onto a half-sheet pan. Remove the parchment. Trim uneven edges and reserve dough scraps. Prick the surface of the dough with a fork and bake at 350°F (180°C) until the dough is light golden, approximately 15 minutes. If cracks develop during the baking process, patch with the leftover dough and return briefly to the oven.

2 Brush the baked dough with egg wash and return to the oven 3 minutes or until the egg wash has set.

3 To prepare the filling, whip the sugar and eggs just until smooth. Whisk in the flour until well combined, then add the lemon juice, milk and salt.

4 Pour the lemon filling into the prebaked shell.

5 Bake at 325°F (160°C) until set, approximately 25 minutes.

6 Cool, then cut into 1½-inch × 1½-inch (4-centimeter × 4-centimeter) squares. Dust liberally with powdered sugar.

Approximate values per cookie: **Calories** 140, **Total fat** 6 g, **Saturated fat** 3 g, **Cholesterol** 40 mg, **Sodium** 80 mg, **Total carbohydrates** 21 g, **Protein** 2 g

CLASSIC PECAN BARS

Yield: 8 Dozen Cookies, 2¹/₂ in. (6 cm) each   **Method:** Bar cookies

Sweet Tart Dough (page 249)	2 lb. 8 oz.	1200 g
Filling:		
Brown sugar	15 oz.	450 g
Unsalted butter	8 oz.	240 g
Honey	14 oz.	420 g
Granulated sugar	3.5 oz.	105 g
Pecans	2 lbs.	960 g
Heavy cream	4 fl. oz.	120 ml

1 Roll the chilled dough out on parchment paper to fit the sides and bottom of a half-sheet pan. Flip the parchment-covered dough onto a half-sheet pan. Remove the parchment. Trim uneven edges and reserve dough scraps. Prick the surface of the dough with a fork and bake at 350°F (180°C) until the dough is light golden, approximately 15 minutes. If cracks develop during the baking process, patch with the leftover dough and return briefly to the oven.

2 To prepare the filling, stir the brown sugar, butter, honey and granulated sugar together in a large saucepan. Bring the mixture to a full rolling boil. Boil the filling 3 minutes.

3 Remove the pan from the heat and stir in the pecans and cream. Pour the filling into the baked crust.

4 Bake at 350°F (180°C) until light brown and bubbling, approximately 15 to 20 minutes.

5 Cool on a wire rack completely before cutting. Cut into 2-inch (5-centimeter) squares, then cut each bar in half on the diagonal to make a triangle shape.

Approximate values per cookie: **Calories** 220, **Total fat** 11 g, **Saturated fat** 4.5 g, **Cholesterol** 50 mg, **Sodium** 105 mg, **Total carbohydrates** 28 g, **Protein** 3 g

MIRROR COOKIES

Yield: 4 Dozen Cookies, 2½ in. (6 cm) each   **Method:** Bar cookies

Shortbread Tart Dough (page 266), made with hazelnuts, chilled	4 lb. 7 oz.	2.1 kg
Almond Macaronnade (recipe follows)	1 lb. 3 oz.	570 g
Red currant jam	1 lb.	480 g

1 On a well-floured surface, roll the chilled hazelnut shortbread dough ¼ inch (6 millimeters) thick.

2 Cut the dough into 2½-inch (6-centimeter) circles. Place the dough circles on paper-lined sheet pans and bake at 375°F (190°C) until pale blond in color, approximately 8 to 10 minutes.

3 Using a pastry bag fitted with a small star tip, pipe a border of Almond Macaronnade along the edge of the baked cookie. Fill the center with red currant jam.

4 Return to the oven and bake until the macaronnade is golden brown, approximately 12 to 14 minutes.

VARIATIONS:

Raspberry Streusel Squares—Omit the Almond Macaronnade. Roll the chilled hazelnut tart dough into a ¼-inch- (6-millimeter)-thick rectangle and place on paper-lined half-sheet pans. Bake at 400°F (200°C) until blond in color, approximately 10 to 12 minutes. Coat with raspberry jam and top with Streusel Topping (page 113). Return to the oven. Reduce temperature to 350°F (180°C) and bake another 10 to 12 minutes until jam is bubbling and streusel is browned. Cool completely, then cut into bars.

Luxembergers—Substitute Coconut Almond Tart Dough (page 267). Roll the chilled dough into a rectangle ³⁄₁₆ inch (5 millimeters) thick. Cut into 12-inch- (30-centimeter-) long strips, 2 inches (5 centimeters) wide. Bake on paper-lined sheet pans at 400°F (200°C) until pale blond in color. Pipe three lines of Almond Macaronnade along the entire length of the strips, one down the center and one along each edge. Pipe a strip on both 2-inch (5-centimeter) ends to contain the jam. Substitute raspberry jam for the red currant jam. Return to the oven and bake until golden brown. Cool, then cut into ¾-inch (2-centimeter) squares.

ALMOND MACARONNADE

Yield: 1 lb. 3 oz. (585 g)

			Almond paste at 100%
Almond paste	12 oz.	360 g	100%
Granulated sugar	5 oz.	150 g	41%
Egg whites	2.5 fl. oz.	75 ml	20%
Total weight:	1 lb. 3 oz.	585 g	161%

1 Blend the almond paste and sugar in the bowl of a mixer fitted with a paddle. Add a quarter of the egg whites. Mix until the dough becomes completely homogenous. Scrape down the bowl and paddle. Gradually add remaining egg whites until the dough is firm but soft enough to pipe.

2 Scrape the dough into a pastry bag fitted with a small plain or star tip. Pipe a border of this dough onto a prebaked cookie or tart crust and bake as directed. Or pipe the dough into 1-inch (2.5-centimeter) circles on paper-lined sheet pans. Bake at 375°F (190°C) until the cookies are golden brown, approximately 12 to 14 minutes.

Approximate values per cookie: **Calories** 200, **Total fat** 15 g, **Saturated fat** 7 g, **Cholesterol** 65 mg, **Sodium** 75 mg, **Total carbohydrates** 24 g, **Protein** 4 g

SUGAR COOKIES

RECIPE 9.17

Yield: 2 Dozen Cookies, approximately 1 oz. (30 g) each

Method: Cut-out cookies

All-purpose flour	12 oz.	360 g	100%
Baking powder	0.3 oz. (2 tsp.)	9 g	2.5%
Mace, ground	0.02 oz. (¼ tsp.)	1 g	0.2%
Unsalted butter, softened	4 oz.	120 g	33%
Granulated sugar	8 oz.	240 g	66%
Vanilla extract	0.15 fl. oz. (1 tsp.)	5 ml	1.2%
Egg	1.6 oz. (1 egg)	50 g	13%
Total weight:	1 lb. 10 oz.	785 g	215%

1 Stir together the flour, baking powder and mace. Set aside.

2 Cream the butter and sugar until light and fluffy. Blend in the vanilla. Add the egg and beat again until fluffy. Gradually add the flour mixture, beating just until well combined.

3 Wrap the dough in plastic wrap and refrigerate until firm, approximately 1 to 2 hours.

4 Work with half of the dough at a time, keeping the remainder refrigerated. On a lightly floured board, roll out the dough to a thickness of approximately ⅛ inch (3 millimeters). Cut as desired with cookie cutters about 3 inches (7.5 centimeters) in diameter. Carefully transfer the cookies to lightly greased baking sheets.

5 Bake at 325°F (160°C) until golden brown, approximately 10 to 12 minutes. Let stand 1 minute, then transfer to wire racks to cool.

Approximate values per cookie: **Calories** 90, **Total fat** 3 g, **Saturated fat** 1.5 g, **Cholesterol** 15 mg, **Sodium** 0 mg, **Total carbohydrates** 14 g, **Protein** 1 g, **Claims**—low fat; low cholesterol; no sodium

LINZER COOKIES

RECIPE 9.18

Yield: 2 Dozen Cookies, 2½ in. (6 cm) each   **Method:** Cut-out cookies

Shortbread Tart Dough (page 266), made with hazelnuts, chilled	4 lb. 7 oz.	2.1 kg
Raspberry jam	1 lb.	480 g

Filling the Linzer cookies with jam.

1 On a well-floured surface, roll the chilled hazelnut shortbread dough ¼ inch (6 millimeters) thick.

2 Cut the dough with a floured cutter into 2½-inch (6-centimeter) circles or ovals. Place the dough cut-outs on paper-lined sheet pans.

3 Using a slightly smaller cookie cutter, remove the center from half of the dough cut-outs. These will be the cookie tops for the sandwich cookies. (Save the dough scraps for more cookies.)

4 Bake at 375°F (190°C) until pale blond in color, approximately 8 to 10 minutes. Cool the cookies completely.

5 Melt 3 ounces (90 grams) of the raspberry jam. Brush the solid cookies with the melted jam. Place the cookie tops on the jam-coated cookies. Using a pastry bag fitted with a small plain tip, fill the center of each cookie with raspberry jam.

Approximate values per cookie: **Calories** 200, **Total fat** 15 g, **Saturated fat** 7 g, **Cholesterol** 65 mg, **Sodium** 75 mg, **Total carbohydrates** 24 g, **Protein** 4 g

RECIPE 9.19

GINGERBREAD COOKIES

Yield: 1 Dozen Cookies, 2⅓ oz. (70 g) each

Method: Cut-out cookies

Unsalted butter, softened	4 oz.	120 g	33%
Brown sugar	4 oz.	120 g	33%
Molasses, dark	6 fl. oz.	180 ml	50%
Egg	1.6 oz. (1 egg)	50 g	13%
All-purpose flour	12 oz.	360 g	100%
Baking soda	0.14 oz. (1 tsp.)	4 g	1%
Salt	0.1 oz. (½ tsp.)	3 g	0.8%
Ginger, ground	0.14 oz. (2 tsp.)	4 g	1%
Cinnamon, ground	0.07 oz. (1 tsp.)	2 g	0.6%
Nutmeg, ground	0.03 oz. (½ tsp.)	1 g	0.2%
Cloves, ground	0.03 oz. (½ tsp.)	1 g	0.2%
Total weight:	1 lb. 12 oz.	845 g	233%

1 Cream the butter and sugar until light and fluffy. Add the molasses and egg and beat to blend well; set aside.

2 Stir together the remaining ingredients. Gradually add the flour mixture to the butter mixture, beating until just blended. Gather the dough into a ball and wrap in plastic wrap; refrigerate at least 1 hour.

3 On a lightly floured board, roll out the gingerbread to a thickness of ¼ inch (6 millimeters). Cut out the cookies with a floured cutter and transfer to greased baking sheets.

4 Bake at 325°F (160°C) until the cookies are lightly browned around the edges and feel barely firm when touched, approximately 10 minutes. Transfer to wire racks to cool, then decorate as desired with Royal Icing (page 361).

Approximate values per cookie: **Calories** 260, **Total fat** 8 g, **Saturated fat** 5 g, **Cholesterol** 40 mg, **Sodium** 220 mg, **Total carbohydrates** 41 g, **Protein** 4 g, **Vitamin A** 8%

RECIPE 9.20

DUTCH ALMOND BUTTER BARS

Yield: 10 Dozen Cookies, 1 × 2 in. (2.5 × 5 cm) each

Method: Cut-out cookies

Pastry flour	11 oz.	330 g	100%
Baking soda	0.14 oz. (1 tsp.)	4 g	1.3%
Cinnamon, ground	0.5 oz.	15 g	0.5%
Unsalted butter, softened	10 oz.	300 g	91%
Brown sugar	8 oz.	240 g	73%
Egg	1.6 oz. (1 egg)	50 g	15%
Salt	0.1 oz. (½ tsp.)	3 g	1%
Egg wash	as needed	as needed	
Sliced almonds	as needed	as needed	
Coarse sugar crystals or granulated sugar	as needed	as needed	
Total dough weight:	1 lb. 15 oz.	942 g	281%

1 Sift together the flour, baking soda and cinnamon. Set aside.

2 Cream the butter and sugar. Add the egg and salt. Add the flour mixture, beating just until well combined. Wrap dough in plastic film and chill until cool, about 2 hours.

3 Divide the dough in half. On a lightly floured surface, roll each piece into a rectangle ⅛ inch (3 millimeters) thick. Cut the dough into 1-inch × 2-inch (2.5 centimeter × 5-centimeter) bars. Place on paper-lined sheet pans.

4 Brush with egg wash, then sprinkle with sliced almonds and sugar.

5 Bake at 350°F (180°C) until golden brown, approximately 12 to 15 minutes.

Approximate values per cookie: **Calories** 35, **Total fat** 2 g, **Saturated fat** 1 g, **Cholesterol** 5 mg, **Sodium** 20 mg, **Total carbohydrates** 4 g, **Protein** 0 g

SPECULAAS (BELGIAN SPICE COOKIES)　　　　RECIPE 9.21

Yield: 11 Dozen Cookies, approximately ⅔ oz. (20 g) each

Method: Cut-out cookies

Unsalted butter, softened	1 lb. 2 oz.	540 g	53%
Brown sugar	1 lb. 13 oz.	870 g	85%
Eggs	4.5 oz. (3 eggs)	135 g	13%
Milk	2 fl. oz.	60 ml	6%
Salt	0.2 oz. (1 tsp.)	6 g	0.6%
Cinnamon, ground	0.25 oz. (3½ tsp.)	8 g	0.7%
Speculaas Spices (recipe follows)	0.5 oz.	15 g	1.4%
Baking soda	0.75 oz.	20 g	2%
Pastry flour, sifted	2 lb. 2 oz.	1020 g	100%
Egg wash	as needed	as needed	
Sliced almonds	as needed	as needed	
Total dough weight:	5 lb. 9 oz.	2674 g	262%

1 Cream the butter and the sugar. Add the eggs, one at a time. Then add the milk, salt, cinnamon, Speculaas Spices and baking soda. Blend in the flour and mix until incorporated. Wrap the dough in plastic and refrigerate overnight.

2 On a lightly floured surface, roll the dough ⅛ inch (3 millimeters) thick. Cut into 3-inch × 1½-inch (7.5-centimeter × 4-centimeter) rectangles. Place on paper-lined sheet pans spaced 1 inch (2 centimeters) apart. Lightly brush with egg wash and sprinkle with sliced almonds.

3 Bake at 350°F (180°C) until the surface of the cookies bounces back when lightly pressed, approximately 18 minutes. Cool, then store in airtight containers. Speculaas will last several weeks.

SPECULAAS SPICES

Yield: 7¾ oz. (232 g)

Cinnamon	4.5 oz.	135 g
Cloves, ground	1.25 oz.	37 g
Ginger, ground	1 oz.	30 g
Cardamom, ground	0.5 oz.	15 g
White pepper	0.5 oz.	15 g

1 Stir the ingredients together. Store in an airtight container in a dark cool place.

Approximate values per cookie: **Calories** 60, **Total fat** 3 g, **Saturated fat** 1.5 g, **Cholesterol** 10 mg, **Sodium** 50 mg, **Total carbohydrates** 10 g, **Protein** 1 g

RECIPE 9.22

MADAGASCARS

Yield: 8 Dozen Cookies, approximately ½ oz. (15 g) each

Method: Cut-out cookies

Unsalted butter, softened	14 oz.	420 g	87%
Powdered sugar	10 oz.	300 g	62%
Eggs	3.3 oz. (2 eggs)	100 g	20%
Vanilla extract	0.15 fl. oz. (1 tsp.)	5 ml	1%
Orange zest, grated fine	0.2 oz. (1 Tbsp.)	5 g	1%
Salt	0.3 oz. (1.5 tsp.)	10 g	2%
Cinnamon, ground	0.2 oz. (1 Tbsp.)	5 g	1%
Pastry flour, sifted	1 lb.	480 g	100%
Almond flour	2 oz.	60 g	12%
Mini chocolate chips	6 oz.	180 g	37%
Total weight:	3 lb. 4 oz.	1565 g	323%

1 Blend the butter and sugar together until thoroughly combined without creaming. Add the eggs one at a time, then stir in the vanilla, orange zest, salt and cinnamon. Mix in the pastry flour and almond flour just until incorporated. Stir in the chocolate chips. Wrap the dough tightly and chill overnight.

2 Roll dough on a lightly floured surface ⅛ inch (3 millimeters) thick.

3 Cut into 2-inch (4.5-centimeter) rounds and place on paper-lined sheet pans.

4 Bake at 375°F (190°C) until golden, approximately 10 to 12 minutes.

Approximate values per cookie: **Calories** 40, **Total fat** 2.5 g, **Saturated fat** 1.5 g, **Cholesterol** 5 mg, **Sodium** 20 mg, **Total carbohydrates** 4 g, **Protein** 0 g

RECIPE 9.23

RUGELACH

Yield: 3 Dozen Cookies, approximately 1½ oz. (45 g) each

Method: Rolled cookies

Pastry flour	15 oz.	450 g	100%
Baking soda	0.07 oz. (½ tsp.)	2 g	0.5%
Cream cheese, room temperature	9 oz.	270 g	60%
Granulated sugar	7 oz.	210 g	46%
Lemon zest, grated fine	0.14 oz. (2 tsp.)	4 g	1%
Unsalted butter, softened	8 oz.	240 g	53%
Salt	0.2 oz. (1 tsp.)	6 g	1.3%
Red currant or apricot jam	12 oz.	360 g	80%
Dried cherries, finely chopped	4 oz.	120 g	26%
Walnuts, chopped coarse	4 oz.	120 g	26%
Cinnamon, ground	as needed	as needed	
Egg wash	as needed	as needed	
Powdered sugar	as needed	as needed	
Total dough weight:	3 lb. 11 oz.	1782 g	394%

1 Sift together the flour and baking soda. Set aside.

2 Blend the cream cheese, sugar and lemon zest on low speed until homogenous. Add the butter and salt and blend well. Mix in the flour until combined. Chill the dough 2 hours.

3 Divide the dough into 12-ounce (360-gram) pieces. On a lightly floured surface, roll each piece of dough into a strip ¼ inch (6 millimeters) thick and 6 inches (15 centimeters) wide. Trim the edges. Spread 4 ounces (120 grams) red currant jam on each strip of dough. Lightly sprinkle with cherries and walnuts, followed by cinnamon.

1 Spreading jam on rugelach dough.

2 Cutting jam-and-nut-topped rugelach dough into triangles.

3 Rolling rugelach before placing on sheet pan and baking.

4 Cut the dough into 2½-inch (6-centimeter) triangles. Roll each piece as for filled croissants (See photo on page 323). Place on paper-lined sheet pans and brush with egg wash.

5 Bake at 375°F (190°C) until golden, approximately 12 to 14 minutes.

6 Lightly dust with powdered sugar.

Approximate values per cookie: **Calories** 160, **Total fat** 10 g, **Saturated fat** 5 g, **Cholesterol** 20 mg, **Sodium** 105 mg, **Total carbohydrates** 17 g, **Protein** 2 g

SWEDISH YULE LOGS   RECIPE 9.24

Yield: 1½ Dozen Cookies, approximately 1½ oz. (45 g) each

Method: Rolled cookies

Unsalted butter, softened	10 oz.	300 g	83%
Powdered sugar	2 oz.	60 g	16%
Vanilla extract	0.25 fl. oz. (1½ tsp.)	7.5 ml	2%
Sherry	1 fl. oz.	30 ml	8%
Cardamom, ground	0.04 oz. (½ tsp.)	1 g	0.3%
All-purpose flour	12 oz.	360 g	100%
Pecans, chopped fine	3.75 oz.	112 g	31%
Powdered sugar	as needed	as needed	
Total weight:	1 lb. 13 oz.	870 g	240%

1 Cream the butter and sugar together until smooth. Stir in the vanilla, sherry and cardamom.

2 Stir the flour and pecans together, then add to the creamed butter mixture, blending well. Cover and chill 30 minutes.

3 Portion the dough into uniform 1½-ounce (45-gram) pieces. Shape each piece into a log, then bend the ends to create a crescent shape. Place on an ungreased baking sheet and bake at 375°F (190°C) until set and very lightly browned, approximately 12 minutes.

4 Sift powdered sugar onto a pan or plate. Cool the baked cookies 5 to 6 minutes, then carefully roll them in the sugar, coating thoroughly. After the cookies are completely cool they may be rerolled in powdered sugar if necessary to form a solid coating.

Approximate values per cookie: **Calories** 240, **Total fat** 17 g, **Saturated fat** 8 g, **Cholesterol** 35 mg, **Sodium** 0 mg, **Total carbohydrates** 18 g, **Protein** 3 g, **Vitamin A** 10%

RECIPE 9.25

SPRITZ COOKIES

Yield: 4 Dozen Cookies, approximately ½ oz. (15 g) each

Method: Pressed cookies

Unsalted butter, softened	8 oz.	240 g	80%
Granulated sugar	4 oz.	120 g	40%
Salt	0.05 oz. (¼ tsp.)	1.5 g	0.5%
Vanilla extract	0.15 fl. oz. (1 tsp.)	5 ml	1.5%
Egg	1.6 oz. (1 egg)	50 g	16%
Cake flour, sifted	10 oz.	300 g	100%
Total weight:	1 lb. 7 oz.	716 g	238%

1 Cream the butter and sugar until light and fluffy. Add the salt, vanilla and egg; beat well.

2 Gradually add the flour, beating until just blended. The dough should be firm but neither sticky nor stiff.

3 Press or pipe the dough onto an ungreased sheet pan, using a cookie press or a piping bag fitted with a large star tip.

4 Bake at 350°F (180°C) until lightly browned around the edges, approximately 10 minutes. Transfer to wire racks to cool.

Approximate values per cookie: **Calories** 40, **Total fat** 2.5 g, **Saturated fat** 1.5 g, **Cholesterol** 10 mg, **Sodium** 10 mg, **Total carbohydrates** 4 g, **Protein** 0 g, **Claims**—low fat; low cholesterol; very low sodium; low calorie

RECIPE 9.26

BUTTER COOKIES

Yield: 2 Dozen Cookies, approximately 1¼ oz. (37 g) each

Method: Pressed cookies

Unsalted butter	9 oz.	270 g	82%
Powdered sugar	6 oz.	180 g	54%
Egg	1.6 oz. (1 egg)	50 g	15%
Vanilla extract	0.5 fl. oz.	15 ml	5%
Orange oil	5 drops	5 drops	
Almond oil	0.15 fl. oz. (1 tsp.)	5 ml	1%
Salt	0.2 oz (1 tsp.)	6 g	2%
Pastry flour	11 oz.	330 g	100%
Pistachios	as needed	as needed	
Dried cherries	as needed	as needed	
Almonds, slivered	as needed	as needed	
Candied orange or grapefruit peel	as needed	as needed	
Total dough weight:	1 lb. 12 oz.	856 g	259%

1 Cream the butter and sugar. Gradually add the egg, vanilla, orange and almond oils and salt. Blend in the flour just until combined.

2 Using a piping bag and a medium-size star tip, pipe 1-inch (2.5-centimeter) rosettes on parchment-lined sheet pans. Place a pistachio, dried cherry, almond sliver and piece of candied peel on each cookie.

3 Bake at 375°F (190°C) until golden, approximately 10 to 12 minutes.

Approximate values per cookie: **Calories** 150, **Total fat** 9 g, **Saturated fat** 5 g, **Cholesterol** 30 mg, **Sodium** 100 mg, **Total carbohydrates** 17 g, **Protein** 2 g

COCONUT RASPBERRY MACAROONS

RECIPE 9.27

Yield: 4 Dozen Cookies, 1 oz. (30 g) each   **Method:** Pressed cookies

			Sugar at 100%
Unsalted butter, melted	as needed	as needed	
Eggs	13.3 oz. (8 eggs)	400 g	83%
Granulated sugar	1 lb.	480 g	100%
Vanilla extract	0.5 fl. oz.	15 ml	3%
Coconut, macaroon type	1 lb.	480 g	100%
Pastry flour	2 oz.	60 g	12%
Raspberry jam	as needed	as needed	
Semisweet chocolate, melted	as needed	as needed	
Total dough weight:	3 lb.	1435 g	298%

1 Brush parchment paper with melted butter. Let the butter solidify.

2 Beat the eggs and sugar in the bowl of a mixer fitted with a paddle. Stir in the vanilla and coconut, followed by the flour.

3 Pipe the mixture into 2-inch (5-centimeter) mounds, using a piping bag fitted with a large plain tip. With gloved hands, indent the center of each cookie, then fill it with raspberry jam.

4 Bake at 425°F (220°C) until golden. Cool on the baking sheet.

5 To decorate, fill a parchment paper cone with melted chocolate and drizzle over the cooled cookies.

Approximate values per cookie: **Calories** 100, **Total fat** 7 g, **Saturated fat** 6 g, **Cholesterol** 35 mg, **Sodium** 15 mg, **Total carbohydrates** 12 g, **Protein** 2 g

ALMOND CRESCENT COOKIES

RECIPE 9.28

Yield: 3 Dozen Cookies, ¾ oz. (20 g) each   **Method:** Pressed cookies

			Almond paste at 100%
Almond paste	1 lb.	480 g	100%
Granulated sugar	8 oz.	240 g	50%
Grapefruit zest, grated fine	0.4 oz. (2 Tbsp.)	12 g	2.5%
Vanilla extract	0.5 fl. oz.	15 ml	3%
Egg whites	4 oz. (4 whites)	120 g	25%
Total weight:	1 lb. 12 oz.	867 g	180%
Almonds, sliced	as needed	as needed	
Egg whites, beaten	as needed	as needed	
Granulated sugar	as needed	as needed	
Semisweet chocolate, tempered	as needed	as needed	

1 In the bowl of a mixer fitted with a paddle, blend the almond paste, sugar and grapefruit zest on low speed until lump-free. Add the vanilla.

2 Beat in the egg whites in four steps, waiting for each addition to be completely incorporated and then scraping down the bowl before adding the next.

3 Spread a thick layer of sliced almonds in a hotel pan. With a large plain tip, pipe the dough into 2-inch (5-centimeter) strips, each weighing about ¾ ounce (20 grams). Pipe the dough directly onto the sliced almonds, then roll the dough into the almonds to coat. Shape each piece of dough into a small crescent, then place the cookie on a clean paper-lined baking sheet.

4 Lightly brush the cookies with beaten egg whites and sprinkle with granulated sugar.

5 Bake at 375°F (190°C) for approximately 15 minutes. Cool completely, then dip the ends of the cookies in tempered semisweet chocolate.

Approximate values per cookie: **Calories** 80, **Total fat** 3.5 g, **Saturated fat** 0 g, **Cholesterol** 0 mg, **Sodium** 5 mg, **Total carbohydrates** 12 g, **Protein** 1 g

RECIPE 9.29

LACY PECAN COOKIES

Yield: 8 Dozen Cookies, 3 in. (7.5 cm) each   **Method:** Wafer cookies

Brown sugar	3 lb.	1300 g	100%
Unsalted butter	2 lb. 8 oz.	1080 g	83%
Dark corn syrup	3 lb. 12 oz.	1625 g	125%
All-purpose flour	3 lb.	1300 g	100%
Pecans, chopped fine	2 lb. 8 oz.	1080 g	83%
Total weight:	14 lb. 12 oz.	6385 g	491%

1 Combine the sugar, butter and corn syrup in a large, heavy saucepan. Bring to a boil.

2 Mix the flour and nuts together.

3 As soon as the sugar mixture comes to a full rolling boil, start timing it. Let it boil 3 minutes. Remove from the heat and stir in the flour-and-nut mixture. Pour into a hotel pan and cool completely.

4 Use a small portion scoop to make equal-sized balls of dough. Flatten out the balls of dough and place on a silicone baking mat or paper-lined sheet pans.

5 Bake at 325°F (160°C) until very dark brown and no longer moist in the center, approximately 15 to 18 minutes. Remove from oven and shape as desired.

Approximate values per serving: **Calories** 320, **Total fat** 17 g, **Saturated fat** 6 g, **Cholesterol** 25 mg, **Sodium** 20 mg, **Total carbohydrates** 38 g, **Protein** 2 g

1 Portioning the dough on a sheet pan lined with a silicone mat.

2 Shaping the baked cookies over a rolling pin while still hot.

RECIPE 9.30

TULIPE COOKIES (TUILE BATTER)

Yield: 30 Cups, approximately 3 in. (7.5 cm) in diameter

Method: Wafer cookies

Unsalted butter	1 lb.	500 g	100%
Powdered sugar	1 lb.	500 g	100%
All-purpose flour	1 lb.	500 g	100%
Egg whites	1 lb. 8 oz.	750 ml	150%
Butter, melted	as needed	as needed	
Total batter weight:	4 lb. 8 oz.	2250 g	450%

1 Melt the butter and place in the bowl of a mixer fitted with a paddle. Add the sugar and blend until almost smooth.

2 Add the flour and blend until smooth. With the mixer running, add the egg whites very slowly. Beat until blended, but do not incorporate air into the batter.

3 Strain the batter through a china cap and set aside to cool completely.

1 Spreading the batter into circles on a sheet pan lined with a silicone mat.

2 Shaping the baked wafer cookies into cups while still hot.

4 Coat several sheet pans with melted butter or line with silicone mats. Spread the batter into 6-inch (15-centimeter) circles on the pans. Bake at 400°F (200°C) until the edges are brown and the batter is dry, approximately 12 to 18 minutes.

5 To shape into cups, lift the hot cookies off the sheet pan one at a time with an offset spatula. Immediately place over an inverted glass and top with a ramekin or small bowl. The cookies cool very quickly, becoming firm and crisp. The cookie bowls can be used for serving ice cream, crème brûlée, fruit or other items.

Approximate values per cookie: **Calories** 240, **Total fat** 12 g, **Saturated fat** 8 g, **Cholesterol** 35 mg, **Sodium** 40 mg, **Total carbohydrates** 37 g, **Protein** 4 g, **Vitamin A** 10%

RUSSIAN CIGARETTES RECIPE 9.31

Yield: 4 Dozen Cookies, approximately ¾ oz. (22 g) each

Method: Wafer cookies

Unsalted butter, softened	10 oz.	300 g	133%
Powdered sugar	11 oz.	330 g	146%
Egg whites	10 oz. (10 whites)	300 g	133%
Orange zest, grated fine	0.2 oz. (1 Tbsp.)	6 g	3%
Vanilla extract	0.15 fl. oz. (1 tsp.)	5 ml	2%
Cake flour	7.5 oz.	225 g	100%
Bittersweet chocolate, melted and tempered	as needed	as needed	
Total batter weight:	2 lb. 6 oz.	1166 g	517%

1 Cream the butter and sugar in the bowl of a mixer fitted with a paddle. Gradually add the egg whites followed by the orange zest and vanilla. Fold in the flour.

2 Spread the batter into 3-inch (8-centimeter) circles on a silicone baking mat or buttered sheet pans, as illustrated above. Bake at 425°F (220°C) until golden and the edges are lightly brown, approximately 4 to 6 minutes.

3 To roll into cigarettes, lift the cookies off the sheet pan one at a time with an offset spatula. Immediately roll each cookie around a ¼-inch (6-millimeter) dowel. (If the cookies have cooled before the shaping process, reheat them until they are very soft, about 3 minutes, and then resume the shaping process.)

4 After cooling, dip the ends in tempered chocolate. Store in airtight containers.

Rolling baked wafer batter around a dowel to make cigarette cookies.

Approximate values per cookie: **Calories** 100, **Total fat** 6 g, **Saturated fat** 3.5 g, **Cholesterol** 15 mg, **Sodium** 15 mg, **Total carbohydrates** 12 g, **Protein** 1 g

RECIPE 9.32   **BISCOTTI**

1 Biscotti dough rolled into log before first baking.

2 Slicing biscotti before second baking.

Italian in origin, biscotti are twice-baked cookies served with coffee, wine or other beverages. The dough is mixed and shaped into a log. The log of dough is baked, then cut on a diagonal into individual cookies, which are returned to the oven to bake further. This twice-baked process ensures that the cookies will have a long-lasting firm, crisp texture.

Yield: 3 Dozen Biscotti, 2 oz. (60 g) each   **Method:** Bar cookies

Cinnamon, ground	0.2 oz. (1 Tbsp.)	4 g	1%
Ammonium carbonate or baking powder	0.3 oz. (2 tsp.)	8 g	1.8%
Hazelnut flour	10 oz.	300 g	62%
Almond flour	3 oz.	90 g	19%
Pastry flour	1 lb.	480 g	100%
Eggs	8.3 oz. (5 eggs)	250 g	52%
Granulated sugar	1 lb.	480 g	100%
Unsalted butter, melted	8 oz.	240 g	50%
Whole hazelnuts	10 oz.	300 g	62%
Chocolate, melted and tempered (optional)	as needed	as needed	
Total dough weight:	4 lb. 8 oz.	2152 g	448%

1 Sift together the cinnamon and ammonium carbonate or baking powder. Stir in the hazelnut, almond and pastry flours. Set aside.

2 In a large bowl, whisk together the eggs and sugar until thick, pale and at least doubled in volume, approximately 3 minutes. Add the butter. Stir in the flour mixture with a rubber spatula, then stir in the hazelnuts.

3 Divide the dough into three equal pieces. Refrigerate until cold.

4 Roll each piece of dough into a 12-inch (30-centimeter) log. Place on a paper-lined sheet pan, leaving at least 3 inches (7.5 centimeters) of space between each log.

5 Bake at 350°F (180°C) until golden in color, approximately 20 minutes. Cool the logs, then slice them into 1-inch- (3-centimeter-) thick slices.

6 Place the sliced cookies upright on paper-lined sheet pans. Place each sheet pan on top of a clean sheet pan to insulate the cookies.

7 Reduce heat to 325°F (160°C) and bake until the biscotti are thoroughly crisp, approximately 40 minutes.

8 Once cool, the biscotti may be dipped in tempered chocolate.

VARIATIONS:

Orange Biscotti—Add 0.5 oz. (15 grams/3%) grated orange zest to the flour mixture.

Anise Biscotti—Add 0.25 ounce (7 grams/1.5%) chopped anise seeds to the flour mixture.

Chocolate Biscotti—Replace 5 ounces (150 grams/31%) of the pastry flour with cocoa powder. Add 0.3 fluid ounces: (9 milligrams/2%) coffee extract and 0.3 ounce (9 grams/2%) cinnamon to the flour mixture.

Approximate values per cookie: **Calories** 260, **Total fat** 17 g, **Saturated fat** 4 g, **Cholesterol** 45 mg, **Sodium** 30 mg, **Total carbohydrates** 26 g, **Protein** 5 g

GERMAN CHOCOLATE LAYERED BROWNIES

RECIPE 9.33

Yield: 8 Dozen 2-in. (5-cm) Squares, 1 Full-Sheet Pan

Method: Bar cookies

Semisweet chocolate	1 lb.	480 g	114%
Unsalted butter	1 lb. 4 oz.	600 g	143%
Vanilla extract	0.5 fl. oz.	15 ml	4%
Eggs	20 oz. (12 eggs)	600 g	143%
Salt	0.1 oz. (½ tsp.)	3 g	0.7%
Granulated sugar	2 lb.	960 g	228%
Cocoa powder	2 oz.	60 g	14%
All-purpose flour	14 oz.	420 g	100%
Pecans, chopped	1 lb.	480 g	114%
Topping:			
Unsalted butter	12 oz.	360 g	86%
Shredded coconut	12 oz.	360 g	86%
Coconut flavoring	0.6 fl. oz. (4 tsp.)	20 ml	5%
Vanilla extract	0.6 fl. oz. (4 tsp.)	20 ml	5%
Powdered sugar	1 lb. 4 oz.	600 g	143%
Cream cheese, softened	1 lb. 8 oz.	720 g	171%
Total weight:	11 lb. 13 oz.	5698 g	1356%

1 Placing coconut topping on brownie batter spread in the sheet pan.

1 Melt the chocolate and butter together and set aside. Stir in the vanilla.

2 Beat the eggs, salt and sugar together in another bowl.

3 In a large bowl stir together the cocoa powder, flour and pecans. Add the egg mixture to the flour, then stir in the melted chocolate.

4 Pour the batter into a greased and floured sheet pan, spreading evenly.

5 To make the topping, melt the butter in a large saucepan, and then stir in the shredded coconut, coconut flavoring, vanilla and sugar. Cook over low heat until the sugar has dissolved and the mixture is creamy.

6 Cream the cream cheese in a mixer or food processor. Add the hot butter mixture and blend until no lumps of cheese remain.

7 Immediately spoon the topping over the unbaked chocolate batter. Spread the topping into a thin layer using an offset spatula.

8 Bake at 300°F (150°C) until the center has set and the surface is golden brown, approximately 1 hour. Cool, then wrap and chill completely overnight before cutting into 2-inch × 2-inch (5-centimeter × 5-centimeter) squares.

2 Spreading topping on layered brownies before baking.

Approximate values per brownie: **Calories** 220, **Total fat** 15 g, **Saturated fat** 8 g, **Cholesterol** 50 mg, **Sodium** 45 mg, **Total carbohydrates** 22 g, **Protein** 2 g

RECIPE 9.34

CHOCOLATE PEANUT BUTTER BROWNIES

Yield: 4 Dozen Brownies, 1½ in. × 3 in. (3.7 cm × 7.5 cm) each, 1 Half-Sheet Pan

Method: Bar cookies

Pastry flour	1 lb.	480 g	100%
Baking powder	0.3 oz. (2 tsp.)	8 g	1.8%
Eggs	8.3 oz. (5 eggs)	250 g	52%
Granulated sugar	12 oz.	360 g	75%
Brown sugar	12 oz.	360 g	75%
Peanut butter	12 oz.	360 g	75%
Vanilla extract	0.5 fl. oz.	15 ml	3%
Unsalted butter, melted	3 oz.	90 g	19%
Peanuts, toasted	6 oz.	180 g	38%
Semisweet chocolate chunks	6 oz.	180 g	38%
Chocolate Ganache (page 362)	1 lb. 8 oz.	720 g	150%
Chocolate Decorations (page 614)	as needed	as needed	
Chopped peanuts	as needed	as needed	
Total batter weight:	6 lb. 4 oz.	3003 g	627%

1 Sift together the flour and baking powder. Set aside.

2 In the bowl of a mixer fitted with a paddle, blend the eggs and sugars. Add the peanut butter and vanilla. Mix until well combined, then beat in the butter. Stir in the flour mixture, peanuts and chocolate chunks.

3 Spread the batter on a paper-lined half-sheet pan. Bake at 350°F (180°C) until set, approximately 35 to 38 minutes.

4 Let cool completely, turn over onto the back of a clean sheet pan and frost the surface with ganache heated to 110°F (43°C).

5 Cut into 1½-inch × 3-inch (3.7-centimeter × 7.5-centimeter) bars and top with chocolate decorations and peanuts.

Approximate values per brownie: **Calories** 250, **Total fat** 13 g, **Saturated fat** 6 g, **Cholesterol** 35 mg, **Sodium** 65 mg, **Total carbohydrates** 31 g, **Protein** 5 g, **Claims**—low fat; low cholesterol; no sodium

RECIPE 9.35

PRALINE SQUARES

Yield: 2½ Dozen Squares, 1 Half-Sheet Pan

Method: Bar cookies

Unsalted butter, softened	8 oz.	240 g	66%
Brown sugar	1 lb. 4 oz.	600 g	166%
Eggs	8.3 oz. (5 eggs)	250 g	69%
Vanilla extract	0.15 fl. oz. (1 tsp.)	5 ml	1.2%
Hazelnut extract	0.15 fl. oz. (1 tsp.)	5 ml	1.2%
All-purpose flour	12 oz.	360 g	100%
Baking powder	0.4 oz. (1 Tbsp.)	11 g	3%
Salt	0.1 oz. (½ tsp.)	3 g	0.8%
Pecans, chopped	8 oz.	240 g	66%
Powdered sugar	as needed	as needed	
Total batter weight:	3 lb. 9 oz.	1714 g	473%

1 In the bowl of a mixer fitted with a paddle, cream the butter and sugar on medium speed until light, approximately 3 minutes.

2 Add the eggs, one at a time, then add the extracts.

3 Stir the dry ingredients together and gradually add them to the creamed mixture on low speed. Stir in the nuts.

4 Spread the batter into a lightly greased pan and bake at 325°F (160°C) until golden brown and set, approximately 40 minutes.

5 Cool in the pan, then cut into squares and dust with powdered sugar.

Approximate values per square: **Calories** 220, **Total fat** 11 g, **Saturated fat** 4.5 g, **Cholesterol** 50 mg, **Sodium** 105 mg, **Total carbohydrates** 28 g, **Protein** 3 g

APPLESAUCE BROWNIES

RECIPE 9.36

This formula offers much of the delicious taste of a great brownie with less fat. The applesauce mimics the fat, creating fudginess. This is the formula to use when a healthier alternative to a classic brownie is required.

Yield: 8 Dozen 2-in. (5-cm) Squares, 1 Full-Sheet Pan

Method: Bar cookies

Unsweetened chocolate	4 oz.	120 g	25%
Cake flour, sifted	1 lb.	480 g	100%
Cocoa powder	9 oz.	270 g	56%
Salt	0.4 oz (2 tsp.)	12 g	2.5%
Egg whites	12 oz. (12 whites)	360 g	75%
Whole eggs	13.3 oz. (8 eggs)	400 g	83%
Granulated sugar	2 lb. 2 oz.	1020 g	212%
Light corn syrup	2 lb.	960 g	200%
Unsweetened applesauce	1 lb. 8 oz.	720 g	150%
Canola oil	7 oz.	210 g	44%
Vanilla extract	1 fl. oz.	30 ml	6%
Total weight:	9 lb. 8 oz.	458 g	953%

1 Coat a sheet pan lightly with vegetable oil.

2 Melt the chocolate over a bain marie and set aside.

3 Sift the flour, cocoa powder and salt together and set aside.

4 Whisk the egg whites and eggs together. Add the sugar, corn syrup, applesauce, oil and vanilla. Whisk in the chocolate.

5 Fold the flour mixture into the egg mixture. Pour into the prepared pan and bake at 350°F (180°C) until a cake tester comes out clean, approximately 25 minutes.

Approximate values per brownie: **Calories** 150, **Total fat** 5 g, **Saturated fat** 0.8 g, **Cholesterol** 19 mg, **Sodium** 82 mg, **Total carbohydrates** 26 g, **Protein** 2 g

THE PIE IS AN ENGLISH INSTITUTION WHICH, PLANTED ON AMERICAN SOIL, FORTHWITH RAN RAMPANT AND BURST FORTH INTO AN UNTOLD VARIETY OF GENERA AND SPECIES.

—Harriet Beecher Stowe, American novelist (1811–1896)

PIES AND TARTS

HOUSTON COMMUNITY COLLEGE, Houston, TX
Pastry Chef Eddy Van Damme

AFTER STUDYING THIS CHAPTER, YOU WILL BE ABLE TO:

▶ prepare a variety of pie crusts and fillings

▶ form and bake a variety of pies and tarts

▶ prepare a variety of dessert and pastry items, incorporating components from other chapters

▶ **pastry** may refer to a group of doughs made primarily with flour, water and fat; pastry can also refer to foods made with these doughs or to a large variety of fancy baked goods

Perhaps the most important (and versatile) building block in pastry making is the dough. The next three chapters examine the different doughs used to form pastries. This chapter focuses on the basic doughs used to make pies and tarts—flaky dough, mealy dough and sweet tart dough. See Table 10.1. This chapter demonstrates how to make, fill, bake and garnish a variety of pies and tarts. Each step is illustrated with step-by-step photographs. The cream, custard and mousse fillings used in some of the recipes at the end of this chapter are discussed in Chapter 15, Custards and Creams. Additional doughs used to make particular kinds of pastry are discussed in Chapter 11, Pastry Doughs, which covers éclair paste, meringues and phyllo dough, and in Chapter 12, Laminated Doughs, which details the methods for making puff pastry, croissant and Danish dough.

▶ PIES AND TARTS

A pie is composed of a sweet or savory filling in a baked crust. It can be made without a top crust or, more typically, topped with a full or lattice crust. A pie is generally made in a round, slope-sided pan and cut into wedges for service. A tart is similar to a pie except it is made in a shallow, straight-sided pan, often with fluted edges. A tart can be almost any shape; round, square, rectangular and petal shapes are the most common. It is usually open-faced and derives much of its beauty from an attractive arrangement of glazed fruit, piped cream or chocolate decorations.

CRUSTS

Pie crusts and tart shells can be made from several types of doughs or crumbs. Flaky dough, mealy dough and crumbs are best for pie crusts; sweet dough is usually used for tart shells. A pie crust or tart shell can be shaped and completely baked before filling (known as baked blind) or filled and baked simultaneously with the filling.

FLAKY AND MEALY DOUGHS

Flaky and mealy pie doughs are quick, easy and versatile. Flaky dough, sometimes known as pâte brisée, takes its name from its final baked texture. It is best for pie top crusts and lattice coverings and may be used for prebaked shells that will be filled with a cooled filling shortly before service. Mealy dough takes its name from its raw texture. It is used whenever a soggy crust would be a problem (for example, as the bottom crust of a custard or fruit pie) because it is sturdier and resists sogginess better than flaky dough. Both flaky and mealy doughs are too delicate for tarts that will be removed from the pan for service. Sweet tart dough, described later, is better for these types of tarts.

Flaky and mealy doughs contain little or no sugar and can be prepared from the same formula with only a slight variation in mixing method. For both types of dough, a cold fat such as butter or shortening is cut into the flour. The amount of flakiness in the baked crust depends on the size of the fat particles

Table 10.1 **CLASSIFICATION OF PIE AND TART DOUGHS**

DOUGH	FRENCH NAME	CHARACTERISTICS AFTER BAKING	USE
Flaky dough	Pâte brisée	Very flaky; not sweet	Prebaked pie shells; pie top crusts
Mealy dough	Pâte brisée	Moderately flaky; not sweet	Custard, cream or fruit pie crusts; quiche crusts
Sweet tart dough	Pâte sucrée	Very rich; crisp; not flaky	Tart and tartlet shells
Shortbread tart dough	Pâte sablée	Very rich; fragile; not flaky	Tart and tartlet shells; cookies

in the dough. The larger the pieces of fat, the flakier the crust will be. This is because the flakes are actually the sides of fat pockets created during baking by the melting fat and steam. When preparing flaky dough, the fat is left in larger pieces, about the size of peas or peanuts. When preparing mealy dough, the fat is blended in more thoroughly, until the mixture resembles coarse cornmeal. Because the resulting fat pockets are smaller, the crust is less flaky.

The type of fat used affects both the dough's flavor and flakiness. Butter contributes a delicious flavor, but does not produce as flaky a crust as other fats. Butter is also more difficult to work with than other fats because of its lower melting point and its tendency to become brittle when chilled. Hydrogenated vegetable shortening produces a flaky crust but contributes nothing to its flavor. The flakiest pastry is made with lard. Because some people dislike its flavor for sweet pies or do not eat pork products, lard is more often used for pâté en croûte or other savory preparations. Some chefs prefer to use a combination of butter with either shortening or lard. Oil is not an appropriate substitute as it disperses too thoroughly throughout the dough; when baked, the crust will be extremely fragile but without any flakiness.

After the fat is cut into the flour, water or milk is added to form a soft dough. Less water is needed for mealy dough because more flour is already in contact with the fat, reducing its ability to absorb liquid. Cold water is normally used for both flaky and mealy doughs. The water should be well chilled to prevent softening the fat. Milk may be used to increase richness and nutritional value. It will produce a darker, less crisp crust, however. If dry milk powder is used, it should be dissolved in water first.

Hand mixing is best for small to moderate quantities of dough. You retain better control over the procedure when you can feel the fat being incorporated. It is very difficult to make flaky dough with an electric mixer or food processor, as machines tend to cut the fat in too thoroughly. (If a food processor is used, the mixing time should be brief.) Overmixing develops too much gluten, making the dough elastic and difficult to use. If an electric mixer must be used for large quantities, use the paddle attachment at the lowest speed and be sure the fat is well chilled, even frozen. Refrigerating pie dough after mixing is recommended to allow the moisture to evenly distribute through the mixture and to firm the fat for ease of handling.

▶ PROCEDURE FOR PREPARING FLAKY AND MEALY DOUGHS

1 Sift flour, salt and sugar (if used) together in a large bowl.

2 Cut the fat into the flour. For flaky dough, the fat should be the size of peas or peanuts. For mealy dough, cut the fat in more thoroughly until the mixture resembles cornmeal.

3 Gradually add a cold liquid, mixing gently until the dough holds together. Do not overmix.

4 Cover the dough with plastic wrap and chill thoroughly before using.

5 Remember that rerolled scraps will be tough and elastic.

INSPIRATION—THE ZEN OF APPLE PIE

I am sitting at a small table sipping Japanese tea at Café Matsunosuke in Kyoto. Through the window I see undulating metal rooftops and the architectural flourishes of the old city framed by modern buildings in the distance . . . the yin and yang of modern Kyoto. Wafting from the kitchen is the unmistakable aroma of apple pie. This American icon is being served to women dressed in kimonos who utter astonished whispers of praise secreted behind delicate hands.

I am here to teach Japanese students how to make apple pie. I once read a passage by M. F. K. Fisher that described her ritual of peeling and eating tangerines. I experience a similar sensation when I teach baking.

As I go through the steps of making a pie, the process becomes a meditation. I see, through the eyes of my students, a ritual unfolding. I become an extension of the dough as I rapidly move my fingertips through the flour and shortening to achieve the perfect texture. The class breathes a collective sigh of knowing as the slow drizzle of ice water miraculously fuses flour and shortening into the promise of a pie. Use your senses. Touch your earlobe. The dough should feel the same. Keep everything cold. Handle the dough with respect. Biological forces are at work. Glutens need to relax. Roll it out with a light touch, just a sprinkling of flour. Carefully fold the circle of dough into

quarters and transport it to a waiting pie tin. Fill the crust to heaping with thinly sliced apples, the perfect blend of spices, and crown with slivers of sweet butter. Add a top crust and begin the ritual of "crimping" the edges. Your fingertips coax the dough into waves lapping to a shore of apples. The pie is ceremoniously carried to the waiting oven. For a few moments, this humble pie becomes the center of the universe, a tranquility meditation, and a link that connects two cultures.

—Cheryl Jean, Chef-Owner and Culinary Educator, 14 Lincoln Street Bed and Breakfast, Niantic, CT

RECIPE 10.1

BASIC PIE DOUGH

Yield: 5 lb. 2 oz. (2277g) dough or approximately 6 shells, 9 in. (22 cm) each

Pastry flour	3 lb.	1440 g	100%
Salt	0.9 oz. (4 tsp.)	27 g	1.9%
Granulated sugar (optional)	2 oz.	60 g	4%
All-purpose shortening	1 lb. 8 oz.	720 g	50%
Water, cold*	8 fl. oz.	230 ml	16%
Total dough weight:	5 lb. 2 oz.	2477 g	172%

1 Sift the flour, salt and sugar together in a large bowl.
2 Cut the shortening into the flour mixture until the desired consistency (flaky or mealy) is reached.
3 Gradually add the cold water, mixing gently until the dough holds together. Do not overmix or add too much water.
4 Cover the dough with plastic wrap and chill thoroughly before using.

*The amount of water needed varies depending on the manner in which the fat is incorporated. Mealy dough will probably not require this entire amount.

Approximate values per 1-oz. (30-g) serving: **Calories** 140, **Total fat** 9 g, **Saturated fat** 2.5 g, **Cholesterol** 0 mg, **Sodium** 120 mg, **Total carbohydrates** 14 g, **Protein** 1 g, **Claims**—no cholesterol; low sodium

1 Cutting the fat into the flour coarsely for flaky dough.

2 Cutting the fat into the flour finely for mealy dough.

3 The finished dough.

SWEET TART DOUGH

Sweet tart dough or pâte sucrée is a rich, nonflaky dough used for sweet tart shells. It is sturdier than flaky or mealy dough because it contains egg yolks and the fat is blended in thoroughly. This mixing technique also prevents air pockets from forming in the baked dough, hence it is not flaky when baked. Since more fat coats the flour, less gluten is formed, making for a tender dough when baked. It is also more cookielike than classic pie dough and has the rich flavor of butter. It creates a crisp but tender crust and is excellent for tartlets as well as for straight-sided tarts that will be removed from their pans before service. Shortbread tart dough or pâte sablée is sweet tart dough with a high percentage of fat, also used, as its name implies, for rich butter cookies. Raw dough may be kept refrigerated up to 2 weeks or frozen up to 3 months.

▶ PROCEDURE FOR PREPARING SWEET TART DOUGH

1 Cream softened butter. Add sugar and beat until the mixture is smooth and lump-free.
2 Slowly add eggs, blending well.
3 Slowly add flour, mixing only until incorporated. Overmixing toughens the dough.
4 Cover the dough with plastic wrap and chill thoroughly before using.
5 Scraps may be rerolled once or twice, provided the dough is still cool, nongreasy and pliable. If too much gluten develops, the crust will shrink and toughen.

SWEET TART DOUGH

RECIPE 10.2

Yield: 7 lb. 8 oz. (3585 g) dough or approximately 10 shells, 9 in. (22 cm) each

Unsalted butter, softened	1 lb. 8 oz.	705 g	42%
Powdered sugar	1 lb. 5 oz.	630 g	37.5%
Egg yolks	1 lb. (26 yolks)	470 g	28%
Eggs	3.3 oz. (2 eggs)	100 g	6%
All-purpose flour	3 lb. 8 oz.	1680 g	100%
Total dough weight:	7 lb. 8 oz.	3585 g	213%

1 Mixing sweet dough.

1 Cream the butter and powdered sugar in the bowl of a large mixer fitted with a paddle.
2 Combine the egg yolks and whole eggs. Slowly add the eggs to the creamed butter. Mix until smooth and free of lumps, scraping down the bowl as needed.
3 With the mixer on low speed, slowly add the flour to the butter-and-egg mixture. Mix only until incorporated; do not overmix. The dough should be firm, smooth and not sticky.
4 Dust a half-sheet pan with flour. Pack the dough into the pan evenly. Wrap well in plastic wrap and chill until firm.
5 Work with a small portion of the chilled dough when shaping tart shells or other products.

2 The finished sweet dough.

VARIATION:

Sweet Coconut Tart Dough—Add 14 ounces (420 grams/25%) desiccated coconut, macaroon type, to the dough with the dry ingredients.

Approximate values per 1-oz. (30-g) serving: **Calories** 120, **Total fat** 5 g, **Saturated fat** 3 g, **Cholesterol** 15 mg, **Sodium** 0 mg, **Total carbohydrates** 16 g, **Protein** 2 g, **Vitamin A** 4%

CRUMB CRUSTS

A quick and tasty bottom crust can be made from finely ground cookie crumbs moistened with melted butter. Crumb crusts can be used for unbaked pies such as those with cream or chiffon fillings, or they can be baked with their fillings, as with cheesecakes.

Chocolate cookies, graham crackers, gingersnaps, vanilla wafers and macaroons are popular choices for crumb crusts. Some breakfast cereals such as corn flakes or bran flakes are also used. Ground nuts and spices can be added for flavor. Whatever cookies or other ingredients are used, be sure they are ground to a fine, even crumb. If packaged crumbs are unavailable, a food processor, blender or rolling pin can be used.

The typical ratio for a crumb crust is one part melted butter, two parts sugar and four parts crumbs. For example, 8 ounces (240 grams) graham crackers mixed with 4 ounces (120 grams) sugar and 2 ounces (60 grams) melted butter produces enough crust to line one 9- or 10-inch (22- or 25-centimeter) pan. The amount of sugar may need to be adjusted depending on the type of crumbs used, however; for example, chocolate sandwich cookies need less sugar than graham crackers. If the mixture is too dry to stick together, gradually add more melted butter. Press the mixture into the bottom of the pan and chill or bake it before filling.

Making a crumb crust.

SHAPING CRUSTS

Crusts are shaped by rolling out the dough to fit into a pie pan or tart shell (mold) or to sit on top of fillings. Mealy, flaky and sweet doughs are all easier to roll out and work with if well chilled, as chilling keeps the fat firm and prevents stickiness. Although an electric dough sheeter (See Chapter 2, Tools and Equipment) will roll out doughs quickly and evenly, sheeters are not available in every kitchen. So any good pastry cook should be comfortable working with all types of dough by hand.

When rolling and shaping the dough, work on a clean, flat surface (wood or marble is best). Lightly dust the work surface, rolling pin and dough with bread or all-purpose flour before starting to roll the dough. (Cake or pastry flour tends to clump and is not recommended.) Also, work only with a manageable amount at a time: usually one crust's worth for a pie or standard-sized tart or enough for 10 to 12 tartlet shells.

Roll out the dough from the center, working toward the edges. Periodically, lift the dough gently and rotate it. This keeps the dough from sticking and helps produce an even thickness. If the dough sticks to the rolling pin or work surface, sprinkle on a bit more flour. Too much flour, however, makes the crust dry and crumbly and causes gray streaks.

▶ PROCEDURE FOR ROLLING AND SHAPING DOUGH FOR DOUBLE-CRUST PIES AND TART SHELLS

1 A typical pie crust or tart shell should be rolled to a thickness of approximately ⅛ inch (3 millimeters); it should also be at least 2 inches (5 centimeters) larger in diameter than the baking pan.

2 Carefully roll the dough up onto a rolling pin. Position the pin over the pie or tart pan and unroll the dough, easing it into the pan. Trim the edges as necessary.

3 When making a double-crust pie, roll the dough out as before, making the circle large enough to hang over the pan's edge. The dough may be lifted into place by rolling it onto the rolling pin, as with the bottom crust. Slits or designs can be cut in the top crust to allow steam to escape.

4 Seal the top crust to the bottom crust with egg wash or water. Crimp as desired.

▶ PROCEDURE FOR ROLLING AND SHAPING DOUGH FOR LATTICE CRUSTS

1 Roll the dough out as before. Using a ruler as a guide, cut even strips of the desired width, typically ½ inch (1.2 centimeters).

2 Using an over-under-over pattern, weave the strips together on top of the filling. Be sure the strips are evenly spaced for an attractive result. Crimp the lattice strips to the bottom crust to seal.

▶ PROCEDURE FOR ROLLING AND SHAPING DOUGH FOR TARTLET SHELLS

1 A typical crust for tartlets should be approximately ⅛ inch (3 millimeters) thick.

2 Roll the dough out as described earlier. Then roll the dough up onto the rolling pin.

1 Lay out a single layer of tartlet shells. Unroll the dough over the shells, pressing the dough gently into each one.

2 Roll the rolling pin over the top of the shells. The edge of the shells will cut the dough. Be sure the dough is pressed against the sides of each shell. Bake or fill as desired.

BAKING CRUSTS

Pie crusts can be filled and then baked, or baked and then filled. Unfilled baked crusts can be stored at room temperature 2 to 3 days or wrapped in plastic wrap and frozen as long as 3 months. Pie crusts that are baked before being filled are said to be **baked blind.** To retain their shape, small holes are pricked in the pie shell dough with a fork or paring knife, a technique known as **docking.** The unbaked pie shell is then lined with parchment or buttered foil and filled with baking (or pie) weights, dry rice or beans. Empty pie pans may be used as a baking weight when making prebaked pie shells. Once the crust has baked long enough to set so it will not puff up, the weights are removed and the shell is returned to the oven to finish baking. To help retain crispness once filled, the crust may be coated with a thin layer of egg wash during the final minutes of baking. A baked crust can also be brushed with a thin layer of caramel or melted chocolate for the same effect. Note that dry rice or beans may be reused several times for future pies or tarts, but may not be used for consumption.

▶ **bake blind** to bake a pie shell or tart shell unfilled, using baking weights or beans to support the crust as it bakes.

▶ **docking** pricking small holes in an unbaked dough or crust to allow steam to escape and to prevent the dough from rising when baked.

▶ PROCEDURE FOR ROLLING AND BAKING UNFILLED TART CRUSTS (BAKED BLIND)

1 Roll the dough out to the desired thickness and line the pie pan or tart ring with the dough.

2 Place a tart ring on a paper-lined sheet pan. Carefully roll the dough up onto a rolling pin. Position the pin over the tart ring and unroll the dough.

3 Ease the dough into the tart ring, pressing to make a smooth edge.

4 Run a rolling pin over the edge of the tart ring to remove excess dough and produce a level edge to the tart. Dock the tart dough with a fork.

5 Cover the dough with heat-resistant plastic, parchment paper or greased aluminum foil (greased side down). Press the plastic, paper or foil against the walls of the shell, allowing a portion of it to extend above the pan. Fill the pan with baking weights or dry rice or beans.

6 Bake the weighted crust at 350°F (180°C) 10 to 15 minutes. Remove the weights and paper.

7 Brush the baked crust with egg wash, then return the crust to the oven. Bake until golden brown and fully cooked, approximately 10 to 15 minutes. Cool, then fill as desired.

FILLINGS

Fillings make pies and tarts distinctive and flavorful. Four types of fillings are discussed here: cream, fruit, custard and chiffon. (Chapter 15, Custards and Creams, includes more custard and cream fillings in detail.) There is no one correct presentation or filling-and-crust combination. The apples in an apple pie, for example, may be sliced, seasoned and topped with streusel; caramelized, puréed and blended with cream; chopped and covered with a flaky dough lattice; or poached, arranged over pastry cream and brushed with a shiny glaze. Only an understanding of the fundamental techniques for making fillings—and some imagination—ensures success. See Table 10.2 for troubleshooting pie making.

CREAM FILLINGS

A cream filling is really nothing more than a flavored pastry cream. Pastry cream is a type of starch-thickened egg custard discussed in Chapter 15, Custards and Creams. When used as a pie filling, pastry cream should be thickened with cornstarch and flour so that it is firm enough to hold its shape when sliced. (Cornstarch provides sheen while the flour ensures firmness.) Popular flavors are chocolate, banana and coconut.

A cream filling is fully cooked on the stovetop, so a prebaked or crumb crust is needed. The crust can be filled while the filling is still warm, or the filling can be chilled and piped into the crust later. A cream pie is often topped with meringue, which is then browned quickly in an oven or under a broiler.

RECIPE 10.3

BASIC CREAM PIE

1 Filling a baked pie shell with chocolate custard.

2 Topping with meringue.

Yield: 3 Pies, 9 in. (22 cm) each   **Method:** Cream filling

Filling:

Granulated sugar	1 lb.	480 g
Milk	2 qt.	1920 ml
Egg yolks	5.3 oz. (8 yolks)	160 g
Eggs	6.75 oz. (4 eggs)	200 g
Flour	4 oz.	120 g
Cornstarch	3 oz.	90 g
Unsalted butter	4 oz.	120 g
Vanilla extract	1 fl. oz.	30 ml
Flaky pie dough shells, baked	3 shells	3 shells
Meringue	as needed	as needed

1 In a heavy saucepan, dissolve 8 ounces (240 grams) of the sugar in the milk. Bring just to a boil.

2 Meanwhile, whisk the egg yolks and eggs together in a large bowl.

3 Sift the flour, the cornstarch and the remaining sugar onto the eggs. Whisk until smooth.

4 Temper the egg mixture with approximately half of the hot milk. Stir the warmed egg mixture back into the remaining milk and return it to a boil, stirring constantly.

5 Whisking constantly and vigorously, allow the cream to boil until thick, approximately 30 seconds. Remove from the heat and stir in the butter and vanilla. Stir until the butter is melted and incorporated.

6 Pour the cream into the pie shells. (Cream may be poured into a bowl, chilled over an ice bath, covered with plastic wrap and stored in the refrigerator up to 2 days before using.)

7 The pies can be topped with meringue while the filling is still warm. The meringue is then lightly browned in a 425°F (220°C) oven. Chill the pies for service.

VARIATIONS:

Chocolate Cream Pie—Melt 12 ounces (360 grams) bittersweet chocolate. Stir the melted chocolate into the hot cream after adding the butter and vanilla.

Banana Cream Pie—Layer 12 ounces (360 grams) sliced bananas (about three medium bananas) into the baked shell with the warm cream. Do not purée the bananas, as this will make the filling runny.

Coconut Cream Pie I—Substitute 12 fluid ounces (360 milliliters) cream of coconut for 12 fluid ounces (360 milliliters) milk and 4 ounces (120 grams) sugar. Top the pie with meringue and shredded coconut.

Coconut Cream Pie II—Stir 8 ounces (240 grams) toasted coconut into the warm cream.

Approximate values per serving: **Calories** 220, **Total fat** 9 g, **Saturated** fat 5 g, **Cholesterol** 130 mg, **Sodium** 55 mg, **Total carbohydrates** 29 g, **Protein** 5 g, **Vitamin A** 10%

FRUIT FILLINGS

A fruit filling is a mixture of fruit, fruit juice, spices and sugar thickened with a starch. Apple, cherry, blueberry and peach are traditional favorites. The fruit can be fresh, frozen or canned. (See Chapter 17, Fruits, for comments on selecting the best fruits for fillings.) The starch can be flour, cornstarch, tapioca or a packaged commercial instant or pregelatinized starch. The ingredients for a fruit filling are most often combined using one of three methods: cooked fruit, cooked juice or baked.

Cooked Fruit Fillings

The cooked fruit filling method is often used when the fruits need to be softened by cooking (for example, apples or rhubarb) or are naturally rather dry, such as dry apricots or raisins. A cooked fruit filling should be combined with a prebaked or crumb crust.

Table 10.2 TROUBLESHOOTING CHART FOR PIES

PROBLEM	CAUSE	SOLUTION
Crust shrinks	Overmixing	Adjust mixing technique
	Overworking dough	Adjust rolling technique
	Not enough fat	Adjust formula
	Dough was stretched or rolled incorrectly	Improve technique
Soggy crust	Wrong dough used	Use mealier dough
	Oven temperature too low	Adjust oven
	Not baked long enough	Adjust baking time
	Filling too moist	Adjust formula
Crumbly crust	Not enough liquid	Adjust formula
	Not enough fat	Adjust mixing technique
	Improper mixing	Correct technique
Tough crust	Not enough fat	Adjust formula
	Overmixing	Adjust mixing technique
Runny filling	Insufficient starch	Adjust formula
	Starch insufficiently cooked	Cook longer
Lumpy cream filling	Starch not incorporated properly	Blend starch with sugar before adding liquid; stir filling while cooking
	Filling overcooked	Adjust cooking time
Custard filling "weeps" or separates	Too many eggs	Reduce egg content or add starch to the filling
	Eggs overcooked	Reduce oven temperature or baking time

▶ PROCEDURE FOR PREPARING COOKED FRUIT FILLINGS

1 Combine the fruit, sugar and some juice or liquid in a heavy, nonreactive saucepan and bring to a boil.

2 Dissolve the starch (usually cornstarch) in a cold liquid, then add to the boiling fruit.

3 Stirring constantly, cook the fruit-and-starch mixture until the starch is clear and the mixture is thickened.

4 Add any other flavorings and any acidic ingredients such as lemon juice. Stir to blend.

5 Remove from the heat and cool before filling a prebaked pie or crumb crust.

RECIPE 10.4

APPLE-CRANBERRY PIE

Yield: 1 Pie, 9 in. (22 cm)   **Method:** Cooked fruit filling

Filling:

Fresh tart apples such as Granny Smiths, peeled, cored and cut in 1-in. (2.5-cm) cubes	1 lb.	480 g
Brown sugar	4 oz.	120 g
Granulated sugar	4 oz.	120 g
Orange zest, grated fine	0.2 oz. (1 Tbsp.)	6 g
Cinnamon, ground	0.07 oz. (1 tsp.)	2 g
Salt	0.05 oz. ($\frac{1}{4}$ tsp.)	1.5 g
Cornstarch	0.18 oz. (2 tsp.)	6 g
Orange juice	3 fl. oz.	90 ml
Fresh cranberries, rinsed	1 pt.	500 ml
Mealy dough pie shell, partially baked	1 shell	1 shell
Streusel Topping (page 113)	4 oz.	120 g

1 Combine the apples, brown sugar, granulated sugar, orange zest, cinnamon and salt in a large, nonreactive saucepan.

2 Dissolve the cornstarch in the orange juice and add it to the apples.

3 Cover and simmer until the apples begin to soften, stirring occasionally. Add the cranberries, cover and continue simmering until the cranberries just begin to soften, approximately 2 minutes.

4 Place the apple-cranberry mixture in the pie shell and cover with the prepared Streusel Topping. Bake at 400°F (200°C) until the filling is bubbling hot and the topping is lightly browned, approximately 20 minutes.

VARIATION:

Apple-Rhubarb Pie—Substitute cleaned rhubarb, cut into 1-inch (2.5-centimeter) chunks, for the cranberries. Add 0.01 ounce ($\frac{1}{8}$ teaspoon/0.3 grams) nutmeg.

Approximate values per serving: **Calories** 290, **Total fat** 8 g, **Saturated fat** 2 g, **Cholesterol** 0 mg, **Sodium** 200 mg, **Total carbohydrates** 53 g, **Protein** 2 g, **Claims**—no cholesterol; good source of fiber

Cooked Juice Fillings

The cooked juice filling method is used for soft, juicy fruits such as berries, especially when they are canned or frozen. This method is also recommended for delicate fruits that cannot withstand cooking, such as strawberries, pineapple and blueberries. Because only the juice is cooked, the fruit retains its shape, color and flavor better. A cooked juice filling should be combined with a prebaked or crumb crust.

▶ PROCEDURE FOR PREPARING COOKED JUICE FILLINGS

1 Drain the juice from the fruit. Measure the juice and add water if necessary to create the desired volume.

2 Combine the liquid with sugar in a nonreactive saucepan and bring to a boil.

3 Dissolve the starch in cold water, then add it to the boiling liquid while whisking constantly to prevent lumps from forming. Boil until the starch is clear and the juice is thickened, about 3 minutes.

4 Add any other flavoring ingredients.

5 Pour the thickened juice over the fruit and stir gently.

6 Cool the filling before placing it in a precooked pie shell.

BLUEBERRY PIE FILLING

RECIPE 10.5

Yield: 8 lb. (3.6 kg)   **Method:** Cooked juice filling

Canned blueberries, #10 can, unsweetened	1	1
Granulated sugar	1 lb. 12 oz.	840 g
Cornstarch	4.5 oz.	135 g
Water	8 fl. oz.	240 ml
Cinnamon, ground	0.04 oz (1/2 tsp.)	1 g
Lemon juice	0.5 fl. oz.	30 ml
Lemon zest, grated fine	0.2 oz. (1 Tbsp.)	6 g

1 Drain the juice from the canned blueberries, reserving both the fruit and the juice.

2 Measure the juice and, if necessary, add enough water to provide 1 quart (1 liter) of liquid. Bring to a boil, add the sugar and stir until dissolved.

3 Dissolve the cornstarch in 8 fluid ounces (240 milliliters) of water.

4 Add the cornstarch to the boiling juice and return to a boil. Cook until the mixture thickens and clears. Remove from the heat.

5 Add the cinnamon, lemon juice, lemon zest and reserved blueberries. Stir gently to coat the fruit with the glaze.

6 Allow the filling to cool to room temperature, then use it to fill prebaked pie shells or other pastry items.

Approximate values per 1-oz. (30-g) serving: **Calories** 40, **Total fat** 0 g, **Saturated fat** 0 g, **Cholesterol** 0 mg, **Sodium** 0 mg, **Total carbohydrates** 10 g, **Protein** 0 g, **Claims**—fat free; no cholesterol; no sodium; low calorie

Baked Fruit Fillings

The baked fruit filling method is a traditional technique in which the fruit, sugar, flavorings and flour or starch are combined in an unbaked shell. The dough and filling are then baked simultaneously. Results are not always consistent with this technique, however, as thickening is difficult to control.

▶ PROCEDURE FOR PREPARING BAKED FRUIT FILLINGS

1 Combine the flour or starch, spices and sugar.

2 Peel, core, cut and drain the fruit as desired or as directed in the recipe.

3 Toss the fruit with the starch mixture, coating well.

4 Add a portion of juice to moisten the fruit. Small lumps of butter are also often added.

5 Fill an unbaked shell with the fruit mixture to just below the rim. Take care not to spill filling on the edge of the pie shell. This can prevent the top crust from sealing properly. Cover with a top crust, lattice or streusel and bake.

RECIPE 10.6

CHERRY PIE

Dotting the cherry filling with butter.

Yield: 2 Pies, 9 in. (22 cm) each, approximately 4 lb. (1920 g) Filling

Method: Baked fruit filling

Filling:

Tapioca	1.5 oz.	45 g
Salt	0.03 oz. (pinch)	0.75 g
Granulated sugar	1 lb.	480 g
Almond extract	0.08 fl. oz. (½ tsp.)	2.5 ml
Canned pitted cherries, drained, liquid reserved	3 lb.	1440 g
Mealy dough pie shells, unbaked	2 shells	2 shells
Unsalted butter	1 oz.	30 g
Egg wash	as needed	as needed
Sanding sugar	as needed	as needed

1 Stir the tapioca, salt and granulated sugar together. Add the almond extract and cherries.

2 Stir in up to 8 fluid ounces (240 milliliters) of the liquid drained from the cherries, adding enough liquid to moisten the mixture thoroughly.

3 Allow the filling to stand 30 minutes. Then stir gently and place the filling in the unbaked pie shells.

4 Cut the butter into small pieces. Dot the filling with the butter.

5 Place a top crust or a lattice crust over the filling; seal and flute the edges. If using a full top crust, cut several slits in the dough to allow steam to escape. Brush the top crust or lattice with egg wash and sprinkle with sanding sugar.

6 Place on a preheated sheet pan and bake at 400°F (200°C) 50 to 60 minutes.

Approximate values per ⅛-pie serving: **Calories** 340, **Total fat** 9 g, **Saturated fat** 3 g, **Cholesterol** 5 mg, **Sodium** 170 mg, **Total carbohydrates** 63 g, **Protein** 2 g

CUSTARD FILLINGS

A custard pie has a soft filling that bakes along with the crust. Popular examples include pumpkin, egg custard and pecan pies. As explained in Chapter 15, Custards and Creams, custards are liquids thickened by coagulated egg proteins. To make a custard pie, an uncooked liquid containing eggs is poured into a pie shell. When baked, the egg proteins coagulate, firming and setting the filling.

The procedure for making custard pies is simple: combine the ingredients and bake. But there is often a problem: baking the bottom crust completely without overcooking the filling. For the best results, start baking the pie near the bottom of a hot oven at 400°F (200°C). After 10 minutes, reduce the heat to 325°F–350°F (160°C–180°C) to finish cooking the filling slowly.

To determine the doneness of a custard pie:

1 Shake the pie gently. It is done if it is no longer liquid. The center should show only a slight movement.

2 Insert a thin knife about 1 inch (2.5 centimeters) from the center. The filling is done if the knife comes out clean.

PUMPKIN PIE

Yield: 4 Pies, 9 in. (22 cm) each, approximately 4 lb. 10 oz. (2220 g) Filling

Method: Custard filling

Filling:

Eggs, beaten slightly	6.75 oz. (4 eggs)	200 g
Pumpkin purée	2 lb.	960 g
Granulated sugar	12 oz.	360 g
Salt	0.2 oz. (1 tsp.)	6 g
Nutmeg, ground	0.04 oz. (½ tsp.)	1 g
Cloves, ground	0.04 oz. (½ tsp.)	1 g
Cinnamon, ground	0.14 oz. (2 tsp.)	4 g
Ginger, ground	0.07 oz. (1 tsp.)	2 g
Evaporated milk	24 fl. oz.	720 ml
Flaky dough pie shells, unbaked	4	4

1 Combine the eggs and pumpkin. Blend in the sugar.

2 Add the salt and spices, and then the evaporated milk. Whisk until completely blended and smooth.

3 Allow the filling to rest 15 to 20 minutes before filling the pie shells. This allows the starch in the pumpkin to begin absorbing liquid, making it less likely to separate after baking.

4 Pour the filling into the unbaked pie shells. Place in the oven on a preheated sheet pan at 400°F (200°C). Bake 15 minutes. Lower the oven temperature to 350°F (180°C) and bake until a knife inserted near the center comes out clean, approximately 40 to 50 minutes.

Approximate values per ⅛-pie serving: **Calories** 210, **Total fat** 10 g, **Saturated fat** 2.5 g, **Cholesterol** 30 mg, **Sodium** 230 mg, **Total carbohydrates** 25 g, **Protein** 4 g, **Vitamin A** 6%

CHIFFON FILLINGS

A chiffon filling is created by adding gelatin to a stirred custard or a fruit purée. Whipped egg whites are then folded into the mixture. The filling is placed in a prebaked crust and chilled until firm. These preparations are the same as those for chiffons, mousses and Bavarians discussed in Chapter 15, Custards and Creams. Any of the chiffons, mousses or Bavarians can be used as a pie filling in a prebaked crust.

ASSEMBLING PIES AND TARTS

The various types of pie fillings can be used to fill almost any crust or shell provided the crust is prebaked as necessary. The filling can then be topped with meringue or whipped cream as desired. Garnishes such as toasted coconut, cookie crumbs and chocolate curls are often added for appearance and flavor. Brushing the inside of a baked-blind tart shell with melted chocolate or a complementary jam adds extra flavor. A thin layer of absorbent spongecake soaked with flavored simple syrup may be placed in the bottom of a baked tart shell to prevent the baked crust from softening. The sponge can then be topped with a cream filling and fruit topping. Table 10.3 offers some suggestions for pie and tart filling and topping combinations.

Table 10.3   SUGGESTIONS FOR ASSEMBLING PIES

FILLING	CRUST	TOPPING	GARNISH
Vanilla or lemon cream	Prebaked flaky dough or crumb	None, meringue or whipped cream	Crumbs from the crust
Chocolate cream	Prebaked flaky dough or crumb	None, meringue or whipped cream	Crumbs from the crust or shaved chocolate
Banana cream	Prebaked flaky dough	Meringue or whipped cream	Dried banana chips
Coconut cream	Prebaked flaky dough	Meringue or whipped cream	Shredded coconut
Fresh fruit	Unbaked mealy dough, or sweet dough if shallow tart	Lattice, full crust or streusel	Sanding sugar or cut-out designs if lattice or top crust is used
Canned or frozen fruit	Unbaked mealy dough	Lattice, full crust or streusel	Sanding sugar or cut-out designs if lattice or top crust is used
Chiffon or mousse	Crumb or prebaked, sweetened flaky dough	None or whipped cream	Crumbs, fruit or shaved chocolate
Custard	Unbaked mealy dough	None	Whipped cream, cinnamon
Vanilla pastry cream	Prebaked sweet dough	Fresh fruit	Glaze
Lemon or citrus curd	Prebaked sweet dough	Fresh fruit, berries	Glaze, Italian meringue

▶ PROCEDURE FOR ASSEMBLING A TART

1 Line tart shells with prepared sweet dough. Bake blind and cool completely.

2 Prepare pastry cream, curd or other filling. Pour filling into prepared crust.

3 Refrigerate or freeze filled tart shells until filling is set.

4 Arrange fresh fruit decoratively over filled tart shell.

5 Warm tart glaze according to manufacturer's directions. Brush over the surface of the fresh fruit. Small tartlets may be placed on an icing screen set over a sheet pan. Ladle warm glaze over the tartlets. Excess glaze captured by the pan may be reheated and reused.

FRESH BERRY TART

Yield: 1 Tart, 9 in. (22 cm)

Sweet Tart Dough (page 249), 9-in. (22-cm) tart shell, fully baked	1 shell	1 shell
Pastry Cream (page 436)	1 pt.	0.5 lt
Fresh berries such as strawberries, blackberries, blueberries or raspberries	3 pt.	1.5 lt
Apricot glaze	as needed	as needed

1 Fill the cool tart shell with Pastry Cream.

2 Arrange the berries over the Pastry Cream in an even layer. Be sure to place the berries so that the Pastry Cream is covered.

3 Heat the apricot glaze and brush over the fruit to form a smooth coating.

Approximate values per ⅙-tart serving: **Calories** 135, **Total fat** 3 g, **Saturated fat** 1 g, **Cholesterol** 2 mg, **Sodium** 62 mg, **Total carbohydrates** 26 g, **Protein** 2 g

TART GLAZE (MIRROR GLAZE)

Tart glaze is a shiny coating applied to tarts, mousse-filled tortes and small pastries. It is spooned over the surface of the product. Once chilled, the product has a mirrorlike smooth surface that protects and enhances the pastry's appearance. Tart glaze may be made with gelatin, simple syrup and flavorings or from a prepared **neutral glaze.** It should flow easily but not be so thin that it would drip off a tart. To test the glaze, pour a few tablespoons of it on a small plate and refrigerate. Check in 5 minutes. It should set without being rubbery. Neutral glaze may be flavored with fruit juice, fruit purée, coffee or another liquid. Use about 40 percent liquid to 60 percent glaze. Fruit preserves may be melted for tart glaze but are not as stable. A recipe for a gelatin-based glaze is included here.

Neutral Glaze

▶ PROCEDURE FOR PREPARING TART GLAZE

1 Heat a simple syrup to 120°F (49°C). Soften or bloom and melt the gelatin.

2 Add gelatin and fruit juice, coffee or other flavorings to the warm syrup. Stir to dissolve.

3 Cool glaze to 70°F (21°C) and apply to product.

TART GLAZE

Yield: Glaze for 4 7-in. (17-cm) tarts

Simple Syrup (page 349)	8 fl. oz.	240 ml
Sheet gelatin, softened	0.3 oz.	9 g
Fruit juice, purée or other flavoring	4 fl. oz.	120 ml

1 Heat the Simple Syrup to 120°F (49°C). Add the softened sheet gelatin to the heated syrup. Stir until dissolved.

2 Add the fruit juice, purée or other liquid. Stir, then cool to 70°F (21°C) before using.

Note: Certain fresh fruits—fig, kiwi, lemon, lime, orange, papaya, pineapple, passion fruit and guava—contain enzymes that prevent gelatin from setting. Boiling the fruit juice or purée before using destroys this enzyme.

Approximate values per ½-fl.-oz. (15-ml) serving: **Calories** 25, **Total fat** 0 g, **Saturated fat** 0 g, **Cholesterol** 0 mg, **Sodium** 5 mg, **Total carbohydrates** 4 g, **Protein** 3 g

CONVENIENCE PRODUCTS

Preformed pie and tart shells in disposable pans are available in a range of sizes and styles, ready to be filled and baked as needed. These are frozen products that, once thawed, must be filled and baked with the same care that scratch pies and tarts require. Deep-dish and double-crust styles are offered as well as products made with pure butter or all-vegetable shortening. The texture of these crusts once baked may be flaky or mealy; manufacturer's specifications indicate the style of the final product. Fully baked ready-to-use pie and tart shells are also available. Most are made with hydrogenated shortenings, though some European manufacturers offer products made with pure butter. These prebaked products have a long shelf life when stored in cool, dry conditions. Once filled, however, they require refrigeration and can become soggy. Like a freshly made tart, these prepared products should be served within 1 or 2 days of preparation.

Prepared or canned pie fillings are available in a variety of fruit and custard flavors. These products offer convenience, consistency and the ability to serve fruit pies out of season. The ratio of fruit to pregelled liquid varies greatly from brand to brand, however. Most commercial fillings are stabilized to permit additional baking that may be needed to assemble the final product. Shelf life tends to be extremely long, often without the need for refrigeration. Dry custard mixes are also available, needing only the addition of water or milk to produce a cream pie filling.

STORING PIES AND TARTS

Pies and tarts filled with cream or custard must be kept refrigerated to retard bacterial growth. Unbaked fruit pies or unbaked pie shells may be frozen up to 2 months. Freezing baked fruit pies is not recommended, but they may be stored 2 to 3 days in the refrigerator. Custard, cream and meringue-topped pies should be stored in the refrigerator no more than 2 to 3 days. They should not be frozen, as the eggs will separate, making the product runny.

CONCLUSION

Pastry making is the backbone of dessert preparation. A wide variety of pastry doughs for pies and tarts can be prepared from simple ingredients—flour, fat and a liquid. Proper mixing, rolling and shaping techniques are crucial to the success of the finished product, however. These doughs can then be filled with numerous pie and tart fillings. Regardless of flavor, most fillings are prepared by properly following a few basic techniques, such as cream fillings, baked custards and cooked or baked fruit. With a selection of properly prepared pie and tart doughs and fillings, you can prepare an endless variety of tempting desserts.

QUESTIONS FOR DISCUSSION

1 How does the type of pie filling influence the selection of a pie crust? What type of crust would be best for a pie made with fresh, uncooked fruit? Explain your answer.
2 Why doesn't sweet tart dough (which contains a high ratio of butter) produce a flaky crust?
3 Explain the difference between a cream pie filling and a custard pie filling. Give two examples of each type of filling.
4 List and describe three ways of preparing fruit fillings for pies.
5 Plan a dessert buffet where four different fruit tarts will be offered. List the combination of fillings and toppings to be used. Describe the fruits you will use and how they will be sourced if they are out of season.

Several of the formulas given in the following pages are combinations of the pies and tarts presented in this chapter and the creams, custards and other dessert products covered in other chapters. For example, the Lemon Curd Tart is made with the Coconut Almond Tart Dough discussed in this chapter, plus the Italian Meringue discussed in Chapter 11, Pastry Doughs, and the Lemon Curd discussed in Chapter 15, Custards and Creams. As a student, your first goal should be to learn to prepare a variety of pastry components. You can then combine and assemble them appropriately into both classic and modern desserts.

CHOCOLATE TART WITH FRESH BERRIES

RECIPE 10.10

Note: This dish appears in the chapter opening photograph.

HOUSTON COMMUNITY COLLEGE, HOUSTON, TX
Pastry Chef Eddy Van Damme

Yield: 2 Tarts, 8 in. (20 cm) each

Shortbread Tart Dough (page 266), made with hazelnut flour	20 oz.	600 g
Egg wash	as needed	as needed
Flourless Chocolate Spongecake (recipe follows), 7 inch (17 centimeter)	2 rounds	2 rounds
Raspberry Ganache (recipe follows)	1 lb. 7 oz.	690 g
Fresh raspberries and strawberries	4–5 pt.	2–2.4 lt
Neutral glaze	1 oz.	30 g

1 Roll out the hazelnut Shortbread Tart Dough to a thickness of ⅛ inch (3 millimeters) and line two 8-inch (20-centimeter) tart rings or pans with it, gently pressing the dough into place.

2 Place paper and pie weights in the shells. Bake at 375°F (190°C) until the edges are lightly golden, approximately 8 minutes. Remove the paper and weights from the shells, brush them with egg wash and bake until golden brown, approximately 12 to 15 minutes. Set aside to cool.

3 Place a 7-inch (17-centimeter) round of Flourless Chocolate Spongecake in the bottom of each cooled tart shell.

4 Using a ladle, fill each tart to the rim with Raspberry Ganache. Refrigerate until set.

5 Cover the entire surface of the tart with fresh berries.

6 Place the neutral glaze in a parchment paper piping and pipe a drop of glaze on each berry to resemble dew drops.

Approximate values per ⅛-tart serving: **Calories** 420, **Total fat** 24 g, **Saturated fat** 13 g, **Cholesterol** 145 mg, **Sodium** 95 mg, **Total carbohydrates** 50 g, **Protein** 6 g, **Vitamin A** 15%, **Vitamin C** 70%, **Iron** 15%

PASTRY CHEF EDDY VAN DAMME
HOUSTON COMMUNITY COLLEGE, HOUSTON, TX

A native of Belgium, Chef Eddy Van Damme knew that his future lay in the pastry shop by the time he was only 7 years old. Inspired by his mother and an uncle, he began baking at home, making cookies, cakes and even éclairs by age 10. He started working weekends in a pastry shop at age 12, where he learned many of the skills that must become second nature to any successful pâtissier. Chef Van Damme has also worked at Bundervoent, one of the finest pastry shops in Belgium; attended pastry school at Piva in Antwerp, Belgium; and has taken many courses at the LeNôtre and Cacao Barry schools in Paris.

When Chef Van Damme moved to the United States in the 1980s, he headed straight for Houston, Texas. He has been in charge of the pastry program at Houston Community College for more than 12 years. His awards include five American Culinary Federation (ACF) gold medals in pastry competitions, Best of Show at the 10th Annual Culinary Classic in Louisiana and the Chancellor's Medallion for teaching excellence. He is co-author of this text.

FLOURLESS CHOCOLATE SPONGECAKE

Yield: 3 Rounds, 7 in. (17 cm) each   **Sugar at 100%**

Egg whites	6 oz. (6 whites)	180 g	92%
Granulated sugar	6.5 oz.	195 g	100%
Egg yolks	4 oz. (6 yolks)	120 g	61%
Vanilla extract	0.15 fl. oz. (1 tsp.)	5 ml	2%
Cocoa powder, sifted	2 oz.	60 g	30%
Total batter weight:	1 lb. 3 oz.	560 g	285%

1 In the bowl of a mixer fitted with a whip, beat the egg whites to soft peaks. Add the sugar and continue whipping to stiff peaks.

2 In a separate bowl, whip the egg yolks to a thick ribbon.

3 When both mixtures have reached the proper consistency, add one-third of the whipped yolks to the egg whites, folding them together using a balloon whisk. Heavy streaks may remain in the batter.

4 Add the remaining egg yolks and gently fold together. Some streaks may remain in the batter.

5 Add the vanilla and cocoa powder and gently fold together until no streaks remain in the batter.

6 Using a piping bag fitted with a large plain tip, pipe the batter onto parchment-lined sheet pans in a tight spiral pattern in order to form three 7-inch- (17-centimeter-) diameter rounds.

7 Bake at 350°F (180°C) until the cake springs back when gently touched, approximately 25 minutes. Cool completely. Any unneeded cake rounds can be wrapped tightly in plastic wrap and frozen for later use.

Approximate values per round: **Calories** 470, **Total fat** 16 g, **Saturated fat** 6 g, **Cholesterol** 545 mg, **Sodium** 115 mg, **Total carbohydrates** 73 g, **Protein** 17 g, **Vitamin A** 15%, **Iron** 25%

RASPBERRY GANACHE

Most ganache formulas call for heavy cream. Raspberry purée takes on the role of the heavy cream in this ganache. The tartness of the fresh berries balances the richness of the chocolate, an intense complement to the buttery crust and fresh fruit topping in this tart.

Yield: 1 lb. 7 oz. (675 g)

Semisweet chocolate	9 oz.	270 g
Raspberry purée, unsweetened, seedless	10 fl. oz.	300 g
Pectin	0.05 oz. (½ tsp.)	0.5 g
Granulated sugar	1.5 oz.	45 g
Unsalted butter, melted	2 oz.	60 g

1 Chop the chocolate into pea-size bits, place in a bowl and set aside.

2 Heat the raspberry purée to 120°F (49°C) in a nonreactive pan.

3 Thoroughly mix the pectin and sugar. Whisk it into the raspberry purée and bring to a boil.

4 Pour approximately 2 fluid ounces (60 milliliters) of the hot purée into the bowl of chocolate. Combine with a spatula, adding the remaining purée in four increments.

5 Stir in the butter. If lumps form or if the chocolate fails to melt completely, place the bowl over a bain marie until completely melted and smooth. Use immediately.

Approximate values per 1-oz. (30-mg) serving: **Calories** 80, **Total fat** 5 g, **Saturated fat** 3 g, **Cholesterol** 5 mg, **Sodium** 0 mg, **Total carbohydrates** 10 g, **Protein** 1 g

PURPLE FIG TART WITH MINTED CHEESE MOUSSE

RECIPE 10.11

Note: This dish appears in the chapter opening photograph.

HOUSTON COMMUNITY COLLEGE, HOUSTON, TX
Pastry Chef Eddy Van Damme

Yield: 12 Tarts, 2½ in. (7.5 cm) each

Shortbread Tart Dough (page 266),		
made with almond flour	24 oz.	720 g
Egg wash	as needed	as needed
Minted Cheese Mousse		
(recipe follows)	1 lb. 10 oz.	780 g
Fresh purple figs	30	30
Neutral glaze	2.5 oz.	75 g
Orange juice	1.5 fl. oz.	45 ml

1 Roll out the almond Shortbread Tart Dough to a thickness of ⅛ inch (3 millimeters). Using a round cutter, cut circles slightly wider than the tart pans. Line the tart pans with the dough, gently pressing the dough into place.

2 Place paper and pie weights in the shells and bake at 375°F (190°C) until the edges of the tarts are lightly golden, approximately 6 minutes. Remove the paper and weights from the shells, brush the shells with egg wash and bake until golden brown, approximately 12 to 15 minutes.

3 Using a pastry bag fitted with a medium plain tip, pipe the Minted Cheese Mousse into the tart shells. Chill until the filling has set.

4 Slice the figs in half and arrange in pyramid style on the tarts.

5 Combine the neutral glaze with the orange juice and brush the fruit with the glaze.

Approximate values per tart: **Calories** 440, **Total fat** 27 g, **Saturated fat** 16 g, **Cholesterol** 110 mg, **Sodium** 140 mg, **Total carbohydrates** 50 g, **Protein** 5 g, **Vitamin A** 25%

MINTED CHEESE MOUSSE

Yield: 1 lb. 10 oz. (795 g)

Cream cheese or mascarpone	10 oz.	300 g
Granulated sugar	4 oz.	120 g
Water	2 fl. oz.	60 ml
Mint compound (or 20 mint leaves)	0.5 fl. oz.	15 ml
Heavy cream	10 fl. oz.	300 ml

1 Cut the cream cheese into medium cubes, place in a bowl and soften in a microwave oven until the cheese is 90°F (32°C).

2 Boil the sugar and water for 1 minute. Remove from the heat and cool, then use a spatula to incorporate into the softened cheese.

3 Whip the mint compound and cream to soft peaks. (Or cut the mint leaves into fine strips, add to the cream and whip to soft peaks.) Fold the cream into the cheese mixture and use immediately.

Approximate values per 1-oz. (30-g) serving: **Calories** 110, **Total fat** 9 g, **Saturated fat** 5 g, **Cholesterol** 70 mg, **Sodium** 10 mg, **Total carbohydrates** 5 g, **Protein** 2 g

RECIPE 10.12   **SHORTBREAD TART DOUGH**

HOUSTON COMMUNITY COLLEGE, HOUSTON, TX
Pastry Chef Eddy Van Damme

Yield: 7 Tart Shells, 8 in. (20 cm) each,
or 46 Tartlet Shells, 2½ in. (7.5 cm) each

Egg yolks, hard-boiled	5 oz. (8 yolks)	150 g	19%
Unsalted butter, softened	1 lb. 8 oz.	720 g	92%
Powdered sugar	11 oz.	330 g	42%
Vanilla extract	0.5 fl. oz.	15 ml	2%
Salt	0.3 oz. (1½ tsp.)	9 g	1.2%
Almond or hazelnut flour	4.5 oz.	135 g	17%
Pastry flour	1 lb. 10 oz.	780 g	100%
Total dough weight:	4 lb. 7 oz.	2139 g	273%

1 Press the egg yolks through a sieve using a plastic pastry scraper. Set aside.
2 In the bowl of a mixer fitted with a paddle, cream the butter. Add the powdered sugar, combining well.
3 Add the vanilla, salt and nut flour, then the sieved egg yolks, and mix until combined.
4 Add the pastry flour and mix on low speed just until combined. Do not overmix.
5 Wrap the dough in plastic and chill several hours or overnight.
6 When ready to use, roll out the chilled dough on a lightly floured board. The dough may be crumbly and difficult to work with, which is normal. Simply press the dough back together with your fingertips.

Approximate values per 2-oz. (60-g) serving: **Calories** 227, **Total fat** 19 g, **Saturated fat** 10 g, **Cholesterol** 93 mg, **Sodium** 103 mg, **Total carbohydrates** 25 g, **Protein** 4 g

RECIPE 10.13   **SWEET ALMOND TART DOUGH**

Yield: 6 Tarts, 8 in. (20 cm) each,
or 42 Tartlets, 2½ in. (7.5 cm) each

Unsalted butter, softened	1 lb.	480 g	59%
Powdered sugar	10 oz.	300 g	37%
Eggs	5 oz. (3 eggs)	150 g	19%
Salt	0.4 oz. (2 tsp.)	12 g	1.5%
Vanilla extract	0.5 fl. oz.	15 ml	2%
Almond flour	4 oz.	120 g	15%
Pastry flour	1 lb. 11 oz.	810 g	100%
Total dough weight:	3 lb. 15 oz.	1887 g	234%

1 In the bowl of a mixer fitted with a paddle, cream the butter. Add the powdered sugar and combine well. Scrape down the bowl.
2 Add the eggs a small amount at a time, then add the salt, vanilla and almond flour and mix until combined.
3 Add the pastry flour and mix on low speed just until combined. Do not overmix.
4 Wrap the dough in plastic and chill several hours or overnight.

VARIATION:

Coconut Almond Tart Dough—Reduce the powdered sugar to 7 ounces (210 grams/26%). Reduce the eggs to 2.5 ounces (75 grams/9%). Reduce the salt to 0.2 oz. (1 teaspoon/6 grams/0.8%). Reduce the pastry flour to 1 pound 2 ounces (510 grams/66%) and add 7 ounces (210 grams/26%) desiccated coconut, macaroon type, with the flour.

Approximate values per 1½-oz. (45-g) serving: **Calories** 180, **Total fat** 11 g, **Saturated fat** 6 g, **Cholesterol** 35 mg, **Sodium** 115 mg, **Total carbohydrates** 21 g, **Protein** 3 g

---

QUICHE DOUGH

RECIPE 10.14

▶ **quiche** a savory tart filled with custard and other ingredients such as cheese, ham and vegetables

Yield: 8 lb. (3840 g) dough, approximately
6 shells, 9 in. (22 cm) each

All-purpose flour	4 lb. 7 oz.	2130 g	100%
Salt	1.5 oz.	45 g	2%
Unsalted butter, cold	2 lb. 4 oz.	1065 g	50%
Eggs	1 lb. 4 oz. (12 eggs)	600 g	28%
Total dough weight:	8 lb.	3840 g	180%

1 Combine the flour and salt in the bowl of a mixer fitted with a paddle. Cut in the butter until the mixture looks like coarse cornmeal.

2 Whisk the eggs together to blend, then add them slowly to the dry ingredients. Blend only until the dough comes together in a ball.

3 Remove from the mixer, cover and chill until ready to use.

Approximate values per 1-oz. (30-g) serving: **Calories** 120, **Total fat** 7 g, **Saturated fat** 4 g, **Cholesterol** 35 mg, **Sodium** 140 mg, **Total carbohydrates** 12 g, **Protein** 2 g

RECIPE 10.15   **LEMON MERINGUE PIE**

Yield: 2 Pies, 9 in. (22 cm) each, approximately 4 lb. (1890 g) Filling

Method: Cream filling

Filling:

Granulated sugar	1 lb. 4 oz.	600 g
Cornstarch	3 oz.	90 g
Salt	pinch	pinch
Water, cold	24 fl. oz.	720 ml
Egg yolks	6.6 oz. (10 yolks)	200 g
Lemon juice, fresh	8 fl. oz.	240 ml
Lemon zest, grated	0.4 oz. (2 Tbsp.)	12 g
Unsalted butter	1 oz.	30 g
Flaky dough pie shells, baked	2 shells	2 shells
Egg whites	8 oz. (8 whites)	240 g
Granulated sugar	8 oz.	240 g

1 To make the filling, combine 1 pound 4 ounces (600 grams) sugar with the cornstarch, salt and water in a heavy saucepan. Cook over medium-high heat, stirring constantly, until the mixture becomes thick and almost clear.

2 Remove from the heat and slowly whisk in the egg yolks. Stir until completely blended. Return to the heat and cook, stirring constantly, until thick and smooth.

3 Stir in the lemon juice and zest. When the liquid is completely incorporated, remove the filling from the heat. Add the butter and stir until melted.

4 Set the filling aside to cool briefly. Fill the pie shells with the lemon filling.

5 To prepare the meringue, whip the egg whites until soft peaks form. Slowly add 8 ounces (240 grams) sugar while whisking constantly. The meringue should be stiff and glossy, not dry or spongy-looking.

6 Mound the meringue over the filling, creating decorative patterns with a spatula. Be sure to spread the meringue to the edge of the crust so that all of the filling is covered with the meringue.

7 Place the pies in a 400°F (200°C) oven until the meringue is golden brown, approximately 5 to 8 minutes. Let cool at room temperature, then refrigerate. Serve the same day.

Approximate values per ⅛-pie serving: **Calories** 400, **Total fat** 12 g, **Saturated fat** 4 g, **Cholesterol** 135 mg, **Sodium** 310 mg, **Total carbohydrates** 67 g, **Protein** 5 g, **Vitamin C** 10%

FRESH STRAWBERRY PIE

Yield: 2 Pies, 9 in. (22 cm) each   **Method:** Cooked juice

Filling:

Granulated sugar	1 lb. 7 oz.	690 g
Water	8 fl. oz.	240 ml
Cornstarch	2.5 oz.	75 g
Water, cold	12 fl. oz.	360 ml
Salt	0.1 oz. (½ tsp.)	3 g
Lemon juice	2 fl. oz.	60 ml
Red food coloring	as needed	as needed
Fresh strawberries, rinsed and sliced in half	2 qt.	2 lt
Flaky dough pie shells, baked	2 shells	2 shells
Crème Chantilly (page 445)	as needed	as needed

1 Bring the sugar and 8 fluid ounces (240 milliliters) of water to a boil.

2 Dissolve the cornstarch in the cold water and add to the boiling liquid. Cook over low heat until clear, approximately 5 minutes.

3 Stir in the salt, lemon juice and enough red food coloring to produce a bright red color.

4 Pour this glaze over the strawberries and toss gently to coat them. Spoon the filling into the prepared pie shells. Chill thoroughly and top with Crème Chantilly for service.

Approximate values per ⅛-pie serving: **Calories** 330, **Total fat** 8 g, **Saturated fat** 2 g, **Cholesterol** 0 mg, **Sodium** 200 mg, **Total carbohydrates** 63 g, **Protein** 2 g, **Vitamin C** 80%

VARIATION:

Fresh Strawberry Pie with Granola Crunch Topping—Sprinkle Granola Crunch Topping (recipe follows) on the whipped cream after garnishing the pie.

GRANOLA CRUNCH TOPPING

Yield: 11 oz. (347 g)

Sliced almonds	3 oz.	90 g
Oats, old-fashioned rolled	2 oz.	60 g
Sesame seeds	1 oz.	30 g
Maple syrup	2 fl. oz.	60 ml
Salt	pinch	pinch
Vanilla extract	0.15 fl. oz. (1 tsp.)	5 ml
Orange zest, grated fine	0.4 oz. (2 tsp.)	12 g
Dried cranberries	3 oz.	90 g

1 Combine the almonds, oats, sesame seeds, maple syrup, salt, vanilla and orange zest.

2 Place on a paper-lined sheet pan and toast in a 375°F (190°C) oven until golden, about 18 to 20 minutes.

3 Cool, then toss in the cranberries. Use as a topping on cream cakes, fruit pies and mousses. Store tightly covered. Will keep 1 week at room temperature.

Approximate values per 1-oz. (30-g) serving: **Calories** 130, **Total fat** 7 g, **Saturated fat** 0.5 g, **Cholesterol** 0 mg, **Sodium** 5 mg, **Total carbohydrates** 16 g, **Protein** 3 g

RECIPE 10.18

FREEFORM APPLE PIES

CONNECTICUT CULINARY INSTITUTE, FARMINGTON, CT
Chef Jamie Roraback

Yield: 4 Pies, 6 in. (15 cm) each   **Method:** Baked fruit

Dough:

Unsalted butter	8 oz.	240 g	100%
All-purpose flour	8 oz.	240 g	100%
Salt	0.2 oz. (1 tsp.)	6 g	2.5%
Water, ice cold	3 fl. oz.	90 ml	37.5%
Total dough weight:	1 lb. 3 oz.	576 g	240%

Filling:

Apples, peeled, cored, large dice	1 lb.	480 g
Unsalted butter	1 oz.	30 g
Granulated sugar	2 oz.	60 g
Cinnamon, ground	0.02 oz. (¼ tsp.)	0.5 g
Vanilla extract	0.5 fl. oz.	15 ml
Apple brandy	2 fl. oz.	60 ml

Egg wash:

Egg	1.6 oz. (1 egg)	50 g
Milk	1 fl. oz.	30 ml
Sanding sugar	as needed	as needed

1 To prepare the dough, cut the butter into medium dice and place it in the freezer 5 minutes. Sift the flour with the salt. Toss the butter with the flour and salt, then place the mixture in the bowl of a food processor. Pulse until the butter chunks are the size of very small peas. Then, in a continuous stream, drizzle in the ice water and pulse just until the dough barely comes together. Do not overmix.

2 Turn the dough out onto a work surface. Knead it gently and quickly. Divide the dough into four small rounds. Place the rounds on a sheet pan, cover them with plastic wrap and refrigerate approximately 20 minutes before rolling out.

3 To prepare the filling, heat a sauté pan over high heat, add the apples and let them brown slightly. Add the butter and let it melt so that it loosens and frees the apples from the bottom of the pan. Then cook approximately 1 minute, add the sugar and let it brown, stirring occasionally. Add the cinnamon and vanilla. Remove from the heat, add the apple brandy, return to the heat and **flambé.** Cool the filling before assembling the pies.

4 Prepare the egg wash by whipping the egg together with the milk.

5 On a floured surface, roll out each round of dough into a circle approximately 8 inches (20 centimeters) wide. Place an appropriate-size plate or other circular object on top of the rolled-out dough and cut out a circle.

6 Place one-quarter of the apple filling in the center of each dough round, leaving exposed 1½ inches (3.7 centimeters) of dough along the edges. Fold this border over the filling in approximately five or six folds, each fold slightly overlapping the previous one. Place the pies on a sheet pan and, using a pastry brush, glaze each pie (dough only) with egg wash. Sprinkle sanding sugar over the pies after glazing.

7 Place the pies in the freezer until frozen. (Freezing will help prevent the butter running from the high-butter-content crust during baking.)

8 Preheat the oven to 400°F (200°C). While the pies are baking, rotate them occasionally. Bake until the apples are tender and the crust is evenly browned, approximately 20 minutes. Serve at room temperature, dusted with powdered sugar and accompanied by whipped cream or ice cream.

▶ **flambé** (flahm-BAY) to ignite brandy, rum or other liqueur added to food in order to remove the alcohol while retaining the taste of the spirits

Approximate values per ½-pie serving: **Calories** 420, **Total fat** 27 g, **Saturated fat** 16 g, **Cholesterol** 95 mg, **Sodium** 300 mg, **Total carbohydrates** 36 g, **Protein** 4 g, **Vitamin A** 20%

OLD NEW ENGLAND FRIED APPLE PIE

14 LINCOLN STREET BED AND BREAKFAST, NIANTIC, CT

Chef-Owner Cheryl Jean

Fried pies were created long ago to serve a practical purpose. Foods were chiefly eaten with the fingers. Therefore, the most popular dishes were those most easily handled—ones wrapped in dough.

Yield: 12 Pastries, 5 in. (12.5 cm) each

Filling:

Unsalted butter	1 oz.	30 g
Apples, peeled, cored and diced	2 lb.	960 g
Cinnamon, ground	0.07 oz. (1 tsp.)	2 g
Nutmeg, ground	0.02 oz. (¼ tsp.)	0.5 g
Granulated sugar	1.5 oz.	45 g
Light brown sugar	2 oz.	60 g
Water	12 fl. oz.	360 ml
Lemon juice	0.15 fl. oz. (1 tsp.)	5 ml
Cornstarch	0.3 oz. (1 Tbsp.)	9 g
Vanilla extract	0.15 fl. oz. (1 tsp.)	5 ml

Dough:

All-purpose flour	8 oz.	240 g	100%
Granulated sugar	1 oz.	30 g	12.5%
Salt	0.3 oz. (1½ tsp.)	9 g	4%
Baking powder	0.04 oz. (¼ tsp.)	1 g	0.05%
Vegetable shortening, chilled	3 oz.	90 g	37.5%
Egg, cold	1.6 oz. (1 egg)	50 g	2%
Whole milk	6 fl. oz.	180 ml	75%
Total dough weight:	1 lb. 3 oz.	600 g	231%
Vegetable oil for frying	as needed	as needed	
Powdered sugar	as needed	as needed	

1 Melt the butter in a heavy saucepan, add the apples and sauté 2 minutes.

2 Stir in the cinnamon, nutmeg and sugars. Sauté 1 more minute, stirring constantly. Add the water and lemon juice and bring to a boil.

3 Dissolve the cornstarch in 0.5 fluid ounces (15 milliliters) cold water and add to the apples with the vanilla. Reduce the heat and simmer the mixture until the apples are soft, approximately 15 to 20 minutes.

4 Remove filling from heat and cool completely.

5 Prepare the dough while the filling is cooling. Sift the flour, sugar, salt and baking powder in a large bowl. Cut in the shortening, breaking into small particles with your fingers until the mixture resembles cornmeal.

6 Beat the egg and milk in a small bowl. Add the egg mixture to the flour gradually, stirring with a fork until the dough clumps together.

7 Divide the dough into 12 equal portions. On a lightly floured surface, roll each piece into a thin round about 5 inches (12.5 centimeters) in diameter. Put 2 ounces (60 grams) of the cool apple mixture in the center of each round. Fold over and crimp the edges with a fork.

8 Fry the pies in deep fat heated to 375°F (191°C), two or three at a time, turning once or twice, until golden brown. Remove from oil and drain on paper towels. Generously sprinkle with powdered sugar.

Approximate values per serving: **Calories** 360, **Total fat** 23 g, **Saturated fat** 5 g, **Cholesterol** 25 mg, **Sodium** 250 mg, **Total carbohydrates** 36 g, **Protein** 3 g

RECIPE 10.20

PECAN PIE WITH OATMEAL STOUT ICE CREAM AND GINGER CARAMEL SAUCE

CAFÉ ALLEGRE, ORLANDO, FL
Chef Kevin Fonzo

Yield: 1 Pie, 10 in. (24 cm)   **Method:** Custard filling

Filling:

Eggs	8.3 oz. (5 eggs)	250 g
Dark corn syrup	1 lb.	480 g
Granulated sugar	9 oz.	270 g
Vanilla extract	0.15 fl. oz. (1 tsp.)	5 ml
Whole butter, melted	1.5 oz.	45 g
Oatmeal stout or dark beer	4 fl. oz.	120 ml
Pecan pieces	12 oz.	360 g
10-inch pie shell, unbaked	1 shell	1 shell
Oatmeal Stout Ice Cream (recipe follows)	as needed	as needed
Ginger Caramel Sauce (recipe follows)	as needed	as needed

1 Beat the eggs thoroughly. Add the corn syrup, sugar, vanilla, butter and stout. Mix until well blended.

2 Fold in the pecans and pour the mixture into the pie crust.

3 Bake at 350°F (180°C) until set, approximately 45 to 55 minutes.

4 Allow the pie to cool completely before service.

5 Cut the pie into 8 portions. Serve each with a scoop of Oatmeal Stout Ice Cream and some Ginger Caramel Sauce.

Approximate values per ⅛-pie serving: **Calories** 800, **Total fat** 45 g, **Saturated fat** 8 g, **Cholesterol** 145 mg, **Sodium** 210 mg, **Total carbohydrates** 91 g, **Protein** 8 g

OATMEAL STOUT ICE CREAM

Yield: 3 qt. (3 lt)

Milk	1 qt.	1 lt
Heavy cream	1 qt.	1 lt
Oatmeal stout or dark beer	8 fl. oz.	240 ml
Dark corn syrup	6 oz.	180 g
Granulated sugar	8 oz.	240 g
Egg yolks	1.3 oz. (2 yolks)	40 g
Vanilla beans, split	2	2

1 In a medium-sized saucepot, heat the milk and cream.

2 In a separate saucepot, bring the oatmeal stout to a boil and reduce by half. Add the corn syrup and remove from heat.

3 In a small mixing bowl, combine the sugar, egg yolks and vanilla beans. Mix well.

4 When the cream mixture comes to a boil, remove it from the heat. Pour one third of the cream into the egg mixture. Whisk in the remaining cream, then strain it.

5 Allow the mixture to cool completely. Gently stir the stout reduction into the cooled custard.

6 Freeze the custard in an ice cream freezer.

Approximate values per ½-c. (120-ml) serving: **Calories** 215, **Total fat** 15 g, **Saturated fat** 9 g, **Cholesterol** 121 mg, **Sodium** 37 mg, **Total carbohydrates** 17 g, **Protein** 3 g, **Vitamin A** 18%

GINGER CARAMEL SAUCE

Yield: 2 pt. (1150 ml)

Granulated sugar	1 lb.	480 g
Water	2.5 fl. oz.	75 ml
Lemon juice	0.08 fl. oz. (½ tsp.)	2.5 ml
Fresh ginger, peeled and chopped	6 oz.	180 g
Heavy cream	12 fl. oz.	360 ml
Unsalted butter	2 oz.	60 g

1 Bring the sugar, water and lemon juice to a boil in a small saucepan.
2 Cook over medium heat until the syrup turns a golden amber color. Add the ginger.
3 Remove the saucepan from the heat and slowly add the cream.
4 Return the pan to the heat and cook 2 to 3 more minutes.
5 Add the butter and stir to melt. Serve the sauce warm.

Approximate values per 1-fl.-oz. (30-ml) serving: **Calories** 90, **Total fat** 4.5 g, **Saturated fat** 3 g, **Cholesterol** 15 mg, **Sodium** 15 mg, **Total carbohydrates** 12 g, **Protein** 0 g

SWEET POTATO PIE

RECIPE 10.21

Yield: 2 Pies, 9 in. (22 cm) each   **Method:** Custard filling

Sweet potatoes, baked and peeled	1 lb.	480 g
Brown sugar	10 oz.	300 g
Salt	0.2 oz. (1 tsp.)	6 g
Cinnamon, ground	0.07 oz. (1 tsp.)	2 g
Ginger, ground	0.14 oz. (2 tsp.)	4 g
Allspice, ground	0.14 oz. (2 tsp.)	4 g
Vanilla extract	0.3 fl. oz. (2 tsp.)	10 ml
Eggs	6.75 oz. (4 eggs)	200 g
Buttermilk	8 fl. oz.	240 ml
Heavy cream	10 fl. oz.	300 ml
Flaky dough or sweet tart dough pie shells, baked	2 shells	2 shells

1 Pass the sweet potatoes through a food mill or ricer. Transfer the sweet potatoes to a mixing bowl and whip until smooth.
2 Add the sugar, salt, cinnamon, ginger, allspice and vanilla.
3 Add the eggs and whisk smooth, followed by the buttermilk and cream.
4 Divide the filling evenly between the two pie shells. Bake at 325°F (160°C) until the filling is set, about 45 minutes.

Approximate values per ⅛-pie serving: **Calories** 310, **Total fat** 16 g, **Saturated fat** 7 g, **Cholesterol** 80 mg, **Sodium** 320 mg, **Total carbohydrates** 37 g, **Protein** 4 g, **Vitamin A** 130%

RECIPE 10.22 ## CHESS PIE

A traditional American pie especially in the South, chess pie is a type of custard pie. Its origins are not clear, but some say "chess" refers to the cheeselike texture of the eggy filling. Others claim that when a southern woman was complimented on the deliciousness of her pie she would reply, "Oh, it's just pie." With a southern accent, "just" becomes "jess."

Yield: 2 Pies, 9 in. (22 cm) each   **Method:** Custard filling

Filling:

Unsalted butter, melted	4 oz.	120 g
Granulated sugar	1 lb. 3 oz.	570 g
Eggs	6.75 oz. (4 eggs)	200 g
Evaporated milk	8 fl. oz.	240 ml
Lemon juice	0.08 fl. oz. (½ tsp.)	2.5 ml
Vanilla extract	0.15 fl. oz. (1 tsp.)	5 ml
All-purpose flour	0.5 oz.	15 g
Flaky dough pie shells, unbaked	2 shells	2 shells
Nutmeg	pinch	pinch

1 Beat the butter, sugar, eggs, milk, lemon juice, vanilla and flour together. Pour into pie shells and sprinkle the top of each pie lightly with nutmeg.

2 Bake at 325°F (160°C) until set and the crust is brown, about 40 minutes.

Approximate values per ⅛-pie serving: **Calories** 350, **Total fat** 16 g, **Saturated fat** 7 g, **Cholesterol** 75 mg, **Sodium** 160 mg, **Total carbohydrates** 47 g, **Protein** 4 g, **Vitamin A** 6%

RECIPE 10.23 ## LEMON CURD TART

Yield: 1 Tart, 8 in. (20 cm)

Raspberry jam	as needed	as needed
Coconut Almond Tart Dough (page 267), 8-in. (20-cm), tart shell, fully baked	1 shell	1 shell
Lemon Curd (page 437)	1 lb. 4 oz.	600 g
Italian Meringue (page 290)	10 oz.	300 g
Lemon juice	1.5 fl. oz.	45 ml
Raspberries	2 oz.	60 g
Neutral glaze	as needed	as needed

1 Spread the raspberry jam on the base of the cooled tart shell.

2 Fill with Lemon Curd.

3 Refrigerate or freeze the tart until the curd is firm, about 1 hour.

4 Prepare the Italian Meringue and flavor it with the lemon juice. Using a piping bag fitted with a **St. Honoré** tip, pipe parallel rows of meringue to cover the surface of the tart.

5 Using a propane torch, brown the surface of the meringue.

6 Scatter the meringue with fresh raspberries. Heat the neutral glaze until flowing. Pour it into a parchment paper cone, then pipe a few drops of neutral tart glaze on each berry to resemble dewdrops.

Approximate values per ⅛-tart serving: **Calories** 520, **Total fat** 30 g, **Saturated fat** 18 g, **Cholesterol** 125 mg, **Sodium** 95 mg, **Total carbohydrates** 61 g, **Protein** 5 g, **Vitamin A** 20%, **Vitamin C** 20%

▶ **St. Honoré** patron saint of the pastry chef; name for a light crisp pastry composed of puff pastry topped with éclair paste filled with custard and coated with hard caramel; also refers to a piping tip that produces a wedge-shaped design, which is often used to pipe in the filling

1 Spreading raspberry jam in the baked tart shell with an offset spatula.

2 Pouring the lemon curd into the tart shell.

3 Piping the Italian meringue with a St. Honoré tip in a freeform pattern over the lemon curd.

4 Browning the surface of the meringue with a blowtorch.

5 Piping drops of neutral tart glaze on the raspberries.

INDIVIDUAL BLACK AND BLUE BERRY TARTS   RECIPE 10.24

Yield: 12 Tartlets, 2½ in. (7.5 cm) each

Crème Brûlée for Tarts (page 457)	2 lb.	960 g
Shortbread Tart Dough (page 266), made with almond flour, 2½-in. (7.5-cm) tart shells, fully baked	12 shells	12 shells
Blackberries	2 pt.	1 lt
Blueberries	1 pt.	0.5 lt
Powdered sugar	as needed	as needed

1 Using a pastry bag fitted with a medium plain tip, pipe the Crème Brûlée for Tarts into each tart shell.

2 Scatter the surface of the cream with the berries. Dust with powdered sugar to garnish.

Approximate values per tart: **Calories** 430, **Total fat** 33 g, **Saturated fat** 19 g, **Cholesterol** 260 mg, **Sodium** 95 mg, **Total carbohydrates** 36 g, **Protein** 6 g, **Vitamin A** 20%, **Vitamin C** 25%

RECIPE 10.25

INDIVIDUAL KEY LIME MANGO TARTS

Yield: 12 Tarts, 2½ in. (7.5 cm) each

Lime Curd (page 437)	1 lb. 4 oz.	600 g
Coconut Almond Tart Dough (page 267), 2½-in. (7.5-cm) tart shells, fully baked	12 shells	12 shells
Mangoes, peeled	6	6
Neutral glaze	5 oz.	150 g
Mango purée	2.5 oz.	75 g
Lime juice	0.5 fl. oz.	15 ml
Chocolate decorations (page 614)	as needed	as needed

1 Using a pastry bag fitted with a medium plain tip, pipe the Lime Curd into the tart shells, filling to the rim of the tarts. Refrigerate or freeze the tarts until the curd is firm, about 1 hour.

2 Cut the mangoes into small dice, ¼ inch (6 millimeters) square. Arrange the mango cubes over the surface of the curd.

3 Dissolve the neutral glaze with the mango purée and the lime juice in a small saucepan over low heat. Cool to lukewarm, then brush the fruit with the glaze.

4 Garnish with chocolate decorations.

Approximate values per tart: **Calories** 430, **Total fat** 26 g, **Saturated fat** 16 g, **Cholesterol** 95 mg, **Sodium** 75 mg, **Total carbohydrates** 51 g, **Protein** 4 g, **Vitamin A** 100%, **Vitamin C** 60%

RECIPE 10.26

INDIVIDUAL STRAWBERRY CREAM TARTS

Yield: 18 Tartlets, 2½- in. (7.5 cm) each

Minted Cheese Mousse (page 265), made without the mint	1 lb. 10 oz.	780 g
Shortbread Tart Dough (page 266), made with hazelnut flour, 2½-in. (7.5-cm) tart shells, fully baked	18 shells	18 shells
Fresh strawberries	2 pts.	1 lt
Neutral glaze	5 oz.	150 g
Strawberry purée	3 oz.	90 g
Pistachios, chopped fine	as needed	as needed

1 Using a pastry bag fitted with a large plain tip, pipe the Minted Cheese Mousse in large mounds in the tart shells.

2 Slice the strawberries lengthwise in half. Press the strawberries into the cream with the cut side facing out pyramid style on the tarts.

3 In a small saucepan over low heat, dissolve the neutral glaze with the strawberry purée. Cool to lukewarm, then brush the fruit with the glaze.

4 Sprinkle chopped pistachios on the neutral glaze along the rim of the tarts.

Approximate values per tart: **Calories** 350, **Total fat** 29 g, **Saturated fat** 17 g, **Cholesterol** 115 mg, **Sodium** 140 mg, **Total carbohydrates** 28 g, **Protein** 5 g, **Vitamin A** 15%, **Vitamin C** 20%

INDIVIDUAL CHOCOLATE MOUSSE CRÈME BRÛLÉE TARTS

RECIPE 10.27

Yield: 24 Tartlets, 2½ in. (7.5 cm) each

Crème Brûlée for Tarts (page 457)	2 lb.	960 g
Shortbread Tart Dough (page 266), made with hazelnut flour, 2½-in. (7.5-cm) tart shells, fully baked	24 shells	24 shells
Chocolate Mousse (page 462)	2 lb. 8 oz.	1200 g
Cocoa Gelée (page 363)	as needed	as needed
Chocolate Fans (page 617)	as needed	as needed

1 Using a pastry bag fitted with a medium plain tip, pipe the tart shells two-thirds full with the Crème Brûlée for Tarts.
2 Using a large plain tip, pipe a dome of Chocolate Mousse on top of the Crème Brûlée for Tarts. (If the mousse is too soft to form a plump dome, chill the product in the refrigerator until it sets a bit.)
3 Place the filled tarts in the freezer at least 1 hour or until the mousse is very firm.
4 Heat the Cocoa Gelée to 120°F (49°C). Stick a paring knife into the bottom of one of the frozen tarts at a 45° angle and about ½ inch (1.5 centimeters) deep. Using the knife as a handle, dip the dome of mousse into the Cocoa Gelée.
5 Remove the knife. Place the tart on a rack to drain and insert a Chocolate Fan or chocolate decoration in the center of the dome.

Approximate values per tart: **Calories** 470, **Total fat** 39 g, **Saturated fat** 21 g, **Cholesterol** 330 mg, **Sodium** 100 mg, **Total carbohydrates** 36 g, **Protein** 8 g, **Vitamin A** 20%

INDIVIDUAL ORANGE MILK CHOCOLATE RUBY RED GRAPEFRUIT TARTS

RECIPE 10.28

Yield: 18 Tartlets, 2½ in. (7.5 cm) each

Orange Milk Chocolate Ganache (page 372)	2 lb. 2 oz.	1020 g
Shortbread Tart Dough (page 266), made with hazelnut flour, 2½-in. (7.5-cm) tart shells, fully baked	18 shells	18 shells
Ruby red grapefruits	3 to 4	3 to 4
Neutral glaze	5 oz.	150 g
Grapefruit juice	3 fl. oz.	90 ml
Red currants or raspberries	as needed	as needed

1 Using a pastry bag fitted with a medium plain tip, pipe the Orange Milk Chocolate Ganache in the tart shells.
2 Segment the grapefruits, saving the juice, and position three to four overlapping segments on top of each tart.
3 Dissolve the neutral glaze with the grapefruit juice and brush evenly over each tart. Garnish each tart with a few currants or raspberries.

Approximate values per tart: **Calories** 370, **Total fat** 27 g, **Saturated fat** 14 g, **Cholesterol** 80 mg, **Sodium** 85 mg, **Total carbohydrates** 41 g, **Protein** 5 g, **Vitamin C** 40%

FLEMISH PEAR CUSTARD TARTS

Yield: 3 Tarts, 8 in. (20 cm) each

Sweet Almond Tart Dough (page 266)	3 lb. 14 oz.	1860 g
Pears	2 lb. (10 pears)	960 g
Filling:		
Eggs	8.3 oz. (5 eggs)	250 g
Brown sugar	10 oz.	300 g
Vanilla extract	0.5 fl. oz.	15 ml
Orange zest, grated fine	0.6 oz.	18 g
Lemon zest, grated fine	0.14 oz. (2 tsp.)	4 g
Salt	0.2 oz. (1 tsp.)	6 g
Cake or potato flour	1.5 oz.	45 g
Unsalted butter, melted	7.5 oz.	225 g
Cocoa Streusel (recipe follows)	1 lb. 8 oz.	720 g

1 Roll out the Sweet Almond Tart Dough to a thickness of ⅛ inch (3 millimeters) and line three 8-inch (20-centimeter) tart rings or pans with it, gently pressing the dough in place.

2 Peel and core the pears and cut into medium dice, ⅜ inch (9 millimeters) square. Divide the fruit between the three pans.

3 Whisk the eggs and sugar in a mixing bowl until well combined. Stir in the vanilla, orange and lemon zest, salt and flour. Cool the melted butter to 120°F (49°C) and add to the egg mixture.

4 Divide the filling, pouring it evenly over the pear cubes. Top with the Cocoa Streusel.

5 Bake at 375°F (190°C) until the center is set, approximately 40 minutes.

Note: Potato flour, not to be confused with potato starch, is found in health food stores. It makes a tender custard. Cake flour may be used in its place.

VARIATION:

Pear Ginger Tart—Cut 2 ounces (60 grams) candied ginger into small dice, ⅛ inch (3 millimeters) square, and toss with the pears.

Approximate values per ⅛-tart serving: **Calories** 320, **Total fat** 18 g, **Saturated fat** 10 g, **Cholesterol** 95 mg, **Sodium** 220 mg, **Total carbohydrates** 39 g, **Protein** 4 g, **Vitamin A** 15%

COCOA STREUSEL

Yield: 1 lb. 8 oz. (747 g)

Unsalted butter, cold	5 oz.	150 g
Brown sugar	7 oz.	210 g
Vanilla extract	0.5 fl. oz.	15 ml
Salt	0.2 oz. (1 tsp.)	6 g
Pastry flour	5 oz.	150 g
Cocoa powder	1 oz.	30 g
Cinnamon, ground	0.2 oz. (1 Tbsp.)	6 g
Hazelnut flour	6 oz.	180 g

1 In the bowl of a mixer fitted with a paddle, blend the butter, sugar, vanilla extract and salt until combined but not creamed.

2 Sift together the pastry flour, cocoa and cinnamon. Stir in the hazelnut flour and add the flour mixture to the butter mixture. Mix very briefly until the mixture resembles coarse meal and lumps form; do not mix until it forms a smooth dough.

3 Sprinkle the streusel on top of custard tarts, butter cakes, coffeecakes or brownies before baking. When refrigerated, this topping keeps 1 month.

Approximate values per 1-oz. (30-g) serving: **Calories** 140, **Total fat** 9 g, **Saturated fat** 3.5 g, **Cholesterol** 15 mg, **Sodium** 200 mg, **Total carbohydrates** 15 g, **Protein** 2 g

FRENCH APPLE TART   RECIPE 10.30

The amount of each ingredient, the yield and the baking time will depend on the capacity and number of tart molds used. This procedure can be used for individual tartlets or large round, rectangular or daisy-shaped tart pans.

Sweet Tart Dough (page 249)	as needed
Almond Cream (page 332)	as needed
Tart apples, peeled, cored and sliced thin	as needed
Unsalted butter, melted	as needed
Granulated sugar	as needed
Apricot glaze	as needed

1 Line the tart pans with Sweet Tart Dough. Do not prick the dough.

2 Pipe in an even layer of Almond Cream.

3 Arrange the apples in overlapping rows, covering the Almond Cream completely.

4 Brush the top of the apples with melted butter and sprinkle lightly with granulated sugar.

5 Bake at 375°F (190°C) until the crust is done and the apples are light brown.

6 Allow the tart to cool to room temperature. Brush the top with apricot glaze.

Approximate values per 4-oz. (120-g) serving: **Calories** 395, **Total fat** 17 g, **Saturated fat** 7 g, **Cholesterol** 234 mg, **Sodium** 98 mg, **Total carbohydrates** 56 g, **Protein** 7 g, **Vitamin A** 12%

RECIPE 10.31

LINZER TART

CHEFS SUSAN FENIGER AND MARY SUE MILLIKEN

Yield: 8–10 Servings

Dough:

Unsalted butter, softened	8 oz.	240 g	73%
Granulated sugar	8 oz.	240 g	73%
Egg yolks	1.3 oz. (2 yolks)	40 g	12%
Orange zest, grated fine	0.4 oz. (2 Tbsp.)	12 g	3.6%
Lemon zest, grated fine	0.2 oz. (1 Tbsp.)	6 g	1.8%
All-purpose flour	11 oz.	330 g	100%
Hazelnuts, ground fine	6 oz.	180 g	54%
Baking powder	0.14 oz. (1 tsp.)	4 g	1.2%
Cinnamon, ground	0.14 oz. (2 tsp.)	4 g	1.2%
Cloves, ground	0.04 oz. ($1/2$ tsp.)	1 g	0.3%
Salt	0.05 oz. ($1/4$ tsp.)	1.5 g	0.5%
Raspberry preserves	6 oz.	180 g	
Total dough weight:	2 lb. 3 oz.	1058 g	320%

1 To make the dough, cream together the butter and sugar until light and fluffy. Add the egg yolks and the orange and lemon zest. Beat until well combined.

2 In another bowl, mix together the flour, hazelnuts, baking powder, cinnamon, cloves and salt. Add the dry mixture all at once to the creamed mixture and mix briefly, until just combined. (This dough looks more like cookie dough than pastry.) Wrap in plastic and chill until firm, at least 4 hours or overnight.

3 Divide the dough in half. On a generously floured board, briefly knead one piece of dough and flatten it with the palm of your hand. Gently roll the dough out $1/4$ inch (6 millimeters) thick and use it to line a 9- or 10-inch (22- or 25-centimeter) tart pan with a removable bottom. This rich dough patches easily. Chill approximately 10 minutes.

4 Roll out the second piece of dough to form a 12-inch × 4-inch (30-centimeter × 10-centimeter) rectangle. Using a sharp knife or pastry wheel, cut lengthwise strips, approximately $1/3$ inch (8 millimeters) wide.

5 Remove the lined tart shell from the refrigerator and spread the raspberry preserves evenly over it. To create the lattice pattern with the pastry strips, first lay some strips in parallel lines, $1/2$ inch (1.2 centimeters) apart. Then lay a second row of strips at a 45-degree angle to the first. Press the strips to the edge of the crust to seal.

6 Bake at 350°F (180°C) until the crust is golden brown and the filling is bubbly in the center, approximately 45 minutes. Set aside to cool.

Approximate values per $1/10$-tart serving: **Calories** 300, **Total fat** 29 g, **Saturated fat** 12 g, **Cholesterol** 90 mg, **Sodium** 65 mg, **Total carbohydrates** 7 g, **Protein** 4 g, **Vitamin A** 20%, **Claims**—low sodium; good source of fiber

ZUPPA INGLESE TART
(ITALIAN TRIFLE TART)

Trifle, the national dessert of the British Isles, is a sponge cake soaked with wine or spirits and then layered with candied fruit or jam and thick custard topped with whipped cream. The Italian version, *Zuppa Inglese,* is not an "English soup" but a génoise sponge cake flavored with rum and filled with pastry cream. Its curious name suggests how popular the dessert was among homesick Britons vacationing in coastal cities including Genoa and Naples, where this dish originated in the late 19th century. Here the trifle ingredients are contained in a pastry shell coated with a thin layer of white chocolate to retain a crisp crust.

Yield: 2 Tarts, 8-in. (20 cm) each

Shortbread Tart Dough (page 266), 8-in. (20-cm) tart shells, fully baked	2 shells	2 shells
White chocolate, melted	6 oz.	120 g
Classic Génoise (page 386), 7-in. (17 cm) rounds	2 rounds	2 rounds
Simple Syrup (page 349)	4 fl. oz.	120 ml
Rum	1 fl. oz.	30 ml
Vanilla extract	0.15 fl. oz. (1 tsp.)	5 ml
Pastry Cream (page 436)	2 pt.	1 lt
Fresh strawberries, sliced in half	1 pt.	0.5 lt
Raspberry jam	as needed	as needed
Crème Chantilly (page 445)	as needed	as needed
Almonds, sliced and toasted	as needed	as needed

1 Brush the inside of the baked and cooled tart shells with the melted white chocolate.

2 Split the Classic Génoise in half and fit one layer in each tart shell.

3 Combine the Simple Syrup, rum and vanilla extract in a small bowl. Moisten the génoise layer with the syrup.

4 Place the Pastry Cream in a pastry bag fitted with a plain tip. Pipe a ¾-inch (1-centimeter) layer of Pastry Cream over the génoise layer in each tart shell.

5 Cover the entire surface of the Pastry Cream with the sliced strawberries, then spread them with raspberry jam.

6 Using a pastry bag with a star tip, pipe rosettes of Crème Chantilly over each tart.

7 Sprinkle the tarts with toasted sliced almonds.

Approximate values per 1/8-tart serving: **Calories** 540, **Total fat** 31 g, **Saturated fat** 15 g, **Cholesterol** 235 mg, **Sodium** 120 mg, **Total carbohydrates** 65 g, **Protein** 10 g

IN COOKING, AS IN ALL THE ARTS, SIMPLICITY IS THE
SIGN OF PERFECTION.

—*Maurice Edmond Sailland (Curnonsky), French
writer and food critic (1872–1956)*

PASTRY DOUGHS

AFTER STUDYING THIS CHAPTER, YOU WILL BE ABLE TO:

▶ prepare a variety of pastries using éclair paste

▶ prepare a variety of meringues

▶ prepare a variety of specialty pastries using phyllo dough

▶ prepare crêpes

▶ prepare a variety of dessert and pastry items, incorporating components from other chapters

▶ **beignets** squares or strips of éclair paste deep-fried and dusted with powdered sugar

▶ **churros** a Mexican and Spanish pastry in which sticks of éclair paste flavored with cinnamon are deep-fried and rolled in sugar while still hot

▶ **croquembouche** a pyramid of small puffs, each filled with pastry cream; a French tradition for Christmas and weddings, it is held together with caramelized sugar and decorated with spun sugar or marzipan flowers

▶ **crullers** a Dutch pastry in which a loop or strip of twisted éclair paste is deep-fried

▶ **éclairs** baked fingers of éclair paste filled with pastry cream; the top is then coated with chocolate glaze or fondant

▶ **gougère** éclair paste flavored with cheese or herbs, baked and served as a savory hors d'oeuvre

▶ **Paris-Brest** rings of baked éclair paste cut in half horizontally and filled with light pastry cream and/or whipped cream; the top is dusted with powdered sugar or drizzled with chocolate glaze

▶ **profiteroles** small baked rounds of éclair paste filled with ice cream and topped with chocolate sauce

One of the enticements of a great bakeshop is the array of different pastries and cakes on display. The secret to such variety is the baker's ability to use a limited number of preparations to make a wide variety of delights. The doughs in this chapter are quick, easy preparations with great versatility. Éclair paste can be baked, poached or deep-fried. When baked, éclair paste becomes its namesake cream-filled pastry as well as sweet puffs, savory appetizers and elaborate cakes such as Paris-Brest and **croquembouche**. Alone or filled with whipped cream, ganache or the mousse and fillings discussed in Chapter 15, Custards and Creams, the meringue is a pastry category of its own. Tender meringue-based nut cakes when filled become pastries that delight the consumer with the pleasure of the contrast between crunch and cream. Many pastry classics are based on the doughs in this chapter.

▶ ÉCLAIR PASTE

Éclair paste, also known as **pâte à choux,** bakes up into golden brown, crisp pastries. Inside these light pastries are mostly air pockets with a bit of moist dough. They can be filled with sweet cream, custard, fruit or even savory mixtures. The dough is most often piped into rounds for **cream puffs,** fingers for **éclairs** or rings for **Paris-Brest.** Éclair paste may also be piped or spooned into specific shapes and deep-fried for doughnut-type products known as **beignets, churros** and **crullers.** And this dough may be flavored with herbs, spices and cheese and made into savory puffs known as **gougères.** Seasoned éclair paste even becomes a savory casserole when pieces of the dough are poached and baked with cheese or a cream sauce.

MAKING ÉCLAIR PASTE

Éclair paste is unique among doughs because it is cooked before baking. The cooking occurs when the flour is added to a boiling mixture of water, milk and butter. This process breaks down the starches in the flour, allowing them to absorb the liquid, speeding gelatinization. Eggs are added to the flour mixture for leavening. The dough produced is batterlike with a smooth, firm texture; it does not have the dry, crumbly texture of other doughs. Without this technique, the dough would not puff up and develop the desired large interior air pockets when baked. Steam is a key leavening agent in baked goods with a large proportion of moisture such as éclair paste, popovers and other pourable batters. To activate the steam before the dough sets, these products are baked at relatively high temperatures, around 400°F (200°C). At this temperature, steam is produced before the egg and other proteins in the formula coagulate.

Table 11.1 **CLASSIFICATION OF PASTRY DOUGHS**

DOUGH	FRENCH NAME	CHARACTERISTICS AFTER BAKING	USE
Éclair paste	Pâte à choux	Hollow with crisp exterior	Cream puffs; éclairs; savory products
Puff pastry	Pâte feuilletée	Rich but not sweet; hundreds of light, flaky layers	Tart and pastry cases; cookies; layered pastries; savory products
Meringue	Meringue	Sweet; light; crisp or soft depending on preparation	Topping or icing; baked as a shell or component for layered desserts, cookies and pastries
Phyllo	Phyllo	Very thin, crisp, flaky layers; bland	Middle Eastern pastries and savory dishes, especially hors d'oeuvre; baklava

▶ PROCEDURE FOR PREPARING ÉCLAIR PASTE

1 Combine the liquid ingredients and butter cut into small cubes. Bring to a boil.

2 As soon as the water-and-butter mixture comes to a boil, add all the flour to the saucepan. If the liquid is allowed to boil, evaporation occurs; this can create an imbalance in the liquid-to-flour ratio.

3 Stir vigorously until the liquid is absorbed. Continue cooking the dough until it forms a ball that comes away from the sides of the pan, leaving only a thin film of dough on the sides of the pan.

4 Transfer the dough to a mixing bowl. Allow it to cool to below 140°F (60°C), then add the eggs one at a time, beating well after each addition. (This may be done in a mixer fitted with a paddle or by hand.) The number of eggs used varies depending on the size of each egg and the moisture content of the flour mixture. Stop adding eggs when the dough just begins to fall away from the beaters.

5 The finished dough should be smooth and pliable enough to pipe through a pastry bag; it should not be runny.

6 Pipe the dough as desired and bake immediately. A high oven temperature is necessary at the start of baking; it is then reduced gradually to finish baking and drying the product. Do not open the oven door during the first half of the baking period.

7 Allow the dough to bake until completely dry. If the products are removed from the oven too soon, they will collapse. Test doneness by breaking open one pastry. If the interior is moist and eggy, continue baking.

8 Baked éclair paste can be stored, unfilled, several days at room temperature or frozen for several weeks. Once filled, the pastry should be served within 2 or 3 hours, as it quickly becomes soggy.

RECIPE 11.1

ÉCLAIR PASTE (PÂTE À CHOUX)

Yield: 2–2½ lb. (1200–1300 g) Dough

Milk*	8 fl. oz.	240 ml	100%
Water	8 fl. oz.	240 ml	100%
Salt	0.3 oz. (1½ tsp.)	9 g	4%
Granulated sugar	0.3 oz. (2 tsp.)	9 g	4%
Unsalted butter	7.5 oz.	225 g	94%
All-purpose flour	8 oz.	240 g	100%
Eggs	8.3–11.5 oz. (5–7 eggs)	250–345 g	103–144%
Total dough weight:	2 lb. 8 oz.– 2 lb. 11 oz.	1213–1308 g	505–546%

1 Preheat the oven to 425°F (220°C). Line a sheet pan with parchment. Have a pastry bag with a large plain tip ready.

2 Place the milk, water, salt, sugar and butter in a saucepan. Bring to a boil. Make sure the butter is fully melted.

3 Remove from the heat and immediately add all the flour. Vigorously beat the dough by hand. Put the pan back on the heat and continue beating the dough until it comes away from the sides of the pan. The dough should look relatively dry and should just begin to leave a film on the saucepan.

4 Transfer the dough to the bowl of a mixer fitted with a paddle and allow it to cool briefly to approximately 130°F (54°C) or lower. Begin beating in the eggs one at a time.

5 Continue to add the eggs one by one until the mixture is shiny but firm. It may not be necessary to use all of the eggs. The dough should pull away from the sides of the bowl in thick threads; it will not clear the bowl.

6 Put a workable amount of dough into the pastry bag and pipe onto the sheet pan in the desired shapes at once. (Spraying the inside of the pastry bag with vegetable cooking spray will help keep the sticky éclair paste from clinging to the inside of the bag and make cleanup easier.)

7 Bake immediately at 425°F (220°C) for 10 minutes, then reduce to 375°F (190°C) and bake another 10 minutes. Continue gradually reducing the oven temperature every few minutes until it reaches about 200°F (90°C) or until the shapes are brown and dry inside. Open the oven door as little as possible, to prevent rapid changes in the oven's temperature.

8 Cool completely, then fill as desired. Leftovers can be frozen or stored at room temperature.

*For a crisper product, replace the milk with water.

Approximate values per 1-oz. (30-g) serving: **Calories** 90, **Total fat** 7 g, **Saturated fat** 4 g, **Cholesterol** 60 mg, **Sodium** 180 mg, **Total carbohydrates** 6 g, **Protein** 2 g, **Vitamin A** 8%

1 Heating the butter and milk.

2 Adding the flour to the hot liquid.

3 Stirring the dough to dry it.

4 The finished batter after the eggs are incorporated.

5 Piping éclairs.

► MERINGUE

Meringue refers to both a basic mixture of egg whites whipped with sugar and a confection or cake baked from this preparation. (See Chapter 4, Bakeshop Ingredients, page 74, for the proper technique for whipping egg whites.) The texture—hard or soft—depends on the ratio of sugar to egg whites. A low sugar content relative to the egg whites creates a **soft meringue.** Soft meringue can be folded into a mousse or Bavarian to lighten it, or used in a spongecake or soufflé. Meringue with only a small amount of sugar will always be soft; it will not become crisp no matter how it is used.

Hard meringue is made with egg whites and an equal part or more, by weight, of sugar. It can be incorporated into a buttercream or pastry cream or used to top a pie or baked Alaska. These toppings are usually placed briefly under a broiler to caramelize the sugar, creating an attractive brown surface.

With twice as much sugar, by weight, as egg whites, hard meringue can be piped into disks or other shapes and dried in an oven. A low oven temperature evaporates the eggs' moisture, leaving a crisp, sugary, honeycomb-like structure. Weather conditions affect meringues. When humid, the meringue may remain soft for a longer period of time. Additional drying time may be necessary. Disks of baked meringue can be used as layers in a torte or cake. Cups or shells of baked meringue can be filled with cream, mousse, ice cream or fruit.

MERINGUE PREPARATIONS

There are three methods for making meringue: **common** (French), **Swiss** and **Italian** (see Table 11.2). Egg whites need to be free of any traces of yolk to foam properly. The whites foam best at room temperature, 70°F to 80°F (21°C to 27°C). Dried egg whites or an acid such as cream of tartar are often added to stabilize the egg whites when making common meringue. (Swiss and Italian meringue do not need stabilizers because the way in which they are prepared ensures stablity.) The formula is 0.3 ounces (10 grams/2 teaspoons) cream of tartar for 1 pound (480 grams) of egg whites. Beating the whites in an unlined copper bowl also helps stability; however, stainless steel will work equally well with the addition of an acid. Aluminum will discolor the product. Regardless of which preparation method is used, the final product should be smooth, glossy and moist. Meringue should never be dry or spongelike. (see Table 11.3)

► **vacherin** a baked meringue disc or cake layered with ice cream

Table 11.2 CLASSIFICATION OF MERINGUES

TYPE	RATIO OF SUGAR TO EGG WHITES BY WEIGHT	PREPARATION	USE
Common—hard	Twice as much or more	Whip or fold sugar into whipped egg whites	Baked
Common—soft	Equal parts or less	Whip or fold sugar into whipped egg whites	Pie topping; soufflé; cake ingredient
Swiss	Varies	Warm egg whites to 100°F (38°C) with sugar, then whip	Buttercream; pie topping; baked
Italian	Varies	Hot sugar syrup poured into whipped egg whites	Buttercream; frosting; crème Chiboust; mousse; baked

COMMON (FRENCH) MERINGUE

Common meringues are made by first beating egg whites until a soft foam capable of holding soft peaks is achieved. Granulated sugar is then slowly beaten or folded into the egg whites. The final product may be hard or soft, depending on the ratio of sugar to egg whites. When baked, this is considered the finest meringue due to its lightness and melt-in-the-mouth quality. Common meringue is less stable than other varieties and should be baked as soon as it is made.

RECIPE 11.2

COMMON (FRENCH) MERINGUE

Yield: 3 Disks, 8 in. (20 cm) each, 1 lb. 8 oz. (720 g) Meringue

Egg whites	8 oz. (8 whites)	240 g
Granulated sugar	1 lb.	480 g
Dried egg whites (optional)	0.3 oz. (2 tsp.)	8 g
Vanilla extract	0.15 fl. oz. (1 tsp.)	5 ml

1 Place the liquid egg whites in the bowl of a mixer fitted with a whip and whip on medium speed until foamy and the mixture holds soft peaks.

2 Sift 8 ounces (240 grams) of the sugar with dried egg whites (if using), then add gradually to the whipped egg whites. Continue to whip the egg whites on medium speed until very stiff and glossy.

3 Remove from the mixer. Fold in the remaining sugar and the vanilla without overmixing.

4 Spread or pipe the meringue into desired shapes on parchment-lined sheet pans.

5 Bake at 225°F (110°C) 1 to 2 hours. Break a baked meringue disk to verify doneness. Check the interior after 30 seconds; if the interior is still sticky and moist, return the meringue to the oven. The baked meringue should be firm, crisp and dry inside but not browned.

6 Once cooled, the baked meringues may be stored in tightly closed plastic bags. Properly wrapped, they will have a long shelf life.

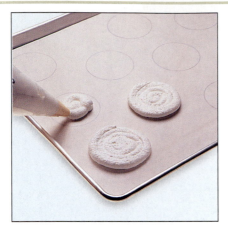

Piping common (French) meringue into individual disks before baking.

VARIATIONS:

Chocolate Meringue—Substitute 8 ounces (240 grams) powdered sugar for the 8 ounces (240 grams) of granulated sugar in Step 2. Sift it with 2 ounces (60 grams) cocoa powder and the dried egg whites (if using). Fold with extra care; because of the fat content in cocoa powder, overfolding will produce runny meringue.

Table 11.3 TROUBLESHOOTING CHART FOR MERINGUES

PROBLEM	CAUSE	SOLUTION
Weeps or beads of sugar syrup are released	Old eggs	Use fresher eggs or add starch or stabilizer
	Egg whites overwhipped	Whip only until stiff peaks form
	Not enough sugar	Increase sugar
	Not baked long enough	Increase baking time
	Browning too rapidly	Do not dust with sugar before baking; reduce oven temperature
	Moisture in the air	Increase baking time
Fails to attain any volume or stiffness	Fat present	Start over with clean bowls and utensils
	Sugar added too soon	Allow egg whites to reach soft peaks before adding sugar
Lumps	Not enough sugar	Add additional sugar gradually or start over
	Overwhipping	Whip only until stiff peaks form
Not shiny	Not enough sugar	Add additional sugar gradually or start over
	Overwhipping	Whip only until stiff peaks form

PAVLOVA, LIGHT AS AIR

As apple pie is to America, pavlova is to Australia and New Zealand: the classic dessert. Both countries claim its invention but what appears certain is that it came into being in the early 1930s after the second Pacific tour of the famed Russian ballerina Anna Pavlova. It is said that Herbert Sachse, the chef at the Esplanade Hotel, where Pavlova stayed during her performances in Perth, created the dish in her honor.

Basically a fruit tart with a meringue base, the classic pavlova is filled with whipped cream decorated with strawberries and/or kiwi fruit, usually topped with a passion fruit purée. When the meringue is garnished with a shell border of whipped cream, the dessert resembles a ballerina's frilled skirt. There are now countless variations of fillings: fruit, mousse, even ice cream. The meringue base should be crisp on the outside, chewy and not too soft inside. Small, individual pavlovas can also be created. The guiding principle is that the pavlova, like its namesake, should be as light as air.

Coffee Meringue—Substitute 0.5 ounce (15 grams) instant coffee powder and 0.5 fluid ounce (15 milliliters) coffee extract for the vanilla. Coffee crystals will be visible in the meringue.

Lemon or Orange Meringue—Omit the vanilla extract. Add 0.14 ounce (4 grams/2 teaspoons) lemon or orange zest to the meringue at the end of the whipping.

Coconut Meringue—Fold in 6 ounces (180 grams) macaroon-type coconut along with the remaining sugar in Step 3.

Almond Meringue—Fold 4 ounces (120 grams) almond flour and 8 ounces (240 grams) toasted chopped almonds into the whipped egg whites with the remaining sugar in Step 3.

Approximate values per 1-oz. (30-g) serving: **Calories** 80, **Total fat** 0 g, **Saturated fat** 0 g, **Cholesterol** 0 mg, **Sodium** 15 mg, **Total carbohydrates** 19 g, **Protein** 1 g

SWISS MERINGUE

Swiss meringue is made by combining unwhipped egg whites with sugar and warming the mixture over a bain marie to a temperature of approximately 100°F (38°C) until the sugar is dissolved. The syrupy solution is then whipped until cool and stiff. The final product may be hard or soft, depending on the ratio of sugar to egg whites. Swiss meringue is extremely stable but rather difficult to prepare. If the mixture gets too hot, it will not whip properly; the result will be syrupy and runny. Another test for Swiss meringue is to feel whether all of the sugar has dissolved. Once it loses all of its graininess, remove the whites from the double boiler and whip. When baked, Swiss meringue does not expand as much as common meringue, making it ideal for decorations. Swiss meringue is often used as a topping or in buttercream (see Chapter 13, Syrups, Icings and Sauces).

SWISS MERINGUE   RECIPE 11.3

Yield: 2 lb. 12 oz. (1320 g)

Egg whites, room temperature	1 lb.	480 g
Granulated sugar	28 oz.	840 g

1 Combine the egg whites and sugar in a stainless steel bowl.

2 Place the bowl over a pan of barely simmering water and whip until the mixture reaches 100°F (38°C).

3 Remove from the heat and whip the mixture until stiff on medium speed.

4 Pipe or spread into desired shapes.

5 Bake at 250°F (120°C) 1½ to 2 hours, checking for doneness as for common meringue.

Approximate values per 1-oz. (30-g) serving: **Calories** 70, **Total fat** 0 g, **Saturated fat** 0 g, **Cholesterol** 0 mg, **Sodium** 15 mg, **Total carbohydrates** 18 g, **Protein** 1 g

ITALIAN MERINGUE

Italian meringue is made by slowly pouring hot sugar syrup into whipped egg whites. The heat from the syrup cooks the egg whites, adding stability. The sugar solution that is poured on egg whites that were whipped to stiff peaks rather than soft-medium peaks may partially cook the egg whites, resulting in tiny white pieces in the meringue. Be sure that the sugar syrup reaches the correct temperature and that it is added to the egg whites in a slow, steady stream. Italian meringue is used in buttercream or may be flavored and used as a cake filling and frosting called boiled icing. It is indispensable in the aeration of mousses and creams such as crème Chiboust (see Chapter 15, Custards and Creams). Furthermore, the human tongue perceives the texture of Italian meringue as velvety and rich; it is therefore an excellent substitute for high-fat whipped cream in reduced-fat preparations.

For many mousses used as torte and tart fillings, Italian meringue may be stabilized with gelatin. (See Chapter 14, Cakes and Tortes, and Chapter 15, Custards and Creams.) The amount of gelatin varies with the application. The softened or melted gelatin is added to the finished meringue when it reaches 120°F (49°C).

RECIPE 11.4

ITALIAN MERINGUE

Yield: Approximately 1 lb. 7 oz. (690 g)

Granulated sugar	13 oz.	390 g
Glucose or corn syrup	2 oz.	60 g
Water	3 fl. oz.	90 ml
Egg whites, room temperature	8 oz. (8 whites)	240 g

1 Place 12 ounces (360 grams) of the sugar in a heavy saucepan with the glucose and water. Attach a candy thermometer to the pan and bring the sugar to a boil over high heat.

2 Place the egg whites in the bowl of a mixer fitted with a whip. As the temperature of the boiling sugar approaches 220°F (104°C), begin whipping the egg whites. When the whites form soft peaks, gradually add the remaining 1 ounce (30 grams) of sugar. Reduce the mixer speed and continue whipping.

3 When the sugar reaches the soft ball stage (240°F/116°C), remove it from the heat. Pour it into the whites, with the mixer running at high speed. Pour in a steady stream between the side of the bowl and the beater. Once all the sugar is incorporated, whip 1 more minute at high speed, then reduce to medium speed and whip until the meringue is cool.

Approximate values per 1-oz. (30-g) serving: **Calories** 70, **Total fat** 0 g, **Saturated fat** 0 g, **Cholesterol** 0 mg, **Sodium** 20 mg, **Total carbohydrates** 17 g, **Protein** 1 g, **Claims**—fat free; no cholesterol; low sodium

NUT MERINGUE PREPARATIONS

Often ground nuts and starch, usually cake flour, are folded into meringue before baking to make various preparations used for pastries and tortes. Since ground nuts can be oily, the small amount of flour helps absorb the oil and makes the meringue more stable. While the names for these preparations vary—dacquoise, progrès, succès and japonais—the formulas are similar. Small changes in the ratio of ingredients create subtle differences in the textures of the finished products. Formulas for three nut meringue cakes—Dacquoise, Succès and Hazelnut and Cherry Meringue Cake—appear at the end of this chapter.

▶ PHYLLO DOUGH

Phyllo (fee-low), also spelled *filo* or *fillo*, is from the Greek *phyllon*, meaning "thin sheet or leaf." Although its name is Greek, its origin is unknown. Indians, Turks, Syrians, Yugoslavs and Austrians all claim it as their own. Somewhat blandly flavored, phyllo sheets are brushed with melted butter or oil, stacked and then used in many Mediterranean, Middle Eastern and Central Asian dishes as a tart crust or a wrapper for various sweet or savory fillings. Shredded phyllo, called kataifi, is also made and used for some Mediterranean and Middle Eastern specialties.

Phyllo dough is made from flour, water, a bit of oil and eggs. The dough must be stretched tissue-paper thin, using techniques that can take years to master. Fortunately, excellent commercially prepared phyllo is available in frozen sheets. Sheets of phyllo can stick together if thawed too quickly, so thaw frozen dough slowly for a day or so in the refrigerator. Then allow the package of dough to sit at room temperature at least 1 hour before opening. (Unused phyllo should not be refrozen; it will keep several days in the refrigerator if tightly wrapped.)

When ready to use, open the package and unfold the stack of leaves. Place them flat on a sheet pan or work surface and cover with a sheet of plastic wrap topped with a damp towel. Remove one leaf at a time from the stack, keeping the remainder well covered to prevent them from drying out. Brush melted butter or oil over the sheet's entire surface. Chopped nuts, sugar, cocoa powder or bread crumbs can be dusted over the butter or oil for additional flavor. Repeat with additional leaves until the desired number of layers have been prepared and stacked together. The number of layers will depend on the thickness of the sheets and their use. Cut the stacked phyllo with scissors or a very sharp knife and use as directed in the formula. Formulas using phyllo dough are found at the end of this chapter.

▶ CRÊPES

Crêpes are thin, delicate, unleavened pancakes. They are made with a very liquid egg batter cooked in a small, very hot sauté pan or crêpe pan. Crêpe batter can be flavored with buckwheat flour, cornmeal or other grains. Crêpes are not eaten as is, but are usually filled and garnished with sautéed fruits, creams or fruit preserves. A crêpe may be filled with any type of soufflé mixture, baked in the oven and served warm. Crêpes can be prepared in advance, then filled and reheated as needed.

A traditional way to serve a number of crêpe desserts is in a preparation known as **crêpes flambées**. The prepared crêpes are reheated in full view of the customer, then flamed with a flavored brandy before plating and serving them. Crêpes Suzette is the most famous of these preparations. A waiter well skilled in tableside service reheats the crêpes with butter and sugar in a decorative sauté pan. Once the sugar begins to caramelize, orange juice and zest are added. An orange-scented liqueur or brandy is added, then carefully ignited. As the alcohol burns off, flames leap from the sauté pan. Then the waiter skillfully folds the crêpes into quarters, placing one or two on each plate. Variations on this type of hot crêpe dish are popular for dessert menus as well as buffet presentations. See Flambéed Pineapple in Crêpes with Blackberry Sorbet (page 519).

Blintzes are crêpes that are cooked on only one side, then filled with cheese, browned in butter and served with sour cream, fruit compote or preserves. A formula for cheese blintzes is provided at the end of this chapter.

▶ PROCEDURE FOR PREPARING CRÊPES

1 Prepare the batter.
2 Heat a well-seasoned crêpe pan or small sauté pan over moderately high heat. Add a small amount of clarified butter.
3 Ladle a small amount of batter into the pan. Tilt the pan so that the batter spreads and coats the bottom evenly.
4 Cook until the crêpe is set and the bottom begins to brown, approximately 1 minute. Flip the crêpe over with a quick flick of the wrist or by lifting it carefully with a spatula.
5 Cook the crêpe for an additional 30 seconds. Slide the finished crêpe from the pan. Crêpes can be stacked between layers of parchment paper for storage.

RECIPE 11.5 — CRÊPES

Yield: 30 Crêpes, 6 in. (15 cm) each

Eggs	10 oz. (6 eggs)	300 g	71%
Egg yolks	4 oz. (6 yolks)	120 g	28%
Water	12 fl. oz.	360 ml	86%
Whole milk	18 fl. oz.	540 ml	129%
Granulated sugar	6 oz.	180 g	43%
Salt	0.2 oz. (1 tsp.)	6 g	1.4%
All-purpose flour	14 oz.	420 g	100%
Unsalted butter, melted	5 oz.	150 g	36%
Total batter weight:	4 lb. 5 oz.	2076 g	494%
Clarified butter	as needed	as needed	

1 Whisk together the eggs, egg yolks, water and milk. Add the sugar, salt and flour; whisk together. Stir in the melted butter. Cover and set aside to rest at least 1 hour before cooking.
2 Heat a small sauté or crêpe pan; brush lightly with clarified butter. Pour in 1–1½ fluid ounces (30–45 milliliters) of batter; swirl to coat the bottom of the pan evenly.
3 Cook the crêpe until set and light brown, approximately 60 seconds. Flip it over and cook 30 seconds longer. Remove from the pan.
4 Cooked crêpes may be used immediately or covered and held briefly in a warm oven. Crêpes can also be wrapped well in plastic wrap and refrigerated for 2 to 3 days or frozen for several weeks.

VARIATION:

Savory Crêpes—Reduce the sugar to 0.45 ounce (13 grams/1 tablespoon/0.3%). Substitute up to 5 ounces (150 grams/36%) buckwheat flour or whole-wheat flour for an equal amount of the all-purpose flour if desired.

Approximate values per 2-oz. (60-g) serving: **Calories** 140, **Total fat** 7 g, **Saturated fat** 3.5 g, **Cholesterol** 95 mg, **Sodium** 100 mg, **Total carbohydrates** 17 g, **Protein** 4 g

1 Coating the bottom of the pan evenly with the batter.

2 Flipping the crêpe. Notice the proper light brown color.

CONVENIENCE PRODUCTS

Various mixes and powders are sold to make many of the products discussed in this chapter. The addition of water and eggs turns powdered éclair mix into batter for éclairs, puffs or profiteroles. While mixes remove the guesswork from measuring and mixing, no mix can make up for a lack of skill in the forming and baking of these products. Éclairs made from mix tend to bake into drier products than those made from scratch.

Meringue powder is made from dried egg whites and may contain sugar, gums and other additives. When water is added, the product may be whipped to make baked meringue or to use in any preparation calling for meringue. Meringue powder bakes into a sweet, dense meringue with less of the lightness associated with a scratch product. Since it is very stable, meringue powder is frequently added to liquid egg whites when whipping them for icings and mousses, as discussed in Chapter 13, Syrups, Icings and Sauces, and Chapter 15, Custards and Creams. Fully cooked meringues come in many sizes, from small cookies to whole tart shells. When stored under dry conditions, these products will keep for several months.

It is the rare bakeshop where phyllo dough is made by hand. Quality fresh or frozen dough is standard.

Powdered crêpe batter to which eggs, water or milk is added is available. Some operations will elect to purchase frozen cooked crêpes, using the time saved to prepare fresh fruit and cream fillings.

CONCLUSION

The simple flour-and-egg paste from which éclairs are made is a useful preparation for classic pastries and modern desserts. Whipped egg whites offer the pastry chef a number of light preparations, including baked meringues, often served with fruit, cream or chocolate fillings or as a stand-alone dessert. Thin-layered doughs like phyllo pastry have varied uses for wrapping fruit desserts or for adding texture when used as a garnish. The classic crêpe is more than a refined pancake and is the basis for a number of hot plated desserts.

QUESTIONS FOR DISCUSSION

1 Why is it said that éclair paste is the only dough that is cooked before it is baked? Why is this step necessary? List three ways of using éclair paste in making classic desserts.

2 Explain the process by which products made from éclair paste are leavened.

3 Explain the differences and similarities between common, Swiss and Italian meringues.

4 Discuss ways in which phyllo dough may be used to make tart or pie products.

5 In which ways might crêpes be served as a hot plated dessert?

Many of the formulas in this section use components that appear in other chapters in this book. For example, Gâteau St. Honoré uses puff pastry dough, discussed in Chapter 12, Laminated Doughs. Your first goal as a student should be to learn to prepare a variety of pastry components. You can then combine and assemble them appropriately into both classic and modern desserts.

RECIPE 11.6

GÂTEAU ST. HONORÉ

CHEFS SUSAN FENIGER AND MARY SUE MILLIKEN

Susan Feniger and Mary Sue Milliken are the chefs and co-owners of Border Grill and Ciudad, both in Los Angeles, California. Culinary graduates, they met in 1978 at Le Perroquet in Chicago, Illinois. After time spent cooking in France, they joined forces in Los Angeles to open City Restaurant, where the food was inspired by the lively flavors of street food found in Latin countries. These two classically trained chefs have been exciting the culinary world of Los Angeles for more than 20 years, turning their vision into critically acclaimed restaurants, cookbooks and the television series *Two Hot Tamales.*

Note: This dish appears in the chapter opening photograph.

Chefs Susan Feniger and Mary Sue Milliken

Yield: 10 Servings

Puff Pastry (page 312)	1 lb.	480 g
Éclair Paste:		
Milk	4 fl. oz.	120 ml
Unsalted butter	1.75 oz.	50 g
Salt	0.03 oz. ($\frac{1}{8}$ tsp.)	1 g
All-purpose flour	2.5 oz.	75 g
Eggs	3.3 oz. (2 eggs)	100 g
Pastry Cream (page 436)	as needed	as needed
Caramel:		
Granulated sugar	10 oz.	300 g
Water	4 fl. oz.	120 ml
City Chocolate (recipe follows)	as needed	as needed
Heavy cream, cold	1 pt.	480 ml
Semisweet chocolate, melted	3 oz.	90 g

1 Roll out the Puff Pastry to form a 10-inch (25-centimeter) square; reserve in the refrigerator.

2 Make the éclair paste by combining the milk, butter and salt in a medium-heavy saucepan. Bring to a boil. Add the flour all at once. Mix quickly with a wooden spoon until a ball forms on the spoon and the flour is evenly moistened. Transfer to a bowl and add the eggs one at a time, beating well after each addition.

3 Fit a piping bag with a large plain tip; fill it with the éclair paste. Line a baking sheet with parchment paper. Pipe the dough onto the baking sheet to form small circles about the size of quarters. With a finger dipped in cold water, flatten the point on top of each puff. Drop the pan on the counter to set the puffs.

4 Bake at 450°F (230°C) until uniformly puffed and golden, approximately 10 minutes. Reduce the heat to 375°F (190°C) and bake an additional 15 to 20 minutes. Test for doneness by opening a puff. The inside should be totally dry. Set aside to cool on a rack.

5 Place the Puff Pastry on a parchment-paper-lined baking sheet and, with a 10-inch (25-centimeter) round cake pan inverted over the dough, trace a circle using a sharp knife. This will be the base for the cake. Remove the excess dough and prick the circle of Puff Pastry all over with a fork; set in the refrigerator to rest for 15 minutes.

6 Bake the Puff Pastry at 425°F (220°C) until puffed and golden, approximately 20 minutes. Reserve at room temperature.

7 Fit a piping bag with a #2 tip; fill it with Pastry Cream. Make a hole in the bottom of each puff using a small paring knife. Fill each puff with Pastry Cream and reserve.

8 To make the caramel, combine the sugar and water in a saucepan and cook until golden brown. Immediately remove from the heat. Using a fork, dip half of each cream puff into the warm caramel and place on a tray lined with parchment paper. When the caramel has set, turn each puff and dip the uncoated half in the caramel. Immediately arrange the puffs, flat side up, along the edge of the cooled puff pastry to form the wall.

9 Spread an even layer of City Chocolate over the center of the pastry.

10 Whip the cream until soft peaks form. Fold half of this cream into the melted chocolate and set aside.

11 Spoon the remaining whipped cream into a pastry bag fitted with a #8 plain tip. Pipe about five rows of kiss-shaped domes over the chocolate filling, leaving even spaces between the rows. Fill the bag with the chocolate-flavored cream and repeat, filling the spaces between rows. Chill until serving time.

Approximate values per ¹⁄₁₀-cake serving: **Calories** 400, **Total fat** 25 g, **Saturated fat** 15 g, **Cholesterol** 115 mg, **Sodium** 65 mg, **Total carbohydrates** 41 g, **Protein** 4 g, **Vitamin A** 25%

CITY CHOCOLATE

Yield: 1 lb. 10 oz. (795 g)

Brandy	0.75 fl. oz.	20 ml
Golden raisins	1.5 oz.	45 g
Semisweet chocolate	9 oz.	270 g
Unsalted butter	7 oz.	210 g
Egg yolks	3.3 oz. (5 yolks)	100 g
Egg whites	5 oz. (5 whites)	150 g

1 Combine the brandy and raisins in a small saucepan and warm over low heat. Reserve.

2 Chop the chocolate into small pieces and melt with the butter over a bain marie. Remove from the heat and stir in the raisins and brandy. Whisk in the egg yolks until combined.

3 Whisk the egg whites until soft peaks form. Gently fold the whites into the chocolate mixture in two stages.

Approximate values per 1-oz. (30-g) serving: **Calories** 120, **Total fat** 9 g, **Saturated fat** 6 g, **Cholesterol** 55 mg, **Sodium** 15 mg, **Total carbohydrates** 7 g, **Protein** 2 g

RECIPE 11.7

CHOCOLATE ÉCLAIRS

1 Using a pastry bag to fill the éclairs with pastry cream.

2 Dipping the éclairs in chocolate glaze.

Yield: 20 Éclairs

Baked éclair shells, 4 in. (10 cm) long, made from Éclair Paste (page 286)	20	20
Pastry Cream (page 436)	1 qt.	1 lt
Chocolate Glaze (page 361), warm	as needed	as needed
White chocolate, melted (optional)	as needed	as needed

1 Use a paring knife or skewer to cut a small hole in the end of each baked, cooled éclair shell.

2 Pipe the Pastry Cream into each shell using a piping bag fitted with a small plain tip. Be sure that the cream fills the full length of each shell. Refrigerate the filled éclairs.

3 In a single, smooth stroke, drag the top of each filled éclair through the warm Chocolate Glaze. Only the very top of each pastry should be coated with chocolate.

4 Melted white chocolate may be piped onto the wet glaze, then pulled into patterns using a toothpick. Keep the finished éclairs refrigerated and serve within 8 to 12 hours.

VARIATION:

Raspberry Cream and Fruit-Filled Éclairs—Prepare the éclairs. Dip the bottom of the cooled pastry shells in Decorating Caramel (see page 352). Slice each éclair in half horizontally. Reserve the caramelized half. With a medium plain tip, fill the other half with Diplomat Cream Filling (see page 453) and garnish with fresh raspberries, blackberries or strawberries. Top with the caramelized side on top. Dust with powdered sugar.

Approximate values per éclair: **Calories** 410, **Total fat** 31 g, **Saturated fat** 17 g, **Cholesterol** 110 mg, **Sodium** 230 mg, **Total carbohydrates** 27 g, **Protein** 5 g, **Vitamin A** 20%

RECIPE 11.8

PARIS-BREST

Named for a famed 19th-century bicycle race between the city of Paris and the country town of Brest, France, the Paris-Brest resembles a puffed bicycle tire. It is filled with a hazelnut pastry cream and may be sprinkled with Hazelnut Crunch (page 583).

Yield: 12 Individual Pastries

Éclair paste (page 286)	2 lb.	1 kg
Egg wash	as needed	as needed
Sliced almonds	1 oz.	30 g
Paris-Brest Cream (recipe follows)	2 lb. 8 oz.	1200 g
Powdered sugar	1 oz.	30 g

1 Using a pastry bag with a large star tip, pipe the Éclair Paste into rings 3½ inches (9 centimeters) in diameter onto a paper-lined sheet pan.

2 Brush the rings lightly with egg wash and then sprinkle with sliced almonds.

3 Bake in a 375°F (190°C) oven until golden brown and the rings' interior are well dried, about 30 minutes. Let cool, then slice the rings in half horizontally.

4 Pipe the Paris-Brest Cream on the bottom half of the baked rings in a connecting chain of rosettes using a medium star tip and pastry bag.

5 Replace the top halves. Dust with powdered sugar.

Approximate values per serving: **Calories** 630, **Total fat** 52 g, **Saturated fat** 29 g, **Cholesterol** 330 mg, **Sodium** 500 mg, **Total carbohydrates** 36 g, **Protein** 9 g, **Vitamin A** 25%

PARIS-BREST CREAM

Yield: 2 lb. 8 oz. (1200 g)

Unsalted butter, softened	12 oz.	360 g
Hazelnut paste, smooth and lump-free	4 oz.	120 g
Pastry Cream (page 436)	1 lb. 8 oz.	720 g

1 In the bowl of a mixer fitted with a paddle, cream the butter until light and fluffy. Add the hazelnut paste and continue the creaming process. Add the Pastry Cream in one step and mix until well combined.

Approximate values per 1-oz. (30-g) serving: **Calories** 110, **Total fat** 10 g, **Saturated fat** 5 g, **Cholesterol** 50 mg, **Sodium** 10 mg, **Total carbohydrates** 5 g, **Protein** 1 g

POPOVERS

RECIPE 11.9

Popovers are crisp hollow muffins made from a rich egg batter. The steam released from the eggs and milk as the popovers bake is trapped in the gluten web of the batter, causing it to rise. Popovers and other products that rely on steam for leavening are baked at a high temperature so that the steam forms quickly before the gluten bond sets. Yorkshire pudding, a popular accompaniment to roasted rib of beef, is made from this same batter. These pastries resemble products baked from éclair paste.

CONNECTICUT CULINARY INSTITUTE, FARMINGTON, CT
Chef Jamie Roraback

Yield: 20 Popovers

Beef fat or vegetable oil	12 fl. oz.	360 ml
All-purpose flour	8 oz.	240 g
Salt	0.2 oz. (1 tsp.)	6 g
Eggs	10 oz. (6 eggs)	300 g
Whole milk	16 fl. oz.	480 ml
Whole butter, melted	3 oz.	90 g

1 Place 20 4-ounce (120-milliliter) greased ramekins or popover tins on a sheet pan and drop 0.5 fluid ounce (15 milliliters) beef fat or vegetable oil in the bottom of each ramekin. Place the ramekins in a 425°F (220°C) oven until the fat smokes.

2 Sift the flour and salt together into a large bowl. In a separate bowl, whisk together the eggs, milk and butter. Pour the liquid ingredients into the dry ingredients and whip until smooth.

3 Remove the ramekins from the oven and fill each approximately two-thirds full with batter. Bake at 425°F (220°C) 20 minutes without opening the oven door. After 20 minutes, reduce the heat to 375°F (190°C) and bake approximately 10 more minutes.

4 Remove the popovers from the oven, unmold and serve.

5 For crisper popovers, slit the sides of the unmolded popovers to allow the steam to escape. Place on a sheet pan and return them to the oven until the tops are firm, crisp and brown, approximately 10 minutes.

VARIATION:

Onion Popovers—Sauté 2 ounces (60 grams) finely chopped onion in 0.5 ounce (15 grams) butter until tender. Sprinkle the onion over the batter just before baking.

Approximate values per popover: **Calories** 250, **Total fat** 21 g, **Saturated fat** 11 g, **Cholesterol** 95 mg, **Sodium** 150 mg, **Total carbohydrates** 10 g, **Protein** 4 g

RECIPE 11.10

CHURROS (FLUTED MEXICAN DOUGHNUT STICKS)

Yield: 2½ Dozen Pastries

Éclair Paste (page 286)	2 lb.	960 g
Granulated sugar	4 oz.	120 g
Cinnamon, ground	0.2 oz. (1 Tbsp.)	6 g
Chocolate Fudge Sauce (page 376)	as needed	as needed

1 Place the Éclair Paste in a pastry bag fitted with a medium star tip.

2 Heat the deep fat to 375°F (191°C). Pipe 6-inch- (15-centimeter-) long strips of Éclair Paste into the fat, cutting the Éclair Paste with a small knife into uniform lengths. Allow the pastries to swim freely in the fat. Deep-fry the dough until golden brown.

3 Combine the sugar and cinnamon in a large bowl. Toss the hot churros in the sugar mixture to coat. Serve the churros while still hot with a cup of warmed Chocolate Fudge Sauce for dipping.

Approximate values per pastry: **Calories** 150, **Total fat** 12 g, **Saturated fat** 5 g, **Cholesterol** 65 mg, **Sodium** 190 mg, **Total carbohydrates** 10 g, **Protein** 2 g

RECIPE 11.11

BAKED MERINGUE

Yield: 6 lb. 8 oz. (3 kg) Batter

Egg whites	2 lb. 3 oz.	1 kg
Granulated sugar	4 lb. 6 oz.	2 kg
Vanilla extract (optional)	2.5 fl. oz.	75 ml

1 Whip the egg whites to soft peaks. With the mixer running at medium speed, slowly add the sugar and continue whipping until very stiff and glossy.

2 Whip in the vanilla (if using).

3 Spread or pipe the meringue into the desired shapes on parchment-lined sheet pans.

4 Bake at 200°F (90°C) 5 hours or overnight in a nonconvection oven. The baked meringues should be firm and crisp but not browned.

5 Use in assembling dessert or pastry items.

VARIATION:

Flavored Meringue—Substitute coffee, lemon, orange, anise or other flavoring for the vanilla extract.

Approximate values per serving: **Calories** 80, **Total fat** 0 g, **Saturated fat** 0 g, **Cholesterol** 0 mg, **Sodium** 15 mg, **Total carbohydrates** 20 g, **Protein** 1 g

RECIPE 11.12

MERVEILLEUX PASTRIES

Yield: 15 Individual Pastries

Crème Chantilly (page 445)	1 qt.	1 lt
Common (French) Meringue (page 288), baked into 2¼-in (6-cm) disks	30 disks	30 disks
Raspberries or wild strawberries	10 oz.	300 g
Chocolate shavings	9 oz.	270 g
Cocoa powder	0.5 oz.	15 g

1 Using a pastry bag fitted with a medium tip, pipe a large rosette of the Crème Chantilly on half of the meringue disks.

2 Place a few berries on the cream and top with an inverted meringue disk.

3 Ice the sides and top of the merveilleux with the remaining Crème Chantilly.
4 Roll the merveilleux, sides and top, in chocolate shavings.
5 Dust lightly with cocoa powder and garnish with more berries.

Approximate values per serving: **Calories** 350, **Total fat** 18 g, **Saturated fat** 11 g, **Cholesterol** 45 mg, **Sodium** 40 mg, **Total carbohydrates** 48 g, **Protein** 3 g, **Vitamin C** 15%

DACQUOISE   RECIPE 11.13

Yield: 3 Rounds, 7 or 8 in. (17 or 20 cm) each, or 1 Half-Sheet Pan, or approximately 35 Individual Rounds, 3 in. (7.5 cm) each

Egg whites	8 oz. (8 whites)	240 g	800%
Dried egg whites (optional)	0.3 oz. (2 tsp.)	10 g	30%
Granulated sugar	9.5 oz.	285 g	950%
Vanilla extract	0.5 fl. oz.	15 ml	50%
Almond flour	7 oz.	210 g	700%
Cake flour	1 oz.	30 g	100%
Total batter weight:	1 lb. 10 oz.	790 g	2630%

1 Whip the liquid egg whites in the bowl of a mixer fitted with a whip on medium speed until foamy. If using the dried egg whites, sift them with 4 ounces (120 grams) of the sugar and add to the foamy egg whites. Whip the egg whites until they hold a firm peak. Fold in the vanilla.
2 Stir the remaining 5.5 ounces (165 grams) of the sugar into the flours. Fold this mixture into the whipped egg whites with a rubber spatula.
3 Place the mixture in a pastry bag fitted with a medium to large tip. Pipe it into three or four 7-inch (17-centimeter) discs on a paper-lined sheet pan. (Or spread on a paper-lined half-sheet pan.)
4 Bake at 350°F (180°C) until done, approximately 30 minutes. Check for doneness by removing part of the crust using a paring knife; the interior should spring back when lightly pressed.
5 This cake is a component in Chocolate Délice (page 301). Or it may be filled with whipped cream or any of the buttercream fillings in Chapter 13, Syrups, Icings and Sauces.

VARIATIONS:

Nougatine Dacquoise—Chop 8 ounces (240 grams/800%) Basic Nougatine (page 633) into fine pieces. Fold into the dacquoise mixture along with the dry ingredients. Because the nougatine may clog a pastry tip, pipe using a pastry bag without a tip.

Dried Apricot and Pistachio Dacquoise—Finely chop 5 ounces (150 grams/500%) dried apricots and 5 ounces (150 grams/500%) pistachios. Fold into the dacquoise mixture along with the dry ingredients. Because the fruit and nuts may clog a tip, pipe using a pastry bag without a tip.

Pistachio Dacquoise—Replace half of the almond flour with pistachio flour.

Chocolate or Macadamia Nut Dacquoise—Fold 10 ounces (300 grams/1000%) finely chopped chocolate chunks or 8 ounces (240 grams/800%) finely chopped macadamia nuts into the dacquoise mixture with the dry ingredients.

Approximate values per 1-oz. (30-g) serving: **Calories** 90, **Total fat** 4 g, **Saturated fat** 0 g, **Cholesterol** 0 mg, **Sodium** 15 mg, **Total carbohydrates** 13 g, **Protein** 3 g

RECIPE 11.14

SUCCÈS (NUT MERINGUE CAKE)

Yield: 3 to 4 Rounds, 6 in. (15 cm) each

Egg whites	8 oz. (8 whites)	240 g	400%
Dried egg whites (optional)	0.3 oz. (2 tsp.)	9 g	15%
Granulated sugar	12 oz.	360 g	600%
Vanilla extract	0.15 fl. oz. (1 tsp.)	5 ml	7.5%
Almond or hazelnut flour or combination	8 oz.	240 g	400%
Cake flour	2 oz.	60 g	100%
Buttercream, Crème Chantilly (page 445) or icing	as needed	as needed	
Total batter weight:	1 lb. 14 oz.	914 g	1523%

1 Whip the liquid egg whites in the bowl of a mixer fitted with a whip on medium speed until foamy. If using the dried egg whites, sift them with 5 ounces (150 grams) of the sugar and add to the whipped egg whites.

2 Whip the egg whites to firm peaks. Fold in the vanilla.

3 Stir the remaining 7 ounces (210 grams) of sugar into the nut and cake flours. Fold the nut-and-flour mixture into the whipped egg whites using a rubber spatula.

4 Pipe the mixture onto a paper-lined sheet pan in three or four 6 inch (15 centimeter) diameter rounds using a medium-large tip.

5 Bake at 350°F (180°C) until golden and crisp, approximately 30 minutes.

6 Cool the cake and fill with buttercream, Crème Chantilly or other icing.

Approximate values per 1-oz. (30-g) serving: **Calories** 100, **Total fat** 4 g, **Saturated fat** 0 g, **Cholesterol** 0 mg, **Sodium** 15 mg, **Total carbohydrates** 14 g, **Protein** 3 g

RECIPE 11.15

HAZELNUT AND CHERRY MERINGUE CAKE

Yield: 3 Half-Sheet Pans

Cake flour, sifted	8 oz.	240 g	100%
Hazelnuts, toasted and coarsely chopped	1 lb. 9 oz.	750 g	312%
Hazelnut flour	9 oz.	270 g	112%
Powdered sugar	14 oz.	420 g	175%
Dried cherries	10 oz.	300 g	125%
Egg whites	2 lb. (32 whites)	960 g	400%
Dried egg whites (optional)	0.5 oz.	15 g	6%
Granulated sugar	1 lb.	480 g	200%
Total batter weight:	7 lb. 2 oz.	3435 g	1430%

1 Stir the cake flour, hazelnuts, hazelnut flour, powdered sugar and dried cherries together in a small bowl. Set aside.

2 Whip the liquid egg whites in the bowl of a mixer fitted with a whip until foaming.

3 Combine the dried egg whites (if using) with the granulated sugar and add the mixture to the whipped egg whites.

4 Whip the egg whites until they hold a firm peak. Fold in the dry ingredients.

5 Spread the mixture using an offset metal spatula over paper-lined sheet pans.

6 Bake at 350°F (180°C) until the cake bounces back when lightly pressed, approximately 40 minutes. Cool completely before using. This cake is a component in Nobilis Torte (page 428). Or it may be filled with whipped cream or any of the buttercream fillings in Chapter 13, Syrups, Icings and Sauces.

Approximate values per 1-oz. (30-g) serving: **Calories** 100, **Total fat** 5 g, **Saturated fat** 0 g, **Cholesterol** 0 mg, **Sodium** 15 mg, **Total carbohydrates** 13 g, **Protein** 3 g

CHOCOLATE DÉLICE   RECIPE 11.16

Yield: 1 Cake, 8 in. (20 cm)

Chocolate Ganache (page 362)	7 oz.	210 g
Dacquoise (page 299),		
8-in. (20-cm) disks	3 disks	3 disks
Crème Chantilly (page 445)	2 qt.	2 lt
Candied Almonds (recipe follows)	as needed	as needed

1 Spread an even layer of soft Chocolate Ganache over two of the Dacquoise disks. (If the ganache has been refrigerated, warm it in a bain marie over simmering water just until it is soft enough to spread easily.)

2 Top one disk with approximately ³⁄₄ cup (170 milliliters) Crème Chantilly. Place the second disk on top, ganache side up. Top with another ³⁄₄ cup (170 milliliters) Crème Chantilly. Position the third disk on top, flat side up.

3 Spread the remaining Crème Chantilly over the top and sides.

4 Sprinkle Candied Almonds over the top and sides of the cake.

5 Freeze to firm the cream, approximately 1 hour. Remove from freezer and refrigerate for service.

Approximate values per ¹⁄₈-cake serving: **Calories** 490, **Total fat** 32.5 g, **Saturated fat** 13 g, **Cholesterol** 50 mg, **Sodium** 35 mg, **Total carbohydrates** 39 g, **Protein** 10 g, **Vitamin A** 16%

1 Piping out the meringue discs.

2 Layering the ganache-covered dacquoise.

CANDIED ALMONDS

Egg whites	2 oz. (2 whites)	60 g
Granulated sugar	2 oz.	60 g
Sliced almonds	8 oz.	240 g

1 Preheat oven to 325°F (160°C).

2 Whisk the egg whites and sugar together. Add the almonds. Toss with a rubber spatula to coat the nuts completely.

3 Spread the nuts in a thin layer on a lightly greased baking sheet. Bake until lightly toasted and dry, approximately 15 to 20 minutes. Watch closely to prevent burning.

4 Stir the nuts with a metal spatula every 5 to 7 minutes during baking.

5 Cool completely. Store in an airtight container up to 10 days.

Approximate values per serving: **Calories** 160, **Total fat** 10 g, **Saturated fat** 1 g, **Cholesterol** 0 mg, **Sodium** 10 mg, **Total carbohydrates** 10 g, **Protein** 6 g, **Claims**—no saturated fat; no cholesterol; very low sodium

3 Frosting the délice.

RECIPE 11.17 — **APPLE STRUDEL**

Yield: 2 Rolls, 12 in. (30 cm) each

Apples, peeled, cored and slivered	1 lb. 8 oz.	720 g
Lemon juice	0.5 fl. oz.	15 ml
Granulated sugar	8 oz.	240 g
Raisins	2 oz.	60 g
Orange zest, grated	0.2 oz. (1 Tbsp.)	6 g
Cinnamon, ground	0.07 oz. (1 tsp.)	2 g
Phyllo dough	12 sheets	12 sheets
Clarified butter, melted	4 fl. oz.	120 ml
Ground almonds	0.6 oz.	18 g

1 Toss the apples with the lemon juice and half of the sugar in a medium bowl. Let stand 30 minutes, then drain off the liquid that forms.

2 Gently combine the drained apples with the raisins, orange zest, cinnamon and the remaining sugar.

3 Prepare the phyllo dough by laying one sheet out on a piece of parchment paper. Brush lightly with clarified butter and top with a second sheet of phyllo. Brush this sheet lightly with butter and sprinkle with about 0.1 oz. (1 teaspoon/3 grams) ground almonds. Top with a third sheet of dough, more butter and nuts and repeat until six sheets of phyllo are stacked.

4 Place half of the apple mixture along the short edge of the assembled dough. Using the paper to assist with rolling the dough, roll the phyllo around the filling tightly.

5 Place the strudel seam side down on a baking sheet. Brush the surface lightly with melted butter. Bake at 375°F (190°C) until golden brown and crisp, approximately 18 minutes.

Approximate values per ⅙-roll serving: **Calories** 260, **Total fat** 10 g, **Saturated fat** 6 g, **Cholesterol** 20 mg, **Sodium** 0 mg, **Total carbohydrates** 42 g, **Protein** 2 g

1 Brushing phyllo sheets with clarified butter.

2 Sprinkling phyllo with chopped nuts before adding another layer of phyllo.

3 Topping the phyllo sheets with the apples.

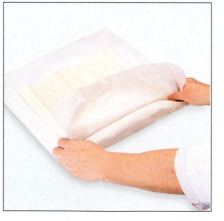

4 Rolling up the strudel.

5 The finished strudel.

GREEK CUSTARD PIE (GALACTOBOUREKO)

SKORPIOS II, LAKE WORTH, FL

Yield: 16 Servings, 1 Pan, 9 in. × 12 in. (22 cm × 30 cm)

Custard:

Milk	1 qt.	1 lt
Granulated sugar	4 oz.	120 g
Semolina flour	4.5 oz.	135 g
Unsalted butter	2 oz.	60 g
Orange zest, grated fine	0.2 oz. (1 Tbsp.)	6 g
Vanilla extract	0.3 fl. oz. (2 tsp.)	10 ml
Eggs, beaten	8.3 oz. (5 eggs)	250 g
Clarified butter	6 fl. oz.	180 ml
Phyllo dough, thawed (approximately 24 sheets)	1 lb.	480 g
Egg wash	as needed	as needed

Spiced syrup:

Water	4 fl. oz.	120 ml
Granulated sugar	4 oz.	120 g
Honey	2 fl. oz.	60 ml
Cinnamon sticks	1	1
Whole cloves	3	3

1 In a large saucepan, combine the milk and sugar. Bring to a boil, stirring to dissolve the sugar. Gradually whisk in the semolina. Continue whisking until the mixture thickens and becomes smooth, approximately 2 minutes.

2 Add the unsalted butter, stirring to melt. Remove from the heat and stir in the orange zest and vanilla. Cool the custard to room temperature, then whisk in the beaten eggs.

3 Brush the baking dish with clarified butter. Spread out the phyllo dough on a work surface and cover with a damp towel and then with plastic wrap to prevent it from drying out. Place one sheet of phyllo in the baking dish. Brush with clarified butter and top with another sheet of phyllo. Repeat until 12 sheets of phyllo have been placed in the baking pan.

4 Spread the custard evenly over the phyllo. Top the custard with the remaining phyllo as in Step 3, brushing clarified butter between each sheet. Brush the top layer with egg wash. Cut through the phyllo top to mark servings.

5 Bake at 350°F (180°C) until the phyllo is a deep golden brown and the custard is set, approximately 55 minutes.

6 Prepare the syrup by combining all the ingredients in a small saucepan. Bring to a simmer, stirring to dissolve the sugar. Allow the syrup to boil 5 minutes. Remove from the heat and set aside to cool, then remove the cinnamon and cloves.

7 When the pie is removed from the oven, immediately begin pouring the syrup slowly over the pie, allowing the syrup to soak in before adding more. Chill the pie before cutting for service.

Approximate values per serving: **Calories** 360, **Total fat** 18 g, **Saturated fat** 10 g, **Cholesterol** 105 mg, **Sodium** 190 mg, **Total carbohydrates** 42 g, **Protein** 7 g, **Vitamin A** 15%

RECIPE 11.19

PEACH AND BLUEBERRY NAPOLEON

PESCE RESTAURANT, HOUSTON, TX
Milan Villavicencio

Yield: 10 Servings

Fresh peaches	2 lb.	960 g
Fresh blueberries	2 pt.	1 lt
Orange Muscat wine	8 fl. oz.	240 ml
Phyllo Crisps (recipe follows)	30	30
Muscat Pastry Cream (recipe follows)	as needed	as needed
Powdered sugar	as needed	as needed
Raspberry Sauce (page 372)	1 pt.	480 ml

1 Split the peaches in half and discard the pits. Cut each half into six wedges.

2 Macerate the peach wedges and blueberries in the wine.

3 To assemble each napoleon, place a Phyllo Crisp in the center of a plate. Pipe Muscat Pastry Cream along the edges of the crisp. Arrange four peach wedges and approximately six blueberries on the crisp and pipe a dollop of pastry cream on top of the fruit. Place another crisp on top of the pastry cream and fruit, pipe more pastry cream and add more fruit to this second layer. Top with a third crisp and dust with powdered sugar.

4 Drizzle Raspberry Sauce around the napoleon on the plate and garnish with additional blueberries and peaches.

Approximate values per serving: **Calories** 790, **Total fat** 31 g, **Saturated fat** 17 g, **Cholesterol** 355 mg, **Sodium** 170 mg, **Total carbohydrates** 111 g, **Protein** 10 g, **Vitamin A** 35%, **Vitamin C** 20%, **Calcium** 15%

PHYLLO CRISPS

Yield: 10 Servings

Whole butter, melted	4 oz.	120 g
Powdered sugar	8 oz.	240 g
Phyllo dough, 12-in. × 17-in. (30-cm × 42-cm) sheets	8	8

1 Line a full-sheet pan with parchment paper and brush with melted butter. Dust with powdered sugar and place two sheets of phyllo dough side by side on the pan.

2 Brush the phyllo sheets with butter and dust with powdered sugar. Place a second phyllo sheet on top of each of the first sheets, brush them with butter and dust with powdered sugar. Continue until there are two stacks of phyllo dough, each four layers high.

3 Using a pastry wheel, cut each stack of phyllo into four columns and four rows, creating 16 small rectangular stacks of phyllo dough from each large stack.

4 Cover the phyllo stacks with parchment paper and another sheet pan. Bake at 325°F (160°C) until brown, approximately 15 minutes. Remove and cool.

Approximate values per crisp: **Calories** 70, **Total fat** 3 g, **Saturated fat** 2 g, **Cholesterol** 10 mg, **Sodium** 25 mg, **Total carbohydrates** 10 g, **Protein** 0 g

MUSCAT PASTRY CREAM

Yield: 10 Servings, 5 fl. oz. (150 ml) each

Milk	1 pt.	500 ml
Vanilla bean, seeded	½	½
Cornstarch	2 oz.	60 g
Granulated sugar	8 oz.	240 g
Salt	0.03 oz. (⅛ tsp.)	1 g
Eggs	3.3 oz. (2 eggs)	100 g
Egg yolks	2.6 oz. (4 yolks)	80 g
Orange Muscat wine	2 fl. oz.	60 ml
Heavy cream, cold	12 fl. oz.	360 ml

1 Reserve 2 fluid ounces (60 milliliters) of the milk. Place the remaining milk in a saucepot and add the vanilla bean and its seeds. Scald the milk.

2 Combine the cornstarch with 7 ounces (210 grams) of the sugar, the salt and the reserved milk and whisk until smooth. Add the eggs and egg yolks and mix until they are incorporated and the mixture is smooth.

3 **Temper** the cornstarch mixture with some of the scalded milk and return the mixture to the saucepot with the remaining scalded milk. Whisk and cook over medium heat until the mixture has thickened and begins to boil.

4 Remove the pastry cream from the heat and pour into a hotel pan. Lay plastic wrap over the surface of the pastry cream and refrigerate until completely cold.

5 Whip the chilled pastry cream until smooth, approximately 1 minute. Add the wine and whip to combine.

6 Whip the cream with the remaining sugar to stiff peaks. Combine the whipped pastry cream and the whipped cream and whip together, scraping down the bowl as necessary. Refrigerate until ready to use.

▶ **tempering** heating gently and gradually; refers to the process of slowly adding a hot liquid to eggs or other foods to raise their temperature without causing them to curdle

Approximate values per 5-fl.-oz. (150-ml) serving: **Calories** 370, **Total fat** 22 g, **Saturated fat** 11 g, **Cholesterol** 330 mg, **Sodium** 90 mg, **Total carbohydrates** 36 g, **Protein** 8 g, **Vitamin A** 20%, **Calcium** 10%

RECIPE 11.20

STRAWBERRY CRÊPES FITZGERALD

BRENNAN'S RESTAURANT, New Orleans, LA
Chef Michael Roussel

Yield: 8 Servings

Cream cheese, room temperature	1 lb.	480 g
Sour cream	2.5 oz.	75 g
Vanilla extract	0.5 fl. oz.	15 ml
Granulated sugar	5 oz.	150 g
Crêpes (page 292)	16	16
Whole butter	0.5 oz.	15 g
Fresh strawberries, sliced	1 lb. 8 oz.	720 g
Fresh lemon juice	0.5 fl. oz.	15 ml
Maraschino liqueur	1 fl. oz.	30 ml

1 Combine the cream cheese, sour cream, vanilla and 1 ounce (30 grams) of the sugar in a mixing bowl and beat until smooth.

2 Place 3 tablespoons (45 milliliters) of the filling on one end of each crêpe; roll the crêpes around the filling and then refrigerate them while preparing the topping.

3 To make the topping, heat the butter and the remaining sugar in a large saucepan. Cook over medium heat, stirring until the sugar dissolves. Add the strawberries and lemon juice.

4 Bring the mixture to a boil, then reduce the heat and simmer until the liquid thickens, approximately 10 to 12 minutes. Add the maraschino liqueur and flambé.

5 To serve, place two crêpes on each plate and spoon approximately 6 fluid ounces (180 milliliters) warm strawberry topping over the crêpes.

Approximate values per serving: **Calories** 630, **Total fat** 37 g, **Saturated fat** 22 g, **Cholesterol** 260 mg, **Sodium** 380 mg, **Total carbohydrates** 65 g, **Protein** 13 g, **Vitamin A** 20%, **Vitamin C** 100%

CHEESE BLINTZES

Yield: 16 Blintzes

Eggs	5 oz. (3 eggs)	150 g
Milk	8 fl. oz.	240 ml
Vegetable oil	1 fl. oz.	30 ml
Salt	0.15 oz. (¾ tsp.)	5 g
Flour	4 oz.	120 g
Clarified butter	as needed	as needed
Ricotta	12 oz.	360 g
Egg yolk	0.6 oz. (1 yolk)	20 g
Lemon juice	0.15 fl. oz. (1 tsp.)	5 ml
Vanilla extract	0.15 fl. oz. (1 tsp.)	5 ml
Whole butter	2 oz.	60 g

1 To make the batter, whisk together the eggs, milk and oil. Add 0.1 ounce (½ teaspoon/3 grams) of the salt. Stir in the flour and mix until smooth. Allow the batter to rest 30 minutes.

2 Heat a crêpe pan and add a small amount of clarified butter.

3 Pour 1 fluid ounce (30 milliliters) of the batter into the pan. Tip the pan so that the batter coats the entire surface in a thin layer.

4 Cook the pancake until browned on the bottom. Remove it from the pan.

5 To make the filling, drain the ricotta in a china cap. Combine the egg yolk, remaining 0.05 ounce (¼ teaspoon/2 grams) salt, lemon juice and vanilla with the cheese and mix well.

6 To assemble, place a pancake on the work surface with the cooked side down. Place 1 ounce (30 grams) of the filling in the center of the pancake. Fold the opposite ends in and then roll up to form a small package.

7 Sauté each blintz in butter until hot. Serve with sour cream or fruit compote as desired.

Approximate values per 2-oz. (60-g) serving: **Calories** 110, **Total fat** 7 g, **Saturated fat** 3.5 g, **Cholesterol** 65 mg, **Sodium** 170 mg, **Total carbohydrates** 7 g, **Protein** 5 g

WHEN YOU HAVE MASTERED PUFF PASTRY YOU WILL FIND IT SUCH A SATISFYING AND SPLENDID ACCOMPLISHMENT THAT YOU WILL BLESS YOURSELF FOR EVERY MOMENT YOU SPENT LEARNING THE TECHNIQUES.

—Julia Child and Simone Beck, Mastering the Art of French Cooking, 1961

LAMINATED DOUGHS

AFTER STUDYING THIS CHAPTER, YOU WILL BE ABLE TO:

▶ prepare puff pastry
▶ prepared croissants and Danish pastries
▶ prepare a variety of pastries using these doughs and other components

▶ **feuilletage** (fuh-yuh-TAHZH) French for flaky; used to describe puff pastry or the process for making puff pastry

Few products distinguish a fine bakeshop more than those made from the types of dough presented in this chapter. Forms of these flaky pastries appear on many continents—the croissant and mille feuille in France, the crescent roll in the United States, the flaky custard-filled sfogliatelle in Italy. Formal pâtisserie and humble bakeries are united in the scent of melting butter and crisping pastry from an oven load of baking croissants. These doughs are produced by lamination, a technique that sandwiches layers of fat between layers of dough. Careful handling of ingredients and repeated rolling and folding produces delicate layers of crisp pastry when baked. Though the techniques necessary to make these products require some practice to master, the results are worth the effort.

Puff pastry, croissant and Danish dough are called rolled-in or laminated doughs. These pastries are so named because the fat is incorporated into the dough through a process of rolling and folding. Products made with laminated dough have a distinctive flaky texture created by the repeated layering of fat and dough. While the formulas for making these products may differ, the techniques for laminating and shaping the dough are similar. This chapter covers the techniques for mixing, laminating, handling and baking a variety of rolled-in doughs and pastries. An understanding of the principles for preparing yeast dough covered in Chapter 7, Yeast Breads, is recommended before working with the techniques discussed here.

▶ PUFF PASTRY

Puff pastry is one of the bakeshop's most elegant and sophisticated products. Also known as pâte feuilletée or mille feuille, it is a rich, buttery dough that bakes into hundreds of light, crisp layers. The classic way of making puff pastry produces more than one thousand layers in the finished dough; hence its name in French is *mille feuille,* meaning "one thousand leaves."

Puff pastry is used for both sweet and savory preparations. It can be baked and then filled, or filled first and then baked. Puff pastry may be used to wrap beef (for beef Wellington), pâté (for pâté en croûte) or almond cream (for an apple tart). It can be shaped into shells or cases known as vol-au-vents or bouchées and filled with shellfish in a cream sauce or berries in a pastry cream. Puff pastry is essential for napoleons, pithiviers and tartes tatin. The Italian pastry sfogliatelle is a type of cream-filled puff pastry shaped like a shell.

Puff pastry does not contain any yeast or chemical leavening agents, unlike croissants and Danish, discussed later in this chapter. Fat is rolled into the dough in horizontal layers; when baked, the fat melts, separating the dough into layers. The fat's moisture turns into steam, which causes the dough to rise and the layers to further separate. The bubbling of the fat as the steam escapes also leavens the pastry, as does steam escaping from the moisture in the dough. To ensure that it rises properly, puff pastry must be baked at high temperatures, usually around 400°F (200°C) to convert the moisture to steam as the fat melts.

MAKING PUFF PASTRY

The procedures described here for making and folding puff pastry dough are just two of several. All methods, however, depend on the proper layering of fat and dough through a series of **turns** to give the pastry its characteristic flakiness and rise. While this dough may be rolled by hand, most commercial establishments will use an electric dough sheeter as illustrated on page 314.

A relatively firm dough base (**détrempe**) is made using flour and water. Often, an acid such as cream of tartar, lemon juice or vinegar is added to the dough to make the gluten more elastic. A minimum of one-third of the dough's weight is used as the roll-in fat, with especially rich products containing up to 80 percent fat. While commercially produced **roll-in** fats are acceptable, and shortening or margarine can be used, unsalted butter is the preferred choice. Butter produces a better flavor and color in the finished product and it has better eating qualities; butter melts at body temperature unlike shortening, which tends to coat the tongue with a layer of grease. But butter lacks plasticity and becomes brittle when cold. (In some formulas, a small quantity of flour is mixed in with the butter to help absorb moisture in the butter.) Since butter is more difficult to handle, margarine and special laminating shortenings may be used. Each has a higher melting point and more plasticity but neither offers the flavor or browning qualities of butter.

In this chapter, two methods for folding and rolling in the fat—the **three fold** or **single book fold** method and the **four fold** or **double book fold** method—are illustrated. In order to ensure that puff pastry rises properly, which is six to eight times its initial volume, the fat must be evenly distributed through the dough. These folding methods help ensure proper fat distribution and the maximum number of layers. Equally important, the fat should be neither absorbed by the dough nor broken up into small lumps by the pulling force of the rolling motion with either the rolling pin or pastry sheeter. To achieve this, the roll-in fat must be the same consistency as the dough. Keeping the dough cool, around 40°F to 60°F (4°C to 16°C), during rolling prevents the dough from absorbing the fat.

Using flour when rolling prevents tearing and shredding, but excess flour should be brushed off before folding so that layers adhere to one another. Work rapidly to keep the dough cool. Refrigerating between turns relaxes the gluten, making the dough easier to roll, and chills the dough and fat layers so they will remain separate. If the dough has been rolled more in one direction than another, shrinkage and distortion can occur in the finished pieces. Maintaining square edges helps ensure proper lamination of the dough. Roll in one direction only with each turn.

Some chefs prefer to prepare a dough called blitz or quick puff pastry. It does not require the extensive rolling and folding procedure used for true puff pastry. Blitz puff pastry is less delicate and flaky but may be perfectly acceptable for some uses. A formula for it is given on page 335.

▶ PROCEDURE FOR PREPARING PUFF PASTRY

1 Prepare the dough base (détrempe) by combining flour, water, salt and a small amount of fat. Do not overmix. Overmixing results in greater gluten formation, and too much gluten can make the pastry undesirably tough.

2 Wrap the détrempe and chill several hours or overnight. This allows the gluten to relax and the flour to absorb the liquid.

3 Shape the butter into a rectangle of even thickness; wrap and chill until ready to use.

4 Allow the détrempe and butter to sit at room temperature until slightly softened and of the same consistency. Butter should be firm and cold but pliable like clay.

5 Roll out the détrempe into a rectangle of even thickness large enough to completely cover the butter rectangle.

▶ **turns** the number of times that laminated dough is rolled and folded

▶ **détrempe** (day-trup-eh) a paste made with flour and water during the first stage of preparing pastry doughs, especially rolled-in doughs

▶ **roll-in** shorthand expression for the butter or other fat used in layering laminated dough; also referred to as lock-in fat

6 Position the butter in the center of the dough. Fold each edge of the dough over the butter to completely encase it in the dough. Press the dough to seal the edges and lock in the butter.

7 Roll out the block of dough and butter into a long, even rectangle. Roll only at right angles so that the layered structure is not destroyed.

8 Fold the dough like a business letter: Fold the bottom third up toward the center so that it covers the center third, then fold the top third down over the bottom and middle thirds. This is the single book fold. This step completes the first turn.

9 Rotate the block of dough one quarter turn (90 degrees) on the work surface. Roll out again into a long, even rectangle.

10 Fold the dough in thirds again, like a business letter. This completes the second turn. Wrap the dough and chill approximately 30 minutes. The resting period allows the gluten to relax; the chilling prevents the butter from becoming too soft.

11 Repeat the rolling and folding process, chilling between every one or two turns, until the dough has been turned a total of five times.

12 Wrap well and chill overnight. Raw dough may be refrigerated a few days or frozen 2 to 3 months.

13 Shape and bake as needed. Baked, unfilled puff pastry can be stored at room temperature 2 to 3 days.

RECIPE 12.1

PUFF PASTRY

Yield: 2 lb. (1 kg)   **Method:** Rolled-in dough

All-purpose flour	13 oz.	390 g	100%
Salt	0.3 oz. (1½ tsp.)	9 g	2.3%
Unsalted butter, cold	3 oz.	90 g	23%
Water, cold	7 fl. oz.	210 ml	54%
Unsalted butter, softened	10 oz.	300 g	77%
Total dough weight:	2 lb. 1 oz.	999 g	256%

1 To form the détrempe, sift the flour and salt together in a large bowl. Cut the cold butter into small pieces and then cut the pieces into the flour until the mixture resembles coarse cornmeal.

2 Make a well in the center of the mixture and add all the water at once. Using a rubber spatula or your fingers, gradually draw the flour into the water. Mix until all the flour is incorporated. Do not knead. The détrempe should be sticky and shaggy-looking.

Note: The détrempe can be made in a food processor. To do so, combine the flour, salt and pieces of cold butter in the bowl of a food processor fitted with a metal blade. Process until a coarse meal is formed. With the processor running, slowly add the water. Turn the machine off as soon as the dough comes together to form a ball. Proceed with the remainder of the recipe.

3 Turn the détrempe out onto a lightly floured surface. Knead the dough a few times by hand, rounding it into a ball. Wrap the dough tightly in plastic and chill overnight.

4 To roll in the butter, first prepare the softened butter by placing it between two sheets of parchment paper or plastic film. Use a rolling pin to roll the softened

1 Mise en place for puff pastry. The détrempe is shown on the left.

2 Folding the dough around the butter.

butter into a rectangle, approximately 5 inches × 8 inches (12.5 centimeters × 20 centimeters). It is important that the détrempe and butter be of almost equal consistency. If necessary, allow the détrempe to sit at room temperature to soften or chill the butter briefly to harden.

5 On a lightly floured board, roll the détrempe into a rectangle approximately 12 inches × 15 inches (30 centimeters × 37.5 centimeters). Lift and rotate the dough as necessary to prevent sticking.

6 Use a dry pastry brush to brush away any flour from the dough's surface. Loose flour can cause gray streaks and can prevent the puff pastry from rising properly when baked.

7 Peel one piece of parchment or plastic film from the butter. Position the butter in the center of the rectangle and remove the remaining plastic. Fold the four edges of the détrempe over the butter, enclosing it completely. Stretch the dough if necessary; it is important that none of the butter be exposed.

8 With the folded side facing up, press the dough several times with a rolling pin. Use a rocking motion to create ridges in the dough. Place the rolling pin in each ridge and slowly roll back and forth to widen the ridge. Repeat until all the ridges are doubled in size.

9 Using the ridges as a starting point, roll the dough out into a smooth, even rectangle approximately 8 inches × 24 inches (20 centimeters × 60 centimeters). Be careful to keep the corners of the dough as right angles.

10 Use a dry pastry brush to remove any loose flour from the dough's surface. Fold the dough in thirds, like a business letter, the single book fold. If one end is damaged or in worse condition, fold it in first; otherwise, start at the bottom. This completes the first turn.

11 Rotate the block of dough 90 degrees so that the folded edge is on your left and the dough faces you like a book. Roll out the dough again, repeating the ridging technique. Once again, the dough should be in a smooth, even rectangle of approximately 8 inches × 24 inches (20 centimeters × 60 centimeters).

12 Fold the dough in thirds again, completing the second turn. Cover the dough with plastic wrap and chill at least 30 minutes.

13 Repeat the rolling and folding technique until the dough has had a total of five turns. Do not perform more than two turns without a resting and chilling period. Cover the dough completely and chill overnight before shaping and baking.

Note: It is not necessary to work with the entire block of dough when making bouchées, cookies or the like. Cut the block into thirds or quarters and work with one of these portions at a time, keeping the rest chilled until needed.

Approximate values per 1-oz. (30-g) serving: **Calories** 120, **Total fat** 9 g, Saturated fat 6 g, **Cholesterol** 25 mg, **Sodium** 110 mg, **Total carbohydrates** 9 g, **Protein** 1 g, **Vitamin A** 8%

3 Rolling out the dough.

4 Folding the dough in thirds.

ROLLING-IN LAMINATED DOUGH

Most bakeshops where puff pastry, croissant and Danish dough are made regularly use an electric sheeter to speed the process and ensure consistent results.

▶ PROCEDURE FOR THINNING LAMINATED DOUGH ON A SHEETER

1 Place a block of dough on the bed of a sheeter. Pass the dough under the rollers to thin the dough.

2 Decrease the height of the roller setting on the sheeter. Pass the dough under the rollers to thin the dough. Continue decreasing the height of the rollers on the sheeter and passing the dough under the rollers until the dough is the desired thickness.

3 Thinned dough ready for use.

▶ PROCEDURE FOR MAKING A SINGLE BOOK FOLD

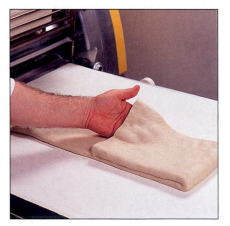 

1 Lift the right side of the dough and fold it over, covering one-third of the dough.

2 Lift the left side of the dough and fold it over to create three uniform layers of dough. Align the edges into a neat packet. This procedure completes one turn.

▶ PROCEDURE FOR MAKING A DOUBLE BOOK FOLD

1 Lift the right side of the dough and fold it over, covering three-quarters of the dough. Pick up the left side of the dough and fold it until the edges touch.

2 Fold both ends of the dough in toward the center again to make four layers. The folded package will resemble a book. This procedure completes one turn.

SHAPING PUFF PASTRY AND LAMINATED DOUGH

Once puff pastry dough is prepared, it can be shaped into containers of various sizes and shapes. **Bouchées** are small puff pastry shells often used for hors d'oeuvre or appetizers. **Vol-au-vents** are larger, deeper shells, often filled with savory mixtures for a main course. Although they may be simply round or square, special vol-au-vent cutters are available in the shape of fish, hearts or petals. **Feuilletées** are square, rectangular or diamond-shaped puff pastry boxes. They can be filled with a sweet or savory mixture.

Use a pastry or rolling cutter to make straight cuts in puff pastry. When a knife must be used, press its tip into the dough and cut by pressing down on the handle. Do not drag the knife through the dough or the layers will be crushed, preventing the dough from rising properly. Sheets of puff pastry to be baked into layers for napoleons (see Strawberry Napoleons page xxx) are docked before baking as are the centers of vol-au-vents and bouchées. Docking with a fork or docker ensures an even rise.

▶ PROCEDURE FOR CUTTING UNIFORM PIECES OF PUFF PASTRY DOUGH

1 Roll out the puff pastry dough into an even rectangle, approximately ⅛ to ¼ inch (3 to 6 millimeters) thick. Square off the edges of the dough using a pastry cutter and a straightedge, reserving the scraps for other uses.

2 Measure horizontally along the top edge of the dough and mark the dough, without cutting through it, with the tip of a knife or pastry cutter spaced every 4 inches (10 centimeters) from the left to right, to use as cutting guides.

3 Repeat this step, measuring the same amount vertically across the dough. Use the straightedge to connect the guides and cut the dough into uniform squares.

▶ **bouchées** (boo-SHAY) small puff pastry shells that can be filled and served as bite-size hors d'oeuvre or petits fours

▶ **vol-au-vents** (vul-oh-vanz) deep, individual portion-sized puff pastry shells, often shaped as a heart, fish or fluted circle; they are filled with a savory mixture and served as an appetizer or main course

▶ **feuilletées** (fuh-yuh-TAY) square, rectangular or diamond-shaped puff pastry boxes; may be filled with a sweet or savory mixture

▶ PROCEDURE FOR SHAPING VOL-AU-VENTS AND BOUCHÉES

1 Roll out the puff pastry dough to a thickness of approximately ¼ inch (6 millimeters).

2 Cut the desired shape and size using a vol-au-vent cutter or rings.

3 Place the vol-au-vent or bouchée on a paper-lined sheet pan. If you used rings, place the base on the paper-lined sheet pan, brush lightly with water, then top it with the dough ring; score the edge with the back of a paring knife. Chill 20 to 30 minutes to allow the dough to relax before baking.

4 Brush with egg wash if desired and dock the center with a fork.

1 A vol-au-vent cutter looks like a double cookie cutter with one cutter about 1 inch (2.5 centimeters) smaller than the other. To cut the pastry, simply position the cutter and press down.

2 To shape the rings, use two rings, one approximately 1 inch (2.5 centimeters) smaller than the other. The larger ring is used to cut two rounds. One will be the base and is set aside. Use the smaller ring to cut out an interior circle from the second round, leaving a border ring of dough.

▶ PROCEDURE FOR SHAPING FEUILLETÉES

1 Roll out the puff pastry dough into an even rectangle, approximately ⅛ to ¼ inch (3 to 6 millimeters) thick. Square off the edges of the dough using a pastry cutter and a straightedge, reserving the scraps for other uses.

2 Using a sharp paring knife or chef's knife, cut squares that are about 2 inches (5 centimeters) larger than the desired interior of the finished feuilletée.

3 Fold each square in half diagonally. Cut through two sides of the dough, about ½ inch (1.2 centimeters) from the edge. Cut a V, being careful not to cut through the corners at the center fold.

4 Open the square and lay it flat. Brush water on the edges to seal the dough. Lift opposite sides of the cut border at the cut corners and cross them.

5 Place the feuilletées on a paper-lined sheet pan.

6 Score the edges with the back of a paring knife. Chill 20 to 30 minutes to allow the dough to relax before baking.

7 Brush with egg wash if desired and dock the center with a fork.

▶ PROCEDURE FOR SHAPING PINWHEELS OR WINDMILLS

1 Roll out the puff pastry dough approximately ⅛ to ¼ inch (3 to 6 millimeters) thick and cut it into even 4-inch (10-centimeter) squares (upper left). Starting at each corner, make four diagonal cuts 1 inch (2.5 centimeters) long in the dough without cutting the dough in half (upper right). Fold one point in each triangular section of dough down toward the center to form the pinwheel shape (lower left and right).

▶ PROCEDURE FOR SHAPING BEAR CLAWS

1 Roll out the puff pastry dough approximately ⅛ to ¼ inch (3 to 6 millimeters) thick and cut it into even 4-inch (10-centimeter) squares (upper left). Place approximately 2 ounces (30 grams) almond paste, frangipane or other filling in the center of the dough (lower left). Moisten the edges of the dough with water, then fold the dough over to enclose the filling (upper right). Seal the edges of the pastry. With a pastry cutter or knife, cut short incisions along one edge of the pastry spaced ½ inch (1.2 centimeters) apart (center right). Curve the pastry slightly before placing on the baking sheet (lower left).

2 Chill the dough 20 to 30 minutes before baking. Brush with egg wash if desired.

3 Bake the bear claw. Brush the baked pastry with glaze.

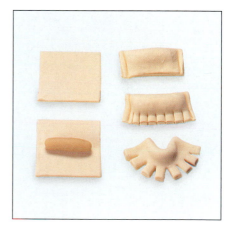

▶ PROCEDURE FOR SHAPING MEDALLIONS

1 Roll out the puff pastry dough approximately ⅛ to ¼ inch (3 to 6 millimeters) thick and cut it into even 4-inch (10-centimeter) squares (upper left). Fold each square in half diagonally. Cut through two sides of the dough, about ½ inch (1.2 centimeters) from the edge. Cut a V, being careful not to cut through the corners (upper right). Pull the sides of the dough out (lower left) and bring the sides of the dough together to form a loop, pinching them together to seal (lower right).

2 Chill the dough 20 to 30 minutes before baking. Brush with egg wash if desired.

3 Bake the pinwheel until golden and well risen. Fill the baked pinwheel with cream filling or jam. Brush the baked pastry with glaze.

▶ PROCEDURE FOR MAKING CHEESE STRAWS

1 Roll out the puff pastry dough approximately ⅛ to ¼ inch (3 to 6 millimeters) thick. The length is not important, but the width should be at least 7 inches (17.5 centimeters). Brush off any flour that clings to the dough. Brush the dough with egg wash or flavored butter and sprinkle with grated hard cheese such as Parmesan, Cheddar or Gruyère.

2 Cut the dough into thin strips measuring about ¾ inch (2 centimeters) wide and 7 inches (17 centimeters) long using a rolling cutter. Pick up each strip and twist both ends three or four times, then place on paper-lined sheet pans.

3 Bake at 400°F (200°C) until the twists are evenly browned, approximately 8 to 12 minutes.

▶ PROCEDURE FOR SHAPING CREAM HORNS

1 Cut puff pastry into narrow strips. Wrap one strip around a conical cream horn form, overlapping each piece slightly. Before baking, press one side of the dough into pearl sugar.

2 The finished cream horns are filled with crème Chantilly.

Puff pastry scraps cannot be rerolled and used for products needing a high rise. The additional rolling destroys the layers. Scraps (known as **rognures**), however, can be used for palmiers (page 337), turnovers, decorative crescents (fleurons), tart shells, napoleons (page 337) or any item for which rise is less important than flavor and flakiness. For best results, press the dough scraps into a 1-inch- (2.5-centimeter-) thick stack to maintain the integrity of the layers. Roll the dough out into an even rectangle. Fold the dough into thirds and refrigerate overnight. The next day, roll, cut and bake as required.

Care should be taken when applying egg wash to puff pastry products. Any wash that drips down the cut sides can prevent rise. For a shiny brown surface, 5 minutes before it finishes baking, brush the puff pastry with simple syrup and return it to the oven.

▶ **rognures** French for trimmings or scraps

Finished puff pastries clockwise from top right: Cheese straws, pinwheel filled with pastry cream and cherry, feuilletée filled with pastry cream and pineapple, bear claw glazed with fondant, two bouchées filled with pastry cream and sliced apples and, in the center, medallion filled with pastry cream and blueberries.

▶ **viennoiserie** the term applied to the category of enriched pastry doughs, which includes brioche, croissants and Danish pastries.

▶ CROISSANT AND DANISH PASTRY

Croissant and Danish doughs are made from yeast dough that, like puff pastry, is laminated with fat. Unlike many sweet doughs discussed in Chapter 8, Enriched Yeast Doughs, croissant and Danish dough have most of their fat added in during the lamination process. These enriched doughs are prepared following most of the 10 production stages for making yeast breads discussed in Chapter 7, Yeast Breads. The principal differences are (1) butter is incorporated through the turning process described earlier in this chapter after the dough base is fermented and punched down; (2) rolled-in doughs are portioned somewhat differently from other yeast doughs; and (3) the portions are shaped without rounding.

The enriched yeast doughs that form the base of croissant and Danish pastry are leavened by the yeast in the dough, the steam escaping from the moisture in the layered fat and eggs, if present, in the formula. These products bake into tender soft-crusted pastries with a distinctive flakiness. The quantity of fat in these doughs is very high, as much as 50 percent of the total dough weight. Because fat and sugar inhibits gluten development, these formulas often use higher-protein flour. Careful handling of the dough in all stages ensures a tender flaky product.

PRODUCTION STAGES FOR YEAST-RAISED ROLLED-IN DOUGHS

The production for yeast-raised rolled-in dough can be divided into 10 stages:

1 Scaling the Ingredients.
2 Preparing the Roll-In Fat.
3 Mixing and Kneading the Dough.
4 Fermenting the Dough.
5 Laminating the Fat in the Dough.
6 Make-up: Portioning the Dough.
7 Filling the Dough.
8 Proofing the Products.
9 Baking the Products.
10 Glazing, Cooling and Storing.

STAGE 1: SCALING THE INGREDIENTS

As with all bakeshop preparations, careful measuring of ingredients helps ensure accurate results. The temperature of the fat should be cool yet not so cold as to harden the fat.

STAGE 2: PREPARING THE ROLL-IN FAT

The roll-in fat used in croissant and Danish dough is softened or conditioned in a mixer before using and should be kept cool during lamination. Or the fat may be softened on a workbench with a dough scraper. The fat should be the same consistency as the dough. As with puff pastry, croissant and Danish dough are best laminated with butter. However, specially formulated shortenings may be used for ease of handling and cost savings.

STAGE 3: MIXING AND KNEADING THE DOUGH

Croissant and Danish dough may be mixed using a straight dough or sponge mixing method. The dough base should not be kneaded too much, as gluten will continue to develop during the rolling and folding process. If the dough is fully developed during kneading, it may be difficult to roll. Retard the dough overnight to relax the gluten before laminating the next day.

Softening the roll-in fat using a dough scraper (right) before forming it into a uniform rectangle (left) to be locked into yeasted laminated dough.

STAGE 4: FERMENTING THE DOUGH

Dough for croissants and Danish is fermented until it doubles in bulk, approximately 1 to 3 hours. Better results are obtained, however, when the dough is retarded overnight before laminating; it enhances the flavor development in the dough, cools it and makes it easier to handle when shaping.

STAGE 5: LAMINATING THE FAT IN THE DOUGH

The dough is rolled out and topped with the roll-in fat prepared earlier. The fat may be spread evenly over the dough or, when formed into a block, wrapped in the dough. The turning and folding process used for croissant and Danish dough is the same as that used to laminate puff pastry illustrated on page 314. The number of turns and type of folds used is according to preference, generally with fewer turns for croissant and Danish dough. Special attention should be paid to the temperature of the dough during roll-in; because yeasted doughs for lamination are softer than the détrempe used for puff pastry, it is essential to chill the dough in the refrigerator or freezer between turns.

An electric dough sheeter is common in bakeshops where these products are made daily, saving time and ensuring product consistency. Croissants and Danish pastries can be made from start to finish in 1 day, but a 2-day process eases the organization schedule of the workplace. Yeasted laminated dough may also be retarded after lamination for convenience and added flavor development in the dough.

The ball of dough is scored (upper left), then flattened into a neat rectangle (lower right). The roll-in fat is wrapped in the dough. Use a rolling pin to seal the edges of the dough and to secure the roll-in fat (upper right).

STAGE 6: MAKE-UP: PORTIONING THE DOUGH

Laminated yeast dough is not rolled and rounded like the yeast doughs in Chapter 7. Instead, to preserve the layers in the dough, it is flattened with a rolling pin or sheeter to an even thickness. The dough is then cut into portions to be formed into unique shapes such as the croissant.

STAGE 7: FILLING THE DOUGH

Laminated doughs are frequently filled with custard, fruit or nut fillings. Uncooked fillings that contain eggs, such as Frangipane (an almond cream filling; see page 331), must be added before the pastries bake. Fillings are added before proofing when the shaping of the dough requires it, such as for bear claws or filled croissants. Some bakers prefer, when possible, to add fillings after the dough is proofed to allow the dough to rise more fully.

STAGE 8: PROOFING THE PRODUCTS

Laminated yeast doughs are proofed at a low temperature, 80°F (27°C) with high humidity if using a proof box, to keep the butter from melting during proofing. Slight underproofing, until the dough expands 70 to 75 percent in volume, ensures a fully risen product after baking. The amount of fat weakens the gluten, making these pastries fragile when fully proofed.

Many bakeshops prepare croissants and Danish pastries once a week. The unbaked products are frozen as soon as they are shaped. Then daily, the frozen units are removed from the freezer (usually in the afternoon) and thawed overnight under refrigeration. The next morning the croissants or Danish pastries are proofed and baked.

STAGE 9: BAKING THE PRODUCTS

Laminated doughs are carefully brushed with egg wash before baking. Croissants and Danish pastries are baked at 375°F to 400°F (190°C to 200°F) to ensure a good rise.

STAGE 10: GLAZING, COOLING AND STORING

Once they are baked, Danish pastries are often coated with thin glazes or icings such as those discussed in Chapter 13. A light wash with a sugar syrup or fondant glaze when the Danish pastries are still hot from the oven sweetens the crust without softening it. Pastries made from laminated yeast dough should cool before packaging to preserve their crisp crust. They may be stored loosely covered in plastic under refrigeration or in the freezer.

A formula for a rich Parisian croissant using a fully developed direct dough illustrates the mixing, rolling and folding technique for croissant dough. Later in this chapter, a variation is offered, a formula with short fermentation times that is retarded overnight after lamination.

▶ PROCEDURE FOR PREPARING YEAST-RAISED ROLLED-IN DOUGHS

1 Mix the dough and allow it to rise.
2 Prepare the butter or shortening.
3 Roll out the dough evenly, then top it with the butter. The butter may be formed into a rectangle to be enclosed in the dough or it may be softened and spread on the dough.
4 Fold the dough around the butter, enclosing it completely.
5 Roll out the dough into a rectangle, approximately ¼ to ½ inch (0.6 to 1.2 centimeters) thick. Always be sure to roll at right angles; do not roll haphazardly or in a circle as for other pastry doughs.
6 Fold the dough in thirds, the single book fold. Be sure to brush off any excess flour from between the folds. Chill the dough 20 to 30 minutes.
7 Roll out the dough and fold it in the same manner a second and third time, allowing the dough to rest between each turn. After completing the third turn, wrap the dough carefully and allow it to rest, refrigerated, several hours or overnight before shaping and baking. (Additional turns may be given to this dough, although four are common.)

RECIPE 12.2

PARISIAN CROISSANTS

1 Rolling out the butter between two sheets of plastic wrap.

Yield: 60 Rolls   **Method:** Rolled-in dough

Fermentation: Approximately 1 hour, chill overnight.

Proofing: 45 minutes.

Bread flour	2 lb. 4 oz.	1080 g	100%
Salt	1 oz.	30 g	3%
Granulated sugar	6 oz.	180 g	17%
Milk	21 fl. oz.	625 ml	58%
Active dry yeast	1 oz.	30 g	3%
Unsalted butter, softened	1 lb. 8 oz.	720 g	67%
Egg wash	as needed	as needed	
Total dough weight:	5 lb. 9 oz.	2665 g	248%

1 Stir the flour, salt and sugar together in the bowl of a mixer fitted with a dough hook.
2 Warm the milk to approximately 90°F (32°C). Stir in the yeast.
3 Add the milk-and-yeast mixture to the dry ingredients. Stir until combined, then knead on medium speed 10 minutes.
4 Place the dough in a large floured bowl, cover and let rise until doubled in size, approximately 1 hour.

2 Folding the dough around the butter, which has been placed in the center.

3 Brushing the excess flour from the rolled-out dough.

4 Folding the dough in thirds.

5 The finished croissant dough.

6 Cutting the dough into triangles.

7 Baked croissants.

5 Prepare the butter while the dough is rising. Place the butter in an even layer between two large pieces of plastic wrap and roll into a flat rectangle, approximately 8 inches × 11 inches (20 centimeters × 27.5 centimeters) and chill.

6 After the dough has risen, punch it down. Roll out the dough into a large rectangle, approximately ½ inch (1.2 centimeters) thick and large enough to enclose the rectangle of butter. Place the unwrapped butter in the center of the dough and fold the dough around the butter, enclosing it completely.

7 Roll out the block of dough into a long rectangle, approximately 1 inch (2.5 centimeters) thick. Fold the dough in thirds, a single book fold. This completes the first turn. Wrap the dough in plastic and chill approximately 20 to 30 minutes.

8 Repeat the rolling and folding process two more times, chilling the dough between each turn. When finished, wrap the dough well and chill it overnight before shaping and baking.

9 To shape the dough into croissant rolls, cut off one-quarter of the block at a time, wrapping the rest and returning it to the refrigerator. Roll each quarter of dough into a large rectangle, approximately ¼ inch (6 millimeters) thick.

10 Cut the dough into uniform triangles. Starting with the large end, roll each triangle into a crescent and place on a paper-lined sheet pan.

11 Brush lightly with egg wash. Proof until doubled, but do not allow the dough to become so warm that the butter melts.

12 Bake at 375°F (190°C) until golden brown, approximately 12 to 15 minutes.

Approximate values per roll: **Calories** 200, **Total fat** 12 g, **Saturated fat** 7 g, **Cholesterol** 40 mg, **Sodium** 230 mg, **Total carbohydrates** 19 g, **Protein** 3 g, **Vitamin A** 10%

SHAPING CROISSANTS

▶ PROCEDURE FOR FORMING CROISSANTS USING A ROLLING CUTTER

Trim the edges of the flattened croissant dough to an even rectangle using a ruler. Use the croissant cutter (upper right) to mark cutting guides on the dough. With a rolling cutter, divide the dough into even triangles using the marks made by the croissant cutter as guidelines. Reserve scraps to be reworked.

▶ PROCEDURE FOR FORMING A FILLED CROISSANT

Cut a ½-inch (1.2-centimeter) slit in the short end of the triangle of croissant dough (upper left). Place a few strips of cooked bacon, ham, cheese or other filling along the scored edge (upper right). Roll up the dough starting from the filled end (lower left). Finish rolling with the pointed end of the dough tucked under the croissant before baking (lower right).

▶ PROCEDURE FOR FORMING A CHOCOLATE-FILLED CROISSANT

Cut the flattened croissant dough into 3-inch × 4-inch (7.5-centimeter × 10-centimeter) rectangles (top left). Place a chocolate batonnet along the bottom edge of the dough (top center) and roll once until the chocolate is covered (top right). Place another chocolate batonnet (bottom left) on the dough and continue rolling until the chocolate is completely covered. Place the rolled dough with the seam tucked underneath (bottom center). Use a dowel or small rolling pin to even the edges of the dough before baking (bottom right).

Assortment of finished croissants, clockwise from upper left: classic curved croissants, savory filled croissant, chocolate-filled croissant cut in half and dusted with powdered sugar after baking and chocolate croissant coated with egg wash.

DANISH PASTRY

According to baking lore, Danish pastry was actually created by a French baker more than 350 years ago. He forgot to knead butter into his bread dough and attempted to cover the mistake by folding in softened butter. This rich, flaky pastry is now popular worldwide for breakfasts, desserts and snacks. The dough may be shaped in a variety of ways and is usually filled with jam, fruit, cream or marzipan. Applying a sugar syrup wash to the pastries when they are hot from the oven adds sheen and flavor.

The butter used to create the flakiness in the layers of Danish pastry may be locked in using the same technique as for croissants, illustrated on page 323. Alternately, the butter may be softened and spread on the dough as illustrated in the following formula.

RECIPE 12.3

DANISH PASTRY DOUGH

Yield: 36 Pastries   **Method:** Rolled-in dough

Fermentation: Dough, 1 to 1½ hours. During lamination, 3 hours.

Proofing: 15 to 20 minutes.

Active dry yeast	0.5 oz.	15 g	2.5%
All-purpose flour	1 lb. 4 oz.	600 g	100%
Granulated sugar	4 oz.	120 g	20%
Water, warm	4 fl. oz.	120 ml	20%
Milk, warm	4 fl. oz.	120 ml	20%
Eggs, room temperature	3.3 oz. (2 eggs)	100 g	16%
Salt	0.2 oz. (1 tsp.)	6 g	1%
Vanilla extract	0.15 fl. oz. (1 tsp.)	5 ml	0.7%
Cinnamon, ground	0.04 oz. (½ tsp.)	1 g	0.2%
Unsalted butter, melted	1.5 oz.	45 g	7.5%
Unsalted butter, cold	1 lb.	480 g	80%
Egg wash	as needed	as needed	
Granulated sugar	as needed	as needed	
Total dough weight:	3 lb. 5 oz.	1612 g	268%

1. In a large bowl, stir together the yeast and 12 ounces (360 grams) of the flour. Add the sugar, water, milk, eggs, salt, vanilla, cinnamon and melted butter. Stir until well combined.

2. Add the remaining flour gradually, kneading the dough by hand or with a mixer fitted with a dough hook. Knead until the dough is smooth and only slightly tacky to the touch, approximately 2 to 3 minutes.

3. Place the dough in a bowl that has been lightly dusted with flour. Cover and refrigerate 1 to 1½ hours.

4. Prepare the remaining butter while the dough is chilling. Start by sprinkling flour over the work surface and placing the cold butter on the flour. Then pound the butter with a rolling pin until the butter softens. Using a pastry scraper or the heel of your hand, knead the butter and flour until the mixture is spreadable. The butter should still be cold. If it begins to melt, refrigerate it until firm. Keep the butter chilled until the dough is ready.

5. On a lightly floured surface, roll out the dough into a large rectangle, about ½ inch (1.2 centimeters) thick. Brush away any excess flour.

6. Spread the chilled butter evenly over two-thirds of the dough. Fold the unbuttered third over the center, then fold the buttered third over the top. Press the edges together to seal in the butter.

1 Kneading the cold butter with the flour.

2 Spreading the butter over two-thirds of the rolled-out dough.

3 Folding the dough in thirds to cover the butter.

4 Rolling out the dough.

5 Folding the dough in thirds to complete a turn.

6 Cutting rectangles of Danish dough.

7 Piping cream cheese filling onto Danish dough.

8 Shaping snails from Danish dough.

7 Roll the dough into a rectangle, about 12 inches × 18 inches (30 centimeters × 45 centimeters). Fold the dough using the single book fold method, for a total of six turns. Chill the dough between turns as necessary. After the final turn, wrap the dough well and retard at least 4 hours or overnight.

8 Shape and fill the Danish dough as desired. Place the shaped pastries on a paper-lined baking sheet and proof approximately 15 to 20 minutes.

9 Brush the pastries with egg wash and sprinkle lightly with sugar if desired. Bake at 400°F (200°C) 5 minutes. Decrease the oven temperature to 350°F (180°C) and bake until light brown, approximately 12 to 15 minutes.

Approximate values per pastry, without filling: **Calories** 85, **Total fat** 1.5 g, **Saturated fat** 0 g, **Cholesterol** 15 mg, **Sodium** 65 mg, **Total carbohydrates** 15.5 g, **Protein** 2 g

Assorted Danish pastries, clockwise from left: braided Danish coffeecake, pretzel Danish filled with lemon filling, twisted fruit Danish filled with lemon filling, candied fruit strip topped with fondant, snail danish filled with lemon and raspberry filling and dusted with powdered sugar and twisted fruit Danish filled with raspberry preserves.

FORMING AND FILLING DANISH PASTRIES

Danish pastries may be rolled and cut in many of the same shapes as for puff pastry illustrated on page 316. The feuilletée, windmill and bear claw shapes illustrated there are also popular Danish pastry forms. For best results, roll Danish pastry dough out to a thickness of ¼ inch (6 millimeters), then cut and fold it into various shapes before proofing.

▶ PROCEDURE FOR MAKING FRUITBASKETS AND TURNOVERS

For fruitbaskets, divide the rolled Danish dough into even 4-inch (10-centimeter) diamonds (upper left). Fold the right and left points into the center of the dough (center left). Fold the top and bottom points into the center (lower left). Proof, bake and fill. For turnovers, divide the Danish dough into 4-inch (10-centimeter) diamonds (upper right). Place a small amount of almond paste, frangipane or cheese filling on the dough (center right). Bring together two points of the dough to cover the filling (lower right), pinching them to seal.

▶ PROCEDURE FOR MAKING TWISTED FRUIT DANISH

Cut the rolled Danish dough into rectangles measuring 2 inches × 4 inches (5 centimeters × 10 centimeters) (top left). Cut a short slit in the center of the dough (top center). Tuck one end of the dough through the opening. Grab it from the other side and pull it through the opening (top right). Flatten slightly. Repeat with the other side (bottom left). Pipe a small amount of pastry cream onto the dough (bottom center) and top with fruit preserves (bottom right).

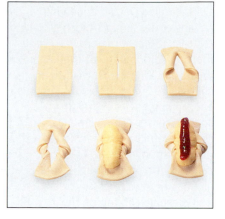

▶ PROCEDURE FOR MAKING CANDIED FRUIT STRIPS

From the left, cut the rolled Danish dough into a rectangle measuring 12 inches × 18 inches (30 centimeters × 45 centimeters). Spread half of the dough with fruit preserves. Sprinkle it with finely chopped candied cherries, lemon peel or other fruit. Cut the dough into strips 1½ inches (3.8 centimeters) wide. Fold the dough over to cover the jam and fruit. Press lightly to seal, then apply egg wash.

▶ PROCEDURE FOR MAKING SNAIL AND PRETZEL DANISH

From the left, cut the rolled Danish dough into strips measuring 10 inches (25 centimeters) long and ¾ inch (2 centimeters) wide. Spread half of each strip with fruit preserves. Fold the dough over so that the preserves are covered between two layers of dough. Then twist the strip. Coil the dough into a tight circle (snail) or pretzel shape.

▶ PROCEDURE FOR MAKING A BRAIDED DANISH COFFEECAKE

Cut the rolled Danish dough into a rectangle measuring 14 inches × 8 inches (35 centimeters × 20 centimeters). Fold the dough over a narrow rolling pin. With a pastry cutter or sharp knife, make incisions along the overlapping edges of the dough spaced ¾ inch (18 millimeters) apart (left). Carefully unroll the dough. Cut a piece of spongecake to fit in the center of the pastry dough. Pipe alternating rows of pastry cream and fruit preserves on top of the spongecake. Fold the dough strips over the filling in a crisscross pattern (right).

FILLINGS FOR DANISH PASTRIES

Danish pastries may be filled with fruit preserves, cream cheese, sweetened farmer's cheese or custard fillings before or after baking. Fillings containing raw eggs must be baked with the dough, however. A light glaze or drizzle of fondant icing may be added after baking to complete the presentation.

RECIPE 12.4

CREAM CHEESE FILLING

Yield: 26 oz. (785 g)

Cream cheese	1 lb.	480 g
Granulated sugar	8 oz.	240 g
Salt	0.05 oz. (¼ tsp.)	1.5 g
Vanilla extract	0.15 fl. oz. (1 tsp.)	5 ml
Flour	1 oz.	30 g
Egg yolk	0.6 oz. (1 yolk)	20 g
Lemon extract	0.15 fl. oz. (1 tsp.)	5 ml
Lemon zest, grated fine	0.14 oz. (2 tsp.)	4 g

1 Beat the cream cheese until light and fluffy. Stir in the remaining ingredients.

Approximate values per 1-oz. (30-g) serving: **Calories** 100, **Total fat** 6 g, **Saturated fat** 4 g, **Cholesterol** 25 mg, **Sodium** 75 mg, **Total carbohydrates** 10 g, **Protein** 1 g

Frangipane

Frangipane is the name used to refer to any number of almond mixtures used to fill Danish pastries and tarts. Coffeecakes and tarts made with firm, tart fruit such as pears and apples are especially good filled with frangipane. (See Fresh Peach Tart with Almond Cream, page 336.) The following three formulas are various types of frangipane filling. When raw eggs are used in the formula, the filling must be added to the pastry before baking.

FRANGIPANE

Yield: 2 lb. 2 oz. (1010 g)

Almond paste	1 lb.	480 g
Granulated sugar	2 oz.	60 g
Unsalted butter, room temperature	7 oz.	210 g
Eggs	6.75 oz. (4 eggs)	200 g
Vanilla extract	0.5 fl. oz.	15 ml
Cake flour	1.5 oz.	45 g

1 In the bowl of a mixer fitted with a paddle, blend the almond paste and sugar on low speed.

2 Gradually add the butter in small amounts, waiting for the previous added amount to be fully incorporated.

3 Gradually add the eggs and mix on medium speed 5 minutes or until the mixture is light and airy. Stir in the vanilla then add the flour.

Approximate values per 1-oz. (30-g) serving: **Calories** 120, **Total fat** 9 g, **Saturated fat** 3.5 g, **Cholesterol** 35 mg, **Sodium** 10 mg, **Total carbohydrates** 9 g, **Protein** 2 g

ALMOND PASTE FILLING

Yield: 2 lb. (973 g)

Almond paste	20 oz.	600 g
Unsalted butter, softened	8 oz.	240 g
Salt	0.1 oz. (½ tsp.)	3 g
Vanilla extract	0.3 fl. oz. (2 tsp.)	10 ml
Egg whites	4 oz. (4 whites)	120 g

1 Blend the almond paste and butter until smooth. Add the salt and vanilla, and then the egg whites. Blend well.

VARIATION:

Pistachio Almond Paste Filling—Combine 6 ounces (180 grams) pistachios and 1.5 ounces (45 grams) pistachio compound in a food processor and blend until smooth. Combine the pistachio mixture with the almond paste, butter, salt and 10 ounces (300 grams) sugar. Omit the vanilla. Moisten with 7 to 8 ounces (210 to 240 grams) egg whites.

Approximate values per 1-oz. (30-g) serving: **Calories** 130, **Total fat** 11 g, **Saturated fat** 4 g, **Cholesterol** 15 mg, **Sodium** 45 mg, **Total carbohydrates** 9 g, **Protein** 2 g

RECIPE 12.7

ALMOND CREAM

VINCENT ON CAMELBACK, Phoenix, AZ

Chef Vincent Guerithault

Yield: 3 lb. (1480 kg)

Unsalted butter, softened	8 oz.	240 g
Granulated sugar	1 lb.	480 g
Eggs	8.3 oz. (5 eggs)	250 g
All-purpose flour	5 oz.	150 g
Almonds, ground	12 oz.	360 g

1 Cream the butter and sugar. Slowly add the eggs, scraping down the bowl as necessary.

2 Stir the flour and almonds together, then add to the butter mixture. Blend until no lumps remain.

3 Almond cream may be stored under refrigeration up to 3 weeks.

Approximate values per 1-oz. (30-g) serving: **Calories** 140, **Total fat** 8 g, **Saturated fat** 3 g, **Cholesterol** 30 mg, **Sodium** 5 mg, **Total carbohydrates** 13 g, **Protein** 2 g

RECIPE 12.8

RICOTTA CHEESE FILLING

Yield: 2 lb. 14 oz. (1395 g)

Cream cheese softened	1 lb. 8 oz.	720 g
Ricotta	10 oz.	300 g
Granulated sugar	5 oz.	150 g
Eggs	3.3 oz. (2 eggs)	100 g
Vanilla extract	0.15 fl. oz. (1 tsp.)	5 ml
Pastry flour	4 oz.	120 g

1 In the bowl of a mixer fitted with a paddle, combine the cream cheese and ricotta on low speed until no lumps remain.

2 Add the sugar, gradually add the eggs and scrape down the bowl between additions.

3 Add the vanilla, followed by the flour, and combine well.

Approximate values per 1-oz. (30-g) serving: **Calories** 90, **Total fat** 6 g, **Saturated fat** 4 g, **Cholesterol** 25 mg, **Sodium** 50 mg, **Total carbohydrates** 6 g, **Protein** 2 g

RECIPE 12.9

THICKENED CHERRIES

Yield: approximately 2 lb. 8 oz. (1245 g)

Cherries, IQF	2 lb.	960 g
Granulated sugar	8 oz.	240 g
Corn or potato starch	0.5 oz.	15 g
Water	1 fl. oz.	30 ml
Almond extract	0.04 fl. oz. (¼ tsp.)	1 ml

1 Defrost the cherries, reserving their juices. Add water to the juice to obtain a total of 8 fluid ounces (240 milliliters).

2 In a nonreactive saucepan, bring the juice and sugar to a boil.

3 Combine the starch and water and pour into the boiling juice. Whisk until thickened.

4 Remove from heat; fold in the cherries and almond extract. Cool before using.

Approximate values 1-oz. (30-g) serving: **Calories** 45, **Total fat** 0 g, **Saturated fat** 0 g, **Cholesterol** 0 mg, **Sodium** 0 mg, **Total carbohydrates** 11 g, **Protein** 0 g

APRICOT FILLING   RECIPE 12.10

Yield: 2 lb. (960 g)

Dried apricots	8 oz.	240 g
Orange juice	1 pt.	480 ml
Granulated sugar	6 oz.	180 g
Salt	0.05 oz. ($^1/_4$ tsp.)	1.5 g
Unsalted butter	2 oz.	60 g

1 Place the apricots and orange juice in a small saucepan. Cover and simmer until the apricots are very tender, approximately 25 minutes. Stir in the sugar and salt. When the sugar is dissolved, add the butter and remove from the heat.

2 Purée the mixture in a blender until smooth. Cool completely before using.

Approximate values per 1-oz. (30-g) serving: **Calories** 60, **Total fat** 1.5 g, **Saturated fat** 1 g, **Cholesterol** 5 mg, **Sodium** 20 mg, **Total carbohydrates** 13 g, **Protein** 0 g, **Vitamin A** 20%, **Vitamin C** 15%, **Claims**—low fat; low sodium; good source of vitamins A and C

Table 12.1   **TROUBLESHOOTING CHART FOR ROLLED-IN DOUGH**

PROBLEM	CAUSE	SOLUTION
Dough tears when rolling	Weak flour	Use higher-protein flour
	Gluten too elastic	Rest dough longer before rolling
Lacks volume when baked	Improper proofing	Proof correctly
	Crust formed before product was baked	Proofer needs more moisture; egg wash before proofing
Product greasy	Too much fat in formula	Adjust formula
	Fat too soft during roll-in	Chill roll-in fat
	Insufficient chilling time between folds	Chill dough longer
	Proofed at too high a temperature	Adjust proofing temperature
Product not flaky	Insufficient fat; shortening used, not butter	Adjust formula; use proper fat
	Dough and fat too warm at outset; insufficient chilling time between folds	Prechill dough and fat; chill dough longer
	Proofed at too high a temperature	Adjust proofing temperature
Product tough	Fat leaks out of product during baking	Proof at proper temperature
Product flattens, spreads during baking	Overproofed	Proof at proper temperature Shorten proofing time

CONVENIENCE PRODUCTS

In bakeshops where space and time does not permit the making of laminated dough, frozen prepared products may be preferred. Frozen puff pastry dough is available in 2- to 10-pound blocks. The dough is thawed in the refrigerator, then rolled, portioned and baked as needed. Frozen sheets of puff pastry dough rolled to a ¼-inch (6-millimeter) thickness and separated by pieces of parchment paper make preparing fresh bouchées, feuilletées, cheese straws and other items possible in even the smallest restaurant kitchen. These sheets thaw quickly under refrigeration. Once the required number of sheets are thawed, they are ready to be portioned and baked. Some bakers thin the sheets further with a rolling pin before portioning and baking.

Manufacturers also sell frozen croissant and Danish dough in bulk blocks or sheets. Because of the yeast, croissant and Danish dough require proofing as well as baking. Croissant and Danish dough are also available portioned and formed into individual pastries before freezing. The pastries are sold filled or to be filled by the baker after baking. Many manufacturers include separate packets of fruit and cheese filling or sugar glazes, designed to be piped directly from their packaging onto the pastries once they are baked.

Bakers can choose products at every stage in the process: formed and frozen; formed, frozen and fully proofed; or formed, frozen, proofed and baked. As with scratch laminated doughs, these frozen products must be glazed with egg wash before baking. For the best flavor and color after baking, select frozen laminated dough products that are made from pure butter.

CONCLUSION

Few techniques in the bakeshop produce the visible and flavorful results that lamination does. Puff pastry demonstrates the wonders of science in the kitchen, that mere steam and fat can leaven dough. The ability to create quality croissants and Danish pastries depends on an understanding of ingredient functions as well as experience with lamination techniques. The information and techniques discussed in this chapter and in Chapter 7, Yeast Breads, will enable any baker to prepare a variety of dessert and breakfast pastry classics.

QUESTIONS FOR DISCUSSION

1 Briefly describe the procedure for making a rolled-in dough, and give two examples of products made from rolled-in doughs.
2 Name the leaveners used in laminated dough.
3 Describe the effect that docking has on puff pastry and why this technique would be used.
4 What can happen if croissants and Danish pastries are proofed at high temperatures?

QUICK PUFF PASTRY

ADAPTED FROM *NICK MALGIERI'S PERFECT PASTRY*

Yield: 1 lb. 3 oz. (591 g)

Unbleached all-purpose flour	6.25 oz.	190 g	100%
Cake flour	1.25 oz.	38 g	20%
Unsalted butter	8 oz.	240 g	128%
Salt	0.1 oz. (½ tsp.)	3 g	1.6%
Water, very cold	4 fl. oz.	120 ml	64%
Total dough weight:	1 lb. 3 oz.	591 g	313%

1 To mix the dough, place the all-purpose flour in a 2-quart (2-liter) mixer bowl and sift the cake flour over it. Thoroughly stir the two flours together.

2 Slice 1 ounce (30 grams) of the butter into thin pieces and add to the bowl. Rub in the butter by hand, tossing and squeezing in the butter until no visible pieces remain.

3 Cut the remaining butter into ½-inch (1.2-centimeter) cubes. Add the butter cubes to the flour mixture. Toss with a rubber spatula just to separate and distribute the butter. Do not rub the butter into the flour.

4 Dissolve the salt in the water. Make a well in the flour-and-butter mixture and add the water. Toss gently with the spatula until the dough is evenly moistened. Add drops of water, if necessary, to complete the moistening. Press and squeeze the dough in a bowl to form a rough cylinder.

5 To turn the dough, first lightly flour the work surface and the dough. Using the palm of your hand, press down on the dough three or four times to shape the dough into a rough rectangle.

6 Press and pound the dough with a rolling pin to form an even rectangle about ½ inch (1.2 centimeters) thick. Roll the dough back and forth along its length once or twice until it is an even rectangle about ¼ inch (6 millimeters) thick. At this stage, pieces of butter are likely to stick to the work surface. If the dough does stick, loosen it with a long spatula or scraper. Clean the surface to minimize further sticking.

7 Fold both ends of the dough in toward the center, then fold them in toward the center again to make four layers, the double book fold. Position the package of dough so that the "spine" is on the left.

8 Lightly flour the work surface and the dough and repeat the pressing as before. Roll the dough along its length as before, then roll several times along its width to form a rectangle, approximately 6 inches × 18 inches (15 centimeters × 45 centimeters). Fold the dough into the double book fold as before. Repeat the process once more so that the dough will have three double turns.

9 Wrap the dough well in plastic and chill at least 1 hour before using.

10 The dough can be refrigerated about 3 days or frozen up to 1 month. Defrost frozen dough in the refrigerator overnight before using it.

Approximate values per 3-oz. (90-g) serving: **Calories** 480, **Total fat** 37 g, **Saturated fat** 23 g, **Cholesterol** 100 mg, **Sodium** 240 mg, **Total carbohydrates** 31 g, **Protein** 5 g, **Vitamin A** 35%

RECIPE 12.12

INDIVIDUAL PUFF PASTRY FRUIT TARTS

Yield: 12 Tarts, 2½ in. (7.5 cm) each

Puff pastry, shaped into bouchées (page 312) and baked	12 bouchées	12 bouchées
Crème Brûlée for Tarts (page 457)	2 lb.	960 g
Strawberries	1 pt.	0.5 lt
Tart Glaze (page 261), flavored with raspberry purée	as needed	as needed
Raspberries	1 pt.	0.5 lt
Red currants	0.5 pt.	0.25 lt
Powdered sugar	as needed	as needed

1 Fill the bouchées two-thirds full with the Crème Brûlée for Tarts.

2 In a circular fashion, place the strawberries cut side up, overlapping one another.

3 Using a pastry brush, glaze the strawberries with the raspberry Tart Glaze.

4 Randomly sprinkle the raspberries and red currants on the strawberries.

5 Dust the edges of the tarts with powdered sugar.

Approximate values per serving: **Calories** 520, **Total fat** 40 g, **Saturated fat** 24 g, **Cholesterol** 250 mg, **Sodium** 250 mg, **Total carbohydrates** 35 g, **Protein** 6 g, **Vitamin A** 25%, **Vitamin C** 60%

RECIPE 12.13

FRESH PEACH TART WITH ALMOND CREAM

VINCENT ON CAMELBACK, PHOENIX, AZ

Chef Vincent Guerithault

Yield: 8 Servings

Puff pastry	6 oz.	180 g
Almond Cream (page 332)	1 lb. 8 oz.	720 g
Fresh peaches, peeled, pitted and sliced	6–8	6–8
Unsalted butter, melted	3 oz.	90 g
Granulated sugar	1 oz.	30 g
Powdered sugar	as needed	as needed

1 Roll out the puff pastry into a strip, approximately 6 inches × 22 inches (15 centimeters × 55 centimeters—the length of a sheet pan); and ⅛ inch (3 millimeters) thick. Lay the dough on a sheet pan lined with parchment paper.

2 Using a large plain tip, pipe four rows of Almond Cream down the length of the puff pastry. Leave a ¾-inch (18-millimeter) margin along both long edges of the dough.

3 Arrange the peach slices over the cream, overlapping slightly.

4 Brush the peaches with the melted butter and evenly sprinkle the granulated sugar over them.

5 Bake at 400°F (200°C) until the dough is done and the peaches are lightly browned, approximately 20 to 30 minutes.

6 Serve warm, dusted with powdered sugar and accompanied by vanilla ice cream.

Approximate values per serving: **Calories** 140, **Total fat** 9 g, **Saturated fat** 5 g, **Cholesterol** 25 mg, **Sodium** 0 mg, **Total carbohydrates** 15 g, **Protein** 1 g, **Vitamin A** 10%

PALMIERS

RECIPE 12.14

Puff pastry	as needed	as needed
Granulated sugar	as needed	as needed

1 Roll out the puff pastry into a very thin rectangle. The length is not important, but the width should be at least 7 inches (17 centimeters).

2 Using a rolling pin, gently press the granulated sugar into the dough on both sides.

3 Make a 1-inch (2.5-centimeter) fold along the long edges of the dough toward the center. Sprinkle on additional sugar.

4 Make another 1-inch (2.5-centimeter) fold along the long edges of the dough toward the center. The two folds should almost meet in the center. Sprinkle on additional sugar.

5 Fold one side on top of the other. Press down gently with a rolling pin or your fingers so that the dough adheres. Chill 1 hour.

6 Cut the log of dough in thin slices. Place the cookies on a paper-lined sheet pan and bake at 400°F (200°C) until the edges are brown, approximately 8 to 12 minutes.

Approximate values per 1-oz. (30-g) serving: **Calories** 130, **Total fat** 5 g, **Saturated fat** 1 g, **Cholesterol** 0 mg, **Sodium** 35 mg, **Total carbohydrates** 19 g, **Protein** 1 g

1 Folding the dough toward the center from both edges.

2 Slicing the log of dough into individual cookies.

STRAWBERRY NAPOLEON

RECIPE 12.15

Yield: 10 Servings

Puff pastry, 4-in. × 15-in. (10-cm × 37-cm)		
strips, docked and baked	3	3
Pastry Cream (page 436)	1 pt.	480 ml
Fresh strawberries, sliced	1 qt.	1 lt
Crème Chantilly (page 445)	1 pt.	480 ml
Basic Sugar Glaze (page 360)	as needed	as needed
Dark chocolate, melted	1 oz.	30 g

1 Allow the puff pastry to cool completely before assembling.

2 Place a strip of puff pastry on a cake cardboard for support. Pipe on a layer of Pastry Cream, leaving a clean margin of almost ½ inch (1.2 centimeters) on all four sides.

3 Top the cream with a layer of strawberries.

4 Spread on a thin layer of Créme Chantilly and top with a second layer of puff pastry. Repeat the procedure for the second layer of puff pastry and chill.

5 Prepare the Basic Sugar Glaze. Place the melted chocolate in a piping cone. When ready to glaze, place the third strip of puff pastry on an icing rack, flat side up. Pour the Basic Sugar Glaze down the length of the pastry and spread evenly with a metal cake spatula. Allow the excess to drip over the sides.

6 Immediately pipe thin lines of chocolate across the glaze. Use a toothpick to pull a spider web pattern in the glaze. Chill to set the glaze, then place the top in position on the napoleon.

Approximate values per 5-oz. (150-g) serving: **Calories** 320, **Total fat** 20 g, **Saturated fat** 9 g, **Cholesterol** 115 mg, **Sodium** 65 mg, **Total carbohydrates** 29 g, **Protein** 4 g, **Vitamin A** 15%, **Vitamin C** 60%

The flakiest croissants are made with the highest percentage of butter. This formula is among the richest, with nearly 30 percent more butter than Parisian Croissants (page 322). To complete the layering in only three turns, this formula uses a combination of the single book fold and the double book fold. For the best flavor development and to ease handling, retard this dough overnight before proofing and baking the finished products.

Yield: 35 Croissants, approximately 2½ oz. (75 g) each

Method: Rolled-in dough

Fermentation: 12 to 15 hours.   **Proofing:** Approximately 1 hour.

Dough:

Granulated sugar	4 oz.	120 g	12%
Salt	1 oz.	30 g	3%
Dry milk powder	1 oz.	30 g	3%
Egg	1.6 oz. (1 egg)	50 g	5%
Water, ice cold	18 fl. oz.	540 ml	56%
Vanilla extract	0.15 fl. oz. (1 tsp.)	5 ml	0.5%
Instant yeast	1 oz.	30 g	3%
Bread flour	2 lb.	960 g	100%
Unsalted butter, softened	1 lb. 14 oz.	900 g	94%
Total dough weight:	5 lb. 8 oz.	2665 g	276%

Egg wash:

Heavy cream	2 fl. oz.	60 ml
Eggs, lightly beaten	3.3 oz. (2 eggs)	100 g

1 Combine the sugar, salt, dry milk powder, egg, water and vanilla in the bowl of a mixer fitted with a dough hook. Stir until blended.

2 Add the yeast, the flour and 2 ounces (60 grams) of the butter to the mixing bowl. Mix 3 to 4 minutes on medium speed to make a smooth but soft dough.

3 Place the dough on a paper-lined sheet pan and refrigerate to chill thoroughly, approximately 30 minutes to 1 hour.

4 Mix the remaining butter in the bowl of a mixer fitted with a paddle on low speed until pliable and lump-free, but still firm. Roll the butter into a 10-inch (25-centimeter) square between two sheets of plastic wrap or parchment paper. Keep the butter cold.

5 After the dough has chilled, place it on a lightly floured work surface and roll it into a rectangle, 11 inches × 21 inches (28 centimeters × 53 centimeters). Place the butter, which should have the same consistency as the dough, on the left side of the dough rectangle. Fold the right side of the dough over the butter and press on the ends to seal them closed.

6 Place the dough with a folded edge parallel to the edge of the table and roll the dough lengthwise until it is $1/2$ inch (1.2 centimeters) thick. Fold the dough into thirds, making a single book fold.

7 Refrigerate until the dough is cold and firm, about 30 minutes to 1 hour. Roll the dough out into a rectangle approximately $1/2$ inch (1.2 centimeters) thick, then fold into a double book fold. Cover well with plastic wrap and refrigerate.

8 Roll out and fold the dough into thirds, making a single book fold again. Refrigerate 1 hour.

9 Position the dough with the seamless side towards you and roll lengthwise to 15 inches (38 centimeters) wide and $1/8$ inch (3 millimeters) thick.

10 Using a pastry wheel, cut the dough lengthwise in half to obtain two strips. Cut the strips into uniform triangles approximately $7^{1}/_{2}$ inches (19 centimeters) long with a base width of $4^{1}/_{2}$ inches (11 centimeters).

11 Roll the croissants from base to point, with the point tucked underneath the croissant, and bend the ends toward the center. Place the croissants on a paper-lined sheet pan. Cover the croissants and retard in the refrigerator overnight.

12 Remove the croissants from the refrigerator and proof them until increased 70 percent in size. Place the croissants in a proof box set to a maximum temperature of 80°F (27°C) with 80% humidity.

13 Combine the heavy cream and beaten eggs. Brush the proofed croissants with the egg wash. Bake at 425°F (220°C) until golden, approximately 18 to 20 minutes.

Approximate values per serving: **Calories** 310, **Total fat** 22 g, **Saturated fat** 13 g, **Cholesterol** 80 mg, **Sodium** 330 mg, **Total carbohydrates** 23 g, **Protein** 5 g, **Vitamin A** 15%

RECIPE 12.17   **ALMOND ORANGE CROISSANTS**

Yield: 35 Croissants

Croissant dough	5 lb. 8 oz.	2640 g
Almond Paste Filling (page 331)	as needed	as needed
Orange marmalade	as needed	as needed
Eggs beaten	3.3 oz. (2 eggs)	100 g
Heavy cream	3 fl. oz.	90 ml
Simple Syrup (page 349)	6 fl. oz.	180 ml
Orange Fondant Glaze (page 370)	as needed	as needed
Sliced almonds, toasted	8 oz.	240 g

1 Roll out the croissant dough and cut into triangles.

2 Fill a pastry bag fitted with a medium plain tip with the Almond Paste Filling. Pipe a strip of paste across the base width of the croissant triangles.

3 Fill another pastry bag fitted with a medium plain tip with the orange marmalade. Pipe a small mound of orange marmalade next to the almond paste.

4 Roll the croissants from base to tip. Place the formed croissants on a paper-lined sheet pan without curving.

5 Proof the formed croissants until increased 70 percent in volume or retard them, covered, up to 24 hours.

6 Combine the eggs and heavy cream. Brush the proofed croissants with the egg wash.

7 Bake at 425°F (220°C) without steam until golden, approximately 18 to 20 minutes.

8 Brush the hot croissants with Simple Syrup. Cool, then brush them with the Orange Fondant Glaze. Sprinkle with the toasted sliced almonds.

VARIATIONS:

Macadamia and Ginger Jam Croissants—Substitute Sugar-Free Mango Ginger Jam (page 555) for the orange marmalade. Sprinkle some chopped macadamia nuts over the jam before rolling the croissants. Sprinkle more chopped macadamia nuts over the proofed croissants before baking. Omit the sliced almonds. Brush the hot croissants with Simple Syrup. Cool, then brush them with the Orange Fondant Glaze.

Chocolate Pistachio Croissants—Substitute Pistachio Almond Paste Filling (page 331) for the Almond Paste Filling. Omit the orange marmalade and the almonds. Pipe a line of paste on each dough triangle. Press a chocolate batonnet into the paste, then roll the dough into a straight log shape. Proof, brush with egg wash and sprinkle with chopped pistachios before baking.

Ham and Cheese Croissants—Slice ham and Gruyère cheese into thin strips (batonnets) and position about 1 ounce (30 grams) ham and ¾ ounce (22 grams) Gruyère cheese at the widest part of each of the dough triangles. Roll, proof and brush with egg wash as for filled croissants. Sprinkle additional grated Gruyère on the surface of the croissants before baking. Omit the Orange Fondant Glaze and Simple Syrup.

Approximate values per serving: **Calories** 350, **Total fat** 26 g, **Saturated fat** 14 g, **Cholesterol** 80 mg, **Sodium** 330 mg, **Total carbohydrates** 26 g, **Protein** 6 g, **Vitamin A** 15%

EUROPEAN DANISH DOUGH

Yield: 5 lb. 1 oz. (2453 grams) dough   **Method:** Rolled-in dough

Fermentation: Dough, 30 minutes. During lamination, 2 to 3 hours.

Proofing: 1 hour.

Instant yeast	1 oz.	30 g	3%
Water (temperature controlled)	14 fl. oz.	420 ml	44%
Bread flour	2 lb.	960 g	100%
Granulated sugar	4 oz.	120 g	12%
Dry milk powder	1.25 oz.	38 g	4%
Vanilla extract	0.5 fl. oz.	15 ml	1.5%
Eggs	3.3 oz. (2 eggs)	100 g	10%
Unsalted butter, softened	3 oz.	90 g	9%
Salt	0.6 oz.	20 g	2%
Unsalted butter, cold	1 lb. 6 oz.	660 g	69%
Total dough weight:	5 lb. 1 oz.	2453 g	254%

1 Dissolve the yeast in the water in the bowl of a mixer fitted with a dough hook. Add the flour, sugar, dry milk powder, vanilla, eggs, softened butter and salt. Mix on low speed until the dough is uniform and smooth, approximately 4 minutes.

2 Flatten the dough onto a paper-lined sheet pan and place in the freezer or refrigerator until thoroughly chilled, approximately 30 minutes to 1 hour.

3 Beat the cold butter in the bowl of a mixer fitted with a paddle on low speed until pliable and lump-free, but still firm.

4 Roll out the dough into a rectangle ½ inch (1.2 centimeters) thick. Spread the butter over half of the dough and fold the dough over to completely cover the buttered dough. Press the edges of the dough with a rolling pin to seal. Place the dough with the seamless side toward you and roll the dough lengthwise ½ inch (1.2 centimeters) thick. Fold dough into thirds, making a single book fold.

5 Refrigerate until dough is cold and firm, approximately 30 minutes to 1 hour. Roll the dough, fold into a double book fold then wrap in plastic and refrigerate 1 hour to complete this second turn.

6 Give the dough a third turn using a single book fold. Wrap in plastic and refrigerate at least 1 hour before using. Dough may be stored in the refrigerator overnight before using. Form, proof and bake as desired.

Approximate values per 2-oz. (60-g) serving: **Calories** 220, **Total fat** 15 g, **Saturated fat** 9 g, **Cholesterol** 45 mg, **Sodium** 190 mg, **Total carbohydrates** 20 g, **Protein** 4 g, **Vitamin A** 10%

RECIPE 12.19   **CUSTARD CHERRY ROLL**

Yield: 42 Pastries

Danish dough, chilled	5 lb. 4 oz.	2520 g
Pastry Cream (page 436)	3 lb.	1440 g
Dried cherries	1 lb.	480 g
Simple Syrup (page 349)	10 fl. oz.	300 ml
Fondant Glaze (page 370)	1 lb. 4 oz.	600 g
Toasted almonds	8 oz.	240 g

1 Position the dough with the seamless side parallel to the edge of the work-bench and roll into a rectangle 14 inches (35 centimeters) wide and $1/8$ inch (3 millimeters) thick.

2 Spread the Pastry Cream over the entire surface of the dough, leaving a $1/2$-inch (1.2-centimeter) border around each edge. Evenly sprinkle with the dried cherries.

3 Starting from the bottom, tightly roll the dough into a spiral.

4 Slice the dough into $1/2$-inch-(1.2-centimeter-) wide pieces using a sharp French knife. Place the dough cut side up on a paper-lined sheet pan. Tuck the end of each piece underneath to prevent the pastries from unraveling.

5 Retard overnight or proof immediately until almost doubled in size.

6 Carefully brush the rolls with egg wash and bake at 400°F (200°C) until well browned, approximately 20 minutes.

7 Brush the hot rolls with a thin coat of Simple Syrup. Cool, then glaze the pastries with a thin coat of Fondant Glaze. Sprinkle immediately with toasted almonds.

VARIATIONS:

Almond Raspberry Bear Claws—Roll out the Danish dough and cut it into rectangles measuring $4^1/2$ inches (11 centimeters) long and $2^1/2$ inches (6.5-centimeters) wide. Brush with egg wash. Omit the Pastry Cream. Pipe a strip of Frangipane (page 331) lengthwise in the center of each dough cutout. Omit the dried cherries. Sprinkle with four or five fresh raspberries and a tablespoon of raspberry jam. Fold the dough in half lengthwise to make a long tube of filled dough. Using a knife or a pastry cutter, make five $1/2$-inch (1.2-centimeter) slits along the seam, as illustrated on page 317. Transfer the pastry to a paper-lined sheet pan, curving slightly to open the cut sides.

Approximate values per serving: **Calories** 400, **Total fat** 21 g, **Saturated fat** 11 g, **Cholesterol** 110 mg, **Sodium** 200 mg, **Total carbohydrates** 49 g, **Protein** 7 g, **Vitamin A** 15%

CHERRY CREAM CHEESE DANISH

The amount of each ingredient and the yield will depend on the amount of Danish dough used.

Danish dough	as needed	as needed
Egg wash	as needed	as needed
Cream Cheese Filling (page 330)	as needed	as needed
Thickened Cherries (page 332)	as needed	as needed
Simple Syrup (page 349)	as needed	as needed
Fondant Glaze (page 370)	as needed	as needed

1 Roll out the dough and cut it into 3½-inch (9-centimeter) feuilletées, as described on page 316. Place the pastry cutouts on paper-lined sheet pans.

2 Brush the edges of the pastry cutouts with egg wash. Pipe some Cream Cheese Filling in the center and top with a few Thickened Cherries.

3 Proof the pastries until nearly doubled, approximately 30 minutes.

4 Bake at 400°F (200°C) until well browned, approximately 20 minutes. Remove from the oven and brush with Simple Syrup. Allow the pastries to cool, then glaze with Fondant Glaze.

Approximate values per serving: **Calories** 420, **Total fat** 28 g, **Saturated fat** 13 g, **Cholesterol** 60 mg, **Sodium** 230 mg, **Total carbohydrates** 39 g, **Protein** 7 g, **Vitamin A** 20%

APRICOT PISTACHIO PINWHEELS

Yield: 40 Pastries

Danish dough	5 lb. 4 oz.	2520 g
Pistachio Almond Paste Filling (page 331)	3 lb.	1440 g
Apricot halves	44	44
Egg wash	as needed	as needed
Simple Syrup (page 349)	8 fl. oz.	240 ml
Fondant Glaze (page 370)	12 oz.	360 g
Pistachios, coarsely chopped	8 oz.	240 g

1 Roll out the dough and cut into 3½-inch (9-centimeter) squares.

2 Form into pinwheel shapes (page 317) and place on a parchment-lined baking sheet.

3 Using a piping bag fitted with a medium piping tip, fill the center with Pistachio Almond Paste Filling. Top with an apricot half.

4 Proof until almost doubled in size, carefully brush with egg wash and bake in a 400°F (200°C) oven, 18 to 20 minutes.

5 Upon removal from the oven, brush with Simple Syrup. Let cool.

6 Brush the pastries with a thin coat of Fondant Glaze and immediately sprinkle with chopped pistachios.

Approximate values per serving: **Calories** 420, **Total fat** 28 g, **Saturated fat** 13 g, **Cholesterol** 60 mg, **Sodium** 230 mg, **Total carbohydrates** 39 g, **Protein** 7 g, **Vitamin A** 20%

RECIPE 12.22   **STRAWBERRY CREAM DANISH**

Yield: 40 Pastries

Danish dough	5 lb. 4 oz.	2520 g
Egg wash	as needed	as needed
Crème Brûlée for Tarts (page 457)	3 lb. 4 oz.	1560 g
Strawberries	2 qt.	2 lt.
Powdered sugar	as needed	as needed

1 Roll out the dough and cut it into 3½-inch (9-centimeter) squares. Place them on a paper-lined sheet pan.

2 Proof until doubled, or cover and retard the dough overnight. Brush the squares of dough with egg wash and bake at 400°F (200°C) until evenly browned, approximately 18 to 20 minutes.

3 Let cool. Slice the pastries in half horizontally. Place the Créme Brûlée for Tarts in a pastry bag with a medium plain tip. Pipe the filling on the bottom half of each pastry.

4 Top the Crème Brûlée for Tarts with strawberries, then replace the top half of the pastry. Dust with powdered sugar.

VARIATION:

Raspberry, Chocolate Ganache and Cream Danish—Dip the top half of each baked pastry square in melted Chocolate Ganache (page 362). Chill until the ganache sets. Split the pastries in half horizontally. Fill with the Crème Brûlée for Tarts and fresh raspberries. Replace the top half of the pastry.

Approximate values per serving: **Calories** 360, **Total fat** 26 g, **Saturated fat** 15 g, **Cholesterol** 145 mg, **Sodium** 210 mg, **Total carbohydrates** 27 g, **Protein** 5 g, **Vitamin A** 20%, **Vitamin C** 20%

CINNAMON ROLLS

Yield: 45 Pastries

Danish dough	5 lb. 4 oz.	2520 g
Cinnamon Roll Paste (recipe follows)	3 lb.	1440 g
Pecans	1 lb.	480 g
Orange Fondant Glaze (page 370)	1 lb. 5 oz.	630 g

1 Roll the dough into a rectangle measuring 14 inches (35 centimeters) wide.

2 Spread the Cinnamon Roll Paste evenly over the rectangle, leaving ½ inch (1 centimeter) of each long edge clear. Sprinkle evenly with pecans.

3 Tightly roll the dough up from the bottom edge into a long tube. Cut ½-inch- (1.2-centimeter-) wide pieces from the dough with a sharp chef's knife.

4 Lay each cut piece flat on a paper-lined sheet pan, with each end tucked underneath the roll.

5 Proof the rolls until increased 90 percent in volume, or cover and retard the pastries.

6 Bake at 400°F (200°C) until evenly browned, approximately 18 to 20 minutes.

7 Cool the rolls, then brush liberally with Orange Fondant Glaze.

Approximate values per serving: **Calories** 430, **Total fat** 29 g, **Saturated fat** 12 g, **Cholesterol** 80 mg, **Sodium** 230 mg, **Total carbohydrates** 39 g, **Protein** 6 g, **Vitamin A** 15%

CINNAMON ROLL PASTE

Yield: 3 lb. (1452 g)

Unsalted butter, softened	8 oz.	240 g
Granulated sugar	9 oz.	270 g
Salt	0.2 oz. (1 tsp.)	6 g
Cinnamon, ground	2 oz.	60 g
Vanilla extract	0.5 fl. oz.	15 ml
Orange oil	5 drops	5 drops
Almond extract	0.04 fl. oz. (¼ tsp.)	1 ml
Eggs	6.75 oz. (4 eggs)	200 g
Almond flour	9 oz.	270 g
Cake flour	1 oz.	30 g
Pastry Cream (page 436)	12 oz.	360 g

1 In the bowl of a mixer fitted with a paddle, mix the butter until creamy. Add the sugar, salt, cinnamon, vanilla, orange oil and almond extract. Scrape down the bowl and add the eggs, beating to combine.

2 Stir in the flours. Scrape down the bowl and fold in the Pastry Cream.

3 Use immediately or refrigerate for later use.

Approximate values per 1-oz. (30-g) serving: **Calories** 110, **Total fat** 8 g, **Saturated fat** 3 g, **Cholesterol** 40 mg, **Sodium** 55 mg, **Total carbohydrates** 10 g, **Protein** 2 g

SUGAR IS THE UNIVERSAL CONDIMENT WHICH NEVER SPOILS ANYTHING.

—Jean-Anthelme Brillat-Savarin, French writer, politician and philosopher, (1755–1826)

SYRUPS, ICINGS AND SAUCES

CHEF JACK SHOOP, CMC, CCE

AFTER STUDYING THIS CHAPTER, YOU WILL BE ABLE TO:

▶ understand the cooking stages of sugar

▶ prepare a variety of sugar syrups and icings that rely on sugar syrup

▶ prepare a variety of buttercream icings and cooked sugar fillings

▶ prepare a variety of dessert sauces

▶ **density** the relationship between the mass and volume of a substance ($D = m/v$); as more and more sugar is dissolved in a liquid, the heavier or denser the liquid will become; sugar density is measured on the Baumé scale using a saccharometer

Using a Baumé hydrometer or saccharometer.

Syrups and icings are not mere garnish but essential components that give many cakes and pastries character and eye appeal. This chapter covers the basic syrups that form, flavor and moisten many cakes and creams. Syrups stabilize egg foams, making meringue, which forms the basis for many types of icing. Mastery of working with sugar as it liquefies and caramelizes is a basic bakeshop skill and a major focus of this chapter.

While an expertly decorated cake is one that will sell, icings and frostings also keep cakes moist and contribute their distinctive flavor. This chapter also covers the elegant sauces that put the finishing touch on plated desserts, adding finesse and refinement. Sauces may be based on fruit, custard, caramel or wine. What guides the pastry chef when making these syrups, icings and sauces is creating a harmonious balance of sweetness, flavor, aroma and appearance.

▶ SUGAR SYRUPS

In the alchemy of the bakeshop, sugar is one of the leading players. It gives color, moisture and flavor to many baked goods. Sugar's ability to dissolve and restructure itself may challenge the uninitiated, but the basic techniques are easily learned with some attention to detail.

Sugar can be incorporated into a prepared item in its dry form or when liquefied into a syrup. Dry granulated sugar and sugar syrups are not used interchangeably, however. Granulated sugar is necessary to create the emulsion necessary for leavening cakes. **Sugar syrups** (not to be confused with liquid sweeteners such as molasses) take two forms: **simple syrups,** which are mixtures of sugar and water, and **cooked syrups,** which are made of melted sugar cooked until it reaches a specific temperature.

SIMPLE SUGAR SYRUPS

Simple or stock syrups are solutions of sugar and water. Often referred to as moistening or dessert syrups, they are used to moisten cakes and to make sauces, sorbets and beverages. The syrup's **density** or concentration is dictated by its intended purpose. Cold water will dissolve up to double its weight in sugar; heating the solution forms denser, more concentrated syrups. A saccharometer or hydrometer, which measures specific gravity and shows degrees of concentration from 0° to 50° on the Baumé scale, is the most accurate guide to density. In 58°F (15°C) water a saccharometer should register 0°. The higher the number, the greater the density of the solution.

Simple syrups can be prepared without the aid of a saccharometer, however. To make a simple sugar syrup, specific amounts of water and sugar are combined in a saucepan and brought to a boil. Once the solution boils, it is important not to stir, as this may cause recrystallization or lumping. For successful simple sugar syrups, the following formulas must be followed precisely.

▶ Light syrup—Boil 2 parts water with 1 part sugar by weight for 1 minute. This concentration should measure 17°–20° on the Baumé scale. A light syrup can be used for making sorbet or moistening spongecake.

▶ Medium syrup—Boil 1½ parts water with 1 part sugar by weight for 1 minute. This concentration should measure 21°–24° on the Baumé scale. A medium syrup can be used for candying citrus peel.

▶ Heavy syrup—Boil equal parts water and sugar for 1 minute. This concentration should measure 28°–30° on the Baumé scale, and the solution should be at 220°F (104°C). Heavy syrup is a basic, all-purpose syrup kept on hand in many bakeshops.

▶ **PROCEDURE FOR MAKING SIMPLE SYRUP**

1 Combine measured amounts of water and sugar in a heavy saucepan. An unlined copper pan may be used.

2 Bring the mixture to a boil without stirring, to prevent the sugar from crystallizing. Boil the syrup 1 minute or until the syrup reaches the proper density reading required for the type of syrup needed.

3 Remove the syrup from the heat. Fresh mint, tea leaves, ground coffee and other aromatics may be steeped in the syrup to flavor. Or the syrup may be flavored with an emulsion, liqueur or extract. The standard ratio of simple syrup to flavoring is 3 parts syrup to 1 part flavoring.

4 Cool, then store under refrigeration.

SIMPLE SYRUP   RECIPE 13.1

Yield: 28 fl. oz. (840 ml)

Water	1 pt.	480 ml
Sugar	1 lb.	480 g

1 Combine the water and sugar in a heavy saucepan. Bring to a full boil.

2 Cook 1 minute or cook to temperature reading for desired syrup.

Approximate values per 1-fl.-oz. (30-ml) serving: **Calories** 80, **Total fat** 0 g, **Saturated fat** 0 g, **Cholesterol** 0 mg, **Sodium** 0 mg, **Total carbohydrates** 20 g, **Protein** 0 g

CONCENTRATED COOKED SUGAR SYRUPS

Meringue, buttercream, candy, caramel sauce and other confections often need liquid sugar that will be firm when cool or have a cooked caramel flavor. For these purposes, sugar needs to be cooked to temperatures far higher than for simple syrups. A small amount of water is generally added at the beginning to help the sugar dissolve evenly. As the mixture boils, the water evaporates, the solution's temperature rises and its density increases. The syrup's concentration depends on the amount of water remaining in the final solution: the less water, the harder the syrup will become when cool.

The sugar's temperature indicates its concentration. If there is a great deal of water present, the temperature will not rise much above 212°F (100°C). As water evaporates, however, the temperature will rise until it reaches 320°F (160°C), the point at which all water is evaporated. At temperatures above 320°F (160°C), the pure sugar begins to brown or caramelize. As sugar caramelizes, its sweetening power decreases dramatically. At approximately 375°F (191°C), sugar will burn, developing a bitter flavor. If allowed to continue cooking, sugar will ignite.

Sugar solutions are unstable because of their molecular structure. They can recrystallize because of agitation or uneven heat distribution. Several steps are taken to prevent recrystallization of a concentrated sugar syrup. The solution is

▶ **interferent** a substance such as glucose or lemon juice that helps stop sugar from recrystallizing when dissolved in a solution

never stirred once it comes to a boil. An interferent may be added when the solution begins to boil. Cream of tartar, vinegar, glucose (a monosaccharide) (see Chapter 4, Bakeshop Ingredients) and lemon juice are known as **interferents** because they interfere with the formation of sugar crystals. Some formulas specify which interferent to use, although most are used in such small quantities that their flavor cannot be detected.

Brushing down the sides of the pan with cold water washes off crystals that may be deposited there. These sugar crystals may seed the solution, causing more crystals (lumps) to form if not removed. Instead of using a brush to wash away crystals, you can cover the pan for a few moments as soon as the solution comes to a boil. Steam will condense on the cover and run down the sides of the pan, washing away the crystals.

The concentration of sugar syrup should be determined with a candy thermometer that measures very high temperatures. If a thermometer is not available, use the traditional but less accurate ice-water test: spoon a few drops of the hot sugar into a bowl of very cold water. Check the hardness of the cooled sugar with your fingertips. Each stage of cooked sugar is named according to its firmness when cool—for example, soft ball or hard crack.

Table 13.1 lists the various stages of cooked sugar and the temperature for each. Each stage is also identified by the ice-water test result. Note that even a few degrees makes a difference in the syrup's concentration.

Preparing concentrated sugar syrups and caramel.

Brushing sugar crystals from the side of the pan.

Soft ball stage.

Hard ball stage.

Hard crack stage.

Table 13.1	**STAGES OF COOKED SUGAR**	
STAGE	**TEMPERATURE**	**ICE-WATER TEST—ONE DROP:**
Thread	236°F (113°C)	Spins a 2-in. (5-cm) thread when dropped
Soft ball	240°F (116°C)	Forms a soft ball
Firm ball	246°F (119°C)	Forms a firm ball
Hard ball	260°F (127°C)	Forms a hard, compact ball
Soft crack	270°F (132°C)	Separates into a hard, but not brittle, thread
Hard crack	300°F (149°C)	Separates into a hard, brittle sheet
Caramel	338°F (170°C)	Liquid turns brown

▶ PROCEDURE FOR PREPARING CONCENTRATED COOKED SUGAR SYRUP

1 Combine granulated sugar and a small amount of water in a heavy saucepan. An unlined copper pan may be used.

2 Stir the solution to make sure all sugar crystals dissolve before it reaches a boil. Cover the pan and bring the mixture to a boil. Do not stir the solution after it begins boiling, however.

3 Once the syrup boils, uncover the pan and add the interferent specified in the formula. Corn syrup, glucose, cream of tartar or lemon juice may be used.

4 Continue cooking the syrup, brushing down the sides of the pan with a clean brush dipped in cold water to wash off crystals that may be deposited there.

5 Cook the syrup to the desired temperature, using a candy thermometer to gauge the syrup's concentration. Wash off the thermometer probe after placing in the syrup; sugar that clings to it can reseed the syrup.

CARAMEL

Sugar that cooks to the caramel stage cools to a hard crack with a distinctive golden hue and smoky flavor. Many pastries, such as Gâteau St. Honoré in Chapter 11, Pastry Doughs, and croquembouche, are dipped in caramel to give their exterior a pleasing crunch. Hard caramel may be drizzled into decorative shapes on oiled parchment or silicone mats, or over oiled bowls to make a caramel cage. When cooled, the caramel is used as a garnish over custards, puddings or mousses.

When making caramel, the same care must be taken to prevent recrystallization of the syrup. Once it begins to caramelize, the syrup will brown quickly if not removed from the heat. Even removing the caramel from the heat doesn't stop browning of the sugar due to carryover cooking. Placing the pan in ice water helps cool the pan and stop caramelization. The procedure for making caramel is illustrated with the formula for Decorating Caramel (page 352). Caramel syrup, when used to dip pastries such as Merveilleux Pastries (page 298) or cream puffs for croquembouche, may include a high percentage of corn syrup or glucose. These liquid sugars keep the caramel pliable longer, making dipping large numbers of pastries possible.

▶ PROCEDURE FOR PREPARING CARAMEL

1 Combine granulated sugar, corn syrup or glucose (if using), and a small amount of water in a heavy saucepan. Unlined copper may be used.

2 Stir the solution to make sure all sugar crystals dissolve before it reaches a boil. Cover the pan and bring the mixture to a boil. Do not stir the solution after it begins boiling, however.

3 Once the syrup boils, add the interferent specified in the formula. Corn syrup, glucose, cream of tartar or lemon juice may be used.

4 Continue cooking the syrup, brushing down the sides of the pan with cold water to wash off crystals that may be deposited there.

5 Cook the syrup to the desired temperature, using a candy thermometer to gauge the syrup's concentration. Wash off the thermometer probe after placing in the syrup; sugar that clings to it can reseed the syrup.

6 Cook the syrup until it begins to caramelize, approximately 338°F (170°C). Remove the pan from the heat as soon as the desired color is reached but before the caramel begins to burn and smoke. Briefly plunge the bottom of the pan in an ice bath to stop the cooking process.

RECIPE 13.2

DECORATING CARAMEL

Yield: 1½ pt. (720 ml)

Granulated sugar	1 lb.	480 g
Glucose or corn syrup	8 fl. oz.	240 ml
Water	8 fl. oz.	240 ml

1 Combine the sugar, glucose or corn syrup and water in a heavy saucepan. Stir the mixture, then cover the pan and bring the mixture to a boil.

2 Once the mixture boils, brush the sides of the pan with a pastry brush dipped in clean water to remove any sugar crystals stuck to the pan.

3 Boil the mixture without stirring until it reaches a golden caramel color, approximately 338°F (170°C).

4 Remove the pan from the heat and dip the bottom of the pan in a bowl of cold water for 30 seconds to stop the cooking process.

5 Use to dip éclairs, cream puffs or other items. This caramel may also be used to make caramel cages and for other decorative caramel work as discussed in Chapter 21, Chocolate and Decorative Work.

Approximate values per 1-fl.-oz. (30-ml) serving: **Calories** 40, **Total fat** 0 g, **Saturated fat** 0 g, **Cholesterol** 0 mg, **Sodium** 15 mg, **Total carbohydrates** 10 g, **Protein** 0 g

▶ ICINGS

Icing, also known as **frosting,** is a sweet decorative coating used as a filling between the layers or as a coating over the top and sides of a cake. It is used to add flavor and to improve a cake's appearance. Icing can also extend a cake's shelf life by forming a protective coating.

There are seven general types of icing: **buttercream, foam, fudge, fondant, glaze, royal icing** and **ganache.** See Table 13.2. Each type can be produced with a number of formulas and in a range of flavorings.

Because icing is integral to the flavor and appearance of many cakes, it should be made carefully using high-quality ingredients and natural flavors and colors. A good icing is smooth; it is never grainy or lumpy (see Table 13.3). It should complement the flavor and texture of the cake without overpowering it.

Table 13.2 **ICINGS**

ICING	PREPARATION	TEXTURE/FLAVOR
Simple buttercream (American)	Mixture of sugar and fat (usually butter); can contain egg yolks or egg whites	Rich but light; smooth; fluffy
Foam	Meringue made with hot sugar syrup	Light, fluffy; very sweet
Fudge	Cooked mixture of sugar, butter and water or milk; applied warm	Heavy, rich and candylike
Fondant	Cooked mixture of sugar and water; applied warm	Thick, opaque; sweet
Glaze	Powdered sugar with liquid	Thin; sweet
Royal icing	Uncooked mixture of powdered sugar and egg whites	Hard and brittle when dry; chalky
Ganache	Blend of melted chocolate and cream; may be poured or whipped	Rich, smooth; intense chocolate flavor

BUTTERCREAM

A buttercream is a light, smooth, fluffy mixture of sugar and fat (butter, margarine or shortening). It may also contain egg yolks for richness or whipped egg whites for lightness. Pasteurized eggs must always be used in buttercreams to ensure food safety. A good buttercream will be sweet, but not cloying; buttery, but not greasy.

Buttercreams are popular and useful for most types of cakes and may be flavored or colored as desired. They may be stored, covered, in the refrigerator for several days but must be softened before use.

The three most popular styles of buttercream, which are discussed here, are **simple, Italian** and **French.**

SIMPLE BUTTERCREAM

Simple buttercream, sometimes known as **American-style buttercream,** is made by creaming butter and powdered sugar together until the mixture is light and smooth. Cream, pasteurized eggs and flavorings may be added as desired. Simple buttercream requires no cooking and is quick and easy to prepare.

If cost is a consideration, hydrogenated all-purpose shortening can be substituted for a portion of the butter, but the flavor and mouth-feel will be different. Buttercream made with shortening tends to feel greasier and heavier because shortening does not melt on the tongue like butter. It will be more stable than buttercream made with pure butter, however, and is necessary when a pure white icing is desired.

▶ PROCEDURE FOR PREPARING SIMPLE BUTTERCREAMS

1 Cream softened butter or shortening until the mixture is light and fluffy.

2 Beat in egg, if desired.

3 Beat in sifted powdered sugar, scraping down the bowl as needed.

4 Beat in the flavoring ingredients.

Table 13.3 **TROUBLESHOOTING CHART FOR ICINGS**

PROBLEM	CAUSE	SOLUTION
Frosting breaks or curdles	Fat added too slowly or eggs too hot when fat was added	Add shortening or sifted powdered sugar
	Butter too cold when added	Soften butter before adding
Icing is lumpy	Powdered sugar not sifted	Sift dry ingredients
	Ingredients not blended	Use softened fats
	Sugar syrup lumps in icing	Add sugar syrups carefully
Icing is too stiff	Not enough liquid	Adjust formula; add small amount of water or milk to thin the icing
	Too cold	Bring icing to room temperature; heat gently over simmering water
Icing will not adhere to cake	Cake too hot	Cool cake completely
	Icing too thin	Adjust icing formula
	Icing too stiff	Adjust icing formula
	Icing too cold	Soften icing at room temperature before using

RECIPE 13.3 **SIMPLE BUTTERCREAM**

Yield: 3 lb. 2 oz. (1510 g)

Lightly salted butter, softened	1 lb.	480 g
Pasteurized egg (optional)	2 oz.	60 g
Powdered sugar, sifted	2 lb.	960 g
Vanilla extract	0.3 fl. oz. (2 tsp.)	10 ml

1 In the bowl of a mixer fitted with a paddle, cream the butter until light and fluffy.
2 Beat in the egg (if using). Gradually add the sugar, frequently scraping down the bowl.
3 Add the vanilla and continue beating until the icing is smooth and light.

VARIATIONS:

Light Chocolate Buttercream—Dissolve 1 ounce (30 grams) sifted cocoa powder in 2 fluid ounces (60 milliliters) cool water. Add to the buttercream along with the vanilla.

Lemon Buttercream—Decrease the vanilla extract to 0.15 fluid ounces (1 teaspoon/5 milliliters). Add 0.15 fluid ounces (1 teaspoon/5 milliliters) lemon extract and 0.2 ounces (6 grams/1 tablespoon) finely grated lemon zest.

Approximate values per 1-oz. (30-g) serving: **Calories** 170, **Total fat** 6 g, **Saturated fat** 4 g, **Cholesterol** 25 mg, **Sodium** 70 mg, **Total carbohydrates** 28 g, **Protein** 0 g, **Vitamin A** 10%

ITALIAN BUTTERCREAM

Italian buttercream, also known as meringue buttercream, is based on an Italian meringue, which is whipped egg whites cooked with hot sugar syrup. (See Chapter 11, Pastry Doughs.) Softened butter is then whipped into the cooled meringue, and the mixture is flavored as desired. This type of buttercream is extremely soft and light. It can be used on most types of cakes and is particularly popular for multilayered genoise and spongecakes.

▶ PROCEDURE FOR PREPARING ITALIAN BUTTERCREAM

1 Whip the egg whites until soft peaks form.

2 Beat granulated sugar into the egg whites and whip until firm and glossy.

3 Meanwhile, combine additional sugar with water and cook to the soft ball stage (240°F/116°C).

4 With the mixer on medium speed, pour the sugar syrup into the whipped egg whites. Pour slowly and carefully to avoid splatters.

5 Continue whipping the egg-white-and-sugar mixture until completely cool.

6 Whip softened, but not melted, butter into the cooled egg-white-and-sugar mixture.

7 Add flavoring ingredients as desired.

1 Adding the sugar syrup to the whipped egg whites.

2 Adding the softened butter to the cooled Italian meringue.

3 The finished Italian buttercream.

RECIPE 13.4   **ITALIAN BUTTERCREAM**

Yield: 5 lb. 5 oz. (2400 g)

Egg whites	14 oz. (14 whites)	400 g
Granulated sugar	1 lb. 11 oz.	750 g
Water	as needed	as needed
Lightly salted butter, softened but not melted	2 lb. 12 oz.	1250 g

1 All ingredients should be at room temperature before beginning.

2 Place the egg whites in a mixer bowl. Have 9 ounces (270 grams) of the sugar nearby.

3 Place 1 pound 2 ounces (540 grams) of the sugar in a heavy saucepan with enough water to moisten. Bring to a boil over high heat.

4 As the sugar syrup's temperature approaches the soft ball stage (240°F/116°C), begin whipping the egg whites. Watch the sugar closely so that the temperature does not exceed 240°F (116°C).

5 When soft peaks form in the egg whites, gradually add the 9 ounces (270 grams) of sugar to them. Reduce the mixer speed to medium and continue whipping the egg whites to stiff peaks.

6 When the sugar syrup reaches the soft ball stage, immediately pour it into the whites while the mixer is running. Pour the syrup in a steady stream between the side of the bowl and the beater. If the syrup hits the beater, it will splatter and cause lumps. Continue beating at medium speed until the egg whites are completely cool. At this point, the product is known as Italian meringue.

7 Gradually add the softened butter to the Italian meringue. When all the butter is incorporated, add flavoring ingredients as desired.

VARIATIONS:

Chocolate Italian Buttercream—Add 0.5 fluid ounces (15 milliliters) vanilla extract to the buttercream, then stir in 10 ounces (300 grams) melted and cooled bittersweet chocolate.

Lemon Italian Buttercream—Add 2 fluid ounces (60 milliliters) lemon extract and 0.4 ounces (2 tablespoons/12 grams) grated lemon zest to the buttercream.

Coffee Italian Buttercream—Add 2 fluid ounces (60 milliliters) coffee extract or strong coffee to the buttercream.

Approximate values per 1-oz. (30-g) serving: **Calories** 175, **Total fat** 13 g, **Saturated fat** 8 g, **Cholesterol** 34 mg, **Sodium** 140 mg, **Total carbohydrates** 16 g, **Protein** 1 g, **Vitamin A** 10%

FRENCH BUTTERCREAM

French buttercream, also known as **mousseline buttercream,** is similar to Italian buttercream except that the hot sugar syrup is whipped into beaten egg yolks (not egg whites). This egg yolk meringue, referred to as *pâte à bombe,* is also used to leaven cakes and mousses, especially those used in still-frozen desserts, discussed in Chapter 16, Ice Cream and Frozen Desserts. Softened butter and flavorings are added when the sweetened egg yolks are fluffy and cool. An Italian meringue such as the one created in the preceding formula is sometimes folded in for additional body and lightness. French buttercream is perhaps the most difficult type of buttercream to master, but it has the richest flavor and smoothest texture. Like a meringue buttercream, mousseline buttercream may be used on almost any type of cake.

▶ PROCEDURE FOR PREPARING FRENCH BUTTERCREAM

1 Prepare a sugar syrup and cook to soft ball stage (240°F/116°C).

2 Beat egg yolks to a thin ribbon.

3 Slowly beat the sugar syrup into the egg yolks.

4 Continue beating until the yolks are pale, stiff and completely cool.

5 Gradually add softened butter to the cooled yolks.

6 Fold in Italian meringue, if using.

7 Stir in flavoring ingredients.

FRENCH MOUSSELINE BUTTERCREAM

RECIPE 13.5

Yield: 2 qt. (2 lt)

Granulated sugar	1 lb. 10 oz.	780 g
Water	8 fl. oz.	240 ml
Egg yolks	10.6 oz. (16 yolks)	320 g
Lightly salted butter, softened		
but not melted	3 lb.	1440 g
Italian Meringue (page 290)	1 lb.	480 g
Vanilla, coffee, lemon or other		
flavoring extract	2 fl. oz.	60 ml

1 Combine the sugar and water in a small saucepan and bring to a boil. Continue boiling until the syrup reaches 240°F (116°C).

2 Meanwhile, beat the egg yolks in the bowl of a mixer fitted with a wire whisk on low speed. When the sugar syrup reaches 240°F (116°C), pour it slowly into the egg yolks, gradually increasing the speed at which they are whipped. Continue beating at medium-high speed until the mixture is very pale, stiff and cool.

3 Gradually add the softened butter to the egg mixture, frequently scraping down the bowl.

4 Fold in the Italian Meringue with a spatula. Fold in the flavoring extract just until well distributed throughout the buttercream.

VARIATION:

Chocolate Mousseline Buttercream—Add 2 fluid ounces (60 milliliters) vanilla extract to the buttercream, then stir in 10 ounces (300 grams) melted and cooled bittersweet chocolate.

Approximate values per 1-oz. (30-g) serving: **Calories** 230, **Total fat** 20 g, **Saturated fat** 12 g, **Cholesterol** 105 mg, **Sodium** 190 mg, **Total carbohydrates** 12 g, **Protein** 1 g, **Vitamin A** 20%

FOAM ICING

Foam or **boiled icing** is simply an Italian meringue (made with hot sugar syrup). Foam icing is light and fluffy but very sweet. It may be flavored with extract, liqueur or melted chocolate. It is frequently used to ice layer cakes and complements lemon, coconut or chocolate cakes especially well.

Foam icing is rather unstable. It should be used immediately and served the day it is prepared. Refrigeration often makes the foam weep beads of sugar. Freezing causes it to separate or melt.

An easy foam icing can be made by following the formula for Italian Meringue (page 290). As soon as the meringue has cooled to room temperature, it can be flavored as desired with an extract or emulsion.

FUDGE ICING

A fudge icing is a warmed mixture of sugar, butter and water or milk. It is heavy, rich and candylike. It is also stable and holds up well. A fudge icing should be applied warm and allowed to dry on the cake or pastry. When dry, it will have a thin crust and a moist interior. A fudge icing can be vanilla- or chocolate-based and is used on cupcakes, layer cakes and sheet cakes.

▶ PROCEDURE FOR PREPARING FUDGE ICINGS

1 Blend sifted powdered sugar with corn syrup, beating until the sugar is dissolved and the mixture is smooth.

2 Blend in warm melted shortening and/or butter.

3 Blend in hot liquids. Add extracts or flavorings.

4 Use fudge icing while still warm.

RECIPE 13.6

Cocoa fudge icing

BASIC FUDGE ICING

Yield: Approximately 4 lb. (2000 g)

Powdered sugar, sifted	3 lb.	1500 g
Salt	0.05 oz. (¼ tsp.)	1.5 g
Light corn syrup	3 oz.	90 g
Shortening, melted	4 oz.	120 g
Water, hot (140°F/60°C)	10 fl. oz.	300 ml
Vanilla extract	1 fl. oz.	30 ml

1 Blend the sugar, salt and corn syrup. Beat until smooth.

2 Add the shortening and blend well.

3 Add the water and vanilla and blend well. If the fudge is too stiff, it may be thinned with a simple sugar syrup. Use before the icing cools.

VARIATION:

Cocoa Fudge Icing—Sift 4 ounces (120 grams) cocoa powder with the powdered sugar. Add 2 ounces (60 grams) melted unsalted butter with the shortening.

Approximate values per 1-oz. (30-g) serving: **Calories** 140, **Total fat** 2.5 g, **Saturated fat** 0.5 g, **Cholesterol** 0 mg, **Sodium** 15 mg, **Total carbohydrates** 30 g, **Protein** 0 g, **Claims**—low fat; low saturated fat; no cholesterol; very low sodium

FONDANT

Fondant is a thick, opaque sugar paste commonly used for glazing napoleons, petits fours and other pastries as well as some cakes. It is a cooked mixture of sugar and water, with glucose or corn syrup added to encourage the correct type of sugar crystallization. Poured over the surface being coated, fondant quickly dries to a shiny, nonsticky coating. It is naturally pure white and can be tinted with food coloring. Fondant can also be flavored with melted chocolate.

Fondant is rather tricky to make, so it is usually purchased prepared either as a ready-to-use paste or a powder to which water is added. To use prepared fondant, thin it with water or simple syrup and carefully warm to 100°F (38°C). Watch the temperature; when overheated, the fondant will lose its opacity and will dry with an uneven appearance. Commercially prepared fondant will keep for several months at room temperature in an airtight container. The surface of the fondant should be coated with simple syrup, however, to prevent a crust from forming.

Rolled fondant is a very stiff doughlike type of fondant that is used for covering cakes and for making flowers and other decorations. As the name implies, it is rolled out to the desired thickness, then draped over a cake or torte to create a very smooth, flat coating. After the fondant dries, the cake may be decorated with royal icing or buttercream according to the procedures discussed in Chapter 14. Rolled fondant is available in a ready-to-use form. It can be flavored or colored if desired. Be sure to keep the rolled fondant tightly wrapped in plastic and stored in an airtight container to prevent it from drying out and cracking.

▶ **rolled fondant** a cooked mixture of sugar, glucose and water with a consistency of a dough; draped over cakes to create a perfectly smooth plaster-like surface

Wedding cake covered with rolled fondant
Cake courtesy of Francis Walsh, Houston, Texas

▶ PROCEDURE FOR APPLYING ROLLED FONDANT

1 Rolling out fondant. Brushing the surface of the cake with melted fruit preserves.

2 Lifting the fondant and draping it over the cake.

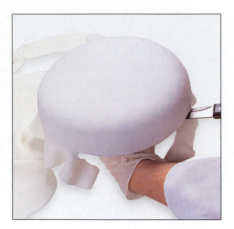

3 The finished cake layer coated with rolled fondant.

GLAZE

A glaze is a thin coating meant to be poured or drizzled onto a cake or pastry. A glaze is usually too thin to apply with a knife or spatula. It is used to add moisture and flavor to cakes on which a heavy icing would be undesirable—for example, a chiffon or angel food cake. Glaze is often tinted with food coloring, the color chosen to reflect the flavor of the cake.

Flat icing or water icing is a specific type of glaze used on Danish pastries and coffeecakes. It is pure white and dries to a firm gloss. A glaze made from fondant is also used for this purpose. The invert sugar in fondant prevents it from crystallizing.

RECIPE 13.7 · **BASIC SUGAR GLAZE**

Yield: 12 oz. (385 g)

Powdered sugar, sifted	9.5 oz.	285 g
Light cream or milk	2 fl. oz.	60 ml
Unsalted butter, melted	1 oz.	30 g
Vanilla, lemon or almond extract	0.3 fl. oz. (2 tsp.)	10 ml

1 Stir all the ingredients together in a small bowl until smooth.

2 Adjust the consistency by adding more cream or milk to thin the glaze if necessary.

3 Adjust the flavor as necessary.

4 Use immediately, before the glaze begins to dry.

VARIATION:

Flavored Sugar Glaze—Stir 0.04 fluid ounces (¼ teaspoon/1 milliliter) lemon or orange oil into the glaze. Fruit juice and other flavorings may be substituted for the vanilla.

Approximate values per 1-oz. (30-g) serving: **Calories** 110, **Total fat** 2 g, **Saturated fat** 1.5 g, **Cholesterol** 5 mg, **Sodium** 0 mg, **Total carbohydrates** 23 g, **Protein** 0 g, **Claims**—low fat; low cholesterol; no sodium

CHOCOLATE GLAZE

RECIPE 13.8

Yield: 13 oz. (390 g)

Unsweetened chocolate	4 oz.	120 g
Semisweet chocolate	4 oz.	120 g
Unsalted butter	4 oz.	120 g
Light corn syrup	1 oz. (4 tsp.)	30 g

1 Melt all the ingredients together over a bain marie. Remove from the heat and allow to cool until slightly thickened, stirring occasionally.

2 Use immediately, before the glaze begins to dry.

Approximate values per 1-oz. (30-g) serving: **Calories** 130, **Total fat** 12 g, **Saturated fat** 7 g, **Cholesterol** 15 mg, **Sodium** 0 mg, **Total carbohydrates** 8 g, **Protein** 1 g

ROYAL ICING

Royal icing, also known as **decorator's icing,** is similar to flat icing except it is much stiffer and becomes hard and brittle when dry. It is an uncooked mixture of powdered sugar and egg whites and can be dyed with food coloring pastes.

Royal icing is used for making decorations, particularly intricate flowers or lace patterns. Prepare royal icing in small quantities, and always keep any unused portion well covered with a damp towel and plastic wrap to prevent hardening.

▶ PROCEDURE FOR PREPARING ROYAL ICING

1 Combine egg white and lemon juice (if using).

2 Beat in sifted powdered sugar until the correct consistency is reached.

3 Beat until very smooth and firm enough to hold a stiff peak.

4 Color as desired with food coloring paste.

5 Store covered with a damp cloth and plastic wrap.

ROYAL ICING

RECIPE 13.9

Yield: 7 oz. (210 g)

Powdered sugar	6 oz.	180 g
Egg white, pasteurized, room temperature	1 oz. (1 white)	30 g
Lemon juice	0.04 fl. oz. (¼ tsp.)	1 ml

1 Sift the sugar and set aside.

2 Place the egg white and lemon juice in a stainless steel bowl.

3 Add 4 ounces (120 grams) of the sugar and beat with an electric mixer or metal spoon until blended. The mixture should fall from a spoon in heavy globs. If it pours, it is too thin and will need the remaining 2 ounces (60 grams) of sugar.

4 Once the consistency is correct, continue beating 3 to 4 minutes. The icing should be white, smooth and thick enough to hold a stiff peak. Food coloring paste can be added at this time if desired.

5 Cover the icing with a damp towel and plastic wrap to prevent it from hardening.

Approximate values per 1-oz. (30-g) serving: **Calories** 120, **Total fat** 0 g, **Saturated fat** 0 g, **Cholesterol** 0 mg, **Sodium** 10 mg, **Total carbohydrates** 28 g, **Protein** 1 g, **Claims**—fat free; no saturated fat; no cholesterol; very low sodium

GANACHE

Ganache is a sublime blending of pure chocolate and cream. It can also include butter, liqueur or other flavorings. Any bittersweet, semisweet or dark chocolate may be used; the choice depends on personal preference and cost considerations.

Depending on its consistency, ganache may be used as a candy (see Chapter 21, Chocolate and Decorative Work) or as a filling, icing or glaze-type coating on cakes or pastries. The ratio of chocolate to cream determines how thick the cooled ganache will be. Equal parts by weight of chocolate and cream generally are best for icings and fillings. Increasing the percentage of chocolate produces a thicker ganache. Warm ganache can be poured over a cake or pastry and allowed to harden as a thin glaze, or it can be cooled and whipped to create a rich, smooth icing. If it becomes too firm, ganache can be remelted over a bain marie.

▶ PROCEDURE FOR PREPARING GANACHE

1 Melt finely chopped chocolate with cream in a double boiler. Alternatively, bring cream just to a boil, then pour it over finely chopped chocolate and allow the cream's heat to gently melt the chocolate. Do not attempt to melt chocolate and then add cool cream. This will cause the chocolate to resolidify and lump.

2 Stir the ganache with a rubber spatula to emulsify the cream and chocolate. (Whisking the ganache using a whip may be quicker, but the ganache will be grainy and less creamy.)

3 Whichever method is used, cool the cream and chocolate mixture over an ice bath, stirring frequently. For poured ganache, cool the cream to 90°F to 100°F (32°C to 38°C), then pour the ganache over the cake or pastry to be iced. For whipped ganache, cool the ganache completely, then incorporate air into the mixture by beating or whipping.

RECIPE 13.10

CHOCOLATE GANACHE

Yield: Approximately 2 lb. (960 g)

Bittersweet chocolate	1 lb.	480 g
Heavy cream	1 pt.	480 ml
Almond or coffee liqueur	1 fl. oz.	30 ml

1 Chop the chocolate into small pieces and place in a large metal bowl.

2 Bring the cream just to a boil, then immediately pour it over the chocolate, stirring with a rubber spatula to blend. Stir gently until all the chocolate has melted.

1 Pouring the hot cream over the chopped chocolate.

2 Cool, firm ganache.

3 Stir in the liqueur.

4 Allow to cool, stirring frequently with a rubber spatula until the desired consistency is achieved.

Approximate values per 1-oz. (30-g) serving: **Calories** 130, **Total fat** 10 g, **Saturated fat** 6 g, **Cholesterol** 20 mg, **Sodium** 5 mg, **Total carbohydrates** 8 g, **Protein** 1 g, **Vitamin A** 6%

COCOA GELÉE

Related to ganache, this luxurious, ebony chocolate glaze incorporates gelatin to give it shine and great covering ability. Use it to glaze the surface of chocolate mousse–filled tarts or tortes, as discussed in Chapter 10, Pies and Tarts, and Chapter 14, Cakes and Tortes.

COCOA GELÉE		RECIPE 13.11

Yield: Approximately 5 lb. (2400g)

Water	16 fl. oz.	480 ml
Granulated sugar	2 lb.	960 g
Heavy cream	21 fl. oz.	630 ml
Cocoa powder, sifted	10 oz.	300 g
Sheet gelatin, softened	1.5 oz.	45 g
Vanilla extract	1.25 fl. oz.	40 ml

1 In a large saucepan bring the water, sugar and cream to a boil.

2 Whisk in the cocoa. Bring the mixture back to a boil and cook 4 minutes, whisking constantly.

3 Remove from the heat and cover the pan with plastic film. Let the mixture cool to 180°F (82°C).

4 Stir the softened sheet gelatin into the warm cocoa mixture. Combine well; re-cover the pan with plastic film and let cool.

5 Add the vanilla.

6 Refrigerate a minimum of 12 hours before using. Heat to 120°F (49°C) for coating tortes, cakes and tarts.

Approximate values per 1-oz. (30-g) serving: **Calories** 80, **Total fat** 3.5 g, **Saturated fat** 2 g, **Cholesterol** 10 mg, **Sodium** 5 mg, **Total carbohydrates** 14 g, **Protein** 1 g

▶ DESSERT SAUCES

Pastries and desserts are often accompanied by sweet sauces. Dessert sauces provide moisture, flavor and texture and enhance plate presentation. Sauces may be based on milk and cream, such as Vanilla Custard Sauce (page 434), the principal dessert sauce. Like any master sauce, it can be flavored and colored with chocolate, coffee extract, liquor or fruit compound as desired. Other dessert sauces include fruit, caramel, butter and wine sauces and chocolate syrup. Sauces should be selected to contrast or complement the dessert or pastry with which they are served. For example, a raspberry soufflé can be complemented by an intense raspberry purée or contrasted with a rich chocolate sauce. Plan on 1 to 2 ounces (30 to 60 milliliters) of sauce per plated dessert.

FRUIT PURÉES

Many types of fruit can be puréed for dessert sauces; strawberries, raspberries, blackberries, apricots, mangoes and papayas are popular choices. They produce thick sauces with strong flavors and colors. Ripe, fresh or individually quick-frozen (IQF) fruits are recommended. Several commercial brands of prepared fruit purées are available. The best use only natural fruits and are excellent for making sauces and sorbets. They provide consistent flavor and color, reduce preparation time, and make out-of-season or hard-to-obtain tropical fruits available at a reasonable price.

Puréed fruit sauces are known as **coulis.** Minimal processing of the best-quality fruit produces pure fresh-tasting sauce. Should thickening be desired, keep in mind that starches require boiling, which can alter the fresh fruit flavor. A thick caramel can be added to tart fruit purées such as strawberry or citrus for sweetening and thickening. Most berries as well as apricots, peaches and other tree fruits are puréed, then mixed with sugar and glucose or corn syrup. A ratio of 20 percent sugar to fruit is recommended, though the amount depends on the fruit's natural sweetness and personal preference. The relatively small amount of sweetener interacts with the fruit acids to enhance the true fruit flavor. Glucose is less sweet than sugar and provides body and an attractive sheen. A small amount of lemon juice or citric acid may be added to enhance fruit flavor. For stone fruits, as much as 2 ounces (60 grams) total weight can be lost per pound of fruit after puréeing. For a seedless berry purée, 28 ounces (840 grams) of whole berries produces approximately 16 ounces (480 grams) of seedless purée. When using purchased fruit purée, taste the product before adding all the sugar in the formula. Adjust the quantity of sugar as needed.

▶ PROCEDURE FOR PREPARING A FRUIT COULIS

1 Wash, peel and chop the fruit if necessary.
2 Purée the fruit in a food mill, blender or food processor. Strain to remove seeds.
3 Combine the purée with flavorings and sweeteners if using.

RECIPE 13.12	**FRUIT COULIS**	

Yield: 1 lb. 4 oz. (600 g)

Fruit purée, strained	16 oz.	480 g
Granulated sugar	2.5 oz.	75 g
Glucose or corn syrup	1 oz.	30 g
Lemon juice	0.5 fl. oz.	15 ml

1 Combine the fruit purée with the sugar and glucose or corn syrup. Add as much lemon juice as needed to balance the flavor of the sauce.
2 Serve warm or cold.

Approximate values per 1-oz. (30-g) serving: **Calories** 35, **Total fat** 0 g, **Saturated fat** 0 g, **Cholesterol** 0 mg, **Sodium** 5 mg, **Total carbohydrates** 8 g, **Protein** 0 g

FRUIT GELÉE

Gelatin may be added to a fruit coulis so that it sets once chilled. This fruit gelée can then be used as a filling in a cake or torte. See the formula for Rubies Torte (page 424) or Palomo Torte (page 426). Enough gelatin is added to a warm fruit juice or purée so that the liquid is firm enough to hold its shape once chilled. The mixture is poured into a container the same shape as the torte or cake. After it is set in the refrigerator or freezer, the fruit gelée is unmolded and placed on top of the mousse or filling in a multilayered torte. The procedure for making a fruit gelée is illustrated by the formula for Raspberry Gelée.

RASPBERRY GELÉE

RECIPE 13.13

Yield: 2 lb. 9 oz. (1230 g)

Seedless raspberry purée	2 lb.	960 g
Granulated sugar	8 oz.	240 g
Sheet gelatin, softened	1 oz.	30 g

1 Heat the purée to 120°F (49°C). Add the sugar and stir until it dissolves.
2 Add the softened sheet gelatin to the warm purée. Stir the mixture until the gelatin dissolves. Immediately pour the mixture into the appropriate mold required as indicated in the formula. Chill or freeze until firm.

Approximate values per 1-oz. (30-g) serving: **Calories** 35, **Total fat** 0 g, **Saturated fat** 0 g, **Cholesterol** 0 mg, **Sodium** 5 mg, **Total carbohydrates** 8 g, **Protein** 1 g

CARAMEL SAUCE

Caramel sauce is a mixture of caramelized sugar and heavy cream. A liqueur or citrus juice may be used for added flavor. Review the material on caramelizing sugar earlier in this chapter. Great care must be taken when caramelizing the sugar and adding the cold cream to the caramel. The sugar can easily spatter and boil over, causing severe burns.

CARAMEL SAUCE

RECIPE 13.14

Yield: 4 qt. (4 lt)

Granulated sugar	4 lb. 8 oz.	2 kg
Water	1 pt.	480 ml
Lemon juice	2 fl. oz.	60 ml
Heavy cream, room temperature	2 qt.	2 lt
Unsalted butter, cut into pieces	5 oz.	150 g

1 Combine the sugar and water in a large heavy saucepan. Stir to moisten the sugar completely. Place the saucepan on the stovetop over high heat and bring to a boil. Brush down the sides of the pan with water to remove any sugar granules.
2 When the sugar comes to a boil, add the lemon juice. Do not stir the sugar, as this may cause lumping. Continue boiling until the sugar caramelizes, turning a dark golden brown and producing a rich aroma.
3 Remove the saucepan from the heat. Gradually add the cream. Be extremely careful, as the hot caramel may splatter. Whisk in the cream to blend.
4 Add the pieces of butter. Stir until the butter melts completely. If necessary, return the sauce to the stove to reheat enough to melt the butter.
5 Strain the sauce and cool completely at room temperature. The sauce may be stored several weeks under refrigeration. Stir before using.

Caramel Sauce

Approximate values per 1-fl.-oz. (30-ml) serving: **Calories** 130, **Total fat** 7 g, **Saturated fat** 4 g, **Cholesterol** 25 mg, **Sodium** 5 mg, **Total carbohydrates** 16 g, **Protein** 0 g, **Vitamin A** 8%

CHOCOLATE SYRUP

Chocolate syrup or sauce can be prepared by adding finely chopped chocolate to warm vanilla custard sauce. A darker syrup can also be made with unsweetened chocolate or cocoa powder. Fudge-type sauces, such as Chocolate Fudge Sauce (page 376), are really just variations on ganache (page 362).

RECIPE 13.15

DARK CHOCOLATE SYRUP

Dark Chocolate Syrup

Yield: 1 pt. (500 ml)

Cocoa powder	2 oz.	60 g
Water	12 fl. oz.	360 ml
Granulated sugar	8 oz.	240 g
Unsalted butter	3 oz.	90 g
Heavy cream	1 fl. oz.	30 ml

1 Mix the cocoa powder with just enough water to make a smooth paste.

2 Bring the sugar and remaining water to a boil in a small, heavy saucepan. Immediately add the cocoa paste, whisking until smooth.

3 Simmer for 15 minutes, stirring constantly, then remove from the heat.

4 Stir the butter and cream into the warm cocoa mixture. Serve warm or at room temperature.

Approximate values per 1-fl.-oz. (30-ml) serving: **Calories** 120, **Total fat** 6 g, **Saturated fat** 3 g, **Cholesterol** 15 mg, **Sodium** 0 mg, **Total carbohydrates** 16 g, **Protein** 1 g, **Vitamin A** 6%

CONVENIENCE PRODUCTS

A wide selection of prepared icings, glazes and toppings are available. Often, chocolate and vanilla fudge-based icings are purchased and then flavored or colored as needed. Foam icings can be purchased in powder form, to which you simply add water and whip. Ready-to-use glazes and flat icings are formulated for many types of applications—brushing over cakes, sweet dough pastries or doughnuts in particular. Even prepared "buttercreams" are available in shelf-stable or frozen forms, although they contain little or no real butter.

Prepared icings are often exceedingly sweet and overpowered by artificial flavors and chemical preservatives. These products save time and offer consistent results but often cost more than their counterparts made from scratch. They should be used only after balancing the disadvantages against the benefits for your particular operation.

Prepared syrups used to flavor coffee drinks may be used in place of simple syrup in a pinch when the syrup is used to moisten a spongecake or torte. The variety of flavors is limitless and exotic; espresso, hazelnut, kiwi or anise, for example. But making sugar syrup from scratch is preferred when making caramel or buttercream. Popular sauces such as caramel, butterscotch, hot fudge and strawberry have been available for many years, usually sold for use at ice cream stands. With the broad appeal of plated desserts, more varieties of sauces and products containing less sugar and more natural ingredients are now available. Convenience reached a new level when fruit sauces for plated desserts became available in ready-to-use plastic applicator bottles.

CONCLUSION

The skilled pastry chef understands the principles of working with sugar syrups to make a variety of fillings, icings and sauces. These items flavor, moisten and embellish cakes and dessert preparations. The techniques for working with these syrups form an important part of the chef's repertoire. Cake decorating, discussed in Chapter 14, Cakes and Tortes, and dessert plating, reviewed in Chapter 20, Restaurant Desserts, rely on the preparations covered in this chapter.

QUESTIONS FOR DISCUSSION

1 Sugar melts at various temperatures. Describe the stages that sugar achieves at various temperatures.

2 Explain why butter should be softened before preparing buttercream icing.

3 Identify three fruits suitable for making into a fruit coulis and describe the procedure to make them.

4 Compare simple buttercream, Italian buttercream and French buttercream. How are they different?

5 What techniques and ingredients are essential to prevent crystallization when making sugar syrups and caramel?

LONGCHAMP

RECIPE 13.16

Chef Jack Shoop, CMC, CMB

Note: This dish appears in the chapter opening photograph.

Yield: 1 Cake, 10 in. (24 cm)

Ladyfingers (page 415)	as needed	as needed
Classic Genoise (page 386), cut into a 10-in. (24-cm) circle	1 layer	1 layer
Kirsch (cherry brandy)	3.5 fl. oz.	105 ml
Simple Syrup (page 349) cool	1 qt.	1 lt
Kirsch Mousse (recipe follows)	as needed	as needed
Fresh raspberries	1 pt.	0.5 lt
Italian Meringue (page 290)	as needed	as needed

1 Place a 10-inch (24-centimeter) metal ring that is 1³/₄ inches (4.5 centimeters) high over a cardboard circle. Line the ring completely with Ladyfingers. Cut the Ladyfingers level with the top of the ring. Place the Classic Genoise inside the ring to form the bottom of the cake.

2 Prepare a Kirsch-flavored syrup by combining the Kirsch and the Simple Syrup. Brush the Classic Genoise and the Ladyfingers with this syrup. Reserve the remaining Kirsch-flavored syrup for another use.

3 Fill the cake with Kirsch Mousse, sprinkling in raspberries as the cake is filled so that the fruit is evenly distributed. The cake should be filled to the top of the ring. Smooth the top of the mousse with an offset spatula.

4 Freeze the cake until set.

5 Spread a thin layer of Italian Meringue over the mousse. Decorate the top of the cake with Italian Meringue piped through a pastry bag fitted with a St. Honoré tip. Pipe the meringue from the center, curving outward to the edge of the cake. Brown the top of the meringue with a propane torch.

6 Remove the metal ring and garnish the cake with fresh raspberries.

Approximate values per ¹/₁₂-cake serving: **Calories** 690, **Total fat** 30 g, **Saturated fat** 17 g, **Cholesterol** 267 mg, **Sodium** 171 mg, **Total carbohydrates** 89 g, **Protein** 10 g, **Vitamin A** 25%, **Vitamin C** 35%, **Calcium** 10%

KIRSCH MOUSSE

Yield: 2 qt. (2 lt)

Kirsch	3.5 fl. oz.	105 ml
Sheet gelatin, softened	1 oz.	30 g
Heavy cream	1 qt.	1 lt
Pastry Cream (page 436)	2 lb.	960 g

1 Bring the Kirsch to a simmer over low heat. Remove from the heat, add the softened sheet gelatin and stir until it is completely dissolved.

2 Stir the gelatin mixture into the heavy cream, then whip the cream to soft peaks.

3 Fold the whipped cream into the Pastry Cream and chill until ready to use.

Approximate values per serving: **Calories** 480, **Total fat** 36 g, **Saturated fat** 22 g, **Cholesterol** 245 mg, **Sodium** 96 mg, **Total carbohydrates** 27 g, **Protein** 8 g, **Vitamin A** 29%, **Vitamin C** 41%, **Calcium** 12%

CHEF JACK SHOOP, CMC, CMB

Chef Shoop is a chef and culinary educator in Destin, Florida, where he is the chef of Bianco Mediterranean Cuisine and Wheat Berries Bakery.

RECIPE 13.17

CREAM CHEESE ICING

Yield: 5 lb. 4 oz. (2535 g)

Unsalted butter, softened	6 oz.	180 g
Cream cheese, softened	1 lb. 8 oz.	720 g
Margarine	6 oz.	180 g
Vanilla extract	0.5 fl. oz.	15 ml
Powdered sugar, sifted	3 lb.	1440 g

1 Cream the butter and cream cheese until smooth. Add the margarine and beat well.

2 Beat in the vanilla. Slowly add the sugar, scraping down the bowl frequently. Beat until smooth.

Approximate values per serving: **Calories** 130, **Total fat** 6 g, **Saturated fat** 3 g, **Cholesterol** 15 mg, **Sodium** 45 mg, **Total carbohydrates** 17 g, **Protein** 1 g, **Vitamin A** 6%

RECIPE 13.18

TRADITIONAL FRENCH BUTTERCREAM

Yield: 3 lb. 12 oz. (1820 g)

Granulated sugar	1 lb. 3 oz.	570 g
Corn syrup or glucose	3 oz.	90 g
Water	6 fl. oz.	180 ml
Eggs	5 oz. (3 eggs)	150 g
Egg yolks	6.6 oz. (10 yolks)	200 g
Unsalted butter, room temperature	1 lb. 10 oz.	780 g
Vanilla extract	1 fl. oz.	30 ml

1 Combine the sugar, corn syrup or glucose and water in a small saucepan and bring to a boil.

2 Meanwhile, place the eggs and egg yolks in the bowl of a mixer fitted with a whip; start whipping the mixture on medium speed the moment the sugar solution begins to boil.

3 Continue boiling until the syrup reaches 250°F (121°C). When the syrup is ready, increase the mixer speed to high and carefully pour the sugar syrup in a steady even stream down the inside of the bowl.

4 Continue whipping until the mixture is cool and mousselike.

5 Reduce the speed to medium and gradually add the butter; whip until light and aerated.

6 Add the vanilla.

VARIATIONS:

Mocha French Buttercream—Omit the vanilla extract. Add 1 fluid ounce (30 milliliters) coffee extract to the buttercream, then stir in 8 ounces (240 grams) melted and cooled bittersweet chocolate.

Pistachio French Buttercream—Omit the vanilla extract. Add 1.5 fluid ounces (45 milliliters) pistachio compound or flavoring and 3 ounces (90 grams) finely ground pistachios to the buttercream.

Citrus French Buttercream—Omit the vanilla extract. Add 0.5 fluid ounces (15 milliliters) orange extract and 0.5 fluid ounces (15 milliliters) lemon extract to the buttercream.

Approximate values per 1-oz. (30-g) serving: **Calories** 140, **Total fat** 11 g, **Saturated fat** 6 g, **Cholesterol** 70 mg, **Sodium** 5 mg, **Total carbohydrates** 10 g, **Protein** 1 g

WHITE CHOCOLATE BUTTERCREAM

Yield: Approximately 5 lb. (2400 g)

Granulated sugar	1 lb. 14 oz.	900 g
Water	8 fl. oz.	240 ml
Egg whites	9 oz. (9 whites)	270 g
Unsalted butter, softened	2 lb. 6 oz.	1140 g
White crème de cacao	3 fl. oz.	90 ml
White chocolate, melted	8 oz.	240 g

1 Cook the sugar and water to 242°F (117°C), then pour into a measuring container with a handle for easier pouring.

2 Start whipping the egg whites when the sugar reaches 235°F (113°C).

3 When the whites are whipped to firm peaks, add the hot sugar syrup slowly while continuing to whip at low speed. Whip until completely cool.

4 Add the butter and whip until smooth.

5 Add the crème de cacao to the white chocolate. Whip until smooth, and then add the chocolate to the buttercream.

Approximate values per 1-oz. (30-g) serving: **Calories** 140, **Total fat** 11 g, **Saturated fat** 7 g, **Cholesterol** 25 mg, **Sodium** 10 mg, **Total carbohydrates** 10 g, **Protein** 1 g, **Vitamin A** 8%

COCONUT PECAN ICING

Yield: 1 lb. 14 oz. (905 g) Icing, enough for 1 three-layer cake

Evaporated milk	8 fl. oz.	240 ml
Granulated sugar	8 oz.	240 g
Egg yolks	2 oz. (3 yolks)	60 g
Unsalted butter	4 oz.	120 g
Vanilla extract	0.15 fl. oz. (1 tsp.)	5 ml
Coconut, flaked	4 oz.	120 g
Pecans, chopped	4 oz.	120 g

1 Combine the milk, sugar, egg yolks and butter in a saucepan over medium heat. Cook, stirring constantly, until the mixture thickens, approximately 12 minutes.

2 Remove from the heat and add the vanilla, coconut and pecans. Beat until cool and spreadable.

Approximate values per 1-oz. (30-g) serving: **Calories** 140, **Total fat** 11 g, **Saturated fat** 7 g, **Cholesterol** 25 mg, **Sodium** 10 mg, **Total carbohydrates** 10 g, **Protein** 1 g, **Vitamin A** 8%

RECIPE 13.21   **CARAMEL NUT FILLING OR ICING**

Use this filling in a cake or torte or as a topping on cheesecake.

Yield: 1 lb. 9 oz. (750 g)

Granulated sugar	6 oz.	180 g
Glucose or corn syrup	1.5 oz.	45 g
Water	3 fl. oz.	90 ml
Honey	2 oz.	60 g
Heavy cream, heated	6 fl. oz.	180 ml
Walnuts	5 oz.	150 g
Pecans	4 oz.	120 g
Vanilla extract	0.5 fl. oz.	15 ml

1 In a deep saucepan, bring the sugar, glucose or corn syrup and water to a boil.

2 Wash down any crystals that cling to the sides of the pan with a brush dipped in water. Cook the mixture without stirring until it turns a golden caramel color, approximately 350°F (177°C).

3 Add the honey and cream; be aware that the caramel mixture will rise when these ingredients are added. Reboil the mixture until it darkens to a medium amber color, approximately 3 to 4 minutes.

4 Remove from heat and add the walnuts and pecans. Let cool to room temperature, then stir in the vanilla. Use immediately to fill or ice a cake or torte (see Eros Torte, page 423) or store in the refrigerator. The filling or icing will keep 2 weeks when refrigerated.

5 Reheat the caramel filling to room temperature in a microwave oven or over a bain marie when it will be used to fill a torte. To use for icing, reheat to approximately 130°F (54°C), then spread on a cooled cheesecake or other cake layers. Let the caramel icing set before cutting.

Approximate values per 1-oz. (30-g) serving: **Calories** 140, **Total fat** 10 g, **Saturated fat** 2.5 g, **Cholesterol** 10 mg, **Sodium** 5 mg, **Total carbohydrates** 12 g, **Protein** 1 g

RECIPE 13.22   **FONDANT GLAZE**

Yield: 12 oz. (365 g)

Fondant	9 oz.	270 g
Water	3 fl. oz.	90 ml
Vanilla extract	0.15 fl. oz. (1 tsp.)	5 ml

1 Combine the fondant and water in a bowl and set it over a pan of simmering water. Heat the fondant to 120°F (49°C) stirring occasionally to ensure even softening of the fondant.

2 Remove the fondant from heat. Stir in the vanilla. Add additional water if needed to obtain the desired consistency.

3 Use the fondant when it is between 110°F and 120°F (43°C and 49°C).

VARIATIONS:

Orange Fondant Glaze—Combine 1 pound (480 grams) fondant with 3 fluid ounces (90 milliliters) orange juice concentrate. Heat as directed. Add 2 fluid ounces (60 milliliters) additional orange juice concentrate and vanilla extract.

Raspberry Fondant Glaze—Substitute 3 ounces (90 grams) raspberry purée for the water. Omit the vanilla extract.

Approximate values per 1-oz. (30-g) serving: **Calories** 80, **Total fat** 0 g, **Saturated fat** 0 g, **Cholesterol** 0 mg, **Sodium** 10 mg, **Total carbohydrates** 20 g, **Protein** 0 g

DECORATIVE COOKIE ICING   RECIPE 13.23

Yield: 1 lb. 6 oz. (665 g)

Powdered sugar	1 lb.	480 g
Lemon juice or water	4 fl. oz.	120 ml
Corn syrup	2 fl. oz.	60 ml
Vanilla extract	0.15 fl. oz. (1 tsp.)	5 ml
Food coloring	as needed	as needed

1 Combine the powdered sugar, lemon juice, corn syrup and vanilla in the bowl of a mixer fitted with a paddle. Blend on low speed until the sugar dissolves and the mixture is smooth. Adjust the consistency of the icing by adding more water if necessary. Color as needed.

2 Apply the icing to cookies and let them air dry until the icing hardens. Cover leftover icing and store it in the refrigerator, where it will keep about 3 weeks.

Approximate values per ¾-oz. (20-g) serving: **Calories** 60, **Total fat** 0 g, **Saturated fat** 0 g, **Cholesterol** 0 mg, **Sodium** 0 mg, **Total carbohydrates** 16 g, **Protein** 0 g

SILKY GANACHE DELUXE   RECIPE 13.24

Some ganache formulas contain just cream and butter; however, the addition of an invert sugar and butter make a ganache unsurpassed in resilience and sheen.

Yield: 3 lb. 2 oz. (1500 g)

Heavy cream	16 fl. oz.	480 ml
Granulated sugar	5 oz.	150 g
Corn syrup or glucose	5 oz.	150 g
Semisweet or bittersweet chocolate	1 lb. 3 oz.	570 g
Unsalted butter	5 oz.	150 g

1 In a large saucepan, bring the cream, sugar and corn syrup or glucose to a boil.

2 Chop the chocolate and butter into walnut-size pieces and place them in a large mixing bowl.

3 When the cream mixture boils, pour one-sixth of it over the chocolate-and-butter mixture. Stir the chocolate with a rubber spatula. Add the remaining cream in five increments, stirring well between additions to emulsify the ganache.

Approximate values per 1-oz. (30-g) serving: **Calories** 120, **Total fat** 80 g, **Saturated fat** 6 g, **Cholesterol** 20 mg, **Sodium** 10 mg, **Total carbohydrates** 12 g, **Protein** 1 g

RECIPE 13.25

ORANGE MILK CHOCOLATE GANACHE

Yield: 2 lb. 2 oz. (1020 g)

Heavy cream	8 fl. oz.	240 ml
Milk	6 fl. oz.	180 ml
Glucose or corn syrup	2 oz.	60 g
Unsalted butter	2 oz.	60 g
Milk chocolate	14 oz.	420 g
Orange oil (not extract)	2–3 drops	2–3 drops
Bittersweet chocolate	2 oz.	60 g

1 Bring the cream and milk to a boil in a large saucepan. Remove from the heat, then whisk in the glucose or corn syrup and butter.

2 Chop the chocolate into walnut-size pieces and place it in a large mixing bowl. Add the orange oil. Pour one-fifth of the boiled cream over the chocolate. Stir with a rubber spatula. Add the remaining cream in four increments, stirring well between additions to emulsify the ganache.

Approximate values per 1-oz. (30-g) serving: **Calories** 110, **Total fat** 8 g, **Saturated fat** 5 g, **Cholesterol** 15 mg, **Sodium** 15 mg, **Total carbohydrates** 9 g, **Protein** 1 g

RECIPE 13.26

RASPBERRY SAUCE

Raspberry Sauce

Yield: 1 qt. (1 lt)

Raspberries, fresh or IQF	2 lb.	1 kg
Granulated sugar	1 lb.	500 g
Lemon juice	1 fl. oz.	30 ml

1 Purée the berries and strain through a fine chinois.

2 Stir in the sugar and lemon juice. Adjust the flavor with additional sugar if necessary.

Approximate values per 1-fl.-oz. (30-ml) serving: **Calories** 70, **Total fat** 0 g, **Saturated fat** 0 g, **Cholesterol** 0 mg, **Sodium** 0 mg, **Total carbohydrates** 17 g, **Protein** 0 g, **Claims**—fat free; no saturated fat; no cholesterol; no sodium

RECIPE 13.27

MINTED PEACH COULIS

Yield: 1 pt. (750 ml)

Peach purée	20 oz.	600 ml
Granulated sugar	5 oz.	150 g
Mint leaves	10	10

1 Blend the ingredients in a blender and process until smooth. Strain if desired.

Approximate values per 1-fl.-oz. (30-ml) serving: **Calories** 35, **Total fat** 0 g, **Saturated fat** 0 g, **Cholesterol** 0 mg, **Sodium** 0 mg, **Total carbohydrates** 9 g, **Protein** 0 g

STRAWBERRY GELÉE

Yield: 1 lb. 13 oz. (888 g)

Strawberry purée	24 oz.	720 g
Granulated sugar	5 oz.	150 g
Sheet gelatin, softened	0.75 oz.	18 g

1 Heat the purée to 120°F (49°C). Stir in the sugar, mixing until it dissolves.

2 Add the gelatin to the purée, stirring until the gelatin dissolves completely. Immediately pour the mixture into the appropriate mold required as indicated in the formula. Chill or freeze until firm.

Approximate values per 1-oz. (30-g) serving: **Calories** 30, **Total fat** 0 g, **Saturated fat** 0 g, **Cholesterol** 0 mg, **Sodium** 5 mg, **Total carbohydrates** 7 g, **Protein** 1 g

CHERRY GELÉE

Yield: 4 lb. (1935 g)

Cherry purée	3 lb.	1440 g
Granulated sugar	15 oz.	450 g
Sheet gelatin, softened	1.75 oz.	45 g

1 Combine the purée and sugar in a nonreactive saucepan and heat the mixture until it reaches 110°F (43°C).

2 Add the gelatin to the purée. Stir until the gelatin dissolves completely. Immediately pour the mixture into the appropriate mold required as indicated in the formula. Chill or freeze until firm.

Approximate values per 1-oz. (30-g) serving: **Calories** 50, **Total fat** 0 g, **Saturated fat** 0 g, **Cholesterol** 0 mg, **Sodium** 5 mg, **Total carbohydrates** 10 g, **Protein** 1 g

PINEAPPLE SAUCE

Yield: Approximately 1 pt. (480 ml)

Ripe pineapple, peeled and cored	1 lb.	480 g
Unsalted butter	4 oz.	120 g
Granulated sugar	4 oz.	120 g
Cider vinegar	0.6 fl. oz.	20 ml
Vanilla bean	1	1

1 Cut the pineapple into pieces and blend in a food processor until finely puréed. Strain the purée through a chinois or sieve. Set aside.

2 Melt the butter in a nonreactive saucepan over low heat without browning. Add the sugar and whisk the mixture while it comes to a boil. Add the vinegar and boil 2 minutes. Remove the pan from heat.

3 Add the pineapple purée. Scrape the seeds from the vanilla bean and add to the pan. Let the sauce sit at least 30 minutes to infuse it with the vanilla flavor. Remove the vanilla bean before serving.

Approximate values per 1-fl.-oz. (30-ml) serving: **Calories** 90, **Total fat** 6 g, **Saturated fat** 3.5 g, **Cholesterol** 15 mg, **Sodium** 0 mg, **Total carbohydrates** 11 g, **Protein** 0 g

RECIPE 13.31   COCONUT SAUCE

Yield: Approximately 20 fl. oz. (600 ml)

Coconut purée or unsweetened		
coconut milk	1 pt.	480 ml
Heavy cream	4 fl.oz.	120 ml
Vanilla extract	0.3 fl. oz. (2 tsp.)	10 ml

1 Combine the coconut purée, cream and vanilla in a small bowl. Blend well with a whisk. Chill before serving.

Approximate values per 1-fl.-oz. (30-ml) serving: **Calories** 60, **Total fat** 7 g, **Saturated fat** 6 g, **Cholesterol** 5 mg, **Sodium** 0 mg, **Total carbohydrates** 1 g, **Protein** 1 g

RECIPE 13.32   WARM WINE SAUCE

Yield: Approximately 1 pt. (500 ml)

Sweet dessert wine	12 fl. oz.	360 ml
Orange zest	0.4 oz. (2 Tbsp.)	12 g
Lemon zest	0.14 oz. (2 tsp.)	4 g
Mint leaves	10	10
Vanilla bean, split	1	1
Corn or tapioca starch	0.3 oz. (1 Tbsp.)	10 g
Granulated sugar	6 oz.	180 g
Water	2 fl. oz.	60 ml

1 In a nonreactive saucepan, bring the wine to a boil. Remove from heat and add the orange and lemon zest, mint leaves and vanilla bean. Cover with plastic film. Infuse 2 hours or overnight.
2 Strain the infusion. Add the starch and bring the mixture to a boil.
3 Cook the sugar and water to a light golden caramel.
4 Carefully pour the heated wine into the caramel. Whisk and reboil the mixture. Remove from heat and chill before serving.

Note: The sauce made with tapioca starch instead of cornstarch will be clearer.

VARIATION:
Cold Wine Sauce—Omit the starch. In step 4, dissolve 0.1 ounce (3 grams) softened sheet gelatin in with the sauce.

Approximate values per 1-fl.-oz. (30-ml) serving: **Calories** 70, **Total fat** 0 g, **Saturated fat** 0 g, **Cholesterol** 0 mg, **Sodium** 0 mg, **Total carbohydrates** 12 g, **Protein** 0 g

BUTTERSCOTCH SAUCE

RECIPE 13.33

Yield: Approximately 2 qt. (2 lt)

Granulated sugar	1 lb. 8 oz.	720 g
Light corn syrup	2 lb. 4 oz.	1080 g
Unsalted butter	4 oz.	120 g
Heavy cream	10 fl. oz.	300 ml
Scotch whisky	4 fl. oz.	120 ml

1 Cook the sugar to a dark brown caramel. Add the corn syrup.

2 Remove the sugar from the heat and slowly add the butter and the cream, stirring until the butter is completely melted.

3 Stir in the Scotch and cool.

Approximate values per 1-fl.-oz. (30-ml) serving: **Calories** 120, **Total fat** 3 g, **Saturated fat** 2 g, **Cholesterol** 23 mg, **Sodium** 20 mg, **Total carbohydrates** 23 g, **Protein** 0 g, **Vitamin A** 4%, **Claims**—low fat; low cholesterol; very low sodium

CLEAR CARAMEL SAUCE

RECIPE 13.34

Yield: Approximately 1 qt. (900 ml)

Granulated sugar	1 lb.	480 g
Glucose or corn syrup	3 fl. oz.	90 ml
Water	19 fl. oz.	570 ml
Orange juice	2 fl. oz.	60 ml
Vanilla bean	1	1

1 Cook the sugar, glucose or corn syrup and 7 fluid ounces (210 milliliters) of the water to a golden-brown caramel.

2 Meanwhile, boil the remaining water with the orange juice and vanilla bean. Add the orange mixture to the caramel.

3 Return to a boil, whisk until homogenous, and remove from heat. Remove the vanilla bean before serving.

Approximate values per 1-fl. oz. (30-ml) serving: **Calories** 70, **Total fat** 0 g, **Saturated fat** 0 g, **Cholesterol** 0 mg, **Sodium** 0 mg, **Total carbohydrates** 17 g, **Protein** 0 g

RECIPE 13.35

FRUITED CARAMEL SAUCE

Yield: Approximately 20 fl. oz. (600 ml)

Granulated sugar	6 oz.	180 g
Water	3 fl. oz.	90 ml
Glucose or corn syrup	3 fl. oz.	90 ml
Lemon, mandarin orange, passion fruit or pineapple juice, strained	12 fl. oz.	360 ml
Pectin	0.2 oz. (2 tsp.)	2 g
Fruit-flavored liqueur (optional)	1 fl. oz.	30 ml

1 Cook the sugar, water and glucose or corn syrup to a golden caramel.
2 Meanwhile, in a nonreactive saucepan, heat the fruit juice to 120°F (49°C) and whisk in the pectin. Bring to a boil.
3 Pour the boiling juice into the caramel; carefully whisk to homogenize and re-boil the mixture.
4 Remove from heat and let cool. Add the fruit liqueur (if using).

Approximate values per 1-fl.-oz. (30-ml) serving: **Calories** 60, **Total fat** 0 g, **Saturated fat** 0 g, **Cholesterol** 0 mg, **Sodium** 10 mg, **Total carbohydrates** 15 g, **Protein** 0 g

RECIPE 13.36

CHOCOLATE FUDGE SAUCE

Yield: Approximately 1 gal. (4 lt)

Heavy cream	2 qt.	2 lt
Light corn syrup	6 fl. oz.	180 ml
Granulated sugar	8 oz.	240 g
Bittersweet chocolate	4 lb.	2000 g

1 Combine the cream, corn syrup and sugar in a saucepan and bring just to a boil, stirring frequently.
2 Chop the chocolate and place in a large bowl.
3 Pour the hot cream over the chocolate and stir until completely melted.
4 Store well covered and refrigerated. Gently rewarm over a bain marie if desired.

VARIATION:

Mint Chocolate Fudge Sauce—Bring the cream to a boil and steep 1 ounce (30 grams) finely chopped fresh mint leaves in the cream 10 minutes. Strain and proceed with the formula.

Approximate values per 1-fl.-oz. (30-ml) serving: **Calories** 130, **Total fat** 9 g, **Saturated fat** 6 g, **Cholesterol** 20 mg, **Sodium** 10 mg, **Total carbohydrates** 10 g, **Protein** 1 g, **Vitamin A** 6%

ESPRESSO SAUCE

RECIPE 13.37

**CHRISTOPHER'S FERMIER BRASSERIE
AND PAOLA'S WINE BAR,** PHOENIX, AZ
Chef-Owner Christopher Gross

Yield: Approximately 1 1/2 pt. (700 ml)

Egg yolks	5.3 oz. (8 yolks)	160 g
Granulated sugar	3.5 oz.	105 g
Half-and-half	1 pt.	480 ml
Espresso beans, whole	3 oz.	90 g
Vanilla bean	1/2	1/2

1 Whisk the egg yolks and sugar together in a medium bowl.

2 Bring the half-and-half, espresso beans and vanilla bean to a simmer in a heavy saucepan.

3 Add a portion of the hot half-and-half to the egg yolks, then return the mixture to the saucepan. Cook over low heat, stirring constantly, until the sauce is thick enough to coat the back of a spoon. Strain and cool over an ice bath.

Approximate values per 1-fl.-oz. (30-ml) serving: **Calories** 60, **Total fat** 4 g, **Saturated fat** 2 g, **Cholesterol** 75 mg, **Sodium** 10 mg, **Total carbohydrates** 5 g, **Protein** 2 g, **Vitamin A** 6%

ANYONE CAN MAKE YOU ENJOY THE FIRST BITE OF A
DISH, BUT ONLY A REAL CHEF CAN MAKE YOU ENJOY
THE LAST.

—*François Minot, French restaurant critic*

14

CAKES AND TORTES

MONTAGE RESORT AND SPA, Laguna Beach, CA
Executive Pastry Chef Richard Ruskell

AFTER STUDYING THIS CHAPTER, YOU WILL BE ABLE TO:

▶ prepare a variety of cakes and tortes

▶ prepare a variety of icings

▶ assemble cakes using basic finishing and decorating techniques

Cakes and tortes are popular in most bakeshops because a wide variety of finished products can be created from only a few basic cake, filling and icing formulas. Many of these components can even be made in advance and assembled into finished desserts as needed. Cakes are also popular because of their versatility: They can be served as unadorned sheets in a high-volume cafeteria or as the elaborate centerpiece of a wedding buffet.

Cake making need not be difficult or intimidating, but it does require an understanding of ingredients and mixing methods. This chapter begins by explaining how typical cake ingredients interact. Each of the traditional mixing methods is then explained and illustrated with a recipe. Information on panning batters, baking temperatures, determining doneness and cooling methods follows. The second portion of this chapter presents methods for assembling and decorating a variety of cakes and tortes using many of the icing formulas discussed in the previous chapter. An array of creams and mousses suitable for filling certain cakes and tortes are discussed in Chapter 15, Custards and Creams. A selection of cake and torte formulas, which can be used throughout this book, concludes the chapter.

▶ CAKES

Most cakes are created from liquid batters with high fat and sugar contents. The baker's job is to combine all the ingredients to create a structure that will support these rich ingredients yet keep the cake as light and delicate as possible. As with other baked goods, it is impossible to taste a cake until it is fully cooked and too late to alter the formula. Therefore, it is extremely important to study any formula before beginning and to follow it with particular care and attention to detail.

INGREDIENTS

Good cakes begin with high-quality ingredients (see Chapter 4, Bakeshop Ingredients); however, even the finest ingredients must be combined in the proper balance. Too much flour and the cake may be dry; too much egg and the cake will be tough and hard. Changing one ingredient may necessitate a change in one or more of the other ingredients.

Each ingredient performs a specific function and has a specific effect on the final product. Cake ingredients can be classified by function as **tougheners, tenderizers, moisteners, driers, leaveners** and **flavorings.** Some ingredients fulfill more than one of these functions. For example, eggs contain water, so they are moisteners, and they contain protein, so they are tougheners. By understanding the function of various ingredients, you should be able to understand why cakes are made in particular ways and why a preparation sometimes fails.

With additional experience, you should be able to recognize and correct flawed formulas and develop your own cake formulas.

TOUGHENERS

Flour, milk and eggs contain protein. Protein provides structure and strengthens the cake once it is baked. Too little protein and the cake may collapse; too much protein and the cake may be tough and coarse.

TENDERIZERS

Sugar, fats and egg yolks interfere with the development of the gluten structure when cakes are mixed. They shorten the gluten strands, making the cake tender and soft. These ingredients also improve the cake's keeping qualities.

MOISTENERS

Liquids such as water, milk, juice and eggs bring moisture to the mixture. Moisture is necessary for gluten formation and starch gelatinization, as well as for improving a cake's keeping qualities.

DRIERS

Flour, starches and milk solids absorb moisture, giving body and structure to the cake.

LEAVENERS

Cakes rise because gases in the batter expand when heated. Cakes are leavened by the air trapped when fat and sugar are creamed together, by carbon dioxide released from baking powder and baking soda and by air trapped in beaten eggs. All cakes rely on natural leaveners—steam and air—to create the proper texture and rise. Because baking soda and baking powder are also used in some cake formulas, reviewing the material on chemical leaveners in Chapter 6, Quick Breads is recommended.

FLAVORINGS

Flavorings such as extracts, cocoa, chocolate, spices, salt, sugar and butter provide cakes with the desired flavors. Acidic flavoring ingredients such as sour cream, chocolate and fruit also provide the acid necessary to activate baking soda.

Cake ingredients should be at room temperature, approximately 70°F (21°C), before mixing begins. If one ingredient is too cold or too warm, it may affect the batter's ability to trap and hold the gases necessary for the cake to rise.

MIXING METHODS

Even the finest ingredients will be wasted if the cake batter is not mixed correctly. When mixing any cake batter, the goals are to combine the ingredients uniformly, incorporate air cells and develop the proper texture.

All mixing methods can be divided into two categories: high fat (those that create a structure that relies primarily on **creamed fat**) and egg foam (those that create a structure that relies primarily on **whipped eggs**). Within these broad categories are several mixing methods or types of cakes. Creamed-fat cakes include **butter cakes** (also known as **creaming-method cakes**) and **high-ratio cakes.** Whipped-egg cakes include **genoise, spongecakes, angel food** cakes and **chiffon** cakes. See Table 14.1, page 384. Although certain general procedures are used to prepare each cake type, there are, of course, numerous variations. Certain European-style cake formulas include both creaming and egg foam

POUNDCAKES

Poundcakes are the original high-fat, creaming-method cake. They are called poundcakes because early formulas specified one pound each of butter, eggs, flour and sugar. Poundcakes should have a close grain and compact texture but still be very tender. They should be neither heavy nor soggy.

As bakers experimented with poundcake formulas, they reduced the amount of eggs and fat, substituting milk instead. These changes led to the development of the modern butter cake.

mixing techniques. Sacher Torte (page 410), for example, is made from a creamed-fat batter into which whipped egg whites are folded before baking. Follow specific formula instructions precisely.

CREAMED FAT

Creamed-fat/high-fat cakes include most of the popular American-style cakes: poundcakes, layer cakes, coffeecakes and even brownies (see Chapter 9, Cookies and Brownies). All are based on high-fat formulas, most containing chemical leaveners. A good high-fat cake has a fine grain, cells of uniform size and a crumb that is moist rather than crumbly. Crusts should be thin and tender.

Creamed-fat/high-fat cakes can be divided into two classes: butter cakes and high-ratio cakes.

Butter Cakes

Butter cakes, also known as creaming-method cakes, begin with softened butter or shortening creamed to incorporate air cells. Because of their high fat content, these cakes usually need the assistance of a chemical leavener to achieve the proper rise.

Modern-day butter cakes—the classic American layer cakes, popular for birthdays and special occasions—are made with the creaming method. These cakes are tender yet sturdy enough to handle rich buttercreams or fillings. High-fat cakes are too soft and delicate, however, to use for roll cakes or to slice into extremely thin layers.

Creaming fat mechanically leavens the cake and creates a mixture in which fats and liquid are suspended. Air cells are trapped in the fat, lightening the mixture. As eggs are mixed into the creamed fat, the mixture emulsifies. Fats and liquids, which normally would not blend, are held in suspension, ensuring that the batter will hold the additional liquids and flour necessary to produce a delectable cake.

Creaming-method cake formulas specify whether to use butter or shortening. Because butter contains approximately 15 percent moisture, when shortening is substituted for butter, additional liquid must be added to replace the liquid lost. An emulsion made with butter cannot support the same quantity of sugar, liquids and flour as one made with shortening. Substituting butter for shortening in a creaming-method cake will require adjustments to the formula.

For butter cakes, the fat should be creamed at low to moderate speeds to prevent raising its temperature. An increased temperature could cause a loss of air cells. All ingredients should be at room temperature, 70°F (21°C), for effective creaming. When the butter is too warm, the soft fat will resist forming air cells. Eggs should be added slowly to keep the emulsion formed when mixed into the creamed mixture. Flour is added alternately with the liquid to prevent development of gluten and to preserve the emulsion.

▶ PROCEDURE FOR PREPARING BUTTER CAKES (CREAMING METHOD)

1 Preheat the oven and prepare the pans.

2 Sift the dry ingredients together and set aside.

3 Cream the butter or shortening until it is light and fluffy. Add the sugar and cream until the mixture is fluffy and smooth. Scrape down the bowl frequently to make certain the entire mixture is well creamed.

4 Add the eggs slowly, beating well after each addition. Scrape down the bowl after each addition.

5 Add the dry and liquid ingredients alternately.
6 Divide the batter into prepared pans and bake immediately.

1 Creaming the butter.

2 Folding in the flour.

3 Panning the batter.

AMERICAN POUNDCAKE

RECIPE 14.1

Yield: 2 Loaves, 8 in. × 4 in. (20 cm × 10 cm), **Method:** Creaming

Cake flour	1 lb.	500 g	100%
Baking powder	0.3 oz. (2 tsp.)	10 g	2%
Salt	0.1 oz. (½ tsp.)	3 g	0.6%
Unsalted butter, softened	1 lb.	500 g	100%
Granulated sugar	12 oz.	375 g	75%
Eggs	15 oz. (9 eggs)	470 g	94%
Vanilla extract	0.15 fl. oz. (1 tsp.)	5 ml	1%
Lemon extract	0.15 fl. oz. (1 tsp.)	5 ml	1%
Total batter weight:	3 lb. 11 oz.	1868 g	374%

1 Sift the cake flour, baking powder and salt together. Set aside.
2 Cream the butter until light and lump-free. Add the sugar and cream until light and fluffy. Add the eggs one at a time, scraping down the bowl frequently and mixing well after each addition. Stir in the extracts.
3 Fold in the dry ingredients by hand. Divide the batter into greased loaf pans.
4 Bake at 325°F (160°C) until golden brown and springy to the touch, approximately 1 hour and 10 minutes.

VARIATION:
French-Style Fruitcake—Add 6 ounces (185 grams/37%) finely diced nuts, raisins and candied fruit to the batter. Substitute vanilla extract for the lemon extract and add 1.5 fluid ounces (45 milliliters/9%) rum to the batter. After baking, brush the warm cake with additional rum.

Approximate values per 3-oz. (90-g) serving: **Calories** 350, **Total fat** 21 g, **Saturated fat** 12 g, **Cholesterol** 145 mg, **Sodium** 90 mg, **Total carbohydrates** 35 g, **Protein** 5 g, **Vitamin A** 20%

High-Ratio Cakes

Commercial bakeries often use a special **two-stage** mixing method to prepare large quantities of a very liquid cake batter with high sugar content. These formulas require special emulsified shortenings to help give the cake its structure. They are known as two-stage cakes because the liquids are added in two stages or portions. If emulsified shortenings are not available, do not substitute all-

Table 14.1 CAKES

CATEGORY	TYPE OF CAKE/ MIXING METHOD	KEY FORMULA CHARACTERISTICS	TEXTURE
Creamed fat (high fat)	Butter (creaming method)	High-fat formula; chemical leavener used	Fine grain; air cells of uniform size; moist crumb; thin and tender crust
	High-ratio (two-stage)	Emulsified shortening; two-part mixing method	Very fine grain; moist crumb; relatively high rise
Whipped eggs	Genoise (egg foam)	Whole eggs are whipped with sugar; no chemical leaveners	Dry and spongy
	Sponge (egg foam)	Egg yolks are mixed with other ingredients, then whipped egg whites are folded in	Moister and more tender than genoise
	Angel food (egg foam)	No fat; large quantity of whipped egg whites; high percentage of sugar	Tall, light and spongy
	Chiffon (egg foam)	Vegetable oil used; egg yolks mixed with other ingredients, then whipped egg whites folded in; baking powder may be added	Tall, light and fluffy; moister and richer than angel food

purpose shortening or butter, as those fats cannot absorb the large amounts of sugar and liquid in the formula.

Because they contain a high ratio of sugar and liquid to flour, these cakes are often known as high-ratio cakes. They have a very fine, moist crumb and relatively high rise. High-ratio cakes can be used interchangeably with modern butter cakes and are most common in high-volume bakeries.

▶ PROCEDURE FOR PREPARING HIGH-RATIO CAKES

1 Preheat the oven and prepare the pans.
2 Place all of the dry ingredients and emulsified shortening into a mixer bowl. Blend on low speed for several minutes.
3 Add approximately half of the liquid ingredients and blend.
4 Scrape down the bowl and add the remaining liquid ingredients. Blend into a smooth batter, scraping down the bowl as necessary.
5 Pour the batter into prepared pans using liquid measurements to ensure uniform division.

RECIPE 14.2

HIGH-RATIO YELLOW CAKE

Yield: 1½ to 2 Full-Sheet Pans   **Method:** Two-stage

Cake flour	2 lb. 8 oz.	1200 g	100%
Granulated sugar	2 lb. 10 oz.	1260 g	105%
Emulsified shortening	1 lb. 4 oz.	600 g	50%
Salt	1 oz.	30 g	2.5%
Baking powder	2 oz.	60 g	5%
Dry milk powder	4 oz.	120 g	10%
Light corn syrup	6 oz.	180 g	15%
Water, cold	36 fl. oz	1080 ml	90%
Eggs	1 lb. 4 oz. (12 eggs)	600 g	50%
Lemon extract	0.5 fl. oz.	15 ml	1.2%
Total batter weight:	10 lb. 11 oz.	5145 g	428%

1 Combine the flour, sugar, shortening, salt, baking powder, dry milk powder, corn syrup and 16 fluid ounces (480 milliliters) cold water in the large bowl of a mixer fitter with a paddle. Beat 5 minutes on low speed.

2 Combine the remaining ingredients in a separate bowl. Add these liquid ingredients to the creamed-fat mixture in three additions. Scrape down the sides of the bowl after each addition.

3 Beat 2 minutes on low speed.

4 Divide the batter into greased and floured pans. Pans should be filled only halfway. One gallon of batter is sufficient for an 18-inch × 24-inch × 2-inch (45-centimeter × 60-centimeter × 5-centimeter) sheet pan. Bake at 340°F (170°C) until a cake tester comes out clean and the cake springs back when lightly touched, approximately 12 to 18 minutes.

Approximate values per 3-oz. (90-g) serving: **Calories** 390, **Total fat** 16 g, **Saturated fat** 5 g, **Cholesterol** 60 mg, **Sodium** 320 mg, **Total carbohydrates** 57 g, **Protein** 5 g, **Calcium** 10%

SPECIFIC GRAVITY

The amount of air in cake batter relates directly to the quality of the finished cake. Too much air creamed into the batter and the grain may be coarse. Too little air creamed into the batter and the grain will be tight, creating a cake with poor volume. In the commercial bakeshop, tracking **specific gravity** can ensure consistent, uniform results in preparation of cakes, fillings and icings.

Specific gravity refers to the weight of an ingredient or a mixture in relation to the weight of water. One pint (16 fluid ounces) of water weighs 1 pound. But other liquids may be lighter than or heavier than water. Specific gravity is calculated by dividing the weight of a volume of an ingredient or mixture by the weight of an equal volume of water.

weight of ingredient ÷ weight of water = specific gravity

For example, a pint of water weights 16 ounces but a pint of honey weighs 24 ounces. Therefore the specific gravity of honey is 1.5 (24/16 = 1.5).

A simple test can be used to determine the specific gravity of a cake batter. Once the specific gravity of a formula has been recorded, it can be used to track future batches. Place a small container on a scale and tare the scale to zero. Fill the container with water to the very top and record the weight. Discard the water and fill the container with the cake batter being tested. Record the weight of the batter. Divide the weight of the cake batter by the weight of water. The result is the specific gravity of the batter. For example, if the container holds 8 ounces of water and 10 ounces of cake batter, the specific gravity of the cake batter is 1.25.

In general, butter/high-fat cakes have a higher specific gravity than egg foam cakes. However, specific gravity of cake batter varies with each formula according to the ingredients and equipment used. A particular brand of butter may contain more liquid, just as a particular type of cake flour may absorb more moisture. For this reason, when developing formulas, bakeshops record the specific gravity for each type of cake in their repertoire and then use these figures to monitor each batch of cake produced thereafter. Each baker will then know what the desired specific gravity of each formula should be. When a butter cake batter has a lower specific gravity, the baker will know that the batter had too much air whipped into it. When a spongecake batter has a higher specific gravity, the baker will know that the batter was deflated during the mixing process. Specific gravity calculations may also be used to monitor consistency in icing and cream formulas.

WHIPPED EGGS

Cakes based on whipped-egg foams include European-style genoise as well as spongecakes, angel food cakes and chiffon cakes. Some formulas contain chemical leaveners, but the air whipped into the eggs (whether whole or separated) is the primary leavening agent. Egg foam cakes contain little or no fat. Genoise and spongecake are pliable; moisture in the eggs develops the protein in the flour, making these cakes springy and elastic. These cakes are well suited for rolling, as for Swiss Jelly Roll (page 389) or Yule Log (page 414), or for cutting into thin layers, lining a torte ring and so on.

Genoise

Genoise is the classic European-style cake. It is based on whole eggs whipped with sugar until very light and fluffy. Chemical leaveners are not used. Slightly warming the egg mixture helps improve the volume of the egg foam. For flavor and moisture a small amount of oil or melted butter is sometimes added to the batter after mixing. Genoise to which fat is added after mixing will bake into a cake that is more tender than a plain genoise because the fat helps shorten gluten strands. Often genoise is baked in a thin sheet and layered with butter-cream, puréed fruit, jam or chocolate filling to create multilayered specialty desserts, sometimes known as torten. Because genoise is rather dry, it is usually soaked with a flavored sugar syrup (see Chapter 13, Syrups, Icings and Sauces) or liqueur for additional flavor and moisture. A basic genoise recipe is included here. Recipes for a richer almond version and the joconde variation are included at the end of this chapter.

▶ PROCEDURE FOR PREPARING GENOISE

1 Preheat the oven and prepare the pans.

2 Sift the flour with any additional dry ingredients.

3 Combine the whole eggs and sugar in a large bowl and warm over a double boiler to 100°F (38°C).

4 Whip the egg-and-sugar mixture until very light and tripled in volume.

5 Fold the sifted flour into the whipped eggs carefully but quickly.

6 Fold in oil or melted butter if desired.

7 Divide into pans and bake immediately.

RECIPE 14.3 | **CLASSIC GENOISE**

Yield: 1 Half-Sheet Pan | **Method:** Egg foam

Cake flour	6 oz.	180 g	100%
Eggs	11 oz. (7 eggs)	330 g	183%
Granulated sugar	6 oz.	180 g	100%
Unsalted butter, melted (optional)	1 oz.	30 g	17%
Total batter weight:	1 lb. 8 oz.	720 g	400%

1 Sift the flour and set aside.

2 Whisk the eggs and sugar together in a large mixer bowl. Place the bowl over a bain marie and warm the eggs to approximately 100°F (38°C). Stir frequently to avoid cooking the eggs.

3 When the eggs are warm, remove the bowl from the bain marie and attach to a mixer fitted with a whip. Whip the egg-and-sugar mixture at medium speed until tripled in volume.

4 Quickly fold the flour into the egg mixture by hand. Be careful not to deflate the batter.

1 Whipped eggs.

2 Folding in the flour.

3 Adding the melted butter.

4 Panning the batter.

5 Pour the melted, cooled butter around the edges of the batter and fold in quickly (if using).

6 Spread the batter immediately onto the paper-lined sheet pan. Bake at 350°F (180°C) until light brown and springy to the touch, approximately 8 minutes.

VARIATION:

Chocolate Genoise—Sift 1 ounce (30 grams/17%) cocoa powder with the flour.

Approximate values per 2-oz. (60-g) serving: **Calories** 140, **Total fat** 4 g, **Saturated fat** 2 g, **Cholesterol** 110 mg, **Sodium** 30 mg, **Total carbohydrates** 21 g, **Protein** 4 g, **Vitamin A** 6%

Spongecakes

Spongecakes (Fr. *biscuits*) are made with separated eggs. A batter is prepared with egg yolks and other ingredients, and then egg whites are whipped with a portion of the sugar to firm but not dry peaks and folded into the batter. Spongecakes are primarily leavened with air, but baking powder may be included in the formula. As with genoise, oil or melted butter may be added if desired.

Spongecakes are extremely versatile. They can be soaked with sugar syrup or a liqueur and assembled with butter cream as a traditional layer cake. Or they can be sliced thinly and layered, like genoise, with a jam, custard, chocolate or cream filling.

▶ PROCEDURE FOR PREPARING SPONGECAKES

1 Preheat the oven and prepare the pans.

2 Sift the dry ingredients together with a portion of the sugar.

3 Separate the eggs. Whip the egg yolks with some of the sugar to the **ribbon stage,** that is, until they fall from the beater in thick ribbons that slowly disappear into the surface. Whip in any flavorings.

4 In a separate bowl of a mixer fitted with a clean whip attachment, whip the egg whites with a portion of the sugar, then carefully fold the whipped yolks and whipped whites together with the remaining sugar.

5 Carefully fold the whipped egg whites into the batter. Then gently fold the sifted dry ingredients into the egg foam in two or three additions.

6 Pour the batter into the pans and bake immediately.

RECIPE 14.4	CLASSIC SPONGECAKE		
Yield: 2 Rounds, 9 in. (22 cm) each		**Method:** Egg foam	
Cake flour, sifted	6 oz.	180 g	100%
Granulated sugar	11 oz.	330 g	183%
Eggs	1 lb. (10 eggs)	480 g	266%
Vanilla extract	0.25 fl. oz. (1½ tsp.)	7.5 ml	4%
Cream of tartar	0.2 oz. (1½ tsp.)	6 g	3%
Total batter weight:	2 lb. 1 oz.	1003 g	556%

1 Line the bottom of two springform pans with parchment. Do not grease the sides of the pans.

2 Sift the flour and 6 ounces (180 grams) of the sugar together and set aside.

3 Separate the eggs, placing the yolks and the whites in separate mixing bowls. Whip the yolks on high speed until thick, pale and at least doubled in volume, approximately 3 to 5 minutes. Whip in the vanilla. The yolks should be whipped until ribbons form.

4 Place the bowl of egg whites on the mixer and, using a clean whip, beat until foamy. Add the cream of tartar and ½ ounce (30 grams) of the sugar. Whip at medium speed until the whites are glossy and stiff but not dry.

5 Remove the bowl from the mixer. Pour the egg yolks onto the whipped whites. Quickly fold the two mixtures together by hand. Sprinkle the remaining sugar over the mixture and fold in lightly.

1 The egg yolks whipped to the ribbon stage.

2 Folding the flour into the batter.

3 Panning the batter.

6 Sprinkle one-third of the sifted flour over the batter and fold in. Repeat the procedure until all the flour is incorporated. Do not overmix; fold just until incorporated.

7 Pour the batter into the prepared pans, smoothing the surface as needed. Bake immediately at 375°F (190°C) until the cake is golden brown and spongy, approximately 30 minutes. A toothpick inserted in the center will be completely clean when removed.

8 Allow the cakes to rest in their pans until completely cool, approximately 2 hours.

9 To remove the cakes from their pans, run a thin metal spatula around the edge of each pan. When the cake is completely cool, it can be frosted or wrapped in plastic film and frozen 2 to 3 months.

VARIATION:

Swiss Jelly Roll—Spread the cake batter onto a paper-lined half sheet pan. Bake at 375°F (190°C) until the cake is golden brown and spongy, approximately 20 minutes. Cool the cake 10 minutes. Invert the warm cake onto a piece of parchment dusted with powdered sugar. Carefully remove the paper on which the cake baked. Spread the warm cake with 8 ounces (235 grams/133%) seedless raspberry or other jam. Roll the cake tightly. Trim the ends and dust with more sugar before serving.

Approximate values per 2-oz. (60-g) serving: **Calories** 130, **Total fat** 2.5 g, **Saturated fat** 1 g, **Cholesterol** 105 mg, **Sodium** 30 mg, **Total carbohydrates** 23 g, **Protein** 4 g, **Claims**—low fat; low saturated fat; very low sodium

Angel Food Cakes

Angel food cakes are tall, light cakes made without fat and leavened with a large quantity of whipped egg whites. As discussed in Chapter 4, Bakeshop Ingredients, egg whites will not foam properly if grease or egg yolk is present in the mixing bowl. Angel food cakes are traditionally baked in ungreased tube pans, but large loaf pans can also be used. The pans are left ungreased so that the batter can cling to the sides as it rises. The cakes should be inverted as soon as they are removed from the oven and left in the pan to cool. This technique allows gravity to keep the cakes from collapsing or sinking as they cool.

Although they contain no fat, angel food cakes are not low in calories, as they contain a high percentage of sugar. The classic angel food cake is pure white, but flavorings, ground nuts or cocoa powder may be added for variety. Although angel food cakes are usually not frosted, they may be topped with a fruit-flavored or chocolate glaze. They are often served with fresh fruit, fruit compote or whipped cream.

▶ PROCEDURE FOR PREPARING ANGEL FOOD CAKES

1 Preheat the oven.
2 Combine the dry ingredients, including a portion of the sugar, in a bowl and set aside.
3 Whip the egg whites with a portion of the sugar until stiff and glossy.
4 Gently fold the dry ingredients into the egg whites.
5 Spoon the batter into an ungreased pan and bake immediately.
6 Allow the cake to cool inverted in its pan.

RECIPE 14.5   **CHOCOLATE ANGEL FOOD CAKE**

Yield: 1 Tube Cake, 10 in. (25 cm)   **Method:** Egg foam

		Sugar at 100%	
Cocoa powder, alkalized	1 oz.	30 g	8%
Water, warm	2 fl. oz.	60 ml	16%
Vanilla extract	0.3 fl. oz. (2 tsp.)	9 ml	2.5%
Granulated sugar	12 oz.	360 g	100%
Cake flour, sifted	3.5 oz.	105 g	29%
Salt	0.05 oz. (¼ tsp.)	1.5 g	0.4%
Egg whites	1 lb. (16 whites)	480 g	133%
Cream of tartar	0.3 oz. (2 tsp.)	9 g	2.5%
Total batter weight:	2 lb. 3 oz.	1055 g	291%

1 Combine the cocoa powder and water in a bowl. Add the vanilla and set aside.
2 In another bowl, combine 5 ounces (150 grams) of the sugar with the flour and salt.

1 Folding the egg-white-and-cocoa mixture into the whipped egg whites.

2 Folding in the flour.

3 Cooling the cake upside down in its pan.

4 Removing the cake from the pan.

3 Whip the egg whites until foamy, add the cream of tartar and beat to soft peaks. Gradually beat in the remaining sugar. Continue beating until the egg whites are stiff but not dry.

4 Whisk a very large spoonful of the whipped egg whites into the cocoa mixture. Fold this into the remaining egg whites.

5 Sift the dry ingredients over the whites and fold in quickly but gently.

6 Pour the batter into an ungreased tube pan and smooth the top with a spatula. Bake immediately at 350°F (180°C) until the cake springs back when lightly touched and a cake tester comes out clean, approximately 40 to 50 minutes. The cake's surface will have deep cracks.

7 Remove the cake from the oven and immediately invert the pan onto the neck of a bottle. Allow the cake to rest upside down until completely cool.

8 To remove the cake from the pan, run a thin knife or spatula around the edge of the pan and the edge of the interior tube. If a two-piece tube pan was used, lift the cake and tube portion out of the pan. Use a knife or spatula to loosen the bottom of the cake, and then invert it onto a cake cardboard or serving platter.

VARIATIONS:

Vanilla Angel Food Cake—Omit the cocoa powder and warm water from the formula. Increase the amount of vanilla extract to 0.5 fluid ounce (15 milliliters/4%) and fold it in at the end of Step 5.

Lemon Angel Food Cake—Omit the cocoa powder and warm water from the formula. Add 0.14 ounces (2 teaspoons/4 grams/1%) fresh lemon zest to the sugar-and-flour mixture. Add 0.15 fluid ounces (1 teaspoon/5 milliliters/1%) lemon extract, folding it and the vanilla extract in at the end of Step 5.

Approximate values per $^1/_{10}$-cake serving: **Calories** 210, **Total fat** 0.5 g, **Saturated fat** 0 g, **Cholesterol** 0 mg, **Sodium** 150 mg, **Total carbohydrates** 44 g, **Protein** 7 g, **Claims**—low fat; no saturated fat; no cholesterol

Chiffon Cakes

Although chiffon cakes are similar to angel food cakes in appearance and texture, the addition of egg yolks and vegetable oil makes them moister and richer. Chiffon cakes are usually leavened with whipped egg whites but may contain baking powder as well. Like angel food cakes, chiffon cakes are baked in an ungreased pan to allow the batter to cling to the pan as it rises. Chiffon cakes can be frosted with a light buttercream or whipped cream or topped with a glaze. Lemon and orange chiffon cakes are the most traditional, but formulas containing chocolate, nuts or other flavorings are also common.

▶ PROCEDURE FOR PREPARING CHIFFON CAKES

1 Preheat the oven.

2 Sift the dry ingredients together. Add the liquid ingredients, including oil.

3 Whip the egg whites with a portion of the sugar until almost stiff.

4 Fold the whipped egg whites into the batter.

5 Spoon the batter into an ungreased pan and bake immediately.

6 Allow the cake to cool inverted in its pan.

A HOLLYWOOD CLASSIC

Chiffon cake is one of the few desserts whose history can be traced with absolute certainty. According to Gerry Schremp in her book *Kitchen Culture: Fifty Years of Food Fads,* a new type of cake was invented by Henry Baker, a California insurance salesman, in 1927. Dubbed chiffon, it was as light as angel food and as rich as poundcake. For years he kept the formula a secret, earning fame and fortune by selling his cakes to Hollywood restaurants. The cake's secret ingredient—vegetable oil—became public knowledge in 1947 when Baker sold the formula to General Mills, which promoted it on packages of cake flour. Chiffon cakes, in a variety of flavors, became extremely popular nationwide.

RECIPE 14.6

ORANGE CHIFFON CAKE

Yield: 1 Tube Cake, 10 in. (25 cm) **Method:** Egg foam

Cake flour, sifted	8 oz.	240 g	100%
Granulated sugar	12 oz.	360 g	150%
Baking powder	0.4 oz. (1 Tbsp.)	12 g	5%
Salt	0.2 oz. (1 tsp.)	6 g	2.5%
Vegetable oil	4 fl. oz.	120 ml	50%
Egg yolks	4 oz. (6 yolks)	120 g	50%
Water, cool	2 fl. oz.	60 ml	25%
Orange juice	4 fl. oz.	120 ml	50%
Orange zest, grated fine	0.2 oz. (1 Tbsp.)	6 g	2.5%
Vanilla extract	0.5 fl. oz.	15 ml	6%
Egg whites	8 oz. (8 whites)	240 g	100%
Glaze:			
Powdered sugar, sifted	3 oz.	90 g	
Orange juice	1 fl. oz.	30 ml	
Orange zest, grated fine	0.14 oz. (2 tsp.)	4 g	
Total batter weight:	2 lb. 11 oz.	1299 g	541%

1 Sift together the flour, 6 ounces (180 grams) of the sugar and the baking powder and salt.

2 In a separate bowl mix the oil, egg yolks, water, orange juice, orange zest and vanilla. Add the liquid mixture to the dry ingredients.

3 In a clean bowl, beat the egg whites until foamy. Slowly beat in the remaining sugar. Continue beating until the egg whites are stiff but not dry.

4 Stir one-third of the egg whites into the batter to lighten it. Fold in the remaining egg whites.

5 Pour the batter into an ungreased 10-inch (25-centimeter) tube pan. Bake at 325°F (160°C) until a toothpick comes out clean, approximately 1 hour.

6 Immediately invert the pan over the neck of a wine bottle. Allow the cake to hang upside down until completely cool, and then remove from the pan.

7 Stir the glaze ingredients together in a small bowl and drizzle over the top of the cooled cake.

VARIATION:

Lemon Chiffon Cake—Substitute 2 fluid ounces (60 milliliters/25%) fresh lemon juice and 2 fluid ounces (60 milliliters/25%) water for the orange juice in the batter. Substitute lemon zest for the orange zest. Top with Basic Sugar Glaze (page 360).

Approximate values per $^1/_{10}$-cake serving: **Calories** 370, **Total fat** 15 g, **Saturated fat** 2.5 g, **Cholesterol** 130 mg, **Sodium** 280 mg, **Total carbohydrates** 54 g, **Protein** 6 g, **Vitamin C** 10%

PANNING, BAKING AND COOLING

PREPARING PANS

To prevent cakes from sticking, pans may be greased or lined with parchment paper or both before baking. (See Chapter 5, Mise en Place.) Pans must be prepared before the cake is finished mixing to prevent air trapped in the emulsion from deflating while pans are being prepared. See Table 14.2. For a bakeshop that frequently needs to grease pans, an all-purpose pan coating suitable for any cake pan requiring greasing and flouring can be made from the formula on page 98.

Pan coating is not appropriate for all cakes, however. Those containing chocolate, raisins or fruit should still be baked in pans lined with parchment paper in order to prevent sticking.

Table 14.2 PAN PREPARATIONS

PAN PREPARATION	USED FOR
Ungreased	Angel food and chiffon cakes
Ungreased sides; paper on bottom	Genoise layers
Greased and papered	High-fat cakes, sponge sheets
Greased and coated with flour	High-fat cakes, chocolate cakes, anything in a Bundt or shaped pan
Greased, floured and lined with paper	Cakes containing melted chocolate, fruit chunks or fruit or vegetable purées

Angel food and chiffon cakes are baked in ungreased, unlined pans because these fragile cakes need to cling to the sides of the pan as they rise. Spongecakes and genoise are often baked in pans with a paper liner on the bottom and ungreased sides. Although the ungreased sides give the batter a surface to cling to, the paper liner makes removing the cake from the pan easier. Flexible silicone pans require little if any greasing.

FILLING PANS

Pans should be filled no more than one-half to two-thirds full. This allows the batter to rise during baking without spilling over the edges. Pans should be filled to uniform depths. High-fat and egg foam cake batters can be ladled into each pan according to weight. High-ratio cake batter is so liquid that it can be measured by volume and poured into each pan (see Table 14.3). Filling the pans uniformly prevents both uneven layers and over- or underfilled pans. When baking multiple layers to be stacked for one presentation with a different amount of batter in each pan, the baking times will vary and the final product will be uneven.

Cake batter should always be spread evenly in the pan. Use an offset spatula. Do not work the batter too much, however, as this destroys air cells and prevents the cake from rising properly.

BAKING

Temperatures

Always preheat the oven before preparing the batter. If the finished batter must wait while the oven reaches the correct temperature, valuable leavening will be lost and the cake will not rise properly.

Most butter cakes are baked at temperatures between 325°F and 375°F (160°C and 190°C). The temperature must be high enough to create steam within the batter and cause that steam and other gases in the batter to expand and rise quickly. If the temperature is too high, however, the cake may rise unevenly and the crust may burn before the interior is completely baked. The temperature must also be low enough so that the batter can set completely and evenly without drying out. If the temperature is too low, however, the cake will not rise sufficiently and may dry out before baking completely. Delicate egg foam cakes and spongecakes may be baked at slightly higher temperatures when panned in thin layers.

If no temperature is given in a formula or you are altering the dimensions of the baking pan from those specified, use common sense in setting the oven temperature. The larger the surface area, the higher the temperature can usually be. Tall cakes, such as Bundt or tube cakes, should be baked at a lower temperature than thin layer or sheet cakes. Tube or loaf cakes take longer to bake than thin sheet cakes; butter cakes, because they contain more liquid, take longer to bake than genoise or spongecake.

Table 14.3 CAKE PAN SIZES

PAN SHAPE AND SIZE	VOLUME OF BATTER	WEIGHT— BUTTER/HIGH-FAT	WEIGHT— EGG FOAM	NO. OF SERVINGS FOR 2-LAYER CAKE
Round, 2 in. deep				
6 in.	1 pt.	8–10 oz.	5–6 oz.	6
8 in.	3 c.	12–16 oz.	8–10 oz.	12
10 in.	1½ qt.	24–32 oz.	16–18 oz.	20
12 in.	1 qt. + 3½ c.	32–36 oz.	18–22 oz.	30
14 in.	2½ qt.	40–48 oz.	24–30 oz.	40
Square, 2 in. deep				
8 in.	1 qt.	16–18 oz.	10–12 oz.	16
10 in.	1½ qt.	24–30 oz.	16–18 oz.	20
12 in.	2½ qt.	40–48 oz.	26–30 oz.	36
14 in.	3 qt. + 1½ c.	48–52 oz.	32–40 oz.	48
Rectangular, 2 in. deep				
6 in. × 8 in.	2½ c.	10–12 oz.	6–8 oz.	12
9 in. × 13 in.	2 qt.	32–36 oz.	20–24 oz.	24
18 in. × 13 in.	2 qt. + 3 c.	3.5–4 lb.	28–32 oz.	48
18 in. × 26 in.	5 qt.	6–8 lb.	2.5–3 lb.	96

*Quantities given are approximate and are based on filling the pans two-thirds full of batter. The weight of cake batter needed to properly fill a pan will vary depending on the type of batter, additional flavor ingredients and the amount of air incorporated during mixing.

Determining Doneness

In addition to following the baking time suggested in a formula, several simple tests can be used to determine doneness. Whichever tests are used, avoid opening the oven door to check the cake's progress. Cold air or a drop in oven temperature can cause the cake to fall. Use a timer to note the minimum suggested baking time. Then, and only then, should you use the following tests to evaluate the cake's doneness:

▶ Appearance—The cake's surface should be a light to golden brown. Unless noted otherwise in the formula, the edges should just begin to pull away from the pan. The cake should not jiggle or move beneath its surface.

▶ Touch—Touch the cake lightly with your finger. It should spring back quickly without feeling soggy or leaving an indentation.

▶ Cake tester—If appearance and touch indicate that the cake is done, test the interior by inserting a toothpick, bamboo skewer or metal cake tester into the cake's center. With most cakes, the tester should come out clean. If wet crumbs cling to the tester, the cake probably needs to bake a bit longer.

If a formula provides particular doneness guidelines, they should be followed. For example, some flourless cakes are fully baked even though a cake tester will not come out clean.

COOLING

Generally, a cake is allowed to cool 10 to 15 minutes in its pan set on a cooling rack after taking it out of the oven. This helps prevent the cake from cracking or breaking when it is removed from its pan.

To remove the partially cooled cake from its pan, run a thin knife or spatula blade between the pan and the cake to loosen it. Place a wire rack, cake card-

Table 14.4 TROUBLESHOOTING CHART FOR CAKES

PROBLEM	CAUSE	SOLUTION
Butter curdles during mixing	Ingredients too warm or too cold	Eggs must be at room temperature and added slowly
	Incorrect fat is used	Use correct ingredients
	Fat inadequately creamed before liquid was added	Add a portion of the flour, then continue adding the liquid
Cake lacks volume	Flour too strong	Use a weaker flour
	Old chemical leavener	Replace with fresh leavener
	Egg foam underwhipped	Use correct mixing method; do not deflate eggs during folding
	Oven too hot	Adjust oven temperature
Crust burst or cracked	Too much flour or too little liquid	Adjust formula; scale accurately
	Oven too hot	Adjust oven temperature
Cake shrinks after baking	Weak internal structure	Adjust formula
	Too much sugar or fat for the batter to support	Adjust formula
	Cake not fully cooked	Test for doneness before removing from oven
Texture is dense or heavy	Too little leavening	Adjust formula
	Too much fat or liquid	Cream fat or whip eggs properly
	Oven too cool	Adjust oven temperature
Texture is coarse with an open grain	Overmixing	Alter mixing method
	Oven too cool	Adjust oven temperature
Poor flavor	Poor ingredients	Check flavor and aroma of all ingredients
	Unclean pans	Do not grease pans with rancid fats
Uneven shape	Butter not incorporated evenly	Incorporate fats completely
	Batter spread unevenly	Spread batter evenly
	Oven rack not level	Adjust oven racks
	Uneven oven temperature	Adjust oven temperature

board or sheet pan over the cake and invert. Then remove the pan. The cake can be left upside down to cool completely or inverted again to cool top side up. Wire racks are preferred for cooling cakes because they allow air to circulate, speeding the cooling process and preventing steam from making the cake soggy.

Angel food and chiffon cakes should be turned upside down immediately after they are removed from the oven. They are left to cool completely in their pans to prevent the cake from collapsing or shrinking. The top of the pan should not touch the countertop, so that air can circulate under the inverted pan.

All cakes should be left to cool away from drafts or air currents that might cause them to collapse. Cakes should not be refrigerated to speed the cooling process, as rapid cooling can cause cracking. Prolonged refrigeration also causes cakes to dry out.

▶ ASSEMBLING AND DECORATING CAKES AND TORTES

Much of a cake's initial appeal lies in its appearance. This is true whether the finished cake is a simple sheet cake topped with swirls of buttercream or an elaborate wedding cake with intricate garlands and bouquets of marzipan roses. Any cake assembled and decorated with care and attention to detail is preferable to a carelessly assembled or garishly overdecorated one.

Thousands of decorating styles or designs are possible, of course. This section describes a few simple options that can be prepared by beginning pastry

OF TARTS AND TORTES

The names given to desserts can be rather confusing. One country or region calls an item a torte while another region calls the same item a gâteau. The following definitions are based on classic terms. You will, no doubt, encounter variations depending on your location and the training of those with whom you work.

Cake–In American and British usages, cake refers to a broad range of pastries, including layer cakes, coffee cakes and gâteaux. Cake may refer to almost everything that is baked, tender, sweet and sometimes frosted. But to the French, *le cake* is a loaf-shaped fruitcake, similar to an American poundcake with the addition of fruit, nuts and rum.

Gâteau–(pl. *gâteaux*) To the French, gâteau refers to various pastry items made with puff pastry, éclair paste, short dough or sweet dough. In America, gâteau often refers to any caketype dessert.

Torte–In Central and Eastern European countries, a torte (pl. *torten*) is a rich cake in which all or part of the flour is replaced with finely chopped nuts or breadcrumbs. Other cultures refer to any round sweet cake as a torte.

cooks using a minimum of specialized tools. In planning a cake's design, consider the flavor, texture and color of the components used as well as the number of guests or portions that must be served. Consider who will be cutting and eating the cake and how long the dessert must stand before service.

ASSEMBLING CAKES

Before a cake can be decorated, it must be assembled and coated with icing or frosting. Formulas and procedures for preparing a variety of icings and glazes for cakes and tortes are detailed in Chapter 13, Syrups, Icings and Sauces. Most cakes can be assembled in a variety of shapes and sizes; sheet cakes, round layer cakes and rectangular layer cakes are the most common. When assembling any cake, the goal is to fill and stack the cake layers evenly and to apply an even coating of icing that is smooth and free of crumbs. (A thin underlayer of icing called a **crumb coat** may be spread on an assembled cake to seal loose surface crumbs before a final decorative layer of icing is applied.)

Most of the photographs used in this section show the assembly and decoration of the wedding cake shown in the photograph at left. The complete formula is found on page 412.

1 Begin by leveling the cake and trimming the edges as needed with a serrated knife.

2 Split the cake horizontally into thin layers if desired. Use cake boards to support each layer as it is removed. Brush away any loose crumbs with a dry pastry brush or your hand.

3 Position the bottom layer on a cake board. Place the layer on a revolving cake stand, if available. Pipe a border of buttercream around the cake, then top the layer with a mound of filling. Use a cake spatula to spread it evenly.

4 Position the next cake layer over the filling and continue layering and filling the cake as desired.

5 Place a mound of icing in the center of the cake top. Push it to the edge of the cake with a cake spatula. Do not drag the icing back and forth or lift the spatula off the icing, as these actions tend to pick up crumbs.

6 Cover the sides with excess icing from the top, adding more as necessary. Hold the spatula upright against the side of the cake and, pressing gently, turn the cake stand slowly. This smoothes and evens the sides. When the sides and top are smooth, the cake is ready to be decorated as desired.

SIMPLE DECORATING TECHNIQUES

An extremely simple yet effective way to decorate an iced cake is with a garnish of chopped nuts, fruit, toasted coconut, shaved chocolate or other foods arranged in patterns or sprinkled over the cake. Be sure to use a garnish that complements the cake and icing flavors or reflects one of the cake's ingredients. For example, finely chopped pecans would be an appropriate garnish for a carrot cake that contains pecans; shaved chocolate would not.

Side masking is the technique of coating only the sides of a cake with garnish. Be sure to apply the garnish while the icing is still moist enough for it to adhere. The top may be left plain or decorated with icing designs or a message.

Stencils can be used to apply patterns of finely chopped garnishes, confectioner's sugar or cocoa powder to the top of a cake. A design can be cut from cardboard, or thin plastic forms can be purchased. Even simple strips of parchment paper can be used to create an attractive pattern. If using a stencil on an iced cake, allow the icing to set somewhat before laying the stencil on top of it. After the garnishes have been sprinkled over the stencil, carefully lift the stencil to avoid spilling the excess garnish and messing the pattern.

Side masking—coating the sides of a carrot cake with chopped pecans.

Stencils—creating a design with confectioner's sugar and strips of parchment paper.

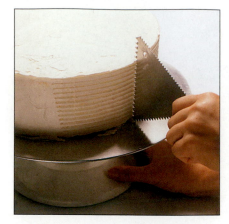

Cake comb—creating a pattern on a frosted cake.

A cake or baker's comb or a serrated knife can be used to create patterns on a cake iced with buttercream, fudge or ganache. Hold the comb against the side of an iced cake and rotate the cake turntable slowly and steadily to create horizontal lines in the icing.

Rolled fondant (page 359) makes an elegant coating on specialty cakes. While not a simple technique, applying rolled fondant is easily mastered. The fondant may be left plain or decorated with piped royal icing according to the procedures discussed later in this chapter.

PIPING TECHNIQUES

More elaborate and difficult decorations can be produced with the aid of a piping bag and an assortment of pastry tips. With these tools, buttercream or royal icing can be used to create borders, flowers and messages. Before applying any decorations, however, plan a design or pattern that is appropriate for the size and shape of the item being decorated.

When used properly, colored icings can bring cake decorations to life. Buttercream, royal icing and fondant are easily tinted using paste food coloring. Liquid food colorings are not recommended as they may thin the icing too much. Always add coloring gradually with a toothpick. Icing colors tend to darken as they sit. It is easy to add more later to darken the color if necessary, but it is difficult to lighten the color if too much is added.

Piping bags made from plastic, nylon or plastic-coated canvas are available in a range of sizes. A disposable piping cone can also be made from parchment paper.

Most decorations and designs are made by using a piping bag fitted with a pastry tip. Pastry tips are available with dozens of different openings and are re-

Tip patterns.

ferred to by standardized numbers. Some commonly used tips are shown in the photo on page 398. You can produce a variety of borders and designs by changing the pressure, the angle of the bag and the distance between the tip and the cake surface.

▶ PROCEDURE FOR MAKING A PARCHMENT-PAPER CONE

1 Begin with an equilateral triangle of uncreased paper. Shape it into a cone as shown.

2 Fold the top edges together to hold the shape.

3 Cut the tip of the filled parchment cone.

▶ PROCEDURE FOR FILLING A PIPING BAG

1 Select the proper size piping bag for your task. Insert the desired tip.

2 Fold down the top of the bag, then fill approximately half full with icing. Do not overfill the bag.

3 Be sure to close the open end tightly before you start piping. Hold the bag firmly in your palm and squeeze from the top. Do not squeeze from the bottom or you may force the contents out the wrong end. Use the fingers of your other hand to guide the bag as you work.

PIPED-ON DECORATING TECHNIQUES

Instead of leaving the sides of an iced cake smooth or coating them with chopped nuts or crumbs, you can pipe on icing designs and patterns. A simple but elegant design is the basket weave, shown on the next page.

Normally, a border pattern will be piped around the base of the cake and along the top edge. Borders should be piped on after nuts or any other garnishes are applied.

Each slice or serving of cake can be marked with its own decoration. For example, a rosette of icing or a whole nut or piece of fruit could be used as shown. This makes it easier to portion the cake evenly.

Delicate flowers such as roses can be piped, allowed to harden, then placed on the cake in attractive arrangements. Royal icing is particularly useful for making decorations in advance because it dries very hard and lasts indefinitely.

The key to success with a piping bag is practice, practice, practice. Use plain all-purpose shortening piped onto parchment paper to practice and experiment with piping techniques. Once you are comfortable using a piping bag, you can apply these newfound skills directly to cakes and pastries.

Applying a basket weave pattern to the sides of the wedding cake.

Applying a shell border to the wedding cake.

Placing royal icing flowers onto cake portions.

▶ PROCEDURE FOR PIPING BUTTERCREAM ROSES

1 Using a #104 tip, pipe a mound of icing onto a rose nail.

2 Pipe a curve of icing around the mound to create the center of the rose.

3 Pipe three overlapping petals around the center.

4 Pipe five more overlapping petals around the first three petals.

5 Place the finished rose on the cake.

ASSEMBLING TORTES

What distinguishes many European-style tortes from American-style cakes is that the latter generally have most of the fat baked into the cake. The European-style torte mainly consists of layers of relatively low-fat, often dry cake that may be moistened with a flavored simple syrup. These layers are then sandwiched with creams, mousses, Bavarians or other fillings discussed in Chapter 15, Custards and Creams. To achieve a well-balanced composition, different types of cake layers may be combined to make an individual torte.

While the elements in pastry making have not changed—genoise and butter cakes have been made for many years—new decorating tools have inspired inventive ways of presenting and assembling these tortes. Ring molds of various sizes, flexible silicone forms and patterned baking mats give tortes a new look, inviting customers to try new desserts. Many popular tortes are made in removable ring molds. Sponge, genoise, meringue and other cake batters may be baked or cut to fit these molds. Fillings include one or a combination of the following: ganache, buttercream, fruit curd and mousse that is stabilized with gelatin. Layers of fruit preserves or fruit coulis that are firmed with gelatin also may be added to provide flavor and color contrast between the cake and soft fillings.

Once lined with cake and then filled, the torte is usually coated with tart glaze. These tortes possess a tailored appearance, requiring little further embellishment, though garnishing with fresh fruits, chocolate decorations or Italian meringue is common. The procedure for assembling a torte is illustrated using a genoise (page 386) layered with Raspberry Mousse (page 463).

▶ PROCEDURE FOR ASSEMBLING A TORTE

1 Prepare the sponge, meringue, ladyfingers or other cake components.

2 Prepare the filling components. Mousses and any fillings that contain gelatin should be made right before filling the molds, as they set quickly.

3 Prepare the flavored simple syrup and finishing glaze or mousse.

4 Line the necessary cake rings with strips of clear acetate, or brush the rings with vegetable oil and dust with granulated sugar. Place the rings on cake cardboards or paper-lined sheet pans. Sheet pan extenders may also be used when making a square or rectangular cake.

5 Trim the cake components to fit inside the chosen mold. Moisten the cake layer with the flavored simple syrup, if desired.

6 Spread a portion of the filling over the cake, leveling it with an offset cake spatula.

7 Top the filling with additional layers of cake and filling as desired.

8 Pour the glaze over the finished torte, spreading to smooth and level. Chill or freeze the torte several hours or overnight before unmolding.

9 Remove the cake ring and acetate strip, if using, and garnish the torte before serving. If the torte has been frozen or thoroughly chilled, a blowtorch may be used to heat the ring for easy removal.

1 Putting the sponge down inside the ring.

2 Spreading raspberry mousse over the sponge with an offset spatula.

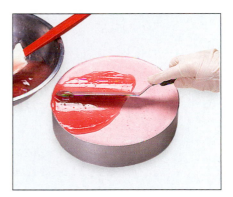

3 Spreading raspberry glaze over the surface of the finished torte.

4 Removing the ring from the finished torte.

STORING CAKES AND TORTES

Plain cake layers or sheets can be stored at room temperature 2 or 3 days if well covered, although they may be easier to handle when chilled. Iced or filled cakes are usually refrigerated to prevent spoilage. Simple buttercreams or sugar glazes made without eggs or dairy products, however, can be left at room temperature 1 or 2 days. Any cake containing custard filling, mousse or whipped cream must be refrigerated. Cakes made with foam-type icing should be eaten the day they are prepared.

Cakes can usually be frozen with great success; this makes them ideal for baking in advance. Unfrosted layers or sheets should be well covered with plastic wrap and frozen at 0°F (−18°C) or lower. High-fat cakes will keep up to 6 months; egg foam cakes begin to deteriorate after 2 or 3 months. Tortes filled with mousses can be frozen several weeks.

Icings and fillings do not freeze particularly well, often losing flavor or changing texture when frozen. Buttercreams made with egg whites or sugar syrups tend to develop crystals and graininess. Foam icings weep, expelling beads of sugar and becoming sticky. Fondant will absorb moisture and separate from the cake. If you must freeze a filled or iced cake, it is best to freeze it unwrapped first, until the icing is firm. The cake can then be covered with plastic wrap without damaging the icing design. Leave the cake wrapped until completely thawed. It is best to thaw cakes in the refrigerator; do not refreeze a thawed cake.

Well-organized pastry shops choose designated times to bake cake and torte components and freeze them until needed for assembly. Baking several batches of cake during one shift saves time and costly mistakes. There will be no need to compensate for different products baking in the ovens at the same times. In a smaller bakeshop, assembly can take place when the oven is not in use, ensuring a cooler work environment, crucial for many creams and mousses.

CONVENIENCE PRODUCTS

Packaged cake mixes are a tremendous time-saver for commercial food service operations. Almost any operation can serve a variety of cakes made by relatively unskilled employees using prepared mixes. The results are consistent and the texture and flavor are acceptable to most consumers. Indeed, a well-prepared packaged cake mix is preferable to a poorly prepared cake made from scratch. Most packaged cake mixes can be adapted to include flavorings, nuts, spices or fruits, which can improve the product's overall quality. The convenience of mixes is not without cost, however. Packaged cake mixes are often more expensive than the ingredients needed for an equal number of cakes made from scratch. Cakes made from mixes are also softer and more cottony than scratch cakes, and their flavor tends to be more artificial.

Cake mixes are blends of flour, shortening, emulsifiers, chemical leavening and flavorings that are moistened with water or other liquid. Some mixes require the addition of eggs, fats and flavorings. Mixing techniques vary, so follow package directions carefully. Most cake mixes are not creamed but simply blended with a paddle. To aerate the batter in an angel food cake mix, a whip may be specified. Some mixes require the addition of liquids in two stages. As with any cake batter, scraping down the bowl frequently in the early stages of mixing ensures that the dry mix is properly moistened. Once the batter is mixed, panning, baking and assembly techniques are the same as for scratch preparations.

The ability to produce good cakes and tortes depends on using the right balance of high-quality ingredients and combining them with the proper techniques. When preparing cakes and tortes, always combine flavors and textures with care; apply icings, garnishes and decorations with care as well. Avoid overly rich, cloyingly sweet or garishly decorated products. With study and practice, you can learn the mixing techniques and assembly skills necessary for producing good cakes. With additional practice, you will develop the decorating and garnishing skills of a fine pastry chef.

1 Cake ingredients can be classified into six categories according to the function they perform. List them and give an example of each.

2 What is the primary leavening agent in cakes made with the egg foam method? How is this similar to or different from cakes made with the creaming method?

3 What is the difference between a spongecake and a classic genoise?

4 Based on the materials presented in this and previous chapters, what different cake and filling components may be used to make a European-style torte?

5 List the steps employed in assembling and icing a three-layer cake.

6 Wedding cakes vary greatly from one region or culture to another. Investigate the various types or styles of cakes traditionally served at weddings in three or four different cultures. Which formulas in this book would be appropriate for a wedding cake?

This section provides a wide variety of formulas, some for complete tortes and others for different types of cakes suitable for baking in many shapes and molds. Some of the finished cakes and tortes rely on formulas for fillings and icings discussed in Chapter 13, Syrups, Icings and Sauces, and Chapter 15, Custards and Creams.

RECIPE 14.7

RICHARD RUSKELL, EXECUTIVE PASTRY CHEF

Chef Richard Ruskell is the executive pastry chef at the Montage Resort and Spa in Laguna Beach, California. He oversees the bakery operations for the resort's three restaurants. Most recently, Chef Ruskell was a baking instructor at the New England Culinary Institute. A graduate of the French Culinary Institute in New York, Chef Ruskell began his professional career in Cannes, France, at the Hotel Gray d'Albion. He has worked at the Peninsula and Stanhope Hotels in New York. For 8 years, he was the executive pastry chef at the Phoenician Resort in Scottsdale, Arizona, where he earned *Chocolatier Magazine*'s Top 10 Pastry Chefs In America award.

CHOCOLATE CARAMEL MAXINE TORTE

MONTAGE RESORT AND SPA, LAGUNA BEACH, CA
Executive Pastry Chef Richard Ruskell

Note: This dish appears in the chapter opening photograph.

Yield: 3 Domed Tortes, 6 in. (15 cm) each, or 38 Individual Tortes, 2½ in. (6 cm) each

Chocolate Caramel Mousse (recipe follows)	6 lb.	2880 g
Caramel Filling (recipe follows)	2 lb. 8 oz.	1200 g
Dark Chocolate Glaze (recipe follows)	3 lb.	1440 g
Chocolate Spongecake (page 416), baked into 6-in. (15-cm) rounds	3 rounds	3 rounds
Chocolate cutouts (page 615)	as needed	as needed

1 Pipe the Chocolate Caramel Mousse into three 6-inch (15-centimeter) molds with approximately 3-quart (3-liter) capacity. Fill the molds approximately three-quarters full.

2 Fill another pastry bag with the Caramel Filling and, inserting the nozzle of the pastry bag into the center of the dome, pipe approximately 12 ounces (360 grams) of Caramel Filling into each mold or just enough to fill the molds. There may be extra mousse or filling.

3 Smooth off the tops of the tortes with an offset spatula. Top with the Chocolate Spongecake, cut slightly smaller than the size of the tortes. Freeze the tortes until completely firm.

4 Remove the tortes from their molds and place on a glazing rack. Pour the Dark Chocolate Glaze over the tortes. Place overlapping squares of Chocolate cutouts along the bottom of each torte as garnish. Serve once thawed.

Approximate values per ⅛-torte serving: **Calories** 740, **Total fat** 47 g, **Saturated fat** 28 g, **Cholesterol** 125 mg, **Sodium** 65 mg, **Total carbohydrates** 88 g, **Protein** 7 g, **Vitamin A** 25%

CHOCOLATE CARAMEL MOUSSE

Yield: 6 lb. 13 oz. (3085 g)

Granulated sugar	1 lb. 5 oz.	590 g
Heavy cream	14 fl. oz.	400 ml
Unsalted butter	7 oz.	200 g
Extra bittersweet chocolate, chopped fine	13 oz.	365 g
Unsweetened chocolate, chopped fine	6 oz.	170 g
Heavy cream, whipped to soft peaks	1½ qt.	1360 ml

1 Place the sugar in a large heavy saucepan. Add enough water to make a wet sand, approximately ½ cup. Place the pan over medium high heat. Cook the sugar to a caramel stage, periodically brushing down the sides of the pot with water to prevent any sugar crystals from building up.

2 Meanwhile, place the cream and butter in a small pot and bring to a boil. Set aside until needed.

3 Combine the chocolates in a large bowl. Set aside.

4 When the caramel reaches a dark brown color, remove from the heat and slowly add the cream-and-butter mixture. Be very careful of the boiling caramel, because serious burns can result. When all of the cream has been added, strain the mixture over the bowl of chopped chocolate. Let the chocolate and cream rest for approximately one minute and then whisk together until the chocolate is fully melted.

5 Set aside the chocolate ganache until cooled to room temperature. Once cooled, whisk in half of the whipped cream. Fold in the remaining cream. Use the mousse immediately.

Approximate values per 1-oz. (30-g) serving: **Calories** 120, **Total fat** 10 g, **Saturated fat** 6 g, **Cholesterol** 25 mg, **Sodium** 5 mg, **Total carbohydrates** 10 g, **Protein** 1 g

CARAMEL FILLING

Yield: 2 lb. 14 oz. (1270 g)

Unsalted butter	2 oz.	30 g
Granulated sugar	1 lb.	450 g
Heavy cream	1 pt.	450 ml
Glucose or corn syrup	12 oz.	340 g

1 Bring the butter, 4 ounces (120 grams) of the sugar and the heavy cream to a boil. Set aside.

2 In a separate large saucepan, warm the glucose or corn syrup until it liquefies. Add the remaining sugar.

3 Continue heating the glucose and sugar until the mixture caramelizes to a dark brown. Turn off the heat.

4 Slowly add the cream mixture to the caramel. Be very careful, as this will bubble wildly. Also, to avoid steam burns, do not place your hands above the boiling caramel. When the boiling begins to subside, stir with a wooden spoon. Repeat this process until all of the cream has been added.

5 Return the pan to the heat and cook to 236°F (113°C). Strain and cool thoroughly before using.

Approximate values per 1-oz. (30-g) serving: **Calories** 100, **Total fat** 4.5 g, **Saturated fat** 3 g, **Cholesterol** 15 mg, **Sodium** 15 mg, **Total carbohydrates** 16 g, **Protein** 0 g

DARK CHOCOLATE GLAZE

Yield: 4 lb. (1870 g)

Evaporated milk	14 oz.	420 g
Glucose or corn syrup	3 oz.	90 g
Simple Syrup (page 349)	14 oz.	420 g
Dark chocolate coating or **pâte à glacer**	17 oz.	480 g
Extra bittersweet chocolate, chopped fine	17 oz.	480 g

▶ **pâte à glacer** a specially formulated chocolate coating compound with vegetable oils designed to retain its shine without tempering; it is used as a coating or icing chocolate

1 Bring the milk, glucose and Simple Syrup to a boil, stirring carefully. Do not whisk vigorously or you will incorporate too much air.

2 In a bowl, combine the dark chocolate coating or pâte à glacer and the bittersweet chocolate.

3 Slowly pour the milk mixture onto the chocolate. Let it sit for approximately a minute. Using a whisk, stir the mixture slowly to incorporate the chocolate and cream.

4 Keep the mixture refrigerated. When ready to use, warm it over a water bath to 100°F (38°C). If the temperature gets any hotter the glaze will loose its shine.

Approximate values per 1-oz. (30-g) serving: **Calories** 90, **Total fat** 6 g, **Saturated fat** 3 g, **Cholesterol** 0 mg, **Sodium** 10 mg, **Total carbohydrates** 12 g, **Protein** 1 g

RECIPE 14.8

CARROT CAKE WITH CREAM CHEESE ICING

Yield: 2 Sheet Cakes or 6 Rounds, 10 in. (25 cm) each

Method: Creaming

Cake:

Vegetable oil	1 lb. 12 oz.	780 g	75%
Granulated sugar	1 lb. 14 oz.	840 g	81%
Eggs	14 oz. (9 eggs)	395 g	38%
Carrots, shredded	2 lb. 4 oz.	1010 g	97%
Crushed pineapple, with juice	1 lb. 9 oz.	700 g	67%
Baking soda	0.75 oz.	20 g	2%
Cinnamon, ground	1 oz.	30 g	3%
Pumpkin pie spice	0.75 oz.	20 g	2%
Salt	0.75 oz.	20 g	2%
Baking powder	0.6 oz. (1.5 Tbsp.)	17 g	1.6%
Cake flour	2 lb. 5 oz.	1040 g	100%
Coconut, shredded	12 oz.	335 g	32%
Walnut pieces	10 oz.	280 g	27%
Total batter weight:	12 lb. 3 oz.	5487 g	528%
Cream Cheese Icing (page 368)	as needed	as needed	

1 Blend the oil and sugar in the large bowl of a mixer fitted with a paddle. Add the eggs, beating to incorporate.

2 Blend in the carrots and pineapple.

3 Sift the baking soda, cinnamon, pumpkin pie spice, salt, baking powder and flour together, then add them to the batter. Stir in the coconut and walnuts.

4 Divide the batter into greased and floured pans.

5 Bake at 340°F (170°C) until springy to the touch and a cake tester comes out almost clean.

6 Allow the cakes to cool, then fill and frost as desired with Cream Cheese Icing.

Approximate values per serving: **Calories** 390, **Total fat** 22 g, **Saturated fat** 4 g, **Cholesterol** 40 mg, **Sodium** 490 mg, **Total carbohydrates** 44 g, **Protein** 5 g, **Vitamin A** 100%

MARBLE CAKE

RECIPE 14.9

Yield: 1 Sheet Cake, 18 in. × 24 in. (45 cm × 60 cm)   **Method:** Creaming

Cake:

Cake flour, sifted	1 lb. 11 oz.	810 g	100%
Baking powder	1 oz.	30 g	4%
Salt	1 oz.	30 g	4%
Unsalted butter, softened	12 oz.	360 g	44%
Granulated sugar	1 lb. 11 oz.	810 g	100%
Milk	24 fl. oz.	720 ml	89%
Vanilla extract	0.15 fl. oz. (1 tsp.)	5 ml	0.5%
Dark chocolate, melted	4.5 oz.	130 g	16%
Baking soda	0.04 oz. (¼ tsp.)	1 g	0.1%
Coffee extract	0.3 fl. oz. (2 tsp.)	8 ml	1%
Egg whites	12 oz. (12 whites)	360 g	44%
Total batter weight:	6 lb. 12 oz.	3264 g	402%
Cocoa Fudge Icing (page 358)	as needed	as needed	

1 Sift the flour, baking powder and salt together. Set aside.
2 Cream the butter and sugar until light and fluffy.
3 Combine the milk and vanilla.
4 Add the dry ingredients alternately with the milk to the creamed butter. Stir the batter only until smooth.
5 Separate the batter into two equal portions. Add the chocolate, baking soda and coffee extract to one portion.
6 Whip the egg whites until stiff but not dry. Fold half of the whites into the vanilla batter and half into the chocolate batter.
7 Spoon the batters onto a greased sheet pan, lined with a pan extender, alternating the two colors. Pull a paring knife through the batter to swirl the colors together.
8 Bake at 350°F (180°C) until a tester comes out clean, approximately 25 minutes.
9 Allow the cake to cool, then cover the top with Cocoa Fudge Icing.

Approximate values per 5-oz. (150-g) serving: **Calories** 480, **Total fat** 17 g, **Saturated fat** 11 g, **Cholesterol** 40 mg, **Sodium** 250 mg, **Total carbohydrates** 75 g, **Protein** 7 g, **Vitamin A** 15%, **Calcium** 15%

RECIPE 14.10   **FLOURLESS CHOCOLATE CAKE**

Yield: 1 Full-Sheet Pan, 18 in. × 24 in. (45 cm × 60 cm)

Method: Creaming

		Sugar at 100%	
Unsalted butter, softened	14 oz.	420 g	78%
Granulated sugar	18 oz.	540 g	100%
Vanilla extract	0.15 fl. oz. (1 tsp.)	5 ml	0.8%
Cocoa powder	2 oz.	60 g	11 %
Egg yolks	8 oz. (12 yolks)	240 g	44%
Eggs	6.75 oz. (4 eggs)	200 g	37%
Semisweet or bittersweet chocolate, melted and held at 110°F (43°C)	1 lb.	480 g	89%
Almond flour	6 oz.	180 g	33%
Egg whites	1 lb. 8 oz. (24 whites)	720 g	133%
Total batter weight:	5 lb. 14 oz.	2845 g	525%

1 Cream the butter and sugar in the bowl of a mixer fitted with a paddle attachment. Add the vanilla and cocoa powder.

2 Add the egg yolks and eggs one at a time, scraping down the bowl well after each addition. Make certain the chocolate is warmed to 110°F (43°C). (This will keep the batter light. Colder chocolate will firm the batter, making it impossible to fold in the whipped egg whites.) Pour in the melted chocolate and mix until well combined. Add the almond flour. Set aside.

3 In a separate mixing bowl, use a clean whip to whip the egg whites and remaining granulated sugar to medium peaks. Quickly fold the whites into the cake batter in three steps.

4 Spread the mixture on a paper-lined sheet pan. Bake at 350°F (180°C) until the top surface of the cake is dry and the interior of the cake is soft but set, approximately 35 to 40 minutes. Test for doneness by removing a bit of the crust and pressing the cake underneath. The crust will be firm but the interior crumb will be soft but not sticky. If the cake is still wet, return it to the oven for a few more minutes.

5 Cool the cake on a wire rack. Cut the cake to line torte rings as needed. (See Eros Torte, page 423). Remove the parchment paper after the cake is cut to keep the cake intact.

VARIATIONS:

White Chocolate Chunk Flourless Chocolate Cake—Fold 10 ounces (300 grams/ 55%) white chocolate chips or chunks into the batter before panning.

Pistachio or Hazelnut Flourless Chocolate Cake—Fold 10 ounces (300 grams/ 55%) coarse chopped pistachios or hazelnuts into the batter before panning.

Approximate values per 1-oz. (30-g) serving: **Calories** 100, **Total fat** 7 g, **Saturated fat** 3.5 g, **Cholesterol** 50 mg, **Sodium** 15 mg, **Total carbohydrates** 9, **Protein** 2g

GERMAN CHOCOLATE CAKE

Yield: 1 Layer Cake, 9 in. (22 cm) **Method:** Creaming

Cake:

Sweet baking chocolate	8 oz.	240 g	80%
Water, boiling	4 fl. oz.	120 ml	40%
Unsalted butter, softened	8 oz.	240 g	80%
Granulated sugar	1 lb.	480 g	160%
Egg yolks	2.6 oz. (4 yolks)	80 g	26%
Vanilla extract	0.15 fl. oz. (1 tsp.)	5 ml	1.5%
Cake flour	10 oz.	300 g	100%
Baking soda	0.14 oz. (1 tsp.)	4 g	1.4%
Salt	0.1 oz. (1/2 tsp.)	3 g	1%
Buttermilk	8 fl. oz.	240 ml	80%
Egg whites	4 oz. (4 whites)	120 g	40%
Total batter weight:	3 lb. 13 oz.	1862 g	620%
Coconut Pecan Icing (page 369)	1 lb. 3 oz.	900 g	

1 Chop the chocolate and melt it with the boiling water over a bain marie.

2 In the bowl of a mixer fitted with a paddle, cream together the butter and sugar until light and fluffy.

3 Add the egg yolks, one at a time, to the butter, then stir in the vanilla and the melted chocolate.

4 Sift the flour, baking soda and salt together and add them alternately with the buttermilk to the batter, beating well after each addition.

5 Whip the egg whites to stiff peaks and fold into the batter.

6 Divide the batter into three 9-inch (22-centimeter) round pans that have been greased and lined with parchment paper.

7 Bake at 350°F (180°C) until set and just beginning to pull away from the sides, approximately 30 to 40 minutes. When the cake has cooled completely, spread the Coconut Pecan Icing between each layer and on top. The sides of this cake are traditionally left plain.

Approximate values per 1/12-cake serving: **Calories** 840, **Total fat** 47 g, **Saturated fat** 24 g, **Cholesterol** 210 mg, **Sodium** 240 mg, **Total carbohydrates** 101 g, **Protein** 10 g, **Vitamin A** 25%, **Calcium** 15%, **Iron** 20%

RECIPE 14.12

SACHER TORTE

Yield: 2 Cakes, 9 in. (22 cm) each   **Method:** Creaming

Cake:

All-purpose flour	10 oz.	300 g	100%
Cocoa powder, alkalized	3 oz.	90 g	30%
Unsalted butter, softened	12.5 oz.	375 g	125%
Granulated sugar	18 oz.	540 g	180%
Egg yolks	8.5 oz. (14 yolks)	255 g	85%
Hazelnuts, toasted and ground	3 oz.	90 g	30%
Egg whites	14 oz. (14 whites)	420 g	140%
Total batter weight:	4 lb. 5 oz.	2070 g	690%
Apricot jam	18 oz.	540 g	
Apricot glaze	as needed	as needed	
Chocolate Glaze (page 361)	as needed	as needed	

1 Grease two 9-inch (22-centimeter) springform pans lightly with butter and line with parchment paper.

2 Sift the flour and cocoa powder together twice. Set aside.

3 Cream the butter and 7 ounces (210 grams) of the sugar together until light and fluffy. Gradually add the egg yolks and beat well.

4 Fold in the sifted flour and cocoa powder and the hazelnuts by hand.

5 Whip the egg whites to soft peaks, then gradually add the remaining sugar and continue whipping until stiff, glossy peaks form.

6 Lighten the batter by folding in approximately one-quarter of the egg whites, then fold in the remaining whites.

7 Pour the batter into the prepared pans and bake at 350°F (180°C) until the cakes are set, approximately 35 to 45 minutes.

8 Cool the cakes 5 minutes before removing from the pans.

9 Cool completely, then cut each cake horizontally into three layers. Spread apricot jam on each layer and restack them, creating two three-layer cakes.

10 Heat the apricot glaze until spreadable. Pour it over the top and sides of each cake.

11 Allow the apricot glaze to cool completely, then pour the Chocolate Glaze over the top and sides of each cake to create a smooth, glossy coating.

Approximate values per $^{1}/_{10}$-cake serving: **Calories** 450, **Total fat** 21 g, **Saturated fat** 10 g, **Cholesterol** 185 mg, **Sodium** 60 mg, **Total carbohydrates** 56 g, **Protein** 7 g, **Vitamin A** 20%

DEVIL'S FOOD CAKE

Yield: 1 Full-Sheet Pan or 10 8-in. (20-cm) Rounds   **Method:** Two-stage

Cake flour	1 lb. 4 oz.	560 g	100%
Granulated sugar	1 lb. 8 oz.	675 g	120%
Emulsified shortening	12 oz.	340 g	60%
Cocoa powder	4 oz.	115 g	20%
Salt	0.6 oz.	17 g	3%
Baking powder	0.75 oz.	20 g	4%
Baking soda	0.5 oz.	15 g	2.5%
Dry milk powder	2.5 oz.	60 g	11%
Vanilla extract	0.5 fl. oz.	15 ml	2.5%
Corn syrup	4 oz.	115 g	20%
Water, cold	18 fl. oz.	500 ml	90%
Eggs	1 lb. (10 eggs)	450 g	80%
Total batter weight:	6 lb. 6 oz.	2882 g	513%

1 Mix the flour, sugar and shortening in the large bowl of a mixer fitted with a paddle on low speed 5 minutes.

2 Add the cocoa powder, salt, baking powder, baking soda, dry milk powder, vanilla, corn syrup and half of the cold water. Blend well, then scrape down the bowl.

3 Combine the eggs with the remaining cold water and add to the batter in three equal parts, blending well and scraping down the bowl after each addition.

4 After all the ingredients are incorporated, blend on low speed 2 minutes.

5 Divide into greased and floured pans, measuring 1 gallon (4 liters) of batter for a full-sheet pan or 1 pound (450 grams) for each 8-inch (20-centimeter) round layer.

6 Bake at 340°F (170°C) until springy and a toothpick inserted in the center comes out clean.

Approximate values per 3.5-oz. (100-g) serving: **Calories** 400, **Total fat** 17 g, **Saturated fat** 5 g, **Cholesterol** 80 mg, **Sodium** 460 mg, **Total carbohydrates** 55 g, **Protein** 6 g, **Calcium** 10%, **Iron** 15%

RECIPE 14.14

VANILLA RASPBERRY WEDDING CAKE WITH WHITE CHOCOLATE BUTTERCREAM

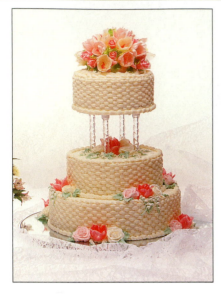

HYATT REGENCY SCOTTSDALE AT GAINEY RANCH, Scottsdale, AZ

Former Executive Pastry Chef Judy Doherty

Yield: 1 Three-Tier Wedding Cake, 80 Servings*   **Method:** Two-stage

Vanilla cake:

Cake flour	1 lb. 14 oz.	900 g	100%
Granulated sugar	2 lb. 8 oz.	1200 g	133%
Baking powder	2.5 oz.	70 g	8%
Eggs	2 lb. 14 oz.		
	(28 eggs)	1380 g	153%
Salt	1 oz.	30 g	3%
Emulsified shortening (Fluid Flex)	1 lb. 4 oz.	595 g	66%
Milk	1 pt.	480 ml	53%
Total batter weight:	9 lb. 11 oz.	4655 g	516%
Simple Syrup (page 349)	1 pt.	500 ml	
Raspberry liquor	2 fl. oz.	60 ml	
Diplomat Cream Filling (page 453)	5 qt.	5 lt	
Fresh raspberries	6 pt.	3 lt	
White Chocolate Buttercream			
(page 369)	15 lb.	7200 g	
Royal icing or pulled sugar roses	as desired	as desired	

1 To prepare the wedding cake pictured here, prepare three cake pans—one 8-inch (20-centimeter) pan, one 10-inch (25-centimeter) pan and one 14-inch (35-centimeter) pan—by spraying with pan release and lining with parchment paper.

2 Combine the flour, sugar, baking powder, eggs and salt in a large mixer bowl. Whip on high speed 8 minutes.

3 Add the Fluid Flex (an emulsifier for spongecakes) and milk. Mix 8 more minutes at medium speed.

4 Divide the batter between the prepared cake pans. Fill each pan halfway.

5 Bake at 350°F (180°C) 35 to 60 minutes, depending on tier size. The cake is done when it springs back when lightly touched in the center. Cool, then remove from the pans and freeze.

6 Working with one cake round at a time, slice each round into three horizontal layers. Combine the Simple Syrup with the raspberry liquor. Brush the bottom layer with the raspberry syrup and then top it with Diplomat Cream Filling and fresh raspberries. Place the middle layer on top of the filled bottom layer and top it with Diplomat Cream Filling and fresh raspberries. Then place the top layer on the middle layer to complete the tier.

7 Repeat with each of the other two cake tiers.

8 Apply a thin coating of White Chocolate Buttercream to the top and sides of each tier. Spread additional buttercream on the tops, smoothing it with a cake spatula. Then pipe additional buttercream onto the sides of each tier in a basketweave design. Pipe a border along the top edge of each tier.

9 Stack the tiers and pipe a border along the bottom edge of each tier. Then decorate the assemblage with icing roses and garlands.

*This assembly is illustrated by photographs appearing throughout this chapter.

Approximate values per 6-oz. (180-g) serving: **Calories** 600, **Total fat** 28 g, **Saturated fat** 7 g, **Cholesterol** 240 mg, **Sodium** 520 mg, **Total carbohydrates** 75 g, **Protein** 10 g, **Vitamin A** 10%, **Calcium** 20%

TRES LECHES CAKE

Yield: 2 Cakes, 8 in. (20 cm) each   **Method:** Spongecake

Cake:

Pastry flour	5 oz.	150 g	100%
Baking powder	0.5 oz.	15 g	10%
Egg yolks	5.3 oz. (8 yolks)	160 g	280%
Granulated sugar	5 oz.	150 g	100%
Egg whites	8 oz. (8 whites)	240 g	160%
Cream of tartar	0.04 oz. ($\frac{1}{8}$ tsp.)	1.5 g	1%
Total batter weight:	1 lb. 7 oz.	716 g	477%

Syrup:

Media crèma*	15 fl. oz.	420 ml
Sweetened condensed milk	28 oz.	790 g
Evaporated milk	24 fl. oz.	700 ml
Vanilla extract	0.3 fl. oz.	9 ml
Rum, dark	4 fl. oz.	120 ml

1 Sift the flour and the baking powder together and set aside.

2 Whip the egg yolks with half of the sugar on high speed until they reach the ribbon stage, approximately 2 minutes.

3 In a separate bowl, use a clean whip to beat the egg whites until foamy. Add the cream of tartar and the remaining sugar. Whip on medium speed until the whites are glossy and stiff but not dry.

4 Fold one-third of the egg whites into the whipped yolks, then fold in the remaining whites.

5 Sprinkle one-third of the sifted flour over the batter and fold in. Repeat until all the flour is incorporated.

6 Divide the batter between greased and floured pans. Bake at 350°F (180°C) until the cake is golden brown and spongy, approximately 30 minutes.

7 Stir the syrup ingredients together in a bowl. Invert the hot cakes onto serving platters. Remove the parchment paper. Ladle the milk mixture over the hot cakes. (If necessary, poke holes in the cakes with a toothpick to allow the cakes to absorb more of the milk syrup.) Let the cakes soak at least 3 hours before serving.

* Media crèma is a canned milk available in the ethnic food section of many markets. If it is unavailable, substitute either crème fraîche flavored with a few drops of vanilla or more evaporated milk.

Approximate values per $\frac{1}{10}$-cake serving: **Calories** 370, **Total fat** 14 g, **Saturated fat** 8 g, **Cholesterol** 130 mg, **Sodium** 220 mg, **Total carbohydrates** 47 g, **Protein** 11 g, **Calcium** 35%

RECIPE 14.16

BÛCHE DE NOËL (YULE LOG)

Yield: 10–12 Servings

Classic Genoise (page 386), freshly baked	1 half sheet	1 half sheet
Simple Syrup (page 349)	as needed	as needed
Buttercream, coffee, chocolate or vanilla	1 qt.	1 lt

1 Roll up the warm Classic Genoise in a spiral, starting with the long side. Wrap in parchment paper and cool.

2 Carefully unroll the cake. Brush the interior with Simple Syrup and coat with buttercream, leaving a 1-inch (2.5-centimeter) unfrosted rim around each edge.

3 Reroll the cake tightly and position it with the seam down on a cake board.

4 Cut one end from the cake on a diagonal. Place the cut piece on top of the log, securing with toothpicks.

5 Pipe additional buttercream onto the cake log using a large star tip. Pipe the buttercream on the ends in a spiral pattern. Decorate as desired with buttercream flowers, baked meringue mushrooms or marzipan figures.

Approximate values per serving: **Calories** 650, **Total fat** 21 g, **Saturated fat** 6 g, **Cholesterol** 0 mg, **Sodium** 330 mg, **Total carbohydrates** 115 g, **Protein** 2 g, **Vitamin C** 70%, **Claims**—no cholesterol

1 Rolling the cake filled with buttercream.

2 Attaching the cut end to the log.

3 Piping on the buttercream.

RECIPE 14.17

ALMOND GENOISE

Yield: 2 Rounds, 7 in. (17 cm) each		**Method:** Egg foam	
Almond paste	3 oz.	90 g	37%
Granulated sugar	6 oz.	180 g	75%
Egg yolk	0.6 oz. (1 yolk)	20 g	8%
Eggs	13 oz. (8 eggs)	390 g	162%
Vanilla extract	0.5 fl. oz.	15 ml	6%
Cake flour, sifted	8 oz.	240 g	100%
Unsalted butter, melted	2.5 oz.	75 g	31%
Total weight:	2 lb. 1 oz.	1010 g	419%

1 In the bowl of a mixer fitted with a paddle, beat the almond paste and the sugar. Add the egg yolk. When fully incorporated, add the eggs and vanilla.

2 Remove the paddle from the mixer and replace it with a whip. Whip the mixture on medium speed 20 minutes.

3 Remove the bowl from the machine and carefully fold in the flour.

4 Remove one-eighth of the batter and mix it with the melted butter in a small bowl. Fold this mixture into the cake batter.

5 Divide the batter between two buttered and floured cake pans. Bake at 375°F (190°C) until the cake bounces back when lightly pressed, approximately 40 minutes.

6 Cool, then fill and ice as desired.

VARIATION:

Pistachio Almond Genoise—Carefully fold in 2 ounces (60 grams/25%) pistachio compound paste and 2 ounces (60 grams/25%) finely chopped pistachios after the butter is added in Step 4.

Approximate values per ⅛-cake serving: **Calories** 190, **Total fat** 8 g, **Saturated fat** 3.5 g, **Cholesterol** 130 mg, **Sodium** 35 mg, **Total carbohydrates** 25 g, **Protein** 5 g

LADYFINGERS

RECIPE 14.18

Ladyfingers are made from a spongecake batter that is piped into finger-length strips. After baking, these soft cakes may be eaten plain as a cookie or petit four. They are equally good when dried out in the oven, like biscotti. These versatile cakes are used to line the mold for a Bavarian dessert. For convenience, the batter may be piped close together to form a strip after baking and used to line a mold or torte ring. See Tiramisu Torte (page 425).

Yield: 80 Cookies, 4 in. (10 cm) each   **Method:** Spongecake

Cornstarch	3 oz.	90 g	75%
Bread flour	4 oz.	120 g	100%
Egg yolks	4 oz. (6 yolks)	120 g	100%
Granulated sugar	6 oz.	180 g	150%
Egg whites	6 oz. (6 whites)	180 g	150%
Lemon juice	0.08 fl. oz. (½ tsp.)	2.5 ml	2%
Total batter weight:	1 lb. 7 oz.	692 g	577%

1 Sift the cornstarch and flour together.

2 Whip the egg yolks with 2 ounces (60 grams) of the sugar until thick and creamy.

3 Whip the egg whites until foamy. Gradually add 2 ounces (60 grams) of the sugar and the lemon juice. Continue whipping to soft peaks, then add the remaining sugar gradually and whip to stiff peaks.

4 Fold approximately one-quarter of the egg whites into the whipped yolks to lighten them, then gently fold in the remaining whites. Fold in the flour mixture.

5 Place the batter into a pastry bag fitted with a large plain tip. Pipe 4-inch- (10-centimeter-) long cookies onto paper-lined sheet pans.

6 Bake immediately at 425°F (220°C) until lightly browned, approximately 8 minutes.

Approximate values per cookie: **Calories** 20, **Total fat** 0 g, **Saturated fat** 0 g, **Cholesterol** 15 mg, **Sodium** 0 mg, **Total carbohydrates** 4 g, **Protein** 1 g, **Claims**—fat free; no saturated fat; low cholesterol; no sodium; low calorie

RECIPE 14.19

VANILLA SPONGECAKE

Yield: 1 Full-Sheet Pan, 18 in. × 24 in. (45 cm × 60 cm)

Method: Spongecake

Eggs	11.5 oz. (7 eggs)	345 g	209%
Egg yolks	4.2 oz. (7 yolks)	125 g	76%
Granulated sugar	10 oz.	300 g	181%
Vanilla extract	1.5 fl. oz.	45 ml	27%
Cake flour, sifted	5.5 oz.	165 g	100%
Egg whites	7 oz. (7 whites)	210 g	127%
Powdered sugar, sifted	2 oz.	60 g	36%
Total batter weight:	2 lb. 9 oz.	1250 g	756%

1 Line a full-sheet pan with parchment. Lightly butter and flour the paper.

2 Whip the eggs, egg yolks, sugar and vanilla in a mixing bowl on medium high speed until the mixture forms thick ribbons.

3 Remove the yolk mixture from the machine and delicately fold in the flour. Set aside.

4 In a separate bowl, use a clean whip to whip the egg whites and powdered sugar to medium-soft peaks.

5 Lighten the yolk mixture with one-third of the whipped egg whites, then fold in the remaining whites.

6 Spread the spongecake batter evenly on the prepared sheet pan using an off-set spatula. Bake at 425°F (220°C) until the cake springs back when lightly touched, approximately 7 to 8 minutes.

VARIATIONS:

Chocolate Spongecake—Reduce the cake flour to 4 ounces (120 grams) and sift it with 1.5 ounces (45 grams) cocoa powder.

Pistachio Spongecake—Add 1.5 ounces (45 grams/27%) pistachio compound to the yolk mixture once it is whipped. Add 3 ounces (90 grams/54%) pistachio flour to the dry ingredients. Fold 5 ounces (150 grams/91%) coarsely chopped pistachios into the batter.

Approximate values per 1-oz. (30-g) serving: **Calories** 70, **Total fat** 2 g, **Saturated fat** 0.5 g, **Cholesterol** 70 mg, **Sodium** 20 mg, **Total carbohydrates** 11 g, **Protein** 2 g, **Claims**—low fat

ALMOND BISCUIT

RECIPE 14.20

Yield: 1 Full-Sheet Pan, 18 in. × 24 in. (45 cm × 60 cm)

Method: Spongecake

Almond flour	8 oz.	240 g	160%
Powdered sugar	8 oz.	240 g	160%
Eggs	5 oz. (3 eggs)	150 g	100%
Egg yolks	3 oz. (5 yolks)	90 g	60%
Vanilla extract	0.3 fl. oz. (2 tsp.)	9 ml	6%
Cake flour	5 oz.	150 g	100%
Egg whites	10 oz. (10 whites)	300 g	200%
Granulated sugar	4.5 oz.	135 g	90%
Almonds, slivered	8 oz.	240 g	160%
Total batter weight:	3 lb. 4 oz.	1554 g	1036%

1 Whip the almond flour, powdered sugar, eggs, egg yolks and vanilla in a mixing bowl until it forms thick ribbons, approximately 10 to 15 minutes.

2 Remove the bowl from the machine. Fold in the cake flour and set aside.

3 Place the egg whites and granulated sugar in a clean bowl and whip them with a clean whip attachment to medium peaks.

4 Quickly fold the whipped egg whites into the batter.

5 Spread the batter onto a paper-lined sheet pan. Sprinkle the surface of the batter with the slivered almonds. Bake at 375°F (190°C) until lightly browned, approximately 18 to 20 minutes.

VARIATIONS:

Almond Biscuit with Hazelnuts—Sprinkle the panned cake batter with 12 ounces (360 grams/240%) coarsely chopped hazelnuts instead of slivered almonds.

Pistachio Biscuit—Reduce the almond flour to 6 ounces (180 grams/120%). Add 3 ounces (90 grams/60%) pistachio flour and 2 ounces (60 grams/40%) pistachio paste to the ingredients in Step 1. Sprinkle the panned cake batter with 8 ounces (240 grams/160%) pistachios before baking.

Approximate values per 1-oz. (30-g) serving: **Calories** 100, **Total fat** 5 g, **Saturated fat** 0.5 g, **Cholesterol** 35 mg, **Sodium** 15 mg, **Total carbohydrates** 11 g, **Protein** 3 g

▶ **biscuit** a French word used to describe any dry, flat cake, whether sweet or savory, usually a spongecake.

JOCONDE

Decorative designs baked into a light spongecake provide an elegant finish to tortes formed in ring molds. A joconde cake batter is used because it bakes into a moist, flexible cake. The cake batter may be tinted or marbleized for further decorative effect. Thanks to silicone baking materials, this batter can be baked on a patterned baking mat, retaining the imprint of the mat when unmolded, as for the Eros Torte (page 423).

This sponge requires attentive baking so that it remains flexible to easily conform to the contours of a torte mold. If underbaked, it will stick to the baking mat. If overbaked, it will dry out. Once cooled, the sponge may be cut into strips to line any shape ring mold. Once unmolded, the sides of the torte need no further embellishment.

Yield: 1 Full-Sheet Pan, 18 in. × 24 in. (45 cm × 60 cm)

Method: Spongecake

Almond flour	5 oz.	150 g	333%
Granulated sugar	6 oz.	180 g	400%
Cake flour	1.5 oz.	45 g	100%
Eggs	7 oz. (4 eggs)	210 g	466%
Egg whites	3.5 oz. (3½ whites)	105 g	233%
Unsalted butter, slightly melted	1.5 oz.	45 g	100%
Total batter weight:	1 lb. 8 oz.	735 g	1632%

1 In the bowl of a mixer fitted with a whip, combine the almond flour, 5 ounces (150 grams) of the sugar, the cake flour and half of the eggs. Whip the mixture 2 minutes. Stop the machine, scrape down the bowl, then whip 3 more minutes.

2 Gradually add the remaining eggs. Whip on medium speed 5 more minutes.

3 In a clean mixing bowl, whip the egg whites and remaining sugar to medium peaks.

4 Remove the bowl of almond mixture from the machine and fold in the melted butter using a spatula.

5 Fold in one-third of the whipped egg whites to lighten the batter, then fold in the remaining whipped egg whites. Do not overmix.

6 Spread the batter over a silicone baking mat placed on a sheet pan. Level it carefully with a long offset spatula. Bake at 450°F (230°C) until the joconde bounces back when lightly pressed, approximately 6 to 8 minutes.

VARIATION:

Fruit and Nut Joconde—Before baking, sprinkle the surface of the joconde batter with 2 ounces (60 grams/133%) of one or more of the following ingredients or any combination: chopped pistachios, chopped apricots, macaroon-type coconut, sun-dried cherries or dried cranberries.

Approximate values per 1-oz. (30-g) serving: **Calories** 90, **Total fat** 4 g, **Saturated fat** 1.5 g, **Cholesterol** 35 mg, **Sodium** 15 mg, **Total carbohydrates** 11 g, **Protein** 2 g

PATTERNED JOCONDE

A rich décor paste is used to create distinct designs on the surface of the baked joconde cake. For this visual effect, the décor paste is made and tinted with a contrasting color or cocoa powder as needed. The décor paste is then spread in a random pattern or stenciled onto a silicone baking mat. After the paste is frozen to ensure that the pattern stays in place, the lighter joconde sponge is spread over the décor paste. Then the cake is baked with care to ensure a flexible cake. Once cooled, the cake is peeled from the baking mat, revealing the distinct pattern. For Bergamot Torte (page 427), a silicone baking mat is finger-painted with cocoa décor paste, then topped with joconde batter before baking.

Yield: 1 Full-Sheet Pan, 18 in. × 24 in. (45 cm × 60 cm)

Method: Spongecake

Décor paste:

Unsalted butter, softened	5.5 oz.	165 g	110%
Granulated sugar	5.5 oz.	165 g	110%
Egg whites	5 oz. (5 whites)	150 g	100%
Pastry flour, sifted	5 oz.	150 g	100%
Food coloring, paste or liquid (optional)	as needed	as needed	
Total paste weight:	1 lb. 5 oz.	630 g	420%
Joconde batter (page 418)	1 lb. 8 oz.	720 g	480%
Total weight:	2 lb. 13 oz.	1350 g	900%

1 Cream the butter and sugar until light and fluffy.

2 Gradually add the egg whites. Fold in the flour. Tint the batter with paste or liquid food coloring (if using).

3 Spread a thin layer of décor paste approximately $1/16$ inch (1 millimeter) thick onto a silicone baking mat using an offset spatula. Pattern the décor paste into lines, wood grain or other patterns as desired.

4 Slide the silicone mat onto a flat sheet pan and freeze until hard.

5 Prepare the Joconde batter. Remove the mat from the freezer. Transfer the Joconde-coated baking mat to a room-temperature sheet pan. (A cold sheet pan prevents the cake from baking properly.) Quickly pour the Joconde batter over the design. Spread the Joconde batter evenly with an offset spatula to completely cover the baking mat.

6 Bake at 450°F (230°C) until the Joconde bounces back when slightly pressed, approximately 6 to 8 minutes.

VARIATION:

Cocoa Décor Paste—Reduce the pastry flour to 3 ounces (90 grams). Add 2 ounces (60 grams) cocoa powder. Sift the cocoa powder with the flour before using.

Approximate values per 1-oz. (30-g) serving: **Calories** 100, **Total fat** 5 g, **Saturated fat** 2.5 g, **Cholesterol** 25 mg, **Sodium** 15 mg, **Total carbohydrates** 12 g, **Protein** 2 g

RECIPE 14.23   **CARAIBE TORTE**

1 Quartering the Caraibe torte.

2 The finished Caraibe torte.

Yield: 4 Tortes, 8 in. × 6 in. (20.5 cm × 15 cm) each

Chocolate Spongecake (page 416), fully baked	3 half sheets	3 half sheets
Simple Syrup (page 349)	14 fl. oz.	420 ml
Jamaican rum	4 fl. oz.	120 ml
Chocolate Buttercream Filling (page 453)	4 lb.	1920 g
Silky Ganache Deluxe (page 371)	as needed	as needed
Chocolate Meringue Sticks (recipe follows)	as needed	as needed
Modeling chocolate roses (page 626)	as needed	as needed

1 Place a rectangular cake frame 16 inches × 12 inches × 2½ inches (41 centimeters × 30 centimeters × 6.5 centimeters) on a flat paper-lined sheet pan.

2 Fit one Chocolate Spongecake layer inside the frame. Flavor the Simple Syrup with the rum and moisten the cake with 6 fluid ounces (180 milliliters) of the rum syrup.

3 Spread half of the Chocolate Buttercream Filling on the cake. Cover the cream with another cake layer, then moisten it with 6 fluid ounces (180 milliliters) of the rum syrup.

4 Spread the remaining Chocolate Buttercream Filling over the cake. Cover with the last cake layer and moisten with the remaining rum syrup.

5 Freeze the torte at least 2 hours.

6 To finish the torte, invert it onto a flat surface and remove the frame and paper. Spread a small layer of room-temperature Silky Ganache Deluxe over the top of the torte. Warm the remaining ganache to 110°F (43°C) and glaze the surface evenly.

7 Once the ganache sets, divide the torte into four equal pieces. Place each piece on a cake board. Garnish the cakes with Chocolate Meringue Sticks and white modeling chocolate roses.

Approximate values per ⅛-torte serving: **Calories** 470, **Total fat** 26 g, **Saturated fat** 15 g, **Cholesterol** 215 mg, **Sodium** 55 mg, **Total carbohydrates** 52 g, **Protein** 7 g, **Vitamin A** 15%

CHOCOLATE MERINGUE STICKS

Yield: Approximately 120 Pieces

Chocolate Meringue (page 289)	1 lb. 8 oz.	720 g

1 Using a small plain tip, pipe the Chocolate Meringue onto a paper-lined sheet pan in strips running the length of the sheet pan.

2 Bake at 225°F (110°C) until crisp, approximately 1 hour.

3 Remove the Chocolate Meringue from the oven and immediately cut the strips into 1½-inch (3.5 centimeter) sticks. Chocolate Meringue Sticks will keep 1 month if stored in a dry place, tightly wrapped in an airtight container.

RIO TORTE

Yield: 2 Tortes, 7 in. (17 cm) each

Coconut Macadamia Cake (recipe follows)	4 rounds	4 rounds
Passion Fruit Crème Chiboust (page 454)	1 lb. 10 oz.	780 g
Pineapple and mango cubes, poached	1 lb.	480 g
Italian Meringue (page 290)	1 lb. 7 oz.	690 g
Tropical fruit	as needed	as needed

1 Lightly oil and sugar two 7-inch (17-centimeter) cake rings. Place them on a paper-lined sheet pan. Place one layer of Coconut Macadamia Cake into each ring.

2 Divide half of the Passion Fruit Crème Chiboust evenly between the rings. Scatter the poached pineapple and mango cubes over the cream. Top with the remaining layers of cake.

3 Fill the rings to the top with more crème chiboust, leveling it to the rim with a long metal spatula. (Since crème Chiboust has a tendency to settle in the ring, reserving some of the cream in the refrigerator and releveling the torte after a few hours is recommended.)

4 Freeze the tortes a minimum of 2 hours.

5 Remove the tortes from the rings and place them on cake boards.

6 Coat the top and sides of each torte with an even layer of Italian Meringue. Decorate the surface of each torte with more Italian Meringue using a pastry bag fitted with a St. Honoré tip. Lightly brown the tortes with a propane torch and decorate with tropical fruit.

Approximate values per ⅛-torte serving: **Calories** 640, **Total fat** 33 g, **Saturated fat** 18 g, **Cholesterol** 260 mg, **Sodium** 95 mg, **Total carbohydrates** 81 g, **Protein** 10 g, **Vitamin A** 25 %, **Vitamin C** 15 %, **Iron** 15%

COCONUT MACADAMIA CAKE

Yield: 4 Rounds, 7 in. (17 cm) each **Method:** Spongecake

Egg yolks	8 oz. (13 yolks)	240 g	200%
Granulated sugar	10 oz.	300 g	250%
Heavy cream	10 fl. oz.	300 ml	250%
Macaroon-type coconut	9 oz.	270 g	225%
Vanilla extract	0.5 fl. oz.	15 ml	12%
Cake flour, sifted	4 oz.	120 g	100%
Macadamia nuts, coarsely chopped	6 oz.	180 g	150%
Egg whites	8 oz. (8 whites)	240 g	200%
Total batter weight:	3 lb. 7 oz.	1665 g	1387%

1 In a large bowl, whisk the egg yolks and sugar until well combined. Add the cream, then the coconut, vanilla and flour. Fold in the macadamias.

2 In a separate bowl, whisk the egg whites to medium stiff peaks. Fold one-third of the whipped egg whites into the coconut mixture, then delicately fold in the rest of the egg whites.

3 Divide the cake batter evenly between buttered and floured cake pans. Bake at 375°F (190°C) until the center of the cake bounces back when lightly pressed, approximately 20 minutes. Cool completely before using.

Approximate values per 1-oz. (30-g) serving: **Calories** 130, **Total fat** 90 g, **Saturated fat** 5 g, **Cholesterol** 70 mg, **Sodium** 15 mg, **Total carbohydrates** 10 g, **Protein** 2 g

RECIPE 14.25

FRAISIR TORTE

Yield: 4 Tortes, 8 in. × 6 in. (20.5 cm × 15 cm) each

Pistachio Spongecake (page 416), fully baked	1 half sheet	1 half sheet
Simple Syrup (page 349)	7.5 fl. oz.	225 ml
Raspberry liqueur	2.5 fl. oz.	75 ml
Raspberry purée	2 oz.	60 g
Raspberry Cream Filling (page 455)	2 lb.	960 g
Fresh strawberries, whole	3 lb.	1500 g
French Mousseline Buttercream (page 357)	as needed	as needed
Marzipan	as needed	as needed
Food coloring (optional)	as needed	as needed
Neutral glaze (optional)	as needed	as needed
Fresh berries (optional)	as needed	as needed
Sugar decorations (optional)	as needed	as needed

1 Place a rectangular cake frame measuring 16 inches × 12 inches × 2½ inches (41 centimeters × 30 centimeters × 6.5 centimeters) on a flat paper-lined sheet pan. Do not oil or sugar the frame.

2 Slice the Pistachio Spongecake in half horizontally and place one layer, cut side facing up, inside the frame.

3 Combine the Simple Syrup with the raspberry liqueur and raspberry purée. Moisten the spongecake with half of the raspberry syrup.

4 Spread a layer of Raspberry Cream Filling ⅛ inch (3 millimeters) thick evenly over the spongecake.

5 Arrange the strawberries upright on the cream, positioning them close together so that their sides touch. Cover the strawberries evenly with the remaining Raspberry Cream Filling. Top with the remaining spongecake layer, cut side facing toward the cream. Moisten it with the remaining raspberry syrup.

6 In order to obtain a clean cut, chill the assembled cake several hours in the refrigerator.

7 Loosen the cake from the frame by running a knife along the inside edge of the frame. Remove the cake frame. Spread a thin layer of French Mousseline Buttercream on the top surface of the cake. Tint the marzipan a pale color. Roll it out ¹⁄₁₆ inch (1 millimeter) thick and position the marzipan on the top surface of the torte, covering the buttercream.

8 With a serrated knife, trim the sides of the torte evenly to expose the strawberries. Quarter the cake, then transfer it to four cake boards. If desired, coat the marzipan with neutral glaze and decorate with fresh berries and sugar decorations.

Approximate values per ⅛-torte serving: **Calories** 685, **Total fat** 48 g, **Saturated fat** 27 g, **Cholesterol** 298 mg, **Sodium** 37 mg, **Total carbohydrates** 60 g, **Protein** 6 g, **Vitamin A** 35%, **Vitamin C** 45%

EROS TORTE

Yield: 3 Tortes, 7 in. (17 cm) each

Joconde (page 418), baked on a patterned mat	1 half sheet	1 half sheet
Dacquoise (page 299), 7-in. (17-cm) disks	3 disks	3 disks
Caramel Nut Filling or Icing (page 370)	1 lb. 9 oz.	750 g
Almond Genoise (page 414), 7-in. (17-cm) round	1 round	1 round
Simple Syrup (page 349)	4.5 fl. oz.	135 ml
Cointreau or orange liqueur	2.5 fl. oz.	75 ml
Poached Pears in Exotic Syrup (page 522)	15	15
Caramel Mousse (page 465)	2 lb. 8 oz.	1200 g
Tart glaze	as needed	as needed
Combed Chocolate Teardrop Ribbons (page 618)	as needed	as needed
Walnut halves	as needed	as needed

1 Oil and sugar three 7-inch (17-centimeter) cake rings and place them on a paper-lined sheet pan. Cut the Joconde into three strips measured to fit the cake rings. Line each ring with a strip of cake, its patterned design facing the ring. Place one Dacquoise disk in the bottom of each ring.

2 Divide the Caramel Nut Filling or Icing evenly between the three rings.

3 Slice the Almond Genoise into three layers. Place one layer in each ring, covering the nut filling. Combine the Simple Syrup and Cointreau and moisten the cake with 2 ounces (60 milliliters) of the syrup.

4 Slice the Poached Pears in Exotic Syrup in half, remove the core and stem and place approximately 10 pear halves in each ring, covering the Almond Genoise layer.

5 Cover the pears with the Caramel Mousse and fill to the rim. Level the top of the tortes by running a long metal spatula over the rim of the ring molds.

6 Freeze the tortes a minimum of 2 hours.

7 Coat the tortes with the tart glaze, then remove the rings. Transfer the tortes onto cake boards. Decorate the tops with Combed Chocolate Ribbons and walnut halves.

Approximate values per 1-oz. (30-g) serving: **Calories** 90, **Total fat** 2.5 g, **Saturated fat** 1 g, **Cholesterol** 45 mg, **Sodium** 15 mg, **Total carbohydrates** 16 g, **Protein** 2 g

RECIPE 14.27

RUBIES TORTE

Yield: 3 Triangular Tortes, 8 in. (20 cm) each

Raspberry Gelée (page 365)	2 lb. 8 oz.	1200 g
Flourless Chocolate Cake (page 408)	1 full sheet	1 full sheet
Raspberry Ganache (page 264)	2 lb. 14 oz.	1380 g
Cocoa Gelée (page 363)	as needed	as needed
White and dark chocolate decorations (page 614)	as needed	as needed
Fresh raspberries	as needed	as needed

1 Cut four 24-inch- (60-centimeter-) long sheets of aluminum foil. For strength, stack the sheets, then fold up the edges to make a rectangular container measuring 8 inches × 16 inches (20 centimeters × 40 centimeters). Place the foil container on a half-sheet pan.

2 Prepare the Raspberry Gelée and pour it into the foil container. Freeze until the gelée sets.

3 Invert the Flourless Chocolate Cake onto a flat surface. Leave the parchment paper attached and cut the cake into three strips measuring approximately 8 inches × 16 inches (20 centimeters × 40 centimeters) each. Transfer one strip of cake, paper side down, to a clean sheet pan.

4 Spread the top of the cake with half of the Raspberry Ganache. Transfer another cake strip, paper side up, onto the ganache. Remove the paper.

5 Spread this layer with half of the remaining ganache. Unwrap the frozen Raspberry Gelée and trim it into a strip measuring 8 inches × 16 inches (20 centimeters × 40 centimeters). Place it onto the ganache-coated cake. Top with the last cake strip, paper side up. Remove the paper and spread the cake layer with the remaining ganache.

6 Freeze until firm, approximately 2 hours.

7 Remove the cake from the freezer and immediately cover it with Cocoa Gelée heated to 120°F (49°C). Cut the cake into three triangular pieces. Place each piece on a cake board and decorate with chocolate decorations and fresh raspberries.

Approximate values per ⅛-torte serving: **Calories** 660, **Total fat** 38 g, **Saturated fat** 20 g, **Cholesterol** 205 mg, **Sodium** 80 mg, **Total carbohydrates** 76 g, **Protein** 13 g, **Vitamin A** 25%, **Vitamin C** 20%, **Iron** 10%

TIRAMISU TORTE

RECIPE 14.28

Yield: 2 Tortes, 7 in. (17 cm) each

Ladyfinger batter (page 415)	2 lb. 14 oz.	1380 g
Simple Syrup (page 349)	9 fl. oz.	270 ml
Coffee or almond liqueur	2 fl. oz.	60 ml
Coffee extract	0.5 fl. oz.	15 ml
Vanilla extract	0.5 fl. oz.	15 ml
Mascarpone Cream Mousse (page 466)	3 lb.	1440 g
Cocoa Gelée (page 363)	as needed	as needed
Hollow molded chocolates (page 624)	as needed	as needed
Chocolate fans or decorations (page 617)	as needed	as needed

1 Butter and flour two paper-lined full-sheet pans. Using a plain medium tip, pipe half of the Ladyfinger batter into four disks measuring 7 inches (17.5 centimeters) in diameter.

2 To make the strips of Ladyfingers to line the ring molds, pipe the remaining batter into Ladyfingers 4 inches (10 centimeters) long, placed close together so they join at the sides and form a strip the entire length of the sheet pan. Bake as directed.

3 Lightly oil and sugar two 7-inch (17-centimeter) torte rings. Place them on a paper-lined sheet pan.

4 Cut the strip of Ladyfingers in half lengthwise. Trim the strips of Ladyfingers on each long edge to fit evenly inside the ring molds.

5 Position the Ladyfinger strips inside the rings, cut to size to make a tight fit. Place a Ladyfinger disk on the bottom of each ring.

6 Combine the Simple Syrup, liqueur, coffee extract and vanilla extract. Moisten the cake with half of this syrup.

7 Divide half of the Mascarpone Cream Mousse between each mold.

8 Place the second Ladyfinger disk in the rings and moisten with the remaining coffee syrup.

9 Fill with the remaining Mascarpone Cream Mousse, leveling it to the rim.

10 Refrigerate or freeze the tortes 2 hours.

11 Remove from freezer and cover the top surface with a thin layer of Cocoa Gelée heated to 120°F (49°C). Or sprinkle lightly with cocoa powder to garnish. Remove the rings, then decorate the tortes with hollow molded chocolates, chocolate fans and other chocolate decorations.

Approximate values per ⅛-torte serving: **Calories** 640, **Total fat** 33 g, **Saturated fat** 18 g, **Cholesterol** 390 mg, **Sodium** 40 mg, **Total carbohydrates** 70 g, **Protein** 17 g, **Vitamin A** 25%

RECIPE 14.29

PALOMO TORTE

Yield: 4 Tortes, 7 in. (17 cm) each

Strawberry Gelée (page 373)	1 lb. 13 oz.	870 g
Fruit and Nut Joconde (page 418), fully baked	1 half sheet	1 half sheet
Pistachio Dacquoise (page 299), 7-in. (17-cm) disks, fully baked	4 disks	4 disks
Mascarpone Cream Mousse (page 466)	4.5 lb.	2160 g
Almond Biscuit (page 417)	1 half sheet	1 half sheet
Simple Syrup (page 349)	7.5 fl. oz.	225 ml
Strawberry liqueur	2.5 fl. oz.	75 ml
Strawberry purée	2 oz.	60 g
Tart Glaze (page 261)	as needed	as needed
White chocolate ribbons (page 618)	as needed	as needed
Strawberries and pistachios	as needed	as needed

1 Prepare the Strawberry Gelée and pour it into four silicone molds or pie tins, slightly smaller than the 7-inch (17-centimeter) torte rings being used. Freeze until needed.

2 Lightly oil and sugar four 7-inch (17-centimeter) torte rings. Place on a paper-lined sheet pan.

3 Cut the Fruit and Nut Joconde into 2-inch- (5-centimeter-) wide strips the length of the sheet pan. Fit the strips tightly into the rings. Place the Pistachio Dacquoise in the bottom of each ring.

4 Spread a small amount of the Mascarpone Cream Mousse in a thin layer on the Pistachio Dacquoise.

5 Cut the Almond Biscuit into four 7-inch (17-centimeter) rounds and place on the Mascarpone Cream Mousse.

6 Combine the Simple Syrup, strawberry liqueur and strawberry purée. Moisten the cake with the strawberry syrup. Cover with a small amount of Mascarpone Cream Mousse.

7 Unmold the frozen Strawberry Gelée by simply pressing it out of the silicone molds, or by briefly placing the pie tins on a heat source, until the disks comes free. Place one molded gelée in each ring.

8 Cover with the remaining Mascarpone Cream Mousse and level to the rim of the ring.

9 Freeze until well chilled, approximately 2 hours.

10 Coat the surface of the tortes with Tart Glaze. Chill until firm, then remove the rings. Place the tortes on cake boards. Garnish with white chocolate ribbons, fresh strawberries and pistachios.

Approximate values per ⅛-torte serving: **Calories** 580, **Total fat** 35 g, **Saturated fat** 15 g, **Cholesterol** 215 mg, **Sodium** 75 mg, **Total carbohydrates** 54 g, **Protein** 15 g, **Vitamin A** 20%, **Vitamin C** 10%, **Calcium** 10%, **Iron** 10%

BERGAMOT TORTE

RECIPE 14.30

Yield: 3 Tortes, 7½ in. (19 cm) each

Patterned Joconde (page 419), fully baked	1 full sheet	1 full sheet
Dacquoise (page 299), 7½-inch (19-centimeter) disks, fully baked	3 disks	3 disks
Orange Bergamot Curd (page 437)	1 lb. 14 oz.	900 g
Almond Genoise (page 414), 7-inch (17-centimeter) rounds, fully baked	2 rounds	2 rounds
Granulated sugar	8 oz.	240 g
Orange juice	8 fl. oz.	240 ml
Bergamot essential oil	5–6 drops	5–6 drops
Orange Milk Chocolate Earl Grey Mousse (page 462)	5 lb.	2400 g
Cocoa gelée	as needed	as needed
Edible gold leaf	as needed	as needed

1 Lightly oil and sugar three 7½-(19-centimeter) torte rings. Place them on a paper-lined sheet pan.

2 Cut the Patterned Joconde into strips ½ inch (1 centimeter) narrower than the height of the rings. Fit the strips tightly into the rings with the design facing the ring. Place a layer of Dacquoise in the bottom of each ring.

3 Spread a small amount of Orange Bergamot Curd on the Dacquoise.

4 Slice the Almond Genoise into three layers and place one in each torte ring.

5 Make a syrup from the sugar, orange juice and bergamot oil and moisten the Almond Genoise with half of the syrup. Spread with the remaining Orange Bergamot Curd.

6 Place the remaining Almond Genoise in each ring and moisten well with the syrup.

7 Top each cake with the Orange Milk Chocolate Earl Grey Mousse, filling the rings to the rim and leveling with a flat metal spatula.

8 Freeze until hard, approximately 2 hours.

9 Remove from the freezer and cover the top surface with a thin layer of Cocoa Gelée.

10 Remove the tortes from the rings, then decorate with edible gold leaf if desired.

Approximate values per ⅛-torte serving: **Calories** 940, **Total fat** 56 g, **Saturated fat** 29 g, **Cholesterol** 380 mg, **Sodium** 135 mg, **Total carbohydrates** 98 g, **Protein** 16 g, **Vitamin A** 35%, **Vitamin C** 25%, **Calcium** 15%, **Iron** 15%

▶ **edible gold leaf** delicate sheets of pure gold used to decorate chocolates and iced cakes; the thin sheets, separated by tissue paper, are sold in packs and are available from cake decorating suppliers. Edible silver leaf, known as *vark,* is also available.

RECIPE 14.31

NOBILIS TORTE

Yield: 4 Tortes, 8 in. × 6 in. (20.5 cm × 15 cm) each

Cherry Gelée (page 373)	4 lb.	1920 g
Hazelnut and Cherry Meringue Cake (page 300)	2 half sheets	2 half sheets
Hazelnut Cream Filling (page 467)	4 lb. 12 oz.	2280 g
Tart Glaze (page 261)	as needed	as needed
Sliced almonds	as needed	as needed
Fresh cherries	as needed	as needed

1 Pour the Cherry Gelée into a 12-inch × 8-inch (30-centimeter × 20-centimeter) pan or silicone mold. (Or place a 12-inch × 8-inch × 2-inch (30-centimeter × 20-centimeter × 5-centimeter) cake frame on a sheet pan that has been lined with a silicone baking mat. Pipe a thin strip of white chocolate along the inner bottom edge of the frame to seal the frame to the baking mat. Pour the Cherry Gelée into the frame.) Freeze until set.

2 Position a half-sheet cake frame measuring 16 inches × 12 inches × 2½ inches (41 centimeters × 30 centimeters × 6.5 centimeters) on a paper-lined sheet pan.

3 Fit one layer of Hazelnut and Cherry Meringue Cake inside the frame.

4 Spread half of the Hazelnut Cream Filling evenly over the surface of the cake.

5 Cover with the Cherry Gelée, then spread half of the remaining Hazelnut Cream Filling over the gelée. Top with the second layer of cake. Cover with plastic wrap and freeze at least 2 hours.

6 Invert the cake onto the back side of a flat sheet pan. Remove the cake frame.

7 Using an offset spatula, spread the remaining Hazelnut Cream Filling over the top of the cake. Spread a thin layer of Tart Glaze on the surface of the tortes.

8 Refrigerate until set. Cut the cake into four equal pieces. Place on cake boards. Decorate with sliced almonds and fresh cherries.

Approximate values per ⅛-torte serving: **Calories** 680, **Total fat** 40 g, **Saturated fat** 15 g, **Cholesterol** 115 mg, **Sodium** 80 mg, **Total carbohydrates** 69 g, **Protein** 14 g, **Vitamin A** 25%, **Vitamin C** 15%, **Calcium** 10%, **Iron** 10%

RECIPE 14.32

EMPRESS TORTE

Yield: 3 Tortes, 7 in. × 2½ in. (17 × 6 cm) each

Nougatine Dacquoise (page 299), 7-in. (17-cm) disks, fully baked	3 disks	3 disks
Lime Curd (page 437)	1 lb. 4 oz.	600 g
Almond Genoise (page 414), 7-in. (17-cm) rounds, fully baked	2 rounds	2 rounds
Simple Syrup (page 349)	7 fl. oz.	210 ml
Raspberry purée	8 fl. oz.	240 ml
Raspberry Mousseline (page 464)	3 lb. 8 oz.	1680 g
Tart Glaze (page 261)	as needed	as needed
Chocolate cutouts (page 615)	as needed	as needed
Raspberries or other fruit	as needed	as needed
Combed chocolate ribbons (page 618)	as needed	as needed
Gerbet Macaroons (page 572)	as needed	as needed

1 Lightly oil and sugar three 7-inch × 2½-inch (17-centimeter × 6-centimeter) torte rings. Place one Nougatine Dacquoise disk in each ring.

2 Spread a small amount of Lime Curd over each Nougatine Dacquoise layer.

3 Slice the Almond Genoise horizontally in three even layers. Place an Almond Genoise round in each ring.

4 Combine the Simple Syrup and raspberry purée and moisten the cake with half of the raspberry syrup. Cover with the remaining Lime Curd.

5 Place another Almond Genoise layer in the ring and moisten with the remaining raspberry syrup.

6 Fill the rings to the rim with the Raspberry Mousseline and level evenly. Freeze until set, approximately 2 hours.

7 Spread a thin layer of Tart Glaze on the surface of the tortes. Let set.

8 Remove the rings and place on cake boards. Carefully heat the sides of the tortes with a blowtorch, then overlap Chocolate cutouts along the sides of the tortes. Decorate with raspberries, chocolate ribbons, Gerbet Macaroons and other fruit.

Approximate values per serving: **Calories** 600, **Total fat** 29 g, **Saturated fat** 13 g, **Cholesterol** 145 mg, **Sodium** 85 mg, **Total carbohydrates** 77 g, **Protein** 14 g, **Vitamin A** 15%, **Vitamin C** 20%, **Iron** 10%

DIVA TORTE
RECIPE 14.33

Yield: 4 Tortes, 8 in. × 6 in. × 2¼ in. (20.5 cm × 15 cm × 6.5 cm), or 1 Half Sheet

Dacquoise (page 299)	1 half sheet	1 half sheet
Apricot Mousse (page 430)	4 lb. 9 oz.	2190 g
Pistachio Spongecake (page 416)	1 half sheet	1 half sheet
Simple Syrup (page 349)	12 fl. oz.	360 ml
Kirsch or brandy	4 fl. oz.	120 ml
Fresh whole apricots, pitted*	40	40
Italian Meringue (page 290)	1 lb. 7 oz.	690 g
Fresh or dried apricots	as needed	as needed
Chopped pistachios	as needed	as needed
Basic Nougatine (page 633), Sesame variation	as needed	as needed
Chocolate cigarettes (page 616)	as needed	as needed

1 Place a rectangular cake frame measuring 16 inches × 12 inches × 2½ inches (41 centimeters × 30 centimeters × 6.5 centimeters) on a flat paper-lined half-sheet pan.

2 Fit the Dacquoise in the frame. Spread a thin layer of Apricot Mousse over the Dacquoise.

3 Split the Pistachio Spongecake in half and position one piece over the Apricot Mousse–covered Dacquoise.

4 Flavor the Simple Syrup with the Kirsch and moisten the spongecake with half of the Kirsch syrup. Halve the apricots. Evenly place them on the moistened spongecake.

5 Spread the remaining Apricot Mousse evenly over the apricots.

6 Top the Apricot Mousse with the remaining Pistachio Spongecake half and moisten with the remaining Kirsch syrup.

7 Refrigerate the assembled torte at least 2 hours. (If canned apricots were used, the torte may be frozen.)

8 Once the Apricot Mousse sets, remove the cake frame and ice the entire surface with a thin layer of Italian Meringue.

9 Divide the large torte into four equal parts. Drag a cake decorating comb over the surface of each torte. Lightly brown the meringue with a propane torch.

10 Garnish with fresh or dried apricots, pistachios and nougatine decorations and chocolate cigarettes.

*One #10 can of whole apricots in heavy syrup may be substituted for the fresh apricots.

Approximate values per ⅛-torte serving: **Calories** 370, **Total fat** 16 g, **Saturated fat** 7 g, **Cholesterol** 125 mg, **Sodium** 55 mg, **Total carbohydrates** 47 g, **Protein** 9 g, **Vitamin A** 60%, **Vitamin C** 15%

LIKE A HOST AT A GOOD PARTY, VANILLA ENCOURAGES ALL THE ELEMENTS PRESENT TO RISE TO THE OCCASION AND MAKE THEIR OWN CONTRIBUTIONS TO THE WHOLE, WITHOUT CALLING UNDUE ATTENTION TO ITSELF.

—Richard Sax, American food writer, cookbook author, and teacher (1954–1995)

15

CUSTARDS AND CREAMS

VINCENT ON CAMELBACK, Phoenix, AZ
Chef Vincent Guerithault

▶ prepare a variety of custards
and creams

▶ prepare a variety of mousses
and other fillings

▶ prepare a variety of hot
dessert soufflés and
cheesecakes

▶ use these products in
preparing and serving other
pastry and dessert items

The bakeshop is responsible for more than just quick breads, yeast breads, pies, pastries, cookies and cakes. It also produces many delightfully sweet creations that use little if any flour and may be cooked on the stove as well as in the oven. These include the sweet creams and custards featured in this chapter. These are stand-alone desserts as well as the foundation of many tortes, pastries and frozen desserts. Sweet custards are cooked mixtures of eggs, sugar and a liquid; flour or cornstarch may be added. Sweet custards can be flavored in a variety of ways and eaten hot or cold. Some are served alone as a dessert or used as a filling, topping or accompaniment for pies, pastries or cakes. Creams include whipped cream and mixtures lightened with whipped cream such as Bavarians, chiffons and mousses.

▶ CUSTARDS

A **custard** is any liquid thickened by the coagulation of egg proteins. (See Chapter 4, Bakeshop Ingredients, for more information on eggs.) A custard's consistency depends on the ratio of eggs to liquid, whether whole eggs or just yolks are used, and the type of liquid used. The more eggs used, the thicker and richer the final product will be. The richer the liquid (cream versus milk, for example), the thicker the final product. Most custards, with the notable exception of pastry creams, are not thickened by starch.

A custard can be stirred or baked. A **stirred custard** tends to be soft, rich and creamy. A **baked custard,** typically prepared in a water bath in the oven, is usually firm enough to unmold and slice.

STIRRED CUSTARDS

A stirred custard is cooked on the stove top either directly in a saucepan or over a double boiler. It must be stirred throughout the cooking process to stabilize the eggs and prevent curdling (overcooking).

A stirred custard can be used as a dessert sauce, incorporated into a complex dessert or eaten alone. The stirred custards most commonly used in food service operations are **vanilla custard sauce** and **pastry cream.** Other popular stirred custards are **curd fillings** (page 437) and **sabayon** (page 438).

VANILLA CUSTARD SAUCE

Vanilla custard sauce (Fr. *crème anglaise*) is made with egg yolks, sugar and milk or half-and-half. Usually flavored with vanilla bean or pure vanilla extract, a custard sauce can also be flavored with liqueur, chocolate, ground nuts or extracts.

Custard sauce is prepared on the stove top over direct heat in a nonreactive saucepan. When making a custard sauce, be extremely careful to stir the mixture continually and not allow it to boil, or it will curdle. Do not allow the temperature to exceed 190°F (88°C) or the custard will break. Use a thermometer to monitor the custard as it cooks, removing it from the heat when it reaches 185°F (85°C). A properly made custard sauce should be smooth and thick enough to coat the back of a spoon. It should not contain any noticeable bits of cooked egg.

A custard sauce can be served with cakes, pastries, fruits and soufflés and is often used for decorating dessert plates. It may be served hot or cold. It is also used as the base for many ice creams.

A very thick version of custard sauce can be made using heavy cream and additional egg yolks. Its consistency is more like a **pudding** than a sauce. This custard is often served over fruit in a small ramekin or other container and then topped with caramelized sugar for a dessert known as **crème brûlée** (burnt cream). See the formula on page 452.

PASTRY CREAM

Pastry cream (Fr. *crème pâtissière*) is a stirred custard made with egg yolks, sugar and milk and thickened with starch (flour, cornstarch or a combination of the two). Because the starch protects the egg yolks from curdling, pastry cream can be boiled. In fact, it must be boiled to fully gelatinize the starch and eliminate the taste of raw starch.

Pastry cream can be flavored with chocolate, liqueurs, extracts or fruits. (Pudding is nothing more than a flavored pastry cream.) It is used for filling éclairs, cream puffs, napoleons, fruit tarts and other pastries. Pastry cream thickened with cornstarch is also the filling for cream pies (see Chapter 10, Pies and Tarts). Pastry cream is thick enough to hold its shape without making pastry doughs soggy.

Pastry cream can be rather heavy. Folding in whipped cream to produce a **mousseline** can lighten it, or Italian meringue can be folded in to produce a **crème Chiboust.**

▶ PROCEDURE FOR PREPARING VANILLA CUSTARD SAUCE AND PASTRY CREAM

1 Place milk and/or cream in a heavy, nonreactive saucepan; add a vanilla bean to **steep** in the cream if desired.

2 In a mixing bowl, whisk together the egg yolks, sugar and starch (if using). Do not use an electric mixer, as it incorporates too much air.

3 Bring the liquid just to a boil. Temper the egg mixture with approximately one-third of the hot liquid.

4 Pour the tempered eggs into the remaining hot liquid and return the mixture to the heat. The stove's temperature can be as hot as you dare: the lower the temperature, the longer the custard will take to thicken; the higher the temperature, the greater the risk of curdling.

5 Cook, stirring constantly, until thickened. Custard sauce should reach a temperature of 185°F (85°C). Pastry cream should be allowed to boil for a few moments.

6 Immediately remove the cooked custard from the hot saucepan to avoid overcooking. Butter or other flavorings can be added at this time.

7 Cool over an ice bath. Store in a clean, shallow container. Cover to prevent pastry cream from developing a thick skin and refrigerate.

▶ PROCEDURE FOR SALVAGING CURDLED VANILLA CUSTARD SAUCE

1 Strain the sauce into a bowl. Place the bowl over an ice bath and whisk vigorously.

2 If this does not smooth out the overcooked sauce, place the sauce in a blender and process for a few moments.

While these steps may reincorporate the curdled eggs, the resulting sauce will be thin and less creamy than a properly prepared vanilla custard sauce.

▶ **pudding** a thick, spoonable dessert custard, usually made with eggs, milk, sugar and flavorings and thickened with flour or another starch

▶ **crème brûlée** (krehm broo-LAY) French for burnt cream; used to describe a rich dessert custard topped with a crust of caramelized sugar

▶ **mousseline** (moos-uh-LEEN) a cream or sauce lightened by folding in whipped cream

▶ **crème chiboust** (krehm chee-BOOS) a vanilla pastry cream lightened by folding in Italian meringue; traditionally used in a gâteau St. Honoré

▶ **steep** to soak a food, especially dry seasonings and spices, in a hot liquid in order to either extract its flavor or soften its texture

VANILLA CUSTARD SAUCE (CRÈME ANGLAISE)

Yield: approximately 40 fl. oz. (1200 ml)   **Method:** Stirred custard

Half-and-half	1 qt.	1 lt
Vanilla bean, split	1	1
Egg yolks	8 oz. (12 yolks)	240 g
Granulated sugar	10 oz.	300 g

1 In a heavy nonreactive saucepan, bring the half-and-half and vanilla bean just to a boil.

2 Whisk the egg yolks and sugar together in a mixing bowl. Temper the egg mixture with approximately one-third of the hot half-and-half, then return the entire mixture to the saucepan with the remaining half-and-half.

3 Cook the sauce over medium heat, stirring constantly, until it is thick enough to coat the back of a spoon. Do not allow the sauce to boil.

4 As soon as the sauce thickens, remove it from the heat and pour it through a fine mesh strainer into a clean bowl. Chill the sauce over an ice bath, then cover and keep refrigerated. The sauce should last 3 to 4 days.

1 Mise en place for vanilla sauce.

2 Tempering the eggs.

3 The properly cooked sauce.

4 Straining the sauce into a bowl.

VARIATIONS:

Chocolate Custard Sauce—Stir 6 ounces (180 grams) finely chopped dark chocolate into the strained custard while it is still warm. The heat of the custard will melt the chocolate.

Coffee Custard Sauce—Add 1 fluid ounce (30 milliliters) coffee extract or compound to the warm custard.

Earl Grey Crème Anglaise—Omit the vanilla bean. Steep four Earl Grey tea bags 4 minutes in the half-and-half. Remove the tea bags, then prepare the sauce as directed.

Frangelico Custard Sauce—Omit the vanilla bean. Stir in 0.08 fluid ounces (2.5 milliliters/½ teaspoon) vanilla extract and 1 to 1.5 fluid ounces (30 to 45 milliliters) Frangelico, to taste.

Ginger Custard Sauce—Omit the vanilla bean. Steep 3 ounces (90 grams) chopped fresh ginger 10 minutes in the half-and-half. Reheat and continue preparing the sauce as directed. The chopped ginger will be strained out in Step 4.

Pistachio Custard Sauce—Omit the vanilla bean. Place 4 ounces (120 grams) finely chopped pistachio nuts in the saucepan with the barely boiling half-and-half. Remove from the heat, cover and steep up to 1 hour. Uncover the mixture, reheat and continue preparing the sauce as directed. The ground nuts will be strained out in Step 4. One fluid ounce (30 milliliters) pistachio compound may be added to intensify the flavor.

Saffron Custard Sauce—Omit the vanilla bean. Steep ⅛ teaspoon (0.5 milliliter) saffron with the half-and-half.

Approximate values per 1-fl.-oz. (30-ml) serving: **Calories** 80, **Total fat** 4.5 g, **Saturated fat** 2.5 g, **Cholesterol** 75 mg, **Sodium** 15 mg, **Total carbohydrates** 8 g, **Protein** 2 g, **Vitamin A** 6%

SAFFRON

Saffron (Fr. *safran*) comes from the dried stigmas of the saffron crocus. Each flower bears only three threadlike stigmas, and each must be picked by hand. It takes approximately 250,000 flowers to produce 1 pound of saffron, making it the most expensive spice in the world. Luckily, a tiny pinch is enough to color and flavor a large quantity of food. Good saffron should be a brilliant orange color, not yellow, with a strong aroma and a bitter, honeylike taste. Saffron produces a yellow dye that diffuses through any warm liquid. It is commonly used with fish and shellfish (a necessity for bouillabaisse), but it makes a colorful and exotic sweet sauce as well.

Saffron

RECIPE 15.2

PASTRY CREAM (CRÈME PÂTISSIÈRE)

Yield: 3½ pt. (1.75 lt)/3 lb. 10 oz. (1740 g)   **Method:** Stirred custard

Cake flour	4 oz.	120 g
Granulated sugar	12 oz.	360 g
Milk	1 qt.	1 lt
Egg yolks	8 oz. (12 yolks)	240 g
Vanilla bean, split	1	1
Unsalted butter	2 oz.	60 g

1 Stirring the pastry cream as it comes to a boil.

2 Folding butter into the cooked pastry cream.

1 Sift the flour and sugar together.

2 Whisk 8 fluid ounces (240 milliliters) of the milk into the egg yolks. Then add the flour and sugar and whisk until completely smooth.

3 Heat the remaining milk with the vanilla bean in a heavy nonreactive saucepan. As soon as the milk comes to a boil, whisk approximately one-third of it into the egg-and-flour mixture and blend completely. Pour the egg mixture into the saucepan with the rest of the milk.

4 Whisk constantly until the custard thickens. As it thickens, the custard will go through a lumpy stage. Although you should not be alarmed, you should increase the speed of your stirring. Continue to stir vigorously, and it will smooth out and thicken just before coming to a boil.

5 Allow the pastry cream to boil approximately 1 minute, stirring constantly.

6 Remove the pastry cream from the heat and immediately pour it into a clean mixing bowl.

7 Fold in the butter until melted. Do not overmix, as this will thin the custard.

8 Cover by placing plastic wrap on the surface of the custard. Chill over an ice bath. Remove the vanilla bean just before using the pastry cream.

VARIATIONS:

Mousseline Pastry Cream—Whip 8 fluid ounces (240 milliliters) plain whipping cream to stiff peaks. Fold into the chilled pastry cream.

Chocolate Pastry Cream—Stir 4 ounces (120 grams) finely chopped dark chocolate into the strained custard while it is still warm. The heat of the custard will melt the chocolate.

Coffee Pastry Cream—Add 1 fluid ounce (30 milliliters) coffee extract or compound to the warm custard.

Coconut Pastry Cream—Replace 16 fluid ounces (480 milliliters) of the milk with an equal amount of unsweetened canned coconut milk.

Approximate values per 1-fl.-oz. (30-ml) serving: **Calories** 110, **Total fat** 4.5 g, **Saturated fat** 2 g, **Cholesterol** 90 mg, **Sodium** 20 mg, **Total carbohydrates** 15 g, **Protein** 2 g, **Vitamin A** 6%

CURD FILLINGS

Curd is a type of stirred custard made with eggs, sugar, butter and fruit juice, usually citrus. It is a popular filling for tarts, cakes, tortes and sandwich cookies. Because of the quantity of sugar used to form the egg-and-butter emulsion, curd is usually flavored with an acid such as lemon or lime juice. A light curd formula follows. A one-step lemon curd formula, which produces a thicker product, appears on page 460.

▶ PROCEDURE FOR PREPARING A FRUIT CURD FILLING

1 Combine sugar and fruit juice in a saucepan. Bring to a boil.

2 Whisk eggs in a nonreactive saucepan, then temper with the boiling sugar mixture. Bring to a boil, whisking constantly. Boil 1 minute.

3 Remove from the heat and whisk over an ice bath to cool to 120°F (49°C).

4 Add butter in several increments, stirring to combine. Immediately pour into pie or tart shells or chill, cover and refrigerate. Curd will keep refrigerated several days.

LEMON CURD   RECIPE 15.3

Yield: 1 lb. 4 oz. (619 g)   **Method:** Stirred custard

Lemon juice	4 fl. oz.	120 ml
Granulated sugar	6.5 oz.	195 g
Lemon zest, grated fine	0.14 oz. (2 tsp.)	4 g
Eggs	4 oz. (2 eggs)	120 g
Unsalted butter, room temperature	6 oz.	180 g

1 Combine the lemon juice, 3 ounces (90 grams) of the sugar and the zest in a nonreactive saucepan. Bring to a boil.

2 Place the eggs and remaining sugar in a nonreactive bowl. Mix well without aerating.

3 Temper the egg mixture with one-quarter of the boiling juice. Add the remaining juice and return to the stove.

4 Bring the mixture to a boil while whisking vigorously. Continue mixing and boil 1 minute.

5 Remove from the heat and chill over an ice bath until the mixture reaches 120°F (49°C).

6 Add the butter in five parts, stirring well with a spatula after each addition.

7 Use immediately to fill a pie or tart shell or chill, cover and refrigerate.

VARIATIONS:

Lime Curd—Substitute lime juice for the lemon juice.

Orange Bergamot Curd—Reduce the lemon juice to 3 fluid ounces (90 milliliters). Add 3 fluid ounces (90 milliliters) orange juice concentrate. Increase the total sugar to 9.5 ounces (285 grams). Omit the lemon zest. Increase the eggs to 6 ounces (180 grams) and the butter to 9 ounces (270 grams). Combine the orange juice concentrate, lemon juice and 5 ounces (150 grams) sugar. Bring to a boil and proceed as in Step 2. Add 10 drops essential oil of bergamot to the finished curd. Yield: 1 pound 14 ounces (915 grams)

Passion Fruit Curd—Reduce the lemon juice to 0.5 fluid ounce (15 milliliters). Increase the total sugar to 8 ounces (240 grams). Increase the eggs to 10 ounces (300 grams/6 eggs). Combine the lemon juice with 5 ounces (150 grams) passion fruit purée and 4 ounces (120 grams) of the sugar. Bring to a boil. Mix the eggs with the remaining 4 ounces (120 grams) sugar. Temper with the passion fruit mixture. Beat in 8 ounces (240 grams) butter. Yield: 2 pounds (945 grams)

Approximate values per 1-oz. (30-g) serving: **Calories** 110, **Total fat** 7 g, **Saturated fat** 4.5 g, **Cholesterol** 40 mg, **Sodium** 5 mg, **Total carbohydrates** 10 g, **Protein** 1 g

SABAYON

Sabayon (sah-bay-OWN; It. *zabaglione*) is a foamy, stirred custard sauce made by whisking eggs, sugar and wine over low heat. The egg proteins coagulate, thickening the mixture, while the whisking incorporates air to make it light and fluffy. Usually a sweet wine is used; marsala and champagne are the most popular choices.

The mixture can be served warm, or it can be chilled and lightened with whipped cream or whipped egg whites. Sabayon may be served alone or as a sauce or topping with fruit or pastries such as spongecake or ladyfingers.

▶ PROCEDURE FOR PREPARING SABAYON

1 Combine egg yolks, sugar and wine in the top of a double boiler.
2 Place the double boiler over low heat and whisk constantly until the sauce is foamy and thick enough to form a ribbon when the whisk is lifted.
3 Remove from the heat and serve immediately, or whisk over an ice bath until cool. If allowed to sit, the hot mixture may separate.
4 Whipped egg whites or whipped cream may be folded into the cooled sabayon.

RECIPE 15.4

The thickened sabayon.

CHAMPAGNE SABAYON

Yield: 1 qt. (1 lt) **Method:** Stirred custard

Egg yolks	5.3 oz. (8 yolks)	160 g
Granulated sugar	4 oz.	120 g
Salt	0.05 oz. (¼ tsp.)	1.5 g
Marsala wine	2 fl. oz.	60 ml
Dry champagne	6 fl. oz.	180 ml
Heavy cream (optional)	8 fl. oz.	240 ml

1 Combine the egg yolks, sugar and salt in a stainless steel bowl.
2 Add the Marsala and champagne to the egg mixture.
3 Place the bowl over a pan of barely simmering water. Whisk vigorously until the sauce is thick and pale yellow, approximately 10 minutes. Serve immediately.
4 To prepare a sabayon mousseline, place the bowl of sabayon over an ice bath and continue whisking until completely cold. Whip the cream to soft peaks and fold it into the cold sabayon.

Approximate values per 1-fl.-oz. (30-ml) serving: **Calories** 50, **Total fat** 4 g, **Saturated fat** 2 g, **Cholesterol** 60 mg, **Sodium** 25 mg, **Total carbohydrates** 4 g, **Protein** 1 g, **Vitamin A** 6%

BAKED CUSTARDS

A baked custard is based on the same principle as a stirred custard: a liquid thickened by the coagulation of egg proteins. However, with a baked custard, the thickening occurs in an oven. The container of custard is usually placed in a water bath (bain marie) to protect the eggs from curdling. Even though the water bath's temperature will not exceed 212°F (100°C), care must be taken not to bake the custards for too long or at too high a temperature. An overbaked custard will be watery or curdled; a properly baked custard should be smooth-textured and firm enough to slice.

Baked custards include simple mixtures of whole eggs or yolks, sugar and milk such as crème caramel, called **flan** in Spain and Mexico. Baked custards also include mixtures in which other ingredients are suspended—for example, cheesecake, rice pudding, bread pudding and quiche.

▶ **flan** a firm custard baked over a layer of caramelized sugar and inverted for service

The texture and flavor of these custards will vary depending on the quantity and types of ingredients used. Whole eggs are used in a simple egg custard such as flan to provide both richness from the fat in the yolk and structure from the protein in the white. This is important in order for the flan to maintain its shape when unmolded. Using heavy cream and additional egg yolks such as in the crème brûlée on page 441 provides added richness and a soft, velvety texture; because the dessert is served in a ramekin, protein strength is not required.

CRÈME CARAMEL

Crème caramel, crème renversée and flan all refer to an egg custard baked over a layer of caramelized sugar and inverted for service. The caramelized sugar produces a golden-brown surface on the inverted custard and a thin caramel sauce. The procedure for preparing crème caramel is illustrated with the formula for Toffee Caramel Flan.

TOFFEE CARAMEL FLAN   RECIPE 15.5

Yield: 10 Ramekins, 6 oz. (180 ml) each   **Method:** Baked custard

Granulated sugar	1 lb. 4 oz.	600 g
Water	8 fl. oz.	240 ml
Milk	24 fl. oz.	720 ml
Heavy cream	24 fl. oz.	720 ml
Cinnamon sticks	2	2
Vanilla bean, split	1	1
Eggs	13.3 oz. (8 eggs)	400 g
Egg yolks	2.6 oz. (4 yolks)	80 g
Brown sugar	6 oz.	180 g
Molasses	0.75 oz.	22 g
Amaretto liqueur	1 fl. oz.	30 ml
Fresh fruit, optional	as needed	as needed
Caramelized almonds, optional	as needed	as needed

Filling the ramekins for flans.

1 Combine the granulated sugar with the water in a small heavy saucepan; bring to a boil. Cook until the sugar reaches a deep golden brown. Immediately pour approximately 2 tablespoons (30 milliliters) of the sugar into each of the ramekins. Tilt each ramekin to spread the caramel evenly along the bottom. Arrange the ramekins in a 2-inch-deep hotel pan and set aside.

2 Combine the milk, cream, cinnamon sticks and vanilla bean in a large saucepan. Bring just to a boil, cover and remove from the heat. Allow this mixture to steep approximately 30 minutes.

3 Whisk the eggs, egg yolks, brown sugar, molasses and amaretto together in a large bowl.

4 Uncover the milk mixture and return it to the stove top. Bring just to a boil. Temper the egg-and-sugar mixture with approximately one-third of the hot milk. Whisk in the remaining hot milk.

5 Strain the custard through a fine mesh strainer. Pour into the caramel-lined ramekins, filling to just below the rim.

6 Pour enough warm water into the hotel pan to reach halfway up the sides of the ramekins. Bake at 325°F (160°C) approximately 30 to 40 minutes. The custards should be almost set, but still slightly soft in the center.

7 Completely chill the baked custards before serving. To unmold, run a small knife around the edge of the custard, invert onto the serving plate and give the ramekin a firm sideways shake. Garnish with fresh fruit or caramelized almonds.

Approximate values per serving: **Calories** 670, **Total fat** 33 g, **Saturated fat** 19 g, **Cholesterol** 355 mg, **Sodium** 120 mg, **Total carbohydrates** 82 g, **Protein** 10 g, **Vitamin A** 40%, **Calcium** 20%

CRÈME BRÛLÉE

Crème brûlée (krehm broo-LAY) can be made as either a stirred or a baked custard. (It is basically a thick version of custard sauce.) Neither version should be considered superior, however; they are simply different. The stirred or stove top method is quicker, but requires constant attention and a practiced feel for the custard's consistency. The finished custard will be heavier, creamier and softer than its baked counterpart. The baked version is served in the ramekin or bowl in which it was baked. Unlike crème caramel or flan, baked crème brûlée is not inverted or removed from its baking dish for service.

Gentle heat is important for both methods. Overcooked stirred custard will curdle, turning into scrambled eggs. Overcooked baked custard will become watery, its texture marred with small bubbles.

Additional flavors and textures can be added to the custard in several ways:

▶ Placing a layer of fresh berries or fruit compote under the custard

▶ Incorporating fruit, nuts or liqueurs directly into the custard

▶ Adding flavoring compounds and extracts to the custard

▶ Infusing the heavy cream with nuts, herbs, spices, tea or other flavorings before making the custard

If fruit purées or other liquids are used, the quantity of cream will have to be adjusted or the custard may be too watery or unable to set properly. A formula for the baked version follows; a stirred version appears on page 452.

A variation of crème brûlée included at the end of this chapter is used as a tart filling. Freezing the baked mixture allows it to be removed from its mold and placed in a tart or torte.

▶ PROCEDURE FOR PREPARING BAKED CRÈME BRÛLÉE

1 Heat cream or half-and-half and flavorings in a saucepan just until warm. Infuse the cream with any flavorings. Reheat the cream if necessary.

2 Blend egg yolks and sugar. Stir in the heated cream.

3 Strain the cream into a pitcher or large measuring cup.

4 Pour the hot cream into the ramekins. They may be partially filled with fresh berries, fruit or nuts.

5 Bake the custards in a water bath until set, barely jiggling in the center.

6 Cool the ramekins, then cover and refrigerate them until chilled.

7 Sprinkle the surface of the ramekins with a thin layer of sugar. Brown the sugar with a blowtorch or salamander without heating the custard.

CLASSIC CUSTARD

James Beard called crème brûlée "one of the greatest desserts in the realm of cooking." The secret to crème brûlée's success probably lies in its comfort-food familiarity. It is a rich, creamy concoction of egg yolks, sugar and cream served very cold and topped with a crisp, crunchy layer of deeply caramelized sugar. The contrast of textures and flavors satisfies multiple taste desires.

Despite its French name, crème brûlée (literally, burnt cream) is most likely a product of Great Britain. Perhaps the earliest recipe for burnt cream appears in a 17th-century cookbook from Dorset, England. Numerous sources credit a member of the faculty at Trinity College in Cambridge, England, with successfully introducing this caramelized custard to his peers in the mid-1800s.

Burnt cream was also popular in America, with recognizable versions appearing in Thomas Jefferson's personal recipe collection and in several cookbooks from the 1800s.

Considered a trendy dessert for upscale American restaurants in the 1980s, crème brûlée now appears on all types of menus and is equally at home in neighborhood diners and four-star, white-tablecloth eateries.

BAKED CRÈME BRÛLÉE

Yield: 10 Servings, 4 oz. (120 g) each   **Method:** Baked custard

Heavy cream	1 qt.	1 lt
Vanilla bean, split	½	½
Granulated sugar	4 oz.	120 g
Egg yolks	6.5 oz. (10 yolks)	200 g
Granulated sugar	as needed	as needed

1 Heat the cream and the vanilla bean in a medium saucepan over medium-high heat until bubbles appear along the sides of the pan.

2 Quickly whisk the sugar into the egg yolks.

3 When the cream is hot, slowly pour it into the yolk mixture. Whisk until well combined.

4 Strain the mixture through a fine sieve into a pitcher or large measuring cup. Scrape the vanilla bean with the tip of a paring knife to remove the remaining seeds; stir the seeds into the custard.

5 Preheat the oven to 325°F (160°C). Arrange the ramekins in a 2-inch- (5-centimeter-) deep hotel pan or baking dish. Pour the custard into the ramekins. Set the pan of ramekins inside the preheated oven, and then carefully pour enough water into the pan to come two-thirds of the way up the sides of the ramekins. Bake until just set, approximately 45 to 50 minutes. Start checking the custards early; baking time will depend on the thickness and depth of your ramekins. The custard should be set, not soupy, with only a small area of jiggle in the center.

6 When the custards are done, carefully remove the baking dish from the oven and allow the ramekins to cool in the water bath. When the ramekins are cool enough to handle, remove them from the water, cover with plastic wrap, and refrigerate at least 4 hours or up to 2 days before service.

7 At service, sprinkle the tops of the custards with granulated sugar, then immediately caramelize the sugar with a blowtorch or broiler.

Approximate values per serving: **Calories** 430, **Total fat** 40 g, **Saturated fat** 24 g, **Cholesterol** 345 mg, **Sodium** 45 mg, **Total carbohydrates** 14 g, **Protein** 5 g, **Vitamin A** 35%

CHEESECAKE

Cheesecakes, which are almost as old as western civilization, have undergone many changes and variations since the ancient Greeks devised the first known recipe. Americans revolutionized the dessert with the development of cream cheese in 1872.

Cheesecake is a baked custard that contains a smooth cheese, usually a soft, fresh cheese such as cream, ricotta, cottage or farmer's cheese. (See Chapter 4, Bakeshop Ingredients.) It is important to work with cheese at room temperature and to mix it on low speed. Mixing or whipping a cheesecake batter on high speed breaks down the cheese, destroying the emulsion of fat and liquid, and will result in a dry textured cheesecake. A cheesecake may be prepared without a crust, or it may have a base or sides of short dough, cookie crumbs, ground nuts or spongecake. The filling can be dense and rich (New York style) or light and fluffy (Italian style). Fruit, nuts and flavorings may also be included in the filling. Cheesecakes are often topped with fruit or sour cream glaze. Formulas for both dense and light cheesecakes are at the end of this chapter.

Some cheesecakes are unbaked and rely on gelatin for thickening; others are frozen. These are not really custards, however, but are more similar to the chiffons or mousses discussed later.

▶ PROCEDURE FOR MAKING CHEESECAKE

1 Soften the cream cheese by gently beating it in the bowl of a mixer fitted with a paddle.

2 Scrape down the bowl, then, on low speed, beat in the sugar and any thickeners (if using). Mix until the cheese is softened but not warm, approximately 4 to 6 minutes.

3 Add the eggs, a small amount at a time, scraping down the bowl frequently to prevent lumps from forming.

4 Stir in additional cream, sour cream or other ingredients and flavorings. Additional ingredients such as dried fruit, nuts or chocolate may be folded into the batter at this time.

5 Butter springform pans or line the bottom and sides of the pans with a crumb crust, if desired. Divide the batter evenly between the pans.

6 Bake the cheesecakes. A water bath may be used for gentle even heat; if using a water bath, make the cheesecakes in regular pans or wrap springform pans in aluminum foil to prevent water from leaking into the cheesecake.

7 Cool the cheesecakes completely at room temperature, then refrigerate overnight before serving.

RECIPE 15.7   **NEW YORK–STYLE CHEESECAKE**

Yield: 2 Cakes, 10 in. (25 cm) each

Cream cheese, softened	3 lb. 6 oz.	1620 g
Cake flour	2 oz.	60 g
Granulated sugar	18 oz.	540 g
Eggs	13.3 oz. (8 eggs)	400 g
Heavy cream	5 fl. oz.	150 ml
Vanilla extract	0.5 fl. oz.	15 ml

1 Beat the cheese until smooth. Beat in the flour and sugar.

2 Blend in the eggs slowly, then add the cream and vanilla.

3 Pour the batter into well-buttered springform pans. Bake at 300°F (150°C) until set, approximately 1 to 1½ hours.

4 Cool completely before removing the sides of each pan.

Approximate values per ¹/₁₀-cake serving: **Calories** 450, **Total fat** 32 g, **Saturated fat** 20 g, **Cholesterol** 180 mg, **Sodium** 260 mg, **Total carbohydrates** 31 g, **Protein** 9 g, **Vitamin A** 40%

BREAD PUDDING

Bread pudding is a home-style dessert in which chunks of bread, flavorings and raisins or other fruit are mixed with an egg custard and baked. The result is somewhat of a cross between a cake and a pudding. It is often served with custard sauce, ice cream, whipped cream or a whiskey-flavored butter sauce. Bread pudding is a delicious way to use stale or leftover bread or overripe fruit. In fact, croissants, brioche, gingerbread, spongecake or a savory product such as cornbread can be used to make sweet or savory bread puddings. A formula for Bread Pudding with Bourbon Sauce appears on page 459.

SOUFFLÉS

A soufflé is made with a custard base, often thickened with flour, that is lightened with whipped egg whites and then baked. The air in the egg whites expands to create a light, fluffy texture and tall rise. A soufflé is not as stable as a cake or other pastry item, however, and will collapse very quickly when removed from the oven.

Soufflés can be prepared in a wide variety of sweet and savory flavors. The flavorings can be incorporated into the custard, as in the following formula. Alternatively, an unflavored pastry cream can be used as the base; the liqueur, fruit or chocolate is then added to each portion separately.

When making a soufflé, the custard base and egg whites should be at room temperature. First, the egg whites will whip to a better volume, and second, if the base is approximately the same temperature as the egg whites, the two mixtures can be more easily incorporated. The egg whites are whipped to stiff peaks with a portion of the sugar for stability. The whipped egg whites are then gently folded into the base immediately before baking.

A soufflé is baked in a straight-sided mold or individual ramekin. Keep the mixture from touching the top edge of the mold so it will rise evenly. The finished soufflé should be puffy with a lightly browned top. It should rise well above the rim of the baking dish. A soufflé must be served immediately, before it collapses. A warm custard sauce (crème anglaise) is often served as an accompaniment to a sweet soufflé.

A frozen soufflé is not a true soufflé. Rather, it is a creamy custard mixture thickened with eggs or gelatin, lightened with whipped egg whites or whipped cream and then frozen before serving. (Frozen dessert soufflés are discussed in Chapter 16, Ice Cream and Frozen Desserts.)

▶ PROCEDURE FOR PREPARING BAKED SOUFFLÉS

1 Butter the mold or ramekins and dust with granulated sugar. Preheat the oven to approximately 425°F (220°C).

2 Prepare the custard base. Add flavorings as desired.

3 Whip the egg whites and sugar to stiff peaks. Fold the whipped egg whites into the base.

4 Pour the mixture into the prepared mold or ramekins and bake immediately.

CHOCOLATE SOUFFLÉS

Yield: 8 Servings

Ingredient	US	Metric
Orange juice	1 pt.	500 ml
Egg yolks	5.3 oz. (8 yolks)	160 g
Granulated sugar	4 oz.	120 g
All-purpose flour	3 oz.	90 g
Bittersweet chocolate, chopped fine	8 oz.	240 g
Orange liqueur	2 fl. oz.	60 ml
Butter, melted	as needed	as needed
Granulated sugar	as needed	as needed
Egg whites	1 lb. (16 whites)	480 g
Powdered sugar, optional	as needed	as needed

1 To prepare the base, heat the orange juice to lukewarm in a heavy saucepan.

2 Whisk the egg yolks with 3 ounces (90 grams) of the sugar in a large mixing bowl. Whisk in the flour and warm orange juice, then return the mixture to the saucepan.

3 Cook over medium-low heat, stirring constantly, until the custard is thick. Do not allow it to boil. Remove from the heat.

4 Stir in the chocolate until completely melted. Stir in the liqueur. Cover this base mixture with plastic wrap to prevent a skin from forming. Hold for use at room temperature. (Unused base can be kept overnight in the refrigerator; it should be brought to room temperature before mixing with the egg whites.)

5 To prepare the soufflés, brush 4-fluid-ounce (120-milliliter) ramekins with melted butter and dust with granulated sugar.

6 Preheat the oven to 425°F (220°C). Place a sheet pan in the oven, onto which you will place the soufflés for baking. (This makes it easier to remove the hot soufflé cups from the oven.)

7 Whip the egg whites to stiff peaks with the remaining 1 ounce (30 grams) of the sugar. Fold the whites into the chocolate base and spoon the mixture into the prepared ramekins. The ramekins should be filled to within ¼ inch (6 millimeters) of the rim. Smooth the top of each soufflé with a spatula and bake immediately.

8 The soufflés are done when well risen and golden brown on top and the edges appear dry, approximately 12 minutes. Do not touch a soufflé to test doneness.

9 Sprinkle the soufflés with powdered sugar if desired and serve immediately.

Approximate values per serving: **Calories** 350, **Total fat** 15 g, **Saturated fat** 8 g, **Cholesterol** 210 mg, **Sodium** 65 mg, **Total carbohydrates** 48 g, **Protein** 10 g, **Vitamin A** 10%, **Vitamin C** 50%

1 Folding the whipped egg whites into the chocolate base.

2 Filling the ramekins.

3 The finished soufflé, ready for service.

▶ CREAMS

Creams (Fr. *crèmes*) include light, fluffy or creamy-textured dessert items made with whipped egg whites or whipped cream. Some, such as **Bavarian creams** and **chiffons,** are thickened with gelatin. Others, such as **mousses** and **crèmes Chantilly,** are softer and lighter. The success of all, however, depends on properly whipping and incorporating egg whites or heavy cream.

Review the material on whipping cream in Chapter 4, Bakeshop Ingredients. Note that whipping cream has a milkfat content of 30 to 36 percent. When preparing any whipped cream, be sure that the cream, the mixing bowl and all utensils are well chilled and clean. A warm bowl can melt the butterfat, destroying the texture of the cream. Properly whipped cream should increase two to three times in volume.

CRÈME CHANTILLY

Crème Chantilly is simply heavy cream whipped to soft peaks and flavored with sugar and vanilla. It can be used for garnishing pastry or dessert items.

When making crème Chantilly, the vanilla extract and sugar should be added after the cream begins to thicken. Either granulated or powdered sugar may be used; there are advantages and disadvantages to both. Granulated sugar assists in forming a better foam than powdered sugar, but it may cause the cream to feel gritty. Powdered sugar dissolves more quickly and completely than granulated sugar, but does nothing to assist with foaming. Whichever sugar is used, it should be added just before the whipping is complete to avoid interfering with the cream's volume and stability. When properly whipped, heavy cream expands two to two and a half times in volume.

CRÈME CHANTILLY (CHANTILLY CREAM)   RECIPE 15.9

Yield: 2–2½ qt. (2–2½ lt)

Ingredient	US	Metric
Heavy cream, chilled	1 qt.	1 lt
Powdered sugar	3 oz.	90 g
Vanilla extract	0.3 fl. oz. (2 tsp.)	10 ml

1 Place the cream in a chilled mixing bowl. Using a balloon whisk, whisk the cream until slightly thickened.
2 Add the sugar and vanilla and continue whisking to the desired consistency. The cream should be smooth and light, not grainy. Do not overwhip.
3 Crème Chantilly may be stored in the refrigerator several hours. If the cream begins to soften, gently rewhip as necessary.

Properly whipped Crème Chantilly.

VARIATION:
Chocolate Chantilly—Melt 1 pound 2 ounces (540 grams) bittersweet chocolate to 120°F (49°C) and remove from the heat. Whip the heavy cream to medium peaks. Whisk one-quarter of the whipped cream into the chocolate vigorously. Gently fold in the remaining cream. This mixture will have the texture of velvety ganache.

Approximate values per 1-fl.-oz. (30-ml) serving: **Calories** 60, **Total fat** 6 g, **Saturated fat** 3.5 g, **Cholesterol** 20 mg, **Sodium** 5 mg, **Total carbohydrates** 2 g, **Protein** 0 g

CHARLOTTE, SWEET CHARLOTTE

The original charlotte was created during the 18th century and named for the wife of King George III of England. It consisted of an apple compote baked in a round mold lined with toast slices. A few decades later, the great French chef Carême adopted the name but altered the concept in response to a kitchen disaster. When preparing a grand banquet for King Louis XVIII, he found that his gelatin supply was insufficient for the Bavarian creams he was making, so Carême steadied the sides of his sagging desserts with ladyfingers. The result became known as charlotte russe, probably due to the reigning fad for anything Russian. A fancier version, known as charlotte royale, is made with pinwheels or layers of spongecake and jam instead of ladyfingers. The filling for either should be a classic Bavarian cream.

BAVARIAN CREAM

A Bavarian cream (Fr. *bavarois*) is prepared by first thickening custard sauce with gelatin, then folding in whipped cream. The final product is poured into a mold and chilled until firm enough to unmold and slice. Although a Bavarian cream can be molded into individual servings, it is often poured into a round mold lined with spongecake or ladyfingers to create the classic dessert known as a **charlotte.**

Bavarians can be flavored by adding chocolate, puréed fruit, chopped nuts, extracts or liquors to the custard sauce base. Layers of fruit or liqueur-soaked spongecake can also be added for flavor and texture.

When thickening a dessert cream with gelatin, it is important to use the correct amount of gelatin. If not enough gelatin is used or it is not incorporated completely, the cream will not become firm enough to unmold. If too much gelatin is used, the cream will be tough and rubbery. An equal amount by weight of sheet gelatin may be substituted for granulated gelatin. Refer to Chapter 4, Bakeshop Ingredients, for information on using gelatin.

▶ PROCEDURE FOR PREPARING BAVARIAN CREAMS

1 Prepare a custard sauce of the desired flavor.
2 While the custard sauce is still quite warm, stir in softened sheet gelatin. (Or, bloom the granulated gelatin in cold water 5 minutes. Melt the gelatin, then pour the melted gelatin into the warm custard sauce.) Make sure the gelatin is completely incorporated.
3 Chill the custard until almost thickened, stirring it from time to time to prevent lumps from forming, then fold in the whipped cream.
4 Pour the Bavarian into a mold or charlotte form. Chill until set.

RECIPE 15.10

FRESH FRUIT BAVARIAN

Yield: 1 qt. (1 lt)

Fresh fruit such as 2 kiwis, 1 banana or ½ pint (¼ liter) raspberries, blueberries or wild strawberries		
Honey	0.75 oz.	22 g
Kirsch or brandy	1 fl. oz.	30 ml
Egg yolks	2.6 oz. (4 yolks)	80 g
Granulated sugar	4 oz.	120 g
Milk	8 fl. oz.	240 ml
Vanilla bean, split	½	½
Sheet gelatin, softened	0.5 oz.	15 g
Heavy cream	12 fl. oz.	360 ml

1 Lightly spray the bottom of a 1-quart (1-liter) mold with spray pan release. If a smooth mold is being used, line it with a sheet of plastic wrap, allowing the wrap to extend beyond the mold's edges.

1 Adding gelatin to the custard base.   **2** Folding in the whipped egg whites.

2 Peel and thinly slice the fruit if necessary. Mix the honey and the Kirsch and pour over the fruit. Chill while preparing the Bavarian cream.

3 Prepare a vanilla custard sauce using the egg yolks, sugar, milk and vanilla bean. Remove from the saucepan.

4 Add softened sheet gelatin to the hot custard. Chill until thick, but do not allow the custard to set.

5 Whip the cream until stiff and fold it into the chilled and thickened custard. Pour approximately one-third of this mixture (the Bavarian cream) into the mold. Arrange half of the fruit on top. Pour half of the remaining Bavarian cream on top of the fruit and top with the remaining fruit. Fill with the rest of the Bavarian cream. Chill until completely set, approximately 2 hours.

6 Unmold onto a serving dish. Garnish the top with additional fruit and whipped cream as desired.

VARIATION:

Charlotte—Line a 1½-quart (1½-liter) charlotte mold with Ladyfingers (page 415), then fill with layers of fruit and Bavarian cream. Invert onto a serving platter when firm and garnish with whipped cream.

Approximate values per 3½-oz. (105-g) serving: **Calories** 230, **Total fat** 15 g, **Saturated fat** 9 g, **Cholesterol** 135 mg, **Sodium** 30 mg, **Total carbohydrates** 19 g, **Protein** 3 g, **Vitamin A** 20%, **Vitamin C** 25%

CHIFFON

A chiffon is similar to a Bavarian except that whipped egg whites instead of whipped cream are folded into the thickened base. The base may be a custard or a fruit mixture thickened with cornstarch. Although a chiffon may be molded like a Bavarian, it is most often used as a pie or tart filling.

▶ PROCEDURE FOR PREPARING CHIFFONS

1 Prepare the base, which is usually a custard or a fruit mixture thickened with cornstarch.

2 Add gelatin to the warm base.

3 Fold in whipped egg whites.

4 Pour into a mold or prebaked pie shell and chill.

RECIPE 15.11

LIME CHIFFON

Yield: 1 Pie, 10 in. (25 cm), 8 Servings

Granulated gelatin	0.25 oz. (2½ tsp.)	7.5 g
Water	5 fl. oz.	150 ml
Granulated sugar	7 oz.	210 g
Fresh lime juice	3 fl. oz.	90 ml
Lime zest, grated fine	0.2 oz. (1 Tbsp.)	6 g
Egg yolks	2.6 oz. (4 yolks)	80 g
Egg whites	4 oz. (4 whites)	120 g

1 Bloom the granulated gelatin in 1 fluid ounce (30 milliliters) of the water.
2 Combine 4 ounces (120 grams) of the sugar, the remaining water, lime juice, lime zest and egg yolks in a bowl over a pan of simmering water.
3 Whisk the egg-and-lime mixture together vigorously until it begins to thicken. Melt the gelatin, then add it to the egg-and-lime mixture. Continue whipping until very thick and foamy.
4 Remove from the heat, cover and refrigerate until cool and as thick as whipping cream.
5 Meanwhile, whip the egg whites to soft peaks. Whip in the remaining sugar and continue whipping until stiff but not dry.
6 Fold the whipped egg whites into the egg-and-lime mixture. Pour into a prepared pie crust or serving dishes and chill for several hours, until firm.

VARIATIONS:

Lemon Chiffon—Substitute lemon juice and lemon zest for the lime juice and lime zest.

Orange Chiffon—Substitute orange juice for the lime juice and for 4 fluid ounces (120 milliliters) of the water. Substitute orange zest for the lime zest. Reduce the amount of sugar in the egg yolk mixture to 1 ounce (30 grams).

Approximate values per serving: **Calories** 140, **Total fat** 2.5 g, **Saturated fat** 1 g, **Cholesterol** 105 mg, **Sodium** 35 mg, **Total carbohydrates** 26 g, **Protein** 4 g, **Claims**—low fat; low saturated fat; low sodium

MOUSSE

The term *mousse* applies to an assortment of dessert creams not easily classified elsewhere. A mousse is similar to a Bavarian or chiffon in that it is lightened with whipped cream, whipped egg whites, whipped egg yolks cooked into a bombe mixture (discussed in Chapter 16, Ice Cream and Frozen Desserts) or all three. A mousse is generally softer than a Bavarian, however, and is generally too soft to mold. A mousse may be served alone as a dessert or used as a filling in pies, cakes, tortes or pastry items. Sweet mousses can be based on a custard sauce, melted chocolate or puréed fruit.

▶ PROCEDURE FOR PREPARING MOUSSES

1 Prepare the base, which is usually a custard sauce, melted chocolate or puréed fruit.
2 If using gelatin, soften it first, then dissolve it in the warm base.
3 Fold in whipped egg whites (if using). If the base is slightly warm when the egg whites are added, their proteins will coagulate, making the mousse firmer and more stable.

4 Allow the mixture to cool completely, then fold in whipped cream (if using). Note that the egg whites are folded in before any whipped cream. Although the egg whites may deflate somewhat during folding, if the cream is added first it may become overwhipped when the egg whites are added, creating a grainy or coarse product.

CLASSIC CHOCOLATE MOUSSE   RECIPE 15.12

Yield: 1½–2 qt. (1½–2 lt)

Bittersweet chocolate	15 oz.	450 g
Unsalted butter	9 oz.	270 g
Egg yolks, pasteurized	4.6 oz. (7 yolks)	140 g
Egg whites, pasteurized	11 oz. (11 whites)	330 g
Granulated sugar	2.5 oz.	75 g
Heavy cream	8 fl. oz.	240 ml

1 Melt the chocolate and butter in a double boiler over low heat. Stir until no lumps remain.

2 Allow the mixture to cool slightly, then whisk in the egg yolks, a small amount at a time.

3 Beat the egg whites until soft peaks form. Slowly beat in the sugar and continue beating until stiff peaks form. Fold the whipped egg whites into the chocolate mixture.

4 Whip the cream to soft peaks. Allow the mousse to cool, then fold in the whipped cream. Make sure no streaks of egg white or cream remain.

5 Spoon the mousse into serving bowls or chill completely and pipe into bowls or baked tartlet shells. The mousse may be used as a cake or pastry filling.

Approximate values per 3-fl.-oz. (90-ml) serving: **Calories** 370, **Total fat** 31 g, **Saturated fat** 18 g, **Cholesterol** 215 mg, **Sodium** 50 mg, **Total carbohydrates** 16 g, **Protein** 7 g, **Vitamin A** 25%

1 Folding in the whipped egg whites.

2 Folding in the whipped cream.

MOUSSE FILLINGS

When a mousse serves as a filling in a layered torte (see Chapter 14, Cakes and Tortes), it may contain a small amount of gelatin to stabilize the mousse. Italian meringue is also used in place of some of the heavy cream. Since it contains no fat, Italian meringue does not interfere with the delicate flavor of a fruit purée.

To ensure the lightest and creamiest mousse, the fruit purée should be slightly warm when folded into the warm Italian meringue. This keeps the mousse light and prevents the gelatin from setting as soon as the cold whipped cream is added in the last step. When made with gelatin, a mousse should be used immediately in its desired application before it cools and sets. The formula for Apricot Mousse (page 450) illustrates the procedure for making a mousse with Italian meringue.

▶ PROCEDURE FOR PREPARING A MOUSSE WITH ITALIAN MERINGUE

1 Prepare the base, which is usually a fruit purée. Make certain the fruit purée is at room temperature, approximately 70°F (21°C). (Overheating the fruit purée may damage its flavor.) This makes for the lightest mousse.

2 Soften and melt gelatin, if necessary.

3 Prepare an Italian meringue. Whip the Italian meringue until it cools down to 120°F (49°C) Add the gelatin to the warm Italian meringue.

4 Fold the room-temperature purée into the Italian meringue in two stages using a balloon whisk. This may require transferring the meringue to a larger bowl.

5 Whip heavy cream to soft peaks. Fold the whipped cream into the meringue. Use the mousse immediately before the gelatin begins to set.

RECIPE 15.13	APRICOT MOUSSE

Yield: 4 lb. 9 oz. (2212 g)

Reduce the amount of gelatin by half if the mousse will not need to be sliced, as in a torte or tart.

Apricot purée	2 lb. 3 oz.	1 k
Egg whites	4 oz. (4 whites)	120 g
Granulated sugar	8 oz.	240 g
Water	3 fl. oz.	90 ml
Sheet gelatin, softened	0.75 oz.	22 g
Heavy cream, whipped to soft peaks	26 oz.	780 g

1 In a heavy saucepan over low heat, warm the apricot purée to room temperature, approximately 70°F (21°C).

2 Prepare an Italian meringue with the egg whites, sugar and water.

3 Add the softened sheet gelatin to the Italian meringue.

4 Transfer the Italian meringue from the mixer into a large bowl.

5 Delicately fold one-quarter of the apricot purée into the Italian meringue with a balloon whisk or rubber spatula. Gradually fold in the remaining apricot purée. Gently fold in the whipped cream, being careful not to overmix.

6 Use immediately. Pipe into serving dishes, tart shells or tortes.

Approximate values per 1-oz. (30-g) serving: **Calories** 60, **Total fat** 4 g, **Saturated fat** 2.5 g, **Cholesterol** 15 mg, **Sodium** 10 mg, **Total carbohydrates** 5 g, **Protein** 1 g, **Vitamin A** 10%

Table 15.1	**CREAM (CRÈME) COMPONENTS**

FOR A:	BEGIN WITH A BASE OF:	THICKEN WITH:	THEN FOLD IN:
Bavarian	Custard	Gelatin	Whipped cream
Chiffon	Custard or starch-thickened fruit	Gelatin	Whipped egg whites
Mousse	Melted chocolate, puréed fruit or custard	Nothing or gelatin	Whipped cream, whipped egg whites, whipped egg yolks or all three

CONVENIENCE PRODUCTS

Commercially prepared powders and mixes can be used to make a wide assortment of puddings, custards, mousses, gelatin desserts and creams. The advantages of these products are speed, quality control and reduced labor costs. Packaged mixes are simply prepared according to the directions provided by the manufacturer. For most mousses, gelatin desserts or creams, milk or other liquid is added to the powder, then it is whipped until the desired consistency is obtained. Cooking is not usually required. The pastry cook can often improve on the final product by adding whipped cream, fruit or an appropriate garnish. Flan, pudding and baked custard mixes may require cooking before serving. As with other convenience products, quality varies from merely adequate to very good. Sample and experiment with several brands to select the best for your operation.

CONCLUSION

If pastry doughs are the backbone of dessert preparations, then custards, creams, mousses and the like are the heart. The skills and techniques presented in this chapter are essential to successful pastry production. Many of these skills, such as whipping cream or preparing custards, are the basis for many great pastries presented in Chapter 10, Pies and Tarts, and Chapter 11, Pastry Doughs. Once you have mastered these skills as well as those discussed in Chapter 14, Cakes and Tortes, you will be able to prepare a wide repertoire of tempting desserts.

QUESTIONS FOR DISCUSSION

1 Eggs and dairy products are susceptible to bacterial contamination. What precautions should be taken to avoid food-borne illnesses when preparing custards?

2 Explain why pastry cream should be boiled and why custard sauce should not be boiled.

3 Identify three desserts that are based on baked custard.

4 Compare a classically prepared Bavarian, chiffon, mousse and soufflé. How are they similar? How are they different?

5 Why should the oven door be kept closed the entire time that a soufflé bakes?

RECIPE 15.14

CRÈME BRÛLÉE

CHEF VINCENT GUERITHAULT

For 17 years, Vincent Guerithault has been the chef owner of Vincent on Camelback, one of the more acclaimed restaurants in Phoenix, Arizona. A native of France, he worked at L'Oustau de Baumaniere in Les Baux de Provence and Maxime's and Fauchon in Paris before coming to the United States. He began his American career in 1976 when he joined Chicago's Le Français as sous-chef. Within 10 years, he had opened his eponymous restaurant. His experience in classic French cooking combined with the unique ingredients of the Southwest to create what patrons call his "bold, intriguing and inspiring" cooking.

VINCENT ON CAMELBACK, PHOENIX, AZ
Chef Vincent Guerithault

Note: This dish appears in the chapter opening photograph.

Yield: 3½ qt. (3½ lt)   **Method:** Stirred custard

Heavy cream	2 qt.	2 lt
Vanilla beans, split	2	2
Egg yolks	33 oz. (50 yolks)	990 g
Granulated sugar	20 oz.	600 g
Fresh berries	as needed	as needed
Tulipe Cookie cups (page 238)	as needed	as needed
Granulated sugar	as needed	as needed

1 Place the cream and the vanilla beans in a large, heavy saucepan. Heat just to a boil.

2 Whisk the egg yolks and sugar together until smooth and well blended.

3 Temper the egg mixture with one-third of the hot cream. Return the egg mixture to the saucepan and cook, stirring constantly, until very thick. Do not allow the custard to boil.

4 Remove from the heat and strain into a clean bowl. Cool over an ice bath, stirring occasionally.

5 To serve, place fresh berries in the bottom of each Tulipe Cookie cup. Top with several spoonfuls of custard.

6 Sprinkle granulated sugar over the top of the custard and caramelize with a propane torch. Serve immediately.

VARIATIONS:

Passion Fruit Crème Brûlée—Replace ½ quart (500 milliliters) of the cream with ½ quart (500 milliliters) frozen, thawed passion fruit purée.

Coffee Crème Brûlée—Omit the vanilla bean. Add 1–1.5 fluid ounces (30–45 milliliters) coffee extract or compound to the finished custard.

Ginger Crème Brûlée—Omit the vanilla bean. Peel and coarsely chop a 2-inch (5-centimeter) piece of fresh ginger. Steep the ginger in the warm cream 30 minutes, and then proceed with the formula. The ginger will be strained out in Step 4.

Approximate values per 5-fl.-oz. (150-ml) serving: **Calories** 460, **Total fat** 36 g, **Saturated fat** 20 g, **Cholesterol** 480 mg, **Sodium** 135 mg, **Total carbohydrates** 26 g, **Protein** 7 g, **Vitamin A** 50%

RECIPE 15.15

PASTRY CREAM FILLING

Because it is thickened with cornstarch, this pastry cream retains more gloss and translucence than one thickened with flour. Use this formula interchangeably with the pastry cream formula on page 436 as a filling for pies, tarts or cakes or in any formula calling for pastry cream.

Yield: 3 lb. (1460 g)   **Method:** Stirred custard

Milk	24 fl. oz.	720 ml
Heavy cream	8 fl. oz.	240 ml
Granulated sugar	7.5 oz.	225 g
Egg yolks	6.6 oz. (10 yolks)	200 g
Cornstarch	2.5 oz.	75 g

1 Boil the milk, cream and 3 ounces (120 grams) of the sugar in a large stainless steel saucepan.

2 Whisk the egg yolks in a mixing bowl and gradually add the remaining sugar. Whisk in the cornstarch to combine.

3 Temper the egg yolk mixture with one-quarter of the boiling milk. Return the egg mixture to the pan and cook, whisking vigorously until the cream boils and is well thickened.

4 Remove the filling from the heat and chill over an ice bath, then cover and keep refrigerated. This cream should keep 3 to 4 days.

VARIATIONS:

Mousseline Cream Filling—Whip 12 fluid ounces (360 milliliters) heavy cream to stiff peaks. Fold into the chilled Pastry Cream Filling.

White Chocolate Mousseline Pastry Cream—Remove the pastry cream from the heat in Step 3 and stir in 10 ounces (300 grams) finely chopped white chocolate and 0.5 fluid ounce (15 milliliters) vanilla extract. Chill the cream to 80°F (27°C), then fold in 8 fluid ounces (360 milliliters) heavy cream whipped to medium peaks. Cover and chill until needed. Yield: 3 pounds 11 ounces (1775 grams)

Chocolate Buttercream Filling—Whip 1 pound (480 grams) butter, 10 ounces (300 grams) powdered sugar and 1 fluid ounce (30 milliliters) vanilla extract in a mixing bowl until light. Add 1 pound 8 ounces (720 grams) cold pastry cream and mix until combined. Turn off the machine and add 14 ounces (420 grams) semisweet chocolate, melted and cooled to 88°F (31°C). Whip until well blended. Yield: 4 pounds (1950 grams)

Approximate values per 1-fl.-oz. (30-ml) serving: **Calories** 70, **Total fat** 3.5 g, **Saturated fat** 2 g, **Cholesterol** 60 mg, **Sodium** 10 mg, **Total carbohydrates** 7 g, **Protein** 1 g

DIPLOMAT CREAM FILLING   RECIPE 15.16

Yield: 5 qt. (5 lt)

Pastry Cream, chilled (page 436)	1 gal.	4 lt
Raspberry liqueur	4 fl. oz.	120 ml
Granulated gelatin	1½ oz.	42 g
Water	6 fl. oz.	170 ml
Whipped cream	1 qt.	1 lt

1 Place the Pastry Cream in a large mixer bowl and whip on high speed until smooth. Add the raspberry liqueur.

2 Bloom the granulated gelatin in the water, then place over a low flame and heat to dissolve.

3 Add one quarter of the raspberry-flavored Pastry Cream to the gelatin. Place over a low flame and whip by hand until smooth and the gelatin is incorporated. Add this mixture to the rest of the Pastry Cream.

4 Fold in the whipped cream.

Approximate values per 1-oz. (30-g) serving: **Calories** 40, **Total fat** 2 g, **Saturated fat** 1 g, **Cholesterol** 30 mg, **Sodium** 10 mg, **Total carbohydrates** 5 g, **Protein** 1 g

RECIPE 15.17

CRÈME CHIBOUST

Yield: 1 pt. (500 ml)   **Method:** Stirred custard

Milk	6 fl. oz.	180 ml
Vanilla bean	½	½
Egg yolks	2 oz. (3 yolks)	60 g
Granulated sugar	1.5 oz.	45 g
Cornstarch	0.6 oz. (2 Tbsp.)	16 g
Sheet gelatin, softened	0.25 oz.	7 g

Italian meringue:

Granulated sugar	6 oz.	180 g
Water	1.5 fl. oz.	45 ml
Egg whites	3 oz. (3 whites)	90 g
Cream of tartar	0.02 oz. (⅛ tsp.)	0.6 g

1 Prepare a pastry cream by heating the milk and vanilla bean just to a boil. Whisk the egg yolks, sugar and cornstarch together. Temper with one-third of the hot milk, then return the mixture to the saucepan and cook over moderate heat until thick. The pastry cream should be allowed to boil briefly to properly gelatinize the starch. Remove the cream from the heat and transfer to a clean bowl.

2 Stir the softened sheet gelatin into the hot cream. Cover and set aside but do not chill or allow the cream to set while preparing the Italian meringue.

3 Prepare an Italian meringue using the remaining ingredients. Whip the meringue just until the hot syrup is incorporated, approximately 1 minute.

4 Quickly and thoroughly incorporate one-third of the hot meringue into the warm pastry cream with a spatula. Gently fold in the remaining meringue.

Approximate values per 1-fl.-oz. (30-ml) serving: **Calories** 80, **Total fat** 1.5 g, **Saturated fat** 0.5 g, **Cholesterol** 40 mg, **Sodium** 20 mg, **Total carbohydrates** 14 g, **Protein** 3 g, **Claims**—low fat; low saturated fat; very low sodium

RECIPE 15.18

PASSION FRUIT CRÈME CHIBOUST

Yield: Approximately 1 lb. 10 oz. (797 g)   **Method:** Stirred custard

Passion fruit juice	6 fl. oz.	180 ml
Heavy cream	3 fl. oz.	90 ml
Egg yolks	3.3 oz. (5 yolks)	100 g
Granulated sugar	8 oz.	240 g
Cornstarch	1 oz.	30 g
Sheet gelatin, softened	0.25 oz.	7 g
Powdered sugar	as needed	as needed
Egg whites	5 oz. (5 whites)	150 g
Water	2 fl. oz.	60 ml

1 Bring the juice and cream to a boil in a large stainless steel saucepan.

2 Whisk the egg yolks and 3 ounces (90 grams) of the sugar to a ribbon, then add the cornstarch. Temper with half of the hot cream.

3 Return the tempered egg mixture to the saucepan and bring to a boil while vigorously whisking. Once the custard has come to a boil and thickened, remove from heat and pour into a clean bowl.

4 Stir the softened sheet gelatin into the cream until it is dissolved and smooth. Scrape down the bowl and lightly dust the surface with powdered sugar to prevent a crust from forming. Do not chill the cream.

5 Meanwhile, prepare an Italian meringue with the egg whites, remaining sugar and water. Delicately fold the Italian meringue into the hot passion fruit cream.

6 Use immediately. Pour the cream into a serving container or torte or other mold before it sets. This will keep refrigerated several days.

Approximate values per 1-oz. (30-g) serving: **Calories** 90, **Total fat** 2.5 g, **Saturated fat** 1 g, **Cholesterol** 45 mg, **Sodium** 15 mg, **Total carbohydrates** 16 g, **Protein** 2 g

RASPBERRY CREAM FILLING   RECIPE 15.19

Yield: 2 lb. (960 g)   **Method:** Stirred custard

Traditional French Buttercream (page 357)	14 oz.	420 g
Pastry Cream (page 436)	12 oz.	360 g
Raspberry purée	5 oz.	150 g
Raspberry compound	1 oz.	30 g

1 Cream the Traditional French Buttercream until light and fluffy. Set aside.

2 Combine the Pastry Cream, raspberry purée and raspberry compound.

3 Delicately fold the Pastry Cream into the Traditional French Buttercream. Use immediately.

Approximate values per 1-oz. (30-g) serving: **Calories** 90, **Total fat** 60 g, **Saturated fat** 3.5 g, **Cholesterol** 55 mg, **Sodium** 10 mg, **Total carbohydrates** 8 g, **Protein** 1 g

APRICOT FLAN   RECIPE 15.20

Yield: 2 lb. 9 oz. (1245 g)   **Method:** Baked custard

Eggs	10 oz. (6 eggs)	300 g
Granulated sugar	5 oz.	150 g
Sour cream	2 fl. oz.	60 ml
Heavy cream	6 fl. oz.	180 ml
Vanilla extract	0.5 fl. oz.	15 ml
Apricot purée	1 lb. 2 oz.	540 g
Fresh fruit (optional)	as needed	as needed
Candied Almonds (optional) (page 301)	as needed	as needed

1 Whisk the eggs and sugar in a mixing bowl until combined. Add the sour cream, heavy cream, vanilla and apricot purée.

2 Brush individual ramekins with melted butter and arrange in a 2-inch- (5-centimeter-) deep hotel pan. Pour the mixture into the prepared ramekins, filling to just below the rim.

3 Pour enough warm water into the hotel pan to reach halfway up the sides of the ramekins. Bake at 325°F (160°C) until the flan no longer makes ripples in the center and is set, approximately 1 hour.

4 Chill thoroughly in refrigerator before unmolding.

5 To unmold, run a small knife around the edge of the custard, invert onto the serving plate and give the ramekin a firm sideways shake. Garnish with fresh fruit or Candied Almonds.

Note: This flan and others may be baked in a variety of containers. Baking time will vary depending on the container used.

Approximate values per 1-fl-oz. (30-ml) serving: **Calories** 50, **Total fat** 3 g, **Saturated fat** 1.5 g, **Cholesterol** 40 mg, **Sodium** 10 mg, **Total carbohydrates** 5 g, **Protein** 1 g, **Vitamin A** 10%

RECIPE 15.21

CHERRY CLAFOUTI

Clafouti is a country-style dessert from the Loire region of France and is similar to a quiche. Stone fruits such as cherries, peaches or plums are baked in an egg custard, then served piping hot or at room temperature.

Yield: 1 Cake, 10 in. (25 cm)

Dark cherries, fresh or canned, pitted	1 lb.	480 g
Eggs	6.75 oz. (4 eggs)	200 g
Milk	12 fl. oz.	360 ml
Granulated sugar	2 oz.	60 g
Vanilla extract	0.15 fl. oz. (1 tsp.)	5 ml
All-purpose flour	2 oz.	60 g
Powdered sugar	as needed	as needed

1 Drain the cherries and pat them completely dry with paper towels. Arrange them evenly on the bottom of a buttered 10-inch (25-centimeter) pan. Do not use a springform pan or removable-bottom tartlet pan.

2 Make the custard by whisking the eggs and milk together. Add the sugar, vanilla and flour and continue whisking until all the lumps are removed.

3 Pour the custard over the cherries and bake at 325°F (160°C) for 1 to 1½ hours. The custard should be lightly browned and firm to the touch when done.

4 Dust with powdered sugar and serve the clafouti while still warm.

Approximate values per ¹/₁₀-cake serving: **Calories** 170, **Total fat** 3.5 g, **Saturated fat** 1.5 g, **Cholesterol** 90 mg, **Sodium** 4.5 mg, **Total carbohydrates** 30 g, **Protein** 5 g, **Vitamin A** 6%

RECIPE 15.22

WARM DOUBLE CHOCOLATE SUN-DRIED CHERRY DIPLOMAT

Yield: 1 Mold, 2 qt. (2 lt)   **Method:** Baked custard

Butter, melted	as needed	as needed
Granulated sugar	as needed	as needed
Classic Spongecake (page 388)	as needed	as needed
Sun-dried cherries	12 oz.	360 g
Flan:		
Eggs	8.3 oz. (5 eggs)	250 g
Egg yolks	3.3 oz. (5 yolks)	100 g
Granulated sugar	7 oz.	210 g
Vanilla extract	0.5 fl. oz.	15 ml
Milk	24 fl. oz.	720 ml
Heavy cream	1 pt.	480 ml
Cocoa powder	2 oz.	60 g
Semisweet or bittersweet chocolate, chopped fine	4 oz.	120 g
Crème Anglaise (page 434)	as needed	as needed

1 Brush a shallow 2-quart (2-liter) mold with melted butter and sprinkle with granulated sugar.

2 Cut the Classic Spongecake in large dice ⅝ inch × ⅝ inch × ⅝ inch (1.5 cm × 1.5 cm × 1.5 cm) and place in the mold, alternating with sun-dried cherries.

3 Prepare the flan mixture. Whisk the eggs, egg yolks, sugar and vanilla in a mixing bowl until combined.

4 Heat the milk and heavy cream to 180°F (82°C) in a large saucepan. Add gradually to the egg mixture. Whisk in the cocoa powder and chocolate.

5 Pour the flan mixture into the mold, covering the spongecake cubes completely.

6 Bake at 325°F (160°C) until set, approximately 60 to 70 minutes. Cooking time will vary depending on the dimensions of the selected mold.

7 Completely chill the mold before serving. To unmold, run a knife around the inner edge of the mold and then invert the flan onto a platter.

8 Slice and serve with Crème Anglaise.

Approximate values per ¹/₁₀-serving: **Calories** 780, **Total fat** 42 g, **Saturated fat** 23 g, **Cholesterol** 530 mg, **Sodium** 150 mg, **Total carbohydrates** 95 g, **Protein** 18 g, **Vitamin A** 50%

CRÈME BRÛLÉE FOR TARTS

RECIPE 15.23

Yield: Approximately 3 lb. (1440 g)   **Method:** Baked custard

Egg yolks	6.6 oz. (10 yolks)	200 g
Eggs	3.3 oz. (2 eggs)	100 g
Brown sugar	7 oz.	210 g
Heavy cream	1 qt.	1 lt
Vanilla extract	1 fl. oz.	30 ml

1 Lightly butter a shallow half-size hotel pan or other container and place it on a sheet pan.

2 Combine the egg yolks and eggs in a mixing bowl. Gently whisk in the brown sugar just to blend. Stir in the cream and vanilla. Mix as little as possible to avoid creating a foamy layer on top the cream.

3 Pour the mixture into the prepared pan to a height of 1 ½ inches (4 centimeters).

4 Place sheet pan in a 325°F (160°C) oven. Fill the sheet pan with water to create a water bath. Bake until set, approximately 30 to 40 minutes.

5 Chill completely before using. Cover and keep refrigerated. This filling will keep 3 days in the refrigerator.

Approximate values per 1-oz. (30-g) serving: **Calories** 100, **Total fat** 8 g, **Saturated fat** 5 g, **Cholesterol** 75 mg, **Sodium** 15 mg, **Total carbohydrates** 5 g, **Protein** 1 g

CHOCOLATE POT DE CRÈME

RECIPE 15.24

Yield: 8 Servings, 4 fl. oz. (120 ml) each   **Method:** Baked custard

Milk	1 pt.	500 ml
Bittersweet chocolate	8 oz.	240 g
Granulated sugar	7 oz.	210 g
Vanilla extract	0.15 fl. oz. (1 tsp.)	5 ml
Coffee liqueur	1 fl. oz.	30 ml
Egg yolks	4.6 oz. (7 yolks)	140 g

1 Heat the milk just to a simmer. Add the chocolate and sugar. Stir constantly until the chocolate melts; do not allow the mixture to boil. Remove from the heat and add the vanilla and liqueur.

2 Whisk the egg yolks together, then slowly whisk them into the chocolate mixture.

3 Pour the custard into ramekins. Place the ramekins in a hotel pan and add enough hot water to reach halfway up the sides of the ramekins.

4 Bake at 325°F (160°C) until the custards are almost set in the center, approximately 30 minutes. Remove from the water bath and refrigerate until thoroughly chilled. Serve garnished with whipped cream and chocolate shavings.

Approximate values per serving: **Calories** 360, **Total fat** 16 g, **Saturated fat** 9 g, **Cholesterol** 195 mg, **Sodium** 40 mg, **Total carbohydrates** 46 g, **Protein** 6 g, **Vitamin A** 10%, **Calcium** 10%

RECIPE 15.25

PISTACHIO CITRUS CHEESECAKE

Yield: 4 Cakes, 10 in. (25 cm) each

Unsalted butter, melted	as needed	as needed
Pistachios, chopped fine	16 oz.	480 g
Cream cheese, softened	6 lb. 10 oz.	3180 g
All-purpose flour	3.5 oz.	105 g
Granulated sugar	2 lb. 5 oz.	1100 g
Eggs	30 oz. (18 eggs)	900 g
Heavy cream	10 fl. oz.	300 ml
Lemon zest, grated fine	0.75 oz.	22 g
Orange zest, grated fine	0.75 oz.	22 g

1 Brush the sides and bottoms of four cake pans (do not use springform pans) with melted butter. Coat with an even layer of pistachio nuts.

2 Beat the cream cheese until smooth. Add the flour and sugar and beat to incorporate completely.

3 Add the eggs slowly, then stir in the cream. Stir in the zests and pour the batter into prepared pans.

4 Place the cake pans in a water bath and bake at 325°F (160°C) until set, approximately 45 minutes.

5 Cool to room temperature before inverting onto a serving tray or cake cardboard. The nut crust becomes the top of the cakes.

Approximate values per $^1/_{10}$-cake serving: **Calories** 470, **Total fat** 34 g, **Saturated fat** 19 g, **Cholesterol** 190 mg, **Sodium** 250 mg, **Total carbohydrates** 32 g, **Protein** 10 g, **Vitamin A** 40%

RECIPE 15.26

INDIVIDUAL VANILLA CHEESECAKES

Yield: 12 Servings

Cream cheese, room temperature	1 lb. 6 oz.	660 g
Granulated sugar	10 oz.	300 g
Eggs	8.3 oz. (5 eggs)	240 g
Sour cream	1 lb. 7 oz.	700 g
Vanilla extract	0.3 fl. oz. (2 tsp.)	10 ml
Fresh fruit	as needed	as needed
Basic Nougatine (page 633)	as needed	as needed
Fruit Coulis (page 364)	as needed	as needed

1 Butter 12 2½-inch (7-centimeter) ramekins and set them on a sheet pan.

2 Blend the cream cheese and sugar in the bowl of a mixer fitted with a paddle on low speed until thoroughly combined. Scrape down the bowl and blend on low another minute until well blended.

3 Add the eggs a small amount at a time, scraping down the bowl and paddle after each addition. Add the sour cream and vanilla.

4 Pour the batter into the prepared ramekins.

5 Place sheet pan in a 325°F (160°C) oven. Fill the sheet pan with water to create a water bath. Bake until set but not cracked on the surface, approximately 45 minutes.

6 Remove from the water bath and chill immediately after removal from oven.

7 To serve, unmold the cheesecakes. Serve them garnished with fresh fruit, Basic Nougatine and Fruit Coulis.

VARIATION:

Cappuccino Cheesecakes—Butter eight 2½-inch (7-centimeter) ramekins. Make the cheesecake batter using 1 pound (480 grams) cream cheese, 4 ounces (120 grams) granulated sugar, 3.3 ounces (100 grams /2 eggs) eggs, 4 ounces (120 grams) sour cream, 1 fluid ounce (30 milliliters) coffee extract and 0.15 fluid ounces (1 teaspoon/ 5 milliliters) vanilla extract. Dust the unmolded cheesecakes with cocoa powder and powdered sugar before serving.

Approximate values per serving: **Calories** 430, **Total fat** 32 g, **Saturated fat** 19 g, **Cholesterol** 170 mg, **Sodium** 210 mg, **Total carbohydrates** 28 g, **Protein** 8 g, **Vitamin A** 25%

BREAD PUDDING WITH BOURBON SAUCE · RECIPE 15.27

Yield: 20 Servings	**Method:** Baked custard	
Raisins	8 oz.	240 g
Brandy	4 fl. oz.	120 ml
Unsalted butter, melted	2 oz.	60 g
White bread, day-old	24 oz.	720 g
Heavy cream	2 qt.	2 lt
Eggs	10 oz. (6 eggs)	300 g
Granulated sugar	1 lb. 10 oz.	780 g
Vanilla extract	1 fl. oz.	30 ml
Bourbon Sauce (recipe follows)	as needed	as needed

1 Combine the raisins and brandy in a small saucepan. Heat just to a simmer, cover and set aside.

2 Use a portion of the butter to thoroughly coat a 2-inch- (5-centimeter-) deep hotel pan. Reserve the remaining butter.

3 Tear the bread into chunks and place in a large bowl. Pour the cream over the bread and set aside until soft.

4 Beat the eggs and sugar until smooth and thick. Add the vanilla, the remaining melted butter and the raisins and brandy.

5 Toss the egg mixture with the bread gently to blend. Pour into the hotel pan and bake at 350°F (180°C) until browned and almost set, approximately 45 minutes.

6 Serve warm with 1–1½ fluid ounces (30–45 milliliters) of Bourbon Sauce per portion.

VARIATION:

Chocolate Bread Pudding—Omit the brandy, raisins and the melted butter. Melt 6 ounces (180 grams) unsalted butter and 12 ounces (360 grams) bittersweet chocolate together. Add the chocolate and butter to the egg mixture in Step 4. Serve with Vanilla Custard Sauce (page 434).

Approximate values per serving: **Calories** 700, **Total fat** 44 g, **Saturated fat** 26 g, **Cholesterol** 270 mg, **Sodium** 260 mg, **Total carbohydrates** 67 g, **Protein** 9 g, **Vitamin A** 50%, **Calcium** 10%, Iron 10%

BOURBON SAUCE

Yield: 1 qt. (1 lt)

Unsalted butter	8 oz.	240 g
Granulated sugar	1 lb.	480 g
Eggs	3.3 oz. (2 eggs)	100 g
Bourbon	8 fl. oz.	240 ml

1 Melt the butter; stir in the sugar and eggs and simmer to thicken.

2 Add the bourbon and hold in a warm place for service.

Approximate values per 1-fl.-oz. (30-ml) serving: **Calories** 150, **Total fat** 8 g, **Saturated fat** 5 g, **Cholesterol** 40 mg, **Sodium** 50 mg, **Total carbohydrates** 19 g, **Protein** 1 g, **Vitamin A** 8%

RECIPE 15.28

HOT LEMON SOUFFLÉ

Yield: 10 Servings

Lemon juice	8 fl. oz.	240 ml
Heavy cream	8 fl. oz.	240 ml
Lemon zest, grated	0.2 oz. (1 Tbsp.)	6 g
Egg yolks	2.6 oz. (4 yolks)	80 g
Granulated sugar	8 oz.	240 g
Cornstarch	1.3 oz.	40 g
Egg whites	12 oz. (12 whites)	360 g
Butter, melted	as needed	as needed
Granulated sugar	as needed	as needed
Powdered sugar	as needed	as needed

1 Prepare a pastry cream by combining the lemon juice and heavy cream in a nonreactive saucepan. Add the lemon zest and bring the cream to a boil.

2 In a mixing bowl, whisk the egg yolks and 4 ounces (120 grams) of the granulated sugar until foamy. Whisk in the cornstarch until well blended.

3 Temper the egg mixture with one-third of the lemon cream. Return the egg mixture to the saucepan. Bring the mixture to a boil, whisking constantly. Remove from the heat when thickened and cover with plastic wrap. Do not chill.

4 Whip the egg whites until foamy, then add the remaining sugar gradually. Whip the mixture until stiff but not dry. Fold the whites into the hot lemon mixture in three additions.

5 To bake the soufflés, brush 10 individual ramekins lightly with melted butter and sprinkle with granulated sugar. Spoon the mixture into the prepared ramekins to within ¼ inch (6 millimeters) of the rim. Bake immediately.

6 Bake at 375°F (190°C) until well puffed and lightly browned, approximately 20 to 25 minutes. Do not touch the soufflé to test doneness.

7 Sift powdered sugar over the top of the soufflés and serve immediately.

Approximate values per serving: **Calories** 230, **Total fat** 11 g, **Saturated fat** 6 g, **Cholesterol** 125 mg, **Sodium** 70 mg, **Total carbohydrates** 29 g, **Protein** 5 g, **Vitamin A** 10%, **Vitamin C** 20%

RECIPE 15.29

ONE-STEP LEMON CURD

Yield: 1½ qt. (1½ lt), approximately 5 lb. (2500 g)

Method: Stirred custard

Eggs	20 oz. (12 eggs)	600 g
Egg yolks	2.6 oz. (4 yolks)	80 g
Granulated sugar	2 lb.	960 g
Unsalted butter, cubed	1 lb.	480 g
Lemon zest, grated	1 oz.	30 g
Fresh lemon juice	12 fl. oz.	360 ml

1 Whisk all of the ingredients together in a large bowl.

2 Place the bowl over a pan of simmering water and cook, stirring frequently, until very thick, approximately 20 to 25 minutes.

3 Strain, cover and chill completely. Serve with scones or use as a filling for tartlets or layer cakes.

Approximate values per 1-fl.-oz. (30-ml) serving: **Calories** 170, **Total fat** 9 g, **Saturated fat** 5 g, **Cholesterol** 90 mg, **Sodium** 20 mg, **Total carbohydrates** 20 g, **Protein** 2 g, **Vitamin A** 10%

WHITE CHOCOLATE FRANGELICO BAVARIAN

RECIPE 15.30

Yield: 4 qt. (4 lt)

Heavy cream	2 qt.	2 lt
White chocolate, chopped	2 lb.	1 kg
Frangelico (hazelnut liqueur)	10 fl. oz.	300 ml
Sheet gelatin, softened	0.75 oz.	24 g
Vanilla extract	0.3 fl. oz. (2 tsp.)	10 ml

1 Bring 1 quart (1 liter) of the cream just to a boil. Immediately pour over the chopped chocolate. Stir until the chocolate melts.

2 Gently heat the Frangelico just to a simmer. Remove from the heat and stir in the softened sheet gelatin.

3 Add the softened gelatin mixture to the chocolate. Stir to blend well. Cool over an ice bath, stirring frequently.

4 Whip the remaining cream with the vanilla to stiff peaks.

5 Fold the whipped cream into the cold white chocolate mixture. Chill until ready to use.

Approximate values per 4-fl.-oz. (120-ml) serving: **Calories** 400, **Total fat** 32 g, **Saturated fat** 21 g, **Cholesterol** 90 mg, **Sodium** 50 mg, **Total carbohydrates** 22 g, **Protein** 5 g, **Vitamin A** 25%

CHOCOLATE CHIFFON PIE

RECIPE 15.31

Yield: 2 Pies, 9 in. (22 cm) each

Milk	20 fl. oz.	600 ml
Unsweetened chocolate	4 oz.	120 g
Granulated sugar	6 oz.	180 g
Salt	0.05 oz. (1/4 tsp.)	1.5 g
Egg yolks	4 oz. (6 yolks)	120 g
Sheet gelatin, softened	0.5 oz.	15 g
Egg whites	6 oz. (6 whites)	180 g
Vanilla extract	0.3 fl. oz. (2 tsp.)	10 ml
Crumb-crust pie shells, 9 in. (22 cm) each	2 shells	2 shells
Whipped cream	as needed for garnish	
Chocolate shavings	as needed for garnish	

1 Combine the milk and chocolate in a heavy saucepan and warm over low heat until the chocolate melts.

2 Add 4 ounces (120 grams) of the sugar, the salt and the egg yolks. Continue cooking, stirring constantly, until the mixture thickens. Do not boil.

3 Remove from the heat and add the softened sheet gelatin, stirring until completely dissolved. Pour the mixture into a bowl and chill until very thick.

4 Whip the egg whites to soft peaks. Add the vanilla and the remaining sugar and whip to stiff peaks. Fold the whites into the chocolate.

5 Mound the chiffon into the pie shells and chill several hours before serving. Garnish with unsweetened whipped cream and chocolate shavings.

Approximate values per 1/10-pie serving: **Calories** 210, **Total fat** 12 g, **Saturated fat** 4.5 g, **Cholesterol** 70 mg, **Sodium** 160 mg, **Total carbohydrates** 21 g, **Protein** 5 g

RECIPE 15.32

CHOCOLATE MOUSSE

Keeping the melted chocolate warm before adding it to the egg mixture preserves the light and creamy texture of this mousse.

Yield: 10 Servings, 4 oz. (120 g) each, 2½ lb. (1210 g) Mousse

Bitter or semisweet chocolate	11 oz.	330 g
Egg yolks	6 oz. (10 yolks)	180 g
Eggs	3.3 oz. (2 eggs)	100 g
Granulated sugar	4 oz.	120 g
Heavy cream, whipped	1 pt.	480 ml

1 In a microwave or over a double boiler, melt the chocolate to 130°F (54°C). Hold at this temperature by placing the bowl in a water bath of 135°F (57°C). Set aside.

2 Place the egg yolks, eggs and sugar in a mixer bowl over a pan of simmering water. Whisk until the mixture reaches 158°F (70°C) and is thickened.

3 Place the bowl on a mixer fitted with a whip. Whip until the mixture cools.

4 Fold one-third of the whipped cream into the warm chocolate. Using a balloon whisk, gently fold in the remaining cream and whipped-egg mixture. Use immediately.

VARIATION:

Flavored Chocolate Mousse—Add 1–2 fluid ounces (30–60 milliliters) liqueur, coffee extract or other extract to the finished mousse.

Approximate values per serving: **Calories** 440, **Total fat** 37 g, **Saturated fat** 20 g, **Cholesterol** 325 mg, **Sodium** 40 mg, **Total carbohydrates** 29 g, **Protein** 7 g, **Vitamin A** 20%

RECIPE 15.33

ORANGE MILK CHOCOLATE EARL GREY MOUSSE

Yield: 16 Servings, approximately 5 lb. (2400 g) Mousse

Milk	5 fl. oz.	150 ml
Heavy cream	5 fl. oz.	150 ml
Earl Grey tea leaves	1 oz.	30 g
Bergamot essential oil	0.5 fl. oz.	15 ml
Orange oil	0.5 fl. oz.	15 ml
Egg yolks	6 oz. (10 yolks)	180 g
Eggs	8.3 oz. (5 eggs)	250 g
Granulated sugar	4.5 oz.	135 g
Heavy cream, softly whipped	1 qt.	1 lt
Milk chocolate, melted and held at 130°F (54°C)	1 lb. 2 oz.	540 g

1 Bring the milk and cream to a boil. Add the tea leaves and steep 3 to 4 minutes. Strain out the tea leaves and add the bergamot and orange oils. Set aside.

2 Place the egg yolks, eggs and sugar in a mixer bowl over a pan of simmering water. Whisk until the mixture reaches 158°F (70°C) and is thickened. Set aside.

3 Stir one-third of the softly whipped cream into the melted chocolate in a large mixing bowl until smooth. Add the tea–cream mixture and combine well.

4 Add the whipped-egg mixture and the remaining tea cream in one step; fold delicately using a balloon whisk.

Approximate values per serving: **Calories** 490, **Total fat** 39 g, **Saturated fat** 23 g, **Cholesterol** 290 mg, **Sodium** 75 mg, **Total carbohydrates** 29 g, **Protein** 7 g, **Vitamin A** 25%, **Calcium** 15%

RASPBERRY MOUSSE

Yield: 1 qt. (1 lt)

Raspberries, puréed	12 oz.	360 g
Granulated sugar	3 oz.	90 g
Raspberry brandy	1 fl. oz.	30 ml
Sheet gelatin, softened	0.25 oz.	7 g
Heavy cream	8 fl. oz.	240 ml

1 Place the raspberry purée, sugar and brandy in a nonreactive saucepan and warm just to dissolve the sugar. Remove from the heat and strain through a fine chinois.

2 Add the softened sheet gelatin, stirring until it is dissolved. Chill the mixture until thick but not set.

3 Whip the cream to soft peaks and fold it into the raspberry mixture.

Approximate values per 3-fl.-oz. (90-ml) serving: **Calories** 180, **Total fat** 11 g, **Saturated fat** 7 g, **Cholesterol** 40 mg, **Sodium** 15 mg, **Total carbohydrates** 16 g, **Protein** 5 g, **Vitamin A** 10%

1 Adding the softened gelatin sheets to the warm raspberry purée.

2 Folding the softly whipped cream into the chilled raspberry purée.

RECIPE 15.35

RASPBERRY MOUSSELINE

Yield: 3 lb. 8 oz. (1680 g)

Raspberry purée	1.5 lb.	720 g
Raspberry liqueur (optional)	1.5 fl. oz.	45 ml
Granulated sugar	9 oz.	270 g
Water	3 fl. oz.	90 ml
Egg whites	5 oz. (5 whites)	150 g
Sheet gelatin, softened	0.5 oz.	15 g
Heavy cream, whipped to soft peaks	1 pt.	480 ml

1 Warm the raspberry purée to 85°F (29°C). Add the liqueur (if using).

2 Prepare an Italian meringue with the sugar, water and egg whites. Bring the sugar and water to a boil. Place the egg whites in the bowl of a mixer fitted with a whip. As the temperature of the boiling sugar approaches 220°F (104°C), begin whipping the egg whites. When the whites reach soft peaks, reduce the mixer speed and continue whipping.

3 When the sugar reaches the firm ball stage (246°F/119°C), remove it from the heat. Pour it into the whites, with the mixer running at high speed. Pour in a steady stream between the side of the bowl and the beater. Once all the sugar is incorporated, whip 1 more minute at high speed, then reduce to medium speed and whip until the meringue cools to approximately 120°F (49°C).

4 Add the softened gelatin to the warm Italian meringue. Stir a few seconds to dissolve the gelatin.

5 Add one-quarter of the raspberry purée to the Italian meringue to temper. Then fold in the remaining purée.

6 Fold in the whipped cream. Use immediately.

Approximate values per 1-oz. (30-g) serving: **Calories** 60, **Total fat** 3 g, **Saturated fat** 2 g, **Cholesterol** 10 mg, **Sodium** 10 mg, **Total carbohydrates** 6 g, **Protein** 1 g

---

RECIPE 15.36

LEMON-LIME MOUSSE

Reduce the amount of gelatin by half if the mousse will not need to be sliced, as in a torte or tart.

Yield: Approximately 2 lb. 14 oz. (1400 g)

Lemon juice	4 fl. oz.	120 ml
Lime juice	4 fl. oz.	120 ml
Grand Marnier	1 fl. oz.	30 ml
Egg whites	4 oz. (4 whites)	120 g
Granulated sugar	7 oz.	210 g
Water	3 fl. oz.	90 ml
Sheet gelatin, softened	0.75 oz.	21 g
Heavy cream, whipped to soft peaks	26 fl. oz.	780 ml

1 Bring the lemon and lime juices to a boil in a nonreactive saucepan to break down the enzyme in the citrus that might interfere with the gelatin. Let cool to room temperature (70°F to 80°F/21°C to 27°C) and set aside. Stir in the Grand Marnier.

2 Prepare an Italian meringue with the egg whites, sugar and water and whip until it cools to 120°F (49°C). Add the softened sheet gelatin to the Italian meringue. Transfer to a large mixing bowl. Fold in the cooled juice mixture.

3 Fold in the whipped cream and use immediately.

Approximate values per 1-oz. (30-g) serving : **Calories** 80, **Total fat** 6 g, **Saturated fat** 3.5 g, **Cholesterol** 20 mg, **Sodium** 10 mg, **Total carbohydrates** 6 g, **Protein** 2 g

CARAMEL MOUSSE

Reduce the amount of gelatin by half if the mousse will not need to be sliced, as in a torte or tart.

Yield: Approximately 2 lb. 8 oz. (1200 g)

Glucose or corn syrup	3.5 oz.	105 g
Granulated sugar	6 oz.	180 g
Water	2.5 fl. oz.	75 ml
Unsalted butter	1.5 oz.	45 g
Heavy cream, boiling	6 fl. oz.	180 ml
Vanilla extract	0.5 fl. oz.	15 ml
Cointreau or orange-flavored liqueur	0.5 fl. oz.	15 ml
Egg yolks	4 oz. (6 yolks)	120 g
Sheet gelatin, softened	0.5 oz.	15 g
Heavy cream, whipped to soft peaks	18 fl. oz.	540 ml

1 Combine the glucose or corn syrup, 4 ounces (120 grams) of the sugar and water in a large, deep saucepan. Stir while bringing the mixture to a boil. Wash away the sugar crystals from the sides of the pan. Without stirring any further, cook the mixture to an amber caramel, approximately 350°F (177°C). Do not let the mixture smoke and burn.

2 Carefully add the butter and the boiling cream to the caramel; be aware that the mixture will rise high in the pan. Stir, then bring back to a boil for 2 minutes. Remove from the heat and let cool to 86°F (30°C). Add the vanilla and liqueur. Set aside.

3 Place the egg yolks in a bowl and whisk in the remaining sugar. Heat the mixture over a bain marie, whisking constantly until it reaches 160°F (71°C), without scorching the yolks.

4 Transfer to the bowl of a mixer fitted with a whip. Add the softened sheet gelatin to the yolk mixture. Whip until lukewarm, approximately 86°F (30°C), then remove the bowl from the mixer.

5 Fold the yolk mixture into the caramel. Then fold in the whipped cream. Use immediately.

Approximate values per 1-oz. (30-g) serving: **Calories** 110, **Total fat** 8 g, **Saturated fat** 5 g, **Cholesterol** 65 mg, **Sodium** 10 mg, **Total carbohydrates** 7 g, **Protein** 1 g

RECIPE 15.38

MASCARPONE CREAM MOUSSE

Reduce the amount of gelatin by half if the mousse will not need to be sliced, as in a torte or tart.

Yield: Approximately 3 lb. (1500 g)

Mascarpone, warmed to 105°F (41°C)	1 lb. 5 oz.	630 g
Egg yolks	6 oz. (9 yolks)	180 g
Granulated sugar	8 oz.	240 g
Water	5 fl. oz.	150 ml
Sheet gelatin, softened	0.5 oz.	15 g
Heavy cream, whipped to soft peaks	1 pt.	480 ml

1 Place the warmed mascarpone in a large bowl.

2 Make a bombe mixture as described on page 477 by whipping the egg yolks in the bowl of a mixer fitted with a whip. Cook the sugar and water in a saucepan until the syrup reaches the soft ball stage (240°F/116°C).

3 Pour the sugar syrup into the yolks, with the mixer running at high speed. Pour in a steady stream between the side of the bowl and the beater. Once all the sugar is incorporated, whip 1 more minute at high speed, then reduce to medium speed and whip until the bombe mixture cools to approximately 110°F (43°C).

4 Add the softened sheet gelatin to the warm bombe batter. Stir until the gelatin dissolves completely.

5 Fold the bombe batter into the mascarpone cream.

6 Fold in the whipped cream. Use immediately.

Approximate values per 1-oz. (30-g) serving: **Calories** 110, **Total fat** 9 g, **Saturated fat** 5 g, **Cholesterol** 70 mg, **Sodium** 10 mg, **Total carbohydrates** 5 g, **Protein** 2 g

RECIPE 15.39

HONEY MOUSSE

Yield: Approximately 2 lb. (915 g)

Egg whites	4 oz. (4 whites)	120 g
Granulated sugar	2 oz.	60 g
Honey	6 oz.	180 g
Water	3 fl. oz.	90 ml
Sheet gelatin, softened	0.5 oz.	15 g
Vanilla extract	1 fl. oz.	30 ml
Grand Marnier	1 fl. oz.	30 ml
Candied citrus rind, diced (optional)	3 oz.	90 g
Heavy cream, whipped to soft peaks	1 pt.	480 ml

1 Prepare an Italian meringue with the egg whites, sugar, honey and water.

2 Add the softened sheet gelatin to the Italian meringue. Transfer it to a large mixing bowl. Fold in the vanilla, Grand Marnier and candied citrus rind, if using.

3 Fold in the whipped cream and use immediately.

Approximate values per 1-oz. (30-g) serving: **Calories** 90, **Total fat** 6 g, **Saturated fat** 3.5 g, **Cholesterol** 20 mg, **Sodium** 10 mg, **Total carbohydrates** 7 g, **Protein** 3 g

HAZELNUT CREAM FILLING

Yield: 4 lb. 12 oz. (2302 g)

Traditional French Buttercream (page 368)	2 lb.	960 g
Hazelnut paste, lump-free	12 oz.	360 g
Sheet gelatin, creamed	0.75 oz.	22 g
Heavy cream, whipped to soft peaks	1 qt.	960 ml

1 Combine the Traditional French Buttercream and hazelnut paste in a mixing bowl. Place over a bain marie of simmering water and whisk constantly to slightly soften the mixture without melting the buttercream. The mixture should be as soft as mayonnaise and approximately 100°F (38°C).

2 Melt the softened sheet gelatin and fold it into the hazelnut mixture.

3 Remove from the heat and fold in the whipped cream. (If the buttercream mixture is too firm or the heavy cream is whipped too stiff, the cream will curdle.) Use immediately.

Approximate values per 1-oz. (30-g) serving: **Calories** 120, **Total fat** 11 g, **Saturated fat** 6 g, **Cholesterol** 50 mg, **Sodium** 10 mg, **Total carbohydrates** 7 g, **Protein** 1 g

I DOUBT WHETHER THE WORLD HOLDS FOR ANYONE
A MORE SOUL-STIRRING SURPRISE THAN THE FIRST
ADVENTURE WITH ICE CREAM.
*—Heywood Campbell Broun, American journalist
and novelist (1888–1939)*

ICE CREAM AND FROZEN DESSERTS

AMBRIA RESTAURANT, Chicago, IL
Executive Pastry Chef Michel Briand

AFTER STUDYING THIS CHAPTER, YOU WILL BE ABLE TO:

▶ understand the churning method for making ice creams and sorbets

▶ understand the still-freezing method for preparing frozen desserts

▶ prepare a variety of ice creams, sorbets, and frozen desserts

Frozen desserts provide a pleasing cold and creamy contrast at the end of a meal. It is no wonder that ice cream is the world's best-selling dessert or that residents of the United States lead the world by consuming more than 5 gallons a year per person. Ice creams and sorbets are important components in the complex desserts served in restaurants discussed in Chapter 20, Restaurant Desserts. This chapter covers the most popular varieties of frozen desserts and the methods for producing them. With or without an ice cream freezer, frozen desserts can be made in any restaurant equipped with a standard freezer. No matter the season, the cool and comforting texture of ice cream and frozen desserts is welcomed by virtually every diner.

▶ ICE CREAM AND FROZEN DESSERTS

Frozen desserts are categorized by the freezing method employed, either churned or still-frozen. **Churned** frozen desserts may be dairy based, made from milk or custard, or nondairy, made from fruit, chocolate or other flavorings combined with sugar. Ice cream, gelato, sorbet and sherbet are all churned. **Still-frozen** desserts, known as semifreddi, are made from custards or mousses that are frozen without churning. These include frozen soufflés and parfaits as well as desserts assembled with ice cream such as **baked Alaska** and Vacherin or **bombes,** molds lined with cake and filled with ice cream, sorbets and frozen mousses and parfaits. Granita is a grainy type of frozen dessert made with fruit juice, wine or other liquids and sugar.

The character of a frozen dessert is determined by the freezing method used and the selection and ratio of ingredients.

CHURN-FROZEN DESSERTS

Ice cream, gelato, sorbet and sherbet are churn-frozen desserts made from a custard base or a fruit juice and sugar syrup. One hallmark of good ice cream, gelato and sorbet is smoothness. The ice crystals that would normally form during freezing are reduced when the mixture is constantly stirred or churned during freezing. The motion of the churn breaks up the crystals while adding air to the mixture. The air causes the mixture to expand in volume and lighten. **Overrun** refers to the additional volume created when air is churned into the product. Overrun is expressed as a percentage. Fifty percent overrun means that the ice cream or sorbet has expanded to one and one half times its original volume; 100 percent overrun is an ice cream or sorbet that has doubled in volume.

Good-quality ice creams and sorbets have enough air to make them light; inferior products often contain excessive overrun. Premium ice creams may have an overrun of up to 20 percent, while an inexpensive product may have 100 percent overrun. The difference becomes obvious when equal volumes are weighed. The type of equipment used to churn the ice cream and the amount placed in the freezer will affect overrun. The amount of milkfat and eggs in a formula will also affect overrun.

The higher fat content of ice cream and gelato as compared to sorbet gives the former a smoother **mouth feel** than the fruit- and sugar-based sorbet. The proper ratio of sugar in frozen mixtures ensures that the product will freeze; too

▶ **overrun** the amount of air churned into an ice cream during freezing

▶ **mouth feel** the sensation, other than flavor, that a food or beverage has in the mouth; a function of the item's body, texture and, to a lesser extent, temperature

ICE CREAM: FROM ANCIENT CHINA TO DOUBLE-FUDGE-BROWNIE-CHOCOLATE-CHIP WITH COOKIE DOUGH AND TOASTED ALMOND SLIVERS

Despite claims to the contrary, it is impossible to identify any one country as having invented ice cream. More likely, it was invented in several places around the world at various times.

Early ancestors of today's ice creams were flavored water ices, which have been popular in China since prehistoric times. They have also been popular in the Mediterranean and Middle East since the Golden Age of Greece. In fact, Alexander the Great had a penchant for wine-flavored ices, made with ice brought down from the mountains by runners. The Roman emperor Nero served his guests mixtures of fruit crushed with snow and honey. The Saracens brought their knowledge of making flavored ices with them when they migrated to Sicily in the 9th century. And 12th-century Crusaders returned to Western Europe with memories of Middle Eastern sherbets.

The Italians are said to have developed gelato from a recipe brought back from China by Marco Polo in the 13th century. Somehow the dish spread to England by the 15th century, where it was recorded that King Henry V served it at his coronation banquet. Catherine de Medici brought the recipe with her when she married the future king of France in 1533. A different flavor was served during each of the 34 days of their marriage festivities.

Ice cream was first sold to the public in Paris during the late 17th century. It was available at fashionable cafés serving another new treat: coffee. French chefs quickly developed many elaborate desserts using ice creams, including bombes, coupes and parfaits.

Many of this country's founders—Thomas Jefferson, Alexander Hamilton and James and Dolley Madison—were confirmed ice cream addicts. George Washington spent more than $200, a very princely sum, for ice cream during the summer of 1790.

The mechanized ice cream freezer was invented in 1846, setting the stage for mass production and wide availability. By the late 19th century, ice cream parlors were popular gathering places. (Some of today's ice cream parlors still take their décor from "Gay Nineties" motifs.)

Despite the disappearance of most ice cream wagons, soda fountains and lunch counters, all of which were popular ice cream purveyors for much of the 20th century, ice cream sales have never waned. Today, more than 80 percent of all ice cream is sold in supermarkets or convenience stores. The public's demand for high-fat, homemade-style "super-premium" ice creams with rich and often-elaborate flavor combinations shows no sign of declining.

much sugar and the mixture will be slushy. Sugar prevents large crystals from forming, resulting in a smoother product.

When making any frozen mixture, remember that cold dulls flavors. Although perfect at room temperature, flavors seem weaker when the mixture is cold. Increased overrun weakens the concentration of flavor. Thus, it may be necessary to oversweeten or overflavor creams, custards or syrups that will be frozen for service. Although liquors and liqueurs are common flavoring ingredients, alcohol drastically lowers a liquid mixture's freezing point. Too much alcohol will prevent the mixture from freezing; thus any liqueurs or liquors must be used in moderation.

Liquid flavorings and purées are added to ice cream or sorbet mixtures before freezing. Solids—diced fresh fruit, chocolate chips and nuts—are mixed in when the mixture is nearly frozen, yet still soft enough to stir. Otherwise these pieces would disintegrate during churning. Fresh and dried fruits and nuts may be conditioned by poaching in sugar syrup to adjust their moisture content, making them remain tender when frozen. Fudge and fruit swirls are folded into ice cream after churning is completed in order to maintain their integrity and visibility in the finished product.

ICE CREAM AND GELATO

Ice cream and gelato are custards that are churned during freezing. The procedure for making an ice cream or gelato base is the same as the procedure for making custard sauce discussed in Chapter 15, Custards and Creams. These custards can be made with milk and/or cream and whole eggs or egg yolks. Milkfat contributes richness and body to the ice cream. High-quality ice creams may contain as much as 24 percent milkfat, resulting in a dense rich product. (A higher fat content could result in a product so dense that it may have difficulty emulsifying and incorporating air during churning, thus limiting its overrun.)

The USDA has established standards for the labeling of frozen products. They require that products labeled "ice cream" contain at least 10 percent milkfat and 20 percent milk solids and have no more than 50 percent overrun.

▶ **baked Alaska** ice cream set on a layer of spongecake and encased in meringue, then baked until the meringue is warm and golden

▶ **bombe** two or more flavors of ice cream, or ice cream and sherbet, shaped in a spherical mold; each flavor is a separate layer that forms the shell for the next flavor

▶ **coupe** an ice cream sundae, especially one served with a fruit topping

▶ **parfait** ice cream served in a long, slender glass with alternating layers of topping or sauce; also the name of the mousselike preparation that forms the basis for some still-frozen desserts

▶ **marquise** a frozen mousselike dessert, usually chocolate

▶ **Neapolitan** a three-layered loaf or cake of ice cream; each layer is a different flavor and a different color, a typical combination being chocolate, vanilla and strawberry

French-style ice creams (frozen custards) contain a higher percentage of egg yolks and cream than standard ice cream. Gelato is an Italian-style ice cream made primarily with milk. While it has a low milkfat content—from 4 to 9 percent—it is denser than American-style products because less air is incorporated during churning.

"Ice milk" refers to products that do not meet the standards for ice cream. Low-fat products made without cream or egg yolks are also available for the calorie-conscious. Frozen yogurt uses yogurt as its base. Although touted as a nutritious substitute for ice cream, frozen yogurt may have whole milk or cream added for richness and smoothness. Alternative ingredients including soy and rice milk make creamy frozen desserts available to those allergic to dairy. A formula for a soy milk–based frozen dessert is provided in Chapter 18, Healthful and Special-Needs Baking.

Stabilizers

In frozen mixtures, some water often remains that does not freeze during churning. **Stabilizers** bind the water and increase the mixture's ability to trap air and expand during churning. Commercially, stabilizers are added to ice creams, sorbets and sherbets to improve their texture and freezing abilities. Stabilizers include the eggs used in a formula as well as gums (guar or locust bean), carageenan, gelatin, pectin and other vegetable-derived ingredients. Inexpensive and mass-produced ice cream products often rely on excessive amounts of stabilizers or gelatin to create texture and aid in the overrun process. Stabilizers are less commonly used in the restaurant industry, where frozen products are made more frequently and in small batches.

Churning

Regardless of the formula, cooling an ice cream base before freezing is essential to ensure a smooth texture in the finished product. The longer a mixture takes to freeze in the machine, the more time it has to develop large ice crystals. A properly chilled ice cream base freezes quickly. An ice cream base that contains eggs should be matured by refrigerating it 24 hours before processing to help it achieve a smooth, creamy texture.

Many food service operations use ice cream makers that have internal freezing units to chill the mixture while churning it. Most commercial machines are suitable for churning either ice cream or sorbet. Follow the manufacturer's directions for using and cleaning any ice cream maker. Once churned, hold ice cream and sorbet in a freezer set to between 0°F and 6°F (−18°C and −15°C) so that it hardens quickly, then store frozen desserts in a freezer set to between 6°F and 14°F (−15°C and −11°C).

▶ PROCEDURE FOR PREPARING ICE CREAMS

1 Prepare a custard sauce. Place the milk and/or cream in a heavy saucepan. Add flavorings such as vanilla beans or ground coffee to infuse the cream at this time.
2 Whisk the egg yolks and sugar together in a mixing bowl.
3 Bring the liquid just to a boil. Temper the egg mixture with approximately one-third of the hot liquid.
4 Pour the tempered eggs into the remaining hot liquid and return the mixture to the heat.
5 Cook, stirring constantly, until warmed to 180°F to 186°F (82°C to 85°C).
6 Remove the cooked custard sauce from the hot saucepan immediately. If left in the hot saucepan, it will overcook. Flavorings may be added at this time.

7 Cool the custard sauce over an ice bath to 40°F (4°C). Store covered and refrigerated at 36°F (2°C) 24 hours to mature the ice cream base.

8 Process according to the machine manufacturer's directions.

ICE CREAM BASE   RECIPE 16.1

Yield: 2½ qt. (2.5 lt)   **Method:** Churned

Whole milk	1½ qt.	1½ lt
Heavy cream	1 pt.	480 ml
Vanilla bean, split (optional)	1	1
Egg yolks	10 oz (16 yolks)	300 g
Granulated sugar	20 oz.	600 g

1 Combine the milk and cream in a heavy saucepan and bring to a boil. Add the vanilla bean (if using).

2 Whisk the egg yolks and sugar together in a mixing bowl.

3 Temper the eggs with one-third of the hot milk. Return the egg mixture to the saucepan.

4 Cook over medium heat until slightly thickened. Pour through a fine mesh strainer into a clean bowl.

5 Chill the cooked ice cream base completely before processing.

6 Pour the mixture into an ice cream/sorbet machine and process according to the manufacturer's directions.

VARIATIONS:

Chocolate Ice Cream—Add approximately 9 ounces (270 grams) finely chopped bittersweet chocolate per quart (liter) of ice cream base. Add the chocolate to the hot mixture after it has been strained. Stir until completely melted.

Cappuccino Ice Cream—Steep the hot milk and cream with the vanilla bean and two or three cinnamon sticks. After the ice cream base is made, stir in 0.5 fluid ounce (30 milliliters) coffee extract.

Brandied Cherry Ice Cream—Drain the liquid from one 16-ounce (480-gram) can of tart, pitted cherries. Soak the cherries in 1.5 fluid ounces (45 milliliters) brandy. Prepare the ice cream base as directed, omitting the vanilla bean. Add the brandy-soaked cherries to the cooled custard before processing.

Approximate values per 6-fl.-oz. (180-ml) serving: **Calories** 370, **Total fat** 20 g, **Saturated fat** 11 g, **Cholesterol** 270 mg, **Sodium** 65 mg, **Total carbohydrates** 41 g, **Protein** 7 g, **Vitamin A** 25%

SORBET AND SHERBET

Sorbet is a churned mixture of sugar, water and fruit juice, wine, liqueurs or other flavorings. (Even some herb and vegetable flavoring are suitable for sorbet.) It is served as a first course, a palate refresher between courses or a dessert.

Sorbet may be made with fresh, frozen or canned fruit. A wide variety of quality, all-natural frozen purées are available for sorbet making. Granulated sugar or sugar syrup is added for flavor and body. Pasteurized egg whites may also be added during churning for improved texture; the protein in the whites coats the water crystals as the sherbet freezes. Often an invert sugar such as glucose or corn syrup replaces some of the granulated sugar to prevent graininess. *Sherbet* is an Americanization of the French word *sorbet,* which has taken on a slightly different meaning on this side of the Atlantic. When it contains fruit juice and sugar, sherbet is identical to sorbet. But milk is often added to the mixture before churning, making it somewhat richer than sorbet and better served at the end of a meal.

The ratio of sugar to fruit purée or juice depends to some extent on the natural sweetness of the specific fruit as well as personal preference. If too much sugar is used, however, the mixture will be soft and syrupy. If too little sugar is used, the sorbet will be very hard and grainy. Following the formula carefully helps avoid this problem. A saccharometer can also be used to measure the concentration of sugar in the mixture before freezing to ensure consistent results.

Measuring Sugar Concentrations

To achieve consistent texture and sweetness, use of a saccharometer is recommended when making sorbet, sherbet or granità. As discussed in Chapter 13, Syrups, Icings and Sauces, heating a solution of sugar and water increases the amount of sugar that will dissolve in the solution. A saccharometer shows the sugar content in a liquid mixture (see page 348).

The saccharometer is a hollow glass tube calibrated with either a density chart, Baumé chart or both. The density reading (D) is obtained where the instrument meets the surface level of the syrup; when a saccharometer is placed in 58°F (14°C) water, it will float exactly at the position marked 1.000 D (0° Baumé). As the percentage of sugar to water increases, the density reading will climb. A simple syrup made from equal amounts of sugar and water will measure 1.2407 D (28° Baumé). Higher temperatures can produce a lower reading, so always measure cold liquids.

Fruit sorbet tastes best at a density between 1.1333 and 1.1425 D (17° and 18° Baumé). Wine, alcohol, tea, coffee and aromatic plant sorbets should have a density reading between 1.1074 and 1.1333 D (13° and 17° Baumé). A sorbet mixture made with too little sugar and a lower-than-ideal density will be grainy and icy. Adding more of the basic sugar syrup called for in the formula will correct this. Water is added when the density reading is too high, thus preventing an overly sweet product. When a saccharometer is not available, follow the formula exactly, cooking the syrup as indicated. Should problems arise, remelt the sorbet, adding more water or sugar syrup as needed.

▶ PROCEDURE FOR PREPARING SHERBET OR SORBET

1 Make a base syrup by combing the water, sugar, invert sugar and stabilizers (if using). Boil 1 minute. Cool completely.

2 Combine the fruit purée or flavorings with the sugar syrup. Check the density. Add more water to reduce the density or add more base syrup to increase the density.

3 Churn according to the manufacturer's directions.

RECIPE 16.2

MANGO SORBET

Yield: 1 qt. (1 lt)	**Method:** Churned	
Water	6 fl. oz.	180 ml
Granulated sugar	3 oz.	90 g
Glucose or corn syrup	2 oz.	60 g
Pectin or stabilizer (optional)	0.1 oz. (1 tsp.)	1 g
Mango purée	17 oz.	510 g

1 Place the water, sugar, glucose or corn syrup and pectin (if using) in a large saucepan. Whisk until well combined. Bring the syrup to a full rolling boil and boil 1 minute.

2 Remove from the heat and let cool completely, then refrigerate, preferably overnight.

3 Combine the fruit purée with the syrup. Check the density. Add water or more sugar syrup to the sorbet base if needed to adjust it to 1.1333 D (17° Baumé).

Table 16.1 **TROUBLESHOOTING CHURNED FROZEN DESSERTS**

PRODUCT	PROBLEM	CAUSE	SOLUTION
Ice cream	Grainy	Custard too warm before freezing	Chill base thoroughly before churning
		Insufficient milkfat	Adjust formula
		Insufficient egg yolk	Adjust formula
		Custard overcooked	Cook properly
	Too dense	Too many eggs; insufficient air incorporated during churning	Adjust formula; churn a smaller volume of custard or sorbet at one time
	Watery	Too few eggs; not enough cream	Adjust formula
		Improperly prepared custard	Cook custard properly to 180°F to 185°F (82°C to 85°C)
Sorbet or sherbet	Too soft when frozen	Too much sugar; too much fruit pulp, too much alcohol added	Remelt and adjust formula, adding water
	Grainy or icy	Too little sugar	Remelt and adjust formula, adding sugar syrup

4 Pour the mixture into an ice cream or sorbet machine and process according to the manufacturer's directions.

5 Remove the sorbet from the machine and freeze at 0°F (−18°C) until needed for service.

VARIATION:

Coconut Sorbet—Use coconut purée in place of the mango purée. Adjust the sorbet mixture to a density reading of 1.1425 D (18° Baumé).

Approximate values per 2½-fl.-oz. (75-ml) serving: **Calories** 100, **Total fat** 0 g, **Saturated fat** 0 g, **Cholesterol** 0 mg, **Sodium** 10 mg, **Total carbohydrates** 26 g, **Protein** 0 g, **Vitamin A** 45%, **Vitamin C** 30%

GRANITA

Granita (Fr. *granité*), which is very similar to an Italian ice, is made with fruit or other flavorings but with less sugar than sorbet. This produces a mixture that will freeze harder than sorbet. Instead of being churned, the granità mixture is frozen in a shallow stainless steel container, then scraped with a fork or spoon to obtain grainy flakes. Or, as the mixture freezes and ice crystals form, the mixture is periodically stirred until granulation is complete.

Granita made with thick fruit purées, such as mango or raspberry, or with wine and liqueurs, requires very cold temperatures to obtain proper granulation. The density reading of a properly prepared granita mixture ranges from 1.0745 to 1.1074 D (10° to 14° Baumé).

▶ PROCEDURE FOR PREPARING GRANITA

1 Make a base syrup by combing the water and sugar. Boil 1 minute. Cool completely.

2 Stir in the fruit juice, coffee, wine or other flavoring liquid. Check the density. Add more water to reduce the density or add more base syrup to increase the density.

3 Pour the mixture into a shallow pan and place in a freezer.

4 Stir the granita mixture with a fork or spoon every 30 minutes as it freezes. The edges of the container will freeze first. As they form, the crystals are stirred into the unfrozen liquid in the center of the pan. This process is repeated until the granulation is complete.

5 Once the granita is completely frozen, scrape the surface of the mixture with a fork to separate the crystals and serve.

RECIPE 16.3

COFFEE GRANITA

Yield: 1½ pt. (720 g)

Water	20 fl. oz.	600 ml
Granulated sugar	5 oz.	150 g
Coffee, ground	0.75 oz.	22 g

1 Bring 4 fluid ounces (120 milliliters) of water and the sugar to a boil. Stir to dissolve the sugar. Remove the syrup from the heat and let cool.

2 Bring the remaining 1 pint (480 milliliters) of the water to a boil. Add the ground coffee and steep 5 minutes. Strain the mixture and set aside to cool.

3 Combine the sugar syrup with the coffee liquid.

4 Check the density. Add water or more sugar syrup to the sorbet base if needed to adjust it to 1.1074 D (14° Baumé). Pour into a shallow stainless steel pan and freeze until the granita begins to harden, approximately 3 hours.

5 Scrape the surface of the granita with a metal fork or spoon to break up the ice crystals. Return the granità to the freezer until firm.

6 Scrape the surface of the frozen granità to loosen the ice crystals. Scoop into serving dishes and serve immediately.

1 When the mixture has begun to freeze, scrape the ice crystals as they form in the granita.

2 Spoon the finished granita into a serving dish and serve immediately.

VARIATION:

Green Tea Granita—Omit the ground coffee. Substitute loose green tea leaves for the ground coffee.

Approximate values per 4-fl.-oz. (120-ml) serving: **Calories** 100, **Total fat** 0 g, **Saturated fat** 0 g, **Cholesterol** 0 mg, **Sodium** 0 mg, **Total carbohydrates** 26 g, **Protein** 0 g, **Vitamin C** 15%

SERVING SUGGESTIONS FOR ICE CREAMS AND SORBETS

Ice creams and sorbets are usually served by the scoop, often in cookie cones or bowls. Toppings and sauces can be added to create coupes, parfaits or sundaes. Many of the sauces in Chapter 13, Syrups, Icings and Sauces, such as Caramel Sauce (page 375), Chocolate Fudge Sauce (page 376), Espresso Sauce (page 377) or any of the fruit sauces work well as ice cream toppings. Crumbled Basic Nougatine (page 633) and Hazelnut Crisps (page 644) as well as toasted nuts, broken bits of candy and chocolate can be blended into churned ice creams to add texture and enhance flavor.

Ice creams and sorbets play an important part in restaurant desserts, as discussed in Chapter 20, Restaurant Desserts. When accompanying a slice of pie or as part of a dessert presentation, figure on 1½ to 2 fluid ounces (45 to 60 milliliters) per person. Figure on 4 to 6 fluid ounces (120 to 180 milliliters) for a single serving of ice cream or sorbet.

Serving frozen desserts at the proper temperature improves their flavor and mouth feel. Ice creams are tempered before serving; that is, they are allowed to warm slightly. In a large operation, ice cream or frozen desserts are transferred from a storage freezer to one set to a slightly warmer temperature. Tempering the desserts at 6°F to 14°F (−15°C to −11°C) for 24 hours makes them soft enough to scoop and cut easily. Special ice cream serving cases used in restaurants or pastry shops will keep ice cream at these softer temperatures for easy scooping. Placing a frozen dessert into the refrigerator for 15 to 30 minutes before serving achieves similar results.

STILL-FROZEN DESSERTS

Still-frozen desserts (It. *semifreddi*) are based on a **bombe mixture,** which is a mousse or a custard mixed with meringue or whipped cream. The bombe mixture (Fr. *pâte à bombe*) is made by stabilizing whipped egg yolks with sugar syrup cooked to the soft ball stage. Because these mixtures are still-frozen without churning, air must be incorporated by folding in relatively large amounts of whipped cream or meringue. The air helps keep the mixture smooth and prevents it from becoming too hard. Because of their air content, these desserts feel less cold than ice creams when frozen.

Frozen soufflés, parfaits, marquise, mousses, Neapolitans and spumoni are some popular frozen desserts. Layers of spongecake and/or fruit may be added for flavor and texture. The word *bombe* also refers to a finished dessert composed of a frozen cream or sorbet molded and layered with meringue or cake layers. If the terminology seems confusing, it is simply because the components for many of these specialty desserts are the creams, mousses and custards discussed in the preceding chapter.

PARFAITS AND FROZEN MOUSSES

In the United States a parfait is the name for a serving of ice cream layered with sauce and served in a tall slender glass. In France and in the pastry kitchen, a parfait is a mixture of cooked whipped egg yolks (bombe mixture) into which whipped cream and flavorings are folded and then frozen. Frozen soufflés (Fr. *soufflés glacés*) are simply frozen mousses molded to resemble baked soufflés.

Sundae with raspberry sauce, Chantilly cream and nuts

► **sundae** a great and gooey concoction of ice cream, sauces (hot fudge, marshmallow and caramel, for example), toppings (nuts, candies and fresh fruit, to name a few) and whipped cream

► **bombe mixture** (Fr. *pâte à bombe*) egg yolks cooked with sugar syrup and whipped, used as a base for still-frozen desserts and cakes

▶ PROCEDURE FOR PREPARING PARFAIT AND FROZEN MOUSSE MIXTURES BASED ON A BOMBE

1 Prepare a bombe mixture. Beat the egg yolks in the bowl of a mixer fitted with a whip. Prepare a sugar syrup and cook to the soft ball stage (240°F/116°C). Pour the hot syrup over the frothed egg yolks. Beat until the bombe mixture cools. Fold in flavorings.
2 Whip heavy cream.
3 Prepare an Italian meringue, if needed.
4 Fold the whipped cream into the bombe mixture, alternating with the Italian meringue.
5 Pour the mixture into molds that have been greased and dusted with granulated sugar. Layer with spongecake, fruits and other fillings if desired.

RECIPE 16.4 | **COFFEE RUM PARFAIT**

Yield: 22 Servings | **Method:** Still-frozen

Granulated sugar	7 oz.	210 g
Glucose or corn syrup	2 oz.	60 g
Water	4 fl. oz.	120 ml
Egg yolks	6 oz. (9 yolks)	180 g
Vanilla extract	0.3 fl. oz. (2 tsp.)	10 ml
Rum	1 fl. oz.	30 ml
Coffee extract	2 fl. oz.	60 ml
Heavy cream, whipped to soft peaks	1 qt.	1 lt
Chocolate shavings, chopped fine	6 oz.	180 g
Powdered sugar	as needed	as needed

1 Cut 22 strips of parchment paper or acetate 2 inches (5 centimeters) wide and long enough to wrap around the ramekins. Fasten the paper or acetate around the top of each ramekin with adhesive tape to form a collar. Lightly oil the ramekins and their collars. Sprinkle with granulated sugar.
2 Make the bombe batter. Place the sugar, glucose or corn syrup and water in a heavy saucepan. Attach a candy thermometer to the pan and bring the sugar to a boil over high heat. Boil until the syrup reaches the soft ball stage (240°F/116°C).

1 Folding the meringue, cream and chocolate shavings into the parfait mixture.

2 Leveling the parfait mixture in the ramekin before freezing.

3 Removing the collar and dusting the finished parfait with powdered sugar before serving.

3 Whip the egg yolks in the bowl of a mixer fitted with a whip until doubled in volume. With the mixer running on slow speed, pour the cooked syrup along the inner wall of the bowl in a slow steady stream. Whip until the yolk mixture cools, approximately 4 to 5 minutes.

4 Add the vanilla, rum and coffee extract and whip on low speed. Remove the bowl from the machine.

5 Using a spatula or balloon whisk, carefully fold in the whipped cream and chocolate shavings.

6 Fill the ramekins to the rim of their collars and level the cream using a metal spatula. Freeze until hardened, approximately 4 to 6 hours.

7 Remove the collars. Decorate the parfaits with chocolate shavings and lightly dust with powdered sugar.

Approximate values per serving: **Calories** 260, **Total fat** 20 g, **Saturated fat** 12 g, **Cholesterol** 145 mg, **Sodium** 25 mg, **Total carbohydrates** 18 g, **Protein** 2 g, **Vitamin A** 15%

FROZEN TORTES AND BOMBES

Frozen tortes and bombes are filled with ice cream, sorbet, and parfait mixtures alone or in combination. Spongecake or genoise, which absorb some of the cream as the dessert melts, or baked meringue layers are used to support the cakes. Frozen tortes are assembled in the same manner as described in Chapter 14, Cakes and Tortes (page 401). Ring molds are lined with cake, then layered with ice cream or parfait mixtures. The traditional bombe is made in a decorative oval mold shaped like a melon, or in a tube pan with a tight-fitting lid. One or more flavors of ice cream, sorbet or parfaits, selected for color and flavor contrast, are packed into the mold, then the mold is sealed before freezing. Handles on the mold facilitate unmolding the frozen bombe by allowing the pastry chef to easily dip the mold into warm water to help release the bombe.

Classic desserts such as Baked Alaska (page 493) and vacherin (see page 603), are always popular and make exciting alternatives to traditional celebration cakes. Individual serving sizes are easy to construct in ramekins, small timbale molds or disposable plastic cups. These desserts may be made ahead and iced with Chantilly cream or Italian meringue before service. The formula for Pistachio Apricot Bombe (page 480) illustrates the procedure for preparing a frozen torte or bombe. As with all frozen products, frozen desserts taste better when slightly softened or tempered before serving.

▶ PROCEDURE FOR PREPARING A FROZEN TORTE OR BOMBE

1 Lightly oil a spherical bombe mold. Pack the mold with churned ice cream or sorbet.

2 Cut a layer of spongecake the same diameter as the bombe mold. Top the ice cream with the cake. Seal the mold tightly with its lid or with plastic wrap.

3 To serve, invert the bombe mold onto a serving platter. Remove the mold and garnish the bombe with crème Chantilly, candied fruit and nuts, chocolate decorations or nougatine. Serve immediately.

Unmolding a frozen bombe.

RECIPE 16.5   **PISTACHIO APRICOT BOMBE**

Yield: 3 Bombes, 1 qt. (1 lt) each

Dacquoise (page 299)	1 half sheet	1 half sheet
Pistachio Ice Cream (page 485)	1½ qt.	1.5 lt
Apricot Sorbet (page 488)	1 qt.	1 lt
Cocoa Gelée (page 363)	as needed	as needed
Gerbet Macaroons (page 572)	60 cookies	60 cookies
Chocolate cutouts (page 615)	as needed	as needed
Pistachios	as needed	as needed

1. Chill the bombe molds in the freezer at least 30 minutes.

2. Cut the Dacquoise into three pieces trimmed to fit the opening of the mold. Set aside.

3. Using a plastic scraper, spread the freshly churned Pistachio Ice Cream to line the molds to a thickness of ¾ inch (2 centimeters). Freeze until hardened.

4. Pack the molds with the Apricot Sorbet, leaving enough space for the Dacquoise to fit level with the rim of the mold.

5. Press the Dacquoise into place. Cover the molds and freeze until hardened.

6. To serve, run the molds briefly under warm water. Unmold them onto icing screens and then return them to the freezer.

7. Heat the Cocoa Gelée until it reaches approximately 130°F (54°C). Pour the Cocoa Gelée over the bombes to cover evenly. Shake the icing screen to remove excess Cocoa Gelée. Transfer the bombes to cake boards.

8. Surround the base of each bombe with a row of overlapping Gerbet Macaroons.

9. Decorate the top of the bombes with chocolate cutouts sprinkled with pistachio nuts.

Approximate values per ⅛-bombe serving: **Calories** 480, **Total fat** 26 g, **Saturated fat** 9 g, **Cholesterol** 120 mg, **Sodium** 65 mg, **Total carbohydrates** 54 g, **Protein** 11 g, **Vitamin A** 25%

CONVENIENCE PRODUCTS

Commercially prepared ice cream, gelato, sherbet and sorbet can be a significant convenience item for the pastry chef. These products are available in 1- and 3-gallon containers in a range of quality grades and flavors. As always, the costs should be evaluated against the cost and effort of producing frozen products in-house. Contemporary pastry chefs often seek unique ice cream flavors that are not available commercially, however. Ice cream mixes allow a variety of different flavored ice creams to be freshly made from one basic preparation. The ingredients in frozen dessert mixes vary by manufacturer. Mixes may be made from milk or cream, eggs and sweeteners and may contain stabilizers, gelatin, gums, flavorings or other additives. Some mixes require the addition of fresh milk, cream or other liquid, however. Most are sold as a refrigerated or frozen liquid in a range of different milkfat contents.

Nondairy mixes are also available, usually in a powdered form to which water or fruit juice is added. The mix is simply placed in an ice cream machine and frozen as needed.

Mixes also come in a neutral flavor to which the pastry chef adds flavorings or fruit purées to customize the ice cream before churning. Prepared flavoring bases are also available in flavors such as French vanilla, butter pecan, pistachio or green tea. The base may also contain additional milkfat and fruit pieces. Mixes and bases are formulated for different styles of ice cream, either hard or soft, and for use in different types of ice cream–making machinery, either in a batch freezer or a continuous-process soft ice cream machine. (See Chapter 2, Tools and Equipment.) Packaging is designed to make one batch of ice cream for the standard-size 20-quart commercial ice cream machine. When purchasing an ice cream mix or base,

select products with the fewest additives and the highest milkfat content appropriate for the equipment in your bakeshop.

Nondairy neutral bases for making sorbet and sherbet are also available. Fresh fruit purées or juices are added as needed. Variegates are specially formulated mixtures designed to be swirled into ice cream after it is frozen. These variegates remain soft when frozen and come in popular flavors such as fudge, caramel, marshmallow and strawberry. Purchasing prepared high-quality ice creams and sorbets lets the pastry chef offer frozen desserts such as baked Alaska or frozen tortes with less preparation time. The pastry chef's creativity can be applied to the flavor combinations and the presentation of the dessert. Some manufacturers will even prepare custom flavored ice cream and sorbet for a small minimum order.

Specialty ice creams and frozen desserts add excitement and variety to the pastry chef's repertoire. With a basic custard sauce or sugar syrup and flavoring, many different types of frozen desserts may be prepared. An understanding of the freezing process and access to quality ingredients allows the chef to prepare still frozen and simple ices such as granità. Expensive ice cream–making machinery is not required to make many specialty frozen desserts discussed in this chapter. Still-frozen tortes and bombes are as convenient to make as any cake or torte. In place of buttercream or mousse, frozen tortes are filled with parfait and bombe mixtures prepared using many basic techniques. Frozen tortes and bombes are a convenient alternative to traditional cakes, their freshness preserved by the necessity of storage in the freezer.

1 Describe the types of ice creams based on frozen custards and their differences.
2 What can be done to ensure that a sorbet mixture will freeze properly?
3 Consider the types of cookie and cake formulas that are available to the pastry chef. Using cookie or cake formulas discussed in previous chapters of this book, create three new frozen desserts that combine a cake or cookie and a frozen mixture from this chapter.
4 Discuss the function of whipped cream and Italian meringue when making frozen parfaits and bombes.

RECIPE 16.6

BRETON SHORTBREAD WITH APPLE CONFIT, BAVARIAN CREAM AND CARAMEL SAUCE

PASTRY CHEF MICHEL BRIAND

A native of La Guerche-de-Bretagne in France, Pastry Chef Michel Briand began working in his family's pastry shop as a young boy. Before coming to the United States in 1991, he worked in numerous pastry shops in Brittany and Paris as well as in Bern, Switzerland. He joined the Rosewood Corporation, working as executive pastry chef at a number of their operations including the Little Dix Resort on the island of Virgin Gorda in the British Virgin Islands. He has been with Ambria since 1994, teaming up with executive chef Gabino Sotelino to produce refined, classic yet modern pastries.

AMBRIA RESTAURANT, CHICAGO, IL
Chef Michel Briand

Note: This dish appears in the chapter opening photograph.

Yield: 24 Desserts, 3 in. × 1½ in. (7.5 cm × 4 cm) each

Breton Shortbread (recipe follows), baked into 3-in. (7.5-cm) disks	24 disks	24 disks
Apple Confit (recipe follows)	2 lb.	960 g
Granulated sugar	9 oz.	270 g
Milk	1 pt.	480 ml
Vanilla bean, split	1	1
Egg yolks	4 oz. (6 yolks)	120 g
Sheet gelatin, softened	0.5 oz.	14 g
Heavy cream, whipped	1 pt.	480 ml
Basic Nougatine (page 633), ground	as needed	as needed
Green Apple Sorbet (recipe follows)	1 qt.	1 lt
Caramel Green Apple Sauce with Cranberries (recipe follows)	1¼ pt.	480 ml
Sour Cream Sorbet (recipe follows)	1 qt.	1 lt

1 Place 24 3-inch (7.5-centimeter) tart rings on a paper-lined sheet pan. Place a baked Breton Shortbread disk in the bottom of each ring. Divide the Apple Confit evenly between the cookie-lined rings. Level it with an offset spatula. Set aside.

2 Caramelize 7 ounces (210 grams) of the sugar. Add the milk and vanilla bean. Heat until the sugar dissolves.

3 Whisk the egg yolks and remaining sugar in a small bowl and temper it with some of the heated caramel milk. Pour the tempered yolks back into the heated milk and cook, stirring constantly, until lightly thickened and the temperature reaches 182°F (83°C).

4 Remove from the heat. Strain the custard then stir in the softened sheet gelatin until dissolved. Chill the bowl of custard over an ice bath to 105°F (41°C), then fold in the whipped cream.

5 Divide the cream mixture between the molds. Level the cream to a height of approximately ½ inch (1.2 centimeters) in each ring. Refrigerate until firm, approximately 2 to 3 hours.

6 To serve, place one ring on each serving plate. Remove the ring.

7 Sprinkle the surface of the cream evenly with ground Basic Nougatine and top with Green Apple Sorbet.

8 Place some of the Caramel Green Apple Sauce with Cranberries on one side of the dessert and a spoon of Sour Cream Sorbet on the other side.

Approximate values per serving: **Calories** 630, **Total fat** 32 g, **Saturated fat** 18 g, **Cholesterol** 170 mg, **Sodium** 160 mg, **Total carbohydrates** 83 g, **Protein** 6 g, **Vitamin A** 25%, **Vitamin C** 10%, **Calcium** 10%

BRETON SHORTBREAD

Yield: 24 Cakes, 3 in. (7.5 cm) each

Unsalted butter, softened	12 oz.	360 g	126%
Powdered sugar	5 oz.	150 g	53%
Egg yolks	2 oz. (3 yolks)	60 g	21%
All-purpose flour	9.5 oz.	285 g	100%
Almond flour	2 oz.	60 g	21%
Salt	0.2 oz. (1 tsp.)	6 g	2%
Baking powder	0.14 oz. (1 tsp.)	4 g	1.5%
Total dough weight:	1 lb. 14 oz.	925 g	325%

1 Blend the butter and sugar until smooth and lump-free. Add the egg yolks, beating well. Then add the flours, salt and baking powder. Blend until a smooth dough is formed. Chill the dough, covered, at least 1 hour or until firm.

2 Line two half-sheet pans with parchment. Place 24 tart rings on the half-sheet pans, 12 on each pan. Divide the cookie dough into 1½-ounce (45-gram) portions. With floured fingertips, press a portion of the dough into an even layer down inside each ring. Bake at 350°F (180°C) until golden brown, approximately 12 minutes.

3 Cool the cakes in the tart rings.

Approximate values per cake: **Calories** 190 **Total fat** 14 g, **Saturated fat** 7 g, **Cholesterol** 60 mg, **Sodium** 115 mg, **Total carbohydrates** 15 g, **Protein** 2 g, **Vitamin A** 10%

APPLE CONFIT

Yield: 2 lb. (960 g)

Rome apples, peeled and cored	8	8
Granulated sugar	4 oz.	120 g
Unsalted butter	4 oz.	120 g
Vanilla beans, split	2	2

1 Slice the apples into wedges approximately ½ inch (1.2 centimeters) thick. Lay evenly in a half-size hotel pan.

2 Stir the sugar and butter in a heavy saucepan over medium heat until it reaches an amber caramel. Add the vanilla bean and pour over the apples. (The caramel may separate, which is normal.)

3 Bake at 400°F (200°C) until nicely caramelized, approximately 45 minutes. Check the apples occasionally as they bake, stirring as needed to keep them from browning unevenly. Remove vanilla bean before using as a filling or topping.

Approximate values per 2-oz. (60-g) serving: **Calories** 70 **Total fat** 3 g, **Saturated fat** 2 g, **Cholesterol** 10 mg, **Sodium** 0 mg, **Total carbohydrates** 12 g, **Protein** 0 g

GREEN APPLE SORBET

Yield: 1 qt. (1 lt)   **Method:** Churned

Water	8 fl. oz.	240 ml
Granulated sugar	3.5 oz.	105 g
Glucose or corn syrup	1 oz.	30 g
Granny Smith apple purée	1 pt.	480 ml

1 Bring the water, sugar and glucose or corn syrup to a boil in a heavy saucepan over high heat. Once the sugar dissolves, boil 1 minute. Cool, then chill before using.

2 Add the apple purée and place in the container of an ice cream machine and process according to the manufacturer's instructions.

Approximate values per 1-fl.oz. (30-ml) serving: **Calories** 20, **Total fat** 0 g, **Saturated fat** 0 g, **Cholesterol** 0 mg, **Sodium** 0 mg, **Total carbohydrates** 5 g, **Protein** 0 g

CARAMEL GREEN APPLE SAUCE WITH CRANBERRIES

Yield: Approximately 1 qt. (1 lt.)

Granulated sugar	3.5 oz.	105 g
Green apple juice, hot	18 fl. oz.	540 ml
Vanilla beans, split	2	2
Simple Syrup (page 349)	11 fl. oz.	330 ml
Dried cranberries	5 oz.	150 g

1 Caramelize the sugar in a heavy nonreactive pan. Add the hot apple juice and vanilla beans. Simmer for 5 minutes. Strain and then stir in the Simple Syrup and dried cranberries.

2 Reduce the mixture to a sauce consistency, approximately 15 to 20 minutes.

Approximate values per 1 1/2-oz. (45-g) serving: **Calories** 80 **Total fat** 0 g, **Saturated fat** 0 g, **Cholesterol** 0 mg, **Sodium** 0 mg, **Total carbohydrates** 21 g, **Protein** 0 g

SOUR CREAM SORBET

Yield: 1 qt. (1 lt)   **Method:** Churned

Half-and-half	8 fl. oz.	240 ml
Sour cream	1 pt.	480 ml
Granulated sugar	12.5 oz.	375 g
Lemon juice	1.5 fl. oz.	45 ml

1 Combine all the ingredients. Place in the container of an ice cream machine and process according to the manufacturer's instructions.

Approximate values per 1-fl.oz. (30-ml) serving: **Calories** 80, **Total fat** 4 g, **Saturated fat** 2.5 g, **Cholesterol** 10 mg, **Sodium** 10 mg, **Total carbohydrates** 12 g, **Protein** 1 g

RECIPE 16.7

FRENCH ICE CREAM BASE

Yield: 1 1/2 qt. (1 1/2 lt)   **Method:** Churned

Whole milk	20 fl. oz.	600 ml
Heavy cream	14 fl. oz.	420 ml
Egg yolks	4 oz. (6 yolks)	120 g
Granulated sugar	7 oz.	210 g
Glucose or corn syrup	1 oz.	30 g
Ice cream stabilizer (optional)	0.3 oz. (2 tsp.)	10 g

1 Bring the milk and cream to a boil in a nonreactive saucepan.

2 Whip the egg yolks, sugar, glucose or corn syrup and ice cream stabilizer (if using) in the bowl of a mixer fitted with a whip until pale and slightly thickened, approximately 3 minutes. Stir one-third of the boiled milk into the yolk mixture.

3 Return the yolk mixture to the saucepan and heat, stirring constantly with a rubber spatula, until it reaches 180°F to 185°F (82°C to 85°C). Remove from the heat and strain into a clean bowl.

4 Quickly chill the ice cream base over an ice bath until it reaches 40°F (4°C). Refrigerate and mature the ice cream base overnight.

5 Pour the mixture into the container of an ice cream machine and process according to the manufacturer's directions.

VARIATIONS:

Anise Ice Cream—Add 0.5 ounce (15 grams) chopped anise seeds and 2 **star anise seeds** to the milk and cream. Prepare the custard, then strain out the seeds before cooling and churning. One fluid ounce (30 milliliters) anise liqueur may be added before churning.

Banana-Nut Ice Cream—Fold in 8 ounces (240 grams) ripe, puréed bananas and 5 ounces (150 grams) crushed nougatine (page 633) when the ice cream is frozen but still soft enough to stir.

Chestnut Ice Cream—Add 1 pound (480 grams) sweetened chestnut purée to the chilled mixture before churning.

Coconut Ice Cream—Add 8 ounces (240 grams) fresh grated or frozen unsweetened coconut to the milk. Strain the custard before churning or place it in a blender and blend until the coconut shavings are small, and leave them in the ice cream. If desired, add 2 fluid ounces (60 milliliters) dark Jamaican rum.

Coffee Ice Cream—Add 1 fluid ounce (30 milliliters) coffee extract to the chilled mixture before churning.

Earl Grey Ice Cream—Steep 10 Earl Grey tea bags in the milk and cream 6 minutes. Remove the tea bags, then finish the custard.

Ginger Ice Cream—Add 3 ounces (90 grams) chopped fresh ginger to the milk and cream.

Hazelnut Ice Cream—Add 6 ounces (180 grams) hazelnut paste to the chilled mixture before churning.

Indian Cardamom and Pistachio Ice Cream—Steep 10 crushed cardamom pods in the milk and cream 10 minutes. Strain the custard. Stir in 2 ounces (60 grams) finely ground pistachios and 0.04 ounce (0.5 teaspoon/1 gram) ground cardamom before churning.

Mint Ice Cream—Steep 40 fresh mint leaves in the milk and cream.

Pistachio Ice Cream—Add 8 ounces (240 grams) chopped pistachio nuts and 1 ounce (30 grams) natural pistachio compound to the custard before churning.

Spiced Chocolate Ice Cream—Increase the milk to 28 fluid ounces (840 milliliters). Place 8 ounces (240 grams) chopped bittersweet or milk chocolate into a bowl. Pour the hot cooked custard base over the chocolate and whisk until the chocolate has melted. Add a pinch of ground white pepper and 0.5 fluid ounce (15 milliliters) coffee extract.

Vanilla Ice Cream—Steep 2 split vanilla beans in the milk and cream.

Approximate values per 4-fl.-oz. (120-ml) serving: **Calories** 250, **Total fat** 17 g, **Saturated fat** 10 g, **Cholesterol** 160 mg, **Sodium** 45 mg, **Total carbohydrates** 22 g, **Protein** 4 g, **Vitamin A** 15%

STAR ANISE

Star anise, also known as Chinese anise, is the dried, star-shaped fruit of a Chinese magnolia tree. Although it is botanically unrelated, its flavor is similar to anise seeds but more bitter and pungent. It lends a licorice-like flavor to aromatic liquids for poaching fruits and for exotic sauces.

Star Anise

RECIPE 16.8

CHOCOLATE ICE CREAM

**CHRISTOPHER'S FERMIER BRASSERIE AND
PAOLA'S WINE BAR, PHOENIX, AZ**
Chef-Owner Christopher Gross

Yield: 10 Servings　　　　　**Method:** Churned

Egg yolks	3.3 oz. (5 yolks)	100 g
Granulated sugar	5 oz.	150 g
Cocoa powder	1.5 oz.	45 g
Milk	1 pt.	480 ml
Heavy cream	3 fl. oz.	90 ml
Semisweet chocolate, chopped	4 oz.	120 g

1 Whisk the egg yolks, sugar and cocoa powder together.
2 Combine the milk and cream and bring to a boil. Temper the egg mixture with a portion of the hot milk; return the mixture to the saucepan and continue cooking, stirring constantly, until the custard thickens.
3 Remove from the heat and add the chocolate. Stir until the chocolate melts, then strain and chill.
4 Process the custard in an ice cream machine according to the manufacturer's directions.

Approximate values per 3-oz. (90-g) serving: **Calories** 210, **Total fat** 11 g, **Saturated fat** 7 g, **Cholesterol** 125 mg, **Sodium** 40 mg, **Total carbohydrates** 27 g, **Protein** 4 g

RECIPE 16.9

HONEY ICE CREAM

BISHOP'S RESTAURANT, VANCOUVER, BC
Chefs Michael Allemeier and Dennis Green

Yield: 1 qt. (1 lt)　　　　　**Method:** Churned

Heavy cream	1 pt.	480 ml
Light cream	1 pt.	480 ml
Egg yolks	5.3 oz. (8 yolks)	160 g
Honey	4 fl. oz.	120 ml

1 In a nonreactive saucepan, combine the heavy and light cream and heat just to a simmer.
2 In a large mixing bowl, beat the egg yolks and honey together until pale, slightly thickened and at the ribbon stage. Slowly add the heated cream, whisking continuously, so as not to cook the yolks.
3 Return the mixture to the saucepan and cook over low heat, stirring constantly, until the mixture coats the back of a spoon.
4 Remove from the heat and cool over an ice bath. Pour into the container of an ice cream machine and process according to the manufacturer's directions.

Approximate values per 3½-fl.-oz. (105-ml) serving: **Calories** 275, **Total fat** 22 g, **Saturated fat** 13 g, **Cholesterol** 210 mg, **Sodium** 48 mg, **Total carbohydrates** 15 g, **Protein** 6 g, **Vitamin A** 30%, **Calcium** 10%

CARAMEL ICE CREAM

Chefs Susan Feniger and Mary Sue Millikin

Yield: 1 ½ qt. (1 ½ lt) **Method:** Churned

Half-and-half	20 fl. oz.	600 ml
Heavy cream	12 fl. oz.	360 ml
Egg yolks	6 oz. (9 yolks)	180 g
Granulated sugar	6 oz.	180 g
Vanilla extract	0.3 fl. oz. (2 tsp.)	10 ml
Sour cream	8 oz.	240 g
Caramel Chunks (recipe follows)	as needed	as needed

1 Combine the half-and-half and heavy cream in a medium-heavy saucepan. Bring to a boil.

2 Whisk together the egg yolks and sugar until thick and pale yellow. Pour into the boiling cream and stir to combine. Remove from the heat.

3 Add the vanilla and stir. Strain into a large container and chill over an ice bath, stirring occasionally.

4 Stir in the sour cream and pour into the container of an ice cream machine and process according to the manufacturer's directions.

5 When the ice cream is frozen but still soft, fold in the Caramel Chunks.

Approximate values per serving: **Calories** 310, **Total fat** 24 g, **Saturated fat** 14 g, **Cholesterol** 225 mg, **Sodium** 45 mg, **Total carbohydrates** 18 g, **Protein** 5 g, **Vitamin A** 30%, **Claims**—low sodium

CARAMEL CHUNKS

Granulated sugar	8 oz.	240 g
Water	4 fl. oz.	120 ml

1 Combine the sugar and water in a heavy saucepan. Cook over moderate heat until the color turns deep brown and the aroma is strong, approximately 10 to 15 minutes.

2 Immediately, and with great care, pour the hot caramel onto a greased sheet pan. Set aside until cool, then crack into ½-inch (1.2-centimeter) pieces.

RECIPE 16.11

APRICOT, PEACH, PEAR OR PINEAPPLE SORBET

Yield: 1 qt. (1 lt)   **Method:** Churned

Water	5 fl. oz.	150 ml
Granulated sugar	4 oz.	120 g
Glucose or corn syrup	2.5 oz.	75 g
Pectin-based ice cream stabilizer (optional)	0.07 oz. (½ tsp.)	1.5 g
Apricot, peach, pear or pineapple purée	17 fl. oz.	500 ml

1 Place the water, sugar, glucose or corn syrup and stabilizer (if using) in a large saucepan. Whisk until well combined, then bring to a full rolling boil.

2 Remove from the heat and cool in a refrigerator several hours or overnight.

3 Combine the fruit purée with the base syrup. Check the density. Add more water or sugar syrup to adjust to 1.1333 D (17° Baumé).

4 Pour the mixture into the container of an ice cream/sorbet machine and process according to the manufacturer's directions.

VARIATIONS:

Lemon or Lime Sorbet—Make the base syrup with 22 fluid ounces (665 milliliters) water, 12 ounces (360 grams) sugar, 3.5 ounces (105 grams) glucose or corn syrup and 0.4 ounce (2⅔ teaspoons/12 grams) stabilizer (if using). Add 17 fluid ounces (0.5 liter) lemon or lime juice.

Basil Lemon Sorbet—Add 20 finely minced basil leaves to the lemon sorbet before churning.

Banana or Kiwi Sorbet—Make the base syrup using 22 fluid ounces (665 milliliters) water, 12 ounces (360 grams) granulated sugar, 3.5 ounces (105 grams) glucose or corn syrup and 0.4 ounce (2⅔ teaspoons /12 grams) stabilizer (if using). Add 17 fluid ounces (0.5 liter) banana or kiwi juice.

Raspberry, Cherry, Blackberry or Three Red Fruit Sorbet—Make the base syrup using 7 fluid ounces (210 milliliters) water, 3.5 ounces (105 grams) granulated sugar, 2.5 ounces (75 grams) glucose or corn syrup and 0.25 ounce (1¾ teaspoons/7.5 grams) stabilizer (if using). Add 17 fluid ounces (0.5 liter) raspberry, cherry, blackberry or any combination fruit purée.

Green Apple or Wild Strawberry Sorbet—Make the base syrup from 8 fluid ounces (240 milliliters) water, 5 ounces (150 grams) sugar, 2.5 ounces (75 grams) glucose or corn syrup and 0.25 ounce (1¾ teaspoons/7.5 grams) stabilizer (if using). Add 17 fluid ounces (0.5 liter) green apple or wild strawberry purée.

Blueberry, Red Currant or Black Currant Sorbet—Make the base syrup from 10 fluid ounces (300 milliliters) water, 6.5 ounces (195 grams) sugar, 2.5 ounces (75 grams) glucose or corn syrup and 0.14 ounce (1 teaspoon/5 grams) stabilizer (if using). Add 17 fluid ounces (0.5 liter) blueberry, red currant or black currant purée.

Passion Fruit Sorbet—Make the base syrup from 20 fluid ounces (600 milliliters) water, 8 ounces (240 grams) sugar, 5 ounces (150 grams) glucose or corn syrup and 0.14 ounce (1 teaspoon/5 grams) stabilizer (if using). Add 17 fluid ounces (0.5 liter) passion fruit purée. Adjust to 1.1425 D (18° Baumé).

Mandarin or Orange Sorbet—Make the base syrup from 6 fluid ounces (180 milliliters) water, 5 ounces (150 grams) sugar, 2 ounces (60 grams) glucose or corn syrup and 0.14 ounce (1 teaspoon/5 grams) stabilizer (if using). Add 17 fluid ounces (0.5 liter) mandarin or orange juice. Adjust to 1.1425 D (18° Baumé).

Verbena Sorbet—Make an infusion from 8 fluid ounces (240 milliliters) water and 0.5 ounce (15 grams) fresh verbena leaves. Steep 30 minutes. Strain, then add the infusion to 8 fluid ounces (240 milliliters) water, 2 fluid ounces (60 milliliters) lemon juice, 5 ounces (150 grams) granulated sugar, 2 ounces (60 grams) glucose or corn syrup and 0.14 ounce (1 teaspoon/5 grams) stabilizer (if using). Chill, then adjust to 1.1425 D (18° Baumé).

Champagne Sorbet—Make the base syrup using 7 fluid ounces (210 milliliters) water, 6 ounces (180 grams) granulated sugar, 1 ounce (30 grams) glucose or corn syrup, 1 ounce (30 grams) orange zest, 1 ounce (30 grams) lemon zest and 0.25 ounce (1¾ teaspoons/7.5 grams) stabilizer (if using). Chill, then add 12 fluid ounces (375 milliliters) champagne. Adjust to 1.1247 D (16° Baumé).

Approximate values per 4-fl.-oz. (120-ml) serving (based on apricot sorbet): **Calories** 110, **Total fat** 0 g, **Saturated fat** 0 g, **Cholesterol** 0 mg, **Sodium** 10 mg, **Total carbohydrates** 28 g, **Protein** 1 g, **Vitamin A** 30%

LEMON SORBET

RECIPE 16.12

VINCENT ON CAMELBACK, PHOENIX, AZ

Chef Vincent Guerithault

Yield: 1½ qt. (1½ lt)		**Method:** Churned
Lemon juice	1 pt.	500 ml
Water	1 pt.	500 ml
Granulated sugar	1 lb.	500 g

1 Combine all the ingredients in a large bowl. Stir until the sugar dissolves completely.

2 Pour the mixture into the container of an ice cream/sorbet machine and process according to the manufacturer's directions.

3 The finished sorbet will be rather soft. Pack it into a storage container and freeze at a temperature of 0°F (−18°C) or lower until firm.

Approximate values per 1½-fl.-oz. (45-ml) serving: **Calories** 25, **Total fat** 0 g, **Saturated fat** 0 g, **Cholesterol** 0 mg, **Sodium** 0 mg, **Total carbohydrates** 6 g, **Protein** 0 g, **Claims**—fat free; no sodium; low calorie

RECIPE 16.13

STRAWBERRY SORBET

THE RITZ-CARLTON, Chicago, IL

Executive Chef George Bumbaris and Chef Sarah Stegner

Yield: 8 Servings | **Method:** Churned

Granulated sugar	4 oz.	120 g
Pectin	0.14 oz. (1 tsp.)	5 g
Medium sugar syrup (page 349)	8 fl. oz.	240 ml
Strawberries, puréed	1 lb.	480 g
Fresh lemon juice	0.5 fl. oz.	15 ml

1 Mix the sugar and pectin together, add the syrup and bring to a boil. Remove from the heat and cool completely.

2 Add the puréed berries and lemon juice; strain. Adjust the flavor with additional sugar or lemon juice as needed.

3 Pour the mixture into the container of an ice cream/sorbet machine and process according to the manufacturer's directions.

Approximate values per 4-fl.-oz. (120-ml) serving: **Calories** 196, **Total fat** 0 g, **Saturated fat** 0 g, **Cholesterol** 0 mg, **Sodium** 1.5 mg, **Total carbohydrates** 48 g, **Protein** 0 g, **Vitamin C** 54%, **Claims**—no fat; no cholesterol; very low sodium; high fiber

RECIPE 16.14

GRAPEFRUIT SORBET

Yield: 1½ qt. (1½ lt) | **Method:** Churned

Fresh grapefruit juice	1 qt.	1 lt
Granulated sugar	8 oz.	240 g

1 Combine the juice and sugar.

2 Process in an ice cream machine according to the manufacturer's directions.

3 Pack into a clean container and freeze until firm.

VARIATION:

Raspberry Sorbet—Combine 2.2 pounds (1 kilogram) puréed, strained raspberries with 1 pound (480 grams) granulated sugar and 1 fluid ounce (30 milliliters) lemon juice.

Approximate values per 3-fl.-oz. (90-ml) serving: **Calories** 94, **Total fat** 0 g, **Saturated fat** 0 g, **Cholesterol** 0 mg, **Sodium** 1 mg, **Total carbohydrates** 23 g, **Protein** 0.5 g, **Vitamin C** 36%, **Claims**—no fat; no cholesterol; very low sodium; low calorie

RECIPE 16.15

COFFEE SHERBET

Yield: 1¾ qt. (1¾ lt) | **Method:** Churned

Water	1 pt.	480 ml
Granulated sugar	1 lb. 4 oz.	600 g
Glucose or corn syrup	4 oz.	120 g
Coffee, ground	1 oz.	30 g
Coffee extract	1 fl. oz.	30 ml
Heavy cream	3.5 fl. oz.	105 ml

1 Bring the water, sugar and glucose or corn syrup to a boil. Boil 1 minute and remove from heat.

2 Add the ground coffee and coffee extract and let the mixture steep 4 minutes. Strain through cheesecloth and discard the grounds.

3 Add the cream to the coffee syrup and then quickly cool the mixture over an ice bath.

4 Check the density of the mixture. Adjust the syrup to 1.1425D (18° Baumé) by adding more base syrup or water as needed.

5 Pour the mixture into the container of an ice cream/sorbet machine and process according to the manufacturer's directions.

Approximate values per 4.-fl.-oz. (120-ml) serving: **Calories** 210, **Total fat** 3 g, **Saturated fat** 1.5 g, **Cholesterol** 10 mg, **Sodium** 15 mg, **Total carbohydrates** 48 g, **Protein** 0 g

CHAMPAGNE SPOOM   RECIPE 16.16

A spoom is a type of sherbet, usually made from champagne or a sweet white wine to which Italian meringue is added after the churning process.

Yield: 2½ qt. (2½ lt)	**Method:** Churned	
Granulated sugar	14 oz.	420 g
Water	14 fl. oz.	420 ml
Glucose or corn syrup	2 oz.	60 g
Whole milk	8 fl. oz.	240 ml
Vanilla bean, split	1	1
Champagne or sparkling wine	24 fl. oz.	750 ml
Italian Meringue (page 290)	12 oz.	360 g

1 Combine the sugar, water, glucose or corn syrup, milk and vanilla bean in a nonreactive saucepan. Boil 1 minute, then chill.

2 Combine the champagne with the chilled base syrup. Check the density of the mixture. Adjust the syrup to 1.1159 D (15° Baumé) by adding more base syrup or water as needed.

3 Pour the mixture into the container of an ice cream machine and process according to the manufacturer's directions.

4 Fold the Italian Meringue into the sherbet as soon as it is churned but still soft enough to stir.

Approximate values per 4-fl.-oz. (120-ml) serving: **Calories** 180, **Total fat** 0 g, **Saturated fat** 0 g, **Cholesterol** 0 mg, **Sodium** 25 mg, **Total carbohydrates** 35 g, **Protein** 1 g, **Claims**—fat free; no cholesterol

PINEAPPLE GRANITA   RECIPE 16.17

Yield: 1½ qt. (1½ lt)	**Method:** Scraped	
Water	2 fl. oz.	60 ml
Granulated sugar	6 oz.	180 g
Pineapple juice	1 qt.	1 lt

1 Combine the water and sugar in a saucepan. Bring to a full boil and boil 1 minute. Remove from the heat and add the pineapple juice. Chill, then check the density. Add water or more sugar syrup to the granita base if needed to adjust it to 1.0907 D (12° Baumé).

2 Pour into a shallow stainless steel pan and freeze until the granita begins to harden, approximately 3 hours.

3 Scrape the surface of the granita with a metal fork or spoon to break up the ice crystals. Return the granita to the freezer until firm.

4 Scrape the surface of the frozen granita to loosen the ice crystals. Scoop into serving dishes and serve immediately.

Approximate values per 4-fl.-oz. (120-ml) cup serving: **Calories** 100, **Total fat** 0 g, **Saturated fat** 0 g, **Cholesterol** 0 mg, **Sodium** 0 mg, **Total carbohydrates** 26 g, **Protein** 0 g, **Vitamin C** 15%

RECIPE 16.18

FROZEN ORANGE SOUFFLÉ

Yield: 15 Servings, 3½-in. (9-cm) ramekins   **Method:** Still-frozen

Egg yolks	5.3 oz. (8 yolks)	160 g
Granulated sugar	4 oz.	120 g
Water	3 fl. oz.	90 ml
Cointreau or orange liqueur	2 fl. oz.	60 ml
Orange or bergamot essential oil	0.15 fl. oz. (1 tsp.)	5 ml
Italian Meringue (page 290)	1 lb. 8 oz.	720 g
Heavy cream, whipped	28 fl. oz.	840 ml
Basic Nougatine (page 633)	as needed	as needed
Powdered sugar	as needed	as needed

1 Cut 15 strips of parchment paper or acetate 2 inches (5 centimeters) wide and long enough to wrap around the top of the ramekins. Fasten the paper or acetate around each ramekin with adhesive tape to form a collar. Lightly oil the ramekins and their collars. Sprinkle with granulated sugar.

2 Prepare a bombe mixture. Beat the egg yolks in the bowl of a mixer fitted with a whip until light and foamy.

3 While the egg yolks whip, bring the sugar and water to a boil in a small saucepan, brushing down the sides of the pan with cold water to wash off crystals that may be deposited there. Cook the syrup to the soft ball stage (240°F/116°C). With the machine running on medium speed, pour the hot syrup into the whipped egg yolks. Increase the speed to high and beat until the bombe mixture cools to room temperature.

4 Remove the bombe mixture from machine; fold in the Cointreau and orange or bergamot oil.

5 In two steps, delicately fold in the Italian Meringue, followed by the whipped cream.

6 Using a ladle, deposit the mixture into the ramekins, leveling it with a metal spatula to the rim of the collar.

7 Freeze until hard.

8 To serve, remove the paper or acetate collars. Garnish with Basic Nougatine or powdered sugar.

Approximate values per serving: **Calories** 300, **Total fat** 16 g, **Saturated fat** 9 g, **Cholesterol** 170 mg, **Sodium** 20 mg, **Total carbohydrates** 38 g, **Protein** 2 g, **Vitamin A** 15%

CHOCOLATE HAZELNUT MARQUISE WITH FRANGELICO SAUCE

RECIPE 16.19

Yield: 12 Servings   **Method:** Still-frozen

Dark chocolate	1 lb.	480 g
Unsalted butter	4 oz.	120 g
Hazelnuts, roasted, skinned and chopped coarse	4 oz.	120 g
Egg yolks	4 oz. (6 yolks)	120 g
Frangelico (hazelnut liqueur)	2 fl. oz.	60 ml
Egg whites	6 oz. (6 whites)	180 g
Salt	0.03 oz. (⅛ tsp.)	1 g
Frangelico Custard Sauce (page 435)	as needed	as needed
Hazelnuts, roasted and chopped coarse	as needed	as needed
Fresh raspberries	as needed	as needed
Fresh mint	as needed	as needed

1 Brush a terrine mold with melted butter and line it with parchment paper.

2 Melt the chocolate and butter over a bain marie. Remove from the heat and stir in the nuts, egg yolks and Frangelico. Set aside to cool to room temperature. Do not use an ice bath, as the chocolate will solidify.

3 Whip the egg whites with the salt until stiff but not dry. Fold the whipped whites into the chocolate mixture.

4 Pour the mixture into the terrine mold and freeze overnight.

5 Remove the marquise from the mold and peel off the paper. (Work quickly because this melts quickly.) While still frozen, use a hot knife to slice the loaf into $1/3$-inch- (8-millimeter-) thick slices. Return the marquise to freeze until just before service.

6 Serve two slices on a pool of Frangelico Custard Sauce. Garnish with coarsely chopped hazelnuts, fresh raspberries and fresh mint.

Approximate values per serving: **Calories** 380, **Total fat** 28 g, **Saturated fat** 14 g, **Cholesterol** 125 mg, **Sodium** 35 mg, **Total carbohydrates** 25 g, **Protein** 6 g, **Vitamin A** 10%

BAKED ALASKA

RECIPE 16.20

Baked Alaska always includes spongecake and Italian Meringue, but the flavor of ice cream and sorbet is a personal choice.

Yield: 20 Servings, 1 Cake

Vanilla Spongecake (page 416)	1 half sheet	1 half sheet
Simple Syrup (page 349)	4 fl. oz	120 ml
Raspberry liqueur	0.5 fl. oz.	15 ml
Vanilla Ice Cream (page 485), churned	$1^1/2$ qt.	1.5 lt
Red Currant Sorbet (page 488)	1 qt.	1 lt
Italian Meringue (page 290)	1 lb. 8 oz.	690 g
Brandy	1–2 fl. oz.	30–60 ml

1 Cut the Vanilla Spongecake into two ovals measuring 6 inches × 11 inches (15 centimeters × 28 centimeters); place the first piece directly on an ovenproof serving tray. Combine the Simple Syrup and the raspberry liqueur. Moisten the cake with half of the raspberry syrup. Place in the freezer 30 minutes.

2 Spread the Vanilla Ice Cream evenly over the chilled cake layer using a plastic scraper. Cover with the second piece of Vanilla Spongecake and moisten with the remaining Raspberry Syrup. Freeze until hard.

3 Spread the Red Currant Sorbet on the top cake layer using a plastic scraper. Freeze hard.

4 Place the Italian Meringue in a pastry bag fitted with a St. Honoré tip. Pipe vertical lines on the sides and a zigzag pattern over the top of the frozen dessert, making certain it is completely covered with Italian Meringue. Return the cake, uncovered, to the freezer. Once it has frozen, cover the cake with plastic wrap. The iced dessert can stay in the freezer up to 1 week before serving.

5 To serve, remove the plastic, place the Baked Alaska in a 500°F (260°C) oven and bake until the meringue is browned, approximately 6 to 9 minutes.

6 Heat the brandy in a small saucepan. Carefully ignite the alcohol and pour it over the cake. Bring the Baked Alaska to the dining room while it is still flaming.

Approximate values per $1/20$-cake serving: **Calories** 110, **Total fat** 12 g, **Saturated fat** 6 g, **Cholesterol** 170 mg, **Sodium** 75 mg, **Total carbohydrates** 64 g, **Protein** 6 g

TALKING OF PLEASURE, THIS MOMENT I WAS
WRITING WITH ONE HAND, AND WITH THE OTHER
HOLDING TO MY MOUTH A NECTARINE—HOW GOOD
HOW FINE. IT WENT DOWN ALL PULPY, SLUSHY,
OOZY, ALL ITS DELICIOUS EMBONPOINT MELTED
DOWN MY THROAT LIKE A LARGE, BEATIFIED
STRAWBERRY.

—*John Keats, English poet (1795–1821)*

FRUITS

BRENNAN'S RESTAURANT, New Orleans, LA
Chef Michael Roussel

Botanically, a fruit is an organ that develops from the ovary of a flowering plant and contains one or more seeds. Culinarily, a fruit is the perfect snack food and a key ingredient in the pastry chef's pantry. No food group offers a greater variety of colors, flavors and textures than fruit. This chapter identifies many of the fruits typically used in the bakeshop. It then addresses general considerations in purchasing fresh and preserved fruits. In the formulas at the end of this chapter, fruits take center stage.

▶ IDENTIFYING FRUITS

This book presents fruits according to the ways most people view them and use them, rather than by rigid botanical classifications. Fruits are divided here into eight categories: berries, citrus, exotics, grapes, melons, pomes, stone fruits and tropicals, according to either their shape, seed structure or natural habitat.

A fruit may have several names, varying from region to region or on a purveyor's whim. Botanists are also constantly reclassifying items to fit new findings. The names given here follow generally accepted custom and usage.

BERRIES

Berries are small, juicy fruits that grow on vines and bushes worldwide. Berries are characterized by thin skins and many tiny seeds that are often so small they go unnoticed. Some of the fruits classified here as berries do not fit the botanical definition (for example, raspberries and strawberries), while fruits that are berries botanically (for example, bananas and grapes) are classified elsewhere.

Berries must be fully **ripened** on the vine, as they will not ripen further after harvesting. Select berries that are plump and fully colored. Avoid juice-stained containers and berries with whitish-gray or black spots of mold. All berries should be refrigerated and used promptly. Do not wash berries until you are ready to use them, as washing removes some of their aroma and softens them.

▶ **ripe** describes fully grown and developed fruit; the fruit's flavor, texture and appearance are at their peak, and the fruit is ready to eat

BLACKBERRIES

Blackberries are similar to raspberries, but are larger and shinier, with a deep purple to black color. Thorny blackberry vines are readily found in the wild; commercial production is limited. Their peak season is mid-June through August. Loganberries, Marionberries, olallie berries and boysenberries are blackberry hybrids.

BLUEBERRIES

Blueberries (Fr. *myrtilles*) are small and firm, with a true blue to almost black skin and a juicy, light gray-blue interior. Cultivated berries (high-bush varieties) tend to be larger than wild (low-bush) ones. Blueberries are native to North America and are grown commercially from Maine to Oregon and along the Atlantic seaboard. Their peak season is short, from mid-June to mid-August.

CRANBERRIES

Cranberries, another native North American food, are tart, firm fruit with a mottled red skin. They grow on low vines in cultivated bogs (swamps) throughout

Massachusetts, Wisconsin and New Jersey. Rarely eaten raw, they are made into sauce or relish or are used in breads, pies or pastries. Cranberries are readily available frozen or made into a jelly-type sauce and canned. Although color does not indicate ripeness, cranberries should be picked over before cooking to remove those that are soft or bruised. Their peak harvesting season is from Labor Day through October, leading to the association of cranberries with Thanksgiving dinner.

CURRANTS

Currants are tiny, tart fruits that grow on shrubs in grapelike clusters. The most common are a beautiful, almost translucent red, but black and golden (or white) varieties also exist. All varieties are used for jams, jellies and sauces, and black currants are made into a liqueur, crème de cassis. Although less commonly grown in the United States, currants are very popular and widely available in Europe, with a peak season during the late summer. (The dried fruits called currants are not produced from these berries; they are a special variety of dried grapes.)

RASPBERRIES

Raspberries (Fr. *framboises*) are perhaps the most delicate of all fruits. They have a tart flavor and velvety texture. Red raspberries are the most common, with black, purple and golden berries available in some markets. When ripe, the berry pulls away easily from its white core, leaving the characteristic hollow center. Because they can be easily crushed and are susceptible to mold, most of the raspberries grown are marketed frozen. They grow on thorny vines in cool climates from Washington State to western New York and are imported from New Zealand and South America. The peak domestic season is from late May through November.

STRAWBERRIES

Strawberries (Fr. *fraises*) are brilliant red, heart-shaped fruits that grow on vines. The strawberry plant is actually a perennial herb. The berry's flesh is covered by tiny black seeds called achenes, which are the plant's true fruits. Select berries with a good red color and intact green leafy hull. (The hulls can be easily removed with a paring knife.) Avoid berries with soft or brown spots. Huge berries may be lovely to look at, but they often have hollow centers and little flavor or juice. Although strawberries are available to some extent all year, fresh California strawberries are at their peak from April through June.

The tiny wild or Alpine berries, known by their French name, *fraises des bois*, have a particularly intense flavor and aroma. They are not widely available in the United States.

CITRUS

Citrus fruits include lemons, limes, grapefruits, tangerines, kumquats, oranges and several hybrids. They are characterized by a thick rind, most of which is a bitter white pith (albedo) with a thin exterior layer of colored skin known as the **zest.** Their flesh is segmented and juicy. Citrus fruits are acidic, with a strong aroma; their flavors vary from bitter to tart to sweet.

Citrus fruits grow on trees and shrubs in tropical and subtropical climates worldwide. All citrus fruits are fully ripened on the tree and will not ripen further after harvesting. They should be refrigerated for longest storage. Select fruits that feel heavy and have thin, smooth skins. Avoid those with large blemishes or moist spots. Organic fruit is recommended whenever the rind will be eaten.

Blackberries

Blueberries

Cranberries

White Currants

Red Currants

Raspberries

Strawberries

▶ **zest** the colored outer portion of the rind of citrus fruit; contains the oil that provides flavor and aroma

White Grapefruits

GRAPEFRUITS

Grapefruits (Fr. *pamplemousse*) are large and round with a yellow skin, thick rind and tart flesh. They are an 18th-century hybrid of the orange and pummelo (a large, coarse fruit used mostly in Middle and Far Eastern cuisines). Two varieties of grapefruit are widely available all year: white-fleshed and pink- or ruby-fleshed. White grapefruits produce the finest juice, although pink grapefruits are sweeter.

Red Grapefruits

KUMQUATS

Kumquats

Kumquats are very small, oval-shaped, orange-colored fruits with a soft, sweet skin and slightly bitter flesh. They can be eaten whole, either raw or preserved in syrup, and may be used in jams and preserves.

LEMONS

Lemons

The most commonly used citrus fruits, lemons (Fr. *citrons*), are oval-shaped, bright yellow fruits available all year. Their strongly acidic flavor makes them unpleasant to eat raw but perfect for flavoring desserts and confections. Lemon zest is candied or used as garnish. Rubbing the skin of a lemon or other citrus fruit with a sugar cube extracts much of the aromatic oil. The cube can then be crushed or dissolved to use in formulas calling for citrus flavor.

LIMES

Limes

Limes (Fr. *limons*) are small fruits with thin skins ranging from yellow-green to dark green. Limes are too tart to eat raw and are often substituted for lemons. Their juice adds its distinctive flavor to ices, curds and sorbet. Lime zest can be grated and used to give color and flavor to a variety of dishes. Limes are available all year; their peak season is during the summer. Key lime is a small tart lime variety native to South Florida and used to make key lime pie.

ORANGES

Oranges (Sp. *naranja*) are round fruits with a juicy, orange-colored flesh and a thin, orange skin. They can be either sweet or bitter.

Valencia oranges and navel oranges (a seedless variety) are the most popular sweet oranges. They can be juiced and the flesh may be eaten raw, cooked in desserts or used as a garnish. The zest may be grated or julienned for sauces or garnish. Sweet oranges are available all year; their peak season is from December to April. Blood oranges are also sweet but are small, with a rough, reddish skin. Their flesh is streaked with a blood-red color. Blood oranges are available primarily during the winter months. When selecting sweet oranges, look for fruits that feel plump and heavy, with unblemished skin. The color of the skin depends on weather conditions; a green rind does not affect the flavor of the flesh.

Valencia Oranges

Navel Oranges

Blood Oranges

Bitter oranges include the Seville and bergamot. They are used primarily for the essential oils found in their zest. Oil of bergamot gives Earl Grey tea its distinctive flavor; oil of Seville is essential to curaçao, Grand Marnier and orange flower water. Seville oranges are also used in marmalades.

Tangerines

TANGERINES

Tangerines, sometimes referred to as mandarins, are small and dark orange. Their rind is loose and easily removed to reveal sweet, juicy, aromatic segments. Tangerines are most often eaten fresh and uncooked, but are available canned as mandarin oranges.

Tangelos are a hybrid of tangerines and grapefruits. They are the size of a medium orange with a bulbous stem end and few to no seeds. Clementines are a hybrid of tangerines and Seville oranges. They are small and sweet with a loose, thin rind.

▶ PROCEDURE FOR SEGMENTING CITRUS FRUITS

1 Citrus segments, known as *supremes,* are made by first carefully cutting off the entire peel (including the bitter white pith) in even slices.

2 Individual segments are then removed by gently cutting alongside each membrane.

▶ PROCEDURE FOR ZESTING CITRUS FRUITS

A five-hole zester is used to remove paper-thin strips of the colored rind.

▶ PROCEDURE FOR CUTTING CITRUS PEELS

Large strips of citrus zest may be used as a garnish or to flavor fruit-poaching liquids.

HYBRIDS AND VARIETIES

Several fruits are extremely responsive to selective breeding and crossbreeding and have been toyed with by botanists and growers since at least the time of ancient Rome. Two distinct products are recognized: hybrids and varieties. **Hybrids** result from crossbreeding fruits from different species that are genetically unalike. The result is a unique product. Citrus is particularly responsive to hybridization. **Varieties** result from breeding fruits of the same species that have different qualities or characteristics. Breeding two varieties of apples, for example, produces a third variety with the best qualities of both parents.

EXOTICS

Improved transportation has led to the increasing availability (although sporadic in some areas) of exotic or unusual fresh fruits such as figs, persimmons, pomegranates, prickly pears, rhubarb and star fruits. Other exotic fruits, such as breadfruit, durian, feijoa, loquat, mangosteen and rambutan are still available only on a limited basis from specialty purveyors and are less commonly used in the bakeshop. They are not discussed here.

FIGS

Figs (Fr. *figues*) are the fruit of ficus trees. They are small, soft, pear-shaped fruits with an intensely sweet flavor and rich, moist texture made crunchy by a multitude of tiny seeds. Fresh figs can be served on tarts or baked, poached and simmered to make jams, preserves or compotes.

Dark-skinned figs, known as Mission figs, are a variety planted at Pacific Coast missions during the 18th century. They have a thin skin and small seeds and are available fresh, canned or dried. The white-skinned figs grown commercially include the White Adriatic, used principally for drying and baking, and the all-purpose Kadota. The most important domestic variety, however, is the Calimyrna. These large figs have a rich yellow color and large nutty seeds. Fresh Calimyrna figs are the finest for eating out of hand; they are also available dried.

For the best flavor, figs should be fully ripened on the tree. Unfortunately, fully ripened figs are very delicate and difficult to transport. Most figs are in season from June through October; fresh Calimyrna figs are available only during June.

Calimyrna Figs

GOOSEBERRIES

Several varieties of gooseberry (Fr. *groseille maquereau*) are cultivated for culinary purposes. One well-known variety is the European gooseberry, a member of the currant family that grows on spiny bushes in cool, moist regions of the Northern Hemisphere. Its berries can be relatively large, like a small plum, but are usually less than 1 inch (2.5 centimeters) in diameter. The skin, which is firm and smooth or only slightly hairy, can be green, white (actually gray-green), yellow or red. The tart berries contain many tiny seeds. They are eaten fresh or used for jellies, preserves, tarts and other desserts. North American gooseberry varieties are smaller, perfectly round, and pink to deep red at maturity. Although more prolific, these varietals lack flavor and are generally considered inferior to European gooseberries.

Cape gooseberries, also known as physalis, ground cherries and poha, are unrelated to European and American gooseberries. Native to Peru, they became popular during the 19th century along Africa's Cape of Good Hope, for which they are named. Australia and New Zealand are currently the largest producers. Cape gooseberries are covered with a paper-thin husk or calyx. About the size of a cherry, they have a waxy, bright orange skin and many tiny seeds. Their flavor is similar to coconut and oranges, but tarter. Cape gooseberries may be eaten raw, made into jam or used in desserts. Fresh, they make an especially striking garnish and are excellent for dipping in tempered chocolate.

Cape Gooseberries

GUAVA

Guava (GWAH-vah) are a small, oval or pear-shaped fruit with a strong fragrance and a mild, slightly grainy flesh. They are excellent juiced and in jams and preserves. Guava paste, a thick, sliceable gel, is a popular treat throughout Central America and the Caribbean. Guava will ripen if stored at room temperature and should be slightly soft and fully ripened for the best flavor.

Guava

LYCHEES

The lychee (LEE-chee), also spelled *litchi* or *leechee,* is the fruit of a large tree native to southern China and Southeast Asia. The fruits, which grow in clusters, are oval to round, red and about 1 inch (2.5 centimeters) in diameter. The tough outer skin encloses juicy, white, almost translucent flesh and one large seed. Neither the skin nor the seed is edible. The fruit travels well and is now cultivated in Florida and Hawaii, so supplies are relatively stable. Lychees are eaten fresh out of hand or juiced, and are widely available canned or dried. Fresh lychees are mild but sweet with a pleasant perfume.

Lychees

PERSIMMONS

Persimmons, sometimes referred to as kaki or Sharon fruits, are a bright orange, acorn-shaped fruit with a glossy skin and a large papery blossom. The flesh is bright orange and jellylike, with a mild but rich flavor similar to honey and plums. Persimmons should be peeled before use; any seeds should be discarded. Select bright orange fruits and refrigerate only after they are completely ripe. When ripe, persimmons will be very soft and the skin will have an almost translucent appearance.

Ripe persimmons are delicious eaten raw, halved and topped with cream or soft cheese or peeled, sliced and added to fruit salads. Persimmon bread, muffins, cakes and pies are also popular. Underripe persimmons are almost inedible, however. They are strongly tannic with a chalky or cottony texture.

Persimmons are tree fruits grown in subtropical areas worldwide, although the Asian varieties—now grown in California—are the most common. Fresh persimmons are available from October through January.

Persimmons

POMEGRANATES

An ancient fruit native to Persia (now Iran), pomegranates (POM-uh-gran-uhtz) have long been a subject of poetry and a symbol of fertility. Pomegranates are round, about the size of a large orange, with a pronounced calyx. The skin forms a hard shell with a pinkish-red color. The interior is filled with hundreds of small red seeds (which are, botanically, the actual fruits) surrounded by juicy red pulp. An inedible yellow membrane separates the seeds into compartments. Pomegranates are sweet-sour, and the seeds are pleasantly crunchy. The bright red seeds make an attractive garnish. Pomegranate juice is a popular beverage in Mediterranean cuisines, and grenadine syrup is made from concentrated pomegranate juice.

Select heavy fruits that are not rock-hard, cracked or heavily bruised. Whole pomegranates can be refrigerated several weeks. Pomegranates are available from September through December; their peak season is in October.

Pomegranates

PRICKLY PEARS

Prickly pear fruits, also known as cactus pears and barbary figs, are actually the berries of several varieties of cactus. They are barrel- or pear-shaped, about the size of a large egg. Their thick, firm skin is green or purple with small sharp pins and nearly invisible stinging fibers. Their flesh is spongy, sweet and a brilliant pink-red, dotted with small black seeds. Prickly pears have the aroma of watermelon and the flavor of sugar water.

Once peeled, prickly pears can be diced and eaten raw, or they can be puréed for making jams, sauces, custards or sorbets, to which they give a vivid pink color. Prickly pears are especially common in Mexican and southwestern cuisines.

Select fruits that are full-colored, heavy and tender, but not too soft. Avoid those with mushy or bruised spots. Ripe prickly pears can be refrigerated a week or more. Prickly pears are grown in Mexico and several southwestern states and are available from September through December.

Prickly Pears

▶ PROCEDURE FOR PEELING PRICKLY PEARS

1 To avoid being stung by a prickly pear, hold it steady with a fork, then use a knife to cut off both ends.

2 Cut a lengthwise slit through the skin. Slip the tip of the knife into the cut and peel away the skin by holding it down while rolling the fruit away.

RHUBARB

Although botanically a vegetable, rhubarb (ROO-barb) is most often prepared as a fruit. It is a perennial plant that grows well in temperate and cold climates. Only the pinkish-red stems are edible; the leaves contain high amounts of oxalic acid, which is toxic.

Rhubarb stems are extremely acidic, requiring large amounts of sugar to create the desired sweet-sour taste. Cinnamon, ginger, orange and strawberry are particularly compatible with rhubarb. It is excellent for pies, cobblers, preserves or stewing. Young, tender stalks of rhubarb do not need to be peeled. When cooked, rhubarb becomes very soft and turns a beautiful light pink color.

Fresh rhubarb is sold as whole stalks, with the leaves removed. Select crisp, unblemished stalks. Rhubarb's peak season is during the early spring, from February through May. Frozen rhubarb pieces are readily available and are excellent for pies, tarts or jams.

Rhubarb

Star Fruits

STAR FRUITS

Star fruits, also known as carambola, are oval, up to 5 inches (12.5 centimeters) long, with five prominent ribs or wings running their length. A cross-section cut is shaped like a star. The edible skin is a waxy orange-yellow; it covers a dry, paler yellow flesh. Its flavor is similar to that of plums, sweet but bland. Star fruits do not need to be peeled or seeded. They are most often sliced and added to fruit salad or used as a garnish.

Color and aroma are the best indicators of ripeness. The fruits should be a deep golden-yellow and there should be brown along the edge of the ribs. The aroma should be full and floral. Green fruits can be kept at room temperature to ripen, then refrigerated up to 2 weeks. Star fruits are cultivated in Hawaii, Florida and California, though some are still imported from the Caribbean. Fresh fruits are available from August to February.

GRAPES

Grapes (Fr. *raisins;* Sp. *uvas*) are the single largest fruit crop in the world, due, of course, to their use in wine making. This section, however, discusses only table grapes, those grown for eating. Grapes are berries that grow on vines in large clusters. California is the world's largest producer, with more than a dozen varieties grown for table use. Grapes are classified by color as white (which are actually green) or black (which are actually red). White grapes are generally blander than black ones, with a thinner skin and firmer flesh.

The grape's color and most of its flavor are found in the skin. Grapes are usually eaten raw, either alone or in fruit salads. They are also used as a garnish or accompaniment to desserts and cheeses. Dried grapes are known as raisins (Fr. *raisins sec*); they are usually made from Thompson Seedless or muscat grapes, currants (made from Black Corinth grapes and labeled Zante currants) or sultanas (made from sultana grapes).

Grapes are available all year because the many varieties have different harvesting schedules. Look for firm, unblemished fruits that are firmly attached to the stem. A surface bloom or dusty appearance is caused by yeasts and indicates recent harvesting. Wrinkled grapes or those with brown spots around the stem are past their prime. All grapes should be rinsed and drained prior to use.

RED FLAME GRAPES

Red Flame grapes are a seedless California hybrid, second only in importance to the Thompson Seedless. Red Flame grapes are large and round with a slightly tart flavor and variegated red color.

Red Flame Grapes

THOMPSON SEEDLESS GRAPES

The most commercially important table grapes are a variety known as Thompson Seedless, which are pale green with a crisp texture and sweet flavor. Their peak season is from June to November. Many are dried in the hot desert sun of California's San Joaquin Valley to produce dark raisins. For golden raisins, Thompson Seedless grapes are treated with sulfur dioxide to prevent browning, then dried mechanically.

Thompson Seedless Grapes

OTHER TABLE GRAPES

Of the table grapes containing seeds, the most important varieties are the Concord, Ribier and Emperor. They range from light red to deep black, and all three are in season during the autumn. Concord grapes, one of the few grape varieties native to the New World, are especially important for making juices and jellies.

Concord Grapes

MELONS

Like pumpkins and cucumbers, melons are members of the gourd family (*Cucurbitaceae*). The dozens of melon varieties can be divided into two general types: sweet (or dessert) melons and watermelons. Sweet melons have a tan, green or yellow netted or farrowed rind and dense, fragrant flesh. Watermelon has a thick, dark green rind surrounding crisp, watery flesh.

Melons are almost 90 percent water, so cooking destroys their texture, quickly turning the flesh to mush. Most are served simply sliced in fruit salads or puréed and made into sorbet.

Melons should be vine-ripened. A ripe melon should yield slightly and spring back when pressed at the blossom end (opposite the stem). It should also give off a strong aroma. Avoid melons that are very soft or feel damp at the stem end. Ripe melons may be stored in the refrigerator, although the flavor will be better at room temperature. Slightly underripe melons can be stored at room temperature to allow flavor and aroma to develop.

CANTALOUPES

American cantaloupes, which are actually muskmelons, are sweet melons with a thick, yellow-green netted rind, a sweet, moist, orange flesh and a strong aroma. (European cantaloupes, which are not generally available in the United States, are more craggy and furrowed in appearance.) As with all sweet melons, the many small seeds are found in a central cavity.

Cantaloupes

Honeydew Melons

Watermelon

Rome

Red Delicious

Granny Smith

Golden Delicious

Gala

Avoid cantaloupes with the pronounced yellow color or moldy aroma that indicates overripeness. Mexican imports ensure a year-round supply, although their peak season is summer.

HONEYDEW MELONS

Honeydew melons are large oval sweet melons with a smooth rind that ranges from white to pale green. Although the flesh is generally pale green, with a mild, sweet flavor, pink- or gold-fleshed honeydews are also available. Like casaba melons, honeydew melons have little to no aroma. They are available almost all year; their peak season is from June through October.

WATERMELONS

Watermelons are large (up to 30 pounds or 13.5 kilograms) round or oval-shaped melons with a thick rind. The skin may be solid green, green-striped or mottled with white. The flesh is crisp and extremely juicy with small, hard, black seeds throughout. Seedless hybrids are available. Most watermelons have pink to red flesh, although golden-fleshed varieties are becoming more common. Watermelons are of a different genus from the sweet melons described earlier. They are native to tropical Africa and are now grown commercially in Texas and several southern states.

POMES

Pomes are tree fruits with thin skin and firm flesh surrounding a central core containing many small seeds called pips or carpels. Pomes include apples, pears and quince.

APPLES

Apples (Fr. *pommes*), perhaps the most common and commonly appreciated of all fruits, grow on trees in temperate zones worldwide. They are popular because of their convenience, flavor, variety and availability. Apples can be eaten raw out of hand, or they can be used in a wide variety of cooked or baked dishes. Apple juice (cider) produces alcoholic and nonalcoholic beverages and cider vinegar.

Of the hundreds of known apple varieties, only 20 or so are commercially significant in the United States. Several varieties and their characteristics are noted in Table 17.1. Most have a moist, creamy white flesh with a thin skin of yellow, green or red. They range in flavor from very sweet to very tart, with an equally broad range of textures, from firm and crisp to soft and mealy.

In Europe, apples are divided into distinct cooking and eating varieties. Cooking varieties are those that disintegrate to a purée when cooked. American varieties are less rigidly classified. Nevertheless, not all apples are appropriate for all types of cooking. Those that retain their shape better during cooking are the best choices where slices or appearance are important. Varieties with a higher malic acid content break down easily, making them more appropriate for applesauce or juicing. Either type may be eaten out of hand, depending on personal preference.

McIntosh

Although not native to North America, apples are now grown commercially in 35 states, with Washington and New York leading in production. Apples are harvested when still slightly underripe, then stored in a controlled atmosphere (temperature and oxygen are greatly reduced) for extended periods until ready for sale. Modern storage techniques make fresh apples available all year, although their peak season is during the autumn.

Table 17.1   APPLE VARIETIES

VARIETY	SKIN COLOR	FLAVOR	TEXTURE	PEAK SEASON	USE
Fiji	Yellow-green with red highlights	Sweet-spicy	Crisp	All year	Eating, in salads
Gala	Yellow-orange with red stripes	Sweet	Crisp	Aug.–March	Eating, in salads, sauce
Golden Delicious	Glossy greenish-gold	Sweet	Semifirm	Sept.–Oct.	In tarts, with cheese, in salads
Granny Smith	Bright green	Tart	Firm and crisp	Oct.–Nov.	Eating, in tarts
Jonathan	Brilliant red	Tart to acidic	Tender	Sept.–Oct.	Eating, all-purpose
McIntosh	Red with green background	Tart to acidic	Soft	Fall	Applesauce, in closed pies
Pippin (Newton)	Greenish-yellow	Tart	Semifirm	Fall	In pies, eating, baking
Red Delicious	Deep red	Sweet but bland	Soft to mealy	Sept.–Oct.	Eating
Rome	Red	Sweet-tart	Firm	Oct.–Nov.	Baking, pies, sauces
Winesap	Dark red with streaks	Tangy	Crisp	Oct.–Nov.	Cider, all-purpose

When selecting apples, look for smooth, unbroken skins and firm fruits, without soft spots or bruises. Badly bruised or rotting apples should be discarded immediately. They emit quantities of ethylene gas that speed spoilage of nearby fruits. (Remember the saying that "one bad apple spoils the barrel.") Store apples chilled up to 6 weeks. Apple peels (the skin) may be eaten or removed as desired, but in either case, apples should be washed just prior to use to remove pesticides and any wax that was applied to improve appearance. Apple slices can be frozen (often with sugar or citric acid added to slow spoilage) or dried.

▶ PROCEDURE FOR CORING APPLES

1 Remove the core from a whole apple with an apple corer by inserting the corer from the stem end and pushing out the cylinder containing the core and seeds.

2 Alternatively, first cut an apple into quarters, then use a paring knife to cut away the core and seeds.

PEARS

Pears (Fr. *poires*) are an ancient tree fruit grown in temperate areas throughout the world. Most of the pears marketed in the United States are grown in California, Washington and Oregon.

Although literally thousands of pear varieties have been identified, only a dozen or so are commercially significant. Several varieties and their characteristics are noted in Table 17.2. Pear varieties vary widely in size, color and flavor. They are most often eaten out of hand, but can be baked or poached. Pears are delicious with cheese, especially blue cheeses, and can be used in fruit salads, compotes or preserves.

Asian pears, also known as Chinese pears or apple-pears, are of a different species than common pears. They have the moist, sweet flavor of a pear and the

Anjou

Bosc

Sekel Pears

Red d'Anjou

Bartlett

Asian Pears

round shape and crisp texture of an apple. They are becoming increasingly popular in the United States, particularly those known as Twentieth Century or Nijisseiki.

When selecting pears, look for fruits with smooth, unbroken skin and an intact stem. Pears will not ripen properly on the tree, so they are picked while still firm and should be allowed to soften before use. Underripe pears may be left at room temperature to ripen. A properly ripened pear should have a good fragrance and yield to gentle pressure at the stem end. Pears can be prepared or stored in the same ways as apples.

QUINCE

Common quince (kwence; Fr. *coing*) resemble large, lumpy yellow pears. Their flesh is hard, with many pips or seeds, and they have a wonderful fragrance. Too astringent to eat raw, quince develop a sweet flavor and pink color when cooked with sugar. Quince are used in breads, jellies, marmalades and pies. They have a

Quince

Table 17.2 PEAR VARIETIES

VARIETY	APPEARANCE	FLAVOR	TEXTURE	PEAK SEASON	USE
Anjou (Beurre d'Anjou)	Greenish-yellow skin; egg-shaped with short neck; red variety also available	Sweet and juicy	Firm, keeps well	Oct.–May	Eating, poaching
Bartlett (Williams)	Thin yellow skin; bell-shaped; red variety also available	Very sweet, buttery, juicy	Tender	Aug.–Dec.	Eating, canning, in salads
Bosc	Golden-brown skin; long tapered neck	Buttery	Dry, holds its shape well	Sept.–May	Poaching, baking
Comice	Yellow-green skin; large and chubby	Sweet, juicy	Smooth	Oct.–Feb.	Eating
Sekel	Tiny; brown to yellow skin	Spicy	Very firm, grainy	Aug.–Dec.	Poaching, pickling

high **pectin** content and may be added to other fruit jams or preserves to encourage gelling.

Fresh quince, usually imported from South America or southeast Europe, are available from October through January. Select firm fruits with a good yellow color. Small blemishes may be cut away before cooking. Quince will keep for up to a month under refrigeration.

STONE FRUITS

Stone fruits, also known as drupes, include apricots, cherries, nectarines, peaches and plums and are related to the almond. They are characterized by a thin skin, soft flesh and one woody stone or pit. Although most originated in China, the shrubs and trees producing stone fruits are now grown in temperate climates worldwide.

The domestic varieties of stone fruits are in season from late spring through summer. They tend to be fragile fruits, are easily bruised and difficult to transport and have a short shelf life. Do not wash them until ready to use, as moisture can cause deterioration. Stone fruits are excellent dried and are often used to make liqueurs and brandies. (The kernel inside the pits of many stone fruits contains amygdalin, a compound that has a bitter almond flavor. Eating the raw kernel can cause digestive discomfort or more serious side effects and should be avoided. When cooked it is harmless and can add flavor to jams and creams.)

APRICOTS

Apricots (Fr. *abricots*) are small, round stone fruits with a velvety skin that varies from deep yellow to vivid orange. Their juicy orange flesh surrounds a dark, almond-shaped pit. Apricots can be eaten out of hand, poached, stewed, baked or candied. Apricots have a short season, peaking during June and July, and do not travel well. Select apricots that are well shaped, plump and fairly firm. Avoid ones that are greenish-yellow or mushy. Fresh apricots will last several days under refrigeration, but the flavor is best at room temperature. If fresh fruits are unavailable, canned apricots are usually an acceptable substitute. Dried apricots and apricot juice (known as nectar) are readily available.

CHERRIES

From the northern states, particularly Washington, Oregon, Michigan and New York, come the two most important types of cherry: the sweet cherry and the sour (or tart) cherry.

Sweet cherries (Fr. *cerises*) are round to heart-shaped, about 1 inch (2.5 centimeters) in diameter, with skin that ranges from yellow to deep red to nearly black. The flesh, which is sweet and juicy, may vary from yellow to dark red. The most common and popular sweet cherries are the dark red Bings. Yellow-red Royal Ann and Rainier cherries are also available in some areas.

Sweet cherries are often marketed fresh, made into maraschino cherries or candied for use in baked goods. Fresh sweet cherries have a very short season, peaking during June and July. Cherries will not ripen further after harvesting. Select fruits that are firm and plump with a green stem still attached. There should not be any brown spots around the stem. A dry or brown stem indicates that the cherry is less than fresh. Once the stem is removed, the cherry will deteriorate rapidly. Store fresh cherries in the refrigerator and do not wash them until ready to use.

Rainier Cherries

Bing Cherries

▶ **pectin** a gelatin-like carbohydrate obtained from certain fruits; used to thicken jams and jellies

HEIRLOOM VARIETIES

Older fruit and vegetable varieties are often less suited to the demands of commercial agriculture. They may bruise easily and be irregular in size and appearance. Many chefs and home gardeners are finding that these heirloom varieties are more flavorful than their photogenic descendants. Seeds and rootstocks from these older varieties are being cultivated in an attempt to preserve the flavors from the past.

Apricots

Remove the stem and place the cherry in the pitter with the indentation facing up. Squeeze the handles together to force out the pit.

Peaches

Nectarines

Santa Rosa Plums

Damson Plums

Sour cherries are light to dark red and are so acidic that they are rarely eaten uncooked. The most common sour cherries are the Montmorency and Morello. Most sour cherries are canned or frozen, or cooked with sugar and starch (usually cornstarch or tapioca) and sold as prepared pastry and pie fillings.

Both sweet and sour varieties are available dried.

PEACHES AND NECTARINES

Peaches (Fr. *pêches*) are moderate-sized, round fruits with a juicy, sweet flesh. Nectarines are a variety of peach, the main difference between the two being their skin. Peaches have a thin skin covered with fuzz, while nectarines have a thin, smooth skin. The flesh of either fruit ranges from white to pale orange. Although their flavors are somewhat different, they may be substituted for each other in most formulas.

Peaches and nectarines are excellent for eating out of hand or in dessert tarts, pastries, ice cream and preserves. Although the skin is edible, peaches are generally peeled before being used. (Peaches are easily peeled if blanched first.)

Peaches and nectarines are either freestones or clingstones. With freestones, the flesh separates easily from the stone; freestone fruits are commonly eaten out of hand. The flesh of clingstones adheres firmly to the stone; they hold their shape better when cooked and are the type most often canned.

Select fruits with a good aroma, an overall creamy, yellow or yellow-orange color and an unwrinkled skin free of blemishes. Red patches are not an indication of ripeness; a green skin indicates that the fruit was picked too early and it will not ripen further. Peaches and nectarines will soften but do not become sweeter after harvesting.

The United States, especially California, is the world's largest producer of peaches and nectarines. Their peak season is through the summer months, with July and August producing the best crop. South American peaches are sometimes available from January to May. Canned and frozen peaches are readily available.

PLUMS

Plums (Fr. *prunes*) are round to oval-shaped fruits that grow on trees or bushes. Dozens of plum varieties are known, although only a few are commercially significant. Plums vary in size from very small to 3 inches (7.5 centimeters) in diameter. Their thin skin can be green, red, yellow or various shades of blue-purple. Plums are excellent for eating out of hand. Plums can also be baked, poached or used in pies, cobblers or tarts.

Fresh plums are widely available from June through October; their peak season is in August and September. When selecting plums, look for plump, smooth fruits with unblemished skin. Generally, they should yield to gentle pressure, although the green and yellow varieties remain quite firm. Avoid plums with moist, brown spots near the stem. Plums may be left at room temperature to ripen, then stored in the refrigerator. Dried plums (prunes), discussed later, are produced by drying special plum varieties, usually the French Agen.

TROPICALS

Tropical fruits are native to the world's hot, tropical or subtropical regions. Most are now readily available throughout the United States thanks to rapid transportation and distribution methods. All can be eaten fresh, without cooking. Their flavors complement each other and are popular in desserts and pastries.

BANANAS

Common yellow bananas (Fr. *bananes*) are actually the berries of a large tropical herb. Grown in bunches called hands, they are about 7 to 9 inches (17 to 22 centimeters) long, with a sticky, soft, sweet flesh. Their inedible yellow skin is easily removed. Baby bananas (Nino, Ladyfinger or Finger Bananas) measure 4 to 5 inches (10 to 12.5 centimeters) long with yellow or red skin. Their flesh is more dense and sweeter than most larger banana varieties and their diminutive size makes them ideal for many dessert applications.

Properly ripened bananas are excellent eaten out of hand or used in salads. Lightly bruised or overripe fruits are best used for breads or muffins. Bananas blend well with other tropical fruits and citrus. Their unique flavor is also complemented by cinnamon, ginger, honey and chocolate.

Fresh bananas are available all year. Bananas are always harvested when still green, because the texture and flavor will be adversely affected if the fruits are allowed to turn yellow on the tree. Unripe bananas are hard, dry and starchy. Because bananas ripen after harvesting, it is acceptable to purchase green bananas if there is sufficient time for final ripening before use. Bananas should be left at room temperature to ripen. A properly ripened banana has a yellow peel with brown flecks. The tip should not have any remaining green coloring. As bananas continue to age, the peel darkens and the starches turn to sugar, giving the fruits a sweeter flavor. Avoid bananas that have large brown bruises or a gray cast (a sign of cold damage).

Plantains, also referred to as cooking bananas, are larger but not as sweet as common bananas. They are frequently cooked as a starchy vegetable in tropical cuisines.

Common Yellow Bananas

DATES

Dates (Fr. *datte*) are the fruit of the date palm tree, which has been cultivated since ancient times. Dates are about 1 to 2 inches (2.5 to 5 centimeters) long, with a paper-thin skin and a single grooved seed in the center. Most are golden to dark brown when ripe.

Although dates appear to be dried, they are actually fresh fruits. They have a sticky-sweet, almost candied texture and rich flavor. Dates provide flavor and moisture for breads, muffins, cookies and tarts. Pitted dates are readily available in several packaged forms: whole, chopped or extruded (for use in baking). Whole unpitted dates are available in bulk. Date juice is also available for use as a natural sweetener in baked goods. Although packaged or processed dates are available all year, peak season for fresh domestic dates is from October through December. When selecting dates, look for those that are plump, glossy and moist.

Medjool Dates

KIWIS

Kiwis, sometimes known as kiwifruits or Chinese gooseberries, are small oval fruits, about the size of a large egg, with a thin, fuzzy brown skin. The flesh is bright green with a white core surrounded by hundreds of tiny black seeds. A golden-fleshed variety is also now available.

Kiwis are sweet, but somewhat bland. They are best used raw, peeled and sliced for fruit salads or garnish. Although kiwis are not recommended for cooking because heat causes them to fall apart, they are a perfect addition to glazed fruit tarts and can be puréed for sorbets, sauces or mousses. Kiwis contain an enzyme similar to that in fresh pineapple and papaya, which prevents gelling.

Kiwis

MANGOES

Mangoes (Fr. *mangue*) are oval or kidney-shaped fruits that normally weigh between 6 ounces and 1 pound (180 grams and 500 grams). Their skin is smooth and thin but tough, varying from yellow to orange-red, with patches of green, red or purple. As mangoes ripen, the green disappears. The juicy, bright orange flesh clings to a large, flat pit.

A mango's unique flavor is spicy-sweet, with an acidic tang. Mangoes can be puréed for use in drinks or sauces, or the flesh can be sliced or cubed for use in salads, pickles, chutneys or desserts.

Mangoes

Although Florida produces some mangoes, most of those available in the United States are from Mexico. Their peak season is from May through August. Select fruits with good color that are firm and free of blemishes. Ripe mangoes should have a good aroma, and should not be too soft or shriveled. Allow mangoes to ripen completely at room temperature, then refrigerate up to 1 week.

▶ PROCEDURE FOR PITTING AND CUTTING MANGOES

1 Cut along each side of the pit to remove two sections.

2 Each section can then be cubed using the "hedgehog" technique: Make crosswise cuts through the flesh, just to the skin; press up on the skin side of the section, exposing the cubes.

3 The mango may be served like this, or the cubes can be cut off to use on tarts or other desserts

PAPAYAS

The papaya (puh-PIE-yuh) is a greenish-yellow fruit shaped rather like a large pear and weighing 1 to 2 pounds (500 to 1000 grams). When halved, it resembles a melon. The flesh is golden to reddish-pink; its center cavity is filled with round, silver-black seeds resembling caviar. Ripe papayas can be eaten raw, with only a squirt of lemon or lime juice. They can also be puréed for sauces or sorbets. Papayas contain **papain,** which breaks down proteins, making them unsuitable for use in gelatins because it inhibits gelling.

Papayas

▶ **papain** an enzyme found in papayas that breaks down proteins; used as the primary ingredient in many commercial meat tenderizers

Papaya seeds are edible, with a peppery flavor and slight crunch. They are occasionally used to garnish fruit dishes.

Papayas are grown in tropical and subtropical areas worldwide. Although they are available year-round, their peak season is from April through June. Select papayas that are plump, with a smooth, unblemished skin. Color is a better determinant of ripeness than is softness: The greater the proportion of yellow to green skin color, the riper the fruit. Papayas may be held at room temperature until completely ripe, then refrigerated up to 1 week.

Red Papayas

PASSION FRUITS

Passion fruits (Fr. *granadillas*) have a firm, almost shell-like purple skin with orange-yellow pulp surrounding large, black, edible seeds. They are about the size and shape of large hen eggs, with a sweet, rich and unmistakable citrusy flavor. The pulp is used in custards, sauces and ice creams.

Select heavy fruits with dark, shriveled skin and a strong aroma. Allow them to ripen at room temperature, if necessary, then refrigerate. Passion fruits are

Passion Fruits

now grown in New Zealand, Hawaii and California and should be available all year, although their peak season is in February and March. Bottles or frozen packs of purée are readily available and provide a strong, true flavor.

Pineapples

PINEAPPLES

Pineapples (Fr. *ananas*) are the fruit of a shrub with sharp spear-shaped leaves. Each fruit is covered with rough, brown eyes, giving it the appearance of a pinecone. The pale yellow flesh, which is sweet and very juicy, surrounds a cylindrical woody core that is edible but too tough for most uses. Most pineapples weigh approximately 2 pounds (1 kilogram), but dwarf varieties are also available.

Pineapples are excellent eaten raw or sautéed. Canned or cooked pineapple can be added to gelatin mixtures, but avoid using fresh pineapple; an enzyme (bromelin) found in fresh pineapple breaks down gelatin.

Pineapples do not ripen after harvesting. They must be left on the stem until completely ripe, at which time they are extremely perishable. The vast majority of pineapples come from Hawaii. Fresh pineapples are available all year, with peak supplies in March through June. Select heavy fruits with a strong, sweet aroma and rich color. Avoid those with dried leaves or soft spots. Pineapples should be used as soon as possible after purchase. Pineapples are also available canned in slices, in cubes or crushed, dried or candied.

▶ PROCEDURE FOR TRIMMING AND SLICING PINEAPPLES

1 Slice off the leaves and stem end. Stand the fruit upright and cut the peel off in vertical strips.

2 Cut the peeled fruit in quarters, then cut away the woody core.

3 The flesh can then be cut as desired.

FRIEDA AND THE KIWIFRUIT

How did a fuzzy brown unknown become a media darling and a hugely viable crop? The answer is, thanks to Frieda Caplan. In 1962 Frieda, founder of Frieda's, Inc., launched her historic worldwide promotion of kiwifruit. Acting on a suggestion that Chinese gooseberries, then grown only in New Zealand, might sell better under the name kiwifruit (the kiwi is the national bird of New Zealand), Frieda unleashed a produce giant. This story of the kiwifruit is studied throughout the world as one of the great successes in food marketing.

In 1980, after 18 years of Frieda's continual, creative, aggressive and expensive marketing, the kiwifruit became a North American star when nouvelle cuisine chefs prominently featured it in their mixes of strawberry, banana, melon and pineapples. Since that time, the question asked most commonly of Frieda's, Inc. is "What will be the next kiwifruit?"

The answer is that there will never be another kiwifruit. When the kiwifruit was accepted into the world's fruit vernacular, there was an unconditional paradigm shift. Today, new specialty produce does not have to go through the rigorous acceptance process inflicted on the kiwifruit. There can never be another kiwifruit because the marketing climate and consumer palate have shifted in a wonderful, irreversible way. Now when a new fruit such as red bananas or yellow seedless watermelon comes onto the market, the consuming public does not react with fear and say "Bananas are supposed to be yellow" or "It really isn't watermelon if there aren't any seeds and it's not red." They respond with positive open minds (much the same as Frieda did when she purchased her first flat of kiwifruit in 1962) and a newfound knowledge that new foods will bring quality and variety, not discord, to their diets.

—Karen Caplan, Frieda's eldest daughter and President of Frieda's, Inc.

▶ PURCHASING FRESH FRUITS

Fresh fruits have not been subjected to any processing (such as canning, freezing or drying). Fresh fruits may be ripe or unripe, depending on their condition when harvested or the conditions under which they have been stored. In order to use fresh fruits to their best advantage, it is important to make careful purchasing decisions. The size of each piece of fruit, its grade or quality, its ripeness on delivery and its nutritional content may affect your ability to use the fruit in an appropriate and cost-effective manner.

GRADING

Fresh fruits traded on the wholesale market may be graded under the USDA's voluntary program. The grades, based on size and uniformity of shape, color and texture as well as the absence of defects, are U.S. Fancy, U.S. No. 1, U.S. No. 2 and U.S. No. 3. Most fruits purchased for food service operations are U.S. Fancy. Fruits with lower grades are suitable for processing into sauces, jams, jellies or preserves.

RIPENING

Several important changes take place in a fruit as it ripens. The fruit reaches its full size; its pulp or flesh becomes soft and tender; its color changes. In addition, the fruit's acid content declines, making it less tart, and its starch content converts into the sugars fructose and glucose, which provide the fruit's sweetness, flavor and aroma.

Unfortunately, these changes do not stop when the fruit reaches its peak of ripeness. Rather, they continue, deteriorating the fruit's texture and flavor and eventually causing spoilage.

Depending upon the species, fresh fruits can be purchased either fully ripened or unripened. Figs and pineapples, for example, ripen only on the plant and are harvested at or just before their peak of ripeness, then rushed to market. They should not be purchased unripened as they will never attain full flavor or texture after harvesting. On the other hand, some fruits, including bananas and pears, continue to ripen after harvesting and can be purchased unripened.

With most harvested fruits, the ripening time as well as the time during which the fruits remain at their peak of ripeness can be manipulated. For instance, ripening can be delayed by chilling. Chilling slows down the fruit's **respiration rate** (fruits, like animals, consume oxygen and expel carbon dioxide). The slower the respiration rate, the slower the conversion of starch to sugar. For quicker ripening, fruit can be stored at room temperature.

Ripening is also affected by ethylene gas, a colorless, odorless hydrocarbon gas. Ethylene gas is naturally emitted by ripening fruits and can be used to encourage further ripening in most fruits. Apples, tomatoes, melons and bananas give off the most ethylene and should be stored away from delicate fruits and vegetables, especially greens. Fruits that are picked and shipped unripened can be exposed to ethylene gas to induce ripening just before sale. Conversely, if you want to extend the life of ripe fruits a day or two, isolate them from other fruits and keep them well chilled.

Fresh fruits will not ripen further once they are cooked or processed. The cooking or processing method applied, however, may soften the fruits or add flavor.

▶ **respiration rate** the speed with which the cells of a fruit use up oxygen and produce carbon dioxide during ripening

PURCHASING

Fresh fruits are sold by weight or by count. They are packed in containers referred to as crates, bushels, cartons, cases, lugs or flats. The weight or count packed in each of these containers varies depending on the type of fruit, the purveyor and the state in which the fruits were packed. For example, Texas citrus is packed in cartons equal to $7/10$ of a bushel; Florida citrus is packed in cartons equal to $4/5$ of a bushel. Sometimes fruit size must be specified when ordering. A 30-pound case of lemons, for example, may contain 96, 112 or 144 individual lemons, depending on their size.

Some fresh fruits, especially melons, pineapples, peaches and berries, are available trimmed, cleaned, peeled or cut. Sugar and preservatives are sometimes added. They are sold in bulk containers, sometimes packed in water. These items offer a consistent product with a significant reduction in labor costs. The purchase price may be greater than that for fresh fruits, and flavor, freshness and nutritional qualities may suffer somewhat from the processing.

▶ PURCHASING AND STORING PRESERVED FRUITS

Preservation techniques are designed to extend the shelf life of fruits in essentially fresh form. These methods include irradiation, acidulation, canning, freezing and drying. Except for drying, these techniques do not substantially change the fruits' texture or flavor. Canning and freezing can also be used to preserve cooked fruits. Preserves such as jellies and jams are cooked products and are discussed later in this chapter.

ACIDULATION

Apples, pears, bananas, peaches and other fruits turn brown when cut. Although this browning is commonly attributed to exposure to oxygen, it is actually caused by the reaction of enzymes.

Immersing cut fruits in an acidic solution such as lemon or orange juice can retard enzymatic browning. This simple technique is sometimes referred to as acidulation. Soaking fruits in water or lemon juice and water (called acidulated water) is not recommended. Unless a sufficient amount of salt or sugar is added to the water, the fruits will just become mushy. But if enough salt or sugar is added to retain texture, the flavor will be affected.

IRRADIATED FRUITS

Some fruits can be subjected to ionizing radiation to destroy parasites, insects and bacteria. The treatment also slows ripening without a noticeable effect on the fruits' flavor and texture. Irradiated fruits must be labeled "treated with radiation," "treated by irradiation" or with the symbol shown here.

CANNED FRUITS

Almost any type of fruit can be canned successfully; pineapple and peaches are the largest sellers. In commercial canning, raw fruits are cleaned and placed in a sealed container, then subjected to high temperatures for a specific amount of time. Heating destroys the microorganisms that cause spoilage, and the sealed environment created by the can eliminates oxidation and retards decomposition. But the heat required by the canning process also softens the texture of most fruits.

In *solid-pack cans,* little or no water is added. The only liquid is from the fruits' natural moisture. *Water-pack cans* have water or fruit juice added, which must be taken into account when determining costs. *Syrup-pack cans* have a sugar syrup—light, medium or heavy—added. The syrup should also be taken into account when determining food costs, and the additional sweetness should be considered when using syrup-packed fruits. Cooked fruit products such as pie fillings are also available canned.

Canned fruits are purchased in cases of standard-sized cans (see Appendix II). Once a can is opened, any unused contents should be transferred to an appropriate storage container and refrigerated. Cans with bulges should be discarded immediately, without opening.

FROZEN FRUITS

Freezing is a highly effective method for preserving fruits. It severely inhibits the growth of microorganisms that cause fruits to spoil. Freezing can alter the appearance or texture of most fruits because of their high water content. This occurs when ice crystals formed from the water in the cells burst the cells' walls.

Many fruits, especially berries and apple and pear slices, are now individually quick-frozen (IQF). This method employs blasts of cold air, refrigerated plates, liquid nitrogen, liquid air or other techniques to chill the produce quickly. Speeding the freezing process can greatly reduce the formation of ice crystals.

Fruits can be trimmed and sliced before freezing and are also available frozen in sugar syrup, which adds flavor and prevents browning. Berries are frozen whole, while stone fruits are usually peeled, pitted and sliced. Fruit purées are also available frozen.

Frozen fruits are graded as U.S. Grade A (Fancy), U.S. Grade B (Choice or Extra Standard), or U.S. Grade C (Standard). The "U.S." indicates that a government inspector has graded the product, but packers may use grade names without an actual inspection if the contents meet the standards of the grade indicated.

IQF fruits can be purchased in bulk by the case. All frozen fruits should be sealed in moisture-proof wrapping and kept at a constant temperature of 0°F (−18°C) or below. Temperature fluctuations can cause freezer burn. Frozen berries such as blueberries and blackberries should not be thawed before adding to batters because their juice can easily discolor the batter.

DRIED FRUITS

Drying is the oldest known technique for preserving fruits, having been used for more than 5000 years. When ripe fruits are dried, they lose most of their moisture. This concentrates their flavors and sugars and dramatically extends shelf life. Although most fruits can be dried, plums (prunes), grapes (raisins, sultanas and currants), apricots and figs are the fruits most commonly dried. The drying method can be as simple as leaving ripe fruits in the sun to dry naturally or the

Golden Raisins

Currants

Kiwis

Apricots

Persimmons

Apples

Pears

more cost-efficient technique of passing fruits through a compartment of hot, dry air to quickly extract moisture.

Dried fruits actually retain 16 to 25 percent residual moisture, which leaves them moist and soft. They are often treated with sulfur dioxide to prevent browning (oxidation) and to extend shelf life. Before use, dried fruits may be softened by steeping them for a short time in a hot liquid such as water, wine, rum, brandy or other liquor. Some dried fruits should be simmered in a small amount of water before use.

Store dried fruits in airtight containers to prevent further moisture loss; keep in a dry, cool area away from sunlight. Dried fruits may mold if exposed to both air and high humidity.

▶ JUICING

Fruit juice is used as a beverage, alone or mixed with other ingredients, and as the liquid ingredient in other preparations. Juice can be extracted from fruits in two ways: pressure and blending.

Pressure is used to extract juice from fruits such as citrus that have a high water content. Pressure is applied by hand-squeezing or with a manual or electric reamer. All reamers work on the same principle: A ribbed cone is pressed against the fruit to break down its flesh and release the juice. Always strain juices to remove seeds, pulp or fibrous pieces.

A blender or an electric juice extractor can be used to liquify less-juicy fruits such as apples and pears. The extractor pulverizes the fruit, then separates and strains the liquid from the pulp with centrifugal force.

Interesting and delicious beverages can be made by combining the juice of one or more fruits: pineapple with orange, apple with cranberry, strawberry with tangerine and papaya with orange. Color should be considered when creating mixed-juice beverages, however. Some combinations can cause rather odd color changes. Although yellow and orange juices are not a problem, those containing red and blue flavonoid pigments (such as Concord grapes, cherries, strawberries, raspberries and blueberries) can create some unappetizing colors. Adding an acid such as lemon juice helps retain the correct red and blue hues.

▶ **juice** the liquid extracted from any fruit or vegetable

▶ **nectar** the diluted, sweetened juice of peaches, apricots, guavas, black currants or other fruits, the juice of which would be too thick or too tart to drink straight

▶ **cider** mildly fermented apple juice; nonalcoholic apple juice may also be labeled cider

▶ APPLYING VARIOUS PREPARATION AND COOKING METHODS

Although most fruits are edible raw and are typically served that way, many fruits are enhanced by macerating them in a flavored syrup or liqueur with added spices and flavorings before using, as discussed in Chapter 5, Mise en Place. When macerating fruits, be certain they are well washed and bruise-free. Drying the fruits after washing prevents dilution of the macerating liquid. Some fruits can also be cooked by broiling and grilling, baking, sautéing, deep-frying, poaching, simmering and preserving.

When cooking fruits, proper care and attention are critical. Even minimal cooking can render fruits overly soft or mushy. To combat this irreversible process, sugar can be added. When fruits are cooked with sugar, the sugar will be absorbed slowly into the cells, firming the fruits. Acids (notably lemon juice) also help fruits retain their structure. (Alkalis, such as baking soda, cause the cells to break down more quickly, reducing the fruits to mush.)

DETERMINING DONENESS

There are so many different fruits with such varied responses to cooking that no one standard for doneness is appropriate. Each item should be evaluated on a formula-by-formula basis. Generally, however, most cooked fruits are done when they are just tender when pierced with a fork or the tip of a paring knife. Simmered fruits, such as compotes, should be softer, cooked just to the point of disintegration.

Avoid overcooking fruits by remembering that some carryover cooking will occur through the residual heat contained in the foods. Always rely on subjective tests—sight, feel, taste and aroma—rather than the clock.

DRY-HEAT COOKING METHODS

BROILING AND GRILLING

Fruits are usually broiled or grilled just long enough to caramelize sugars; cooking must be done quickly in order to avoid breaking down the fruits' structure. Good fruits to broil or grill are pineapples, apples, grapefruits, bananas, persimmons and peaches. The fruits may be cut into slices, chunks or halves as appropriate. A coating of sugar, honey or liqueur adds flavor, as do lemon juice, cinnamon and ginger.

When broiling fruits, use an oiled sheet pan or broiling platter. When grilling fruits, use a clean grill grate or thread the pieces onto skewers. Only thick fruit slices will need to be turned or rotated to heat fully.

▶ PROCEDURE FOR BROILING OR GRILLING FRUITS

1 Select ripe fruits and peel, core or slice as necessary.

2 Top with sugar or honey to add flavor and aid caramelization.

3 Place the fruits on the broiler platter, sheet pan or grill grate.

4 Broil or grill at high temperatures, turning as necessary to heat the fruits thoroughly but quickly.

BROILED GRAPEFRUIT

RECIPE 17.1

Yield: 8 Servings   **Method:** Broiling

Ruby grapefruits	4	4
Sweet sherry	1 fl. oz.	30 ml
Brown sugar	2 oz.	60 g

1 Cut each grapefruit in half (perpendicular to the segments), then section with a sharp knife, carefully removing any visible seeds.

2 Sprinkle the grapefruit halves with the sherry and sugar.

3 Arrange on a baking sheet and place under a preheated broiler. Cook briefly, only until well heated and the sugar caramelizes. Serve immediately alone or with ice cream or sherbet.

Approximate values per serving: **Calories** 70, **Total fat** 0 g, **Saturated fat** 0 g, **Cholesterol** 0 mg, **Sodium** 0 mg, **Total carbohydrates** 16 g, **Protein** 1 g, **Vitamin C** 80%, **Claims**—fat free; no sodium

BAKING

After washing, peeling, coring or pitting, most pomes, stone fruits and tropicals can be baked to create hot, flavorful desserts. Fruits with sturdy skins, particularly apples and pears, are excellent for baking alone, as their skin (peel) holds in moisture and flavor. They can also be used as edible containers by filling the cavity left by coring with a variety of sweet mixtures.

Combinations of fruits can also be baked successfully; try mixing fruits for a balance of sweetness and tartness (for example, strawberries with rhubarb or apples with plums).

Several baked desserts are simply fruits (fresh, frozen or canned) topped with a crust (called a cobbler), streusel (called a crumple or crisp) or batter (called a buckle). Fruits, sometimes poached first, can also be baked in a wrapper of puff pastry, flaky dough or phyllo dough to produce an elegant dessert.

▶ PROCEDURE FOR BAKING FRUITS

1 Select ripe but firm fruits and peel, core, pit or slice as necessary.

2 Add sugar or any flavorings.

3 Wrap the fruits in pastry dough if desired or directed in the formula.

4 Place the fruits in a baking dish and bake uncovered in a moderate oven until tender or properly browned.

RECIPE 17.2

BAKED APPLES

Yield: 8 Servings   **Method:** Baking

Red Delicious or Golden Delicious Apples	8	8
Raisins	6 oz.	180 g
Orange zest	0.3 oz. (1½ Tbsp.)	10 g
Brown sugar	4 oz.	120 g

1 Rinse and core each apple. The peels should be scored or partially removed to allow the pulp to expand without bursting the skin during baking.

2 Plump the raisins by soaking them in boiling water 10 minutes. Drain the raisins thoroughly.

3 Combine the raisins, orange zest and brown sugar. Fill the cavity of each apple with this mixture.

4 Stand the apples in a shallow baking dish. Add enough water to measure about ½ inch (1.2 centimeters) deep.

5 Bake the apples at 375°F (190°C) 15 minutes. Reduce the temperature to 300°F (150°C) and continue baking until the apples are tender but still hold their shape, approximately 1 hour. Occasionally baste the apples with liquid from the baking dish.

Approximate values per apple: **Calories** 220, **Total fat** 0.5 g, **Saturated fat** 0 g, **Cholesterol** 0 mg, **Sodium** 10 mg, **Total carbohydrates** 52 g, **Protein** 1 g, **Vitamin C** 15%, **Claims**—low fat, no cholesterol, very low sodium, good source of fiber

SAUTÉING

Fruits develop a rich, syrupy flavor when sautéed briefly in butter, sugar and, if desired, spices or liqueur. The sugar caramelizes, creating a syrup or glaze. Cherries, bananas, apples, pears and pineapples are good choices. They should be peeled, cored and seeded as necessary and cut into uniform pieces before sautéing. The fruits and syrup can be used to fill crêpes or to top spongecakes or ice creams. Liquor may be added and the mixture flamed (flambéed) in front of diners, as with Bananas Foster (page 525).

▶ PROCEDURE FOR SAUTÉING FRUITS

1 Peel, pit and core the fruits as necessary and cut into uniform pieces.

2 Melt the fat in a hot sauté pan.

3 Add the fruit pieces and any flavoring ingredients. Do not crowd the pan, as this will cause the fruit to stew in its own juices.

4 Cook quickly over high heat.

FLAMBÉED PINEAPPLE IN CRÊPES
WITH BLACKBERRY SORBET

Yield: 2 Servings   **Method:** Sautéing

Unsalted butter	1 oz.	30 g
Fresh pineapple, ½-inch (1.2-centimeter) slices, cored	4	4
Granulated sugar	1 oz.	30 g
Lemon juice	0.15 fl. oz. (1 tsp.)	5 ml
Orange juice	1 fl. oz.	30 ml
Sambuca or Kirsch liqueur	0.5 fl. oz.	15 ml
Crêpes (page 292)	2	2
Blackberry Sorbet (page 488)	4 oz.	120 g
Fresh blackberries	as needed	as needed

1 Melt the butter over medium-high heat in a sauté pan large enough to hold the pineapple slices. When the butter stops sizzling, add the pineapple slices and cook approximately 1 to 2 minutes on each side, until the slices are lightly browned.

2 While the pineapple cooks, in a medium-sized saucepan cook the sugar, lemon juice and orange juice to a golden caramel. Stop the cooking process by placing the bottom of the pan in a bowl of cold water.

3 Add the pineapple slices to the caramel. Reheat until the syrup is warm and flowing.

4 Add the liqueur and carefully ignite.

5 Heat the Crêpes in a 350°F (180°C) oven. Place one on each serving plate. Place the pineapple slices on one half of each warm Crêpe.

6 Fold the Crêpes to close and decorate each plate with some Blackberry Sorbet and fresh blackberries. Pour the warm sauce over the Crêpes and serve immediately.

Approximate values per serving: **Calories** 330, **Total fat** 12 g, **Saturated fat** 11 g, **Cholesterol** 125 mg, **Sodium** 110 mg, **Total carbohydrates** 56 g, **Protein** 1 g, **Vitamin A** 10%, **Vitamin C** 45%

DEEP-FRYING

Deep-fried batter-coated fresh fruit makes a delectable dessert or a garnish on a complex plated presentation. Apples, bananas, pears, pineapples and firm peaches mixed in or coated with batter work best for deep-frying. These fruits should be peeled, cored, seeded and cut into evenly sized slices or chunks. They may also need to be dried with paper towels so that the batter or coating can adhere. **Fritters** are spooned or dropped directly into the hot fat; they form a crust as they cook. Once cooked and drained, they are served sprinkled with powdered or granulated sugar alone or accompanied by ice cream or whipped cream.

▶ **fritters** deep-fried sweet or savory cakes often made from chopped fruits or vegetables coated in batter

▶ PROCEDURE FOR DEEP-FRYING FRUIT—FRITTERS

1 Cut, chop and otherwise prepare the food to be made into fritters.

2 Precook any ingredients if necessary.

3 Prepare the batter as directed.

4 Scoop the fritters into deep fat at 350°F (180°C) allowing them to swim freely in the oil. Once browned, flip the fritters with tongs or a spider to finish cooking on the other side.

5 Cook until done. The fritters should be golden brown on the outside and moist but set on the inside.

6 Remove the fritters from the fat and hold them over the fryer, allowing the excess fat to drain off. Transfer the food to a hotel pan either lined with absorbent paper or fitted with a rack. Serve hot.

7 If the fritters are to be held for later service, place them under a heat lamp.

RECIPE 17.4

APPLE FRITTERS

Yield: 100 Fritters, 2 in. (5 cm) each | **Method:** Deep-frying

Egg yolks	4 oz. (6 yolks)	120 g
Milk	1 pt.	480 ml
Flour	1 lb.	480 g
Baking powder	0.4 oz. (1 Tbsp.)	12 g
Salt	0.2 oz. (1 tsp.)	6 g
Granulated sugar	2 oz.	60 g
Cinnamon, ground	0.04 oz. (½ tsp.)	1 g
Apples, peeled, cored, medium dice	1 lb. 8 oz.	700 g
Egg whites	6 oz. (6 whites)	180 g
Powdered sugar	as needed	as needed

1 Combine the egg yolks and milk.

2 Sift together the flour, baking powder, salt, sugar and cinnamon. Add the dry ingredients to the milk-and-egg mixture; mix until smooth.

3 Allow the batter to rest 1 hour.

4 Stir the apples into the batter.

5 Just before the fritters are to be cooked, whip the egg whites to soft peaks and fold into the batter.

6 Scoop the fritters into deep fat at 350°F (180°C). Once browned on one side, flip the fritters in the fat to cook until done.

7 Dust with powdered sugar and serve hot.

VARIATION:

Banana Fritters—Omit the cinnamon and apples. Add 0.6 ounces (18 grams) finely grated orange zest, 4 fluid ounces (120 milliliters) orange juice and 2 large bananas, peeled and diced (not puréed).

Approximate values per fritter: **Calories** 60, **Total fat** 4 g, **Saturated fat** 1 g, **Cholesterol** 15 mg, **Sodium** 5 mg, **Total carbohydrates** 6 g, **Protein** 1 g

1 Adding the dry ingredients to the liquids.

2 Folding the egg whites into the batter.

3 Dropping the fritters into the deep fat.

4 Dusting the fritters with powdered sugar.

MOIST-HEAT COOKING METHODS
POACHING

One of the more popular cooking methods for fruits is poaching. Poaching softens and tenderizes fruits and infuses them with additional flavors such as spices or wine. Poached fruit can be served hot or cold and used in tarts or pastries or as a light dessert on its own.

The poaching liquid can be water, wine, liquor or sugar syrup. (As noted earlier, sugar helps fruits keep their shape, although it takes longer to tenderize fruits poached in sugar syrup.) The low poaching temperature (185°F/85°C) allows fruits to soften gradually. The agitation created at higher temperatures would damage them. When boiled, some fruits, especially pears, can overcook on the outside and be underdone on the inside. Underdone areas of the fruit may discolor.

Cooked fruits should be allowed to cool in the flavored poaching liquid or syrup. Most poaching liquids can be used repeatedly. If they contain sufficient sugar, they can be reduced to a sauce or glaze to accompany the poached fruits.

▶ PROCEDURE FOR POACHING FRUITS

1 Peel, core and slice the fruits as necessary.

2 In a sufficiently deep, nonreactive saucepan, combine the poaching liquid (usually water or wine) with sugar, spices, citrus zest and other ingredients as desired or as directed in the formula.

3 Submerge the fruits in the liquid. Place a circle of parchment paper over the fruits to help them stay submerged.

4 Place the saucepan on the stove top over a medium-high flame; bring to a boil.

5 As soon as the liquid boils, reduce the temperature. Simmer gently.

6 Poach until the fruits are tender enough for the tip of a small knife to be easily inserted. Cooking time depends on the type of fruit used, its ripeness and the cooking liquid.

7 Remove the saucepan from the stove top and allow the liquid and fruits to cool. Or remove the fruits from the syrup immediately and let them cool separately.

8 Remove the fruits from the liquid and then refrigerate. The liquid can be returned to the stove top and reduced until thick enough to use as a sauce or glaze or refrigerated for later use.

RECIPE 17.5

SPICED POACHED PEARS

Yield: 15 Poached Pears   **Method:** Poaching

Pears	15	15
Water	48 fl. oz.	1440 ml
White wine	36 fl. oz.	1080 ml
Granulated sugar	2 lb. 12 oz.	1320 g
Cinnamon	0.5 oz.	15 g
Star anise pods	3	3
Ground cardamom	0.07 oz. (1 tsp.)	2 g
Anise seeds	0.5 oz.	15 g
Lemon zest, grated fine	0.4 oz. (2 Tbsp.)	12 g
Orange zest, grated fine	0.6 oz. (3 Tbsp.)	18 g
Mint leaves	30	30
Vanilla beans	1½	1½

1 Peel the pears, leaving the stems intact. Set aside.

2 Bring the remaining ingredients to a boil in a large stainless steel saucepan.

3 Add the peeled pears to the mixture. Cut a piece of parchment to fit inside the pan on top of the pears. Place the paper over the pears, then fit a lid inside the saucepan so that it weighs down the fruit, keeping it submerged in the liquid.

4 Reduce the heat to very low. Cook the pears in the barely simmering liquid until tender, approximately 45 minutes to 1 hour 15 minutes depending on the variety of pear.

5 Remove the pears from the poaching liquid and return the liquid to the stove top. Reduce until the liquid is thick enough to coat the back of a spoon, then strain.

VARIATION:

Poached Pears in Exotic Syrup—Omit the cinnamon, star anise, cardamom and anise seeds and replace with 4 fluid ounces (120 milliliters) passion fruit juice.

Approximate values per serving: **Calories** 480, **Total fat** 1 g, **Saturated fat** 0 g, **Cholesterol** 0 mg, **Sodium** 0 mg, **Total carbohydrates** 110 g, **Protein** 1 g, **Vitamin C** 15%, **Claims**—low fat, no cholesterol, no sodium, good source of fiber

SIMMERING

Simmering techniques are used to make stewed fruits and compotes. Fresh, frozen, canned and dried fruits can be simmered or stewed. As with any moist-heat cooking method, simmering softens and tenderizes fruits. The liquid used can be water, wine or the juices naturally found in the fruits. Sugar, honey and spices may be added as desired. Stewed or simmered fruits can be served hot or cold, as a dessert with cookies or an accompaniment to ice cream and cakes.

▶ PROCEDURE FOR SIMMERING FRUITS

1 Peel, core, pit and slice the fruits as necessary.

2 Add sugar or other sweeteners as desired or as directed in the formula.

3 Bring the fruits and cooking liquid, if used, to a simmer. Cook until the fruit is tender.

DRIED FRUIT COMPOTE

RECIPE 17.6

Yield: 2 lb. (1 kg) **Method:** Simmering

Dried apricots	5 oz.	150 g
Dried plums (prunes), pitted	5 oz.	150 g
Dried pears or apples	5 oz.	150 g
Dried peaches	5 oz.	150 g
Water, hot	24 fl. oz.	720 ml
Cinnamon stick	1	1
Light corn syrup	12 fl. oz.	360 ml
Cointreau or orange liqueur	2 fl. oz.	60 ml

1 Coarsely chop the fruits. Place the pieces in a nonreactive saucepan and add the water and cinnamon stick.

2 Bring the mixture to a simmer, cover and cook until tender, approximately 12 to 15 minutes.

3 Add the corn syrup and liqueur. Simmer uncovered until thoroughly heated. Serve warm or refrigerate for longer storage.

Approximate values per 1-oz. (30-g) serving: **Calories** 60, **Total fat** 0 g, **Saturated fat** 0 g, **Cholesterol** 0 mg, **Sodium** 15 mg, **Total carbohydrates** 15 g, **Protein** 0 g, **Claims**—fat free; very low sodium

Apple Jelly

Apricot Jam

Orange Marmalade

PRESERVING

Fresh fruits can be preserved with sugar if the fruit-and-sugar mixture is concentrated by evaporation to the point that microbial spoilage cannot occur. The added sugar retards the growth of, but does not destroy, microorganisms.

Pectin, a substance present in varying amounts in all fruits, can cause cooked fruits to form a semisolid mass known as a gel. Fruits that are visually unattractive but otherwise of high quality can be made into gels, which are more commonly known as **jams, jellies, marmalades** and **preserves.**

The essential ingredients of a fruit gel are fruit, pectin, acid (usually lemon juice) and sugar. They must be carefully combined in the correct ratio for the gel to form. For fruits with a low pectin content (such as strawberries) to form a gel, pectin must be added, either by adding a fruit with a high pectin content (for example, apples or quince) or by adding packaged pectin.

▶ **concentrate** also known as a fruit paste or compound; a reduced fruit purée, without a gel structure, used as a flavoring

▶ **jam** a fruit gel made from fruit pulp and sugar

▶ **jelly** a fruit gel made from fruit juice and sugar

▶ **marmalade** a citrus jelly that also contains unpeeled slices of citrus fruit

▶ **preserve** a fruit gel that contains large pieces or whole fruits

Fruits, whether fresh, frozen, canned or dried, are one of the most versatile and popular bakeshop ingredients. Fruits can be used uncooked or incorporated into breads, pastries, cakes, muffins or used as the centerpiece in a plated dessert. When selecting fresh fruits, it is important to consider seasonal availability, storage conditions and ripeness. When using fruits it is important that they be at their peak of ripeness for the best flavor, texture, aroma and appearance.

QUESTIONS FOR DISCUSSION

1 Define ripeness and explain why ripe fruits are most desirable. How does the ripening process affect the availability of some fruits?

2 Describe the proper storage conditions for most fruits. Which fruits emit ethylene gas, and why is this a consideration when storing fruits?

3 Explain why some apple varieties are preferred for cooking, while other varieties are preferred for eating. Which variety is generally preferred for making applesauce?

4 Which types of fruits are best for dry-heat cooking methods? Explain your answer. Why is sugar usually added when cooking any type of fruit?

5 List and describe three ways to prepare fruits for extended storage.

6 Research a tropical or exotic fruit that is not available in your local area. Create a dessert preparation using this type of fruit. What handling procedures will be necessary when working with this ingredient? Discuss the type of bakeshop preparation to which this fruit is best suited and why.

BANANAS FOSTER

RECIPE 17.7

BRENNAN'S RESTAURANT, NEW ORLEANS, LA
Chef Michael Roussel

Note: This dish appears in the chapter opening photograph.

Bananas Foster was created in 1951 by Brennan's chef Paul Blangé to promote New Orleans' role as the major port of entry for bananas arriving from Central and South America. The dish was named for Richard Foster, chairman of the New Orleans Crime Commission, a civic group working to clean up the French Quarter. Foster was a good friend to Owen Edward Brennan and a frequent customer at his restaurant. Today Brennan's flambés some 35,000 pounds of bananas each year for this world-famous dessert.

Yield: 4 Servings	**Method:** Sautéing	
Whole butter	2 oz.	60 g
Brown sugar	8 oz.	240 g
Cinnamon, ground	0.04 oz. (½ tsp.)	1 g
Banana liqueur	2 fl. oz.	60 ml
Bananas, cut into quarters	4	4
White rum	2 fl. oz.	60 ml
Vanilla ice cream	4 scoops	4 scoops

1 Combine the butter, sugar and cinnamon in a sauté or flambé pan. Cook over low heat, stirring until the sugar dissolves.

2 Stir in the banana liqueur, then place the bananas in the pan. When the bananas soften and begin to brown, carefully add the rum.

3 Place one scoop of ice cream on each serving plate. Continue to cook the bananas until the rum is hot, then tip the pan slightly to ignite the rum. When the flames subside, lift the bananas out of the pan and place four pieces over each portion of ice cream. Spoon the warm sauce over the ice cream and serve immediately.

Approximate values per serving: **Calories** 640, **Total fat** 23 g, **Saturated fat** 14 g, **Cholesterol** 70 mg, **Sodium** 65 mg, **Total carbohydrates** 103 g, **Protein** 4 g, **Vitamin A** 20%, **Vitamin C** 20%, **Calcium** 15%, **Iron** 10%, **Claims**—good source of fiber, vitamins A and C, calcium and iron

BRENNAN'S RESTAURANT

After World War II, Owen Edward Brennan, then owner of the French Quarter's Old Absinthe House Saloon, became determined to have the best French and Creole restaurant in New Orleans. Many believe that he succeeded when, in 1946, he opened Brennan's Restaurant on Bourbon Street. This culinary Mecca served breakfast, lunch and dinner to Hollywood stars, national politicians, syndicated columnists and assorted celebrities. Owen's personal success was cut short by his sudden death in 1955, just before Brennan's Restaurant moved into a renovated mansion on Royal Street.

Still located at 417 Royal Street, Brennan's now features 12 elegantly decorated dining rooms with some 550 seats, and the mansion's former slave quarters houses an award-winning wine cellar. Owen's three sons—Pip, Jimmy and Ted—remain the sole owners and operators of their father's world-famous restaurant.

Owen Brennan is credited with popularizing the concept of a formal breakfast in a public restaurant through his "Breakfast at Brennan's" promotion. Not a traditional juice-and-toast meal, however, a typical Brennan's breakfast begins with a gin fizz and includes lamb chops with béarnaise, champagne, shrimp rémoulade, hot French bread, bread pudding and café diable. Through the years, Brennan's chefs have created and popularized some of this country's best known dishes: Eggs Hussarde, Oysters 2-2-2, Crêpes Fitzgerald (strawberry) and Bananas Foster.

Chef Paul Blangé was the ingenious creator of many of Brennan's signature dishes. Today, Chef Michael Roussel maintains Brennan's rich culinary traditions from the kitchen he has called home for 43 years.

RECIPE 17.8

FIGS WITH BERRIES AND HONEY MOUSSE

GREENS, SAN FRANCISCO, CA
Chef Annie Somerville

Yield: 4 Servings

Fresh raspberries or blackberries	1 pt.	0.5 lt
Fresh figs such as Black Mission, Kadota or Calimyrna	1 pt.	0.5 lt
Honey	6 oz.	180 g
Egg yolks	2.6 oz. (4 yolks)	80 g
Salt	0.03 oz. (1/8 tsp.)	1 g
Heavy cream	1 pt.	0.5 lt
Fresh mint	as needed for garnish	

1 Pick through the berries, but do not rinse them because water will dilute their flavor.

2 Rinse the figs and cut them in half, leaving the stem attached.

3 To make the mousse, whisk the honey, egg yolks and salt together in a bowl over a pan of barely simmering water. Whisk the mixture continuously for 8 minutes. After 5 minutes, the mousse will begin to thicken and the texture will become creamy. Whisk vigorously until the mousse leaves thick ribbons on its surface when poured over itself. Set aside to cool. The texture of the cooled mousse will be stiff and sticky.

4 Whisk 1 fluid ounce (30 milliliters) of the cream into the mousse, working it until it loosens.

5 Whip the remaining cream until it is firm, fold it into the mousse until it is just incorporated, then whisk the two together. The texture will be light and creamy.

6 Loosely arrange the figs on a platter, sprinkle with the berries, garnish with mint and serve with the mousse.

Approximate values per serving: **Calories** 680, **Total fat** 47 g, **Saturated fat** 28 g, **Cholesterol** 370 mg, **Sodium** 200 mg, **Total carbohydrates** 57 g, **Protein** 6 g, **Vitamin A** 60%, **Vitamin C** 25%

RECIPE 17.9

SWEET RICOTTA AND MASCARPONE MOUSSE WITH FRESH BERRIES

Yield: 8 Servings, 3 lb. 6 oz. (1590 g) Mousse

Whole-milk ricotta	24 oz.	720 g
Mascarpone	12 oz.	360 g
Granulated sugar	2 oz.	60 g
Orange zest, grated	0.4 oz. (2 Tbsp.)	12 g
Vanilla extract	0.15 fl. oz. (1 tsp.)	5 ml
Heavy cream	1 pt.	480 ml
Powdered sugar	1 oz.	30 g
Fresh strawberries, cleaned and quartered	1 pt.	0.5 lt
Fresh raspberries	1 pt.	0.5 lt
Fresh blackberries	1 pt.	0.5 lt
Fresh mint	8 sprigs	8 sprigs

1 Process the ricotta, mascarpone and sugar in the bowl of a food processor until smooth and creamy. Transfer to a mixing bowl. Stir the zest and vanilla into the ricotta.

2 Whip the heavy cream with the powdered sugar to stiff peaks.

3 Stir a small amount of the whipped cream into the ricotta mixture to lighten it. Add the remaining whipped cream and gently fold together until well combined.

4 Layer the mousse with the berries in eight large wine glasses. Garnish with berries and a mint sprig. Refrigerate up to 1 hour before serving.

Approximate values per serving: **Calories** 630, **Total fat** 53 g, **Saturated fat** 31 g, **Cholesterol** 180 mg, **Sodium** 120 mg, **Total carbohydrates** 27 g, **Protein** 15 g, **Vitamin A** 40%, **Vitamin C** 70%, **Calcium** 30%

BLACKBERRY COBBLER

RECIPE 17.10

A cobbler is a home-style baked fruit dessert, usually made with a top crust of flaky pie dough, biscuit dough or streusel topping. The finished product will be slightly runny and is often served warm in a bowl or rimmed dish, accompanied by whipped cream or ice cream.

Yield: 10 Servings

Method: Baked fruit

Blackberries, IQF	2 qt.	2 lt
Granulated sugar	8 oz.	240 g
Instant tapioca	2 oz.	60 g
Water	10 fl. oz.	300 ml
Unsalted butter	2 oz.	60 g
Lemon zest, grated	0.2 oz. (1 Tbsp.)	6 g
Streusel (page 113)	16 oz.	480 g
Egg wash	as needed	as needed

1 Combine the berries, sugar, tapioca, water, butter and lemon zest, tossing the berries gently until well coated with the other ingredients.

2 Transfer to a lightly buttered half-size hotel pan, then set aside at least 30 minutes before baking.

3 Cover the top of the cobbler with an even layer of Streusel.

4 Bake at 350°F (180°C) until the berry mixture bubbles and the crust is appropriately browned, approximately 40 to 50 minutes.

Approximate values per 6-oz. (180-g) serving: **Calories** 210, **Total fat** 5 g, **Saturated fat** 3 g, **Cholesterol** 20 mg, **Sodium** 10 mg, **Total carbohydrates** 39 g, **Protein** 1 g, **Vitamin C** 45%

GRATIN OF FRESH BERRIES
WITH CRÈME FRAÎCHE

RECIPE 17.11

Yield: 1 Serving

Method: Broiling

Assorted fresh berries, such as raspberries, strawberries and blackberries	4 oz.	120 g
Crème fraîche	2 fl. oz.	60 ml
Orange liqueur	0.15 fl. oz. (1 tsp.)	5 ml
Brown sugar	0.5 oz.	15 g

1 Arrange the berries in an even layer in a shallow, heatproof serving dish.

2 Stir the crème fraîche and orange liqueur together. Spoon this mixture over the berries.

3 Sprinkle the brown sugar over the crème fraîche. Place under a broiler or salamander just until the sugar melts. Serve immediately.

Approximate values per serving: **Calories** 210, **Total fat** 7 g, **Saturated fat** 4 g, **Cholesterol** 20 mg, **Sodium** 30 mg, **Total carbohydrates** 33 g, **Protein** 3 g, **Vitamin C** 40%, **Claims**—very low sodium; high fiber

RECIPE 17.12

WARM BAKED PEACHES OR NECTARINES

Yield: 8 Servings	**Method:** Baked Fruit	
Freestone peaches or nectarines	4	4
Vanilla bean	1	1
Granulated sugar	2 oz.	60 g
Lemon	1	1
Unsalted butter	2 oz.	60 g

1 Cut the peaches or nectarines in half. Remove the pits. Place them cut side up in a well-buttered half-size hotel pan or an ovenproof dish.

2 Split the vanilla bean and scrape the seeds into the sugar. Juice the lemon and sprinkle the fruit with the sugar and lemon juice.

3 Place a small piece of the butter in the center of each fruit half and bake at 350°F (180°C) until tender and lightly browned, approximately 20 minutes. Serve warm with ice cream or custard.

Approximate values per serving: **Calories** 100, **Total fat** 6 g, **Saturated fat** 3.5 g, **Cholesterol** 15 mg, **Sodium** 0 mg, **Total carbohydrates** 13 g, **Protein** 0 g, **Vitamin A** 10%, **Vitamin C** 10%, **Claims**—low calorie, no sodium

RECIPE 17.13

GRILLED FRUIT KEBABS

Yield: 8 Skewers	**Method:** Grilling	
Cantaloupe	1/2	1/2
Honeydew melon	1/4	1/4
Pineapple	1/2	1/2
Fresh strawberries	8	8
Brown sugar	2 oz.	60 g
Lime juice	4 fl. oz.	120 ml
Cinnamon, ground	0.02 oz. (1/4 tsp.)	0.5 g

1 Remove the rind and cut the melons and pineapple into 1-inch (2.5-centimeter) cubes. Hull the strawberries and leave whole.

2 Make a sugar glaze by combining the sugar, lime juice and cinnamon, stirring until the sugar dissolves.

3 Heat the grill and clean the grate thoroughly.

4 Thread the fruits onto kebab skewers, alternating colors for an attractive appearance.

5 Brush the fruits with the sugar glaze. Grill, rotating the skewers frequently to develop an evenly light brown surface.

6 Serve immediately.

Approximate values per skewer: **Calories** 70, **Total fat** 0 g, **Saturated fat** 0 g, **Cholesterol** 0 mg, **Sodium** 10 mg, **Total carbohydrates** 16 g, **Protein** 1 g, **Vitamin C** 50%, **Claims**—fat free; very low sodium

BRAISED RHUBARB AND APPLES

RECIPE 17.14

Yield: 10 lb. (4.5 kg)   **Method:** Braising

Tart green apples, peeled and cubed	2 lb. 8 oz.	1.1 kg
Rhubarb, IQF pieces	7 lb.	3.2 kg
Unsalted butter	4 oz.	120 g
Sweet white wine	8 fl. oz.	240 ml
Brown sugar	14 oz.	420 g
Vanilla extract	0.3 fl. oz. (2 tsp.)	10 ml
Cinnamon, ground	0.2 oz. (1 Tbsp.)	6 g
Nutmeg, ground	0.02 oz. (¼ tsp.)	0.5 g
Orange juice	2 fl. oz.	60 ml
Salt	0.1 oz. (½ tsp.)	3 g

1 Sauté the apples and rhubarb in the butter until they begin to soften.

2 Add the wine and reduce by half. Add the remaining ingredients. Simmer until the rhubarb is very tender.

3 Serve at room temperature in prebaked pastry cups, topped with crème Chantilly, or serve warm over ice cream.

Approximate values per 1-oz. (30-g) serving: **Calories** 60, **Total fat** 2 g, **Saturated fat** 0.5 g, **Cholesterol** 0 mg, **Sodium** 25 mg, **Total carbohydrates** 11 g, **Protein** 0 g, **Claims**—low fat; no cholesterol; very low sodium

STRAWBERRY CHUTNEY

RECIPE 17.15

Yield: 10–12 Servings, 1 lb. 14 oz. (900 g)   **Method:** Simmering

Fresh strawberries	2 qt.	2 lt
Balsamic vinegar	2 fl. oz.	60 ml
Ginger, grated fine	0.5 oz.	15 g
Lime juice	0.5 fl. oz.	15 ml
Black pepper, coarsely cracked	0.07 oz. (1 tsp.)	2 g
Vanilla bean, split	1	1
Cinnamon stick	½	½
Simple Syrup (page 349)	8 fl. oz.	240 ml
Strawberry purée	4 oz.	120 g

1 In a nonreactive saucepan bring the strawberries, balsamic vinegar, ginger, lime juice, pepper, vanilla bean and cinnamon stick to a boil. Cook 1 minute, stirring occasionally. Reduce heat to medium-low and simmer 10 to 15 minutes.

2 Add the Simple Syrup and cook another 10 minutes. Remove from the heat and add the Strawberry Purée. Serve this chutney as a garnish on vanilla ice cream, plain cheesecake or baked custard.

Approximate values per 2-oz. (60-g) serving: **Calories** 45, **Total fat** 0 g, **Saturated fat** 0 g, **Cholesterol** 0 mg, **Sodium** 0 mg, **Total carbohydrates** 12 g, **Protein** 0 g, **Vitamin C** 50%, **Claims**—fat free, no cholesterol, no sodium

RECIPE 17.16   **BERRY COMPOTE**

Yield: 1 pt. (480 ml)   **Method:** Simmering

Berries, fresh or frozen	1 pt.	0.5 lt
Granulated sugar	4 oz.	120 g
Oranges	2	2
Honey	3 fl. oz.	90 ml
Cinnamon stick	1	1
Brandy	1.5 fl. oz.	45 ml

1 Select an assortment of fresh or frozen berries—strawberries, blueberries, raspberries, blackberries and cherries can be used, depending on availability.

2 Place the fruits and sugar in a nonreactive saucepan. Add the juice from the two oranges. Bring to a simmer over low heat; cook until the fruits are soft but still intact.

3 Strain the mixture, reserving both the fruits and the liquid. Return the liquid to the saucepan. Add the finely grated zest from one orange and the honey, cinnamon stick and brandy.

4 Bring to a boil and reduce until the mixture thickens enough to coat the back of a spoon. Remove from the heat and cool to room temperature.

5 Gently stir the reserved fruits into the sauce, cover and chill. Serve with ice cream, poundcake or cheesecake.

VARIATION:

Sweet Red Wine Berry Compote—Combine the assortment of fruits in a saucepan with 4 fluid ounces (120 milliliters) sweet red wine. Omit the oranges and simmer over low heat to cook the fruits. Strain the mixture, reserving the fruits. Add 1 vanilla bean, split and seeds scraped. Bring to a boil and cook until the mixture thickens. Stir in the reserved fruits, cover and chill.

Approximate values per 1-oz. (30-g) serving: **Calories** 70, **Total fat** 0 g, **Saturated fat** 0 g, **Cholesterol** 0 mg, **Sodium** 0 mg, **Total carbohydrates** 16 g, **Protein** 0 g, **Vitamin C** 15%, **Claims**—fat free; no sodium

SUN-DRIED FRUIT COMPOTE WITH HONEY ICE CREAM

RECIPE 17.17

BISHOP'S RESTAURANT, Vancouver, BC
Chefs Michael Allemeier and Dennis Green

Yield: 6 Servings   **Method:** Boiling/Steeping

Zinfandel wine	12 fl. oz.	360 ml
Water	1 pt.	480 ml
Granulated sugar	12 oz.	360 g
Sundried fruits, such as apples, cherries and apricots, whole	12 oz.	360 g
Cinnamon stick	1	1
Cloves, whole	2	2
Nutmeg, ground	0.4 oz. (½ tsp.)	1 g
Vanilla bean, split	½	½
Black peppercorns	6	6
Fresh ginger, 1-in. (2.5-cm) piece, sliced	1	1
Honey Ice Cream (page 486)	as needed	as needed

1 In a nonreactive saucepan, combine the wine, water and sugar. Bring to a boil, skim off any scum that forms and add the fruit and spices.

2 Bring to a boil again and remove from the heat.

3 Allow the compote to sit for several hours to allow the fruit to absorb some of the syrup.

4 To serve, warm the compote, and top each portion with a scoop of Honey Ice Cream.

Approximate values per 5-oz. (150-g) serving, without ice cream: **Calories** 290, **Total fat** 0 g, **Saturated fat** 0 g, **Cholesterol** 0 mg, **Sodium** 30 mg, **Total carbohydrates** 71 g, **Protein** 1 g, **Claims**—no fat; no cholesterol; very low sodium; good source of fiber

RECIPE 17.18

APPLESAUCE

Yield: 1 qt. (1 lt) **Method:** Simmering

McIntosh apples	4 lb.	1.8 kg
Cinnamon sticks	2	2
Granulated sugar	5 oz.	150 g
Lemon juice	0.5 fl. oz.	15 ml

1 Peel, core and quarter the apples. Place in a saucepan with just enough cold water to cover the bottom of the pan. Add the cinnamon sticks.

2 Bring to a simmer, cover and cook until the apples are tender, approximately 15 minutes.

3 Add the sugar and lemon juice. Simmer 10 minutes.

4 Remove the cinnamon sticks and press the apples through a food mill.

Approximate values per 1-oz. (30-g) serving: **Calories** 50, **Total fat** 0 g, **Saturated fat** 0 g, **Cholesterol** 0 mg, **Sodium** 0 mg, **Total carbohydrates** 13 g, **Protein** 0 g, **Claims**—fat free; no sodium

RECIPE 17.19

FRESH CRANBERRY-ORANGE SAUCE

Yield: 3 qt. (3 lt) **Method:** Simmering

Granulated sugar	1 lb.	480 g
Orange juice	4 fl. oz.	120 ml
Water	8 fl. oz.	240 ml
Fresh or frozen cranberries	1 lb. 8 oz.	720 g
Cinnamon stick	1	1
Orange liqueur	2 fl. oz.	60 ml
Orange zest, grated fine	0.4 oz. (2 Tbsp.)	12 g
Orange segments	20	20

1 Combine the sugar, orange juice and water in a nonreactive saucepan; bring to a boil.

2 Add the cranberries and cinnamon stick and simmer uncovered until the berries begin to burst, approximately 15 minutes. Skim off any foam that rises to the surface.

3 Add the orange liqueur and orange zest and simmer another 5 minutes.

4 Remove from the heat and remove the cinnamon stick. Add the orange segments. Cool and refrigerate.

Approximate values per 1-oz. (30-g) serving: **Calories** 25, **Total fat** 0 g, **Saturated fat** 0 g, **Cholesterol** 0 mg, **Sodium** 0 mg, **Total carbohydrates** 6 g, **Protein** 0 g, **Claims**—fat free; no sodium; low calorie

COINTREAU CHERRIES

RECIPE 17.20

Yield: Approximately 2½ lb. (1200 g)   **Method:** Preserving

Fresh pitted cherries	1 lb.	480 g
Granulated sugar	12 oz.	360 g
Cointreau or brandy	12–14 fl. oz.	360–420 ml

1 Select one or two narrow deep stainless steel containers such as a quarter-size hotel pan. Sterilize the pans by placing them in a large pot of boiling water. Remove the pans after 2 minutes.

2 Place the pitted cherries in the sterilized containers.

3 Combine the sugar and Cointreau. Pour this mixture over the cherries, making certain that the fruit is completely covered by the liquid, adding more liqueur as needed to completely cover the fruit. Cover with plastic wrap and macerate the cherries at least 1 week in the refrigerator. The cherries are then ready to use as a topping on ice cream, in cakes and tortes. They will keep 6 months.

Approximate values per 1-oz. (30-g) serving: **Calories** 70, **Total fat** 0 g, **Saturated fat** 0 g, **Cholesterol** 0 mg, **Sodium** 0 mg, **Total carbohydrates** 14 g, **Protein** 0 g, **Claims**—fat free, no sodium

FRESH RASPBERRY JAM

RECIPE 17.21

Although made with frozen berries, this is a fresh jam because it contains approximately 30 percent less sugar than a normal jam and must be refrigerated to maintain freshness. Use it in any formula calling for raspberry jam.

Yield: Approximately 6 lb. (2700 g)   **Method:** Preserving

Raspberries, IQF, defrosted	3 lb.	1440 g
Apples, cored, unpeeled, chopped	1 lb. 6 oz.	630 g
Granulated sugar	2 lb.	960 g
Lemon juice	2 oz.	60 g
Pectin	1.5 oz.	45 g
Citric acid	0.6 oz. (1 Tbsp.)	18 g
Water	0.5 fl. oz.	15 ml

1 Drain the raspberries, reserving the juice. Set aside the raspberries. Combine the raspberry juice with the apple pieces and purée the mixture until fine. Purée the raspberries and strain the seeds, if desired, and then add the strained raspberry purée to the apple purée.

2 Place the fruit mixture in a nonreactive pan with 1 pound 14 ounces (900 grams) of the sugar and the lemon juice. Heat to 120°F (49°C).

3 Mix the pectin with the remaining sugar and add to the warm fruit mixture.

4 Bring the mixture to a boil and cook 3 minutes, stirring constantly.

5 Remove from heat. Combine the citric acid and water and add to the jam. Cool, then refrigerate. This jam keeps 2 to 3 weeks under refrigeration.

Approximate values per 1-oz. (30-g) serving: **Calories** 50, **Total fat** 0 g, **Saturated fat** 0 g, **Cholesterol** 0 mg, **Sodium** 0 mg, **Total carbohydrates** 12 g, **Protein** 0 g, **Claims**—fat free, no sodium, no cholesterol

RECIPE 17.22

CANDIED CITRUS RIND

Oranges, lemons, grapefruits or tangerines may be used. Organic produce is recommended.

Yield: 50–100 Candied Strips	**Method:** Preserving	
Citrus fruit	5 to 10 fruits	5 to 10 fruits
Water	1 qt.	1 lt
Salt	0.1 oz. (½ tsp.)	3 g
Granulated sugar	1 lb.	480 g
Glucose or corn syrup	7 oz.	210 g

1 Wash the fruits. With a sharp knife, cut large, thin pieces of the peel from the citrus fruits. Remove as much of the white pith from the peel as possible.

2 Cut the peel into long, thin strips, approximately ¼ inch (6 millimeters) wide.

3 Bring 1 pint (480 milliliters) of the water and the salt to boil in a saucepan large enough to hold the citrus rind. Add the rind and simmer 2 minutes. Drain.

4 Bring the remaining 1 pint (450 milliliters) of water, the sugar and glucose or corn syrup to a boil. Add the blanched citrus rind and reduce the heat to a low simmer. Cook the rinds approximately 15 to 20 minutes until they are translucent and tender. Store the rinds in the syrup in the refrigerator. Or drain the rinds on a screen until cool. Sprinkle the drained rinds with granulated sugar and store in an airtight container.

Approximate values per piece: **Calories** 35, **Total fat** 0 g, **Saturated fat** 0 g, **Cholesterol** 0 mg, **Sodium** 20 mg, **Total carbohydrates** 9 g, **Protein** 0 g

RECIPE 17.23

CARAMELIZED APPLE CRISPS

Yield: 20–30 Slices	**Method:** Preserving	
Granny Smith apples	3	3
Powdered sugar	as needed	as needed

1 Thoroughly wash and dry the apples. Using a mandoline slicer or a meat slicer, cut the apples horizontally through the core into paper-thin slices. Place the apple slices on silicone mats or paper-lined sheet pans. Dust the slices lightly with powdered sugar on both sides.

2 Place the sliced apples in a 175°F (80°C) oven and dry them completely, approximately 3 hours. Check after 1 hour. If the apples are browning too quickly, reduce the heat to 150°F (65°C).

3 Remove the pans from the oven. Let the apples cool, then store them in an airtight container.

Approximate values per piece: **Calories** 5, **Total fat** 0 g, **Saturated fat** 0 g, **Cholesterol** 0 mg, **Sodium** 0 mg, **Total carbohydrates** 2 g, **Protein** 0 g

DRIED PINEAPPLE SLICES

Yield: 30–40 Slices   **Method:** Preserving

Water	1 qt.	1 lt
Granulated sugar	10 oz.	300 g
Vanilla bean, split	1	1
Pineapple, large	1	1
Powdered sugar	as needed	as needed

1 Bring the water, sugar and vanilla bean to a boil. Cook a few minutes, until the sugar dissolves. Remove from the heat and let cool.

2 Remove the base and crown and peel the pineapple. Slice the pineapple into thin slices, $1/32$ inch (1 millimeter) thick using a meat slicer. Remove the center core from each slice using a small round cookie cutter.

3 Place the slices in a hotel pan and cover with the syrup. Marinate approximately 12 hours.

4 Thoroughly drain the slices and lightly dust both sides with powdered sugar. Place the slices without overlapping on silicone baking mats or paper-lined sheet pans.

5 Dry the slices in a 275°F (135°C) oven 30 minutes or until parts of the slices are light amber in color.

6 Immediately drape the warm slices over an oiled rolling pin or press them into oiled tart pans to form small cups. When cool, store in airtight containers.

Approximate values per slice: **Calories** 40, **Total fat** 0 g, **Saturated fat** 0 g, **Cholesterol** 0 mg, **Sodium** 0 mg, **Total carbohydrates** 11 g, **Protein** 0 g

IF WE COULD GIVE EVERY INDIVIDUAL THE RIGHT AMOUNT OF NOURISHMENT AND EXERCISE, NOT TOO LITTLE AND NOT TOO MUCH, WE WOULD HAVE FOUND THE SAFEST WAY TO HEALTH.

—Hippocrates, Greek physician, founder of the study of medicine (460–377 B.C.)

HEALTHFUL AND SPECIAL-NEEDS BAKING

AFTER STUDYING THIS
CHAPTER, YOU WILL BE
ABLE TO:

▶ recognize dietary conditions
that affect today's consumers

▶ understand how to adapt
bakeshop formulas to meet
dietary needs

Although Americans are becoming increasingly health conscious, the pleasures of the dessert table still call to them. Because of national health concerns about overconsumption leading to obesity, cardiovascular disease and diabetes, Americans are looking for baked goods and desserts to satisfy their sweet tooth in a healthier way. At the same time, people with certain health conditions that limit the intake of sugar, fat or wheat are looking for foods that will taste good and meet their diet regimens.

Modifying or adapting formulas for those with special dietary needs presents a challenge even to the most experienced professional because of the exacting nature of baking. In baking more than in any other form of cooking, many of the ingredients provide an important function other than flavor. Healthy baking demands a thorough knowledge of the principles of baking to ensure an appealing product.

Rather than being a complete primer, this chapter is designed to introduce the reader to a variety of healthful baking options and illustrate ways a small bakeshop or restaurant can offer products for those with special dietary requirements.

For a variety of personal and medical reasons, many consumers are concerned about avoiding certain foods or foods containing certain ingredients or additives. For some, it is a matter of preference: they would rather eat a lower-fat cookie or a food prepared with organic ingredients. For others, avoiding a particular ingredient is not a choice but a necessity because consuming or even touching the ingredient can be a matter of life and death. People who are allergic to peanuts, for instance, can develop a life-threatening reaction after eating even a minute amount of peanut or peanut product such as peanut oil. The concern is not why customers require a special product. The goal is to provide the tastiest products that meet their dietary needs.

Chefs and bakers who prepare food for public consumption must be aware of these needs and be willing and able to prepare products that are suitable for customers with special requirements. The challenge is that many of the ingredients that raise concerns are widely used in bakeshop products including wheat flour (gluten), sugar, fats, eggs, soy products, dairy products and flavorings such as peanuts, tree nuts, alcoholic beverages and chocolate. Customers who are concerned about ingredients will usually ask how a dish is prepared. Waiters, cooks, and other food service workers should take the guest's inquiries seriously. Failure to do so could result in severe illness or death.

Chefs, bakers, managers and restaurateurs can improve customer relations and build a new clientele base by developing and promoting strategies that adequately address the health concerns of their patrons. To do so requires a two-phase program. In the first phase, all the staff who come in contact with the public must be made aware of, or have access to, a list of all ingredients in all products. Post notices or label products appropriately if peanuts or other potential **allergens** (substances that may cause allergic reactions in some people) are present. For instance, know when alcohol has been used to prepare a dish;

▶ **allergens** substances that may cause allergic reactions in some people

SHARON B. SALOMON, MS, RD

This chapter was written and researched by Sharon Salomon, a registered dietitian with a master of science degree in clinical nutrition. As an undergraduate at Queens College in Flushing, New York, Ms. Salomon majored in cultural anthropology and traveled to Mexico, Turkey and Europe as part of her education. On these trips she enjoyed the benefits of living with local people in their homes, where she spent most of her free time in the families' kitchens learning authentic preparations of their native cuisines. Ms. Salomon has also studied at La Varenne Cooking School in Burgundy, France, and attended the Culinary Institute of America at Greystone for certification in nutritional cuisine. Ms. Salomon has combined her love of food and cooking with her nutrition education in a variety of ways. She has taught nutrition and culinary education courses and has worked as a caterer as well as a spokesperson for the Arizona Beef Council, the National Pork Producers Council and the California Kiwi Association. She appears regularly on Phoenix-area television and has written magazine and newspaper columns on sports nutrition and cooking with children.

learn whether the chocolate used contains a soy-based emulsifier; be aware of where peanuts have been used in the kitchen and if the oil used in a formula is peanut, soy or other vegetable-based oil.

In the second phase, build a repertoire of products that have a reduced fat, sugar, wheat or dairy content. The baker should not expect to be able to adjust all formulas based on a reading of this chapter, but should become more aware of potential issues. The chef should also be able to offer customers an alternative bread or dessert on a regular basis, or at least when a special request is made. Finally, chefs and bakers should be familiar with some of the newer products available that can be used to alter or modify baking formulas. These include alternative sweeteners, low- and nonfat dairy products, nongluten flours and fruit and vegetable purées. Most manufacturers of commercial products have valuable information on their Web sites. In researching techniques for healthier baking, the Internet is a good place to start.

▶ SPECIAL DIETARY CONCERNS

For many people, personal conviction drives their desire for a modified version of a favorite dessert: weight control, avoiding additives or eating less processed foods, for example. Weight loss regimens in vogue today run the gamut from high-protein, low-carbohydrate to the long-established reduced-calorie diets. For others, specific physical conditions prevent them from enjoying a traditional bakeshop item. Many Americans are on low-cholesterol and low-fat diets as well as sodium- (salt-) controlled diets to treat cardiovascular disease. Others must pay attention to their intake of calories and carbohydrates because they have diabetes.

Allergies to wheat, dairy, nuts, eggs and soy are widespread, affecting millions of consumers. The challenge for the pastry chef is to know the function of the ingredient in the bakeshop formula and understand how to alter the formula to meet dietary needs. In the case of peanut allergy, mise en place should be considered as well as removing peanuts from a given formula. No peanuts or peanut products should even be near the area where the preparation is taking place. Avoiding peanut oil or peanut oil–containing products means that pans must be prepared with an alternative oil and utensils may not come in contact with peanut products or even peanut dust.

Another common food component of concern to the public is lactose. **Lactose** is a natural sugar found in milk and dairy products. People who are lactose intolerant have a digestive problem that causes intestinal discomfort if the milk sugar is consumed, sometimes even in small amounts. Since many bakeshop products use dairy products, finding a suitable substitute is important.

▶ **cholesterol** fat found only in foods of animal origin. Since the human body produces adequate cholesterol for its own needs, consumption of excess cholesterol is discouraged.

▶ **carbohydrates** a group of compounds composed of oxygen, hydrogen and carbon; the human body's primary source of energy (4 calories per gram); carbohydrates are classified as simple (including certain sugars) and complex (including starches and fiber)

GLUTEN ALLERGY

Celiac disease, the inability to digest gluten, is one of the few diseases that is treated exclusively with diet. By removing all wheat, rye and barley from the diet, people with celiac disease return to living a normal, healthy life. However, the most minute amount of gluten can cause symptoms to return. The problem is the gluten protein that is present in wheat, rye and barley.

Staying gluten-free is quite a challenge and requires a quick education about foods and ingredients. Gluten is hidden in many places, including soy sauce (fermented with wheat), sauces, soups and even some spice blends. Wheat is also used in the glue on most en-velopes. Many different flours are safe: rice flour, corn flour, cornstarch, potato flour and potato starch, tapioca starch, quinoa, soy, sorghum, bean flours, buckwheat, millet and amaranth. Teff and oats can be safe as long as the source is free of cross-contamination from wheat.

Baking without gluten defies most of the principles of food chemistry. It's best to use a blend of two to three different gluten-free flours and starches, usually rice flour, sorghum, buck-wheat or millet with the addition of at least 30 percent starch—corn, potato or tapioca. Some of the protein and elasticity of gluten can be re-placed with gums—xanthan, guar or locust bean gum. Usually 1 teaspoon per cup is used for pastries and 3 teaspoons per cup is recom-mended for creating a blend that is used for bread flour. The addition of eggs helps build up the protein in the mixture. Also, adding a small amount of a flour that is high in protein (ama-ranth, soy or other bean flour) helps to produce moisture in the final product.

Although gluten-free baking takes a bit of extra effort, the rewards outweigh the chal-lenges, as gluten-free consumers are very ap-preciative and will remain customers for life!

—BETH HILSON, founder and CEO, The Gluten-Free Pantry

In addition to allergic customers and those who have digestive intolerances, others are looking for lower-fat or lower-calorie items. There are also a growing number of people who just want to eat healthier food. These individuals might want a dessert that offers more fiber or is higher in certain vitamins or minerals or lower in sugar because they perceive these foods to be healthier. Many peo-ple are trying to avoid eating processed foods containing chemical additives. Their preference might be to choose foods prepared with organic ingredients. Meeting their needs requires creativity and as much vigilance as preparing foods for those with special health conditions.

▶ DEVELOPING AND MODIFYING FORMULAS

When conceiving and creating healthier bread, pastry and dessert formulas, be-gin by selecting naturally healthy ingredients. Choose foods that are naturally lower in calories, fat, cholesterol and sugar and higher in fiber, vitamins and min-erals. For example, a fruit salad or fruit compote garnished with a fruit sorbet might be offered in place of a more traditional item such as a fruit pie garnished with ice cream. This book includes many formulas for desserts and baked goods that are naturally healthy, indicated by the pyramid icon.

When modifying a traditional formula, there are three principles to be followed: Reduce, Replace or Eliminate.

▶ *Reduce* the quantity of an ingredient when the reduction will have little or no effect on the taste, texture or appearance of the final product but will result in a healthier profile for the product.

▶ *Replace* the ingredient or the cooking method with an alternative that will do the least to change the flavor, texture or appearance of the final product.

▶ *Eliminate* an ingredient if doing so does not appreciably change the product.

Chefs use these concepts when developing more healthy alternatives to tradi-tional pastry and dessert offerings. In other cases a chef may alter a basic for-mula by reducing the amount of one or more ingredients, often with little serious change to the taste or quality of the finished product. The formulas at the end of this chapter illustrate the various ways that formulas may be changed to meet the needs of certain types of dietary conditions. Some use al-ternative ingredients, others substitutes to produce items that meet nutritional guidelines.

ALTERNATIVE INGREDIENTS AND SUBSTITUTES

In choosing ingredients for healthful desserts, the flavor, appearance and texture of the final product should be the guiding criteria. It is important to know the function an ingredient serves in a formula before a substitute or alternative is chosen. Does the ingredient affect flavor, structure, texture or appearance? When eggs are used as a binder, for example, substitutions may include flax seeds, tofu, puréed fruits or commercial egg replacements. On the other hand, if the eggs are acting as leaveners, then baking powder mixed with oil and water may be used. If the egg is serving as an emulsifier, adding commercially available liquid or granular **lecithin** will substitute for the emulsification properties of the egg.

The successful substitution of many commonly used bakeshop ingredients may require a change in the method of preparation, such as increasing or decreasing the amount of mixing or beating, varying the order in which the ingredients are combined, and decreasing the temperature for baking as well as the time the product is baked. The following are suggestions for ingredient substitutions or formula modifications to create healthier and alternative baked goods.

▶ **lecithin** fat found in egg yolks, a natural emulsifier

FAT

Some desserts are naturally fat-free or low in fat. Angel food cake, meringues and meringue cake layers are naturally fat-free since they are made with egg whites, sugar and white flour. Fruit cobblers can be low in fat, especially if the topping is made with a high-fiber cereal and a small amount of melted butter or oil, with fruit juice to substitute for some of the fat.

The simplest solution to reducing the fat content of a formula is to reduce the amount of fat used by up to 30 percent. If the formula calls for flour, switch to cake flour to ensure a tender result. Most quick breads can be reduced to 1 ounce (30 grams) of fat per 4 ounces (120 grams) of flour and still produce good results. If butter is being used for flavor and nothing else, then substituting powdered butter-flavored granules for the butter may work. The best course of action, however, might be to just reduce the amount of butter used.

There are many choices for replacing fat in formulas; some will affect the flavor, appearance and texture of the finished product. Adding fruit purées in place of some of the fat in cakes, cookies and muffins is a common practice. Some fruit purées will affect the flavor in a negative way while others will enhance the flavor. Prune purée seems to blend well with chocolate desserts, while applesauce does not. Applesauce does, however, work well in "neutral" cakes and muffins and quick breads. Mashed bananas make an excellent substitute for fat and/or eggs but will add a distinct banana flavor. Other fruit and vegetable substitutes include puréed cooked pumpkin, puréed cooked yellow or orange squash, puréed cooked apricots and mashed ripe bananas. Pumpkin and squash will not affect the flavor as much as the apricots and banana will. Fruit purées also change the texture and color of the baked good. Using a fruit purée to replace some or all of the fat results in a moister, stickier baked good that will get moister during storage.

If the butter is also crucial to the structure, then reducing the amount of butter and replacing some of it with a fruit purée will usually work well. Some bakers combine butter with low-fat cream cheese in place of some of the butter in cookies and cakes. Be wary of using margarines in place of butter. Substituting margarine for butter in a formula will reduce the **saturated fat** but will not reduce the calories. Choose a margarine that does not contain **hydrogenated fats** because hydrogenated fats are not considered a healthy alternative to butter. Fat-free margarines usually do not perform well in baked goods.

Using a vegetable oil to substitute for butter will not reduce the amount of fat in a formula, either. Liquid and solid fats have similar amounts of fat; only their composition is different. Solid fats have more saturated fat. Liquid fats have more

▶ **saturated fats** fats found mainly in animal products such as milk, butter, cheese, eggs and meat as well as in tropical oils such as coconut and palm; usually solid at room temperature. Research suggests that high-fat diets, especially those high in saturated fat, may be linked to heart disease, obesity and certain forms of cancer

▶ **hydrogenated fats** unsaturated, liquid fats that are chemically altered to remain solid at room temperature, such as solid shortening or margarine

▶ **unsaturated fats** fats that are normally liquid (oils) at room temperature, they may be monounsaturated (from plants such as olives and avocados) or polyunsaturated (from grains and seeds such as corn, soybeans and safflower as well as from fish)

unsaturated components. Using a vegetable oil for some or all of the butter in a formula will also reduce the amount of saturated fat. Substituting liquid oil for a solid fat may alter the texture and appearance of a baked product.

Replacing melted butter or melted shortening with a more healthy liquid fat such as olive oil or canola oil is one simple way to reduce the amount of saturated fat in baked goods. Oils made from nuts, including almonds, hazelnuts and walnuts, will also add a unique flavor and can work well in muffin and cookie formulas. Using vegetable oil in place of melted butter such as in a crêpe batter or for sautéing will only slightly alter the taste. Substituting a liquid oil in a formula that requires a solid fat, however, will alter the product dramatically. Piecrust made with olive oil, for instance, may be difficult to roll out and will bake into a mealy tough crust. For piecrusts, margarine may make a suitable substitute.

DAIRY PRODUCTS

Dairy products add color, texture and flavor to baked goods. They may be the basic liquid in a mixture, such as milk in a cake batter. Dairy products such as cream cheese or sour cream may add body, fat and texture to baked goods. To find an appropriate substitute, first determine if the fat in the dairy food is necessary for the success of the end product. If it is, try a low-fat or fat-free substitute combined with additional ingredients to substitute for some of the fat lost by using a fat-free dairy product. If the formula calls for whole milk, cream, sour cream, cream cheese or other cheese, a low-fat dairy alternative will usually work.

Reduced-fat milk such as 2%, 1% or skim milk can often be substituted on an equal basis for whole or regular milk. In some instances, evaporated skim milk might be a better choice, although it could add an off-flavor. Evaporated milk often imparts a "burnt" flavor because of the way it is processed. Light cream cheese (Neufchâtel) can be undetectable in baked goods when it replaces full-fat cream cheese. Using it to replace mascarpone cheese may require some other manipulation such as beating until light and fluffy with the addition of milk and and/or a small amount of sour cream. Fat-free cream cheese is not usually a suitable substitute for full-fat cream cheese.

Buttermilk, a by-product of churning cream into butter, is a naturally low-fat dairy product and a good substitute for other full-fat dairy products. Keep in mind that buttermilk is acidic, so using it may require some alteration in leavening ingredients. Low-fat and fat-free sour cream make suitable substitutions for full-fat sour cream in most preparations. Fat-free yogurt, made without gelatin, can be drained to remove excess liquid and used in place of sour cream. If the mixture is to be heated for a sauce or custard, adding a small amount of cornstarch will prevent curdling. Low-fat cottage cheese that has been blended in a food processor until smooth and creamy can be substituted for some of the full-fat cream cheese in a cheesecake formula. Use low-fat cream cheese for the remainder.

EGGS

Eggs add flavor and color; contribute to structure; incorporate air when beaten; provide liquid, fat and protein; and emulsify fat with liquid ingredients. Eggs contain fat as well as cholesterol. Determine how much fat and cholesterol the eggs are adding to each serving of the finished product before deciding to modify the formula. If a cake formula that will serve 8 to 10 people requires 3 ounces (120 grams) or two eggs, it might not be necessary to make any changes, as the per-serving impact of the fat and cholesterol from this small amount of eggs will be low. Two ounces (60 grams) or two egg whites can substitute for one whole egg in a formula. It is best, however, to include some whole eggs both for color and texture. Commercial egg substitutes may not be lower in fat. Read the label to determine the suitability of the egg substitute.

When the eggs are used as a binder, certain combinations of ingredients can provide a similar structural component. For one egg, some possible substitutes include the following:

▶ 1 tablespoon (15 milliliters) ground flax seed with 1.5 fluid ounces (45 milliliters) warm water

▶ 3.5 ounces (105 grams) mashed soft tofu

▶ 1.5 ounces (45 grams) puréed fruit

▶ 2 ounces (60 grams) puréed unflavored cooked beans

▶ unflavored mashed potatoes thinned a bit with warm water

LACTOSE

For those allergic to lactose, the sugar in milk, both true dairy products and plant sources of "milk" may be suitable. Commercially available lactose-free dairy products will work well in most preparations. Lactose is not usually necessary for the successful outcome of a formula. Some lactose-reduced and lactose-free dairy products may taste a bit sweeter to the sensitive palate.

Soy milk, either unflavored or flavored, may be substituted for milk although there may be a detectable flavor difference. Soy milk tends to brown prematurely; therefore, baking temperatures should be reduced and baking times shortened when soy milk is used. A milky substance can be made from nuts such as almonds or walnuts that are ground in water. However, those with a nut allergy would not be able to consume this product. The ration of nuts to water is 3 ounces (90 grams) nuts ground in 8 fluid ounces (240 milliliters) water.

GLUTEN

Wheat flour is the basis for many bakeshop products. Without it, making cookies, muffins, cakes and bread poses specific challenges. Baked goods will be less elastic and may crumble. Developing formulas that do not use gluten-forming flours involves making a number of changes to basic formulas. Alternative flours made from non-gluten-forming proteins combined with starches can make satisfactory gluten-free baked goods. The addition of stabilizers such as starches and gums, as discussed in Chapter 16, Ice Cream and Frozen Desserts, binds the batters into a homogeneous baked product. Available in powdered forms, gums and pectin can be adapted for use in the commercial kitchen. Since fruits are sources of gums and pectin, the addition of fruit purée to a formula for a gluten-free baked product is worth trying. For best results, mix several gluten-free flours together.

Gluten-free substitutes for wheat flour include flours made from arrowroot, **buckwheat,** corn, potato, rice, tapioca, soy, **amaranth, beans** such as chickpea, **flax** meal, **millet, quinoa, sorghum** and ground nuts. Commercially available gluten-free baking flours ease the preparation of suitable gluten-free products.

SUGAR

Sugar and other sweeteners add structure, texture and volume to baked goods. They retain moisture, contribute to a product's shelf life and help in the caramelization and browning of baked items. Because sugar provides flavor, color and tenderness to baked goods, finding an alternative that can provide all functions may be difficult. Most of the suitable substitutes for white table sugar are simply other kinds of sugar (such as fructose, which is fruit sugar). Using another kind of sugar will not reduce calories or carbohydrate content.

For consumers who simply prefer not to consume refined white table sugar, natural sweeteners from other sources may be used. Date and maple sugars can be used in baking and desserts but will impart a distinct flavor, which may actually be preferable to the sweetness of white table sugar. Date sugar works especially well as a sweetener when sprinkled on top of a baked good before

▶ **amaranth** tiny oval seeds of a type of annual herb plant native to South America; used as a cooked grain and flour

▶ **bean flour** cooked beans, including chickpeas, soybeans and white beans, that are dried, then ground into a fine powder; many bean flours, especially soy with its 50 percent protein content, are added to wheat flour mixtures to boost protein content

▶ **buckwheat flour** dark, nutty-tasting flour milled from the seeds of the buckwheat plant and used for centuries in Middle Eastern and Asian countries to make bread, cereals and baked goods

▶ **flax** a grain plant also known as linseed, rich in omega-3 fatty acids; flax hulls and seeds are crushed into a meal or flour to release beneficial compounds

▶ **millet** high-protein cereal grain cooked and eaten like rice; ground and used in combination with wheat flour in conventional baking

▶ **quinoa** (KEEN-wa) tiny, spherical seeds of a plant native to South America, cooked like grain or ground and used like flour

▶ **sorghum** grain harvested from a plant that resembles corn, used primarily for animal feed and food processing applications; also called milo; when ground, sorghum may be blended with other flours to make gluten-free preparations

baking. Brown rice syrup is a liquid sweetener that is not as sweet as sugar but works well in baking, especially in cookies and granola bars.

Honey is often used to replace some or all the sugar in a formula. If the formula calls for a small amount of honey, no adjustments to the liquid ingredients should be necessary when additional honey is used in place of granulated sugar. But if granulated sugar represents a large proportion of the ingredients, then some reduction of the liquid ingredients will have to be made to compensate for the extra liquid if honey is being substituted. Often reducing the amount of white table sugar instead of attempting to find an alternative is the best solution. Most desserts and baked goods will not be affected when the total sugar in the formula is reduced by up to one-third. To compensate for the reduced sweetness in these formulas, add additional flavor with extracts or spices such as nutmeg, mace, allspice and cinnamon.

The more challenging aspect of reducing the granulated sugar in formulas is replacing the carbohydrate with a noncarbohydrate sweetener. Noncaloric or very-low-calorie sugar alternatives such as **aspartame** (sold under the brands NutraSweet and Equal) or **saccharin** (sold under the brand name Sweet'n Low) may not be good substitutes for white table sugar in baking. Although they will sweeten the dessert, neither possesses any of the structural qualities that sugar imparts. Also, aspartame loses its sweetness when heated, so it can be used only in cold foods. For people on low-carbohydrate regimens, **sucralose** (sold under the brand name Splenda) may be the best substitute since it can be used measure for measure like white table sugar and stands up well to heat. Cakes and cookies baked with sucralose will not brown because it does not caramelize. As with all modifications, check for doneness before baking time has elapsed.

SALT

Reducing or eliminating added salt or sodium is usually successful in baked goods. Although chocolate desserts benefit from a dash of salt, most people will not notice that it is gone. Keep in mind that some leavening agents contain sodium, but there are sodium-free alternatives. Salt substitutes impart a bitter off-flavor and are not recommended. Be aware that skim milk has slightly higher sodium content than regular milk.

▶ **fiber** also known as dietary fiber; indigestible carbohydrates found in the seeds and cell walls of fruits, vegetables and cereal grains; fiber aids digestion

FIBER

Fiber is an important component in the diet, one in which Americans are lacking. Found in whole grains, fruits and vegetables, fiber may easily be added to baked goods. Ways in which additional fiber may be added to bakeshop formulas include the following:

▶ Replace some of the white flour (1 to 2 ounces/30 to 60 grams) per half pound (240 grams) with whole-wheat flour. Use whole-wheat pastry flour if substituting more than 2 ounces (60 grams).
▶ Add ground flax seed to any bakeshop formula in small amounts. Sprinkle flax seed over muffins and quick breads.
▶ Replace up to 2 ounces (60 grams) white flour per half pound (240 grams) with oat bran, oatmeal or bran cereal.
▶ Add a portion of fruit or vegetable purée to the formula to increase the fiber content.

Table 18.1 lists a number of ingredients and some common substitutions. Use it as a general guide. Appropriate substitutions depend on the function of the ingredient in the specific formula. Experimentation is the key to success.

Table 18.1 COMMON INGREDIENT SUBSTITUTES AND ALTERNATIVES

INSTEAD OF	USE	IN THESE APPLICATIONS
Butter	Powdered butter-flavored granules plus liquid (either fat-free milk or water)	Muffins, quick bread, and in place of melted butter in batters
	Butter-flavored or vegetable oil sprays	Pan coating, sautéing
	Vegetable and nut oils	In place of melted butter in batters and piecrusts (mealy dough, not flaky); may affect taste and texture
	Dried fruit or cooked vegetable purées	Quick breads, cookies and general baking; may affect color, taste and texture
Chocolate	Cocoa powder (vegetable oil may be added as needed)	General baking, icings; not suitable as a substitute in ganache or for coating chocolate
Cream cheese	Reduced-fat cream cheese or fat-free cream cheese	Cheesecake, icings
Granulated sugar	Other natural, granular sugars; date sugar; unrefined cane sugar	All applications; may darken cakes
	Liquid sugar, honey, rice syrup	All applications; reduce liquid in formula to balance additional moisture
	Sugar substitutes such as aspartame, saccharin or sucralose	For sweetening syrups, custards, creams, compotes
	Sucralose	In baked goods, cakes, quick breads, muffins where granulated sugar would provide structure
Light cream	Equal portions of low-fat milk and fat-free evaporated milk	Custards, creams, frozen desserts, general baking
Milk	Low-fat or skim milk	Most applications
	Soy or other grain- or nut-based beverage	Sauces, custards, frozen desserts; general baking; reduce baking temperatures
Salt	Ground spices including allspice, cinnamon, nutmeg; citrus juice and extracts	Any formula where salt is not needed to assist leavening
Sour cream	Reduced-fat or nonfat sour cream; drained reduced-fat or nonfat plain yogurt without gelatin	Topping, icings, in cakes, quick breads and muffins and for general baking
Whole eggs	Liquid egg substitutes; use 1 egg white for every third whole egg called for in formula	Batters
	Fruit purées alone or combined with starches	Batters when eggs are used to moisten; other binder may be necessary
Whipped cream	Whipped chilled evaporated fat-free milk; the milk and beaters need to be very cold (needs to be stabilized with gelatin)	Topping
	Italian meringue	To aerate mousses, frozen soufflés and creams
Wheat flour	Blends of non-gluten-forming flours and starches, including rice flour, corn flour, cornstarch, potato flour and potato starch, tapioca starch, quinoa, soy, sorghum, bean flours, buckwheat, millet and amaranth	Quick breads, yeast breads, muffins, cookies, cakes and brownies; mix gently

VEGETARIAN PREPARATIONS

There are several different forms of **vegetarianism,** eating a plant-based diet. Some vegetarians eat eggs (ovo vegetarians), some eat dairy (lacto vegetarians) and some eat both (lacto-ovo vegetarians). Strict vegetarians, called vegans, do not consume any animal products including gelatin—a common ingredient made from animal sources. Use the plant-based substitutes in each category

▶ **vegetarianism** eating a plant-based diet; ovo vegetarians will eat eggs; lacto vegetarians will eat some dairy; ovo-lacto vegetarians will eat eggs and dairy; vegans will consume no animal products of any kind

when developing a formula for a vegan. Avoid using honey in vegan formulas; vegans consider honey an animal by-product. Often vegetarians are particularly concerned with food additives and consuming processed foods. Their foods of choice are often organically grown, minimally processed foods.

WEIGHT LOSS DIETS

Many Americans are following low-carbohydrate diets for weight loss. Both flour and sugar are strictly controlled, as are fruits, but fat is usually not restricted. Suitable desserts for people on these diets include cakes made with ground nut flours, sucralose as the sweetener and egg whites and/or whole eggs. Cheesecake and meringue-type cookies made with sucralose would also conform to a low-carbohydrate diet.

CONCLUSION

Today's consumers are aware of nutritional recommendations and the healthful properties of the foods they eat. Customers may make food requests based on medical needs (such as allergies, diabetes or heart disease) or personal choice (such as avoiding processed foods). Taking into consideration the appropriateness of the methods used to modify or create a formula will guide the baker to prepare a palatable healthier product.

This chapter looked at ways the pastry chef and baker can adapt formulas to address dietary concerns. This overview introduced the student to the basic concepts of modifying and creating healthier formulas based on sound nutritional concepts. The formulas that follow put into practice some of the concepts presented.

QUESTIONS FOR DISCUSSION

1 Select a formula from those at the end of this chapter and compare it with a similar formula from one of the previous chapters. Note the nutritional differences. Discuss the ingredients that might account for these differences.
2 Using a traditional chocolate chip cookie formula, make suggestions for reducing fat and for increasing fiber.
3 Suggest ways to make a cheesecake for someone who must avoid lactose; for someone who is a vegan; for someone who must reduce the saturated fat in his or her diet.

4 You have been hired to develop a menu for a school cafeteria where some of the students have nut and gluten allergies. Use the Internet to obtain information on these two conditions. Then develop a week's worth of dessert menu items that can be offered in a school setting.

The formulas in this chapter were created specifically to address certain dietary requirements. The formula title or headnote indicates for which application such a dish would be used. Formulas throughout this book that conform to recommended dietary guidelines are indicated with the pyramid icon.

PEARS POACHED IN RED WINE   RECIPE 18.1

Note: This dish appears in the chapter opening photograph.

Yield: 8 Servings   **Method:** Poaching

Ripe pears, Anjou or Bartlett	8	8
Zinfandel wine	52 fl. oz.	1500 ml
Whole black peppercorns	8–10	8–10
Vanilla bean	1	1
Granulated sugar	12 oz.	360 g
Fresh basil, chopped	1 oz.	30 g
Orange zest	from 1 orange	from 1 orange

1 Peel and core the pears, leaving the stems intact.

2 Combine the remaining ingredients in a large nonreactive saucepan. Arrange the pears in the liquid in a single layer.

3 Place the pears on the stove top over a medium-high flame. Bring to just below a boil, then immediately reduce the heat and allow the liquid to simmer gently. Cover with a round of parchment paper if necessary to keep the pears submerged.

4 Continue poaching the pears until tender, approximately 1 to 1½ hours. Remove the saucepan from the stove and allow the pears to cool in the liquid.

5 Remove the pears from the poaching liquid. Strain the poaching liquid, then return it to the stove top. Reduce until the liquid is thick enough to coat the back of a spoon, then strain.

6 Serve the pears chilled or at room temperature in a pool of the reduced wine syrup.

Approximate values per 7-oz. (210-g) serving: **Calories** 410, **Total fat** 1.5 g, **Saturated fat** 0 g, **Cholesterol** 0 mg, **Sodium** 35 mg, **Total carbohydrates** 91 g, **Protein** 6 g, **Vitamin A** 40%, **Calcium** 90%, **Iron** 110%, **Claims**—low fat; no cholesterol; low sodium; high fiber

RECIPE 18.2   **NONFAT MANGO MOUSSE**

Yield: 10 Servings, 3¾ oz. (115 g) each, 2 lb. 6 oz. (1140 g) Mousse

Yogurt, nonfat and unsweetened	14 oz.	420 g
Mango purée	1 lb.	480 g
Egg whites	3 oz. (3 whites)	90 g
Granulated sugar	5 oz.	150 g
Water	2 fl. oz.	60 ml
Sheet gelatin, softened	0.75 oz.	20 g

1 Place the yogurt in a cheesecloth-lined strainer set over a bowl to collect the liquid. Drain the yogurt 2 to 3 hours in the refrigerator before using. Discard the liquid.

2 Combine the mango purée and the drained yogurt in a bowl. Lightly warm the mixture over a bain marie to 85°F (29°C). Set aside.

3 Prepare an Italian meringue with the egg whites, sugar and water. Melt the gelatin and add it to the meringue.

4 Fold one-quarter of the mango-yogurt mixture into the meringue using a balloon whisk. Add another one-quarter of the mixture and combine well. Fold in the remaining meringue.

5 Portion into serving dishes or fill a torte immediately before the gelatin sets.

Approximate values per 3¾-oz. (115-g) serving: **Calories** 120, **Total fat** 0 g, **Saturated fat** 0 g, **Cholesterol** 0 mg, **Sodium** 50 mg, **Total carbohydrates** 25 g, **Protein** 5 g, **Vitamin A** 35%, **Vitamin C** 20%, **Claims**—fat free, low sodium

RECIPE 18.3   **PIE OR TART DOUGH MADE WITH OLIVE OIL**

This crust has no cholesterol and less saturated fat than one made with animal fat or hydrogenated shortening.

Yield: 1 lb. 4 oz. (600 g) Dough for one 8-in. (20-cm) double-crust pie

Olive oil	5.25 fl. oz.	158 ml
Vanilla extract	0.15 fl. oz. (1 tsp.)	5 ml
Molasses	1 oz.	30 g
Almond extract	0.15 fl. oz. (1 tsp.)	5 ml
Pastry flour	9 oz.	270 g
Oats, quick-cooking	4 oz.	120 g
Salt	0.2 oz. (1 tsp.)	6 g
Cinnamon	0.2 oz. (1 Tbsp.)	6 g

1 Combine the olive oil, vanilla, molasses and almond extract in a measuring cup. Set aside.

2 Place the flour, oats, salt and cinnamon in the bowl of a food processor. With the machine running, pour in the olive oil mixture. Mix until the dough forms a ball, approximately 30 to 40 seconds. Wrap the dough and refrigerate approximately 1 hour before using.

Approximate values per 1-oz. (30-g) serving: **Calories** 140, **Total fat** 8 g, **Saturated fat** 1 g, **Cholesterol** 0 mg, **Sodium** 115 mg, **Total carbohydrates** 15 g, **Protein** 2 g

PASSION FRUIT TART

This tart represents a lower-calorie dessert when compared with some options.

Yield: 2 Tarts, 7 in. (17 cm) each

Orange juice	1 pt.	480 ml
Passion fruit juice	8 fl. oz.	240 ml
Lemon juice	2 fl. oz.	60 ml
Fructose or granulated sugar	8 oz.	240 g
Eggs	6.75 oz. (4 eggs)	200 g
Egg yolks	1.3 oz. (2 yolks)	40 g
Granulated sugar	6 oz.	180 g
Cornstarch	2.25 oz.	68 g
Unsalted butter, softened	2 oz.	60 g
Nut Tart/Pie Dough (recipe follows), 7-in. (17-cm) shells, fully baked	2 shells	2 shells
Fresh strawberries	1 lb. 4 oz.	600 g
Neutral glaze	5 oz.	150 g
Strawberry purée	3 oz.	90 g

1 Combine the orange juice, passion fruit juice, lemon juice and fructose in a large saucepan. Bring to a boil.

2 Meanwhile whisk together the eggs, egg yolks and granulated sugar. Stir in the cornstarch.

3 Temper the egg batter with one-quarter of the boiling fruit juice. Pour the tempered egg mixture into the remaining boiling juice. Whisk vigorously until the mixture boils and is well thickened.

4 Remove from the heat and stir in the butter, then pour the filling into the baked tart shells. Let cool.

5 Cut the strawberries in half and arrange cut side down on the tarts. Melt the neutral glaze with the strawberry purée. Cool slightly, then brush the glaze over the strawberries. Chill.

Approximate values per 1/8-tart serving: **Calories** 390, **Total fat** 15 g, **Saturated fat** 4.5 g, **Cholesterol** 105 mg, **Sodium** 210 mg, **Total carbohydrates** 59 g, **Protein** 8 g, **Vitamin A** 15%, **Vitamin C** 60%, **Iron** 10%

NUT TART/PIE DOUGH

This crust has less saturated fat than one made with animal fats or hydrogenated shortening.

Yield: 1 lb. 9 oz. (750 g) dough

Pastry flour, sifted	4 oz.	120 g
Whole white-wheat flour	2 oz.	60 g
Almond flour	4 oz.	120 g
Hazelnut flour	4 oz.	120 g
Brown sugar	6 oz.	180 g
Reduced-fat cream cheese	6 oz.	180 g
Egg	1.6 oz. (1 egg)	50 g
Egg white	1 oz. (1 white)	30 g
Vanilla extract	0.15 fl. oz. (1 tsp.)	5 ml
Salt	0.2 oz. (1 tsp.)	6 g

1 Combine the pastry, whole-wheat, almond and hazelnut flours. Set aside.
2 Cream the brown sugar and cream cheese until fluffy.
3 Gradually add the egg and egg white, then the vanilla and salt to the creamed mixture.
4 Mix in the flour mixture until just combined.
5 Chill the dough before using.

Approximate values per 1-oz. (30-g) serving: **Calories** 110, **Total fat** 6 g, **Saturated fat** 1 g, **Cholesterol** 10 mg, **Sodium** 105 mg, **Total carbohydrates** 12 g, **Protein** 3 g

RECIPE 18.5

REDUCED-FAT CHOCOLATE MOUSSE TORTE

Yield: 3 Tortes, 7 in. × 2½ in. (17 cm × 6 cm) each

Reduced-Fat Chocolate Cake (recipe follows)	1 round	1 round
Reduced-Fat Chocolate Mousse (recipe follows)	3 lb. 12 oz.	1800 g
Cocoa Gelée (page 363)	10 oz.	300 g
Fresh raspberries	15	15

1 Lightly oil and sugar three 7-inch (17-centimeter) torte rings. Or line the rings with strips of clear acetate. Place on a paper-lined sheet pan.
2 Slice the Reduced-Fat Chocolate Cake horizontally into three even layers and place one in each ring. Set aside.
3 Prepare the Reduced-Fat Chocolate Mousse and fill to the edge of the ring. Level the mousse with a long metal spatula.
4 Place the tortes in a refrigerator and let set, approximately 2 hours.
5 Warm the Cocoa Gelée to 120°F (49°C) and cover the surface of each torte with the gelée. Let the gelée firm.
6 Gently heat the sides of the ring using a propane torch to facilitate the removal of the ring.
7 Place the tortes on cake boards and decorate with the raspberries.

Approximate values per ⅑-cake serving: **Calories** 350, **Total fat** 12 g, **Saturated fat** 5 g, **Cholesterol** 15 mg, **Sodium** 90 mg, **Total carbohydrates** 55 g, **Protein** 8 g

REDUCED-FAT CHOCOLATE CAKE

Yield: 1 Cake, 7 in. (17 cm)

Method: Creaming

Fruit paste or prune purée	5.5 oz.	165 g
Granulated sugar	9.5 oz.	285 g
Olive oil	3 fl. oz.	90 ml
Egg	1.6 oz. (1 egg)	50 g
Buttermilk	3 fl. oz.	90 ml
Vanilla extract	0.3 fl. oz. (2 tsp.)	10 ml
Salt	0.05 oz. (¼ tsp.)	1.5 g
Hazelnut flour, toasted	2 oz.	60 g
Cake flour, sifted	2.75 oz.	85 g
Cocoa powder	2.75 oz.	85 g
Baking powder	0.07 oz. (½ tsp.)	2 g
Egg whites	3 oz. (3 whites)	90 g

1 In the bowl of a mixer fitted with a paddle, blend the fruit paste and 4 ounces (120 grams) of the sugar.

2 Gradually add the olive oil. Scrape down the bowl, then add the egg, buttermilk and vanilla. Scrape down the bowl, then stir in the salt, flours, cocoa powder and baking powder just until mixed into the batter.

3 In a separate clean bowl, whip the egg whites and the remaining sugar to medium peaks and fold one-third of the whipped egg whites into the cake batter. Once combined, delicately fold in the remaining whipped egg whites. Do not overfold.

4 Pour the batter into a greased 7-inch (17-centimeter) cake pan and bake at 375°F (190°C) until the center of the cake bounces back when lightly pressed, approximately 25 minutes. Cool the cake before slicing and filling.

Approximate values per 1-oz. (30 g) serving: **Calories** 90, **Total fat** 4 g, **Saturated fat** 0.5 g, **Cholesterol** 5 mg, **Sodium** 35 mg, **Total carbohydrates** 14 g, **Protein** 2 g

REDUCED-FAT CHOCOLATE MOUSSE

Yield: Approximately 3 lb. 12 oz. (1800 g)

Fat-free ricotta cheese	12 oz.	360 g
Fat-free sour cream	12 oz.	360 g
Low-fat sweetened condensed milk	6 oz.	180 g
Bittersweet chocolate	15 oz.	450 g
Egg whites	9 oz. (9 whites)	270 g
Granulated sugar	15 oz.	450 g
Water	5 fl. oz.	150 ml

1 Whisk together the ricotta cheese, sour cream and sweetened condensed milk until smooth. Warm the mixture to 95°F (35°C) over simmering water. Hold the mixture at this temperature while preparing the remaining ingredients.

2 In a separate bowl melt the chocolate to 95°F (35°C). Hold the chocolate at this temperature while preparing the remaining ingredients.

3 Prepare an Italian meringue with the egg whites, sugar and water.

4 Once the Italian meringue is prepared, whisk together the cheese mixture and the melted chocolate. Immediately fold in one-third of the Italian meringue. Once combined, fold in the remaining Italian meringue. Use immediately.

Approximate values per 1-oz. (30 g) serving: **Calories** 70, **Total fat** 2 g, **Saturated fat** 1.5 g, **Cholesterol** 0 mg, **Sodium** 15 mg, **Total carbohydrates** 11 g, **Protein** 2 g

REDUCED-FAT THREE BERRY TORTE

This dessert has less total fat and less saturated fat when compared with a traditional cream-filled cake.

Yield: 2 Tortes, 7 in. × 2½ in. (17 cm × 6 cm) each

Dacquoise (page 299), 7-in. (17-cm) disks	4 disks	4 disks
Reduced-Fat Vanilla Cream (recipe follows)	3 lb. 11 oz.	1770 g
Fresh raspberries	6 oz.	180 g
Fresh blueberries	6 oz.	180 g
Fresh blackberries	6 oz.	180 g
Italian Meringue (page 290)	1 lb. 8 oz.	720 g
Red Fruit Gelée (recipe follows)	1 lb.	480 g

1 Lightly oil and sugar two 7-inch (17-centimeter) torte rings. Or line the rings with strips of clear acetate. Place on a paper-lined sheet pan.

2 Place one Dacquoise disk in each torte ring.

3 Cover each Dacquoise disk with a 1-inch- (2.5-centimeter-) thick layer of Reduced-Fat Vanilla Cream. Scatter half of the berries over the cream.

4 Trim the two remaining Dacquoise disks slightly to fit inside the torte rings. Place them on top of the cream, then top them with another 1-inch- (2.5-centimeter-) thick layer of the cream and the remaining berries. Cover the berries with the remaining cream, leveling it off with a long metal spatula. Refrigerate the tortes until set, approximately 2 hours.

5 Gently heat the sides of the ring using a propane torch to facilitate the removal of the ring. Place on a cake board.

6 Ice the tortes with a thin layer of Italian Meringue. Using a pastry bag fitted with a medium star tip or a St. Honoré tip, pipe a connecting meringue border along the edge of the torte. Brown the meringue using a propane torch.

7 Prepare the Red Fruit Gelée and pour inside the meringue border.

Approximate values per ⅛-cake serving: **Calories** 510, **Total fat** 10 g, **Saturated fat** 1.5 g, **Cholesterol** 5 mg, **Sodium** 240 mg, **Total carbohydrates** 91 g, **Protein** 18 g, **Vitamin C** 25%, **Calcium** 15%

REDUCED-FAT VANILLA CREAM

Yield: 3 lb. 11 oz. (1770 g)

Fat-free cottage cheese	1 lb. 8 oz.	720 g
Fat-free sour cream	10 oz.	300 g
Low-fat sweetened condensed milk	13 oz.	390 g
Vanilla extract	0.5 fl. oz.	15 ml
Sheet gelatin, softened	0.75 oz.	21 g
Fresh raspberries	4 oz.	120 g
Fresh blueberries	3 oz.	90 g
Fresh blackberries	4 oz.	120 g

1 Blend the cottage cheese, sour cream, sweetened condensed milk and vanilla in a food processor until smooth.

2 Scrape the mixture into a bowl set over simmering water and warm to 95°F (35°C). Set aside.

3 Melt the gelatin and whisk it into the cheese mixture. Fold in the berries and use immediately.

Approximate values per 1-oz. (30 g) serving: **Calories** 35, **Total fat** 0 g, **Saturated fat** 0 g, **Cholesterol** 0 mg, **Sodium** 45 mg, **Total carbohydrates** 5 g, **Protein** 2 g

RED FRUIT GELÉE

Yield: Approximately 1 lb. (480 g)

Raspberry purée	5 oz.	150 g
Blueberry purée	5 oz.	150 g
Blackberry purée	5 oz.	150 g
Granulated sugar	5 oz.	150 g
Sheet gelatin, softened	0.75 oz.	21 g

1 In a nonreactive saucepan, combine and heat the fruit purées to 110°F (43°C). Whisk in the sugar. Melt the gelatin and add to the fruit purée.

2 Use immediately to coat the top of a tart or torte.

Approximate values per 1-oz. (30 g) serving: **Calories** 50, **Total fat** 0 g, **Saturated fat** 0 g, **Cholesterol** 0 mg, **Sodium** 5 mg, **Total carbohydrates** 11 g, **Protein** 1 g

REDUCED-FAT STRAWBERRY AND MANGO TRIFLE

RECIPE 18.7

Yield: 12 Servings

Fresh strawberries, quartered	12 oz.	360 g
Granulated sugar	2 oz.	60 g
Mangoes, cubed	12 oz.	360 g
Reduced-Fat Trifle Cream (recipe follows)	1 lb. 3 oz.	570 g
Reduced-Fat Poundcake (recipe follows)	1 cake	1 cake
Granola Crunch Topping (page 269)	6 oz.	180 g

1 Purée 4 ounces (120 grams) of the strawberries with 1 ounce (30 grams) of the sugar. Fold in the remaining strawberries and set aside.

2 Purée 4 ounces (120 grams) of the mangoes with 1 ounce (30 grams) of the sugar. Fold in the remaining mango cubes and set aside.

3 Spoon approximately ½ ounce (15 grams) of the Reduced-Fat Trifle Cream into the bottom of each of 12 tall parfait glasses.

4 Cut the Reduced-Fat Poundcake into 12 thin slices. Cut each slice in half and fit one in each parfait glass.

5 Evenly divide the strawberry mixture between the 12 parfait glasses. Top with ½ ounce (15 grams) of the Reduced-Fat Trifle Cream.

6 Place the remaining pieces of Reduced-Fat Poundcake in each parfait glass, covering the Reduced-Fat Trifle Cream.

7 Evenly divide the mango mixture between the 12 parfait glasses.

8 Fill the glasses with the remaining Reduced-Fat Trifle Cream. Sprinkle each glass with Granola Crunch Topping.

Approximate values per serving: **Calories** 420, **Total fat** 14 g, **Saturated fat** 4 g, **Cholesterol** 50 mg, **Sodium** 250 mg, **Total carbohydrates** 67 g, **Protein** 10 g, **Vitamin A** 30%, **Vitamin C** 40%

REDUCED-FAT TRIFLE CREAM

Yield: 1 lb. 3 oz. (570 g)

Fat-free ricotta cheese	8 oz.	240 g
Low-fat cottage cheese	6 oz.	180 g
Low-fat sweetened condensed milk	5 oz.	150 g
Vanilla extract	0.15 fl. oz. (1 tsp.)	5 ml
Peppermint oil (optional)	0.08 fl. oz. (½ tsp.)	2.5 ml
Sheet gelatin, softened	0.125 oz. (1 sheet)	3 g

1 Combine the ricotta cheese, cream cheese, sweetened condensed milk, vanilla and peppermint oil (if using) in the bowl of a food processor. Blend until smooth.

2 Warm the mixture in a double boiler or microwave to 100°F (38°C). Stir in the softened gelatin. Use immediately.

Approximate values per 1-oz. (30-g) serving: **Calories** 40, **Total fat** 0.5 g, **Saturated fat** 0 g, **Cholesterol** 0 mg, **Sodium** 85 mg, **Total carbohydrates** 5 g, **Protein** 3 g

REDUCED-FAT POUNDCAKE

Yield: 1 Loaf, 8½ in. × 4½ in. (21.2 cm × 11.2 cm)

Pastry flour	7 oz.	210 g
Baking soda	0.04 oz. (¼ tsp.)	1 g
Baking powder	0.07 oz. (½ tsp.)	2 g
Fruit paste or prune purée	1.5 oz.	45 g
Unsalted butter, softened	2 oz.	60 g
Olive oil	2 fl. oz.	60 ml
Granulated sugar	10 oz.	300 g
Salt	0.05 oz. (¼ tsp.)	1.5 g
Vanilla extract	0.15 fl. oz. (1 tsp.)	5 ml
Almond extract	0.15 fl. oz. (1 tsp.)	5 ml
Orange zest, grated fine	0.2 oz. (1 Tbsp.)	6 g
Egg yolks	1.3 oz. (2 yolks)	40 g
Fat-free sour cream	3 oz.	180 g
Egg whites	2 oz. (2 whites)	60 g

1 Sift together the pastry flour, baking soda and baking powder. Set aside.

2 Cream the fruit paste and butter until fluffy. Gradually add the olive oil. Scrape down the bowl and add 8 ounces (240 grams) of the sugar, mixing well. Stir in the salt, vanilla, almond extract and orange zest. Mix in the egg yolks.

3 Add half of the sour cream, alternating with half of the flour mixture, mixing well after each addition. Repeat with the remaining sour cream and the flour.

4 In a separate clean bowl, whip the egg whites and the remaining sugar to medium peaks and fold into the batter.

5 Bake at 350°F (180°C) until the cake bounces back when lightly pressed in the center, approximately 1 hour. Cool completely before slicing.

Approximate values per 1-oz. (30 g) serving: **Calories** 100, **Total fat** 4 g, **Saturated fat** 1.5 g, **Cholesterol** 20 mg, **Sodium** 45 mg, **Total carbohydrates** 17 g, **Protein** 1 g

NO-SUGAR-ADDED HAZELNUT SHORTBREAD   RECIPE 18.8

Yield: 24 Cookies, 1¾ oz. (50 g) each   **Method:** Icebox

Unsalted butter, softened	8 oz.	240 g
Sucralose	0.75 oz.	22 g
Salt	0.2 oz. (1 tsp.)	6 g
Fat-free sour cream	4 oz.	120 g
Orange zest, grated fine	0.2 oz. (1 Tbsp.)	6 g
Hazelnuts, toasted and chopped coarse	5 oz.	150 g
Pastry flour	8 oz.	240 g
Rice flour	2 oz.	60 g

1 Cream the butter, sucralose and salt.

2 Add the sour cream, orange zest and hazelnuts. Mix well.

3 Add the flours and mix until just combined. Form the dough into a long bar measuring 2 inches × 2 inches (5 centimeters × 5 centimeters) square. Chill the bar in the freezer until hard.

4 When ready to bake, cut the bar into ½-inch- (1.2-centimeter-) thick slices.

5 Position slices on a paper-lined sheet pan and bake at 375°F (190°C) until golden brown, approximately 25 minutes.

Approximate values per cookie: **Calories** 150, **Total fat** 12 g, **Saturated fat** 5 g, **Cholesterol** 20 mg, **Sodium** 100 mg, **Total carbohydrates** 12 g, **Protein** 2 g

SUGAR-FREE MANGO GINGER JAM   RECIPE 18.9

Yield: 14 oz. (420 g)

Ginger, grated	0.4 oz. (1 Tbsp.)	12 g
Orange juice concentrate	2 fl. oz.	60 ml
Mango, cubed	14 oz.	420 g
Sucralose	0.14 oz. (2 Tbsp.)	4 g
Citric acid, powdered (optional)	pinch	pinch

1 Boil the ginger and orange juice concentrate in a nonreactive pan. Remove from the heat, cover and let sit 10 minutes. Add the remaining ingredients. Bring the mixture to a boil, stirring constantly. Cook 3 to 5 minutes until the mixture thickens.

2 Remove from the heat and let cool.

Approximate values per 1-oz. (30-g) serving: **Calories** 25, **Total fat** 0 g, **Saturated fat** 0 g, **Cholesterol** 0 mg, **Sodium** 0 mg, **Total carbohydrates** 7 g, **Protein** 0 g, **Vitamin A** 20%, **Vitamin C** 20%

► **citric acid** acid found in citrus fruit juice, used to enhance flavor in foods and to prevent crystallization of sugar syrups; available in liquid or powdered form

RECIPE 18.10

NO-SUGAR-ADDED REDUCED-FAT APPLE-ALMOND POUNDCAKE

Yield: 2 Cakes, 9 in. × 4 in. (22 cm × 10 cm)

Cake flour	8 oz.	240 g
Baking powder	0.3 oz. (2 tsp.)	8 g
Baking soda	0.14 oz. (1 tsp.)	4 g
Cinnamon, ground	1 oz.	30 g
Ginger, ground	0.14 oz. (2 tsp.)	4 g
Dry buttermilk powder	1 oz.	30 g
Almond flour	4.5 oz.	135 g
Fat-free sour cream	10 oz.	300 g
Sucralose	1.5 oz.	45 g
Salt	0.2 oz. (1 tsp.)	6 g
Olive oil	10 fl. oz.	300 ml
Vanilla extract	0.15 fl. oz. (1 tsp.)	5 ml
Almond extract	0.3 fl. oz. (2 tsp.)	10 ml
Eggs	5 oz. (3 eggs)	150 g
Golden Delicious apples, medium dice	3	3
Walnut pieces	6 oz.	180 g
Egg whites	4 oz. (4 whites)	120 g

1 Sift together the cake flour, baking powder, baking soda, cinnamon, ginger and dry milk powder. Add the almond flour and set aside.

2 In the bowl of a mixer fitted with a paddle, blend the sour cream, sucralose and salt until well combined. Gradually add the olive oil, then the vanilla and almond extracts.

3 Add the eggs one at a time, waiting for the previous egg to be fully incorporated before adding the next one. Fold in the dry ingredients. Stir in the apples and walnut pieces.

4 In a separate clean bowl, whip the egg whites to soft peaks. Fold one-third of the whipped egg whites into the cake batter, then fold in the remaining whipped egg whites.

5 Divide the cake batter evenly between two greased 9-inch × 4-inch (22-centimeter × 10-centimeter) pans.

6 Bake at 375°F (190°C) until the cake bounces back when lightly pressed, approximately 20 to 22 minutes.

Approximate values per 2-oz. (60 g) serving: **Calories** 190, **Total fat** 14 g, **Saturated fat** 2 g, **Cholesterol** 20 mg, **Sodium** 150 mg, **Total carbohydrates** 12 g, **Protein** 4 g

RECIPE 18.11

GLUTEN-FREE BUCKWHEAT BREAD

Yield: 4 Loaves, 1 lb. 2 oz. (540 g) each   **Method:** Straight dough

Fermentation: Approximately 1 hour.

Water at 75°F (24°C)	1 pt.	480 ml
Soy milk at 75°F (24°C)	14 fl. oz.	420 ml
Salt	0.75 oz.	22 g
Brown sugar	0.5 oz.	15 g
Eggs	5 oz. (3 eggs)	150 g
Instant yeast	0.5 oz.	15 g
Xanthan gum*	0.4 oz. (1 Tbsp.)	12 g
Buckwheat flour	1 lb.	480 g
Rice flour	11 oz.	330 g

1 In the bowl of a mixer fitted with a whip, combine the water, soy milk, salt, sugar, eggs, yeast and xanthan gum.

2 On low speed, gradually add the flours.

3 Pour the batter into paper-lined or well-buttered loaf pans measuring 8½ inches × 4½ inches × 2½ inches (21.2 centimeters × 11.2 centimeters × 6.2 centimeters). The pans should be nearly half full.

4 Let the batter ferment until increased 50 percent in volume, approximately 1 hour.

5 Bake at 425°F (220°C) until the bread sounds hollow when lightly tapped on the bottom, 35 to 40 minutes.

*Xanthan gum is produced by fermenting the sugars in corn. It is used to thicken, stabilize and emulsify prepared sauces, dairy products, ice creams and baked goods.

Approximate values per ⅑-loaf serving: **Calories** 90, **Total fat** 1 g, **Saturated fat** 0 g, **Cholesterol** 20 mg, **Sodium** 240 mg, **Total carbohydrates** 17 g, **Protein** 3 g

GLUTEN-FREE FUDGE BROWNIES   RECIPE 18.12

Yield: 48 Brownies, 2 in. (5 cm) each, 1 Half-Sheet Pan

Method: Bar cookie

Rice flour	6 oz.	180 g
Tapioca flour	2 oz.	60 g
Cornstarch	2 oz.	60 g
Cocoa powder	1 oz.	30 g
Baking powder	0.14 oz. (1 tsp.)	4 g
Unsalted butter	8 oz.	240 g
Semisweet or bittersweet chocolate	1 lb.	480 g
Maple syrup	6 oz.	120 g
Eggs	8.3 oz. (5 eggs)	250 g
Granulated sugar	1 lb.	480 g
Vanilla extract	0.5 fl. oz.	15 ml
Almond extract	0.15 fl. oz. (1 tsp.)	5 ml
Salt	0.2 oz. (1 tsp.)	6 g
Walnuts, chopped	12 oz.	360 g
Silky Ganache Deluxe (page 371)	1 lb.	480 g
Cocoa powder for garnish	as needed	as needed
Walnut halves for garnish	48	48

1 Sift together the rice flour, tapioca, cornstarch, cocoa powder and baking powder. Set aside.

2 Combine the butter and chocolate in a bowl over simmering water. Melt the mixture to 110°F (43°C). Set aside.

3 Whip the maple syrup, eggs, sugar, vanilla and almond extract until well combined. Stir in the melted chocolate mixture, then the walnuts.

4 Spread the mixture on a paper-lined half-sheet pan.

5 Bake at 350°F (180°C) until the brownies are set and bounce back when lightly pressed, approximately 35 minutes.

6 Cool the brownies, then refrigerate or freeze until firm.

7 Loosen the edge of the brownies from the pan with a plastic scraper. Invert the pan onto the backside of a sheet pan. If the brownies stick, hold the pan briefly over a heat source to release. Remove the paper.

8 Heat the Silky Ganache Deluxe to 110°F (43°C) and spread it over the brownies. Let firm, then cut into 2-inch × 2-inch (5-centimeter × 5-centimeter) squares.

9 Dust the brownies with cocoa powder and place a walnut half in the center of each square.

Approximate values per brownie: **Calories** 260, **Total fat** 17 g, **Saturated fat** 7 g, **Cholesterol** 40 mg, **Sodium** 65 mg, **Total carbohydrates** 27 g, **Protein** 4 g

RECIPE 18.13

GLUTEN-FREE PIE DOUGH

Yield: 1 lb. 5 oz. (630 g), Dough for one 8-in. (20-cm) double-crust pie

Buttermilk	1.5 fl. oz.	45 ml
Egg	1.6 oz. (1 egg)	50 g
Salt	0.2 oz. (1 tsp.)	6 g
Brown sugar	1 oz.	30 g
Vanilla extract	0.15 fl. oz. (1 tsp.)	5 ml
Almond extract	0.15 fl. oz. (1 tsp.)	5 ml
Rice flour	7 oz.	210 g
Cornstarch	2 oz.	60 g
Tapioca flour	2 oz.	60 g
Xanthan gum	0.05 oz. (½ tsp.)	1 g
Unsalted butter, cold	6 oz.	180 g

1 Whisk together the buttermilk, egg, salt, sugar, vanilla and almond extracts. Set aside.

2 Combine the rice flour, cornstarch, tapioca flour and xanthan gum in a large bowl. Cut the butter into medium dice, ⅜ inch × ⅜ inch (9 millimeters × 9 millimeters), then cut it into the flour mixture until the pieces are the size of a pea.

3 Add the buttermilk mixture and mix just until the dough comes together. Wrap the dough in plastic and chill at least 1 hour before using.

VARIATION:

Gluten- and Lactose-Free Pie Dough—Substitute soy margarine for the butter and soy milk for the buttermilk.

Approximate values per 1-oz. (30-g) serving: **Calories** 120, **Total fat** 7 g, **Saturated fat** 4 g, **Cholesterol** 25 mg, **Sodium** 110 mg, **Total carbohydrates** 13 g, **Protein** 1 g

RECIPE 18.14

GLUTEN-FREE ITALIAN CREAM CAKE

Yield: 2 Cakes, 8 in. (20 cm) each

Rice flour	10 oz.	300 g
Tapioca flour	2 oz.	60 g
Potato starch	2 oz.	60 g
Cornstarch	1 oz.	30 g
Baking soda	0.3 oz. (2 tsp.)	8 g
Baking powder	0.14 oz. (1 tsp.)	4 g
Xanthan gum	0.15 oz. (1½ tsp.)	1.5 g
Unsalted butter, softened	5 oz.	150 g
Granulated sugar	10 oz.	300 g
Salt	0.2 oz. (1 tsp.)	6 g
Egg yolks	2.6 oz. (4 yolks)	80 g
Olive oil	2 fl. oz.	60 ml
Buttermilk	4 fl. oz.	120 ml
Vanilla extract	0.5 fl. oz.	15 ml
Pecan pieces	1 lb.	480 g
Coconut flakes	7 oz.	210 g
Egg whites	4 oz. (4 whites)	120 g
Granulated sugar	2 oz.	60 g
Reduced-Fat Cream Cheese Icing (recipe follows)	2 lb.	960 g

1 Combine and sift together the rice flour, tapioca flour, potato starch, corn-starch, baking soda, baking powder and xanthan gum. Set aside.

2 In the bowl of a mixer fitted with a paddle, cream the butter and sugar. Add the salt, then add the egg yolks in two additions. Stir in the olive oil, buttermilk and vanilla.

3 Stir in the dry ingredients just until mixed, then stir in 8 ounces (240 grams) of the pecan pieces and 3 ounces (120 grams) of the coconut flakes.

4 In a separate clean bowl, whip the egg whites and sugar to soft peaks and fold one-third of the whipped whites into the batter using a rubber spatula. Fold in another third and then the remaining whipped whites.

5 Pour the batter into two 8-inch (20-centimeter) greased pans. Bake at 375°F (190°C) until the cake bounces back when lightly pressed, approximately 35 minutes.

6 Cool the cakes completely, then slice each one into three equal layers. Spread each layer with a thin coating of the cream cheese icing.

7 Ice the cakes with the remaining icing and surround the bottom edge of the cake with the remaining pecan pieces. Decorate the top with the remaining co-conut flakes.

Approximate values per 1/8-cake serving: **Calories** 710, **Total fat** 44 g, **Saturated fat** 15 g, **Cholesterol** 95 mg, **Sodium** 510 mg, **Total carbohydrates** 73 g, **Protein** 10 g, **Vitamin A** 15%, **Calcium** 10%, **Iron** 10%

REDUCED-FAT CREAM CHEESE ICING

Yield: Approximately 2 lb. (960 g)

Reduced-fat cream cheese, room temperature	1 lb. 8 oz.	720 g
Powdered sugar	9 oz.	270 g
Lemon zest, grated fine	0.07 oz. (1 tsp.)	2 g
Orange zest, grated fine	0.14 oz. (2 tsp.)	4 g
Vanilla extract	0.5 fl. oz.	15 ml

1 In the bowl of a mixer fitted with a paddle, mix the cream cheese on low speed until smooth.

2 Add the powdered sugar and mix until well combined.

3 Add the lemon zest, orange zest and vanilla.

Approximate values per ounce (30 g): **Calories** 80, **Total fat** 4 g, **Saturated fat** 2.5 g, **Cholesterol** 10 mg, **Sodium** 65 mg, **Total carbohydrates** 10 g, **Protein** 2 g

VARIATION:

No-Sugar-Added Reduced-Fat Cream Cheese Icing—Substitute 0.5 ounce (15 grams) sucralose for the powdered sugar. Add 4 fluid ounces (120 mil-liliters) buttermilk in Step 2.

Approximate values per ounce (30 g): **Calories** 60, **Total fat** 4 g, **Saturated fat** 2.5 g, **Cholesterol** 15 mg, **Sodium** 75 mg, **Total carbohydrates** 2 g, **Protein** 3 g

RECIPE 18.15

SOYNUT TOFU ICE CREAM

ADAPTED FROM *SOY DESSERTS* BY PATRICIA GREENBERG, CCP

ReganBooks, 2000

Yield: 1½ qt. (1½ lt), 12 Servings

▶ **soynuts** soaked soybeans that are dried or roasted and consumed as a snack food in place of higher-fat alternatives such as roasted tree nuts or peanuts

Soynuts	7 oz.	210 g
Soft tofu	2 lb.	1 kg
Granulated sugar	5 oz.	150 g
Soy milk	12 fl. oz.	360 ml
Almond extract	0.15 fl. oz. (1 tsp.)	5 ml

1 In a food processor, grind the soynuts to a coarse consistency. Add the tofu and sugar and purée.

2 With the processor running, add the soy milk and almond extract and continue to process until the mixture is smooth. Pour into the container of an ice cream machine and process according to the manufacturer's directions.

VARIATION:

Lemon-Ginger-Soy Ice Cream—Omit the soynuts and the almond extract. Add 2 ounces (60 grams) crystallized ginger, the zest of 3 lemons and 0.8 fluid ounces (2.5 milliliters/½ teaspoon) lemon extract. Process the ginger and lemon zest with the tofu as directed in Step 2.

Approximate values per 4-oz. (120 g) serving: **Calories** 200, **Total fat** 7 g, **Saturated fat** 1 g, **Cholesterol** 0 mg, **Sodium** 15 mg, **Total carbohydrates** 23 g, **Protein** 13 g

RECIPE 18.16

LACTOSE-FREE PECAN ICE CREAM

Yield: 1½ pt. (¾ lt)

Soy milk creamer	1 pt.	480 ml
Egg yolks	2.6 oz. (4 yolks)	80 g
Maple syrup	4 oz.	120 g
Caramelized Pecans (recipe follows)	4 oz.	120 g

1 Bring the soy milk creamer to a boil.

2 In a separate bowl, whisk together the egg yolks and the maple syrup. Temper the egg mixture with one-quarter of the soy milk creamer.

3 Pour the tempered egg yolk mixture into the soymilk creamer and heat to 183°F (83°C) while constantly stirring with a rubber spatula.

4 Strain through a chinois and chill in an ice bath. Refrigerate overnight.

5 Process in an ice cream machine. Once the ice cream starts to firm, add the Caramelized Pecans.

Approximate values per 3½-oz. (109-g) serving: **Calories** 260, **Total fat** 16 g, **Saturated fat** 3 g, **Cholesterol** 120 mg, **Sodium** 45 mg, **Total carbohydrates** 26 g, **Protein** 3 g

CARAMELIZED PECANS

Yield: 6 oz. (120 g)

Granulated sugar	2 oz.	60 g
Water	1 fl. oz.	30 ml
Vanilla extract	0.15 fl. oz. (1 tsp.)	5 ml
Pecan pieces	4 oz.	120 g

1 Bring the sugar and the water to a full boil. Add the vanilla and pecans. Stir until the sugar coats the pecans and becomes grainy.

2 Reduce the heat to low and stir the pecans until the sugar starts to caramelize. Cool, then store in an airtight container until ready to use.

Approximate values per 1-oz. (30-g) serving: **Calories** 170, **Total fat** 14 g, **Saturated fat** 1 g, **Cholesterol** 0 mg, **Sodium** 0 mg, **Total carbohydrates** 12 g, **Protein** 4 g

LACTOSE-FREE CRÈME BRÛLÉE   RECIPE 18.17

Yield: 4 Servings

Egg yolks	2 oz. (3 yolks)	60 g
Eggs	3.3 oz. (2 eggs)	100 g
Brown sugar	4 oz.	120 g
Vanilla bean	1	1
Soy milk creamer	1 pt.	480 ml
Granulated raw sugar	2 oz.	60 g

1 Whisk together the egg yolks, eggs and brown sugar in a bowl until smooth. Scrape the seeds of the vanilla bean into the mixture and add the soy milk creamer.

2 Strain through a chinois and pour into shallow ceramic ramekins.

3 Place the ramekins in a hotel pan and fill with hot water halfway up the sides of the ramekins. Bake at 325°F (160°C) until set, approximately 30 minutes.

4 Let cool in a refrigerator.

5 To serve, sprinkle the crème brûlée with the sugar and caramelize the sugar with a blowtorch.

Approximate values per serving: **Calories** 390, **Total fat** 16 g, **Saturated fat** 4.5 g, **Cholesterol** 265 mg, **Sodium** 125 mg, **Total carbohydrates** 56 g, **Protein** 6 g

RECIPE 18.18   **LACTOSE-FREE SOY CHOCOLATE SILK PIE**

Yield: 1 Pie, 7 in. (17 cm)

Soy milk	1 pt.	480 ml
Cocoa powder	1.5 oz.	45 g
Brown sugar	5 oz.	150 g
Egg	1.6 oz. (1 egg)	50 g
Egg white	2 oz. (2 whites)	60 g
Cornstarch	1 oz.	30 g
Lactose-Free Pie Dough (recipe follows),		
7-in. (17-cm) shell, fully baked	1 shell	1 shell
Vanilla extract	0.15 fl. oz. (1 tsp.)	5 ml
Bitter or semisweet chocolate, chopped	3 oz.	90 g
Chocolate shavings	2 oz.	60 g

1 Combine the soy milk, cocoa powder and 2 ounces (60 grams) of the brown sugar in a large saucepan. Bring to a boil.

2 In a separate bowl, whisk together the egg and egg whites. Add the remaining brown sugar and mix to form a smooth batter. Stir in the cornstarch.

3 Temper the egg batter with one-quarter of the boiling soy milk.

4 Add the tempered egg mixture to the remaining boiling milk. Whisk vigorously over medium high heat until the cream boils and is well thickened.

5 Remove from heat. Add the vanilla and chocolate, stirring until the chocolate is melted. Pour the filling into the baked shell.

6 Cool until set, then sprinkle with chocolate shavings.

Approximate values per $\frac{1}{8}$-pie serving: **Calories** 390, **Total fat** 20 g, **Saturated fat** 6 g, **Cholesterol** 25 mg, **Sodium** 320 mg, **Total carbohydrates** 50 g, **Protein** 10 g, **Vitamin A** 10%, **Iron** 15%

LACTOSE-FREE PIE DOUGH

Yield: 1 lb. 4 oz. (600 g), Dough for one 8-in. (20-cm) double-crust pie

Soy milk, chilled	2 fl. oz.	60 ml
Egg white	1 oz. (1 white)	30 g
Salt	0.2 oz. (1 tsp.)	6 g
Brown sugar	0.5 oz.	15 g
Vanilla extract	0.15 fl. oz. (1 tsp.)	5 ml
Vinegar	0.5 fl. oz.	15 ml
White wheat flour	3 oz.	90 g
Oat flour or oats ground into flour	6 oz.	180 g
Soy flour	1 oz.	30 g
Soy margarine, cold	7 oz.	210 g

1 Whisk together the soy milk, egg white, salt, sugar, vanilla and vinegar. Set aside.

2 Combine the wheat, oat and soy flours in a large bowl. Cut the margarine into medium dice, $\frac{3}{8}$ inch × $\frac{3}{8}$ inch (9 millimeters × 9 millimeters), then cut it into the flour until the pieces are the size of peas.

3 Add the soy milk mixture. Mix just until combined.

4 Wrap the dough in plastic and chill at least 1 hour before using.

Approximate values per 1-oz. (30-g) serving: **Calories** 130, **Total fat** 9 g, **Saturated fat** 1.5 g, **Cholesterol** 0 mg, **Sodium** 200 mg, **Total carbohydrates** 10 g, **Protein** 3 g

I WOULD STAND TRANSFIXED BEFORE THE WINDOWS OF THE CONFECTIONERS' SHOPS, FASCINATED BY THE LUMINOUS SPARKLE OF CANDIED FRUITS, THE CLOUDY LUSTRE OF JELLIES, THE KALEIDOSCOPE INFLORESCENCE OF ACIDULATED FRUITDROPS—RED, GREEN, ORANGE, VIOLET: I COVETED THE COLOURS THEMSELVES AS MUCH AS THE PLEASURE THEY PROMISED ME.

—*Simone de Beauvoir, French existentialist and writer (1908–1986)*

PETITS FOURS

On the glass tray, starting from the left: White Chocolate Mousse Bites (page 580), Gerbet Macaroon (page 572), San Diegos (page 577), Lemon Tartlets (page 578), Petit Four Glacé (page 570) and Cappuccino Cheesecake (page 578)

In the background, clockwise starting from the left of the tray: Chocolate Pecan Cake (page 579), Chocolate Raspberry Mousse Bites (page 580), Irish Cream Crème Brûlée (page 581), Apricot Passion Fruit Ganache Tartlets (page 581) and l'Opéra (page 582)

HOUSTON COMMUNITY COLLEGE, Houston, TX
Pastry Chef Eddy Van Damme

AFTER STUDYING THIS CHAPTER, YOU WILL BE ABLE TO:

▶ understand the uses of the petit four

▶ prepare an assortment of traditional petits fours

▶ create petits fours using components from other chapters in this book

▶ **friandise** a small pastry or sweet delicacy often served between or after meals; petit four

▶ **marzipan** (MAHR-sih-pan) a paste of ground almonds, sugar and glucose used to fill and decorate pastries

Petits fours are any number of small pastries, cookies and miniature desserts that are served after a meal or with afternoon tea. According to British culinary authority Alan Davidson, these pastries may take their name from the small ovens (Fr. *petits fours*) in which these pastries were baked in the 18th century. Long a favorite at receptions and buffets, the petit four is having a renaissance. As pastry chefs work to develop their signature creations, more attention is being paid to the petit four as a way to express the style of the restaurant and its cuisine. Today, petits fours are often served at the end of a meal or as a dessert on their own when accompanied by ice cream, sorbet, crème brûlée or other creamy products.

▶ PETITS FOURS—MINIATURE PASTRIES

Petits fours are any type of pastry small enough to be consumed in one to two mouthfuls. They may also be referred to as **friandises.** Made fresh in fine pâtisserie, petits fours offer the host of a large, stand-up gathering the possibility of serving a sweet after a meal. Petits fours also appeal to those seeking dainty, small-scale sweets. Afternoon tea, bridal showers and traditional ladies' luncheons frequently feature petits fours, long a symbol of elegance and refinement.

Meticulously prepared miniature cookies such as cigarettes, langues de chat, mirroirs, almond macaroons, miniature éclairs and meringues are traditional petits fours. But it is common practice for a pastry chef to make smaller versions of frequently made pastries to create petits fours. For example, when a mousse or cream is prepared for a torte, extra can be made and piped into small tart shells or chocolate cups. This method saves time when the production schedule is well organized.

When preparing petits fours, attention to detail is paramount. Uniformity in size and shape, and consistency of finishing details count a great deal for the eye appeal of petits fours. Thanks to the invention of silicone molds, the production of petits fours has become easier, faster and therefore more profitable than ever. "New-style" petits fours have emerged due to the flexibility of silicone molds. Cheesecake batter, crème brûlée and other creams and mousses can be poured into these molds, baked and then frozen. Once hardened, the pastries are easily removed and can be placed on prebaked disks made from nougatine, tart dough or chocolate. Petits fours based on rich buttercream and **marzipan** have become less popular, but whole new realms of petits fours have been introduced to the discerning guest.

Petits fours should:

▶ be no more than one or two small bites. Most should measure no more than 1.5 to 2 inches (3.7 to 5 centimeters) in length.
▶ represent a variety of textures and flavors.
▶ be visually attractive.
▶ complement whatever foods precede or accompany them without duplicating their flavors.

Fancy Cake I

Fancy Cake II

Fancy Cake III

Fancy Cake IV

Fancy Cake V

Bouchée De Dame

Railroad Cake

Diamond Dainty

Styles of petits fours have endured for many years, as this illustration from 1926 demonstrates. From The Henry Heide Company, New York, NY, 1926.

PETIT FOUR VARIETIES

Petits fours are divided into five broad categories based upon preparation method, texture or principal ingredient—dry, fresh, iced, almond and glazed fruit. Chocolates and truffles may be served along with petits fours and are discussed in Chapter 21, Chocolate and Decorative Work. These categories assist the bakery and pastry chef in planning the proper assortment of products suitable to the occasion. (See Table 19.1)

DRY PETITS FOURS

Dry petits fours (Fr. *petits fours sec*) are any number of fragile, crunchy dainty cookies. The most common are cookies such as Tulipe Cookies (page 238), Checkerboard Cookies (page 230), nut meringues and small butter cookies or puff pastry products made without a cream filling. These cookies may also be filled with or dipped in chocolate (see Cherry-Almond Florentines [page 576] or Langue de Chat [Cat's Tongues, page 574]). Be aware that, when filled, these brittle cookies may become moist and soften in a few hours.

FRESH PETITS FOURS

Fresh petits fours (Fr. *petits fours frais*) are moist miniatures that may contain fruit and fillings such as buttercream, citrus curd, ganache or various mousses. Miniature tartlets or **barquettes** filled with pastry cream and topped with fresh berries, grapes or apricot halves are examples of this type. Nearly all the tarts in this book can be miniaturized and served as petits fours. Diminutive cups made from tempered chocolate, sweet dough (pâte sucrée) baked into small shells, miniature rum babas and cream puffs (pâte à choux) make excellent containers for cream-filled petits fours. The formulas for Cappuccino Cheesecakes (page 578) and Chocolate Raspberry Mousse Bites (page 580) illustrate the procedure for making fresh petits fours.

▶ **barquette** a small boat-shaped pastry shell used for miniature cakes or tarts served as canapés or petits fours

▶ PROCEDURE FOR MAKING BARQUETTE SHELLS

1 Roll out the pastry dough ⅛ inch (3 millimeters) thick.

2 Press the dough into the barquette shells.

3 Prick the dough with a fork to allow steam to escape during baking.

4 Place a second barquette shell on top of the dough to prevent it from rising as it bakes.

Table 19.1 RECOMMENDED PETIT FOUR COMPONENTS

BASE	SHAPE	FILLING	GARNISH
Baked shortbread or sweet dough	Tartlets, disks, barquettes	Buttercreams, custards, curds, ganache, frozen parfaits, mousses and chiffons	Berries, fruit slices, chocolate ornaments, toasted nuts
Baked meringue or nut meringue	Piped cookies, shells, discs	Crème Chantilly, buttercreams, curds, ganache, frozen parfaits, mousses and chiffons	Chopped pistachios, candied citrus rind, shaved chocolate
Baked éclair paste	Mini éclairs, puffs	Crème Chantilly, curds, frozen parfaits, mousses	Chocolate or fondant glaze, caramel, powdered sugar

(Continued)

Table 19.1 CONTINUED

BASE	SHAPE	FILLING	GARNISH
Tulipe (tuile batter)	Rolled, cup	crème Chantilly, white chocolate mousse	Dip in chocolate, then in toasted nuts
Wafer cookies	Piped, then baked	Buttercreams, curds, ganache, jams	Filled and sandwiched together, ends dipped in chocolate
Joconde or other firm spongecake	Filled and layered	Buttercreams, jam, marzipan, ganache	Fondant glaze, decorated with piping gel or chocolate
Poundcake	Sliced and cut out, baked in mini pans	Buttercreams, curds, crème Chantilly, jam	Fondant glaze or chocolate glaze
Chocolate	Molded cups or disks	Mousses, ganache, ice creams, crème Chantilly, hazelnut cream	Berries, fruit slices, candied fruit or nuts, mint leaves

ICED PETITS FOURS

Iced petits fours (Fr. *petits fours glacé*) are small cakes, cookies or biscuits iced with fondant or glaze. They are most frequently made from a firm cake such as a joconde that is baked into thin sheets. The thin cake is then layered with jam, ganache or various buttercreams, and often topped with a layer of rolled marzipan. Perhaps because of their frequent appearance in holiday mail order catalogs, many in the United States think that this style of cake is the definitive petit four.

Iced petits fours should not exceed 1 inch (2.5 centimeters) in height. Different shapes may be cut as long as they can be consumed in two mouthfuls. A rolling cutter, knife dipped in hot water or petit four cutter ensures uniform pieces. After cutting, the petit four is usually coated with heated fondant, often pastel tinted. See Chapter 13, Syrups, Icings and Sauces (page 359). The fondant is thinned until it is just thick enough to coat the petit four. A long **dipping fork,** such as that used when coating chocolates, is inserted into the cut petit four to hold the layers together when immersing the cakes in the melted fondant. Fondant seals the petits fours, helping them retain moisture but also making them rather sweet. Select a filling that will balance the sweetness. For example, petits fours filled with jam and coated with fondant will remain moist several days when stored in an airtight container under refrigeration. Tinted royal icing or chocolate is usually piped into delicate flowers or fine scrolling designs on top of the glazed petit four. Of course these petits fours can also be made without the final glazing process, with the lightest coating of jam or icing on top perhaps more appropriate for the taste preferences of today's consumer.

► **dipping fork** utensil used to hold chocolate or small pastries for dipping into chocolate or other coating; consists of a narrow handle with two, three or four long, thin prongs, which are easily inserted into small pastries

► PROCEDURE FOR PREPARING AN ICED PETIT FOUR

1 Bake a thin, flexible spongecake such as a joconde. Using a serrated or cake knife, trim the edges then cut the cake into four uniform pieces.

2 Generously moisten one layer of the cake with flavored simple syrup. Spread it with one or more fillings chosen to complement the flavors in the cake, such as raspberry jam, lemon curd or vanilla buttercream.

3 Continue layering cake, moistened with syrup, and filling, ending with a final layer of cake.

4 Top the cake with a thin sheet of marzipan.

5 Freeze the cake, then cut it into small uniform squares or shapes.

6 Prepare fondant or glaze. Thin until it is thick enough to coat the cake but the layers of spongecake can be seen through the fondant. Dip the cut pieces of cake into the glaze and place on a cake screen to drain. Alternatively, spoon the coating over the cut cakes placed on an icing screen.

7 Allow the fondant or glaze to dry, then decorate with piped chocolate or royal icing.

RECIPE 19.1

PETIT FOUR GLACÉ

Yield: 72 Petits Fours, 1³/₄ in. (4.5 cm) each   **Type:** Iced petit four

Joconde (page 418)	1 full sheet	1 full sheet
Simple Syrup (page 349)	4 fl. oz.	120 ml
Raspberry liqueur or purée	2 fl. oz.	60 ml
Raspberry jam	as needed	as needed
Fondant	3 lb.	1440 g
Chocolate decorations (page 615)	as needed	as needed
Fresh raspberries	1¹/₂ pt.	0.75 lt

1 Cut the baked Joconde crosswise into four equal strips. Place one of the Joconde strips on a paper-lined sheet pan. Combine the Simple Syrup and raspberry liqueur and moisten the cake with 1¹/₂ fluid ounces (45 milliliters) of this syrup.

2 Spread a thin even layer of raspberry jam on the moistened cake.

3 Cover with another sheet of Joconde. Moisten with 1¹/₂ fluid ounces (45 milliliters) raspberry syrup and coat with more raspberry jam. Cover with another sheet of Joconde and once again repeat the moistening and jam process. Top with the last Joconde layer. Freeze until firm.

4 Trim the cake, then cut into small squares or triangles measuring approximately 1³/₄ inches (4.5 centimeters).

5 Gently heat the fondant to 100°F (38°C) over a bain marie. Remove from the heat and thin the fondant slightly with a small amount of the remaining raspberry syrup. Strain the fondant through a fine sieve to remove any crumbs.

6 Place the cake pieces on an icing screen. Coat with warm fondant, using a large spoon or a pastry bag with a plain small to medium tip. After coating the petits fours, the layers of joconde should still be visible through the fondant.

7 Decorate with chocolate decorations and fresh raspberries.

VARIATION:

Raspberry Petit Four—Omit the fondant and top the cake with neutral glaze before cutting the cake into small triangles as shown in the chapter opening photograph.

Approximate values per piece: **Calories** 120, **Total fat** 10 g, **Saturated fat** 0 g, **Cholesterol** 10 mg, **Sodium** 15 mg, **Total carbohydrates** 26 g, **Protein** 1 g

ALMOND PETITS FOURS

Almond petits fours are small cookies made from raw almond paste or almond flour such as macaroons and other piped cookies. The dough might use almond paste or flour, egg whites or yolks and granulated or powdered sugar. Use of invert sugar in the formula adds to their keeping properties. The dough may be piped or formed like an icebox cookie, rolled in nuts, then sliced before baking. Almond Crescent Cookies (page 237) make an excellent petit four when piped with a small plain tip into 2-inch (5-centimeter) strips, rolled into finely diced almonds, curved and baked into miniature cookies.

Almond Macaroons

Almond macaroons are a simple yet refined cookie that is made in a number of styles. Those made with almond paste are especially moist and chewy. But other types of almond macaroons resemble a crunchy baked meringue with a moist interior. The technique for making macaroons is illustrated here with the formula for Gerbert Macaroons, which is a smooth-topped macaroon made with blanched almond flour and usually filled with jam or buttercream.

▶ PROCEDURE FOR PREPARING ALMOND MACAROONS

1 Have all ingredients at room temperature.

2 Beat the egg whites and sugar until stiff.

3 Fold in blanched almond flour and powdered sugar until the mixture develops a sheen. (Overmixed batter will be runny. Undermixed batter will result in macaroons with a cracked surface.)

4 Using a small or medium plain tip, pipe the batter onto silicone baking mats or paper-lined sheet trays. Let the piped batter sit 10 minutes to ensure a smooth surface.

5 Bake the macaroons at 400°F (200°C) until lightly browned, approximately 10 to 12 minutes. Or bake the macaroons at 400°F (200°C) 2 to 3 minutes, then reduce the heat to 350°F (180°C) and bake until done, approximately 7 to 10 additional minutes. Baking at a lower temperature during the last stages of baking ensures that the macaroons do not overly darken.

6 Cool the macaroons before removing them from the silicone mat or baking paper. Or pour a few drops of water under the silicone mat or baking paper when the macaroons are removed from the oven. The steam created may help release the macaroons.

7 Sandwich two macaroons together with a small amount of jam, curd or buttercream.

Turban Macaroon   *Kiss Macaroon*

Twin Macaroons   *Jelly Macaroon*

Souffle or Case Macaroon   *Frascati Cake*

Chocolate Macaroon   *Lemon Macaroon*

Almond petits fours. From The Henry Heide Company, New York, NY, 1926.

GERBET MACAROONS

Note: This petit four appears in the chapter opening photograph.

Yield: 120 Cookies, approximately ½ in. (1.2 cm) each

Type: Almond petit four

Granulated sugar	1 oz.	30 g
Dried egg whites	0.45 oz. (1 Tbsp.)	14 g
Egg whites	7 fl. oz. (7 whites)	210 ml
Almond flour	8 oz.	240 g
Powdered sugar	1 lb.	480 g
Liquid food coloring (optional)	as needed	as needed
Buttercream, lemon curd, jam, ganache or other filling	as needed	as needed

1 Sift the granulated sugar and dried egg whites together, add to the liquid egg whites and whip to stiff peaks.

2 Sift the almond flour and powdered sugar together to combine well.

3 Fold the almond flour mixture into the whipped egg whites. Add a few drops of food coloring (if using). If the mixture looks dull, continue to fold until the batter develops a shine.

4 Using a pastry bag fitted with a medium plain tip, pipe the batter onto a silicone mat or paper-lined sheet pan. Each macaroon should measure ½ inch (1.2 centimeters) wide and ¼ inch (6 millimeters) tall. If the mark left by the piping tip does not dissolve within 1 minute, stir the batter a little more, then continue piping.

5 Rest 10 minutes before baking.

6 Bake at 400°F (200°C) until golden brown, approximately 12 minutes.

7 Allow the cookies to cool, then remove them from the silicone mat or sheet pan.

8 Spread a thin layer of buttercream, lemon curd, jam or ganache on the bottom (pan side) of one cookie and gently press another cookie onto the filling, top side out.

Approximate values per cookie: **Calories** 30, **Total fat** 1 g, **Saturated fat** 0 g, **Cholesterol** 0 mg, **Sodium** 0 mg, **Total carbohydrates** 4 g, **Protein** 1 g

GLAZED FRUIT

Glazed fruit coated with caramel or sugar syrup cooked to the hard crack stage complements any assortment of petits fours. Grapes, strawberries, blackberries, pineapple pieces, citrus segments and many other small pieces of fruit hold up well when coated in crunchy sugar. Often dried fruit such as dates or apricots or conserved fruits such as candied chestnuts (Fr. *marrons glacés*) and kumquats will be stuffed with a nugget of tinted marzipan, then rolled in granulated sugar or coated with melted fondant before serving. The formula for Caramel Dipped Fruits (page 583) illustrates a glazed fruit petit four.

SERVING AND PRESENTING PETITS FOURS

Whether served at the conclusion of a formal dinner, as the centerpiece of an afternoon tea or passed on butlered trays during a wedding reception, petits fours must be properly selected and presented to maintain eye appeal. In a fine-dining restaurant, waiters may present each table with small trays of petits fours as a dessert course or when the check is presented. An attractive assortment of petits fours may be included in a dessert buffet or passed on decorated trays in butler-style service. Often individual petits fours are placed in fluted paper cases. This makes them easy to pick up and leaves the serving tray looking clean and neat.

For presentation platters, the composition of the assortment and the way it is positioned on the tray must be visually pleasing. A classic presentation is to line up parallel rows of the same item so that the guest may select from many types of petits fours without having to reach across the tray. In this arrangement, the waiter monitoring the buffet may easily refill the tray. Footed and tiered trays offer the opportunity to create visual excitement in a limited amount of space. Each level of the tiered tray may contain a different petit four. Intensely flavored and smaller items, such as chocolates or small glazed fruits, may be offered from graduated tiered trays while larger pieces such as miniature tartlets or éclairs are served from flat trays.

CONVENIENCE PRODUCTS

Miniature tart shells, barquettes and chocolate cups are popular products sold to facilitate making fresh petits fours in a busy kitchen. Using prepared miniature tart shells adds to the cost of the final product, but it frees up the chef's time. The pastry chef can focus on creating intriguing fillings and garnishes when using prepared shells and cups. While ready-to-serve iced petits fours (*petits fours glacés*) are available for purchase from many commercial vendors, making the effort to prepare custom fillings is within the scope of most operations.

CONCLUSION

Petits fours complete a meal or offer an elegant yet convenient way to serve something sweet for a large number of guests. While preparing an elaborate assortment of these dainties may seem to consume vast staff resources, newer ways of preparing petits fours make this feasible. Many of the preparations made in the pastry kitchen, such as cakes, small cookies, mousses and chocolates, can be used to create delightful small treats to offer as petits fours.

QUESTIONS FOR DISCUSSION

1 What are the different types of petits fours and under what circumstances would each type be appropriate?
2 Discuss the techniques you might use to cut iced petits fours to ensure uniform products.
3 What procedures should the pastry chef observe in order to ensure uniformity of product when making petits fours?
4 Using some of the recommended petit four combinations in Table 19.1, plan an assortment of small pastries to be served after a formal banquet. Take into consideration what might be offered as the dessert and explain the reasoning for your selection.

Several of the following formulas are combinations of formulas presented in this chapter and other dessert products covered in other chapters. For example, White Chocolate Mousse Bites are made with Shortbread Tart Dough, discussed in Chapter 10, Pies and Tarts. Many of these petits fours use components including nougatine, simple syrup and ganache, discussed elsewhere in this book.

RECIPE 19.3

Piping batter for Cat's Tongue Cookies onto buttered parchment paper.

LANGUE DE CHAT (CAT'S TONGUE COOKIES)

Yield: 65 Sandwich Cookies, 3 in. (7.5 cm) each **Type:** Dry petit four

Unsalted butter, melted	as needed	as needed
Unsalted butter, softened	8 oz.	240 g
Powdered sugar	13 oz.	390 g
Egg whites	9 fl. oz. (9 whites)	270 g
Vanilla extract	0.15 fl. oz. (1 tsp.)	5 ml
Cake flour	10 oz.	300 g
Pistachios, chopped	5 oz.	150 g
Semisweet chocolate, melted	as needed	as needed

1 Lightly brush melted butter on a sheet of parchment paper. Allow the butter to solidify. Set aside.

2 Cream the solid unsalted butter and powdered sugar. Gradually add the egg whites, then the vanilla. Fold in the flour using a rubber spatula.

3 In a pastry bag fitted with a plain medium tip, pipe the batter into 3-inch-(7.5-centimeter-) long strips. Sprinkle with chopped pistachios.

4 Bake at 400°F (200°C) until light golden, approximately 9 to 10 minutes.

5 Cool the cookies. Spread melted semisweet chocolate on the underside of one cookie, then sandwich it with a second cookie. Dip the ends of each cookie sandwich in additional chocolate.

VARIATION:

Lemon Sandwich Cookies—Omit the melted chocolate. Fill the cookies with Lemon Curd (page 437).

Approximate values per cookie: **Calories** 80, **Total fat** 4 g, **Saturated fat** 2 g, **Cholesterol** 10 mg, **Sodium** 10 mg, **Total carbohydrates** 10 g, **Protein** 1 g

MADELEINES

Madeleines are cookies made from spongecake or genoise batter. They are traditionally shaped as small fluted fans using special molds. Madeleines are popular petits fours to serve with tea or coffee, as their somewhat dry, spongy texture is excellent for dipping into a hot beverage. Unlike the classic that launched Marcel Proust on his *Remembrance of Things Past*, this formula incorporates brown butter (beurre noisette) for additional flavor.

1 Piping the batter into greased and floured molds.

Yield: 12 Cookies, approximately 1 oz. (30 g) each   **Method:** Spongecake

Type: Dry petit four

Unsalted butter	4 oz.	120 g
Eggs	3.3 oz. (2 eggs)	100 g
Granulated sugar	3 oz.	90 g
Lemon zest, grated fine	0.07 oz (1 tsp.)	2 g
Lemon juice	0.04 fl. oz. (1/4 tsp.)	1 ml
Vanilla extract	0.04 fl. oz. (1/4 tsp.)	1 ml
Baking powder	0.02 oz. (1/8 tsp.)	0.5 g
Cake flour, sifted	3 oz.	90 g

1 Melt the butter over medium heat; continue cooking until the milk solids turn a golden-brown color. Set aside to cool.

2 Whisk the eggs and sugar over a bain marie until warm (98°F/37°C). Remove from the heat and whisk in the lemon zest, lemon juice and vanilla.

3 Sift the baking powder and flour together; stir into the egg mixture. Stir in the melted butter. Cover the bowl and allow the batter to rest 1 hour at room temperature.

4 Butter and flour the madeleine shells. Spoon or pipe the batter into the shells, filling each three-fourths full.

5 Bake at 450°F (230°C) until the cookies rise in the center and are very light brown on the bottom and edges, approximately 3 to 4 minutes for 1 1/2-inch (3.7-centimeter) madeleines and 10 to 12 minutes for 3-inch (7.5-centimeter) madeleines. They should spring back when touched lightly in the center. Remove the madeleines from the oven, invert the pan over a wire cooling rack, and tap lightly to release the cookies from the pan.

2 The finished madeleines.

Approximate values per cookie: **Calories** 110, **Total fat** 7 g, **Saturated fat** 4 g, **Cholesterol** 45 mg, **Sodium** 10 mg, **Total carbohydrates** 10 g, **Protein** 1 g, **Vitamin A** 6%

RECIPE 19.5

CHERRY-ALMOND FLORENTINES

Yield: 40 Cookies, 2 in. (5 cm) each   **Type:** Dry petit four

Sweet Tart Dough (page 249), chilled	1 lb.	480 g
Granulated sugar	6 oz.	180 g
Glucose or corn syrup	2 oz.	60 g
Water	3 fl. oz.	90 ml
Unsalted butter, cubed	5 oz.	150 g
Honey	2.5 oz.	75 g
Heavy cream, boiling	3 fl. oz.	90 ml
Vanilla extract	0.15 fl. oz. (1 tsp.)	5 ml
Almonds, sliced, toasted	11 oz.	330 g
Dried cherries	2 oz.	60 g
Semisweet chocolate, tempered	as needed	as needed

1 Roll the chilled Sweet Tart Dough ⅛ inch (3 millimeters) thick and slightly larger than a half-sheet pan. Line the bottom and sides of the sheet pan with the dough. Prick the dough with a fork.

2 Bake blind at 375°F (190°C) until blond in color, approximately 8 to 11 minutes. Remove from the oven and set aside to cool.

3 Boil the sugar, glucose or corn syrup and water to a golden caramel, approximately 325°F (160°C). Add the butter and honey to the caramel, then add the boiling cream. Bring the mixture to a full boil.

4 Remove from heat and add the vanilla, almonds and cherries. While still warm, spread the mixture onto the prebaked crust in a thin, even layer.

5 Bake at 375°F (190°C) approximately 20 minutes or until the center has set and is golden brown.

6 Cool completely, trim the edges, then cut into 2-inch (5-centimeter) squares. Excess trimmed from the edges may be ground and used to side mask frosted cakes.

7 Dip one corner of each piece in tempered semisweet chocolate.

Approximate values per cookie: **Calories** 160, **Total fat** 10 g, **Saturated fat** 3.5 g, **Cholesterol** 15 mg, **Sodium** 0 mg, **Total carbohydrates** 15 g, **Protein** 3 g

1 Spreading the cherry-almond mixture over the baked dough.

2 Cutting the cookies.

3 Dipping the finished Cherry-Almond Florentines in chocolate.

SAN DIEGOS

Note: This petit four appears in the chapter opening photograph.

Yield: 65 Petits Fours, 1½ in. (3.7 cm) each   **Type:** Fresh petit four

Sweet Almond Tart Dough (page 266)	1 lb. 8 oz.	720 g
Hazelnut paste	13 oz.	390 g
Heavy cream	2 fl. oz.	60 ml
Eggs	5 oz. (3 eggs)	150 g
Egg yolks	6.5 oz. (11 yolks)	195 g
Almond paste	1 lb. 5 oz.	630 g
Granulated sugar	5 oz.	150 g
Pistachio compound	2 oz.	60 g
Pistachios, blended to a paste*	3 oz.	90 g
Unsalted butter, melted	9 oz.	270 g
Simple Syrup (page 349)	4 fl. oz.	120 ml
Kirsch	2 fl. oz.	60 ml
Pistachios, finely chopped	10 oz.	300 g
Chocolate decorations (page 615)	as needed	as needed

1 Roll the Sweet Almond Tart Dough ⅛ inch (3 millimeters) thick. Line the bottom and sides of a paper-lined half-sheet pan with the dough. Prick the dough with a fork.

2 Bake blind at 375°F (190°C) until blond in color, approximately 10 minutes.

3 In the bowl of a mixer fitted with a paddle, blend the hazelnut paste and cream. Beat in one-third of the eggs. Scrape down the bowl and beat in 1½ ounces (45 grams) of the egg yolks.

4 Spread the hazelnut mixture on the baked tart dough.

5 In the bowl of a mixer fitted with a paddle, combine the almond paste, sugar and pistachio compound. Add the blended pistachio paste. Add the remaining eggs, in two additions. Add the remaining egg yolks and melted butter.

6 Spread the cake batter over the hazelnut mixture. Bake at 350°F (180°C) until the cake bounces back when lightly pressed, approximately 35 to 38 minutes. Let cool.

7 Combine the Simple Syrup and Kirsch. Moisten the cake with the syrup, then cut it into 1½-inch (3.7-centimeter) squares.

8 Dip the top surface of each petit four in the chopped pistachios. Decorate with a chocolate decoration.

*Pistachio paste is made by blending pistachio nuts in a food processor until a smooth paste is formed.

Approximate values per cookie: **Calories** 210, **Total fat** 14 g, **Saturated fat** 4.5 g, **Cholesterol** 65 mg, **Sodium** 35 mg, **Total carbohydrates** 17 g, **Protein** 4 g

RECIPE 19.7

LEMON TARTLETS

Note: This petit four appears in the chapter opening photograph.

Yield: 40 Tartlets, 2 in. (4.5 cm) each   **Type:** Fresh petit four

Sesame Seed Nougatine (page 633)	1 lb. 12 oz.	840 g
Lemon Curd (page 437)	1 lb. 4 oz.	600 g
Fresh blackberries	2 pt.	1 lt
Gold leaf (optional)	as needed	as needed

1 Lightly oil 40 small tartlet pans or petit four molds.
2 Roll the Sesame Seed Nougatine very thin. Cut it into circles the size of the tartlet or petit four molds. Line them with the nougatine. Remove the shells from the molds as soon as they hold their shape.
3 Pipe chilled Lemon Curd into the nougatine cups.
4 Place a blackberry in the center of the cream.
5 Garnish each blackberry with a small piece of gold leaf.

Approximate values per 1-oz. (30-g) serving: **Calories** 180, **Total fat** 10 g, **Saturated fat** 3.5 g, **Cholesterol** 20 mg, **Sodium** 20 mg, **Total carbohydrates** 23 g, **Protein** 3 g

RECIPE 19.8

CAPPUCCINO CHEESECAKES

Note: This petit four appears in the chapter opening photograph.

Yield: 40 Tartlets, 1½ in. (4 cm) each   **Type:** Fresh petit four

Cream cheese, room temperature	1 lb.	480 g
Granulated sugar	4 oz.	120 g
Eggs	3.3 oz. (2 eggs)	100 g
Sour cream	4 oz.	120 g
Coffee extract	1 fl. oz.	30 ml
Vanilla extract	0.15 fl. oz. (1 tsp.)	5 ml
Sesame Seed Nougatine (page 633), 2-in. (5-cm) disks, fully baked	40 disks	40 disks
Coffee beans	as needed	as needed
White chocolate decorations (page 614)	as needed	as needed
Cocoa powder, optional	as needed	as needed

1 Beat the cream cheese and sugar on low speed in the bowl of a mixer fitted with a paddle. Scrape down the bowl and beat until no lumps remain.
2 Add the eggs one at a time, waiting for each egg to be fully incorporated before adding the next. Add the sour cream then the coffee and vanilla extracts.
3 Place a silicone petit four mold on a sheet pan and divide the batter evenly between the molds.
4 Pour water on the sheet pan to create a water bath and bake at 325°F (160°C) until the cheesecakes have set, approximately 25 minutes. Let cool, then freeze until hard.
5 Unmold each cheesecake onto a Sesame Seed Nougatine disk. Decorate with a coffee bean and white chocolate or dust lightly with cocoa powder.

Approximate values per tartlet: **Calories** 120, **Total fat** 7 g, **Saturated fat** 3.5 g, **Cholesterol** 25 mg, **Sodium** 45 mg, **Total carbohydrates** 12 g, **Protein** 2 g

CHOCOLATE PECAN CAKES

Note: This petit four appears in the chapter opening photograph.

Yield: 40 Petits Fours, 1¼ in. × 2 in. (3 cm × 5 cm) each

Type: Fresh petit four

Unsalted butter, softened	3.5 oz.	105 g
Powdered sugar	3 oz.	90 g
Eggs	3.3 oz. (2 eggs)	100 g
Cake flour	1.75 oz.	50 g
Bittersweet chocolate, melted to 110°F (43°C)	2.5 oz.	75 g
Pecans, coarsely chopped	3 oz.	90 g
Silky Ganache Deluxe (page 371), room temperature	1 lb. 4 oz.	600 g
Pecan halves	20	20
Chocolate mesh (page 614)	as needed	as needed

1. Cream the butter and sugar in the bowl of a mixer fitted with a paddle. Gradually add the eggs. Scrape down the bowl.
2. On low speed add the cake flour. Once it is incorporated, add the melted chocolate and the chopped pecans.
3. Pipe the batter into silicone molds or buttered and floured petit four molds.
4. Bake at 375°F (190°C) until the cake bounces back when lightly pressed, approximately 12 minutes. Let cool, then remove the cakes from the molds.
5. Pipe a rosette of Silky Ganache Deluxe onto each cake. Cut the pecan pieces in half. Insert a piece of chocolate mesh and a pecan piece into the ganache.

Approximate values per tartlet: **Calories** 100, **Total fat** 8 g, **Saturated fat** 4 g, **Cholesterol** 20 mg, **Sodium** 0 mg, **Total carbohydrates** 7 g, **Protein** 1 g

RECIPE 19.10

WHITE CHOCOLATE MOUSSE BITES

Note: This petit four appears in the chapter opening photograph.

Yield: 40 Petits Fours, approximately 1½ in. (4 cm) each

Type: Fresh petit four

Heavy cream	5 fl. oz.	150 ml
White chocolate	14 oz.	420 g
Egg yolks	2 oz. (3 yolks)	60 g
Granulated sugar	1 oz.	30 g
Sheet gelatin, softened	0.3 oz.	9 g
Shortbread Tart Dough (page 266), made with almond flour, 1½-in. (4-cm) disks, fully baked	40 disks	40 disks
Red seedless grapes	1 pt.	0.5 lt
White chocolate cutouts (page 615)	as needed	as needed

1 Whip the cream to soft peaks and set aside.

2 Melt the chocolate to 110°F (43°C) and hold it at this temperature.

3 Place the egg yolks and sugar in a bowl over simmering water. Whip the yolks constantly until they form a thick ribbon and the temperature reaches 158°F (70°C).

4 Remove the yolks from the heat and whip them over an ice bath until they cool to 120°F (49°C). Add the softened gelatin to the yolk mixture, then fold it into the melted chocolate. Fold in the whipped cream using a whisk until just incorporated.

5 Pour the mixture into 1½-inch (4-centimeter) silicone molds. Level the mousse with an offset spatula.

6 Freeze until hard, then unmold each mousse onto a Shortbread Tart Dough disk.

7 Decorate with a few small grapes and a white chocolate cutout.

Approximate values per piece: **Calories** 190, **Total fat** 15 g, **Saturated fat** 8 g, **Cholesterol** 70 mg, **Sodium** 50 mg, **Total carbohydrates** 17 g, **Protein** 3 g

RECIPE 19.11

CHOCOLATE RASPBERRY MOUSSE BITES

Note: This petit four appears in the chapter opening photograph.

Yield: 40 Petits Fours, 1¾ in. (4.5 cm) each   **Type:** Fresh petit four

Raspberry purée, seedless	5 oz.	150 g
Semisweet chocolate, melted	6 oz.	180 g
Heavy cream	10 fl. oz.	300 ml
Granulated sugar	1 oz.	30 g
Shortbread Tart Dough (page 266), made with hazelnut flour, 1¾-in. (4.5-cm) disks, fully baked	40 disks	40 disks
Fresh raspberries for garnish	as needed	as needed
Chocolate decorations (page 615)	as needed	as needed

1 Warm the raspberry purée until it reaches 75°F (24°C). Stir it into the melted chocolate and set aside until completely cool. Whip the cream and sugar to soft peaks. Fold the whipped cream into the chocolate-and-raspberry mixture.

2 Pour the mixture into 1¾-inch (4.5-centimeter) silicone molds. Level the mousse with an offset spatula. Freeze until hard, then unmold the mousses onto the Shortbread Tart Dough disks.

3 Garnish with fresh raspberries and chocolate decorations.

Approximate values per piece: **Calories** 130, **Total fat** 10 g, **Saturated fat** 6 g, **Cholesterol** 40 mg, **Sodium** 35 mg, **Total carbohydrates** 13 g, **Protein** 2 g

IRISH CREAM CRÈME BRÛLÉE

Note: This petit four appears in the chapter opening photograph.

Yield: 40 Petits Fours, 1½ in. (4 cm) each   **Type:** Fresh petit four

Egg yolks	3.3 oz. (5 yolks)	100 g
Brown sugar	3 oz.	90 g
Heavy cream	1 pt.	480 ml
Milk chocolate, chopped fine	3 oz.	90 g
Sheet gelatin, softened	0.25 oz.	7 g
Irish whiskey	1.5 fl. oz.	45 ml
Coffee extract	0.15 fl. oz. (1 tsp.)	5 ml
Vanilla extract	1 fl. oz.	30 ml
Shortbread Tart Dough (page 266), 1½-in. (4.5-cm) disks, fully baked	40 disks	40 disks
Chocolate decorations (page 615)	as needed	as needed

1 Combine the egg yolks and sugar in a large bowl. Whisk until smooth. Set aside.

2 Heat the cream and milk chocolate until it reaches 150°F (66°C) and whisk it into the yolk mixture.

3 Add the softened gelatin to the cream mixture along with the whiskey and extracts.

4 Place a silicone petit four mold on a sheet pan and divide the cream mixture evenly between the molds.

5 Pour water onto the sheet pan to create a water bath and bake at 325°F (160°C) until the custards have set, approximately 30 minutes. Let cool, then freeze until hard.

6 Unmold the frozen crème brûlée onto the prebaked Shortbread Tart Dough disks. Garnish each with a chocolate decoration.

Approximate values per piece: **Calories** 160, **Total fat** 13 g, **Saturated fat** 7 g, **Cholesterol** 80 mg, **Sodium** 45 mg, **Total carbohydrates** 13 g, **Protein** 2 g

APRICOT PASSION FRUIT GANACHE TARTLETS

Note: This petit four appears in the chapter opening photograph.

Yield: 40 Tartlets, 1½ in. (3.7 cm) each   **Type:** Fresh petit four

Apricot purée	5 oz.	150 g
Passion fruit purée	2 oz.	60 g
Granulated sugar	3 oz.	90 g
Honey	1 oz.	30 g
Milk chocolate, chopped fine	5 oz.	150 g
Semisweet chocolate, chopped fine	5 oz.	150 g
Unsalted butter, room temperature	2 oz.	60 g
Shortbread Tart Dough shells (page 266), made with almond flour, 1½-in. (3.7-cm) disks, fully baked	40 disks	40 disks
Dried apricots, sliced thin	3 oz.	90 g
Gold leaf (optional)	as needed	as needed

1 In a nonreactive saucepan heat the apricot and passion fruit purées, sugar and honey to 120°F (49°C).

2 Combine the milk chocolate and semisweet chocolate and melt them to 90°F (32°C). Stir the fruit purée mixture into the melted chocolate until well blended. Stir in the soft butter.

3 Pipe the ganache into the Shortbread Tart Dough shells, filling them to the rim.

4 Refrigerate the tarts until set, then garnish with a slice of dried apricot and gold leaf.

Approximate values per tartlet: **Calories** 160, **Total fat** 9 g, **Saturated fat** 5 g, **Cholesterol** 25 mg, **Sodium** 65 mg, **Total carbohydrates** 19 g, **Protein** 2 g

RECIPE 19.14

L'OPÉRA

Note: This petit four appears in the chapter opening photograph.

One of pastry chef Gaston Lenôtre's creations, the Opéra cake should be generously moistened with coffee syrup. This intensifies the flavor and improves the cake's keeping properties.

Yield: 75 Petits Fours, 1 in. × 1½ in. (2.5 cm × 3.7 cm) each

Type: Iced petit four

Simple Syrup (page 349)	4 fl. oz.	120 ml
Coffee liqueur	1 fl. oz	30 ml
Coffee extract	1 fl. oz.	30 ml
Vanilla extract	0.3 fl. oz. (2 tsp.)	10 ml
Joconde (page 418)	1 full sheet	1 full sheet
Silky Ganache Deluxe (page 371), room temperature	14 oz.	420 g
Traditional French Buttercream (page 368)	1 lb.	480 g
Chocolate decorations (page 615)	as needed	as needed

1 Combine the Simple Syrup, coffee liqueur, 1 tablespoon (15 milliliters) of the coffee extract and the vanilla. Set aside.

2 Cut the Joconde crosswise into three equal strips. Place one of the Joconde strips on a paper-lined sheet pan and moisten with 2 fluid ounces (60 milliliters) of the coffee-vanilla syrup.

3 Evenly spread a thin layer of Silky Ganache Deluxe over the moistened cake. Cover with another sheet of Joconde and moisten with 2 fluid ounces (60 milliliters) of the coffee-vanilla syrup.

4 Combine the Traditional French Buttercream with the remaining coffee extract and spread evenly over the cake. Cover with another sheet of Joconde and moisten with the remaining syrup.

5 Freeze until hard.

6 Invert the frozen cake onto a sheet pan. Trim the edges. Coat the cake with a thin layer of Silky Ganache Deluxe to seal. Heat the remaining ganache to 120°F (49°C), then spread it evenly over the cake with an offset spatula. Let the ganache harden.

7 Cut the cake into small squares, triangles or rectangles measuring approximately 1 inch × 1½ inches (2.5 centimeters × 3.7 centimeters). Garnish with chocolate decorations.

Approximate values per piece: **Calories** 90, **Total fat** 5 g, **Saturated fat** 3 g, **Cholesterol** 30 mg, **Sodium** 10 mg, **Total carbohydrates** 8 g, **Protein** 1 g

RECIPE 19.15

HAZELNUT FOCUS

Yield: 60 Petits Fours, 1½ in. (3.7 cm) each　　**Type:** Iced petit four

Granulated sugar	13 oz.	390 g
Hazelnut flour	6 oz.	180 g
Cake flour	4 oz.	120 g
Egg whites	10 oz. (10 whites)	300 g
Butter, melted	10 oz.	300 g
Vanilla extract	0.15 fl. oz. (1 tsp.)	5 ml
Silky Ganache Deluxe (page 371)	10 oz.	300 g
Hazelnut paste, room temperature	2.5 oz.	75 g
Hazelnut Crunch (recipe follows)	9 oz.	270 g

1 In the bowl of a mixer fitted with a whip, combine the sugar, hazelnut flour and cake flour.

2 Add the egg whites and mix 5 minutes on medium speed.

3 With the mixer running on low speed, gradually add the butter and vanilla.

4 Pipe the batter into silicone molds or buttered and floured petit four molds.

5 Bake at 375°F (190°F) until cakes bounce back when lightly pressed, approximately 13 minutes. Let cool.

6 Combine the Silky Ganache Deluxe with the hazelnut paste. Pipe a small rosette of hazelnut ganache on each petit four.

7 Sprinkle the rosettes with Hazelnut Crunch.

Approximate values per piece: **Calories** 140, **Total fat** 9 g, **Saturated fat** 4.5 g, **Cholesterol** 15 mg, **Sodium** 25 mg, **Total carbohydrates** 13 g, **Protein** 2 g

HAZELNUT CRUNCH

Yield: Approximately 9 oz. (270 g)

Milk chocolate	4 oz.	120 g
Cocoa butter	1.5 oz.	45 g
Hazelnut paste	1.5 oz.	45 g
Puffed rice cereal	2.5 oz.	75 g

1 Combine the chocolate and the cocoa butter and temper.

2 Add the hazelnut paste and the puffed rice cereal.

3 Sprinkle the chocolate-coated cereal onto petits fours or cakes before the chocolate hardens. The mixture may also be spread on a parchment-lined sheet pan and then broken up into tiny pieces once the chocolate hardens.

Approximate values per 1-oz. (30-g) serving: **Calories** 150, **Total fat** 9 g, **Saturated fat** 5 g, **Cholesterol** 5 mg, **Sodium** 90 mg, **Total carbohydrates** 16 g, **Protein** 2 g

CARAMEL-DIPPED FRUITS

RECIPE 19.16

Yield: 30 Pieces **Type:** Glazed fruit

Glucose or corn syrup	1 lb.	480 g
Fondant	12 oz.	360 g
Strawberries, kumquats, seedless grapes, orange segments or fresh figs	30	30

1 Place the glucose or corn syrup in a heavy saucepan over medium-high heat. Bring to a boil without stirring.

2 Carefully add the fondant to the glucose without stirring. Boil until the mixture reaches a golden caramel.

3 Remove from the heat. Immediately dip the bottom of the pot in a bowl of room-temperature water to stop the cooking process.

4 Using tongs, dip each piece of fruit in the caramel and place on a silicone baking mat or onto a lightly oiled sheet pan to harden.

Note: Decorating Caramel (page 352) used for dipped éclairs may be substituted in this formula; however, caramel made with glucose or corn syrup and fondant is superior at resisting humidity.

Approximate values per piece: **Calories** 90, **Total fat** 0 g, **Saturated fat** 0 g, **Cholesterol** 0 mg, **Sodium** 25 mg, **Total carbohydrates** 23 g, **Protein** 0 g (Values vary depending on fruit selected.)

THE DESSERT CROWNS THE DINNER. TO CREATE A
FINE DESSERT, ONE HAS TO COMBINE THE SKILLS OF
A CONFECTIONER, A DECORATOR, A PAINTER, AN
ARCHITECT, AN ICE-CREAM MANUFACTURER, A
SCULPTOR, AND A FLORIST. THE SPLENDOR OF SUCH
CREATIONS APPEALS ABOVE ALL TO THE EYE—
THE REAL GOURMAND ADMIRES THEM WITHOUT
TOUCHING THEM!

*—Eugene Briffault, French humorist and food
writer (1799–1854)*

RESTAURANT DESSERTS

RESTAURANT HUGO, Houston, TX
Pastry Chef Ruben Ortega

AFTER STUDYING THIS
CHAPTER, YOU WILL BE
ABLE TO:

▶ understand the basic
principles of plate
presentation

▶ use a variety of techniques to
add visual appeal to plated
desserts

A great source of excitement in restaurants today is the interest in presenting desserts with the same care and attention to detail as the main meal. Desserts and the pastry chefs who create them are getting top billing along with the heretofore more prominent chefs de cuisine. Plated desserts may include several sweets on one plate presented in a manner that is visually stunning. A main item may be served hot accompanied by a contrasting cold garnish and something acidic or crunchy as a contrast. Today's restaurant desserts are a far cry from a humble slice of apple crisp and scoop of ice cream, although a well-crafted pie using ripe fruit in season cannot be beat.

Today's restaurant customer, whether in a fine-dining establishment or a fast service bakery café, expects great desserts that are attractively presented. This chapter looks at ways to create and present desserts appropriate for a number of restaurant settings. Elements from topics covered throughout this book are used to create exciting sweets suitable for ending any great meal.

The moment of truth for the pastry chef is when his or her creation is served and presented to the guest. **Service** is the process of delivering foods to diners in the proper fashion, appropriately prepared and presented at the correct time. Cold desserts should be served properly chilled and on cold plates. Ice cream should be cold and hold its shape in its bowl, not be runny and melted. A hot soufflé should be served soon after it is removed from the oven and arrive hot at the guest's table. Piecrusts should be crisp, not mushy.

Chefs work to present food in a manner that enhances its appeal. **Presentation** is the process of offering the selected foods to diners in a manner that is visually pleasing. When presenting foods, always bear in mind that diners consume first with their eyes and then with their mouths. The colors, textures and shapes on the plate should work together to form a harmonious balance on the plate.

Presentation techniques are divided into two broad categories: those applied to specific desserts and those applied to the plate as a whole. Many of the techniques discussed here are illustrated with desserts that appear elsewhere in this book.

▶ THE DESSERT

The most attractive desserts are those that are well prepared and whose appeal is enhanced by proper presentation. Desserts must be properly portioned both for the economics of the business and for the pleasure of the customer. Frosted cakes should be cut into neat slices. The knife should be held so as not to crush the cake when slicing. A clean knife is used each time a cake, pie, cheesecake or other dessert is portioned. Lemon filling should not mar the meringue in a lemon meringue pie because the knife used to slice it was not cleaned after cutting the previous portion. The meringue should be evenly browned, the crust golden and in one piece. Portions of cakes and bar cookies should be uniformly sliced into crisp-edged pieces; each guest should receive the same size piece.

Fruit-filled pies and tarts, when sliced, should arrive with their filling intact; pieces of fruit should not tumble onto the serving plate.

Any decorative touches, such as sauces and garnishes, should be placed with thought and care. Whipped cream should be carefully piped. Most important, plates should be neat and spotless. Inspect each plate before it leaves the kitchen. Wipe fingerprints, specks of sauce and stray crumbs from their rims with a clean towel.

CREATING THE RESTAURANT DESSERT

While pastry chefs seek out new ideas for their menus, most are based on staples in their baking repertoire. Rarely is there enough time for new formulas to be developed for each dessert to be served. Restaurant desserts are based on combining the various preparations from the pastry kitchen to create specific dishes appropriate for the restaurant. By carefully changing the shape of basic preparations, new desserts are created. Pastry chefs save time by using one formula to prepare a number of items.

SHAPING DESSERTS

By varying the shape and size of baking pans specified in a formula, the pastry chef may create a variety of presentations. Cakes and batters may be baked in diverse forms, adjusting the baking time according to the size and type of pan used. A shallow baking sheet or baking sheet with a pan extender will make one large flat cake. From this basic rectangle, many shapes of cake may be cut. The cake can be frosted and cut into individual square portions. The whole sheet cake can be divided into four rectangles, each to be filled and frosted to make four rectangular cakes. Alternately, before frosting, the sheet cake may be cut into individual rounds using a biscuit cutter, filled, then frosted for individual cakes. (Cake trim is saved and ground to use to mask the sides of a cake.) Cakes as well as muffin batters may be baked in greased muffin tins or loaf pans normally used for breads. Pie dough can be used to line shallow muffin pans. Once filled with fruit, these muffin-shaped pies can be baked and served as individual deep-dish pies. Pie and tart pans come in a myriad of sizes and shapes, from round tartlets to narrow rectangular tarts or square shapes.

The same formula for Basic Pie Dough (page 248) or Shortbread Tart Dough (page 266) can be baked in any number of forms beyond the standard round pie pan. A whole apple or peach may be wrapped in pie dough and baked on a baking sheet. The dough can be rolled out and used to make a freeform pie as on page 270. The size of the freeform pie can be small enough so that each serves one person or equivalent to a full-size pie that is then cut into wedges for serving. Pastry chefs often bake miniature pastries, using two or three on a plate to complete one serving. Baked meringues, éclairs, fruit fritters, churros and beignets lend themselves to this type of presentation.

CHANGING COMPONENTS

Changing the look of a traditional dessert is as simple as changing the type of crust used in a pie or tart. Choux paste and meringue shells can be formed and baked into tart shells. Shortcake is generally made with a type of biscuit that absorbs the juices from the fruit layered on it, as in the Shortcakes formula on page 114. But the pastry chef is not limited; various cakes could be sliced and used to make a type of layered fruit shortcake, including Lemon Tea Bread (page 121), Almond Genoise (page 414) or Coconut Macadamia Cake (page 421).

MOLDING CUSTARDS, MOUSSES AND CREAMS

Some desserts, particularly custards, mousses and creams, can be molded into attractive shapes by using small ramekins, silicone molds, ice cream scoops or ice cube containers. These mixtures are placed into the molds before they set so that, once ready for service, they take the shape of their container.

USING COMPONENTS IN DIFFERENT PREPARATIONS

Proper preparation of a quality dessert requires skill, attention to detail and the proper amount of time to complete the work. Pressed for time in a commercial bakeshop and restaurant kitchen, the pastry chef looks for ways to be efficient. Using the same formulas in multiple preparations eases the work. Here are several examples of the ways in which three basic preparations—classic Spongecake (page 388), Shortbread Tart Dough (page 266), and Chocolate Mousse (page 462)—can be used to create six different desserts. (The amount of each ingredient, the yield and the baking time will depend on the pans used. These procedures are guidelines only.)

INDIVIDUAL RASPBERRY MOUSSE CAKES

Classic Spongecake (page 388)
Raspberry Mousse (page 463)

1 Bake the Spongecake batter in individual pans or muffin cups, adjusting the time according to the size of the pan selected.
2 Slice the cooled cakes in half and fill each with Raspberry Mousse.

MOCHA TORTE

Classic Spongecake (page 388)
Simple Syrup (page 349)
Coffee extract
Caramel Mousse (page 465)
Chocolate Mousse (page 462)
Chocolate Ganache, warm (page 362)
Toasted coconut
Chopped nuts

1 Bake the Classic Spongecake in 8-inch (20-centimeter) round pans.
2 Slice the cooled cakes into three layers each. Moisten the sponge with Simple Syrup flavored with coffee extract.
3 Fill alternating layers of the cake with Caramel Mousse and Chocolate Mousse.
4 Coat the cakes with a thin layer of melted Chocolate Ganache. Mask the sides of the cake with toasted coconut or chopped nuts.

FRESH STRAWBERRY TARTLETS

Shortbread Tart Dough (page 266)
Raspberry Mousse (page 463)
Fresh strawberries, sliced
Tart glaze

1 Make individual tarts with the Shortbread Tart Dough. Bake them blind.
2 Fill the baked shells with Raspberry Mousse and top with fresh strawberries. Coat with tart glaze.

CHOCOLATE MOUSSE NAPOLEON

Shortbread Tart Dough (page 266)
Chocolate Mousse (page 462)
Powdered sugar

1 Roll out the Shortbread Tart Dough. Cut it into uniform rectangles. Bake the rectangles.
2 Place one piece of baked shortbread on a serving plate. Top with Chocolate Mousse. Top with another layer of shortbread and more mousse. Top with a piece of shortbread dusted with powdered sugar.

APRICOT CHARLOTTE

Classic Spongecake (page 388)
Apricot jam
Apricot Mousse (page 430)
Tart glaze

1 Bake the spongecake batter in a half-sheet pan. Spread the cake with apricot jam and roll tightly as for a jelly roll. Cut the cake into $1/2$-inch-(1.2-centimeter) thick slices and line the bottom and sides of an 8-inch (20-centimeter) cake pan or mold with the slices of cake.
2 Fill the cake-lined pan with the Apricot Mousse. Let the mousse set until firm. Coat the surface of the charlotte with tart glaze. Chill, then unmold.

CINNAMON "BREAD" PUDDING

Classic Spongecake (page 388)
Custard from Bread Pudding with Bourbon Sauce (page 459)
Cinnamon
Chocolate Mousse (page 462)

1 Cut the Classic Spongecake, especially any trimming left from other uses, into cubes.
2 Place the cake cubes in a rectangular mold, top with the custard mixture and sprinkle generously with cinnamon.
3 Bake as for bread pudding. Serve with spoonfuls of Chocolate Mousse.

▶ THE PLATE

With the care that has been taken in creating a dessert, equal care must be taken to present it to the customer. Desserts that combine several components and are presented in a manner similar to that of the main meal are called **plated desserts.** The way in which a dessert is placed on a plate is part of the appeal of a plated dessert. The **composition** of the plate should be balanced and harmonious. The main dessert item, the way it is shaped, the items that accompany the dessert and the plate on which it is placed all contribute to the diner's perception of its quality.

▶ **composition** a completed plate's structure of colors, shapes and arrangements

CHOOSING PLATES

Restaurant china designed to withstand the rigors of repeated use is available in many shapes, colors and styles. It is often the chef's responsibility to select the china appropriate for the food being served. Frequently, specific plates will be used for specific dishes, such as a tulip sundae glass for an ice cream dish.

SIZE AND SHAPE

Most plates are round, but oval, rectangular, square and triangular plates are becoming more common. Plates are available in a variety of sizes, from a small

Chewy Date Bars with Caramel Ice
Cream

Lemon Sorbet

Mango Sorbet

4-inch (10-centimeter) bread plate to a huge 14-inch (35-centimeter) charger or
base plate. Plates are typically concave; their depths may vary within a limited
range of about 1 inch (2.5 centimeters). Most plates have rims; rim diameters also
vary. Soup bowls can be rimmed or rimless. Soup plates are usually larger and
shallower than soup bowls and have wide rims. There are also dozens of plates
and bowls intended for a specific purpose, such as tall, narrow glasses for ice
cream parfaits.

Choose plates large enough to hold the food comfortably without overcrowding or spilling. Oversized, rimmed soup plates are popular for serving ice
creams and sorbets or other moist desserts with a sauce. Be careful when using
oversized plates, however, as the food may look sparse, creating poor value
perception.

Whether the plates are round, oval or less conventionally shaped, be sure to
choose one with a size and shape that best highlights the food and supports the
composition. For example, in the photograph to the left, the rectangular dish
with round corners and raised rim accentuates the geometrically simple yet effective composition of the square date bar and spherical scoop of ice cream.

COLORS AND PATTERNS

White and cream are by far the most common colors for restaurant china; almost
any food looks good on these neutral colors. Colored and patterned plates can
be used quite effectively to accent food, however. The obvious choice is to contrast dark plates with bright- or light-colored foods and light plates with dark-
colored foods. The food should always be the focal point of any plate. The colors
and shapes in the pattern should blend well and harmonize with the foods
served. The lacy green vine and pale blue floral motif on the rim of the plate to
the left artfully balances the crisp, toasty color of the wafer cookie cup and the
frosty pale sorbet punctuated with bright bursts of red raspberries.

ARRANGING DESSERTS ON PLATES

Plates should be composed to make the dessert appetizing to the customer. Strive
for a well-balanced composition, which can be achieved with careful consideration of the shape, size, colors, textures and arrangement of foods on the plate.

SHAPES

For visual interest or pure drama, combine a variety of shapes on the plate when
composing a plated dessert. It is exciting to the eye and can make a bold statement. The diamond shape of the Tulipe Cookie perched on top of a triangular
wedge of sorbet in the photograph to the left is a bold geometric statement, crisp
modern lines that match the snap of the cookie and the bright flavor of the
mango sorbet. Adding some height is amusing and can be an effective addition
when plating a pastry. Attention should be paid to how the guest will eat the
dessert, however. Some creations may be too complicated for the guest to eat
comfortably.

COLORS

Foods come in a rainbow of colors and to the extent appropriate, foods of different colors should be presented together. Generally, the colors should provide
balance and contrast. But no matter how well prepared or planned, some
desserts simply have dull and boring colors. If so, try adding another ingredient
or garnish for a splash of color.

TEXTURES

Pastry chefs strive to include a variety of textures in their desserts. Texture refers
to the sensation perceived when eating the product as well as the appearance

of the surface of the food. It may be crisp, crumbly, grainy, flaky, smooth or creamy. Many historically popular pastries, such as a well-made éclair, offer a wonderful balance between crisp pastry and creamy filling. The preparations included on a plated dessert should offer a harmonious balance of textures. The trio of chocolate desserts shown to the right offer a similar flavor palate made more interesting by the striking textural contrasts on this sparse, elegant plate. From the right, a fragile wafer cookie contrasts with the cold ice cream, a brittle chocolate box holds a light fluid custard and a gooey cake is coated with a melting chocolate essence.

The pages of this book are filled with formulas for toppings cookies, and garnishes that can add a pleasing textural contrast to a plated dessert.

A trio of miniature chocolate desserts offers complementary tastes and contrasting textures on one plate.

▶ Candied Citrus Rind (page 534)
▶ Caramelized Apple Crisps (page 534)
▶ Dried Pineapple Slices (page 535)
▶ Candied Almonds (page 301)
▶ Palmiers (page 337)
▶ Puff Pastry (page 312), dusted with coarse sugar, cut in strips and baked
▶ Chocolate Meringue Sticks (page 420)
▶ Granola Crunch Topping (page 269)
▶ Chocolate Cut-Outs (page 615)
▶ Basic Nougatine (page 633)
▶ Banana Twists (page 602)

FLAVOR

Use judgment in combining elements on the dessert plate so that the flavors of the components will harmonize on the palate. For best results, limit the number of different flavorings in an individual preparation; too many different tastes confuse the palate and muddy flavors. Flavors may be **complementary** or **contrasting.** Complementary flavors are those that are similar to the other flavors in a dish. Chocolate and cocoa are complementary flavors, different variations of the same flavor. Consider layering flavors in a dish by combining similar flavors of different intensities.

Contrasting flavors are those that are very different, such as sweet and sour, sweet and bitter or fat and acid. Oatmeal Stout Ice Cream, shown to the right, is a perfect example of the contrast between the bitter beer and the sweet cream. When paired with a sugary pecan pie, the hint of bitterness balances the sugary pecan filling.

Classic flavor combinations are illustrated throughout this book; cinnamon in apple pie and chocolate and mint are two common examples. Table 20.1 lists some other companion flavors. Taste is to a large extent a personal preference. These combinations are time-tested based on the experience of pastry chefs and confectioners. Experimentation will lead to new taste combinations. This table is a place to begin.

Closely related to the flavor of food is the temperature at which it is served. Warm foods have a more intense flavor than cold foods. The diner will perceive the aroma of a warm dish before it is tasted. Hot and cold foods served together on a dessert plate please the palate.

Pecan Pie with Oatmeal Stout Ice Cream

ARRANGEMENTS

Having decided on the color, texture and shapes of the foods that will go on the plate, next the pastry chef must decide where to place each individual item to achieve a balanced and unified composition. Mostly this takes judgment and style, but there are a few general guidelines.

Table 20.1 CLASSIC FLAVOR COMBINATIONS

DOMINANT FLAVOR	FORMS	COMPLEMENTS
Chocolate	Bittersweet or dark	Coffee, cinnamon, orange Fresh berry flavors, particularly those with some acidity: cherry, strawberry, raspberry Mint, spearmint or peppermint Fruit liqueurs or rum Dry fruit Coconut
	Milk chocolate	Toasted nuts, caramel
	Cocoa	Espresso, vanilla, whiskey
Spices	Allspice	Pears, apples, tree fruit
	Anise or licorice	Almonds and sweet cream
	Cinnamon	Chocolate, apples, pears, caramel
	Ginger	Most fruit and berries, especially apricot, pear and lemon
	Peppermint	Chocolate, sweet cream
	Spearmint	Chocolate, cherries, strawberries, peaches, melon
Citrus (lemon, lime, mandarin, orange)	Juice	Almonds and almond flavor Cream and cream cheese Other citrus, honey Mint
	Zest	Chocolate Sweet or tart creamy products, sour cream, cream cheese
Caramel		Most spices, toasted nuts Sweet or tart creamy products Apples, pears
Nuts	Raw	Fruits and berries Sweet or tart creams Citrus juice or rind
	Toasted	Buttery pastry, caramel and chocolate, coffee

Warm Peaches with Champagne Rose Sorbet

Guidelines for Arranging Foods on a Plate

▶ Strike a balance between overcrowding the plate and leaving large gaps of space. Foods should not touch the plate rim nor necessarily be confined in the very center.

▶ Choose a focal point for the plate—that is, the point to which the eye is drawn. This is usually the highest point on the plate. Design the plate with the highest point to the rear or center. Avoid placing foods of equal heights around the edge of the plate, leaving a hole in the center—the eye will naturally be drawn to that gap.

▶ The plate's composition should flow naturally. For example, make the highest point the back of the plate and have the rest of the food become gradually shorter toward the front of the plate. Slicing and fanning fruits or scattering the plate with berries can bring the eye down and help establish flow.

The baked peach on which a cookie is artfully perched shown here elegantly illustrates these principles. The triangular cookie brings height and humor to the composition and the theme. The design is visually amusing because it demonstrates the concept of balance in a literal way. The dark color of the blackberry brings the eye to its placement and the scroll of lace cookie is a whimsical contrast to the formality of the geometric and round shapes on the plate.

DECORATING PLATES

Nothing adds more polish to a plated dessert than a bit of plate decorating and garnish. The colors, textures, shapes and arrangements of foods on a plate can be improved or highlighted by decorating a plate with candied fruit, herbs, spices and other garnishes and sauce. If any of these are to be applied after the food is plated, plan to do so quickly so that the dessert stays hot or cold when it reaches the table.

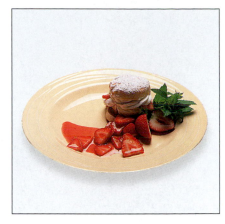

A dessert garnished with fresh mint and berries.

GARNISHING DESSERTS WITH HERBS AND EDIBLE FLOWERS

Using a sprig of fresh mint or other mild herb or a fresh flower is one easy way to add color and flow to the design of a dessert plate. Whether the herb is an ingredient in the dish or merely a decoration, it should always complement the dessert and be consistent with the flavorings on the plate. Sprigs of fresh green mint (often with a fresh berry or two or a strawberry cut into a fan) are often the perfect decoration for a dessert plate. Candied citrus rind or toasted or candied nuts add sparkle and crunch to ice cream and custard presentations.

PLATE DUSTING

An attractive method for decorating dessert plates is to cover the entire plate with a dusting of powdered sugar, cocoa powder or both before placing the dessert on the plate. Ground cinnamon, nutmeg or citrus rind can be used if appropriate and used sparingly. Use sugar on dark-colored plates and cocoa on light-colored plates. These items can be dusted onto the plate with a shaker can or sifter in a freeform fashion or into any desired pattern by using a template. The template can be a doily or a stencil placed over the plate before it is dusted.

▶ PROCEDURE FOR DUSTING PLATES

1 Place a template over the plate. Dust the sugar or cocoa over the template.

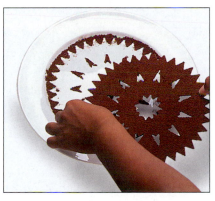

2 Carefully remove the template.

DECORATING PLATES WITH SAUCES

Sauce is an integral part of many deserts. It adds flavor and moisture; it also adds color, texture and flow to the plate. One or more colored sauces can also be used to paint plates. One technique is simply to drizzle or splatter the sauce onto the plate. In the photograph shown to the right, the sauce is rustically dotted and drizzled on the plate.

Peach and Blueberry Napoleon

Vanilla Cream Bavarian with Red Fruit
Lime Gel

Alternatively, one or more colored sauces can be applied to a plate using squirt bottles to create abstract patterns or representational designs. Painting the plates with colored sauces also facilitates the visual flow of the design and adds color. In the photograph shown to the left, the geometric design of the custard sauce is offset by the dramatic dots of raspberry purée. The intricate plate decoration contrasts nicely with the simple circular shape of the dessert. This technique is used with cold sauces such as vanilla, caramel, chocolate and fruit-flavored sauces. The sauces must be thick enough to hold the pattern once it is created and they should be the same viscosity.

▶ PROCEDURE FOR PAINTING A DESIGN WITH SAUCES

 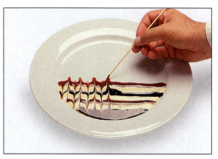

1 Apply the sauces to the plate in parallel lines of alternating colors.

2 Carefully pull a toothpick through the sauces, perpendicular to the parallel lines in the sauces.

▶ PROCEDURE FOR PAINTING A SPIDER WEB DESIGN

1 Pool one sauce evenly across the entire base of the plate, then apply a contrasting sauce onto the base sauce in a spiral.

2 Draw a thin-bladed knife or a toothpick through the sauce from the center point toward the edge. Then, leaving a 1/2-inch (1.2-centimeter) space along the edge, draw a knife blade or toothpick from the edge to the center.

Other patterns can be produced by squirting the sauces onto the plate in different patterns or by pulling the knife or toothpick through the sauce in different directions. As shown to the left, a circle of chocolate and raspberry-sauce dots in a pool of vanilla sauce is pulled to create a border of hearts.

CONCLUSION

Employing the technical skills learned in the classroom bakeshop and the techniques discussed in this chapter, the student pastry chef can create a variety of desserts and pastry presentations. Using basic bakeshop formulas, a complete dessert menu can be created by varying the size, shape, fillings and presentation of the pastry. The excitement for the pastry department comes in creating new combinations of flavors and components to make desserts that reflect the creativity of the chef and the style and theme of the restaurant. A complete restaurant dessert designed to be served after a main meal must complement the entire dining experience. A restaurant dessert may be as simple as a slice of pie and whipped cream garnish. For many types of restaurants a straightforward combination may be appropriate. Once the practical and economic considerations are addressed, the pastry chef approaches the exciting aspect of the job, creating the actual desserts that will be served to the guests.

QUESTIONS FOR DISCUSSION

1 Select a basic formula from any of the preceding chapters in this book. Using that one formula, create three different plated dessert presentations.
2 List and describe three different plating techniques for a cut portion of dessert.
3 Discuss the impact that size of kitchen staff has on serving plated desserts. Discuss which components are best suited to including on a dessert plate when kitchen staff is limited.
4 Describe various ways a sauce may be used to decorate a plated dessert.

RECIPE 20.1

DULCE DE LECHE MOUSSE

BACKSTREET CAFÉ, PREGO AND HUGO'S, HOUSTON, TX
Pastry Chef Ruben Ortega

Note: This dish appears in the chapter opening photograph.

Yield: 10 Servings

Milk	1 pt.	480 ml
Baking soda	0.05 oz. (¼ tsp.)	1.5 g
Granulated sugar	8 oz.	240 g
Vanilla extract	0.5 fl. oz.	15 ml
Sheet gelatin, softened	0.25 oz.	6 g
Heavy cream, whipped to soft peaks	14 fl. oz.	420 ml
Silky Ganache Deluxe (page 371), softened	5 oz.	150 g
Traditional Shortbread (page 225), 3¼-in. (8-cm) disks, fully baked	10	10
Chocolate for spraying	as needed	as needed
Coffee Custard Sauce (page 435)	as needed	as needed
Chocolate decorations (page 617)	as needed	as needed

1 Bring the milk to a boil in a heavy saucepan. Add the baking soda, sugar and vanilla. Simmer this mixture over medium heat, stirring occasionally.

2 Once the mixture begins to darken and caramelize, stir more frequently. Remove from the heat when the mixture has the consistency of maple syrup and a deep honey color, approximately 10 to 12 minutes. Let cool to 120°F (49°C).

3 Melt the softened gelatin and add it to the warm caramel cream.

4 Immediately fold in the whipped cream.

5 Using a ladle, fill 3¼-inch (8-centimeter) dome-shaped silicone molds or ramekins halfway with the mousse.

6 Using a piping bag, pipe approximately 1 Tablespoon (15 milliliters) of the Ganache in the center of the mousse.

7 Fill the molds or ramekins with the remaining mousse. Place a disk of Traditional Shortbread on the mousse. Freeze until hard, approximately 2 hours.

8 Unmold the desserts onto an icing screen. Place them in the freezer until very cold.

9 Warm the chocolate for spraying to approximately 120°F (49°C) and pour into a chocolate sprayer. Spray the domes evenly (see page 619).

10 Serve each dome with Coffee Custard Sauce and chocolate decorations.

Approximate values per serving: **Calories** 550, **Total fat** 40 g, **Saturated fat** 23 g, **Cholesterol** 160 mg, **Sodium** 170 mg, **Total carbohydrates** 54 g, **Protein** 7 g, **Vitamin A** 15%

WARM PEACHES WITH
CHAMPAGNE-ROSE SORBET

RECIPE 20.2

Yield: 10 Servings

Warm Baked Peaches (page 528)	10	10
Tulipe Cookies (page 238), baked into rectangular and triangular shapes	20 cookies	20 cookies
Champagne-Rose Sorbet (recipe follows)	28 fl. oz.	840 ml
Lace Cookies (recipe follows)	10 cookies	10 cookies
Grapefruit Coulis (page 364)	as needed	as needed
Fresh currants	as needed	as needed

1 Remove the Warm Baked Peaches from the oven. Place one on each serving plate.

2 Place a diamond-shaped Tulipe Cookie on top of each peach.

3 Unmold a piece of Champagne-Rose Sorbet and center it on the Tulipe Cookie. Insert a triangular Tulipe Cookie into the sorbet.

4 Surround the peach with a curved Lace Cookie, some of the Grapefruit Coulis and fresh currants.

Approximate values per serving: **Calories** 440, **Total fat** 19 g, **Saturated fat** 9 g, **Cholesterol** 40 mg, **Sodium** 25 mg, **Total carbohydrates** 63 g, **Protein** 4 g, **Vitamin A** 10% **Vitamin C** 15%

CHAMPAGNE-ROSE SORBET

Yield: Approximately 28 fl. oz. (840 ml)

Water	8 fl. oz.	240 ml
Granulated sugar	6 oz.	180 g
Glucose or corn syrup	2 oz.	60 g
Rose petals, organic	10 petals	10 petals
Rose liqueur	1 fl. oz.	30 ml
Champagne	12.5 fl. oz.	375 ml

1 Bring the water, sugar and glucose or corn syrup to boil in a small saucepan. Remove from the heat and add the rose petals. Let cool.

2 Pour the mixture in a blender and purée until the petals are finely chopped. Add the liqueur and champagne. If necessary, adjust the mixture to 1.1074 D (14° Baumé). Chill the mixture completely, then process in an ice cream machine.

3 Once the sorbet has been churned, pack it in individual 2-ounce (60-gram) molds. Freeze until firm.

Approximate values per ½ cup serving: **Calories** 100, **Total fat** 0 g, **Saturated fat** 0 g, **Cholesterol** 0 mg, **Sodium** 10 mg, **Total carbohydrates** 26 g, **Protein** 0 g

LACE COOKIES

Yield: 1 lb. 5 oz. (610 g)   **Method:** Wafer cookie

Unsalted butter, softened	3 oz.	90 g
Granulated sugar	6 oz.	120 g
Almonds, chopped	7 oz.	210 g
Blackberry purée	4 fl. oz.	120 ml
Cake flour	1.6 oz.	50 g

1 Make a stencil by cutting a 10-inch × ½-inch (25-centimeter × 1.2-centimeter) rectangular hole out of a rigid piece of thin cardboard or plastic. Line a sheet tray with a silicone baking mat. Set aside.

2 Cream the butter in the bowl of a mixer until lump-free. Add the sugar and incorporate well. Add the almonds and the blackberry purée. Mix well, then add the cake flour.

3 Place the stencil on the silicone baking mat. Spread the wafer batter the same thickness as the stencil. Move the stencil and repeat until the sheet tray is covered with stenciled cookie better.

4 Bake at 400°F (200°C) until the cookies are firm and lightly brown, approximately 6 minutes.

5 As soon as the cookies are removed from the oven, wrap the strips of warm dough around an oiled tube or French-style rolling pin. Once cooled, slide the cookie from the form. Store the cookies tightly sealed in a plastic container.

Approximate values per serving: **Calories** 440, **Total fat** 19 g, **Saturated fat** 9 g, **Cholesterol** 40 mg, **Sodium** 25 mg, **Total carbohydrates** 63 g, **Protein** 4 g, **Vitamin A** 10%, **Vitamin C** 15%

VANILLA CREAM BAVARIAN WITH RED FRUIT LIME GEL

RECIPE 20.3

AMBRIA RESTAURANT, Chicago, IL
Pastry Chef Michel Briand

Yield: 24 Desserts

Milk	1 pt.	480 ml
Vanilla bean, split	1	1
Egg yolks	5.3 oz. (8 yolks)	160 g
Granulated sugar	9 oz.	270 g
Sheet gelatin, softened	1.5 oz.	45 g
Heavy cream, whipped	1 pt.	480 ml
Red berries: raspberries, currants, strawberries, or any combination	24 oz.	720 g
Simple Syrup (page 349), warm	20 fl. oz.	300 ml
Lime juice	6 fl. oz.	180 ml
Lime zest	0.2 oz. (1 Tbsp.)	6 g
Crème Anglaise (page 434)	24 fl. oz.	720 ml
Breton Shortbread (page 483) baked into 3-in. (7.5-cm) disks	24 disks	24 disks
Red Fruit Sorbet (recipe follows)	2 qt.	2 lt
Tulipe Cookies (page 238)	24 cookies	24 cookies
Raspberry purée	as needed	as needed
Rose Powder or raspberry powder	as needed	as needed

1 To make the Bavarian cream, bring the milk and vanilla bean to a boil.

2 Whisk the egg yolks and sugar in a small bowl and temper with some of the heated milk. Add back to the mixture and cook the cream, stirring constantly until lightly thickened.

▶ **rose powder** fresh rose petals, dried and then ground into a fine powder used to flavor chocolates, fillings and toppings

3 Remove from the heat. Stir 0.5 ounces (15 grams) of the softened gelatin into the cream. Cool, then fold in the whipped cream.

4 Place 24 3-inch (7.5-centimeter) ring molds on paper-lined sheet pans. Divide the Bavarian cream between the molds. Level the cream to a height of approximately ½ inch (1.2 centimeters) in each ring. Chill in the refrigerator until firm, approximately 2 hours.

5 Divide the assorted red fruits evenly between the rings, covering the firm Bavarian cream to a height of ½ inch (1.2 centimeters).

6 Add the remaining gelatin to the Simple Syrup with the lime juice and lime zest.

7 Pour the lime gel over the fruits to cover and refrigerate until set.

8 To serve, spoon some Crème Anglaise in the center of each serving plate. Position a Breton Shortbread disk on top of the sauce. Unmold a Bavarian onto each disk. Spoon Red Fruit Sorbet on top of the Bavarian. Garnish with a Tulipe Cookie, some raspberry purée and rose or raspberry powder.

Approximate values per serving: **Calories** 600, **Total fat** 31 g, **Saturated fat** 17 g, **Cholesterol** 250 mg, **Sodium** 170 mg, **Total carbohydrates** 77 g, **Protein** 9 g, **Vitamin A** 20%, **Vitamin C** 30%

RED FRUIT SORBET

Yield: 2 qt. (2 lt)

Water	18 fl. oz.	540 ml
Granulated sugar	10 oz.	300 g
Glucose or corn syrup	3 oz.	90 g
Red fruit purée	2 lb.	960 g

1 Make a simple syrup from the water, sugar and glucose or corn syrup. Chill, then add the red fruit purée. Process in an ice cream machine.

LEMON CURD MERINGUE TARTS
WITH MANGO COULIS

RECIPE 20.4

Yield: 12 Tarts, 2½ in. (7.5 cm) each

Mango purée	20 oz.	600 g
Granulated sugar	5 oz.	150 g
Common (French) Meringue (page 288),		
2½-in. (7.5-cm) shells, fully baked	12 shells	12 shells
White chocolate, melted	as needed	as needed
Lemon Curd (page 437)	1 lb. 4 oz.	600 g
Fresh lychees	24	24
Neutral glaze	as needed	as needed
Fresh blackberries	36	36

1 Combine the mango purée and sugar in a blender and process until smooth. Strain if desired. Set aside.

2 Using a pastry brush, gently brush the interior of the meringue shells with tempered white chocolate.

3 Using a pastry bag fitted with a medium plain piping tip, fill the meringue shell to the edge with Lemon Curd.

4 Place the lychees in the center of the tarts. Using a pastry brush, glaze the lychees with the tart glaze.

5 Surround the lychees with blackberries. Dot the plate with some of the mango purée.

Approximate values per serving: **Calories** 520, **Total fat** 30 g, **Saturated fat** 18 g, **Cholesterol** 125 mg, **Sodium** 95 mg, **Total carbohydrates** 61 g, **Protein** 5 g, **Vitamin A** 20%, **Vitamin C** 20%

RECIPE 20.5

CHOCOLATE SOUFFLÉ CAKE WITH PEANUT BUTTER HONEY CENTER AND BURNT BLOOD-ORANGE SAUCE

THE BROWN PALACE HOTEL, Denver, CO

Pastry Chef Sky Goble

Yield: 6 Servings

Chocolate Soufflé Cake (recipe follows)	6 cakes	6 cakes
Grand Marnier Flambé Bananas (recipe follows)	as needed	as needed
Candied Orange Peel (recipe follows)	24 pieces	24 pieces
Burnt Blood-Orange Sauce (recipe follows)	9 fl. oz.	270 ml
Banana Twists (recipe follows)	6	6

1 Heat the Chocolate Soufflé Cakes in a 350°F (180°C) oven until warm, approximately 5 to 10 minutes.

2 For each serving, place nine Grand Marnier Flambé Banana disks in one layer in the center of a plate and place the warm Chocolate Soufflé Cake on top of them.

3 Place small piles of diced flambé bananas at 12, 3, 6 and 9 o'clock positions on the plate. Place a Candied Orange Peel on top of each pile of bananas.

4 Drizzle Burnt Blood-Orange Sauce between the piles of bananas. Garnish each plate with a Banana Twist.

Approximate values per serving: **Calories** 1080, **Total fat** 48 g, **Saturated fat** 24 g, **Cholesterol** 185 mg, **Sodium** 140 mg, **Total carbohydrates** 160 g, **Protein** 12 g, **Vitamin A** 20%, **Vitamin C** 40%, **Iron** 20%

CHOCOLATE SOUFFLÉ CAKE WITH PEANUT BUTTER HONEY CENTER

Yield: 6 Servings	**Method:** Creaming	
Peanut butter honey center:		
Peanut butter	3 oz.	90 g
Honey	2.25 oz. (3 Tbsp.)	70 g
Peanut oil	0.75 oz. (1 Tbsp.)	22 g
Chocolate soufflé cake:		
Pastry flour	4 oz.	120 g
Salt	pinch	pinch
Whole butter, softened	4 oz.	120 g
Egg yolks	2 oz. (3 yolks)	60 g
Dark chocolate, melted	9 oz.	270 g
Strong coffee	2 fl. oz.	60 ml
Vanilla extract	0.25 fl. oz. (1½ tsp.)	7.5 ml
Egg whites	3.5 oz. (3½ whites)	105 g
Granulated sugar	3.75 oz.	110 g

1 Combine the peanut butter, honey and peanut oil and mix well. Freeze the mixture overnight. Remove from the freezer, form the mixture into six balls and return them to the freezer.

2 Cream the flour, salt and butter. Blend in the egg yolks. Add the melted chocolate, then the coffee and vanilla.

3 Whip the egg whites to soft peaks, then add the sugar and continue whipping to medium-firm peaks. Fold the whites into the batter.

4 Grease six molds, approximately 2½ inches × 2½ inches (7 centimeters × 7 centimeters). Fill each mold halfway with soufflé batter. Add a frozen ball of the peanut butter mixture and then fill each mold to the top with soufflé batter. Bake at 350°F (180°C) until done, approximately 15 minutes. Chill and remove from the molds.

GRAND MARNIER FLAMBÉ BANANAS

Yield: 6 Servings

Bananas	3	3
Granulated sugar	2 oz.	60 g
Water	0.5 fl. oz.	15 ml
Whole butter	0.5 oz.	15 g
Half-and-half	2 fl. oz.	60 ml
Grand Marnier	2 fl. oz.	60 ml

1 Peel the bananas. Cut a total of 54 thin slices, then dice the remainder.

2 Combine the sugar and water. Bring to a boil and cook until it caramelizes. Add the butter and half-and-half and stir very carefully.

3 Add the sliced and diced bananas. Add the Grand Marnier and flambé. Remove from the heat and set aside.

CANDIED ORANGE PEEL

Yield: 24 Pieces

Water	1 pt.	0.5 lt
Granulated sugar	8 oz.	240 g
Oranges	as needed	as needed

1 Combine 8 fluid ounces (240 milliliters) of the water with the sugar in a small saucepan.

2 Bring the remaining water to a boil in a second small saucepan. Cut 24 strips of orange zest with a channel knife. Blanch the zest in the boiling water 30 seconds, drain and add the orange peel to the sugar mixture and simmer until the peel is translucent, approximately 15 minutes.

3 Remove the peel from the liquid and spread on a sheet pan to cool.

BURNT BLOOD-ORANGE SAUCE

Yield: 9 fl. oz. (270 ml)

Granulated sugar	4 oz.	120 g
Corn syrup	1.5 oz. (2 Tbsp.)	45 g
Water	0.5 fl. oz.	15 ml
Fresh lemon juice	0.04 fl. oz. (1/4 tsp.)	1 ml
Whole butter	1 oz.	30 g
Blood orange purée	3 oz.	90 g

1 Combine the sugar, corn syrup, water and lemon juice over low heat until the sugar is dissolved. Turn the heat to high and boil the mixture, occasionally brushing the sides of the pan with the liquid to prevent crystals from forming. Cook the sugar to a caramel stage.

2 Add the butter. Carefully add the blood orange purée. Stir until well combined and set aside to cool.

Approximate values per 1-fl.-oz. (30-ml) serving: **Calories** 80, **Total fat** 2.5 g, **Saturated fat** 1.5 g, **Cholesterol** 5 mg, **Sodium** 0 mg, **Total carbohydrates** 16 g, **Protein** 0 g

BANANA TWISTS

Banana, green-tip	1	1

1 Peel the banana. Slice the banana lengthwise in very thin slices using an electric slicer or mandoline. Place the slices on a sheet pan lined with a silicone mat or parchment paper and dry in a 200°F (90°C) oven 1½ to 2 hours.

2 While they are still warm, wrap the banana slices around a clean piece of PVC pipe and allow to cool.

RECIPE 20.6

PALMIERS WITH BAKED NECTARINES, PEACH SORBET AND CHAMPAGNE SABAYON

Yield: 6 Servings

Palmiers (page 337)	12 cookies	12 cookies
Peach Sorbet (page 488)	as needed	as needed
Warm Baked Nectarines (page 528)	6	6
Champagne Sabayon (page 438)	1 qt.	1 lt
Chocolate decorations (page 615)	as needed	as needed

1 Place a Palmier on the center of a plate. Place a scoop of Peach Sorbet in the center of the Palmier. Stand another Palmier upright behind the scoop of sorbet.

2 Split a Warm Baked Nectarine in half, then cut each piece in two. Arrange the cut slices of nectarine around the sorbet. Surround the dessert with Champagne Sabayon and garnish the plate with pieces of chocolate decorations.

Approximate values per serving: **Calories** 480, **Total fat** 26 g, **Saturated fat** 9 g, **Cholesterol** 120 mg, **Sodium** 65 mg, **Total carbohydrates** 54 g, **Protein** 11 g

RECIPE 20.7

VANILLA CHEESECAKE WITH SESAME SEED NOUGATINE, COCONUT SAUCE AND SORBET

Yield: 12 Servings

Individual Vanilla Cheesecakes (page 458)	12	12
Sesame Seed Nougatine (page 633), 2-in. (5-cm) disks	24 disks	24 disks
Tulipe Cookies (page 238), shaped into small cups	24 cups	24 cups
Raspberry Sorbet (page 488)	as needed	as needed
Mango Sorbet (page 474)	as needed	as needed
Coconut Sauce (page 374)	as needed	as needed

1 Place an Individual Vanilla Cheesecake onto a plate. Stand two Sesame Seed Nougatine disks upright next to the cheesecake.

2 Place two Tulipe Cookie cups next to the cheesecake, then fill one with a scoop of Raspberry Sorbet and the other with a scoop of Mango Sorbet.

3 Drizzle Coconut Sauce on the plate.

Approximate values per serving: **Calories** 430, **Total fat** 32 g, **Saturated fat** 19 g, **Cholesterol** 170 mg, **Sodium** 210 mg, **Total carbohydrates** 28 g, **Protein** 8 g, **Vitamin A** 25%

HOT LEMON SOUFFLÉ WITH RASPBERRY
SORBET SERVED IN TULIPE COOKIE BASKETS

RECIPE 20.8

Yield: 10 Servings

Hot Lemon Soufflé (page 460)	10 soufflés	10 soufflés
Tulipe Cookies (page 238), baked into cups	10 cups	10 cups
Raspberry Sorbet (page 488)	1 qt.	1 lt
Fresh mint leaves	as needed	as needed
Fresh raspberries	1 pt.	0.5 lt

1 Place a baked Hot Lemon Soufflé on a plate. Position a Tulipe Cookie cup next to the soufflé. Quickly place a scoop of Raspberry Sorbet in the cup. Decorate the sorbet with fresh mint leaves and fresh raspberries.

Approximate values per serving: **Calories** 230, **Total fat** 11 g, **Saturated fat** 6 g, **Cholesterol** 125 mg, **Sodium** 70 mg, **Total carbohydrates** 29 g, **Protein** 5 g, **Vitamin A** 10%, **Vitamin C** 20%

INDIVIDUAL BRANDIED CHERRY VACHERIN
WITH MINTED PEACH COULIS

RECIPE 20.9

Yield: 12 Servings

Common (French) Meringue (page 288), 1½-inch (4-cm) disks, baked	24 disks	24 disks
Brandied Cherry Ice Cream (page 473)	as needed	as needed
Minted Peach Coulis (page 372)	1½ pt.	750 ml
Basic Nougatine (page 633), crushed	as needed	as needed
Toasted almonds	as needed	as needed

1 Place 12 individual tart rings, approximately 2½ inches (6 centimeters) in diameter, on a paper-lined sheet pan.

2 Fit a baked Common (French) Meringue disk into each ring.

3 Spoon or pipe a small amount of Brandied Cherry Ice Cream into each ring. Place another meringue disk on top of the ice cream. Cover the meringue disk with the remaining ice cream, leveling it to the edge of the ring. Freeze until hard.

4 To serve, unmold a vacherin onto a serving plate. Surround it with Minted Peach Coulis. Sprinkle the top of the dessert with crushed Basic Nougatine or toasted almonds.

Approximate values per serving: **Calories** 480, **Total fat** 26 g, **Saturated fat** 9 g, **Cholesterol** 120 mg, **Sodium** 65 mg, **Total carbohydrates** 54 g, **Protein** 11 g, **Vitamin A** 25%

CHOCOLATE IS A PERFECT FOOD, AS WHOLESOME AS IT IS DELICIOUS, A BENEFICENT RESTORER OF EXHAUSTED POWER. IT IS THE BEST FRIEND OF THOSE ENGAGED IN LITERARY PURSUITS.

—*Baron Justus von Liebig, German chemist (1803–1873)*

CHOCOLATE AND DECORATIVE WORK

HOUSTON COMMUNITY COLLEGE, Houston, TX
Pastry Chef Eddy Van Damme

AFTER STUDYING THIS CHAPTER, YOU WILL BE ABLE TO:

▶ identify a variety of chocolate products

▶ understand the various procedures for tempering chocolate

▶ prepare simple and complex chocolate decorations and candies

▶ prepare marzipan and nougatine

▶ use spun sugar and other decorations

▶ **showpiece** decorative sculpture made from chocolate, sugar or other confections used as table displays and to demonstrate the skills of the pastry chef

Chocolate work, candy making and sugar confectionery are specialties within the baking industry. Entire books have been written about these products. The intention of this chapter is to provide a solid grounding in the most popular products. Many students are attracted to the culinary arts for the possibility of artistic expression. Products such as chocolate, marzipan and nougatine afford the pastry chef an opportunity to use delicious food products to sculpt and mold edible treats. With its enticing aroma, silken texture and complex taste, chocolate is a seductive ingredient, appealing to most everyone. In the right hands chocolate can be transformed into an artistic expression comparable to any piece of sculpture. While the procedures for handling chocolate may seem complex at first, many are easily mastered. Piping chocolate decorations and making truffles is well within the grasp of most pastry cooks.

This chapter covers chocolate as well as marzipan, nougatine (a type of sugar and nut confection) and simple sugar work used to make edible decorations. These techniques are the basis for more complex sugar work and crafting of chocolate and sugar **showpieces,** which is beyond the scope of this book.

▶ CHOCOLATE

Few need to be told of the myriad uses for chocolate in the bakeshop. Chocolate appears in everything from croissants and foamy puddings to cakes, frostings and candies. It flavors foods, enhances texture, holds moisture and helps build emulsions. And it tastes delicious.

CHOCOLATE PRODUCTION

Chocolate (Fr. *chocolat*) begins as yellow fruit pods dangling from the trunk and main branches of the tropical cacao tree. A native species of the Amazon rainforest, the cacao tree is found in the Caribbean, parts of Africa, Asia and Latin America. Each pod contains about 40 almond-sized cocoa beans. After the pods ripen, the beans are scooped out and placed in the sun for several days to dry and ferment. While time consuming, this process helps develop the aroma and essential oils in the beans. They are then cleaned, dried, cured and roasted to develop flavor and reduce bitterness. Next, the beans are crushed to remove their shells, yielding the prized chocolate **nib.**

Like coffee beans, chocolate beans are blended to the specifications of the chocolate manufacturer to obtain the desired flavor and aroma of their end product, a trade secret closely guarded unless the finest beans are used. Nibs are shipped to manufacturers worldwide where they can be further roasted.

They are crushed into a thick (nonalcoholic) paste known as **chocolate liquor** or **chocolate mass.** Chocolate mass contains about 53 percent fat, known as **cocoa butter.** The chocolate mass is further refined depending on the

Cocoa Beans

desired product. If **cocoa powder** is to be produced, virtually all the cocoa butter is removed. Adding more cocoa butter, sugar, milk solids and flavorings to the chocolate mass creates a variety of other products.

Most manufacturers of fine chocolates use the Swiss technique of **conching** to increase smoothness. Conching involves stirring large vats of blended chocolate with a heavy granite roller or paddle to smooth out sugar crystals and mellow the flavor, a process that may last from 12 hours to 3 days. The particle size of unconched chocolate is between 50 and 70 microns in size (one micron is 0.001 millimeter or 0.000039 inch). Fully conched chocolate has a particle size of 18 to 20 microns, resulting in a superior product. Once conched, chocolate is tempered, molded and wrapped for shipping and sale.

▶ **conching** stirring melted chocolate with large stone or metal rollers to create a smooth texture in the finished chocolate

TASTING CHOCOLATES

There are three types of cocoa beans: a very hardy, abundant African variety used as a base bean, and two flavorful, aromatic varieties used for flavor. Unlike wine or coffee, you cannot taste processed chocolate and tell which beans were used. Most chocolates are blends, created by their manufacturer to be unique yet consistent. Varietal chocolates, those made from one type of bean grown in one specific area, have become trendy, though expensive, for both chocolate bars and baking chocolates.

Roasting greatly affects the final flavor of chocolate. Generally, German and Spanish manufacturers use a high (or strong) roast; Swiss and American makers use a low (or mild) roast.

Refining is also a matter of national taste. Swiss and German chocolate are the smoothest, followed by English chocolates. American chocolate is noticeably grainier.

Chocolate quality is actually the product of several factors besides flavor. All these factors should be evaluated when selecting chocolates:

▶ Appearance—color should be even and glossy, without any discoloration.
▶ Smell—should be chocolatey with no off-odors or staleness.
▶ Break—should snap cleanly without crumbling.
▶ Texture—should melt quickly and evenly on the tongue.

TYPES OF CHOCOLATE

Unsweetened Chocolate
Unsweetened chocolate is pure hardened chocolate liquor without any added sugar or milk solids. It is frequently used in baking and is sometimes referred to as "baking chocolate." Unsweetened chocolate is approximately 53 percent cocoa butter and 47 percent cocoa solids. Its flavor is pure and chocolatey, but the absence of sugar makes it virtually inedible as is.

Bittersweet and Semisweet Chocolates
Both bittersweet and semisweet chocolates contain at least 35 percent chocolate liquor plus additional cocoa butter, sugar, flavorings and sometimes emulsifiers. Generally, semisweet chocolate will be sweeter than bittersweet chocolate, but there are no precise definitions, so flavor and sweetness will vary from brand to brand. Both are excellent eating chocolates and can usually be substituted measure for measure in any formula.

Couverture
Couverture (koo-vehr-TYOOR) refers to high-quality chocolate containing at least 32 percent cocoa butter. Professional chocolatiers generally prefer couverture chocolate, which has

Clockwise from lower left; semisweet chips, disks of chocolate liquor, block of bittersweet chocolate, block of milk chocolate, disks of white chocolate, alkalized cocoa powder

FROM CACAO TO CHOCOLATE CHIPS

To understand the history of chocolate, a chef or chocoholic must first understand the fundamental difference between its original use as a beverage and its later transformation into a candy.

The cacao tree (called *theobroma cacao*, meaning "food of the gods") originated in the river valleys of South America and was carried into what is now Mexico by the Mayans before the 7th century A.D. It was cultivated by Mayans, Aztecs and Toltecs not only as a source of food but also as currency. Chocolate was consumed only as a treasured drink. Cacao beans were roasted, crushed to a paste and steeped in water, then thickened with corn flour to create a cold, bitter beverage. Sometimes honey, vanilla or spices, including chiles, were added. The Aztec emperor Montezuma was so enamored with the beverage that he reportedly consumed 50 cups at each meal.

Columbus brought cacao beans to Spain from his fourth voyage to the New World in 1504. (The common term *cocoa* is actually a western European mispronunciation of the proper term *cacao*, caused by confusion with another New World delicacy, the coconut.) But almost 20 years passed before Spanish conquistadors, led by Cortez, understood the beans' value. With Montezuma's encouragement, Cortez and his soldiers slowly acquired a taste for the bitter beverage, spurred on by the intoxicating effects of caffeine.

Cortez's most important contribution to the history of chocolate was to take beans with him when he left Mexico. He planted them on the islands he passed on his return to Spain: Trinidad, Haiti and Fernando Po, from which the giant African cocoa industry grew. Through Cortez's farsighted efforts, Spain controlled all aspects of the cocoa trade until well into the 18th century.

The Spanish began drinking chocolate at home during the 16th century. It was usually mixed with two other expensive imports, sugar and vanilla, and frothed with a carved wooden swizzle stick known as a *molinet*. This thick, cold drink was made from tablets of crushed cocoa beans produced and sold by monks. The Spanish believed that cocoa cured all ills and supplied limitless stamina. In the early 17th century, cocoa beverages, now served hot, crept into France via royal marriages.

Cocoa spread through the rest of Europe by different routes. The Dutch, who had poached on Spanish trade routes for many years, eventually realized the value of the unusual beans they found on Spanish ships. Holland soon became the most important cocoa port outside of Spain. From there, a love of cocoa spread to Germany, Scandinavia and Italy. In 1655, England acquired Jamaica and its own cocoa plantations.

Until the Industrial Revolution, cocoa was made by hand using mortar and pestle or stone-grinding disks to crush the cocoa nibs. By the 1700s, cocoa factories had opened throughout Europe. James Baker opened the first cocoa factory in the United States in 1765.

Conrad van Houten, a Dutch chemist, patented "chocolate powder" in 1825. His work marked the beginning of a shift from drinking to eating chocolate. It also paved the way for everything we know as chocolate today. Van Houten developed a screw press that removed most of the cocoa butter from the bean, leaving a brown, flaky powder, essentially the same substance as modern cocoa powder.

Eventually, it was discovered that the extra cocoa butter resulting from the production of

Chocolate Chef, sculpted by Pastry Chef Rubin Foster

cocoa powder could be added to ground beans to make the paste more malleable, smoother and more tolerant of added sugar. The English firm of Fry and Sons introduced the first eating chocolate in 1847. Their recipe was the same then as today: crushed cocoa beans, cocoa butter and sugar.

In 1876, Swiss chocolatier Daniel Peter invented solid milk chocolate using the new condensed milk created by baby food manufacturer Henri Nestlé. Pennsylvania cocoa manufacturer Milton Hershey introduced his milk chocolate bars in 1894, followed by Hershey's Kisses in 1907. Nestlé Foods introduced the chocolate chip, perfect for cookies, in 1939.

a higher fluidity than other chocolates when melted. It is available in a range of flavors—bittersweet, semisweet and milk chocolate, for example. Couverture has a glossy appearance and can be used to create a thin, smooth coating on confections and pastries.

Sweet Chocolate

Government standards require that sweet chocolate contain not less than 15 percent chocolate liquor and varying amounts of sugar, milk solids, flavorings and emulsifiers. As the name implies, sweet chocolate is sweeter, and thus less chocolatey, than semisweet chocolate.

Milk Chocolate

The favorite eating chocolate in the United States is milk chocolate. It contains sugar, vanilla, perhaps other flavorings and, of course, milk solids. The milk solids that make the chocolate milder and sweeter than other chocolates also make it less suitable for baking purposes. Do not substitute milk chocolate for dark chocolate in any product that must be baked, as the milk solids tend to burn. If melted slowly and carefully, milk chocolate can be used in glazes, mousses or candies.

Chocolate Chips, Chunks and Pistoles

Chocolate chips are drops of chocolate available in count sizes from 14 to 160 per ounce (the average chips are 800 to 1000 per pound). They are easy additions to cookies, muffins and cakes. Like the larger chocolate chunks, chips are available in many flavors including white chocolate, butterscotch, peanut butter and other fruit flavors. Pistoles or calets are small round pieces of chocolate, often the finest couverture, designed to eliminate the need for chopping chocolate in the bakeshop, especially useful when tempering.

Chocolate Pistoles

Cocoa Powder

The brown powder left after the fat (cocoa butter) is removed from cocoa beans is known as cocoa powder. It does not contain any sweeteners or flavorings and is used primarily in baked goods. Alkalized or Dutch-processed cocoa powder has been treated with an alkaline solution, such as potassium carbonate, to raise the powder's pH from 5.5 to 7 or 8. Alkalized powder is darker and milder than nonalkalized powder and has a reduced tendency to lump. Either can be used in baked goods, however.

Dutch-Processed Cocoa Powder (left) and American-Style Non-Alkalized Cocoa Powder

Cocoa Butter

Chocolate liquor is approximately 53 percent fat, known as cocoa butter. Cocoa butter has long been prized for its resistance to rancidity and its use as a cosmetic. Cocoa butter has a very precise melting point, just below body temperature. Fine chocolatiers use high percentages of cocoa butter to give their chocolates melt-in-the-mouth quality.

White Chocolate

This ivory-colored substance is not the product of an albino cocoa bean. It is actually a confectionery product that does not contain any chocolate solids or liquor. (Thus it is usually labeled white confectionery or coating in the United States.) The finest white chocolate couverture contains a minimum of 31 percent cocoa butter, a maximum of 55 percent sugar, 20 percent milk solids and, vanilla or other flavors. Other products replace all or part of the cocoa butter with vegetable oils. These confectionery products will be less expensive than those containing pure cocoa butter, but their flavor and texture will be noticeably inferior. White chocolate melts at a lower temperature than dark chocolate and burns easily. It is excellent for mousses, sauces and candy making but is less often used in baked products.

Gianduja

Gianduja (jan-DOO-yah) is a blend of ground roasted hazelnuts and chocolate containing 25 to 38 percent cocoa mass, milk solids and sugar. Used in candy production, mousses and buttercreams, gianduja is a prized confection in Italy.

Imitation Chocolate or Chocolate-Flavored Coating

A less-expensive product substituted in many prepared foods, imitation chocolate is made with hydrogenated vegetable oils instead of cocoa butter, as little as 8 percent defatted cocoa powder and as much as 55 percent sugar, plus

MELTING CHOCOLATE

Two important rules for melting chocolate:

1　Chocolate must never exceed 120°F (49°C) or there will be a loss of flavor.
2　Water—even a drop in the form of steam—must never touch the chocolate.

When a droplet of water enters melted chocolate, the chocolate becomes lumpy (a process called *seizing*). There must be a minimum of 1/2 fluid ounce (15 millileters) of water per ounce (30 grams) of chocolate to keep this from happening. If seizing does occur, the addition of fat such as vegetable shortening, clarified butter, or cocoa butter will somewhat restore the chocolate to a workable condition.

For melting chocolate, unlined copper is the traditional "chocolate pot" because it is so responsive to changes in temperature. Aluminum or heatproof glass also works well. Ideally, chocolate should be heated to 120°F (49°C), the point at which all the different fat fractions in the cocoa butter are melted.

When melting chocolate or cocoa butter, temperatures exceeding 120°F (49°C) adversely affect the flavor. There are many acceptable methods for melting dark chocolate. If the heat source does not exceed 120°F (49°C) it is fine to add the dark chocolate in large pieces and leave it to melt unmonitored. When the heat source is capable of bringing the chocolate over 120°F (49°C), however, the chocolate should be finely chopped or grated to ensure uniformity of melting. The chocolate must be carefully watched and stirred to avoid overheating. If using a double boiler, water in the lower container should not exceed 140°F (60°C) and the upper container should not touch the water. The chocolate should be stirred constantly.

Milk chocolate and white chocolate must always be stirred frequently while melting because they contain milk solids that seed (lump) if left undisturbed.

Remove chocolate from the heat source when it reaches 115°F (46°C), as the temperature may continue to rise, and stir vigorously to prevent overheating and to distribute the cocoa butter evenly.

Always melt chocolate uncovered as moisture could condense on the lid, drop back into the chocolate, and cause seizing.

–from *The Cake Bible* by Rose Levy Beranbaum

emulsifiers, flavorings and perhaps milk solids. The resulting product melts at a higher temperature and requires no tempering. Imitation chocolates have an inferior taste and leave a waxy feel in the mouth, though when quality is no concern they may be used in most cases when chocolate is required. Products containing imitation chocolate should be labeled "chocolate flavored."

STORING CHOCOLATES

All chocolates should be stored at a cool, consistent temperature, away from strong odors and moisture. Dark chocolate, white chocolate and cocoa powder can be kept up to 1 year without loss of flavor. Milk chocolate will not keep as well because it contains milk solids.

TEMPERING CHOCOLATE

In order to create chocolate candies with a high gloss and a crisp sharp snap when eaten, chocolate must be tempered. **Tempering** chocolate is a controlled process of melting, cooling and reheating chocolate within set temperature ranges. (See Table 21.1) High cocoa butter chocolate such as couverture chocolate consists of fat molecules and solid crystals that, when heated above a certain temperature—approximately 90°F (32°C) for dark couverture chocolate and 87°F (30.5°C) for milk and white couverture—unchain and become unstable. Tempering the chocolate rechains these molecules and stabilizes the cocoa butter crystals, making the chocolate homogenous again. Chocolate melted for mousses, creams, ganache and baking requires no tempering. When chocolate is not tempered, it will be crumbly and streaked with gray and will not snap. It takes a long time to set and sticks to candy molds.

Several methods are used to temper chocolate manually—*seeding, tabling* and *microwave oven* methods. Each method relies on melting chocolate and heating it to a certain temperature, then cooling it. The chocolate must be chopped into small, uniform pieces so that it melts evenly. When melting chocolate, make certain that that chocolate bowl makes no contact with water to avoid overheating. Equally important, steam or water should not enter the chocolate because this would cause it to seize. When stirring chocolate during tempering, avoid incorporating excess air into the mass, which makes the chocolate thick and unmanageable. Reheating and retempering will restore the chocolate's fluidity.

Table 21.1 TEMPERATURE RANGES FOR TEMPERING CHOCOLATE

	MELT	COOL	TEMPER
Dark chocolate couverture	113–120°F (45–48°C)	78°F (25°C)	86–90°F (29–32°C)
Milk or white chocolate couverture	104–115°F (40–46°C)	78°F (25°C)	87°F (30.5°C)

The ideal room temperature when working with tempered chocolate is between 68°F and 72°F (20°C and 22°C) with low humidity. Always wear gloves when handling chocolate. Gloves are sanitary and keep chocolate from melting as quickly with body temperature.

For tempering, use only couverture chocolate or add more cocoa butter; chocolate with a low cocoa butter content, such as chocolate chips made for cookies, will not melt properly. Chocolate manufacturers recommend various temperatures best suited for tempering their blend of chocolate. Follow these temperatures even if they differ from those provided in this book.

Do not heat chocolate over 120°F (49°C) since it may cause the cocoa butter to break down and make proper tempering impossible. When one of the tempering techniques has been executed but the temperature of the couverture is above that of the tempered range, repeating the entire process is necessary.

SEEDING METHOD

Tempering chocolate using the seeding method requires tempered chocolate as it comes from the manufacturer. Two-thirds of the chocolate is melted either in the microwave or over a bain marie. When the melted portion reaches 118°F (48°C), the remaining chocolate is added and the chocolate is stirred until it melts. This is the seeding process. The crystals in the solid chocolate melt gently without unchaining, thus tempering the entire mass.

▶ PROCEDURE FOR TEMPERING CHOCOLATE BY SEEDING

Place two-thirds of the chopped couverture chocolate or pistoles to be tempered in a dry bowl. Melt the chocolate in a microwave or over barely simmering water. When the chocolate couverture is melted to 118°F (48°C) (115°F [46°C] for milk or white chocolate) remove from the heat and seed with the remaining one-third of the chocolate. Stir the mixture using a rubber spatula until lumps are dissolved. Or use an immersion blender, holding the blade  well under the melted chocolate. Check the temperature with an instant-read thermometer. The chocolate must stay below recommended temperatures; dark couverture chocolate needs to be below 90°F (32°C). Milk and white couverture chocolate needs to be below 87°F (30.5°C).

TABLING METHOD

The tabling method is the classic method, performed by the most experienced chocolatiers but one that requires practice to master. First the chocolate is melted, then a portion of the chocolate is poured onto a marble slab or cool sanitary surface. The pastry chef stirs the chocolate with a spatula, working it back and forth over the marble, performing the tabling process until it cools. Once the chocolate reaches the desired temperature, the tabled chocolate is heated to 86°F to 90°F (29°C to 32°C) for dark couverture chocolate. Milk and white couverture chocolate are reheated to 87°F (30.5°C). Chocolate tempered successfully by tabling retains its shine and crispness longer than with other methods.

When using this method to temper chocolate, wipe the outside of the bowl before pouring out the chocolate so that no water drips onto the marble. When reheating the chocolate after it has been tabled, its temperature will climb in seconds. If overheated, the chocolate will lose temper, requiring the process to be repeated.

▶ PROCEDURE FOR TEMPERING CHOCOLATE BY TABLING

1 Place the chopped couverture pieces in a dry stainless steel bowl over a pot of barely simmering water (bain marie). Melt the chocolate to approximately 120°F (49°C) for dark couverture chocolate, and 115°F (46°C) for milk or white couverture chocolate while constantly stirring with a rubber spatula. Pour two-thirds of the melted chocolate onto a clean, dry marble slab. Work the chocolate with a bench scraper or palette knife, scraping and turning the mass to cool it.

2 Work the chocolate until it reaches 78°F (25°C), using an instant-read thermometer to check the temperature. The chocolate will thicken as it is worked. Scrape the cooled chocolate back into the bowl of melted chocolate. Reheat it over the bain marie until the chocolate reaches 86°F to 90°F (29°C to 32°C) for dark couverture chocolate. Milk and white couverture chocolate are reheated to 87°F (30.5°C). Couverture will climb to this temperature in seconds; do not heat above recommended temperatures or the couverture will lose temper, requiring the process to be repeated.

MICROWAVE OVEN METHOD

Chocolate that has already been tempered may be melted in a microwave oven as long as the chocolate is not heated above temperatures that would unchain the fat molecules. Simply heat the chocolate using the lowest power setting, checking every 10 seconds so as not to exceed the maximum allowed temperatures. The chocolate is then ready for use. This is a simple, quick and hygienic method, but it may require some practice to determine the power range suitable for different microwave ovens. Chocolate tempered using this method may not hold its temper as long as chocolate tempered in other methods.

▶ PROCEDURE FOR TEMPERING CHOCOLATE IN A MICROWAVE
OVEN

1 Place the chopped chocolate in a dry bowl. Place the bowl in the microwave oven. Heat on medium 10 to 12 seconds. Remove the bowl from the microwave and gently stir the chocolate without incorporating any air bubbles into the chocolate. Repeat this process as needed until all pieces are melted.

2 Check the temperature of the melted chocolate to make certain it stays below 90°F (32°C) to hold its temper. Milk and white couverture chocolate needs to stay below 87°F (30.5°C).

HANDLING TEMPERED CHOCOLATE

Incorrectly tempered or improperly stored chocolate may develop a grayish white surface known as **bloom.** Two types of bloom can develop on chocolate. **Fat bloom** occurs when cocoa butter crystals rise and crystallize on the chocolate's surface. Chocolate stored above 70°F (21°C) will develop fat bloom over time. Since fat bloom has no effect on taste, tempering the product will remedy the problem. **Sugar bloom** occurs when moisture collects on the surface of the chocolate and blends with the sugar in the chocolate, leaving a white sugar film. The result is a gritty chocolate that cannot be improved by tempering. Chocolate should never be stored under refrigeration.

Cool melted chocolate in a room at 65°F (18°C). Cookies dipped in chocolate couverture and decorations made of chocolate couverture should cool and harden at this same temperature. Temperatures above 75°F (24°C) may slow the hardening process and cause the chocolate to bloom. Refrigerating the chocolates to harden will make the couverture softer and less crisp. Improperly wrapped chocolate stored under refrigeration causes sugar bloom. Store chocolate work in a cool dry place with low humidity below 70°F (21°C). A temperature range of 56°F–60°F (13°C–16°C) is ideal for storing all types of chocolate and chocolate candies.

Properly tempered chocolate, lower left, retains its shine. Improperly tempered chocolate, upper right, changes texture, blooms and loses its shine.

CHOCOLATE DECORATIONS

Tempered chocolate lends itself to being piped, shaped and formed into tempting decorations to garnish cakes, tarts, petits fours, ice creams and just about anything in the bake shop. Strips of tempered chocolate may also be used to cover cakes and tortes and to enhance plated desserts.

For most of these items, tempered chocolate is piped or spread with a palette knife over a marble slab or thin sheets of acetate. Once cooled, the pieces can

▶ **chocolate comb** utensil made from hard plastic or rubber with sharp teeth carved into one or more of its sides; used to create patterns in chocolate and icings

be stored for use as needed. Plastic **chocolate combs** (see page 618), some designed to create a marbleized effect, bubble wrap and silk screens, are useful tools to create textural effects with chocolate. Chocolate cutouts employ the most basic techniques and are recommended for beginners. Chocolate cigars, curls, shavings and fans require more practice but are simple once mastered. (For chocolate cigars, start using one type of couverture before attempting the two-toned version.) When chocolate sticks to the scraper, let it harden more on the marble before proceeding. If the chocolate flakes into pieces while being scraped off the marble, it has cooled too much. Try rubbing a gloved hand over the chocolate to warm it slightly. There is no waste when making chocolate decorations. Scraps and broken pieces of chocolate may be melted for use in brownies, ganache, icings and other items.

▶ PROCEDURE FOR PIPING CHOCOLATE DECORATIONS

Fill a parchment paper cone with melted chocolate. Snip the tip with a sharp knife. Pipe chocolate filigree patterns onto sheets of acetate or parchment paper.

▶ PROCEDURE FOR PIPING CHOCOLATE MESH

Fill a parchment paper cone with melted chocolate. Snip the tip with a sharp knife. Pipe freestyle patterns to make small or large pieces of chocolate mesh.

▶ PROCEDURE FOR MAKING CHOCOLATE LEAVES

1 Brush the underside of a clean, dry lemon leaf with tempered couverture. Place the leaf on a wire cooling rack and allow the chocolate to set.

2 Once the chocolate has set, peel off the lemon leaf.

▶ PROCEDURE FOR MAKING MARBLED CHOCOLATE CUTOUTS

1 In a bowl of tempered white couverture chocolate, randomly deposit small amounts of dark tempered couverture. Do not mix together. Pour a row of marbled chocolate onto a sheet of acetate.

2 As the white chocolate flows onto the acetate, the dark chocolate forms contrasting ribbons.

3 Spread the marbled chocolate with an offset spatula into a wide band approximately ¹⁄₁₆ inch (1 millimeter) thick. Pushing the chocolate enhances the marbleized effect.

4 Allow the marbled chocolate to set, just until the surface of the chocolate loses some of its gloss, then cut into desired shapes with a paring knife or circular cutter. Allow the chocolate to harden completely, then peel the pieces from the acetate.

▶ PROCEDURE FOR MAKING CHOCOLATE BOXES

1 Cut a clean sponge into 2-inch (5-centimeter) cubes. Cut 4-inch (10-centimeter) squares of plastic wrap. Place a sponge on a square of plastic and gather up the sides, twisting the top to completely enclose the sponge.

2 Dip the plastic-wrapped sponge three quarters of the way into tempered chocolate. Drain the excess chocolate, then place it onto a paper-lined sheet pan or silicone baking mat. Cool and dip again. When hardened, loosen the plastic and remove the sponge. Then peel the plastic off to reveal the chocolate box.

▶ PROCEDURE FOR MAKING CHOCOLATE CIGARETTES

Spread a thin layer of tempered couverture on a clean, dry marble slab. When the couverture has set slightly and the chocolate loses some of its gloss, position a metal dough scraper along one edge of the chocolate. Holding it at a 45-degree angle, push the scraper in a short motion, moving forward approximately 1 inch (2.5 centimeters) to produce uniform curls.

VARIATION:
Two-Toned Chocolate Cigarettes—Spread couverture over an acetate strip. Quickly comb the couverture into stripes. Scrape away excess couverture on the sides of the combed strip. Once the strips have set but have not hardened, cover with a thin layer of contrasting-color tempered couverture.

▶ PROCEDURE FOR MAKING TEMPERED CHOCOLATE SHAVINGS

1 Spread tempered couverture chocolate evenly on a marble slab. Allow to set slightly.

2 Using a metal dough scraper, scrape chocolate forward in a 90-degree angle with a quick motion. If chocolate smears on the scraper, wait a few seconds. If it flakes, it has cooled too much. Rub a gloved hand over the chocolate surface to slightly soften it.

▶ PROCEDURE FOR MAKING UNTEMPERED CHOCOLATE SHAVINGS

1 Select a new, totally flat sheet pan. Warm the sheet pan to 80°F (27°C) by placing it in a warm oven. Spread nontempered melted couverture chocolate on the back of the sheet pan.

2 Refrigerate the sheet pan until the couverture has hardened.

3 Remove from the refrigerator. Let the chocolate soften slightly. Hold a plastic scraper at a 90-degree angle to the sheet pan and scrape 1-inch (2.5-centimeter) curls from the pan.

4 Transfer the shavings directly onto the cake, tart or pastry. Serve as soon as possible, since the untempered chocolate will bloom under refrigeration.

▶ PROCEDURE FOR MAKING CHOCOLATE FANS

1 Combine 20 ounces (600 grams) tempered couverture with 2 fluid ounces (60 milliliters) peanut oil to make it spread easily and remain pliable when set.

2 Spread the chocolate on a marble slab. Allow it to cool slightly, just until the surface of the chocolate loses some of its gloss.

3 If right-handed, hold a metal scraper in your right hand at a 90-degree angle to the marble in front of chocolate.

4 Position the middle finger of your left hand on the lower left corner of the scraper, partially touching the chocolate. In a fast motion, scrape forward. The pressure of your left hand will help form the ruffles of chocolate. (Reverse directions if left-handed.)

5 Place fans immediately on cakes to decorate, or store them in an airtight container in a cool dry area below 70°F (21°C).

Scraping lightly cooled chocolate with a flat metal scraper to make chocolate fans.

▶ PROCEDURE FOR MAKING COMBED CHOCOLATE RIBBONS

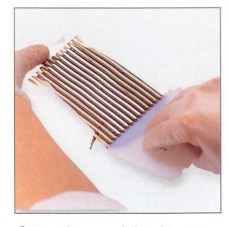

1 Spread tempered chocolate onto a 5-inch × 2-inch (13-centimeter × 5-centimeter) strip of acetate using an offset spatula. Run a chocolate comb over the acetate to form parallel lines in the band of chocolate.

2 Pipe a thin border of couverture across each end of the combed chocolate to keep the thin strips of chocolate connected once the chocolate hardens.

3 Roll a clean sheet of acetate to make a tube measuring 5 inches (13 centimeters) long with a 2-inch (5-centimeter) opening. Secure with adhesive tape. Carefully slide the chocolate-coated sheet of piped chocolate into the tube, twisting gently as it enters the tube. Place in a cool place until hardened and release by cutting the clear tape.

▶ PROCEDURE FOR MAKING CHOCOLATE TEARDROP RIBBONS

1 Spread tempered chocolate on a 5-inch × 2-inch (13-centimeter × 5-centimeter) strip of acetate. Comb to create lines in the chocolate. Fold the ends of the acetate together with the chocolate inside. Press the ends together and secure with adhesive tape. Place in a cool place until firm.

2 Remove the acetate from the chocolate ribbon, clockwise from upper right. Using a paring knife, separate the strips of chocolate and gently arrange the chocolate loops into a lacy bow.

SPRAYING CHOCOLATE

Pastry chefs find their tools in unlikely places, including the home improvement store. Mason's scrapers and trowels and bubble wrap become decorating tools for spreading icing or creating textured chocolate. One indispensable tool, the heavy-duty paint sprayer, is the secret to applying an elegant chocolate finish on a torte, frozen dessert or chocolate showpiece.

To prepare chocolate for spraying, melt an equal weight of semisweet or bittersweet chocolate and cocoa butter to 120°F (49°C) in a microwave or over a double boiler. The chocolate should be tempered for coating a chocolate showpiece, but tempering is not necessary when spraying tortes or frozen desserts. Pour the chocolate mixture into the clean canister of a new heavy-duty paint sprayer or one sold expressly for spraying chocolate.

Use the same precautions spraying chocolate as for spraying paint. Cover the workbench with parchment paper or silicone mats. Create an enclosed area in which to spray to minimize cleanup. Three sheet pans or three sheets of hard plastic standing upright on a workbench make an open-sided box in which to work. Place the torte or other item to be sprayed on a cake turntable inside the enclosed area created on the workbench. Hold the sprayer a minimum of 18 inches (45 centimeters) away from the torte. Rotate the turntable with one hand while moving the sprayer gently back and forth over the torte. Spray a thin layer of the chocolate over the entire surface one section at a time. To achieve a matte finish, freeze the torte a minimum of two hours and apply the chocolate when the torte is still frozen. Products that are oversprayed become shiny instead of matte. Chocolate is more forgiving than enamel; simply freeze and spray the object again.

CHOCOLATE CANDIES

Without a doubt, chocolates are one of the most luxurious items created by the pastry chef. Fillings may be based on buttercream, marzipan, ganache, fondant, liqueur or a combination. Chocolate candies are divided into two categories based on the way they are made: dipped or molded.

Dipped chocolates are made when firm candy centers such as pieces of marzipan, caramel or firm ganache are cut or piped into bite-size pieces and dipped into tempered chocolate. **Molded** chocolates are made when solid plastic or metal molds are coated with chocolate, filled, then sealed with more chocolate. Because the molds hold the chocolate's shape, molded chocolates can be filled with soft creams, mousses, even liqueur syrups.

In general, chocolates made with fresh cream and butter have a shorter shelf life than chocolates made with marzipan, fondant or liqueur. Glucose helps extend the keeping quality of a cream or butter filling; however, not every preparation allows this ingredient.

DIPPED CHOCOLATES

Fillings for dipped chocolates, also known as **centers,** may be fruit jellies, marzipan, firm ganache or nut clusters. Fillings may be poured or spread on silicone baking mats or wax paper. Metal bars called **candy rulers** contain the filling while it sets, then the fillings are cut to size with a knife or a wire cutting device.

The centers are dipped when sufficiently set. Ideally, the temperature of the centers is near 70°F (21°C) for dipping. Specialized dipping forks with two or more long thin prongs may be used to remove the dipped chocolates from the coating. Softer fillings may be piped onto disks of chocolate, marzipan or nougatine before dipping. The dipping fork is inserted into the disk, not the gooey center, making dipping easier. The forks are also used to create patterns on the chocolates after dipping. Ring-shaped dipping spoons help hold round candies like truffles when dipping (see the photograph on page 620).

Chocolates can be garnished using nuts, gold leaf or coffee beans; decorated or streaked with chocolate, candies or violets; imprinted with a dipping fork; and decorated with silk-screened designs. The procedure for dipping chocolates is illustrated by Dark Chocolate Truffles (page 620).

Chocolate Truffles

Chocolate truffles take their name from the rough, black, highly prized fungus they resemble, but there the similarity ends. Chocolate truffles should have a rich, creamy ganache center with a well-balanced, refined flavor.

▶ **centers** the firm or soft filling for chocolate candies

▶ **candy rulers** steel or aluminum bars of varying lengths and thicknesses used to contain fillings for candies; the metal bars may also be used to roll a pastry to a uniform thickness

To prepare chocolate truffles a firm ganache is flavored as desired, then piped or allowed to harden. Once firm, the ganache is rolled in cocoa powder, confectioner's sugar or melted chocolate. The classic French truffle is a small, irregularly shaped ball of bittersweet chocolate dusted with cocoa powder. Americans, however, seem to prefer larger candies, coated with melted chocolate and decorated with nuts or additional chocolate, toasted sliced almonds, chocolate shavings or candied citrus peel. The following formula can be prepared in either style.

RECIPE 21.1

DARK CHOCOLATE TRUFFLES

Yield: 150 Medium-Sized Truffles, 4 lb. 4 oz. (2040 g)

Dark chocolate	2 lb.	960 g
Unsalted butter	1 lb.	480 g
Heavy cream	1 pt.	480 ml
Brandy, bourbon or liqueur	4 fl. oz.	120 ml

1 Chop the chocolate and butter into small pieces and place in a large metal bowl.
2 Bring the cream to a boil. Immediately pour the hot cream over the chocolate and butter. Stir until the chocolate and butter are completely melted.
3 Stir in the brandy. Pour the ganache into a flat, shallow, ungreased pan and chill until firm.
4 Shape the ganache into rough balls using a melon ball cutter. Immediately drop each ball into a pan of sifted cocoa powder or confectioner's sugar, rolling it around to coat completely.
5 Truffles can be stored in the refrigerator 7 to 10 days. Allow them to soften slightly at room temperature before serving.

Approximate values per truffle: **Calories** 70, **Total fat** 6 g, **Saturated fat** 3.5 g, **Cholesterol** 10 mg, **Sodium** 0 mg, **Total carbohydrates** 4 g, **Protein** 0 g

1 Shaping chocolate truffles with a melon ball scoop and coating with cocoa powder.

2 Alternatively, chocolate truffles may be dipped into tempered chocolate using a dipping spoon.

3 After dipping in tempered chocolate, truffles may also be coated with chopped toasted nuts.

MOLDING CHOCOLATES

Chocolate lends itself to being molded into small candies or larger, three-dimensional pieces. Chocolates are molded in several stages. A thin layer of chocolate is built up in the mold by filling it with melted chocolate, then pouring out the excess. This is repeated a second time, then the molds are chilled—the **first cooling.** Fillings are poured or piped into the chilled shells then they are sealed with a thin layer of tempered chocolate. The **second cooling** is the stage when the finished chocolates are chilled before unmolding.

Chocolate molds come in a wide range of designs, sizes and materials. Those made from a polycarbonate material are preferred because they are easy to use and provide superior chocolate sheen. Tin molds rust easily and generally produce less glossy chocolates. Hobbyists usually work with molds made of thin, flexible plastic.

Before using, new or soiled molds are washed in warm water no higher than 120°F (49°C) with a mild unscented detergent. Buffing with cotton balls is usually sufficient to remove any chocolate residue that remains, so molds are not washed after each use. An abrasive is never used to clean chocolate molds, as this would scratch the delicate surface and mar the finished chocolates.

Accurate temperatures and properly prepared molds are needed to ensure success when making molded chocolates. The melted chocolate should be held at the recommended temperatures (see page 611) throughout the molding process. The temperature of the fillings should not exceed 70°F (21°C) to prevent melting the chocolate shells. The molds should also be held at the proper temperatures to ensure successful molding—70°F (21°C) for polycarbonate molds, 78°F (25°C) for metal molds.

When molding chocolates, a large quantity of melted, tempered chocolate is necessary to coat the insides of the shells completely. Not all of the chocolate specified in each formula will be used to make the batch of molded chocolate. Excess can be reserved for use in other bakeshop items or for reuse once it is retempered. The amount of molded candies each batch produces varies according to the size and depth of molds used. Each formula in this book is calculated using either the molds in the procedural photographs or those in the chapter opening photograph on page 605. Overfilled chocolate shells will be impossible to close neatly. Remove excess filling with a spoon or the suction from a clean squeeze bottle.

▶ PROCEDURE FOR MOLDING CHOCOLATES

1 Ladle tempered chocolate onto the mold. Spread the chocolate over the surface of the mold with an offset spatula, filling each cavity. Tap the mold on the table a few times to remove any air bubbles.

2 Turn the mold upside down, then tap the sides of the mold with a rubber hammer or a spatula to remove the excess chocolate. The coating should be no thicker than 1/16 inch (1 millimeter).

3 Invert the mold and scrape the excess couverture from its surface with a metal spatula. Place the mold, chocolate side up, on a paper-lined sheet pan and cool it in a low-humidity refrigerator at 50° F (10° C). Leave the molds in the refrigerator only until the chocolate shells loosen.

4 Remove the molds from the refrigerator. Using a pastry bag fitted with a small plain tip, carefully pipe the filling into the shells to just within 1/16 inch (1 millimeter) of the rim.

5 Cover the filled shells with tempered couverture melted to its highest allowed temperature.

6 Scrape excess chocolate from the surface of the mold with an offset spatula.

7 After the chocolate has hardened and the shells have shrunk slightly from the sides of their molds, the chocolates are ready for unmolding. Firmly tap a corner of the mold on the table to loosen the chocolates, then invert the mold.

NOBLE (RASPBERRY GANACHE CHOCOLATES)

RECIPE 21.2

Yield: Ganache for 48 Candies, 1 lb. 11 oz. (825 g) Ganache

Method: Molded

Raspberry purée	10 oz.	300 g
Glucose or corn syrup	2 oz.	60 g
Semisweet couverture chocolate, chopped fine	10 oz.	300 g
Raspberry liquor	1.5 fl. oz.	45 ml
Natural raspberry compound (optional)	0.5 oz.	30 g
Trimoline or honey	1 oz.	30 g
Unsalted butter, room temperature	2 oz.	60 g
Semisweet or bittersweet couverture for coating molds	3 lb.	1440 g

▶ **trimoline** invert sugar syrup used commercially to prevent crystallization in candies and fondant fillings

1 Boil the raspberry purée and glucose or corn syrup in a nonreactive saucepan over medium-high heat.

2 Remove from the heat. Add the purée to the chopped chocolate in five increments, stirring between each addition to create an emulsion.

3 Add the liquor and raspberry compound (if using), then the trimoline or honey and the butter. Let cool to 70°F (21°C).

4 Coat the molds using tempered semisweet or bittersweet couverture. Allow the chocolate-filled molds to sit in the refrigerator until the shells shrink from the sides of the molds.

5 Fill the molds with the cooled ganache to within $1/16$ inch (1 millimeter) from the top. When the filling is sufficiently firm, cover with tempered couverture. Chill, then unmold.

Approximate values per candy: **Calories** 80, **Total fat** 4.5 g, **Saturated fat** 3 g, **Cholesterol** 5 mg, **Sodium** 0 mg, **Total carbohydrates** 11 g, **Protein** 1 g

Hollow Chocolate Figure Molding

Three-dimensional chocolate figures are made in two-sided molds with either a closed or an open bottom. In a **closed-bottom mold,** there are two separate molds, one a mirror image of the other. Each mold is filled, then chilled until the chocolate pieces are unmolded. The finished three-dimensional candy is made when two matching pieces are attached together. Closed-bottom chocolate molding is illustrated by the white chocolate dolphins shown on page 624. **Open-bottom molds** are two mirror-image molds hinged or attached together with clips. The molds are coated inside, then closed or clipped together. When the chocolate sets and contracts from the molds, the clips and sides are removed to reveal the completed three-dimensional piece.

As with all tempered chocolate work, a room temperature of 68°F (20°C) with low humidity is recommended. Having the molds at the proper temperature provides consistent results. Chilling molded chocolates in a room or refrigerator at 52°F (11°C) helps the chocolate set and unmold quickly.

▶ PROCEDURE FOR CLOSED-BOTTOM CHOCOLATE MOLDING

1 Pipe or brush areas of the mold requiring highlighting with tinted tempered couverture chocolate.

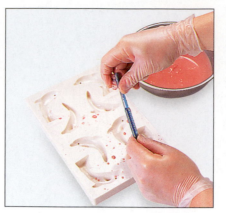

2 Speckle additional details into the mold with tinted chocolate.

3 Fill the mold with tempered white chocolate couverture. Scrape excess chocolate from the surface of the mold before allowing it to harden.

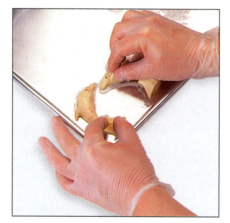

4 Once the chocolates are unmolded, slightly soften the flat sides of each piece by placing them on a sheet tray that has been warmed in a hot oven.

5 Press two matching chocolate pieces together to form the three-dimensional dolphin-shaped candy.

▶ PROCEDURE FOR MOLDING A CHOCOLATE BOWL

1 With gloved hands, rub the inside of a bowl-shaped mold with tinted white chocolate. Ladle tempered white chocolate couverture into the mold. Tilt the mold to evenly coat it with the chocolate. Scrape excess couverture from the surface of the mold and place in a cool place until the chocolate hardens and shrinks from the sides of the mold.

2 Rap the side of the mold on a table to loosen the chocolate. Unmold the white chocolate bowl once it sets to reveal its patterned surface.

MODELING CHOCOLATE

Modeling chocolate is a type of edible modeling clay used for making cake decorations. Made from melted chocolate, sugar syrup and invert sugar such as glucose or corn syrup, modeling chocolate has a smoother texture than marzipan, making it ideal for delicate work. Lifelike chocolate roses are made by tinting white modeling chocolate pink, then sandwiching it between two layers of white modeling chocolate. This creates a delicate mottled material. Modeling chocolate is also used to add small details to chocolate showpieces. Modeling chocolate keeps 6 months when wrapped tightly in plastic and stored in the refrigerator.

▶ PROCEDURE FOR MAKING MODELING CHOCOLATE

1 Have all ingredients at room temperature.
2 Melt dark or white chocolate couverture in a microwave or over a bain marie until it reaches 90°F (32°C).
3 Heat simple syrup to 180°F (82°C) and combine it with glucose or corn syrup.
4 Stir the syrup mixture into the melted chocolate. Add coloring (if using).
5 Cool the mixture at room temperature several hours.
6 Knead the mixture thoroughly until well blended. If the cocoa butter separates from the mass, chill the modeling chocolate before kneading.
7 Let the modeling chocolate rest, wrapped in plastic and stored in the refrigerator overnight before using to make it easier to handle.

Dark and White Modeling Chocolate

RECIPE 21.3

DARK MODELING CHOCOLATE

Yield: 1 lb. 8 oz. (720 g)

Bittersweet chocolate (50 to 56% cocoa butter)	1 lb.	480 g
Simple Syrup (page 349)	3 fl. oz.	90 ml
Glucose or corn syrup	5 oz.	150 g

1 Finely chop the chocolate and melt to 90°F (32°C).

2 Heat the Simple Syrup to 180°F (82°C) and combine it with the glucose or corn syrup.

3 Stir the syrup mixture into the melted chocolate.

4 Let cool at room temperature a few hours.

5 Knead the mass until well blended and elastic. Wrap the modeling chocolate in plastic wrap and store in the refrigerator before using.

Approximate values per ¹/₂-oz. (15-g) serving: **Calories** 60, **Total fat** 25 g, **Saturated fat** 1.5 g, **Cholesterol** 0 mg, **Sodium** 0 mg, **Total carbohydrates** 9 g, **Protein** 1 g

RECIPE 21.4

WHITE MODELING CHOCOLATE

Yield: 4 lb. (1920 g)

Cocoa butter	8 oz.	240 g
Powdered sugar, sifted	1 lb. 8 oz.	720 g
Fondant, room temperature	1 lb.	480 g
Glucose or corn syrup	1 lb.	480 g

1 Melt the cocoa butter over a double boiler until it reaches 90°F (32°C).

2 Place the powdered sugar, fondant and glucose or corn syrup in the bowl of a mixer fitted with a paddle. Add the melted cocoa butter and mix on low speed until well combined, approximately 5 to 7 minutes.

3 If the cocoa butter separates from the mixture during mixing, let it cool 15 to 30 minutes and mix again. Wrap the modeling chocolate in plastic wrap and store in the refrigerator before using.

Approximate values per ¹/₂-oz. (15-g) serving: **Calories** 60, **Total fat** 2 g, **Saturated fat** 1 g, **Cholesterol** 0 mg, **Sodium** 5 mg, **Total carbohydrates** 11 g, **Protein** 0 g

▶ PROCEDURE FOR MAKING MODELING CHOCOLATE ROSES AND LEAVES

1 Divide the white modeling chocolate into three uniform pieces. Tint one section with pink food coloring, kneading it to distribute the color evenly. Dust a worktable lightly with powdered sugar and roll out each piece of modeling chocolate into an 8-inch × 10-inch (20-centimeter × 25-centimeter) block. Stack the three layers so that the layer of pink modeling chocolate is sandwiched between the two white layers.

2 Flatten the modeling chocolate with a rolling pin to ¹/₁₆ inch (1 millimeter) thick. Cut 2-inch (5-centimeter) circles out of the dough with a cookie cutter and place them on a sheet of heavy-gauge plastic spaced 2 inches (5 centimeters) apart. Cover the circles with another sheet of heavy-gauge plastic. Thin the upper edges of the discs evenly using a flexible metal spatula to make realistic rose petals.

3 Roll a scrap of the dough into a 2-inch- (5-centimeter-) tall cone with a narrow tip. Wrap a petal completely around the cone with the upper edge of the petal flush with the top of the cone. Attach another petal around the cone, positioning it at the exact height of the center tip. Fold part of the petal back. Attach the next petal, overlapping the previous petal by approximately ¹/₄ inch (6 millimeters). Continue adding petals until the desired size rose is obtained. Cut excess dough from the bottom with scissors.

4 Flatten additional white modeling chocolate with a rolling pin until it is ¹/₈ inch (3 millimeters) thick. Cut the modeling chocolate into leaf shapes using a small paring knife. Use the back of a knife or modeling tools to indent veins in the leaves. Drape the leaves over a dowel or rolling pin to obtain a curved shape and let dry overnight.

5 Attach the leaves to the finished rose with simple syrup.

▶ MARZIPAN

Marzipan is a mixture of almond paste, sugar and glucose or corn syrup that may be colored and used like modeling clay for sculpting small fruits, flowers or other objects. Because of its plasticity, marzipan can also be rolled out and cut into various shapes or used to cover cakes and pastries. It is widely used as an ingredient in chocolate candies and petits fours.

The best-quality marzipan is made from equal parts by weight of fresh almonds and sugar by weight, with liquid sugar for pliability. With their high fat content (50 percent), almonds need sugar to bring out their delicate flavor. A higher amount of sugar creates a sweeter marzipan that may be more difficult to handle. Quality marzipan is ivory in color, subtle in almond flavor, short textured, not sticky and should hold its shape when modeled.

Make the paste in a stainless steel bowl rather than aluminum to prevent discoloration. Wrap marzipan tightly in plastic and then place it in a thick black plastic bag. Proper wrapping keeps the paste from drying out; opaque or black plastic prevents fading from exposure to light. Properly prepared and stored marzipan retains optimum freshness 2 to 3 months.

Marzipan exposed to air will form a crust; therefore, only the amount needed should be removed from the plastic bag. To cover tortes, wedding cakes and pastries the paste is rolled to approximately ⅛ inch (3 millimeters) thick. Special rolling pins are available to create various patterns on the marzipan sheet. Powdered sugar is used to prevent the marzipan from sticking, as flour may ferment marzipan and cannot be used.

RECIPE 21.5

MARZIPAN

Yield: 2 lb. 4 oz. (1080 g)

Almond paste	1 lb.	480 g
Glucose or corn syrup	4 oz.	120 g
Powdered sugar, sifted	1 lb.	480 g

1 In the stainless steel bowl of a mixer fitted with a paddle, blend the almond paste and glucose on low speed until well combined.

2 Continuing on low speed, gradually add just enough of the powdered sugar to make a pliable paste that is not oily. Wrap the marzipan tightly in plastic and store in a dry place until ready to use.

Approximate values per ½-oz. (15-g) serving: **Calories** 60, **Total fat** 2 g, **Saturated fat** 0 g, **Cholesterol** 0 mg, **Sodium** 0 mg, **Total carbohydrates** 10 g, **Protein** 1 g

MARZIPAN MODELING

Marzipan is the perfect medium for making edible decorations. Children's birthday cakes enchant when topped with whimsical animals and balloons. When tinted orange, marzipan can be rolled into Lilliputian carrots used to mark individual portions of carrot cake. When modeling marzipan, color the paste with liquid food coloring before modeling. The marzipan may also be hand-painted or sprayed with edible food coloring after it has been shaped. For either method, water-soluble colors are used. Light brown shades are obtained by adding coffee extract, chocolate tones with cocoa powder. (Sugar syrup might be needed to compensate for the cocoa drying action.) Marzipan roses may be made according to the instructions on page 626 for modeling chocolate roses. All-white roses accented with gold leaf combined with green tinted leaves make a dramatic and elegant combination.

Assortment of
Marzipan Fruit

For marzipan production, uniformity and fine detail is the hallmark of good craftsmanship. **Serial work** refers to modeling identical pieces of molded candies such as marzipan. To create a series of figures of identical weight, calculate the total weight of marzipan to be used. For example, if 10 pears each weighing 1 ounce (30 grams) are needed, scale 10 ounces (300 grams) of marzipan. Tint the paste, if desired, then roll the marzipan into a cylinder measuring 10 inches (25 centimeters) long. Cut the cylinder into 1-inch (2.5-centimeter) segments to obtain 10 pieces of marzipan of identical size and weight. Use this technique to prepare each part of a multipart marzipan figure such as the Happy Pig (page 630) and Hunter the Dog (page 631).

Sugar syrup is used to attach separate pieces of marzipan together to make a complete figure. (Even though egg whites work equally well for assembling, the safety of this practice is questionable.) The basic marzipan figure is based on a pear shape to which other pieces are attached to form details such as leaves for fruits and arms, legs, ears and other features for animal shapes. Additional details are made from melted chocolate, royal icing, dried fruit or other edible decoration.

Proper placement of decorative details makes the difference between an appealing marzipan sculpture and a dull one. When making animal figures, eyes are one of the most important features. The eye indentions should be sufficiently deep to allow for a good amount of royal icing. Eyes should be flush with the face and not bulging too much. Tempered chocolate may be used to add eye details. Placing the pupils of the eyes off to one side, on the left or right or looking up make a lively figure. Place the eyes, ears, nose and mouth relatively close together to create a young and appealing figure.

A light spray with cocoa butter once the figures are finished slows the drying process. It also protects colored marzipan from fading and provides an attractive luster. Cocoa butter may be melted to 90°F (32°C), placed in a pressure sprayer and applied to the figure or brushed on. **Edible food lacquer** may be sparingly used to provide extra shine. Marzipan figures may be made several months ahead and stored in an airtight container in a cool place before serving.

▶ PROCEDURE FOR MAKING MARZIPAN FIGURES

1 Determine the number of finished pieces required.

2 Scale the marzipan. Tint the marzipan if necessary. Then roll and divide the pieces evenly according to the amount needed for each part, if necessary.

3 Shape the different pieces required for the marzipan figure. Attach the pieces together if necessary, using sugar syrup as the glue. Allow the pieces to set approximately 30 minutes.

4 Apply decorative details using marzipan sculpting tools or a small knife.

5 Paint or airbrush colors on the finished pieces. Add decorative details such as royal icing eyes. Spray or brush the finished pieces with cocoa butter or edible food lacquer.

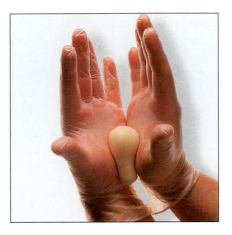

Rolling marzipan into a basic pear shape.

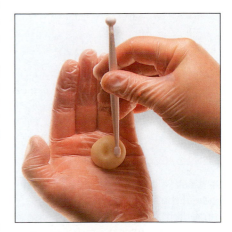

Indenting the marzipan with a sculpting tool to form the eyes for a marzipan figure.

▶ **edible food lacquer** a composition of fats, lecithin and other edible ingredients used to create a shine on marzipan and other confections

RECIPE 21.6

MARZIPAN PEAR

Yield: 1 Pear Figure

| Marzipan | 0.5 oz. | 15 g |

1 Form the marzipan into a round ball. Roll one end of the ball between your palms to form a pear shape.
2 Airbrush or paint color onto the surface of the marzipan.
3 Attach the pear to a disk of marzipan using sugar syrup.
4 Cut out a leaf shape from tinted marzipan. Attach it to the pear using a marzipan modeling tool or wooden skewer.

Approximate values per ½-oz. (15-g) serving: **Calories** 60, **Total fat** 2 g, **Saturated fat** 0 g, **Cholesterol** 0 mg, **Sodium** 0 mg, **Total carbohydrates** 10 g, **Protein** 1 g

Form the marzipan into a smooth ball (left foreground). Taper the marzipan into a pear shape (center foreground). Indent the tip of the figure with a sculpting tool. Insert a stem and leaf (right) into the marzipan pear. Airbrush or paint the finished pear with food coloring. The finished marzipan pears are shown at the top.

RECIPE 21.7

HAPPY PIG

Start with a ball of marzipan. Form the body of the figure and its two legs (upper left). Going counterclockwise: attach two front legs; attach ears onto the head, which has been sculpted with details; two views of the finished pig after it has been airbrushed with color.

Yield: 1 Pig Figure

Marzipan	5 ounces	150 grams
Simple Syrup (page 349)	as needed	as needed
Liquid food coloring	as needed	as needed
Cocoa butter	as needed	as needed
Royal Icing (page 361)	as needed	as needed
Chocolate, melted	as needed	as needed
Chocolate cutouts (page 615)	as needed	as needed

1 For the body, roll 2½ ounces (75 grams) of the marzipan into a ball. Form an oval shape with two blunt ends by rolling the marzipan between gloved palms. Curve the marzipan so that the extensions form the hind legs. Cut a slit into one end of each piece to form the hooves.
2 For the front legs, divide ⅓ ounce (10 grams) of the marzipan into two equal pieces. Roll each piece into tubes ½ inch (1.2 centimeters) long. Indent one end of each rope with a knife or marzipan tool to indicate the hooves. Attach the marzipan to each side of the figure to form the front legs.
3 Roll 1½ ounces (45 grams) marzipan into a pear shape. Flatten the narrow end of the pear shape on the work surface to create a pig snout. Indent two holes for the nose and make a small cut for the mouth. Make indentions for the eyes. Attach the head to the body with a small amount of Simple Syrup.

4 For the ears, divide ⅓ ounce (10 grams) of the marzipan in half. Roll each piece of the marzipan into a small ball, then taper the marzipan into a cone 1 inch (2.5 centimeters) in length. Flatten the cones slightly, then attach them to the head, bending the tips down toward the eyes.

5 For the tail, roll a small amount of marzipan into a thin rope, tapered slightly at the end. Curl and attach it to the body.

6 Airbrush details onto the pig with red food color. Spray the finished figure with cocoa butter. Fill a pastry bag with a small plain tip with Royal Icing. Fill the indentations for the eyes with royal icing. Use a toothpick dipped in melted chocolate to add details to the eyes.

7 Place the finished marzipan pig on a chocolate cutout.

Approximate values per ½-oz. (15-g) serving: **Calories** 60, **Total fat** 2 g, **Saturated fat** 0 g, **Cholesterol** 0 mg, **Sodium** 0 mg, **Total carbohydrates** 10 g, **Protein** 1 g

HUNTER THE DOG

RECIPE 21.8

Yield: 1 Dog Figure

Marzipan	4 ounces	120 grams
Simple Syrup (page 349)	as needed	as needed
Cocoa butter	as needed	as needed
Royal Icing (page 361)	as needed	as needed
Chocolate, melted	as needed	as needed

1 For the body, roll 1⅔ ounces (50 grams) of the marzipan into a ball. Taper the ball into a pear shape by rolling the marzipan between gloved hands.

2 Roll ⅓ ounce (10 grams) of the marzipan into a 3-inch- (7.5-centimeter-) long rope. Cut the rope in half, then curve each piece to form the hind legs. Attach each piece of marzipan to the sides of the body with Simple Syrup. Use a modeling tool or toothpick to indent the marzipan to resemble the paws.

3 Roll ⅓ ounce (10 grams) of the marzipan into a 2-inch- (5-centimeter-) long rope. Curve the marzipan rope and place it on the front of the figure to form the front legs.

4 For the tail, roll a small amount of the marzipan into a seamless ball. Taper the marzipan into a pear shape, then attach the narrow end under the figure.

5 For the head, roll 1 ounce (30 grams) of the marzipan into a smooth ball. Taper it into a blunt pear shape. Curve the tapered end slightly to form a turned-up nose. Indent the eyes and mouth with a modeling tool or toothpick. Attach the head to the body of the figure with Simple Syrup.

6 For the ears, divide ⅓ ounce (10 grams) of the marzipan into two equal pieces. Roll into balls. Taper one end to make the pear shape and flatten the tapered end. Attach the marzipan to each side of the head of the figure.

7 Spray the finished figure with cocoa butter. Fill a pastry bag with a small plain tip with Royal Icing. Fill the indentations for the eyes and snout with Royal Icing. Use a toothpick dipped in melted chocolate to add details to the eyes.

Start with a ball of marzipan (center left); roll into a cone for the body (left). Roll small pieces of marzipan to form the rear and front legs (lower left). Form another piece of marzipan into a pear shape for the head (foreground). Use a modeling tool to indent the cone to make the eye and nose. Attach the cone to the marzipan body (right). Pipe Royal Icing to add decorative details. Two views of the finished marzipan figure are shown at the top.

Approximate values per ½-oz. (15-g) serving: **Calories** 60, **Total fat** 2 g, **Saturated fat** 0 g, **Cholesterol** 0 mg, **Sodium** 0 mg, **Total carbohydrates** 10 g, **Protein** 1 g

▶ NOUGATINE

Nougatine is a blend of melted caramelized sugar, sliced toasted almonds and butter. (Closely related is **nougat** candy, the same composition to which egg whites are added.) Nougatine is used as an ingredient in petits fours, chocolates, creams and mousses. When still warm, nougatine is pliable and may be formed into edible dessert containers. Croquembouche is often displayed on an elaborate nougatine showpiece. Unlike other sugar decorations, such as pastillage or gum paste, nougat remains deliciously edible.

Like all nut brittle and sugar candies, nougatine softens under humid conditions. Using cocoa butter in the formula helps it resist stickiness. Specialty ingredients used by pastry chefs can be used to help nougatine stay crisp longer and resist crystallization. **Powdered glucose** may be substituted for 10 percent of the sugar in the formula for this purpose. In all cases, nougatine should be stored in well-sealed containers. A **drying agent** such as **silica gel** may be placed in the storage container, especially under humid conditions or when storing the product for more than 1 week. Edible food lacquer, sold by specialty vendors, sprayed on the pieces will help them resist weeping.

As with other types of sugar work, oiled parchment paper or silicone baking mats are recommended. Oil all tools and work surfaces to be used when making nougatine. A constant warm temperature makes rolling, cutting and shaping nougatine easier; working over a heated surface such as a flat-top stove is recommended. Otherwise, work near a warm oven on a silicone mat or an oiled marble slab. Pieces of nougatine may be assembled into simple or elaborate showpieces. Attach the pieces together using caramel sugar (page 352) or nougatine made without the nuts. Nougatine formulas are versatile and may be made by replacing all or some of the almonds with sliced toasted hazelnuts, walnuts, cocoa nibs, coffee beans or toasted sesame seeds.

▶ PROCEDURE FOR MAKING NOUGATINE

1 Oil all cooking surfaces, tools, knives, rolling pins and molds with vegetable oil.

2 Melt the sugars, corn syrup, fondant and glucose in a pot, preferably copper, over medium heat.

3 Cook the syrup until caramelized, approximately 320°F to 330°F (160°C to 166°C). Remove from the heat.

4 Carefully stir in the nuts or other ingredients, then the fat.

5 Pour the mass onto a silicone baking mat, oiled marble or oiled parchment paper. Let cool slightly.

6 Roll the mass to the desired thickness. Cut into desired shapes and form immediately. Should it harden before cutting, reheat nougatine in a warm oven, 275°F (135°C).

7 Store nougatine away from heat and humidity. Excess scraps may be reused or ground for a crunchy topping or an addition to mousses, chocolates or a frozen dessert known as **nougat glacé.**

▶ **nougat** a candy made from caramelized sugar, almonds and egg whites known as *turrón* in Spain and *torrone* in Italy

▶ **powdered glucose** the dried form of glucose syrup.

▶ **drying agent** any of several products used to remove humidity from the air, particularly useful when storing sugar work, nougatine and other dry cookies, which soften under moist conditions; packets of drying agents are placed in storage containers for such confections; reusable envelopes of silica gel are sold for this purpose

SAFETY ALERT

Caramelizing sugar can cause serious burns. Use rubber gloves and take proper precautions to avoid hot sugar coming into direct contact with your skin.

▶ **nougat glacé** a still-frozen dessert composed of whipped cream, Italian meringue, chopped nougatine and candied fruits

BASIC NOUGATINE

This formula stands up to humidity and is recommended for those working in a humid environment.

Yield: 3 lb. 8 oz. (1680 g)

Glucose or corn syrup	14 oz.	420 g
Fondant	1 lb. 3 oz.	570 g
Almonds, sliced, toasted and warm	1 lb. 5 oz.	630 g
Unsalted butter or cocoa butter	2 oz.	60 g

1 Over medium-high heat, bring the glucose or corn syrup to a boil in a heavy saucepan without stirring.

2 Add the fondant and let it dissolve without stirring. Cook until the syrup turns a golden amber color, approximately 320°F to 330°F (160°C to 166°C).

3 Remove from the heat. Quickly add the almonds, then stir in the butter or cocoa butter.

4 Pour the cooked nougatine out on a silicone baking mat or a lightly oiled marble slab. Wait a few moments before rolling the nougatine to prevent it from sticking to the rolling pin.

5 Roll the mixture to approximately $1/16$ inch (1 millimeter) thick for most uses, slightly thicker for showpieces.

6 If the nougatine hardens before the required thickness is reached, place it on a silicone mat or lightly oiled sheet pan and reheat in a 275°F (135°C) oven. Nougatine rolled to $1/8$-inch (3-millimeter) thickness will take approximately 8 to 10 minutes to soften. Reheat the nougatine anytime during the cutting or shaping process.

7 When the nougatine is rolled evenly thin, quickly flip the baking mat, nougatine side down, onto a sheet of parchment. (Or lift the nougatine with a spatula and flip onto the paper.) Immediately cut into shapes and press into molds.

8 Leftover nougatine scraps can be stored in an airtight container. Scraps can be reheated and reworked at a later time. Slightly overlap the pieces on a paper-lined sheet pan and place in a 300°F (150°C) oven. Remove the warm nougatine and roll to form a uniform sheet.

Approximate values per 1-oz. (30-g) serving: **Calories** 100, **Total fat** 40 g, **Saturated fat** 1 g, **Cholesterol** 0 mg, **Sodium** 15 mg, **Total carbohydrates** 15 g, **Protein** 1 g

VARIATIONS:

Hazelnut or Walnut Nougatine—Increase the fondant to 1 pound 6 ounces (660 grams). Substitute 1 pound 5 ounces (630 grams) finely chopped, hot toasted hazelnuts or walnuts for the almonds.

Cocoa Nougatine—Reduce the glucose or corn syrup to 7 ounces (210 grams). Reduce the fondant to 11 ounces (330 grams). Replace the almonds with 8 ounces (240 grams) cocoa nibs and $1/2$ ounce (15 grams) cocoa powder. Cook the glucose or corn syrup and fondant until it reaches an amber caramel, then add the cocoa nibs and cocoa powder. Reduce butter or cocoa butter to 1 ounce (30 grams) and stir it into the nougatine.

Sesame Seed Nougatine—Reduce the glucose or corn syrup to 7 ounces (210 grams). Reduce the fondant to 11 ounces (330 grams) Substitute 10 ounces (300 grams) hot, toasted sesame seeds for the almonds. Reduce butter or cocoa butter to 1 ounce (30 grams).

Coffee Nougatine—Increase the fondant to 1 pound 6 ounces (660 grams). Reduce the almonds to 8 ounces (240 grams). Add 8 ounces (240 grams) finely chopped toasted hazelnuts, 4 ounces (120 grams) hot toasted sesame seeds, and 1 ounce (30 grams) instant coffee to the mixture along with the hot almonds once it caramelizes.

▶ DECORATIVE SUGAR WORK

Sugar can be used to create a number of doughs, pastes and syrups used for artistic and decorative work. **Spun sugar** is long, fine, hairlike threads of sugar made by flicking a hot concentrated sugar syrup rapidly across dowels. Mounds or wreaths of these threads are used to decorate ice cream desserts, croquembouche and gâteaux.

Making spun sugar is a messy process. The workstation used to prepare spun sugar should be covered with paper to catch sugar that flies around in the process. Some chefs will cut the curved ends from a whisk to make a tool for spinning sugar, although a pair of forks may be used instead. Use Decorating Caramel (page 352) to make spun sugar. Remove the pan from the heat and stop the cooking process by immersing the bottom of the pan in cool water for a few seconds. Should the caramel harden, reheat it by placing it over low heat. These fragile threads absorb moisture and soften easily, so they are best used the same day they are made, stored in an airtight container until needed.

Spun Sugar Threads

▶ PROCEDURE FOR MAKING SPUN SUGAR

1 Lightly oil two 18-inch (45-centimeter) wooden dowels or wooden-handled spoons. Place them spaced 12 inches (30 centimeters) apart on a clean worktable so that they extend off the edge of the table approximately 12 inches (30 centimeters). Line a few sheet pans with paper and place them under the dowels to catch drips.

2 Prepare a batch of Decorating Caramel (page 352).

3 To make the gossamer threads, dip a whisk approximately 3 inches (7.5 centimeters) into the caramel. With a quick flick of the wrist, shake the whisk back and forth over the ends of the dowels. Repeat the process until a mass of threads collects on the dowels.

4 Collect the threads and coil into a nest or other shape. Use to garnish ice cream, cakes or other desserts.

ADVANCED PÂTISSERIE

Although formulas and preparation methods are beyond the scope of this book, it is important that all pastry cooks be able to recognize and identify certain decorative sugar products. Mastering even some of these products takes years of experience and practice.

Blown sugar—a boiled mixture of sucrose, glucose and tartaric acid that is colored and shaped (in a manner very similar to glass blowing) using an air pump. It is used for making pieces of fruit and containers such as bowls and vases.

Gum paste—a smooth dough made of sugar and gelatin; it dries relatively slowly, becoming very firm and hard. The paste can be colored and rolled out, cut and shaped, or molded. It is used for making flowers, leaves and small figures.

Pastillage—a paste made with sugar, cornstarch and gelatin. It can be rolled into sheets, then cut into shapes. It dries in a very firm and sturdy form, like plaster. Naturally pure white, it can be painted with cocoa or food colorings. Pastillage is used for showpieces and large decorative items.

Pulled sugar—a doughlike mixture of sucrose, glucose and tartaric acid that is colored, then shaped by hand. Pulled sugar is used for making birds, flowers, leaves, bows and other items.

CONVENIENCE PRODUCTS

In many food service establishments, space, staffing and time do not permit making chocolates and decorative sugar confections on site. Because chocolate confectionery is such a specialized craft, many high-quality chocolate products are available to fill this need. Prepared chocolate shells come in many forms, from miniature tart shells to unusual molded containers such as miniature swans, pianos and even tiny ovens designed to be filled with fruit, creams or mousses. Hollow molded chocolate shells used to make truffles and other chocolate candies are sold. They come in disposable plastic trays, handy for filling with a signature ganache or other soft center. Chocolate decorations come in various shapes—fans, swirls, circles, triangles and many more, some with designs stenciled on their surface. When purchasing prepared chocolate products, select those made from the highest-quality chocolate, with the highest percentage of cocoa butter and solids and the lowest amount of hydrogenated fat and artificial flavorings. As with all tempered chocolate products, these prepared items require careful storage in a cool dry place.

White or dark chocolate modeling paste made with cocoa powder, cocoa butter and other fats, emulsifiers, milk powder and flavorings is available. Piping chocolate, formulated so it resists blooming, makes decorating cakes with chocolate feasible when tempering chocolate might be difficult. Ganache is available in 5-pound (2.5 kilo) tubs, a shelf-stable product that may contain hydrogenated fats in place of natural dairy ingredients such as cream or butter. Such products are used to make candy centers and may be customized with the addition of fruit compounds, liqueurs or other flavorings.

Nougatine powder to which water is added is available for making nougatine cups, disks and decorations. Premade nougatine cups and plates on which to serve ice cream or sorbets are also available. Specialty ingredient catalogs are full of simple and elaborate decorations made from marzipan and sugar. Marzipan plaques on which a greeting may be piped, figures made from colored royal icing and ready-made sculpted marzipan fruit are a few of the many items that may be purchased. Such convenience products allow the pastry chef the freedom to spend more time creating desserts; however, no amount of elaborate garnish will compensate for a poorly executed creation.

CONCLUSION

Like a silk scarf or elegant tie, the decorative items discussed in this chapter finish off a dessert, adding a touch of drama, whimsy or elegance. Chocolate confectionery offers many opportunities for the pastry chef to enhance a dessert menu. Many of the specialized skills necessary to create chocolate candies and sugar decorations take years to master. However, this should not deter the student from the satisfaction of making many of the products covered in this chapter. Chocolate truffles, modeling chocolate and marzipan roses and figures are fun to make and might inspire a student to pursue a career in candy making and chocolate confectionery.

QUESTIONS FOR DISCUSSION

1 What are the basic types of chocolates and their common uses in the pastry kitchen?

2 Why must couverture chocolate be tempered? When is it not necessary to temper chocolate?

3 Discuss the three methods for tempering couverture and discuss the precautions that must be taken when preparing the chocolate.

4 Imagine that you have been asked to prepare a celebration cake for a special event. Describe the type of event and the ways you might use decorative marzipan, nougatine and other items in this chapter to create an appropriate motif.

RECIPE 21.10

HAVANA (MILK CHOCOLATE AND RUM GANACHE CHOCOLATES)

Yield: Ganache for 56 Candies, 1 lb. 13 oz. (885 g) Ganache

Method: Molded

Milk chocolate, chopped fine	8 oz.	240 g
Semisweet couverture, chopped fine	5 oz.	150 g
Heavy cream	8 fl. oz.	240 ml
Glucose or corn syrup	6 oz.	180 g
Coffee extract	0.5 fl. oz.	15 ml
Jamaican rum	1 fl. oz.	30 ml
Tahitian vanilla extract	1 fl. oz.	30 ml
Semisweet or bittersweet couverture, tempered for coating molds	3 lb.	1440 g

1 Combine the chopped chocolate and chopped couverture and melt to 90°F (32°C). Set aside.

2 Boil the heavy cream. Remove from the heat and whisk in the glucose or corn syrup until thoroughly combined.

3 Add the cream to the melted chocolate in five increments, stirring with a rubber spatula after each addition. Add the coffee extract, rum and vanilla.

4 Let cool to 70°F (21°C).

5 Coat the molds with the tempered couverture and give the chocolate the first cooling.

6 Fill the molds with the ganache to within $1/16$ inch (1 millimeter) of the top. When the ganache has set sufficiently, cover it with tempered couverture to seal.

7 Chill the chocolates in a cool area until set, then unmold.

Approximate values per candy: **Calories** 100, **Total fat** 6 g, **Saturated fat** 3.5 g, **Cholesterol** 5 mg, **Sodium** 10 mg, **Total carbohydrates** 11 g, **Protein** 1 g

RECIPE 21.11

FAUN (HAZELNUT GANACHE CHOCOLATES)

Yield: Ganache for 56 Candies, 1 lb. 9 oz. (750 g) Ganache

Method: Molded

Gianduja	12 oz.	360 g
Hazelnut paste	13 oz.	390 g
Bittersweet couverture, tempered for coating molds	3 lb.	1440 g

1 Melt the gianduja to 110°F (43°C).

2 Remove from the heat and stir in the hazelnut paste. Let cool to 72°F (22°C).

3 Coat the molds with the tempered couverture and give the chocolate the first cooling.

4 Fill the molds with the ganache to within ¹/₁₆ inch (2 millimeters) of the top. When the ganache has set sufficiently, cover it with tempered couverture to seal.

5 Chill the chocolates in a cool area until set, then unmold.

Approximate values per candy: **Calories** 100, **Total fat** 7 g, **Saturated fat** 2.5 g, **Cholesterol** 0 mg, **Sodium** 0 mg, **Total carbohydrates** 10 g, **Protein** 1 g

CEYLON (MILK CHOCOLATE AND CINNAMON GANACHE CHOCOLATES)

RECIPE 21.12

Yield: Ganache for 56 Candies, 1 lb. 9 oz. (765 g) Ganache

Method: Molded

Milk chocolate couverture, chopped fine	8 oz.	240 g
Bittersweet couverture, chopped fine	5 oz.	150 g
Heavy cream	9 fl. oz.	270 ml
Ceylon cinnamon sticks, crushed	0.5 oz.	15 g
Glucose or corn syrup	3 oz.	90 ml
Milk chocolate couverture, tempered for coating molds	3 lb.	1440 g

1 Combine the chopped chocolates in a large bowl. Set aside.

2 Bring the cream and cinnamon to a boil. Remove from the heat, cover with plastic film and infuse 20 minutes.

3 Strain the cream and discard the cinnamon. Add the glucose or corn syrup and return to a boil.

4 Add the cream to the chopped chocolate in five increments, stirring after each addition with a rubber spatula to form an emulsion.

5 Let the cinnamon ganache cool to 70°F (21°C).

6 Coat the molds with the tempered couverture and give the chocolate the first cooling.

7 Fill the molds with the ganache to within ¹/₁₆ inch (1 millimeter) of the top. When the ganache has set sufficiently, cover it with tempered couverture to seal. Chill the chocolates in a cool area until set, then unmold.

Approximate values per candy: **Calories** 90, **Total fat** 6 g, **Saturated fat** 4 g, **Cholesterol** 10 mg, **Sodium** 10 mg, **Total carbohydrates** 10 g, **Protein** 1 g

RECIPE 21.13

PONA (ORANGE CREAM–FILLED CHOCOLATES)

Yield: Filling for 48 Candies, 1 lb. 11 oz. (810 g) Filling   **Method:** Molded

Fondant	1 lb. 6 oz.	660 g
Orange marmalade	4 oz.	120 g
Grand Marnier or other orange liqueur	1 fl. oz.	30 ml
Semisweet or bittersweet couverture, tempered for coating molds	3 lb.	1440 g

1 In the bowl of a mixer fitted with a paddle, combine the fondant, marmalade and liqueur.

2 Coat the molds with the tempered couverture, and give the chocolate the first cooling.

3 While the chocolate cools, warm the fondant mixture in a bain marie over simmering water to 80°F (25°C). Fill the molds with the fondant mixture to within $1/16$ inch (1 millimeter) from the top.

4 When the filling has lightly crusted over, after approximately 10 minutes, cover it with tempered couverture. Chill the chocolates in a cool area until set, then unmold.

Approximate values per candy: **Calories** 90, **Total fat** 25 g, **Saturated fat** 1.5 g, **Cholesterol** 0 mg, **Sodium** 5 mg, **Total carbohydrates** 17 g, **Protein** 1 g

RECIPE 21.14

CARAVELLE (MARZIPAN, RASPBERRY AND HAZELNUT CHOCOLATES)

Yield: Filling for 48 Candies, 1 lb. 12 oz. (480 g) Filling

Method: Molded

Marzipan (page 628)	10 oz.	300 g
Fondant	4 oz.	120 g
Raspberry compound	1 oz.	30 g
Raspberry liqueur	1 fl. oz.	30 ml
Hazelnuts, toasted	48	48
Semisweet or bittersweet couverture, tempered for coating molds	3 lb.	1440 g

1 Combine the marzipan, fondant and raspberry compound in the bowl of a mixer fitted with a paddle and mix until the mixture is lump-free.

2 Gradually add the raspberry liqueur.

3 Coat the molds with the tempered couverture and give the chocolate the first cooling.

4 Fill the molds with a small amount of filling and place a toasted hazelnut in each mold.

5 Pipe the remaining filling to within $1/16$ inch (1 millimeter) from the top. Cover the filling with tempered couverture. Chill the chocolates in a cool area until set, then unmold.

Approximate values per candy: **Calories** 80, **Total fat** 3 g, **Saturated fat** 1.5 g, **Cholesterol** 0 mg, **Sodium** 0 mg, **Total carbohydrates** 12 g, **Protein** 1 g

PASSION (WHITE CHOCOLATE AND PASSION FRUIT GANACHE CHOCOLATES)

RECIPE 21.15

Yield: Ganache for 56 Candies, 1 lb. 11 oz. (795 g) Ganache

Method: Molded

Granulated sugar	4 oz.	120 g
Passion fruit purée, warm	8 fl. oz.	240 ml
Heavy cream	2 fl. oz.	60 ml
Vanilla bean, split	1/2	1/2
White chocolate, chopped fine	11 oz.	330 g
Unsalted butter	1.5 oz.	45 g
Semisweet or bittersweet couverture, tempered for coating molds	3 lb.	1440 g

1 Cook the sugar in a heavy saucepan over medium-high heat stirring constantly until it forms a golden caramel.

2 Add the passion fruit purée and cream to the caramel. Bring the mixture to a boil, then remove it from the heat.

3 Stir the vanilla bean into the cream with a whisk. Infuse the cream with the vanilla bean 5 minutes, then remove the bean.

4 Add the caramel cream to the chopped white chocolate in five increments, stirring well after each addition. Add the butter, then let the ganache cool to 70°F (21°C).

5 Coat the molds with the tempered couverture and give the chocolate the first cooling.

6 Fill the molds with the cooled ganache to within 1/16 inch (1 millimeter) from the top.

7 When the filling has sufficiently firmed, cover it with tempered couverture. Chill the chocolates in a cool area until set, then unmold.

Approximate values per candy: **Calories** 90, **Total fat** 5 g, **Saturated fat** 3 g, **Cholesterol** 5 mg, **Sodium** 5 mg, **Total carbohydrates** 11 g, **Protein** 1 g

SEVILLE (MILK CHOCOLATE, HAZELNUT AND ORANGE GANACHE CHOCOLATES)

RECIPE 21.16

Yield: Ganache for 56 Candies, 1 lb. 13 oz. (870 g) Ganache

Method: Molded

Milk chocolate couverture, chopped fine	10 oz.	300 g
Cocoa butter or additional milk chocolate, chopped fine	2 oz.	60 g
Heavy cream	10 fl. oz.	300 ml
Hazelnut paste	3 oz.	90 g
Candied orange peel, chopped fine	3 oz.	90 g
Grand Marnier or orange liqueur	1 fl. oz.	30 ml
Semisweet couverture, tempered for coating molds	3 lb.	1440 g

1 Combine the chopped chocolate and cocoa butter (if using) in a large bowl. Set aside.
2 Boil the cream. Add it to the chocolate mixture in five increments, stirring with a rubber spatula after each addition.
3 Stir in the hazelnut paste, candied orange peel and liqueur.
4 Coat the molds with the tempered couverture and give the chocolate the first cooling.
5 Fill the molds with the ganache to within $1/16$ inch (1 millimeter) from the top.
6 When the filling has sufficiently set, cover it with tempered couverture to seal. Chill the chocolates in a cool area until set, then unmold.

Approximate values per candy: **Calories** 100, **Total fat** 7 g, **Saturated fat** 4 g, **Cholesterol** 10 mg, **Sodium** 5 mg, **Total carbohydrates** 10 g, **Protein** 1 g

BAHO (GINGER, LIME AND CARAMEL CREAM–FILLED CHOCOLATES)

RECIPE 21.17

Yield: Filling for 56 Candies, 1 lb. 11 oz. (825 g) Filling

Method: Molded

Heavy cream	7 fl. oz.	210 ml
Ginger, chopped fine	2 oz.	60 g
Lime zest, grated	0.2 oz. (1 Tbsp.)	6 g
Granulated sugar	10 oz.	300 g
Unsalted butter	4.5 oz.	135 g
Glucose or corn syrup	4 oz.	120 g
Chocolate couverture, tempered for coating molds	3 lb.	1440 g

1 Boil the cream in a nonreactive saucepan. Add the ginger and lime zest, and infuse the cream 20 minutes, then strain. Discard the ginger and zest and keep the cream warm.
2 Stir the sugar over medium-high heat in a large saucepan using a whisk until a golden caramel is obtained. Remove the caramel from the heat and add the butter.

3 Slowly pour the infused cream into the caramel, whisking constantly. Bring the cream back to a boil and cook stirring constantly until no lumps of caramel remain.

4 Remove from the heat and add the glucose or corn syrup. Cool the filling to 70°F (21°C) before molding the chocolates.

5 Coat the molds with the tempered couverture.

6 Pipe the filling to within $1/16$ inch (1 millimeter) from the edge.

7 Carefully cover the filling with tempered couverture to seal. Chill the chocolates in a cool area until set, then unmold.

Approximate values per candy: **Calories** 90, **Total fat** 5 g, **Saturated fat** 3.5 g, **Cholesterol** 10 mg, **Sodium** 5 mg, **Total carbohydrates** 11 g, **Protein** 0 g

SAMBA (ANISE GANACHE
AND NOUGATINE CHOCOLATES)

RECIPE 21.18

Yield: Filling for 70 Candies, 1 lb. 13 oz. (892 g) Filling   **Method:** Dipped

Heavy cream	9 fl. oz.	270 ml
Glucose or corn syrup	1.5 oz.	45 g
Anise seeds, chopped fine	0.25 oz. (4 tsp.)	7.5 g
Semisweet couverture, chopped fine	1 lb. 2 oz.	540 g
Sambuca or anise liqueur	1 fl. oz.	30 ml
Basic Nougatine (page 633), baked into disks $1/16$ inch (1 millimeter) thick and $3/4$ inch (1.8 centimeters) in diameter	70 disks	70 disks
Bittersweet couverture, tempered for dipping	3 lb.	1440 g

1 Boil the cream and glucose or corn syrup in a nonreactive saucepan. Remove from the heat and add the anise seeds. Cover with plastic film and steep 20 minutes.

2 Strain the mixture and discard the seeds.

3 Melt the chopped couverture until half of the mass is melted.

4 Reheat the infused cream to 180°F (82°C) and pour into the half-melted chocolate. Whisk until thoroughly combined.

5 Let the ganache cool to 80°F (26°C) and add the liqueur.

6 When the mixture starts to set, pipe $1/3$-ounce (10-gram) spheres of ganache onto silicone mats or wax paper.

7 Place a nougatine disk flat on the center of each piped sphere.

8 When the chocolates have set, dip in the tempered couverture.

Approximate values per candy: **Calories** 100, **Total fat** 7 g, **Saturated fat** 4 g, **Cholesterol** 5 mg, **Sodium** 5 mg, **Total carbohydrates** 12 g, **Protein** 1 g

VIONI (MILK CHOCOLATE AND VANILLA SQUARES)

Yield: Approximately 144 Candies, 1 in. (2.5 cm) each   **Method:** Dipped

Milk chocolate couverture, chopped fine	1 lb. 4 oz.	600 g
Glucose or corn syrup	1 oz.	30 g
Granulated sugar	10 oz.	300 g
Heavy cream	7 fl. oz.	210 ml
Vanilla bean, split	1	1
Unsalted butter, room temperature	2 oz.	60 g
Milk chocolate couverture, tempered for dipping	3 lb.	1440 g

1 Place the chopped couverture in a large bowl. Set aside.

2 In a nonreactive saucepan, bring the glucose or corn syrup to a boil. Add the sugar gradually and stir until it reaches an amber caramel.

3 While the sugar cooks, boil the cream with the vanilla bean and whisk to release the seeds.

4 Deglaze the caramel with the boiling cream. Bring the mixture to a full boil and remove from the heat. Discard the vanilla bean.

5 Add the caramel cream to the chopped couverture in five increments, stirring after each addition with a rubber spatula to form an emulsion. Add the butter.

6 Pour the ganache into a candy frame or between candy rulers spaced to form a 12-inch (30-centimeter) square $\frac{1}{2}$ inch (1.2 centimeters) thick. Let the ganache set.

7 Spread a very thin layer of tempered couverture over the ganache.

8 Cut the ganache into 1-inch (2.5-centimeter) squares.

9 Dip in tempered couverture and imprint a diagonal line using a dipping fork.

Approximate values per candy: **Calories** 100, **Total fat** 4.5 g, **Saturated fat** 1.5 g, **Cholesterol** 0 mg, **Sodium** 5 mg, **Total carbohydrates** 16 g, **Protein** 1 g

IRISH CREAM (CHOCOLATE GANACHE, COFFEE AND WHISKEY SQUARES)

Yield: Approximately 144 Candies, 1 in. (2.5 cm) each   **Method:** Dipped

Milk chocolate couverture, chopped fine	1 lb.	480 g
Semisweet couverture, chopped fine	2 oz.	60 g
Heavy cream	8 fl. oz.	240 ml
Coffee extract	0.3 fl. oz.	10 ml
Whiskey	4 fl. oz.	120 ml
Trimoline or honey	0.5 oz.	15 g
Chocolate couverture, tempered	as needed	as needed
Milk chocolate couverture, tempered for dipping	3 lb.	1440 g

1 Combine the chopped couvertures in a large mixing bowl. Set aside.

2 Boil the cream. Add it to the chopped couverture in five increments, stirring with a rubber spatula after each addition to form an emulsion.

3 Stir in the coffee extract, whiskey and trimoline or honey.

4 Pour the chocolate ganache into a candy frame or between candy rulers spaced to form a 12-inch (30-centimeter) square a thickness of ¹/₂ inch (1.2 centimeters). Let the ganache set.

5 Spread a very thin layer of tempered couverture over the ganache. Once the chocolate sets, cut the candy into 1-inch (2.5-centimeter) squares.

6 Coat the individual chocolates with tempered milk chocolate couverture and imprint 3 lines using a dipping fork.

Approximate values per candy: **Calories** 45, **Total fat** 2.5 g, **Saturated fat** 1.5 g, **Cholesterol** 5 mg, **Sodium** 0 mg, **Total carbohydrates** 4 g, **Protein** 0 g

ROCHERS (CARAMEL, ALMOND AND ORANGE CHOCOLATES)

RECIPE 21.21

Yield: 70 Candies		**Method:** Dipped
Slivered almonds	1 lb.	480 g
Granulated sugar	4 oz.	120 g
Water	2 fl. oz.	60 ml
Vanilla bean, split	¹/₂	¹/₂
Milk chocolate couverture, chopped fine	11 oz.	330 g
Candied Orange Peel (page 601), fine dice	4 oz.	120 g

1 Toast the almonds to light golden brown. Set aside.

2 Boil the sugar and water to 240°F (116°C). Remove from the heat. Scrape the vanilla bean into the syrup. Add the toasted almonds. Stir the mixture until the sugar crystallizes on the almonds.

3 Pour one-third of the crystallized almonds into a sauté pan and stir over medium heat until the sugar coating caramelizes. Spread them on a silicone baking mat or oiled parchment paper. Separate the almonds using an oiled fork. Repeat with the remaining almonds. Let cool.

4 Temper the milk chocolate couverture and mix in the caramelized almonds and Candied Orange Peel.

5 Using two spoons, shape the mixture into uniform mounds and place the chocolates on a silicone baking mat or paper-lined sheet pan. Let the chocolates harden before storing.

Approximate values per ¹/₂-oz. (15-g) candy: **Calories** 70, **Total fat** 4.5 g, **Saturated fat** 1 g, **Cholesterol** 0 mg, **Sodium** 5 mg, **Total carbohydrates** 7 g, **Protein** 2 g

RECIPE 21.22

HAZELNUT CRISPS

Yield: 7 oz. (210 g)

Milk chocolate, chopped	1 oz.	30 g
Cocoa butter, chopped fine	1 oz.	30 g
Unsalted butter	0.5 oz.	15 g
Hazelnut paste	3 oz.	90 g
Puffed rice cereal	1.5 oz.	45 g

1 Combine the chocolate and cocoa butter. Melt in the microwave or a bain marie over simmering water to 120°F (49°C).

2 Remove from the heat and add the butter and hazelnut paste in one step. Mix well with a whisk.

3 Fold in the puffed rice cereal.

4 Drop the chocolate-coated cereal by teaspoonfuls onto a silicone mat or paper-lined sheet pan. Or, sprinkle the candy while still soft directly onto cakes, tortes or wherever it is to be used.

Approximate values per ¹/₂-oz. (15-g) serving: **Calories** 80, **Total fat** 5 g, **Saturated fat** 2.5 g, **Cholesterol** 5 mg, **Sodium** 35 mg, **Total carbohydrates** 7 g, **Protein** 1 g

RECIPE 21.23

SUGAR-BASED NOUGATINE

Yield: 3 lb. 13 oz. (1830 g)

Glucose or corn syrup	5 oz.	150 g
Granulated sugar	2 lb.	960 g
Almonds, sliced, toasted and hot	1 lb. 5 oz.	630 g
Unsalted butter or cocoa butter	3 oz.	90 g

1 Bring the glucose or corn syrup to a boil in a heavy saucepan over medium-high heat.

2 Stir 4 ounces (120 grams) of the sugar into the glucose or corn syrup. Once the sugar has dissolved, add another 4 ounces (120 grams) of the sugar. Gradually add the remaining sugar when most of the sugar has dissolved. Continue stirring to evenly cook the mixture, approximately 3 to 4 minutes.

3 Reduce the heat. Brush down any sugar crystals that may have stuck to the sides of the pan with a clean brush dipped in clean water. Stir constantly until the mixture caramelizes to a light amber color, approximately 5 to 9 minutes.

4 When the mixture is amber, add the hot toasted almonds at once. Stir rapidly to coat the almonds, then cook 1 more minute. Remove from the heat and stir in the butter or cocoa butter.

5 Roll and form the nougatine as needed.

VARIATIONS:

Hazelnut or Walnut Nougatine—Substitute 1 pound 5 ounces (630 grams) finely chopped, hot toasted hazelnuts or walnuts for the almonds.

Coffee Nougatine—Reduce the almonds to 8 ounces (240 grams). Add 8 ounces (240 grams) finely chopped toasted hazelnuts, 4 ounces (120 grams) hot toasted sesame seeds, and 1 ounce (30 grams) instant coffee to the mixture along with the hot almonds once it caramelizes. Reduce the butter or cocoa butter to 2 ounces (60 grams).

Approximate values per ¹/₂-oz. (15-g) serving: **Calories** 70, **Total fat** 3 g, **Saturated fat** 0.5 g, **Cholesterol** 0 mg, **Sodium** 0 mg, **Total carbohydrates** 9 g, **Protein** 1 g

APPENDIX I

▶ MEASUREMENT AND CONVERSION CHARTS

MEASUREMENT CONVERSION CHART— FORMULAS FOR EXACT MEASURES

	WHEN YOU KNOW:	MULTIPLY BY:	TO FIND:
Mass (weight)	ounces	28.35	grams
	pounds	0.45	kilograms
	grams	0.035	ounces
	kilograms	2.2	pounds
Volume (capacity)	teaspoons	5.0	milliliters
	tablespoons	15.0	milliliters
	fluid ounces	29.57	milliliters
	cups	0.24	liters
	pints	0.47	liters
	quarts	0.95	liters
	gallons	3.785	liters
	milliliters	0.034	fluid ounces
Temperature	Fahrenheit	$5/9$ (after subtracting 32)	Celsius
	Celsius	$9/5$ (then add 32)	Fahrenheit

ROUNDED MEASURES FOR QUICK REFERENCE

1 oz.		= 30 g
4 oz.		= 120 g
8 oz.		= 240 g
16 oz.	= 1 lb.	= 480 g
32 oz.	= 2 lb.	= 960 g
36 oz.	= 2¼ lb.	= 1000 g (1 kg)
¼ tsp.	= $1/24$ fl. oz.	= 1 ml
½ tsp.	= $1/12$ fl. oz.	= 2.5 ml
1 tsp.	= $1/6$ fl. oz.	= 5 ml
1 Tbsp.	= ½ fl. oz.	= 15 ml
1 c.	= 8 fl. oz.	= 240 ml
2 c. (1 pt.)	= 16 fl. oz.	= 480 ml
4 c. (1 qt.)	= 32 fl. oz.	= 960 ml
4 qt. (1 gal.)	= 128 fl. oz.	= 3¾ lt
32°F	= 0°C	
122°F	= 50°C	
212°F	= 100°C	

CONVERSION GUIDELINES

1 gallon	=	4 quarts 8 pints 16 cups (8 fluid ounces) 128 fluid ounces
1 fifth bottle	=	approximately 1½ pints or exactly 26.5 fluid ounces
1 measuring cup	=	8 fluid ounces (a coffee cup generally holds 6 fluid ounces)
1 large egg white	=	1 ounce (average)
1 lemon	=	1 to 1¼ fluid ounces of juice
1 orange	=	3 to 3½ fluid ounces of juice

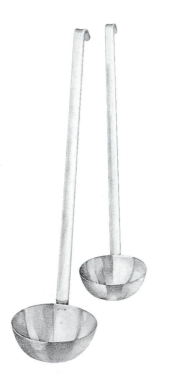

SCOOP SIZES

SCOOP MEASURE	LEVEL MEASURE
6	⅔ cup
8	½ cup
10	⅖ cup
12	⅓ cup
16	¼ cup
20	3⅕ tablespoons
24	2⅔ tablespoons
30	2⅕ tablespoons
40	1⅗ tablespoons

Note: The number of the scoop determines the number of servings in each quart of a mixture; for example, with a No. 16 scoop, one quart of mixture will yield 16 servings.

LADLE SIZES

SIZE	PORTION OF A CUP	NUMBER PER QUART	NUMBER PER LITER
1 fl. oz.	⅛	32	34
2 fl. oz.	¼	16	17
2⅔ fl. oz.	⅓	12	13
4 fl. oz.	½	8	8.6
6 fl. oz.	¾	5⅓	5.7

CANNED-GOOD SIZES

SIZE	NO. OF CANS PER CASE	AVERAGE WEIGHT	AVERAGE NO. CUPS PER CAN
No. $\frac{1}{2}$	8	8 oz.	1
No. 1 tall (also known as 303)	2 & 4 doz.	16 oz.	2
No. 2	2 doz.	20 oz.	$2\frac{1}{2}$
No. $2\frac{1}{2}$	2 doz.	28 oz.	$3\frac{1}{2}$
No. 3	2 doz.	33 oz.	4
No. 3 cylinder	1 doz.	46 oz.	$5\frac{2}{3}$
No. 5	1 doz.	3 lb. 8 oz.	$5\frac{1}{2}$
No. 10	6	6 lb. 10 oz.	13

Various standard cans—(left to right, front row) No. $\frac{1}{2}$ flat, No. $\frac{1}{4}$; (middle row) No. 300, No. 1 tall, No. $\frac{1}{2}$; (back row) No. 10, No. 3 cylinder, No. 5

APPROXIMATE VOLUME AND WEIGHT CONVERSIONS OF KEY BAKESHOP INGREDIENTS

ITEM	APPROXIMATE VOLUME EQUIVALENTS			APPROXIMATE WEIGHT EQUIVALENTS				
	1 OUNCE	$\frac{1}{4}$ OUNCE	1 POUND	1 TSP. OUNCES	1 TSP. GRAMS	1 TBSP. OUNCES	1 TBSP. GRAMS	1 CUP
Butter	2 Tbsp.	$1\frac{1}{2}$ tsp.	2 cups	0.17 oz.	5	0.5 oz.	15	8 oz.
Flour, all-purpose	$3\frac{1}{2}$ Tbsp.	$2\frac{2}{3}$ tsp.	$3\frac{1}{2}$ cups	0.09 oz.	3	0.28 oz.	9	4.5 oz.
Honey, corn syrup and molasses	4 tsp.	1 tsp.	$1\frac{1}{3}$ cups	0.25 oz.	8	0.75 oz.	24	12 oz.
Shortening, solid	7 tsp.	$1\frac{3}{4}$ tsp.	$2\frac{1}{4}$ cups	0.15 oz.	4	0.45 oz.	12	7.1 oz.
Sugar, granulated	7 tsp.	$1\frac{3}{4}$ tsp.	$2\frac{1}{4}$ cups	0.15 oz.	4	0.45 oz.	12	7 oz.
Sugar, brown	2 Tbsp.	$1\frac{1}{2}$ tsp.	2 cups	0.16 oz.	5	0.5 oz.	15	8 oz.
Sugar, powdered	$\frac{1}{4}$ cup	1 Tbsp.	4 cups	0.08 oz.	2.5	0.25 oz.	7	4 oz.
Baking powder, baking soda and cream of tartar	7 tsp.	$1\frac{3}{4}$ tsp.		0.14 oz.	4	0.4 oz.	12	
Cornstarch	11 tsp.	$2\frac{3}{4}$ tsp.		0.09 oz.	3	0.3 oz.	9	
Dried egg whites	$1\frac{3}{4}$ tsp.	$\frac{1}{2}$ tsp.		0.15 oz.	4	0.45 oz.	12	
Gelatin, powdered	10 tsp.	$2\frac{1}{2}$ tsp.		0.1 oz.	3	0.10 oz.	1	
Lemon peel	14 tsp.	$3\frac{1}{2}$ tsp.		0.07 oz.	2	0.2 oz.	6	
Salt, table	5 tsp.	$1\frac{1}{4}$ tsp.		0.21 oz.	6	0.6 oz.	18	
Salt, kosher	2 Tbsp.	$1\frac{1}{2}$ tsp.		0.17 oz.	5	0.5 oz.	15	
Seeds (anise, caraway, dill)	14 tsp.	$3\frac{1}{2}$ tsp.		0.07 oz.	2	0.2 oz.	6	
Spices, dry ground	14 tsp.	$3\frac{1}{2}$ tsp.		0.07 oz.	2	0.2 oz.	6	
Yeast, active dry	7 tsp.	$1\frac{3}{4}$ tsp.		0.14 oz.	4	0.4 oz.	12	
Yeast, fresh compressed	2 Tbsp.	$1\frac{1}{2}$ tsp.		0.17 oz.	5	0.5 oz.	15	
Vanilla extract and other extracts	2 Tbsp.	$1\frac{1}{2}$ tsp.		0.15 oz.	5	0.5 oz.	15	

APPENDIX II

▶ HIGH-ALTITUDE BAKING

Altitude affects the temperatures at which foods cook. The decreased atmospheric pressure at altitudes above 3000 feet affects the creation of steam and the expansion of hot air in dough and cake batters. These factors must be considered when making breads and cakes. Because gases expand more easily at higher altitudes, breads and cakes may rise so much that their structure cannot support the weight and the bread or cake collapses.

Therefore, the amount of leavening should be decreased at higher altitudes. Chemical leaveners should usually be reduced by one-third at 3500 feet and by two-thirds at altitudes over 5000 feet. Eggs should be underwhipped to avoid incorporating too much air, which would also create too much rise. For yeast-leavened products, bake them before they are fully proofed or reduce the yeast by 20 percent when baking over 5000 feet. In general, oven temperatures should also be increased by 25°F (4°C) at altitudes over 3500 feet to help set the product's structure rapidly.

Because the boiling point decreases at higher altitudes, more moisture will evaporate from baked goods in the oven. This may cause dryness and an excessive proportion of sugar, which shows up as white spots on a cake's surface. Correct this by reducing every 8 ounces (240 grams) of sugar by ½ ounce (15 grams) at 3000 feet and by 1½ ounces (45 grams) at 7000 feet.

Attempting to adjust typical (that is, sea-level) formulas for high altitudes is somewhat risky, especially in a commercial operation. Furthermore, different types of baked goods will need different adjustment techniques. Try to find and use formulas developed especially for your area, or contact the local offices of your state's department of agriculture or the agricultural extension service for detailed assistance.

APPENDIX III

▶ FRESH FRUIT AVAILABILITY CHART

The following chart is intended as only a general guide to the best availability of freshly harvested fruit grown in the continental United States. State departments of agri- culture can provide charts of local produce availability and information on local farmer's markets and sustain- able agriculture programs.

PRODUCT	JAN.	FEB.	MAR.	APR.	MAY	JUN.	JUL.	AUG.	SEP.	OCT.	NOV.	DEC.
	WINTER DEC. 21–MAR. 19		SPRING MAR. 20–JUN. 20			SUMMER JUN. 21–SEP. 21			AUTUMN SEP. 22–DEC. 20			
Apples								X	X	X	X	
Apricots						X	X					
Blueberries					X	X	X	X				
Cantaloupe						X	X	X	X			
Cherries					X	X	X	X				
Chestnuts									X	X	X	X
Citrus	X	X	X	X	X	X			X	X	X	X
Cranberries									X	X	X	X
Dates										X	X	X
Figs						X	X	X	X	X		
Grapes						X	X	X	X	X	X	
Lychees						X	X					
Mangos					X	X	X	X				
Papayas			X	X	X	X						
Peaches					X	X	X	X				
Pears	X	X	X	X						X	X	X
Pecans											X	X
Persimmons										X	X	X
Pineapples			X	X	X	X	X	X				
Plums						X	X	X	X			
Pomegranates									X	X	X	X
Prickly pears									X	X	X	X
Pumpkins									X	X	X	
Raspberries						X	X	X	X			
Rhubarb		X	X	X	X							
Strawberries		X	X	X	X	X						
Watermelons						X	X	X				

APPENDIX IV

▶ PROFESSIONAL ORGANIZATIONS

American Culinary Federation, Inc. (ACF)

10 San Bartola Drive
St. Augustine, FL 32086
800-624-9458
http://www.acfchefs.org

American Dietetic Association (ADA)

120 South Riverside Plaza, Suite 2000
Chicago, IL 60606-6995
800-877-1600
http://www.eatright.org

American Institute of Baking (AIB)

P.O. Box 3999
Manhattan, KS 66505-3999
800-633-5137
http://www.aibonline.com

American Institute of Wine and Food (AIWF)

304 West Liberty Street, Suite 201
Louisville, KY 40202
800-274-2493
http://www.aiwf.org

Bread Bakers Guild of America

3203 Maryland Avenue
North Versailles, PA 15137
412-823-2080
http://www.bbga.org

Chefs Collaborative

262 Beacon Street
Boston, MA 02116
617-236-5200
http://www.chefscollaborative.org

International Association of Culinary Professionals (IACP)

304 West Liberty Street, Suite 201
Louisville, KY 40202
502-581-9786
http://www.iacp.com

James Beard Foundation

167 West 12th Street
New York, NY 10011
800-36-BEARD
http://www.jamesbeard.org

Les Dames d'Escoffier International

P.O. Box 4961
Louisville, KY 40204
502-456-1851
http://www.ldei.org

National Restaurant Association

1200 17th Street NW
Washington, DC 20036
202-331-5900
http://www.restaurant.org

Oldways Preservation and Exchange Trust

266 Beacon Street
Boston, MA 02116
617-421-5500
http://www.oldwayspt.org

Personal Chefs Network

877-905-CHEF
http://www.personalchefsnetwork.com

Retailer's Bakery Association (RBA)

14239 Park Center Drive
Laurel, MD 20707-5261
800-638-0924
http://www.rbanet.com

Share Our Strength (SOS)

733 15th Street NW, Suite 640
Washington, DC 20005
800-969-4767
http://www.strength.org

Slow Food USA

434 Broadway, 6th Floor
New York, NY 10013
212-965-5640
http://www.slowfoodusa.org

U.S. Personal Chef Association

481 Rio Rancho Blvd. NE
Rio Rancho, NM 87124
800-995-2138
http://www.uspca.com

Women Chefs and Restaurateurs (WCR)

304 West Liberty Street, Suite 201
Louisville, KY 40202
877-927-7787
http://www.womenchefs.org

BIBLIOGRAPHY
and Recommended Reading

General Interest

Bickel, Walter, ed. and trans. *Hering's Dictionary of Classical and Modern Cookery.* 13th English ed. London: Virtue, 1994.

Davidson, Alan. *The Oxford Companion to Food.* Oxford, England: Oxford University Press, 1999.

Escoffier, Auguste. *The Escoffier Cook Book and Guide to the Fine Art of Cookery for Connoisseurs, Chefs, Epicures.* (Trans. of *Le Guide culinaire.*) New York: Crown, 1969.

Kamman, Madeleine. *The New Making of a Cook.* New York: Morrow, 1997.

Labensky, Steven, Gaye G. Ingram, and Sarah R. Labensky. *Webster's New World Dictionary of Culinary Arts.* 2nd Ed. Upper Saddle River, N.J.: Prentice Hall, 2001.

Larousse Gastronomique. English ed. New York: Potter, 2001.

Molt, Mary. *Food for Fifty.* 11th ed. Upper Saddle River, N.J.: Prentice Hall, 2001.

Pépin, Jacques. *The Art of Cooking.* New York: Knopf, 1987.

———. *La Technique.* New York: Pocket Books, 1987.

Peterson, James. *Essentials of Cooking.* New York: Artisan, 2000.

Point, Fernand. *Fernand Point: Ma Gastronomie.* English ed. Wilton, Conn.: Lyceum Books, 1974.

Saulnier, Louis. *Le Répertoire de la Cuisine.* Revised ed. New York: Barron's Educational Series, 1976.

Willan, Anne. *La Varenne Pratique.* New York: Crown, 1989.

Food History

Assire, Jérome. *The Book of Bread.* New York: Flammarion, 1996.

Coe, Sophie D., and Michael D. Coe. *The True History of Chocolate.* New York: Thames and Hudson, 1996.

Cooper, Ann. *A Woman's Place Is in the Kitchen: The Evolution of Women Chefs.* Stamford, Conn.: Thomson, 1997.

David, Elizabeth. *Harvest of the Cold Months: Social History of Ice and Ices.* New York: Viking, 1994.

Dupaigne, Bernard. *The History of Bread.* New York: Abrams, 1999.

Lovegren, Sylvia. *Fashionable Food: Seven Decades of Food Fads.* New York: Macmillan General Reference, 1995.

Mintz, Sidney W. *Sweetness and Power: The Place of Sugar in Modern History.* New York: Viking Press, 1995.

Norman, Barbara. *Tales of the Table: A History of Western Cuisine.* Englewood Cliffs, N.J.: Prentice Hall, 1972.

Revel, Jean-François. *Culture and Cuisine.* (Trans. of *Un Festin en paroles.*) New York: Da Capo Press, 1982.

Schlossberg, Eli W. *The World of Orthodox Judaism.* Northvale, N.J.: Aronson, 1996.

Tannahill, Reay. *Food in History.* Revised ed. New York: Crown, 1995.

Toussaint-Samat, Maguelonne. *A History of Food.* Trans. by Anthea Bell. Cambridge, Mass.: Blackwell, 1992.

Wheaton, Barbara Ketcham. *Savoring the Past: The French Kitchen and Table from 1300 to 1789.* Reprint ed. New York: Touchstone Books, 1996.

Willan, Anne. *Great Cooks and Their Recipes: From Taillevent to Escoffier.* Boston: Little, Brown, 1992.

Sanitation and Safety

International Life Sciences Institute. *A Simple Guide to Understanding and Applying the Hazard Analysis Critical Control Point Concept.* Washington, D.C.: ILSI Press, 1993.

Loken, Joan K. *The HACCP Food Safety Manual.* New York: Wiley, 1995.

McSwane, David, Nancy Rue and Richard Linton. *Essentials of Food Safety and Sanitation.* Updated 2nd ed. Upper Saddle River, N.J.: Prentice Hall, 2002.

National Assessment Institute. *Handbook for Safe Food Service Management.* 2nd ed. Upper Saddle River, N.J.: Prentice Hall, 1998.

National Restaurant Association Educational Foundation. *ServSafe Coursebook.* New York: Wiley, 2001.

Healthful Baking and Nutrition

Baskette, Michael, and Eleanor Mainella. *The Art of Nutritional Cooking.* 2nd ed. Upper Saddle River, N.J.: Prentice Hall, 1999.

Egan, Maureen, and Susan Davis Allen. *Healthful Quantity Baking.* New York: Wiley, 1992.

Freyberg, Nicholas, and Willis A. Gortner. *The Food Additives Book.* New York: Bantam Books, 1982.

Tools

Bridge, Fred, and Jean F. Tibbetts. *The Well-Tooled Kitchen.* New York: Morrow, 1991.

Williams, Chuck, ed. *Williams-Sonoma Kitchen Companion.* New York: Time-Life Books, 2000.

Wolf, Burton, ed. *The New Cooks' Catalogue.* New York: Knopf, 2000.

General Ingredients

DeMers, John. *The Community Kitchen's Complete Guide to Gourmet Coffee.* New York: Simon & Schuster, 1986.

Dowell, Philip, and Adrian Bailey. *Cook's Ingredients.* New York: Morrow, 1980.

Greenburg, Patricia. *The Whole Soy Cookbook.* New York: Random House, 1998.

Jenkins, Steven. *Steven Jenkins' Cheese Primer.* New York: Workman, 1996.

Jordan, Michele Anna. *The Good Cook's Book of Oil & Vinegar.* Reading, Mass.: Addison-Wesley, 1992.

Lambert, Paula. *The Cheese Lover's Cookbook & Guide.* New York: Simon & Schuster, 2000.

Morris, Sallie, and Lesley Mackley. *The Spice Ingredients Cookbook.* New York: Lorenz Books, 1997.

Norman, Jill. *The Complete Book of Spices.* New York: Viking Studio Books, 1991.

Ortiz, Elisabeth Lambert. *The Encyclopedia of Herbs, Spices and Flavorings.* New York: Dorling Kindersley, 1992.

Schapira, Joel, and Karl Schapira. *The Book of Coffee and Tea.* New York: St. Martin's Press, 1975.

Ward, Susie, Claire Clifton, and Jenny Stacey. *The Gourmet Atlas.* New York: Macmillan, 1997.

Food Science

Corriher, Shirley O. *Cookwise.* New York: Morrow, 1997.

McGee, Harold. *On Food and Cooking.* New York: Scribner, 1984.

McWilliams, Margaret. *Foods: Experimental Perspectives.* 4th ed. Upper Saddle River, N.J.: Prentice Hall, 2001.

Parsons, Russ. *How to Read a French Fry.* Boston: Houghton Mifflin, 2001.

Custards, Creams and Sauces

Eggcyclopedia, 3rd ed. Park Ridge, Ill.: American Egg Board, 1999.

Fox, Margaret S., and John Bear. *Morning Food from Café Beaujolais.* Berkeley, Calif.: Ten Speed Press, 1994.

Larousse, David Paul. *The Sauce Bible: Guide to the Saucier's Craft.* New York: Wiley, 1993.

Peterson, James. *Sauces: Classical and Contemporary Sauce Making.* 2nd ed. New York: Van Nostrand Reinhold, 1998.

Fruits

Brown, Marlene. *International Produce Cookbook and Guide.* Los Angeles: HP Books, 1989.

Davidson, Alan. *Fruit: A Connoisseur's Guide and Cookbook.* New York: Simon & Schuster, 1991.

Murdich, Jack. *Buying Produce.* New York: Morrow, 1986.

Payne, Rolce Redard, and Dorrit Speyer Senior. *Cooking with Fruit.* New York: Crescent Books, 1995.

Routhier, Nicole. *Nicole Routhier's Fruit Cookbook.* New York: Workman, 1996.

Schmidt, Jimmy. *Cooking for All Seasons.* New York: Macmillan, 1991.

Schneider, Elizabeth. *Uncommon Fruits and Vegetables: A Commonsense Guide.* New York: Morrow, 1998.

Quick Breads, Yeast Breads and Laminated Doughs

Albright, Barbara, and Leslie Weiner. *Mostly Muffins.* New York: St. Martin's Press, 1984.

Alston, Elizabeth. *Biscuits and Scones.* New York: Potter, 1988.

Amendola, Joseph. *The Bakers' Manual.* 4th ed. New York: Wiley, 1993.

Clayton, Bernard. *Bernard Clayton's New Complete Book of Breads.* Revised ed. New York: Fireside Books, 1995.

David, Elizabeth. *English Bread and Yeast Cookery.* Notes by Karen Hess. New York: Viking Press, 1980.

Hanneman, L. J. *Bakery: Bread & Fermented Goods.* London: Heinemann, 1980.

Leader, Daniel, and Judith Blahnik. *Bread Alone.* New York: Morrow, 1993.

Ortiz, Joe. *The Village Baker: Classic Regional Breads from Europe and America.* Berkeley, Calif.: Ten Speed Press, 1993.

Neuhaus, Tom. *The Informed Baker.* Trumansburg, New York: Neuhaus Features, 1997.

Power, Kenneth. *Power Baking: A Contemporary American Baking Manual.* Oklahoma City, Okla.: Ycart, 1991.

Pyler, E. J. *Handbook of Basic Technical Baking Terminology.* Kansas City, Mo.: Sosland, 1994.

Reinhart, Peter. *Bread Baker's Apprentice.* Berkeley, Calif.: Ten Speed Press, 2002.

———. *Crust & Crumb.* Berkeley, Calif.: Ten Speed Press, 1998.

Schunemann, Claus. *Baking, the Art and Science: A Practical Handbook for the Baking Industry.* Calgary, Canada: Baker Tech, 1988.

Pastries and Desserts

Bloom, Carole. *The International Dictionary of Desserts, Pastries, and Confections.* New York: Hearst Books, 1995.

Braker, Flo. *The Simple Art of Perfect Baking.* Shelburne, Vt.: Chapters, 1992.

Daley, Regan. *In the Sweet Kitchen: The Definitive Baker's Companion.* New York: Artisan, 2001.

Fletcher, Helen S. *The New Pastry Cook.* New York: Morrow, 1986.

Friberg, Bo. *The Professional Pastry Chef.* 4th ed. New York: Wiley, 2002.

Healy, Bruce, and Paul Bugat. *Mastering the Art of French Pastry.* Woodbury, N.Y.: Barron's, 1984.

Heatter, Maida. *Maida Heatter's Book of Great Desserts.* Kansas City, Kans.: Andrews & McMeel, 1999.

Hyman, Philip, and Mary Hyman, trans. *The Best of Gaston Lenôtre's Desserts.* Woodbury, N.Y.: Barron's, 1983.

———. *Lenôtre's Ice Creams and Candies.* Woodbury, N.Y.: Barron's, 1979.

London, Sheryl, and Mel London. *Fresh Fruit Desserts: Classic and Contemporary.* New York: Prentice Hall, 1990.

Maglieri, Nick. *Nick Maglieri's Perfect Pastry.* New York: Macmillan, 1989.

Patent, Greg. *Baking in America.* Boston: Houghton Mifflin, 2002.

Purdy, Susan G. *A Piece of Cake.* Reprint. New York: Macmillan, 1993.

Silverton, Nancy. *Desserts by Nancy Silverton.* New York: Harper & Row, 1986.

Chocolate, Sugar and Decorative Work

Minifie, Bernard W. *Chocolate, Cocoa, and Confectionery: Science and Technology.* 3rd ed. Gaithersburg, Maryland: Aspen Publishers, 1989.

Prescilla, Maricel. *The New Taste of Chocolate.* Berkeley, Calif.: Ten Speed Press, 2001.

Teubner, Christian, ed. *The Chocolate Bible.* New York: Penguin Studio, 1997.

Books by Contributing Chefs

Beranbaum, Rose Levy. *The Cake Bible.* New York: Morrow, 1988.

Bishop, John. *Bishop's: The Cookbook.* Vancouver, Canada: Douglas & McIntyre, 1997.

Brennan, Pip, Jimmy Brennan and Ted Brennan. *Breakfast at Brennan's and Dinner, Too.* New Orleans, La.: Brennan's Inc., 1994.

Gand, Gale, and Julia Moskin. *Gale Gand's Just a Bite.* New York: Clarkson Potter, 2001.

Guerithault, Vincent. *Vincent's Cookbook.* Berkeley, Calif.: Ten Speed Press, 1994.

Malgieri, Nick. *Nick Malgieri's Perfect Pastry.* New York: Macmillan, 1989.

Medrich, Alice. *Cocolat.* New York: Warner Books, 1990.

Milliken, Mary Sue, and Susan Feniger. *City Cuisine.* New York: Morrow, 1989.

GLOSSARY

absorption—the ability of flour to absorb moisture when mixed into a dough; varies according to protein content, growing and storage conditions of the flour

acid—foods such as citrus juice, vinegar and wine that have a sour or sharp flavor (most foods are slightly acidic); acids have a pH of less than 7

acidulation—the browning of cut fruit caused by the reaction of an enzyme (polyphenoloxidase) with the phenolic compounds present in these fruits; this browning is often mistakenly attributed to exposure to oxygen

additives—substances added to many foods to prevent spoilage or to improve appearance, texture, flavor or nutritional value; may be synthetic materials copied from nature (for example, sugar substitutes) or naturally occurring substances (for example, lecithin); some food additives may cause allergic reactions in sensitive people

aerate—(1) to whip air into a mixture to lighten it, such as beating egg whites to a foam; (2) to incorporate air into a mixture through sifting and mixing

aging—the period during which freshly milled flour is allowed to rest so that it will whiten and produce less sticky doughs; the aging of flour can be chemically accelerated

albumen—the principal protein found in egg whites

allergens—substances that may cause allergic reactions in some people

amaranth—tiny oval seeds of a type of annual herb plant native to South America; used as a cooked grain and flour

artisan—a person who works in a skilled craft or trade; one who works with his or her hands; applied to bread bakers and confectioners who prepare foods using traditional methods

baba—a small, light yeast cake soaked in rum syrup; traditionally baked in an individual cylindrical mold, giving the finished product a mushroom shape

bacteria—single-celled microorganisms, some of which can cause diseases, including food-borne diseases

bagel—a dense, donut-shaped yeast roll; it is cooked in boiling water, then baked, which gives it a shiny glaze and chewy texture

bain marie—(bane mah-ree) (1) a hot-water bath used to gently cook food or keep cooked food hot; (2) a container for holding food in a hot-water bath

bake blind—process of baking a pie shell or tart shell unfilled using baking weights or beans to support the crust as it bakes

bake-off—the procedure of cooking a prepared dough or other pastry item that has been produced elsewhere and is merely finished on site

baked Alaska—an ice cream dessert set on a layer of spongecake and encased in meringue, then baked until the meringue is warm and golden

baker's peel—flat-handled paddle used to slide food, particularly bread and pizza, into a deck oven

baker's percentage—a system for measuring ingredients in a formula by expressing them as a percentage of the total flour weight

baking—a dry-heat cooking method in which foods are surrounded by hot, dry air in a closed environment; similar to roasting, the term baking is usually applied to breads, pastries, vegetables and fish

baking powder—a mixture of sodium bicarbonate and one or more acids, generally cream of tartar and/or sodium aluminum sulfate, used to leaven baked goods; it releases carbon dioxide gas if moisture is present in a formula; single-acting baking powder releases carbon dioxide gas in the presence of moisture only; double-acting baking powder releases some carbon dioxide gas upon contact with moisture, and more gas is released when heat is applied

baking soda—sodium bicarbonate, an alkaline compound that releases carbon dioxide gas when combined with an acid and moisture; used to leaven baked goods

baking weights—small ceramic or metal disks used to keep pie crust from bubbling up during baking; used when baking an unfilled pie or tart shell; also known as pie weights

banneton——(BAN-tahn) a traditional woven basket, often lined with canvas, in which yeast bread is placed to rise before baking

barquette—a small boat-shaped pastry shell used for miniature cakes or tarts served as canapés or petits fours

base—a mixture of one or more dry ingredients to which flour, water and yeast are added; see **concentrate** and **mix**

batter—(1) a semiliquid mixture containing flour or other starch used to make cakes and breads; the gluten development is minimized and the liquid forms the continuous medium in which other ingredients are dispersed; generally contains more fat, sugar and liquids than a dough; (2) a semiliquid mixture of liquid and starch used to coat foods for deep-frying

Baumé scale—(boh-may) see **hydrometer**

Bavarian cream—a sweet dessert mixture made by thickening custard sauce with gelatin and then folding in whipped cream; the final product is poured into a mold and chilled until firm

bean flour—cooked beans, including chickpeas, soybeans and white beans, that are dried, then ground into a fine powder; used in place of gluten-forming wheat flours

beating—a mixing method in which foods are vigorously agitated to incorporate air or develop gluten; a spoon or electric mixer fitted with a paddle is used

beignets—squares or strips of éclair paste deep-fried and dusted with powdered sugar

bench—a bakeshop worktable made with a stainless or wooden top

bergamot—a member of the citrus family, resembling an orange with inedible flesh; edible oil extracted from its skin gives a mellow orange flavor to candies, chocolates, and Earl Grey tea

berry—(1) the kernel of certain grains such as wheat; (2) a small, juicy fruit that grows on vines and bushes

biological hazard—a danger to the safety of food caused by disease-causing microorganisms such as bacteria, molds, yeasts, viruses or fungi

biscuit—(1) a small, flaky quickbread leavened with baking soda or baking powder for a light, tender texture; the dough is rolled out and cut into circles or dropped from a spoon; (2) any dry, flat cake, usually leavened with baking powder and/or baking soda; (3) (bee-SQUEE) a type of dry sponge cake used to make multilayered tortes

biscuit method—a mixing method used to make biscuits, scones and flaky doughs; it involves cutting cold fat into the flour and other dry ingredients before any liquid is added

blanching—very briefly and partially cooking a food in boiling water or hot fat; used to assist preparation (for example, to loosen peels from fruits or veg-

etables), as part of a combination cooking method, to remove undesirable flavors or to prepare a food for freezing

blending—a mixing method in which two or more ingredients are combined just until they are evenly distributed

bloom—(1) a white, powdery layer that sometimes appears on chocolate; (2) to soften granulated gelatin in a liquid before melting and using

boiling—a moist-heat cooking method that uses convection to transfer heat from a hot (approximately 212°F/100°C) liquid to the food submerged in it

bombe—two or more flavors of ice cream, or ice cream and sherbet, shaped in a spherical mold; each flavor is a separate layer that forms the shell for the next flavor

bombe mixture—(Fr. *pâte à bombe*) egg yolks cooked with sugar syrup and whipped, used as a base for still-frozen desserts and cakes

bouchées—(boo-SHAY) small puff pastry shells that can be filled and served as bite-size hors d'oeuvre or petits fours

boulanger—French for a baker

bowl knife—a flexible plastic spatula used to scrape ingredients from a mixing bowl

bran—the tough outer layer of a cereal grain and the part highest in fiber

brandy—an alcoholic beverage made by distilling the fermented mash of grapes or other fruits

bread flour—blended flour made from hard winter wheat with a protein content between 12 and 15 percent

brigade—a system of staffing a kitchen so that each worker is assigned a set of specific tasks; these tasks are often related by cooking method, equipment or the types of foods being produced

brioche—(bree-OHSH) a rich yeast bread containing large amounts of eggs and butter

broiling—a dry-heat cooking method in which foods are cooked by heat radiating from an overhead source

brotform—(BROT-form) a traditional basket made from coiled willow in which yeast bread is placed to rise before baking; the basket leaves circular marks in the dough; heavy plastic versions are available for commercial food service use

buckwheat flour—dark, nutty-tasting flour milled from the seeds of the buckwheat plant and used to make bread, cereals and baked goods

bun—any of a variety of small, round yeast rolls; may be sweet or savory

butler service—restaurant service in which servers pass foods (typically hors d'oeuvre) or drinks arranged on trays

buttercream—a light, smooth, fluffy frosting of sugar, fat and flavorings; egg yolks or whipped egg whites are sometimes added; the three principal kinds are simple, Italian and French

caffeine—an alkaloid found in coffee beans, tea leaves and cocoa beans that acts as a stimulant

cake—in American usage, refers to a broad range of pastries, including layer cakes, coffeecakes and gâteaux; can refer to almost anything that is baked, tender, sweet and sometimes frosted

cake comb—a utensil made from hard plastic, metal or rubber with sharp teeth carved into one of more of its sides; used to create patterns in icings and chocolate

cake flour—a finely milled soft wheat flour with a protein content of less than 8 percent; designed to produce tender products

calorie—a unit of energy measured by the amount of heat required to raise 1000 grams of water 1 degree Celsius; it is also written as kilocalorie or kcal and is used as a measure of food energy

candy rulers—steel or aluminum bars of varying lengths and thicknesses used to contain fillings for candies; the metal bars may also be used to roll a pastry to a uniform thickness

cannoli—an Italian pastry made from a dough shell curled into a tube, deep-fried and filled with sweetened ricotta cheese

caramelization—the process of cooking sugars; the browning of sugar enhances the flavor and appearance of foods

carbohydrates—a group of compounds composed of oxygen, hydrogen and carbon, the human body's primary source of energy (4 calories per gram); carbohydrates are classified as simple (including certain sugars) and complex (including starches and fiber)

carryover cooking/baking—the cooking that occurs after a food is removed from a heat source; it is accomplished by the residual heat remaining in the food

centers—the firm or soft filling for chocolate candies

chalazae cords—thick, twisted strands of egg white that anchor the yolk in place

charlotte—a dessert made in a mold lined with ladyfingers and filled with a custard cream stabilized with gelatin

cheesecloth—a light, fine mesh gauze used to strain liquids and make sachets

chef de cuisine—(shef duh quizine) also known simply as chef; the person responsible for all kitchen operations, developing menu items and setting the kitchen's tone and tempo

chef's knife—an all-purpose knife used for chopping, slicing and mincing; its tapering blade is 8–14 inches (20–35 centimeters) long

china cap—a cone-shaped strainer made of perforated metal

chocolate comb—*see* cake comb

cholesterol—a fatty substance found in foods derived from animal products and in the human body; in excess, it has been linked to heart disease

chop—to cut an item into small pieces where uniformity of size and shape is neither feasible nor necessary

choux pastry—(shoo) see **éclair paste**

churros—a Mexican and Spanish pastry in which sticks of éclair paste flavored with cinnamon are deep-fried and rolled in sugar while still hot

cider—mildly fermented apple juice; nonalcoholic apple juice may also be labeled cider

citric acid—acid found in citrus fruit juice, used to enhance flavor in foods and to prevent crystallization of sugar syrups; available in liquid or powdered form

citrus—fruits characterized by a thick rind, most of which is a bitter white pith (albedo) with a thin exterior layer of colored skin (zest); their flesh is segmented and juicy and varies from bitter to tart to sweet

clarified butter—purified butterfat; the butter is melted and the water and milk solids are removed

classic cuisine—a late 19th- and early 20th-century refinement and simplification of French *grande cuisine;* classic (or classical) cuisine relies on the thorough exploration of culinary principles and techniques, and emphasizes the refined preparation and presentation of superb ingredients

clean—to remove visible dirt and soil

club roll—a small oval-shaped roll made of crusty French bread

coagulation—the irreversible transformation of proteins from a liquid or semiliquid state to a drier, solid state; usually accomplished through the application of heat

cocoa butter—the fat found in cocoa beans and used in fine chocolates

coconut cream—(1) a coconut-flavored liquid made like coconut milk but with less water; it is creamier and thicker than coconut milk; (2) the thick fatty portion that separates and rises to the top of canned or frozen coconut milk. Do not substitute cream of coconut for true coconut cream.

coconut milk—a coconut-flavored liquid made by pouring boiling water over shredded coconut; may be sweetened or unsweetened. Do not substitute cream of coconut for coconut milk.

coconut water—the thin, slightly opaque liquid contained within a fresh coconut

cold spot—area in an oven where heat is not evenly distributed; opposite is hot spot

composition—a completed plate's structure of colors, shapes and arrangements

concentrate—also known as a fruit paste or compound; a reduced fruit purée, without a gel structure, used as a flavoring

conching—stirring melted chocolate with large stone or metal rollers to create a smooth texture in the finished chocolate

conduction—the transfer of heat from one item to another through direct contact

confectionery—transforming sugar into sweets; also refers to the trade of candy making

contaminants—biological, chemical or physical substances that can be harmful when consumed in sufficient quantities

contamination—the presence, generally unintentional, of harmful organisms or substances

convection—the transfer of heat caused by the natural movement of molecules in a fluid (whether air, water or fat) from a warmer area to a cooler one; mechanical convection is the movement of molecules caused by stirring

conversion factor—(C.F.) the number used to increase or decrease ingredient quantities and formula yields

cookery—the art, practice or work of cooking

cookies—small, sweet, flat pastries; usually classified by preparation or make-up techniques as drop, icebox, bar, cutout, pressed and wafer

cooking—(1) the transfer of energy from a heat source to a food; this energy alters the food's molecular structure, changing its texture, flavor, aroma and appearance; (2) the preparation of food for consumption

cooking medium—the air, fat, water or steam in which a food is cooked

coring—the process of removing the seeds or pit from a fruit or fruit-vegetable

coulibiac—(koo-LEE-bee-yack) a creamy mixture of salmon fillet, rice, hard-cooked eggs, mushrooms, shallots and dill enclosed in a pastry envelope usually made of brioche dough

count—the number of individual items in a given measure of weight or volume

coupe—(koop) an ice cream sundae, especially one served with a fruit topping

cracking—a milling process in which grains are broken open

cream filling—a pie filling made of flavored pastry cream thickened with cornstarch

cream of coconut—a canned commercial product consisting of thick, sweetened coconut-flavored liquid; used for baking and in beverages

creaming—a mixing method in which softened fat and sugar are vigorously combined to incorporate air

creams—also known as crèmes; include light, fluffy or creamy-textured dessert foods made with whipped cream or whipped egg whites, such as Bavarian creams, chiffons, mousses and crème Chantilly

crème anglaise—(khrem ahn-GLEHZ) also known as crème à l'anglaise; see **vanilla custard sauce**

crème brûlée—(krehm broo-LAY) French for burnt cream; used to describe a rich dessert custard topped with a crust of caramelized sugar

crème caramel—(khrem kair-ah-MEHL) like crème renversée (rehn-vehr-SAY) and flan, a custard baked over a layer of caramelized sugar and inverted for service

crème Chantilly—(khrem shan-TEE) heavy cream whipped to soft peaks and flavored with sugar and vanilla; used to garnish pastries or desserts or folded into cooled custard or pastry cream for fillings

crème Chiboust—(khrem chee-BOOS) a vanilla pastry cream lightened by folding in Italian meringue; traditionally used in gâteau St. Honoré

crème pâtissière—(khrem pah-tees-SYEHR) see **pastry cream**

crêpe—(krayp) a thin, delicate unleavened griddlecake made with a very thin egg batter cooked in a very hot sauté pan; used in sweet and savory preparations

croissant—(krwah-SAHN) a crescent-shaped roll made from a rich, rolled-in yeast dough

croquembouche—(krow-kem-BOOSH) a pyramid of small choux puffs, each filled with pastry cream; a French tradition for Christmas and weddings, it is held together with caramelized sugar and decorated with spun sugar or marzipan flowers

cross-contamination—the transfer of bacteria or other contaminants from one food, work surface or piece of equipment to another

croûte, en—(awn KROOT) describes a food encased in a bread or pastry crust

cruller—a Dutch pastry in which a loop or strip of twisted éclair paste is deep fried

crumb—the interior of bread or cake; may be elastic, aerated, fine or coarse grained

crumb coat—a thin layer of icing applied to a cake to seal loose surface crumbs before a final decorative layer of icing is applied

cuisine—the ingredients, seasonings, cooking procedures and styles attributable to a particular group of people; the group can be defined by geography, history, ethnicity, politics, culture or religion

curd—(1) the solid portion of milk when it separates; what becomes cheese; (2) a stirred custard made from eggs, sugar, butter and fruit juice, usually citrus

curdling—the separation of milk or egg mixtures into solid and liquid components; caused by overcooking, high heat or the presence of acids

custard—any liquid thickened by the coagulation of egg proteins; its consistency depends on the ratio of eggs to liquid and the type of liquid used; custards can be baked in the oven or cooked in a bain marie or on the stove top

cutting—(1) reducing a food to smaller pieces; (2) a mixing method in which solid fat is incorporated into dry ingredients until only lumps of the desired size remain

dairy products—include cow's milk and foods produced from cow's milk such as butter, yogurt, sour cream and cheese; sometimes other milks and products made from them are included (such as goat's-milk cheese)

deck oven—an oven with stationary, individually heated shelves; products can be baked on each deck's floor (hearth) either in or out of pans.

decorator's icing—see **royal icing**

deep-frying—a dry-heat cooking method that uses convection to transfer heat to a food submerged in hot fat; foods to be deep-fried are usually first coated in batter or breading

density—the relationship between the mass and volume of a substance ($D = m/v$); as more and more solids are dissolved in a liquid, the heavier or denser the liquid will become; sugar density is measured on the Baumé scale using a saccharometer

détrempe—(day-trup-eh) a paste made with flour and water during the first stage of preparing pastry doughs, especially rolled-in doughs

develop—to mix dough to the point when the protein bond in the flour forms gluten and the dough becomes smooth and elastic

dipping fork—a utensil used to hold chocolate or small pastries for dipping into chocolate or other coating; consists of a narrow handle with two, three or four long, thin prongs, which are easily inserted into small foods

direct contamination—the contamination of raw foods in their natural setting or habitat

direct method—see **straight dough method**

divider—device that mechanically cuts portions of bread dough before forming

docker—a hand tool designed to pierce holes in the surface of bread, cracker, pastry and pizza dough before baking to release air bubbles so the product bakes evenly

docking—pricking small holes in an unbaked dough or crust to allow steam to escape and to prevent the dough from rising when baked

dough—a mixture of flour and other ingredients used in baking; has a low moisture content, and gluten forms the continuous medium into which other ingredients are embedded; it is often stiff enough to cut into shapes

dough conditioner—enzymes, emulsifiers and yeast foods added to bread dough to improve gluten development or to soften the dough for faster mixing and shorter fermentation times; available as a powdered blend

dough hook—mixer attachment used when kneading bread dough or other heavy products

dry-heat cooking methods—cooking methods, principally broiling, grilling, roasting and baking, sautéing, pan-frying and deep-frying, that use air or fat to transfer heat through conduction and convection; dry-heat cooking methods allow surface sugars to caramelize

drying agent—products such as silica gel used to remove humidity from the air for storing sugar work, nougatine and other dry cookies, which soften under moist conditions

dumpling—any of a variety of small starchy products made from doughs or batters that are simmered or steamed; can be plain or filled

durum wheat—a species of very hard wheat with a particularly high amount of protein; it is used to make couscous or milled into semolina, which is used for making pasta

dusting—lightly coating the surface of an unbaked dough product with a powdery substance such as flour or cornmeal, usually to prevent sticking or to give the product a decorative finish

éclair paste—(ay-clayr) also known as pâte à choux; a soft dough that produces hollow baked products with crisp exteriors; used for making éclairs, cream puffs and savory products

edible food lacquer—a composition of fats, lecithin and other edible ingredients used to create a shine on marzipan and other confections

egg wash—a mixture of beaten eggs (whole eggs, yolks or whites) and a liquid, usually milk or water, used to coat doughs before baking to add sheen

emulsification—the process by which generally unmixable liquids, such as oil and water, are forced into a uniform distribution

emulsifier—a substance, natural or chemical, added to a mixture to assist in the binding of unmixable liquids; lecithin found in egg yolks or mono- and diglycerides are commonly used emulsifiers

emulsify—the process of combining a fat and a liquid into a homogeneous mixture, accomplished by proper blending of ingredients

emulsion—(1) a uniform mixture of two unmixable liquids; (2) flavoring oils such as orange and lemon, mixed into water with the aid of emulsifiers

endosperm—the largest part of a cereal grain and a source of protein and carbohydrates (starch); the part used primarily in milled products

enzymes—proteins that aid specific chemical reactions in plants and animals

essential nutrients—nutrients that must be provided by food because the body cannot or does not produce them in sufficient quantities

essential oils—pure oils extracted from the skins, peels and other parts of plants used to give their aroma and taste to flavoring agents in foods, cosmetics and other products

evaporation—the process by which heated water molecules move faster and faster until the water turns to a gas (steam) and vaporizes; evaporation is responsible for the drying of foods during cooking

extracts—concentrated mixtures of ethyl alcohol and flavoring oils such as vanilla, almond and lemon

fancy—a quality grade for fruits, especially canned or frozen

fats—(1) a group of compounds composed of oxygen, hydrogen and carbon atoms that supply the body with energy (9 calories per gram); fats are classified as saturated, monounsaturated or polyunsaturated; (2) the general term for butter, lard, shortening, oil and margarine used as cooking media or ingredients

fermentation—the process by which yeast converts sugar into alcohol and carbon dioxide; it also refers to the time that yeast dough is left to rise, that is, the time it takes for carbon dioxide gas cells to form and become trapped in the gluten network

feuilletage—(fuh-yuh-TAHZH) French for flaky; used to describe puff pastry or the process for making puff pastry

feuilletées—(fuh-yuh-TAY) square, rectangular or diamond-shaped puff pastry boxes; may be filled with a sweet or savory mixture

fiber—also known as dietary fiber; indigestible carbohydrates found in grains, fruits and vegetables; fiber aids digestion

flambé—(flahm-BAY) food served flaming; produced by igniting brandy, rum or other liquor so that the alcohol burns off and the flavor of the liquor is retained

flan—a firm custard baked over a layer of caramelized sugar and inverted for service

flash-frozen—describes food that has been frozen very rapidly using metal plates, extremely low temperatures or chemical solutions

flat icing—an opaque white sugar glaze used to decorate Danish pastry and coffeecakes

flavoring—an item that adds a new taste to a food and alters its natural flavors; flavorings include herbs, spices, vinegars and condiments; the terms *seasoning* and *flavoring* are often used interchangeably

flax—a grain plant also known as linseed, rich in omega-3 fatty acids; flax hulls and seeds are crushed into a meal of flour to release beneficial compounds

fleuron—(fluh-rawng) a crescent-shaped piece of puff pastry used as a garnish

flour—a powdery substance of varying degrees of fineness made by milling grains such as wheat, corn or rye

foam icing—a coating for cakes made from meringue; made with a hot sugar syrup

fold—a measurement of the strength of vanilla extract

folding—a mixing method in which light, airy ingredients are incorporated into heavier ingredients by gently moving them from the bottom of the bowl up over the top in a circular motion, usually with a rubber spatula

fondant—(FAHN-dant) a sweet, thick opaque sugar paste commonly used for glazing pastries such as napoleons or making candies

formula—a recipe; the term is most often used in the bakeshop

frangipane—(fran-juh-pahn) a sweet almond and egg filling cooked inside pastry

French buttercream—a cake icing or filling made with egg yolks into which a hot sugar syrup is beaten before butter and flavorings are added; also known as **mousseline buttercream**

friable—easily crumbled; said of a baked good with a low

moisture and high fat content such as a butter cookie

friandises—a small pastry or sweet delicacy often served between or after meals; petits fours

frosting—also known as icing; a sweet decorative coating used as a filling between the layers or as a coating over the top and sides of a cake

fruit—the edible organ that develops from the ovary of a flowering plant and contains one or more seeds (pips or pits)

frying—a dry-heat cooking method in which foods are cooked in hot fat; includes sautéing and stir-frying, pan-frying and deep-frying

fudge—a cooked mixture of sugar, corn syrup, butter or cream and flavorings made into a soft candy or thick icing

fusion cuisine—the blending or use of ingredients and/or preparation methods from various ethnic, regional or national cuisines in the same dish; also known as transnational cuisine

ganache—(ga-nosh) a rich blend of chocolate and heavy cream and, optionally, flavorings, used as a pastry or candy filling or frosting

garnish—(1) food used as an attractive decoration; (2) a subsidiary food used to add flavor or character to the main ingredient in a dish

gastronomy—the art and science of eating well

gâteau—(gah-toe) (1) in American usage, refers to any cake-type dessert; (2) in French usage, refers to various pastry items made with puff pastry, éclair paste, short dough or sweet dough

gelatin—a natural product derived from collagen, an animal protein, used to thicken liquids when chilled; available in two

forms: granulated gelatin and sheet (also called leaf) gelatin

gelatinization—the process by which starch granules are cooked; they absorb moisture when placed in a liquid and heated; as the moisture is absorbed, the product swells, softens and clarifies slightly

gelato—(jah-laht-to) an Italian-style ice cream that is denser than American-style ice cream

genoise—(zhen-waahz) (1) a form of whipped-egg cake that uses whole eggs whipped with sugar; (2) a French spongecake

germ—the smallest portion of a cereal grain and the only part that contains fat

glaçage—(glah-sahge) browning or glazing a food, usually under a salamander or broiler

glaze—(1) any shiny coating applied to food or created by browning; (2) a thin, flavored coating poured or dripped onto a cake or pastry

gliaden—see **gluten**

glucose—(1) an important energy source for the body; also known as blood sugar; (2) a thick, sweet syrup made from cornstarch, composed primarily of dextrose; light corn syrup can usually be substituted for it in baked goods or candy making; also sold in a powdered form

gluten—an elastic network of proteins created when wheat flour is moistened and manipulated; it gives structure and strength to baked goods and is responsible for their volume, texture and appearance; the proteins necessary for gluten formation are glutenin and gliaden

glutenin—*see* **gluten**

gold leaf—delicate sheets of gold used to decorate chocolate and iced cakes; the thin sheets, separated by tissue paper, are sold in packs available from cake decorating suppliers. Edible silver leaf, known as vark, is also available

gougère—éclair paste flavored with cheese or herbs, baked and served as a savory hors d'oeuvre

gourmand—a connoisseur of fine food and drink, often to excess

gourmet—a connoisseur of fine food and drink

gourmet foods—foods of the highest quality, perfectly prepared and beautifully presented

grading—a series of voluntary programs offered by the U.S. Department of Agriculture to designate a food's overall quality

grains—(1) grasses that bear edible seeds, including corn, rice and wheat; (2) the fruit (that is, the seed or kernel) of such grasses

gram—the basic unit of weight in the metric system; equal to approximately $1/30$ of an ounce

grande cuisine—the rich, intricate and elaborate cuisine of the 18th- and 19th-century French aristocracy and upper classes; it is based on the rational identification, development and adoption of strict culinary principles

grind—to pulverize or reduce food to small particles using a mechanical grinder or food processor

grinding—a milling process in which grains are reduced to a powder; the powder can be of differing degrees of fineness or coarseness

gum paste—a smooth dough of sugar and gelatin that can be colored and used to make decorations, especially for pastries

Hazard Analysis Critical Control Points (HACCP)—a rigorous system of self-inspection used to manage and maintain sanitary conditions in all types of food service operations; it fo-

cuses on the flow of food through the food service facility to identify any point or step in preparation (known as a critical control point) where some action must be taken to prevent or minimize a risk or hazard

hearth—the heated bottom surface of a baking oven on which foods are directly baked

hearth oven—an oven whose floor is made from stone or masonry; bread, pizzas or other items are baked directly on its heated stone surface; also known as a deck oven

herb—any of a large group of aromatic plants whose leaves, stems or flowers are used as a flavoring; used either dried or fresh

high-ratio cake—a form of creamed-fat cake that uses emulsified shortening and has a two-stage mixing method

homogenization—the process by which milkfat is prevented from separating out of milk products

hotel pan—a rectangular, stainless steel pan with a lip allowing it to rest in a storage shelf or steam table; available in several standard sizes

hull—also known as the husk; the outer covering of a fruit, seed or grain

humectant—a substance such as corn syrup, glucose or honey that absorbs moisture, making baked goods soft and tender

hybrid—the result of cross-breeding genetically different species; often a unique product

hydrogenated fat—unsaturated, liquid fats that are chemically altered to remain solid at room temperature, such as solid shortening or margarine

hydrogenation—the process used to harden oils; hydrogen

atoms are added to unsaturated fat molecules, making them partially or completely saturated and thus solid at room temperature

hydrometer—a device used to measure specific gravity; it shows degrees of concentration on the Baumé scale; also known as a saccharometer

hygroscopic—describes a food that readily absorbs moisture from the air

icing—*see* **frosting**

infuse—to flavor a liquid by steeping it with ingredients such as tea, coffee, herbs or spices

instant-read thermometer—a thermometer used to measure the internal temperature of foods; the stem is inserted in the food, producing an instant temperature readout

interferent—a substance such as glucose or lemon juice that helps stop sugar from recrystallizing when dissolved in a solution

IQF (individually quick-frozen)—describes the technique of rapidly freezing each individual item of food such as slices of fruit, berries or pieces of fish before packaging; IQF foods are not packaged with syrup or sauce

Italian buttercream—a cake icing or filling made from whipped egg white meringue cooked with hot sugar syrup into which butter and flavorings are beaten

jam—a fruit gel made from fruit pulp and sugar

jelly—a fruit gel made from fruit juice and sugar

juice—the liquid extracted from any fruit or vegetable

Kaiser roll—a large round yeast roll with a crisp crust and a curved pattern stamped on the top; used primarily for sandwiches

kneading—a mixing method in which dough is worked to develop gluten

kosher—describes food prepared in accordance with Jewish dietary laws

kuchen—(KOO-ken) a German-style cake, often yeasted

kugelhopf—(KOO-guhl-hopf) a light, buttery yeast cake studded with nuts and raisins and baked in a special fluted mold; a specialty of Germany, the Alsace region of France and other central European countries

lactose—a disaccharide that occurs naturally in mammalian milk; milk sugar

lamination—incorporating fat such as butter into a pastry dough to create hundreds of crisp layers as for puff pastry and croissants

leavener—an ingredient or process that produces or incorporates gases in a baked product in order to increase volume, provide structure and give texture

lecithin—a natural emulsifier found in egg yolks and soybeans

levain—the French term for leavening; dough made from a sourdough culture that forms the basis for French-style sourdough bread

Linzer torte—a nut crust and jam tart from Austria

liqueur—a strong, sweet, syrupy alcoholic beverage made by mixing or redistilling neutral spirits with fruits, flowers, herbs, spices or other flavorings; also known as a cordial

liquor—an alcoholic beverage made by distilling grains, vegetables or other foods; includes rum, whiskey and vodka

liter—the basic unit of volume in the metric system, equal to slightly more than a quart

macerate—to soak foods in a flavorful liquid, usually alcoholic, to soften them

make-up—the cutting, shaping and forming of dough products before baking

mandoline—a stainless steel, hand-operated slicing device with adjustable blades

marmalade—a citrus jelly that contains unpeeled slices of citrus fruit

marquise—a frozen mousselike dessert, usually chocolate

Marsala—(mar-SAH-lah) a flavorful fortified sweet-to-semidry Sicilian wine

marzipan—(MAHR-sih-pan) a paste of ground almonds, sugar and glucose used to fill and decorate pastries

master baker—a professional title given exclusively to highly skilled and experienced bakers who have demonstrated their professional knowledge in written and practical exams

meal—the coarsely ground seeds of any edible grain such as corn or oats

melting—the process by which certain foods, especially those high in fat, gradually soften and then liquefy when heated

menu—a list of foods and beverages available for purchase

meringue—(muh-reng) a foam made of beaten egg whites and sugar

meter—the basic unit of length in the metric system, equal to slightly more than 1 yard

metric system—a measurement system based on decimal units in which the gram, liter and meter are the basic units of weight, volume and length, respectively

microorganisms—single-celled organisms as well as tiny plants and animals that can be seen only through a microscope

microwave cooking—a heating method that uses radiation generated by a special oven to penetrate the food; it agitates water molecules, creating friction and heat; this energy then spreads throughout the food by conduction (and by convection in liquids)

millet—high-protein cereal grain cooked and eaten like rice; ground and used in combination with wheat flour in baking

milling—the process by which grain is ground into flour or meal

minerals—inorganic micronutrients necessary for regulating body functions and proper bone and tooth structures

mise en place—(meez on plahs) French for putting in place; refers to the preparation and assembly of all necessary ingredients and equipment

mix—(1) to combine ingredients in such a way that they are evenly dispersed throughout the mixture; (2) a blend of dry ingredients to which liquid, eggs and other ingredients are added in order to make a batter or dough

moist-heat cooking methods—cooking methods, principally simmering, poaching, boiling and steaming, that use water or steam to transfer heat through convection; moist-heat cooking methods are used to emphasize the natural flavors of foods

molder—a mechanical device that shapes divided bread dough into forms before proofing and baking

molding—the process of shaping foods, particularly custards, tortes and mousses, into attractive, hard-edged shapes by using metal rings, circular cutters or other forms

molds—(1) algaelike fungi that form long filaments or strands; for the most part, molds affect only food appearance and flavor; (2) containers used for shaping foods

monounsaturated fats—*see* **unsaturated fats**

mortar and pestle—a hard bowl (the mortar) in which foods such as spices are ground or pounded into a powder with a club-shaped tool (the pestle)

mousse—(moose) a soft, creamy food, either sweet or savory, lightened by adding whipped cream, beaten egg whites or both

mousseline—(moose-uh-leen) a cream or sauce lightened by folding in whipped cream

mousseline buttercream—*see* **French buttercream**

mouth feel—the sensation, other than flavor, that a food or beverage has in the mouth; a function of the item's body, texture and, to a lesser extent, temperature

muffin method—a mixing method used to make quick-bread batters; it involves combining liquid fat with other liquid ingredients before adding them to the dry ingredients

napoleon—many-layered pastry made from baked sheets of puff pastry filled with pastry cream or whipped cream

Neapolitan—a three-layered loaf or cake of ice cream; each layer is a different flavor and a different color, a typical combination being chocolate, vanilla and strawberry

nectar—the diluted, sweetened juice of peaches, apricots, guavas, black currants or other fruits, the juice of which would be too thick or too tart to drink straight

new American cuisine—a late-20th-century movement that began in California but has spread across the United States; it stresses the use of fresh, locally grown, seasonal produce and high-quality ingredients prepared simply in a fashion that preserves and emphasizes natural flavors

noisette—French for hazelnut

no-time dough—yeast dough formulated with additional yeast and dough conditioners to accelerate fermentation to 15 to 30 minutes

nougat—a candy made from caramelized sugar, almonds and egg whites; known as *turrón* in Spain and *torrone* in Italy

nougat glacé—a frozen dessert composed of crumbled nougatine folded into Italian meringue and whipped cream

nougatine—a confection made from toasted nuts and caramelized sugar used as a decoration, as an ingredient or in showpieces

nouvelle cuisine—French for new cooking; a mid-20th-century movement away from many classic cuisine principles and toward a lighter cuisine based on natural flavors, shortened cooking times and innovative combinations

nut—(1) the edible single-seed kernel of a fruit surrounded by a hard shell; (2) generally, any seed or fruit with an edible kernel in a hard shell

nutrients—the chemical substances found in food that nourish the body by promoting growth, facilitating body functions and providing energy; the six categories of nutrients are proteins, carbohydrates, fats, water, minerals and vitamins

nutrition—the science that studies nutrients

oil—a type of fat that remains liquid at room temperature

oven spring—the rapid rise of yeast goods when first placed in a hot oven; results from the temporary increase in yeast activity and the expansion of trapped gases

overrun—the amount of air churned into an ice cream during freezing

pan-frying—a dry-heat cooking method in which food is cooked in a moderate amount of hot fat

panettone—(pan-eh-TONE-nay) sweet Italian yeast bread filled with raisins, candied fruits, anise seeds and nuts; traditionally baked in a rounded cylindrical mold and served as a breakfast bread or dessert during the Christmas holidays

papain—an enzyme found in papayas that breaks down proteins; used as the primary ingredient in many commercial meat tenderizers

par-baked—bread that has been baked until the gluten structure is set and yeast activity has stopped but without browning; a frequent procedure for preparing bread that will be frozen for resale

parboiling—partially cooking a food in boiling or simmering liquid; similar to blanching but the cooking time is longer

parchment (paper)—heat-resistant paper used throughout the bakeshop for tasks such as lining baking pans, making pastry cones for piping and covering foods during shallow poaching

parfait—ice cream served in a long, slender glass with alternating layers of topping or sauce; also the name of the mousselike preparation that forms the basis for some still-frozen desserts

paring knife—a short knife used for detail work, especially cutting fruits and vegetables; it has a rigid blade approximately 2–4 inches (5–10 centimeters) long

Paris-Brest—rings of baked éclair paste cut in half horizontally and filled with light pastry cream and/or whipped cream; the top is dusted with powdered sugar or drizzled with chocolate glaze

Parisienne; Parisian—(1) the smaller scoop on a two-scoop melon ball cutter; (2) small spheres of fruit or vegetables cut with a tiny melon ball cutter

pasteurization—the process of heating something to a prescribed temperature for a specific period in order to destroy pathogenic bacteria

pastillage—(pahst-tee-azh) a paste made of sugar, cornstarch and gelatin; it may be cut or molded into decorative shapes

pastry bag—a cone-shaped cloth, plastic or parchment bag used to control the application of icings, fillings and batters

pastry cream—also known as crème pâtissière; a stirred custard made with egg yolks, sugar and milk and thickened with starch; used for pastry and pie fillings

pâte—(paht) French for dough

pâte à bombe—*see* **bombe mixture**

pâte à choux—(paht ah shoo) see **éclair paste**

pâte à glacer—(paht-ah-glasay) a specially formulated chocolate coating compound made with vegetable oils; designed to retain its shine without tempering

pâte brisée—(paht bree-zay) a dough that produces a very flaky baked product containing little or no sugar; flaky dough is used for prebaked pie shells or crusts; mealy dough is a less flaky product used for custard, cream or fruit pie crusts

pâte feuilletée—(paht fuh-yuh-tay) also known as puff pastry; a rolled-in dough used for pastries, cookies and savory products; it produces a rich and buttery but not sweet baked product with hundreds of light, flaky layers

pâte sucrée—(paht soo-kray) a dough containing sugar that produces a very rich, crisp (not flaky) baked product; also known as sweet dough, it is used for tart shells

pathogen—any organism that causes disease; usually refers to bacteria

pâtissier—(pah-tees-ee-yay) a pastry chef; the person responsible for all baked items, including breads, pastries and desserts

pearl sugar—large-grain sugar formed into opaque pellets for decorating cookies and breads

pearling—a milling process in which all or part of the hull, bran and germ are removed from the grain

pectin—a gelatin-like carbohydrate obtained from certain fruits; used to thicken jams and jellies

peel—*see* **baker's peel**

pH—a measurement of the acid or alkali content of a solution, expressed on a scale of 0 to 14.0. A pH of 7.0 is considered neutral or balanced. The lower the pH value, the more acidic the substance. The higher the pH value, the more alkaline the substance

physical hazard—a danger to the safety of food caused by particles such as glass chips, metal shavings, bits of wood or other foreign matter

pie weights—*see* **baking weights**

pigment—any substance that gives color to an item

poaching—a moist-heat cooking method that uses convection to transfer heat from a hot (approximately 160°F–180°F, [71°C–82°C]) liquid to the food submerged in it; used for whole fruits such as apricots, peaches and pears

polyunsaturated fats—*see* **unsaturated fats**

pomes—members of the *Rosaceae* family; tree fruits with a thin skin and firm flesh surrounding a central core containing many small seeds (called pips or carpels); include apples, pears and quince

powdered glucose—*see* **glucose**

pot de crème—(1) rich French egg and cream custard; (2) ceramic or porcelain cup in which the rich custard is baked and served

potentially hazardous foods—foods on which bacteria can thrive

preserve—(1) a fruit gel that contains large pieces or whole fruits; (2) to extend the shelf life of a food by subjecting it to a process such as irradiation, canning, vacuum-packing, drying or freezing and/or by adding preservatives

professional cooking—a system of cooking based on a knowledge of and appreciation for ingredients and procedures

profiterole—(pro-feet-uh-roll) small round pastry made from éclair paste filled with a savory filling and served as an hors d'oeuvre or filled with ice cream topped with sauce and served as a dessert

proof box—a heat- and humidity-controlled cabinet in

which yeast-leavened dough is put to rise immediately before baking

proofing—the rise given to shaped yeast products just prior to baking

proteins—a group of compounds composed of oxygen, hydrogen, carbon and nitrogen atoms necessary for manufacturing, maintaining and repairing body tissues and as an alternative source of energy (4 calories per gram); protein chains are constructed of various combinations of amino acids

pudding—a thick, spoonable dessert custard, usually made with eggs, milk, sugar and flavorings and thickened with flour or another starch

puff pastry—*see* **pâte feuilletée**

pulled sugar—a doughlike mixture of sucrose, glucose and tartaric acid that can be colored and shaped by hand

Pullman—a long rectangular loaf of bread for slicing; also, the pan in which this bread is baked

pumpernickel—(1) coarsely ground rye flour; (2) bread made with this flour

punch—to fold dough after it has fermented and risen in order to reactivate the yeast, allowing gases to escape

purée—(pur-ray) (1) to process food to achieve a smooth pulp; (2) food that is processed by mashing, straining or fine chopping to achieve a smooth pulp

quark—a fresh white curd cheese, with the texture and flavor of sour cream, commonly eaten in Germany

quiche—a savory tart filled with custard and other ingredients such as cheese, ham and vegetables

quick bread—a bread, including loaves and muffins, leavened by chemical leaveners or steam rather than yeast

quinoa—(keen-wa) tiny, spherical seeds of a plant native to South America, cooked like grain or ground and used as flour

rack oven—an oven in which multiple trays of baked goods are loaded onto racks rolled directly into the oven

ramekin—a small, ovenproof dish, usually ceramic

rancidity—a chemical change in fats caused by exposure to air, light or heat that results in objectionable flavors and odors

recipe—a set of written instructions for producing a specific food or beverage; also known as a formula

reduction—a liquid cooked until a portion of it evaporates, reducing the volume of the liquid; used to concentrate flavor and thicken liquids

refreshing—*see* **shocking**

respiration rate—the speed with which the cells of a fruit use up oxygen and produce carbon dioxide during ripening

retardation—chilling a yeasted dough product under refrigeration to slow yeast activity and to extend fermentation or proofing time

ricer—a sievelike utensil with small holes through which soft food is forced; it produces particles about the size of a grain of rice

ripe—(1) describes fully grown and developed fruit; the fruit's flavor, texture and appearance are at their peak and the fruit is ready to eat; (2) describes an unpleasant odor indicating that a food, especially meat, poultry, fish or shellfish, may be past its prime

rognures—French for trimmings or scraps

roll-in—(1) shorthand expression for the butter or other fat used in layering laminated dough; also referred to as lock-in fat (2) the procedure of incorporating fat such as butter into a pastry dough to create hundreds of crisp layers

rolled fondant—a cooked mixture of sugar, glucose and water formulated to drape over cakes

rolled-in dough—a dough in which a fat is incorporated in many layers by using a rolling and folding procedure; it is used for flaky baked goods such as croissants, puff pastry and Danish pastry; also called laminated dough

rose powder—fresh rose petals, dried and then ground into a fine powder used to flavor chocolates, fillings and toppings

roulade—(roo-lahd) a filled and rolled spongecake

rounding—the process of shaping dough into smooth, round balls; used to stretch the outside layer of gluten into a smooth coating

royal icing—also known as decorator's icing; an uncooked mixture of confectioner's sugar and egg whites that becomes hard and brittle when dry; used for making intricate cake decorations

sabayon—(sa-by-on) also known as zabaglione; a foamy, stirred custard sauce made by whisking eggs, sugar and wine over low heat

saccharometer—*see* **hydrometer**

salamander—a small broiler used primarily for browning or glazing the tops of foods

sanding sugar—granulated sugar with a large, coarse crystal structure that prevents it from dissolving easily; used for decorating cookies and pastries

sanitation—the creation and maintenance of conditions that will prevent food contamination or food-borne illness

sanitize—to reduce pathogenic organisms to safe levels

saturated fats—fats found mainly in animal products and tropical oils; usually solid at room temperature; the body has more difficulty breaking down saturated fats than either monounsaturated or polyunsaturated fats

sauce—generally, a thickened liquid used to flavor and enhance other foods

sautéing—(saw-tay-ing) a dry-heat cooking method that uses conduction to transfer heat from a hot pan to food with the aid of a small amount of hot fat; cooking is usually done quickly over high temperatures

savarin—rich, yeasted cake prepared from baba dough baked into a small round ring, the center of which may be filled with whipped cream and candied fruit

savory—(1) describes spiced or seasoned, as opposed to sweet, foods; (2) (savoury) a highly seasoned last course of a traditional English dinner

scald—to heat a liquid, usually milk, to just below the boiling point

scale up (down)—to increase (decrease) a recipe or formula mathematically

scaling—measuring ingredients on a scale before mixing a batter or dough

score—to cut shallow gashes across the surface of a food before cooking

season—(1) traditionally, to enhance flavor by adding salt; (2) more commonly, to enhance

flavor by adding salt and/or pepper as well as herbs and spices; (3) to prepare a pot, pan or other cooking surface to prevent sticking

seasoning—an item added to enhance the natural flavors of a food without dramatically changing its taste; salt is the most common seasoning, although all herbs and spices are often referred to as seasonings

semifreddi—(seh-mee-frayd-dee) also known as still-frozen desserts; items made with frozen mousse, custard or cream into which large amounts of whipped cream or meringue are folded in order to incorporate air; layers of spongecake and/or fruits may be added for flavor and texture; includes frozen soufflés, marquise, mousses and neapolitans

semolina—*see* **durum wheat**

sfoglia—(sfo-glee-ah) a thin, flat sheet of pasta dough that can be cut into ribbons, circles, squares or other shapes

sheeter—a machine for rolling out dough between rollers set over a canvas surface

sherbet—a frozen mixture of fruit juice or fruit purée that contains milk and/or eggs for creaminess

shocking—also called refreshing; the technique of quickly chilling blanched or parcooked foods in ice water; prevents further cooking and sets colors

shortening—(1) a white, flavorless, solid fat formulated for baking or deep-frying; (2) any fat used in baking to tenderize the product by shortening gluten strands

showpiece—decorative sculpture made from chocolate, sugar or other confections; used as a table display and to demonstrate the skills of the pastry chef

shred—to cut into thin but irregular strips

side masking—the technique of coating only the sides of a cake with garnish

sifting—passing one or more dry ingredients through a wire mesh to remove lumps, combine and aerate

simmering—(1) a moist-heat cooking method that uses convection to transfer heat from a hot (approximately 185°F–205°F [85°C–96°C]) liquid to the food submerged in it; (2) maintaining the temperature of a liquid just below the boiling point

simple syrup—a mixture of sugar dissolved in water used in icings, mousses, frozen desserts and confectionery

slice—to cut an item into relatively broad, thin pieces

smoke point—the temperature at which a fat begins to break down and smoke

solid pack—describes canned fruits or vegetables with little or no water added

sorbet—(sore-bay) a frozen mixture of fruit juice or fruit purée; similar to sherbet but without milk products

sorghum—grain harvested from a plant that resembles corn, used primarily for animal feed and food processing applications; also called milo; when ground, sorghum may be blended with other flours to make gluten-free preparations

soufflé—(soo-flay) either a sweet or savory fluffy dish made with a custard base lightened with whipped egg whites and then baked; the whipped egg whites cause the dish to puff when baked

sour—a fermented mixture of flour and water added to dough for leavening and flavoring

sous-chef—(soo-shef) a cook who supervises food production and who reports to the executive chef; he or she is second in command of a kitchen

soy nuts—soaked soybeans that are dried or roasted and consumed as a snack food in place of higher-fat alternatives such as roasted tree nuts or peanuts

specific gravity—the weight of an ingredient or a mixture in relation to the weight of water

specifications; specs—standard requirements to be followed in procuring items from suppliers

spice—any of a group of strongly flavored or aromatic portions of plants (other than leaves) used as flavorings, condiments or aromatics; usually used in dried form, either whole or ground

sponge method—a yeast dough mixing method in which flour, yeast and water are premixed and allowed to ferment; after the sponge has fermented, the remainder of the formula ingredients are mixed in

spread—the flattening of cookie dough when it heats and bakes, controlled by the formula, ingredients and temperature; spread is determined by the amount of crystalline sugar in the cookie mix; adding granulated sugar increases spread

springform pan—a circular baking pan with a separate bottom and a side wall held together with a clamp that is released to free the baked product

spun sugar—a decoration made by flicking dark caramelized sugar rapidly over a dowel to create long, fine, hairlike threads

staling—*see* **starch retrogradation**

standardized recipe—a recipe producing a known quality and

quantity of food for a specific operation

starch—(1) complex carbohydrates from plants that are edible and either digestible or indigestible (fiber); (2) a rice, grain, pasta or potato accompaniment to a meal

starch retrogradation—also known as staling; a change in the distribution and location of water molecules within baked products; stale products are firmer, drier and more crumbly than fresh baked goods

steaming—a moist-heat cooking method in which heat is transferred from steam to the food being cooked by direct contact; the food to be steamed is placed in a basket or rack above a boiling liquid in a covered pan

steel—a tool, usually made of steel, used to hone or straighten knife blades

steep—to soak food in a hot liquid in order to either extract its flavor or impurities or soften its texture

sterilize—to destroy all living microorganisms

St. Honoré—the patron saint of the pastry chef; also the name for a light, crisp pastry composed of puff pastry topped with éclair paste baked and then filled with custard and coated with hard caramel; the name for a piping tip that produces a wedge-shaped design, which is often used to pipe in the filling

stirring—a mixing method in which ingredients are gently mixed by hand until evenly blended, usually with a spoon, whisk or rubber spatula

stone fruits—members of the genus *Prunus,* also known as drupes; tree or shrub fruits with a thin skin, soft flesh and one woody stone or pit; include apri-

cots, cherries, nectarines, peaches and plums

straight dough method—a mixing method for yeast breads in which all ingredients are simply combined and mixed; also known as direct method

strain—to pour foods through a sieve, mesh strainer or cheesecloth to separate or remove the liquid component

streusel—(stroo-zel) a crumbly mixture of fat, flour, sugar and sometimes nuts and spices; used to top baked goods

sucrose—the chemical name for refined or table sugar, it is refined from the raw sugars found in the large tropical grass called sugar cane and the root of the sugar beet; a disaccharide composed of one molecule each of glucose and fructose

sugar—a carbohydrate that provides the body with energy and gives a sweet taste to foods

sugar syrups—either simple syrups (thin mixtures of sugar and water) or cooked syrups (melted sugar cooked until it reaches a specific temperature)

sundae—a great and gooey concoction of ice cream, sauces (hot fudge, marshmallow and caramel, for example), toppings (nuts, candies and fresh fruit, to name a few) and whipped cream

supreme—an intact segment of citrus fruit with all membrane removed

syrup—sugar that is dissolved in liquid, usually water, and often flavored with spices or citrus zest

syrup pack—describes canned fruits with a light, medium or heavy syrup added

tang—the portion of a knife's blade that extends inside the handle

tart—a sweet or savory filling in a baked crust made in a shallow, straight-sided pan without a top crust

tartlet—a small, single-serving tart

temperature danger zone—the broad range of temperatures between 40°F and 140°F (4°C and 60°C) at which bacteria multiply rapidly

tempering—(1) heating gently and gradually; refers to the process of slowly adding a hot liquid to eggs or other foods to raise their temperature without causing them to curdle; (2) a process for melting chocolate during which the temperature of the cocoa butter is carefully stabilized; this keeps the chocolate smooth and glossy

thickening agents—ingredients used to thicken sauces; include starches (flour, cornstarch and arrowroot) and gelatin

toque—(toke) the tall white hat worn by chefs

torte—in Central and Eastern European usage, refers to a rich cake in which all or part of the flour is replaced with finely chopped nuts or bread crumbs; also refers to any multilayered sweet cake

trimoline—invert sugar syrup used commercially to prevent crystallization in candies and fondant fillings

truffles—(1) rich chocolate candies made with ganache; (2) an edible fungus considered a delicacy

tube pan—a deep round baking pan with a hollow tube in the center

tunneling—the holes that may form in baked goods as the result of overmixing

turns—the number of times that laminated dough is rolled and folded

unsaturated fats—fats that are normally liquid (oils) at room temperature; they may be monounsaturated (from plants such as olives and avocados) or polyunsaturated (from grains and seeds such as corn, soybeans and safflower as well as from fish)

vacherin—a baked meringue disk or cake layered with ice cream

vanilla custard sauce—also known as crème anglaise; a stirred custard made with egg yolks, sugar and milk or half-and-half and flavored with vanilla; served with or used in dessert preparations

vanillin—(1) whitish crystals of vanilla flavor that often develop on vanilla beans during storage; (2) synthetic vanilla flavoring

vegetarian—a person who does not eat any meat, poultry, game, fish, shellfish or animal by-products such as gelatin or animal fats; may not eat dairy products and eggs

vegetarianism—eating a plant-based diet; ovo vegetarians eat eggs; lacto vegetarians eat some dairy; ovo-lacto vegetarians eat eggs and dairy; vegans consume no animal products of any kind

vent—(1) to allow the circulation or escape of a liquid or gas; (2) to cool a pot of hot liquid by setting the pot on blocks in a cold water bath and allowing cold water to circulate around it

Viennoiserie—(Vienneh-wah-zer-ee) the term applied to the category of enriched pastry doughs, which includes brioche, croissants and Danish pastries

vinegar—a thin, sour liquid used as a preservative, cooking ingredient and cleaning solution

viruses—the smallest known form of life; they invade the living cells of a host and take over those cells' genetic material, causing the cells to produce more viruses; some viruses can enter a host through the ingestion of food contaminated with those viruses

vitamins—compounds present in foods in very small quantities; they do not provide energy but are essential for regulating body functions

vol-au-vents—(vul-oh-vanz) deep, individual portion-sized puff pastry shells; often filled with a savory mixture and served as an appetizer or a main course

volume—the space occupied by a substance; volume measurements are commonly expressed as liters, teaspoons, tablespoons, cups, pints and gallons

wash—a glaze applied to dough before baking; a commonly used wash is made with whole egg and water

water bath—see **bain marie**

water pack—describes canned fruit with water or fruit juice added

weight—the mass or heaviness of a substance; weight measurements are commonly expressed as grams, ounces and pounds

whetstone—a dense, grained stone used to sharpen or hone a knife blade

whipping—a mixing method in which foods are vigorously beaten to incorporate air; a whisk or electric mixer fitted with a whip is used

whole butter—butter that is not clarified, whipped or reduced in fat content; it may be salted or unsalted

windowpane test—a procedure to check that yeast dough has been properly kneaded; a piece of the kneaded dough is pulled apart to see if it stretches without breaking apart

wine—an alcoholic beverage made from the fermented juice of grapes; may be sparkling (effervescent) or still (noneffervescent) or fortified with additional alcohol

work section—see **work station**

work station—a work area in the kitchen dedicated to a particular task, such as broiling or salad making; work stations us-ing the same or similar equipment for related tasks are grouped together into work sections

yeasts—microscopic fungi whose metabolic processes are responsible for fermentation; they are used for leavening bread and in cheese, beer and wine making

yield—the total amount of a product produced by a formula expressed in total weight, volume or number of units of the product

zabaglione—see **sabayon**

zest—the thin, colored outer portion of the rind of citrus fruit; contains the oil that provides flavor and aroma

RECIPE INDEX

Boldface page numbers indicate pages on which the main recipe appears.

SUBJECT INDEX

Recipe titles and their page numbers are in **boldface** type and may be listed under main ingredient(s), category, or cooking method. Thus, **Lemon Poppy Seed Muffins** is found under Lemons, Poppy seeds, Muffins, and Quick breads. Some recipes, such as **Conchas,** are also listed as unique entries. A complete list of recipes alphabetically by title begins on page 671.

SINGLE PC LICENSE AGREEMENT AND LIMITED WARRANTY

READ THIS LICENSE CAREFULLY BEFORE OPENING THIS PACKAGE. BY OPENING THIS PACKAGE, YOU ARE AGREEING TO THE TERMS AND CONDITIONS OF THIS LICENSE. IF YOU DO NOT AGREE, DO NOT OPEN THE PACKAGE. PROMPTLY RETURN THE UNOPENED PACKAGE AND ALL ACCOMPANYING ITEMS TO THE PLACE YOU OBTAINED THEM FOR A FULL REFUND OF ANY SUMS YOU HAVE PAID FOR THE SOFTWARE. THESE TERMS APPLY TO ALL LICENSED SOFTWARE ON THE CD-ROM EXCEPT THAT THE TERMS FOR USE OF ANY SHAREWARE OR FREEWARE ON THE CD-ROM ARE AS SET FORTH IN THE ELECTRONIC LICENSE LOCATED ON THE CD:

1. GRANT OF LICENSE and OWNERSHIP: The enclosed computer programs and data ("Software") are licensed, not sold, to you by Prentice-Hall, Inc. ("We" or the "Company") and in consideration of your payment of the license fee, which is part of the price you paid and your agreement to these terms. We reserve any rights not granted to you. You own only the disk(s) but we and/or our licensors own the Software itself. This license allows you to use and display your copy of the Software on a single computer (i.e., with a single CPU) at a single location for academic use only, so long as you comply with the terms of this Agreement. You may make one copy for back up, or transfer your copy to another CPU, provided that the Software is usable on only one computer.

2. RESTRICTIONS: You may not transfer or distribute the Software or documentation to anyone else. Except for backup, you may not copy the documentation or the Software. You may not network the Software or otherwise use it on more than one computer or computer terminal at the same time. You may not reverse engineer, disassemble, decompile, modify, adapt, translate, or create derivative works based on the Software or the Documentation. You may be held legally responsible for any copying or copyright infringement which is caused by your failure to abide by the terms of these restrictions.

3. TERMINATION: This license is effective until terminated. This license will terminate automatically without notice from the Company if you fail to comply with any provisions or limitations of this license. Upon termination, you shall destroy the Documentation and all copies of the Software. All provisions of this Agreement as to limitation and disclaimer of warranties, limitation of liability, remedies or damages, and our ownership rights shall survive termination.

4. LIMITED WARRANTY AND DISCLAIMER OF WARRANTY: Company warrants that for a period of 60 days from the date you purchase this SOFTWARE (or purchase or adopt the accompanying textbook), the Software, when properly installed and used in accordance with the Documentation, will operate in substantial conformity with the description of the Software set forth in the Documentation, and that for a period of 30 days the disk(s) on which the Software is delivered shall be free from defects in materials and workmanship under normal use. The Company does not warrant that the Software will meet your requirements or that the operation of the Software will be uninterrupted or error-free. Your only remedy and the Company's only obligation under these limited warranties is, at the Company's option, return of the disk for a refund of any amounts paid for it by you or replacement of the disk. THIS LIMITED WARRANTY IS THE ONLY WARRANTY PROVIDED BY THE COMPANY AND ITS LICENSORS, AND THE COMPANY AND ITS LICENSORS DISCLAIM ALL OTHER WARRANTIES, EXPRESS OR IMPLIED, INCLUDING WITHOUT LIMITATION, THE IMPLIED WARRANTIES OF MERCHANTABILITY AND FITNESS FOR A PARTICULAR PURPOSE. THE COMPANY DOES NOT WARRANT, GUARANTEE OR MAKE ANY REPRESENTATION REGARDING THE ACCURACY, RELIABILITY, CURRENTNESS, USE, OR RESULTS OF USE, OF THE SOFTWARE.

5. LIMITATION OF REMEDIES AND DAMAGES: IN NO EVENT, SHALL THE COMPANY OR ITS EMPLOYEES, AGENTS, LICENSORS, OR CONTRACTORS BE LIABLE FOR ANY INCIDENTAL, INDIRECT, SPECIAL, OR CONSEQUENTIAL DAMAGES ARISING OUT OF OR IN CONNECTION WITH THIS LICENSE OR THE SOFTWARE, INCLUDING FOR LOSS OF USE, LOSS OF DATA, LOSS OF INCOME OR PROFIT, OR OTHER LOSSES, SUSTAINED AS A RESULT OF INJURY TO ANY PERSON, OR LOSS OF OR DAMAGE TO PROPERTY, OR CLAIMS OF THIRD PARTIES, EVEN IF THE COMPANY OR AN AUTHORIZED REPRESENTATIVE OF THE COMPANY HAS BEEN ADVISED OF THE POSSIBILITY OF SUCH DAMAGES. IN NO EVENT SHALL THE LIABILITY OF THE COMPANY FOR DAMAGES WITH RESPECT TO THE SOFTWARE EXCEED THE AMOUNTS ACTUALLY PAID BY YOU, IF ANY, FOR THE SOFTWARE OR THE ACCOMPANYING TEXTBOOK. BECAUSE SOME JURISDICTIONS DO NOT ALLOW THE LIMITATION OF LIABILITY IN CERTAIN CIRCUMSTANCES, THE ABOVE LIMITATIONS MAY NOT ALWAYS APPLY TO YOU.

6. GENERAL: THIS AGREEMENT SHALL BE CONSTRUED IN ACCORDANCE WITH THE LAWS OF THE UNITED STATES OF AMERICA AND THE STATE OF NEW YORK, APPLICABLE TO CONTRACTS MADE IN NEW YORK, AND SHALL BENEFIT THE COMPANY, ITS AFFILIATES AND ASSIGNEES. HIS AGREEMENT IS THE COMPLETE AND EXCLUSIVE STATEMENT OF THE AGREEMENT BETWEEN YOU AND THE COMPANY AND SUPERSEDES ALL PROPOSALS OR PRIOR AGREEMENTS, ORAL, OR WRITTEN, AND ANY OTHER COMMUNICATIONS BETWEEN YOU AND THE COMPANY OR ANY REPRESENTATIVE OF THE COMPANY RELATING TO THE SUBJECT MATTER OF THIS AGREEMENT.

If you are a U.S. Government user, this Software is licensed with "restricted rights" as set forth in subparagraphs (a)-(d) of the Commercial Computer-Restricted Rights clause at FAR 52.227-19 or in subparagraphs (c)(1)(ii) of the Rights in Technical Data and Computer Software clause at DFARS 252.227-7013, and similar clauses, as applicable.